SUPREME COURT POLICYMAKING AND CONSTITUTIONAL LAW

SUPREME COURT POLICYMAKING AND CONSTITUTIONAL LAW

S. Sidney Ulmer

University of Kentucky

McGRAW-HILL BOOK COMPANY

New York   St. Louis   San Francisco   Auckland   Bogotá
Hamburg   Johannesburg   London   Madrid   Mexico   Montreal   New Delhi
Panama   Paris   São Paulo   Singapore   Sydney   Tokyo   Toronto

This book was set in Times Roman by University Graphics, Inc. (ECU).
The editors were David V. Serbun and Barry Benjamin;
the cover was designed by Laura Stover;
the production supervisor was Leroy A. Young.
R. R. Donnelley & Sons Company was printer and binder.

**SUPREME COURT POLICYMAKING AND
CONSTITUTIONAL LAW**

1 2 3 4 5 6 7 8 9 0 DOCDOC 8 9 8 7 6 5

ISBN 0-07-065747-5

Library of Congress Cataloging in Publication Data
Ulmer, S. Sidney.
   Supreme court policymaking and constitutional law.

   Includes bibliographies.
     1. United States—Constitutional law—Cases.
2. United States. Supreme Court. I. Title.
KF4549.U53 1986   342.73   85-6689
ISBN 0-07-065747-5   347.302

CONTENTS

PREFACE

This book is designed primarily for the beginning student in constitutional law. It makes no assumptions about previous exposure to case law or other explanatory materials on the Supreme Court. The book is divided into two parts. Part I explores the structure of governmental power as outlined in the Constitution and the development of that power through Supreme Court decisions. In Part II, we survey the various interfaces between governmental power and individual rights. In general, the cases included in Part II impose restrictions on the use of governmental power. But a number of the cases—by holding against the individual claim—teach us that the constitutional rights of persons and their governments are balanced in a legal, political, and social medium via appropriate Supreme Court decisions.

The cases in each part of this book are preceded by introductory essays (Chapters 1 and 6). In Chapter 1, the student is introduced to many of the basic concepts used by the Court in determining decisions in cases. While this chapter is no substitute for a study of judicial decision-making, attention is called to many of the leading concepts or theoretical considerations employed by those who write about decision-making. At the least, this chapter should alert the student to the fact that Supreme Court decisions are not made in a vacuum. Nor are they decisions guided solely by legal considerations or decisions automatically implemented in exactly the fashion intended by the Court. And they are certainly not decisions that, once made, are never modified or overruled.

In Chapter 6, we explore two momentous developments that have given the constitutional protection of civil liberties the significance it has today. One is the nationalization of the Bill of Rights, specifically Amendments I through VIII. This evolutionary change has enhanced and insulated the protections accorded individuals in the criminal justice system. It has also led to a dramatic expansion of the rights of individuals to participate in the political process, to criticize that process, and to engage in political expression—all facets of freedom of expression generally. Of great importance in this development has been the metamorphosis of freedom of speech to include many kinds of expression of a nonverbal nature.

The second phenomenal change given emphasis in Chapter 6 pertains to the constitutional rights of blacks in the United States. While individual cases certifying or enlarging such rights are included in this text, Chapter 6 attempts to impart a developmental sense of some of the approaches used by the Court to reshape black rights. In the process, the student is also introduced to some of the major concepts employed by the Court in this veritable explosion of constitutional rights under the Civil War amendments, particularly the Fourteenth Amendment. The concepts mentioned in Chapter 6 will be repeatedly encountered in the cases that follow.

In using this text, students will become aware that while Supreme Court cases may, in one sense, be isolated events, a better view sees the Court's cases as representing a constant process or flow of events which we may intersect for cross-sectional analysis but can best understand by considering its dynamic and longitudinal characteristics. Chapter 6 and the introductory statements preceding each section of the text should underscore this perspective for the student.

The commentary that precedes each case or set of cases is designed to provide a sense of continuity to case decisions. Each case decided comes with a background of cases and a background of cultural, historical, and political precedents. Each is decided in a particular social context at a particular point in time. In offering these introductory notes, we have sought to emphasize how a current case or cases is related to earlier cases, primarily in a subject matter and doctrinal sense. For although the justices often make policy, they almost always attempt to justify their decisions by pointing to continuity with the past or consistency between current principles of constitutional law and decision in an instant case. While the ostensible reasons for a decision may mask the "real" reasons (e.g., policy preferences), the reasons given in the justices' opinions are often the reasons motivating the justices' votes—to the extent that they are conscious of such motivations.

Apart from that consideration, the student should be alert to the developmental aspects of constitutional law principles, whatever their initial source. For these principles guide decisions to litigate and the arguments and concepts employed in litigation. Moreover, the priorities, doctrines, and concepts that make up the language of constitutional law operate as restraints on the ability of the justices to exercise attitudinal or policy preferences in deciding Court cases. In the notes section, we combine attention to both doctrinal and policy-making considerations, thereby spotlighting those areas in which social, political, or economic policy preferences were or might have been of some relevance for decisional outcome. In sum, then, our introductory comments are a reminder that formulating a Supreme Court decision is not the equivalent of building a ship in a bottle. Such decisions do frequently consist of many elements painstakingly crafted to make a work of science or art. But many considerations not seen through the glass contribute to making the ship, if not watertight, at least sufficiently seaworthy to make port. Or at least that is the Court's aim.

With a few exceptions, the cases are edited to highlight a single primary question. But a principal goal has been to emphasize the ideas employed by the justices and the fact that beliefs, values, policy preferences, and interpretations of the Constitution vary from one justice to another. To that end, over-editing of the cases is avoided. Dicta, comments by a justice that are not necessary for resolving the issue in dispute, are frequently left in where they make a contribution to the contrasting of the policies and theories to which different justices subscribe. For similar reasons, we include excerpts from many dissenting opinions and some concurrences. In particular, we have sought to include commentary bearing on the structure of our political and governmental systems and the contrasting views of the justices pertaining to such questions. Such material will undoubtedly make the point that the meaning of a constitutional provision is not to be ascertained merely by reading it.

The questions and comments that follow the cases are designed to promote discussions that will stimulate the students' interest and possibly enlarge their understanding of the subject matter. While some of the questions can be answered from a mere reading of the case excerpts, many require analysis, and some may require the reading of additional cases. In many instances, there are no pat answers to the questions posed. Such questions call for the exercise of analytical skills and an exchange of views in the classroom.

In general, the involvement and leadership of the instructor is likely to be required in the use of the material appearing under "Questions and Comments." Of course, instructors are free to skip over this material or to pick and choose whatever material will promote the goals they have set for a particular class.

I would like to express my thanks for the many useful comments and suggestions provided by colleagues who reviewed this text during the course of its development, especially to Robert S. Gerstein, University of California, Los Angeles; Jerry Goldman, Northwestern University; Milton Heumann, Rutgers University; Charles M. Lamb, SUNY, Buffalo, who read the entire manuscript and whose detailed comments on Chapters 1 and 6 led to substantial improvement of the book; William P. McLauchlan, Purdue University; Jeffrey Morris, University of Pennsylvania; David Neubauer, University of New Orleans; David M. O'Brian, University of Virginia; Susan M. Olson, University of Minnesota; Richard S. Randall, New York University; C. K. Rowland, University of Kansas; Elliot E. Slotnick, Ohio State University; Kenneth A. Wagner, California State University, Los Angeles; and Thomas G. Walker, Emory University, who read the entire book and offered suggestions that were of great value to me. Thanks also go to Kathy Stanwix-Hay, Betty Pasley, and Carolyn England for assistance in preparing various parts of the book. And special thanks to Kim Hayden, who cheerfully and expertly typed much of the manuscript.

Finally, I wish to recognize and express my gratitude for the assistance, support, and encouragement provided by my wife, Margaret L. Ulmer. Margaret was crucial to this endeavor in more ways than I can mention. But other authors will readily understand the indebtedness I acknowledge here.

S. Sidney Ulmer

PART ONE

THE POWERS OF GOVERNMENT

CHAPTER 1

THE SUPREME COURT IN THEORY AND IN PRACTICE

Remarkable though it may be, over 200 million Americans are currently being governed by a Constitution adopted for a nation of less than 5 million persons almost 200 years ago. When one considers the complexities of social and political life today, as compared to 1787, two thoughts come quickly to mind. The first is that the document must have been susceptible to and must have undergone considerable change since its inception. Secondly, the 1787 Constitution must have outlined an unusually effective governmental system—one based on unusual insights into human nature and its corresponding social and political needs.

The first of these hypotheses is certainly true. The Constitution may be amended by a two-thirds vote of both Houses of Congress subject to approval by three-fourths of the states.[1] As of January 1, 1984, twenty-six amendments had been adopted—the last in 1971. Even more important, the meaning of the document has been changed dramatically over the 197 years of its existence by the process of interpretation and reinterpretation of its general and sometime ambiguous provisions. In the process of using this text, one will become acutely aware of the changes wrought by this process and by Supreme Court justices who have had the courage to conform the Constitution to evolving political and economic standards of social life and intercourse.

Our second hypothesis is equally appealing given the longevity of our democratic form of government. The founding fathers constructed a system based on two fundamental concepts—separation of powers and federalism. These concepts have served us well.

SEPARATION OF POWERS/CHECKS AND BALANCES

Those who subscribe to separation-of-powers theory favor the division of governmental power among executive, legislative, and judicial branches. They argue that such a division of power is the best safeguard against its abuse, implying, in turn, that concentration of government power invites its misuse. The doctrine, insofar as legislative and executive departments are concerned, stems from seventeenth-century England. It was clearly articulated and widely disseminated by the English philosopher John Locke[2] and by the French aristocrat Montesquieu.[3] But the doctrine of checks and balances was implicitly set forth even earlier by an Italian philosopher, Machiavelli.[4]

In any event, these ideas were well known to the framers of our Constitution. A typical American expression of them is found in the following statement by James Madison.

> The great security against a gradual concentration of the several powers in the same department, consists in giving to those who administer each department the necessary constitutional means and personal motives to resist encroachments of the others. . . . Ambition must be made to counteract ambition. The interest of the man must be connected with the constitutional rights of the Place. It may be a reflection on human nature, that such devices should be necessary to control the abuses of government. But what's government itself? If men were angels, no government would be necessary. If angels were to govern men, neither external nor internal controls on government would be necessary. . . . A dependence on the people is, no doubt, the primary control on government; but experience has taught mankind the necessity of auxiliary precautions. This policy of supplying, by opposite and rival interests, the defect of better motives, might be traced through the whole system of human affairs, private as well as public. We see it particularly displayed in all the subordinate distributions of power, where the conscious aim is to divide and arrange the several offices in such a manner as that each may be a check on the other—that the private interest of every individual may be a sentinel over the public rights. These inventions of prudence cannot be less requisite in the distributions of the supreme powers of the State.[5]

The 1787 Constitution implicitly adopts the Madisonian position, since it divides the federal government into legislative (Article I), executive (Article II), and judicial (Article III) branches. Left unsettled either explicitly or implicitly, however, is how to settle conflicts that might arise among the three branches. John Locke thought that such conflicts could only be settled by God. But, as we shall see, another way has been found.

FEDERALISM

The framers of the federal Constitution did not write on a clean slate. The 1787 Convention was called by the states, each of which had its own functioning governmental system, and was attended by delegates from the states. Independence from Great Britain had been declared in 1776, and the Articles of Confederation were adopted in 1781. Under the Articles, the United States government was merely a weak legislature. Congress could make declarations and pass resolutions, but generally, it lacked the power to enforce its will on the states. Under the Articles, each of the thirteen states remained sovereign and independent. Each retained all the powers of a sovereign except those expressly delegated to the Congress. In short, it was a confederate rather than a federal government.

In an absolute monarchy, the king is sovereign, i.e., he exercises supreme power or dominion over the body politic. A sovereign state, on the other hand, is one that is independent and autonomous. In a confederacy, each state retains its sovereignty, its freedom, its independence. Every power and right associated with sovereignty is also retained unless expressly delegated to the confederate government. A consequence of such an arrangement is that every act of a confederacy must have the approval of each of its sovereign members.

Thus, government by confederacy is slow, ponderous, and in many instances, incapable of taking action until the action itself has become irrelevant. One of the major factors helping to seal the fate of the southern confederacy in the Civil War was the confederate form of government chosen by those states and the slow reactions of that government occasioned by conflicts among the confederate states. But unlike the southern confederacy, the impotence of the Continental Congress did not prove to be fatal. Recognizing the problem early, representatives from the states met in Philadelphia in 1787 and replaced the continental confederation with a federal system of government.

In a federal system, the central government remains a government of delegated powers. Theoretically, all power not delegated is reserved to the states or to the people. A significant difference, when compared to a confederation, is that the powers delegated are considerably more extensive, and their exercise does not require the consent of individual states. Under our Constitution, the states are not sovereign. However, they possess "reserved" powers—all those not "delegated." While the federal government can only exercise powers delegated to it in the Constitution, it operates on persons directly, rather than through state governments, and is thus a truly national government.

In a system of the type we have described, conflict among the branches of government is consciously structured into the political system via separation of powers and check and balances. Conflict is also inevitable on such questions as: (1) What are the delegated powers and the reserved powers? (2) What is the scope of the powers in each sphere? (3) What are the proper spheres of action for each of the three branches of the federal government? and (4) How is conflict about such matters to be resolved? Theory, for all its great value, does not resolve conflict. It only furnishes a framework within which discussion and debate may legitimately occur. The answers to the questions posed, therefore, are likely to change over time, while theory remains constant. And at any given time the answers are likely to reflect the configurations of political power then in existence. However, this does not relieve us of the necessity of adopting structures that will provide answers, for a time, to all questions regarding the distribution of governmental power. Early philosophers did not find this a simple matter. John Locke seemed to think that no person could judge such a conflict—possibly implying settlement by force. But the framers of the Constitution and those who have implemented their work have provided a better solution to the problem.

JUDICIAL REVIEW

One way of resolving conflict is by means of third-party intervention. Where conflicting interpretations of the Constitution arise between Congress and the President, or an interpretation of either is questioned, one might reasonably expect that third party to be the United States Supreme Court. This is not to suggest that Congress and the Executive do not have the responsibility to interpret the Constitution. When each acts, it must always trace its power to do so to some provision of the Constitution which appropriately delegates the power used. President Ford could pardon former President Nixon in 1973 because Article II, Section 2, gave him the power to pardon for offenses against the United States. Similarly, Congress could regulate the wages of state hospital employees in 1968 under the power granted it in the commerce clause (*Maryland v. Wirtz,* 192 U.S. 183). But when congressional or presidential understandings of the Constitution are questioned, some final and authoritative interpretation is needed. That final authority, the power of *judicial review,* now rests with the Supreme Court. It is not at all clear that the framers intended the Court to possess the power to invalidate the acts of a President or a Congress when those acts were thought to be in conflict with one or more constitutional provisions. The best that can be said is that most of the framers probably intended to vest such a power in the Court. But, in any event, any doubt that existed was resolved with a bold seizure of power by John Marshall in 1803. Momentarily, we shall see just how that was done, in the case of *Marbury v. Madison.*[6]

The related question—the power of the Supreme Court to nullify state laws in conflict with the Constitution—was less in doubt. Article VI, Section 2 binds state judges to give the Constitution precedence over state statutes or state constitutions. As early as 1792, federal circuit courts were holding state laws null and void when in conflict with the Constitution (*Champion v. Casey,* U.S. Cir. Ct. for Rhode Island). In 1810, the Supreme Court made initial use of its power to overrule state legislative acts in the case of *Fletcher v. Peck.*[7] And after decisions in *Martin v. Hunter's Lessee*[8] and *Cohens v. Virginia,*[9] the Court's authority to nullify state legislation was generally conceded, though initially the decisions caused some political controversy.

If the Supreme Court is to be granted the power of *judicial review*—the power to nullify actions of Congress, the President, or the states in conflict with the Constitution—structures and procedures for carrying out such a function must be established.

THE SUPREME COURT IN THE AMERICAN COURT SYSTEM

The American court system as a whole involves both state and federal laws. State courts deal primarily with state law, and federal courts with federal laws. But for purposes of federal constitutional law, state and federal courts combine to form a single court system, with final and ultimate authority to interpret the Constitution vested in the U.S. Supreme Court. Thus, many cases commencing in state courts are subsequently brought to the Supreme Court for final resolution. Such cases must, at a minimum, involve a question of federal statutory, constitutional, or treaty law.

Figure 1 arrays legislative courts, constitutional courts, and state courts—all of which furnish cases for Supreme Court decision. The United States claims court and the court of military appeals constitute two examples of courts established by Congress under Article I of the Constitution, the legislative article. Thus, they are known as "legislative courts." The courts of appeals and district courts are based on the power granted Congress in the judicial article (III) to establish "inferior courts." These are known as "constitutional courts." The important distinction is that judges on constitutional courts serve for good behavior (essentially life), while judges on legislative courts serve at the pleasure of Congress. Moreover, the compensation of judges on constitutional courts may not be reduced during their continuance in office. These provisions are intended to promote the independence of constitutional court judges from the vagaries of political pressure or influence. As Figure 1 makes clear, cases from four of the five courts portrayed may come directly to the Supreme Court, while cases from district courts (the federal trial court) must usually pass through one of twelve courts of appeals.

For purposes of generating cases for Supreme Court Review, the claims court, the court of military appeals, and other legislative courts are not significant. As for cases coming from federal constitutional courts and state courts,

FIGURE 1

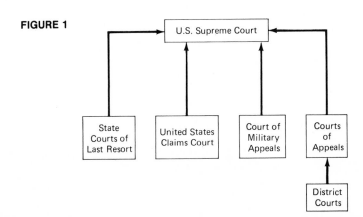

many knock on the Supreme Court's door but few gain admittance. For to open the lock, one must have the appropriate jurisdictional key.

SUPREME COURT JURISDICTION

The most important concept in determining the parameters of the Court's powers is that of jurisdiction. The Constitution does not empower the justices to resolve any and all conflicts that might catch their eye. Instead, the Court must sit and wait for cases to be brought to it, i.e., it is by design a reactive institution. Nonetheless, the Court selects the cases it will review from a larger number of requests, and the case pool usually includes issues pressing for social or legal resolution, as well as issues which, for whatever reason, the justices are anxious to resolve. But this power should not be exaggerated, for the Court's own rules and decisions severely limit the number of cases that can be heard in each Court term—usually the months of October through June.

Original and Appellate Jurisdiction

Cases involving specific issues may be brought to the Court in two major ways. Article III of the Constitution permits particular types of cases affecting certain officers of foreign governments and certain cases involving a state as a party to actually begin (or originate) in the Supreme Court. In all other appropriate cases, at least one federal or state court must have decided the case—a decision that may then be brought to the Supreme Court for review. A case falling in this category may be reviewed by the Court under its "appellate" jurisdiction, as contrasted to the Court's "original" jurisdiction mentioned above.

The Court's original jurisdiction is specified in Article III. The same article grants the Court appellate jurisdiction but subject to such "Exceptions, and under such Regulations as the Congress shall make." Under this provision, Congress has on occasion diminished the Court's jurisdiction to hear certain kinds of cases. Thus, after the decision *Ex Parte McCardle*,[10] Congress successfully repealed a statute conferring jurisdiction on the Court to review the authority of federal military commissions. As a consequence, a southern newspaper editor was denied review of his claim that he could not be legally tried by such commissions. Nevertheless, the scope of congressional control over Supreme Court jurisdiction is somewhat unclear. At the margin, it would not appear that Congress could accomplish via control of appellate jurisdiction substantive ends that it otherwise lacks the power to reach.

Obligatory Jurisdiction The appellate jurisdiction of the Court may be described as obligatory and discretionary. The obligatory jurisdiction is referred to as "appeals jurisdiction." Such jurisdiction stems from various congressional statutes which require the Supreme Court to review certain kinds of cases coming from federal and state courts. In such cases, the losing party below has the "right" to appeal the lower court decision to the Supreme

Court. But this is a statutory, not a constitutional, right. Examples of holdings subject to obligatory jurisdiction would include: (1) a decision by a court of appeals that a state statute violates the Constitution, (2) a decision by a court of appeals or a district court that a federal statute is unconstitutional in a civil case brought against the United States, and (3) a decision by a state court declaring a federal treaty invalid or upholding a state statute against a charge of unconstitutionality.

Although the Supreme Court is required to review cases coming under its appeals jurisdiction, it must decide for every appeals case whether jurisdiction is properly invoked, i.e., whether the case comes within the requirements set forth in the statute establishing jurisdiction. Obviously, one does not possess a right granted by statute unless one meets the conditions established by the statute to acquire the right. Generally, however, this consideration has not been a problem for appellants, insofar as the explicit statutory requirements are concerned.

More troublesome is a requirement imposed by the Court itself. Appeals must not only raise a federal question, they must raise a "substantial" federal question.[11] This means that the federal question must not be frivolous or devoid of merit and that it must not have been decided in earlier Supreme Court cases. Since the meaning of such terms as "frivolous," "devoid of merit," and "substantial" is relatively subjective, the obligatory jurisdiction of the Court is more discretionary than meets the eye, thereby giving the Court greater latitude as to which cases it will fully review. Finally, it may be noted that one who seeks to have the Court exercise its obligatory jurisdiction is known as the "appellant," while the other party to the case is the "appellee." Since the Court frequently refers to the parties in such a fashion, understanding of these terms will make it easier to follow the arguments presented in Court opinions.

Discretionary Jurisdiction   The discretionary jurisdiction of the Court also has a statutory basis, the so-called Judge's Bill of 1925 as amended.[12] Over 90 percent of the Court's docket in a given term consists of requests for a writ of certiorari. The writ is nothing more than an order from a higher court to a lower court to send up the records and papers in a case so that it may be properly reviewed. The granting of the writ at the Supreme Court level is entirely discretionary. If the writ is issued, the case will normally be given review "on the merits," i.e., the substantive legal question in the case will be considered and a formal decision usually made. Those who petition the Court for writs of certiorari are referred to by the Court as "petitioners," while the second party to the case is the "respondent."

It should be clear at this point that the Supreme Court makes two kinds of significant decisions: (1) whether to grant review of a case, and (2) if review is granted, how to decide the substantive legal issue which the case raises or suggests. While in this text we will be concerned primarily with cases falling in the second category, the importance of the first class of decisions should be underlined. If the Court cannot be persuaded to review an appellant's case, it matters little whether right or justice is on the appellant's side. But, given the extreme time constraints under which the Court must work and the limits on human capabilities, the Court does not and cannot sit to correct all the mistakes that might be made by lower court judges ruling on federal questions.

In exercising the Court's discretionary jurisdiction, the justices play a political role in which they select for review 150 to 200 of the thousands of cases presented each term. More often than not, these are cases raising social, economic, and political issues that are national in scope. All this puts in perspective the so-called right to have one's case decided by the Supreme Court. For all practical purposes, no such right exists. One who is successful in having a case reviewed by the Court has been accorded a rare privilege indeed. In this sense, the justices perform more of a political than a legal role, leaving it to lower courts to provide "justice" in most cases presenting "merely legal" claims.

SOME LIMITATIONS ON THE EXERCISE OF JURISDICTION

We have noted that the granting and denying of plenary or full review are discretionary decisions in the Supreme Court. Yet, that is not to say that such decisions are made without guidelines or that the Court's discretion is unlimited. In fact, a number of restrictions on the use of jurisdictional power are to be found either in the Constitution or in the internal rules and practices of the Court itself.

Cases and Controversies

Article III specifically limits the Court to deciding cases and controversies arising under the Constitution, laws, and treaties of the United States. Such cases raise what is called a "federal question," the presence of which is necessary to invoke Supreme Court jurisdiction. A case of controversy must involve adverse litigants with real interests. There must be an actual injury to the complaining party; the injury must have already occurred or be certain of occurring. Moreover, the injury must be of a personal nature[13] and must result in the violation of a legal right.[14] The determination of whether such requirements have been met is a matter for the Supreme Court itself to decide on a case-by-case basis. That means that decisions have gone both ways, a not unusual fact in and of itself. The Court, for example, has held that a mere listing of "Communist" organizations by the attorney general is sufficient to meet the injury requirement, since such a listing, even with no formally associated punishment, interferes with recruitment and other rights of such organizations.[15]

The Court has held that an impairment of the effectiveness of a citizen's vote by a state meets the injury requirement.[16] It has also held that a merchant forced to close on Sunday has been sufficiently damaged economically to challenge the constitutionality of the action.[17] However, the same merchant could not challenge such a law as a violation of the right to exercise one's religion freely unless Sunday closing was claimed and shown to constitute such an interference.[18] This would seem easier to establish if one worships on Sunday rather than on some other day of the week—i.e., the injury requirement in this context might be more readily established under the "free exercise of religion" clause of the First Amendment by a Protestant or a Catholic than by an Orthodox member of the Jewish faith.

Standing

An appellant who cannot establish the requisite conditions under the cases or controversies rule is said to lack the "standing" to litigate. If one lacks standing, one cannot legally challenge governmental action even though a constitutional right might have been violated. To establish the standing necessary to the pursuit of any claim against the government, an appellant must meet the requirements of adverse interests and personal injury, and also show that the issue is historically capable of resolution by a court of law. This latter condition is the condition or requirement of "justiciability." The concept of standing is central to two cases in Chapter 2, *Massachusetts v. Mellon* and *Flast v. Cohen.* The concept of justiciability is addressed at length in *Baker v. Carr* and in the section below on political questions.

Political Questions

At the very outset of its existence, the Supreme Court suggested that it would not accept jurisdiction of cases involving political questions.[19] There is no clearcut definition that will allow one to know a political question when one sees one, and the justices have a great deal of discretion in identifying such questions. The determinations are made on an ad hoc, case-by-case basis. Questions arising in the field of foreign affairs have most frequently been categorized as "political" and not reviewable by the Supreme Court. However, the doctrine does have and has had domestic applications, as seen in *Luther v. Borden,* a case included in Chapter 2.

Generally, where it is considered wiser to attribute finality to a decision of a political branch of government, the Court will do so. An example is the reluctance of the Court to interfere with decisions by a Congress or a President that a war has ended.[20] The Court has also declined to decide whether a treaty has been broken[21] and whether the President has correctly called out the militia.[22] Under the political-question doctrine, the Court more recently has denied review of the following matters:

1 The administration of public lands.[23]
2 The guarantee of a "republican form of government.[24]
3 The formal recognition of the Soviet Union.[25]

4 Federal control over the 3-mile marginal ocean belt.[26]
5 Federal policy regarding aliens.[27]

Since 1962, the Court has addressed a number of questions—e.g., apportionment of legislative seats,[28] congressional control over seating members of Congress,[29] and state restrictions on new political parties[30]—that might have been thought to be political questions. This implies a possible weakening of the doctrine, but that implication should not be accepted too quickly. For the device serves political purposes; it enables the Court to either decide an issue or dodge it. The inclination to do one or the other is bound to vary with the personnel—the justices—who sit on that high bench. More experience is needed to determine whether recent decisions on political questions represent something other than a temporary departure from earlier practices, particularly given the fact that the Court itself says that the doctrine of political questions is very much alive.[31]

Mootness and Abatement

A case becomes moot when the conflict under which it arose has been ended or abated—i.e., there is no longer a live case or controversy. The Supreme Court has traditionally declined to exercise jurisdiction in mooted cases. Indeed, the Court may refuse to hear a moot case even if the Court itself is responsible for producing that condition. In *Atherton Mills v. Johnston,*[32] Gene Johnston sued to prevent the company from discharging a minor in order to avoid violation of the Child Labor Act. That act imposed a tax on corporations employing minors between ages 14 and 16 more than eight hours per day. The Court held the case for over thirty months, and required that it be argued twice. By that time, Johnston had reached the age of 16. This had the effect of mooting the issue, and the Court then declined to decide it on that basis. One effect of this action was to avoid having to rule on the constitutionality of the statute, though we cannot know whether that was the Court's motivation.

In *DeFunis v. Odegaard* (416 U.S. 312), the Court declined to reach a claim that Marco DeFunis had been illegally denied admission to law school after a lower court forced his admission and graduation was assured, even though these developments resulted from an order barring the school from ejecting DeFunis until the Supreme Court had heard and decided the case. This case is particularly relevant for political science students since Justice Douglas's issuance of such an order suggests the possibility of using legitimate legal procedures to accomplish political or legally extraneous ends. But since DeFunis's case was based on his claim of reverse discrimination, one cannot rule out the possibility that the Court was simply not ready to decide such an issue at that time. In that event, mootness would be a rationalization of the failure to reach the merits of the issue.

Under some conditions, the Court will proceed to hear a mooted case, as in *Roe v. Wade.*[33] Jane Roe challenged a Texas abortion statute which limited abortions to those performed on advice of a medical doctor to save the mother's life. Roe was successful in getting the district court to declare the statute a violation of the Ninth and Fourteenth Amendments, but the court declined to enjoin enforcement. Jane Roe was a single pregnant female when she started her suit, but by the time the issue was heard in the district court, her pregnancy had apparently terminated. On review, the Supreme Court proceeded to decide the case in spite of mootness, saying that, though the general rule is that an actual controversy must exist at the review stage, pregnancy is an act capable of repetition and the case would be heard irrespective of mootness. The practical reason for making such exceptions lies in the economic use of judicial resources. If a mooted issue is likely to be recurring, there is little point in declining to rule on it, thereby inviting additional litigation to test the question. At the same time, one cannot rule out the possibility that political and social considerations persuaded the Court to rule on abortion at this time. Abatement may occur for a number of reasons, including, under appropriate circumstances, death of a party to the case, withdrawal of a legal action, settlement of the case out of court, repeal of a relevant statute, or when the conduct at issue occurs before the case is heard. If the event mooting a case occurs after the Supreme Court has granted review, the Court may revoke its action as improvidently taken. If mootness occurs before review has been granted but while the case is pending on the Court's docket, the Court will usually grant review, vacate or reverse the judgment below, and send the case back down for dismissal by the lower court.

It is evident that at the Supreme Court level, mootness and abatement are related to the case or controversy and standing requirements. When an issue has been mooted, i.e., no real conflict of interests continues to exist, there is no case or controversy and no standing to sue.

The Supreme Court is not bound by any determination of mootness except its own. A party must suggest dismissal of a case for mootness or a lower court judge may actually base a decision on a finding of mootness. But the Supreme Court will decide for itself on the question, as well as on what to do about mootness if present. Thus, the concept must be included among the political doors that the Court may open when it feels the occasion so warrants.

Advisory Opinions

It follows from our discussion of the threshold requirement of cases and controversies that the Supreme Court may not issue advisory opinions, i.e., an opinion on a point of law not raised in some concrete case. Yet, the Constitution does not forbid advisory opinions, and in the first few years after adoption of the Constitution, it was thought that the President could legitimately consult the Court on questions of law. It is easy to understand why the executive and legislative branches of government might wish to consult the justices about the legality of an action or program before that action or program is instigated. If the Court pronounces illegality after a program is implemented, great social, political, and economic costs may be entailed. It is much better to avoid all that by discovering in advance whether a planned action or program will pass muster. Such advance advice would also undercut opponents of a measure who might argue that the measure is unconstitutional as a means of defeating its passage or who burden the courts with litigation on the matter after passage.

Convenient as it might be, however, we have a system of separated powers and a constitutional requirement that the Supreme Court limit itself to cases and controversies. In the earlier period, the idea of manipulating these concepts in order to justify reaching preferred political/legal decisions was not as readily acceptable as it came to be in a later day. There was some doubt in President Washington's mind when, in the first historically known request for an advisory opinion, he directed his secretary of state to address twenty-nine questions to the justices in 1793—even though Jefferson himself thought the Court would respond to them.[34] The questions pertained to the appropriate interpretation of the laws and treaties of the United States as they related to international law stemming from the French Revolution.

In a reply authored by Chief Justice Jay on August 18, 1793, the Court declined to answer Washington's questions on separation-of-powers grounds. This put in place at the outset a practice that has served American democracy well. If the Court judges political questions only when "forced"—i.e., only when the questions arise between parties with a real conflict and a real interest—politically based suspicion and hostility toward the Court is less likely to be engendered. It may be noted that individual justices have communicated with the President and the Congress on occasion and that these communications sometimes discuss the constitutionality of pending or proposed action. Chief Justice Hughes, for example, wrote Senator Wheeler that President Franklin Roosevelt's 1937 plan to increase the number of justices on the Court was unconstitutional.[35] And earlier, Chief Justice Taney advised the secretary of the treasury privately that a tax levied on the salaries of judges was unconstitutional.[36] But it is still accurate to say that the Supreme Court as a court will not issue advisory opinions.

SUPREME COURT PROCEDURES

Like all courts, the Supreme Court proceeds in an orderly and structured fashion. A general familiarity with the Court's structure and procedures will enhance one's understanding of its workways and sensitize one to the discretion-points available to the justices as they go about their daily business.

Terms

The Supreme Court sits for a term that begins on the first Monday in October and usually runs until it has disposed of all cases available in that term. Ordinarily, this means from October to late June or early July. This is known as the "October term" and is designated by the year in which October falls. Thus, the October 1982 term began on October 4, 1982, and ended on July 6, 1983.

Summer and special terms may also be scheduled when necessary, though the Court generally avoids exercising this option. The justices need the summer months to review the steady stream of certiorari petitions and other applications for relief, which knows no letup from January through December. Without the summer recess, each justice would likely begin the new term each October with a backlog of several thousand cases to review, and even working relatively long hours does not resolve the backlog problems of the justices. While continuing to sit in the summer months would enable the Court to grant full review to a greater number of cases, it is not at all clear that the tradeoff would represent an improvement in the Court's efficient handling of its workload.

An added consideration is the need of the justices for some rest and relaxation during the summer and Christmas periods. Their job is probably as physically and mentally burdensome as any position in government, with the exception of the presidency. And even the President is not meting out justice to individual citizens on a day-to-day basis. The daily making of decisions which may send people to prison or to the executioner's block is psychologically taxing—especially when done over the long term. Clearly, the Supreme Court justice is a unique decision-maker among all the public officials who operate our governmental system.

Jurisdictional Briefs

Before the Supreme Court can make a jurisdictional decision or a decision on the substantive issue in a case, it must reasonably inform itself about the issues and the legal or social reasons for providing one decision or another. This is accomplished in part through printed briefs. A party that petitions the Court for certiorari is required to submit a printed statement composed and organized in strict accordance with Supreme Court rules. At present, this statement, or brief, must address the opinion or decision of the lower court in summary form, the particular kind of jurisdiction the Supreme Court is being asked to exercise, the question or questions which the case represents, the statutory or constitutional provisions of relevance, the facts of the case, and the reasons why review should be granted. These matters are then followed by a concluding section and an appendix containing the opinion and judgment of the court below.

The brief of the opposing party, by comparison, is only required to inform the Court as to why review should be denied. The party requesting review is also permitted the option of a short "reply brief." If the case falls under the Court's appeals jurisdiction, the appellant's brief must address, in addition to the matters sketched above, the federal question at issue and convince the justices that the question is "substantial"—a concept that gives the justices great leeway in accepting and rejecting appeals.

In addition to the briefs of direct-party litigants, the Court may also receive the jurisdictional briefs of amici curiae. An amicus is formally a "friend of the court" with an interest in a case who believes that he or she can assist the Court in making a proper decision by submitting argument or information not otherwise available to the justices. Permission to submit an amicus brief is conditioned on the consent of the direct parties in the case or the permission of the Court itself.

The Rule of Four

Once the jurisdictional briefs are in hand and enough cases have accumulated, the Court schedules an internal conference at which the justices will decide who is to be granted and who denied review. These decisions will be made in accordance with the Rule of Four. Under that rule, if as many as four of the nine justices wish to grant review, it will be granted. This is true for both appeals and certiorari cases, a fact which underscores our earlier suggestion that the Court has wide discretion in exercising its "obligatory" jurisdiction.

If the number of justices participating in a case is sufficiently low, the Rule of Four may become the Rule of Three. This can occur in two ways. Should a case, for example, garner three votes for review in a six-member Court, one of the justices voting against review may change his or her vote to grant review. Or the Court may simply decide in advance of decision in a reduced Court to use the Rule of Three in a particular case. The reasoning is that four is not a magic number. The intention is to grant review when a "substantial" number of justices believe the case important enough to warrant full consideration. While four is a substantial portion of nine, a substantial portion of a reduced Court may be less than four.

Recusal

Since a quorum in the Court is six justices, cases may be decided by anywhere from six to nine justices. Individual justices sometimes "recuse" themselves, i.e., decline to participate in a particular case, for various reasons. It may be that one of the attorneys in the case is related to a justice, is a former law partner of the justice, or is a member of the justice's former law firm. Or the justice may own stock in a corporate litigant, or may have participated in the same case as a lower judge or as a prosecutor. All of these are sound reasons for recusal in a given case. But when recusal is exercised, it is purely voluntary and requires no explanation from the justice. Justices may also be absent from the Court for reasons of illness, or, on occasion, because of assignment outside the country.[37]

Conference and Preconference Procedures

All requests for review will not be considered and voted on in conference. The reason is clear. The Court receives thousands of briefs each term and over 4,500 appeals or petitions for certiorari. Many of these cases are frivolous or, in the eyes of the Court, devoid of merit, and others are too politically sensitive to be accepted for review, in which case the Court may use as an excuse that the case is not justiciable. The Court's workload generally produces pressure for administrative practices that will facilitate the processing of cases. One way of reserving conference time for the more important cases is by use of a "discuss list."

Copies of all petitions for certiorari and all appeals are routinely routed to each of the nine justices, who in turn assign some of the work to their clerks. During the 1972 term, five of the justices (Burger, Blackmun, Powell, Rehnquist, and White) formed a "certiorari pool"—i.e., they decided to pool their clerks and divide the petitions among all five justice's chambers. The memoranda prepared by each justice's clerks are sent to all five justices. The maximum result of such a procedure would be to reduce the time committed to the screening of certiorari petitions by 80 percent. As Justice Powell has pointed out, each of the five justices remains ultimately responsible for the decision he makes on each certiorari petition, no matter who does the preparatory staff work or how the work is divided administratively.

As this is being written, it is safe to say that the certiorari pool is still operative and that the original five members are still participating. What is not known is whether that number has grown in the past thirteen years. When the pool was initially formed, Brennan vehemently opposed the idea, and Marshall also declined to join. Given that the five original pool members were and continue to be more conservative on many matters than Justices Brennan and Marshall, and that conservative and liberal justices may not see eye to eye on what cases to select for review, it is likely that Justices Brennan and Marshall remain outside the pool. We do not know, however, whether Justices Stevens and O'Conner have joined the certiorari pool since coming to the Court in 1975 and 1982, respectively.

Prior to conference, the Chief Justice prepares a discuss list and circulates it to the associate justices. The list contains the name of each case considered worthy of conference discussion—usually about 30 percent of the total cases requesting review. A justice who wishes to add a case to the list may do so by notifying the Chief Justice. All cases not on the final discuss list are automatically denied review without the benefit of conference discussion. This is not to say that cases not reaching conference are not thoroughly reviewed by individual justices (with the help of their law clerks) in their chambers. However, such cases do not receive the benefit of collective discussion and debate which the conference setting permits. In the *U.S. Reports,* the cases denied review after conference discussion are not differentiated from other cases denied review. Thus, with rare exceptions, we are not able to identify the cases reaching conference.

At conference, the justices may take any number of actions in disposing of a petition for review or an appeal. But, in most instances, a case is either denied or granted full or plenary review. When review is granted, it may be summary or plenary. If summary, the Court will make a decision on the merits of issue. The decision will be made at the same or a later conference. It will be published without opinion.

Briefs on the Merits

If the Court grants plenary review, additional procedures are called into play. First of all, decision on the merits will be made at a later conference. Prior to that decision, litigating parties are required to brief the legal issues in the case. The "brief on the merits" must provide an index and table of cases at the outset. Then follow, in order, a statement regarding the opinions of the lower courts, a statement of the jurisdictional grounds involved, and the questions which are to be resolved on review. The selection and framing of these questions are of crucial importance. For although the justices have the discretion to decide what issues will be addressed in cases accepted for review, they usually will not address any questions not identified at this stage. If the Court gives no guidance, the attorney for a petitioner or appellant is free to develop the questions as he or she wishes, subject to the constraints flowing from the questions posed in the jurisdictional brief. In all cases, the attorney must decide how many questions to pose, what they should be, and exactly how they should be formulated, i.e., whether in broad, general terms or in narrow, specific terms. How the attorney goes about this task may be influenced by the justices with whom he or she is dealing and by recent policy trends of Court majorities on related issues.

Recent evidence indicates that as the number of questions increases, the possibility that "issue fluidity" will occur increases.[38] Issue fluidity occurs when the Court ignores an issue posed by an attorney or addresses some issue not posed in deciding the case on the merits. Attorneys also might be influenced by the extent to which they perceive the Court as liberal or conservative. For example, if the Court is liberal on civil rights, the attorney may pose a civil rights question as broadly as possible. If, on the other hand, the Court majority is viewed as unsympathetic to a certain class of claims, the attorney may present the narrowest question possible so to control the damage should the Court rule against the appellant.[39] Finally, the Court majority itself may, in granting plenary review, either (1) specify the questions to be briefed or (2) require the attorney to brief issues not mentioned in the jurisdictional brief.[40]

After the identification of questions, the brief on the merits must include reference to the statutes or constitutional provisions involved, a statement of the case and identification of materials relevant to its resolution, a summary of the argument, the argument itself, and a conclusion which specifies precisely the relief requested and the names of counsel. The brief of the respondent or appellee at this stage may be limited generally to a statement of the case, the arguments, and the conclusion. Yet, many attorneys choose to follow the same format as the party requesting relief—an option that the Court leaves open to them.

It is evident that the justices direct the development of information that will assist them in deciding a case with dispatch. By requiring all parties to follow the same organizational format, to present certain crucial information, and to present it in summary as well as extended form, the justices hope to reduce the time necessary to read and digest the briefs on the merits. Certainly these organizational schemes reduce the redundancy, triviality, irrelevancy, and simple long-windedness that sometimes threaten to characterize the arguments of petitioning attorneys. The burden is thereby reduced for the justices. These procedures also lighten the load of the law clerks who, on request, provide memoranda on cases to the justices.

Oral Argument

While it is possible to decide a case "on the briefs," plenary review normally implies oral argument before the Court by attorneys for both sides after the briefs have been read and analyzed. Normally, each side is permitted to argue for 30 minutes, though the Court may extend the time at its option, especially when issues are of great importance, as in *Brown v. Board of Education,* the school desegregation case. No attorney is permitted to simply stand and state a position. As soon as the clock begins to run, the justices will pepper the attorney with questions, often following up the answers with more questions. Thus, in many cases, the oral argument is actually a question-and-answer session which the justices use to familiarize themselves further with the case and to explore possible social or other ramifications not discussed in the written briefs.

Supreme Court Opinions

After oral argument, the argued cases will be discussed and voted on in conference. A member of the majority will then be assigned to write the Court's opinion in the case. This assignment is made by the Chief Justice if he or she votes as a member of the majority. Otherwise, the justice in the majority with the greatest number of years on the Court makes the assignment. The justice receiving the assignment then prepares a draft which is printed and circulated among the other justices. The draft opinion will usually state the facts of the case, the issue to be resolved, the Court's decision on the issue, and the Court's explanation of or justification for the decision it has reached. If more than one issue has been decided, a justification for the decision on each will normally be included.

The structure and reasoning of an opinion "for the Court" obviously invites disagreement. The justices may agree as to the relief to be granted or denied a litigant but disagree as to the justification for it. They may agree in all respects

with the opinion's treatment of some issues but not with the treatment accorded others. They may even disagree with the opinion's statement of the "facts" of the case. This is possible because, technically, a case is decided on the "legally relevant" facts only. Thus, should the Supreme Court be confronted with an allegedly illegal, warrantless search of a black married woman's luggage in her parked pale-magenta Buick, marriage status would clearly be irrelevant, as would the color of her automobile, her race, and her sex. The fact that the search was conducted without a warrant would clearly be legally relevant. But the facts of (1) a *luggage* search, (2) in an *automobile,* (3) that was *parked,* may or may not be facts essential to the settlement of the procedural issue in dispute. The ability to choose one's relevant facts not only may lead to disagreement among the justices, it contributes to their ability to reflect policy preferences in the decisions they make.

The draft opinion, at a minimum, strives to get agreement from the justices voting with the majority. But defections may make that impossible after the majority justices have closely examined the draft. If a majority of the justices find the draft opinion unacceptable, some bargaining and compromise may then ensue in an attempt to negotiate a majority opinion. If that fails, the case may be transferred to another justice to see whether he or she can produce an opinion that the majority will support. That, however, is a rare occurrence. A more likely outcome is that there will be no majority opinion in the case. The "opinion of the Court" will be a plurality opinion, i.e., an opinion subscribed to by less than a majority of the participating justices.

In addition to the opinion for the Court, the justices who disagree may write concurring or dissenting opinions at their discretion. A justice who writes a concurring opinion agrees with the majority as to how the case should be decided but disagrees about the proper legal basis or reasoning for the decision. In a concurrence, the justice explains the justification for the decision he or she has made. The writer of a dissenting opinion, by comparison, disagrees with the Court about the decision itself. In such an opinion, the justice will usually argue for a different outcome and explain why the outcome he or she prefers should be favored by the Court. A justice may also use a dissent to dissect and analyze the Court's opinion (plurality or majority), or other opinions written by his or her colleagues. These dissenting opinions are often of great value in helping the student understand what the Court majority has omitted, why it has taken the action it has, the legal and social consequences of the action, and the general shortcomings of the Court's logic and analysis of the problem presented in the case. The dissenting opinion has become quite prevalent since World War II, and during any recent term of the Court there is likely to be at least one dissent in a majority of cases. Therefore, we have included many dissenting opinions in this text, and students are encouraged to read them.

The Court's decisions in cases given plenary review and the accompanying opinions are generally presented in open court with all the justices present. Until that time, all votes and opinions are tentative and subject to change. The presentation of the decision in public occurs on what is known as "opinion day." This rubric reflects the fact that in addition to announcing the decision, the opinion for the Court is read or summarized by the justice who authored it. Where several opinions are ready for presentation, a reverse order of seniority in terms of years on the Court determines the order of the justices presenting the opinions. Beyond the opinions for the Court, any author of a concurring or dissenting opinion may read or summarize that opinion if he or she wishes.

The opinions reported in this text are edited versions of the full opinions. Should you wish to read the complete version in any given case, the full citations provided with each case will enable you to quickly find the case in your library. Cases should always be cited by title to the *U.S. Reports* unless that citation is not available. While the year of decision is not formally a part of a case citation, it is often useful information and should be included if possible.

SUPREME COURT DECISION-MAKING

Two aspects of Supreme Court decision-making may be differentiated: jurisdictional decision-making and decision-making on the merits.

Jurisdictional Decision-Making

Since the Court's decisions to grant or deny jurisdiction are almost totally discretionary, with no recorded vote or opinion explaining Court action, we are severely challenged to isolate and identify the appropriate decisional basis. Yet, it is important to try—to attempt to understand the factors that "tend" to motivate the majority of the justices to grant review in specific case situations. This is important from the standpoint of knowledge per se. It also has a practical side. To appeal a case or petition the Supreme Court for a writ of certiorari is costly, both in time and money. If one is totally without financial resources (which is the condition of most prison inmates who appeal), the Court may modify its rules or foot the bill for materials, legal fees, and other charges associated with an appeal or a petition. The Court does this by granting the complaining party the status of "in forma pauperis"—literally, "the manner or character of a pauper."

A litigant who is not proceeding in forma pauperis must pay all the costs associated with an appeal or petition—thousands of dollars in a typical case. Some clients may be so well off financially or so emotionally involved in a case that money is no object. However, this is not the case for most litigants. Most are desirous of knowing, before committing substantial resources to an application for Supreme Court review, just what the chance of actually receiving review is likely to be. It is a legitimate function of the client's attorney to provide such information in specific cases. In order to so serve, the attorney must understand the conditions under which review is granted or denied. Only then can the attorney assess the client's case in the context of knowledge of Supreme Court decision-making and offer appropriate advice. The problem is that when the Court exercises discretionary jurisdiction, it is not required to, and normally does not, explain the basis of its action.

In recognition of the interest of the bar in such matters, the Court offers its internal rule 17 as a guide. That rule, after reiterating that review on a writ of certiorari is not a matter of right, states that:

> The following, while neither controlling nor fully measuring the Court's discretion, indicate the character of reasons that will be considered.
>
> **a** When a federal court of appeals has rendered a decision in conflict with the decision of another court of appeals on the same matter; or has decided a federal question in a way in conflict with a state court of last resort; or has so far departed from the accepted and usual course of judicial proceedings, or so far sanctioned such a departure by a lower court, as to call for an exercise of this Court's power of supervision.
>
> **b** When a state court of last resort has decided a federal question in a way in conflict with the decision of another state court of last resort or of a federal court of appeals.
>
> **c** When a state court or a federal court of appeals has decided an important question of federal law which has not been, but should be settled by this Court, or has decided a federal question in a way in conflict with applicable decisions of this Court.[41]

Since the reviewing of appeals also has a discretionary component, the references here to certiorari undoubtedly cover, in most instances, the factors that may motivate the Court in appeals cases. But, in any event, the rule does not tell us the conditions under which review will be granted or denied. The rule primarily emphasizes "conflict" between courts as a reason for Supreme Court review.[42] Such an emphasis should come as no surprise. In a federal system in which federal law is subject to interpretation by over 100 major federal courts and 50 different state courts of last resort, such conflict is inevitable. At the same time, the uniformity of federal law is a prerequisite for a stable legal and political system.

There is an intuitive appeal to the notion that federal laws, treaties, and the Constitution should have the same meaning in all parts of the United States. The Supreme Court, which usually has the final say on that meaning, can make a valuable contribution by resolving conflicting interpretations in the lower courts as they occur. Unfortunately, there appear to be more conflicts each term than the Court can possibly review. It is estimated that in the first eight terms of the Burger Court (1969–1976) there were, on the average, 172 conflicts with Supreme Court precedents and 155 conflicts between the rulings of courts of appeal per term which the Supreme Court declined to review. These figures do not cover conflicts between state courts of last resort or conflicts between state courts and federal courts of appeals. Since the Supreme Court clearly cannot review more than 150 to 200 cases per year in plenary fashion, many conflicts are simply left to stand.

The factors which are used to weed out reviewable conflicts from those to be denied review are not stated in rule 17. Nor has the Court offered elsewhere to share its knowledge of them. The importance of this knowledge, however, has motivated political scientists and others to seek to identify such factors by inference. The procedure generally is to examine the factors associated with cases granted review and the factors associated with those denied review and develop a theory based upon distinctions between the two sets of cases. Following that approach, it has been found that in addition to conflict, the presence of the federal government as the party requesting review and the type of case are important predictors of Supreme Court decisions to grant or deny review.

Decision on the Merits

The cases included in this text represent disputes in which review was granted. The opinions excerpted represent attempts by the majority of the justices to explain the reason or reasons for the decision taken in each case. Research in Court opinions and other sources of information suggests a number of factors that influence decisions on the merits. While no list can be exhaustive, the following would be included on any list of such factors:

1 Facts and law.
2 Stare decisis.
3 The idiosyncratic characteristics of the justices.
4 Law clerks.
5 Small-group factors.
6 The historical, social, and political environment of the Court at the time a decision is made.

Facts and Law   Supreme Court decision-making on the merits always begins with a consideration of facts and law. A case before the Court always represents a conflict between two parties. At the trial court level, there may be a conflict over the facts, but at the appellate level, the conflict is almost always over the law and what it requires in a given factual situation. Factual questions are decided by trial court juries and/or judges, and the Supreme Court almost always accepts the finding of fact made below.

In some cases, it is quite simple to read the facts, read the relevant law or constitutional provision, and determine the appropriate decision on the substantive issue raised by the facts. For example, Article I, Section 3 of the Constitution allows each state to be represented in the United States Senate by two senators. Imagine the following situation: The state of Illinois had two senators sitting in the Senate in 1965. In 1966, it elected a third person, Mr. Push, and sent him to Washington to be seated as a third senator from the state. Acting under its authority to determine who is qualified to sit as a senator (Article I, Section 5 of the Constitution), and citing Article I, Section 3, the Senate refused to seat Mr. Push. Push reacted to the refusal by suing the clerk of the Senate and assorted Senate officers in the federal district court for the District of Columbia, asserting a violation of his constitutional rights. The district court denied relief, but the federal court of appeals for the District of Columbia held that Mr. Push was entitled to the seat. The United States requested and was granted review by the Supreme Court. In such a situation, the Court would merely have to know the basic facts and the relevant constitutional provision. The appropriate decision would then be forced on the justices. The decision would be unanimous. The opinion for the Court would be short and unanimous—to wit: the Constitution permits each state two senators; Illinois is attempting to have three; Illinois is a state; three is not two; Mr. Push is rightfully denied a seat in the Senate and no violation of his constitutional rights has occurred. The court of appeals is reversed.

This trivial and oversimplified example makes one point absolutely clear. There are situations in which mere knowledge of facts and law is sufficient to determine the appropriate, indeed the required, decision on a legal issue raised by a set of facts. Having made that point, we may now draw a somewhat different picture of the role of facts and law in Supreme Court decision-making.

First off, such clearcut and obvious violations of the Constitution are not likely to occur. If they occur, they are likely to be quickly disposed of by lower courts. Thus, the U.S. Supreme Court simply accepts no such cases.

More typical is the following situation. It is 3:00 in the morning on a dark September night in Selma, Alabama. Within 30 minutes of that hour, a black man awakens two women in their bedrooms, attempting to pull a sheet off one and to rip the panties off another. Five years pass. Another woman in Selma is raped in her bed at knife point. About a month later, the mayor's daughter is attacked. However, after a struggle, a rape is avoided. On May 16, eight months after the initial attack, police arrest a man they think connected with all of the intrusions—William Earle Fikes. After questioning by police on four separate days, including a nine-hour session on the fourth day, Fikes confesses to the rape and burglary and signs a written statement to that effect.

In Alabama, the penalty for rape ran from 10 years to death. A jury brought in a guilty verdict but recommended (assessed) a 99-year sentence. Subsequently, Fikes was charged with entering the home of the mayor's daughter with the intent to commit rape—a capital offense. After conviction on this charge, Fikes was sentenced to death. The conviction was based largely on Fikes's signed confession. On petition, the U.S. Supreme Court granted certiorari.[43] Prior to this time, the Court had established that a coerced confession violates the due process clause of the Fourteenth Amendment.[44] But what is coercion? Is a confession coerced only if the prisoner has been beaten? Should psychological coercion be relevant? Is psychological coercion to be measured by merely counting the hours, days, or frequency of interrogatory sessions? Is access to family and friends or counsel after arrest pertinent to identifying coercion? Is it worth noting that Fikes was not arraigned for a week after his arrest—being subject to interrogation during this period?

At trial, Fikes did not testify about his confession, and the police testified that Fikes was told of his right to remain silent and that the confession had to be voluntary. Is the unchallenged testimony of the police to be believed? There was no evidence that Fikes's signing of the confession was anything but voluntary. Could one simply assume that police officers lie? Fikes had a record of mental illness, though he was mentally able to stand trial. Should the Court consider such facts in deciding whether coercion occurred? The Alabama Supreme Court found no coercion. Should the U.S. Supreme Court give credibility to that finding?

These and other questions presented the Court with something other than an open-and-shut case, a case that could turn on a single fact, such as a disparity between the number of senators authorized a state and the number claimed by Illinois in our hypothetical example. Indeed, in the Fikes case the Court could find no single fact or cluster of a limited set of facts on which the decision could turn. Instead, the conviction was reversed on the totality of the facts, which, when viewed collectively, convinced six justices that coercion had occurred. Yet, on the same facts, three justices found no illegal coercion. Writing for the dissenters, Justice Harlan said:

> I find nothing here beyond a state of facts upon which reasonable men might differ in their conclusions as to whether the confessions had been coerced. In the absence of anything in the conduct of the state authorities which "shocks the conscience" or does "more than offend some fastidious squeamishness or private sentimentalism about combatting crime too energetically, . . . " [we should] let Alabama's judgment stand.[45]

Obviously, Fikes's case is one that could have been decided either way. It illustrates the myriad of questions that the Court might be faced with routinely in disposing of cases on its plenary docket. It also illustrates that the same justices looking at the same facts can reach different conclusions about what the law or Constitution requires.

In 1966 the Court, in *Miranda v. Arizona*,[46] decided to narrow the subjective leeway available to the justices in responding to claims of unconstitutional coercion. *Miranda* requires that arrested persons be given certain warnings about their rights at the time of arrest and prior to interrogation, and that they may exercise these rights unless they choose to waive them. Waiver, moreover, is to be established by the interrogators. If the warning is not given and the rights are not waived, the testimony or confession cannot be used. However, one who reads cases dealing with claims of coercion in more recent years will find that subjective judgment has not been eliminated. Multiple questions arise and must be faced in such cases. Examples might include: Were the *Miranda* rights waived? If a claim of waiver is made, was the waiver free from coercion? Was the suspect in a physical and mental condition sufficient to give a waiver freely? If *Miranda* warnings were given, were they understood by the suspect? Was the suspect interrogated? Was the suspect interrogated in the absence of *Miranda* warnings? What is interrogation? Where did the interrogation occur?

Under what time and place constraints are *Miranda* warnings required by the Constitution? And so on.

Clearly, when dealing with such a complexity of fact and interpretation of fact, knowledge of fact and law will not provide a computerlike answer to the issue or issues posed by a case. Indeed, it is the very complexity of Supreme Court decision-making, and of understanding when and why the Court overtly makes policy, that makes it so interesting to study. The same factor suggests that although the antecedents of Supreme Court decisions certainly include fact and law, other factors may be of great importance. As noted earlier, some facts are legally relevant and some are not. How are the legally relevant facts to be selected from the total fact situation of a case? Which provision of the Constitution is to be employed to produce a decision in the case? In Fikes's case, there was a question about the racial composition of the grand jury, but the Supreme Court did not conceptualize the case in racial-discrimination terms even though Fikes was a black. So, there is often a choice both as to fact and as to law. To understand, to some extent, how these and other choices are influenced requires attention to additional considerations.

Stare Decisis   We have noted previously that the "opinion for the Court" in a given case may be a majority opinion or a plurality opinion. Whether a majority or a plurality opinion is produced has great consequences. In general, the Court follows the rule of stare decisis—i.e., the Court decides any given case consistent with its earlier rulings in similar cases. "Stare decisis" is a Latin term meaning "let the decision stand." Courts which follow this rule are said to "follow precedent." The Supreme Court, unlike lower courts ruling on federal questions, is not bound by its own precedents. Thus, on occasion, the Court will overrule an earlier precedent explicitly or will simply rule contrary to established precedent without reference to it. In the latter case, the Court engages in what is known as "overruling sub silentio," a procedure that may be used to avoid political or other types of criticism.

All of this is relevant for opinion writing. For while votes decide cases, opinions define and state the law—the legal basis of the decision. Written opinions are crucial for stare decisis, since the precedent in a case—the rule of the case—consists of the principle on which the case decision rests. This principle can only be derived from the written opinion. And clearly, the evolution in the law or in the meaning of the Constitution that occurs as precedents are weakened, modified, questioned, or overruled can only be derived from the written opinions of the Court. One must be careful to note that written opinions may or may not attract a majority of the justices. If no majority joins the opinion, it is known as a "plurality opinion" and technically carries no precedential weight. In this text, unless otherwise noted, the first vote given at the beginning of each case represents the number of justices subscribing to the reported opinion.

We have described stare decisis primarily in formal and traditional terms. The Supreme Court today continues to be influenced by the traditional perspective. But, in recent years, some writers have asserted that stare decisis has other components. Fred Kort has suggested that stare decisis may operate not through the principles or doctrines gleaned from past cases, but through Court decisions viewed as responses to facts. In such a case, the consistency sought is the same or similar decisional response whenever the same or similar fact situations are encountered, which may or may not entail doctrinal consistency.[47]

The present author has shown that Supreme Court decisions in cases challenging the exclusion of blacks from state jury systems in the period 1935–1977 can be readily explained as reactions to particular fact situations. In such cases, the complainant asserts that blacks have been systematically underrepresented in the trial or grand jury pools from which jurors in the jurisdiction are drawn and that the underrepresentation is based solely on race. This, it is alleged, violates the equal protection clause of the Fourteenth Amendment. The Supreme Court has held that purposeful and intentional racial discrimination in the selection of jurors is unconstitutional.[48] Yet, the Fourteenth Amendment does not tell us how purposeful and intentional discrimination is to be differentiated from that which occurs by chance. Chance discrimination, according to the Court, violates no constitutional right.[49]

An examination of the cases between 1935 and 1977 revealed that the Court found purposeful and intentional discrimination on a number of occasions, but in some cases the alleged discrimination was attributed to chance. These differences could not be effectively explained by traditional stare decisis. They are subject to explanation, however, via analysis of a single fact—the disparity between the percentage of blacks in the jury pool and the percentage of blacks in the population from which the jury pool was selected. The hypothetical explanation was that if the disparities were of a magnitude expected by chance, less than five times in a hundred, the Court would draw the inference of purposeful, intentional racial discrimination in violation of the Fourteenth Amendment. Otherwise, no violation would be found. This model accounted for 87 percent of the decisions made in this area in the period 1935–1977, i.e., twenty of twenty-three cases.[50]

A third view of stare decisis is reflected in the work of Martin Shapiro.[51] According to Shapiro, traditional stare decisis has broken down. To apply the traditional doctrine strictly, the facts of the present case and the past case from which the precedent is drawn must be identical. Since this is never the case, analogy must be employed. Since analogy can be tight or strained or anything in between, there is vast room for avoiding the restraints of past cases where that is thought desirable.

Shapiro points out other difficulties with applying the traditional model. The opinion in the precedent case may be vaguely written. The facts may not be completely or clearly stated. Identification of the legally relevant facts may have gone amiss. Later judges interpreting the precedent case may have provided differing interpretations. Clearly, determining the precedent to be derived from a case is not a simple matter. If determined, its application to a different set of facts (always the case) may be even more complex. As a consequence, Shapiro argues that the legal profession is not concerned with how judges get from fact to decision, but how they would have done so if the rules of stare decisis had been clearly and correctly followed.

In spite of all this, Shapiro thinks that consistency, the concern for the status quo which underlies stare decisis, is obtained in a slightly different fashion, i.e., via something called "incremental decision-making." A case before the Supreme Court inevitably involves a litigant who disagrees with the interpretation of a law or constitutional provision provided by a lower court judge. That interpretation represents the status quo, or, presumably, the intention of the framers of law or the Constitution. The complaining party in the Supreme Court is asking the high court to alter the situation, to "change" the meaning of the statute or the constitutional provision to provide the relief sought. Consistent with traditional stare decisis, however, Shapiro sees the Court as a defender of the status quo—the past way of doing business or governing relationships—and as generally reluctant to bring change to the social and political system.

When faced with a demand for change, the Court, says Shapiro, may either (a) deny the demand or (b) provide incremental change. It will depart from the status quo on occasion, but only at the margin, only enough to take care of the problem immediately at hand. Subsequently, the Court will observe how its proffered solution has been received. If litigation on the problem continues to surface, additional incremental adjustments will be made until the social tension which the problem has produced reaches some acceptable level. At that point, the status quo will be defended—for a while—against further requests for change. This is Shapiro's view. We do not have to credit it entirely or think it holds in all areas to believe that in some areas of case-law development the theory has appeal as an explanation.

As a description of case decision, incremental theory seems most adequate in the development of obscenity law.[52] Here the Court has determined what is obscene and, therefore, not protected by the First Amendment on a case-by-case basis, making minor changes from one case to the next. Likewise, in the abortion cases,[53] though the initial change was fairly dramatic, subsequent development of constitutional law in that area has been incremental. One must be careful, however, not to view as incremental change the mere fleshing out publicly of decisions taken earlier in private. In the area of racial segregation, for example, the prohibitions applied to various areas of social intercourse through a long series of cases could be viewed as incremental change fed by feedback from each earlier decision in the series. But if the Court had actually decided in *Brown v. Board of Education*[54] to eliminate all racial segregation in the same areas, but to announce it bit by bit as relevant cases came to the Court, the incremental theory of policy-making would not be descriptive.

As you study the opinions of the Court presented in this text, perhaps you will get a feel for the extent to which the Court is responding to traditional principles of stare decisis, to the dictates of incrementalism, or is merely reacting consistently to the fact-patterns encountered in the cases. At the same time, one should also be aware that other factors can and do influence the decisional and policy-making behavior of the justices.

Idiosyncratic Characteristics of the Justices   By idiosyncratic factors, we refer to factors that are unique to the Supreme Court in a given time period. These factors are psychological and ideological at the level of the individual justice and are situational or contextual for the composition of the Court at any point in time. In short, we suggest that the justices differ in their values, outlooks, policy preferences, legal training, and experience. These differences are often manifested in their decisional patterns and in the opinions they write, and in some cases are equally or more important than traditional legal considerations in determining how a majority of the justices vote.

Attitudes   The cases coming before the Court can be conceptualized as posing questions which the justices are required to answer. The answers to many of these questions cannot be derived clearly and directly from the Constitution. As noted earlier, if the question is a simple one (such as, how many senators are permitted each state?), the issue is unlikely to get into the court system. If it does, it will be decided at some level below that of the Supreme Court. Our highest court can plenarily review only relatively few of the thousands of cases it is asked to consider each term. Thus, a very selective process is imposed on the Court. Research shows that the selective process is used largely to treat difficult cases, cases in which some ambiguous provision of the Constitution must be interpreted. Given a tough question and a vague provision of law, the justices often have the option of deciding the case in several different ways. In such cases, the choice may turn on or be influenced by the attitudes of the justices toward the issue of the case.

When the Court is asked, it must do more than merely examine the Constitution or past cases to find answers to such questions as: (1) Is insurance a matter of interstate commerce?[55] (2) In promoting the general welfare, can Congress use tax revenues to maintain the social security system of old age benefits?[56] and (3) Does one have a constitutional right to have an abortion performed?[57] As for these particular questions, the first was answered in the negative, the second and third in the affirmative. It is a fair hypothesis that the justices were influenced in these cases by their attitudes toward abortion, state-federal relations, and the need to care for the elderly in our midst. Thus, policy-making often occurs as a result of the justices' value preferences.

The hypothesis that personal values and attitudes influence case decision has been extensively explored by means of Guttman scales.[58] Scale theory maintains that if the votes of the justices in a series of cases can be explained by the different attitudes of the justices, a consistent scale of the votes should result. This approach assumes that attitudes and values are slow to change, and that attitudes and values govern behavior. If one were to select a group of cases raising questions about the deprivation of civil liberties and arrange them so that each succeeding case represented a greater degree of deprivation, a justice deciding such cases on the basis of his or her attitudes toward such depriva-tions would be expected to reveal a consistent voting pattern. Thus, if a dep-rivation of rank 1 was unacceptable to the justice, consistency would require that all greater degrees of deprivation be unacceptable. A vote for the civil lib-erty claimant in case one would be followed by a vote for the claimant in each succeeding case. On the other hand, a justice may find the deprivation accept-able in the first five cases, but unacceptable in all the following cases. Such consistency is said to support the hypothesis that the justices are voting their attitudes toward deprivation of civil liberty.

Different justices will make the switch from acceptable deprivation to non-acceptable deprivation at different points on the scale. These differences are said to reflect attitudinal differences among the justices. Employing a Guttman Scalogram, Lawrence Baum has found that on "freedom issues," the most lib-eral (proclaimant) justices on the Supreme Court in 1978 were Brennan, Mar-shall, and Stevens, while the most conservative (anticlaimant) were Blackmun, Burger, and Rehnquist.[59] Baum interpreted these findings to mean that the jus-tices' "personal views of policy issues are a crucial factor in their decisions."[60] Such a conclusion is hard to resist when one notes that while the three most liberal justices disapproved the deprivation of freedom from 75 to 100 percent of the time, the three most conservative justices disapproved it in only 8 to 17 percent of the cases.

When justices sitting in the same cases are exposed to the same facts, apply the same law or constitutional provision to these facts, and then disagree about the outcome to the extent reflected in the freedom-issue cases, one may rea-sonably think that mere facts and law are not determinitive of the justices' votes. A more appealing explanation would focus on the attitudes of the jus-tices toward personal freedom. Students of constitutional law should be con-sciously aware that justices make decisions on the basis of law—plus other, legally extraneous considerations.

Activism and Restraint   A related consideration involving the values of the justices on the Supreme Court at any given time involves the concepts of activ-ism and restraint. Basically, these terms refer to the tendency and willingness of individual justices to "legislate"—to go beyond the mere strict application of law to facts and impose their own values and policy preferences on the development of constitutional law in the United States. The historical meaning of judicial restraint has been nicely encapsulated by Charles Lamb. He lists six characteristics or notions embodied by the concept.[61] They are:

1 That the justices refrain from reading their personal preferences into the law and make a serious effort to reflect the intent of the framers in the Court's decisions.

2 That the justices overrule the policies of state and federal governments only when strictly legal grounds require it.

3 That the justices avoid constitutional questions when possible.

4 That the justices hew closely to the requirement that litigants must pres-ent real cases and controversies—i.e., have standing to sue.

5 That the Court issue no advisory opinions.

6 That the Court decide no political question.

Activism is generally defined as the absence of restraint. However, as we shall see momentarily, the concept has been redefined in recent years.

The ideas contained in Professor Lamb's list strongly reflect the discretion available to the justices in deciding cases. The intent of the framers can be relatively ignored by the justices if their view of their role is to keep the Constitution up to date. Indeed, a justice with such a view may make little effort to determine that intent even when ostensibly basing a decision on it. A misreading of intent, of course, may be just as consequential as paying no attention to it at all.

Since the Court possesses the power of judicial review, it may nullify any action taken by state or federal governments which, in its view, is in conflict with the Constitution. A determination of such conflict is not the simple matter suggested by Justice Roberts in 1936.[62] According to Roberts, one can determine whether a congressional statute is in conflict with the Constitution by placing the statute alongside the relevant constitutional provision. A conflict will then be either evident or not evident. If evident, the statute is null and void. Roberts tells us that the justices do no more than make this mechanical judgment when they rule in a case alleging conflict between statutes and the Constitution.

Without going into the history of judicial review before and after 1936, suffice it to say that Roberts's description of decision-making would satisfy few today. Through 1977, the Court held over 1,000 acts of state or local government unconstitutional. In the same period, the Court nullified acts of Congress over 100 times. In each of these cases, the Court had to decide which provision of the Constitution was called into play and the meaning of the provision selected, which is not necessarily the one emphasized by attorneys in the case. Given that the justices in a collegial court can be expected to disagree vigorously about such matters, and have indeed done so, and that the Courts sitting in these cases covered almost 200 years and involved over 100 different justices, one can fairly say that Roberts was trying to perpetuate a standard myth that persists to some extent even today, or that he is guilty at the least of oversimplification.

A few illustrations make the point. In 1870, the Court decided that Congress lacked the authority to make United States notes legal tender in payment of all debts, public and private.[63] However, three justices disagreed with this conclusion, and a year later a majority overruled the precedent.[64] In 1936, an attempt by New York State to require minimum wages for female workers was struck down by the Court as a violation of freedom to contract and due process law. Four justices, including the Chief Justice, dissented.[65] The next year, this precedent was overruled in *West Coast Hotel v. Parrish*,[66] and state minimum-wage laws are quite constitutional today. In 1921, the Court decided that Congress could not limit the amount to be spent in a primary-election campaign by a candidate for the United States Senate or, more broadly, that the power of Congress over elections did not extend to the regulation of primary elections.[67] Yet 20 years later, the Court declared in *United States v. Classic* that Congress did possess such a power.[68]

Exhibiting a bold lack of restraint in *Classic,* the Court conceded that the framers knew nothing of primary elections. Nevertheless, Chief Justice Stone, writing for five justices, maintained that

> . . . we are now concerned with the question whether the right to choose at a primary election, a candidate for election as representative, is embraced in the right to choose representatives secured by Article I, § 2 [of the Constitution]. We may assume that the framers of the Constitution in adopting that section, did not have specifically in mind the selection and elimination of candidates for Congress by the direct primary any more than they contemplated the application of the commerce clause to interstate telephone, telegraph and wireless communication which are concededly within it . . . in determining whether a provision of the Constitution applies to a new subject matter, it is of little significance that it is one with which the framers were not familiar.[69]

This is not to imply, Stone wrote, that the Constitution is like a legislative code which is subject to "continuous revision with the changing course of events." But, where the subject matter was unknown to the framers and its constitutionality is challenged, "we cannot rightly prefer, of the possible meanings of [the Constitution's] words, that which will defeat rather than effectuate the Constitutional purpose."[70]

All the justices did not see "constitutional purpose" in the same light. Justices Douglas, Murphy, and Black, while conceding that Congress might regulate primary elections, denied that the Constitution guaranteed the right of citizens to vote in such elections. Since the statute in *Classic* only penalized conspiracies to "injure, oppress, threaten, or intimidate any citizen in the free exercise or enjoyment of any right or privilege secured to him by the Constitution or laws of the United States," the dissenters thought Classic, who "stuffed a ballot box" in a primary election in Louisiana, not within the reach of the statute.

Since such illustrations could be multiplied many times, it is evident that Roberts's model of decision-making in nullification cases is, at the least, inadequate.

Justice Roberts is not the only justice to define or explain the judicial-restraint model. In 1935, Justice Brandeis outlined seven principles of judicial self-restraint, which he defined as a series of rules for cases confessedly within the Court's jurisdiction. These seven rules are:

> **1** The Court will not pass upon the constitutionality of legislation in a friendly, nonadversary, proceeding, declining because to decide such questions is legitimate only in the last resort, and as a necessity in the determination of real, earnest, and vital controversy between individuals. . . .
> **2** The Court will not "anticipate a question of constitutional law in advance of the necessity of deciding it.". . .

3 The Court will not "formulate a rule of constitutional law broader than is required by the precise facts to which it is to be applied.". . .

4 The Court will not pass upon a constitutional question although properly presented by the record, if there is also present some other ground upon which the case may be disposed of. . . .

5 The Court will not pass upon the validity of a statute upon complaint of one who fails to show that he is injured by its operation. . . .

6 The Court will not pass upon the constitutionality of a Statute at the instance of one who has availed himself of its benefits . . . and

7 When the validity of an act of the Congress is drawn in question and even if a serious doubt of constitutionality is raised, it is a cardinal principle that this Court will first ascertain whether a construction of the statute is fairly possible by which the question may be avoided.[71]

It may be noted that these seven principles incorporate almost all of the principles mentioned by Lamb. They boil down to the suggestion that the Court decide only cases and controversies—as required by the Constitution—and in doing so, exert great effort to avoid deciding constitutional questions. It does not appear that Brandeis's rule 1 is an internal rule for cases confessedly in the Court's jurisdiction. For the Court has no jurisdiction in a "friendly, nonadversary proceeding." However, the rule also has a political component, since if followed, it would be more difficult to test the actions of Congress or state legislative bodies in the Supreme Court. Thus, rule 1 relates to the doctrine of political questions, at least tangentially.

The admonition to avoid constitutional questions recognizes the fact that the Constitution may be changed through Supreme Court interpretation. It cannot be changed in such a fashion, however, in a case in which no constitutional issue is decided. Thus, as do courts generally, the admonition favors the status quo. Since cases are decided on statutory grounds where possible, losing litigants are left with political options that are foreclosed when the Court bases a decision on the Constitution. A losing party who does not like a statute or the interpretation of a statute provided by the Supreme Court may appeal to the political arena and attempt to get the statute changed. Moreover, if one chooses not to do that, the probability that some subsequent Supreme Court majority will modify or reverse an earlier interpretation is greater if the issue has not been decided by interpretation of a constitutional provision. If the Court decides constitutional questions only when it cannot avoid doing so and makes its rulings in such cases as narrow as possible, it would reflect the kind of incremental change in constitutional law attributed earlier to Shapiro. Thus, we see that Brandeis's admonitions speak to the kind of political system we have and to the Court's role in that system and in bringing change to the system.

Having said all this, we must underscore the fact that Brandeis developed his rules in a concurring opinion. They have not been adopted formally by the Court. They represent admonitions of self-restraint, Brandeis's notion of how the Court should operate. The rules have appeal to, and have been followed in part or in whole by, the justices who believe in a restrained Court—one which attempts to construe the Constitution narrowly and give great deference to the political branches of government.

While probably most of the 102 Supreme Court justices have leaned toward restraint, the best-known proponents of judicial restraint in the modern day were Justices Holmes, Brandeis, Stone, and Frankfurter. Yet, these "restraintists" (1) were not restrained to the same degree, (2) in many instances were not restrained at all, and (3) were restrained more in some subject areas than in others.[72] Anthony Champagne and Stuart Nagel have measured restraint by isolating the dissenting votes of these justices in cases in which the Court nullified a municipal, state, or federal statute. A justice was considered more restraintist when he objected to such interference by casting a dissenting vote.

Using the dissent percentage of each justice in nullification cases, as compared to the rest of the Court, measures of restraint were derived. It turns out that Holmes was most restrained when the restraint was antilabor. The same was true of Brandeis and Stone. But Frankfurter was most restrained when the restraint was antibusiness. In nullifications benefiting conservative interests, Holmes, Brandeis, and Stone cast not a single dissent. Frankfurter, on the other hand, took the position of restraint 27 percent of the time. These variations suggest that even for justices who value judicial self-restraint, there are numerous occasions when other values predominate and determine decisions. This might cause some cynics to argue that judicial self-restraint is nonexistent. However, such a position would be too radical. Better is the comment by Harold Spaeth and Stuart Teger that "judicial deference is a sometimes thing."[73] For though the so-called restraintists are not always restrained when interpreting the Constitution and state and federal law, they are clearly more restrained than the activists.

Activism is, among other things, the absence of judicial restraint. Bradley Canon, in a seminal work, has specified six major dimensions to activism.

1 Majoritarianism—a measure of the extent to which democratically adopted policies are nullified by the Supreme Court.

2 Interpretive Stability—a measure of the extent to which the Court's decisions, doctrines, or interpretations are modified or overruled.

3 Interpretive Fidelity—a measure of the extent to which provisions of the Constitution are given strained interpretations or interpretations which violate the intentions of the framers.

4 Substance-Democratic Process Distinction—a measure of the extent to which the Supreme Court makes substantive policies without appreciable effect on the maintenance of the democratic process.

5 Specificity of Policy—a measure of the extent to which the Supreme Court makes detailed policies in contrast to general policies with the discretion to fill in the details left to other governmental branches or agencies.

6 Availability of Alternate Policy Maker—a measure of the extent to which Supreme Court decisions seriously deprive other governmental policy makers of the opportunity to consider the problems to which the policies are addressed.[74]

Using this framework, Canon suggests the surprising conclusion that in selected cases the Burger Court has been more activist than the Warren Court. However, on the dimension of interpretive stability—i.e., the changing of earlier doctrines or principles—the Warren Court was considerably more activist. This reflects the fact that the Warren Court overruled Supreme Court precedents, in whole or in part, that were established in sixty-two earlier cases—all within a 16-year period. All previous Courts, spanning 164 years, overruled only slightly more precedents in eighty-eight cases.

To understand judicial activism as something other than mere absence of restraint, one must be sensitive to how activism is carried out. The central question is not so much who are the activists and who the restraintists, or the "interpretists," as they are sometimes called. All justices reflect activism and restraint in their decisions over time. The important inquiries have to do with the timing of activism and restraint and the dimensions on which the behavior occurs.

The dimensional question relates directly to the kind of governmental system we have—separation of powers, federalism—and to the general role of the Supreme Court in American politics. From that standpoint, Canon's six conceptual dimensions are not precisely equal.[75] Behavior on one dimension is not equal to behavior on another insofar as impact on the governmental process is concerned.

Least intrusive on the political process are decisions involving interpretive stability and interpretive fidelity. The Supreme Court is not bound by its own precedents, and when it overrules or changes earlier Court doctrine, it is clearly within its prerogatives as our high Court. Such activism may have little or no impact as an intrusion into political life or process. As for interpretive fidelity, the Court is the final interpreter of the intent of the framers. While on many occasions it may be charged with straying from that intent, such arguments are often not reducible to probative judgment. Since the framers shaped a living Constitution, it can be argued that they did not expect their "intent" to be abided for all eternity. Moreover, activism measured on this dimension need not involve political or governmental process.

Next-least intrusive is the activism classified on the dimensions of substance-democratic process distinction and specificity of policy. Both involve policy-making by the Court. However, the first, by definition, does not affect the preservation of the democratic process. The latter, which recognizes the degree to which the Court details its policy pronouncements, intrudes to some extent on the ability of other individuals or agencies to provide such details. Yet, we do not know whether the details of the policy would be any different if the Court made a general policy and others were left with the discretion to implement it. Presumably those implementing a Supreme Court policy are under compulsion to follow the direction and pursue the ends which the Supreme Court had in view in announcing the policy in the first place. If this is not done, new litigation is likely to be initiated. And, of course, reducing the discretion of those who implement policy will have little to do with political or governmental process unless the policy itself is so directed.

The remaining categories—majoritarianism and availability of an alternate policymaker—are clearly the most intrusive dimensions of activism insofar as impact on, or interference with, the political or democratic process is concerned. If a majority of an elected legislative body adopts a policy, it is fair to assume that the policy is preferred by a majority of the people[76] or a majority of those for whom the policy has relevance. When the Supreme Court, through judicial review, nullifies such a policy, it intrudes directly into the political process. It says to the democratically elected representatives of the people: You may prefer this policy, but you cannot have it. If we assume equal good faith on the part of the Court and the legislative bodies that pass our laws, judicial review results in the imposition of the Court's interpretation of the Constitution (often the policy preferences of the justices) for the good faith interpretation of elected legislators.

The extent to which a Court nullifies legislation or executive action via judicial review speaks directly to the nature of the governmental system. At one extreme, the Court may never engage in such a practice, thus maximizing government by democratic process. At the other, the Court may engage in nullification frequently, thus shading the political process toward government by a bevy of Platonic guardians—justices not elected who serve for good behavior (i.e., life).

When the Court moves to settle issues which can be handled by other agencies of government, it can change the processes associated with democratic government. In a democracy, one has the right to think that basic social and political issues will be decided by elected representatives. If this right is usurped by the Supreme Court in a situation in which decisions would have been forthcoming from other agencies of government, we recognize a form of action that is highly intrusive on, and fundamentally related to, the political process. For it touches the question of who shall decide. A reading of the debates at the 1787 Constitutional Convention will quickly remind us that no question was of greater concern to the framers—time after time—than the question of who will make policy for the polity.

Law Clerks   At present each justice is entitled to have four clerks furnished at Court expense, though a justice may use fewer than that number if desired. The clerks read cases, applications for review, briefs submitted by litigants, and other material as requested by their justices. They may draft opinions and submit written recommendations as to appropriate action to take on any pending legal matter. They may also discuss cases or other legal questions with their respective justices. How justices use their clerks depends on the individual justice. Some justices involve their clerks heavily in the day-to-day business of the Court. Others do not. One of the current justices has told the author that it all depends on whether he thinks discussion with his clerks will do any good. "If I have been around the track more than the clerk, there will be no discussion. I am not interested in educating the clerk. In general, clerks are not interested in presenting different views on issues with which I am very familiar."

However, the same justice noted that "some clerks do disagree with me from time to time."

As for the drafting of opinions, we cannot say that all justices use their clerks in that way.[77] While some of the less able justices have given their clerks the responsibility for writing most of their opinions, some of the better justices have also used clerks for opinion drafting. Justice Frankfurter employed his clerks to draft opinions, and his famous dissent in *Baker v. Carr,* the legislative reapportionment case, was drafted by his clerks.

Chief Justice Warren also assigned significant responsibilities to his clerks. After *Brown v. Board of Education* was decided unanimously in May 1954, a question arose as to who should write the opinion. Frankfurter suggested that the opinion be issued "per curiam," i.e., unsigned. The justices voted 8 to 1, however, to have Warren write for the Court. Warren then proceeded to prepare an outline which was given to his clerk Earl Pollock. Pollock, working straight through for 24 hours, then wrote the first draft of the *Brown* opinion. That draft was basically the opinion that appears in the *U.S. Reports.*

Subsequent to the Court's decision in May 1954, Warren had six clerks prepare a research report on desegregation and recommendations for an enforcement decree. The decree was handed down in the second *Brown* case in 1955. One who reads the Court's opinion in the second *Brown* case will be struck by the similarity between that opinion and the recommendations of the clerks.

None of this establishes, of course, that clerks influence justices. The justices, after all, have the final say and a veto power over all that the clerks, individually or collectively, might propose. But one must recognize the potential for influence inherent in the working relationships between justices and their clerks.

Small-Group Considerations   Supreme Court policy-making cannot avoid being influenced by the fact that the Court is collegial in nature. Nine justices must, in deciding a case, produce a majority of at least five who agree on case outcome. And, if the legal system is to function, majority opinions to guide the bar and the users of the law must be fashioned. Since each justice has an equal vote, conflict, discussion, compromise, and bargaining are important components of the process that produces decision and, thus, policy.

The concept of the small group was developed in the field of social psychology. It suggests that certain common kinds of behavior will occur in small, face-to-face decision-making groups. Small-group theory maintains that these behaviors flow from the context of "groupness" and are behaviors that would not occur if decision-making were centralized in one individual. Research with this theory has led to a number of inferences: for example, groups are now thought to be more accurate than individuals in making objective decisions; individual group members are influenced by the views held by the majority of the group's members even if the individual initially thinks the majority mistaken; group members soon recognize and follow the group norm for behavior of various kinds; and the size of a group affects the behavior of members of the group.[78]

In transferring this kind of analysis to the Supreme Court, we cannot match the research of social psychologists in their laboratories. Social psychologists are able to control the environment in which research is conducted and to isolate the variables of interest from the many factors that might contaminate the inferential process. They do this by working with artificial groups given assigned and limited tasks in a tightly controlled situation. By varying groups, members, environment, and inquiry, it is possible to reach fairly reliable inferences regarding the influence of group factors on member behavior.

By contrast, when we view collegial courts as small groups, we are dealing with real-life groups which cannot be manipulated, in environments that cannot be controlled to suit the demands of good research design. We cannot directly observe the Court's decision-making process, which is secret in the conference room, but we can analyze the personal papers and memoirs of justices to determine influence in small-group interplay.

One group characteristic that is of great interest in judicial settings is that of group size. A question sometimes addressed is whether the size of a decision-making group (such as a jury or a collegial court) makes any difference. That question was addressed almost 100 years ago by the Supreme Court. In 1895, a fellow named Bates killed John Nordquist with a wooden pole and was convicted of the crime by an eight-member jury.[79] However, the conviction came in 1896 in the *state* of Utah, while the crime was committed in 1895 in the *territory* of Utah. Had Bates been tried in the territory, he would have been entitled to a twelve-member jury. The reduction in the number of peers by whom he was tried from twelve to eight was alleged to violate Bates's constitutional rights, under the ex post facto provision of Article I, Section 9. Under that provision, one cannot be punished for an act defined as criminal that was not so defined at the time the act was committed. Punishment, in this context, is defined as the deprivation of a substantial right. Bates argued that reducing the number of jurors from twelve to eight deprived him of a substantial right involved in his liberty—i.e., that the size of the decision-making group "makes the difference." The Utah Supreme Court rejected this argument, concluding that eight were as likely to reach a truthful verdict as twelve, and that twelve was not a magic number.

Shortly after the Bates decision, the U.S. Supreme Court decided *Thompson v. Utah.*[80] In the same year that Bates committed murder with a wooden pole, Thompson stole Heber Wilson's calf. Thompson was first convicted by a jury of twelve but, having been granted a new trial, was retried by a jury of eight. After exhausting his remedies in the Utah courts, he appealed to the Supreme Court, arguing, as did Bates, a violation of the ex post facto clause of the Constitution. Confronting the same question as the Utah Supreme Court in *Bates,* the U.S. Supreme Court reached a different conclusion, saying:

> If in respect to felonies committed in Utah while it was a territory, it was competent for the state to prescribe a jury of eight persons, it could just as well have prescribed a jury of four or two, and, perhaps, have dispensed altogether with a jury, and provided for a trial before a single judge. . . . But, the wise men who framed the Consti-

tution of the United States and the people who approved it were of the opinion that life and liberty, when involved in criminal prosecutions, would not be adequately secured except through the unanimous verdict of twelve jurors. It was not for the state . . . to dispense with that guaranty simply because its people had reached a conclusion that the truth could be as well ascertained . . . by eight as by twelve jurors in a criminal case.[81]

In short, the Court thought that the size of decision-making groups did make a difference, the opinion of Utah to the contrary notwithstanding. It went on to find a violation of the ex post facto clause in Utah's reduction in jury size. In more recent years, the Court has dealt extensively with the question of jury size as well as with the size of decisional majorities in the jury setting. While exhibiting some uncertainty about the numbers required by the Constitution, it has nevertheless now reached the firm conclusion that some aspects of the group context—i.e., the size of the jury and the size of the majority required for decision—do "make a difference."

Group size has also figured in research on Supreme Court voting patterns. C. Herman Pritchett revealed as early as 1948 that the nine justices on the Supreme Court frequently split into voting blocs or subgroups.[82] Certain justices showed pronounced tendencies to agree with certain of their colleagues, and disagreed consistently with certain others. Pritchett labeled these voting blocs as right, center, and left. And while Pritchett studied only cases decided on the merits, voting blocs have also been observed when the Court makes jurisdictional decisions.[83]

Pritchett suggested that voting blocs reflected differences in the attitudes of the justices toward issues of public policy. Such an explanation is more appealing when the decision is a public policy choice and less appealing when the question is merely a jurisdictional one or one in which public policy is not a major consideration. In any event, without the group context of Supreme Court decision-making, such groupings would be impossible. Moreover, when groups of justices consistently vote together over time, the tendency to vote as a bloc rather than individually is constantly being reinforced, thereby enhancing the "group" influence on decision-making.

The kind of bloc observed by Pritchett has continued to be observed right up to the present time. The membership of the Court changes from time to time, as does the composition of blocs or subgroups of justices. But the bloc phenomenon continues to exist. In the present Court, Justices Marshall and Brennan frequently vote as one, as do Justices Rehnquist and O'Connor, and Chief Justice Burger. Justices White, Blackmun, Powell, and Stevens are found to shift around a bit between the two poles but are often at the center of the Court on key issues.

Eloise Snyder and others, using Pritchett's work as a point of departure, have looked at other aspects of the group phenomenon.[84] Snyder, after studying over 10,000 opinions, concluded that the Supreme Court had a strong tendency to split into three subgroups. Another study reports that the subgroups may vary in number from one to five but suggests that the size of such blocs tends to be five or less.[85] Snyder defined her three blocs as conservative, pivotal, and liberal. The conservative bloc was composed of justices who resist constitutional change, the liberal bloc welcomed constitutional change, and the pivotal bloc was a swing group that aligned sometimes with the conservatives and sometimes with the liberals. Analysis led her to conclude that new justices tend to align initially with the pivotal bloc, moving later to a conservative or liberal bloc. She also reported that any change of a justice from one bloc to another was very likely to be a contiguous bloc, i.e., movement was incremental rather than radical, and that the direction of movement tended to be from liberal to conservative rather than vice versa.

With the exception of the three-bloc structure, Snyder's findings have been supported by subsequent research and by information from inside the Court. Justice Douglas has written that there were three evangelizers or proselytizers in the Court while he sat there: Stone, Black, and Frankfurter. And Douglas has also described himself, Rutledge, Murphy, and Black as somewhat of a voting bloc.[86] The close personal relationship between Murphy and Rutledge made them a voting clique, even when not joined by other members of this foursome.[87]

A further consequence of the Court's collegial structure is that the justices are forced to interact with each other to reach a group decision. This means that appropriate personal relations must be developed. To the extent that good working relationships are not accomplished, personality variables and lack of respect for colleagues may impact on decisional choice. Sometimes the influence of one justice or several can be extreme. Though it does not presently seem to be accurate, Justice Harry Blackmun was once referred to as "Hip Pocket Harry" by Court clerks who believed Blackmun too often persuaded by Chief Justice Burger.[88] Others have thought former Justice Stewart too much influenced by Justice Rehnquist.[89] Justice Marshall has been called "Mr. Justice Brennan-Marshall" to reflect the alleged influence of Justice Brennan.[90] On the negative side, Justice Stone had little use for Justice Black,[91] and Justice Frankfurter is said to have been contemptuous of Justice Murphy's intellect.[92] And from the decision in the case of *Bridges v. Wixon*[93] until he resigned from the Court, Justice Roberts did not robe with, speak to, or shake hands with Justices Douglas, Black, and Murphy.[94]

Group context may impinge on the decisional process in still further ways. It is reported that in the case of *Thornhill v. Alabama,*[95] in order to assemble a majority in agreement with him, Justice Murphy had to bargain away two-thirds of the opinion he had drafted in the case.[96] A single judge who wishes to reinterpret the Constitution has his conscience as his guide. But in a collegial court, others must be persuaded. Justice Frankfurter once remarked to Justice Douglas that if we can get Hughes on our side, there is no limit to the extent to which we can rewrite the Constitution.[97]

Clearly, the mere existence of a group context for all decision-making introduces elements that have a potential for influencing Supreme Court decisions. We do not suggest, of course, that such considerations are ever solely determinative of case outcomes. But they are components in the decision-making process that loom large or small across the cases. As other factors shade toward equality, these components exert a greater influence.

Social and Historical Contexts   Just as we cannot be oblivious to the fact that the Supreme Court is composed of nine justices who make their decisions as a group, we cannot ignore the larger environment in which these decisions are made. We do not have to take literally the notion that the Supreme Court follows the election returns to recognize that the justices are influenced by various factors in their social environment. Supreme Court justices are appointed by the President with the consent of the Senate. They serve for good behavior, which in effect means life. While they can be impeached, no justice has ever met that fate. Given all this job security, one might think the justices would be immune to criticisms or complaints from the consumers of their product— their decisions. Yet, such is not at all the case. While the Court does possess the independence, technically, to make its decisions free of outside influence, the relationship of decisions to environmental factors is more complex.

In the first place, while the justices are interested in carrying out their assigned functions efficiently and effectively, they do not function in a vacuum. The Court's budget and its appellate jurisdiction, legally, are controlled by the Congress. It depends on the executive branch to enforce its orders and decisions, since it has no enforcement powers itself. Few justices, no matter how safe their jobs, would have an interest in serving on the Court if its jurisdiction was reduced to trivialities and its decisions were haphazardly enforced or ignored at the whim of the President. In short, the Court requires support and cooperation of the legislative and executive branches and must, therefore, be sensitive to the wishes and interests of those who control these branches of government. This is true in spite of the fact that legislative and executive powers are rarely used to "curb" the Court. For the potential is there, and it is that potential to which the Court is responsive.

Since the political branches are elected and are sensitive to societal groups whose support is valued, the values of these groups have indirect relevance for the work of the Supreme Court. If the Court gets too far out of line with the preferences of the political branches, it risks such frontal attacks as Franklin D. Roosevelt's attempt to increase the size of the Court to fifteen justices in 1937, President Nixon's attempt to change the Court's direction by appointing justices sympathetic to his point of view, and the many threats by Congress to curb the Court by reversing particular decisions (either by statute or constitutional amendment) or by reducing appellate jurisdiction. While such threats may not always be carried out, they may be effective in persuading the Court to mend its ways.

Roosevelt did not succeed with his plan to "pack" the Court in 1937, but the threat was enough (combined with some appointments) to improve substantially the chances of New Deal legislation that met with a constitutional challenge in the Court after 1937.[98] President Nixon succeeded, by his four appointments, in producing a Court considerable less sympathetic to the claims of criminal suspects than the Warren Court had been.[99]

We cannot tell, as yet, whether in the long run protection for civil and political rights will be greater or lesser given the Warren Court's dramatic expansion of those rights in the period 1953–1969. That expansion, in other words, produced a backlash which could not only undo the gains brought by Warren and his colleagues, but actually regress on some dimensions. More likely, however, is a slowing of the rate at which rights have been expanding and perhaps a stoppage of that growth altogether on some dimensions. The point is that the Court is in the social flow. What it does, how it does it, and when it does it all have consequences, the contours of which can only be seen over the long run.

Congress has generally not been successful in passing bills to curb Supreme Court jurisdiction. It has had more success in reversing Supreme Court decisions through political action. Robert Dahl reports that of thirty-eight instances in which the Court held congressional legislation unconstitutional within four years of enactment, Congress reversed the decision in nineteen.[100] However, success in curbing the Court does not depend on passing bills designed to do that. The threat that a Court-curbing bill may pass is frequently enough to influence the direction being taken by the Court on some dimension of interest to Congress or executive. Nagel suggests that the influence of a Court-curbing bill on the Court increases dramatically once it gets out of committee. Other correlates of success in curbing the Court are identified by Nagel as: (1) whether the majority party sponsored the bill, (2) whether Congress and Court are dominated by different political parties, (3) whether a social crisis is being exacerbated by Court decisions, (4) whether the Court has the support of the public or of subpublics in the polity, (5) whether the attack is sponsored in northern states, (6) whether the bill is introduced in the House or Senate, (7) whether the purpose of the bill is limited, and (8) whether the President and Congress are both desirous of curbing the Court.[101]

It is fair to say that should a Democratic President and Congress wish to curb a Court composed largely of Republicans that is exacerbating a social crisis, and should they have convinced the public generally of the need to do so, a limited bill introduced in the Senate (the body that approves appointments to the Court) would certainly succeed. Yet, all these factors need not be present. Nagel reports that of 101 Democratic-sponsored bills to curb the Court, 12.8 percent were successful. Of 41 Republican-sponsored curbing bills, 29.9 percent were successful. Given all this, the Court is unlikely to ignore the reaction in political and social circles to the decisions that it makes.

In making a decision in any particular case, the Court technically decides between direct-party litigants. It will normally be decided that one party is to receive some kind of relief or remedy, and the Court opinion will flesh out the details of the remedy. But while the Court technically resolves a dispute only between the parties to a case, its ruling may have widespread implications for other persons and interests in the social system. In making a decision the Court will, therefore, wish to assess the ramifications of the various alternatives that might be available to it.

First of all, the Court may not wish to rule in such a way as to destroy the losing party. If it denies an appeal from a prison inmate languishing on death row, it may be argued that it destroys the losing litigant. But such instances are limited. On the whole, the Court wishes to provide a remedy to a meritorious claimant which imposes a cost on the respondent or appellee, but a cost which does not impose irreparable damage. Thus, a majority of the justices would not wish to rule against General Motors in a civil liability case in such a way as to force the company into bankruptcy. Even assuming that a case could be brought that would warrant such an outcome, the Court would surely avoid it because the social costs of such a result would be unacceptable.

The interest of the justices in levying costs that are reparable is justified from another perspective. As indicated above, the Court needs the support and protection of the people. It also needs the support of those who end up as losing parties before the Court. We cannot depend on U.S. marshals or military forces to enforce Supreme Court decisions. Such an arrangement would obviously be unworkable. The Court system works only because losing parties voluntarily obey Court decisions. They will do so only so long as decisions are viewed as fair and just. Such an accommodation would be short-lived indeed if every conflict before the Supreme Court was a "killed or be killed" situation in which the Court decided who is to die—in the figurative sense.

Beyond all that, the Court is highly concerned with the costs that may be imposed on third parties when a conflict between party litigants is resolved. An example may be drawn from the Court's decisions establishing the right to counsel of criminal indigents in state cases. At the time *Gideon v. Wainwright*[102] was decided—1963—no such right existed. Gideon was charged in Florida with breaking and entering a poolroom, a felony in that state. He had no money and no counsel and asked the state to provide counsel. The state declined, and Gideon went to prison. On certiorari, the U.S. Supreme Court could have declined to review or, if granting jurisdiction, could simply have followed stare decisis and ruled that no such right existed. Instead, it ruled that such a right should exist and overruled one of its earlier cases in the process.[103]

Nine years laters, the Court extended the right to misdemeanors where a jail sentence is a possible punishment.[104] In doing so, the justices clearly examined the social costs of making such a decision. In a concurring opinion, Chief Justice Burger remarked on one social consequence of the decision, saying: "This will mean not only that more defense counsel must be provided, but also additional prosecutors and better facilities for securing information about the accused as it bears on the probability of a decision to confine."[105] Justices Brennan, Douglas, and Stewart responded in another concurrence by suggesting that law students might be used as an important source of counsel for indigents, thus reducing the costs to the states.

The solicitor general of the United States, in his amicus brief, predicted a "massive pile up in state courts" if mandatory requirement of counsel in misdemeanor cases were adopted. He foresaw "chaos," and suggested the possibility of using "clergymen, social workers, probation officers, and other persons of that type . . . as counsel in certain types of cases."[106]

Justices Douglas, Blackmun, and Marshall, taking note of the social consequences of the decision, estimated that between 1,575 and 2,300 full-time counsel would be needed to represent indigents brought within the new rule. However, they said, there were already 355,200 attorneys in the United States, and they suggested that the number would double by 1985. Thus, they thought the problem insignificant.

This was directly challenged by Justices Powell and Rehnquist, who pointed out that while there might be 355,200 attorneys in the country, they were not all available to serve as counsel for indigents. Moreover, they did not think 2,300 attorneys would be sufficient to serve the new need being created by the Court. They pointed to overburdened courts and the varying ability of states to furnish counsel. They favored right to counsel in misdemeanor cases at the discretion of the trial judge, in order to reduce the impact of the new rule on the criminal justice system.

The new rule was adopted by a majority—seven of nine justices. Thus, after considering the social costs, the change was made anyway. The point is that all nine justices did consider and debate the cost and instituted the rule change only after satisfying themselves that the problems to be created by the rule change were manageable and the costs justified. Two clearly did not think the expanded right worth the price of the social ticket. All this should disabuse the student of any notion that the Court is concerned only with the Constitution, à la Justice Roberts, in making decisions.

Following up our discussions of stare decisis and incremental decision-making, we may take note of how social and historical context relates to such considerations. Given that Supreme Court decisions frequently have broad ramifications that extend far beyond the interests of the parties in conflict before the Court, it is not surprising to find the Court adhering to past precedent, i.e., the status quo. One who argues for change—a new rule, as in *Argersinger v. Hamlin*—must convince the Court that a problem exists that can no longer be ignored. The Court's initial impulse is to make no change, because it, like other political institutions, can never foresee all the implications of any change it might adopt in constitutional law.

This reluctance to move can be overcome by convincing the Court that if the requested change in law is not forthcoming, the consequences will be socially intolerable. It is possible that a set of relationships socially tolerable at one point in time is not acceptable at a later point. Illustrative here are cases dealing with racial segregation and legislative malapportionment. In 1896, "separate but equal" facilities for the races in rail transportation were held to violate no provision of the Constitution.[107] The doctrine was subsequently applied to the separation of the races in public schools. Through the years, the

Supreme Court, while slowly modifying its posture toward racial segregation, resisted all efforts to overrule the separate-but-equal doctrine.

The Court believed, apparently, that the problems occasioned by sticking with the doctrine were less serious than those that would accompany its reversal. Pressure for change was handled by making incremental adjustments which had the effect of making it increasingly difficult to meet the requirements of equality across separate facilities. In 1954, the Court decided that the situation had become intolerable and overruled the separate-but-equal doctrine in the famous case of *Brown v. Board of Education of Topeka, Kansas.*[108] Before doing so, the Court was well aware of the implications of its actions, but simply indicated its belief that any new problems that might arise would be better than the problems entailed in sticking to the status quo.[109]

Similarly, between 1946 and 1962, the Court studiously avoided a decision on the constitutionality of malapportioned legislative bodies by defining such an issue as a "political question." One of the reasons for avoiding the issue was the inability of the Court to foresee all the implications of entering what Justice Frankfurter referred to as a "political thicket."[110] This uncertainty was coupled with the failure of petitioners and appellants to convince the Court that to weight the vote of some citizens at ten times that of others was more of a problem than would be entailed were the Court to require relative equality in voting. However, due in part to the political tendencies and attitudes of its justices, the Court did become so convinced in 1962—at which point what had previously been a "political question" became a justiciable issue which the Court then proceeded to decide.[111] The decision to require "one man one vote" in electoral systems has been implemented with some success, as have decisions which have moved us toward the elimination of racial segregation in public life. And although perfection has not been achieved, it appears that the Court understood fairly well the relative problems associated with sticking with or changing the status quo and made the proper social choices. Whether the timing of the choices was defensible is, however, a matter for debate.

By contrast, the Court does not appear to have read the social scene adequately when it changed the law in the *Dred Scott* case,[112] i.e., the Court seemingly failed to anticipate the reaction its decision would engender. Scott was a slave in Missouri who was taken by his owner into the free state of Illinois and the free territory of Wisconsin. He was later returned to Missouri and sold as a slave (in an arranged case) to a man in New York. Scott sued in a federal court, arguing that by virtue of being taken into a free territory, he was no longer a slave. On a negative verdict, he appealed to the Supreme Court. In 1857, by a 7–2 vote, the Court denied Scott standing to sue on the ground that a Negro could not be a citizen of the United States, adding that Congress had no power, in any event, to prohibit slavery in the territories. Did the Court correctly foresee the consequences of this decision? One must think not. Legally, the decision made slavery a national rather than a local institution. Politically, it erected the property rights of slaveholders over the right of local constituencies to ban it. And via media hype and some distortion by the Court's critics the decision became an important factor in bringing on the Civil War in 1860; i.e., the decision so entrenched the institution of slavery legally that the abolitionists were encouraged to think that only war could change the institution. Thus, the Court can make mistakes. But this fact in no way diminishes its interest in knowing, before major social decisions are made, the consequences of acting or not. The historical and social context of a decision will significantly influence the action to be taken and its timing.

THE IMPACT OF SUPREME COURT DECISIONS

The fact that the Supreme Court has decided a conflict between two parties and carefully spelled out its reasons in a written opinion does not inform us as to what happens next. A Supreme Court decision is most properly seen as an event in a continuous flow of events which begins with the initial legal action, and proceeds through trial and intermediate courts to the Supreme Court. But the process continues after the Supreme Court decision. All relevant parties must be notified of the Court's decision. If specific orders to litigants are handed down, someone must interpret those orders, decide what action is to be taken, who is to take the action, its timing, and the methods of proceeding. Additional questions arise if the Supreme Court decision entails a "class" of persons rather than two parties in conflict. This occurs when the case is defined as a "class action." Rule 23 of the *Federal Rules of Civil Procedure* allows a class of persons to be sued by suing a representative of the class. Conversely, a class representative may bring a suit on behalf of the class. In both cases it is unnecessary for members of the class to be directly joined individually to the suit.

In a case before the Supreme Court, the final decision to grant or deny class-action status will be made by the Court itself. Once a case is granted class-action status, the decision in the case will bind not just the directly litigating parties but all members of the class. Thus, in the 1954 case of *Brown v. Board of Education of Topeka, Kansas,* the Court's decision bound not only the five school districts that were parties to the suit, but also all other school districts nationwide in which illegal discrimination based on race was in existence. This subsequently entailed multiple determinations of who was in the class and what action was required on the part of class members.

In some cases, a school district may define itself as a member of the class sued and modify its policies voluntarily. If, on the other hand, a citizen believed that his or her district was a member of the class sued, and the district authorities disagreed and continued their segregational practices, the citizen's remedy would lie in the federal district court and injunctive relief. In that event, the district court judge would determine class status. However, the appeals process could then begin all over again. Likewise the implementation of any Supreme Court decision can trigger new litigation. Thus, we see, the

Supreme Court decision is not always the end of the process. Even if the decision puts an end to legal proceedings, losing parties may repair to one or another political arena in an attempt to recoup their losses.

Research on what happens after a Supreme Court decision is known as "impact research." A brief illustration of that research will help fix in the mind the concept of impact and some of the considerations which influence or shape it in real-life situations. In 1980, the Supreme Court decided the so-called Ten Commandments Case.[113] This case stemmed from a Kentucky law requiring the posting of the Ten Commandments in public school classrooms if enough voluntary donations could be secured to pay for the necessary materials.

The U.S. Supreme Court found this to be in violation of the establishment clause of the First Amendment, a provision that forbids governmental aid to an establishment of religion. In 1981, the attorney general of Kentucky interpreted the Supreme Court's opinion to mean that the Commandments could not be posted and that those posted would have to be taken down. If one could simply assume that Supreme Court decisions are automatically self-enforcing, one could be assured that shortly after the attorney general's opinion, if not sooner, no Commandments would be found in any public school classrooms in Kentucky. However, given our earlier remarks on impact, we know that automatic self-enforcement cannot safely be assumed.

To know what has happened in Kentucky schoolrooms since the decision in *Stone v. Graham,* one must seek additional information. In the spring of 1982, research identified eighty-two school districts in which the Commandments had been posted prior to *Stone v. Graham.* Of these eighty-two districts, the Commandments were taken down in twenty-eight as a result of decision in *Stone*—a noncompliance rate of approximately 66 percent.[114] Further investigation revealed that the discrepancy between complying and noncomplying districts was significantly correlated with (1) public support for posting the Commandments, and (2) whether the decision to continue or discontinue posting was made by the superintendent of education, the local board of education, or others. In addition, decisions made by the superintendents were apparently influenced by (1) the extent to which they considered the decision political meddling and (2) the extent to which their reading of the Supreme Court's opinion led them to believe that voluntarily posting was not ruled out. Thus, to understand the case of *Stone v. Graham* and its significance, we must go beyond the decision of the Court and ask about its impact on relevant parties. When we do so, we find that impact to be considerably less than one might have imagined from merely reading the Court's decision and opinion.

One might ask at this point how fifty-four school districts in Kentucky can continue to post the Commandments when the Court has ruled the practice unconstitutional. The answer lies in the particular features of our judicial system. A ruling of the Supreme Court often only binds the direct parties to a suit or the class covered in a class-action suit. Thus, if one or more persons who are not direct or class litigants initiate action or continue practices held unconstitutional, new suits or legal actions must be initiated to stop them. Even for direct parties, failure to abide by a Supreme Court ruling may be perfectly safe if no one raises any question about it.

To enforce any orders that might be encompassed or implied in *Stone v. Graham* would require new legal actions in the federal district court, a subsequent violation of which would lead to court-imposed penalties. One approach might be for the Kentucky Civil Liberties Union to ask the federal court to order the Commandments taken down and left down in each public school. But this request may or may not be honored, since the Supreme Court itself inserted no such order in its opinion in the case. It merely held that requiring the posting of the Commandments was unconstitutional, and orders issued by a district court are subject to review by appellate courts. Thus, the Kentucky Civil Liberties Union may or may not be able to get such relief in this situation.

Putting all this together, it is easy to see that the impact of a Supreme Court decision is very difficult to forecast from the content of decision and opinion alone. Serious students of Supreme Court decision-making, therefore, always go the further step to see what action was taken after a decision, by whom, and how quickly. Only in this way can the true significance of the Court's work be determined.

NOTES

1 Article II, U.S. Constitution. In addition, if two-thirds of the states so petition Congress, a constitutional convention will be called. Amendments proposed at the convention must be approved by three-fourths of the state legislatures or by three-fourths of the states in convention, as directed by Congress.

2 *Treatise on Government* (1690).

3 *Spirit of the Laws* (1748).

4 *Discourses* (1513).

5 *The Federalist: A Commentary on the Constitution of the United States,* Random House, Modern Library, New York, 1937, p. 337.

6 5 U.S. (1 Cranch) 137. (Note: The official source for Supreme Court cases is the *United States Reports,* published by the U.S. Government Printing Office.) The number 5 in the above citation refers to the volume of the *U.S. Reports* in which *Marbury v. Madison* appears. The number 137 identifies the page on which the case begins. The (1 Cranch) refers to volume 1 of the Reports prepared by Cranch, the Supreme Court's official reporter in 1803. Cases decided through volume 90 (1874) of the *U.S. Reports* include the name of the reporter and the volume number of the reports issued by him. Beginning with volume 91, the official citation omits reference to the Court reporter.

In addition to the *U.S. Reports,* Supreme Court cases may be found in two unofficial reporters: the *Supreme Court Reporter,* published by West Publishing Co., and the *Lawyers Edition of the United States Reports,* published by the Lawyers Cooperative Publishing Co. The unofficial reporters follow the same citation practices as those sketched above. Thus, for example, the case of *Horn v. Mitchell* would be cited as 243 U.S. 247 in the *United States Reports,* 37 S. Ct. 293 in the *Supreme Court Reporter,* and 61 L. Ed. 700 in the *Lawyers Edition.*

The decisions and opinions are reported identically in all three publications, but the unofficial reporters contain headnotes and other supplementary materials that differ from or are omitted from the *U.S. Reports.* The *Supreme Court Reporter* began its coverage with volume 106 of the *U.S. Reports.* The *Lawyers Edition* commences coverage in 1791, and is now in its second series. A citation to a case falling in the second series will be identified by 2d, as in 22 L. Ed. 2d 133.

7 10 U.S. (6 Cranch) 87.

8 14 U.S. (1 Wheat.) 304.

9 19 U.S. (6 Wheat.) 264.

10 74 U.S. (7 Wall.) 506.

11 Since 1928, the Supreme Court has required that a party appealing under statute must provide a statement justifying jurisdiction (*Supreme Court Rules,* 12 and 15). The Court has long felt free to dismiss appeals on technical grounds or when the questions presented for review were not "substantial . . . in character" (*Zucht v. King,* 260 U.S. 174; *Sugarman v. United States,* 249 U.S. 182). In its Revised Rules of 1980, the Court requires "a statement of the reasons why the questions presented are so substantial as to require plenary consideration, with briefs on the merits and oral argument, for their resolution" (Rule 15h).

12 See 28 U.S.C. 81.

13 *Braxton v. County Court of West Virginia,* 208 U.S. 192 (1908).

14 *City of Chicago v. Atchinson, Topeka, and Santa Fe Railway,* 357 U.S. 77 (1958).

15 *Joint Anti-Fascist Refugee Committee v. McGrath,* 341 U.S. 123 (1951).

16 *Baker v. Carr,* 368 U.S. 186 (1962).

17 *McGowan v. Maryland,* 366 U.S. 420 (1961).

18 Ibid.

19 *Marbury v. Madison,* 5 U.S. (1 Cranch) 137.

20 *Commercial Trust Co. v. Miller,* 262 U.S. 51 (1923).

21 *Ware v. Hylton,* 3 U.S. (3 Dallas) 199 (1796).

22 *Martin v. Mott,* 25 U.S. (12 Wheat.) 19 (1827).

23 *United States v. City and County of San Francisco,* 310 U.S. 16 (1940).

24 *Cochran v. Louisiana,* 281 U.S. 370 (1930).

25 *United States v. Pink,* 315 U.S. 203 (1942).

26 *United States v. California,* 332 U.S. 19 (1947).

27 *Harisiades v. Shaughnessy,* 342 U.S. 580 (1952).

28 *Wesberry v. Sanders,* 376 U.S. 1; *Reynolds v. Sims,* 377 U.S. 533 (1964); *Avery v. Midland County, Texas,* 390 U.S. 474 (1968).

29 *Powell v. McCormack,* 395 U.S. 486 (1969).

30 *Williams v. Rhodes,* 393 U.S. 23 (1968).

31 *Gilligan v. Morgan,* 413 U.S. 1 (1973).

32 259 U.S. 13 (1922).

33 410 U.S. 113 (1973).

34 Charles Warren, *The Supreme Court in United States History,* Little-Brown, Boston, 1923, vol. I, p. 108.

35 *Hearings Before the Senate Judiciary Committee on S. 1392,* 75th Congress, 1st Sess., 1937, pt. 3, p. 491.

36 S. Tyler, *Memoirs of Roger B. Taney,* J. Murphy, Baltimore, 1876, pp. 432–435.

37 For example, in 1946 Justice Robert H. Jackson served as chief U.S. prosecutor at the Nuremberg trials of Nazi war criminals and took leave from the Supreme Court during that period.

38 See Ulmer, "Issue Fluidity in the U.S. Supreme Court: A Conceptual Analysis," in Stephen C. Halpern and Charles M. Lamb (eds.), *Supreme Court Activism and Restraint,* Heath, Lexington, Mass., 1982, pp. 319–350.

39 This merely recognizes that lower court decisions are only regionally binding, whereas a Supreme Court decision has precedential value at the national level.

40 For a recent example, see *Illinois v. Gates* (51 LW 3415), where, in restoring the case to the calendar for reargument, the Court said: "In addition to the question presented in the petition for certiorari and previously argued here, the parties are requested to address the question whether the rule requiring the exclusion at a criminal trial of evidence obtained in violation of the Fourth Amendment . . . should to any extent be modified, so as, for example, not to require the exclusion of evidence obtained in the reasonable belief that the search and seizure at issue was consistent with the Fourth Amendment" (p. 3415).

41 48 LW 4344.

42 For an extended treatment of this matter, see Ulmer, "The Supreme Court's Certiorari Decisions: 'Conflict' as a Predictive Variable," *American Political Science Review,* vol. 78, December 1984, pp. 901–911.

43 *Fikes v. Alabama,* 352 U.S. 191 (1957).

44 *Bram v. United States,* 168 U.S. 532 (1897).

45 *Fikes v. Alabama,* p. 201.

46 384 U.S. 436 (1966).

47 Fred Kort, "Quantitative Analysis of Fact Patterns in Cases," in S. Sidney Ulmer (ed.), *Courts, Law, and Judicial Processes,* Free Press, New York, 1981, pp. 324–330.

48 *Smith v. Texas,* 311 U.S. 128 (1940).

49 *Cassell v. Texas,* 339 U.S. 282 (1950).

50 S. Sidney Ulmer, "The Supreme Court and Jury Selection Facts," in S. Sidney Ulmer (ed.), *Courts, Law, and Judicial Processes,* Free Press, New York, 1981, pp. 330–339.

51 Martin Shapiro, "Incremental Decision Making," in Ulmer, *Courts, Law, and Judicial Processes,* pp. 313–323.

52 See *Miller v. California,* 413 U.S. 15 (1973) and cases cited.

53 *Bigelow v. Virginia,* 421 U.S. 809 (1975) and *Planned Parenthood v. Danforth,* 428 U.S. 52 (1976) enlarging abortion rights; *Maher v. Roe,* 432 U.S. 464 (1977) and *Poelker v. Doe,* 432 U.S. 519 (1977) declining to enlarge such rights further.

54 349 U.S. 294 (1955).

55 *Paul v. Virginia,* 75 U.S. (8 Wall) 168 (1869).

56 *Helvering v. Davis,* 301 U.S. 619 (1937).

57 *Roe v. Wade,* 410 U.S. 113 (1973).

58 Cf. Glendon A. Schubert, *Quantitative Analysis of Judicial Behavior,* Free Press, Glencoe, Ill., 1959, chap. 5, and Harold J. Spaeth, *Supreme Court Policy Making,* Freeman, San Francisco, 1979, chap. 5.

59 Lawrence Baum, *The Supreme Court,* Congressional Quarterly Press, Washington, D.C., 1981, p. 128.

60 Ibid., p. 129.

61 Charles M. Lamb, "Judicial Restraint on the Supreme Court," in Halpern and Lamb, op. cit., pp. 7–36.

62 *U.S. v. Butler,* 297 U.S. 1 (1936).

63 *Hepburn v. Griswold,* 755 U.S. (8 Wall) 603 (1870).

64 *Knox v. Lee,* 78 U.S. (12 Wall) 457 (1871).

65 *Morehead v. New York ex rel Tipaldo,* 298 U.S. 587 (1936).

66 300 U.S. 379 (1937).

67 *Newberry v. United States,* 256 U.S. 232 (1921).

68 313 U.S. 299 (1941).

69 Ibid., pp. 315–316.

70 Ibid.

71 *Ashwander v. T.V.A.,* 297 U.S. 288 (1938).

72 We rely here on Anthony Champagne and Stuart S. Nagel, "The Advocates of Restraint: Holmes, Brandeis, Stone, and Frankfurter," in Halpern and Lamb, op. cit., pp. 303–318.

73 "Activism and Restraint: A Cloak for the Justices' Policy Preferences," in Halpern and Lamb, op. cit., p. 296.

74 Bradley C. Canon, "A Framework for the Analysis of Judicial Activism," in Halpern and Lamb, op. cit., pp. 386–387.

75 Canon does not suggest otherwise.

76 Robert Dahl has made this assumption. See "The Supreme Court and Majority Control," in S. Sidney Ulmer (ed.), *Courts, Law, and Judicial Processes,* Free Press, New York, 1981, pp. 213–229.

77 The account that follows relies primarily on Bernard Schwartz, *Super Chief: Earl Warren and His Supreme Court—A Judicial Biography,* unabridged ed., New York University Press, New York, 1983, pp. 96–97, and the author's own reading of material in the papers of Harold Burton and Felix Frankfurter, Manuscript Division, Library of Congress.

78 For an overview of research on courts within a group framework, see S. Sidney Ulmer, *Courts as Small and Not So Small Groups,* Van Nostrand, New York, 1971.

79 *Utah v. Bates,* 14 Utah 293 (1896).

80 *Thompson v. Utah,* 170 U.S. 343 (1898).

81 Ibid., p. 353.

82 *The Roosevelt Court: A Study in Judicial Politics and Values 1937–1947,* Macmillan, New York, 1948.

83 S. Sidney Ulmer, "Bloc Voting and Access to the U.S. Supreme Court: 1947–56 Terms," *Jurimetrics Journal,* vol. 16 (Fall 1975), pp. 6–13.

84 "The Supreme Court as a Small Group," *Social Forces,* vol 36 (1958), pp. 232–238.

85 S. Sidney Ulmer, "Toward a Theory of Subgroup Formation in the U.S. Supreme Court," *Journal of Politics,* vol. 27 (1965), pp. 133–152.

86 William O. Douglas, *The Court Years: 1939–1975,* Random House, New York, 1980, p. 28.

87 J. Woodford Howard, *Mr. Justice Murphy,* Princeton University Press, Princeton, N.J., 1968, p. 426.

88 Bob Woodward and Scott Armstrong, *The Brethren,* Simon & Schuster, New York, 1979, p. 122.

89 Ibid., p. 421.

90 Ibid., p. 48.

91 Ibid., p. 157.

92 Howard, op. cit., p. 268.

93 326 U.S. 135 (1945).

94 Douglas, op. cit., p. 33. As Douglas reports it: "It is customary for the Justices to come to the Robing Room, shake hands with one another, line up in the Conference Room and then walk into Court. Roberts refused to go to the Robing Room. He would have the messenger come out in the hall and robe him, there he would stand in the hall waiting for the line to come by, and then step into his proper place so as to avoid shaking hands."

95 310 U.S. 88 (1940).

96 Howard, op. cit., p. 259.

97 Douglas, op. cit., pp. 7–8.

98 Cf. Robert H. Jackson, *The Supreme Court in the American System of Government,* Harvard, Cambridge, Mass., 1958; Sheldon Goldman and Thomas P. Jahnige, *The Federal Courts as a Political System,* 2d ed., Harper & Row, New York, 1976, pp. 8–11.

99 S. Sidney Ulmer and John A. Stookey, "Nixon's Legacy to the Supreme Court: A Statistical Analysis of Judicial Behavior," *Florida State University Law Review,* vol. 3 (Summer 1975), pp. 331–347.

100 Dahl, op. cit.

101 Stuart Nagel, *The Legal Process from a Behavioral Perspective,* Dorsey, Homewood, Ill., 1969, pp. 260–279.

102 372 U.S. 335 (1963).

103 *Betts v. Brady,* 316 U.S. 455 (1942).

104 *Argersinger v. Hamlin,* 407 U.S. 25 (1972).

105 Ibid., p. 43.

106 Ibid., p. 56.

107 *Plessy v. Ferguson,* 163 U.S. 537 (1896).

108 349 U.S. 294 (1954).

109 See S. Sidney Ulmer, "Earl Warren and the Brown Decision," *Journal of Politics,* vol. 33 (1971), pp. 689–702.

110 *Colegrove v. Green,* 328 U.S. 549 (1946).

111 *Baker v. Carr,* 368 U.S. 186 (1962).

112 *Scott v. Sandford,* 60 U.S. (19 How.) 393 (1857).

113 *Stone v. Graham,* 449 U.S. 39 (1980).

114 S. Sidney Ulmer and Wiley S. Rutledge, "Moses in the Classroom: The Impact of Stone v. Graham" (Unpublished paper, 1983).

CHAPTER 2

THE USES OF SUPREME COURT POWER

To Challenge Congress

Marbury v. Madison (1803)

Massachusetts v. Mellon (1923)

Flast v. Cohen (1968)

As one branch of our tripartite governmental system the Supreme Court possessed great power from the very moment of its establishment. But exactly how broad the Court's authority was and how that authority was to be used were questions left for another day. Great power not used is unlikely to attract much attention. Great power used for trivial purposes is likely to meet a similar fate. But great power used for great purposes not only becomes a focus of attention but also, over time, helps define an institution's role and the impact of that role on the lives of all subject to its jurisdiction. The power, status, and significance of the Supreme Court today are in large part a consequence of the fact that interested parties have attempted to use the power of the Court to further particular ends.

An early question for our federal system of separated powers was the precise contours of authority vested in the states and in each of the three branches of the federal government. Who is to decide whether, in specific situations, the power reserved to the states or the authority delegated to a branch of the federal government has been constitutionally exceeded? Justice Iredell expressed the view in 1798 that the Supreme Court could nullify any state or federal legislation found to contravene the Constitution. But he went on to say that since the power to void legislation "is of a delicate and awful nature, the court will never resort to that authority, but in a clear and urgent case."[1] While others shared Iredell's view of the Court's power, some did not. And the question remained controversial until that "clear and urgent case" presented itself in *Marbury v. Madison*—a case involving the authority of Congress to expand the Supreme Court's original jurisdiction.

William Marbury v. James Madison, Secretary of State of the United States

1 Cranch 137 (1803)
Vote: Unanimous

One of President Adams's last acts before leaving office was to appoint William Marbury as a justice of the peace for the District of Columbia. Though this "midnight appointment" had been signed, the commission had not been delivered when Thomas Jefferson assumed the presidency. Jefferson proceeded to order his secretary of state, James Madison, to withhold the commission. At the request of Marbury, the Supreme Court ordered Madison to "show cause" why an order requiring delivery of the commission should not be issued. When Madison ignored this order, the Court proceeded to consider Marbury's application for the order.

Mr. Chief Justice MARSHALL delivered the opinion of the court. . . .

In the order in which the court has viewed this subject, the following questions have been considered and decided.

1 Has the applicant a right to the commission he demands?

2 If he has a right, and that right has been violated, do the laws of his country afford him a remedy?

3 If they do afford him a remedy, is it a mandamus issuing from this court?

[The Court then decided that Marbury had a right to the commission and that the laws of his country afforded him a remedy.]

It remains to be inquired whether, . . .

He is entitled to the remedy for which he applies. This depends on,

1 The nature of the writ applied for. And,

2 The power of the court.

1 The nature of the writ.

Blackstone, in the third volume of his Commentaries, page 110, defines a mandamus to be, "a command issuing in the king's name from the court of king's bench, and directed to any person, corporation, or inferior court of judicature within the king's dominions, requiring them to do some particular thing therein specified which appertains to their office and duty, and which the court of king's bench has previously determined, or at least supposes, to be consonant to right and justice. . . ."

This writ, if awarded, would be directed to an officer of government, and its mandate to him would be, to use the words of Blackstone, "to do a particular thing therein specified, which appertains to his office and duty, and which the court has previously determined or at least supposes to be consonant to right and justice." Or, in the words of Lord Mansfield, the applicant, in this case, has a right to execute an office of public concern, and is kept out of possession of that right.. . .

[After further analysis, Marshall concluded that mandamus was the appropriate writ in this case, and proceeded to discuss the power of the Court to issue the writ.]

The secretary of state, being a person, holding an office under the authority of the United States, is precisely within the letter of the description; and if this court is not authorized to issue a writ of mandamus to such an officer, it must be because the law is unconstitutional, and therefore absolutely incapable of conferring the authority, and assigning the duties which its words purport to confer and assign.

The constitution vests the whole judicial power of the United States in one supreme court, and such inferior courts as congress shall, from time to time, ordain and establish. This power is expressly extended to all cases arising under the laws of the United States; and consequently, in some form, may be exercised over the present case; because the right claimed is given by the law of the United States.

In the distribution of this power, it is declared that "the supreme court shall have original jurisdiction in all cases affecting ambassadors, other public ministers and counsuls, and those in which a state shall be a party. In all other cases, the supreme court shall have appellate jurisdiction."

*   *   *

When an instrument organizing fundamentally a judicial system, divides it into one supreme, and so many inferior courts as the legislature may ordain and establish; then enumerates its powers, and proceeds so far to distribute them, as to define the jurisdiction of the supreme court by declaring the cases in which it shall take appellate jurisdiction, the plain import of the words seems to be, that in one class of cases its jurisdiction is original, and not appellate; in the other it is appellate, and not original. If any other construction would render the clause inoperative, that is an additional reason for rejecting such other construction, and for adhering to the obvious meaning.

To enable this court then to issue a mandamus, it must be shown to be an exercise of appellate jurisdiction, or to be necessary to enable them to exercise full appellate jurisdiction.

*   *   *

It is the essential criterion of appellate jurisdiction, that it revises and corrects the proceedings in a cause already instituted, and does not create that case. Although, therefore, a mandamus may be directed to courts, yet to issue such a writ to an officer for the delivery of a paper, is in effect the same as to sustain an original action for that paper, and therefore seems not to belong to appellate, but to original jurisdiction. Neither is it necessary in such a case as this, to enable the court to exercise its appellate jurisdiction.

The authority, therefore, given to the supreme court, by the act establishing the judicial courts of the United States, to issue writs of mandamus to public officers, appears not to be warranted by the constitution; and it becomes necessary to inquire whether a jurisdiction, so conferred, can be exercised.

The question, whether an act, repugnant to the constitution, can become the law of the land, is a question deeply interesting to the United States; but, happily, not of an intricacy proportioned to its interest. It seems only necessary to recognise certain principles, supposed to have been long and well established, to decide it.

That the people have an original right to establish, for their future government, such principles as, in their opinion, shall most conduce to their own happiness, is the basis on which the whole American fabric has been erected. The exercise of this original right is a very great exertion; nor can it nor ought it to be frequently repeated. The principles, therefore, so established are deemed fundamental. And as the authority, from which they proceed, is supreme, and can seldom act, they are designed to be permanent.

This original and supreme will organizes the government, and assigns to different departments their respective powers. It may either stop here; or establish certain limits not to be transcended by those departments.

The government of the United States is of the latter description. The powers of the legislature are defined and limited; and that those limits may not be mistaken or forgotten, the constitution is written. To what purpose are powers limited, and to what purpose is that limitation committed to writing; if these limits may, at any time, be passed by those intended to be restrained? The distinction between a government with limited and unlimited powers is abolished, if those limits do not confine the persons on whom they are imposed, and if acts prohibited and acts allowed are of equal obligation. It is a proposition too plain to be contested, that the constitution controls any legislative act repugnant to it; or, that the legislature may alter the constitution by an ordinary act.

Between these alternatives there is no middle ground. The constitution is either a superior, paramount law, unchangeable by ordinary means, or it is on a level with ordinary legislative acts, and like other acts, is alterable when the legislature shall please to alter it.

If the former part of the alternative be true, then a legislative act contrary to the constitution is not law: if the latter part be true, then written constitutions are absurd attempts, on the part of the people, to limit a power in its own nature illimitable.

Certainly all those who have framed written constitutions contemplate them as forming the fundamental and paramount law of the nation, and consequently the theory of every such government must be, that an act of the legislature repugnant to the constitution is void.

This theory is essentially attached to a written constitution, and is consequently to be considered by this court as one of the fundamental principles in our society. It is not therefore to be lost sight of in the further consideration of this subject.

If an act of the legislature, repugnant to the constitution, is void, does it, notwithstanding its invalidity, bind the courts and oblige them to give it effect? Or, in other words, though it be not law, does it constitute a rule as operative as if it was a law? This would be to overthrow in fact what was established in theory; and would seem, at first view, an absurdity too gross to be insisted on. It shall, however, receive a more attentive consideration.

It is emphatically the province and duty of the judicial department to say what the law is. Those who apply the rule to particular cases, must of necessity expound and interpret that rule. If two laws conflict with each other, the courts must decide on the operation of each.

So if a law be in opposition to the constitution: if both the law and the constitution apply to a particular case, so that the court must either decide that case conformably to the law, disregarding the constitution; or conformably to the constitution, disregarding the law: the court must determine which of these conflicting rules governs the case. This is of the very essence of judicial duty.

If then the courts are to regard the constitution; and the constitution is superior to any ordinary act of the legislature; the constitution, and not such ordinary act, must govern the case to which they both apply.

Those then who controvert the principle that the constitution is to be considered, in court, as a paramount law, are reduced to the necessity of maintaining that courts must close their eyes on the constitution, and see only the law.

This doctrine would subvert the very foundation of all written constitutions. It would declare that an act, which, according to the principles and theory of our government, is entirely void, is yet, in practice, completely obligatory. It would declare, that if the legislature shall do what is expressly forbidden, such act, notwithstanding the express prohibition, is in reality effectual. It would be giving to the legislature a practical and real omnipotence with the same breath which professes to restrict their powers within narrow limits. It is prescribing limits, and declaring that those limits may be passed at pleasure.

That it thus reduces to nothing what we have deemed the greatest improvement on political institutions—a written constitution, would of itself be sufficient, in America where written constitutions have been viewed with so much reverence, for rejecting the construction. But the peculiar expressions of the constitution of the United States furnish additional arguments in favour of its rejection.

The judicial power of the United States is extended to all cases arising under the constitution.

Could it be the intention of those who gave this power, to say that, in using it, the constitution should not be looked into? That a case arising under the constitution should be decided without examining the instrument under which it arises?

This is too extravagant to be maintained.

In some cases then, the constitution must be looked into by the judges. And if they can open it at all, what part of it are they forbidden to read, or to obey?

There are many other parts of the constitution which serve to illustrate this subject.

It is declared that "no tax or duty shall be laid on articles exported from any state." Suppose a duty on the export of cotton, of tobacco, or of flour; and a suit instituted to recover it. Ought judgment to be rendered in such a case? ought the judges to close their eyes on the constitution, and see only the law.

The constitution declares that "no bill of attainder or ex post facto law shall be passed."

If, however, such a bill should be passed and a person should be prosecuted under it, must the court condemn to death those victims whom the constitution endeavours to preserve?

"No person," says the constitution, "shall be convicted of treason unless on the testimony of two witnesses to the same overt act, or on confession in open court."

Here the language of the constitution is addressed especially to the courts. It prescribes, directly for them, a rule of evidence not to be departed from. If the legislature should change that rule, and declare *one* witness, or a confession *out* of court, sufficient for conviction, must the constitutional principle yield to the legislative act?

From these and many other selections which might be made, it is apparent, that the framers of the constitution contemplated that instrument as a rule for the government of *courts,* as well as of the legislature.

Why otherwise does it direct the judges to take an oath to support it? This oath certainly applies, in an especial manner, to their conduct in their official character. How immoral to impose it on them, if they were to be used as the instruments, and the knowing instruments, for violating what they swear to support!

The oath of office, too, imposed by the legislature, is completely demonstrative of the legislative opinion on this subject. It is in these words: "I do solemnly swear that I will administer justice without respect to persons, and do equal right to the poor and to the rich; and that I will faithfully and impartially discharge all the duties incumbent on me as according to the best of my abilities and understanding, agreeably to the constitution and laws of the United States."

Why does a judge swear to discharge his duties agreeably to the constitution of the United States, if that constitution forms no rule for his government? If it is closed upon him and cannot be inspected by him.

If such be the real state of things, this is worse than solemn mockery. To prescribe, or to take this oath, becomes equally a crime.

It is also not entirely unworthy of observation, that in declaring what shall be the supreme law of the land, the constitution itself is first mentioned; and not the laws of the United States generally, but those only which shall be made in pursuance of the constitution, have that rank.

Thus, the particular phraseology of the constitution of the United States confirms and strengthens the principle, supposed to be essential to all written constitutions, that a law repugnant to the constitution is void, and that courts, as well as other departments, are bound by that instrument.

The rule must be discharged.

QUESTIONS AND COMMENTS

1 While the power of the Supreme Court to nullify congressional acts has never been successfully challenged, it has been subjected to endless critiques. No one denies that the power exists, but the intention of the framers and the wisdom of vesting such power in the Court remain topics of debate. Can the power of judicial review be derived from the Constitution, or did Marshall merely manufacture it out of whole cloth? In a democratic political system, should a court be given such power over the other branches of government?

2 In this case, William Marbury wanted his commission and was denied it. How important are these facts in the context of John Marshall's decision?

3 *Marbury v. Madison* was a case brought under the Supreme Court's original jurisdiction. What does that mean, and how significant is it?

4 John Marshall was President Adams's last secretary of state. That being so, should he have recused himself in *Marbury v. Madison* on conflict-of-interest grounds?

5 What if the Court had ordered mandamus to issue and Madison declined to deliver the commission to Marbury? What should Marshall and his Court have done about it? What would be the significance of such a refusal? Do you think such considerations might have influenced Marshall and his Court?

6 In his opinion, Marshall poses three questions which he then proceeds to answer. Are all three necessary to the decision ultimately reached in the case? Do you see any significance in the order in which Marshall poses these questions?

* * * * * *

In *Marbury v. Madison,* we saw that Marbury invoked the original jurisdiction of the Supreme Court. And while the Court ruled that it lacked jurisdiction to grant the relief Marbury sought, it did hear his complaint and ruled it a valid complaint—i.e., Marbury presented a true "case or controversy." A person who attempts to question the validity of a statute in the Supreme Court must meet several conditions. In general, one must show that the statute is being applied to one's disadvantage,[2] and that the right of which one is deprived is *substantial.*[3] But one need not wait until the harm has actually occurred.

If one has a clear intention to engage in an act, and the highly probable action of government is to impose a sanction for that act, standing is available to challenge the constitutionality of the statute under which government acts.[4] The question of standing, then, is not so much the issue the litigant wants litigated but whether the Supreme Court is a forum in which he can get his issue heard. Denial of standing means that the Court will impose no restrictions on or interfere with the governmental action challenged. But the granting of standing does not ensure that the Court will decide for the petitioner or appellant on the merits.

Many challenges to the exercise of governmental power have foundered on the shoals of standing. For example, banks have been held to lack standing to make Fifth Amendment claims regarding the reporting requirements of the Bank Security Act.[5] And a taxpayer has no standing to challenge Bible reading in public classrooms.[6] Illustrative cases in which the Court has granted standing include recent holdings that a pregnant woman has standing to challenge a state ban on abortion,[7] and that one has standing to question a state statute barring him from giving vaginal foam to a woman.[8] *Massachusetts v. Mellon* and *Flast v. Cohen* illustrate some of the theoretical considerations associated with the concept of standing in real case situations.

Commonwealth of Massachusetts v. Mellon, Secretary of the Treasury, et al.

262 U.S. 447; 43 S. Ct. 597; 13 L. Ed. 1078 (1923)
Vote: Unanimous

The facts are provided in the opinion.

MR. JUSTICE SUTHERLAND delivered the opinion of the Court.

[*Massachusetts v. Mellon,* no. 24, and *Frothingham v. Mellon,* no. 962.] were argued and will be considered and disposed of together. The first is an original suit in this Court. The other was brought in the Supreme Court of the District of Columbia. That court dismissed the bill and its decree was affirmed by the District Court of Appeals. Thereupon the case was brought here by appeal. Both cases challenge the constitutionality of the Act of November 23, 1921, commonly called the Maternity Act. Briefly, it provides for an initial appropriation and thereafter annual appropriations for a period of five years, to be apportioned among such of the several States as shall accept and comply with its provisions, for the purpose of coöperating with them to reduce maternal and infant mortality and protect the health of mothers and infants. It creates a bureau to administer the act in coöperation with state agencies, which are required to make such reports concerning their operations and expenditures as may be prescribed by the federal bureau. Whenever that bureau shall determine that funds have not been properly expended in respect of any State, payments may be withheld.

It is asserted that these appropriations are for purposes not national, but local to the States, and together with numerous similar appropriations constitute an effective means of inducing the States to yield a portion of their sovereign rights. It is further alleged that the burden of the appropriations provided by this act and similar legislation falls unequally upon the several States, and rests largely upon the industrial States, such as Massachusetts; that the act is a usurpation of power not granted to Congress by the Constitution—an attempted exercise of power of local self-government reserved to the States by the Tenth Amendment; and that the defendants are proceeding to carry the act into operation. In the *Massachusetts* case it is alleged that the plaintiff's rights and powers as a sovereign State and the rights of its citizens have been invaded and usurped by these expenditures and acts; and that, although the State has not accepted the act, its constitutional rights are infringed by the passage thereof and the imposition upon the State of an illegal and unconstitutional option either to yield to the Federal Government a part of its reserved rights or lose the share which it would otherwise be entitled to receive of the moneys appropriated. In the *Frothingham* case plaintiff alleges that the effect of the statute will be to take her property, under the guise of taxation, without due process of law.

We have reached the conclusion that the cases must be disposed of for want of jurisdiction without considering the merits of the constitutional questions.

In the first case, the State of Massachusetts presents no justiciable controversy either in its own behalf or as the representative of its citizens. The appellant in the second suit has no such interest in the subject-matter, nor is any such injury inflicted or threatened, as will enable her to sue.

First. The State of Massachusetts in its own behalf, in effect, complains that the act in question invades the local concerns of the State, and is a usurpation of power, viz: the power of local self government reserved to the States.

Probably it would be sufficient to point out that the powers of the State are not invaded, since the statute imposes no obligation but simply extends an option which the State is free to accept or reject. But we do not rest here. Under Article III, § 2, of the Constitution, the judicial power of this Court extends "to controversies . . . between a State and citizens of another State" and the Court has original jurisdiction "in all cases . . . in which a State shall be party." The effect of this is not to confer jurisdiction upon the Court merely because a State is a party, but only where it is a party to a proceeding of judicial cognizance. Proceedings not of a justiciable character are outside the contemplation of the constitutional grant. . . .

What, then, is the nature of the right of the State here asserted and how is it affected by this statute? Reduced to its simplest terms, it is alleged that the statute constitutes an attempt to legislate outside the powers granted to Congress by the Constitution and within the field of local powers exclusively reserved to the States. Nothing is added to the force or effect of this assertion by the further incidental allegations that the ulterior purpose of Congress thereby was to induce the States to yield a portion of their sovereign rights; that the burden of the appropriations falls unequally upon the several States; and that there is imposed upon the States an illegal and unconstitutional option either to yield to the Federal Government a part of their reserved rights or lose their share of the moneys appropriated. But what burden is imposed upon the States, unequally or otherwise? Certainly there is none, unless it be the burden of taxation, and that falls upon their inhabitants, who are within the taxing power of Congress as well as that of the States where they reside. Nor does that statute require the States to do or to yield anything. If Congress enacted it with the ulterior purpose of tempting them to yield, that purpose may be effectively frustrated by the simple expedient of not yielding.

In the last analysis, the complaint of the plaintiff State is brought to the naked contention that Congress has usurped the reserved powers of the several States by the mere enactment of the statute, though nothing has been done and nothing is to be done without their consent; and it is plain that the question, as it is thus presented, is political and not judicial in character, and therefore is not a matter which admits of the exercise of the judicial power.

* * *

. . . in so far as the case depends upon the assertion of a right on the part of the State to sue in its own behalf we are without jurisdiction. In that aspect of the case we are called upon to adjudicate, not rights of person or property, not rights of dominion over physical domain, not quasi-sovereign rights actually invaded or threatened, but abstract questions of political power, of sovereignty, of government. No rights of the State falling within the scope of the judicial power have been brought within the actual or threatened operation of the statute and this Court is as much without authority to pass abstract opinions upon the constitutionality of acts of Congress as it was held to be, in *Cherokee Nation v. Georgia,* [1831], of state statutes. If an alleged attempt by congressional action to annul and abolish an existing state government "with all its constitutional powers and privileges," presents no justiciable issue, as was ruled in *Georgia v. Stanton,* [1867], no reason can be suggested why it should be otherwise where the attempt goes no farther, as it is here alleged, than to propose to share with the State the field of state power.

We come next to consider whether the suit may be maintained by the State as the representative of its citizens. To this the answer is not doubtful. We need not go so far as to say that a State may never intervene by suit to protect its citizens against any form of enforcement of unconstitutional acts of Congress; but we are clear that the right to do so does not arise here. Ordinarily, at least, the only way in which a State may afford protection to its citizens in such cases is through the enforcement of its own criminal statutes, where that is appropriate, or by opening its courts to the injured persons for the maintenance of civil suits or actions. But the citizens of Massachusetts are also citizens of the United States. It cannot be conceded that a State, as *parens patriae,* may institute judicial proceedings to protect citizens of the United States from the operation of the statutes thereof. While the State, under some circumstances, may sue in that capacity for the protection of its citizens (*Missouri v. Illinois,* [1901]) it is no part of its duty or power to enforce their rights in respect of their relations with the Federal Government. In that field it is the United

States, and not the State, which represents them as *parens patriae,* when such representation becomes appropriate; and to the former, and not to the latter, they must look for such protective measures as flow from that status.

Second. The attack upon the statute in the *Frothingham* case is, generally, the same, but this plaintiff alleges in addition that she is a taxpayer of the United States; and her contention, though not clear, seems to be that the effect of the appropriations complained of will be to increase the burden of future taxation and thereby take her property without the due process of law. The right of a taxpayer to enjoin the execution of a federal appropriation act, on the ground that it is invalid and will result in taxation for illegal purposes, has never been passed upon by this Court. . . . The interest of a taxpayer of a municipality in the application of its moneys is direct and immediate and the remedy by injunction to prevent their misuse is not inappropriate. It is upheld by a large number of state cases and is the rule of this Court. . . .

But the relation of a taxpayer of the United States to the Federal Government is very different. His interest in the moneys of the Treasury—partly realized from taxation and partly from other sources—is shared with millions of others; is comparatively minute and indeterminable; and the effect upon future taxation, of any payment out of the funds, so remote, fluctuating and uncertain, that no basis is afforded for an appeal to the preventive powers of a court of equity.

The administration of any statute, likely to produce additional taxation to be imposed upon a vast number of taxpayers, the extent of whose several liability is indefinite and constantly changing, is essentially a matter of public and not of individual concern. If one taxpayer may champion and litigate such a cause, then every other taxpayer may do the same, not only in respect of the statute here under review but also in respect of every other appropriation act and statute whose administration requires the outlay of public money, and whose validity may be questioned. The bare suggestion of such a result, with its attendant inconveniences, goes far to sustain the conclusion which we have reached, that a suit of this character cannot be maintained. It is of much significance that no precedent sustaining the right to maintain suits like this has been called to our attention, although, since the formation of the government, as an examination of the acts of Congress will disclose, a large number of statutes appropriating or involving the expenditure of moneys for non-federal purposes have been enacted and carried into effect.

The functions of government under our system are apportioned. To the legislative department has been committed the duty of making laws; to the executive the duty of executing them; and to the judiciary the duty of interpreting and applying them in cases properly brought before the courts. The general rule is that neither department may invade the province of the other and neither may control, direct or restrain the action of the other. We are not now speaking of the merely ministerial duties of the officials.

We have no power *per se* to review and annul acts of Congress on the ground that they are unconstitutional. That question may be considered only when the justification for some direct injury suffered or threatened, presenting a justiciable issue, is made to rest upon such an act. Then the power exercised is that of ascertaining and declaring the law applicable to the controversy. It amounts to little more than the negative power to disregard an unconstitutional enactment, which otherwise would stand in the way of the enforcement of a legal right. The party who invokes the power must be able to show not only that the statute is invalid but that he has sustained or is immediately in danger of sustaining some direct injury as the result of its enforcement, and not merely that he suffers in some indefinite way in common with people generally. If a case for preventive relief be presented the court enjoins, in effect, not the execution of the statute, but the acts of the official, the statute notwithstanding. Here the parties plaintiff have no such case. Looking through forms of words to the substance of their complaint, it is merely that officials of the executive department of the government are executing and will execute an act of Congress asserted to be unconstitutional; and this we are asked to prevent. To do so would be not to decide a judicial controversy, but to assume a position of authority over the governmental acts of another and co-equal department, an authority which plainly we do not possess.

No. 24, Original, dismissed.
No. 962 affirmed.

Flast, et al. v. Cohen, Secretary of Health, Education, and Welfare, et al.

392 U.S. 83; 88 S. Ct. 1942; 20 L. Ed. 2d 947 (1968)
Vote: 8–1

The facts are provided in the opinion below.

MR. CHIEF JUSTICE WARREN delivered the opinion of the Court.

In *Frothingham v. Mellon,* (1923), this Court ruled that a federal taxpayer is without standing to challenge the constitutionality of a federal statute. That ruling has stood for 45 years as an impenetrable barrier to suits against Acts of Congress brought by individuals who can assert only the interest of federal taxpayers. In this case, we must decide whether the *Frothingham* barrier should be lowered when a taxpayer attacks a federal statute on the ground that it violates the Establishment and Free Exercise Clause of the First Amendment.

Appellants filed suit in the United States District Court for the Southern District of New York to enjoin the allegedly unconstitutional expenditure of federal funds under Titles I and II of the Elementary and Secondary Education Act of 1965.

The complaint alleged that seven appellants had as a common attribute that "each pay[s] income taxes of the United States," and it is clear from the complaint that the appellants were resting their standing to maintain the action solely on their status as federal taxpayers. The appellees, who are charged by Congress with administering the Elementary and Secondary Education Act of 1965, were sued in their official capacities.

The gravamen of the appellants' complaint was that federal funds appropriated under the Act were being used to finance instruction in reading, arithmetic, and other subjects in religious schools, and to purchase textbooks and other instructional materials for use in such schools. Such expenditures were alleged to be in contravention of the Establishment and Free Exercise Clauses of the First Amendment. . . .

The Government moved to dismiss the complaint on the ground that appellants lacked standing to maintain the action. District Judge Frankel, who considered the motion, recognized that *Frothingham v. Mellon,* provided "powerful" support for the Government's position, but he ruled that the standing question was of sufficient substance to warrant the convening of a three-judge court to decide the question. The three-judge court received briefs and heard arguments limited to the standing question, and the court ruled on the authority of *Frothingham* that appellants lacked standing. Judge Frankel dissented.

From the dismissal of their complaint on that ground, appellants appealed directly to this Court, and we noted probable jurisdiction.

For reasons explained at length below, we hold that appellants do have standing as federal taxpayers to maintain this action, and the judgment below must be reversed. . . .

This Court first faced squarely the question whether a litigant asserting only his status as a taxpayer has standing to maintain a suit in a federal court in *Frothingham v. Mellon, supra,* and that decision must be the starting point for analysis in this case. The taxpayer in *Frothingham* attacked as unconstitutional the Maternity Act of 1921, which established a federal program of grants to those States which would undertake programs to reduce maternal and infant mortality. The taxpayer alleged that Congress, in enacting the challenged statute, had exceeded the powers delegated to it under Article I of the Constitution and had invaded the legislative province reserved to the several States by the Tenth Amendment. The taxpayer complained that the result of the allegedly unconstitutional enactment would be to increase her future federal tax liability and "thereby take her property without due process of law." The Court noted that a federal taxpayer's "interest in the moneys of the Treasury . . . is comparatively minute and indeterminable" and that "the effect upon future taxation, of any payment out of the [Treasury's] funds, . . . [is] remote, fluctuating and uncertain." As a result, the Court ruled that the taxpayer had failed to allege the type of "direct injury" necessary to confer standing.

Although the barrier *Frothingham* erected against federal taxpayer suits has never been breached, the decision has been the source of some confusion and the object of considerable criticism. The confusion has developed as commentators have tried to determine whether *Frothingham* establishes a constitutional bar to taxpayer suits or whether the Court was simply imposing a rule of self-restraint which was not constitutionally compelled.

* * *

The opinion delivered in *Frothingham* can be read to support either position. The concluding sentence of the opinion states that, to take jurisdiction of the taxpayer's suit, "would be not to decide a judicial controversy, but to assume a position of authority over the governmental acts of another and co-equal department, an authority which plainly we do not possess."

Yet the concrete reasons given for denying standing to a federal taxpayer suggest that the Court's holding rests on something less than a constitutional foundation. For example, the Court conceded that standing had previously been conferred on municipal taxpayers to sue in that capacity. However, the Court viewed the interest of a federal taxpayer in total federal tax revenues as "comparatively minute and indeterminable" when measured against a municipal taxpayer's interest in a smaller city treasury.

This suggests that the petitioner in *Frothingham* was denied standing not because she was a taxpayer but because her tax bill was not large enough. In addition, the Court spoke of the "attendant inconveniences" of entertaining that taxpayer's suit because it might open the door of the federal courts to countless such suits "in respect of every other appropriation act and statute whose administration requires the outlay of public money, and whose validity may be questioned." Such a statement suggests pure policy considerations.

To the extent that *Frothingham* has been viewed as resting on policy considerations, it has been criticized as depending on assumptions not consistent with modern conditions. For example, some commentators have pointed out that a number of corporate taxpayers today have a federal tax liability running into hundreds of millions of dollars, and such taxpayers have a far greater monetary stake in the Federal Treasury than they do in any municipal treasury. To some degree, the fear expressed in *Frothingham* that allowing one taxpayer to sue would inundate the federal courts with countless similar suits has been mitigated by the ready availability of the devices of class actions and joinder under the Federal Rules and Civil Procedure, adopted subsequent to the decision in *Frothingham.* Whatever the merits of the current debate over *Frothingham,* its very existence suggests that we should undertake a fresh examination of the limitations upon standing to sue in a federal court and the application of those limitations to taxpayer suits.

* * *

Standing is an aspect of justiciability and, as such, the problem of standing is surrounded by the same complexities and vagaries that inhere in justiciability. Standing has been called one of "the most amorphous [concepts] in the entire domain of public law." Some of the complexities peculiar to standing problems result because standing "serves, on occasion, as a shorthand expression for all the various elements of justiciability." In addition, there are at work in the standing doctrine the many subtle pressures which tend to cause policy considerations to blend into constitutional limitations.

Despite the complexities and uncertainties, some meaningful form can be given to the jurisdictional limitations placed on federal court power by the concept of standing. The fundamental aspect of standing is that it focuses on the party seeking to get his complaint before a federal court and not on the issues he wishes to have adjudicated. The "gist of the question of standing" is whether the party seeking relief has "alleged such a personal stake in the outcome of the controversy as to assure that concrete adverseness which sharpens the presentation of issues upon which the court so largely depends for illumination of difficult constitutional questions." *Baker v. Carr,* (1962). In other words, when standing is placed in issue in a case, the question is whether the person whose standing is challenged is a proper party to request an adjudication of a particular issue and not whether the issue itself is justiciable. . . .

When the emphasis in the standing problem is placed on whether the person invoking a federal court's jurisdiction is a proper party to maintain the action, the weakness of the Government's argument in this case becomes apparent. The question whether a particular person is a proper party to maintain the action does not, by its own force, raise separation of powers problems related to improper judicial interference in areas committed to other branches of the Federal Government. Such problems arise, if at all, only from the substantive issues the individual seeks to have adjudicated. Thus, in terms of Article III limitations on federal court jurisdiction, the question of standing is related only to whether the dispute sought to be adjudicated will be presented in an adversary context and in a form historically viewed as capable of judicial resolution. It is for that reason that the emphasis in standing problems is on whether the party invoking federal court jurisdiction has "a personal stake in the outcome of the controversy," *Baker v. Carr, supra,* and whether the dispute touches upon "the legal relations of parties having adverse legal interest." *Aetna Life Insurance Co. v. Haworth,* [1937]. A taxpayer may or may not have the requisite personal stake in the outcome, depending upon the circumstances of the particular case. Therefore, we find no absolute bar in Article III to suits by federal taxpayers challenging allegedly unconstitutional federal taxing and spending programs. There remains, however, the problem of determining the circumstances under which a federal taxpayer will be deemed to have the personal stake and interest that impart the necessary concrete adverseness to such litigation so that standing can be conferred on the taxpayer *qua* taxpayer consistent with the constitutional limitations of Article III . . . our decisions establish that, in ruling on standing, it is both appropriate and necessary to look to the substantive issues for another purpose, namely, to determine whether there is a logical nexus between the status asserted and the claim sought to be adjudicated. . . .

The nexus demanded of federal taxpayers has two aspects to it. First, the taxpayer must establish a logical link between that status and the type of legislative enactment attacked. Thus, a taxpayer will be a proper party to allege the unconstitutionality only of exercises of congressional power under the taxing and spending clause of Art. I, § 8, of the Constitution. . . . Secondly, the taxpayer must establish a nexus between the status and the precise nature of the constitutional infringement alleged. Under this requirement, the taxpayer must show that the alleged enactment exceeds specific constitutional limitations imposed upon the exercise of a congressional taxing and spending power and not simply that the enactment is generally beyond the powers delegated to Congress by Art. I, § 8. . . .

The taxpayer-appellants in this case have satisfied both nexuses to support their claim of standing under the test we announce today. Their constitutional challenge is made to an exercise by Congress of its power under Art. I, § 8, to spend for the general welfare, and the challenged program involves a substantial expenditure of federal tax funds. In addition, appellants have alleged that the challenged expenditures violate the Establishment and Free Exercise Clauses of the First Amendment.

* * *

The allegations of the taxpayer in *Frothingham v. Mellon, supra,* were quite different from those made in this case, and the result in *Frothingham* is consistent with the test of taxpayer standing announced today. The taxpayer in *Frothingham* attacked a federal spending program and she, therefore, established the first nexus required. However, she lacked standing because her constitutional attack was not based on an allegation that Congress, in enacting the Maternity Act of 1921, had breached a specific limitation upon its taxing and spending power. . . .

We have noted that the Establishment Clause of the First Amendment does not specifically limit the taxing and spending power conferred by Art. I, § 8. Whether the Constitution contains other specific limitations can be determined only in the context of future cases. However, whenever such specific limitations are found, we believe a taxpayer will have a clear stake as a taxpayer in assuring that they are not breached by Congress. Consequently, we hold that a taxpayer will have standing consistent with Article III to invoke federal judicial power when he alleges that congressional action under the taxing and spending clause is in derogation of those constitutional provisions which operate to restrict the exercise of the taxing and spending power. The taxpayer's allegation in such cases would be that his tax money is being extracted and spent in violation of specific constitutional protections against such abuses of legislative power. Such an injury is appropriate for judicial redress, and the taxpayer has established the necessary nexus between his status and the nature of the allegedly unconstitutional action to support his claim of standing to secure judicial review. . . .

While we express no view at all on the merits of appellants' claims in this case, their complaint contains sufficient allegations under the criteria we have outlined to give them standing to invoke a federal court's jurisdiction for an adjudication on the merits.

Reversed.

* * *

MR. JUSTICE HARLAN, dissenting.

* * *

I cannot accept the standing doctrine [that the Court] . . . substitutes for *Frothingham,* for it seems to me that this new doctrine rests on premises that do not withstand analysis. Accordingly, I respectfully dissent. . . .

The lawsuits here and in *Frothingham* are fundamentally different. They present the question whether federal taxpayers *qua* taxpayers may, in suits in which they do not contest the validity of their previous or existing tax obligations, challenge the constitutionality of the uses for which Congress has authorized the expenditure of public funds. These differences in the purposes of the cases are reflected in differences in the litigants' interests. An action brought to contest the validity of tax liabilities assessed to the plaintiff is designed to vindicate interests that are personal and proprietary. The wrongs alleged and the relief sought by such a plaintiff are unmistakably private; only secondarily are his interests representative of those of the general population. I take it that the Court, although it does not pause to examine the question, believes that the interests of those who as taxpayers challenge the constitutionality of public expenditures may, at least in certain circumstances, be similar. Yet this assumption is surely mistaken. . . .

It seems to me clear that public actions, whatever the constitutional provisions on which they are premised, may involve important hazards for the continued effectiveness of the federal judiciary. Although I believe such actions to be within the jurisdiction conferred upon the federal courts by Article III of the Constitution, there surely can be little doubt that they strain the judicial function and press to the limit judicial authority. There is every reason to fear that unrestricted public actions might well alter the allocation of authority among the three branches of the Federal Government. . . .

Presumably the Court recognizes at least certain of these hazards, else it would not have troubled to impose limitations upon the situations in which, and purposes for which, such suits may be brought. Nonetheless, the limitations adopted by the Court are, as I have endeavored to indicate, wholly untenable. This is the more unfortunate because there is available a resolution of this problem that entirely satisfies the demands of the principle of separation of powers. This Court has previously held that individual litigants have standing to represent the public interest, despite their lack of economic or other personal interests, if Congress has appropriately authorized such suits. See especially *Oklahoma v. Civil Service Comm'n,* [1947]. I would adhere to that principle. Any hazards to the proper allocation of authority among the three branches of the Government would be substantially diminished if public actions had been pertinently authorized by Congress and the President. I appreciate that this Court does not ordinarily await the mandate of other branches of the Government, but it seems to me that the extraordinary character of public actions, and of the mischievous, if not dangerous, consequences they involve for the proper functioning of our constitutional system, and in particular of the federal courts, makes such judicial forbearance the part of wisdom. It must be emphasized that the implications of these questions of judicial policy are of fundamental significance for the other branches of the Federal Government.

Such a rule could readily be applied in this case. Although various efforts have been made in Congress to authorize public actions to contest the validity of federal expenditures in aid of religiously affiliated schools and other institutions, no such authorization has yet been given.

This does not mean that we would, under such a rule, be enabled to avoid our constitutional responsibilities, or that we would confine to limbo the First Amendment or any other constitutional command. The question here is not, despite the Court's unarticulated premise, whether the religious clauses of the First Amendment are hereafter to be enforced by the federal courts; the issue is simply whether plaintiffs of an *additional* category, heretoafter excluded from those courts, are to be permitted to maintain suits. The recent history of this Court is replete with illustrations, including even one announced today that questions involving the religious clauses will not, if federal taxpayers are prevented from contesting federal expenditures, be left "unacknowledged, unresolved, and undecided."

Accordingly, for the reasons contained in this opinion, I would affirm the judgment of the District Court.

QUESTIONS AND COMMENTS

1 We have indicated that, in general, one has no standing to assert the rights of another. The Court normally requires "injury in fact" to the party asserting the claim. The Court has indicated [*Sierra Club v. Morton,* 405 U.S. 737 (1972)] that purely ideological interests in the environment are not enough to establish standing to challenge governmental action which a litigant believes will be injurious or environmentally harmful. But environmental injury may serve to establish "injury in fact." If, for example, government wished to level a mountain which the litigant used for climbing, and such climbing gave the litigant aesthetic pleasure, "injury in fact" might be found. Do you think the distinction made here is defensible?

2 What is the relationship of *Mellon v. Massachusetts* to *Flast v. Cohen?*

3 Given your study of *Massachusetts v. Mellon* and *Flast v. Cohen,* in which of the following situations do you think the Court granted standing?

　a Where a litigant claimed that a railroad rate increase would decrease the use of recyclable goods, thereby causing increased litter everywhere [*United States v. Scrap,* 412 U.S. 669 (1973)].

   b Where an individual claimed that a member of Congress is ineligible to hold a commission in the armed forces while he or she is a member of Congress [*Schlesinger v. Reservists Committee to Stop the War,* 418 U.S. 208 (1974)].

   c Where an indigent claimed that IRS regulations cutting the level of free care necessary to enable a hospital to qualify as a tax-exempt charity were unconstitutional [*Simon v. Eastern Kentucky Welfare Rights Organization,* 426 U.S. 26 (1976)].

   d Where a Negro guest challenged the constitutionality of private club regulations barring the service of nonmember Negro guests [*Moose Lodge No. 107 v. Irvis,* 407 U.S. 163 (1972)].

4 Should we make it easy or difficult for taxpayers to challenge the acts of the federal government or its agencies? Why?

To Decide Abstract Questions of Law

Muskrat v. United States (1911)

Though English courts issued advisory opinions as early as 1770, it is a well-established principle in the United States that the Supreme Court will not do so. The late Felix Frankfurter suggested some of the reasons underlying the principle. According to Frankfurter,[9] to issue advisory opinions would involve the Court in decision-making without any assurance that all relevant facts have been developed and presented—a function accomplished by the adversary system. Moreover, Frankfurter suggests, there is danger in too much reliance on the judiciary. For example, once Congress has passed a statute, it is likely to defend it against challenge with great vigor. Thus Congress may be more creative and exercise a greater voice in national policy-making if it is denied the opinion of the Court in a noncase context. In *Muskrat v. United States* the Court explains its position on advising Congress about the constitutionality of legislation absent a challenge via a real case or controversy.

Muskrat v. United States

219 U.S. 346; 31 S. Ct. 250; 55 L. Ed. 246 (1911)
Vote: Unanimous

The facts are stated in the opinion.

MR. JUSTICE DAY delivered the opinion of the court.

   These cases arise under an act of Congress undertaking to confer jurisdiction upon the Court of Claims, and upon this court on appeal, to determine the validity of certain acts of Congress hereinafter referred to.

Case No. 330 was brought by David Muskrat and J. Henry Dick in their own behalf and in behalf of others in a like situation to determine the constitutional validity of the act of Congress of April 26, 1906, ... as amended by the act of June 21, ... and to have the same declared invalid in so far as the same undertook to increase the number of persons entitled to share in the final distribution of lands and funds of the Cherokees beyond those enrolled on September 1, 1902, in accordance with the act of Congress passed July 1, 1902. ... The acts subsequent to that of July 1, 1902, have the effect to increase the number of persons entitled to participate in the division of the Cherokee lands and funds, by permitting the enrollment of children who were minors living on March 4, 1906, whose parents had theretofore been enrolled as members of the Cherokee tribe or had applications pending for that purpose.

* * *

The first question in these cases, as in others, involves the jurisdiction of this court to entertain the proceeding, and that depends upon whether the jurisdiction conferred is within the power of Congress, having in view the limitations of the judicial power as established by the Constitution of the United States.

Section 1 of Article III of the Constitution provides:

The judicial power of the United States shall be vested in one Supreme Court and in such inferior courts as the Congress may from time to time ordain and establish.

Section 2 of the same Article provides:

The judicial power shall extend to all cases, in law and equity, arising under this Constitution, the laws of the United States, and treaties made, or which shall be made, under their authority;—to all cases affecting ambassadors, other public ministers, and consuls;—to all cases of admiralty and maritime jurisdiction;—to controversies to which the United States shall be a party; to controversies between two or more States;—between a State and citizens of another State;—between citizens of different States;—between citizens of the same State claiming lands under grants of different States, and between a State, or the citizens thereof, and foreign states, citizens or subjects.

* * *

As ... seen by the express terms of the Constitution, the exercise of the judicial power is limited to "cases" and "controversies." Beyond this it does not extend, and unless it is asserted in a case or controversy within the meaning of the Constitution, the power to excercise it is nowhere conferred.

What, then, does the Constitution mean in conferring this judicial power with the right to determine "cases" and "controversies"? A "case" was defined by Mr. Chief Justice Marshall as early as the leading case of *Marbury v. Madison,* [1803], to be a suit instituted according to the regular course of judicial procedure. And what more, if anything, is meant in the use of the term "controversy"? That question was dealt with by Mr. Justice Field, at the circuit, in

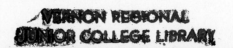

the case of *In re Pacific Railway Commission,* 32 Fed. Rep. 241, 255. Of these terms that learned Justice said:

"The judicial article of the Constitution mentions cases and controversies. The term 'controversies,' if distinguishable at all from 'cases,' is so in that it is less comprehensive than the latter, and includes only suits of a civil nature. *Chisholm v. Georgia,* [1793.] By cases and controversies are intended the claims of litigants brought before the courts for determination by such regular proceedings as are established by law or custom for the protection or enforcement of rights, or the prevention, redress, or punishment of wrongs. Whenever the claim of a party under the Constitution, laws, or treaties of the United States takes such a form that the judicial power is capable of acting upon it, then it has become a case. The term implies the existence of present possible adverse parties whose contentions are submitted to the court for adjudication."

The power being thus limited to require an application of the judicial power to cases and controversies, is the act which undertook to authorize the present suits to determine the constitutional validity of certain legislation within the constitutional authority of the court? This inquiry in the case before us includes the broader question, When may this court, in the exercise of the judicial power, pass upon the constitutional validity of an act of Congress? That question has been settled for the early history of the court, the leading case on the subject being *Marbury v. Madison, supra.*

. . . in the case of *Cohens v. Virginia,* [1821] Chief Justice Marshall, amplifying and reasserting the doctrine of *Marbury v. Madison,* recognized the limitations upon the right of this court to declare an act of Congress unconstitutional, and granting that there might be instances of its violation which could not be brought within the jurisdiction of the courts, and referring to a grant by a State of a patent of nobility as a case of that class, and conceding that the court would have no power to annul such a grant, said, p. 405:

"This may be very true; but by no means justifies the inference drawn from it. The article does not extend the judicial power to every violation of the Constitution which may possibly take place, but to 'a case in law or equity' in which a right under such law is asserted in a court of justice. If the question cannot be brought into court, then there is no case in law or equity, and no jurisdiction is given by the words of the article. But if, in any controversy depending in a court, the cause should depend on the validity of such a law, that would be a case arising under the Constitution, to which the judicial power of the United States would extend. . . .

Applying the principles thus long settled by the decisions of this court to the act of Congress undertaking to confer jurisdiction in this case, we find that David Muskrat and J. Henry Dick, for themselves and representatives of all Cherokee citizens enrolled as such for allotment as of September 1, 1902, are authorized and empowered to institute suits in the Court of Claims to determine the validity of acts of Congress passed since the act of July 1, 1902, in so far as the same attempt to increase or extend the restrictions upon alienation, encumbrance, or the right to lease the allotments of lands of Cherokee citizens, or to increase the number of persons entitled to share in the final distribution of lands and funds of the Cherokees beyond those enrolled for allotment as of September 1, 1902, and provided for in the said act of July 1, 1902.

The jurisdiction was given for that purpose first in the Court of Claims and then upon appeal to this court. That is, the object and purpose of the suit is wholly comprised in the determination of the constitutional validity of certain acts of Congress; and furthermore, in the last paragraph of the section, should a judgment be rendered in the Court of Claims or this court, denying the constitutional validity of such acts, then the amount of compensation to be paid to attorneys employed for the purpose of testing the constitutionality of the law is to be paid out of funds in the Treasury of the United States belonging to the beneficiaries, the act having previously provided that the United States should be made a party and the Attorney General be charged with the defense of the suits.

It is therefore evident that there is neither more nor less in this procedure than an attempt to provide for a judicial determination, final in this court, of the constitutional validity of an act of Congress. Is such a determination within the judicial power conferred by the Constitution, as the same has been interpreted and defined in the authoritative decisions to which we have referred? We think it is not. That judicial power, as we have seen, is the right to determine actual controversies arising between adverse litigants, duly instituted in courts of proper jurisdiction. The right to declare a law unconstitutional arises because an act of Congress relied upon by one or the other of such parties in determining their rights is in conflict with the fundamental law. The exercise of this, the most important and delicate duty of this court, is not given to it as a body with revisory power over the action of Congress, but because the rights of the litigants in justiciable controversies require the court to choose between the fundamental law and a law purporting to be enacted within constitutional authority, but in fact beyond the power delegated to the legislative branch of the Government. This attempt to obtain a judicial declaration of the validity of the act of Congress is not presented in a "case" or "controversy," to which, under the Constitution of the United States, the judicial power alone extends. It is true the United States is made a defendant to this action, but it has no interest adverse to the claimants. The object is not to assert a property right as against the Government, or to demand compensation for alleged wrongs because of action upon its part. The whole purpose of the law is to determine the constitutional validity of this class of legislation, in a suit not arising between parties concerning a property right necessarily involved in the decision in question, but in a proceeding against the Government in its sovereign capacity, and concerning which the only judgment required is to settle the doubtful character of the legislation in question. Such judgment will not conclude private parties, when actual litigation brings to the court the question of the constitutionality of such legislation. In a legal sense the judgment could not be executed, and amounts in fact to no more than an expression of opinion upon the validity of the acts in question. Confining the jurisdiction of this court within the limitations conferred by the Constitution, which the court has hitherto been careful to observe, and whose boundaries it has refused to transcend, we think the Congress, in the act of March 1, 1907, exceeded the limitations of legislative authority, so far as it required of this court action not judicial in its nature within the meaning of the Constitution.

For the reasons we have stated, we are constrained to hold that these actions present no justiciable controversy within the authority of the court, acting within the limitations of the Constitution under which it was created.

The judgments will be reversed and the cases remanded to the Court of Claims, with directions to dismiss the petitions for want of jurisdiction.

QUESTIONS AND COMMENTS

1 Are Frankfurter's arguments against the advisory opinion weakened or refuted by the following considerations?

a Though the adversary context is usually missing when the Court is asked for an advisory decision, must it be? Could Congress or the Court appoint lawyers to brief and argue both sides of an issue prior to an advisory opinion? If so, would the adversary system and its advantages be adequately simulated?

b An advisory opinion about proposed legislation would be given, normally, without any national experience with the legislative policy. Is it better to require the passing of a statute and experience with its consequences before having the Supreme Court rule on the policy's constitutionality? Should the consequences of a policy have anything to do with whether it is constitutionally valid?

To Challenge the Structure and Exercise of State Power

Luther v. Borden (1949)

Baker v. Carr (1962)

Article IV, Section 4 of the Constitution guarantees to every state "a republican form of government." Query: What is guaranteed, and who should determine when the "republican" requirement has been met? An answer to this question is suggested to the Court in *Luther v. Borden,* where we are introduced also to the "political question" doctrine.

Martin Luther v. Luther M. Borden et al.

7 How 1 (1849)
Vote: 8–1

The facts are given in the opinion.

Mr. Chief Justice TANEY delivered the opinion of the court.

This case has arisen out of the unfortunate political differences which agitated the people of Rhode Island in 1841 and 1842.

It is an action of trespass brought by Martin Luther, the plaintiff in error, against Luther M. Borden and others, the defendants, in the Circuit Court of the United States for the District of Rhode Island, for breaking and entering the plaintiff's house. . . .

The evidence shows that the defendants, in breaking into the plaintiff's house and endeavouring to arrest him, as stated in the pleadings, acted under the authority of the government which was established in Rhode Island at the time of the Declaration of Independence, and which is usually called the charter government. For when the separation from England took place, Rhode Island did not, like the other States, adopt a new constitution, but continued the form of government established by the charter of Charles the Second in 1663; making only such alterations, by acts of the legislature, as were necessary to adapt it to their condition and rights as an independent State. It was under this form of government that Rhode Island united with the other States in the Declaration of Independence, and afterwards ratified the Constitution of the United States and became a member of this Union; and it continued to be the established and unquestioned government of the State until the difficulties took place which have given rise to this action.

* * *

For some years previous to the disturbances of which we are now speaking, many of the citizens became dissatisfied with the charter government, and particularly with the restriction upon the right of suffrage. Memorials were addressed to the legislature upon this subject, urging the justice and necessity of a more liberal and extended rule. But they failed to produce the desired effect. And thereupon meetings were held and associations formed by those who were in favor of a more extended right of suffrage, which finally resulted in the election of a convention to form a new constitution to be submitted to the people for their adoption or rejection. This convention was not authorized by any law of the existing government. It was elected at voluntary meetings and by those citizens only who favored this plan of reform; those who were opposed to it, or opposed to the manner in which it was proposed to be accomplished, taking no part in the proceedings. The persons chosen as above mentioned came together and framed a constitution, by which the right of suffrage was extended to every male citizen of twenty-one years of age, who had resided in the State for one year, and in the town in which he offered to vote for six months, next preceding the election. The convention also prescribed the manner in which this constitution should be submitted to the decision of the people,—permitting every one to vote on that question who was an American citizen, twenty-one years old, and who had a permanent residence or home in the State, and directing the votes to be returned to the convention.

Upon the return of the votes, the convention declared that the constitution was adopted and ratified by a majority of the people of the State, and was the paramount law and constitution of Rhode Island. And it communicated this decision to the governor under the charter government, for the purpose of being laid before the legislature; and directed elections to be held for a governor, members of the legislature, and other officers under the new constitution. These elections accordingly took place, and the governor, lieutenant-governor, secretary of state, and senators and representatives thus appointed assembled at the city of Providence on May 3d, 1842, and immediately proceeded to organize the new government, by appointing the officers and passing the laws necessary for that purpose.

The charter government did not, however, admit the validity of these proceedings, nor acquiesce in them. On the contrary, in January, 1842, when this new constitution was communicated to the governor, and by him laid before the legislature, it passed resolutions declaring all acts done for the purpose of imposing that constitution upon the State to be an assumption of the powers of government, in violation of the rights of the existing government and of the people at large: and that it would maintain its authority and defend the legal and constitutional rights of the people.

In adopting this measure, as well as in all others taken by the charter government to assert its authority, it was supported by a large number of the citizens of the State, claiming to be a majority, who regarded the proceedings of the adverse party as unlawful and disorganizing, and maintained that, as the existing government had been established by the people of the State, no convention to frame a new constitution could be called without its sanction; and that the times and places of taking the votes, and the officers to receive them, and the qualification of the voters, must be previously regulated and appointed by law.

But, notwithstanding the determination of the charter government, and of those who adhered to it to maintain its authority, Thomas W. Dorr, who had been elected governor under the new constitution, prepared to assert the authority of that government by force, and many citizens assembled in arms to support him. The charter government thereupon passed an act declaring the State under martial law, and at the same time proceeded to call out the militia, to repel the threatened attack and to subdue those who were engaged in it. In this state of the contest, the house of the plaintiff, who was engaged in supporting the authority of the new government, was broken and entered in order to arrest him. The defendants were, at the time, in the military service of the old government, and in arms to support its authority.

* * *

The plaintiff contends that the charter government was displaced, and ceased to have any lawful power, after the organization, in May, 1842, of the government which he supported, and although that government never was able to exercise any authority in the State, nor to command obedience to its laws or to its officers, yet he insists that it was the lawful and established government, upon the ground that it was ratified by a large majority of the male people of the State of the age of twenty-one and upwards, and also by a majority of those who were entitled to vote for general officers under the then existing laws of the State. . . .

The Circuit Court . . . instructed the jury that the charter government and laws under which the defendants acted were, at the time the trespass is alleged to have been committed, in full force and effect as the form of government and paramount law of the State, and constituted a justification of the acts of the defendants as set forth in their pleas.

It is this opinion of the Circuit Court that we are now called upon to review. It is set forth more at large in the exception, but is in substance as above stated; and the question presented is certainly a very serious one. For, if this court is authorized to enter upon this inquiry as proposed by the plaintiff, and it should be decided that the charter government had no legal existence during the period of time above mentioned,—if it had been annulled by the adoption of the opposing government,—then the laws passed by its legislature during that time were nullities; its taxes wrongfully collected; its salaries and compensation to its officers illegally paid; its public accounts improperly settled; and the judgments and sentences of its courts in civil and criminal cases null and void, and the officers who carried their decisions into operation answerable as trespassers, if not in some cases as criminals.

When the decision of this court might lead to such results, it becomes its duty to examine very carefully its own powers before it undertakes to exercise jurisdiction.

Certainly, the question which the plaintiff proposed to raise by the testimony he offered has not heretofore been recognized as a judicial one in any of the State courts. In forming the constitutions of the different States, after the Declaration of Independence, and in the various changes and alterations which have since been made, the political department has always determined whether the proposed constitution or amendment was ratified or not by the people of the State, and the judicial power has followed its decision. . . .

Upon what ground could the Circuit Court of the United States which tried this case have departed from this rule, and disregarded and overruled the decisions of the courts of Rhode Island? Undoubtedly the courts of the United States have certain powers under the Constitution and laws of the United States which do not belong to the State courts. But the power of determining that a State government has been lawfully established, which the courts of the State disown and repudiate, is not one of them. Upon such a question the courts of the United States are bound to follow the decisions of the State tribunals, and must therefore regard the charter government as the lawful and established government during the time of this contest.

Besides, if the Circuit Court had entered upon this inquiry, by what rule could it have determined the qualification of voters upon the adoption or rejection of the proposed constitution, unless there was some previous law of the State to guide it? It is the province of a court to expound the law, not to make it. And certainly it is no part of the judicial functions of any court of the United States to prescribe the qualification of voters in a State, giving the right to those to whom it is denied by the written and established constitution and laws of the State, or taking it away from those to whom it is given; nor has it the right to determine what political privileges the citizens of a State are entitled to, unless there is an established constitution or law to govern its decision.

. . . the Constitution of the United States, as far as it has provided for an emergency of this kind, and authorized the general government to interfere in the domestic concerns of a State, has treated the subject as political in its nature, and placed the power in the hands of that department.

The fourth section of the fourth article of the Constitution of the United States provides that the United States shall guarantee to every State in the Union a republican form of government, and shall protect each of them against invasion; and on the application of the legislature or of the executive (when the legislature cannot be convened) against domestic violence.

Under this article of the Constitution it rests with Congress to decide what government is the established one in a State. For as the United States guarantee to each State a republican government, Congress must necessarily decide what government is established in the State before it can determine whether it is republican or not. And when the senators and representatives of a State are admitted into the councils of the Union, the authority of the government under which they are appointed as well as its republican character, is recognized by the proper constitutional authority. And its decision is binding on every other department of the government, and could not be questioned in a judicial tribunal. It is true that the contest in this case did not last long enough to bring the matter to this issue; and as no senators or representatives were elected under the authority of the government of which Mr. Dorr was the head, Congress was not called upon to decide the controversy. Yet the right to decide is placed there, and not in the courts.

* * *

Upon the whole, we see no reason for disturbing the judgment of the Circuit Court. The admission of evidence to prove that the charter government was the established government of the State was an irregularity, but is not material to the judgment. A Circuit Court of the United States sitting in Rhode Island is presumed to know the constitution and law of the State. And in order to make up its opinion upon that subject, it seeks information from any authentic and available source, without waiting for the formal introduction of testimony to prove it, and without confining itself to the process which the parties may offer. But this error of the Circuit Court does not affect the result. For whether this evidence was or was not received, the Circuit Court, for the reasons herein before stated, was bound to recognize that government as the paramount and established authority of the State.

Much of the argument on the part of the plaintiff turned upon political rights and political questions, upon which the court has been urged to express an opinion. We decline doing so. The high power has been conferred on this court of passing judgment upon the acts of the State sovereignties, and of the legislative and executive branches of the federal government, and of determining whether they are beyond the limits of power marked out for them respectively by the Constitution of the United States. This tribunal, therefore, should be the last to overstep the boundaries which limit its own jurisdiction. And while it should always be ready to meet any question confided to it by the Constitution, it is equally its duty not to pass beyond its appropriate sphere of action, and to take care not to involve itself in discussions which properly belong to other forums. No one, we believe, has ever doubted the proposition, that, according to the institutions of this country, the sovereignty in every State resides in the people of the State, and that they may alter and change their form of government at their own pleasure. But whether they have changed it or not by abolishing an old government, and establishing a new one in its place, is a question to be settled by the political power. And when that power has decided, the courts are bound to take notice of its decision, and to follow it.

The judgment of the Circuit Court must therefore be affirmed.

* * *

QUESTIONS AND COMMENTS

1 Do you think the Court's decision in *Luther v. Borden* was influenced more by the ambiguity of the "guaranty clause" or by the political ramifications of deciding the issue raised? Why?
2 Could Luther have presented his claim more successfully under some other clause of the Constitution? What if Luther's case arose in 1968?

* * * * * *

Baker v. Carr deals with the time-honored position of the Court that questions of legislative redistricting or reapportionment are political in nature and not subject to Supreme Court jurisdiction. In 1946, in *Colegrove v. Green,* the Court dismissed a challenge to an Illinois statute apportioning congressional districts.[10]

In 1950, in *South v. Peters,* a challenge to Georgia's "county unit" system met the same fate.[11] Under the Georgia scheme, each county was allotted a number of unit votes—from six to two—with the candidate receiving the highest popular vote in a primary election being awarded all the county's unit votes. County unit votes determined the statewide outcome. Voters in Fulton County, Georgia's most populous, maintained that a vote in another county would be worth over 120 times as much as theirs, with lesser discrepancies in other counties. They claimed a violation of Fourteenth and Seventeenth Amendment rights. The district court dismissed the claim. The Supreme Court affirmed, saying: "Federal Courts consistently refuse to exercise their equity powers in cases posing political issues arising from a state's geographical distribution of electoral strength among its political subdivisions."[12]

The Court had reached similar conclusions in similar cases raising this kind of issue between *Colegrove* and *South.*[13] Ten years after *South v. Peters,* the court held that the disenfranchising of Negroes was a justiciable question.[14] This ruling turned on the Fifteenth Amendment. But ruling out a gerrymander that diluted the votes of Negroes undoubtedly set the stage for the Court's decision in *Baker v. Carr* two years later.

Baker et al. v. Carr et al.

369 U.S. 186; 82 S. Ct. 691; 7 L. Ed. 2d 663 (1962)
Vote: 6–2

Baker and others challenged a 1901 Tennessee statute which apportioned the seats in the General Assembly among the state's ninety-five counties. The complaint alleged that the apportionment had been capricious and arbitrary, and that it had not been corrected subsequently in spite of substantial growth and redistribution of the state's population. The result, they argued, debased their votes, thereby denying them equal protection of the law under the Fourteenth Amendment. The federal district court dismissed the complaint for lack of jurisdiction of the subject matter. The Supreme Court granted review.

MR. JUSTICE BRENNAN delivered the opinion of the Court.

* * *

In 1901 the General Assembly abandoned separate enumeration in favor of reliance upon the Federal Census and passed the Apportionment Act here in controversy. In the more than 60 years since that action, all proposals in both Houses of the General Assembly for reapportionment have failed to pass.

Between 1901 and 1961. Tennessee has experienced substantial growth and redistribution of her population. In 1901 the population was 2,020,616, of whom 487,380 were eligible to vote. The 1960 Federal Census reports the

State's population at 3,567,080, of whom 2,092,891 are eligible to vote. The relative standings of the counties in terms of qualified voters have changed significantly. It is primarily the continued application of the 1901 Apportionment Act to this shifted and enlarged voting population which gives rise to the present controversy.

* * *

I THE DISTRICT COURT'S OPINION AND ORDER OF DISMISSAL

After noting that the plaintiffs challenged the existing legislative apportionment in Tennessee under the Due Process and Equal Protection Clauses, and summarizing the supporting allegations and the relief requested, the ... [district court] proceeded to explain its action as turning on the case's presenting a "question of the distribution of political strength for legislative purposes." For example:

> From a review of [numerous Supreme Court] ... decisions there can be no doubt that the federal rule, as enunciated and applied by the Supreme Court, is that the federal courts, whether from a lack of jurisdiction or from the inappropriateness of the subject matter for judicial consideration, will not intervene in cases of this type to compel legislative reapportionment. . . .

In light of the District Court's treatment of the case, we hold today only (a) that the court possessed jurisdiction of the subject matter; (b) that a justiciable cause of action is stated upon which appellants would be entitled to appropriate relief; and (c) because appellees raise the issue before this Court, that the appellants have standing to challenge the Tennessee apportionment statutes. Beyond noting that we have no cause at this stage to doubt the District Court will be able to fashion relief if violations of constitutional rights are found, it is improper now to consider what remedy would be most appropriate if appellants prevail at the trial.

II JURISDICTION OF THE SUBJECT MATTER

The District Court was uncertain whether our cases withholding federal judicial relief rested upon a lack of federal jurisdiction or upon the inappropriateness of the subject matter for judicial consideration—what we have designated "nonjusticiability." The distinction between the two grounds is significant. In the instance of nonjusticiability, consideration of the cause is not wholly and immediately foreclosed; rather, the Court's inquiry necessarily proceeds to the point of deciding whether the duty asserted can be judicially identified and its breach judicially determined, and whether protection for the right asserted can be judicially molded. In the instance of lack of jurisdiction the cause either does not "arise under" the Federal Constitution, laws or treaties (or fall within one of the other enumerated categories of Art. III, § 2), or is not a "case or controversy" within the meaning of that section: or the cause is not one described by any jurisdictional statute. Our conclusion . . . that this cause presents no nonjusticiable "political question" settles the only possible doubt that it is a case or controversy. Under the present heading of "Jurisdiction of the Subject Matter" we hold only that the matter set forth in the complaint does arise under the Constitution and is within 28 U.S.C. § 1343.

Article III, § 2, of the Federal Constitution provide that "The judicial Power shall extend to all Cases, in Law and Equity, arising under this Constitution, the Laws of the United States, and Treaties made, or which shall be made, under their Authority. . . ." It is clear that the cause of action is one which "arises under" the Federal Constitution. The complaint alleges that the 1901 statute effects an apportionment that deprives the appellants of the equal protection of the laws in violation of the Fourteenth Amendment. Dismissal of the complaint upon the ground of lack of jurisdiction of the subject matter would, therefore, be justified only if that claim were "so attenuated and unsubstantial as to be absolutely devoid of merit." *Newburyport Water Co. v. Newburyport,* [1904], or "frivolous," *Bell v. Hood,* [1946]. That the claim is unsubstantial must be "very plain." *Hart v. Keith Vaudeville Exchange,* [1921]. Since the District Court obviously and correctly did not deem the asserted federal constitutional claim unsubstantial and frivolous, it should not have dismissed the complaint for want of jurisdiction of the subject matter. And of course no further consideration of the merits of the claim is relevant to a determination of the court's jurisdiction of the subject matter.

*   *   *

Since the complaint plainly sets forth a case arising under the Constitution, the subject matter is within the federal judicial power defined in Art. III, § 2, and so within the power of Congress to assign to the jurisdiction of the District Courts. Congress has exercised that power in 28 U.S.C. § 1343 (3):

*   *   *

An unbroken line of our precedents sustains the federal courts' jurisdiction of the subject matter of federal constitutional claims of this nature. . . .

The appellees refer to *Colegrove v. Green,* [1946], as authority that the District Court lacked jurisdiction of the subject matter. Appellees misconceive the holding of that case. The holding was precisely contrary to their reading it. Seven members of the Court participated in the decision. Unlike many other cases in this field which have assumed without discussion that there was jurisdiction, all three opinions filed in *Colegrove* discussed the question. Two of the opinions expressing the views of four of the Justices, a majority, flatly held that there was jurisdiction of the subject matter. . . .

We hold that the District Court has jurisdiction of the subject matter of the federal constitutional claim asserted in the complaint.

III STANDING

A federal court cannot "pronounce any statute, either of a State or of the United States, void, because irreconcilable with the Constitution, except as it is called upon to adjudge the legal rights of litigants in actual controversies." *Liverpool Steamship Co. v. Commissioners of Emigration,* [1884]. Have the appellants alleged such a personal stake in the outcome of the controversy as to assure that concrete adverseness which sharpens the presentation of issues upon which the court so largely depends for illumination of difficult constitutional questions? This is the gist of the question of standing. It is, of course, a question of federal law.

* * *

We hold that the appellants do have standing to maintain this suit. Our decisions plainly support this conclusion. Many of the cases have assumed rather than articulated the premise in deciding the merits of similar claims. And *Colegrove v. Green, supra,* squarely held that voters who allege facts showing disadvantage to themselves as individuals have standing to sue. . . .

The injury which appellants assert is that . . . [the statutory] classification disfavors the voters in the counties in which they reside, placing them in a position of constitutionally unjustifiable inequality *vis-à-vis* voters in irrationally favored counties. . . .

It would not be necessary to decide whether appellants' allegations of impairment of their votes by the 1901 apportionment will, ultimately, entitle them to any relief, in order to hold that they have standing to seek it. If such impairment does produce a legally cognizable injury, they are among those who have sustained it. They are asserting "a plain, direct and adequate interest in maintaining the effectiveness of their votes," *Coleman v. Miller,* [1939]. . . . They are entitled to a hearing and to the District Court's decision on their claims.

* * *

IV JUSTICIABILITY

In holding that the subject matter of this suit was not justiciable, the District Court relied on *Colgrove v. Green, supra,* and subsequent *per curiam* cases. . . .

We understand the District Court to have read the cited cases as compelling the conclusion that since the appellants sought to have a legislative apportionment held unconstitutional, their suit presented a "political question" and was therefore nonjusticiable. We hold that this challenge to an apportionment presents no nonjusticiable "political question.". . .

Of course the mere fact that the suit seeks protection of a political right does not mean it presents a political question. Such an objection "is little more than a play upon words." *Nixon v. Herndon,* [1927]. Rather, it is argued that apportionment cases, whatever the actual wording of the complaint, can involve no federal constitutional right except one resting on the guaranty of a republican form of government, and that complaints based on that clause have been held to present political questions which are nonjusticiable.

We hold that the claim pleaded here neither rests upon nor implicates the Guaranty Clause and that its justiciability is therefore not foreclosed by our decisions of cases involving that clause. The District Court misinterpreted *Colegrove v. Green* and other decisions of this Court on which it relied. Appellants' claim that they are being denied equal protection is justiciable, and if "discrimination is sufficiently shown, the right to relief under the equal protection clause is not diminished by the fact that the discrimination relates to political rights." *Snowden v. Hughes,* [1944]. . . . in the Guaranty Clause cases and in the other "political question" cases, it is the relationship between the judiciary and the coordinate branches of the Federal Government, and not the federal judiciary's relationship to the States, which gives rise to the "political question."

We have said that "In determining whether a question falls within [the political question] category, the appropriateness under our system of government of attributing finality to the action of the political departments and also the lack of satisfactory criteria for a judicial determination are dominant considerations." *Coleman v. Miller.*

The nonjusticiability of a political question is primarily a function of the separation of powers. Much confusion results from the capacity of the "political question" label to obscure the need for case-by-case inquiry. Deciding whether a matter has in any measure been committed by the Consitution to another branch of government, or whether the action of that branch exceeds whatever authority has been committed, is itself a delicate exercise in constitutional interpretation and is a responsibility of this Court as ultimate interpreter of the Constitution. . . .

[After reviewing a number of "political question" cases, the Court continued.]

We come, finally, to the ultimate inquiry whether our precedents as to what constitutes a nonjusticiable "political question" bring the case before us under the umbrella of that doctrine. A natural beginning is to note whether any of the common characteristics which we have been able to identify and label descriptively are present. We find none: The question here is the consistency of state action with the Federal Constitution. We have no question decided, or to be decided, by a political branch of government coequal with this Court. Nor do we risk embarrassment of our government abroad, or grave disturbance at home if we take issue with Tennessee as to the constitutionality of her action here challenged. Nor need the appellants, in order to succeed in this action, ask the Court to enter upon policy determination for which judicially manageable standards are lacking. Judicial standards under the Equal Protection Clause are well developed and familiar, and it has been open to courts since the enactment of the Fourteenth Amendment to determine, if on the particular facts they must, that a discrimination reflects *no* policy, but simply arbitrary and capricious action.

This case does, in one sense, involve the allocation of political power within a State, and the appellants might conceivably have added a claim under the Guaranty Clause. Of course, as we have seen, any reliance on that clause would be futile. But because any reliance on the Guaranty Clause could not have succeeded it does not follow that appellants may not be heard on the equal protection claim which in fact they tender. True, it must be clear that the Fourteenth Amendment claim is not so enmeshed with those political question elements which render Guaranty Clause claims nonjusticiable as actually to present a political question itself. But we have found that not to be the case here. . . .

We conclude that the complaint's allegations of a denial of equal protection present a justiciable constitutional cause of action upon which appellants are entitled to a trial decision. The right asserted is within the reach of judicial protection under the Fourteenth Amendment.

The judgment of the District Court is reversed and the cause is remanded for further proceedings consistent with this opinion.

Reversed and remanded.

* * *

MR. JUSTICE FRANKFURTER, whom MR. JUSTICE HARLAN joins, dissenting.

The Court today reverses a uniform course of decision established by a dozen cases, including one by which the very claim now sustained was unanimously rejected only five years ago. The impressive body of rulings thus cast aside reflected the equally uniform course of our political history regarding the relationship between population and legislative representation—a wholly different matter from denial of the franchise to individuals because of race, color, religion or sex. Such a massive repudiation of the experience of our whole past in asserting destructively novel judicial power demands a detailed analysis of the role of this Court in our constitutional scheme. Disregard of inherent limits in the effective exercise of the Court's "judicial Power" not only presages the futility of judicial intervention in the essentially political conflict of forces by which the relation between population and representation has time out of mind been and now is determined. It may well impair the Court's position as the ultimate organ of "the supreme Law of the Land" in that vast range of legal problems, often strongly entangled in popular feeling, on which this Court must pronounce. The Court's authority—possessed of neither the purse nor the sword—ultimately rests on sustained public confidence in its moral sanction. Such feeling must be nourished by the Court's complete detachment, in fact and in appearance, from political entanglements and by abstention from injecting itself into the clash of political forces in political settlements.

* * *

We were soothingly told at the bar of this Court that we need not worry about the kind of remedy a court could effectively fashion once the abstract constitutional right to have courts pass on a state-wide system of electoral districting is recognized as a matter of judicial rhetoric, because legislatures would heed the Court's admonition. This is not only a euphoric hope. It implies a sorry confession of judicial impotence in place of a frank acknowledgment that there is not under our Constitution a judicial remedy for every political mischief, for every undesirable exercise of legislative power. The Framers carefully and with deliberate forethought refused so to enthrone the judiciary. In this situation, as in others of like nature, appeal for relief does not belong here. Appeal must be to an informed, civically militant electorate. In a democratic society like ours, relief must come through an aroused popular conscience that sears the conscience of the people's representatives. In any event there is nothing judicially more unseemly nor more self-defeating than for this Court to make *in terrorem* pronouncements, to indulge in merely empty rhetoric, sounding a word of promise to the ear, sure to be disappointing to the hope.

* * *

What . . . is this question of legislative apportionment? Appellants invoke the right to vote and to have their votes counted. But they are permitted to vote and their votes are counted. They go to the polls, they cast their ballots, they send their representatives to the state councils. Their complaint is simply that the representatives are not sufficiently numerous or powerful—in short, that Tennessee has adopted a basis of representation with which they are dissatisfied. Talk of "debasement" or "dilution" is circular talk. One cannot speak of "debasement" or "dilution" of the value of a vote until there is first defined a standard of reference as to what a vote should be worth. What is actually asked of the Court in this case is to choose among competing bases of representation—ultimately, really, among competing theories of political philosophy—in order to establish an appropriate frame of government for the State of Tennessee and thereby for all the States of the Union.

In such a matter, abstract analogies which ignore the facts of history deal in unrealities; they betray reason. This is not a case in which a State has, through a device however oblique and sophisticated, denied Negroes or Jews or red-headed persons a vote, or given them only a third or a sixth of a vote. That was *Gomillion v. Lightfoot,* [1960].

What Tennessee illustrates is an old and still widespread method of representation—representation by local geographical division, only in part respective of population—in preference to others, others, forsooth, more appealing. Appellants contest this choice and seek to make this Court the arbiter of the disagreement. They would make the Equal Protection Clause the charter of adjudication, asserting that the equality which it guarantees comports, if not the assurance of equal weight to every voter's vote, at least the basic conception that representation ought to be proportionate to population, a standard by reference to which the reasonableness of apportionment plans may be judged.

To find such a political conception legally enforceable in the broad and unspecific guarantee of equal protection is to rewrite the Constitution. . . .

Dissenting opinion of MR. JUSTICE HARLAN, whom MR. JUSTICE FRANKFURTER joins. . . .

I can find nothing in the Equal Protection Clause or elsewhere in the Federal Constitution which expressly or impliedly supports the view that state legislatures must be so structured as to reflect with approximate equality the voice of every voter. Not only is that proposition refuted by history, as shown by my Brother FRANKFURTER, but it strikes deep into the heart of our federal system. Its acceptance would require us to turn our backs on the regard which this Court has always shown for the judgment of state legislatures and courts on matters of basically local concern.

In the last analysis, what lies at the core of this controversy is a difference of opinion as to the function of representative government. It is surely beyond argument that those who have the responsibility for devising a system of representation may permissibly consider that factors other than bare numbers should be taken into account. The existence of the United States Senate is proof enough of that. To consider that we may ignore the Tennessee Legislature's judgment in this instance because that body was the product of an asymmetrical electoral apportionment would in effect be to assume the very conclusion here disputed. Hence we must accept the present form of the Tennessee Legislature as the embodiment of the State's choice, or, more realistically, its compromise, between competing political philosophies. The federal courts have not been empowered by the Equal Protection Clause to judge whether this resolution of the State's internal political conflict is desirable or undesirable, wise or unwise.

. . . there is nothing in the Federal Constitution to prevent a State, acting not irrationally, from choosing any electoral legislative structure it thinks best suited to the interests, temper, and customs of its people. I would have thought this proposition settled by *MacDougall v. Green,* [1948], in which the Court observed (at p. 283) that to "assume that political power is a function exclusively of numbers is to disregard the practicalities of government," and reaffirmed by *South v. Peters,* [1950]. A State's choice to distribute electoral strength among geographical units, rather than according to a census of population, is certainly no less a rational decision of policy than would be its choice to levy a tax on property rather than a tax on income. Both are legislative judgments entitled to equal respect from this Court.

* * *

In conclusion, it is appropriate to say that one need not agree, as a citizen, with what Tennessee has done or failed to do, in order to deprecate, as a judge, what the majority is doing today. Those observers of the Court who see it primarily as the last refuge for the correction of all inequality or injustice, no matter what its nature or source, will no doubt applaud this decision and its break with the past. Those who consider that continuing national respect for the Court's authority depends in large measure upon its wise exercise of self-restraint and descipline in constitutional adjudication, will view the decision with deep concern.

I would affirm.

* * *

QUESTIONS AND COMMENTS

1 It has been said that the malapportionment of legislative bodies is incompatible with democracy. If that is true, does the Supreme Court have a duty to strike down all electoral schemes that result in such malapportionment? If the answer is yes, does that mean the Court should decide "political questions"? What of the dangers described by Justice Frankfurter in *Baker v. Carr?* Is there a "judicial remedy for every political mischief"? Should there be?

2 Today, how would you assess the concerns expressed by Frankfurter in 1962 and earlier? Was he right or wrong?

3 How does *Baker v. Carr* relate to the doctrine of "judicial restraint" or "judicial activism"? On which of Canon's six dimensions would you place *Baker v. Carr?*

4 In 1977, the Supreme Court was asked to invalidate a New York redistricting law which diluted the value of the franchise for Hasidic Jews in order to create a majority of 65 percent in some districts. Why did the Court not view this as a political question? On the basis of *Baker v. Carr,* what decision would you anticipate? (See *United Jewish Organizations v. Carey,* 430 U.S. 144.)

NOTES

1 *Calder v. Bull,* 3 Dallas 386, 399 (1798).
2 *Rindge Co. v. Los Angeles County,* 262 U.S. 700 (1923).
3 *Jenkins v. McKeithen,* 395 U.S. 411 (1969).
4 *Babbitt v. United Farm Workers,* 442 U.S. 289 (1979).
5 *California Banker's Association v. Schultz,* 416 U.S. 21 (1974).
6 *Doremus v. Board of Education,* 342 U.S. 429 (1952).
7 *Doe v. Bolton,* 410 U.S. 179 (1973).
8 *Eisenstadt v. Baird,* 405 U.S. 438 (1972).
9 Felix Frankfurter, "Note on Advisory Opinions," 37 *Harvard Law Review* 1002 (1924).
10 *Colegrove v. Green,* 328 U.S. 549 (1946).
11 *South v. Peters,* 339 U.S. 276 (1950).
12 Ibid., p. 277.
13 *McDougall v. Green,* 335 U.S. 281 (1948); *Cook v. Fortson,* 329 U.S. 675 (1946).
14 *Gomillion v. Lightfoot,* 364 U.S. 339 (1960).

CHAPTER 3

THE SCOPE OF STATE POWER

To Burden Interstate Commerce

Gibbons v. Ogden (1824)

Cooley v. Board of Wardens (1851)

South Carolina Highway Department v. Barnwell Brothers (1938)

California v. Thompson (1941)

Southern Pacific v. Arizona (1945)

Morgan v. Virginia (1946)

Ray v. Atlantic Richfield Co. (1978)

It was the practice in some states in the early part of the nineteenth century to grant exclusive rights to steam navigation on certain waters within the boundaries of the state. New York, Louisiana, Massachusetts, and Georgia were among the states granting such monopolies. Naturally, would-be competitors sought ways to break these monopolies so that they too might ply the lucrative market for moving people and goods by steamboat. One way to break such monopolies would be to attack the power of states to grant these monopolies in the first place. This line of attack not only appealed to prospective commercial competitors, it also attracted believers in a strong federal government who wanted to enhance the control of commerce by the Congress. States'-righters, on the other hand, were natural supporters of the monopolies—that is to say, supporters of the states' power to grant such privileges.

Congress is delegated the power to "regulate commerce . . . among the several states" in the Constitution, but in the early years showed little interest in adopting specific regulations. Thus, in 1824, when *Gibbons v. Ogden* came to the Court, the definition of interstate commerce subject to control by Congress was somewhat fuzzy. One view was that "commerce among the states" meant all commerce in the United States. A competing view held that Congress only had power to control commerce between two or more states. Under this second definition, commerce occurring within a single state would not be subject to congressional control. In *Gibbons v. Ogden,* the Marshall-led Court effectively chose between these competing conceptualizations. In so doing, the Marshall opinion made important contributions to the question of relative state and federal power.

Gibbons v. Ogden

22 U.S. (9 Wheat.) 1 (1824)
Vote: Unanimous

The state of New York granted exclusive navigational rights on its waters to
Robert Fulton and Robert R. Livingston. The right to navigate the waters
between New York City and places in New Jersey was later assigned to John
R. Livingston and by him to Aaron Ogden. Thomas Gibbons owned two
steamboats, the *Stoudinger* and the *Bellona,* and operated them between
New York and Elizabethtown, New Jersey, in alleged violation of Ogden's
exclusive grant. Ogden obtained an injunction to stop Gibbons's trafficking
on New York waters, in spite of the fact that Gibbons's boats were licensed
for the coasting trade by an act of Congress. After the highest state court of
jurisdiction upheld the injunction, the Supreme Court granted review.

MARSHALL, C. J., delivered the opinion of the court, and, after stating the case,
proceeded as follows:—

The appellant contends that this decree is erroneous, because the laws which
purport to give the exclusive privilege it sustains, are repugnant to the Constitution and laws of the United States.

They are said to be repugnant—

1 To that clause in the constitution which authorizes congress to regulate
commerce.

2 To that which authorizes congress to promote the progress of science and
useful arts.

. . . [The Constitution] contains an enumeration of powers expressly granted
by the people to their government. It has been said that these powers ought to
be construed strictly. But why ought they to be so construed? Is there one sentence in the constitution which gives countenance to this rule? In the last of
the enumerated powers, that which grants, expressly, the means for carrying
all others into execution, congress is authorized "to make all laws which shall
be necessary and proper" for the purpose. But this limitation on the means
which may be used, is not extended to the powers which are conferred; nor is
there one sentence in the constitution, which has been pointed out by the
gentlemen of the bar, or which we have been able to discern, that prescribes
this rule. We do not, therefore, think ourselves justified in adopting it. What
do gentlemen mean by a strict construction? If they contend only against that
enlarged construction, which would extend words beyond their natural and
obvious import, we might question the application of the term, but should not
controvert the principle. If they contend for that narrow construction which,
in support of some theory not to be found in the constitution, would deny to
the government those powers which the words of the grant, as usually understood, import, and which are consistent with the general views and objects of

the instrument; for that narrow construction, which would cripple the government, and render it unequal to the objects for which it is declared to be instituted, and to which the powers given, as fairly understood, render it competent; then we cannot perceive the propriety of this strict construction, nor adopt it as the rule by which the constitution is to be expounded. As men whose intentions require no concealment, generally employ the words which most directly and aptly express the ideas they intend to convey, the enlightened patriots who framed our constitution, and the people who adopted it, must be understood to have employed words in their natural sense, and to have intended what they have said. . . .

The words are: "Congress shall have power to regulate commerce with foreign nations, and among the several States, and with the Indian tribes."

The subject to be regulated is commerce; and our constitution being, as was aptly said at the bar, one of enumeration, and not of definition, to ascertain the extent of the power, it becomes necessary to settle the meaning of the word. The counsel for the appellee would limit it to traffic, to buying and selling, or the interchange of commodities, and do not admit that it comprehends navigation. This would restrict a general term, applicable to many objects, to one of its significations. Commerce, undoubtedly, is traffic, but it is something more: it is intercourse. It describes the commercial intercourse between nations, and parts of nations, in all its branches, and is regulated by prescribing rules for carrying on that intercourse. The mind can scarcely conceive a system for regulating commerce between nations, which shall exclude all laws concerning navigation, which shall be silent on the admission of the vessels of the one nation into the ports of the other, and be confined to prescribing rules for the conduct of individuals, in the actual employment of buying and selling, or of barter.

If commerce does not include navigation, the government of the Union has no direct power over that subject, and can make no law prescribing what shall constitute American vessels, or requiring that they shall be navigated by American seamen. Yet this power has been exercised from the commencement of the government, has been exercised with the consent of all, and has been understood by all to be a commercial regulation. All America understands, and has uniformly understood, the word "commerce," to comprehend navigation. It was so understood, and must have been so understood, when the constitution was framed. The power over commerce, including navigation, was one of the primary objects for which the people of America adopted their government, and must have been contemplated in forming it. The convention must have used the word in that sense, because all have understood it in that sense; and the attempt to restrict it comes too late.

*   *   *

The word used in the constitution, then, comprehends, and has been always understood to comprehend, navigation, within its meaning; and a power to regulate navigation is as expressly granted as if that term had been added to the word "commerce."

To what commerce does this power extend? The constitution informs us, to commerce "with foreign nations, and among the several States, and with the Indian tribes."

It has, we believe, been universally admitted that these words comprehend every species of commercial intercourse between the United States and foreign nations. No sort of trade can be carried on between this country and any other, to which this power does not extend. It has been truly said that commerce, as the word is used in the constitution, is a unit, every part of which is indicated by the term.

If this be the admitted meaning of the word, in its application to foreign nations, it must carry the same meaning throughout the sentence, and remain a unit, unless there be some intelligible cause which alters it.

The subject to which the power is next applied, is to commerce "among the several States." The word "among" means intermingled with. A thing which is among others, is intermingled with them. Commerce among the States, cannot stop at the external boundary line of each State, but may be introduced into the interior.

It is not intended to say that these words comprehend that commerce which is completely internal, which is carried on between man and man in a State, or between different parts of the same State, and which does not extend to or affect other States. Such a power would be inconvenient, and is certainly unnecessary.

Comprehensive as the word "among" is, it may very properly be restricted to that commerce which concerns more States than one. The phrase is not one which would probably have been selected to indicate the completely interior traffic of a State, because it is not an apt phrase for that purpose; and the enumeration of the particular classes of commerce to which the power was to be extended, would not have been made, had the intention been to extend the power to every description. The enumeration presupposes something not enumerated; and that something, if we regard the language, or the subject of the sentence, must be the exclusively internal commerce of a State. . . . The completely internal commerce of a State, then, may be considered as reserved for the State itself.

But, in regulating commerce with foreign nations, the power of congress does not stop at the jurisdictional lines of the several States. It would be a very useless power, if it could not pass those lines. The commerce of the United States with foreign nations, is that of the whole United States. Every district has a right to participate in it. The deep streams which penetrate our country in every direction, pass through the interior of almost every State in the Union, and furnish the means of exercising this right. If congress has the power to regulate it, that power must be exercised whenever the subject exists. If it exists within the States, if a foreign voyage may commence or terminate at a port within a State, then the power of congress may be exercised within a state. . . .

The power of congress, then, whatever it may be, must be exercised within the territorial jurisdiction of the several States. The sense of the nation on this subject, is unequivocally manifested by the provisions made in the laws for transporting goods, by land, between Baltimore and Providence, between New York and Philadelphia, and between Philadelphia and Baltimore.

We are now arrived at the inquiry—what is this power?

It is the power to regulate; that is, to prescribe the rule by which commerce is to be governed. This power, like all others vested in congress, is complete in itself, may be exercised to its utmost extent, and acknowledges no limitations other than are prescribed in the constitution. These are expressed in plain terms, and do not affect the questions which arise in this case, or which have been discussed at the bar. . . .

The power of congress . . . comprehends navigation within the limits of every State in the Union, so far as that navigation may be, in any manner, connected with "commerce with foreign nations, or among the several States, or with the Indian tribes." It may, of consequence, pass the jurisdictional line of New York, and act upon the very waters to which the prohibition now under consideration applies.

But it has been urged with great earnestness that, although the power of congress to regulate commerce with foreign nations, and among the several States, be coextensive with the subject itself, and have no other limits than are prescribed in the constitution, yet the States may severally exercise the same power, within their respective jurisdictions. In support of this argument, it is said that they possessed it as an inseparable attribute of sovereignty, before the formation of the constitution, and still retain it, except so far as they have surrendered it by that instrument; that this principle results from the nature of the government, and is secured by the tenth amendment; that an affirmative grant of power is not exclusive, unless in its own nature it be such that the continued exercise of it by the former possessor is inconsistent with the grant, and that this is not of that description.

* * *

In discussing the question whether this power is still in the States, in the case under consideration, we may dismiss from it the inquiry, whether it is surrendered by the mere grant to congress, or is retained until congress shall exercise the power. We may dismiss that inquiry because it has been exercised, and the regulations which congress deemed it proper to make, are now in full operation. The sole question is, can a State regulate commerce with foreign nations and among the States, while congress is regulating it?

* * *

In our complex system, presenting the rare and difficult scheme of one general government, whose action extends over the whole, but which possesses only certain enumerated powers; and of numerous state governments, which retain and exercise all powers not delegated to the Union, contests respecting power must arise. Were it even otherwise, the measures taken by the respective governments to execute their acknowledged powers, would often be of the same description, and might, sometimes, interfere. This, however, does not prove that the one is exercising, or has a right to exercise, the powers of the other.

* * *

It has been said that the act of August 7, 1789, acknowledges a concurrent power in the States to regulate the conduct of pilots, and hence is inferred as admission of their concurrent right with congress to regulate commerce with foreign nations, and amongst the States. But this inference is not, we think, justified by the fact.

Although congress cannot enable a State to legislate, congress may adopt the provisions of a State on any subject. When the government of the Union was brought into existence, it found a system for the regulation of its pilots in full force in every State. The act which has been mentioned, adopts this system, and gives it the same validity as if its provisions had been specially made by congress. But the act, it may be said, is prospective also, and the adoption of laws to be made in future, presupposes the right in the maker to legislate on the subject.

The act unquestionably manifests an intention to leave this subject entirely to the States, until congress should think proper to interpose; but the very enactment of such a law indicates an opinion that it was necessary; that the existing system would not be applicable to the new state of things, unless expressly applied to it by congress. But this section is confined to pilots within the "bays, inlets, rivers, harbors, and ports of the United States," which are, of course, in whole or in part, also within the limits of some particular State. The acknowledged power of a State to regulate its police, its domestic trade, and to govern its own citizens, may enable it to legislate on this subject, to a considerable extent; and the adoption of its system by congress, and the application of it to the whole subject of commerce, does not seem to the court to imply a right in the States so to apply it of their own authority. But the adoption of the state system being temporary, being only "until further legislative provision shall be made by congress," shows, conclusively, an opinion that congress could control the whole subject, and might adopt the system of the States, or provide one of its own.

* * *

It has been contended, by the counsel for the appellant, that, as the word to "regulate" implies in its nature full power over the thing to be regulated, it excludes, necessarily, the action of all others that would perform the same operation on the same thing. That regulation is designed for the entire result, applying to those parts which remain as they were, as well as to those which are altered. It produces a uniform whole, which is as much disturbed and deranged by changing what the regulating power designs to leave untouched, as that on which it has operated.

There is great force in this argument, and the court is not satisfied that it has been refuted. Since, however, in exercising the power of regulating their

own purely internal affairs, whether of trading or police, the States may sometimes enact laws, contrary to, an act of congress passed in pursuance of the
constitution, the court will enter upon the inquiry, whether the laws of New
York, as expounded by the highest tribunal of that State, have, in their application to this case, come into collision with an act of congress, and deprived a
citizen of a right to which that act entitles him. Should this collision exist, it
will be immaterial whether those laws were passed in virtue of a concurrent
power "to regulate commerce with foreign nations and among the several
States," or, in virtue of a power to regulate their domestic trade and police. In
one case and the other, the acts of New York must yield to the law of congress;
and the decision sustaining the privilege they confer, against a right given by a
law of the Union, must be erroneous.

* * *

The questions, then, whether the conveyance of passengers be a part of the
coasting trade, and whether a vessel can be protected in that occupation by a
coasting license, are not, and cannot be, raised in this case. The real and sole
question seems to be, whether a steam machine, in actual use, deprives a vessel
of the privileges conferred by a license. . . . But all inquiry into this subject
seems to the court to be put completely at rest, by the act already mentioned,
entitled, "An act for the enrolling and licensing of steam-boats."

This act authorizes a steam-boat employed, or intended to be employed,
only in a river or bay of the United States, owned wholly or in part by an alien,
resident within the United States, to be enrolled and licensed as if the same
belonged to a citizen of the United States.

This act demonstrates the opinion of congress, that steam-boats may be
enrolled and licensed, in common with vessels using sails. They are, of course,
entitled to the same privileges, and can no more be restrained from navigating
waters, and entering ports which are free to such vessels, than if they were
wafted on their voyage by the winds, instead of being propelled by the agency
of fire. The one element may be as legitimately used as the other, for every
commercial purpose authorized by the laws of the Union; and the act of a State
inhibiting the use of either to any vessel having a license under the act of congress, comes, we think, in direct collision with that act. As this decides the
cause, it is unnecessary to enter in an examination of that part of the constitution which empowers congress to promote the progress of science and the
useful arts.

* * *

Powerful and ingenious minds, taking as postulates that the powers
expressly granted to the government of the Union, are to be contracted by construction into the narrowest possible compass, and that the original powers of
the States are retained, if any possible construction will retain them, may, by
a course of well-digested but refined and metaphysical reasoning founded on
these premises, explain away the constitution of our country, and leave it a
magnificent structure, indeed, to look at, but totally unfit for use. They may so

entangle and perplex the understanding, as to obscure principles which were before thought quite plain, and induce doubts where, if the mind were to pursue its own course, none would be perceived. In such a case, it is peculiarly necessary to recur to safe and fundamental principles to sustain those principles, and, when sustained, to make them the tests of the arguments to be examined.

* * *

Decree. . . .

This court is, therefore, of opinion that the decree of the court of New York for the trial of impeachments and the correction of errors, affirming the decree of the chancellor of that State, which perpetually enjoins the said Thomas Gibbons, the appellant, from navigating the waters of the State of New York with the steam-boats The Stoudinger and The Bellona, by steam or fire, is erroneous, and ought to be reversed, and the same is hereby reversed and annulled: and this court doth further direct, order, and decree, that the bill of the said Aaron Ogden be dismissed, and the same is hereby dismissed accordingly.

QUESTIONS AND COMMENTS

1 In choosing between competing theories of congressional control over commerce, does Marshall hold directly or by implication that Congress may regulate strictly intrastate commerce if it *affects* commerce in another state? What evidence can be cited in support of your answer?

2 What relationship does Marshall see between federal commerce power and state police power?

3 What does Marshall say in his opinion that supports a states'-rights point of view? How do you square such support with Marshall's reputation as a "nationalist"?

4 Would you classify Marshall as a practitioner of judicial activism or of judicial restraint? Why?

5 Under Marshall's definition of "commerce among the states," which of the following would involve an unconstitutional burden on interstate commerce?

   a A state erects a dam across a navigable creek [*Willson v. Blackbird Creek Marsh Co.,* 27 U.S. (2 Peters) 245 (1829)].

   b A state regulates the business of piping natural gas from one state to another [*Missouri ex rel Barrett v. Kansas Gas Co.,* 265 U.S. 298 (1924)].

   c A state forbids the shipment of shrimp taken in its tidal waters unless the heads and hulls have been removed [*Foster-Fountain Packing Co. v. Haydel,* 278 U.S. 1 (1928)].

   d A state law prohibits the sale of convict-made goods imported from other states and still in the original package [*Whitfield v. Ohio,* 297 U.S. 431 (1936)].

6 What phase of Marshall's opinion do you think caused the greatest consternation among advocates of state sovereignty in the south? Why?

* * * * *

When a state law conflicts with a federal statute, the state law must fall. Thus, in *Gibbons v. Ogden,* New York's steamboat monopoly law was found in conflict with acts of Congress regulating vessels employed in the coasting trade and was therefore declared unconstitutional. While this makes clear that a state may not regulate interstate commerce in conflict with congressional regulation of the same subject matter, *Gibbons v. Ogden* does not hold that all state regulation of interstate commerce is illegitimate. The Court has never given credence to the view that when congressional power to regulate commerce is dormant, a state may not act. Sometimes it may. Sometimes it may not. In certain situations, Congress is given exclusive power over commerce. In others, both Congress and the states may regulate commerce as long as state regulation neither conflicts with that of Congress nor imposes an undue burden on interstate commerce.

When exclusivity is to prevail and when concurrent jurisdiction is a matter that has occupied the Court on many occasions. In *Cooley v. Board of Wardens,* the Court enunciates a standard for determining the validity of state efforts to regulate commerce.

Aaron B. Cooley v. Board of Wardens of the Port of Philadelphia

53 U.S. 299; 13 L. Ed. 996 (1851)
Vote: 7–2

In 1803, the Pennsylvania legislature passed a statute which set up a system of regulation for pilotage in the port of Philadelphia. Under the regulations, a vessel refusing to take on a pilot when leaving the port was required to pay one-half the regular pilotage fee, the proceeds to be used for the relief of "Distressed and Decayed Pilots, Their Widows and Children."

The Philadelphia Board of Wardens sued Cooley to recover the one-half pilotage fee owed on a vessel which had sailed from Philadelphia without a pilot when one might have been had. All Pennsylvania courts ruled against Cooley, who appealed to the U.S. Supreme Court.

CURTIS, J., delivered the opinion of the court.

[It is urged that the Pennsylvania statute] . . . is repugnant to the third clause of the eighth section of the first article. "The congress shall have power to regulate commerce with foreign nations and among the several States, and with the Indian tribes."

That the power to regulate commerce includes the regulation of navigation, we consider settled. And when we look to the nature of the service performed by pilots, to the relations which that service and its compensations bear to navigation between the several States, and between the ports of the United States and foreign countries, we are brought to the conclusion, that the regulation of the qualifications of pilots, of the modes and times of offering and rendering their services, of the responsibilities which shall rest upon them, of the powers they shall possess, of the compensation they may demand, and of the penalties by which their rights and duties may be enforced, do constitute regulations of navigation, and consequently of commerce, within the just meaning of this clause of the constitution.

The power to regulate navigation is the power to prescribe rules in conformity with which navigation must be carried on. It extends to the persons who conduct it, as well as to the instruments used. Accordingly, the first congress assembled under the constitution passed laws, requiring the masters of ships and vessels of the United States to be citizens of the United States, and established many rules for the government and regulation of officers and seamen.

These have been from time to time added to and changed, and we are not aware that their validity has been questioned.

Now, a pilot, so far as respects the navigation of the vessel in that part of the voyage which is his pilotage-ground, is the temporary master charged with the safety of the vessel and cargo, and of the lives of those on board, and intrusted with the command of the crew. He is not only one of the persons engaged in navigation, but he occupies a most important and responsible place among those thus engaged. And if congress has power to regulate the seamen who assist the pilot in the management of the vessel, a power never denied, we can perceive no valid reason why the pilot should be beyond the reach of the same power. It is true that, according to the usages of modern commerce on the ocean, the pilot is on board only during a part of the voyage between ports of different States, or between ports of the United States and foreign countries; but if he is on board for such a Purpose and during so much of the voyage as to be engaged in navigation, the power to regulate navigation extends to him while thus engaged, as clearly as it would if he were to remain on board throughout the whole passage, from port to port. For it is a power which extends to every part of the voyage, and may regulate those who conduct or assist in conducting navigation in one part of a voyage as much as in another part, or during the whole voyage.

Nor should it be lost sight of, that this subject of the regulation of pilots and pilotage has an intimate connection with, and an important relation to, the general subject of commerce with foreign nations and among the several States, over which it was one main object of the constitution to create a national control. . . .

The act of congress of the 7th of August, 1789, § 4, is as follows:

> That all pilots in the bays, inlets, rivers, harbors, and ports of the United States shall continue to be regulated in conformity with the existing laws of the States, respectively, wherein such pilots may be, or with such laws as the States may respectively hereafter enact for the purpose, until further legislative provision shall be made by congress. . . .

If the States were divested of the power to legislate on this subject by the grant of the commercial power to congress, it is plain this act could not confer upon them power thus to legislate. If the constitution excluded the States from making any law regulating commerce, certainly congress cannot regrant, or in any manner reconvey to the States that power. And yet this act of 1789 gives its sanction only to laws enacted by the States. This necessarily implies a constitutional power to legislate; for only a rule created by the sovereign power of a State acting in its legislative capacity, can be deemed a law, enacted by a State; and if the State has so limited its sovereign power that it no longer extends to a particular subject, manifestly it cannot, in any proper sense, be said to enact laws thereon. Entertaining these views, we are brought directly and unavoidably to the consideration of the question, whether the grant of the commercial power to congress, did *per se* deprive the States of all power to regulate pilots. This question has never been decided by this court, nor, in our judgment, has any case depending upon all the considerations which must govern this one, come before this court. The grant of commercial power to congress does not contain any terms which expressly exclude the States from exercising an authority over its subject-matter. If they are excluded, it must be because the nature of the power, thus granted to congress, requires that a similar authority should not exist in the States. If it were conceded on the one side, that the nature of this power, like that to legislate for the District of Columbia, is absolutely and totally repugnant to the existence of similar power in the States, probably no one would deny that the grant of the power to congress, as effectually and perfectly excludes the States from all future legislation on the subject, as if express words had been used to exclude them. And on the other hand, if it were admitted that the existence of this power in congress, like the power of taxation, is compatible with the existence of a similar power in the States, then it would be in conformity with the contemporary exposition of the constitution, (Federalist, No. 32), and with the judicial construction, given from time to time by this court, after the most deliberate consideration, to hold that the mere grant of such a power to congress, did not imply a prohibition on the States to exercise the same power; that it is not the mere existence of such a power, but its exercise by congress, which may be incompatible with the exercise of the same power by the States, and that the States may legislate in the absence of congressional regulations. . . . Now, the power to regulate commerce, embraces a vast field, containing not only many, but exceedingly various subjects, quite unlike in their nature; some imperatively demanding a single uniform rule, operating equally on the commerce of the United States in every port; and some, like the subject now in question, as imperatively demanding that diversity, which alone can meet the local necessities of navigation.

Either absolutely to affirm, or deny that the nature of this power requires exclusive legislation by congress, is to lose sight of the nature of the subjects of this power, and to assert concerning all of them, what is really applicable but to a part. Whatever subjects of this power are in their nature national, or admit only of one uniform system, a plan of regulation, may justly be said to be of such a nature as to require exclusive legislation by congress. That this cannot be affirmed of laws for the regulation of pilots and pilotage, is plain. The act of

1789 contains a clear and authoritative declaration by the first congress, that the nature of this subject is such, that until congress should find it necessary to exert its power, it should be left to the legislation of the States; that it is local and not national; that it is likely to be the best provided for, not by one system, or plan of regulations, but by as many as the legislative discretion of the several States should deem applicable to the local peculiarities of the ports within their limits.

* * *

It is the opinion of a majority of the court that the mere grant to congress of the power to regulate commerce, did not deprive the States of power to regulate pilots, and that although congress has legislated on this subject, its legislation manifests an intention, with a single exception, not to regulate this subject, but to leave its regulation to the several States. To these precise questions, which are all we are called on to decide, this opinion must be understood to be confined. It does not extend to the question what other subjects under the commercial power, are within the exclusive control of congress, or may be regulated by the States in the absence of all congressional legislation; nor to the general question, how far any regulation of a subject by congress, may be deemed to operate as an exclusion of all legislation by the States upon the same subject. We decide the precise questions before us, upon what we deem sound principles, applicable to this particular subject in the State in which the legislation of congress has left it. We go no further.

* * *

We are of opinion that this state law was enacted by virtue of a power, residing in the State to Legislate, that it is not in conflict with any law of congress; that it does not interfere with any system which congress has established by making regulations, or by intentionally leaving individuals to their own unrestricted action; that this law is therefore valid, and the judgment of the supreme court of Pennsylvania in each case must be affirmed.

* * *

QUESTIONS AND COMMENTS

1 In exercising their power to promote the general welfare of their citizens (the police power), states frequently adopt rules and regulations which impinge upon interstate commerce. The Supreme Court must then decide whether the state's action violates an exclusive prerogative of Congress or, if not, whether the burden imposed on interstate commerce is permissible. This necessarily entails a balancing of interests—i.e., political considerations. Should Supreme Court decisions be guided by such factors?

2 Did the framers of the Constitution intend for jurisdiction over interstate commerce to be differentiated as concurrent and exclusive? What evidence can you use to support your answer?

3 Would it be better in a democratic political system to have Congress, the Interstate

Commerce Commission, or some other agency determine those areas of commerce in which only national regulation is to be permitted?

* * * * * *

Recent cases dealing with state regulation of interstate commerce involve (1) situations in which Congress has not acted and in which states have concurrent regulatory power, (2) situations in which Congress has not acted and in which Congress has exclusive jurisdiction, and (3) situations in which Congress has acted and has, in effect, preempted the field. *South Carolina Highway Department v. Barnwell Brothers* falls in the first category, as does *California v. Thompson. Southern Pacific Railway Co. v. Arizona* and *Morgan v. Virginia* illustrate the concepts encompassed in the second classification. *Ray v. Atlantic Richfield* turns on the third concept in our list.

South Carolina State Highway Department et al. v. Barnwell Brothers, Inc. et al.

303 U.S. 177; 58 S. Ct. 510; 82 L. Ed. 734 (1938)
Vote: 7–0

South Carolina prohibited use of the state's highways by motor trucks and trailers whose width exceeded 90 inches and whose weight exceeded 20,000 pounds. Barnwell Brothers (and others) sued to prevent enforcement of the restrictions, claiming a violation of rights under the commerce and due process clauses of the Constitution. The district court rejected the due process claim but held the width and weight provisions of the statute to be an unlawful burden on interstate commerce on certain state highways. Barnwell Brothers appealed directly to the Supreme Court.

MR. JUSTICE STONE delivered the opinion of the Court.

* * *

The commerce clause, by its own force, prohibits discrimination against interstate commerce, whatever its form or method, and the decisions of this Court have recognized that there is scope for its like operation when state legislation nominally of local concern is in point of fact aimed at interstate commerce, or by its necessary operation is a means of gaining a local benefit by throwing the attendant burdens on those without the state.

* * *

But the present case affords no occasion for saying that the bare possession of power by Congress to regulate the interstate traffic forces the states to conform to standards which Congress might, but has not adopted, or curtails their power to take measures to insure the safety and conservation of their highways which may be applied to like traffic moving intrastate. Few subjects of state regulation are so peculiarly of local concern as is the use of state highways. There are few, local regulation of which is so inseparable from a substantial effect on interstate commerce. Unlike the railroads, local highways are built, owned and maintained by the state or its municipal subdivisions. The state has a primary and immediate concern in their safe and economical administration. The present regulations, or any others of like purpose, if they are to accomplish their end, must be applied alike to interstate and intrastate traffic both moving in large volume over the highways. The fact that they affect alike shippers in interstate and intrastate commerce in large number within as well as without the state is a safeguard against their abuse. . . .

The nature of the authority of the state over its own highways has often been pointed out by this Court. It may not, under the guise of regulation, discriminate against interstate commerce. But "In the absence of national legislation especially covering the subject of interstate commerce, the State may rightly prescribe uniform regulations adapted to promote safety upon its highways and the conservation of their use, applicable alike to vehicles moving in interstate commerce and those of its own citizens." This formulation has been repeatedly affirmed, and never disapproved. This Court has often sustained the exercise of that power although it has burdened or impeded interstate commerce. It has upheld weight limitations lower than those presently imposed, applied alike to motor traffic moving interstate and intrastate. Restrictions favoring passenger traffic over the carriage of interstate merchandise by truck have been similarly sustained, as has the exaction of a reasonable fee for the use of the highways.

In each of these cases regulation [has involved] . . . a burden on interstate commerce. But so long as the state action does not discriminate, the burden is one which the Constitution permits because it is an inseparable incident of the exercise of a legislative authority, which, under the Constitution, has been left to the states.

Congress, in the exercise of its plenary power to regulate interstate commerce, may determine whether the burdens imposed on it by state regulation, otherwise permissible, are too great, and may, by legislation designed to secure uniformity or in other respects to protect the national interest in the commerce, curtail to some extent the state's regulatory power. But that is a legislative, not a judicial function, to be performed in the light of the Congressional judgment of what is appropriate regulation of interstate commerce, and the extent to which, in that field, state power and local interests should be required to yield to the national authority and interest. In the absence of such legislation the judicial function, under the commerce clause as well as the Fourteenth Amendment, stops with the inquiry whether the state legislature in adopting regulations such as the present has acted within its province, and whether the means of regulation chosen are reasonably adapted to the end sought.

Here the first inquiry has already been resolved by our decisions that a state may impose non-discriminatory restrictions with respect to the character of motor vehicles moving in interstate commerce as a safety measure and as a means of securing the economical use of its highways. In resolving the second, courts do not sit as legislatures, either state or national. They cannot act as Congress does when, after weighing all the conflicting interests, state and national, it determines when and how much the state regulatory power shall yield to the larger interests of a national commerce. And in reviewing a state highway regulation where Congress has not acted, a court is not called upon, as are state legislatures, to determine what, in its judgment, is the most suitable restriction to be applied to those that are possible, or to choose that one which in its opinion is best adapted to all the diverse interests affected.

When the action of a legislature is within the scope of its power, fairly debatable questions as to its reasonableness, wisdom and propriety are not for the determination of courts, but for the legislative body, on which rests the duty and responsibility of decision.

* * *

Since the adoption of one weight or width regulation, rather than another, is a legislative not a judicial choice, its constitutionality is not to be determined by weighing in the judicial scales the merits of the legislative choice and rejecting it if the weight of evidence presented in court appears to favor a different standard. Being a legislative judgment it is presumed to be supported by facts known to the legislature unless facts judicially known or proved preclude that possibility. Hence, in reviewing the present determination we examine the record, not to see whether the findings of the court below are supported by evidence, but to ascertain upon the whole record whether it is possible to say that the legislative choice is without rational basis. Not only does the record fail to exclude that possibility, but it shows affirmatively that there is adequate support for the legislative judgment.

* * *

Before adoption of its weight limitation South Carolina had had experience with higher weight limits. In 1924 it had adopted a combined gross weight limit of 20,000 pounds for vehicles of four wheels or less, and an axle weight limit of 15,000 pounds. In 1930 it had adopted a combined gross weight limit of 12½ tons with a five ton axle weight limit for vehicles having more than two axles. In 1931 it appointed a commission to investigate motor transportation in the state, to recommend legislation, and to report in 1932. The present weight limitation was recommended by the commission after a full consideration of relevant data, including a report by the state engineer who had constructed the concrete highways of the state and who advised a somewhat lower limitation as necessary for their preservation. The fact that many states have adopted a different standard is not persuasive. The conditions under which highways must be built in the several states, their construction and the demands made upon them, are not uniform. The road building art, as the record shows, is far from having attained a scientific certainty and precision, and scientific precision is not the criterion for the exercise of the constitutional regulatory power of the states. The legislature, being free to exercise its own judgment, is not bound by that of other legislatures. It would hardly be contended that if all the states had adopted a single standard none, in the light of its own experience and in the exercise of its judgment upon all the complex elements which enter into the problem, could change it.

Only a word need be said as to the width limitation. . . . The 90 inch limitation has been in force in South Carolina since 1920 and the concrete highways which it has built appear to be adapted to vehicles of that width. The record shows without contradiction that the use of heavy loaded trucks on the highways tends to force other traffic off the concrete surface onto the shoulders of the road adjoining its edges and to increase repair costs materially. It appears also that as the width of trucks is increased it obstructs the view of the highway, causing much inconvenience and increased hazard in its use. It plainly cannot be said that the width of trucks used on the highways in South Carolina is unrelated to their safety and cost of maintenance, or that a 90 inch width limitation adopted to safeguard the highways of the State, is not within the range of the permissible legislative choice.

The regulatory measures taken by South Carolina are within its legislative power. They do not infringe the Fourteenth Amendment, and the resulting burden on interstate commerce is not forbidden.

Reversed.

* * *

California v. Thompson

313 U.S. 109; 61 S. Ct. 930; 85 L. Ed. 1219 (1941)
Vote: Unanimous

The facts are provided in the opinion below.

MR. JUSTICE STONE delivered the opinion of the Court.

A statute of California defines a transportation agent as one who "sells or offers to sell or negotiate for" transportation over the public highways of the state, and requires every such agent to procure a license from the State Railroad Commission authorizing him so to act. . . . Prerequisites to the license are determination by the Commission of the applicant's fitness to exercise the licensed privilege, the payment of a license fee of $1.00, and the filing by the applicant of a bond in the sum of $1,000, conditioned upon the faithful performance of the transportation contracts which he negotiates. . . . any person acting as a transportation agent without a license is guilty of a misdemeanor. The question for decision is whether the statutory exaction of the license and bond infringes the Commerce Clause of the Constitution when applied to one who negotiates for the transportation interstate of passengers over the public highways of the state.

Respondent was convicted of violation of the statute by arranging for the transportation by motor vehicle, of passengers from Los Angeles, California, to Dallas, Texas, by one who, so far as appears, made only the single trip in question. The state appellate court reversed the judgment of conviction, holding . . . that the statute as applied infringes the Commerce Clause. We granted certiorari. . . .

Congress has not undertaken to regulate the acts for which respondent was convicted or the interstate transportation to which they related. The Motor Carrier Act of 1935, which applies to certain classes of common and contract interstate carriers by motor vehicle, excludes from its operation the casual or occasional transportation by motor vehicle of passengers in interstate commerce by persons not engaged in such transportation as a regular occupation or business, . . . Hence we are concerned here only with the constitutional authority of the state to regulate those who, within the state, aid or participate in a form of interstate commerce over which Congress has not undertaken to exercise its regulatory power.

The statute is not a revenue measure. It applies alike to transportation agents who negotiate for transportation intrastate as well as interstate and so does not discriminate against interstate commerce. It does not appear that the regulation will operate to increase the cost of the transportation or in respects not already indicated affect interstate commerce. It is not shown to be other than what on its face it appears to be, a measure to safeguard the members of the public desiring to secure transportation by motor vehicle, who are peculiarly unable to protect themselves from fraud and overreaching of those engaged in a business notoriously subject to those abuses.

As this Court has often had occasion to point out, the Commerce Clause, in conferring on Congress power to regulate commerce, did not wholly withdraw from the states the power to regulate matters of local concern with respect to which Congress has not exercised its power, even though the regulation affects interstate commerce. Ever since *Willson* v. *Black Bird Creek Marsh Co.,* [1829], and *Cooley* v. *Board of Port Wardens,* [1851], it has been recognized that there are matters of local concern, the regulation of which unavoidably involves some regulation of interstate commerce, but which because of their local character and their number and diversity may never be adequately dealt with by Congress. Because of their local character, also, there is wide scope for local regulation without impairing the uniformity of control of the national commerce in matters of national concern and without materially obstructing the free flow of commerce which were the principal objects sought to be secured by the Commerce Clause. Notwithstanding the Commerce Clause, such regulation in the absence of Congressional action has, for the most part, been left to the states by the decisions of this Court, subject only to other applicable constitutional restraints. . . .

The present case is not one of prohibiting interstate commerce or licensing it on conditions which restrict or obstruct it. For here the regulation is applied to one who is not himself engaged in the transportation but who acts only as broker or intermediary in negotiating a transportation contract between the passengers and the carrier. The license required of those engaged in such business is not conditioned upon any control or restriction of the movement of the traffic interstate but only on the good character and responsibility of those engaged locally as transportation brokers.

Fraudulent or unconscionable conduct of those so engaged which is injurious to their patrons, is peculiarly a subject of local concern and the appropriate subject of local regulation. In every practical sense regulation of such conduct is beyond the effective reach of Congressional action. Unless some measure of local control is permissible, it must go largely unregulated. In any case, until Congress undertakes its regulation, we can find no adequate basis for saying that the Constitution, interpreted as a working instrument of government, has foreclosed regulation, such as the present, by local authority.

In *Di Santo v. Pennsylvania,* this Court took a different view. Following what is conceived to be the reasoning of *McCall v. California,* [1890], it held that a Pennsylvania statute requiring others than railroad or steamship companies, who engage in the intrastate sale of steamship tickets or of orders for transportation to and from foreign countries, to procure a license by giving proof of good moral character and filing a bond as security against fraud and misrepresentation to purchasers, was an infringement of the Commerce Clause. Since the decision in that case this Court has been repeatedly called upon to examine the constitutionality of numerous local regulations affecting interstate motor vehicle traffic. It has uniformly held that in the absence of pertinent Congressional legislation there is constitutional power in the states to regulate interstate commerce by motor vehicle wherever it affects the safety of the public or the safety and convenient use of its highways, provided only that the regulation does not in any other respect unnecessarily obstruct interstate commerce.

If there is authority in the state, in the exercise of its police power, to adopt such regulations affecting interstate transportation, it must be deemed to possess the power to regulate the negotiations for such transportation where they affect matters of local concern which are in other respects within state regulatory power, and where the regulation does not infringe the national interest in maintaining the free flow of commerce and in preserving uniformity in the regulation of the commerce in matters of national concern.

The decision in the *Di Santo* case was a departure from this principle which has been recognized since *Cooley v. Board of Port Wardens, supra.* It cannot be reconciled with later decisions of this Court which have likewise recognized and applied the principle, and it can no longer be regarded as controlling authority.

Reversed.

QUESTIONS AND COMMENTS

1 Did the Supreme Court use the Cooley test in *South Carolina Highway Department v. Barnwell Brothers* and *California v. Thompson?* What is the evidence for your answer?

Southern Pacific Railway Co. v. Arizona ex rel. Sullivan, Attorney General

325 U.S. 761; 65 S. Ct. 1515; 89 L. Ed. 1915 (1945)
Vote: 7–2

The facts are given in the opinion below.

MR. CHIEF JUSTICE STONE delivered the opinion of the Court.

The Arizona Train Limit Law of May 16, 1912, Arizona Code Ann., 1939 § 69–119, makes it unlawful for any person or corporation to operate within the state a railroad train of more than fourteen passenger or seventy freight cars, and authorizes the state to recover a money penalty for each violation of the Act. The questions for decision are whether Congress has, by legislative enactment, restricted the power of the states to regulate the length of interstate trains as a safety measure and, if not, whether the statute contravenes the commerce clause of the Federal Constitution.

In 1940 the State of Arizona brought suit in the Arizona Superior Court against appellant, the Southern Pacific Company, to recover the statutory penalties for operating within the state two interstate trains, one a passenger train of more than fourteen cars, and one a freight train of more than seventy cars. Appellant answered, admitting the train operations, but defended on the ground that the statute offends against the commerce clause and the due process clause of the Fourteenth Amendment and conflicts with federal legislation. After an extended trial, without a jury, the court made detailed findings of fact on the basis of which it gave judgment for the railroad company. The Supreme Court of Arizona reversed and directed judgment for the state.

The Supreme Court left undisturbed the findings of the trial court and made no new findings. It held that the power of the state to regulate the length of interstate trains had not been restricted by Congressional action. It sustained the Act as a safety measure to reduce the number of accidents attributed to the operation of trains of more than the statutory maximum length, enacted by the state legislature in the exercise of its "police power." This power the court held extended to the regulation of the operations of interstate commerce in the interests of local health, safety and well-being. It thought that a state statute, enacted in the exercise of the police power, and bearing some reasonable relation to the health, safety and well-being of the people of the state, of which the state legislature is the judge, was not to be judicially over-turned, notwithstanding its admittedly adverse effect on the operation of interstate trains.

* * *

Congress, in enacting legislation within its constitutional authority over interstate commerce, will not be deemed to have intended to strike down a state statute designed to protect the health and safety of the public unless its purpose to do so is clearly manifested, or unless the state law, in terms or in its practical administration, conflicts with the Act of Congress, or plainly and palpably infringes its policy.

The contention, faintly urged, that the provisions of the Safety Appliance Act, providing for brakes on trains, and of § 25 of Part I of the Interstate Commerce Act, permitting the Commission to order the installation of train stop and control devices, operate of their own force to exclude state regulation of train lengths, has even less support. Congress, although asked to do so, has declined to pass legislation specifically limiting trains to seventy cars. We are therefore brought to appellant's principal contention, that the state statute contravenes the commerce clause of the Federal Constitution.

* * *

For a hundred years it has been accepted constitutional doctrine that the commerce clause, without the aid of Congressional legislation, affords some protection from state legislation inimical to the national commerce, and that in such cases, where Congress has not acted, this Court, and not the state legislature, is under the commerce clause the final arbiter of the competing demands of state and national interests. . . .

Hence the matters for ultimate determination here are the nature and extent of the burden which the state regulation of interstate trains, adopted as a safety measure, imposes on interstate commerce, and whether the relative weights of the state and national interests involved are such as to make inapplicable the rule, generally observed, that the free flow of interstate commerce and its freedom from local restraints in matters requiring uniformity of regulation are interests safeguarded by the commerce clause from state interference.

While this Court is not bound by the findings of the state court, and may determine for itself the facts of a case upon which an asserted federal right depends, the facts found by the state trial court showing the nature of the interstate commerce involved, and the effect upon it of the train limit law, are not seriously questioned.

* * *

The findings show that the operation of long trains, that is trains of more than fourteen passenger and more than seventy freight cars, is standard practice over the main lines of the railroads of the United States, and that, if the length of trains is to be regulated at all, national uniformity in the regulation adopted, such as only Congress can prescribe, is practically indispensable to the operation of an efficient and economical national railway system.

* * *

The unchallenged findings leave no doubt that the Arizona Train Limit Law imposes a serious burden on the interstate commerce conducted by appellant. It materially impedes the movement of appellant's interstate trains through that state and interposes a substantial obstruction to the national policy proclaimed by Congress, to promote adequate, economical and efficient railway transportation service.

Enforcement of the law in Arizona, while train lengths remain unregulated or are regulated by varying standards in other states, must inevitably result in an impairment of uniformity of efficient railroad operation because the railroads are subjected to regulation which is not uniform in its application. Compliance with a state statute limiting train lengths requires interstate trains of a length lawful in other states to be broken up and reconstituted as they enter each state according as it may impose varying limitations upon train lengths. The alternative is for the carrier to conform to the lowest train limit restriction of any of the states through which its trains pass, whose laws thus control the carriers' operations both within and without the regulating state.

Although the seventy car maximum for freight trains is the limitation which has been most commonly proposed, various bills introduced in the state legislatures provided for maximum freight train lengths of from fifty to one hundred and twenty-five cars, and maximum passenger train lengths of from ten to eighteen cars. With such laws in force in states which are interspersed with those having no limit on train lengths, the confusion and difficulty with which interstate operations would be burdened under the varied system of state regulation and the unsatisfied need for uniformity in such regulation, if any, are evident.

* * *

If one state may regulate train lengths, so may all the others, and they need not prescribe the same maximum limitation. The practical effect of such regulation is to control train operations beyond the boundaries of the state exacting it because of the necessity of breaking up and reassembling long trains at the nearest terminal points before entering and after leaving the regulating state. The serious impediment to the free flow of commerce by the local regulation of train lengths and the practical necessity that such regulation, if any, must be prescribed by a single body having a nation-wide authority are apparent.

The trial court found that the Arizona law had no reasonable relation to safety, and made train operation more dangerous. Examination of the evidence and the detailed findings makes it clear that this conclusion was rested on facts found which indicate that such increased danger of accident and personal injury as may result from the greater length of trains is more than offset by the increase in the number of trains when train lengths are reduced. In considering the effect of the statute as a safety measure, therefore, the factor of controlling significance for present purposes is not whether there is basis for the conclusion of the Arizona Supreme Court that the increase in length of trains beyond the statutory maximum has an adverse effect upon safety of operation. The decisive question is whether in the circumstances the total effect of the law as a safety measure in reducing accidents and casualties is so slight or problematical as not to outweigh the national interest in keeping interstate commerce free from interferences which does not have a uniform effect on the interstate train journey which it interrupts.

* * *

We think, as the trial court found, that the Arizona Train Limit Law, viewed as a safety measure, affords at most slight and dubious advantage, if any, over unregulated train lengths, because it results in an increase in the number of trains and train operations and the consequent increase in train accidents of a character generally more severe than those due to slack action. Its undoubted effect on the commerce is the regulation, without securing uniformity, of the length of trains operated in interstate commerce, which lack is itself a primary cause of preventing the free flow of commerce by delaying it and by substantially increasing its cost and impairing its efficiency. . . .

Appellees . . . rely on the full train crew cases, and also on *South Carolina Highway Dept. v. Barnwell Bros.,* [1938], as supporting the state's authority to regulate the length of interstate trains. While the full train crew laws undoubtedly placed an added financial burden on the railroads in order to serve a local interest, they did not obstruct interstate transportation or seriously impede it. They had no effects outside the state beyond those of picking up and setting down the extra employees at the state boundaries; they involved no wasted use of facilities or serious impairment of transportation efficiency, which are among the factors of controlling weight here. In sustaining those laws the Court considered the restriction a minimal burden on the commerce comparable to the law requiring the licensing of engineers as a safeguard against those of reckless and intemperate habits, sustained in *Smith v. Alabama,* [1888], or those afflicted with color blindness, upheld in *Nashville, C. & St. L. R. Co. v. Alabama,* [1888], and other similar regulations.

South Carolina Highway Dept. v. Barnwell Bros., supra, was concerned with the power of the state to regulate the weight and width of motor cars passing interstate over its highways, a legislative field over which the state has a far more extensive control than over interstate railroads. In the case, . . . we were at pains to point out that there are few subjects of state regulation affecting interstate commerce which are so peculiarly of local concern as is the use of the state's highways. Unlike the railroads local highways are built, owned and maintained by the state or its municipal subdivisions. The state is responsible for their safe and economical administration. Regulations affecting the safety of their use must be applied alike to intrastate and interstate traffic. The fact that they affect alike shippers in interstate and intrastate commerce in great numbers, within as well as without the state, is a safeguard against regulatory abuses. Their regulation is akin to quarantine measures, game laws, and like local regulations of rivers, harbors, piers, and docks, with respect to which the state has exceptional scope for the exercise of its regulatory power, and which, Congress not acting, have been sustained even though they materially interfere with interstate commerce . . .

The contrast between the present regulation and the full train crew laws in point of their effects on the commerce, and the like contrast with the highway safety regulations, in point of the nature of the subject of regulation and the state's interest in it, illustrate and emphasize the considerations which enter into a determination of the relative weights of state and national interests where state regulation affecting interstate commerce is attempted. Here examination of all the relevant factors makes it plain that the state interest is outweighed by the interest of the nation in an adequate, economical and efficient railway transportation service, which must prevail.

Reversed.

MR. JUSTICE RUTLEDGE concurs in the result.

MR. JUSTICE BLACK, dissenting.

. . . the determination of whether it is in the interest of society for the length of trains to be governmentally regulated is a matter of public policy. Someone must fix that policy—either the Congress, or the state, or the courts. A century and a half of constitutional history and government admonishes this Court to leave that choice to the elected legislative representatives of the people themselves, where it properly belongs both on democratic principles and the requirements of efficient government. . . .

The history of congressional consideration of this problem leaves little if any room to doubt that the choice of Congress to leave the state free in this field was a deliberate choice, which was taken with a full knowledge of the complexities of the problems and the probable need for diverse regulations in different localities. I am therefore compelled to reach the conclusion that today's decision is the result of the belief of a majority of this Court that both the legislature of Arizona and the Congress made wrong policy decisions in permitting a law to stand which limits the length of railroad trains. I should at least give the Arizona statute the benefit of the same rule which this Court said should be applied in connection with state legislation under attack for violating the Fourteenth Amendment, that is, that legislative bodies have "a wide range of legislative discretion, . . . and their conclusions respecting the wisdom of their legislative acts are not reviewable by the courts."

* * *

MR. JUSTICE DOUGLAS, dissenting.

. . . we are dealing here with state legislation in the field of safety where the propriety of local regulation has long been recognized. . . . Whether the question arises under the Commerce Clause or the Fourteenth Amendment, I think the legislation is entitled to a presumption of validity. If a State passed a law prohibiting the hauling of more than one freight car at a time, we would have a situation comparable in effect to a state law requiring all railroads within its borders to operate on narrow gauge tracks. The question is one of degree and calls for a close appraisal of the facts. I am not persuaded that the evidence adduced by the railroads overcomes the presumption of validity to which this train-limit law is entitled. For the reasons stated by MR. JUSTICE BLACK, Arizona's train-limit law should stand as an allowable regulation enacted to protect the lives and limbs of the men who operate the trains.

QUESTIONS AND COMMENTS

1 In the Arizona Train Case, the Court decided that the harm likely to be caused by "slack movement" in trains was less than the harm likely to be caused by "short trains." What is the evidence for this conclusion? Should this be a matter for judges to decide? Would engineers be a better source for judging such matters? Would Congress be? Since Congress had declined to pass legislation limiting trains to seventy cars, why did the Court not conclude that Congress did not think a national policy on the point necessary? If Congress has refused to establish a national policy, what is the source of the Court's conclusion that train length should either be unregulated or regulated nationally? If left unregulated, train length would be subject to determination by train operators. Is that in the public interest?

Morgan v. Virginia

328 U.S. 373; 66 S. Ct. 1050; 90 L. Ed. 1317 (1946)
Vote: 7–1

The facts are included in the opinion below.

MR. JUSTICE REED delivered the opinion of the Court.

This appeal brings to this Court the question of the constitutionality of an act of Virginia, which requires all passenger motor vehicle carriers, both interstate and intrastate, to separate without discrimination the white and colored passengers in their motor buses so that contiguous seats will not be occupied by persons of different races at the same time. A violation of the requirement of separation by the carrier is a misdemeanor. The driver or other person in charge is directed and required to increase or decrease the space allotted to the respective races as may be necessary or proper and may require passengers to change their seats to comply with the allocation. The operator's failure to enforce the provisions is made a misdemeanor.

These regulations were applied to an interstate passenger, this appellant, on a motor vehicle then making an interstate run or trip. According to the statement of fact by the Supreme Court of Appeals of Virginia, appellant, who is a Negro, was traveling on a motor common carrier, operating under the above-mentioned statute, from Gloucester County, Virginia, through the District of Columbia, to Baltimore, Maryland, the destination of the bus. There were other passengers, both white and colored. On her refusal to accede to a request of the driver to move to a back seat, which was partly occupied by other colored passengers, so as to permit the seat that she vacated to be used by white passengers, a warrant was obtained and appellant was arrested, tried and convicted of a violation of § 4097dd of the Virginia Code. On a writ of error the conviction was affirmed by the Supreme Court of Appeals of Virginia. . . .

The errors of the Court of Appeals that are assigned and relied upon by appellant are in form only two. The first is that the decision is repugnant to Clause 3, § 8, Article I of the Constitution of the United States, and the second the holding that powers reserved to the states by the Tenth Amendment include the power to require an interstate motor passenger to occupy a seat restricted for the use of his race. Actually, the first question alone needs consideration for, if the statute unlawfully burdens interstate commerce, the reserved powers to the state will not validate it.

*   *   *

On appellant's journey, this statute required that she sit in designated seats in Virginia. Changes in seat designation might be made "at any time" during the journey when "necessary or proper for the comfort and convenience of passengers." This occurred in this instance. Upon such change of designation, the statute authorizes the operator of the vehicle to require, as he did here, "any passenger to change his or her seat as it may be necessary or proper." An interstate passenger must if necessary repeatedly shift seats while moving in Virginia to meet the seating requirements of the changing passenger group. On arrival at the District of Columbia line, the appellant would have had freedom to occupy any available seat and so to the end of her journey.

Interstate passengers traveling via motor buses between the north and south or the east and west may pass through Virginia on through lines in the day or in the night. The large buses approach the comfort of pullmans and have seats convenient for rest. On such interstate journeys the enforcement of the requirements for reseating would be disturbing.

Appellant's argument, properly we think, includes facts bearing on interstate motor transportation beyond those immediately involved in this journey under the Virginia statutory regulations. To appraise the weight of the burden of the Virginia statute on interstate commerce, related statutes of other states are important to show whether there are cumulative effects which may make local regulation impracticable. Eighteen states, it appears, prohibit racial separation on public carriers. Ten require separation on motor carriers. Of these, Alabama applies specifically to interstate passengers with an exception for interstate passengers with through tickets from states without laws on separation of passengers. The language of the other acts, like this Virginia statute before the Court of Appeals' decision in this case, may be said to be susceptible to an interpretation that they do or do not apply to interstate passengers.

In states where separation of races is required in motor vehicles, a method of identification as white or colored must be employed. This may be done by definition. Any ascertainable Negro blood identifies a person as colored for purposes of separation in some states. In the other states which require the separation of the races in motor carriers, apparently no definition generally applicable or made for the purposes of the statute is given. Court definition or further legislative enactments would be required to clarify the line between the races. Obviously there may be changes by legislation in the definition.

* * *

In weighing the factors that enter into our conclusion as to whether this statute so burdens interstate commerce or so infringes the requirements of national uniformity as to be invalid, we are mindful of the fact that conditions vary between northern or western states such as Maine or Montana, with practically no colored population; industrial states such as Illinois, Ohio, New Jersey and Pennsylvania with a small, although appreciable, percentage of colored citizens; and the states of the deep south with percentages of from twenty-five to nearly fifty per cent colored, all with varying densities of the white and colored races in certain localities. Local efforts to promote amicable relations in difficult areas by legislative segregation in interstate transportation emerge from the latter racial distribution. As no state law can reach beyond its own border nor bar transportation of passengers across its boundaries, diverse seating requirements for the races in interstate journeys result. As there is no federal act dealing with the separation of races in interstate transportation, we must decide the validity of this Virginia statute on the challenge that it interferes with commerce, as a matter of balance between the exercise of the local police power and the need for national uniformity in the regulations for interstate travel. It seems clear to us that seating arrangements for the different races in interstate motor travel require a single, uniform rule to promote and protect national travel. Consequently, we hold the Virginia statute in controversy invalid.

Reversed.

* * *

MR. JUSTICE BURTON, dissenting.

On the application of the interstate commerce clause of the Federal Constitution to this case, I find myself obliged to differ from the majority of the Court. I would sustain the Virginia statute against that clause. The issue is neither the desirability of the statute nor the constitutionality of racial segregation as such. The opinion of the Court does not claim that the Virginia statute, regulating seating arrangements for interstate passengers in motor vehicles, violates the Fourteenth Amendment or is in conflict with a federal statute. The

Court holds this statute unconstitutional for but one reason. It holds that the burden imposed by the statute upon the nation's interest in interstate commerce so greatly outweighs the contribution made by the statute of the State's interest in its public welfare as to make it unconstitutional.

The undue burden upon interstate commerce thus relied upon by the Court is not complained of by the Federal Government, by any state, or by any carrier. This statute has been in effect since 1930. The carrier concerned is operating under regulations of its own which conform to the statute. The statute conforms to the policy adopted by Virginia as to steamboats (1900), electric or street cars and railroads (1902–1904). Its validity has been unanimously upheld by the Supreme Court of Appeals of Virginia. The argument relied upon by the majority of this Court to establish the undue burden of this statute on interstate commerce is the lack of uniformity between its provisions and those of the laws of other states on the subject of the racial separation of interstate passengers on motor vehicles.

If the mere diversity between the Virginia statute and comparable statutes of other states is so serious as to render the Virginia statute invalid, it probably means that the comparable statutes of those other states, being diverse from it and from each other, are equally invalid. This is especially true under that assumption of the majority which disregards sectional interstate travel between neighboring states having similar laws, to hold "that seating arrangements for the different races in interstate motor travel require a *single, uniform rule to promote and protect national travel.*" (Italics supplied.) More specifically, the opinion of the Court indicates that the laws of the 10 contiguous states of Virginia, North Carolina, South Carolina, Georgia, Alabama, Mississippi, Louisiana, Arkansas, Texas and Oklahoma require racial separation of passengers on motor carriers, while those of 18 other states prohibit racial separation of passengers on public carriers. On the precedent of this case, the laws of the 10 states requiring racial separation apparently can be invalidated because of their sharp diversity from the laws in the rest of the Union, or, in a lesser degree, because of their diversity from one another. Such invalidation, on the ground of lack of nation-wide uniformity, may lead to questioning the validity of the laws of the 18 states now prohibiting racial separation of passengers, for those laws likewise differ sharply from laws on the same subject in other parts of the Union and, in a lesser degree, from one another. In the absence of federal law, this may eliminate state regulation of racial separation in the seating of interstate passengers on motor vehicles and leave the regulation of the subject to the respective carriers. . . .

The Court relies largely upon the recital of a nation-wide diversity among state statutes on this subject without a demonstration of the factual situation in those states, and especially in Virginia. The Court therefore is not able in this case to make that necessary "appraisal and accommodation of the competing demands of the state and national interests involved" which should be the foundation for passing upon the validity of a state statute of long standing and of important local significance in the exercise of the state police power.

The Court makes its own further assumption that the question of racial separation of interstate passengers in motor vehicle carriers requires national uniformity of treatment rather than diversity of treatment at this time. The inaction of Congress is an important indication that, in the opinion of Congress, this issue is better met without nationally uniform affirmative regulation than with it. Legislation raising the issue long has been, and is now, pending before Congress but has not reached the floor of either House. The fact that 18 states have prohibited in some degree racial separation in public carriers is important progress in the direction of uniformity. The fact, however, that 10 contiguous states in some degree require, by state law, some racial separation of passengers on motor carriers indicates a different appraisal by them of the needs and conditions in those areas than in others. The remaining 20 states have not gone equally far in either direction. This recital of existing legislative diversity is evidence against the validity of the assumption by this Court that there exists today a requirement of a single uniform national rule on the subject.

It is a fundamental concept of our Constitution that where conditions are diverse the solution of problems arising out of them may well come through the application of diversified treatment matching the diversified needs as determined by our local governments. Uniformity of treatment is appropriate where a substantial uniformity of conditions exists.

QUESTIONS AND COMMENTS

1 What does the Supreme Court mean by the proposition that "the seating arrangements for the different cars in interstate motor travel require a single uniform rule to promote and protect national travel"? What is the basis for this requirement insofar as impact on interstate commerce is concerned?

2 Was the Court's decision in *Morgan,* a precursor of *Brown v. Board of Education?* Cf. *Bob-Lo Excursion Co. v. Michigan,* 333 U.S. 28 (1948).

Dixie Lee Ray, Governor of Washington, et al. v. Atlantic Richfield Co. and Seatrains-Lever Incorporated

435 U.S. 148; 98 S. Ct. 988; 55 L. Ed. 2d 179 (1978)
Vote: The votes in this case varied across several different issues.

The facts are given in the opinion below.

MR. JUSTICE WHITE delivered the opinion of the Court.

Pursuant to the Ports and Waterways Safety Act of 1972 (PWSA), navigation in Puget Sound, a body of inland water lying along the northwest coast of the State of Washington, is controlled in major respects by federal law. The PWSA also subjects to federal rule the design and operating characteristics of oil tankers.

This case arose when ch. 125, 1975 Wash. Laws, (Tanker Law), was adopted with the aim of regulating in particular respects the design, size, and movement of oil tankers in Puget Sound. . . .

[Three operative provisions are involved: (1) a requirement (§ 88.16.180) that both enrolled and registered oil tankers of at least 50,000 deadweight tons (DWT) carry a Washington-licensed pilot while navigating the Sound; (2) a requirement (§ 88.16.190(2)) that enrolled and registered oil tankers of from 40,000 to 125,000 DWT satisfy certain design or safety standards, or else use tug escorts while operating in the Sound; and (3) a ban on the operation in the Sound of any tanker exceeding 125,000 DWT (§ 88.16.190(1)).]

On the day the Tanker Law became effective, ARCO brought suit in the United States District Court for the Western District of Washington, seeking a judgment declaring the statute unconstitutional and enjoining its enforcement. Seatrain was later permitted to intervene as a plaintiff. Named as defendants were the state and local officials responsible for the enforcement of the Tanker Law. The complaint alleged that the statute was pre-empted by federal law, in particular the PWSA, and that it was thus invalid under the Supremacy Clause. It was also alleged that the law imposed an undue burden on interstate commerce in violation of the Commerce Clause, Art. I, § 8, cl. 3, and that it interfered with the federal regulation of foreign affairs. . . .

[A three-judge District Court adjudged the statute void in its entirety, upholding appellees' contentions that all the Tanker Law's operative provisions were pre-empted by federal law particularly the Ports and Waterways Safety Act of 1972 (PWSA), which is designed to insure vessel safety and the protection of navigable waters and adjacent shore areas from tanker oil spillage.]

[2]   The Court's prior cases indicate that when a State's exercise of its police power is challenged under the Supremacy Clause, "we start with the assumption that the historic police powers of the States were not to be superseded by the Federal Act unless that was the clear and manifest purpose of Congress." *Rice v. Santa Fe Elevator Corp.,* (1947). Under the relevant cases, one of the legitimate inquiries is whether Congress has either explicitly or implicitly declared that the States are prohibited from regulating the various aspects of oil-tanker operations and design with which the Tanker Law is concerned. As the Court noted in *Rice, supra,*

> [The congressional] purpose may be evidenced in several ways. The scheme of federal regulation may be so pervasive as to make reasonable the inference that Congress left no room for the States to supplement it.

or the Act of Congress may touch a field in which the federal interest is so dominant that the federal system will be assumed to preclude enforcement of state laws on the same subject. *Hines v. Davidowitz,* [1941]. Likewise, the object sought to be obtained by the federal law and the character of obligations imposed by it may reveal the same purpose.

Even if Congress has not completely foreclosed state legislation in a particular area, a state statute is void to the extent that it actually conflicts with a valid federal statute. A conflict will be found "where compliance with both federal and state regulations is a physical impossibility . . . " *Florida Lime & Avocado Growers, Inc. v. Paul,* (1963), or where the state "law stands as an obstacle to the accomplishment and execution of the full purposes and objectives of Congress."

* * *

[3]   With these principles in mind, we turn to an examination of each of the three operative provisions of the Tanker Law. We address first Wash.Rev.Code § 88.16.180 (Supp.1975), which requires both enrolled and registered oil tankers of at least 50,000 DWT to take on a pilot licensed by the State of Washington while navigating Puget Sound. The District Court held that insofar as the law required a tanker "enrolled in the coastwise trade" to have a local pilot on board, it was in direct conflict with 46 U.S.C. §§ 215, 364. We agree.

Section 364 provides that "every coastwise seagoing steam vessel subject to the navigation laws of the United States, . . . not sailing under register, shall, when under way, . . . be under the control and direction of pilots licensed by the Coast Guard.". . .

The Court has long held that . . . [federal statutes] give the Federal Government exclusive authority to regulate pilots on enrolled vessels and that they preclude a State from imposing its own pilotage requirements upon them.

* * *

While the opinion of the court below indicated that the pilot provision of the Tanker Law was void only to the extent that it applied to tankers enrolled in the coastwise trade, the judgment itself declared the statute null and void in its entirety. No part of the statute was excepted from the scope of the injunctive relief. The judgment was overly broad, for just as it is clear that States may not regulate the pilots of enrolled vessels, it is equally clear that they are free to impose pilotage requirements on registered vessels entering and leaving their ports. Not only does 46 U.S.C. § 215 so provide, as was noted above, but so also does § 101(5) of the PWSA, which authorizes the Secretary of Transportation to "require pilots on self-propelled vessels engaged in the foreign trades in areas and under circumstances where a pilot is not otherwise required by State law to be on board until the State having jurisdiction of an area involved establishes a requirement for a pilot in that area or under the circumstances involved. . . . " Accordingly, as appellees now agree, the State was free to require registered tankers in excess of 50,000 DWT to take on a state-licensed pilot upon entering Puget Sound.

We next deal with § 88.16.190(2) of the Tanker Law, which requires enrolled and registered oil tankers of from 40,000 to 125,000 DWT to possess [certain safety features.]

* * *

This section contains a proviso, . . . stating that if the "tanker is in ballast or is under escort of a tug or tugs with an aggregate shaft horsepower equivalent to five percent of the deadweight tons of that tanker . . . ," the design requirements are not applicable. The District Court held invalid this alternative design/tug requirement of the Tanker Law. We agree insofar as we hold that the foregoing design requirements, standing alone, are invalid in the light of the PWSA and its regulatory implementation. . . . Congress, insofar as design characteristics are concerned, has entrusted to the Secretary the duty of determining which oil tankers are sufficiently safe to be allowed to proceed in the navigable waters of the United States. This indicates to us that Congress intended uniform national standards for design and construction of tankers that would foreclose the imposition of different or more stringent state requirements. In particular, as we see it, Congress did not anticipate that a vessel found to be in compliance with the Secretary's design and construction regulations and holding a Secretary's permit, or its equivalent, to carry the relevant cargo would nevertheless be barred by state law from operating in the navigable waters of the United States on the ground that its design characteristics constitute an undue hazard.

* * *

Enforcement of the state requirements would at least frustrate what seems to us to be the evident congressional intention to establish a uniform federal regime controlling the design of oil tankers. The original Tank Vessel Act, amended by Title II, sought to effect a "reasonable and uniform set of rules and regulations concerning ship construction . . . ," and far from evincing a different purpose, the Title II amendments strongly indicate that insofar as tanker design is concerned, Congress anticipated the enforcement of federal standards that would pre-empt state efforts to mandate different or higher design requirements.

That the Nation was to speak with one voice with respect to tanker-design standards is supported by the legislative history of Title II, particularly as it reveals a decided congressional preference for arriving at international standards for building tank vessels. . . .

[6]   Of course, that a tanker is certified under federal law as a safe vessel inso-far as its design and construction characteristics are concerned does not mean that it is free to ignore otherwise valid state or federal rules or regulations that do not constitute design or construction specifications. Registered vessels, for example, as we have already indicated, must observe Washington's pilotage requirement. In our view, both enrolled and registered vessels must also com-ply with the provision of the Tanker Law that requires tug escorts for tankers over 40,000 DWT that do not satisfy the design provisions specified in § 88.16.190(2).

* * *

The relevant inquiry under Title I with respect to the State's power to impose a tug-escort rule is thus whether the Secretary has either promulgated his own tug requirement for Puget Sound tanker navigation or has decided that no such requirement should be imposed at all. It does not appear to us that he has yet taken either course. He has, however, issued an advance notice of pro-posed rulemaking, to amend his Navigation Safety Regulations issued under Title I, so as to require tug escorts for certain vessels operating in confined waters. The notice says that these rules, if adopted, "are intended to provide uniform guidance for the maritime industry and Captains of the Port."

It may be that rules will be forthcoming that will pre-empt the State's pres-ent tug-escort rule, but until that occurs, the State's requirement need not give way under the Supremacy Clause.

* * *

[9]   We cannot arrive at the same conclusion with respect to the remaining provision of the Tanker Law at issue here. Section 88.16.190(1) excludes from Puget Sound under any circumstances any tanker in excess of 125,000 DWT. In our view, this provision is invalid in light of Title I and the Secretary's actions taken thereunder.

[10]   We begin with the premise that the Secretary has the authority to estab-lish "vessel size and speed limitations," § 1221(3)(iii), and that local Coast Guard officers have been authorized to exercise this power on his behalf. . . .

The pertinent inquiry at this point thus becomes whether the Secretary, through his delegate, has addressed and acted upon the question of size limi-tations. Appellees and the United States insist that he has done so by his local navigation rule with respect to Rosario Strait: The rule prohibits the passage of more than one 70,000 DWT vessel through Rosario Strait in either direction at any given time, and in periods of bad weather, the "size limitation" is reduced to approximately 40,000 DWT. On the record before us, it appears sufficiently clear that federal authorities have indeed dealt with the issue of size and have determined whether and in what circumstances tanker size is to limit navigation in Puget Sound. The Tanker Law purports to impose a general ban on large tankers, but the Secretary's response has been a much more limited one. Because under § 1222(b) the State may not impose higher safety standards than those prescribed by the Secretary under Title I, the size limitation of § 88.16.190(1) may not be enforced. . . .

This being the case, we conclude that Washington is precluded from enforcing the size limitation contained in the Tanker Law. . . .

[11] We reject appellees' additional constitutional challenges to the State's tug escort requirement for vessels not satisfying its design standards. Appellees contend that this provision, even if not preempted by the PWSA, violates the Commerce Clause because it is an indirect attempt to regulate the design and equipment of tankers, an area of regulation that appellees contend necessitates a uniform national rule. We have previously rejected this claim, concluding that the provision may be viewed as simply a tug-escort requirement since it does not have the effect of forcing compliance with the design specifications set forth in the provision. So viewed, it becomes apparent that the Commerce Clause does not prevent a State from enacting a regulation of this type. Similar in its nature to a local pilotage requirement, a requirement that a vessel take on a tug escort when entering a particular body of water is not the type of regulation that demands a uniform national rule. See *Cooley v. Board of Wardens,* (1852). Nor does it appear from the record that the requirement impedes the free and efficient flow of interstate and foreign commerce, for the cost of the tug escort for a 120,000 DWT tanker is less than one cent per barrel of oil and the amount of oil processed at Puget Sound refineries has not declined as a result of the provision's enforcement. Accordingly, we hold that § 88.16.190(2) of the Tanker Law is not invalid under the Commerce Clause.

[12] Similarly, we cannot agree with the additional claim that the tug-escort provision interferes with the Federal Government's authority to conduct foreign affairs. Again, appellees' argument is based on the contention that the overall effect of § 88.16.190(2) is to coerce tanker owners into outfitting their vessels with the specified design requirements. Were that so, we might agree that the provision constituted an invalid interference with the Federal Government's attempt to achieve international agreement on the regulation of tanker design. The provision as we view it, however, does no more than require the use of tug escorts within Puget Sound, a requirement with insignificant international consequences. We, therefore, decline to declare § 88.16.190(2) invalid for either of the additional reasons urged by appellees.

Accordingly, the judgment of the three judge District Court is affirmed in part and reversed in part, and the case is remanded for further proceedings consistent with this opinion.

It is so ordered.

To Impair Contracts

Dartmouth College v. Woodward (1819)

Although state power could have been restricted severely by the Bill of Rights, it was not the intention of the framers to do so. On the other hand, the original Constitution imposes a number of direct limits on the power of the states. These limits are found in Article I, Section 10. Among them is the proviso that no state shall pass any "law impairing the obligation of contracts." In the Commerce Cases, we have noted the tension between the police power of the states and the protection of property interests. Property interests were given protection against state encroachment by the Supreme Court's interpretation of the commerce clause. But even prior to *Gibbons v. Ogden,* the Court attempted to place some limits on state police power via the contract clause.

The framers inserted the commerce clause primarily to prevent state interference with the relationships of debtors and creditors. Debtor movements in several states had shown the dangers which democracy posed for economic interests, and the contract clause was in part a reaction or defensive response to these movements. Under the guidance of John Marshall, however, the Supreme Court found even broader uses for the clause. The first case in which a state law was held unconstitutional turned on the contract clause. But it did not involve the debtor-creditor relationship. The case was *Fletcher v. Peck,* decided in 1910.[1]

The Fletcher Case involved a grant of 35 million acres of land by the state of Georgia to four land companies, including the Georgia Company. It later developed that the legislators who made the grant had been bribed, and the grant was revoked. In the interim, however, the Georgia Company had sold the land. The buyers argued that Georgia could not revoke their title under the Constitution. The conflict was transferred to Congress in 1802 when the land in controversy was ceded to the federal government. Efforts at getting compensation from Congress having failed, the claimants then arranged a test case, *Fletcher v. Peck.* In holding that Georgia could not revoke the original grants without violating the contract clause, Marshall gave notice of the potential in the clause for protecting vested property interests in a more general fashion than originally intended. This potential was further revealed in 1814 in the Dartmouth College Case, a case involving not a contract between debtors and creditors but the rights of those who held a charter from George III.

The Trustees of Darthmouth College v. Woodward

4 Wheaton 518 (1819)
Vote: 5–1

In 1769, the British Crown granted a charter of incorporation to Dartmouth College. The charter gave the trustees of the college the permanent right to govern the college. The board itself was made self-perpetuating by granting it the right to choose a president and fill vacancies as needed. In 1816, New Hampshire sought to convert the institution from private to public by placing it under a board of overseers appointed by the state's governor. The legislation establishing this structure was challenged by the trustees in New Hampshire courts to no avail. The U.S. Supreme Court granted review.

MARSHALL, C. J., delivered the opinion of the court as follows:

   . . . it has been argued, that the word "contract," in its broadest sense, would comprehend the political relations between the government and its citizens, would extend to offices held within a State for state purposes, and to many of those laws concerning civil institutions, which must change with circumstances, and be modified by ordinary legislation; which deeply concern the public, and which, to preserve good government, the public judgment must control. That even marriage is a contract, and its obligations are affected by the laws respecting divorces. That the clause in the constitution, if construed in its greatest latitude, would prohibit these laws. Taken in its broad unlimited sense, the clause would be an unprofitable and vexatious interference with the internal concerns of a State, would unnecessarily and unwisely embarrass its legislation, and render immutable those civil institutions which are established for purposes of internal government, and which, to subserve those purposes, ought to vary with varying circumstances. That as the framers of the constitution could never have intended to insert in that instrument a provision so unnecessary, so mischievous, and so repugnant to its general spirit, the term "contract" must be understood in a more limited sense. That it must be understood as intended to guard against a power of at least doubtful utility, the abuse of which had been extensively felt; and to restrain the legislature in future from violating the right to property. That anterior to the formation of the constitution, a course of legislation had prevailed in many, if not in all, of the States, which weakened the confidence of man in man, and embarrassed all transactions between individuals, by dispensing with a faithful performance of engagements. To correct this mischief, by restraining the power which produced it, the State legislatures were forbidden "to pass any law impairing the obligation of contracts," that is, of contracts respecting property, under which some individual could claim a right to something beneficial to himself; and that since the clause in the constitution must, in construction, receive some limitation, it may be confined, and ought to be confined, to cases of this description; to cases within the mischief it was intended to remedy.

The general correctness of these observations cannot be controverted. That the framers of the constitution did not intend to restrain the States in the regulation of their civil institutions, adopted for internal government, and that the instrument they have given us is not to be so construed, may be admitted. The provision of the constitution never has been understood to embrace other contracts than those which respect property, or some object of value, and confer rights which may be asserted in a court of justice. It never has been understood to restrict the general right of the legislature to legislate on the subject of divorces. Those acts enable some tribunal, not to impair a marriage contract, but to liberate one of the parties because it has been broken by the other. When any State Legislature shall pass an act annulling all marriage contracts, or allowing either party to annul it without the consent of the other, it will be time enough to inquire whether such an act be constitutional.

The parties in this case differ less on general principles, less on the true construction of the constitution in the abstract, than on the application of those principles of this case, and on the true construction of the charter of 1769. This is the point on which the cause essentially depends. If the act of incorporation be a grant of political power, if it create a civil institution to be employed in the administration of the government, or if the funds of the college be public property, or if the State of New Hampshire, as a government, be alone interested in its transactions, the subject is one in which the legislature of the State may act according to its judgment, unrestrained by any limitation of its power imposed by the Constitution of the United States.

* * *

. . . it appears, that Dartmouth College is an eleemosynary institution, incorporated for the purpose of perpetuating the application of the bounty of the donors, to the specified objects of that bounty; that its trustees or governors were originally named by the founder; and invested with the power of perpetuating themselves; that they are not public officers, nor is it a civil institution, participating in the administration of government; but a charity school, or a seminary of education, incorporated for the preservation of its property, and the perpetual application of that property to the objects of its creation.

Yet a question remains to be considered, of more real difficulty, on which more doubt has been entertained than on all that have been discussed. The founders of the college, at least those whose contributions were in money, have parted with the property bestowed upon it, and their representatives have no interest in that property. The donors of land are equally without interest, so long as the corporation shall exist. Could they be found, they are unaffected by any alteration in its constitution, and probably regardless of its form, or even of its existence. The students are fluctuating, and no individual among our youth has a vested interest in the institution, which can be asserted in a court of justice. Neither the founders of the college, nor the youth for whose benefit it was founded, complain of the alteration made in its charter, or think themselves injured by it. The trustees alone complain, and the trustees have no beneficial interest to be protected. Can this be such a contract as the constitution intended to withdraw from the power of State legislation?. . .

This is plainly a contract to which the donors, the trustees, and the crown, (to whose rights and obligations New Hampshire succeeds,) were the original parties. It is a contract made on a valuable consideration. It is a contract for the security and disposition of property. It is a contract, on the faith of which, real and personal estate has been conveyed to the corporation. It is then a contract within the letter of the constitution, and within its spirit also, unless the fact that the property is invested by the donors in trustees, for the promotion of religion and education, for the benefit of persons who are perpetually changing, though the objects remain the same, shall create a particular exception, taking this case out of the prohibition contained in the constitution. . . .

On what safe and intelligible ground can this exception stand. There is no expression in the constitution, no sentiment delivered by its contemporaneous expounders, which would justify us in making it. In the absence of all authority of this kind, is there, in the nature and reason of the case itself, that which would sustain a construction of the constitution, not warranted by its words? Are contracts of this description of a character to excite so little interest, that we must exclude them from the provisions of the constitution, as being unworthy of the attention of those who framed the instrument? Or does public policy so imperiously demand their remaining exposed to legislative alteration, as to compel us, or rather permit us to say, that these words, which were introduced to give stability to contracts, and which, in their plan import, comprehend this contract, must yet be so construed as to exclude it?

Almost all eleemosynary corporations, those which are created for the promotion of religion, of charity, or of education, are of the same character. The law of this case is the law of all.

* * *

The opinion of the court, after mature deliberation, is, that this is a contract, the obligation of which cannot be impaired, without violating the constitution of the United States. This opinion appears to us to be equally supported by reason, and by the former decisions of this court.

2. We next proceed to the inquiry, whether its obligation has been impaired by those acts of the legislature of New Hampshire, to which the special verdict refers.

From the review of this charter, which has been taken, it appears that the whole power of governing the college, of appointing and removing tutors, of fixing their salaries, of directing the course of study to be pursued by the students, and of filling up vacancies created in their own body, was vested in the trustees. On the part of the crown, it was expressly stipulated that this corporation, thus constituted, should continue forever; and that the number of trustees should forever consist of twelve, and no more. By this contract, the crown was bound, and could have made no violent alteration in its essential terms, without impairing its obligation.

By the Revolution, the duties as well as the powers of government devolved on the people of New Hampshire. It is admitted, that among the latter was comprehended the transcendent power of parliament, as well as that of the executive department. It is too clear to require the support of argument, that all contracts and rights, respecting property, remained unchanged by the Revolution. The obligations, then, which were created by the charter to Dartmouth College, were the same in the new that they had been in the old government. The power of the government was also the same. A repeal of this charter at any time prior to the adoption of the present constitution of the United States, would have been an extraordinary and unprecedented act of power, but one which could have been contested only by the restrictions upon the legislature, to be found in the constitution of the State. But the constitution of the United States has imposed this additional limitation, that the legislature of a State shall pass no act "impairing the obligation of contracts."

It has been already stated, that the act "to amend the charter, and enlarge and improve the corporation of Dartmouth College," increases the number of trustees to twenty-one, gives the appointment of the additional members to the executive of the State, and creates a board of overseers, to consist of twenty-five persons, of whom twenty-one are also appointed by the executive of New Hampshire, who have power to inspect and control the most important acts of the trustees.

On the effect of this law, two opinions cannot be entertained. Between acting directly, and acting through the agency of trustees and overseers, no essential difference is perceived. The whole power of governing the college is transferred from trustees, appointed according to the will of the founder, expressed in the charter, to the executive of New Hampshire. The management and application of the funds of this eleemosynary institution, which are placed by the donors in the hands of trustees named in the charter, and empowered to perpetuate themselves, are placed by this act under the control of the government of the State. The will of the State is substituted for the will of the donors, in every essential operation of the college. This is not an immaterial change. The founders of the college contracted, not merely for the perpetual application of the funds which they gave, to the objects for which those funds were given; they contracted also, to secure that application by the constitution of the corporation. They contracted for a system, which should, as far as human foresight can provide, retain forever the government of the literary institution they had formed, in the hands of persons approved by themselves. This system is totally changed. The charter of 1769 exists no longer. It is reorganized; and reorganized in such a manner, as to convert a literary institution, moulded according to the will of its founders, and placed under the control of private literary men, into a machine entirely subservient to the will of government. This may be for the advantage of this college in particular, and may be for the advantage of literature in general; but it is not according to the will of the donors, and is subversive of that contract, on the faith of which their property was given.

In the view which has been taken of this interesting case, the court has confined itself to the rights possessed by the trustees, as the assignees and representatives of the donors and founders, for the benefit of religion and literature. Yet it is not clear, that the trustees ought to be considered as destitute of such beneficial interest in themselves, as the law may respect. In addition to their being the legal owners of the property, and to their having a freehold right in the powers confided to them, the charter itself countenances the idea that trustees may also be tutors, with salaries. The first president was one of the original trustees; and the charter provides, that in case of vacancy in that office, "the senior professor or tutor, being one of the trustees, shall exercise the office of president, until the trustees shall make choice of, and appoint a president." According to the tenor of the charter, then, the trustees might, without impropriety, appoint a president and other professors from their own body. This is a power not entirely unconnected with an interest. Even if the proposition of the counsel for the defendant were sustained; if it were admitted, that those contracts only are protected by the constitution, a beneficial interest in which is vested in the party who appears in court to assert that interest; yet it is by no means clear, that the Trustees of Dartmouth College have no beneficial interest in themselves.

But the court has deemed it unnecessary to investigate this particular point, being of opinion, on general principles, that in these private eleemosynary institutions, the body corporate, as possessing the whole legal and equitable interest, and completely representing the donors, for the purpose for executing the trust, has rights which are protected by the constitution.

It results from this opinion, that the acts of the legislature of New Hampshire, which are stated in the special verdict found in this cause, are repugnant to the constitution of the United States; and that the judgment on this special verdict ought to have been for the plaintiffs. The judgment of the state court must, therefore, be reversed.

QUESTIONS AND COMMENTS

1 In *Fletcher v. Peck,* we noted that the corruption of legislators is a distinct possibility. Did the holding in *Dartmouth* that a corporate charter is a contract protected from state impairment by the contract clause tend to increase or decrease the probability of such corruption?

2 What do you think would be the effect of the ruling in *Dartmouth* on the willingness of holders of capital to invest in needed industries? In which industries would investments most likely be enhanced? Is it the Supreme Court's function to consider such matters?

3 In *Charles River Bridge v. Warren Bridge* [11 Peters 420 (1837)], the Supreme Court held that no state can validly contract away rights and privileges by implication. Is this ruling consistent with the ruling in *Dartmouth?* Would such a ruling constitute a broadening or a narrowing of the implications flowing from *Dartmouth?*

4 The Court has held that a state may not contract away its police power, its power of eminent domain, or any of its other vital powers. Could a state validly exempt a corporation from property tax in exchange for locating a plant at a selected state site? Cf. *New Jersey v. Willson,* 7 Cranch 164 (1812).

To Tax

McCulloch v. Maryland (1819)

When Congress exercises a power, as when it passes particular legislation, that power must be traceable to some particular provision of the Constitution. For the federal government is a government of delegated powers only. In 1791, Congress chartered the First Bank of the United States. Since the Constitution nowhere explicitly delegates such a power to Congress, questions were raised as to the source of congressional authority. The ostensible answer was that Congress not only possessed the powers expressly delegated in Article I, Section 8 of the Constitution but also those powers "necessary and proper for carrying [the listed powers] into execution." While the answer did not please all critics, the issue was not so intense as to produce any legal action prior to the expiration of the bank's charter in 1811.

When the Second Bank of the United States was chartered in 1816, the situation was somewhat more politicized, and the reaction to the bank, as a consequence, somewhat different. The bank was thought to be under the influence of Federalists who used it for their own political purposes—an alleged result being that many people suffered financial losses directly traceable to bank policy and operations. In response to public pressure, some states attempted to exert some control over the operations of the Second Bank. Maryland's effort in that direction led to the celebrated case of *McCulloch v. Maryland,* in which John Marshall spelled out the doctrine of implied powers and uttered his oft-quoted words that "the power to tax involves the power to destroy."

McCulloch v. The State of Maryland

4 Wheaton 316; 4 L. Ed. 579 (1819)
Vote: Unanimous

In 1816, Congress incorporated the Bank of the United States and located a branch in Baltimore. A Maryland statute imposed a tax on the issuance of bank notes. The cashier of the Baltimore branch of the bank issued bank notes without paying the tax. Maryland sued to recover the penalties for such violations established by its law.

MARSHALL, Chief Justice, delivered the opinion of the court.—In the case now to be determined, the defendant, a sovereign state denies the obligation of a law enacted by the legislature of the Union, and the plaintiff, on his part, contests the validity of an act which has been passed by the legislature of that state. The constitution of our country, in its most interesting and vital parts, is to be considered; the conflicting powers of the government of the Union and of its members, as marked in that constitution, are to be discussed; and an opinion given, which may essentially influence the great operations of the government.

. . . The powers of the general government, it has been said, are delegated by the states, who alone are truly sovereign; and must be exercised in subordination to the states, who alone possess supreme dominion. It would be difficult to sustain this proposition. The convention which framed the constitution was indeed elected by the state legislatures. But the instrument, when it came from their hands, was a mere proposal, without obligation, or pretensions to it. It was reported to the then existing congress of the United States, with a request that it might "be submitted to a convention of delegates, chosen in each state by the people thereof, under the recommendation of its legislature, for their assent and ratification." This mode of proceeding was adopted; and by the convention, by congress, and by the state legislatures, the instrument was submitted to the *people.* They acted upon it in the only manner in which they can act safely, effectively and wisely, on such a subject, by assembling in convention. It is true, they assembled in their several states—and where else should they have assembled? No political dreamer was ever wild enough to think of breaking down the lines which separate the states, and of compounding the American people into one common mass. Of consequence, when they act, they act in their states. But the measures they adopt do not, on that account, cease to be the measures of the people themselves, or become the measures of the state government.

. . . The government of the Union . . . is emphatically and truly, a government of the people. In form, and in substance, it emanates from them. Its powers are granted by them, and are to be exercised directly on them, and for their benefit.

This government is acknowledged by all, to be one of enumerated powers. The principle, that it can exercise only the powers granted to it, would seem too apparent, to have required to be enforced by all those arguments, which its enlightened friends, while it was depending before the people, found it necessary to urge; that principle is now universally admitted. But the question respecting the extent of the powers actually granted, is perpetually arising, and will probably continue to arise, so long as our system shall exist. In discussing these questions, the conflicting powers of the general and state governments must be brought into view, and the supremacy of their respective laws, when they are in opposition, must be settled.

If any one proposition could command the universal assent of mankind, we might expect it would be this—that the government of the Union, though limited in its powers, is supreme within its sphere of action. This would seem to result, necessarily, from its nature. It is the government of all; its powers are delegated by all; it represents all, and acts for all. Though any one state may be willing to control its operations, no state is willing to allow others to control them. The nation, on those subjects on which it can act, must necessarily bind its component parts. But this question is not left to mere reason: the people have, in express terms, decided it, by saying, "this constitution, and the laws of the United States, which shall be made in pursuance thereof," "shall be the supreme law of the land," and by requiring that the members of the state legislatures, and the officers of the executive and judicial departments of the states, shall take the oath of fidelity to it. The government of the United States, then, though limited in its powers, is supreme; and its laws, when made in pursuance of the constitution, form the supreme law of the land, "anything in the constitution or laws of any state to the contrary notwithstanding."

* * *

Although, among the enumerated powers of government, we do not find the work "bank" or "incorporation," we find the great powers, to lay and collect taxes; to borrow money; to regulate commerce; to declare and conduct a war; and to raise and support armies and navies. The sword and the purse, all the external relations, and no inconsiderable portion of the industry of the nation, are intrusted to its government. It can never be pretended, that these vast powers draw after them others of inferior importance, merely because they are inferior. Such an idea can never be advanced. But it may with great reason be contended, that a government, intrusted with such ample powers, on the due execution of which the happiness and prosperity of the nation so vitally depends, must also be intrusted with ample means for their execution. The power being given, it is the interest of the nation to facilitate its execution. It can never be their interest, and cannot be presumed to have been their intention, to clog and embarrass its execution, by withholding the most appropriate means. . . .

It is not denied, that the powers given to the government imply the ordinary means of execution. That, for example, of raising revenue, and applying it to national purposes, is admitted to imply the power of conveying money from place to place, as the exigencies of the nation may require, and of employing the usual means of conveyance. But it is denied, that the government has its choice of means; or, that it may employ the most convenient means, if, to employ them, it be necessary to erect a corporation. On what foundation does this argument rest? on this alone: the power of creating a corporation, is one appertaining to sovereignty, and is not expressly conferred on congress. This is true. But all legislative powers appertain to sovereignty. The original power of giving the law on any subject whatever, is a sovereign power; and if the government of the Union is restrained from creating a corporation, as a means for performing its functions, on the single reason that the creation of a corporation is an act of sovereignty; if the sufficiency of this reason be acknowledged, there would be some difficulty in sustaining the authority of congress to pass other laws for the accomplishment of the same objects. The government which has a right to do an act, and has imposed on it, the duty of performing that act, must according to the dictates of reason, be allowed to select the means; and those who contend that it may not select any appropriate means, that one particular mode of effecting the object is excepted, take upon themselves the burden of establishing that exception.

But the constitution of the United States has not left the right of congress to employ the necessary means, for the execution of the powers conferred on the government, to general reasoning. To its enumeration of powers is added, that of making "all laws which shall be necessary and proper, for carrying into execution the foregoing powers, and all other powers vested by this constitution, in the government of the United States, or in any department thereof." The counsel for the state of Maryland have urged various arguments, to prove that this clause, though, in terms, a grant of power, is not so, in effect; but is really restrictive of the general right, which might otherwise be implied, of selecting means for executing the enumerated powers. In support of this proposition, they have found it necessary to contend, that this clause was inserted for the purpose of conferring on congress the power of making laws. That, without it, doubts might be entertained, whether congress could exercise its powers in the form of legislation.

But could this be the object for which it was inserted?

... That a legislature, endowed with legislative powers, can legislate, is a proposition too self-evident to have been questioned.

But the argument on which most reliance is placed, is drawn from that peculiar language of this clause. Congress is not empowered by it to make all laws, which may have relation to the powers conferred on the government, but such only as may be *"necessary and proper"* for carrying them into execution. The word *"necessary"* is considered as controlling the whole sentence, and as limiting the right to pass laws for the execution of the granted powers, to such as are indispensable, and without which the power would be nugatory. That it excludes the choice of means, and leaves to congress, in each case, that only which is most direct and simple.

Is it true, that this is the sense in which the word "necessary" is always used? Does it always import an absolute physical necessity, so strong, that one thing to which another may be termed necessary, cannot exist without that other? We think it does not. If reference be had to its use, in the common affairs of the world, or in approved authors, we find that it frequently imports no more than that one thing is convenient, or useful, or essential to another. To employ the means necessary to an end, is generally understood as employing any means calculated to produce the end, and not as being confined to those single means, without which the end would be entirely unattainable. Such is the character of human language, that no word conveys to the mind, in all situations, one single definite idea; and nothing is more common than to use words in a figurative sense. Almost all compositions contain words, which taken in their rigorous sense, would convey a meaning different from that which is obviously intended. It is essential to just construction, that many words which import something excessive, should be understood in a more mitigated sense—in that sense which common usage justifies. The word "necessary" is of this description. It has not a fixed character, peculiar to itself. It admits of all degrees of comparison; and is often connected with other words, which increase or diminish the impression the mind receives of the urgency it imports. A thing may be necessary, very necessary, absolutely or indispensably necessary. To no mind would the same idea be conveyed by these several phrases. The comment on the word is well illustrated by the passage cited at the bar, from the 10th section of the 1st article of the constitution. It is, we think, impossible to compare the sentence which prohibits a state from laying "imposts, or duties on imports or exports, except what may be *absolutely* necessary for executing its inspection laws," with that which authorizes congress "to make all laws which shall be necessary and proper for carrying into execution" the powers of the general government, without feeling a conviction, that the convention understood itself to change materially the meaning of the word "necessary," by prefixing the word "absolutely." This word, then, like others, is used in various senses; and, in its construction, the subject, the context, the intention of the person using them, are all to be taken into view.

Let this be done in the case under consideration. The subject is the execution of those great powers on which the welfare of a nation essentially depends. It must have been the intention of those who gave these powers, to insure, so far as human prudence could insure, their beneficial execution. This could not be done by confiding the choice of means to such narrow limits as not to leave it in the power of congress to adopt any which might be appropriate, and which were conducive to the end. This provision is made in a constitution, intended to endure for ages to come, and consequently, to be adapted to the various *crises* of human affairs. To have prescribed the means by which government should, in all future time, execute its powers, would have been to change, entirely, the character of the instrument, and give it the properties of a legal code. It would have been an unwise attempt to provide, by immutable rules, for exigencies which, if foreseen at all, must have been seen dimly, and which can be best provided for as they occur. To have declared, that the best means shall not be used, but those alone, without which the power given would be nugatory, would have been to deprive the legislature of the capacity to avail itself of experience, to exercise its reason, and to accommodate its legislation to circumstances.

* * *

In ascertaining the sense in which the word "necessary" is used in this clause of the constitution, we may derive some aid from that with which it is associated. Congress shall have power "to make all laws which shall be necessary and proper to carry into execution" the powers of the government. If the word "necessary" was used in that strict and rigorous sense for which the counsel for the state of Maryland contend, it would be an extraordinary departure from the usual course of the human mind, as exhibited in composition, to add a word, the only possible effect of which is, to qualify that strict and rigorous meaning; to present to the mind the idea of some choice of means of legislation, not strained and compressed within the narrow limits for which gentlemen contend.

* * *

The result of the most careful and attentive consideration bestowed upon this clause is, that if it does not enlarge, it cannot be construed to restrain the powers of congress, or to impair the right of the legislature to exercise its best judgment in the selection of measures to carry into execution the constitutional powers of the government. If no other motive for its insertion can be suggested, a sufficient one is found in the desire to remove all doubts respecting the right to legislate on that vast mass of incidental powers which must be involved in the constitution, if that instrument be not a splendid bauble.

We admit, as all must admit, that the powers of the government are limited, and that its limits are not to be transcended. But we think the sound construction of the constitution must allow to the national legislature that discretion, with respect to the means by which the powers it confers are to be carried into execution, which will enable that body to perform the high duties assigned to it, in the manner most beneficial to the people. Let the end be legitimate, let it be within the scope of the constitution, and all means which are appropriate, which are plainly adapted to that end, which are not prohibited, but consistent with the letter and spirit of the constitution, are constitutional.

That a corporation must be considered as a means not less usual, not of higher dignity, nor more requiring a particular specification than other means, has been sufficiently proved. . . . Had it been intended to grant this power, as one which should be distinct and independent, to be exercised in any case whatever, it would have found a place among the enumerated powers of the government. But being considered merely as a means, to be employed only for the purpose of carrying into execution the given powers, there could be no motive for particularly mentioning it.

* * *

After the most deliberate consideration, it is the unanimous and decided opinion of this court, that the act to incorporate the Bank of the United States is a law made in pursuance of the constitution, and is a part of the supreme law of the land.

The branches, proceeding from the same stock, and being conducive to the complete accomplishment of the object, are equally constitutional. It would have been unwise, to locate them in the charter, and it would be unnecessarily inconvenient, to employ the legislative power in making those subordinate arrangements. The great duties of the bank are prescribed; those duties require branches; and the bank itself may, we think, be safely trusted with the selection of places where those branches shall be fixed; reserving always to the government the right to require that a branch shall be located where it may be deemed necessary.

* * *

It being the opinion of the court that the act incorporating the bank is constitutional; and that the power of establishing a branch in the State of Maryland might be properly exercised by the bank itself, we proceed to inquire:—

2. Whether the State of Maryland may, without violating the Constitution, tax that branch?

That the power of taxation is one of vital importance; that it is retained by the States; that it is not abridged by the grant of a similar power to the government of the Union; that it is to be concurrently exercised by the two governments: are truths which have never been denied. But, such is the paramount character of the Constitution, that its capacity to withdraw any subject from the action of even this power, is admitted. The States are expressly forbidden to lay any duties on imports or exports, except what may be absolutely necessary for executing their inspection laws. If the obligation of this prohibition must be conceded—if it may restrain a State from the exercise of its taxing power on imports and exports; the same paramount character would seem to restrain, as it certainly may restrain, a State from such other exercise of this power, as is in its nature incompatible with, and repugnant to, the constitutional laws of the Union. A law, absolutely repugnant to another, as entirely repeals that other as if express terms of repeal were used.

On this ground the counsel for the bank place its claim to be exempted from the power of a State to tax its operations. There is no express provision for the case, but the claim has been sustained on a principle which so entirely pervades the Constitution, is so intermixed with the materials which compose it, so interwoven with its web, so blended with its texture, as to be incapable of being separated from it, without rending it into shreds.

This great principle is, that the Constitution and the laws made in pursuance thereof are supreme; that they control the Constitution and laws of the respective States, and cannot be controlled by them. From this, which may be almost termed an axiom, other propositions are deduced as corollaries, on the truth or error of which, and on their application to this case, the cause has been supposed to depend. These are, 1st. That a power to create implies a power to preserve. 2d. That a power to destroy, if wielded by a different hand, is hostile to, and incompatible with, these powers to create and preserve. 3d. That where this repugnancy exists, that authority which is supreme must control, not yield to that over which it is supreme. . . .

That the power to tax involves the power to destroy; that the power to destroy may defeat and render useless the power to create; that there is a plain repugnance, in conferring on one government a power to control the constitutional measures of another, which other, with respect to those very measures, is declared to be supreme over that which exerts the control, are propositions not to be denied. But all inconsistencies are to be reconciled by the magic of the word "confidence." Taxation, it is said, does not necessarily and unavoidably destroy. To carry it to the excess of destruction would be an abuse, to presume which, would banish that confidence which is essential to all government.

But is this a case of confidence? Would the people of any one State trust those of another with a power to control the most insignificant operations of their State government? We know they would not. Why, then, should we suppose that the people of any one State should be willing to trust those of another with a power to control the operations of a government to which they have confided their most important and most valuable interests? In the legislature of the Union alone, are all represented. The legislature of the Union alone, therefore, can be trusted by the people with the power of controlling measures which concern all, in the confidence that it will not be abused. This, then, is not a case of confidence, and we must consider it as it really is.

If we apply the principle for which the State of Maryland contends, to the Constitution generally, we shall find it capable of changing totally the character of that instrument. We shall find it capable of arresting all the measures of the government, and of prostrating it at the foot of the States. The American people have declared their Constitution, and the laws made in pursuance thereof, to be supreme; but this principle would transfer the supremacy, in fact, to the States.

If the States may tax one instrument, employed by the government in the execution of its powers, they may tax any and every other instrument. They may tax the mail; they may tax the mint; they may tax patent rights; they may tax the papers of the custom-house; they may tax judicial process; they may tax all the means employed by the government, to an excess which would defeat all the ends of government. This was not intended by the American people. They did not design to make their government dependent on the States. . . .

It has also been insisted, that, as the power of taxation in the general and State governments is acknowledged to be concurrent, every argument which would sustain the right of the general government to tax banks chartered by the States, will equally sustain the right of the States to tax banks chartered by the general government.

But the two cases are not on the same reason. The people of all the States have created the general government, and have conferred upon it the general power of taxation. The people of all the States, and the States themselves, are represented in Congress, and, by their representatives, exercise this power. When they tax the chartered institutions of the States, they tax their constituents; and these taxes must be uniform. But when a State taxes the operations of the government of the United States, its acts upon institutions created, not by their own constituents, but by people over whom they claim no control. It acts upon the measures of a government created by others as well as themselves, for the benefit of others in common with themselves. The difference is that which always exists, and always must exist, between the action of the whole on a part, and the action of a part on the whole—between the laws of a government declared to be supreme, and those of a government which, when in opposition to those laws, is not supreme.

But if the full application of this argument could be admitted, it might bring into question the right of Congress to tax the State banks, and could not prove the right of the States to tax the Bank of the United States.

The court has bestowed on this subject its most deliberate consideration. The result is a conviction that the States have no power, by taxation or otherwise, to retard, impede, burden or in any manner control, the operations of the constitutional laws enacted by Congress to carry into execution the powers vested in the general government. This is, we think, the unavoidable consequence of that supremacy which the Constitution has declared.

We are unanimously of opinion, that the law passed by the legislature of Maryland, imposing a tax on the Bank of the United States, is unconstitutional and void.

This opinion does not deprive the States of any resources which they originally possessed. It does not extend to a tax paid by the real property of the bank, in common with the other real property within the State, nor to a tax imposed on the interest which the citizens of Maryland may hold in this institution, in common with other property of the same description throughout the State. But this is a tax on the operations of the bank, and is, consequently, a tax on the operation of an instrument employed by the government of the Union to carry its powers into execution. Such a tax must be unconstitutional. . . .

QUESTIONS AND COMMENTS

1 *McCulloch v. Maryland* constituted the first step in developing the doctrine of "intergovernmental tax immunity"—by protecting federal government activities from state taxation. In 1871, *Collector v. Day* [78 U.S. (11 Wallace) 113] established state immunity from federal taxation by holding that the salary of a Massachusetts judge was immune from the federal income tax. However, *Collector v. Day* was overruled in 1938 [*Helvering v. Gerhardt* 304 U.S. 405], or at least heavily modified, when the Court declined to interfere with the imposition of the federal income tax on employees of the Port of New York Authority. Since 1938, the intergovernmental tax immunity doctrine has undergone drastic weakening, though it is not yet dead. Cf. *Graves v. New York ex rel O'Keefe*, 306 U.S. 466 (1937); *New York v. United States*, 326 U.S. 572 (1946); *Oklahoma Tax Commission v. Texas*, 336 U.S. 342 (1939).

2 In 1928, Justice Holmes remarked that the "power to tax is not the power to destroy while this Court sits" [*Panhandle Oil Co. v. Mississippi*, 277 U.S. 218, dissenting opinion]. Was Holmes, in effect, responding to Marshall in *McCulloch v. Maryland?*

What is the implication of Holmes's comment for Marshall's argument in *McCulloch?* Note: *Panhandle* was reversed in *Alabama v. King and Boozer,* 314 U.S. 1 (1941).

3 While the Court was preparing to issue its judgment in the McCulloch Case, a debate over a bill to repeal the bank's charter occurred in the House of Representatives. Representative McLane of Delaware argued against repeal on the ground that a charter was a contract and not annullable under the ruling in the Dartmouth College Case. What is wrong with McLane's argument?

4 Critics of the 1819 decision in the Bank Case argued that the decision went far to strip the states of their sovereignty and leave them prostrate at the feet of the national government. They foresaw a gradual invasion of states' rights and a centralization of power in the federal government. Can you find any evidence in Marshall's opinion to support such fears? Were these fears realistic, exaggerated, or foolish?

5 Subsequent to decision in *McCulloch,* the Court avoided unduly antagonizing critical states by exercising its jurisdiction with extreme care. Cf. *Miller v. Nicholls,* 4 Wheaton 311 (1819). Should the jurisdiction of the Court be dependent on such considerations? Why or why not?

To Discriminate Between Residents and Nonresidents

Edwards v. California (1941)

Hicklin v. Orbeck (1978)

While the commerce clause may be used to restrict state interference with interstate commerce, it may also be used as an instrument of public policy. When a state acts to protect the public welfare, and the impact on interstate commerce is incidental, the Supreme Court is unlikely to interfere.[2] But what if a state attempts to regulate not the movement of goods, or the transportation industry, or highway travel, but the actual freedom of people to move from one state to another?

In all periods of economic stress, the movement of people from one state to another is very likely to increase. For the unemployed, the hungry, and the destitute are likely to wonder whether the grass is greener in some other place. They travel to find out—often with great hope which is frequently not justified. States whose economies are in relatively better condition or whose welfare policies are relatively more generous are likely to attract a number of indigents who then become a burden on the host state. California was such a state during the great depression of the thirties. To hold down the cost of its welfare rolls, it adopted the so-called Okie law, so named because of the large number of Oklahomans who were fleeing the dust-bowl conditions present in that part of the country and who gravitated in large numbers to California. *Edwards v. California* tests that law, although in this case the "Okie law" was applied to a Texan. The opinion by Justice Jimmy Byrnes has been characterized as the only outstanding opinion he wrote while on the Court.[3]

Edwards v. California

314 U.S. 160; 62 S. Ct. 104; 86 L. Ed. 119 (1941)
Vote: Unanimous

The facts are given in the opinion.

MR. JUSTICE BYRNES delivered the opinion of the Court.

The facts of this case are simple and are not disputed. Appellant is a citizen of the United States and a resident of California. In December, 1939, he left his home in Marysville, California, for Spur, Texas, with the intention of bringing back to Marysville his wife's brother, Frank Duncan, a citizen of the United States and a resident of Texas.

When he arrived in Texas, appellant learned that Duncan had last been employed by the Works Progress Administration. Appellant thus became aware of the fact that Duncan was an indigent person and he continued to be aware of it throughout the period involved in this case. The two men agreed that appellant should transport Duncan from Texas to Marysville in appellant's automobile. Accordingly, they left Spur on January 1, 1940, entered California by way of Arizona on January 3, and reached Marysville on January 5. When he left Texas, Duncan had about $20. It had all been spent by the time he reached Marysville. He lived with appellant for about ten days until he obtained financial assistance from the Farm Security Administration. During the ten day interval, he had no employment.

In Justice Court a complaint was filed against appellant under § 2615 of the Welfare and Institutions Code of California, which provides: "Every person, firm or corporation or officer or agent thereof that brings or assists in bringing into the State any indigent person who is not a resident of the State, knowing him to be an indigent person, is guilty of a misdemeanor." On demurrer to the complaint, appellant urged that the Section violated several provisions of the Federal Constitution. The demurrer was overruled, the cause was tried, appellant was convicted and sentenced to six months imprisonment in the county jail, and sentence was suspended.

On appeal to the Superior Court of Yuba County, the facts as stated above were stipulated. The Superior Court, although regarding as "close" the question of the validity of the Section, felt "constrained to uphold the statute as a valid exercise of the police power of the State of California." Consequently, the conviction was affirmed. No appeal to a higher state court was open to appellant. We noted probable jurisdiction early last term, and later ordered reargument which has been held.

* * *

Article I, § 8 of the Constitution delegates to the Congress the authority to regulate interstate commerce. And it is settled beyond question that the transportation of persons is "commerce," within the meaning of that provision. It is nevertheless true, that the States are not wholly precluded from exercising their police power in matters of local concern even though they may thereby affect interstate commerce.

The issue presented in this case, therefore, is whether the prohibition embodied in § 2615 against the "bringing" or transportation of indigent persons into California is within the police power of that State. We think that it is not, and hold that it is an unconstitutional barrier to interstate commerce.

The grave and perplexing social and economic dislocation which this statute reflects is a matter of common knowledge and concern. We are not unmindful of it. We appreciate that the spectacle of large segments of our population constantly on the move has given rise to urgent demands upon the ingenuity of government. Both the brief of the Attorney General of California and that of the Chairman of the Select Committee of the House of Representatives of the United States, as *amicus curiae,* have sharpened this appreciation. The State asserts that the huge influx of migrants into California in recent years has resulted in problems of health, morals, and especially finance, the proportions of which are staggering. It is not for us to say that this is not true. We have repeatedly and recently affirmed, and we now reaffirm, that we do not conceive it our function to pass upon "the wisdom, need, or appropriateness" of the legislative efforts of the States to solve such difficulties.

But this does not mean that there are no boundaries to the permissible area of State legislative activity. There are. And none is more certain than the prohibition against attempts on the part of any single State to isolate itself from difficulties common to all of them by restraining the transportation of persons and property across its borders. It is frequently the case that a State might gain a momentary respite from the pressure of events by the simple expedient of shutting its gates to the outside world. But, in the words of Mr. Justice Cardozo: "The Constitution was framed under the dominion of a political philosophy less parochial in range. It was framed upon the theory that the peoples of the several States must sink or swim together, and that in the long run prosperity and salvation are in union and not division." *Baldwin v. Seelig,* [1935].

It is difficult to conceive of a statute more squarely in conflict with this theory than the Section challenged here. Its express purpose and inevitable effect is to prohibit the transportation of indigent persons across the California border. The burden upon interstate commerce is intended and immediate; it is the plain and sole function of the statute. Moreover, the indigent nonresidents who are the real victims of the statute are deprived of the opportunity to exert political pressure upon the California legislature in order to obtain a change in policy.

We think this statute must fail under any known test of the validity of State interference with interstate commerce.

It is urged, however, that the concept which underlies § 2615 enjoys a firm basis in English and American history. This is the notion that each community should care for its own indigent, that relief is solely the responsibility of local government.

* * *

... the record in this very case illustrates the inadequate basis in fact for the theory that relief is presently a local matter. Before leaving Texas, Duncan had received assistance from the Works Progress Administration. After arriving in California he was aided by the Farm Security Administration, which, as we have said, is wholly financed by the Federal government. This is not to say that our judgment would be different if Duncan had received relief from local agencies in Texas and California. Nor is it to suggest that the financial burden of assistance to indigent persons does not continue to fall heavily upon local and State governments. It is only to illustrate that in not inconsiderable measure the relief of the needy has become the common responsibility and concern of the whole nation.

* * *

... it would be a virtual impossibility for migrants and those who transport them to acquaint themselves with the peculiar rules of admission of many States. "This Court has repeatedly declared that the grant [the commerce clause] established the immunity of interstate commerce from the control of the States respecting all those subjects embraced within the grant which are of such a nature as to demand that, if regulated at all, their regulation must be prescribed by a single authority." *Milk Control Board v. Eisenberg Farm Products,* [1939]. We are of the opinion that the transportation of indigent persons from State to State clearly falls within this class of subjects. The scope of Congressional power to deal with this problem we are not now called upon to decide.

There remains to be noticed only the contention that the limitation upon State power to interfere with the interstate transportation of persons is subject to an exception in the case of "paupers." It is true that support for this contention may be found in early decisions of this Court. In *City of New York v. Miln,* it was said that it is "as competent and as necessary for a State to provide precautionary measures against the moral pestilence of paupers, vagabonds, and possibly convicts, as it is to guard against the physical pestilence, which may arise from unsound and infectious articles imported, ... " This language has been casually repeated in numerous later cases up to the turn of the century.

In none of these cases, however, was the power of a State to exclude "paupers" actually involved.

Whether an able-bodied but unemployed person like Duncan is a "pauper" within the historical meaning of the term is open to considerable doubt.

But assuming that the term is applicable to him and to persons similarly situated, we do not consider ourselves bound by the language referred to. *City of New York v. Miln* was decided in 1837. Whatever may have been the notion then prevailing, we do not think that it will now be seriously contended that because a person is without employment and without funds he constitutes a "moral pestilence." Poverty and immorality are not synonymous.

We are of the opinion that § 2615 is not a valid exercise of the police power of California; that it imposes an unconstitutional burden upon interstate commerce, and that the conviction under it cannot be sustained. In the view we have taken it is unnecessary to decide whether the Section is repugnant to other provisions of the Constitution.

Reversed.

* * *

MR. JUSTICE JACKSON, *concurring:*

I concur in the result reached by the Court, and I agree that the grounds of its decision are permissible ones under applicable authorities. But the migrations of a human being, of whom it is charged that he possesses nothing that can be sold and has no wherewithal to buy, do not fit easily into my notions as to what is commerce. To hold that the measure of his rights is the commerce clause is likely to result eventually either in distorting the commercial law or in denaturing human rights. I turn, therefore, away from principles by which commerce is regulated to that clause of the Constitution by virtue of which Duncan is a citizen of the United States and which forbids any State to abridge his privileges or immunities as such.

. . . For nearly three-quarters of a century this Court rejected every plea to the privileges and immunities clause. The judicial history of this clause and the very real difficulties in the way of its practical application to specific cases have been too well and recently reviewed to warrant repetition.

While instances of valid "privileges or immunities" must be but few, I am convinced that this is one. . . .

This Court should . . . hold squarely that it is a privilege of citizenship of the United States, protected from state abridgement, to enter any state of the Union, either for temporary sojourn or for the establishment of permanent residence therein and for gaining resultant citizenship thereof. If national citizenship means less than this, it means nothing.

* * *

The right of the citizen to migrate from state to state which, I agree with MR. JUSTICE DOUGLAS, is shown by our precedents to be one of national citizenship, is not, however, an unlimited one. In addition to being subject to all constitutional limitations imposed by the federal government, such citizen is subject to some control by state governments. He may not, if a fugitive from justice, claim freedom to migrate unmolested, nor may he endanger others by carrying contagion about. These causes, and perhaps others that do not occur to me now, warrant any public authority in stopping a man where it finds him and arresting his progress across a state line quite as much as from place to place within the state.

It is here that we meet the real crux of this case. Does "indigence" as defined by the application of the California statute constitute a basis for restricting the freedom of a citizen, as crime or contagion warrants its restriction? We should say now, and in no uncertain terms, that a man's mere property status, without more, cannot be used by a state to test, qualify, or limit his rights as a citizen of the United States. "Indigence" in itself is neither a source of rights nor a basis for denying them. The mere state of being without funds is a neutral fact—constitutionally an irrelevance, like race, creed, or color. I agree with what I understand to be the holding of the Court that cases which may indicate the contrary are overruled.

Any measure which would divide our citizenry on the basis of property into one class free to move from state to state and another class that is poverty-bound to the place where it has suffered misfortune is not only at war with the habit and custom by which our country has expanded, but is also a short-sighted blow at the security of property itself. Property can have no more dangerous, even if unwitting, enemy than one who would make its possession a pretext for unequal or exclusive civil rights. Where those rights are derived from national citizenship no state may impose such a test, and whether the Congress could do so we are not called upon to inquire.

I think California had no right to make the condition of Duncan's purse, with no evidence of violation by him of any law or social policy which caused it, the basis of excluding him or of punishing one who extended him aid.

QUESTIONS AND COMMENTS

1 In writing the opinion in *Edwards,* Justice Byrnes analogizes people to livestock. Is that analogy apt?

2 Byrnes argues that being poor does not constitute "moral pestilence." Can a state bar the entry of persons who represent moral pestilence? Should they be allowed to do so? How might such persons be identified?

3 Why does Byrnes choose to rest his argument on the commerce clause rather than on the privileges and immunities clause of the Fourteenth Amendment?

4 Justice Douglas has characterized Frank Duncan as a man who wanted to enter California to get the sun on his back and reduce his cost of living (William O. Douglas, *The Court Years 1939–1975,* Random House, New York, 1980, p. 27). Are these constitutional rights? Should they be?

*   *   *   *   *   *

While dire conditions may motivate a state to try to protect its own citizens, good times may stimulate similar behavior. That is, if a state suddenly finds that it is unusually advantaged and people from other states are coming in unusually large numbers, it may seek to stop or drastically curtail such "people traffic." The discovery of Alaskan oil and its subsequent development produced just such results in the seventies, as reflected in the "Alaska Hire" statute tested in *Hicklin v. Orbeck.*

Hicklin et al. v. Orbeck, Commissioner, Department of Labor of Alaska, et al.

437 U.S. 518; 98 S. Ct. 2482; 57 L. Ed. 2d 397 (1978)
Vote: 9–0

The facts are given in the opinion below.

MR. JUSTICE BRENNAN delivered the opinion of the Court.

In 1972, professedly for the purpose of reducing unemployment in the State, the Alaska Legislature passed an Act entitled "Local Hire Under State Leases." The key provision of "Alaska Hire," as the Act has come to be known, is the requirement that "all oil and gas leases, easements or right-of-way permits for oil or gas pipeline purposes, unitization agreements, or any renegotiation of any of the preceding to which the state is a party" contain a provision "requiring the employment of qualified Alaska residents" in preference to nonresidents. This employment preference is administered by providing persons meeting the statutory requirements for Alaskan residency with certificates of residence—"resident cards"—that can be presented to an employer covered by the Act as proof of residency. Appellants, individuals desirous of securing jobs covered by the Act but unable to qualify for the necessary resident cards, challenge Alaska Hire as violative of both the Privileges and Immunities Clause of Art. IV, § 2, and the Equal Protection Clause of the Fourteenth Amendment.

* * *

Appellants' principal challenge to Alaska Hire is made under the Privileges and Immunities Clause of Art. IV, § 2: "The Citizens of each State shall be entitled to all Privileges and Immunities of Citizens in the several States." That provision, which "appears in the so-called States' Relations Article, the same Article that embraces the Full Faith and Credit Clause, the Extradition Clause, . . . the provisions for the admission of new States, the Territory and Property Clause, and the Guarantee Clause, . . . establishes a norm of comity," *Austin v. New Hampshire,* (1975), that is to prevail among the States with respect to their treatment of each other's residents. The purpose of the Clause, as described in *Paul v. Virginia,* (1869), is

> to place the citizens of each State upon the same footing with citizens of other States, so far as the advantages resulting from citizenship in those States are concerned. It

relieves them from the disabilities of alienage in other States; it inhibits discriminating legislation against them by other States; it gives them the right of free ingress into other States, and egress from them; it insures to them in other States the same freedom preserved by the citizens of those states in the acquisition and enjoyment of property and in the pursuit of happiness; and it secures to them in other States the equal protection of their laws. It has been justly said that no provision in the Constitution has tended so strongly to constitute the citizens of the United States one people as this.

Appellants' appeal to the protection of the Clause is strongly supported by this Court's decisions holding violative of the Clause state discrimination against nonresidents seeking to ply their trade, practice their occupation, or pursue a common calling within the State. For example, in *Ward v. Maryland,* (1871), a Maryland statute regulating the sale of most goods in the city of Baltimore fell to the privileges and immunities challenge of a New Jersey resident against whom the law discriminated. . . .

Again, *Toomer v. Witsell,* (1948), the leading modern exposition of the limitations the Clause places on a State's power to bias employment opportunities in favor of its own residents, invalidated a South Carolina statute that required nonresidents to pay a fee 100 times greater than that paid by residents for a license to shrimp commercially in the three-mile maritime belt off the coast of that State. The Court reasoned that although the Privileges and Immunities Clause "does not preclude disparity of treatment in the many situations where there are perfectly valid independent reasons for it, . . . [it] does bar discrimination against citizens of other States where there is no substantial reason for the discrimination beyond the mere fact that they are citizens of other States." A "substantial reason for the discrimination" would not exist, the Court explained, "unless there is something to indicate that non-citizens constitute a peculiar source of the evil at which the [discriminatory] statute is aimed." Moreover, even where the presence or activity of nonresidents causes or exacerbates the problem the State seeks to remedy, there must be a "reasonable relationship between the danger represented by non-citizens, as a class, and the . . . discrimination practiced upon them.". . .

Even assuming that a State may validly attempt to alleviate its unemployment problem by requiring private employers within the State to discriminate against nonresidents—an assumption made at least dubious by *Ward* it is clear that under the *Toomer* analysis . . . Alaska Hire's discrimination against nonresidents cannot withstand scrutiny under the Privileges and Immunities Clause. For although the statute may not violate the Clause if the State shows something to indicate that non-citizens constitute a peculiar source of the evil at which the statute is aimed, . . . and, beyond this, the State has no burden to prove that its laws are not violative of the . . . Clause, . . . certainly no showing was made on this record that nonresidents were "a peculiar source of the evil" Alaska Hire was enacted to remedy, namely, Alaska's "uniquely high unemployment."

What evidence the record does contain indicates that the major cause of

Alaska's high unemployment was not the influx of nonresidents seeking employment, but rather the fact that a substantial number of Alaska's jobless residents—especially the unemployed Eskimo and Indian residents—were unable to secure employment either because of their lack of education and job training or because of their geographical remoteness from job opportunities; and that the employment of nonresidents threatened to deny jobs to Alaska residents only to the extent that jobs for which untrained residents were being prepared might be filled by nonresidents before the residents' training was completed.

Moreover, even if the State's showing is accepted as sufficient to indicate that nonresidents were "a peculiar source of evil," . . . Alaska Hire nevertheless fails to pass constitutional muster. For the discrimination the Act works against nonresidents does not bear a substantial relationship to the particular "evil" they are said to present. Alaska Hire simply grants all Alaskans, regardless of their employment status, education, or training, a flat employment preference for all jobs covered by the Act. A highly skilled and educated resident who has never been unemployed is entitled to precisely the same preferential treatment as the unskilled, habitually unemployed Arctic Eskimo enrolled in a job-training program. If Alaska is to attempt to ease its unemployment problem by forcing employers within the State to discriminate against nonresidents—again, a policy which may present serious constitutional questions—the means by which it does so must be more closely tailored to aid the unemployed the Act is intended to benefit. Even if a statute granting an employment preference to unemployed residents or to residents enrolled in job-training programs might be permissible, Alaska Hire's across-the-board grant of a job preference to all Alaskan residents clearly is not.

* * *

Although appellants raise no Commerce Clause challenge to the Act, the mutually reinforcing relationship between the Privileges and Immunities Clause of Art. IV, § 2, and the Commerce Clause—a relationship that stems from their common origin in the Fourth Article of the Articles of Confederation and their shared vision of federalism, . . . —renders several Commerce Clause decisions appropriate support for our conclusion. *West v. Kansas Natural Gas,* (1911), struck down an Oklahoma statutory scheme that completely prohibited the out-of-state shipment of natural gas found within the State. The Court reasoned that if a State could so prefer its own economic well-being to that of the Nation as a whole, "Pennsylvania might keep its coal, the Northwest its timber, [and] the mining States their minerals," so that "embargo may be retaliated by embargo" with the result that "commerce [would] be halted at state lines." *West* was held to be controlling in *Pennsylvania v. West Virginia,* (1923), where a West Virginia statute that effectively required natural gas companies within the State to satisfy all fuel needs of West Virginia residents before transporting any natural gas out of the State was held to violate the Commerce Clause. *West* and *Pennsylvania v. West Virginia* thus established that the location in a given State of a resource bound for interstate commerce is an insufficient basis for preserving the benefits of the resource exclusively or even principally for that State's residents. *Foster Packing Co. v. Haydel,* 278 U.S. 1 (1928), went one step further; it limited the extent to which a State's purported *ownership* of certain resources could serve as a justification for the State's economic discrimination in favor of residents. There, in the face of Louisiana's claim that the State owned all shrimp within state waters, the Court invalidated a Louisiana law that required the local processing of shrimp taken from Louisiana marshes as a prerequisite to their out-of-state shipment. The Court observed that "by permitting its shrimp to be taken and all the products thereof to be shipped and sold in interstate commerce, the State necessarily releases its hold and, as to the shrimp so taken, definitely terminates its control."

West, Pennsylvania v. West Virginia, and *Foster Packing* thus establish that the Commerce Clause circumscribes a State's ability to prefer its own citizens in the utilization of natural resources found within its borders, but destined for interstate commerce. Like Louisiana's shrimp in *Foster Packing,* Alaska's oil and gas here are bound for out-of-state consumption. Indeed, the construction of the Trans-Alaska Pipeline, on which project appellants' nonresidency has prevented them from working, was undertaken expressly to accomplish this end. Although the fact that a state-owned resource is destined for interstate commerce does not, of itself, disable the State from preferring its own citizens in the utilization of that resource, it does inform analysis under the Privileges and Immunities Clause as to the permissibility of the discrimination the State visits upon nonresidents based on its ownership of the resource. Here, the oil and gas upon which Alaska hinges its discrimination against nonresidents are of profound national importance. On the other hand, the breadth of the discrimination mandated by Alaska Hire goes far beyond the degree of resident bias Alaska's ownership of the oil and gas can justifiably support. The confluence of these realities points to but one conclusion: Alaska Hire cannot withstand constitutional scrutiny. As Mr. Justice Cardozo observed in *Baldwin v. G.A.F. Seelig, Inc.,* (1935), the Constitution "was framed upon the theory that the peoples of the several states must sink or swim together, and that in the long run prosperity and salvation are in union and not division."

Reversed.

QUESTIONS AND COMMENTS

1 In *Hicklin,* Alaska argued that the evil it sought to affect was high unemployment in the state. If that unemployment was caused entirely by the movement of nonresidents into the state, what decision would be required under *Edwards v. California?* What decision would Brennan have reached?

2 How does *Hicklin v. Orbeck* differ from *Edwards v. California?*

3 Why was *Hicklin* decided on the privileges and immunities clause and *Edwards* based on the commerce clause?

4 Can a state ever discriminate against nonresidents? How can we tell when the discrimination passes muster and when it fails to do so?

To Legislate for the "Public Good"

The Slaughterhouse Cases (1873)

Home Building and Loan v. Blaisdell (1934)

West Coast Hotel v. Parrish (1937)

Hines v. Davidowitz (1941)

Perez v. Campbell (1971)

The first three cases in this section involve the restrictions imposed on state police power by the Fourteenth Amendment, primarily the due process clause. In the Slaughterhouse Cases, the public good was public health. The Mississippi River was cholera-laden, and slaughterhouses were thought responsible. In *Home Building and Loan v. Blaisdell,* the public good was thought to entail preserving the homes of delinquent mortgagees. In *West Coast Hotel v. Parrish,* it was the maintenance of a living wage for those who worked for a living.

The significance of the Slaughterhouse Cases goes far beyond the immediate issues in the case. The cases presented the Court, in 1873, with the first opportunity to interpret not only the due process clause but also the equal protection and the privileges and immunities Clauses. Indeed, the chief claim of the butchers in *Slaughterhouse* was a privileges and immunities claim. In ruling on the various claims the Court limited due process to its procedural dimensions, differentiated national and state citizenship, maintained the ability of states to regulate private property interests, and supported the balance between state and federal authority then prevailing.

In *Home Building and Loan,* we are in an entirely different era. Between 1890 and 1937, the Court had used the due process clause of the Fourteenth Amendment to restrict state regulation of property interests, though the extent to which this was done has been exaggerated. In *Lochner v. New York,*[4] the Court struck an attempt by the state to regulate working conditions in its baking industry. The statute, inter alia, set a 10-hour day and a 60-hour week as maxima not to be exceeded in the industry. The Court thought such legislation not an essential health measure. In 1923, the Court voided a Washington, D.C., minimum wage law for women[5] and followed this up at the state level in *Morehead v. New York ex rel. Tipaldo*[6] in 1936. Thus, the use of due process to restrict the substance of state legislation ran into the era of Franklin Roosevelt.

Roosevelt was not passionately concerned over the restrictions imposed on the states. But beginning in January 1935, the Court nullified at least eight federal statutes or provisions of statutes over the next year and a half. In early 1937, President Roosevelt proposed to reorganize the judiciary, and more specifically to increase the size of the Supreme Court to as many as fifteen justices from the then current nine. This so-called Court-packing plan was not successful, but it may have contributed to the more favorable posture toward governmental regulation of economic interests that the Court soon adopted—both as to federal and state regulation of such interests. A hint of a turn had surfaced in *Home Building and Loan v. Blaisdell,* but *West Coast Hotel v. Parrish* clearly signaled the beginning of the new era.

The Slaughterhouse Cases

16 Wallace 36; 21 L. Ed. 394 (1873)
Vote: 5–4

On March 8, 1869, the Louisiana legislature granted a monopoly of the slaughterhouse business to the Crescent City Live Stock Landing and Slaughterhouse Company. Under the act, slaughtering for New Orleans was restricted to an area outside New Orleans. Penalties were established for violations. The act also required the monopoly to permit other butchers to use the monopoly's facilities upon payment of certain fees. The butchers of New Orleans challenged the legislation as a violation of their constitutional rights to ply their trade. The Louisiana Supreme Court upheld the statute.

Mr. Justice MILLER, now, April 14th, 1873, delivered the opinion of the court.
. . .
The plaintiffs in error . . . allege that the statute is a violation of the Constitution of the United States in these several particulars:

That it creates an involuntary servitude forbidden by the thirteenth article of amendment;

That it abridges the privileges and immunities of citizens of the United States:

That it denies to the plaintiffs the equal protection of the laws; and,

That it deprives them of their property without due process of law; contrary to the provisions of the first section of the fourteenth article of amendment.

This court is thus called upon for the first time to give construction to these articles.

* * *

[The two short sections of the Thirteenth Amendment] . . . seem hardly to admit of construction, so vigorous is their expression and so appropriate to the purpose we have indicated.

1 Neither slavery nor involuntary servitude, except as a punishment for crime, whereof the party shall have been duly convicted, shall exist within the United States or any place subject to their jurisdiction.

2 Congress shall have power to enforce this article by appropriate legislation.

To withdraw the mind from the contemplation of this grand yet simple declaration of the personal freedom of all the human race within the jurisdiction of this government—a declaration designed to establish the freedom of four millions of slaves—and with a microscopic search endeavor to find in it a reference to servitudes, which may have been attached to property in certain localities, requires an effort, to say the least of it.

That a personal servitude was meant is proven by the use of the word "involuntary," which can only apply to human beings. The exception of servitude as a punishment for crime gives an idea of the class of servitude that is meant. The word servitude is of larger meaning than slavery, as the latter is popularly understood in this country, and the obvious purpose was to forbid all shades and conditions of African slavery. It was very well understood that in the form of apprenticeship for long terms, as it had been practiced in the West India Islands, on the abolition of slavery by the English government, or by reducing the slaves to the condition of serfs attached to the plantation, the purpose of the article might have been evaded, if only the word slavery had been used. The case of the apprentice slave, held under a law of Maryland, liberated by Chief Justice Chase, on a writ of habeas corpus under this article, illustrates this course of observation.* And it is all that we deem necessary to say on the application of that article to the statute of Louisiana, now under consideration.

. . . [After the Civil War, among] the first acts of legislation adopted by several of the States in the legislative bodies which claimed to be in their normal relations with the Federal government, were laws which imposed upon the colored race onerous disabilities and burdens, and curtailed their rights in the pursuit of life, liberty, and property to such an extent that their freedom was of little value, while they had lost the protection which they had received from their former owners from motives both of interest and humanity.

They were in some States forbidden to appear in the towns in any other character than menial servants. They were required to reside on and cultivate the soil without the right to purchase or own it. They were excluded from many occupations of gain, and were not permitted to give testimony in the courts in any case where a white man was a party. It was said that their lives were at the mercy of bad men, either because the laws for their protection were insufficient or were not enforced.

These circumstances, whatever of falsehood or misconception may have been mingled with their presentation, forced upon the statesmen who had conducted the Federal government in safety through the crisis of the rebellion, and who supposed that by the thirteenth article of amendment they had secured the result of their labors, the conviction that something more was necessary in the way of constitutional protection to the unfortunate race who had suffered so much. They accordingly passed through Congress the proposition for the

*Matter of Turner, 1 Abbott United States Reports, 84.

fourteenth amendment, and they declined to treat as restored to their full participation in the government of the Union the States which had been in insurrection, until they ratified that article by a formal vote of their legislative bodies. . . .

. . . the fifteenth amendment . . . declares that "the right of a citizen of the United States to vote shall not be denied or abridged by any State on account of race, color, or previous condition of servitude." The negro having, by the fourteenth amendment, been declared to be a citizen of the United States, is thus made a voter in every State of the Union.

. . . in the light of this recapitulation of events, almost too recent to be called history, but which are familiar to us all; and on the most casual examination of the language of these amendments, no one can fail to be impressed with the one pervading purpose found in them all, lying at the foundation of each, and without which none of them would have been even suggested; we mean the freedom of the slave race, the security and firm establishment of that freedom, and the protection of the newly-made freeman and citizen from the oppressions of those who had formerly exercised unlimited dominion over him. It is true that only the fifteenth amendment, in terms, mentions the negro by speaking of his color and his slavery. But it is just as true that each of the other articles was addressed to the grievances of that race, and designed to remedy them as the fifteenth.

* * *

The first section of the fourteenth article, to which our attention is more specially invited, opens with a definition of citizenship—not only citizenship of the United States, but citizenship of the States. . . .

All persons born or naturalized in the United States, and subject to the jurisdiction thereof, are citizens of the United States and of the State wherein they reside.

. . . this clause . . . declares that persons may be citizens of the United States without regard to their citizenship of a particular State, and it overturns the Dred Scott decision by making *all persons* born within the United States and subject to its jurisdiction citizens of the United States. That its main purpose was to establish the citizenship of the negro can admit of no doubt. The phrase, "subject to its jurisdiction" was intended to exclude from its operation children of ministers, consuls, and citizens or subjects of foreign States born within the United States.

The next observation is more important in view of the arguments of counsel in the present case. It is, that the distinction between citizenship of the United States and citizenship of a State is clearly recognized and established. Not only may a man be a citizen of the United States without being a citizen of a State, but an important element is necessary to convert the former into the latter. He must reside within the State to make him a citizen of it, but it is only necessary that he should be born or naturalized in the United States to be a citizen of the Union.

It is quite clear, then, that there is a citizenship of the United States, and a citizenship of a State, which are distinct from each other, and which depend upon different characteristics or circumstances in the individual.

We think this distinction and its explicit recognition in this amendment of great weight in this argument, because that next paragraph of this same section, which is the one mainly relied on by the plaintiffs in error, speaks only of privileges and immunities of citizens of the United States, and does not speak of those of citizens of the several States. The argument, however, in favor of the plaintiffs rests wholly on the assumption that the citizenship is the same, and the privileges and immunities guaranteed by the clause are the same.

The language is, "No State shall make or enforce any law which shall abridge the privileges or immunities of citizens of *the United States.*" It is a little remarkable, if this clause was intended as a protection to the citizen of a State against the legislative power of his own State, that the word citizen of the State should be left out when it is so carefully used, and used in contradistinction to citizens of the United States, in the very sentence which precedes it. It is too clear for argument that the change in phraseology was adopted understandingly and with a purpose.

Of the privileges and immunities of the citizen of the United States, and what they respectively are, we will presently consider; but we wish to state here that it is only the former which are placed by this clause under the protection of the Federal Constitution, and that the latter, whatever they may be, are not intended to have any additional protection by this paragraph of the amendment.

The first occurrence of the words "privileges and immunities" in our constitutional history, is to be found in the fourth of the articles of the old Confederation. . . .

In the Constitution of the United States, which superseded the Articles of Confederation, the corresponding provision is found in section two of the fourth article, in the following words: "The citizens of each State shall be entitled to all the Privileges and immunities of citizens of the several States. . . ."

Fortunately we are not without judicial construction of this clause of the Constitution. The first and the leading case on the subject is that of *Corfield v. Coryell,* decided by Mr. Justice Washington in the Circuit Court for the District of Pennsylvania in 1823.

"The inquiry," he says, "is, what are the privileges and immunities of citizens of the several States? We feel no hesitation in confining these expressions to those privileges and immunities which are *fundamental,* which belong of right to the citizens of all free governments, and which have at all times been enjoyed by citizens of the several States which compose this Union, from the time of their becoming free, independent, and sovereign. What these fundamental principles are, it would be more tedious than difficult to enumerate.

They may all, however, be comprehended under the following general heads: protection by the government, with the right to acquire and possess property of every kind, and to pursue and obtain happiness and safety, subject, nevertheless, to such restraints as the government may prescribe for the general good of the whole."

This definition of the privileges and immunities of citizens of the States is adopted in the main by this court in the recent case of *Ward v. The State of Maryland,* [1871], while it declines to undertake an authoritative definition beyond what was necessary to that decision. The description, when taken to include others not named, but which are of the same general character, embraces nearly every civil right for the establishment and protection of which organized government is instituted. They are, in the language of Judge Washington, those rights which are fundamental. Throughout his opinion, they are spoken of as rights belonging to the individual as a citizen of a State. They are so spoken of in the constitutional provision which he was construing. And they have always been held to be the class of rights which the State governments created to establish and secure.

In the case of *Paul v. Virginia,* the court, in expounding this clause of the Constitution, says that "the privileges and immunities secured to citizens of each State in the several States, by the provision in question, are those privileges and immunities which are common to the citizens in the latter States under their constitution and laws by virtue of their being citizens."

The constitutional provision there alluded to did not create those rights, which it called privileges and immunities of citizens of the States. It threw around them in that clause no security for the citizen of the State in which they were claimed or exercised. Nor did it profess to control the power of the State governments over the rights of its own citizens.

Its sole purpose was to declare to the several States, that whatever those rights, as you grant or establish them to your own citizens, or as you limit or qualify, or impose restrictions on their exercise, the same, neither more nor less, shall be the measure of the rights of citizens of other States within your jurisdiction.

It would be the vainest show of learning to attempt to prove by citations of authority, that up to the adoption of the recent amendments, no claim or pretence was set up that those rights depended on the Federal government for their existence or protection, beyond the very few express limitations which the Federal Constitution imposed upon the States—such, for instance, as the prohibition against ex post facto laws, bills of attainder, and laws impairing the obligation of contracts. But with the exception of these and a few other restrictions, the entire domain of the privileges and immunities of citizens of the States, as above defined, lay within the constitutional and legislative power of the States, and without that of the Federal government. Was it the purpose of the fourteenth amendment, by the simple declaration that no State should make or enforce any law which shall abridge the privileges and immunities of *citizens of the United States,* to transfer the security and protection of all the civil rights which we have mentioned, from the States to the Federal government? And where it is declared that Congress shall have the power to enforce that article, was it intended to bring within the power of Congress the entire domain of civil rights heretofore belonging exclusively to the States?

All this and more must follow, if the proposition of the plaintiffs in error be sound. . . .

We are convinced that no such results were intended by the Congress which proposed these amendments, nor by the legislatures of the States which ratified them.

Having shown that the privileges and immunities relied on in the argument are those which belong to citizens of the states as such, and that they are left to the State governments for security and protection, and not by this article placed under the special care of the Federal government, we may hold ourselves excused from defining the privileges and immunities of citizens of the United States which no State can abridge, until some case involving those privileges may make it necessary to do so.

But lest it should be said that no such privileges and immunities are to be found if those we have been considering are excluded, we venture to suggest some which owe their existence to the Federal government, its National character, its Constitution, or its laws.

One of these is well described in the case of *Crandall v. Nevada,* [1868].

It is said to be the right of the citizen of this great country, protected by implied guarantees of its Constitution, "to come to the seat of government to assert any claim he may have upon that government, to transact any business he may have with it, to seek its protection, to share its offices, to engage in administering its functions. He has the right of free access to its seaports, through which all operations of foreign commerce are conducted, to the subtreasuries, land offices, and courts of justice in the several States." And quoting from the language of Chief Justice Taney in another case, it is said "that *for all the great purposes for which the Federal government* was established, we are one people, with one common country, *we are all citizens of the United States;*" and it is, as such citizens, that their rights are supported in this court in *Crandall v. Nevada.*

Another privilege of a citizen of the United States is to demand the care and protection of the Federal government over his life, liberty, and property when on the high seas or within the jurisdiction of a foreign government. Of this there can be no doubt, nor that the right depends upon his character as a citizen of the United States. The right to peaceably assemble and petition for redress of grievances, the privilege of the writ of *habeas corpus,* are rights of the citizen guaranteed by the Federal Constitution. The right to use the navigable waters of the United States, however they may penetrate the territory of the several States, all rights secured to our citizens by treaties with foreign nations, are dependent upon citizenship of the United States, and not citizenship of a State.

One of these privileges is conferred by the very article under consideration. It is that a citizen of the United States can, of his own volition, become a citizen of any State of the Union by a *bonâ fide* residence therein, with the same rights as other citizens of that State. To these may be added the rights secured by the thirteenth and fifteenth articles of amendment, and by the other clause of the fourteenth, next to be considered.

* * *

The argument has not been much pressed in these cases that the defendant's charter deprives the plaintiffs of their property without due process of law, or that it denies to them the equal protection of the law. The first of these paragraphs has been in the Constitution since the adoption of the fifth amendment, as a restraint upon the Federal power. It is also to be found in some form of expression in the constitutions of nearly all the States, as a restraint upon the power of the States. This law, then, has practically been the same as it now is during the existence of the government, except so far as the present amendment may place the restraining power over the States in this matter in the hands of the Federal government.

We are not without judicial interpretation, therefore, both State and National, of the meaning of this clause. And it is sufficient to say that under no construction of that provision that we have ever seen, or any that we deem admissible, can the restraint imposed by the State of Louisiana upon the exercise of their trade by the butchers of New Orleans be held to be a deprivation of property within the meaning of that provision.

* * *

In the light of the history of these amendments, and the pervading purpose of them, which we have already discussed, it is not difficult to give a meaning to this clause. The existence of laws in the States where the newly emancipated negroes resided, which discriminated with gross injustice and hardship against them as a class, was the evil to be remedied by this clause, and by it such laws are forbidden.

If, however, the States did not conform their laws to its requirements, then by the fifth section of the article of amendment Congress was authorized to enforce it by suitable legislation. We doubt very much whether any action of a State not directed by way of discrimination against the negroes as a class, or on account of their race, will ever be held to come within the purview of this provision. It is so clearly a provision for that race and that emergency, that a strong case would be necessary for its application to any other. But as it is a State that is to be dealt with, and not alone the validity of its laws, we may safely leave that matter until Congress shall have exercised its power, or some case of State oppression, by denial of equal justice in its courts, shall have claimed a decision at our hands. We find no such case in the one before us, and do not deem it necessary go over the argument again, as it may have relation to this particular clause of the amendment.

* * *

The judgments of the Supreme Court of Louisiana in these cases are

Affirmed.

* * *

Home Building and Loan Association v. Blaisdell

290 U.S. 398; 54 S. Ct. 231; 78 L. Ed. 413 (1934)
Vote: 5–4

The 1933 Minnesota Mortgage Moratorium Law provided that during declared emergencies, a district court could grant a moratorium from a mortgage foreclosure sale and extend the period during which foreclosed property could be redeemed. Home foreclosed and sold land belonging to Blaisdell after Blaisdell defaulted on his mortgage payments. Proceeding under the Minnesota Mortgage Moratorium Law, Blaisdell petitioned the court to extend the redemption period. At a hearing on this motion, Home argued the unconstitutionality of the law and moved that the petition be dismissed. The motion was granted, but the Minnesota Supreme Court reversed. Appeal was taken to the U.S. Supreme Court.

MR. CHIEF JUSTICE HUGHES delivered the opinion of the Court.

* * *

In determining whether the . . . [Minnesota Mortgage Moratorium Act] exceeds the power of the State by reason of the clause in the Federal Constitution prohibiting impairment of the obligations of contracts, we must consider the relation of emergency to constitutional power, the historical setting of the contract clause, the development of the jurisprudence of this Court in the construction of that clause, and the principles of construction which we may consider to be established.

Emergency does not create power. Emergency does not increase granted power or remove or diminish the restrictions imposed upon power granted or reserved. The Constitution was adopted in a period of grave emergency. Its grants of power to the Federal Government and its limitations of the power of the States were determined in the light of emergency and they are not altered by emergency. What power was thus granted and what limitations were thus imposed are questions which have always been, and always will be, the subject of close examination under our constitutional system.

While emergency does not create power, emergency may furnish the occasion for the exercise of power. "Although an emergency may not call into life a power which has never lived, nevertheless emergency may afford a reason for the exertion of a living power already enjoyed."

The constitutional question presented in the light of an emergency is whether the power possessed embraces the particular exercise of it in response to particular conditions. Thus, the war power of the Federal Government is not created by the emergency of war, but it is a power given to meet that emergency. It is a power to wage war successfully, and thus it permits the harnessing of the entire energies of the people in a supreme cooperative effort to preserve the nation. But even the war power does not remove constitutional limitations safeguarding essential liberties.[5] When the provisions of the Constitution, in grant or restriction, are specific, so particularized as not to admit of construction, no question is presented. Thus, emergency would not permit a State to have more than two Senators in the Congress, or permit the election of President by a general popular vote without regard to the number of electors to which the States are respectively entitled, or permit the States to "coin money" or to "make anything but gold and silver coin a tender in payment of debts." But where constitutional grants and limitations of power are set forth in general clauses, which afford a broad outline, the process of construction is essential to fill in the details. That is true of the contract clause. . . .

In the construction of the contract clause, the debates in the Constitutional Convention are of little aid. But the reasons which lead to the adoption of that clause, and of the other prohibitions of Section 10 of Article I, are not left in doubt and have frequently been described with eloquent emphasis. The widespread distress following the revolutionary period, and the plight of debtors, had called forth in the States an ignoble array of legislative schemes for the defeat of creditors and the invasion of contractual obligations. Legislative interferences had been so numerous and extreme that the confidence essential to prosperous trade had been undermined and the utter destruction of credit was threatened. "The sober people of America" were convinced that some "thorough reform" was needed which would "inspire a general prudence and industry, and give a regular course of the business of society." *The Federalist,* No. 44. It was necessary to interpose the restraining power of a central authority in order to secure the foundations even of "private faith." The occasion and general purpose of the contract clause are summed up in the terse statement of Chief Justice Marshall in *Ogden v. Saunders,* [1827]

> The power of changing the relative situation of debtor and creditor, of interfering with contracts, a power which comes home to every man, touches the interest of all, and controls the conduct of every individual in those things which he supposes to be proper for his own exclusive management, had been used to such an excess by the state legislatures, as to break in upon the ordinary intercourse of society, and destroy all confidence between man and man. This mischief had become so great, so

alarming, as not only to impair commercial intercourse, and threaten the existence of credit, but to sap the morals of the people, and destroy the sanctity of private faith. To guard against the continuance of the evil was an object of deep interest with all the truly wise, as well as the virtuous, of this great community, and was one of the important benefits expected from a reform of the government.

*   *   *

[But] the legislature cannot "bargain away the public health or the public morals." Thus, the constitutional provision against the impairment of contracts was held not to be violated by an amendment of the state constitution which put an end to a lottery theretofore authorized by the legislature. The lottery was a valid enterprise when established under express state authority, but the legislature in the public interest could put a stop to it. A similar rule has been applied to the control by the State of the sale of intoxicating liquors. The States retain adequate power to protect the public health against the maintenance of nuisances despite insistence upon existing contracts. . . .

The economic interests of the State may justify the exercise of its continuing and dominant protective power notwithstanding interference with contracts. In *Manigault v. Springs,* [1905], riparian owners in South Carolina had made a contract for a clear passage through a creek by the removal of existing obstructions. Later, the legislature of the State, by virtue of its broad authority to make public improvements, and in order to increase the taxable value of the lowlands which would be drained, authorized the construction of a dam across the creek. The Court sustained the statute upon the ground that the private interests were subservient to the public right. . . .

[It is argued] that the state power may be addressed directly to the prevention of the enforcement of contracts only when these are of a sort which the legislature in its discretion may denounce as being in themselves hostile to public morals, or public health, safety or welfare, or where the prohibition is merely of injurious practices; that interference with the enforcement of other and valid contracts according to appropriate legal procedure, although the interference is temporary and for a public purpose, is not permissible. This is but to contend that in the latter case the end is not legitimate in the view that it cannot be reconciled with a fair interpretation of the constitutional provision.

Undoubtedly, whatever is reserved of state power must be consistent with the fair intent of the constitutional limitation of that power. The reserved power cannot be construed so as to destroy the limitation, nor is the limitation to be construed to destroy the reserved power in its essential aspects. They must be construed in harmony with each other. This principle precludes a construction which would permit the State to adopt as its policy the repudiation of debts or the destruction of contracts or the denial of means to enforce them. But it does not follow that conditions may not arise in which a temporary restraint of enforcement may be consistent with the spirit and purpose of the constitutional provision and thus be found to be within the range of the reserved power of the State to protect the vital interests of the community. It cannot be maintained that the constitutional prohibition should be so construed as to prevent limited and temporary interpositions with respect to the enforcement of contracts if made necessary by a great public calamity such as fire, flood, or earthquake.

The reservation of state power appropriate to such extraordinary conditions may be deemed to be as much a part of all contracts, as is the reservation of state power to protect the public interest in the other situations to which we have referred. And if state power exists to give temporary relief from the enforcement of contracts in the presence of disasters due to physical causes such as fire, flood or earthquake, that power cannot be said to be non-existent when the urgent public need demanding such relief is produced by other and economic causes.

* * *

It is manifest from [a] . . . review of our decisions that there has been a growing appreciation of public needs and of the necessity of finding ground for a rational compromise between individual rights and public welfare. The settlement and consequent contraction of the public domain, the pressure of a constantly increasing density of population, the interrelation of the activities of our people and the complexity of our economic interests, have inevitably led to an increased use of the organization of society in order to protect the very bases of individual opportunity. Where, in earlier days, it was thought that only the concerns of individuals or of classes were involved, and that those of the State itself were touched only remotely, it has later been found that the fundamental interests of the State are directly affected; and that the question is no longer merely that of one party to a contract as against another, but of the use of reasonable means to safeguard the economic structure upon which the good of all depends.

It is no answer to say that this public need was not apprehended a century ago, or to insist that what the provision of the Constitution meant to the vision of that day it must mean to the vision of our time. If by the statement that what the Constitution meant at the time of its adoption it means to-day, it is intended to say that the great clauses of the Constitution must be confined to the interpretation which the framers, with the conditions and outlook of their time, would have placed upon them, the statement carries its own refutation. It was to guard against such a narrow conception that Chief Justice Marshall uttered the memorable warning—"We must never forget that it is *a constitution* we are expounding" (*McCulloch v. Maryland,* [1819])—"a constitution intended to endure for ages to come, and consequently, to be adapted to the various *crises* of human affairs." When we are dealing with the words of the Constitution, said this Court in *Missouri v. Holland,* [1920] "we must realize that they have called into life a being the development of which could not have been foreseen completely by the most gifted of its begetters . . . The case before us must be considered in the light of our whole experience and not merely in that of what was said a hundred years ago."

* * *

Applying the criteria established by our decisions we conclude:

1 An emergency existed in Minnesota which furnished a proper occasion for the exercise of the reserved power of the State to protect the vital interests of the community. The declarations of the existence of this emergency by the legislature and by the Supreme Court of Minnesota cannot be regarded as a subterfuge or as lacking in adequate basis. . . .

2 The legislation was addressed to a legitimate end, that is, the legislation was not for the mere advantage of particular individuals but for the protection of a basic interest of society.

3 In view of the nature of the contracts in question—mortgages of unquestionable validity—the relief afforded and justified by the emergency, in order not to contravene the constitutional provision, could only be of a character appropriate to that emergency and could be granted only upon reasonable conditions.

4 The conditions upon which the period of redemption is extended do not appear to be unreasonable. . . . The legislature was entitled to deal with the general or typical situation. The relief afforded by the statute has regard to the interest of mortgagees as well as to the interest of mortgagors. The legislation seeks to prevent the impending ruin of both by a considerate measure of relief. . . .

5 The legislation is temporary in operation. It is limited to the exigency which called it forth. . . .

We are of the opinion that the Minnesota statute as here applied does not violate the contract clause of the Federal Constitution. Whether the legislation is wise or unwise as a matter of policy is a question with which we are not concerned.

What has been said on that point is also applicable to the contention presented under the due process clause.

Nor do we think that the statute denies to the appellant the equal protection of the laws. The classification which the statute makes cannot be said to be an arbitrary one.

The judgment of the Supreme Court of Minnesota is affirmed.

Judgment affirmed.

MR. JUSTICE SUTHERLAND, dissenting.

* * *

Chief Justice Taney, in *Dred Scott v. Sandford,* 19 How. 393, 426, said that while the Constitution remains unaltered it must be construed now as it was understood at the time of its adoption; that it is not only the same in words but the same in meaning, "and as long as it continues to exist in its present form, it speaks not only in the same words, but with the same meaning and intent with which it spoke when it came from the hands of its framers, and was voted on and adopted by the people of the United States. Any other rule of construction would abrogate the judicial character of this court, and make it the mere reflex of the popular opinion or passion of the day. . . ."

. . . What a court is to do, therefore, is *to declare the law as written*, leaving it to the people themselves to make such changes as new circumstances may require. The meaning of the constitution is fixed when it is adopted, and it is not different at any subsequent time when a court has occasion to pass upon it."

The whole aim of construction, as applied to a provision of the Constitution, is to discover the meaning, to ascertain and give effect to the intent, of its framers and the people who adopted it. . . .

An application of these principles to the question under review removes any doubt, if otherwise there would be any, that the contract impairment clause denies to the several states the power to mitigate hard consequences resulting to debtors from financial or economic exigencies by an impairment of the obligation of contracts of indebtedness. . . .

The present exigency is nothing new. From the beginning of our existence as a nation, periods of depression, of industrial failure, of financial distress, of unpaid and unpayable indebtedness, have alternated with years of plenty. The vital lesson that expenditure beyond income begets poverty, that public or private extravagance, financed by promises to pay, either must end in complete or partial repudiation or the promises be fulfilled by self-denial and painful effort, though constantly taught by bitter experience, seems never to be learned; and the attempt by legislative devices to shift the misfortune of the debtor to the shoulders of the creditor without coming into conflict with the contract impairmant clause has been persistent and oft-repeated.

* * *

It is quite true that an emergency may supply the occasion for the exercise of power, depending upon the nature of the power and the intent of the Constitution with respect thereto. The emergency of war furnishes an occasion for the exercise of certain of the war powers. This the Constitution contemplates, since they cannot be exercised upon any other occasion. The existence of another kind of emergency authorizes the United States to protect each of the states of the Union against domestic violence. Const. Art. IV, § 4. But we are here dealing not with a power granted by the Federal Constitution, but with the state police power, which exists in its own right. Hence the question is not whether an emergency furnishes the occasion for the exercise of that state power, but whether an emergency furnishes an occasion for the relaxation of the restrictions upon the power imposed by the contract impairment clause; and the difficulty is that the contract impairment clause forbids state action under any circumstances, if it have the effect of impairing the obligation of contracts. That clause restricts every state power in the particular specified, no matter what may be the occasion. It does not contemplate that an emergency shall furnish an occasion for softening the restriction or making it any the less a restriction upon state action in that contingency than it is under strictly normal conditions.

* * *

If what has now been said is sound, as I think it is, we come to what really is the vital question in the case: Does the Minnesota statute constitute an impairment of the obligation of the contract now under review? . . . As this court has well said, whatever tends to postpone or retard the enforcement of a contract, to that extent weakens the obligation. According to one latin proverb, "He who gives quickly, gives twice," and according to another, "He who pays too late, pays less." "Any authorization of the postponement of payment, or of means by which such postponement may be effected, is in conflict with the constitutional inhibition." *Louisiana v. New Orleans,* 102 U.S. 203, 207. I am not able to see any real distinction between a statute which in substantive terms alters the obligation of a debtor-creditor contract so as to extend the time of its performance for a period of two years, and a statute which, though in terms acting upon the remedy, is aimed at the obligation (as distinguished, for example, from the judicial procedure incident to the enforcement thereof) and which does in fact withhold from the creditor, for the same period of time, the stipulated fruits of his contract.

* * *

West Coast Hotel v. Parrish

300 U.S. 379; 57 S. Ct. 578; 81 L. Ed. 703 (1937)
Vote: 5–4

The facts are given in the opinion.

MR. CHIEF JUSTICE HUGHES delivered the opinion of the Court.

* * *

The appellant conducts a hotel. The appellee Elsie Parrish was employed as a chambermaid and (with her husband) brought this suit to recover the difference between the wages paid her and the minimum wage fixed pursuant to the state law. The minimum wage was $14.50 per week of 48 hours. The appellant challenged the act as repugnant to the due process clause of the Fourteenth Amendment of the Constitution of the United States. The Supreme Court of the State, reversing the trial court, sustained the statute and directed judgment for the plaintiffs. The case is here on appeal.

The appellant relies upon the decision of this Court in *Adkins v. Children's Hospital,* [1923], which held invalid the District of Columbia Minimum Wage Act, which was attacked under the due process clause of the Fifth Amendment. . . .

The Supreme Court of Washington has upheld the minimum wage statute of that State. It has decided that the statute is a reasonable exercise of the police power of the State. In reaching that conclusion the state court has invoked principles long established by this Court in the application of the Fourteenth Amendment. The state court has refused to regard the decision in the *Adkins* case as determinative and has pointed to our decisions both before and since that case as justifying its position. We are of the opinion that this ruling of the state court demands on our part a reexamination of the *Adkins* case. The importance of the question, in which many States having similar laws are concerned, the close division by which the decision in the *Adkins* case was reached, and the economic conditions which have supervened, and in the light of which the reasonableness of the exercise of the protective power of the State must be considered, make it not only appropriate, but we think imperative, that in deciding the present case the subject should receive fresh consideration.

*   *   *

The principle which must control our decision is not in doubt. The constitutional provision invoked is the due process clause of the Fourteenth Amendment governing the States, as the due process clause invoked in the *Adkins* case governed Congress. In each case the violation alleged by those attacking minimum wage regulation for women is deprivation of freedom of contract. What is this freedom? The Constitution does not speak of freedom of contract. It speaks of liberty and prohibits the deprivation of liberty without due process of law. In prohibiting that deprivation the Constitution does not recognize an absolute and uncontrollable liberty. Liberty in each of its phases has its history and connotation. But the liberty safeguarded is liberty in a social organization which requires the protection of law against the evils which menace the health, safety, morals and welfare of the people. Liberty under the Constitution is thus necessarily subject to the restraints of due process, and regulation which is reasonable in relation to its subject and is adopted in the interests of the community is due process.

This essential limitation of liberty in general governs freedom of contract in particular. More than twenty-five years ago we set forth the applicable principle in these words, after referring to the cases where the liberty guaranteed by the Fourteenth Amendment had been broadly described:

"But it was recognized in the cases cited, as in many others, that freedom of contract is a qualified and not an absolute right. There is no absolute freedom to do as one wills or to contract as one chooses. The guaranty of liberty does not withdraw from legislative supervision that wide department of activity which consists of the making of contracts, or deny to government the power to provide restrictive safeguards. Liberty implies the absence of arbitrary restraint, not immunity from reasonable regulations and prohibitions imposed in the interests of the community." *Chicago, B. & Q. R. Co. v. McGuire,* [1911].

This power under the Constitution to restrict freedom of contract has had many illustrations. That it may be exercised in the public interest with respect to contracts between employer and employee is undeniable. Thus statutes have been sustained limiting employment in underground mines and smelters to eight hours a day (*Holden v. Hardy,* [1898]); in requiring redemption in cash of store orders or other evidences of indebtedness issued in the payment of wages (*Knoxville Iron Co. v. Harbison,* [1901]); in forbidding the payment of seamen's wages in advance (*Patterson v. Bark Eudora,* [1903]); in making it unlawful to contract to pay miners employed at quantity rates upon the basis of screened coal instead of the weight of the coal as originally produced in the mine (*McLean v. Arkansas,* [1909]); in prohibiting contracts limiting liability for injuries to employees (*Chicago, B. & Q. R. Co. v. McGuire, supra*); in limiting hours of work of employees in manufacturing establishments (*Bunting v. Oregon,* [1917]); and in maintaining workmen's compensation laws (*New York Central R. Co. v. White,* [1917]).

In dealing with the relation of employer and employed, the legislature has necessarily a wide field of discretion in order that there may be suitable protection of health and safety, and that peace and good order may be promoted through regulations designed to insure wholesome conditions of work and freedom from oppression.

The point that has been strongly stressed that adult employees should be deemed competent to make their own contracts was decisively met nearly forty years ago in *Holden v. Hardy,* where we pointed out the inequality in the footing of the parties. . . .

With full recognition of the earnestness and vigor which characterize the prevailing opinion in the *Adkins* case, we find it impossible to reconcile that ruling with these well-considered declarations. What can be closer to the public interest than the health of women and their protection from unscrupulous and overreaching employers? And if the protection of women is a legitimate end of the exercise of state power, how can it be said that the requirement of the payment of a minimum wage fairly fixed in order to meet the very necessities of existence is not an admissible means to that end? The legislature of the State was clearly entitled to consider the situation of women in employment, the fact that they are in the class receiving the least pay, that their bargaining power is relatively weak, and that they are the ready victims of those who would take advantage of their necessitous circumstances. The legislature was entitled to adopt measures to reduce the evils of the "sweating system," the exploiting of workers at wages so low as to be insufficient to meet the bare cost of living, thus making their very helplessness the occasion of a most injurious competition. The legislature had the right to consider that its minimum wage requirements would be an important aid in carrying out its policy of protection. The adoption of similar requirements by many States evidences a deepseated conviction both as to the presence of the evil and as to the means adapted to check it. Legislative response to that conviction cannot be regarded as arbitrary or capricious, and that is all we have to decide. Even if the wisdom of the policy be regarded as debatable and its effects uncertain, still the legislature is entitled to its judgment.

There is an additional and compelling consideration which recent economic experience has brought into a strong light. The exploitation of a class of workers who are in an unequal position with respect to bargaining power and are thus relatively defenceless against the denial of a living wage is not only detrimental to their health and well being but casts a direct burden for their support upon the community. What these workers lose in wages the taxpayers are called upon to pay. The bare cost of living must be met. We may take judicial notice of the unparalleled demands for relief which arose during the recent period of depression and still continue to an alarming extent despite the degree of economic recovery which has been achieved. It is unnecessary to cite official statistics to establish what is of common knowledge through the length and breadth of the land. While in the instant case no factual brief has been presented, there is no reason to doubt that the State of Washington has encountered the same social problem that is present elsewhere. The community is not bound to provide what is in effect a subsidy for unconscionable employers. The community may direct its law-making power to correct the abuse which springs from their selfish disregard of the public interest. The argument that the legislation in question constitutes an arbitrary discrimination, because it does not extend to men, is unavailing. This Court has frequently held that the legislative authority, acting within its proper field, is not bound to extend its regulation to all cases which it might possibly reach. The legislature "is free to recognize degrees of harm and it may confine its restrictions to those classes of cases where the need is deemed to be clearest." If "the law presumably hits the evil where it is most felt, it is not to be overthrown because there are other instances to which it might have been applied." There is no "doctrinaire requirement" that the legislation should be couched in all embracing terms.

This familiar principle has repeatedly been applied to legislation which singles out women, and particular classes of women, in the exercise of the State's protective power.

Their relative need in the presence of the evil, no less than the existence of the evil itself, is a matter for the legislative judgment. Our conclusion is that the case of *Adkins v. Children's Hospital, supra,* should be, and it is, overruled. The judgment of the Supreme Court of the State of Washington is

Affirmed.

MR. JUSTICE SUTHERLAND, dissenting:

MR. JUSTICE VAN DEVANTER, MR. JUSTICE MCREYNOLDS, MR. JUSTICE BUTLER and I think the judgment of the court below should be reversed.

* * *

Under our form of government, where the written Constitution, by its own terms, is the supreme law, some agency, of necessity, must have the power to say the final word as to the validity of a statute assailed as unconstitutional. The Constitution makes it clear that the power has been intrusted to this court when the question arises in a controversy within its jurisdiction; and so long as the power remains there, its exercise cannot be avoided without betrayal of the trust.

It has been pointed out many times, as in the *Adkins* case, that this judicial duty is one of gravity and delicacy; and that rational doubts must be resolved in favor of the constitutionality of the statute. But whose doubts, and by whom resolved? Undoubtedly it is the duty of a member of the court, in the process of reaching a right conclusion, to give due weight to the opposing views of his associates; but in the end, the question which he must answer is not whether such views seem sound to those who entertain them, but whether they convince him that the statute is constitutional or engender in his mind a rational doubt upon that issue. The oath which he takes as a judge is not a composite oath, but an individual one. And in passing upon the validity of a statute, he discharges a duty imposed upon *him,* which cannot be consummated justly by an automatic acceptance of the views of others which have neither convinced, nor created a reasonable doubt in, his mind. If upon a question so important he thus surrender his deliberate judgment, he stands forsworn. He cannot subordinate his convictions to that extent and keep faith with his oath or retain his judicial and moral independence.

The suggestion that the only check upon the exercise of the judicial power, when properly invoked, to declare a constitutional right superior to an unconstitutional statute is the judge's own faculty of self-restraint belongs in the domain of will and not of judgment. The check upon the judge is that imposed by his oath of office, by the Constitution and by his own conscientious and informed convictions; and since he has the duty to make up his own mind and adjuge accordingly, it is hard to see how there could be any other restraint. This court acts as a unit. It cannot act in any other way; and the majority (whether a bare majority or a majority of all but one of its members), therefore, establishes the controlling rule as the decision of the court, binding, so long as it remains unchanged, equally upon those who disagree and upon those who subscribe to it. Otherwise, orderly administration of justice would cease. But it is the right of those in the minority to disagree, and sometimes, in matters of grave importance, their imperative duty to voice their disagreement at such length as the occasion demands—always, of course, in terms which, however forceful, do not offend the proprieties or impugn the good faith of those who think otherwise.

It is urged that the question involved should now receive fresh consideration, among other reasons, because of "the economic conditions which have supervened"; but the meaning of the Constitution does not change with the ebb and flow of economic events. We frequently are told in more general words that the Constitution must be construed in the light of the present. If by that it is meant that the Constitution is made up of living words that apply to every new condition which they include, the statement is quite true. But to say, if that be intended, that the words of the Constitution mean today what they did not mean when written—that is, that they do not apply to a situation now to which they would have applied then—is to rob that instrument of the essential element which continues it in force as the people have made it until they, and not their official agents, have made it otherwise.

* * *

The judicial function is that of interpretation; it does not include the power of amendment under the guise of interpretation. To miss the point of difference between the two is to miss all that the phrase "supreme law of the land" stands for and to convert what was intended as inescapable and enduring mandates into mere moral reflections.

If the Constitution, intelligently and reasonably construed in the light of these principles, stands in the way of desirable legislation, the blame must rest upon that instrument, and not upon the court for enforcing it according to its terms. The remedy in that situation—and the only true remedy—is to amend the Constitution.

* * *

QUESTIONS AND COMMENTS

1 The attempt in *Slaughterhouse* to free economic interests from state interference and centralize power in the federal government via appropriate interpretation of the privilege and immunities clause failed by one vote. The consequences of the Slaughterhouse Cases for future constitutional development is, therefore, attributable to one man—a fact that points up the importance of the personnel on the Court and the "historical accident" that led to the particular composition of the Court in 1873.

2 Is the list of rights associated with national citizenship in *Slaughterhouse* exhaustive? Cf. *Twining v. New Jersey,* 211 U.S. 78 (1908),

3 In the twentieth century, the Court has used the privileges and immunities clause sparingly. Why do you think the Court has refrained from using the clause to expand the rights and liberties guaranteed by the Constitution?

4 Maximum hours for female employees were upheld in 1908 (*Muller v. Oregon,* 208 U.S. 412). *Lochner v. New York* was overruled in 1917 (*Bunting v. Oregon,* 243 U.S. 426).

5 How does the role perception of the Court held by Chief Justice Hughes differ from that of Justice Sutherland in *Home Building and Loan?* Do these perceptions have anything to do with the way that case was decided? Sutherland had no previous bench experience, while Hughes had been a federal judge before coming to the Court. Is that distinction relevant? Why or why not?

6 Mortgage moratoria are still valid under the Constitution. See *El Paso v. Simmons,* 379 U.S. 497 (1965), and *East New York Savings Bank v. Hahn,* 326 U.S. 230 (1945).

7 The hotel owner in *West Coast* relied on the Court's decision in *Adkins v. Children's Hospital.* But that case involved a federal statute, while *West Coast* involved a state statute. Does that make any difference? Why or why not?

8 Is *Adkins* still good law?

9 What view of the judicial role is taken by the dissenting justices in *West Coast Hotel v. Parrish?* Who on the present Supreme Court might be most comfortable with this view? Who least comfortable?

10 What argument would you offer against the dissenters' view that the Constitution should be changed by amendment only?

11 Are all the justices consistent in the positions taken in *Home Building and Loan* and *West Coast Hotel?*

* * * * * *

The last two cases in this section, *Hines v. Davidowitz* and *Perez v. Campbell,* turn on the "supremacy clause." Article VI of the Constitution makes the Constitution, the laws of the United States, and all treaties to which the United States is a party, the supreme law of the land. This means that any state law or constitutional provision in conflict with any federal law or treaty must fall when challenged in the courts. Moreover, the Supreme Court has interpreted the supremacy clause to deny the states the right to legislate in any area in which Congress has "occupied the field." This is the so-called preemption doctrine. It holds that when Congress wishes, or thinks it wise, it may legislate some comprehensive scheme of regulation that preempts the field and bars all state regulation of the same subject matter. This bar on the states does not turn on conflict. The only question is whether Congress has, in fact, occupied the field.

In answering this question, the Court has usually asked three questions: (1) Is the congressional act so all-encompassing as to support the inference that Congress intended to preempt the field? (2) Does the federal statute deal with a matter of such overriding importance to the federal system that Congress could reasonably be assumed to want the states kept out of it? (3) Is state administration of a nonconflicting statute in the field likely to conflict with the federal act or administration of the federal act?

Hines v. Davidowitz specifically focuses on the question of preemption, while *Perez v. Campbell* addresses an Arizona statute said to be in conflict with the Federal Bankruptcy Act.

Hines, Secretary of Labor and Industry of Pennsylvania, et al. v. Davidowitz et al.

312 U.S. 52; 61 S. Ct. 399; 85 L. Ed. 581 (1941)
Vote: 6–3

The facts are given in the opinion below.

MR. JUSTICE BLACK delivered the opinion of the Court.

This case involves the validity of an Alien Registration Act adopted by the Commonwealth of Pennsylvania. The Act, passed in 1939, requires every alien 18 years or over, with certain exceptions, to register once each year; provide such information as is required by the statute, plus any "other information and details" that the Department of Labor and Industry may direct; pay $1 as an annual registration fee; receive an alien identification card and carry it at all times; show the card whenever it may be demanded by any police officer or any agent of the Department of Labor and Industry; and exhibit the card as a condition precedent to registering a motor vehicle in his name or obtaining a license to operate one. The Department of Labor and Industry is charged with the duties of classifying the registrations for "the purpose of ready reference," and furnishing a copy of the classification to the Pennsylvania Motor Police. Nonexempt aliens who fail to register are subject to fine of not more than $100 or imprisonment for not more than 60 days, or both. For failure to carry an identification card or for failure to show it upon proper demand, the punishment is a fine of not more than $10, or imprisonment for not more than 10 days, or both.

A three-judge District Court enjoined enforcement of the Act, holding that it denied aliens equal protection of the laws, and that it encroached upon legislative powers constitutionally vested in the federal government. It is that judgment we are here called upon to review. But in 1940, after the court had held the Pennsylvania Act invalid, Congress enacted a federal Alien Registration Act. We must therefore pass upon the state Act in the light of the Congressional Act. . . .

The basic subject of the state and federal laws is identical—registration of aliens as a distinct group. Appellants urge that the Pennsylvania law "was constitutional when passed," and that "The only question is whether the state act is in abeyance or whether the state and Federal Government have concurrent jurisdiction to register aliens for the protection of inhabitants and property." Appellees, on the other hand, contend that the Pennsylvania Act is invalid, for the reasons that it (1) denies equal protection of the laws to aliens residing in the state; (2) violates § 16 of the Civil Rights Act of 1870; (3) exceeds Pennsylvania's constitutional power in requiring registration of aliens without Congressional consent. Appellees' final contention is that the power to restrict, limit, regulate and register aliens as a distinct group is not an equal and continuously existing concurrent power of state and nation, but that even if the state can legislate on this subject at all, its power is subordinate to supreme national law. Appellees conclude that by its adoption of a comprehensive, integrated scheme for regulation of aliens—including its 1940 registration act—Congress has precluded state action like that taken by Pennsylvania.

In the view we take it is not necessary to pass upon appellees' first, second, and third contentions, and so we pass immediately to their final question, expressly leaving open all of appellees' other contentions, including the argument that the federal power in this field, whether exercised or unexercised, is exclusive. Obviously the answer to appellees' final question depends upon an analysis of the respective powers of state and national governments in the regulation of aliens as such, and a determination of whether Congress has, by its action, foreclosed enforcement of Pennsylvania's registration law.

First. That the supremacy of the national power in the general field of foreign affairs, including power over immigration, naturalization and deportation, is made clear by the Constitution, was pointed out by the authors of The Federalist in 1787, and has since been given continuous recognition by this Court. When the national government by treaty or statute has established rules and regulations touching the rights, privileges, obligations or burdens of aliens as such, the treaty or statute is the supreme law of the land. No state can add to or take from the force and effect of such treaty or statute, for Article VI of the Constitution provides that "This Constitution, and the Laws of the United States which shall be made in Pursuance thereof; and all Treaties made, or which shall be made, under the Authority of the United States, shall be the supreme Law of the Land; and the Judges in every State shall be bound thereby, any Thing in the Constitution or Laws of any State to the Contrary notwithstanding." The Federal Government, representing as it does the collective interests of the forty-eight states, is entrusted with full and exclusive responsibility for the conduct of affairs with foreign sovereignties. "For local interests the several States of the Union exist, but for national purposes, embracing our relations with foreign nations, we are but one people, one nation, one power." Our system of government is such that the interest of the cities, counties and states, no less than the interest of the people of the whole nation, imperatively requires that federal power in the field affecting foreign relations be left entirely free from local interference.

* * *

One of the most important and delicate of all international relationships, recognized immemorially as a responsibility of government, has to do with the protection of the just rights of a country's own nationals when those nationals are in another country. Experience has shown that international controversies of the gravest moment, sometimes even leading to war, may arise from real or imagined wrongs to another's subjects inflicted, or permitted, by a government. This country, like other nations, has entered into numerous treaties of amity and commerce since its inception—treaties entered into under express constitutional authority, and binding upon the states as well as the nation. Among those treaties have been many which not only promised and guaranteed broad rights and privileges to aliens sojourning in our own territory, but secured reciprocal promises and guarantees for our own citizens while in other lands.

. . . It cannot be doubted that both the state and the federal registration laws belong "to that class of laws which concern the exterior relation of this whole nation with other nations and governments." Consequently the regulation of aliens is so intimately blended and intertwined with responsibilities of the national government that where it acts, and the state also acts on the same subject, "the act of Congress, or the treaty, is supreme; and the law of the State, though enacted in the exercise of powers not controverted, must yield to it." And where the federal government, has enacted a complete scheme of regulation and has therein provided a standard for the registration of aliens, states cannot, inconsistently with the purpose of Congress, conflict or interfere with, curtail or complement, the federal law, or enforce additional or auxiliary regulations. There is not—and from the very nature of the problem there cannot be—any rigid formula or rule which can be used as a universal pattern to determine the meaning and purpose of every act of Congress. This Court, in considering the validity of state laws in the light of treaties or federal laws touching the same subject, has made use of the following expressions: conflicting; contrary to; occupying the field; repugnance; difference; irreconcilability; inconsistency; violation; curtailment; and interference. But none of these expressions provides an infallible constitutional test or an exclusive constitutional yardstick. In the final analysis, there can be no one crystal clear distinctly marked formula. Our primary function is to determine whether, under the circumstances of this particular case, Pennsylvania's law stands as an obstacle to the accomplishment and execution of the full purposes and objectives of Congress. And in that determination, it is of importance that this legislation is in a field which affects international relations, the one aspect of our government that from the first has been most generally conceded imperatively to demand broad national authority. Any concurrent state power that may exist is restricted to the narrowest of limits; the state's power here is not bottomed on the same broad base as is its power to tax. And it is also of importance that this legislation deals with the rights, liberties, and personal freedoms of human beings, and is in an entirely different category from state tax statutes or state pure food laws regulating the labels on cans.

Our conclusion is that appellee is correct in his contention that the power to restrict, limit, regulate, and register aliens as a distinct group is not an equal and continuously existing concurrent power of state and nation, but that whatever power a state may have is subordinate to supreme national law. We proceed therefore to an examination of Congressional enactments to ascertain whether or not Congress has acted in such manner that its action should preclude enforcement of Pennsylvania's law.

* * *

When Congress passed the Alien Registration Act of 1940, . . . [its] purpose, as announced by the chairman of the Senate subcommittee which drafted the final bill, was to "work . . . the new provisions into the existing [immigration and naturalization] laws, so as to make a harmonious whole." That "harmonious whole" included the "Uniform Rule of Naturalization" the Constitution empowered the Congress to provide. And as a part of that "harmonious whole," under the federal Act aliens need not carry cards, and can only be punished for willful failure to register. Further, registration records and fingerprints must be kept secret and cannot be revealed except to agencies—such as a state—upon consent of the Commissioner and the Attorney General.

We have already adverted to the conditions which make the treatment of aliens, in whatever state they may be located, a matter of national moment. And whether or not registration of aliens is of such a nature that the Constitution permits only of one uniform national system, it cannot be denied that the Congress might validly conclude that such uniformity is desirable. The legislative history of the Act indicates that Congress was trying to steer a middle path, realizing that any registration requirement was a departure from our traditional policy of not treating aliens as a thing apart, but also feeling that the Nation was in need of the type of information to be secured. Having the constitutional authority so to do, it has provided a standard for alien registration in a single integrated and all-embracing system in order to obtain the information deemed to be desirable in connection with aliens. When it made this addition to its uniform naturalization and immigration laws, it plainly manifested a purpose to do so in such a way as to protect the personal liberties of law-abiding aliens through one uniform national registration system, and to leave them free from the possibility of inquisitorial practices and police surveillance that might not only affect our international relations but might also generate the very disloyalty which the law has intended guarding against. Under these circumstances, the Pennsylvania Act cannot be enforced. Accordingly, the judgment below is

Affirmed.

MR. JUSTICE STONE, dissenting:

I think the judgment below should be reversed.

Undoubtedly Congress, in the exercise of its power to legislate in aid of powers granted by the Constitution to the national government may greatly enlarge the exercise of federal authority and to an extent which need not now be defined, it may, if such is its will, thus subtract from the powers which might otherwise be exercised by the states. Assuming, as the Court holds, that Congress could constitutionally set up an exclusive registration system for aliens, I think it has not done so and that it is not the province of the courts to do that which Congress has failed to do.

* * *

It is conceded that the federal act in operation does not at any point conflict with the state statute, and it does not by its terms purport to control or restrict state authority in any particular. But the government says that Congress by passing the federal act, has "occupied the field" so as to preclude the enforcement of the state statute and that the administration of the latter might well conflict with Congressional policy to protect the civil liberty of aliens against the harassments of intrusive police surveillance.

Little aid can be derived from the vague and illusory but often repeated formula that Congress "by occupying the field" has excluded from it all state legislation. Every Act of Congress occupies some field, but we must know the boundaries of that field before we can say that it has precluded a state from the exercise of any power reserved to it by the Constitution. To discover the boundaries we look to the federal statute itself, read in the light of its constitutional setting and its legislative history.

...We must take it that Congress was not unaware that some nineteen states have statutes or ordinances requiring some form of registration for aliens, seven of them dating from the last war. The repeal of this legislation is not to be inferred from the silence of Congress in enacting a law which at no point conflicts with the state legislation and is harmonious with it.

* * *

The Fourteenth Amendment guarantees the civil liberties of aliens as well as of citizens against infringement by state action in the enactment of laws and their administration as well. Again we are pointed to nothing in the Federal Alien Registration Act or in the records of its passage through Congress to indicate that Congress thought those guarantees inadequate or that in acquiring registration of all aliens it undertook to prevent the states from passing any registration measure otherwise constitutional. True, it was careful to bring the new legislation into harmony with existing federal statutes and to avoid, so far as consistent with its purposes, any harsh or oppressive requirements, but in all this there is to be found no warrant for saying that there was a Congressional purpose to curtail the exercise of any constitutional power of the state over its alien residents or to protect the alien from state action which the Constitution prohibits and which the federal courts stand ready to prevent. See *Hague v. C.I.O.,* [1939].

Here compliance with the state law does not preclude or even interfere with compliance with the act of Congress. The enforcement of both acts involves no more inconsistency, no more inconvenience to the individual, and no more embarrassment to either government than do any of the laws, state and national, such as revenue laws, licensing laws, or police regulations, where interstate commerce is involved, which are equally applied to the citizen because he is subject, as are aliens, to a dual sovereignty.

The CHIEF JUSTICE and MR. JUSTICE MCREYNOLDS concur in this opinion.

Perez v. Campbell

402 U.S. 637; 91 S. Ct. 1704; 29 L. Ed. 2d 233 (1971)
Vote: Unanimous (four justices dissented in part)

The facts are given in the opinion below.

MR. JUSTICE WHITE delivered the opinion of the Court.

This case raises an important issue concerning the construction of the Supremacy Clause of the Constitution—whether . . . Arizona's Motor Vehicle Safety Responsibility Act, is invalid under that clause as being in conflict with the mandate of § 17 of the Bankruptcy Act, 11 U. S. C. § 35, providing that receipt of a discharge in bankruptcy fully discharges all but certain specified judgments. The courts below, concluding that this case was controlled by *Kesler v. Department of Public Safety,* (1962), and *Reitz y. Mealay,* (1941), two earlier opinions of this Court dealing with alleged conflicts between the Bankruptcy Act and state financial responsibility laws, ruled against the claim of conflict and upheld the Arizona statute.

On July 8, 1965, petitioner Adolfo Perez, driving a car registered in his name, was involved in an automobile accident in Tucson, Arizona. The Perez automobile was not covered by liability insurance at the time of the collision. The driver of the second car was the minor daughter of Leonard Pinkertor and in September 1966 the Pinkertons sued Mr. and Mrs. Perez in state court for personal injuries and property damage sustained in the accident. On October 31, 1967, the petitioners confessed judgment in this suit, and a judgment order was entered against them on November 8, 1967, for $2,425.98 plus court costs.

Mr. and Mrs. Perez each filed a voluntary petition in bankruptcy in Federal District Court on November 6, 1967. Each of them duly scheduled the judgment debt to the Pinkertons. The District Court entered orders on July 8, 1968, discharging both Mr. and Mrs. Perez from all debts and claims provable against their estates, including the Pinkerton judgment.

During the pendency of the bankruptcy proceedings, the provisions of the Arizona Motor Vehicle Safety Responsibility Act came into play. . . .

Article 4 of the Arizona Act, which includes the only provision at issue here, deals with suspension of licenses and registrations for nonpayment of judgments. Interestingly, it is only when the judgment debtor is an automobile accident lawsuit—usually an owner-operator like Mr. Perez—fails to respond to a judgment entered against him that he must overcome two hurdles in order to regain his driving privileges. Section 28–1161, the first section of Art. 4, requires the state court clerk or judge, when a judgment has remained unsatisfied for 60 days after entry, to forward a certified copy of the judgment to the superintendent. This was done in the present case, and on March 13, 1968, Mr. and Mrs. Perez were served with notice that their drivers' licenses and registration were suspended pursuant to § 28–1162 (A).

. . . [The Perezes] asserted several constitutional violations, and also alleged that § 28–1163 (B) was in direct conflict with the Bankruptcy Act and was thus violative of the Supremacy Clause of the Constitution. In support of their complaint, Mr. and Mrs. Perez filed affidavits stating that the suspension of their licenses and registration worked both physical and financial hardship upon them and their children. The District Judge granted the petitioners leave to proceed *in forma pauperis,* but thereafter granted the respondents' motion to dismiss the complaint for failure to state a claim upon which relief could be granted, citing *Kesler* and *Reitz.* The Court of Appeals affirmed, relying on the same two decisions. We granted certiorari.

Deciding whether a state statute is in conflict with a federal statute and hence invalid under the Supremacy Clause is essentially a two-step process of first ascertaining the construction of the two statutes and then determining the constitutional question whether they are in conflict. In the present case, both statutes have been authoritatively construed. In *Schecter v. Killingsworth,* (1963), the Supreme Court of Arizona held that "[t]he Financial Responsibility Act has for its principal purpose the protection of the public using the highways from financial hardship which may result from the use of automobiles by financially irresponsible persons. . . ."

Turning to the federal statute, the construction of the Bankruptcy Act is similarly clear. This Court on numerous occasions has stated that "[o]ne of the primary purposes of the bankruptcy act" is to give debtors "a new opportunity in life and a clear field for future effort, unhampered by the pressure and discouragement of preexisting debt. . . ."

With the construction of both statutes clearly established, we proceed immediately to the constitutional question whether a state statute that protects judgment creditors from "financially irresponsible persons" is in conflict with a federal statute that gives discharged debtors a new start "unhampered by the pressure and discouragement of preexisting debt." As early as *Gibbons v. Ogden,* (1824) , Chief Justice Marshall stated the governing principle—that "acts of the State Legislatures . . . [which] *interfere with,* or are contrary to the laws of Congress, made in pursuance of the constitution," are invalid under the Supremacy Clause.

Three decades ago MR. JUSTICE BLACK, after reviewing the precedents, wrote in a similar vein that, while "[t]his Court, in considering the validity of state laws in the light of treaties or federal laws touching the same subject, ha[d] made use of the following expressions: conflicting; contrary to; occupying the field; repugnance; difference; irreconcilability; inconsistency; violation; curtailment; and interference[,] . . . [i]n the final analysis," our function is to determine whether a challenged state statute "stands as an obstacle to the accomplishment and execution of the full purposes and objectives of Congress." *Hines v. Davidowitz,* (1941). Since *Hines* the Court has frequently adhered to this articulation of the meaning of the Supremacy Clause. . . .

Both *Kesler* and *Reitz,* however, ignored this controlling principle. . . .

We can no longer adhere to the aberrational doctrine of *Kesler* and *Reitz* that state law may frustrate the operation of federal law as long as the state legislature in passing its law had some purpose in mind other than one of frustration. Apart from the fact that it is at odds with the approach taken in nearly all our Supremacy Clause cases, such a doctrine would enable state legislatures to nullify nearly all unwanted federal legislation by simply publishing a legislative committee report articulating some state interest or policy—other than frustration of the federal objective—that would be tangentially furthered by the proposed state law. In view of the consequences, we certainly would not apply the *Kesler* doctrine in all Supremacy Clause cases. Although it is possible to argue that *Kesler* and *Reitz* are somehow confined to cases involving either bankruptcy or highway safety, analysis discloses no reason why the States should have broader power to nullify federal law in these fields than in others. Thus, we conclude that *Kesler* and *Reitz* can have no authoritative effect to the extent they are inconsistent with the controlling principle that any state legislation which frustrates the full effectiveness of federal law is rendered invalid by the Supremacy Clause.

* * *

From the foregoing, we think it clear that § 28–1163 (B) of the Arizona Safety Responsibility Act is constitutionally invalid. The judgment of the Court of Appeals is reversed and the case is remanded for further proceedings consistent with this opinion.

It is so ordered.

MR. JUSTICE BLACKMUN, joined by THE CHIEF JUSTICE, MR. JUSTICE HARLAN, and MR. JUSTICE STEWART.

I concur in the result as to petitioner Emma Perez and dissent as to petitioner Adolfo Perez.

* * *

. . . it is a matter of deep concern to me that today the Court lightly brushes aside and overrules two cases where it had upheld a representative attempt by the States to regulate traffic and where the Court had considered and rejected the very Supremacy Clause argument that it now discovers to be so persuasive.

* * *

I am not prepared to overrule those two cases and to undermine their control over Adolfo Perez' posture here. I would adhere to the rulings and I would hold that the States have an appropriate and legitimate concern with highway safety; that the means Arizona has adopted with respect to one in Adolfo's position (that is, the driver whose negligence has caused harm to others and whose judgment debt based on that negligence remains unsatisfied) in its attempt to assure driving competence and care on the part of its licensees, as well as to protect others, is appropriate state legislation; and that the Arizona statute, . . . despite the tangential effect upon bankruptcy, does not operate in derogation of the Bankruptcy Act or conflict with it to the extent it may rightly be said to violate the Supremacy Clause.

Other factors of significance are also to be noted:

* * *

2. Arizona's § 28–1163 (B) also has its counterparts in the statutes of no less than 44 other States. It is, after all, or purports to be, a *uniform* Act. I suspect

the Court's decision today will . . . astonish the legislatures of those 44 States that absorbed assurance from *Reitz* and *Kesler* that the provision withstands constitutional attack. . . .

4. While *stare decisis* "is no immutable principle," as a glance at the Court's decisions over the last 35 years, or over almost any period for that matter, will disclose, it seems to me that the principle does have particular validity and application in a situation such as the one confronting the Court in this case. . . . I fear that the Court today makes *stare decisis* meaningless and downgrades it to the level of a tool to be used or cast aside as convenience dictates. I doubt if Justices Roberts, Stone, Reed, Frankfurter, Murphy, Warren, Clark, HARLAN, BRENNAN, and STEWART, who constituted the respective majorities on the merits in *Reitz* and *Kesler,* were all that wrong. . . .

QUESTIONS AND COMMENTS

1 While the first "suppression test" we mentioned above involves the "intent" of Congress, the Supreme Court is called on to decide many cases in which congressional intent is unclear or in which new developments since the passage of a federal statute pose questions to which Congress gave no thought. In such cases, the Court must decide, basically, what "good policy" requires. It does so by looking at the *nature* of the regulated field and deciding what the effects of state statutes are likely to be on congressional oversight of the field. Obviously, the Court, in making such judgments, is "making policy" at the national level. Is the Supreme Court the best source of such judgments in the federal system? Can you justify this role in theoretical terms? Can you think of a better way of handling this problem in the kind of democratic system represented by the United States?

2 The Tenth Amendment reserves to the states, or to the people, all powers not delegated to the national government. In the early years, the Court interpreted this to mean that the police powers are vested totally in the states—i.e., that there is no "federal police power." If that is so, how can Congress adopt legislation involving social security, labor relations, and consumer-protection statutes without violating the Tenth Amendment?

3 The doctrine of dual federalism holds that there are two levels of government—state and federal—each supreme within its constitutional areas of operation. This doctrine was strongly supported by the Taney Court and by the Courts sitting in the period 1890–1937. The doctrine represents a view in conflict with the national-supremacy posture reflected in the work of the Marshall Court. Since 1937, the Marshall view has regained considerable lost ground. Indeed, it is said that the notion of dual federalism is no longer tenable in the modern-day Court. What influences on Supreme Court decision-making does this development suggest to you?

4 What response can you make to Justice Stone's comment in *Hines* that "every Act of Congress occupies some field," and thus, to verbalize that formula is of little use in determining congressional intent?

5 The three tests of suppression referred to are stated in *Pennsylvania v. Nelson* (350 U.S. 497), a 1956 case. *Hines* was decided in 1941. Are all three of the *Nelson* tests met in *Hines*? Or did the Court develop new tests subsequent to *Hines*? What is the source of these tests anyhow?

6 Which is the more important social goal—to give debtors "a new opportunity in life and a clear field for future effort" or to give creditors some assurance that they will be compensated for damage or harm illegally inflicted upon them? Why?

NOTES

1 10 U.S. (6 Cranch) 87 (1810).
2 *Parker v. Brown,* 317 U.S. 341 (1943).
3 William O. Douglas, *The Court Years: 1939–1975,* Random House, New York, 1980, p. 27.
4 198 U.S. 45 (1905).
5 *Adkins v. Children's Hospital,* 261 U.S. 525 (1923).
6 298. U.S. 587 (1936).

CHAPTER 4

THE POWER OF CONGRESS

To Regulate Interstate Commerce

In Pursuance of Social and Moral Policies

Champion v. Ames (1903)

Southern Railway Co. v. United States (1911)

Clark Distilling Co. v. Western Maryland Railway Co. (1916)

Hammer v. Dagenhart (1918)

Brooks v. United States (1925)

Heart of Atlanta Motel v. United States (1964)

To say that Congress has the power to regulate interstate commerce is, without more, not very informative. To find the meaning of such a statement we must look to the many interpretive decisions of the Supreme Court involving this congressional prerogative. When we do so, we find, as reported earlier, that the power has been a serious restriction on the acts of the states. The "flip side" is that the commerce clause has been used dramatically to expand the power of Congress not only to regulate economic enterprise or free it from undue encroachment by the states but also to impose social policy preferred by the Congress and the Court. These social policies are intermixed with moral and economic issues. We first consider the use of the commerce power to promote certain moral choices. The moral choices covered by the six cases in this section might be stated as:

1 Whether lotteries should be permitted.
2 Whether the safety of railroad employees should be nationally protected.
3 Whether to discourage the use of intoxicating liquor.
4 Whether to discourage child labor.
5 Whether to discourage auto theft.
6 Whether to discourage racial discrimination.

We do not suggest that these are the legal questions posed in our six cases. But the decision in each case spoke directly to the issues we have framed, and the motivation behind the congressional acts in each case had little to do with the intention of the framers to free commerce from undue governmental burdens. In the process of responding to these social-moral questions, the Supreme Court revealed a broadened scope for congressional power under the commerce clause. Thus, in the Lottery Case, Harlan, for the Court, announced that the power to regulate commerce is the power to prohibit it. Moreover, the prohibition need not be related to any effect on the efficient movement of commerce. The moral ground is sufficient. This holding has been of great significance, for it enabled Congress later to prohibit the use of adulterated foods,[1] and concubinage if the woman is to be transported across state lines.[2] In the Concubine Case, a man bought a ticket on an interstate bus in order that his mistress could join him in Reno, Nevada. This was found to be a violation of the Mann "White Slave" Act, which bars the interstate transportation of women for "immoral purposes." Also prohibited under the commerce power is the taking of kidnap victims[3] and plural wives across state lines.[4] In the Plural-Wives Case, a Mormon was barred from taking his several wives from one state to the next on the ground that polygamy is "immoral" use of women barred by the Mann Act.

Champion v. Ames

188 U.S. 321; 23 S. Ct. 321; 47 L. Ed. 492 (1903)
Vote: 5–4

In 1895, Congress passed a statute prohibiting lottery traffic through national and interstate commerce and barring the use of the mails to such traffic. C. F. Champion was indicted under this statute for transporting tickets of the Pan American Lottery Company from Dallas, Texas, to Fresno, California. Subsequent to his arrest on the charge, Champion sued for a writ of habeas corpus on the ground that his constitutional rights were being violated.

MR. JUSTICE HARLAN . . . delivered the opinion of the court.

The appellant insists that the carrying of lottery tickets from one State to another State by an express company engaged in carrying freight and packages from State to State, although such tickets may be contained in a box or package, does not constitute, and cannot by any act of Congress be legally made to constitute, *commerce* among the States within the meaning of the clause of the Constitution of the United States providing that Congress shall have power "to regulate commerce with foreign nations, and among the several States, and with the Indian tribes;" consequently, that Congress cannot make it an offence to cause such tickets to be carried from one State to another.

The Government insists that express companies when engaged, for hire, in the business of transportation from one State to another, are instrumentalities of commerce among the States; that the carrying of lottery tickets from one State to another is commerce which Congress may regulate; and that as a means of executing the power to regulate interstate commerce Congress may make it an offence against the United States to cause lottery tickets to be carried from one State to another.

* * *

We are of opinion that lottery tickets are subjects of traffic and therefore are subjects of commerce, and the regulation of the carriage of such tickets from State to State, at least by independent carriers, is a regulation of commerce among the several States.

But it is said that the statute in question does not regulate the carrying of lottery tickets from State to State, but by punishing those who cause them to be so carried Congress in effect prohibits such carrying; that in respect of the carrying from one State to another of articles or things that are, in fact, or according to usage in business, the subjects of commerce, the authority given Congress was not to *prohibit,* but only to *regulate.* This view was earnestly pressed at the bar by learned counsel, and must be examined.

It is to be remarked that the Constitution does not define what is to be deemed a legitimate regulation of interstate commerce. In *Gibbons v. Ogden* it was said that the power to regulate such commerce is the power to prescribe the rule by which it is to be governed. But this general observation leaves it to be determined, when the question comes before the court, whether Congress in prescribing a particular rule has exceeded its power under the Constitution. While our Government must be acknowledged by all to be one of enumerated powers, *McCulloch v. Maryland*, [1821], the Constitution does not attempt to set forth all the means by which such powers may be carried into execution. It leaves to Congress a large discretion as to the means that may be employed in executing a given power. The sound construction of the Constitution, this court has said, "must allow to the national legislature that discretion, with respect to the means by which the powers it confers are to be carried into execution, which will enable that body to perform the high duties assigned to it, in the manner most beneficial to the people. Let the end be legitimate, let it be within the scope of the Constitution, and all means which are appropriate, which are plainly adapted to that end, which are not prohibited, but consist with the letter and spirit of the Constitution, are constitutional."

We have said that the carrying from State to State of lottery tickets constitutes interstate commerce, and that the regulation of such commerce is within the power of Congress under the Constitution. Are we prepared to say that a provision which is, in effect, a *prohibition* of the carriage of such articles from State to State is not a fit or appropriate mode for the *regulation* of that particular kind of commerce? If lottery traffic, *carried on through interstate commerce,* is a matter of which Congress may take cognizance and over which its power may be exerted, can it be possible that it must tolerate the traffic, and simply regulate the manner in which it may be carried on? Or may not Congress, for the protection of the people of all the States, and under the power to regulate interstate commerce, devise such means, within the scope of the Constitution, and not prohibited by it, as will drive that traffic out of commerce among the States?

In determining whether regulation may not under some circumstances properly take the form or have the effect of prohibition, the nature of the interstate traffic which it was sought by the act of May 2, 1895, to suppress cannot be overlooked. When enacting that statute Congress no doubt shared the views upon the subject of lotteries heretofore expressed by this court. In *Phalen v. Virginia*, [1850], after observing that the suppression of nuisances injurious to public health or morality is among the most important duties of Government, this court said: "Experience has shown that the common forms of gambling are comparatively innocuous when placed in contrast with the widespread pestilence of lotteries. The former are confined to a few persons and places, but the latter infests the whole community; it enters every dwelling; it reaches every class; it preys upon the hard earnings of the poor; it plunders the ignorant and simple. . . ."

If a State, when considering legislation for the suppression of lotteries within its own limits, may properly take into view the evils that inhere in the raising of money, in that mode, why may not Congress, invested with the power to regulate commerce among the several States, provide that such commerce shall not be polluted by the carrying of lottery tickets from one State to another? In this connection it must not be forgotten that the power of Congress to regulate commerce among the States is plenary, is complete in itself, and is subject to no limitations except such as may be found in the Constitution. What provision in that instrument can be regarded as limiting the exercise of the power granted? What clause can be cited which, in any degree, countenances the suggestion that one may, of right, carry or cause to be carried from one State to another that which will harm the public morals? We cannot think of any clause of that instrument that could possibly be invoked by those who assert their right to send lottery tickets from State to State except the one providing that no person shall be deprived of his liberty without due process of law. We have said that the liberty protected by the Constitution embraces the right to be free in the enjoyment of one's faculties; "to be free to use them in all lawful ways; to live and work where he will; to earn his livelihood by any lawful calling; to pursue any livelihood or avocation, and for that purpose to enter into all contracts that may be proper." *Allgeyer v. Louisiana,* [1897]. But surely it will not be said to be a part of any one's liberty, as recognized by the supreme law of the land, that he shall be allowed to introduce into commerce among the States an element that will be confessedly injurious to the public morals.

If it be said that the act of 1895 is inconsistent with the Tenth Amendment, reserving to the States respectively or to the people the powers not delegated to the United States, the answer is that the power to regulate commerce among the States has been expressly delegated to Congress.

Besides, Congress, by that act, does not assume to interfere with traffic or commerce in lottery tickets carried on exclusively within the limits of any State, but has in view only commerce of that kind among the several States. It has not assumed to interfere with the completely internal affairs of any State, and has only legislated in respect of a matter which concerns the people of the United States. As a State may, for the purpose of guarding the morals of its own people, forbid all sales of lottery tickets within its limits, so Congress, for the purpose of guarding the people of the United States against the "widespread pestilence of lotteries" and to protect the commerce which concerns all the States, may prohibit the carrying of lottery tickets from one State to another. In legislating upon the subject of the traffic in lottery tickets, as carried on through interstate commerce, Congress only supplemented the action of those States—perhaps all of them—which, for the protection of the public morals, prohibit the drawing of lotteries, as well as the sale or circulation of lottery tickets, within their respective limits. It said, in effect that it would not permit the declared policy of the States, which sought to protect their people against the mischiefs of the lottery business, to be overthrown or disregarded by the agency of interstate commerce. We should hesitate long before adjudging that an evil of such appalling character, carried on through interstate commerce, cannot be met and crushed by the only power competent to that end. . . .

It is said, however, that if, in order to suppress lotteries carried on through interstate commerce, Congress may exclude lottery tickets from such commerce, that principle leads necessarily to the conclusion that Congress may arbitrarily exclude from commerce among the States any article, commodity or thing, of whatever kind or nature, or however useful or valuable, which it may choose, no matter with what motive, to declare shall not be carried from one State to another. It will be time enough to consider the constitutionality of such legislation when we must do so. The present case does not require the court to declare the full extent of the power that Congress may exercise in the regulation of commerce among the States. We may, however, repeat, in this connection, what the court has heretofore said, that the power of Congress to regulate commerce among the States, although plenary, cannot be deemed arbitrary, since it is subject to such limitations or restrictions as are prescribed by the Constitution. This power, therefore, may not be exercised so as to infringe rights secured or protected by that instrument. It would not be difficult to imagine legislation that would be justly liable to such an objection as that stated, and be hostile to the objects for the accomplishment of which Congress was invested with the general power to regulate commerce among the several States. But, as often said, the possible abuse of a power is not an argument against its existence. There is probably no governmental power that may not be exerted to the injury of the public. If what is done by Congress is manifestly in excess of the powers granted to it, then upon the courts will rest the duty of adjudging that its action is neither legal nor binding upon the people. But if what Congress does is within the limits of its power, and is simply unwise or injurious, the remedy is that suggested by Chief Justice Marshall in *Gibbons v. Ogden,* when he said: "The wisdom and the discretion of Congress, their identity with the people, and the influence which their constituents possess at elections, are, in this, as in many other instances, as that, for example, of declaring war, the sole restraints on which they have relied, to secure them from its abuse. They are the restraints on which the people must often rely solely, in all representative governments."

The whole subject is too important, and the questions suggested by its consideration are too difficult of solution, to justify any attempt to lay down a rule for determining in advance the validity of every statute that may be enacted under the commerce clause. We decide nothing more in the present case than that lottery tickets are subjects of traffic among those who choose to sell or buy them; that the carriage of such tickets by independent carriers from one State to another is therefore interstate commerce; that under its power to regulate commerce among the several States Congress—subject to the limitations imposed by the Constitution upon the exercise of the powers granted—has plenary authority over such commerce, and may prohibit the carriage of such tickets from State to State; and that legislation to that end, and of that character, is not inconsistent with any limitation or restriction imposed upon the exercise of the powers granted to Congress.

The judgment is

Affirmed.

Mr. Chief Justice Fuller, with whom concur Mr. Justice Brewer, Mr. Justice Shiras and Mr. Justice Peckham, dissenting.

* * *

The naked question is whether the prohibition by Congress of the carriage of lottery tickets from one State to another by means other than the mails is within the powers vested in that body by the Constitution of the United States. That the purpose of Congress in this enactment was the suppression of lotteries cannot reasonably be denied. That purpose is avowed in the title of the act, and is its natural and reasonable effect, and by that its validity must be tested.

The power of the State to impose restraints and burdens on persons and property in conservation and promotion of the public health, good order and prosperity is a power originally and always belonging to the States, not surrendered by them to the General Government nor directly restrained by the Constitution of the United States, and essentially exclusive, and the suppression of lotteries as a harmful business falls within this power, commonly called of police.

It is urged, however, that because Congress is empowered to regulate commerce between the several States, it, therefore, may suppress lotteries by prohibiting the carriage of lottery matter. Congress may indeed make all laws necessary and proper for carrying the powers granted to it into execution, and doubtless an act prohibiting the carriage of lottery matter would be necessary and proper to the execution of a power to suppress lotteries; but that power belongs to the States and not to Congress. To hold that Congress has general police power would be to hold that it may accomplish objects not entrusted to the General Government, and to defeat the operation of the Tenth Amendment, declaring that: "The powers not delegated to the United States by the Constitution, nor prohibited by it to the States, are reserved to the States respectively, or to the people. . . ."

If a lottery ticket is not an article of commerce, how can it become so when placed in an envelope or box or other covering, and transported by an express company? To say that the mere carrying of an article which is not an article of commerce in and of itself nevertheless becomes such the moment it is to be transported from one state to another, is to transform a non-commercial article into a commercial one simply because it is transported. I cannot conceive that any such result can properly follow.

It would be to say that everything is an article of commerce the moment it is taken to be transported from place to place, and of interstate commerce if from state to state.

An invitation to dine, or to take a drive, or a note of introduction, all become articles of commerce under the ruling in this case, by being deposited with an express company for transportation. This in effect breaks down all the differences between that which is, and that which is not, an article of commerce, and the necessary consequence is to take from the states all jurisdiction over the subject so far as interstate communication is concerned. It is a long step in the direction of wiping out all traces of state lines, and the creation of a centralized government.

Does the grant to Congress of the power to regulate interstate commerce import the absolute power to prohibit it?

* * *

The Constitution gives no countenance to the theory that Congress is vested with the full powers of the British Parliament, and that, although subject to constitutional limitations, it is the sole judge of their extent and application; and the decisions of this court from the beginning have been to the contrary.

"To what purpose are powers limited, and to what purpose is that limitation committed to writing, if these limits may, at any time, be passed by those intended to be restrained?" asked Marshall, in *Marbury v. Madison,* [1803].

"Should Congress," said the same great magistrate in *McCulloch v. Maryland,* [1819], "under the pretext of executing its powers, pass laws for the accomplishment of objects not entrusted to the Government; it would become the painful duty of this tribunal, should a case requiring such a decision come before it, to say that such an act was not the law of the land.". . .

It is argued that the power to regulate commerce among the several States is the same as the power to regulate commerce with foreign nations, and with the Indian tribes. But is its scope the same?

. . . the power to regulate commerce with foreign nations and the power to regulate interstate commerce, are to be taken *diverso intuitu,* for the latter was intended to secure equality and freedom in commercial intercourse as between the States, not to permit the creation of impediments to such intercourse; while the former clothed Congress with that power over international commerce, pertaining to a sovereign nation in its intercourse with foreign nations, and subject, generally speaking, to no implied or reserved power in the States. The laws which would be necessary and proper in the one case, would not be necessary or proper in the other.

* * *

. . . the right of passage of persons and property from one State to another cannot be prohibited by Congress. But that does not challenge the legislative power of a sovereign nation to exclude foreign persons or commodities, or place an embargo, perhaps not permanent, upon foreign ships or manufactures.

The power to prohibit the transportation of diseased animals and infected goods over railroads or on steamboats is an entirely different thing, for they would be in themselves injurious to the transaction of interstate commerce, and, moreover, are essentially commercial in their nature. And the exclusion of diseased persons rests on different ground, for nobody would pretend that persons could be kept off the trains because they were going from one State to another to engage in the lottery business. However enticing that business may be, we do not understand these pieces of paper themselves can communicate bad principles by contact.

* * *

I regard this decision as inconsistent with the views of the framers of the Constitution, and of Marshall, its great expounder. Our form of government may remain notwithstanding legislation or decision, but, as long ago observed, it is with governments, as with religions, the form may survive the substance of the faith.

In my opinion the act in question in the particular under consideration is invalid, and the judgments below ought to be reversed, and my brothers BRE-WER, SHIRAS and PECKHAM concur in this dissent.

QUESTIONS AND COMMENTS

1 *Champion v. Ames* was argued three times and decided by a 5–4 vote. What does this suggest about the policy-making role of the Supreme Court?

2 In *Champion,* the Court established that the power to regulate interstate commerce encompasses the power to prohibit it entirely. Since that power has been used frequently to support the exercise of state police power, does *Champion* represent an expansion of state power or of the power of Congress?

3 Does *Champion* establish a federal police power? Explain your answer.

4 Could Congress, under its commerce power, prevent the shipment across state lines of a mini-atomic bomb? How about pure, unadulterated milk from healthy, disease-free cows? What constitutional justification can be offered for your answer in each case?

* * * * * *

In *Southern Railway v. United States,* unlike the cases mentioned above, the *effect* on commerce was of some concern. But safety was the primary motivation for the act involved in that case. This is seen in the fact that the statute covered not only trains moving in interstate commerce, but also trains restricted to in-state movement only.

Southern Railway Co. v. United States

222 U.S. 20; 32 S. Ct. 2; 56 L. Ed. 72 (1911)
Vote: 9–0

The facts are included in the opinion below.

Mr. Justice Van Devanter delivered the opinion of the court.

This was a civil action to recover penalties for the violation in specified instances of the Safety Appliance Acts of Congress. The Government prevailed in the District Court and the defendant sued out this direct writ of error.

Briefly stated, the case is this: The defendant, while operating a railroad which was "a part of a through highway" over which traffic was continually being moved from one State to another, hauled over a part of its railroad, during the month of February, 1907, five cars, the couplers upon which were defective and inoperative. Two of the cars were used at the time in moving interstate traffic and the other three in moving intrastate traffic; but it does not appear that the use of the three was in connection with any car or cars used in interstate commerce. The defendant particularly objected to the assessment of any penalty for the hauling of the three cars, and insisted, first, that such a hauling in intrastate commerce, although upon a railroad over which traffic was continually being moved from one State to another, was not within the prohibition of the Safety Appliance Acts of Congress, and, second, that, if it was, those acts should be pronounced invalid as being in excess of the power of Congress under the commerce clause of the Constitution. But the objection was overruled, and error is assigned upon that ruling.

* * *

. . . it must be held that the original act as enlarged by the amendatory one is intended to embrace all locomotives, cars and similar vehicles used on any railroad which is a highway of interstate commerce.

We come then to the question whether these acts are within the power of Congress under the commerce clause of the Constitution, considering that they are not confined to vehicles used in moving interstate traffic, but embrace vehicles used in moving intrastate traffic. The answer to this question depends upon another, which is, Is there a real or substantial relation or connection between what is required by these acts in respect of vehicles used in moving intrastate traffic and the object which the acts obviously are designed to attain, namely, the safety of interstate commerce and of those who are employed in its movement? Or, stating it in another way. Is there such a close or direct relation or connection between the two classes of traffic, when moving over the same railroad, as to make it certain that the safety of the interstate traffic and of those who are employed in its movement will be promoted in a real or substantial sense by applying the requirements of these acts to vehicles used in moving the traffic which is intrastate as well as to those used in moving that which is interstate? If the answer to this question, as doubly stated, be in the affirmative, then the principal question must be answered in the same way. And this is so, not because Congress possesses any power to regulate intrastate commerce as such, but because its power to regulate interstate commerce is plenary and competently may be exerted to secure the safety of the persons and property transported therein and of those who are employed in such transportation, no matter what may be the source of the dangers which threaten it. That is to say, it is no objection to such an exertion of this power that the dangers intended to be avoided arise, in whole or in part, out of matters connected with intrastate commerce.

Speaking only of railroads which are highways of both interstate and intrastate commerce, these things are of common knowledge: Both classes of traffic are at times carried in the same car and when this is not the case the cars in which they are carried are frequently commingled in the same train and in the switching and other movements at terminals. Cars are seldom set apart for exclusive use in moving either class of traffic, but generally are used interchangeably in moving both; and the situation is much the same with trainmen, switchmen and like employés, for they usually, if not necessarily, have to do with both classes of traffic. Besides, the several trains on the same railroad are not independent in point of movement and safety, but are interdependent, for whatever brings delay or disaster to one, or results in disabling one of its operatives, is calculated to impede the progress and imperil the safety of other trains. And so the absence of appropriate safety appliances from any part of any train is a menace not only to that train but to others.

These practical considerations make it plain, as we think, that the questions before stated must be answered in the affirmative.

Affirmed.

*   *   *   *   *   *

The year 1919 saw the adoption of the Eighteenth Amendment, prohibiting the "manufacture, sale, or transportation of intoxicating liquors" in the United States. But Congress had been concerned about the "liquor problem" somewhat earlier, as reflected in the Webb-Kenyon Act, discussed in *Clark Distilling.* In *Clark,* the Court makes it clear that if Congress may, under the commerce clause, *prohibit* the interstate shipment of intoxicants, it could certainly impose regulations of a less restrictive nature on the interstate movement of such intoxicants. In the Twenty-first Amendment (repealing the Eighteenth) the control over intoxicants is clearly vested in the states. But if a state thinks it desirable to remain "dry"—a moral issue—the amendment lends support via the constitutional provision and federal laws implementing the provision. The effect of all this is to remove the bar to state action against interstate commerce if that commerce violates state liquor laws.

Clark Distilling Co. v. Western Maryland Railway Co. and the State of West Virginia

242 U.S. 311; 37 S. Ct. 180; 61 L. Ed. 326 (1916)
Vote: 7–2

The facts are given in the opinion.

MR. CHIEF JUSTICE WHITE delivered the opinion of the court.

* * *

West Virginia in February, 1913, enacted a prohibition law to go into effect on July 1st of the following year.

. . . the law forbade "the manufacture, sale, keeping or storing for sale in this state, or offering or exposing for sale" intoxicating liquors, and the intoxicants embraced were comprehensively defined. . . . There was no express prohibition against the individual right to use intoxicants and none implied unless that result arose (a) from the prohibition in universal terms of all sales and purchases of liquor within the State, (b) from the clause providing that every delivery made in the State by a common or other carrier of the prohibited intoxicants should be considered as a consummation of a sale made in the State at the point of delivery, and (c) from the prohibitions which the statute contained against solicitations made to induce purchases of liquor and against the publication in the State of all circulars, advertisements, price-lists, etc., which might tend to stimulate purchases of liquor.

Under this statute and in reliance upon the provisions of the act of Congress known as the Webb-Kenyon Law the State of West Virginia in one of its courts sued the Western Maryland Railway Company and the Adams Express Company to enjoin them from carrying from Maryland into West Virginia liquor in violation of law. In substance it was charged that very many shipments had been taken by the carriers contrary to the law both as to solicitations and as to the use for which the liquor was intended. Preliminary injunctions were issued restraining the carrying of liquor into the State subject to many conditions as to investigation, etc., etc. With these injunctions in force, these suits were commenced by the Clark Distilling Company to compel the carriers to take a shipment of liquor which it was asserted was ordered for personal use and deliver it in West Virginia, on the ground that the Act of Congress to Regulate Commerce imposed the duty to receive and carry and that besides the West Virginia prohibition law when rightly construed did not forbid it. . . .

[The district court dismissed the suits, and direct appeal was taken to the Supreme Court.]

2 *The power of the State to enact the prohibition law consistently with the due process clause of the Fourteenth Amendment and the exclusive power of Congress to regulate commerce among the several States.*

That government can, consistently with the due process clause, forbid the manufacture and sale of liquor and regulate its traffic, is not open to controversy; and that there goes along with this power full police authority to make it effective, is also not open. Whether the general authority includes the right to forbid individual use, we need not consider, since clearly there would be power, as an incident to the right to forbid manufacture and sale, to restrict the means by which intoxicants for personal use could be obtained, even if such use was permitted. This being true, there can be no doubt that the West Virginia prohibition law did not offend against the due process clause of the Fourteenth Amendment.

But that it was a direct burden upon interstate commerce and conflicted with the power of Congress to regulate commerce among the several States, and therefore could not be used to prevent interstate shipments from Maryland into West Virginia, has been not open to question since the decision in *Leisy v. Hardin,* [1890]. And this brings us to consider whether the Webb-Kenyon Law has so regulated interstate commerce as to give the State the power to do what it did in enacting the prohibition law and cause its provisions to be applicable to shipments of intoxicants in interstate commerce, thus saving that law from repugnancy to the Constitution of the United States, which is the third proposition for consideration.

3 *Assuming the constitutionality of the Webb-Kenyon Act, what is its true meaning and its operation upon the prohibitions contained in the West Virginia law?*

Omitting words irrelevant to the subject now under consideration, the title and text of the Webb-Kenyon Act are as follows:

> "An Act Diverting intoxicating liquors of their interstate character in certain cases. . . . That the shipment or transportation, in any manner or by any means whatsoever, of any spirituous, vinous, malted, fermented, or other intoxicating liquor of any kind, from one State, Territory, or District of the United States, . . . into any other State, Territory, or District of the United States, . . . which said spirituous, vinous, malted, fermented, or other intoxicating liquor is intended, by any person interested therein, to be received, possessed, sold, or in any manner used, either in the original package or otherwise, in violation of any law of such State, Territory, or District of the United States, . . . is hereby prohibited."

As the state law forbade the shipment into or transportation of liquor in the State whether from inside or out, and all receipt and possession of liquor so transported without regard to the use to which the liquor was to be put, and as the Webb-Kenyon Act prohibited the transportation in interstate commerce of all liquor "intended . . . to be received, possessed, sold, or in any manner used, either in the original package or otherwise, in violation of any law of such State," there would seem to be no room for doubt that the prohibitions of the state law were made applicable by the Webb-Kenyon Law. If that law was valid, therefore, the state law was not repugnant to the commerce clause. . . .

[The purpose of Webb-Kenyon] . . . was to prevent the immunity characteristic of interstate commerce from being used to permit the receipt of liquor through such commerce in States contrary to their laws, and thus in effect afford a means by subterfuge and indirection to set such laws at naught. In this light it is clear that the Webb-Kenyon Act, if effect is to be given to its text, but operated so as to cause the prohibitions of the West Virginia law against shipment, receipt and possession to be applicable and controlling irrespective of whether the state law did or did not prohibit the individual use of liquor. That such also was the embodied spirit of the Webb-Kenyon Act plainly appears since if that be not true, the coming into being of the act is wholly inexplicable. . . .

The movement of liquor in interstate commerce and the receipt and possession and right to sell prohibited by the state law having been in express terms divested by the Webb-Kenyon Act of their interstate commerce character, it follows that if that act was within the power of Congress to adopt, there is no possible reason for holding that to enforce the prohibitions of the state law would conflict with the commerce clause of the Constitution; and this brings us to the last question, which is:

4 *Did Congress have power to enact the Webb-Kenyon Law?*

We are not unmindful that opinions adverse to the power of Congress to enact the law were formed and expressed in other departments of the government. Opinion of the Attorney General, 30 Op. A. G. 88; Veto Message of the President, Cong. Rec., vol. 49, pt. 5, p. 4291. We are additionally conscious, therefore, of the responsibility of determining these issues and of their serious character.

It is not in the slightest degree disputed that if Congress had prohibited the shipment of all intoxicants in the channels of interstate commerce and therefore had prevented all movement between the several States, such action would have been lawful because within the power to regulate which the Constitution conferred.

The issue, therefore, is not one of an absence of authority to accomplish in substance a more extended result than that brought about by the Webb-Kenyon Law, but of a want of power to reach the result accomplished because of the method resorted to for that purpose. . . .

The mistaken assumption that the accidental considerations which cause a subject on the one hand to come under state control in the absence of congressional regulation, and other subjects on the contrary to be free from state control until Congress has acted, are the essential criteria by which to test the question of the power of Congress to regulate and the mode in which the exertion of that power may be manifested. The two things are widely different, since the right to regulate and its scope and the mode of exertion must depend upon the power possessed by Congress over the subject regulated. Following the unerring path pointed out by that great principle we can see no reason for saying that although Congress in view of the nature and character of intoxicants had a power to forbid their movement in interstate commerce, it had not the authority to so deal with the subject as to establish a regulation (which is what was done by the Webb-Kenyon Law) making it impossible for one State to violate the prohibitions of the laws of another through the channels of interstate commerce. Indeed, we can see no escape from the conclusion that if we accepted the proposition urged, we would be obliged to announce the contradiction in terms that because Congress had exerted a regulation lesser in power than it was authorized to exert, therefore its action was void for excess of power. Or, in other words, stating the necessary result of the argument from a concrete consideration of the particular subject here involved, that because Congress in adopting a regulation had considered the nature and character of our dual system of government, State and Nation, and instead of absolutely prohibiting, had so conformed its regulation as to produce coöperation between the local and national forces of government to the end of preserving the rights of all, it had thereby transcended the complete and perfect power of regulation conferred by the Constitution. And it is well again to point out that this abnormal result to which the argument leads concerns a subject as to which both State and Nation in their respective spheres of authority possessed the supremest authority before the action of Congress which is complained of, and hence the argument virtually comes to the assertion that in some undisclosed way by the exertion of congressional authority, power possessed has evaporated.

It is only necessary to point out that the considerations which we have stated dispose of all contentions that the Webb-Kenyon Act is repugnant to the due process clause of the Fifth Amendment, since what we have said concerning that clause in the Fourteenth Amendment as applied to state power is decisive.

Before concluding we come to consider what we deem to be arguments of inconvenience which are relied upon, that is, the dread expressed that the power by regulation to allow state prohibitions to attach to the movement of intoxicants lays the basis for subjecting interstate commerce in all articles to state control and therefore destroys the Constitution. The want of force in the suggested inconvenience becomes patent by considering the principle which after all dominates and controls the question here presented, that is, the subject regulated and the extreme power to which that subject may be subjected. The fact that regulations of liquor have been upheld in numberless instances which would have been repugnant to the great guarantees of the Constitution but for the enlarged right possessed by government to regulate liquor, has never that we are aware of been taken as affording the basis for the thought that government might exert an enlarged power as to subjects to which under the constitutional guarantees such enlarged power could not be applied. In other words, the exceptional nature of the subject here regulated is the basis upon which the exceptional power exerted must rest and affords no ground for any fear that such power may be constitutionally extended to things which it may not, consistently with the guarantees of the Constitution, embrace.

Affirmed.

QUESTIONS AND COMMENTS

1 Assume that the Interstate Commerce Commission established maximum freight rates for railroads running between Louisiana and Texas. Assume further that the commission's action was challenged as a violation of due process and defended as a valid exercise of the commerce power. Does *Southern Railway* furnish a precedent that could be effectively used by the Supreme Court in deciding such a case? Explain your answer. See *The Shreveport Case,* 234 U.S. 342 (1914).

2 When the Webb-Kenyon Act reached the desk of President Taft, the attorney general of the United States advised him that it unconstitutionally delegated congressional power over interstate commerce to the states. Taft thereupon vetoed the measure, but the bill was passed over Taft's veto. Which interpretation of the Constitution do you think closest to the intention of the framers, that of Congress or that of the President? Why? Did the later adoption of the Twenty-first Amendment shed any light on the question? What do you conclude from all this?

3 *Brooks v. United States* and later cases made it crystal-clear that *Clark Distilling* was not an aberration. To put it another way, transportation and use of intoxicants is not such a unique evil that only it may be restricted or discouraged via the use of the commerce clause.

* * * * * *

If Congress may prohibit the shipment of any goods in interstate commerce, can it also prohibit any practices that touch those goods at any point in the process leading up to shipment? In *Hammer v. Dagenhart,* the relevant practices apparently offended the moral sensibilities of Congress, since child labor, which Congress proposed to ban as related to goods manufactured for interstate shipment, is not a matter that necessarily interferes with commerce. It is a matter which many people would consider morally offensive. The Hammer Case delineates local from interstate activity and reminds us that in 1918, the Tenth Amendment still had its supporters in the Court.

Hammer, United States Attorney for the Western District of North Carolina v. Dagenhart, et al.

247 U.S. 251; 38 S. Ct. 529; 62 L. Ed. 1101 (1918)
Vote: 5–4

The facts are given in the opinion below.

MR. JUSTICE DAY delivered the opinion of the court.

A bill was filed in the United States District Court for the Western District of North Carolina by a father in his own behalf and as next friend of his two minor sons, one under the age of fourteen years and the other between the ages of fourteen and sixteen years, employees in a cotton mill at Charlotte, North

Carolina, to enjoin the enforcement of the act of Congress intended to prevent interstate commerce in the products of child labor. Act of Sept. 1, 1916, c. 432, 39 Stat. 675.

The District Court held the act unconstitutional and entered a decree enjoining its enforcement. This appeal brings the case here. The first section of the act is in the margin.*

Other sections of the act contain provisions for its enforcement and prescribe penalties for its violation.

The attack upon the act rests upon three propositions: First: It is not a regulation of interstate and foreign commerce; Second: It contravenes the Tenth Amendment to the Constitution; Third: It conflicts with the Fifth Amendment to the Constitution.

The controlling question for decision is: Is it within the authority of Congress in regulating commerce among the States to prohibit the transportation in interstate commerce of manufactured goods, the product of a factory in which, within thirty days prior to their removal therefrom, children under the age of fourteen have been employed or permitted to work, or children between the ages of fourteen and sixteen years have been employed or permitted to work more than eight hours in any day, or more than six days in any week, or after the hour of seven o'clock P.M. or before the hour of 6 o'clock A.M.?

The power essential to the passage of this act, the Government contends, is found in the commerce clause of the Constitution which authorizes Congress to regulate commerce with foreign nations and among the States.

In *Gibbons v. Ogden,* [1824]. Chief Justice Marshall, speaking for this court, and defining the extent and nature of the commerce power, said, "It is the power to regulate; that is, to prescribe the rule by which commerce is to be governed." In other words, the power is one to control the means by which commerce is carried on, which is directly the contrary of the assumed right to forbid commerce from moving and thus destroy it as to particular commodities. But it is insisted that adjudged cases in this court establish the doctrine that the power to regulate given to Congress incidentally includes the authority to prohibit the movement of ordinary commodities and therefore that the subject is not open for discussion. The cases demonstrate the contrary. They rest upon the character of the particular subjects dealt with and the fact that the scope of governmental authority, state or national, possessed over them is such that the authority to prohibit is as to them but the exertion of the power to regulate.

---

*That no producer, manufacturer, or dealer shall ship or deliver for shipment in interstate or foreign commerce any article or commodity the product of any mine or quarry, situated in the United States, in which within thirty days prior to the time of the removal of such product therefrom children under the age of sixteen years have been employed or permitted to work, or any article or commodity the product of any mill, cannery, workshop, factory, or manufacturing establishment, situated in the United States, in which within thirty days prior to the removal of such product therefrom children under the age of fourteen years have been employed or permitted to work, or children between the ages of fourteen years and sixteen years have been employed or permitted to work more than eight hours in any day, or more than six days in any week, or after the hour of seven o'clock postmeridian, or before the hour of six o'clock antemeridian.

The first of these cases is *Champion v. Ames,* [1903], the so-called *Lottery Case,* in which it was held that Congress might pass a law having the effect to keep the channels of commerce free from use in the transportation of tickets used in the promotion of lottery schemes. In *Hipolite Egg Co. v. United States,* [1910], this court sustained the power of Congress to pass the Pure Food and Drug Act which prohibited the introduction into the States by means of interstate commerce of impure foods and drugs. In *Hoke v. United States,* [1913], this court sustained the constitutionality of the so-called "White Slave Traffic Act" whereby the transportation of a woman in interstate commerce for the purpose of prostitution was forbidden. . . .

In *Caminetti v. United States,* [1917], we held that Congress might prohibit the transportation of women in interstate commerce for the purposes of debauchery and kindred purposes. In *Clark Distilling Co. v. Western Maryland Ry. Co.,* [1917], the power of Congress over the transportation of intoxicating liquors was sustained. . . .

In each of these instances the use of interstate transportation was necessary to the accomplishment of harmful results. In other words, although the power over interstate transportation was to regulate, that could only be accomplished by prohibiting the use of the facilities of interstate commerce to effect the evil intended.

This element is wanting in the present case. The thing intended to be accomplished by this statute is the denial of the facilities of interstate commerce to those manufacturers in the States who employ children within the prohibited ages. The act in its effect does not regulate transportation among the States, but aims to standardize the ages at which children may be employed in mining and manufacturing within the States. The goods shipped are of themselves harmless. The act permits them to be freely shipped after thirty days from the time of their removal from the factory. When offered for shipment, and before transportation begins, the labor of their production is over, and the mere fact that they were intended for interstate commerce transportation does not make their production subject to federal control under the commerce power.

Commerce "consists of intercourse and traffic . . . and includes the transportation of persons and property, as well as the purchase, sale and exchange of commodities." The making of goods and the mining of coal are not commerce, nor does the fact that these things are to be afterwards shipped or used in interstate commerce, make their production a part thereof.

Over interstate transportation, or its incidents, the regulatory power of Congress is ample, but the production of articles, intended for interstate commerce, is a matter of local regulation.

* * *

It is further contended that the authority of Congress may be exerted to control interstate commerce in the shipment of child-made goods because of the effect of the circulation of such goods in other States where the evil of this class of labor has been recognized by local legislation, and the right to thus employ child labor has been more rigorously restrained than in the State of production. In other words, that the unfair competition, thus engendered, may be controlled by closing the channels of interstate commerce to manufacturers in those States where the local laws do not meet what Congress deems to be the more just standard of other States.

There is no power vested in Congress to require the States to exercise their police power so as to prevent possible unfair competition. Many causes may coöperate to give one State, by reason of local laws or conditions, an economic advantage over others. The Commerce Clause was not intended to give to Congress a general authority to equalize such conditions. . . .

The grant of power to Congress over the subject of interstate commerce was to enable it to regulate such commerce, and not to give it authority to control the States in their exercise of the police power over local trade and manufacture.

The grant of authority over a purely federal matter was not intended to destroy the local power always existing and carefully reserved to the States in the Tenth Amendment to the Constitution.

* * *

In interpreting the Constitution it must never be forgotten that the Nation is made up of States to which are entrusted the powers of local government. And to them and to the people the powers not expressly delegated to the National Government are reserved.

The power of the States to regulate their purely internal affairs by such laws as seem wise to the local authority is inherent and has never been surrendered to the general government. To sustain this statute would not be in our judgment a recognition of the lawful exertion of congressional authority over interstate commerce, but would sanction an invasion by the federal power of the control of a matter purely local in its character, and over which no authority has been delegated to Congress in conferring the power to regulate commerce among the States.

We have neither authority nor disposition to question the motives of Congress in enacting this legislation. The purposes intended must be attained consistently with constitutional limitations and not by an invasion of the powers of the States. This court has no more important function than that which devolves upon it the obligation to preserve inviolate the constitutional limitations upon the exercise of authority, federal and state, to the end that each may continue to discharge, harmoniously with the other, the duties entrusted to it by the Constitution.

In our view the necessary effect of this act is, by means of a prohibition against the movement in interstate commerce of ordinary commercial commodities, to regulate the hours of labor of children in factories and mines within the States, a purely state authority. Thus the act in a twofold sense is repugnant to the Constitution. It not only transcends the authority delegated to Congress over commerce but also exerts a power as to a purely local matter to which the federal authority does not extend. The far reaching result of upholding the act cannot be more plainly indicated than by pointing out that if Congress can thus regulate matters entrusted to local authority by prohibition of the movement of commodities in interstate commerce, all freedom of commerce will be at an end, and the power of the States over local matters may be eliminated, and thus our system of government be practically destroyed.

For these reasons we hold that this law exceeds the constitutional authority of Congress. It follows that the decree of the District Court must be

Affirmed.

MR. JUSTICE HOLMES, dissenting.

* * *

The question ... is ... whether the exercise of its otherwise constitutional power by Congress can be pronounced unconstitutional because of its possible reaction upon the conduct of the States in a matter upon which I ... [admit] that they are free from direct control. I should have thought that that matter had been disposed of so fully as to leave no room for doubt. I should have thought that the most conspicuous decisions of this Court had made it clear that the power to regulate commerce and other constitutional powers could not be cut down or qualified by the fact that it might interfere with the carrying out of the domestic policy of any State.

The manufacture of oleomargarine is as much a matter of state regulation as the manufacture of cotton cloth. Congress levied a tax upon the compound when colored so as to resemble butter that was so great as obviously to prohibit the manufacture and sale. ... Fifty years ago a tax on state banks, the obvious purpose and actual effect of which was to drive them, or at least their circulation, out of existence, was sustained, although the result was one that Congress had no constitutional power to require. ...

The Pure Food and Drug Act which was sustained in *Hipolite Egg Co. v. United States,* [1910], with the intimation that "no trade can be carried on between the States to which it [the power of Congress to regulate commerce] does not extend," applies not merely to articles that the changing opinions of the time condemn as intrinsically harmful but to others innocent in themselves, simply on the ground that the order for them was induced by a preliminary fraud.

It does not matter whether the supposed evil precedes or follows the transportation. It is enough that in the opinion of Congress the transportation encourages the evil. ...

The notion that prohibition is any less prohibition when applied to things now thought evil I do not understand. But if there is any matter upon which civilized countries have agreed—far more unanimously than they have with regard to intoxicants and some other matters over which this country is now emotionally aroused—it is the evil of premature and excessive child labor. I should have thought that if we were to introduce our own moral conceptions where in my opinion they do not belong, this was preëminently a case for upholding the exercise of all its powers by the United States.

But I had thought that the propriety of the exercise of a power admitted to exist in some cases was for the consideration of Congress alone and that this Court always had disavowed the right to intrude its judgment upon questions of policy or morals. It is not for this Court to pronounce when prohibition is necessary to regulation if it ever may be necessary—to say that it is permissible as against strong drink but not as against the product of ruined lives.

The act does not meddle with anything belonging to the States. They may regulate their internal affairs and their domestic commerce as they like. But when they seek to send their products across the state line they are no longer within their rights. If there were no Constitution and no Congress their power to cross the line would depend upon their neighbors. Under the Constitution such commerce belongs not to the States but to Congress to regulate. It may carry out its views of public policy whatever indirect effect they may have upon the activities of the States. Instead of being encountered by a prohibitive tariff at her boundaries the State encounters the public policy of the United States which it is for Congress to express. The public policy of the United States is shaped with a view to the benefit of the nation as a whole. If, as has been the case within the memory of men still living, a State should take a different view of the propriety of sustaining a lottery from that which generally prevails, I cannot believe that the fact would require a different decision from that reached in *Champion v. Ames.* Yet in that case it would be said with quite as much force as in this that Congress was attempting to intermeddle with the State's domestic affairs. The national welfare as understood by Congress may require a different attitude within its sphere from that of some selfseeking State. It seems to me entirely constitutional for Congress to enforce its understanding by all the means at its command.

MR. JUSTICE MCKENNA, MR. JUSTICE BRANDEIS and MR. JUSTICE CLARKE concur in this opinion.

QUESTIONS AND COMMENTS

1 Identify the part of the Court's opinion in *Hammer v. Dagenhart* that relates to dual federalism.

2 In his opinion, Justice Day distinguishes the power to prohibit the use of interstate transportation to accomplish a harmful effect from the power to forbid the harm or evil itself. How does Holmes deal with that distinction? How effective is Holmes's analysis?

3 A cost-benefit analysis might suggest that the cost of the Court's decision in *Hammer* is that children under 14 years of age were permitted to work more than eight hours a day, seven days a week, and at night if it suited an employer's purposes. What benefit can be identified which justified such a social cost?

4 *Hammer v. Dagenhart* was overruled by *United States v. Darby,* 312 U.S. 100 (1941).

Brooks v. United States

267 U.S. 432; 45 S. Ct. 345; 69 L. Ed. 699 (1925)
Vote: Unanimous

Rae Brooks was convicted on two counts for violating the National Motor Vehicle Act of 1919. That act made it a crime to transport stolen vehicles in interstate commerce. Brooks owned a garage in Sioux Falls, South Dakota. In Sioux City, Iowa, he obtained two automobiles which had been stolen and took them to Sioux Falls. At trial, Brooks maintained that the 1919 statute was not authorized under the commerce clause of the Constitution.

MR. CHIEF JUSTICE TAFT delivered the opinion of the Court.

* * *

The objection to the Act can not be sustained. Congress can certainly regulate interstate commerce to the extent of forbidding and punishing the use of such commerce as an agency to promote immorality, dishonesty or the spread of any evil or harm to the people of other States from the State of origin. In doing this it is merely exercising the police power, for the benefit of the public, within the field of interstate commerce.

In *Reid v. Colorado,* [1902], it was held that Congress could pass a law excluding diseased stock from interstate commerce in order to prevent its use in such a way as thereby to injure the stock of other States. In the *Lottery Case,* [1903], it was held that Congress might pass a law punishing the transmission of lottery tickets from one State to another, in order to prevent the carriage of those tickets to be sold in other States and thus demoralize, through a spread of the gambling habit, individuals who were likely to purchase. In *Hipolite Egg Co. v. United States,* [1910], it was held that it was within the regulatory power of Congress to punish the transportation in interstate commerce of adulterated articles which, if sold in other States than the one from which they were transported, would deceive or injure persons who purchased such articles. In *Caminetti v. United States,* [1917], the so-called White Slave Traffic Act, which was construed to punish any person engaged in enticing a woman from one State to another for immoral ends, whether for commercial purposes or otherwise, was valid because it was intended to prevent the use of interstate commerce to facilitate prostitution or concubinage, and other forms of immorality. In *Clark Distilling Co. v. Western Maryland Railway Co.,* [1917], it was held that Congress had power to forbid the introduction of intoxicating liquors into any State in which their use was prohibited, in order to prevent the use of interstate commerce to promote that which was illegal in the State. In *Weber v. Freed,* [1915], it was held that Congress had power to prohibit the importation of pictorial representations of prize fights designed for public exhibition, because of the demoralizing effect of such exhibitions in the State of destination.

In *Hammer v. Dagenhart,* [1918], it was held that a federal law forbidding the transportation of articles manufactured by child labor in one State to another was invalid, because it was really not a regulation of interstate commerce but a congressional attempt to regulate labor in the State of origin, by an embargo on its external trade. Articles made by child labor and transported into other States were harmless, and could be properly transported without injurying any person who either bought or used them. In referring to the cases already cited, upon which the argument for the validity of the Child Labor Act was based, this Court pointed out that, in each of them, the use of interstate commerce had contributed to the accomplishment of harmful results to people of other States, and that the congressional power over interstate transportation in such cases could only be effectively exercised by prohibiting it. The clear distinction between authorities first cited and the *Child Labor Case* leaves no doubt where the right lies in this case. It is known of all men that the radical change in transportation of persons and goods effected by the introduction of the automobile, the speed with which it moves, and the ease with which evil-minded persons can avoid capture, have greatly encouraged and increased crimes. One of the crimes which have been encouraged is the theft of the automobiles themselves and their immediate transportation to places remote from homes of the owners. Elaborately organized conspiracies for the theft of automobiles and the spiriting them away into some other State, and their sale or other disposition far away from the owner and his neighborhood, have roused Congress to devise some method for defeating the success of these widely spread schemes of larceny. The quick passage of the machines into another State helps to conceal the trail of the thieves, gets the stolen property into another police jurisdiction and facilitates the finding of a safer place in which to dispose of the booty at a good price. This is a gross misuse of interstate commerce. Congress may properly punish such interstate transportation by any one with knowledge of the theft, because of its harmful result and its defeat of the property rights of those whose machines against their will are taken into other jurisdictions.

* * *

The judgment of the District Court is

Affirmed.

* * * * * *

The Motel Case, *Heart of Atlanta Motel v. United States,* falls in a different era. Does the commerce clause cover the movement of people? In *Edwards v. California,* the Court said yes. Thus, California could not bar indigents who possessed less than $20. In *Heart,* the question is not whether a state can bar transients but how may they be treated while moving in interstate commerce. In order to allay any doubts about this, Congress passed the 1964 Civil Rights Act to protect blacks moving in interstate commerce. By basing

the act on the commerce power, Congress was able to reach private as well as
state action. It was not concerned with the relationship of racial segregation
in hotels to interstate commerce. And no congressional findings about that
relationship were introduced in connection with the bill. Congress considered
the deprivation of public accommodations on account of race, origin, or
color bad or immoral, and the commerce power was an effective means to
get at the evil.

Heart of Atlanta Motel, Inc. v. United States et al.

379 U.S. 241; 85 S. Ct. 348; 13 L. Ed. 2d 258 (1964)
Vote: Unanimous

The facts are given in the opinion below.

MR. JUSTICE CLARK delivered the opinion of the Court.

This is a declaratory judgment action, attacking the constitutionality of Title
II of the Civil Rights Act of 1964. . . .

In addition to declaratory relief the complaint sought an injunction restraining the enforcement of the Act and damages against appellees based on allegedly resulting injury in the event compliance was required. Appellees counter-
claimed for enforcement under § 206 (a) of the Act and asked for a three-judge
district court under § 206 (b). A three-judge court, empaneled under § 206 (b)
as well as 28 U. S. C. § 2282 (1958 ed.), sustained the validity of the Act and
issued a permanent injunction on appellees' counterclaim restraining appellant
from continuing to violate the Act which remains in effect on order of MR.
JUSTICE BLACK. We affirm the judgment.

THE FACTUAL BACKGROUND AND CONTENTIONS OF THE PARTIES

The case comes here on admissions and stipulated facts. Appellant owns and
operates the Heart of Atlanta Motel which has 216 rooms available to transient
guests. The motel is located on Courtland Street, two blocks from downtown
Peachtree Street. It is readily accessible to interstate highways 75 and 85 and
state highways 23 and 41. Appellant solicits patronage from outside the State
of Georgia through various national advertising media, including magazines
of national circulation; it maintains over 50 billboards and highway signs
within the State, soliciting patronage for the motel; it accepts convention trade
from outside Georgia and approximately 75% of its registered guests are from
out of State. Prior to passage of the Act the motel had followed a practice of

refusing to rent rooms to Negroes, and it alleged that it intended to continue to do so. In an effort to perpetuate that policy this suit was filed.

The appellant contends that Congress in passing this Act exceeded its power to regulate commerce under Art. I, § 8, cl. 3, of the Constitution of the United States; that the Act violates the Fifth Amendment because appellant is deprived of the right to choose its customers and operate its business as it wishes, resulting in a taking of its liberty and property without due process of law and a taking of its property without just compensation; and, finally, that by requiring appellant to rent available rooms to Negroes against its will, Congress is subjecting it to involuntary servitude in contravention of the Thirteenth Amendment.

The appellees counter that the unavailability to Negroes of adequate accommodations interferes significantly with interstate travel, and that Congress, under the Commerce Clause, has power to remove such obstructions and restraints; that the Fifth Amendment does not forbid reasonable regulation and that consequential damage does not constitute a "taking" within the meaning of that amendment; that the Thirteenth Amendment claim fails because it is entirely frivolous to say that an amendment directed to the abolition of human bondage and the removal of widespread disabilities associated with slavery places discrimination in public accommodations beyond the reach of both federal and state law.

At the trial the appellant offered no evidence, submitting the case on the pleadings, admissions and stipulation of facts; however, appellees proved the refusal of the motel to accept Negro transients after the passage of the Act. The District Court sustained the constitutionality of the sections of the Act under attack (§§ 201 (a), (b) (1) and (c) (1)) and issued a permanent injunction on the counterclaim of the appellees. It restrained the appellant from "[r]efusing to accept Negroes as guests in the motel by reason of their race or color" and from "[m]aking any distinction whatever upon the basis of race or color in the availability of the goods, services, facilities, privileges, advantages or accommodations offered or made available to the guests of the motel, or to the general public, within or upon any of the premises of the Heart of Atlanta Motel, Inc."

* * *

THE BASIS OF CONGRESSIONAL ACTION

While the Act as adopted carried no congressional findings the record of its passage through each house is replete with evidence of the burdens that discrimination by race or color places upon interstate commerce.

* * *

The power of Congress to deal with these obstructions depends on the meaning of the Commerce Clause. Its meaning was first enunciated 140 years ago by the great Chief Justice John Marshall in *Gibbons v. Ogden,* (1824), in these words:

> The subject to be regulated is commerce; and . . . to ascertain the extent of the power, it becomes necessary to settle the meaning of the word. The counsel for the appellee would limit it to traffic, to buying and selling, or the interchange of commodities . . . but it is something more: it is intercourse . . . between nations, and parts of nations, in all its branches, and is regulated by prescribing rules for carrying on that intercourse. . . .

That the "intercourse" of which the Chief Justice spoke included the movement of persons through more States than one was settled as early as 1849, in the *Passenger Cases,* [1849], where Mr. Justice McLean stated: "That the transportation of passengers is a part of commerce is not now an open question." Again in 1913 Mr. Justice McKenna, speaking for the Court, said: "Commerce among the States, we have said, consists of intercourse and traffic between their citizens, and includes the transportation of persons and property." *Hoke v. United States,* [1913]. And only four years later in 1917 in *Caminetti v. United States,* [1917], Mr. Justice Day held for the Court:

> The transportation of passengers in interstate commerce, it has long been settled, is within the regulatory power of Congress, under the commerce clause of the Constitution, and the authority of Congress to keep the channels of interstate commerce free from immoral and injurious uses has been frequently sustained, and is no longer open to question.

Nor does it make any difference whether the transportation is commercial in character. In *Morgan v. Virginia,* (1946), Mr. Justice Reed observed as to the modern movement of persons among the States:

> The recent changes in transportation brought about by the coming of automobiles [do] not seem of great significance in the problem. People of all races travel today more extensively than in 1878 when this Court first passed upon state regulation of racial segregation in commerce.

* * *

In framing Title II of this Act Congress was . . . dealing with what it considered a moral problem. But that fact does not detract from the overwhelming evidence of the disruptive effect that racial discrimination has had on commercial intercourse. It was this burden which empowered Congress to enact appropriate legislation, and, given this basis for the exercise of its power, Congress was not restricted by the fact that the particular obstruction to interstate commerce with which it was dealing was also deemed a moral and social wrong.

It is said that the operation of the motel here is of a purely local character. But, assuming this to be true, "[i]f it is interstate commerce that feels the pinch, it does not matter how local the operation which applies the squeeze. . . ." the power of Congress to promote interstate commerce also includes the power to regulate the local incidents thereof, including local activities in both the States of origin and destination, which might have a substantial and harmful effect upon that commerce. . . .

Congress may—as it has—prohibit racial discrimination by motels serving travelers, however "local" their operations may appear.

Nor does the Act deprive appellant of liberty or property under the Fifth Amendment. The commerce power invoked here by the Congress is a specific and plenary one authorized by the Constitution itself. The only questions are: (1) whether Congress had a rational basis for finding that racial discrimination by motels affected commerce, and (2) if it had such a basis, whether the means it selected to eliminate that evil are reasonable and appropriate. If they are, appellant has no "right" to select its guests as it sees fit, free from governmental regulation.

There is nothing novel about such legislation. Thirty-two States now have it on their books either by statute or executive order and many cities provide such regulation. Some of these Acts go back fourscore years. It has been repeatedly held by this Court that such laws do not violate the Due Process Clause of the Fourteenth Amendment.

*   *   *

It is doubtful if in the long run appellant will suffer economic loss as a result of the Act. Experience is to the contrary where discrimination is completely obliterated as to all public accommodations. But whether this be true or not is of no consequence since this Court has specifically held that the fact that a "member of the class which is regulated may suffer economic losses not shared by others . . . has never been a barrier" to such legislation. Likewise in a long line of cases this Court has rejected the claim that the prohibition of racial discrimination in public accommodations interferes with personal liberty.

*   *   *

Neither do we find any merit in the claim that the Act is a taking of property without just compensation. The cases are to the contrary. See *Legal Tender Cases,* (1870); *United States v. Central Eureka Mining Co.,* (1958).

We find no merit in the remainder of appellant's contentions, including that of "involuntary servitude." As we have seen, 32 States prohibit racial discrimination in public accommodations. These laws but codify the common-law innkeeper rule which long predated the Thirteenth Amendment. It is difficult to believe that the Amendment was intended to abrogate this principle.

*   *   *

We, therefore, conclude that the action of the Congress in the adoption of the Act as applied here to a motel which concededly serves interstate travelers is within the power granted it by the Commerce Clause of the Constitution, as interpreted by this Court for 140 years. It may be argued that Congress could have pursued other methods to eliminate the obstructions it found in interstate commerce caused by racial discrimination. But this is a matter of policy that rests entirely with the Congress not with the courts. How obstructions in commerce may be removed—what means are to be employed—is within the sound and exclusive discretion of the Congress. It is subject only to one caveat—that the means chosen by it must be reasonably adapted to the end permitted by the Constitution. We cannot say that its choice here was not so adapted. The Constitution requires no more.

Affirmed.

QUESTIONS AND COMMENTS

1 In *Heart,* the Court states that Title II of the Civil Rights Act, which requires motels to rent to blacks, deals with a "moral problem," which Congress considered to be a "moral and social wrong." Does the ruling in this case mean that if Congress can identify what it thinks is a moral wrong, it may constitutionally move to forbid it? Explain your answer.

2 The Court in *Heart* assumes that racial discrimination in renting to transients unduly burdens interstate commerce in that it has an obvious impact upon blacks traveling interstate. Does such discrimination against blacks also impact on white transients, thereby burdening commerce?

3 What if the Heart of Atlanta Motel served no interstate transients? Could a black resident of Atlanta who was refused a room bring a challenge under the 1964 act, and if so, would such a complainant be likely to win the case? Why or why not?

4 Section 201 (6) (4) (d) of the 1964 act assumes "state action" if racial discrimination is the "custom" in the state. Can you explain the linkage here? What role did state action play in shaping the Court's decision in *Heart?* Why do you think Congress inserted a section dealing with state action?

5 In recent cases, the Court has upheld the power of Congress to regulate strip-mining (*Hodel v. Virginia Surface Mining and Reclamation Association,* 452 U.S. 264 [1981]) and the way in which states regulate the energy-producing utilities within state boundaries (*Federal Energy Regulatory Commission v. Mississippi,* 50 LW 4566 [1982]). The social goal in the first case was protection of the environment, in the second the preservation of energy. In 1983, the Court upheld a California ban on the construction of nuclear plants (*Pacific Gas and Electric Co. v. State Resources Conservation and Development Commission,* 51 LW 4449 [1983]). This appears to conflict with the Atomic Energy Act of 1954, through which Congress sought to promote safety in the production and use of nuclear energy. However, California avoided a clash with the "supremacy power" by justifying its restriction in economic terms—i.e., the high costs associated with disposing of nuclear wastes. It hardly needs noting that the California moratorium and the Supreme Court's approval of it, while germane to the economic argument, were also consistent with the politics surrounding the construction and operation of nuclear plants in California in 1983.

6 In *Katzenbach v. McClung* [379 U.S. 294 (1964)], the Court upheld a racial discrimination claim under the Civil Rights Act against Ollie's Barbecue, a restaurant in Alabama. The purchase of $70,000 worth of meat which originated out of state was enough to bring the practices of the restaurant under the commerce power.

In Pursuance of Social and Economic Policies

N.L.R.B. v. Jones and Laughlin Steel Co. (1937)

United States v. Darby Lumber Co. (1941)

Wickard v. Filburn (1942)

National League of Cities v. Usery (1976)

The first three of these cases represent an era of marked change in the thrust of Supreme Court decisions touching the power of Congress under the commerce clause. We have previously noted the tension between two views of the commerce power: (1) the view that the Tenth Amendment reserved the police powers to the states and that such powers could not be used by the Congress, and (2) the view that the commerce power is plenary and is not restricted by the fact that its use may impinge upon state policy. As we moved into the 1930s, the first view was in a strong phase. Congress was permitted to regulate commerce generally only if the subject matter had a relatively direct effect on commercial transactions across state lines. Such restrictions on the Congress assumed unusual importance in the thirties because of the great depression and President Roosevelt's determination to revitalize the economy. Roosevelt had no shortage of advisers, economic and otherwise, to tell him what was needed. A question, however, was whether he could get his measures through Congress and whether Congress had the power to adopt the programs proposed.

Though not always without difficulty, Roosevelt generally succeeded in getting his bills passed—so-called New Deal measures. His election in 1932 and his overwhelming mandate in 1936 suggested that the country wanted change. And most people were not too concerned with the legal niceties at that moment. However, some parties did not welcome the economic change being sought and proceeded to challenge administration measures, one after the other, in the courts. Many of these challenges reached the Supreme Court, where Roosevelt's luck had clearly run out.

The Court in 1932 was composed of Justices Hughes (C.J.), Van Devanter, Cardozo, McReynolds, Brandeis, Butler, Sutherland, Roberts, and Stone. It is often said that this Court was aged and conservative. But what transpired in the New Deal Cases cannot be attributed totally to such a fact. For the Court had, for fifty years, been narrowing the powers of government to control the use of private economic power. In the process it carved out areas in which neither Congress nor the states could adequately control economic activities that created grievous social problems. We have seen how, in *Hammer v. Dagenhart,* Congress was denied the right to regulate or prohibit child labor. Earlier the Court had denied Congress the power to regulate labor relations.[5] And in 1923, Congress was told that it could not fix minimum wages in the District of Columbia.[6]

Roosevelt and his advisers were well aware of all this. In the first term of his administration, he was temporarily cheered by the Court's decision in *Home Building and Loan Association v. Blaisdell,*[7] upholding the Minnesota

Moratorium Law, and *Nebbia v. New York,*[8] approving the regulation of the milk industry in New York. But these were cases upholding state power. Federal power was to meet a different fate.

Roosevelt's strategy in restructuring the economy was to use the commerce and taxing powers delegated to Congress in the Constitution. One statute based on the commerce power was the Railroad Retirement Act. That act established a fund to which all interstate railroads were required to contribute. The fund was used to pay pensions to retired railroad workers. In 1935, the Supreme Court decided that the act was not a legitimate use of the commerce power and held it unconstitutional.[9] In the same year, the Court struck certain provisions of the National Recovery Act, in part on the ground that the act could not be justified as a valid exercise of the commerce power.[10]

In short order the Court proceeded in 1936 to nullify (1) the Agricultural Adjustment Act, regulating farm surpluses, on the ground that agriculture was a local or intrastate activity,[11] (2) the Bituminous Coal Conservation Act, which regulated coal prices, collective bargaining, and wages/hours of employees, on the ground, inter alia, that the mining of coal was a local activity and did not meet the requirements of interstate commerce,[12] and (3) the New York State Minimum Wage Law.[13] While the New York Case involved neither federal power nor the commerce clause, it reflected the social and political philosophy that had buttressed the Tenth Amendment restrictions on the commerce power in earlier cases.

Apparently losing all hope of salvaging his program with the Court as then composed, Roosevelt set out to change its personnel. He sought to increase its membership. At this time, the Court contained four advocates of entrepreneurial liberty, Sutherland, Butler, McReynolds, and Van Devanter, justices who did not look kindly on congressional regulation of commerce to accomplish social and political goals. It also contained three liberals, Brandeis, Stone, and Cardozo, who could generally be counted on to support Roosevelt's efforts to bring change to the system. In the middle were Chief Justice Hughes and Associate Justice Roberts, who were usually found voting with the conservatives. Both were Republicans from the conservative wing of that party.

Since Congress determines the size of the Court, the easiest way to increase the probability of getting New Deal measures past the justices was to add justices friendly to the President's plans. Roosevelt proposed, therefore, that for every federal judge who did not retire within six months of reaching the age of 70, having served ten years or more, one additional judge be appointed to the Court on which the aged judge sat. At this time, seven of the Supreme Court justices had served at least ten years and attained the age of 70. But since Roosevelt proposed that the Supreme Court not be expanded beyond fifteen members, his plan would have enabled him to add six new justices to the Court. The expansion in Court size could be avoided, of course, to the extent that the aged justices resigned. But had all seven done so, Roosevelt would have been rid of all but Roberts and Cardozo—one liberal, Brandeis, but five conservatives, Sutherland, Butler, Van Devanter, McReynolds, and Hughes. While Roosevelt's proffered justification for his measure was to provide assistance to aged justices, no one was fooled.

The attempt to "pack the Court," as it came to be known, stimulated the opposition of all those individuals, groups, and professional organizations (such as the American Bar Association) that valued the separation of powers and the independence of the Court from the political branches of the government. The "independence" argument rallied the American people, and Roosevelt was unsuccessful in getting his proposal enacted. The irony, perhaps, is that the Court's insulation from political influence was the very point at issue for both sides; Roosevelt's opponents mobilized to defend the concepts, and it was the President's desire to exercise political influence on the Court that motivated him to propose his plan in the first place.

Now, lest we jump to the conclusion that Roosevelt's ultimate goal—to get Supreme Court approval of his administration's economic measures—was lost in the defeat of his bill, it must be quickly said that the contrary is true. The "attack" on the Court appeared to influence some of the justices. Several are alleged to have become more sympathetic to the New Deal overnight. Furthermore, one of Roosevelt's strongest opponents on the Court, Van Devanter, announced his resignation in May 1937, thereby enabling the President to appoint an ardent New Deal senator—Hugo Black. Thus, in the latter part of 1937 we find a Court composed of conservatives Sutherland, McReynolds, and Butler; liberals Black, Stone, Cardozo, and Brandeis; plus Roberts and Hughes—who now proceeded to give Roosevelt 5–4 and 6–3 majorities in support of his regulatory measures. The first three cases in this section illustrate some of the rulings of the Court in the period 1937–1942.

National Labor Relations Board v. Jones and Laughlin Steel Corporation

301 U.S. 1; 57 S. Ct. 615; 81 L. Ed. 2d 893 (1937)
Vote: 5–4

The facts are given in the opinion below.

MR. CHIEF JUSTICE HUGHES delivered the opinion of the Court.

In a proceeding under the National Labor Relations Act of 1935, the National Labor Relations Board found that the respondent, Jones & Laughlin Steel Corporation, had violated the Act by engaging in unfair labor practices affecting commerce. The proceeding was instituted by the Beaver Valley Lodge No. 200, affiliated with the Amalgamated Association of Iron, Steel and Tin Workers of America, a labor organization. The unfair labor practices charged were that the corporation was discriminating against members of the union with regard to hire and tenure of employment, and was coercing and intimidating its employees in order to interfere with their self-organization. The discriminatory and coercive action alleged was the discharge of certain employees.

The National Labor Relations Board, sustaining the charge, ordered the corporation to cease and desist from such discrimination and coercion, to offer reinstatement to ten of the employees named, to make good their losses in pay, and to post for thirty days notices that the corporation would not discharge or discriminate against members, or those desiring to become members, of the labor union. As the corporation failed to comply, the Board petitioned the Circuit Court of Appeals to enforce the order. The court denied the petition, holding that the order lay beyond the range of federal power.

We granted certiorari.

* * *

Contesting the ruling of the Board, the respondent argues (1) that the Act is in reality a regulation of labor relations and not of interstate commerce; (2) that the Act can have no application to the respondent's relations with its production employees because they are not subject to regulation by the federal government; and (3) that the provisions of the Act violate § 2 of Article III and the Fifth and Seventh Amendments of the Constitution of the United States.

* * *

First. The scope of the Act.—The Act is challenged in its entirety as an attempt to regulate all industry, thus invading the reserved powers of the States over their local concerns. It is asserted that the references in the Act to interstate and foreign commerce are colorable at best; that the Act is not a true regulation of such commerce or of matters which directly affect it but on the contrary has the fundamental object of placing under the compulsory supervision of the federal government all industrial labor relations within the nation. . . .

We think it clear that the National Labor Relations Act may be construed so as to operate within the sphere of constitutional authority. The jurisdiction conferred upon the Board, and invoked in this instance, is found in § 10 (a), which provides:

"SEC. 10 (a). The Board is empowered, as hereinafter provided, to prevent any person from engaging in any unfair labor practice (listed in section 8) affecting commerce."

The critical words of this provision, prescribing the limits of the Board's authority in dealing with the labor practices, are "affecting commerce. . . ."

"The term 'affecting commerce' means in commerce, or burdening or obstructing commerce or the free flow of commerce, or having led or tending to lead to a labor dispute burdening or obstructing commerce or the free flow of commerce. . . ."

Whether or not particular action does affect commerce in such a close and intimate fashion as to be subject to federal control, and hence to lie within the authority conferred upon the Board, is left by the statute to be determined as individual cases arise. We are thus to inquire whether in the instant case the constitutional boundary has been passed.

* * *

Third. The application of the Act to employees engaged in production.—The principle involved.—Respondent says that whatever may be said of employees engaged in interstate commerce, the industrial relations and activities in the manufacturing department of respondent's enterprise are not subject to federal regulation. The argument rests upon the proposition that manufacturing in itself is not commerce. *Schechter Corp. v. United States,* [1935]; *Carter v. Carter Coal Co.,* [1936].

The Government distinguishes these cases. The various parts of respondent's enterprise are described as interdependent and as thus involving "a great movement of iron ore, coal and limestone along well-defined paths to the steel mills, thence through them, and thence in the form of steel products into the consuming centers of the country—a definite and well-understood course of business." It is urged that these activities constitute a "stream" or "flow" of commerce, of which the Aliquippa manufacturing plant is the focal point, and that industrial strife at that point would cripple the entire movement.... Respondent says that the Aliquippa plant is extensive in size and represents a large investment in buildings, machinery and equipment. The raw materials which are brought to the plant are delayed for long periods and, after being subjected to manufacturing processes, "are changed substantially as to character, utility and value." The finished products which emerge "are to a large extent manufactured without reference to pre-existing orders and contracts and are entirely different from the raw materials which enter at the other end." Hence respondent argues that "If importation and exportation in interstate commerce do not singly transfer purely local activities into the field of congressional regulation, it should follow that their combination would not alter the local situation." *Arkadelphia Milling Co. v. St. Louis Southwestern Ry. Co.,* [1919].

* * *

Although activities may be intrastate in character when separately considered, if they have such a close and substantial relation to interstate commerce that their control is essential or appropriate to protect that commerce from burdens and obstructions, Congress cannot be denied the power to exercise that control. *Schechter Corp. v. United States, supra.* Undoubtedly the scope of this power must be considered in the light of our dual system of government and may not be extended so as to embrace effects upon interstate commerce so indirect and remote that to embrace them, in view of our complex society, would effectually obliterate the distinction between what is national and what is local and create a completely centralized government. The question is necessarily one of degree. As the Court said in *Chicago Board of Trade v. Olsen,* [1923]. . .

Whatever amounts to more or less constant practice, and threatens to obstruct or unduly to burden the freedom of interstate commerce is within the regulatory power of Congress under the commerce clause and it is primarily for Congress to consider and decide the fact of the danger and meet it.

* * *

The close and intimate effect which brings the subject within the reach of federal power may be due to activities in relation to productive industry although the industry when separately viewed is local. This has been abundantly illustrated in the application of the federal Anti-Trust Act. . . .

. . . the Anti-Trust Act has been applied to the conduct of employees engaged in production. *Coronado Coal Co. v. United Mine Workers,* [1925]; . . .

It is thus apparent that the fact that the employees here concerned were engaged in production is not determinative. The question remains as to the effect upon interstate commerce of the labor practice involved. In the *Schechter* case, *supra,* we found that the effect there was so remote as to be beyond the federal power. To find "immediacy or directness" there was to find it "almost everywhere," a result inconsistent with the maintenance of our federal system.

* * *

Giving full weight to respondent's contention with respect to a break in the complete continuity of the "stream of commerce" by reason of respondent's manufacturing operations, the fact remains that the stoppage of those operations by industrial strife would have a most serious effect upon interstate commerce. In view of respondent's far-flung activities, it is idle to say that the effect would be indirect or remote. It is obvious that it would be immediate and might be catastrophic. We are asked to shut our eyes to the plainest facts of our national life and to deal with the question of direct and indirect effects in an intellectual vacuum. Because there may be but indirect and remote effects upon interstate commerce in connection with a host of local enterprises throughout the country, it does not follow that other industrial activities do not have such a close and intimate relation to interstate commerce as to make the presence of industrial strife a matter of the most urgent national concern. When industries organize themselves on a national scale, making their relation to interstate commerce the dominant factor in their activities, how can it be maintained that their industrial labor relations constitute a forbidden field into which Congress may not enter when it is necessary to protect interstate commerce from the paralyzing consequences of industrial war? We have often said that interstate commerce itself is a practical conception. It is equally true that interferences with that commerce must be appraised by a judgment that does not ignore actual experience.

Experience has abundantly demonstrated that the recognition of the right of employees to self-organization and to have representatives of their own choosing for the purpose of collective bargaining is often an essential condition of industrial peace. Refusal to confer and negotiate has been one of the most prolific causes of strife. This is such an outstanding fact in the history of labor disturbances that it is a proper subject of judicial notice and requires no citation of instances.

* * *

The steel industry is one of the great basic industries of the United States, with ramifying activities affecting interstate commerce at every point. The Government aptly refers to the steel strike of 1919–1920 with its far-reaching consequences. The fact that there appears to have been no major disturbance in that industry in the more recent period did not dispose of the possibilities of future and like dangers to interstate commerce which Congress was entitled to foresee and to exercise its protective power to forestall. It is not necessary again to detail the facts as to respondent's enterprise. Instead of being beyond the pale, we think that it presents in a most striking way the close and intimate relation which a manufacturing industry may have to interstate commerce and we have no doubt that Congress had constitutional authority to safeguard the right of respondent's employees to self-organization and freedom in the choice of representatives for collective bargaining.

*Fifth. The means which the Act employs.—Questions under the due process clause and other constitutional restrictions.—*Respondent asserts its right to conduct its business in an orderly manner without being subjected to arbitrary restraints. What we have said points to the fallacy in the argument. . . .

The Act does not compel agreements between employers and employees. It does not compel any agreement whatever. It does not prevent the employer "from refusing to make a collective contract and hiring individuals on whatever terms" the employer "may by unilateral action determine." . . . The Act does not interfere with the normal exercise of the right of the employer to select its employees or to discharge them. The employer may not, under cover of that right, intimidate or coerce its employees with respect to their self-organization and representation, and, on the other hand, the Board is not entitled to make its authority a pretext for interference with the right of discharge when that right is exercised for other reasons than such intimidation and coercion. The true purpose is the subject of investigation with full opportunity to show the facts. It would seem that when employers freely recognize the right of their employees to their own organizations and their unrestricted right of representation there will be much less occasion for controversy in respect to the free and appropriate exercise of the right of selection and discharge.

* * *

We construe the procedural provisions as affording adequate opportunity to secure judicial protection against arbitrary action in accordance with the well-settled rules applicable to administrative agencies set up by Congress to aid in the enforcement of valid legislation. It is not necessary to repeat these rules which have frequently been declared. None of them appears to have been transgressed in the instant case. Respondent was notified and heard. It had opportunity to meet the charge of unfair labor practices upon the merits, and by withdrawing from the hearing it declined to avail itself of that opportunity. The facts found by the Board support its order and the evidence supports the findings. Respondent has no just ground for complaint on this score. . . .

Our conclusion is that the order of the Board was within its competency and that the Act is valid as here applied. The judgment of the Circuit Court of Appeals is reversed and the cause is remanded for further proceedings in conformity with this opinion.

Reversed.

MR. JUSTICE McREYNOLDS delivered the following dissenting opinion in the cases preceding:

MR. JUSTICE VAN DEVANTER, MR. JUSTICE SUTHERLAND, MR. JUSTICE BUTLER and I are unable to agree with the decisions just announced.

* * *

The Court, as we think, departs from well-established principles followed in *Schechter Corp. v. United States,* (1935) and *Carter v. Carter Coal Co.,* (1936). Upon the authority of those decisions, the Circuit Courts of Appeals of the Fifth, Sixth and Second Circuits in the causes now before us have held the power of Congress under the commerce clause does not extend to relations between employers and their employees engaged in manufacture, and therefore the Act conferred upon the National Labor Relations Board no authority in respect of matters covered by the questioned orders.

* * *

We are told that Congress may protect the "stream of commerce" and that one who buys raw material without the state, manufactures it therein, and ships the output to another state is in that stream. Therefore it is said he may be prevented from doing anything which may interfere with its flow.

This, too, goes beyond the constitutional limitations heretofore enforced. If a man raises cattle and regularly delivers them to a carrier for interstate shipment, may Congress prescribe the conditions under which he may employ or discharge helpers on the ranch? The products of a mine pass daily into interstate commerce; many things are brought to it from other states. Are the owners and the miners within the power of Congress in respect of the miners' tenure and discharge? May a mill owner be prohibited from closing his factory or discontinuing his business because so to do would stop the flow of products to and from his plant in interstate commerce? May employees in a factory be restrained from quitting work in a body because this will close the factory and thereby stop the flow of commerce? May arson of a factory be made a Federal offense whenever this would interefere with such flow? If the business cannot continue with the existing wage scale, may Congress command a reduction? If the ruling of the Court just announced is adhered to these questions suggest some of the problems certain to arise.

And if this theory of a continuous "stream of commerce" as now defined is correct, will it become the duty of the Federal Government hereafter to suppress every strike which by possibility may cause a blockade in that stream? *In re Debs,* [1895]. Moreover, since Congress has intervened, are labor relations between most manufacturers and their employees removed from all control by the state?

There is no ground on which reasonably to hold that refusal by a manufacturer, whose raw materials come from states other than that of his factory and whose products are regularly carried to other states, to bargain collectively with employees in his manufacturing plant, directly affects interstate commerce. In such business, there is not one but two distinct movements or streams in interstate transportation. The first brings in raw material and there ends. Then follows manufacture, a separate and local activity. Upon completion of this, and not before, the second distinct movement or stream in interstate commerce begins and the products go to other states. Such is the common course for small as well as large industries. It is unreasonable and unprecedented to say the commerce clause confers upon Congress power to govern relations between employers and employees in these local activities. In *Schechter's* case we condemned as unauthorized by the commerce clause assertion of federal power in respect of commodities which had come to rest after interstate transportation. And, in *Carter's* case, we held Congress lacked power to regulate labor relations in respect of commodities before interstate commerce has begun.

It is gravely stated that experience teaches that if an employer discourages membership in "any organization of any kind" "in which employees participate, and which exists for the purpose in whole or in part of dealing with employers concerning grievances, labor disputes, wages, rates of pay, hours of employment or conditions of work," discontent may follow and this in turn may lead to a strike, and as the outcome of the strike there may be a block in the stream of interstate commerce. Therefore Congress may inhibit the discharge! Whatever effect any cause of discontent may ultimately have upon commerce is far too indirect to justify Congressional regulation. Almost anything—marriage, birth, death—may in some fashion affect commerce.

* * *

The right to contract is fundamental and includes the privilege of selecting those with whom one is willing to assume contractual relations. This right is unduly abridged by the Act now upheld. A private owner is deprived of power to manage his own property by freely selecting those to whom his manufacturing operations are to be entrusted. We think this cannot lawfully be done in circumstances like those here disclosed.

It seems clear to us that Congress has transcended the powers granted.

United States v. F. W. Darby Lumber Co.

312 U.S. 100; 61 S. Ct. 451; 85 L. Ed. 609 (1941)
Vote: Unanimous

The Fair Labor Standards Act of 1938 provided for the fixing of minimum wages and maximum hours for employees engaged in interstate commerce, and mandated increased compensation for overtime. Appropriate records were required to be kept by employers covered by the act. Fines and/or imprisonment could be imposed on any employers found to be in violation of these provisions. Darby was indicted for violating the act. The district court quashed (voided) the indictment. The Supreme Court granted review.

MR. JUSTICE STONE delivered the opinion of the Court.

* * *

[The appellee] challenged the validity of the Fair Labor Standards Act under the Commerce Clause and the Fifth and Tenth Amendments. The district court quashed the indictment in its entirety upon the broad grounds that the Act, which it interpreted as a regulation of manufacture within the states, is unconstitutional. It declared that manufacture is not interstate commerce and that the regulation by the Fair Labor Standards Act of wages and hours of employment of those engaged in the manufacture of goods which it is intended at the time of production "may or will be" after production "sold in interstate commerce in part or in whole" is not within the congressional power to regulate interstate commerce.

The effect of the court's decision and judgment is thus to deny the power of Congress to prohibit shipment in interstate commerce of lumber produced for interstate commerce under the proscribed substandard labor conditions of wages and hours, its power to penalize the employer for his failure to conform to the wage and hour provisions in the case of employees engaged in the production of lumber which he intends thereafter to ship in interstate commerce in part or in whole according to the normal course of his business and its power to compel him to keep records of hours of employment as required by the statute and the regulations of the administrator.

* * *

While manufacture is not of itself interstate commerce, the shipment of manufactured goods interstate is such commerce and the prohibition of such shipment by Congress is indubitably a regulation of the commerce. The power to regulate commerce is the power "to prescribe the rule by which commerce is governed." *Gibbons v. Ogden,* [1824]. . . .

But it is said that [while] the present . . . prohibition is nominally a regulation of the commerce its motive or purpose is regulation of wages and hours of persons engaged in manufacture, the control of which has been reserved to the states and upon which Georgia and some of the states of destination have placed no restriction; that the effect of the present statute is not to exclude the proscribed articles from interstate commerce in aid of state regulation as in *Kentucky Whip & Collar Co. v. Illinois Central R. Co.,* [1937], but instead, under the guise of a regulation of interstate commerce, it undertakes to regulate wages and hours within the state contrary to the policy of the state which has elected to leave them unregulated. . . .

The motive and purpose of the present regulation are plainly to make effective the Congressional conception of public policy that interstate commerce should not be made the instrument of competition in the distribution of goods produced under substandard labor conditions, which competition is injurious to the commerce and to the states from and to which the commerce flows. The motive and purpose of a regulation of interstate commerce are matters for the legislative judgment upon the exercise of which the Constitution places no restriction and over which the courts are given no control. *McCray v. United States,* [1904]. "The judicial cannot prescribe to the legislative department of the government limitations upon the exercise of its acknowledged power." *Veazie Bank v. Fenno,* [1869]. Whatever their motive and purpose, regulations of commerce which do not infringe some constitutional prohibition are within the plenary power conferred on Congress by the Commerce Clause. Subject only to that limitation, presently to be considered, we conclude that the prohibition of the shipment interstate of goods produced under the forbidden substandard labor conditions is within the constitutional authority of Congress.

In the more than a century which has elapsed since the decision of *Gibbons v. Ogden,* these principles of constitutional interpretation have been so long and repeatedly recognized by this Court as applicable to the Commerce Clause, that there would be little occasion for repeating them now were it not for the decision of this Court twenty-two years ago in *Hammer v. Dagenhart,* [1918]. In that case it was held by a bare majority of the Court over the powerful and now classic dissent of Mr. Justice Holmes setting forth the fundamental issues involved, that Congress was without power to exclude the products of child labor from interstate commerce. The reasoning and conclusion of the Court's opinion there cannot be reconciled with the conclusion which we have reached, that the power of Congress under the Commerce Clause is plenary to exclude any article from interstate commerce subject only to the specific prohibitions of the Constitution.

Hammer v. Dagenhart has not been followed. The distinction on which the decision was rested that Congressional power to prohibit interstate commerce is limited to articles which in themselves have some harmful or deleterious property—a distinction which was novel when made and unsupported by any provision of the Constitution—has long since been abandoned. *Mulford v. Smith,* [1939]. The thesis of the opinion that the motive of the prohibition or its effect to control in some measure the use or production within the states of the article thus excluded from the commerce can operate to deprive the regulation of its constitutional authority has long since ceased to have force. *United States v. Carolene Products Co.,* [1938]. And finally we have declared "The authority of the federal government over interstate commerce does not differ in extent or character from that retained by the states over intrastate commerce." *United States v. Rock Royal Co-operative,* [1939].

The conclusion is inescapable that *Hammer v. Dagenhart,* was a departure from the principles which have prevailed in the interpretation of the Commerce Clause both before and since the decision and that such vitality, as a precedent, as it then had has long since been exhausted. It should be and now is overruled.

Validity of the wage and hour requirements. Section 15 (a) (2) and §§ 6 and 7 require employers to conform to the wage and hour provisions with respect to all employees engaged in the production of goods for interstate commerce. As appellee's employees are not alleged to be "engaged in interstate commerce" the validity of the prohibition turns on the question whether the employment, under other than the prescribed labor standards, of employees engaged in the production of goods for interstate commerce is so related to the commerce and so affects it as to be within the reach of the power of Congress to regulate it.

To answer this question we must at the outset determine whether the particular acts charged in the counts which are laid under § 15 (a) (2) as they were construed below, constitute "production for commerce" within the meaning of the statute. . . .

Without attempting to define the precise limits of the phrase, we think the acts alleged in the indictment are within the sweep of the statute. The obvious purpose of the Act was not only to prevent the interstate transportation of the proscribed product, but to stop the initial step toward transportation, production with the purpose of so transporting it.

*   *   *

There remains the question whether such restriction on the production of goods for commerce is a permissible exercise of the commerce power. The power of Congress over interstate commerce is not confined to the regulation of commerce among the states. It extends to those activities intrastate which so affect interstate commerce or the exercise of the power of Congress over it as to make regulation of them appropriate means to the attainment of a legitimate end, the exercise of the granted power of Congress to regulate interstate commerce. . . .

. . . Long before the adoption of the National Labor Relations Act this Court had many times held that the power of Congress to regulate interstate commerce extends to the regulation through legislative action of activities intrastate which have a substantial effect on the commerce or the exercise of the Congressional power over it.

*   *   *

Congress, having by the present Act adopted the policy of excluding from interstate commerce all goods produced for the commerce which do not conform to the specified labor standards, it may choose the means reasonably adapted to the attainment of the permitted end, even though they involve control of intrastate activities. Such legislation has often been sustained with respect to powers, other than the commerce power granted to the national government, when the means chosen, although not themselves within the granted power, were nevertheless deemed appropriate aids to the accomplishment of some purpose within an admitted power of the national government.

*   *   *

Our conclusion is unaffected by the Tenth Amendment which provides: "The powers not delegated to the United States by the Constitution, nor prohibited by it to the States, are reserved to the States respectively, or to the people." The amendment states but a truism that all is retained which has not been surrendered. There is nothing in the history of its adoption to suggest that it was more than declaratory of the relationship between the national and state governments as it had been established by the Constitution before the amendment or that its purpose was other than to allay fears that the new national government might seek to exercise powers not granted, and that the states might not be able to exercise fully their reserved powers.

*   *   *

Validity of the wage and hour provisions under the Fifth Amendment. Both provisions are minimum wage requirements compelling the payment of a minimum standard wage with a prescribed increased wage for overtime of "not less than one and one-half times the regular rate" at which the worker is employed. Since our decision in *West Coast Hotel Co. v. Parrish,* [1937], it is no longer open to question that the fixing of a minimum wage is within the legislative power and that the bare fact of its exercise is not a denial of due process under the Fifth more than under the Fourteenth Amendment. Nor is it any longer open to question that it is within the legislative power to fix maximum hours. *Muller v. Oregon,* [1908], *Bunting v. Oregon,* [1917]. Similarly the statute is not objectionable because applied alike to both men and women.

The Act is sufficiently definite to meet constitutional demands. One who employs persons, without conforming to the prescribed wage and hour conditions, to work on goods which he ships or expects to ship across state lines, is warned that he may be subject to the criminal penalties of the Act. No more is required.

We have considered, but find it unnecessary to discuss other contentions.

Reversed.

Wickard, Secretary of Agriculture, et al. v. Filburn

317 U.S. 111; 63 S. Ct. 82; 87 L. Ed. 122 (1942)
Vote: Unanimous

The facts are given in the opinion below.

MR. JUSTICE JACKSON delivered the opinion of the Court.

The appellee filed his complaint against the Secretary of Agriculture of the United States, three members of the County Agricultural Conservation Committee for Montgomery County, Ohio, and a member of the State Agricultural Conservation Committee for Ohio. He sought to enjoin enforcement against himself of the marketing penalty imposed by the amendment of May 26, 1941, to the Agricultural Adjustment Act of 1938, upon that part of his 1941 wheat crop which was available for marketing in excess of the marketing quota established for his farm. He also sought a declaratory judgment that the wheat marketing quota provisions of the Act as amended and applicable to him were unconstitutional because not sustainable under the Commerce Clause or consistent with the Due Process Clause of the Fifth Amendment.

[A three-judge district court permanently enjoined the secretary of agriculture and others from enforcing penalties against Filburn.]

The appellee for many years past has owned and operated a small farm in Montgomery County, Ohio, maintaining a herd of dairy cattle, selling milk, raising poultry, and selling poultry and eggs. It has been his practice to raise a small acreage of winter wheat, sown in the Fall and harvested in the following July; to sell a portion of the crop; to feed part to poultry and livestock on the farm, some of which is sold; to use some in making flour for home consumption; and to keep the rest for the following seeding. The intended disposition of the crop here involved has not been expressly stated.

In July of 1940, pursuant to the Agricultural Adjustment Act of 1938, as then amended, there were established for the appellee's 1941 crop a wheat acreage allotment of 11.1 acres and a normal yield of 20.1 bushels of wheat an acre. He was given notice of such allotment in July of 1940, before the planting of his 1941 crop of wheat, and again in July of 1941, before it was harvested. He sowed, however, 23 acres, and harvested from his 11.9 acres of excess acreage 239 bushels, which under the terms of the Act as amended on May 26, 1941, constituted farm marketing excess, subject to a penalty of 49 cents a bushel, or $117.11 in all. The appellee has not paid the penalty and he has not postponed or avoided it by storing the excess under regulations of the Secretary of Agriculture, or by delivering it up to the Secretary. The Committee, therefore, refused him a marketing card, which was, under the terms of Regulations promulgated by the Secretary, necessary to protect a buyer from liability to the penalty and upon its protecting lien.

* * *

It is urged that under the Commerce Clause of the Constitution, Article I, § 8, clause 3, Congress does not possess the power it has in this instance sought to exercise. The question would merit little consideration since our decision in *United States v. Darby,* [1941], sustaining the federal power to regulate production of goods for commerce, except for the fact that this Act extends federal regulation to production not intended in any part for commerce but wholly for consumption on the farm. The Act includes a definition of "market" and its derivatives, so that as related to wheat, in addition to its conventional meaning, it also means to dispose of "by feeding (in any form) to poultry or livestock which, or the products of which, are sold, bartered, or exchanged, or to be so disposed of." Hence, marketing quotas not only embrace all that may be sold without penalty but also what may be consumed on the premises. Wheat produced on excess acreage is designated as "available for marketing" as so defined, and the penalty is imposed thereon. Penalties do not depend upon whether any part of the wheat, either within or without the quota, is sold or intended to be sold. The sum of this is that the Federal Government fixes a quota including all that the farmer may harvest for sale or for his own farm needs, and declares that wheat produced on excess acreage may neither be disposed of nor used except upon payment of the penalty, or except it is stored as required by the Act or delivered to the Secretary of Agriculture.

Appellee says that this is a regulation of production and consumption of wheat. Such activities are, he urges, beyond the reach of Congressional power under the Commerce Clause, since they are local in character, and their effects upon interstate commerce are at most "indirect." In answer the Government argues that the statute regulates neither production nor consumption, but only marketing; and, in the alternative, that if the Act does go beyond the regulation of marketing it is sustainable as a "necessary and proper" implementation of the power of Congress over interstate commerce.

* * *

It was not until 1887, with the enactment of the Interstate Commerce Act, that the interstate commerce power began to exert positive influence in American law and life. This first important federal resort to the commerce power was followed in 1890 by the Sherman Anti-Trust Act and, thereafter, mainly after 1903, by many others. These statutes ushered in new phases of adjudication, which required the Court to approach the interpretation of the Commerce Clause in the light of an actual exercise by Congress of its power thereunder.

. . . It was soon demonstrated that the effects of many kinds of intrastate activity upon interstate commerce were such as to make them a proper subject of federal regulation. In some cases sustaining the exercise of federal power over intrastate matters the term "direct" was used for the purpose of stating, rather than of reaching, a result; in others it was treated as synonymous with "substantial" or "material"; and in others it was not used at all. Of late its use has been abandoned in cases dealing with questions of federal power under the Commerce Clause.

* * *

The Court's recognition of the relevance of the economic effects in the application of the Commerce Clause, . . . has made the mechanical application of legal formulas no longer feasible. Once an economic measure of the reach of the power granted to Congress in the Commerce Clause is accepted, questions of federal power cannot be decided simply by finding the activity in question to be "production," nor can consideration of its economic effects be foreclosed by calling them "indirect.". . .

Whether the subject of the regulation in question was "production," "consumption," or "marketing" is, therefore, not material for purposes of deciding the question of federal power before us. That an activity is of local character may help in a doubtful case to determine whether Congress intended to reach it. The same consideration might help in determining whether in the absence of Congressional action it would be permissible for the state to exert its power on the subject matter, even though in so doing it to some degree affected interstate commerce. But even if appellee's activity be local and though it may not be regarded as commerce, it may still, whatever its nature, be reached by Congress if it exerts a substantial economic effect on interstate commerce, and this irrespective of whether such effect is what might at some earlier time have been defined as "direct" or "indirect."

* * *

The wheat industry has been a problem industry for some years. Largely as a result of increased foreign production and import restrictions, annual exports of wheat and flour from the United States during the ten-year period ending in 1940 averaged less than 10 per cent of total production, while during the 1920's they averaged more than 25 per cent. The decline in the export trade has left a large surplus in production which, in connection with an abnormally large supply of wheat and other grains in recent years, caused congestion in a number of markets; tied up railroad cars; and caused elevators in some instances to turn away grains, and railroads to institute embargoes to prevent further congestion. . . .

In the absence of regulation, the price of wheat in the United States would be much affected by world conditions. During 1941, producers who coöperated with the Agricultural Adjustment program received an average price on the farm of about $1.16 a bushel, as compared with the world market price of 40 cents a bushel.

Differences in farming conditions, however, make these benefits mean different things to different wheat growers. There are several large areas of specialization in wheat, and the concentration on this crop reaches 27 per cent of the crop land, and the average harvest runs as high as 155 acres. Except for some use of wheat as stock feed and for seed, the practice is to sell the crop for cash. Wheat from such areas constitutes the bulk of the interstate commerce therein.

On the other hand, in some New England states less than one per cent of the crop land is devoted to wheat, and the average harvest is less than five acres per farm. In 1940 the average percentage of the total wheat production that was sold in each state, as measured by value, ranged from 29 per cent thereof in Wisconsin to 90 per cent in Washington. Except in regions of large-scale production, wheat is usually grown in rotation with other crops; for a nurse crop for grass seeding; and as a cover crop to prevent soil erosion and leaching. Some is sold, some kept for seed, and a percentage of the total production much larger than in areas of specialization is consumed on the farm and grown for such purpose. Such farmers, while growing some wheat, may even find the balance of their interest on the consumer's side.

The effect of consumption of home-grown wheat on interstate commerce is due to the fact that it constitutes the most variable factor in the disappearance of the wheat crop. Consumption on the farm where grown appears to vary in an amount greater than 20 per cent of average production. The total amount of wheat consumed as food varies but relatively little, and use as seed is relatively constant.

The maintenance by government regulation of a price for wheat undoubtedly can be accomplished as effectively by sustaining or increasing the demand as by limiting the supply. The effect of the statute before us is to restrict the amount which may be produced for market and the extent as well to which one may forestall resort to the market by producing to meet his own needs. That appellee's own contribution to the demand for wheat may be trivial by itself is not enough to remove him from the scope of federal regulation where, as here, his contribution, taken together with that of many others similarly situated, is far from trivial.

It is well established by decisions of this Court that the power to regulate commerce includes the power to regulate the prices at which commodities in that commerce are dealt in and practices affecting such prices. One of the primary purposes of the Act in question was to increase the market price of wheat, and to that end to limit the volume thereof that could affect the market. It can hardly be denied that a factor of such volume and variability as home-consumed wheat would have a substantial influence on price and market conditions. This may arise because being in marketable condition such wheat overhangs the market and, if induced by rising prices, tends to flow into the market and check price increases. But if we assume that it is never marketed, it supplies a need of the man who grew it which would otherwise be reflected by purchases in the open market. Home-grown wheat in this sense competes with wheat in commerce. The stimulation of commerce is a use of the regulatory function quite as definitely as prohibitions or restrictions thereon. This record leaves us in no doubt that Congress may properly have considered that wheat consumed on the farm where grown, if wholly outside the scheme of regulation, would have a substantial effect in defeating and obstructing its purpose to stimulate trade therein at increased prices.

* * *

The statute is also challenged as a deprivation of property without due process of law contrary to the Fifth Amendment, both because of its regulatory effect on the appellee and because of its alleged retroactive effect. . . .

That appellee is the worse off for the aggregate of this legislation does not appear; it only appears that, if he could get all that the Government gives and do nothing that the Government asks, he would be better off than this law allows. To deny him this is not to deny him due process of law. Cf. *Mulford v. Smith*, [1939].

Reversed.

QUESTIONS AND COMMENTS

1 Conceptually, does "stream of commerce" differ from the "indirect" effect on commerce which the Court found outside the powers of Congress to regulate in earlier cases? Where does the Tenth Amendment fit in all this? Is the operation of a steel mill less of a local activity than the coal mines in *Carter v. Carter Coal*? Does *N.L.R.B. v. Jones and Laughlin Steel* bring all manufacturing industries into the ambit of the commerce power? Cf. *N.L.R.B. v. Friedman-Harry Marks Clothing Co.*, (1937).

2 Can you identify any justices who changed positions between *Carter Coal* and *N.L.R.B. v. Jones and Laughlin Steel*?

3 What role did the possibility of strikes or other forms of industrial strife play in the Court's decision in *N.L.R.B. v. Jones and Laughlin Steel*? What do such considerations have to do with interpreting the Constitution?

4 How would you explain the fact that *N.L.R.B. v. Jones and Laughlin Steel* was decided by a 5–4 vote while *United States v. Darby* was decided unanimously?

5 Would it be correct to say that *United States v. Darby* overruled *Hammer v. Dagenhart* sub silentio? Why or why not?

6 Would John Marshall have voted with the majority in *United States v. Darby*? Why do you say so? Would Marshall have joined the rationale of the majority to support his decision? Why do you say so?

7 What is the relationship of *Brooks v. United States* to *United States v. Darby*?

8 After *Wickard v. Filburn*, is it possible to distinguish intrastate and interstate commerce? How would you make the distinction?

9 Is marijuana grown in indoor pots for consumption only by the grower subject to the power of Congress to regulate interstate commerce? What cases would you cite for your answer? Why?

10 After *Wickard v. Filburn*, what checks on the commerce power remained? Be specific.

After the Court's decision in *Wickard,* Congress seemed to possess the power, under the commerce clause, to indirectly regulate or prohibit activities which occurred solely within the boundaries of a single state. The fact that the activities might be noncommercial was not a bar as long as they had a substantial relationship to interstate commerce. The key word is *substantial,* and the cases subsequent to 1936 indicate a great reluctance on the part of the Court to question congressional determination of its meaning. The prevailing view up to 1976 was that the reach of Congress under the commerce clause was plenary and extended to any activity that might affect interstate commerce at present or in the future. The apparent "local" nature of the activity had no effect on this principle. In 1976, however, the Court decided *National League of Cities v. Usery,* a case in which we learn that as broad as the Court has interpreted the commerce power of Congress to be, it is not totally without limits.

National League of Cities, et al. v. Usery, Secretary of Labor

426 U.S. 833; 96 S. Ct. 2465; 49 L. Ed. 2d 245 (1976)
Vote: 5–4

The facts are given in the opinion below.

Mr. Justice Rehnquist delivered the opinion of the Court.

Nearly 40 years ago Congress enacted the Fair Labor Standards Act, and required employers covered by the Act to pay their employees a minimum hourly wage and to pay them at one and one-half times their regular rate of pay for hours worked in excess of 40 during a workweek. By this Act covered employers were required to keep certain records to aid in the enforcement of the Act, and to comply with specified child labor standards. This Court unanimously upheld the Act as a valid exercise of congressional authority under the commerce power in *United States v. Darby,* (1941). . . .

The original Fair Labor Standards Act passed in 1938 specifically excluded the States and their political subdivisions from its coverage. In 1974, however, Congress enacted the most recent of a series of broadening amendments to the Act. By these amendments Congress has extended the minimum wage and maximum hour provisions to almost all public employees employed by the States and by their various political subdivisions. Appellants in these cases include individual cities and States, the National League of Cities, and the National Governors' Conference; they brought an action in the District Court for the District of Columbia which challenged the validity of the 1974 amendments. . . .

In a series of amendments beginning in 1961 Congress began to extend the provisions of the Fair Labor Standards Act to some types of public employees. The 1961 amendments to the Act extended its coverage to persons who were employed in "enterprises" engaged in commerce or in the production of goods for commerce. And in 1966, with the amendment of the definition of employers under the Act, the exemption heretofore extended to the States and their political subdivisions was removed with respect to employees of state hospitals, institutions, and schools. We nevertheless sustained the validity of the combined effect of these two amendments in *Maryland v. Wirtz,* (1968). . . .

[In the present case] . . . appellants sought both declaratory and injunctive relief against the amendments' application to them, and a three-judge court was accordingly convened pursuant to 28 U. S. C. § 2282. That court, after hearing argument on the law from the parties, granted appellee Secretary of Labor's motion to dismiss the complaint for failure to state a claim upon which relief might be granted. The District Court stated it was "troubled" by appellants' contentions that the amendments would intrude upon the States' performance of essential governmental functions. The court went on to say that it considered their contentions

> substantial and that it may well be that the Supreme Court will feel it appropriate to draw back from the far-reaching implications of [*Maryland v. Wirtz, supra*]; but that is a decision that only the Supreme Court can make, and as a Federal district court we feel obliged to apply the Wirtz opinion as it stands. . . .

We agree with the District Court that the appellants' contentions are substantial. Indeed upon full consideration of the question we have decided that the "far-reaching implications" of *Wirtz* should be overruled, and that the judgment of the District Court must be reversed.

* * *

Appellants in no way challenge . . . decisions establishing the breadth of authority granted Congress under the commerce power. Their contention, on the contrary, is that when Congress seeks to regulate directly the activities of States as public employers, it transgresses an affirmative limitation on the exercise of its power akin to other commerce power affirmative limitations contained in the Constitution. Congressional enactments which may be fully within the grant of legislative authority contained in the Commerce Clause may nonetheless be invalid because found to offend against the right to trial by jury contained in the Sixth Amendment, *United States v. Jackson,* (1968), or the Due Process Clause of the Fifth Amendment, *Leary v. United States,* (1969). Appellants' essential contention is that the 1974 amendments to the Act, while undoubtedly within the scope of the Commerce Clause, encounter a similar constitutional barrier because they are to be applied directly to the States and subdivisions of States as employers.

This Court has never doubted that there are limits upon the power of Congress to override state sovereignty, even when exercising its otherwise plenary powers to tax or to regulate commerce which are conferred by Art. I of the Constitution. In *Wirtz,* for example, the Court took care to assure the appellants that it had "ample power to prevent . . . 'the utter destruction of the State as a sovereign political entity,'" which they feared. Appellee Secretary in this case, both in his brief and upon oral argument, has agreed that our federal system of government imposes definite limits upon the authority of Congress to regulate the activities of the States as States by means of the commerce power.

In *Fry v. United States,* [1975], the Court recognized that an express declaration of this limitation is found in the Tenth Amendment:

> While the Tenth Amendment has been characterized as a 'truism,' stating merely that 'all is retained which has not been surrendered,' *United States v. Darby,* (1941), it is not without significance. The Amendment expressly declares the constitutional policy that Congress may not exercise power in a fashion that impairs the States' integrity or their ability to function effectively in a federal system. . . .

One undoubted attribute of state sovereignty is the States' power to determine the wages which shall be paid to those whom they employ in order to carry out their governmental functions, what hours those persons will work, and what compensation will be provided where these employees may be called upon to work overtime. The question we must resolve here, then, is whether these determinations are " 'functions essential to separate and independent existence,'". . .so that Congress may not abrogate the States' otherwise plenary authority to make them.

In their complaint appellants advanced estimates of substantial costs which will be imposed upon them by the 1974 amendments. Since the District Court dismissed their complaint, we take its well-pleaded allegations as true, although it appears from appellee's submissions in the District Court and in this Court that resolution of the factual disputes as to the effect of the amendments is not critical to our disposition of the case.

Judged solely in terms of increased costs in dollars, these allegations show a significant impact on the functioning of the governmental bodies involved. The Metropolitan Government of Nashville and Davidson County, Tenn., for example, asserted that the Act will increase its costs of providing essential police and fire protection, without any increase in service or in current salary levels, by $938,000 per year. Cape Girardeau, Mo., estimated that its annual budget for fire protection may have to be increased by anywhere from $250,000 to $400,000 over the current figure of $350,000. The State of Arizona alleged that the annual additional expenditures which will be required if it is to continue to provide essential state services may total $2.5 million. The State of California, which must devote significant portions of its budget to fire-suppression endeavors, estimated that application of the Act to its employment practices will necessitate an increase in its budget of between $8 million and $16 million.

Increased costs are not, of course, the only adverse effects which compliance with the Act will visit upon state and local governments, and in turn upon the citizens who depend upon those governments. In its complaint in intervention, for example, California asserted that it could not comply with the overtime costs (approximately $750,000 per year) which the Act required to be paid to California Highway Patrol cadets during their academy training program. California reported that it had thus been forced to reduce its academy training program from 2,080 hours to only 960 hours, a compromise undoubtedly of substantial importance to those whose safety and welfare may depend upon the preparedness of the California Highway Patrol.

This type of forced relinquishment of important governmental activities is further reflected in the complaint's allegation that the city of Inglewood, Cal., has been forced to curtail its affirmative action program for providing employment opportunities for men and women interested in a career in law enforcement. The Inglewood police department has abolished a program for police trainees who split their week between on-the-job training and the classroom. The city could not abrogate its contractual obligations to these trainees, and it concluded that compliance with the Act in these circumstances was too financially burdensome to permit continuance of the classroom program. The city of Clovis, Cal., has been put to a similar choice regarding an internship program it was running in cooperation with a California state university. According to the complaint, because the interns' compensation brings them within the purview of the Act the city must decide whether to eliminate the program entirely or to substantially reduce its beneficial aspects by doing away with any pay for the interns.

* * *

It may well be that as a matter of economic policy it would be desirable that States, just as private employers, comply with these minimum wage requirements. But it cannot be gainsaid that the federal requirement directly supplants the considered policy choices of the States' elected officials and administrators as to how they wish to structure pay scales in state employment. . . .

The degree to which the FLSA amendments would interfere with traditional aspects of state sovereignty can be seen even more clearly upon examining the overtime requirements of the Act. The general effect of these provisions is to require the States to pay their employees at premium rates whenever their work exceeds a specified number of hours in a given period. The asserted reason for these provisions is to provide a financial disincentive upon using employees beyond the work period deemed appropriate by Congress. According to appellee:

> This premium rate can be avoided if the [State] uses other employees to do the overtime work. This, in effect, tends to discourage overtime work and to spread employment, which is the result Congress intended.

We do not doubt that this may be a salutary result, and that it has a sufficiently rational relationship to commerce to validate the application of the overtime provisions to private employers. But, like the minimum wage provisions, the vice of the Act as sought to be applied here is that it directly penalizes the States for choosing to hire governmental employees on terms different from those which Congress has sought to impose.

* * *

Our examination of the effect of the 1974 amendments, as sought to be extended to the States and their political subdivisions, satisfies us that both the minimum wage and the maximum hour provisions will impermissibly interfere with the integral governmental functions of these bodies. We earlier noted some disagreement between the parties regarding the precise effect the amendments will have in application. We do not believe particularized assessments of actual impact are crucial to resolution of the issue presented, however. For even if we accept appellee's assessments concerning the impact of the amendments, their application will nonetheless significantly alter or displace the States' abilities to structure employer-employee relationships in such areas as fire prevention, police protection, sanitation, public health, and parks and recreation. These activities are typical of those performed by state and local governments in discharging their dual functions of administering the public law and furnishing public services. Indeed, it is functions such as these which governments are created to provide, services such as these which the States have traditionally afforded their citizens. If Congress may withdraw from the States the authority to make those fundamental employment decisions upon which their systems for performance of these functions must rest, we think there would be little left of the States' " 'separate and independent existence.' "

Thus, even if appellants may have overestimated the effect which the Act will have upon their current levels and patterns of governmental activity, the dispositive factor is that Congress has attempted to exercise its Commerce Clause authority to prescribe minimum wages and maximum hours to be paid by the States in their capacities as sovereign governments. In so doing, Congress has sought to wield its power in a fashion that would impair the States' "ability to function effectively in a federal system."

This exercise of congressional authority does not comport with the federal system of government embodied in the Constitution. We hold that insofar as the challenged amendments operate to directly displace the States' freedom to structure integral operations in areas of traditional governmental functions, they are not within the authority granted Congress by Art. I, § 8, cl. 3.

* * *

One final matter requires our attention. Appellee has vigorously urged that we cannot, consistently with the Court's decisions in *Maryland v. Wirtz,* (1968), and *Fry, supra,* rule against him here. It is important to examine this contention so that it will be clear what we hold today, and what we do not.

With regard to *Fry,* we disagree with appellee. There the Court held that the Economic Stabilization Act of 1970 was constitutional as applied to temporarily freeze the wages of state and local government employees.

* * *

We think our holding today quite consistent with *Fry.* The enactment at issue there was occasioned by an extremely serious problem which endangered the well-being of all the component parts of our federal system and which only collective action by the National Government might forestall. The means selected were carefully drafted so as not to interfere with the States' freedom beyond a very limited, specific period of time. The effect of the across-the-board freeze authorized by that Act, moreover, displaced no state choices as to how governmental operations should be structured, nor did it force the States to remake such choices themselves. Instead, it merely required that the wage scales and employment relationships which the States themselves had chosen be maintained during the period of the emergency. Finally, the Economic Stabilization Act operated to reduce the pressures upon state budgets rather than increase them. These factors distinguish the statute in *Fry* from the provisions at issue here. The limits imposed upon the commerce power when Congress seeks to apply it to the States are not so inflexible as to preclude temporary enactments tailored to combat a national emergency. "[A]lthough an emergency may not call into life a power which has never lived, nevertheless emergency may afford a reason for the exertion of a living power already enjoyed." *Wilson v. New,* (1917).

With respect to the Court's decision in *Wirtz,* we reach a different conclusion. Both appellee and the District Court thought that decision required rejection of appellants' claims. Appellants, in turn, advance several arguments by which they seek to distinguish the facts before the Court in *Wirtz* from those presented by the 1974 amendments to the Act. There are undoubtedly factual distinctions between the two situations, but in view of the conclusions expressed earlier in this opinion we do not believe the reasoning in *Wirtz* may any longer be regarded as authoritative.

Wirtz relied heavily on the Court's decision in *United States v. California,* (1936). The opinion quotes the following language from that case:

> [We] look to the activities in which the states have traditionally engaged as marking the boundary of the restriction upon the federal taxing power. But there is no such limitation upon the plenary power to regulate commerce. The state can no more deny the power if its exercise has been authorized by Congress than can an individual.

But we have reaffirmed today that the States as States stand on a quite different footing from an individual or a corporation when challenging the exercise of Congress' power to regulate commerce. We think the dicta from *United States v. California,* simply wrong. Congress may not exercise that power so as to force directly upon the States its choices as to how essential decisions regarding the conduct of integral governmental functions are to be made. . . . We are therefore persuaded that *Wirtz* must be overruled.

* * *

The judgment of the District Court is accordingly reversed, and the cases are remanded for further proceedings consistent with this opinion.

So ordered.

* * *

MR. JUSTICE BRENNAN, with whom MR. JUSTICE WHITE and MR. JUSTICE MARSHALL join, dissenting.

* * *

My Brethren do not successfully obscure today's patent usurpation of the role reserved for the political process by their purported discovery in the Constitution of a restraint derived from sovereignty of the States on Congress' exercise of the commerce power. Mr. Chief Justice Marshall recognized that limitations "prescribed in the constitution," *Gibbons v. Ogden,* [1824], restrain Congress' exercise of the power. Thus laws within the commerce power may not infringe individual liberties protected by the First Amendment, *Mabee v. White Plains Publishing Co.,* (1946); the Fifth Amendment, *Leary v. United States,* (1969); or the Sixth Amendment, *United States v. Jackson,* (1968). But there is no restraint based on state sovereignty requiring or permitting judicial enforcement anywhere expressed in the Constitution; our decisions over the last century and a half have explicitly rejected the existence of any such restraint on the commerce power. . . .

My Brethren thus have today manufactured an abstraction without substance, founded neither in the words of the Constitution nor on precedent. An abstraction having such profoundly pernicious consequences is not made less so by characterizing the 1974 amendments as legislation directed against the "States *qua* States." Of course, regulations that this Court can say are not regulations of "commerce" cannot stand, *Santa Cruz Fruit Packing Co. v. NLRB,* (1938), and in this sense "[t]he Court has ample power to prevent . . . 'the utter destruction of the State as a sovereign political entity.'" *Maryland v. Wirtz,* (1968). But my Brethren make no claim that the 1974 amendments are not regulations of "commerce"; rather they overrule *Wirtz* in disagreement with historic principles that *United States v. California, supra,* reaffirmed: "[W]hile the commerce power has limits, valid general regulations of commerce do not cease to be regulations of commerce because a State is involved. If a State is engaging in economic activities that are validly regulated by the Federal Government when engaged in by private persons, the State too may be forced to conform its activities to federal regulation." Clearly, therefore, my Brethren are also repudiating the long line of our precedents holding that a judicial finding that Congress has not unreasonably regulated a subject matter of "commerce" brings to an end the judicial role. . . .

The only analysis even remotely resembling that adopted today is found in a line of opinions dealing with the Commerce Clause and the Tenth Amendment that ultimately provoked a constitutional crisis for the Court in the 1930's. *E. g., Carter v. Carter Coal Co.,* (1936); *United States v. Butler,* (1936); *Hammer v. Dagenhart,* (1918).

We tend to forget that the Court invalidated legislation during the Great Depression, not solely under the Due Process Clause, but also and primarily under the Commerce Clause and the Tenth Amendment. It may have been the eventual abandonment of that overly restrictive construction of the commerce power that spelled defeat for the Court-packing plan, and preserved the integrity of this institution, see, e.g., *United States v. Darby,* (1941); *Mulford v. Smith,* (1939); *NLRB v. Jones & Laughlin Steel Corp.,* (1937), but my Brethren today are transparently trying to cut back on that recognition of the scope of the commerce power. . . .

My Brethren do more than turn aside longstanding constitutional jurisprudence that emphatically rejects today's conclusion. More alarming is the startling restructuring of our federal system, and the role they create therein for the federal judiciary. This Court is simply not at liberty to erect a mirror of its own conception of a desirable governmental structure. . . .

It is unacceptable that the judicial process should be thought superior to the political process in this area. Under the Constitution the Judiciary has no role to play beyond finding that Congress has not made an unreasonable legislative judgment respecting what is "commerce." My Brother BLACKMUN suggests that controlling judicial supervision of the relationship between the States and our National Government by use of a balancing approach diminishes the ominous implications of today's decision. Such an approach, however, is a thinly veiled rationalization for judicial supervision of a policy judgment that our system of government reserves to Congress.

* * *

My Brethren's disregard for precedents recognizing these long-settled constitutional principles is painfully obvious in their cavalier treatment of *Maryland v. Wirtz.* Without even a passing reference to the doctrine of *stare decisis, Wirtz*—regarded as controlling only last Term, *Fry v. United States,* [1975], and as good law in *Employees v. Missouri Public Health Dept.,* [1973],—is by exercise of raw judicial power overruled.

No effort is made to distinguish the FLSA amendments sustained in *Wirtz* from the 1974 amendments. We are told at the outset that "the 'far-reaching implications' of *Wirtz* should be overruled." Later it is said that the "reasoning in *Wirtz*" is no longer "authoritative." My Brethren then merely restate their essential-function test and say that *Wirtz* must "therefore" be overruled. There is no analysis whether *Wirtz* reached the correct result, apart from any flaws in reasoning, even though we are told that "there are obvious differences" between this case and *Wirtz.* Are state and federal interests being silently balanced, as in the discussion of *Fry,*. . .The best I can make of it is that the 1966 FLSA amendments are struck down and *Wirtz* is overruled on the basis of the

conceptually unworkable essential-function test; and that the test is unworkable is demonstrated by my Brethren's inability to articulate any meaningful
distinctions among state-operated railroads, state-operated schools and hospitals, and state-operated police and fire departments.

We are left then with a catastrophic judicial body blow at Congress' power
under the Commerce Clause. Even if Congress may nevertheless accomplish
its objectives—for example, by conditioning grants of federal funds upon compliance with federal minimum wage and overtime standards,—there is an ominous portent of disruption of our constitutional structure implicit in today's
mischievous decision. I dissent.

QUESTIONS AND COMMENTS

1 How does the Court's view of the Tenth Amendment in *National League of Cities*
differ from the view taken of that amendment in *United States v. Darby*?

2 In deciding *National League of Cities,* has the Court altered its approach to deciding
cases arising under the commerce clause? Do the three other cases in this section still
constitute good law? Explain your answer.

3 The dissenting justices in *National League of Cities* accuse the majority of usurping
a role reserved for the political process. Can this charge be probatively sustained?
How?

4 Subsequent to *National League of Cities v. Usery,* the Supreme Court's decision in
E.E.O.C. v. Wyoming (1983) suggested that the Court had not abandoned its decades-
long willingness to construe the commerce powers of Congress broadly. In the Wyoming Case, the Court held that Congress could legitimately forbid states to practice
age discrimination in dealing with state employees or prospective employees. Such a
restriction on the states was found constitutional on its face and as applied, and was
not precluded by the external constraints of the Tenth Amendment.

The Court distinguished the principles of *National League of Cities* as follows.
A state's Tenth Amendment immunity, as conferred in *National League of Cities,* is
available only if, through the use of its commerce powers, Congress attempts to (1)
regulate a state as a state, (2) regulate matters that are clearly attributed to state sovereignty, and (3) impose compliance procedures that would impair the state's ability
to "structure integral operations in areas of traditional governmental functions"
(*Hodel v. Virginia Surface Mining and Reclamation Associations,* 452 U.S. 264, 287–
288). The facts in *E.E.O.C.* were found not to meet these three conditions, particularly condition 3.

National League of Cities was overruled in 1985 by a 5–4 vote in *Garcia v. San
Antonio Metropolitan Transit Authority.*

To Tax

In Pursuance of Revenue

Pollock v. Farmer's Loan and Trust Co. (1895)

Article I of the Constitution gives Congress the power to tax. However, no
direct tax is to be levied except in proportion to population. Prior to 1895, it
was generally agreed that the term "direct taxes," as employed in the
Constitution, referred to real estate, poll, and capitation taxes. Thus taxes on

carriages[14] and bank notes[15] were held not to be direct taxes. And in 1880, the Supreme Court decided that the Civil War income tax was an excise tax and therefore not subject to the apportionment requirement.[16] But five years later the Court reviewed the income tax levied via the Wilson-Gorman Tariff Act and reached some startling conclusions. Indeed, the decision was so surprising and produced such vehement criticism that an amendment was added to the Constitution to reverse the Court's decision—i.e., the Sixteenth or so-called Income Tax Amendment. The case of *Pollock v. Farmer's Loan and Trust Co.* is commonly referred to as the Income Tax Case.

Pollock v. Farmer's Loan and Trust Co.

158 U.S. 601; 15 S. Ct. 912; 39 L. Ed. 1108 (1895)
Vote: 5–4

In 1894, Congress passed a proportional income tax on incomes in excess of $4,000 derived, inter alia, from real estate, stocks, and bonds of municipal corporations. The tax was levied on individuals and corporations alike. Farmers Loan and Trust Company was a corporation whose income was subject to the tax. Charles Pollock was a stockholder in the company. He sued the company to prevent payment of the tax, arguing that the tax was unconstitutional.

MR. CHIEF JUSTICE FULLER delivered the opinion of the court.

* * *

The Constitution prohibits any direct tax, unless in proportion to numbers as ascertained by the census; and, in the light of the circumstances to which we have referred, is it not an evasion of that prohibition to hold that a general unapportioned tax, imposed upon all property owners as a body for or in respect of their property, is not direct, in the meaning of the Constitution, because confined to the income therefrom?

Whatever the speculative views of political economists or revenue reformers may be, can it be properly held that the Constitution, taken in its plain and obvious sense, and with due regard to the circumstances attending the formation of the government, authorizes a general unapportioned tax on the products of the farm and the rents of real estate, although imposed merely because of ownership and with no possible means of escape from payment, as belonging to a totally different class from that which includes the property from whence the income proceeds?

There can be but one answer, unless the constitutional restriction is to be treated as utterly illusory and futile, and the object of its framers defeated. We find it impossible to hold that a fundamental requisition, deemed so important as to be enforced by two provisions, one affirmative and one negative, can be refined away by forced distinctions between that which gives value to property, and the property itself.

Nor can we perceive any ground why the same reasoning does not apply to capital in personalty held for the purpose of income or ordinarily yielding income, and to the income therefrom. All the real estate of the country, and all its invested personal property, are open to the direct operation of the taxing power if an apportionment be made according to the Constitution. The Constitution does not say that no direct tax shall be laid by apportionment on any other property than land; on the contrary, it forbids all unapportioned direct taxes; and we know of no warrant for excepting personal property from the exercise of the power, or any reason why an apportioned direct tax cannot be laid and assessed, as Mr. Gallatin said in his report when Secretary of the Treasury in 1812, "upon the same objects of taxation on which the direct taxes levied under the authority of the State are laid and assessed."

* * *

Nor are we impressed with the contention that, because in the four instances in which the power of direct taxation has been exercised, Congress did not see fit, for reasons of expediency, to levy a tax upon personalty, this amounts to such a practical construction of the Constitution that the power did not exist, that we must regard ourselves bound by it. We should regret to be compelled to hold the powers of the general government thus restricted, and certainly cannot accede to the idea that the Constitution has become weakened by a particular course of inaction under it.

The stress of the argument is thrown, however, on the assertion that an income tax is not a property tax at all; that it is not a real estate tax, or a crop tax, or a bond tax; that it is an assessment upon the taxpayer on account of his moneyspending power as shown by his revenue for the year preceding the assessment; that rents received, crops harvested, interest collected, have lost all connection with their origin, and although once not taxable have become transmuted in their new form into taxable subject-matter; in other words, that income is taxable irrespective of the source from whence it is derived. [But] in *Weston v. Charleston* [1829] the Court rejected it. . . .

We have unanimously held in this case that, so far as this law operates on the receipts from municipal bonds, it cannot be sustained, because it is a tax on the power of the States, and on their instrumentalities to borrow money, and consequently repugnant to the Constitution. But if, as contended, the interest when received has become merely money in the recipient's pocket, and taxable as such without reference to the source from which it came, the question is immaterial whether it could have been originally taxed at all or not. This was admitted by the Attorney General with characteristic candor; and it follows that, if the revenue derived from municipal bonds cannot be taxed because the source cannot be, the same rule applies to revenue from any other source not subject to the tax; and the lack of power to levy any but an apportioned tax on real and personal property equally exists as to the revenue therefrom.

Admitting that this act taxes the income of property irrespective of its source, still we cannot doubt that such a tax is necessarily a direct tax in the meaning of the Constitution.

* * *

We have considered the act only in respect of the tax on income derived from real estate, and from invested personal property, and have not commented on so much of it as bears on gains or profits from business, privileges, or employments, in view of the instances in which taxation on business, privileges, or employments has assumed the guise of an excise tax and been sustained as such.

Being of opinion that so much of the sections of this law as lays a tax on income from real and personal property is invalid, we are brought to the question of the effect of that conclusion upon these sections as a whole.

It is elementary that the same statute may be in part constitutional and in part unconstitutional, and if the parts are wholly independent of each other, that which is constitutional may stand while that which is unconstitutional will be rejected. And in the case before us there is no question as to the validity of this act, except sections twenty-seven to thirty-seven, inclusive, which relate to the subject which has been under discussion; and as to them we think the rule laid down by Chief Justice Shaw in *Warren v. Charlestown*, . . . applicable, that if the different parts "are so mutually connected with and dependent on each other, as conditions, considerations or compensations for each other, as to warrant a belief that the legislature intended them as a whole, and that, if all could not be carried into effect, the legislature would not pass the residue independently, and some parts are unconstitutional, all the provisions which are thus dependent, conditional or connected, must fall with them."

* * *

Our conclusions may, therefore, be summed up as follows:

First. We adhere to the opinion already announced, that, taxes on real estate being indisputably direct taxes, taxes on the rents or income of real estate are equally direct taxes.

Second. We are of opinion that taxes on personal property, or on the income of personal property, are likewise direct taxes.

Third. The tax imposed by sections twenty-seven to thirty-seven, inclusive, of the act of 1894, so far as it falls on the income of real estate and of personal property, being a direct tax within the meaning of the Constitution, and, therefore, unconstitutional and void because not apportioned according to representation, all those sections, constituting one entire scheme of taxation, are necessarily invalid.

The decrees hereinbefore entered in this court will be vacated; the decrees below will be reversed, and the cases remanded, with instructions to grant the relief prayed.

MR. JUSTICE HARLAN dissenting.

*   *   *

Let us examine the grounds upon which the decision of the majority rests, and look at some of the consequences that may result from the principles now announced. I have a deep, abiding conviction, which my sense of duty compels me to express, that it is not possible for this court to have rendered any judgment more to be regretted than the one just rendered.

Assuming it to be the settled construction of the Constitution that the general government cannot tax *lands, co nomine,* except by apportioning the tax among the States according to their respective numbers, does it follow that a tax on *incomes* derived from *rents* is a *direct* tax *on the real estate* from which such rents arise?

In my judgment a tax on *income* derived from real property ought not to be, and until now has never been, regarded by any court as a direct tax on such property within the meaning of the Constitution. As the great mass of lands in most of the States do not bring any rents, and as incomes from rents vary in the different States, such a tax cannot possibly be apportioned among the States on the basis merely of numbers with any approach to equality of right among taxpayers, any more than a tax on carriages or other personal property could be so apportioned. And, in view of former adjudications, beginning with the *Hylton case* and ending with the *Springer case,* a decision now that a tax on income from real property can be laid and collected only by apportioning the same among the States, on the basis of numbers, may, not improperly, be regarded as a judicial revolution, that may sow the seeds of hate and distrust among the people of different sections of our common country. . . .

In determining whether a tax on income from rents is a direct tax, within the meaning of the Constitution, the inquiry is not whether it may in some way indirectly affect the land or the land owner, but whether it is a *direct* tax *on the thing taxed, the land.* The circumstance that such a tax may possibly have the effect to diminish the value of the use of the land is neither decisive of the question nor important. While a tax *on the land* itself, whether at a fixed rate applicable to all lands without regard to their value, or by the acre or according to their market value, might be deemed a direct tax within the meaning of the Constitution as interpreted in the *Hylton case,* a duty on rents is a duty on something distinct and entirely separate from, although issuing out of, the land.

*   *   *

It has been well observed, on behalf of the government, that rents have nothing in common with land: that taking wrongful possession of land is trespass, while the taking of rent may, under some circumstances, be stealing; that the land goes to the heir while the rent-money goes to the personal representative; one has a fixed *situs*; that of the other may be determined by law, but generally is that of the owner; that one is taxed, and can be taxed only, by the sovereignty within which it lies, while the other may be taxed, and can be taxed only, by the sovereignty under whose dominion the owner is; that a tax on land is generally a *lien* on the land, while that on personalty almost universally is not; and that, in their nature, lands and rents arising from land have not a single attribute in common. A tax on land reaches the land itself, whether it is rented or not. The citizen's residence may be reached by a land tax, although he derives no rent from it. But a duty on rents will not reach him, unless he rents his residence to some one else and receives the rent. A tax with respect to the money that a landlord receives for rent is personal to him, because it relates to his revenue from a designated source, and does not, in any sense— unless it be otherwise provided by statute—rest on the land. The tax in question was laid without reference to the land of the taxpayer; for the amount of rent is a subject of contract, and is not always regulated by the intrinsic value of the source from which the rent arises. In its essence it is a tax with reference only to income received.

* * *

In my judgment—to say nothing of the disregard of the former adjudications of this court, and of the settled practice of the government—this decision may well excite the gravest apprehensions. It strikes at the very foundations of national authority, in that it denies to the general government a power which is, or may become, vital to the very existence and preservation of the Union in a national emergency, such as that of war with a great commercial nation, during which the collection of all duties upon imports will cease or be materially diminished. It tends to reëstablish that condition of helplessness in which Congress found itself during the period of the Articles of Confederation, when it was without authority by laws operating directly upon individuals, to lay and collect, through its own agents, taxes sufficient to pay the debts and defray the expenses of government, but was dependent, in all such matters, upon the good will of the States, and their promptness in meeting requisitions made upon them by Congress. . . .

But this is not all. The decision now made may provoke a contest in this country from which the American people would have been spared if the court had not overturned its former adjudications, and had adhered to the principles of taxation under which our government, following the repeated adjudications of this court, has always been administered. Thoughtful, conservative men have uniformly held that the government could not be safely administered except upon principles of right, justice, and equality—without discrimination against any part of the people because of their owning or not owning visible property, or because of their having or not having incomes from bonds and stocks. But, by its present construction of the Constitution the court, for the first time in all its history, declares that our government has been so framed that, in matters of taxation for its support and maintenance those who have incomes derived from the renting of real estate or from the leasing or using of tangible personal property, or who own invested personal property, bonds, stocks and investments of whatever kind, have privileges that cannot be accorded to those having incomes derived from the labor of their hands, or the exercise of their skill, or the use of their brains.

It was said in argument that the passage of the statute imposing this income tax was an assault by the poor upon the rich, and by much eloquent speech this court has been urged to stand in the breach for the protection of the just rights of property against the advancing hosts of socialism. With the policy of legislation of this character, this court has nothing to do. That is for the legislative branch of the government. It is for Congress to determine whether the necessities of the government are to be met, or the interests of the people subserved, by the taxation of incomes. With that determination, so far as it rests upon grounds of expediency or public policy, the courts can have no rightful concern. The safety and permanency of our institutions demand that each department of government shall keep within its legitimate sphere as defined by the supreme law of the land. We deal here only with questions of law. Undoubtedly, the present law contains exemptions that are open to objection, but, for reasons to be presently stated, such exemptions may be disregarded without invalidating the entire law and the property so exempted may be reached under the general provisions of the statute.

If it were true that this legislation, in its important aspects and in its essence, discriminated against the rich, because of their wealth, the court, in vindication of the equality of all before the law, might well declare that the statute was not an exercise of the power of *taxation,* but was repugnant to those principles of natural right upon which our free institutions rest, and, therefore, was legislative spoliation, under the guise of taxation. But it is not of that character. There is no foundation for the charge that this statute was framed in sheer hostility to the wealth of the country. The provisions most liable to objection are those exempting from taxation large amounts of accumulated capital, particularly that represented by savings banks, mutual insurance companies, and loan associations. Surely such exemptions do not indicate sympathy on the part of the legislative branch of the government with the pernicious theories of socialism, nor show that Congress had any purpose to despoil the rich. . . .

We are told in argument that the burden of this income tax, if collected, will fall, and was imposed that it might fall, almost entirely upon the people of a few States, and that it has been imposed by the votes of Senators and Representatives of States whose people will pay relatively a very small part of it. This suggestion, it is supposed, throws light upon the construction to be given to the Constitution, and constitutes a sufficient reason why this court should strike down the provision that Congress has made for an income tax. It is a suggestion that ought never to have been made in a court of justice. But it seems to have received some consideration; for, it is said that the grant of the power to lay and collect direct taxes was, in the belief of the framers of the

Constitution, that it would not be exercised "unfairly and discriminately, as to particular States or otherwise, by a mere majority vote, possibly of those whose constituents were intentionally not subjected to any part of the burden." It is cause for profound regret that it has been deemed appropriate to intimate that the law now before us had its origin in a desire upon the part of a majority in the two Houses of Congress to impose undue burdens upon the people of particular States.

I am unable to perceive that the performance of our duty should depend, in any degree, upon an inquiry as to the residence of the persons who are required by the statute to pay this income tax.

... Arguments that rest upon favoritism by the law-making power to particular sections of the country and to mere property, or to particular kinds of property, do not commend themselves to my mind; for, they cannot but tend to arouse a conflict that may result in giving life, energy, and power as well to those in our midst who are eager to array section against section as to those, unhappily not few in number, who are without any proper idea of our free institutions, and who have neither respect for the rights of property nor any conception of what is liberty regulated by law.

* * *

I cannot assent to an interpretation of the Constitution that impairs and cripples the just powers of the National Government in the essential matter of taxation, and at the same time discriminates against the greater part of the people of our country.

The practical effect of the decision to-day is to give to certain kinds of property a position of favoritism and advantage inconsistent with the fundamental principles of our social organization, and to invest them with power and influence that may be perilous to that portion of the American people upon whom rests the larger part of the burdens of the government, and who ought not to be subjected to the dominion of aggregated wealth any more than the property of the country should be at the mercy of the lawless.

I dissent from the opinion and judgment of the court.

QUESTIONS AND COMMENTS

1 What is a capitation tax?

2 In 1937, the Supreme Court held that taxes on income from real estate are not taxes on real estate (*New York ex rel Cohn v. Graves*). In *Pollock,* on the other hand, Chief Justice Fuller says that "taxes on real estate being ... direct taxes, taxes on the rents or incomes of real estate are equally direct taxes." The effect of the 1937 ruling is to overrule *Pollock.* Does this mean that the Sixteenth Amendment was not needed and that it was a mistake to adopt it?

3 Since *Pollock,* the Court has identified federal taxes on gifts, tobacco, estates, and sugar refining as "indirect" or excise taxes not subject to the apportionment requirement.

In Pursuance of Social and Economic Policies

McCray v. United States (1904)

United States v. Doremus (1919)

United States v. Butler (1936)

Helvering v. Davis (1937)

When Congress raises revenue through the use of its taxing power, that revenue goes into the United States Treasury for general spending purposes. On the other hand, Congress may wish to earmark the receipts accruing under a particular tax measure for a specific social purpose. If the purpose of a tax is to raise revenue, no question is likely to arise, given the clear delegation of that power in Article I. The use of the taxing power to accomplish a legislative goal may be another matter. The provisions of the Constitution granting the taxing power do not specify that it may be used for nonrevenue purposes. While the necessary and proper clause may imply the power to tax in order to raise and maintain armies, to coin money, to establish post offices, or to carry out any of the other explicitly delegated powers, the earmarking of tax receipts for social purposes not even dreamed of by the framers raises a different kind of question.

This "new" use of the taxing power may seek to operate on either the civil or the criminal side of the law. In *United States v. Doremus,* Congress was concerned with narcotics. In *United States v. Kahriger,* it was concerned with gambling. In such cases, the Court is likely to give Congress considerable leeway. Crime is always a problem, and national crime is a national problem. If Congress can invent a new and reasonable means to deal with such problems, the Court is unlikely to naysay it. This is quite consistent with the cases noted earlier in which Congress was allowed the use of the commerce clause to deal with a national "evil."

When we turn to matters other than traditional crime, the issue becomes more controversial. The evil nature of the act which Congress seeks to discourage or eliminate may not be so clear. Is it evil, for example, to color oleomargarine yellow, for a farmer to produce more of a certain crop than Congress thinks is in the national interest, or for employers to shirk the responsibility for their employees' old age pensions? These are matters discussed in *McCray v. United States, United States v. Butler,* and *Helvering v. Davis.* In each, Congress attempts to use its taxing power to stop or discourage certain practices which it believes not in the social interest. The raising of revenue in each instance is strictly a secondary goal.

The constitutional problem with such a concept relates to the notion of delegated and reserved powers. A reading of the Constitution reminds us that each power delegated to Congress is the power to do something. That something is specified in the assignment itself or, as the Court has held, is implied as a necessary, essential, or reasonable means of realizing a delegated function. This is not troubling if strictly applied. If Congress may coin money, it certainly is free to hire the persons who operate the presses and build the buildings in which to house them. If it may establish post offices, it certainly may issue stamps and do all the other things reasonably associated with operating a postal service. None of this would give the framers pause. But there is no evidence that as the framers delegated each power to accomplish a certain end, they debated, understood, and approved all the unnamed purposes to which a specific power might be put.

Certainly in adopting the power to tax, the framers did not understand themselves to be delegating the power to use taxing authority to accomplish any governmental end that fertile minds could conjure up. Such a conception would be incompatible with the notion of delegated powers—a contradiction in terms. If the extent to which a power may be used to accomplish something other than its designated purpose is not all-inclusive, choices must be made and justified in particular instances. The cases in this section reveal some of those choices and the justifications accompanying them.

McCray v. United States
195 U.S. 27; 24 S. Ct. 769; 49 L. Ed. 78 (1904)
Vote: 6–3

The Oleomargarine Act of 1886, as amended in 1902, imposed a tax of 0.25 percent on oleomargarine when the product was free of artificial coloring causing it to look like butter. Otherwise, the tax was 10 percent. McCray purchased for resale a 50-pound block of yellow oleomargarine without the 10 percent tax stamps affixed as required by the statute. The United States sued for the statutory penalty of 50 percent, alleging that the oleomargarine was artificially colored to "look like butter." In his defense, McCray maintained that the yellow came not from any artificial color but from creamery butter, which constituted over 36 percent of the formula used for the margarine. This butter had previously been "yellowed" by adding a substance known as "Wells-Richardson's improved butter color." In any event, McCray alleged, the statute was in violation of the Fifth and Tenth Amendments.

MR. JUSTICE WHITE . . . delivered the opinion of the court.

* * *

Whilst, as a result of our written constitution, it is axiomatic that the judicial department of the government is charged with the solemn duty of enforcing the Constitution, and therefore in cases properly presented, of determining whether a given manifestation of authority has exceeded the power conferred by that instrument, no instance is afforded from the foundation of the government where an act, which was within a power conferred, was declared to be repugnant to the Constitution, because it appeared to the judicial mind that the particular exertion of constitutional power was either unwise or unjust. To announce such a principle would amount to declaring that in our constitutional system the judiciary was not only charged with the duty of upholding the Constitution but also with the responsibility of correcting every possible abuse arising from the exercise by the other departments of their conceded authority. So to hold would be to overthrow the entire distinction between the legislative, judicial and executive departments of the government, upon which our system is founded, and would be a mere act of judicial usurpation.

It is, however, argued if a lawful power may be exerted for an unlawful purpose, and thus by abusing the power it may be made to accomplish a result not intended by the Constitution, all limitations of power must disappear, and the grave function lodged in the judiciary, to confine all the departments within the authority conferred by the Constitution, will be of no avail. This, when reduced to its last analysis, comes to this, that, because a particular department of the government may exert its lawful powers with the object or motive of reaching an end not justified, therefore it becomes the duty of the judiciary to restrain the exercise of a lawful power wherever it seems to the judicial mind that such lawful power has been abused. But this reduces itself to the contention that, under our constitutional system, the abuse by one department of the government of its lawful powers is to be corrected by the abuse of its powers by another department.

The proposition, if sustained, would destroy all distinction between the powers of the respective departments of the government, would put an end to that confidence and respect for each other which it was the purpose of the Constitution to uphold, and would thus be full of danger to the permanence of our institutions. . . .

The decisions of this court from the beginning lend no support whatever to the assumption that the judiciary may restrain the exercise of lawful power on the assumption that a wrongful purpose or motive has caused the power to be exerted. As we have previously said, from the beginning no case can be found announcing such a doctrine, and on the contrary the doctrine of a number of cases is inconsistent with its existence. . . .

[After reviewing the relevant cases, the Court continued.]

It being thus demonstrated that the motive or purpose of Congress in adopting the acts in question may not be inquired into, we are brought to consider the contentions relied upon to show that the acts assailed were beyond the power of Congress, putting entirely out of view all considerations based upon purpose or motive.

1. Undoubtedly, in determining whether a particular act is within a granted power, its scope and effect are to be considered. Applying this rule to the acts assailed, it is self-evident that on their face they levy an excise tax. That being their necessary scope and operation, it follows that the acts are within the grant of power. The argument to the contrary rests on the proposition that, although the tax be within the power, as enforcing it will destroy or restrict the manufacture of artificially colored oleomargarine, therefore the power to levy the tax

did not obtain. This, however, is but to say that the question of power depends, not upon the authority conferred by the Constitution, but upon what may be the consequence arising from the exercise of the lawful authority.

Since, as pointed out in all the decisions referred to, the taxing power conferred by the Constitution knows no limits except those expressly stated in that instrument, it must follow, if a tax be within the lawful power, the exertion of that power may not be judicially restrained because of the results to arise from its exercise.

* * *

2. The proposition that where a tax is imposed which is within the grant of powers, and which does not conflict with any express constitutional limitation, the courts may hold the tax to be void because it is deemed that the tax is too high, is absolutely disposed of by the opinions in the cases hitherto cited, and which expressly hold, to repeat again the language of one of the cases, (*Spencer v. Merchant,*) that "The judicial department cannot prescribe to the legislative department limitations upon the exercise of its acknowledged powers. The power to tax may be exercised oppressively upon persons; but the responsibility of the legislature is not to the courts, but to the people by whom its members are elected."

3. Whilst undoubtedly both the Fifth and Tenth Amendments qualify, in so far as they are applicable, all the provisions of the Constitution, nothing in those amendments operates to take away the grant of power to tax conferred by the Constitution upon Congress. The contention on this subject rests upon the theory that the purpose and motive of Congress in exercising its undoubted powers may be inquired into by the courts, and the proposition is therefore disposed of by what has been said on that subject.

The right of Congress to tax within its delegated power being unrestrained, except as limited by the Constitution, it was within the authority conferred on Congress to select the objects upon which an excise should be laid. It therefore follows that, in exerting its power, no want of due process of law could possibly result, because that body chose to impose an excise on artificially colored oleomargarine and not upon natural butter artificially colored. The judicial power may not usurp the functions of the legislative in order to control that branch of the government in the performance of its lawful duties. This was aptly pointed out . . . in *Treat v. White,* [1900].

But it is urged that artificially colored oleomargarine and artificially colored natural butter are in substance and in effect one and the same thing, and from this it is deduced that to lay an excise tax only on oleomargarine artificially colored and not on butter so colored is violative of the due process clause of the Fifth Amendment, because, as there is no possible distinction between the two, the act of Congress was a mere arbitrary imposition of an excise on the one article and not on the other, although essentially of the same class. Conceding merely for the sake of argument that the due process clause of the Fifth Amendment, would avoid an exertion of the taxing power which, without any basis for classification, arbitrarily taxed one article and excluded an article of the same class, such concession would be wholly inapposite to the case in hand. The distinction between natural butter artificially colored, and oleomargarine artificially colored so as to cause it to look like butter, has been pointed out in previous adjudications of this court.

* * *

4. Lastly we come to consider the argument that, even though as a general rule a tax of the nature of the one in question would be within the power of Congress, in this case the tax should be held not to be within such power, because of its effect. This is based on the contention that, as the tax is so large as to destroy the business of manufacturing oleomargarine artificially colored, to look like butter, it thus deprives the manufacturers of that article of their freedom to engage in a lawful pursuit, and hence, irrespective of the distribution of powers made by the Constitution, the taxing laws are void, because they violate those fundamental rights which it is the duty of every free government to safeguard, and which, therefore, should be held to be embraced by implied though none the less potential guaranties, or in any event to be within the protection of the due process clause of the Fifth Amendment.

Let us concede, for the sake of argument only, the premise of fact upon which the proposition is based. Moreover, concede for the sake of argument only, that even although a particular exertion of power by Congress was not restrained by any express limitation of the Constitution, if by the perverted exercise of such power so great an abuse was manifested as to destroy fundamental rights which no free government could consistently violate, that it would be the duty of the judiciary to hold such acts to be void upon the assumption that the Constitution by necessary implication forbade them.

Such concession, however, is not controlling in this case. This follows when the nature of oleomargarine, artificially colored to look like butter, is recalled. As we have said, it has been conclusively settled by this court that the tendency of that article to deceive the public into buying it for butter is such that the States may, in the exertion of their police powers, without violating the due process clause of the Fourteenth Amendment, absolutely prohibit the manufacture of the article. It hence results, that even although it be true that the effect of the tax in question is to repress the manufacture of artificially colored oleomargarine, it cannot be said that such repression destroys rights which no free government could destroy, and, therefore, no ground exists to sustain the proposition that the judiciary may invoke an implied prohibition, upon the theory that to do so is essential to save such rights from destruction. And the same considerations dispose of the contention based upon the due process clause of the Fifth Amendment. That provision, as we have previously said, does not withdraw or expressly limit the grant of power to tax conferred upon Congress by the Constitution. From this it follows, as we have also previously declared, that the judiciary is without authority to avoid an act of Congress exerting the taxing power, even in a case where to the judicial mind it seems that Congress had in putting such power in motion abused its lawful authority by levying a tax which was unwise or oppressive, or the result of the enforcement of which might be to indirectly affect subjects not within the powers delegated to Congress.

Let us concede that if a case was presented where the abuse of the taxing power was so extreme as to be beyond the principles which we have previously stated, and where it was plain to the judicial mind that the power had been called into play not for revenue but solely for the purpose of destroying rights which could not be rightfully destroyed consistently with the principles of freedom and justice upon which the Constitution rests, that it would be the duty of the courts to say that such an arbitrary act was not merely an abuse of a delegated power, but was the exercise of an authority not conferred. This concession, however, like the one previously made, must be without influence upon the decision of this cause for the reasons previously stated; that is, that the manufacture of artificially colored oleomargarine may be prohibited by a free government without a violation of fundamental rights.

Affirmed.

The CHIEF JUSTICE, MR. JUSTICE BROWN and MR. JUSTICE PECKHAM dissent.

QUESTIONS AND COMMENTS

1 In *McCray,* Justice White says that "the manufacture of artificially colored oleomargarine may be prohibited by a free government without a violation of fundamental rights." What rights is he talking about? Where does he get these rights?
2 What if the tax on oleomargarine colored yellow had been 90 percent instead of 10 percent? Any different decision?
3 Compare the treatment of the Tenth Amendment in *McCray* with that in *Hammer v. Dagenhart.*

United States v. Doremus

249 U.S. 86; 39 S. Ct. 214; 63 L. Ed. 493 (1919)
Vote: 5–4

Doremus, a physician, was indicted for violation of Section 2 of the Narcotic Drug Act of 191. That act required those who knowingly sell or give away certain drugs to register and pay a special tax. Moreover, any dispensation of the prescribed drugs was limited to persons who presented appropriate forms issued by the commissioner of internal revenue. Those providing drugs under the act were also required to keep specified records and follow the reporting provisions of the act. The act exempted physicians in cases of "personal attendance upon a patient; and . . . [the sale] of the drugs by a dealer upon a prescription issued by a physician."

Doremus allegedly dispensed 500 heroin tablets to one Ameris, a person known by Doremus to be a drug addict. He was charged with doing so, not in pursuit of his professional practice, but for the purpose of satisfying the drug appetite of a habitual drug-user. Doremus persuaded a district court to strike Section 2 of the statute employed against him as unconstitutional. The Supreme Court granted review.

MR. JUSTICE DAY delivered the opinion of the court.

* * *

This statute purports to be passed under the authority of the Constitution, Article I, § 8, which gives the Congress power "To lay and collect taxes, duties, imposts and excises, to pay the debts and provide for the common defence and general welfare of the United States; but all duties, imposts and excises shall be uniform throughout the United States."

The only limitation upon the power of Congress to levy excise taxes of the character now under consideration is geographical uniformity throughout the United States. This court has often declared it cannot add others. Subject to such limitation Congress may select the subjects of taxation, and may exercise the power conferred at its discretion. *License Tax Cases,* [1867]. Of course Congress may not in the exercise of federal power exert authority wholly reserved to the States. Many decisions of this court have so declared. And from an early day the court has held that the fact that other motives may impel the exercise of federal taxing power does not authorize the courts to inquire into that subject. If the legislation enacted has some reasonable relation to the exercise of the taxing authority conferred by the Constitution, it cannot be invalidated because of the supposed motives which induced it. *Veazie Bank v. Fenno,* [1869], in which case this court sustained a tax on a state bank issue of circulating notes. *McCray v. United States,* [1904], where the power was thoroughly considered, and an act levying a special tax upon oleomargarine artificially colored was sustained. . . .

Nor is it sufficient to invalidate the taxing authority given to the Congress by the Constitution that the same business may be regulated by the police power of the State. *License Tax Cases,* [1867].

The act may not be declared unconstitutional because its effect may be to accomplish another purpose as well as the raising of revenue. If the legislation is within the taxing authority of Congress—that is sufficient to sustain it.

The legislation under consideration was before us in a case concerning § 8 of the act, and in the course of the decision we said: "It may be assumed that the statute has a moral end as well as revenue in view, but we are of opinion that the District Court, in treating those ends as to be reached only through a revenue measure and within the limits of a revenue measure, was right." *United States v. Jin Fuey Moy,* [1915]. Considering the full power of Congress over excise taxation the decisive question here is: Have the provisions in question any relation to the raising of revenue? That Congress might levy an excise tax upon such dealers, and others who are named in § 1 of the act, cannot be successfully disputed. The provisions of § 2, to which we have referred, aim to confine sales to registered dealers and to those dispensing the drugs as physicians, and to those who come to dealers with legitimate prescriptions of physicians. Congress, with full power over the subject, short of arbitrary and unreasonable action which is not to be assumed, inserted these provisions in an act specifically providing for the raising of revenue. Considered of themselves, we think they tend to keep the traffic aboveboard and subject to inspection by those authorized to collect the revenue. They tend to diminish the opportunity of unauthorized persons to obtain the drugs and sell them clandestinely without paying the tax imposed by the federal law. This case well illustrates the possibility which may have induced Congress to insert the provisions limiting sales to registered dealers and requiring patients to obtain these drugs as a medicine from physicians or upon regular prescriptions. Ameris, being as the indictment charges an addict, may not have used this great number of doses for himself. He might sell some to others without paying the tax, at least Congress may have deemed it wise to prevent such possible dealings because of their effect upon the collection of the revenue.

We cannot agree with the contention that the provisions of § 2, controlling the disposition of these drugs in the ways described, can have nothing to do with facilitating the collection of the revenue, as we should be obliged to do if we were to declare this act beyond the power of Congress acting under its constitutional authority to impose excise taxes. It follows that the judgment of the District Court must be reversed.

Reversed.

THE CHIEF JUSTICE dissents because he is of opinion that the court below correctly held the act of Congress, in so far as it embraced the matters complained of, to be beyond the constitutional power of Congress to enact because to such extent the statute was a mere attempt by Congress to exert a power not delegated, that is, the reserved police power of the States.

MR. JUSTICE MCKENNA, MR. JUSTICE VAN DEVANTER and MR. JUSTICE MCREYNOLDS concur in this dissent.

As we have noted earlier, *United States v. Butler* came in the Roosevelt era and was one of the cases prompting the President to propose his notorious Court Reform Plan. But the case is also noted for its statement of dual federalism by Justice Roberts. It is also well known as the case in which Roberts spelled out what is sometimes referred to as the "slot machine" theory of judicial decision-making—at least insofar as the decision pertains to the power of Congress under the Constitution. In Roberts's oft-quoted words:

There should be no misunderstanding as to the function of this court. . . . It is sometimes said that the court assumes a power to overrule or control the action of the people's representatives. This is a misconception. The Constitution is the supreme law of the land ordained and established by the people. All legislation must conform to the principles it lays down. When an act of Congress is appropriately challenged in the courts as not conforming to the constitutional mandate, the judicial branch of the Government has only one duty—to lay the article of the Constitution which is invoked beside the statute which is challenged and decide whether the latter squares with the former. All the Court does, or can do, is to announce its considered judgement upon the question. The only power it has, if such it may be called, is the power of judgement. The Court neither approves nor condemns any legislative policy. Its delicate and difficult office is to ascertain and declare whether the legislation is in accordance with, or in contravention of, the provisions of the Constitution; and having done that, its duty ends.

Few students of the Court today would agree with all that Roberts says here. But few would characterize the statement as totally false either.

United States v. Butler, et al., Receivers of Hoosac Mills Corp.

297 U.S. 1; 56 S. Ct. 312; 80 L. Ed. 477 (1936)
Vote: 6–3

The Agricultural Adjustment Act of 1933 sought to persuade farmers to reduce production of certain farm products in order to improve the prices of such products in the marketplace. Encouragement was provided in the form of crop-reduction payments directly to farmers participating in the crop-reduction program. To provide funds for these payments, processing and "floor-stock" taxes were placed on certain processors of farm products, one of which was Hoosac Cotton Mills. Although Hoosac was bankrupt, a district court ordered the receiver for the corporation to pay the taxes owed under the act. A court of appeals reversed. The Supreme Court granted certiorari.

MR. JUSTICE ROBERTS delivered the opinion of the Court.

* * *

First. At the outset the United States contends that the respondents have no standing to question the validity of the tax. The position is that the act is merely a revenue measure levying an excise upon the activity of processing cotton,—a proper subject for the imposition of such a tax,—the proceeds of which go into the federal treasury and thus become available for appropriation for any purpose. It is said that what the respondents are endeavoring to do is to challenge the intended use of the money pursuant to Congressional appropriation when, by confession, that money will have become the property of the Government and the taxpayer will no longer have any interest in it. *Massa-*

chusetts v. Mellon, [1923], is claimed to foreclose litigation by the respondents or other taxpayers, as such, looking to restraint of the expenditure of government funds. That case might be an authority in the petitioners' favor if we were here concerned merely with a suit by a taxpayer to restrain the expenditure of the public moneys. It was there held that a taxpayer of the United States may not question expenditures from its treasury on the ground that the alleged unlawful diversion will deplete the public funds and thus increase the burden of future taxation. Obviously the asserted interest of a taxpayer in the federal government's funds and the supposed increase of the future burden of taxation is minute and indeterminable. But here the respondents who are called upon to pay moneys as taxes, resist the exaction as a step in an unauthorized plan. This circumstance clearly distinguishes the case. . . .

It is inaccurate and misleading to speak of the exaction from processors prescribed by the challenged act as a tax, or to say that as a tax it is subject to no infirmity. A tax, in the general understanding of the term, and as used in the Constitution, signifies an exaction for the support of the Government. The word has never been thought to connote the expropriation of money from one group for the benefit of another. We may concede that the latter sort of imposition is constitutional when imposed to effectuate regulation of a matter in which both groups are interested and in respect of which there is a power of legislative regulation. But manifestly no justification for it can be found unless as an integral part of such regulation. The exaction cannot be wrested out of its setting, denominated an excise for raising revenue and legalized by ignoring its purpose as a mere instrumentality for bringing about a desired end. To do this would be to shut our eyes to what all others than we can see and understand. *Child Labor Tax Case,* [1922].

We conclude that the act is one regulating agricultural production; that the tax is a mere incident of such regulation and that the respondents have standing to challenge the legality of the exaction.

Second. The Government asserts that even if the respondents may question the propriety of the appropriation embodied in the statute their attack must fail because Article I, § 8 of the Constitution authorizes the contemplated expenditure of the funds raised by the tax. This contention presents the great and the controlling question in the case. We approach its decision with a sense of our grave responsibility to render judgment in accordance with the principles established for the governance of all three branches of the Government.

There should be no misunderstanding as to the function of this court in such a case. It is sometimes said that the court assumes a power to overrule or control the action of the people's representatives. This is a misconception. The Constitution is the supreme law of the land ordained and established by the people. All legislation must conform to the principles it lays down. When an act of Congress is appropriately challenged in the courts as not conforming to the constitutional mandate the judicial branch of the Government has only one duty,—to lay the article of the Constitution which is invoked beside the statute which is challenged and to decide whether the latter squares with the former. All the court does, or can do, is to announce its considered judgment upon the question. The only power it has, if such it may be called, is the power of judgment. This court neither approves nor condemns any legislative policy. Its delicate and difficult office is to ascertain and declare whether the legislation is in accordance with, or in contravention of, the provisions of the Constitution; and, having done that, its duty ends.

* * *

Article I, § 8, of the Constitution vests sundry powers in the Congress. But two of its clauses have any bearing upon the validity of the statute under review.

The third clause endows the Congress with power "to regulate Commerce . . . among the several States." Despite a reference in its first section to a burden upon, and an obstruction of the normal currents of commerce, the act under review does not purport to regulate transactions in interstate or foreign commerce. . . .

The clause thought to authorize the legislation, . . . confers upon the Congress power "to lay and collect Taxes, Duties, Imposts and Excises, to pay the Debts and provide for the common Defence and general Welfare of the United States. . . ." It is not contended that this provision grants power to regulate agricultural production upon the theory that such legislation would promote the general welfare. The Government concedes that the phrase "to provide for the general welfare" qualifies the power "to lay and collect taxes." The view that the clause grants power to provide for the general welfare, independently of the taxing power, has never been authoritatively accepted. Mr. Justice Story points out that if it were adopted "it is obvious that under color of the generality of the words, to 'provide for the common defence and general welfare,' the government of the United States is, in reality, a government of general and unlimited powers, notwithstanding the subsequent enumeration of specific powers." The true construction undoubtedly is that the only thing granted is the power to tax for the purpose of providing funds for payment of the nation's debts and making provision for the general welfare.

Nevertheless the Government asserts that warrant is found in this clause for the adoption of the Agricultural Adjustment Act. The argument is that Congress may appropriate and authorize the spending of moneys for the "general welfare"; that the phrase should be liberally construed to cover anything conducive to national welfare; that decision as to what will promote such welfare rests with Congress alone, and the courts may not review its determination; and finally that the appropriation under attack was in fact for the general welfare of the United States.

* * *

From the accepted doctrine that the United States is a government of delegated powers, it follows that those not expressly granted, or reasonably to be implied from such as are conferred, are reserved to the states or to the people.

To forestall any suggestion to the contrary, the Tenth Amendment was adopted. The same proposition, otherwise stated, is that powers not granted are prohibited. None to regulate agricultural production is given, and therefore legislation by Congress for that purpose is forbidden.

It is an established principle that the attainment of a prohibited end may not be accomplished under the pretext of the exertion of powers which are granted.

> Should Congress, in the execution of its powers, adopt measures which are prohibited by the constitution; or should Congress, under the pretext of executing its powers, pass laws for the accomplishment of objects not intrusted to the government; it would become the painful duty of this tribunal, should a case requiring such a decision come before it, to say that such an act was not the law of the land. *McCulloch v. Maryland,* [1819].
>
> Congress cannot, under the pretext of executing delegated power, pass laws for the accomplishment of objects not entrusted to the Federal Government. And we accept as established doctrine that any provision of an act of Congress ostensibly enacted under power granted by the Constitution, not naturally and reasonably adapted to the effective exercise of such power but solely to the achievement of something plainly within power reserved to the States, is invalid and cannot be enforced.

These principles are as applicable to the power to lay taxes as to any other federal power. Said the court, in *McCulloch v. Maryland, supra,* 421:

> Let the end be legitimate, let it be within the scope of the constitution, and all means which are appropriate, which are plainly adapted to that end, which are not prohibited, but consist with the letter and spirit of the constitution, are constitutional.

The power of taxation, which is expressly granted, may, of course, be adopted as a means to carry into operation another power also expressly granted. But resort to the taxing power to effectuate an end which is not legitimate, not within the scope of the Constitution, is obviously inadmissible.

* * *

Third. If the taxing power may not be used as the instrument to enforce a regulation of matters of state concern with respect to which the Congress has no authority to interfere, may it, as in the present case, be employed to raise the money necessary to purchase a compliance which the Congress is powerless to command? The Government asserts that whatever might be said against the validity of the plan if compulsory, it is constitutionally sound because the end is accomplished by voluntary cooperation. There are two sufficient answers to the contention. The regulation is not in fact voluntary. The farmer, of course, may refuse to comply, but the price of such refusal is the loss of benefits. The amount offered is intended to be sufficient to exert pressure on him to agree to the proposed regulation. The power to confer or withhold unlimited benefits is the power to coerce or destroy. If the cotton grower elects not to accept the benefits, he will receive less for his crops; those who receive payments will be able to undersell him. The result may well be financial ruin. The coercive purpose and intent of the statute is not obscured by the fact that it has not been perfectly successful. It is pointed out that, because there still remained a minority whom the rental and benefit payments were insufficient to induce to surrender their independence of action, the Congress has gone further and, in the Bankhead Cotton Act, used the taxing power in a more directly minatory fashion to compel submission. This progression only serves more fully to expose the coercive purpose of the so-called tax imposed by the present act. It is clear that the Department of Agriculture has properly described the plan as one to keep a non-coöperating minority in line. This is coercion by economic pressure. The asserted power of choice is illusory.

* * *

It is said that Congress has the undoubted right to appropriate money to executive officers for expenditure under contracts between the government and individuals; that much of the total expenditures is so made. But appropriations and expenditures under contracts for proper purposes cannot justify contracts which are not within federal power. And contracts for the reduction of acreage and the control of production are outside the range of that power. An appropriation to be expended by the United States under contracts calling for violation of a state law clearly would offend the Constitution. Is a statute less objectionable which authorizes expenditure of federal moneys to induce action in a field in which the United States has no power to intermeddle? The Congress cannot invade state jurisdiction to compel individual action; no more can it purchase such action.

We are referred to numerous types of federal appropriation which have been made in the past, and it is asserted no question has been raised as to their validity. We need not stop to examine or consider them. As was said in *Massachusetts v. Mellon, supra* (p. 487):

> . . . as an examination of the acts of Congress will disclose, a large number of statutes appropriating or involving the expenditure of moneys for non-federal purposes have been enacted and carried into effect.

As the opinion points out, such expenditures have not been challenged because no remedy was open for testing their constitutionality in the courts.

We are not here concerned with a conditional appropriation of money, nor with a provision that if certain conditions are not complied with the appropriation shall no longer be available. By the Agricultural Adjustment Act the amount of the tax is appropriated to be expended only in payment under contracts whereby the parties bind themselves to regulation by the Federal Government. There is an obvious difference between a statute stating the conditions upon which moneys shall be expended and one effective only upon assumption of a contractual obligation to submit to a regulation which otherwise could not be enforced. Many examples pointing the distinction might be cited. We are referred to appropriations in aid of education, and it is said that no one has doubted the power of Congress to stipulate the sort of education for which money shall be expended. But an appropriation to an educational institution which by its terms is to become available only if the beneficiary enters into a contract to teach doctrines subversive of the Constitution is clearly bad. An affirmance of the authority of Congress so to condition the expenditure of an appropriation would tend to nullify all constitutional limitations upon legislative power.

But it is said that there is a wide difference in another respect, between compulsory regulation of the local affairs of a state's citizens and the mere making of a contract relating to their conduct; that, if any state objects, it may declare the contract void and thus prevent those under the state's jurisdiction from complying with its terms. The argument is plainly fallacious. The United States can make the contract only if the federal power to tax and to appropriate reaches the subject matter of the contract. If this does reach the subject matter, its exertion cannot be displaced by state action. . . .

Congress has no power to enforce its commands on the farmer to the ends sought by the Agricultural Adjustment Act. It must follow that it may not indirectly accomplish those ends by taxing and spending to purchase compliance. The Constitution and the entire plan of our government negative any such use of the power to tax and to spend as the act undertakes to authorize. It does not help to declare that local conditions throughout the nation have created a situation of national concern; for this is but to say that whenever there is a widespread similarity of local conditions, Congress may ignore constitutional limitations upon its own powers and usurp those reserved to the states. If, in lieu of compulsory regulation of subjects within the states' reserved jurisdiction, which is prohibited, the Congress could invoke the taxing and spending power as a means to accomplish the same end, clause 1 of § 8 of Article I would become the instrument for total subversion of the governmental powers reserved to the individual states.

* * *

The judgment is

Affirmed.

MR. JUSTICE STONE, dissenting.
I think the judgment should be reversed.

* * *

. . . we should direct our attention to the pivot on which the decision of the Court is made to turn. It is that a levy unquestionably within the taxing power of Congress may be treated as invalid because it is a step in a plan to regulate agricultural production and is thus a forbidden infringement of state power. . . .

Here regulation, if any there be, is accomplished not by the tax but by the method by which its proceeds are expended, and would equally be accomplished by any like use of public funds, regardless of their source.

The method may be simply stated. Out of the available fund payments are made to such farmers as are willing to curtail their productive acreage, who in fact do so and who in advance have filed their written undertaking to do so with the Secretary of Agriculture. . . .

Although the farmer is placed under no legal compulsion to reduce acreage, it is said that the mere offer of compensation for so doing is a species of economic coercion which operates with the same legal force and effect as though the curtailment were made mandatory by Act of Congress.

* * *

Of the assertion that the payments to farmers are coercive, it is enough to say that no such contention is pressed by the taxpayer, and no such consequences were to be anticipated or appear to have resulted from the administration of the Act. The suggestion of coercion finds no support in the record or in any data showing the actual operation of the Act. Threat of loss, not hope of gain, is the essence of economic coercion. Members of a long depressed industry have undoubtedly been tempted to curtail acreage by the hope of resulting better prices and by the proffered opportunity to obtain needed ready money. But there is nothing to indicate that those who accepted benefits were impelled by fear of lower prices if they did not accept, or that at any stage in the operation of the plan a farmer could say whether, apart from the certainty of cash payments at specified times, the advantage would lie with curtailment of production plus compensation, rather than with the same or increased acreage plus the expected rise in prices which actually occurred.

* * *

It is upon the contention that state power is infringed by purchased regulation of agricultural production that chief reliance is placed. It is insisted that, while the Constitution gives to Congress, in specific and unambiguous terms, the power to tax and spend, the power is subject to limitations which do not find their origin in any express provision of the Constitution and to which other expressly delegated powers are not subject.

The Constitution requires that public funds shall be spent for a defined purpose, the promotion of the general welfare. Their expenditure usually involves payment on terms which will insure use by the selected recipients within the limits of the constitutional purpose. Expenditures would fail of their purpose and thus lose their constitutional sanction if the terms of payment were not such that by their influence on the action of the recipients the permitted end would be attained. The power of Congress to spend is inseparable from persuasion to action over which Congress has no legislative control. . . .

Courts are not the only agency of government that must be assumed to have capacity to govern. Congress and the courts both unhappily may falter or be mistaken in the performance of their constitutional duty. But interpretation of our great charter of government which proceeds on any assumption that the responsibility for the preservation of our institutions is the exclusive concern of any one of the three branches of government, or that it alone can save them from destruction is far more likely, in the long run, "to obliterate the constituent members" of "an indestructible union of indestructible states" than the frank recognition that language, even of a constitution, may mean what it says: that the power to tax and spend includes the power to relieve a nationwide economic maladjustment by conditional gifts of money.

MR. JUSTICE BRANDEIS and MR. JUSTICE CARDOZO join in this opinion.

QUESTIONS AND COMMENTS

1 Take each sentence of Roberts's description of judicial decision-making and indicate whether you agree or disagree, and why.
2 What is the relationship between the power to tax and the power to spend?
3 One view is that the general welfare power is limited only to the enumerated powers and those powers that can be implied from them. Another view is that the general welfare clause confers a separate and distinct power to legislate for the common good irrespective of the enumerated powers. Which view does Roberts adopt?
4 How would you evaluate Roberts's assumptions about human behavior and motivation in this case?
5 Relatively few cases in the Supreme Court have involved the power to spend. Can you guess why? Consider *Massachusetts v. Mellon,* 262 U.S. 447 (1923).
6 Did Justice Stone accept: (a) Roberts's conception of the general welfare power? or (b) his theory of judicial decision-making?

*   *   *   *   *   *

In *Steward Machine Co. v. Davis,* the Supreme Court upheld a payroll tax imposed on employers of eight or more persons. The proceeds were to go, without earmarking, into the general treasury. However, if the taxpayer made contributions to a state unemployment fund established and operated in accordance with established federal criteria, he was to receive a tax credit equivalent to 90 percent of his contributions. The Court reasoned that no one was coerced by this tax statute. Though states might have been tempted to establish unemployment funds, the Court thought the main purpose of the tax was to safeguard federal revenues. But in a companion case challenging old age pension provisions of the Social Security Act, the Court found a provision of the Constitution which justified the use of the taxing power for new and novel social goals.

Helvering, Commissioner of Internal Revenue, et al. v. Davis

301 U.S. 619; 57 S. Ct. 904; 81 L. Ed. 1307 (1937)
Vote: 7–2

Title II of the Social Security Act provided for old age benefits for persons who had attained the age of 65. Title VIII imposed taxes on employers and employees to finance the benefits. Davis, a stockholder in Edison Electric Company, sought an injunction in the district court to prevent the company from complying with the tax requirements of the act. The district court denied the injunction and dismissed the case. The court of appeals reversed. The Supreme Court granted certiorari.

MR. JUSTICE CARDOZO delivered the opinion of the Court.

* * *

This suit is brought by a shareholder of the Edison Electric Illuminating Company of Boston, a Massachusetts corporation, to restrain the corporation from making the payments and deductions called for by the act, which is stated to be void under the Constitution of the United States. The bill tells us that the corporation has decided to obey the statute, that it has reached this decision in the face of the complainant's protests, and that it will make the payments and deductions unless restrained by a decree. The expected consequences are indicated substantially as follows: The deductions from the wages of the employees will produce unrest among them, and will be followed, it is predicted, by demands that wages be increased. If the exactions shall ultimately be held void, the company will have parted with moneys which as a practical matter it will be impossible to recover. Nothing is said in the bill about the promise of indemnity. The prediction is made also that serious consequences will ensue if there is a submission to the excise. The corporation and its shareholders will suffer irreparable loss, and many thousands of dollars will be subtracted from the value of the shares. The prayer is for an injunction and for a declaration that the act is void. . . .

We were asked to determine: (1) "whether the tax imposed upon employers by § 804 of the Social Security Act is within the power of Congress under the Constitution," and (2) "whether the validity of the tax imposed upon employees by § 801 of the Social Security Act is properly in issue in this case, and if it is, whether that tax is within the power of Congress under the Constitution."

* * *

The scheme of benefits created by the provisions of Title II is not in contravention of the limitations of the Tenth Amendment.

Congress may spend money in aid of the "general welfare." Constitution, Art. I, section 8; *Steward Machine Co. v. Davis,* [1937]. There have been great statesmen in our history who have stood for other views. We will not resurrect the contest. It is now settled by decision.

The conception of the spending power advocated by Hamilton and strongly reinforced by Story has prevailed over that of Madison, which has not been lacking in adherents. Yet difficulties are left when the power is conceded. The line must still be drawn between one welfare and another, between particular and general. Where this shall be placed cannot be known through a formula in advance of the event. There is a middle ground or certainly a penumbra in which discretion is at large. The discretion, however, is not confided to the courts. The discretion belongs to Congress, unless the choice is clearly wrong, a display of arbitrary power, not an exercise of judgment. This is now familiar law.

* * *

Congress did not improvise a judgment when it found that the award of old age benefits would be conducive to the general welfare. The President's Committee on Economic Security made an investigation and report, aided by a research staff of Government officers and employees, and by an Advisory Council and seven other advisory groups. Extensive hearings followed before the House Committee on Ways and Means, and the Senate Committee on Finance. A great mass of evidence was brought together supporting the policy which finds expression in the act. . . .

The problem [of old age security] is plainly national in area and dimensions. Moreover, laws of the separate states cannot deal with it effectively. Congress, at least, had a basis for that belief. States and local governments are often lacking in the resources that are necessary to finance an adequate program of security for the aged. This is brought out with a wealth of illustration in recent studies of the problem. Apart from the failure of resources, states and local governments are at times reluctant to increase so heavily the burden of taxation to be borne by their residents for fear of placing themselves in a position of economic disadvantage as compared with neighbors or competitors. . . .

Only a power that is national can serve the interests of all.

Whether wisdom or unwisdom resides in the scheme of benefits set forth in Title II, it is not for us to say. The answer to such inquiries must come from Congress, not the courts. Our concern here, as often, is with power, not with wisdom. Counsel for respondent has recalled to us the virtues of self-reliance and frugality. There is a possibility, he says, that aid from a paternal government may sap those sturdy virtues and breed a race of weaklings. If Massachusetts so believes and shapes her laws in that conviction, must her breed of sons be changed, he asks, because some other philosophy of government finds favor in the halls of Congress? But the answer is not doubtful. One might ask with equal reason whether the system of protective tariffs is to be set aside at will in one state or another whenever local policy prefers the rule of *laissez faire.* The issue is a closed one. It was fought out long ago. When money is spent to promote the general welfare, the concept of welfare or the opposite is shaped by Congress, not the states. So the concept be not arbitrary, the locality must yield. Constitution, Art. VI, Par. 2. . . .

The decree of the Court of Appeals should be reversed and that of the District Court affirmed.

Reversed.

Mr. Justice McReynolds and Mr. Justice Butler are of opinion that the provisions of the act here challenged are repugnant to the Tenth Amendment, and that the decree of the Circuit Court of Appeals should be affirmed.

QUESTIONS AND COMMENTS

1 How can we demarcate the powers of the states to legislate for the general welfare of their citizens (police powers, Tenth Amendment) and the power of Congress to do the same? If the necessary and proper clause is combined with the general welfare clause in Article I, Section 8, what is the limit of congressional power to regulate the lives of American citizens? Who determines whether a particular congressional act promotes the general welfare?

2 In deciding *Helvering v. Davis,* was the Court, in effect, passing on the wisdom of the policy adopted by Congress? What evidence can you cite for your answer?

To Freely Debate

Gravel v. United States (1972)

Doe v. McMillan (1973)

Hutchinson v. Proxmire (1979)

In order that Congress be free to legislate, the framers of the Constitution granted its members immunity from civil arrest while participating in a legislative session. Indeed, members of Congress cannot be arrested while going to or returning from a legislative session. But the framers were not content to merely provide protection against physical interference with the legislative process. The political system they established assumed that legislation would be the end result of free and open discussion on the floors of the House and Senate. In order to protect that assumption, they also included in the Constitution the so-called speech and debate clause. That clause provides that "for any Speech or Debate in either House, [the Senators and Representatives] . . . shall not be questioned in any other place."

This clause has presented several fundamental questions for those who would interpret it: (1) Is the protection absolute? (2) Does it protect members of Congress in both civil and criminal proceedings? (3) Does it protect members of Congress only, or does it extend to congressional aides and other staff personnel?

In *Kilbourn v. Thompson,*[18] the Court suggested that the speech and debate clause does not provide absolute protection and that it does not extend to all employees of Congress. More recent cases provide needed clarification in this area. In 1951, the Court held that legislative committee members cannot be sued in a civil proceeding for their committee activities.[19] But in this and later cases, the Court has indicated that protection is not afforded to all employees of Congress who carry out the orders of Congress or its committees.[20]

Protection is provided in criminal as well as civil cases, though in *United States v. Brewster*[21] the protection was denied Senator Brewster—on trial for taking a bribe—for another reason. That other reason was the Court's determination that the speech and debate clause protects only legislative activities. A legislative activity was defined as an act done in relation to legislative business—i.e., those things said or done in the performance of official congressional business. The taking of a bribe is obviously not within the ambit of this definition.

In *Brewster,* the Court developed a distinction between legislative acts (protected) and political acts (not protected), a distinction further developed in *Gravel v. United States.* In *Doe v. McMillan,* the Court addresses the distinction between members of Congress and congressional employees and others who assist in preparing and reporting the legislative product. Some fine-line-drawing is evident here. The case of Senator Proxmire delineates the role of press releases and newsletters in the life of a senator and determines whether such activities are protected by the speech and debate clause.

Gravel v. United States

408 U.S. 606; 92 S. Ct. 2614; 33 L. Ed. 2d 583 (1972)
Vote: 5–4

The facts are contained in the opinion below.

Opinion of the Court by MR. JUSTICE WHITE, announced by MR. JUSTICE BLACKMUN.

These cases arise out of the investigation by a federal grand jury into possible criminal conduct with respect to the release and publication of a classified Defense Department study entitled History of the United States Decision-Making Process on Viet Nam Policy. This document, popularly known as the Pentagon Papers, bore a Defense security classification of Top Secret-Sensitive. The crimes being investigated included the retention of public property or records with intent to convert; the gathering and transmitting of national defense information; the concealment or removal of public records or documents; and conspiracy to commit such offenses and to defraud the United States.

Among the witnesses subpoenaed were Leonard S. Rodberg, an assistant to Senator Mike Gravel of Alaska and a resident fellow at the Institute of Policy Studies, and Howard Webber, Director of M. I. T. Press. Senator Gravel, as intervenor, filed motions to quash the subpoenas and to require the Government to specify the particular questions to be addressed to Rodberg. He asserted that requiring these witnesses to appear and testify would violate his privilege under the Speech or Debate Clause of the United States Constitution, Art. I, § 6, cl. 1.

It appeared that on the night of June 29, 1971, Senator Gravel, as Chairman of the Subcommittee on Buildings and Grounds of the Senate Public Works Committee, convened a meeting of the subcommittee and there read extensively from a copy of the Pentagon Papers. He then placed the entire 47 volumes of the study in the public record. Rodberg had been added to the Senator's staff earlier in the day and assisted Gravel in preparing for and conducting the hearing. Some weeks later there were press reports that Gravel had arranged for the papers to be published by Beacon Press and that members of Gravel's staff had talked with Webber as editor of M. I. T. Press.

The District Court overruled the motions to quash and to specify questions but entered an order proscribing certain categories of questions. . . .

The Court of Appeals affirmed the denial of the motions to quash but modified the protective order to reflect its own views of the scope of the congressional privilege. . . .

As modified by the Court of Appeals, the protective order to be observed by prosecution and grand jury was:

> **1** No witness before the grand jury currently investigating the release of the Pentagon Papers may be questioned about Senator Mike Gravel's conduct at a meeting of the Subcommittee on Public Buildings and Grounds on June 29, 1971, nor, if the questions are directed to the motives or purposes behind the Senator's conduct at that meeting, about any communications with him or with his aides regarding the activities of the Senator or his aides during the period of their employment, in preparation for and related to said meeting.
>
> **2** Dr. Leonard S. Rodberg may not be questioned about his own actions in the broadest sense, including observations and communications, oral or written, by or to him or coming to his attention while being interviewed for, or after having been engaged as a member of Senator Gravel's personal staff to the extent that they were in the course of his employment.

The United States petitioned for certiorari challenging the ruling that aides and other persons may not be questioned with respect to legislative acts and that an aide to a Member of Congress has a common-law privilege not to testify before a grand jury with respect to private publication of materials introduced into a subcommittee record. Senator Gravel also petitioned for certiorari seeking reversal of the Court of Appeals insofar as it held private publication unprotected by the Speech or Debate Clause and asserting that the protective order of the Court of Appeals too narrowly protected against inquiries that a grand jury could direct to third parties. We granted both petitions.

* * *

[The Speech or Debate] Clause provides Members of Congress with two distinct privileges. Except in cases of "Treason, Felony and Breach of the Peace," the Clause shields Members from arrest while attending or traveling to and from a session of their House. History reveals, and prior cases so hold, that this part of the Clause exempts Members from arrest in civil cases only.

* * *

In recognition, no doubt, of the force of this part of § 6, Senator Gravel disavows any assertion of general immunity from the criminal law. But he points out that the last portion of § 6 affords Members of Congress another vital privilege—they may not be questioned in any other place for any speech or debate in either House. The claim is not that while one part of § 6 generally permits prosecutions for treason, felony, and breach of the peace, another part nevertheless broadly forbids them. Rather, his insistence is that the Speech or Debate Clause at the very least protects him from criminal or civil liability and from questioning elsewhere than in the Senate, with respect to the events occurring at the subcommittee hearing at which the Pentagon Papers were introduced into the public record. To us this claim is incontrovertible.

The Speech or Debate Clause was designed to assure a co-equal branch of the government wide freedom of speech, debate, and deliberation without intimidation or threats from the Executive Branch. It thus protects Members against prosecutions that directly impinge upon or threaten the legislative process. We have no doubt that Senator Gravel may not be made to answer—either in terms of questions or in terms of defending himself from prosecution—for the events that occurred at the subcommittee meeting. . . .

Even so, the United States strongly urges that because the Speech or Debate Clause confers a privilege only upon "Senators and Representatives," Rodberg himself has no valid claim to constitutional immunity from grand jury inquiry. In our view, both courts below correctly rejected this position. We agree with the Court of Appeals that for the purpose of construing the privilege a Member and his aide are to be "treated as one," or, as the District Court put it: the "Speech or Debate Clause prohibits inquiry into things done by Dr. Rodberg as the Senator's agent or assistant which would have been legislative acts, and therefore privileged, if performed by the Senator personally."

Both courts recognized what the Senate of the United States urgently presses here: that it is literally impossible, in view of the complexities of the modern legislative process, with Congress almost constantly in session and matters of legislative concern constantly proliferating, for Members of Congress to perform their legislative tasks without the help of aides and assistants; that the day-to-day work of such aides is so critical to the Members' performance that they must be treated as the latter's alter egos; and that if they are not so recognized, the central role of the Speech or Debate Clause—to prevent intimidation of legislators by the Executive and accountability before a possibly hostile judiciary—will inevitably be diminished and frustrated.

*   *   *   *

The United States fears the abuses that history reveals have occurred when legislators are invested with the power to relieve others from the operation of otherwise valid civil and criminal laws. But these abuses, it seems to us, are for the most part obviated if the privilege applicable to the aide is viewed, as it must be, as the privilege of the Senator, and invocable only by the Senator or by the aide on the Senator's behalf, and if in all events the privilege available to the aide is confined to those services that would be immune legislative conduct if performed by the Senator himself. This view places beyond the Speech or Debate Clause a variety of services characteristically performed by aides for

Members of Congress, even though within the scope of their employment. It likewise provides no protection for criminal conduct threatening the security of the person or property of others, whether performed at the direction of the Senator in preparation for or in execution of a legislative act or done without his knowledge or direction. Neither does it immunize Senator or aide from testifying at trials or grand jury proceedings involving third-party crimes where the questions do not require testimony about or impugn a legislative act. Thus our refusal to distinguish between Senator and aide in applying the Speech or Debate Clause does not mean that Rodberg is for all purposes exempt from grand jury questioning.

We are convinced also that the Court of Appeals correctly determined that Senator Gravel's alleged arrangement with Beacon Press to publish the Pentagon Papers was not protected speech or debate within the meaning of Art. I, § 6, cl. 1, of the Constitution.

* * *

The heart of the Clause is speech or debate in either House. Insofar as the Clause is construed to reach other matters, they must be an integral part of the deliberative and communicative processes by which Members participate in committee and House proceedings with respect to the consideration and passage or rejection of proposed legislation or with respect to other matters which the Constitution places within the jurisdiction of either House. As the Court of Appeals put it, the courts have extended the privilege to matters beyond pure speech or debate in either House, but "only when necessary to prevent indirect impairment of such deliberations."

Here, private publication by Senator Gravel through the cooperation of Beacon Press was in no way essential to the deliberations of the Senate; nor does questioning as to private publication threaten the integrity or independence of the Senate by impermissibly exposing its deliberations to executive influence. The Senator had conducted his hearings; the record and any report that was forthcoming were available both to his committee and the Senate. Insofar as we are advised, neither Congress nor the full committee ordered or authorized the publication. We cannot but conclude that the Senator's arrangements with Beacon Press were not part and parcel of the legislative process. . . .

Similar considerations lead us to disagree with the Court of Appeals insofar as it fashioned, tentatively at least, a nonconstitutional testimonial privilege protecting Rodberg from any questioning by the grand jury concerning the matter of republication of the Pentagon Papers. This privilege, thought to be similar to that protecting executive officials from liability for libel, see *Barr v. Matteo*, [1959], was considered advisable "[t]o the extent that a congressman has responsibility to inform his constituents. . . ."

But we cannot carry a judicially fashioned privilege so far as to immunize criminal conduct proscribed by an Act of Congress or to frustrate the grand jury's inquiry into whether publication of these classified documents violated a federal criminal statute. The so-called executive privilege has never been applied to shield executive officers from prosecution for crime, the Court of Appeals was quite sure that third parties were neither immune from liability nor from testifying about the republication matter, and we perceive no basis for conferring a testimonial privilege on Rodberg as the Court of Appeals seemed to do.

We must finally consider, in the light of the foregoing, whether the protective order entered by the Court of Appeals is an appropriate regulation of the pending grand jury proceedings.

Focusing first on paragraph two of the order, we think the injunction against interrogating Rodberg with respect to any act, "in the broadest sense," performed by him within the scope of his employment, overly restricts the scope of grand jury inquiry. Rodberg's immunity, testimonial or otherwise, extends only to legislative acts as to which the Senator himself would be immune. The grand jury, therefore, if relevant to its investigation into the possible violations of the criminal law, and absent Fifth Amendment objections, may require from Rodberg answers to questions relating to his or the Senator's arrangements, if any, with respect to republication or with respect to third-party conduct under valid investigation by the grand jury, as long as the questions do not implicate legislative action of the Senator. Neither do we perceive any constitutional or other privilege that shields Rodberg, any more than any other witness, from grand jury questions relevant to tracing the source of obviously highly classified documents that came into the Senator's possession and are the basic subject matter of inquiry in this case, as long as no legislative act is implicated by the questions.

Because the Speech or Debate Clause privilege applies both to Senator and aide, it appears to us that paragraph one of the order, alone, would afford ample protection for the privilege if it forbade questioning any witness, including Rodberg: (1) concerning the Senator's conduct, or the conduct of his aides, at the June 29, 1971, meeting of the subcommittee; (2) concerning the motives and purposes behind the Senator's conduct, or that of his aides, at that meeting; (3) concerning communications between the Senator and his aides during the term of their employment and related to said meeting or any other legislative act of the Senator; (4) except as it proves relevant to investigating possible third-party crime, concerning any act, in itself not criminal, performed by the Senator, or by his aides in the course of their employment, in preparation for the subcommittee hearing. We leave the final form of such an order to the Court of Appeals in the first instance, or, if that court prefers, to the District Court.

The judgment of the Court of Appeals is vacated and the cases are remanded to that court for further proceedings consistent with this opinion.

So ordered.

MR. JUSTICE STEWART, dissenting in part.

* * *

Under the Court's ruling, a Congressman may be subpoenaed by a vindictive Executive to testify about informants who have not committed crimes and who have no knowledge of crime. Such compulsion can occur, because the judiciary has traditionally imposed virtually no limitations on the grand jury's broad investigatory powers; grand jury investigations are not limited in scope to specific criminal acts, and standards of materiality and relevance are greatly relaxed. But even if the Executive had reason to believe that a Member of Congress had knowledge of a specific probable violation of law, it is by no means clear to me that the Executive's interest in the administration of justice must *always* override the public interest in having an informed Congress. Why should we not, given the tension between two competing interests, *each* of constitutional dimensions, balance the claims of the Speech or Debate Clause against the claims of the grand jury in the particularized contexts of specific cases? And why are not the Houses of Congress the proper institutions in most situations to impose sanctions upon a Representative or Senator who withholds information about crime acquired in the course of his legislative duties?

I am not prepared to accept the Court's rigid conclusion that the Executive may always compel a legislator to testify before a grand jury about sources of information used in preparing for legislative acts. For that reason, I dissent from that part of the Court's opinion that so inflexibly and summarily decides this vital question.

MR. JUSTICE DOUGLAS, dissenting.

I would construe the Speech or Debate Clause to insulate Senator Gravel and his aides from inquiry concerning the Pentagon Papers, and Beacon Press from inquiry concerning publication of them, for that publication was but another way of informing the public as to what had gone on in the privacy of the Executive Branch concerning the conception and pursuit of the so-called "war" in Vietnam. Alternatively, I would hold that Beacon Press is protected by the First Amendment from prosecution or investigations for publishing or undertaking to publish the Pentagon Papers.

* * *

MR. JUSTICE BRENNAN, with whom MR. JUSTICE DOUGLAS, and MR. JUSTICE MARSHALL, join, dissenting.

* * *

In my view, today's decision so restricts the privilege of speech or debate as to endanger the continued performance of legislative tasks that are vital to the workings of our democratic system. . . .

. . . the Court excludes from the sphere of protected legislative activity a function that I had supposed lay at the heart of our democratic system. I speak, of course, of the legislator's duty to inform the public about matters affecting the administration of government. That this "informing function" falls into the class of things "generally done in a session of the House by one of its members in relation to the business before it," *Kilbourn v. Thompson,* (1881), was explicitly acknowledged by the Court in *Watkins v. United States,* (1957). In speaking of the "power of the Congress to inquire into and publicize corruption, maladministration or inefficiency in agencies of the Government," the Court noted that "[f]rom the earliest times in its history, the Congress has assiduously performed an 'informing function' of this nature."

* * *

Unlike the Court, therefore, I think that the activities of Congressmen in communicating with the public are legislative acts protected by the Speech or Debate Clause. I agree with the Court that not every task performed by a legislator is privileged; intervention before Executive departments is one that is not. But the informing function carries a far more persuasive claim to the protections of the Clause. It has been recognized by this Court as something "generally done" by Congressmen, the Congress itself has established special concessions designed to lower the cost of such communication, and, most important, the function furthers several well-recognized goals of representative government. To say in the face of these facts that the informing function is not privileged merely because it is not necessary to the internal deliberations of Congress is to give the Speech or Debate Clause an artificial and narrow reading unsupported by reason. . . .

Doe et al. v. McMillan et al.

412 U.S. 306; 93 S. Ct. 2018; 36 L. Ed. 2d 912 (1973)
Vote: 5–4

The facts are given in the opinion below.

Mr. Justice White delivered the opinion of the Court.

This case concerns the scope of congressional immunity under the Speech or Debate Clause of the United States Constitution. Art. I, § 6, cl. 1, as well as the reach of official immunity in the legislative context.

By resolution adopted February 5, 1969, the House of Representatives authorized the Committee on the District of Columbia or its subcommittee "to conduct a full and complete investigation and study of . . . the organization, management, operation, and administration" of any department or agency of the government of the District of Columbia or of any independent agency or instrumentality of government operating solely within the District of Columbia. The Committee was given subpoena power and was directed to "report to the House as soon as practicable . . . the results of its investigation and study together with such recommendations as it deems advisable." On December 8, 1970, a Special Select Subcommittee of the Committee on the District of Columbia submitted to the Speaker of the House a report, represented to be a summary of the Subcommittee's investigation and hearings devoted to the public school system of the District of Columbia. On the same day, the report was referred to the Committee of the Whole House on the State of the Union and was ordered printed.

Thereafter, the report was printed and distributed by the Government Printing Office. . . .

The 450-page report included among its supporting data some 45 pages that are the gravamen of petitioners' suit. Included in the pertinent pages were copies of absence sheets, lists of absentees, copies of test papers, and documents relating to disciplinary problems of certain specifically named students.* The report stated that these materials were included to "give a realistic view" of a troubled school and "the lack of administrative efforts to rectify the multitudinous problems there," to show the level of reading ability of seventh graders who were given a fifth-grade history test, and to illustrate suspension and disciplinary problems. . . . [Shortly after the issuance of the report, petitioners sued in federal district court.]

The District Court, after a hearing on motions for a temporary restraining order and for an order against further distribution of the report, dismissed the action against the individual defendants on the ground that the conduct complained of was absolutely privileged. A divided panel of the United States Court of Appeals for the District of Columbia Circuit affirmed. Without determining whether the complaint stated a cause of action under the Constitution or any applicable law, the majority held that the Members of Congress, the Committee staff employees, and the Public Printer and Superintendent of Documents were immune from the liability asserted against them because of the Speech or Debate Clause and that the official immunity doctrine recognized in *Barr v. Matteo*, [1959], barred any liability on the part of the District of Columbia officials as well as the legislative employees. We granted certiorari. . . .

The proper scope of our inquiry . . . is whether the Speech or Debate Clause affords absolute immunity from private suit to persons who, with authorization from Congress, distribute materials which allegedly infringe upon the rights of individuals. The respondents insist that such public distributions are protected, that the Clause immunizes not only publication for the information

---

*The Court of Appeals' opinion terms the material "somewhat derogatory." The absentee lists named students who were frequent "class cutters." Of the 29 test papers published in the report, 21 bore failing grades; all included the name of the student being tested. The letters, memoranda, and other documents relating to disciplinary problems detailed conduct of specifically named students. Some of the deviant conduct described involved sexual perversion and criminal violations.

and use of Members in the performance of their legislative duties but also must be held to protect "publications to the public through the facilities of Congress." Public dissemination, it is argued, will serve "the important legislative function of informing the public concerning matters pending before Congress. . . ."

We do not doubt the importance of informing the public about the business of Congress. However, the question remains whether the act of doing so, simply because authorized by Congress, must always be considered "an integral part of the deliberative and communicative processes by which Members participate in committee and House proceedings" with respect to legislative or other matters before the House. *Gravel v. United States,* [1972]. A Member of Congress may not with impunity publish a libel from the speaker's stand in his home district, and clearly the Speech or Debate Clause would not protect such an act even though the libel was read from an official committee report. The reason is that republishing a libel under such circumstances is not an essential part of the legislative process and is not part of that deliberative process "by which Members participate in committee and House proceedings." By the same token, others, such as the Superintendent of Documents or the Public Printer or legislative personnel, who participate in distribution of actionable material beyond the reasonable bounds of the legislative task, enjoy no Speech or Debate Clause immunity.

Members of Congress are themselves immune for ordering or voting for a publication going beyond the reasonable requirements of the legislative function, *Kilbourn v. Thompson,* [1881], but the Speech or Debate Clause no more insulates legislative functionaries carrying out such nonlegislative directives than it protected the Sergeant at Arms in *Kilbourn v. Thompson* when, at the direction of the House, he made an arrest that the courts subsequently found to be "without authority." The Clause does not protect "criminal conduct threatening the security of the person or property of others, whether performed at the direction of the Senator in preparation for or in execution of a legislative act or done without his knowledge or direction."

Neither, we think, does it immunize those who publish and distribute otherwise actionable materials beyond the reasonable requirements of the legislative function.

Thus, we cannot accept the proposition that in order to perform its legislative function Congress not only must at times consider and use actionable material but also must be free to disseminate it to the public at large, no matter how injurious to private reputation that material might be. We cannot believe that the purpose of the Clause—"to prevent intimidation of legislators by the Executive and accountability before a possibly hostile judiciary,"—will suffer in the slightest if it is held that those who, at the direction of Congress or otherwise, distribute actionable material to the public at large have no automatic immunity under the Speech or Debate Clause but must respond to private suits to the extent that others must respond in light of the Constitution and applicable laws. To hold otherwise would be to invoke gratuitous injury to citizens for little if any public purpose. We are unwilling to sanction such a result, at least absent more substantial evidence that, in order to perform its legislative function, Congress must not only inform the public about the fundamentals of its business but also must distribute to the public generally materials otherwise actionable under local law.

* * *

That the Speech or Debate Clause has finite limits is important for present purposes. The complaint before us alleges that the respondents caused the Committee report "to be distributed to the public," that "distribution of the report continues to the present," and that, "unless restrained, defendants will continue to distribute and publish" damaging information about petitioners and their children. It does not expressly appear from the complaint, nor is it contended in this Court, that either the Members of Congress or the Committee personnel did anything more than conduct the hearings, prepare the report, and authorize its publication. As we have stated, such acts by those respondents are protected by the Speech or Debate Clause and may not serve as a predicate for a suit. The complaint was therefore properly dismissed as to these respondents. Other respondents, however, are alleged to have carried out a public distribution and to be ready to continue such dissemination.

In response to these latter allegations, the Court of Appeals, after receiving sufficient assurances from the respondents that they had no intention of seeking a republication or carrying out further distribution of the report, concluded that there was no basis for injunctive relief. But this left the question whether any part of the previous publication and public distribution by respondents other than the Members of Congress and Committee personnel went beyond the limits of the legislative immunity provided by the Speech or Debate Clause of the Constitution. Until that question was resolved, the complaint should not have been dismissed on threshold immunity grounds, unless the Court of Appeals was correct in ruling that the action against the other respondents was foreclosed by the doctrine of official immunity, a question to which we now turn.

The official immunity doctrine, which "has in large part been of judicial making," confers immunity on Government officials of suitable rank for the reason that "officials of government should be free to exercise their duties unembarrassed by the fear of damage suits in respect of acts done in the course of those duties—suits which would consume time and energies which would otherwise be devoted to governmental service and the threat of which might appreciably inhibit the fearless, vigorous, and effective administration of policies of government.". . .

Because the Court has not fashioned a fixed, invariable rule of immunity but has advised a discerning inquiry into whether the contributions of immunity to effective government in particular contexts outweigh the perhaps recurring harm to individual citizens, there is no readymade answer as to whether the remaining federal respondents—the Public Printer and the Superintendent of Documents—should be accorded absolute immunity in this case. Of course, to the extent that they serve legislative functions, the performance of which would be immune conduct if done by Congressmen, these officials enjoy the protection of the Speech or Debate Clause. Our inquiry here, however, is whether, if they participate in publication and distribution beyond the legislative sphere, and thus beyond the protection of the Speech or Debate Clause, they are nevertheless protected by the doctrine of official immunity.

* * *

Congress has conferred no express statutory immunity on the Public Printer or the Superintendent of Documents. Congress has not provided that these officials should be immune for printing and distributing materials where those who author the materials would not be. We thus face no statutory or constitutional problems in interpreting this doctrine of "judicial making."

We do, however, write in the shadow of *Board of Regents of State Colleges v. Roth,* (1972), and *Wisconsin v. Constantineau,* (1971), where the Court advised caution "[w]here a person's good name, reputation, honor, or integrity is at stake because of what the government is doing to him. . ." We conclude that, for the purposes of the judicially fashioned doctrine of immunity, the Public Printer and the Superintendent of Documents are no more free from suit in the case before us than would be a legislative aide who made copies of the materials at issue and distributed them to the public at the direction of his superiors. . . .

Because we think the Court of Appeals applied the immunities of the Speech or Debate Clause and of the doctrine of official immunity too broadly, we must reverse its judgment and remand the case for appropriate further proceedings. . . .

MR. JUSTICE BLACKMUN, with whom THE CHIEF JUSTICE joins, concurring in part and dissenting in part.

I join MR. JUSTICE REHNQUIST's opinion.

* * *

Although the Court in the present case holds that the gathering of information, the preparation of a report, and the voting on a resolution authorizing the printing of a committee report are protected activities under the Speech or Debate Clause, it renders that protection for Members of Congress and legislative personnel less than meaningful by further holding that the authorized public distribution of a committee document may be enjoined and those responsible for the distribution held liable when the document contains materials "otherwise actionable under local law." The Court's holding thus imposes on Congress the onerous burden of justifying, apparently by "substantial evidence," the inclusion of allegedly actionable material in committee documents.

This, unfortunately, ignores the realities of the "deliberative and communicative processes," by which legislative decisionmaking takes place.

Although it is regrettable that a person's reputation may be damaged by the necessities or the mistakes of the legislative process, the very act of determining judicially whether there is "substantial evidence" to justify the inclusion of "actionable" information in a committee report is a censorship that violates the congressional free speech concept embodied in the Speech or Debate Clause and is, as well, the imposition of this Court's judgment in matters textually committed to the discretion of the Legislative Branch by Art. I of the Constitution. I suspect that Mr. Chief Justice Marshall and his concurring Justices would be astonished to learn that the time-honored doctrine of judicial review they enunciated in *Marbury v. Madison,* (1803), has been utilized to foster the result reached by the Court today.

Stationing the federal judiciary at the doors of the Houses of Congress for the purpose of sanitizing congressional documents in accord with this Court's concept of wise legislative decisionmaking policy appears to me to reveal a lack of confidence in our political processes and in the ability of Congress to police its own members. It is inevitable that occasionally, as perhaps in this case, there will be unwise and even harmful choices made by Congress in fulfilling its legislative responsibility. That, however, is the price we pay for representative government. I am firmly convinced that the abuses we countenance in our system are vastly outweighed by the demonstrated ability of the political process to correct overzealousness on the part of elected representatives.

MR. JUSTICE REHNQUIST, with whom THE CHIEF JUSTICE and MR. JUSTICE BLACKMUN join, and with whom MR. JUSTICE STEWART joins [in part] . . . concurring in part and dissenting in part.

I concur in the Court's holding that the respondent Members of Congress and their committee aides and employees are immune under the Speech or Debate Clause for preparation of the Committee report for distribution within the halls of Congress. I dissent from the Court's holding that Members of Congress might be held liable if they were in fact responsible for public dissemination of a committee report, and that therefore the Public Printer or the Superintendent of Documents might likewise be liable for such distribution. And quite apart from the immunity which I believe the Speech or Debate Clause confers upon congressionally authorized public distribution of committee reports, I believe that the principle of separation of powers absolutely prohibits any form of injunctive relief in the circumstances here presented.

* * *

I agree with the Court that the Public Printer and the Superintendent of Documents have no "official immunity" under the authority of *Barr v. Matteo,* (1959).

There is no immunity there when officials are simply carrying out the directives of officials in the other branches of Government, rather than performing any discretionary function of their own. But for this very reason, if the body directing the publication or its Members would themselves be immune from publishing and distributing, the Public Printer and the Superintendent should be likewise immune. I do not understand the Court to hold otherwise. Because I would hold the Members immune had they undertaken the public distribution. I would likewise hold the Superintendent and the Public Printer immune for having done so under the authority of the resolution and statute. The Court's contrary conclusion, perhaps influenced by the allegations of serious harm to the petitioners contained in their complaint, unduly restricts the privilege. . . .

Entirely apart from the immunity conferred by the Speech or Debate Clause on these respondents, I believe that the principle of separation of powers forbids the granting of injunctive relief by the District Court in a case such as this. We have jurisdiction to review the completed acts of the Legislative and Executive Branches.

But the prospect of the District Court's enjoining a committee of Congress, which, in the legislative scheme of things, is for all practical purposes Congress itself, from undertaking to publicly distribute one of its reports in the manner that Congress has by statute prescribed that it be distributed, is one that I believe would have boggled the minds of the Framers of the Constitution.

* * *

Hutchinson v. Proxmire et al.

443 U.S. 111; 99 S. Ct. 2675; 61 L. Ed. 2d 411 (1979)
Vote: 7–2

In March 1975, Senator William Proxmire initiated the "Golden Fleece of the Month Award" to publicize what he considered to be unusual examples of wasteful governmental spending. Ronald Hutchinson was a behavioral scientist whose research on "why monkeys clench their jaws" was funded at various times by the National Science Foundation, the Office of Naval Research, and the National Aeronautics and Space Agency—to the tune of about a half a million dollars. In April 1975, Proxmire gave these agencies his Golden Fleece Award for funding Hutchinson's research. On April 18, the senator made a speech in the Senate in which he said (inter alia):

> The funding of this nonsense makes me almost angry enough to scream and kick or even clench my jaw. It seems to me it is outrageous.
> Dr. Hutchinson's studies should make the taxpayers as well as his monkeys grind

their teeth. In fact, the good doctor has made a fortune from his monkeys and in the process made a monkey out of the American taxpayer.

It is time for the Federal Government to get out of this "monkey business." In view of the transparent worthlessness of Hutchinson's study of jaw-grinding and biting by angry or hard-drinking monkeys, it is time we put a stop to the bite Hutchinson and the bureaucrats who fund him have been taking of the taxpayer.

Copies of the speech were sent to 275 members of the news media throughout the United States and abroad. In May 1975, the essence of the speech and press release was repeated in a newsletter sent to about 100,000 people. Finally, in February 1976, Proxmire distributed a newsletter which, while not mentioning Hutchinson by name, stated that:

—The NSF, the Space Agency, and the Office of Naval Research won the "Golden Fleece" for spending jointly $500,000 to determine why monkeys clench their jaws.

All the studies on why monkeys clench their jaws were dropped. No more monkey business.

Hutchinson brought a libel action on April 17, 1976, in a federal district court. He alleged that the actions of Proxmire (and his assistant, Swartz) had caused him (Hutchinson) to "suffer a loss of respect in his profession, . . . injury to his feelings, . . . extreme mental anguish and physical illness and pain to his person." He also claimed that Proxmire's conduct had deprived him of the ability to secure funding of his research and that his rights of privacy, peace, and tranquility had been violated.

The district court held that the speech and debate clause afforded absolute immunity for Proxmire's speech to the Senate and the press release covering the speech. The court of appeals affirmed.

MR. CHIEF JUSTICE BURGER delivered the opinion of the Court. . . .

The purpose of the Speech or Debate Clause is to protect Members of Congress "not only from the consequences of litigation's results but also from the burden of defending themselves." *Dombrowski v. Eastland,* (1967). If the respondents have immunity under the Clause, no other questions need be considered for they may "not be questioned in any other Place."

. . . [Respondents] contend that impetus for the Speech or Debate Clause privilege in our Constitution came from the history of parliamentary efforts to protect the right of members to criticize the spending of the Crown and from the prosecution of a Speaker of the House of Commons for publication of a report outside of Parliament. Respondents also contend that in the modern day very little speech or debate occurs on the floor of either House; from this they argue that press releases and newsletters are necessary for Members of Congress to communicate with other Members. For example, in his deposition Proxmire testified:

I have found in 19 years in the Senate that very often a statement on the floor of the Senate or something that appears in the Congressional Record misses the attention of most members of the Senate, and virtually all members of the House, because they don't read the Congressional Record. If they are handed a news release or something, that is going to call it to their attention. . . .

Respondents also argue that an essential part of the duties of a Member of Congress is to inform constituents, as well as other Members, of the issues being considered.

* * *

Literal reading of the Clause would, of course, confine its protection narrowly to a "Speech or Debate *in* either House." But the Court has given the Clause a practical rather than a strictly literal reading which would limit the protection to utterances made within the four walls of either Chamber. Thus, we have held that committee hearings are protected, even if held outside the Chambers; committee reports are also protected.

The gloss going beyond a strictly literal reading of the Clause has not, however, departed from the objective of protecting only legislative activities. . . .

Whatever imprecision there may be in the term "legislative activities," it is clear that nothing in history or in the explicit language of the Clause suggests any intention to create an absolute privilege from liability or suit for defamatory statements made outside the Chamber. [In United States v. Brewster (1972)], we observed:

> The immunities of the Speech or Debate Clause were not written into the Constitution simply for the personal or private benefit of Members of Congress, but to protect the integrity of the legislative process by insuring the independence of individual legislators.

Claims under the Clause going beyond what is needed to protect legislative independence are to be closely scrutinized. In *Brewster* we took note of this:

> The authors of our Constitution were well aware of the history of both the need for the privilege *and the abuses that could flow from too sweeping safeguards.* In order to preserve other values, they wrote the privilege so that it tolerates and protects behavior on the part of Members not tolerated and protected when done by other citizens, *but the shield does not extend beyond what is necessary to preserve the integrity of the legislative process.* (Emphasis added.)

Indeed, the precedents abundantly support the conclusion that a Member may be held liable for republishing defamatory statements originally made in either House. We perceive no basis for departing from that long-established rule.

* * *

In *Gravel v. United States,* [1972] we recognized that the doctrine denying immunity for republication had been accepted in the United States:

> [P]rivate publication by Senator Gravel . . . was in no way essential to the deliberations of the Senate; nor does questioning as to private publication threaten the integ-

rity or independence of the Senate by impermissibly exposing its deliberations to executive influence.

We reaffirmed that principle in *Doe v. McMillan,* [1973]:

A Member of Congress may not with impunity publish a libel from the speaker's stand in his home district, and clearly the Speech or Debate Clause would not protect such an act even though the libel was read from an official committee report. The reason is that republishing a libel under such circumstances is not an essential part of the legislative process and is not part of that deliberative process "by which Members participate in committee and House proceedings."

We reach a similar conclusion here. A speech by Proxmire in the Senate would be wholly immune and would be available to other Members of Congress and the public in the Congressional Record. But neither the newsletters nor the press release was "essential to the deliberations of the Senate" and neither was part of the deliberative process. . . .

We therefore reverse the judgment of the Court of Appeals and remand the case to the Court of Appeals for further proceedings consistent with this opinion.

Reversed and remanded.

* * *

Mr. Justice Brennan, dissenting.

I disagree with the Court's conclusion that Senator Proxmire's newsletters and press releases fall outside the protection of the speech or debate immunity. In my view, public criticism by legislators of unnecessary governmental expenditures, whatever its form, is a legislative act shielded by the Speech or Debate Clause. I would affirm the judgment below for the reasons expressed in my dissent in *Gravel v. United States,* (1972).

QUESTIONS AND COMMENTS

1 Which of the following would be protected from questioning under the speech and debate clause?

  a A senator votes for an appropriations bill.

  b A member of the House of Representatives argues about a pending bill with the mayor of Toledo on the steps of the Capitol Building.

  c In a televised conversation with a Defense Department official concerning a defense appropriations measure, a senator calls the governor of New York a son of a bitch.

  d A member of the House arranges for a constituent to have access to the files of a House committee for research on a book being written by the constituent.

  e An aide to a senator, in an interview with the press, expounds at length on the senator's legislative effectiveness.

  f An aide to a representative, without being requested to do so, consults several members of the House about an upcoming vote and reports the result to the representative.

Provide an explanation (and evidence, if available) for each answer.

2 What justification can you offer for distinguishing political and legislative activities in applying the speech and debate clause protection? Would members of Congress not be more "free" if their political activities were made immune from civil and criminal suit?

3 What are the implications of the *Gravel, Doe,* and *Hutchinson* cases for the values articulated in the First Amendment? For the right of privacy?

4 In *Hutchinson v. Proxmire,* the Court held, in effect, that a defamatory statement made on the floor of the House or Senate and published in the *Congressional Record* is immune from civil suit. But that immunity is lost if the statement is reprinted in a press release. Can you think of any arguments for and against this distinction other than those included in the case excerpt?

5 What if Proxmire's statements about the "monkey research" had been made on the telephone? Different decision?

6 What if the statements published by Proxmire in his press release were (a) not defamatory in fact, or (b) not known by him to be defamatory at the time he made them? Different decision?

To Investigate

Watkins v. United States (1957)

Barenblatt v. United States (1959)

Eastland v. United States Servicemen's Fund (1975)

For a period of about fifteen years after World War II, the United States and the Soviet Union were engaged in what came to be known as the "cold war." One consequence was a growing concern with Soviet spies, domestic Communists, and Communist sympathizers who allegedly served Soviet interests. The primary Soviet interest was thought to be the use of subversion, espionage, and assorted conspiratorial tactics designed to overthrow the government of the United States by force. Indeed, that concern had been evident even earlier when Congress adopted the Smith Act in 1940. That statute banned advocating and teaching that the government should be overthrown by violence and conspiring to commit acts leading to its overthrow. While the Smith Act was not explicitly anti-Communist, its provisions lent themselves to use against Communist activities. As the cold war heated up in the fifties, the "advocacy" section became a major tool of the government in its prosecutions of Communists and alleged Communists.

Other internal security statutes, explicitly directed to the "Communist menace," were enacted in 1950 (the Internal Security Act) and in 1954 (the Communist Control Act). In addition, Presidents Truman and Eisenhower issued a number of executive orders designed to ensure the loyalty of federal employees. Many states also adopted state loyalty programs of one kind or another. Much of this activity was driven by Senator Joseph McCarthy's tactics in publicizing the alleged presence of Communists in government.

The imposition of various restrictions on individuals inevitably raised questions of personal liberty under the Constitution. The resolution of these questions was the prerogative of the Supreme Court, and the Court addressed them in a number of cases in the fifties and sixties. The Court, in this period, was headed by Chief Justice Earl Warren, who served from 1953 through the 1968 term. Joined by other libertarian justices, Warren's overall thrust was to restrict Congress and the executive in dealing with the "Communist menace"—i.e., to maintain the protection for civil liberties provided in the Constitution. But, initially, Warren could count only on Justices Black, Brennan, and Douglas to vote the libertarian position. On occasion Harlan or Frankfurter or Whittaker would join the group. But sometimes the liberals were not able to have their way.

The first two cases in this section deal with a small but very important aspect of the "subversion" problem—the power of Congress to investigate so-called un-American activities. One of these cases upholds congressional power and one does not. In the case upholding the power, Harlan joined an opinion written by Warren. But in the case denying the power, Harlan wrote the Court's opinion, while Warren, Black, Douglas, and Brennan dissented. After Goldberg replaced Justice Frankfurter (1962) and Fortas replaced Justice Whittaker (1965), the liberals in the Court had a comfortable majority. As a consequence, the partial dilution of the threat to civil liberties posed by the various anti-Communist statutes and executive orders was made more encompassing.[22]

Watkins v. United States

354 U.S. 178; 77 S. Ct. 1173; 1 L. Ed. 2d 1273 (1957)
Vote: 6–1

The facts are given in the opinion below.

MR. CHIEF JUSTICE WARREN delivered the opinion of the Court.

* * *

On April 29, 1954, petitioner appeared as a witness in compliance with a subpoena issued by a Subcommittee of the Committee on Un-American Activities of the House of Representatives. The Subcommittee elicited from petitioner a description of his background in labor union activities. He had been an employee of the International Harvester Company between 1935 and 1953. During the last eleven of those years, he had been on leave of absence to serve as an official of the Farm Equipment Workers International Union, later merged into the United Electrical, Radio and Machine Workers. He rose to the position of President of District No. 2 of the Farm Equipment Workers, a district defined geographically to include generally Canton and Rock Falls, Illinois, and Dubuque, Iowa. In 1953, petitioner joined the United Automobile Workers International Union as a labor organizer.

Petitioner's name had been mentioned by two witnesses who testified before the Committee at prior hearings. In September 1952, one Donald O. Spencer admitted having been a Communist from 1943 to 1946. He declared that he had been recruited into the Party with the endorsement and prior approval of petitioner, whom he identified as the then District Vice-President of the Farm Equipment Workers. Spencer also mentioned that petitioner had attended meetings at which only card-carrying Communists were admitted. A month before petitioner testified, one Walter Rumsey stated that he had been recruited into the Party by petitioner. Rumsey added that he had paid Party dues to, and later collected dues from, petitioner, who had assumed the name, Sam Brown. Rumsey told the Committee that he left the Party in 1944.

Petitioner answered these allegations freely and without reservation. . . .

The Subcommittee . . . was apparently satisfied with petitioner's disclosures. After some further discussion elaborating on the statement, counsel for the Committee turned to another aspect of Rumsey's testimony. Rumsey had identified a group of persons whom he had known as members of the Communist Party, and counsel began to read this list of names to petitioner. Petitioner stated that he did not know several of the persons. Of those whom he did know, he refused to tell whether he knew them to have been members of the Communist Party. He explained to the Subcommittee why he took such a position:

> I am not going to plead the fifth amendment, but I refuse to answer certain questions that I believe are outside the proper scope of your committee's activities. I will answer any questions which this committee puts to me about myself. I will also answer questions about those persons whom I knew to be members of the Communist Party and whom I believe still are. I will not, however, answer any questions with respect to others with whom I associated in the past. I do not believe that any law in this country requires me to testify about persons who may in the past have been Communist Party members or otherwise engaged in Communist Party activity but who to my best knowledge and belief have long since removed themselves from the Communist movement.
>
> I do not believe that such questions are relevant to the work of this committee nor do I believe that this committee has the right to undertake the public exposure of persons because of their past activities. I may be wrong, and the committee may have this power, but until and unless a court of law so holds and directs me to answer, I most firmly refuse to discuss the political activities of my past associates.

[For his refusal, Watkins was convicted of contempt of Congress, fined, given a suspended sentence, and put on probation.]. . .

An appeal was taken to the Court of Appeals for the District of Columbia. The conviction was reversed by a three-judge panel, one member dissenting.

Upon rehearing *en banc,* the full bench affirmed the conviction with the judges of the original majority in dissent. We granted certiorari because of the very important questions of constitutional law presented.

We start with several basic premises on which there is general agreement. The power of the Congress to conduct investigations is inherent in the legislative process. That power is broad. It encompasses inquiries concerning the administration of existing laws as well as proposed or possibly needed statutes. It includes surveys of defects in our social, economic or political system for the purpose of enabling the Congress to remedy them. It comprehends probes into departments of the Federal Government to expose corruption, inefficiency or waste. But, broad as is this power of inquiry, it is not unlimited. There is no general authority to expose the private affairs of individuals without justification in terms of the functions of the Congress. This was freely conceded by the Solicitor General in his argument of this case. Nor is the Congress a law enforcement or trial agency. These are functions of the executive and judicial departments of government. No inquiry is an end in itself; it must be related to, and in furtherance of, a legitimate task of the Congress.

. . . [Moreover,] . . . an investigation is subject to the command that the Congress shall make no law abridging freedom of speech or press or assembly. While it is true that there is no statute to be reviewed, and that an investigation is not a law, nevertheless an investigation is part of lawmaking. It is justified solely as an adjunct to the legislative process. The First Amendment may be invoked against infringement of the protected freedoms by law or by lawmaking. . . .

The Court recognized the restraints of the Bill of Rights upon congressional investigations in *United States v. Rumely,* [1953]. The magnitude and complexity of the problem of applying the First Amendment to that case led the Court to construe narrowly the resolution describing the committee's authority. It was concluded that, when First Amendment rights are threatened, the delegation of power to the committee must be clearly revealed in its charter.

Accommodation of the congressional need for particular information with the individual and personal interest in privacy is an arduous and delicate task for any court. We do not underestimate the difficulties that would attend such an undertaking. It is manifest that despite the adverse effects which follow upon compelled disclosure of private matters, not all such inquiries are barred. *Kilbourn v. Thompson* teaches that such an investigation into individual affairs is invalid if unrelated to any legislative purpose. That is beyond the powers conferred upon the Congress in the Constitution. *United States v. Rumely* makes it plain that the mere semblance of legislative purpose would not justify an inquiry in the face of the Bill of Rights. The critical element is the existence of, and the weight to be ascribed to, the interest of the Congress in demanding disclosures from an unwilling witness. We cannot simply assume, however, that every congressional investigation is justified by a public need that overbalances any private rights affected. To do so would be to abdicate the responsibility placed by the Constitution upon the judiciary to insure that the Congress does not unjustifiably encroach upon an individual's right to privacy nor abridge his liberty of speech, press, religion or assembly.

Petitioner has earnestly suggested that the difficult questions of protecting these rights from infringement by legislative inquiries can be surmounted in this case because there was no public purpose served in his interrogation. His conclusion is based upon the thesis that the Subcommittee was engaged in a program of exposure for the sake of exposure. The sole purpose of the inquiry, he contends, was to bring down upon himself and others the violence of public reaction because of their past beliefs, expressions and associations. In support of this argument, petitioner has marshalled an impressive array of evidence that some Congressmen have believed that such was their duty, or part of it.

We have no doubt that there is no congressional power to expose for the sake of exposure. The public is, of course, entitled to be informed concerning the workings of its government. That cannot be inflated into a general power to expose where the predominant result can only be an invasion of the private rights of individuals. But a solution to our problem is not to be found in testing the motives of committee members for this purpose. Such is not our function. Their motives alone would not vitiate an investigation which had been instituted by a House of Congress if that assembly's legislative purpose is being served.

* * *

It is the responsibility of the Congress, in the first instance, to insure that compulsory process is used only in furtherance of a legislative purpose. That requires that the instructions to an investigating committee spell out that group's jurisdiction and purpose with sufficient particularity. Those instructions are embodied in the authorizing resolution. That document is the committee's charter. Broadly drafted and loosely worded, however, such resolutions can leave tremendous latitude to the discretion of the investigators. The more vague the committee's charter is, the greater becomes the possibility that the committee's specific actions are not in conformity with the will of the parent House of Congress.

The authorizing resolution of the Un-American Activities Committee was adopted in 1938 when a select committee, under the chairmanship of Representative Dies, was created. Several years later, the Committee was made a standing organ of the House with the same mandate. It defines the Committee's authority as follows:

> The Committee on Un-American Activities, as a whole or by subcommittee, is authorized to make from time to time investigations of (1) the extent, character, and objects of un-American propaganda activities in the United States, (2) the diffusion within the United States of subversive and un-American propaganda that is instigated from foreign countries or of a domestic origin and attacks the principle of the form of government as guaranteed by our Constitution, and (3) all other questions in relation thereto that would aid Congress in any necessary remedial legislation.

It would be difficult to imagine a less explicit authorizing resolution. Who can define the meaning of "un-American"? What is that single, solitary "principle of the form of government as guaranteed by our Constitution"? There is no need to dwell upon the language, however. . . . No one could reasonably deduce from the charter the kind of investigation that the Committee was directed to make.

* * *

The problem attains proportion when viewed from the standpoint of the witness who appears before a congressional committee. He must decide at the time the questions are propounded whether or not to answer. As the Court said in *Sinclair v. United States,* [1929], the witness acts at his peril. He is " . . . bound rightly to construe the statute." An erroneous determination on his part, even if made in the utmost good faith, does not exculpate him if the court should later rule that the questions were pertinent to the question under inquiry.

It is obvious that a person compelled to make this choice is entitled to have knowledge of the subject to which the interrogation is deemed pertinent. That knowledge must be available with the same degree of explicitness and clarity that the Due Process Clause requires in the expression of any element of a criminal offense. The "vice of vagueness" must be avoided here as in all other crimes.

* * *

The Government believes that the topic of inquiry before the Subcommittee concerned Communist infiltration in labor. In his introductory remarks, the Chairman made reference to a bill, then pending before the Committee, which would have penalized labor unions controlled or dominated by persons who were, or had been, members of a "Communist-action" organization, as defined in the Internal Security Act of 1950. The Subcommittee, it is contended, might have been endeavoring to determine the extent of such a problem.

This view is corroborated somewhat by the witnesses who preceded and followed petitioner before the Subcommittee. Looking at the entire hearings, however, there is strong reason to doubt that the subject revolved about labor matters. The published transcript is entitled: Investigation of Communist Activities in the Chicago Area, and six of the nine witnesses had no connection with labor at all.

The most serious doubts as to the Subcommittee's "question under inquiry," however, stem from the precise questions that petitioner has been charged with refusing to answer. Under the terms of the statute, after all, it is these which must be proved pertinent. Petitioner is charged with refusing to tell the Subcommittee whether or not he knew that certain named persons had been members of the Communist Party in the past. The Subcommittee's counsel read the list from the testimony of a previous witness who had identified them as Communists. Although this former witness was identified with labor, he had not stated that the persons he named were involved in union affairs. Of the thirty names propounded to petitioner, seven were completely unconnected with organized labor. One operated a beauty parlor. Another was a watchmaker. Several were identified as "just citizens" or "only Communists." When almost a quarter of the persons on the list are not labor people, the inference becomes strong that the subject before the Subcommittee was not defined in terms of Communism in labor.

* * *

Unless the subject matter has been made to appear with undisputable clarity, it is the duty of the investigative body, upon objection of the witness on grounds of pertinency, to state for the record the subject under inquiry at that time and the manner in which the propounded questions are pertinent thereto. To be meaningful, the explanation must describe what the topic under inquiry is and the connective reasoning whereby the precise questions asked relate to it.

The statement of the Committee Chairman in this case, in response to petitioner's protest, was woefully inadequate to convey sufficient information as to the pertinency of the questions to the subject under inquiry. Petitioner was thus not accorded a fair opportunity to determine whether he was within his rights in refusing to answer, and his conviction is necessarily invalid under the Due Process Clause of the Fifth Amendment.

* * *

The judgment of the Court of Appeals is reversed, and the case is remanded to the District Court with instructions to dismiss the indictment.

It is so ordered.

* * *

Barenblatt v. United States

360 U.S. 109; 79 S. Ct. 1081; 3 L. Ed. 2d 1115 (1959)
Vote: 5–4

The facts are given in the opinion below.

MR. JUSTICE HARLAN delivered the opinion of the Court.

Once more the Court is required to resolve the conflicting constitutional claims of congressional power and of an individual's right to resist its exercise. . . .

Broad as it is, the power is not, however, without limitations. Since Congress may only investigate into those areas in which it may potentially legislate or appropriate, it cannot inquire into matters which are within the exclusive province of one of the other branches of the Government. Lacking the judicial power given to the Judiciary, it cannot inquire into matters that are exclusively the concern of the Judiciary. Neither can it supplant the Executive in what exclusively belongs to the Executive. And the Congress, in common with all branches of the Government, must exercise its powers subject to the limitations placed by the Constitution on governmental action, more particularly in the context of this case the relevant limitations of the Bill of Rights.

* * *

We here review petitioner's conviction under 2 U.S.C. § 192 for contempt of Congress, arising from his refusal to answer certain questions put to him by a Subcommittee of the House Committee on Un-American Activities during the course of an inquiry concerning alleged Communist infiltration into the field of education.

The case is before us for the second time. Petitioner's conviction was originally affirmed in 1957 by a unanimous panel of the Court of Appeals.

This Court granted certiorari, vacated the judgment of the Court of Appeals, and remanded the case to that court for further consideration in light of *Watkins v. United States,* [1957], which had reversed a contempt of Congress conviction, and which was decided after the Court of Appeals' decision here had issued. Thereafter the Court of Appeals, sitting *en banc,* reaffirmed the conviction by a divided court. We again granted certiorari, to consider petitioner's statutory and constitutional challenges to his conviction, and particularly his claim that the judgment below cannot stand under our decision in the *Watkins* case.

Pursuant to a subpoena, and accompanied by counsel, petitioner on June 28, 1954, appeared as a witness before this congressional Subcommittee. After answering a few preliminary questions and testifying that he had been a graduate student and teaching fellow at the University of Michigan from 1947 to 1950 and an instructor in psychology at Vassar College from 1950 to shortly before his appearance before the Subcommittee, petitioner objected generally to the right of the Subcommittee to inquire into his "political" and "religious" beliefs or any "other personal and private affairs" or "associational activities," upon grounds set forth in a previously prepared memorandum which he was allowed to file with the Subcommittee. Thereafter petitioner specifically declined to answer each of the following five questions:

Are you now a member of the Communist Party? . . .

Have you ever been a member of the Communist Party? . . .

Now, you have stated that you knew Francis Crowley. Did you know Francis Crowley as a member of the Communist Party? . . .

Were you ever a member of the Haldane Club of the Communist Party while at the University of Michigan? . . .

Were you a member while a student of the University of Michigan Council of Arts, Sciences, and Professions? . . .

In each instance the grounds of refusal were those set forth in the prepared statement. Petitioner expressly disclaimed reliance upon "the Fifth Amendment."

* * *

Petitioner's various contentions resolve themselves into three propositions: First, the compelling of testimony by the Subcommittee was neither legislatively authorized nor constitutionally permissible because of the vagueness of Rule XI of the House of Representatives, Eighty-third Congress, the charter of authority of the parent Committee. Second, petitioner was not adequately apprised of the pertinency of the Subcommittee's questions to the subject matter of the inquiry. Third, the questions petitioner refused to answer infringed rights protected by the First Amendment.

SUBCOMMITTEE'S AUTHORITY TO COMPEL TESTIMONY

At the outset it should be noted that Rule XI authorized this Subcommittee to compel testimony within the framework of the investigative authority conferred on the Un-American Activities Committee. Petitioner contends that *Watkins v. United States, supra,* nevertheless held the grant of this power in all circumstances ineffective because of the vagueness of Rule XI in delineating the Committee jurisdiction to which its exercise was to be appurtenant. . . .

The *Watkins* case cannot properly be read as standing for such a proposition. . . .

Petitioner also contends, independently of *Watkins,* that the vagueness of Rule XI deprived the Subcommittee of the right to compel testimony in this investigation into Communist activity. We cannot agree with this contention, which in its furthest reach would mean that the House Un-American Activities Committee under its existing authority has no right to compel testimony in any circumstances. Granting the vagueness of the Rule, we may not read it in isolation from its long history in the House of Representatives. Just as legislation is often given meaning by the gloss of legislative reports, administrative interpretation, and long usage, so the proper meaning of an authorization to a congressional committee is not to be derived alone from its abstract terms unrelated to the definite content furnished them by the course of congressional actions. The Rule comes to us with a "persuasive gloss of legislative history," which shows beyond doubt that in pursuance of its legislative concerns in the domain of "national security" the House has clothed the Un-American Activities Committee with pervasive authority to investigate Communist activities in this country. . . .

We are urged, however, to construe Rule XI so as at least to exclude the field of education from the Committee's compulsory authority. . . . [But there is] . . . no indication that the House ever viewed the field of education as being outside the Committee's authority under Rule XI, . . . [and] the legislative history affirmatively evinces House approval of this phase of the Committee's work. . . .

PERTINENCY CLAIM

Undeniably a conviction for contempt under 2 U.S.C. § 192 cannot stand unless the questions asked are pertinent to the subject matter of the investigation. *Watkins v. United States,* [1957].

* * *

[But] . . . it goes without saying that the scope of the Committee's authority was for the House, not a witness, to determine, subject to the ultimate reviewing responsibility of this Court. What we deal with here is whether petitioner was sufficiently apprised of "the topic under inquiry" thus authorized "and the connective reasoning whereby the precise questions asked relate[d] to it."

. . . The subject matter of the inquiry had been identified at the commencement of the investigation as Communist infiltration into the field of education. Just prior to petitioner's appearance before the Subcommittee, the scope of the day's hearings had been announced as "in the main communism in education and the experiences and background in the party by Francis X. T. Crowley. It will deal with activities in Michigan, Boston, and in some small degree, New York." Petitioner had heard the Subcommittee interrogate the witness Crowley along the same lines as he, petitioner, was evidently to be questioned, and had listened to Crowley's testimony identifying him as a former member of an alleged Communist student organization at the University of Michigan while they both were in attendance there. Further, petitioner had stood mute in the face of the Chairman's statement as to why he had been called as a witness by the Subcommittee. And, lastly, unlike Watkins, petitioner refused to answer questions as to his own Communist Party affiliations, whose pertinency of course was clear beyond doubt.

Petitioner's contentions on this aspect of the case cannot be sustained.

CONSTITUTIONAL CONTENTIONS

* * *

The precise constitutional issue confronting us is whether the Subcommittee's inquiry into petitioner's past or present membership in the Communist Party transgressed the provisions of the First Amendment, which of course reach and limit congressional investigations.

* * *

The first question is whether this investigation was related to a valid legislative purpose, for Congress may not constitutionally require an individual to disclose his political relationships or other private affairs except in relation to such a purpose.

That Congress has wide power to legislate in the field of Communist activity in this Country, and to conduct appropriate investigations in aid thereof, is hardly debatable. The existence of such power has never been questioned by this Court, and it is sufficient to say, without particularization, that Congress has enacted or considered in this field a wide range of legislative measures, not a few of which have stemmed from recommendations of the very Committee whose actions have been drawn in question here. In the last analysis this power rests on the right of self-preservation, "the ultimate value of any society," *Dennis v. United States,* [1951]. Justification for its exercise in turn rests on the long and widely accepted view that the tenets of the Communist Party include the ultimate overthrow of the Government of the United States by force and violence, a view which has been given formal expression by the Congress.

* * *

We think that investigatory power in this domain is not to be denied Congress solely because the field of education is involved. . . .

Indeed we do not understand petitioner here to suggest that Congress in no circumstances may inquire into Communist activity in the field of education. Rather, his position is in effect that this particular investigation was aimed not at the revolutionary aspects but at the theoretical classroom discussion of communism.

In our opinion this position rests on a too constricted view of the nature of the investigatory process, and is not supported by a fair assessment of the record before us. An investigation of advocacy of or preparation for overthrow certainly embraces the right to identify a witness as a member of the Communist Party, and to inquire into the various manifestations of the Party's tenets. . . .

The record discloses considerable testimony concerning the foreign domination and revolutionary purposes and efforts of the Communist Party. That there was also testimony on the abstract philosophical level does not detract from the dominant theme of this investigation—Communist infiltration furthering the alleged ultimate purpose of overthrow. And certainly the conclusion would not be justified that the questioning of petitioner would have exceeded permissible bounds had he not shut off the Subcommittee at the threshold.

Nor can we accept the further contention that this investigation should not be deemed to have been in furtherance of a legislative purpose because the true objective of the Committee and of the Congress was purely "exposure." So long as Congress acts in pursuance of its constitutional power, the Judiciary lacks authority to intervene on the basis of the motives which spurred the exercise of that power. *Arizona v. California,* [1931].

* * *

Finally, the record is barren of other factors which in themselves might sometimes lead to the conclusion that the individual interests at stake were not subordinate to those of the state. There is no indication in this record that the Subcommittee was attempting to pillory witnesses. Nor did petitioner's appearance as a witness follow from indiscriminate dragnet procedures, lacking in probable cause for belief that he possessed information which might be helpful to the Subcommittee. And the relevancy of the questions put to him by the Subcommittee is not open to doubt.

We conclude that the balance between the individual and the governmental interests here at stake must be struck in favor of the latter, and that therefore the provisions of the First Amendment have not been offended.

We hold that petitioner's conviction for contempt of Congress discloses no infirmity, and that the judgment of the Court of Appeals must be

Affirmed.

* * *

MR. JUSTICE BLACK, with whom THE CHIEF JUSTICE and MR. JUSTICE DOUGLAS concur, dissenting.

* * *

The Court—while not denying the vagueness of Rule XI—nevertheless defends its application here because the questions asked concerned communism, a subject of investigation which had been reported to the House by the Committee on numerous occasions. If the issue were merely whether Congress intended to allow an investigation of communism, or even of communism in education, it may well be that we could hold the data cited by the Court sufficient to support a finding of intent. But that is expressly not the issue. On the Court's own test, the issue is whether Barenblatt can know with sufficient certainty, at the time of his interrogation, that there is so compelling a need for his replies that infringement of his rights of free association is justified. The record does not disclose where Barenblatt can find what that need is. There is certainly no clear congressional statement of it in Rule XI. . . .

I would hold that Rule XI is too broad to be meaningful and cannot support petitioner's conviction.

* * *

To apply the Court's balancing test under such circumstances is to read the First Amendment to say "Congress shall pass no law abridging freedom of speech, press, assembly and petition, unless Congress and the Supreme Court reach the joint conclusion that on balance the interest of the Government in stifling these freedoms is greater than the interest of the people in having them exercised." This is closely akin to the notion that neither the First Amendment nor any other provision of the Bill of Rights should be enforced unless the Court believes it is *reasonable* to do so. Not only does this violate the genius of our *written* Constitution, but it runs expressly counter to the injunction to Court and Congress made by Madison when he introduced the Bill of Rights. . . .

But even assuming what I cannot assume, that some balancing is proper in this case, I feel that the Court after stating the test ignores it completely. At most it balances the right of the Government to preserve itself, against Barenblatt's right to refrain from revealing Communist affiliations. Such a balance, however, mistakes the factors to be weighed. In the first place, it completely leaves out the real interest in Barenblatt's silence, the interest of the people as a whole in being able to join organizations, advocate causes and make political "mistakes" without later being subjected to governmental penalties for having dared to think for themselves. It is this right, the right to err politically, which keeps us strong as a Nation. For no number of laws against communism can have as much effect as the personal conviction which comes from having heard its arguments and rejected them, or from having once accepted its tenets and later recognized their worthlessness.

* * *

Finally, I think Barenblatt's conviction violates the Constitution because the chief aim, purpose and practice of the House Un-American Activities Committee, as disclosed by its many reports, is to try witnesses and punish them because they are or have been Communists or because they refuse to admit or deny Communist affiliations. The punishment imposed is generally punishment by humiliation and public shame. There is nothing strange or novel about this kind of punishment. It is in fact one of the oldest forms of governmental punishment known to mankind; branding, the pillory, ostracism and subjection to public hatred being but a few examples of it. . . .

It is no answer to all this to suggest that legislative committees should be allowed to punish if they grant the accused some rules of courtesy or allow him counsel. For the Constitution proscribes *all* bills of attainder by State or Nation, not merely those which lack counsel or courtesy.

* * *

It is the protection from arbitrary punishments through the right to a judicial trial with all these safeguards which over the years has distinguished America from lands where drumhead courts and other similar "tribunals" deprive the weak and the unorthodox of life, liberty and property without due process of law. It is this same right which is denied to Barenblatt, because the Court today fails to see what is here for all to see—that exposure and punishment is the aim of this Committee and the reason for its existence. To deny this is to ignore the Committee's own claims and the reports it has issued ever since it was established. I cannot believe that the nature of our judicial office requires us to be so blind, and must conclude that the Un-American Activities Committee's "identification" and "exposure" of Communists and suspected Communists, like the activities of the Committee in *Kilbourn v. Thompson,* amount to an encroachment on the judiciary which bodes ill for the liberties of the people of this land.

Ultimately all the questions in this case really boil down to one—whether we as a people will try fearfully and futilely to preserve democracy by adopting totalitarian methods, or whether in accordance with our traditions and our Constitution we will have the confidence and courage to be free.

I would reverse this conviction.

QUESTIONS AND COMMENTS

1 Can you find the congressional power to investigate in the Constitution? If so, give the appropriate citation. If not, what is the source of the power?
2 In *Watkins,* Warren says that "there is no congressional power to expose for the sake of exposure." Is there a power to expose for any other reasons? If the answer is affirmative, identify the reasons. Whatever your answer, should Congress be allowed to inform the public, i.e., expose via investigations or other methods, whenever it thinks the public should "know"?
3 What is the Court's method for determining whether a congressional inquiry is "pertinent" to a legislative purpose?
4 What if Barenblatt had refused to answer the committee's questions re party membership on Fifth Amendment grounds (i.e., protection against self-incrimination)? Different decision?

* * * * * *

In *Eastland v. United States Servicemen's Fund,* we have a case dealing with a fundamental concept: separation of powers. In this instance, the relationship between the speech and debate clause, the investigatory power of Congress, and judicial power is explored.

Eastland et al. v. United States Servicemen's Fund et al.

421 U.S. 491; 95 S. Ct. 1813; 44 L. Ed. 2d 324 (1975)
Vote: 8–1

The facts are given in the opinion below.

MR. CHIEF JUSTICE BURGER delivered the opinion of the Court.

We granted certiorari to decide whether a federal court may enjoin the issuance by Congress of a subpoena *duces tecum* that directs a bank to produce the bank records of an organization which claims a First Amendment privilege status for those records on the ground that they are the equivalent of confidential membership lists. The Court of Appeals for the District of Columbia Circuit held that compliance with the subpoena "would invade the constitutional rights" of the organization, and that judicial relief is available to prevent implementation of the subpoena.

In early 1970 the Senate Subcommittee on Internal Security was given broad authority by the Senate to "make a complete and continuing study and investigation of . . . the administration, operation, and enforcement of the Internal Security Act of 1950. . . ."

The authority encompassed discovering the "extent, nature, and effect of subversive activities in the United States," and the resolution specifically directed inquiry concerning "infiltration by persons who are or may be under the domination of the foreign government. . . ."

Pursuant to that mandate the Subcommittee began an inquiry into the activities of respondent United States Servicemen's Fund, Inc. (USSF).

USSF describes itself as a nonprofit membership corporation supported by contributions. Its stated purpose is "to further the welfare of persons who have served or are presently serving in the military." To accomplish its declared purpose USSF has engaged in various activities directed at United States servicemen. It established "coffeehouses" near domestic military installations, and aided the publication of "underground" newspapers for distribution on American military installations throughout the world. The coffeehouses were meeting places for servicemen, and the newspapers were specialized publications which USSF claims dealt with issues of concern to servicemen. Through these operations USSF attempted to communicate to servicemen its philosophy and attitudes concerning United States involvement in Southeast Asia. USSF claims the coffeehouses and newspapers became "the focus of dissent and expressions of opposition within the military toward the war in [Southeast Asia]."

*   *   *

[In the course of its investigation, the subcommittee issued a subpoena to the bank where USSF had an account.] The subpoena commanded the bank to produce by June 4, 1970:

> any and all records appertaining to or involving the account or accounts of [USSF]. Such records to comprehend papers, correspondence, statements, checks, deposit slips and supporting documentation, or microfilm thereof within [the bank's] control or custody or within [its] means to produce. . . .

Before the return date, USSF and two of its members brought this action to enjoin implementation of the subpoena *duces tecum*. [The district court dismissed the action, but the court of appeals reversed on First Amendment grounds.]

The question to be resolved is whether the actions of the petitioners fall within the "sphere of legitimate legislative activity." If they do, the petitioners "shall not be questioned in any other Place" about those activities since the prohibitions of the Speech or Debate Clause are absolute.

Without exception, our cases have read the Speech or Debate Clause broadly to effectuate its purposes. The purpose of the Clause is to insure that the legislative function the Constitution allocates to Congress may be performed independently.... In our system "the clause serves the additional function of reinforcing the separation of powers so deliberately established by the Founders."...we have long held that, when it applies, the Clause provides protection against civil as well as criminal actions, and against actions brought by private individuals as well as those initiated by the Executive Branch. *Kilbourn v. Thompson,* [1881]. . . .

In determining whether particular activities other than literal speech or debate fall within the "legitimate legislative sphere" we look to see whether the activities took place "in a session of the House by one of its members in relation to the business before it."

More specifically, we must determine whether the activities are

> an integral part of the deliberative and communicative processes by which Members participate in committee and House proceedings with respect to the consideration and passage or rejection of proposed legislation or with respect to other matters which the Constitution places within the jurisdiction of either House. *Gravel v. United States,* [1972].

The power to investigate and to do so through compulsory process plainly falls within that definition.

* * *

The particular investigation at issue here is related to and in furtherance of a legitimate task of Congress. *Watkins v. United States,* [1957]. On this record the pleadings show that the actions of the Members and the Chief Counsel fall within the "sphere of legitimate legislative activity." The Subcommittee was acting under an unambiguous resolution from the Senate authorizing it to make a complete study of the "administration, operation, and enforcement of the Internal Security Act of 1950. . . ."

That grant of authority is sufficient to show that the investigation upon which the Subcommittee had embarked concerned a subject on which "legislation could be had." *McGrain v. Daugherty,* [1927].

* * *

We conclude that the Speech or Debate Clause provides complete immunity for the Members for issuance of this subpoena. We draw no distinction between the Members and the Chief Counsel. In *Gravel, supra,* we made it clear that "the day-to-day work of such aides is so critical to the Members' performance that they must be treated as [the Members'] alter egos. . . ."

Here the complaint alleges that the "Subcommittee members and staff caused the . . . subpoena to be issued . . . under the authority of Senate Resolution 366. . . ." The complaint thus does not distinguish between the activities of the Members and those of the Chief Counsel. . . .

Since the Members are immune because the issuance of the subpoena is "essential to legislating," their aides share that immunity.

Respondents rely on language in *Gravel v. United States, supra,* at 621:

> [N]o prior case has held that Members of Congress would be immune if they executed an invalid resolution by themselves carrying out an illegal arrest, or if, in order to secure information for a hearing, themselves seized the property or invaded the privacy of a citizen. Neither they nor their aides should be immune from liability or questioning in such circumstances.

From this respondents argue that the subpoena works an invasion of their privacy, and thus cannot be immune from judicial questioning. The conclusion is unwarranted. The quoted language from *Gravel* referred to actions which were *not* "essential to legislating. . . .

Quite the contrary is the case with a routine subpoena intended to gather information about a subject on which legislation may be had.

Respondents also contend that the subpoena cannot be protected by the speech or debate immunity because the "sole purpose" of the investigation is to force "public disclosure of beliefs, opinions, expressions and associations of private citizens which may be unorthodox or unpopular." Respondents view the scope of the privilege too narrowly. Our cases make clear that in determining the legitimacy of a congressional act we do not look to the motives alleged to have prompted it.

* * *

If the mere allegation that a valid legislative act was undertaken for an unworthy purpose would lift the protection of the Clause, then the Clause simply would not provide the protection historically undergirding it. "In times of political passion, dishonest or vindictive motives are readily attributed to legislative conduct and as readily believed." The wisdom of congressional approach or methodology is not open to judicial veto. *Doe v. McMillan,* [1973]. Nor is the legitimacy of a congressional inquiry to be defined by what it produces. The very nature of the investigative function—like any research— is that it takes the searchers up some "blind alleys" and into nonproductive enterprises. To be a valid legislative inquiry there need be no predictable end result.

Finally, respondents argue that the purpose of the subpoena was to "harass, chill, punish and deter" them in the exercise of their First Amendment rights, App. 16, and thus that the subpoena cannot be protected by the Clause. Their theory seems to be that once it is alleged that First Amendment rights may be infringed by congressional action the Judiciary may intervene to protect those rights; the Court of Appeals seems to have subscribed to that theory. That approach, however, ignores the absolute nature of the speech or debate protection and our cases which have broadly construed that protection.

* * *

For us to read the Clause as respondents suggest would create an exception not warranted by the language, purposes, or history of the Clause. Respondents make the familiar argument that the broad protection granted by the Clause creates a potential for abuse. That is correct, and . . . [earlier] we noted that the risk of such abuse was "the conscious choice of the Framers" buttressed and justified by history. Our consistently broad construction of the Speech or Debate Clause rests on the belief that it must be so construed to provide the independence which is its central purpose.

This case illustrates vividly the harm that judicial interference may cause. A legislative inquiry has been frustrated for nearly five years, during which the Members and their aide have been obliged to devote time to consultation with their counsel concerning the litigation, and have been distracted from the purpose of their inquiry. The Clause was written to prevent the need to be confronted by such "questioning" and to forbid invocation of judicial power to challenge the wisdom of Congress' use of its investigative authority.

Reversed and remanded.

* * *

MR. JUSTICE MARSHALL, with whom MR. JUSTICE BRENNAN and MR. JUSTICE STEWART join, concurring in the judgment.

I agree with the Court that the Speech or Debate Clause protects the actions of the Senate petitioners in this case from judicial interference, and that the House aspects of this case should be reconsidered by the District Court. As our cases have consistently held, however, the Speech or Debate Clause protects legislators and their confidential aides from suit; it does not immunize congressional action from judicial review. I write today only to emphasize that the Speech or Debate Clause does not entirely immunize a congressional subpoena from challenge by a party not in a position to assert his constitutional rights by refusing to comply with it. . . .

Modern legislatures, and particularly the Congress, may legislate on a wide range of subjects. In order to discharge this function, and their related informing function, they may genuinely need a great deal of information in the exclusive possession of persons who would not make it available except under the compulsion of a subpoena. When duly subpoenaed, however, such a person does not shed his constitutional right to withhold certain classes of information. If he refuses to testify or to produce documents and invokes a pertinent privilege, he still runs the risk that the legislature will cite him for contempt. At trial he may defend on the basis of the constitutional right to withhold information from the legislature, and his right will be respected along with the legitimate needs of the legislature.

* * *

The Speech or Debate Clause cannot be used to avoid meaningful review of constitutional objections to a subpoena simply because the subpoena is served on a third party. Our prior cases arising under the Speech or Debate Clause indicate only that a Member of Congress or his aide may not be called upon to defend a subpoena against constitutional objection, and not that the objection will not be heard at all.

* * *

This case does not present the questions of what would be the proper procedure, and who might be the proper parties defendant, in an effort to get before a court a constitutional challenge to a subpoena *duces tecum* issued to a third party. As respondent's counsel conceded at oral argument, this case is at an end if the Senate petitioners are upheld in their claim of immunity, as they must be.

MR. JUSTICE DOUGLAS, dissenting.

I would affirm the judgment below. . . .

Under our federal regime that delegates, by the Constitution and Acts of Congress, awesome powers to individuals, those powers may not be used to deprive people of their First Amendment or other constitutional rights. It is my view that no official, no matter how high or majestic his or her office, who is within the reach of judicial process, may invoke immunity for his actions for which wrongdoers normally suffer. There may be few occasions when, on the merits, it would be appropriate to invoke such a remedy. But no regime of law that can rightfully claim that name may make trustees of these vast powers immune from actions brought by people who have been wronged by official action.

QUESTIONS AND COMMENTS

1 In *Eastland,* it is alleged in effect that while the subpoena may be related to a legitimate task of Congress, its purpose is to "harass, chill, punish, and deter"—i.e., that Congress had a "bad" motive in issuing the subpoena. The Supreme Court has been extremely reluctant to inquire into legislative motive as long as the investigation can

be rationally related to a legitimate legislative purpose—real or imagined. *Cf. Watkins v. United States,* (1957).

To Delegate Legislative Authority

Schechter Poultry Corp. v. United States (1935)

This is the so-called Sick Chicken Case. The Congress legislates, the executive implements or enforces the law, the Supreme Court adjudicates questions that might arise concerning the actions of the other two branches. Power to govern, in short, is separated. And it makes a fine theory. But were separation of power to be viewed as an absolute, the governmental system would undoubtedly grind to a halt. This was well understood at the outset. Thus, we have always permitted Congress to legislate broad policy, with executive agencies permitted, under appropriate conditions, to issue rules and regulations in implementing the congressional policy. However, legislative power may not be delegated to the President. Whether such a delegation has occurred in a particular instance is for the courts to decide. And the Supreme Court decided several such cases during the period in which President Roosevelt's New Deal measures were receiving short shrift in the Court. The Schechter Case was one of these. Since this case also deals with the commerce power, the second part of the opinion may be read in conjunction with the section on interstate commerce.

A. L. A. Schechter Poultry Corp. et al. v. United States

295 U.S. 495; 55 S. Ct. 837; 79 L. Ed. 1570 (1935)
Vote: Unanimous

The National Industrial Recovery Act of 1933 provided, inter alia, for "codes of fair competition" covering wages and prices, trade practices, etc. The codes were to be drafted by trade and industrial groups and promulgated by the President—given his approval. Once promulgated, these codes constituted "law" in the full sense. Schechter Poultry Corporation was convicted of violating code wage and hour provisions limiting the work week to 40 hours and minimum pay to 50 cents per hour. The corporation was also convicted of violating the code's "straight killing" provision which prohibited selected selling of individual chickens and the selling of a "sick chicken." The corporation challenged the code as unconstitutional; the court of appeals sustained the conviction on all charges except the wages and hours allegation. The Supreme Court granted certiorari.

Mr. Chief Justice Hughes delivered the opinion of the Court.

* * *

First. Two preliminary points are stressed by the Government with respect to the appropriate approach to the important questions presented. We are told that the provision of the statute authorizing the adoption of codes must be viewed in the light of the grave national crisis with which Congress was confronted. Undoubtedly, the conditions to which power is addressed are always to be considered when the exercise of power is challenged. Extraordinary conditions may call for extraordinary remedies. But the argument necessarily stops short of an attempt to justify action which lies outside the sphere of constitutional authority. Extraordinary conditions do not create or enlarge constitutional power. The Constitution established a national government with powers deemed to be adequate, as they have proved to be both in war and peace, but these powers of the national government are limited by the constitutional grants. Those who act under these grants are not at liberty to transcend the imposed limits because they believe that more or different power is necessary. Such assertions of extra-constitutional authority were anticipated and precluded by the explicit terms of the Tenth Amendment,—"The powers not delegated to the United States by the Constitution, nor prohibited by it to the States, are reserved to the States respectively, or to the people."

The further point is urged that the national crisis demanded a broad and intensive coöperative effort by those engaged in trade and industry, and that this necessary coöperation was sought to be fostered by permitting them to initiate the adoption of codes. But the statutory plan is not simply one for voluntary effort. It does not seek merely to endow voluntary trade or industrial associations or groups with privileges or immunities. It involves the coercive exercise of the law-making power. The codes of fair competition which the statute attempts to authorize are codes of laws. If valid, they place all persons within their reach under the obligation of positive law, binding equally those who assent and those who do not assent. Violations of the provisions of the codes are punishable as crimes.

Second. The question of the delegation of legislative power. We recently had occasion to review the pertinent decisions and the general principles which govern the determination of this question. *Panama Refining Co. v. Ryan,* [1935]. The Constitution provides that "All legislative powers herein granted shall be vested in a Congress of the United States, which shall consist of a Senate and House of Representatives." Art. I, § 1. And the Congress is authorized "To make all laws which shall be necessary and proper for carrying into execution" its general powers. Art. I, § 8, par. 18. The Congress is not permitted to abdicate or to transfer to others the essential legislative functions with which it is thus vested. We have repeatedly recognized the necessity of adapting legislation to complex conditions involving a host of details with which the national legislature cannot deal directly. We pointed out in the *Panama Company* case that the Constitution has never been regarded as denying to Congress the necessary resources of flexibility and practicality, which will enable it to perform its function in laying down policies and establishing standards, while leaving to selected instrumentalities the making of subordinate rules within prescribed limits and the determination of facts to which the policy as declared by the legislature is to apply. But we said that the constant recognition of the necessity and validity of such provisions, and the wide range of administrative authority which has been developed by means of them, cannot be allowed to obscure the limitations of the authority to delegate, if our constitutional system is to be maintained.

* * *

The question, then, turns upon the authority which § 3 of the Recovery Act vests in the President to approve or prescribe. If the codes have standing as penal statutes, this must be due to the effect of the executive action. But Congress cannot delegate legislative power to the President to exercise an unfettered discretion to make whatever laws he thinks may be needed or advisable for the rehabilitation and expansion of trade or industry. See *Panama Refining Co. v. Ryan, supra,* and cases there reviewed.

Accordingly we turn to the Recovery Act to ascertain what limits have been set to the exercise of the President's discretion. *First,* the President, as a condition of approval, is required to find that the trade or industrial associations or groups which propose a code, "impose no inequitable restrictions on admission to membership" and are "truly representative." That condition, however, relates only to the status of the initiators of the new laws and not to the permissible scope of such laws. *Second,* the President is required to find that the code is not "designed to promote monopolies or to eliminate or oppress small enterprises and will not operate to discriminate against them." And, to this is added a proviso that the code "shall not permit monopolies or monopolistic practices." But these restrictions leave virtually untouched the field of policy envisaged by section one, and, in that wide field of legislative possibilities, the proponents of a code, refraining from monopolistic designs, may roam at will and the President may approve or disapprove their proposals as he may see fit. That is the precise effect of the further finding that the President is to make— that the code "will tend to effectuate the policy of this title." While this is called a finding, it is really but a statement of an opinion as to the general effect upon the promotion of trade or industry of a scheme of laws. These are the only findings which Congress has made essential in order to put into operation a legislative code having the aims described in the "Declaration of Policy."

Nor is the breadth of the President's discretion left to the necessary implications of this limited requirement as to his findings. As already noted, the President in approving a code may impose his own conditions, adding to or taking from what is proposed, as "in his discretion" he thinks necessary "to effectuate the policy" declared by the Act. Of course, he has no less liberty when he prescribes a code on his own motion or on complaint, and he is free to prescribe one if a code has not been approved. The Act provides for the creation by the President of administrative agencies to assist him, but the action or reports of such agencies, or of his other assistants,—their recommendations and findings in relation to the making of codes—have no sanction beyond the will of the President, who may accept, modify or reject them as he pleases. Such recommendations or findings in no way limit the authority which § 3 undertakes to vest in the President with no other conditions than those there specified. And this authority relates to a host of different trades and industries, thus extending the President's discretion to all the varieties of laws which he may deem to be beneficial in dealing with the vast array of commercial and industrial activities throughout the country.

* * *

To summarize and conclude upon this point: Section 3 of the Recovery Act is without precedent. It supplies no standards for any trade, industry or activity. It does not undertake to prescribe rules of conduct to be applied to particular states of fact determined by appropriate administrative procedure. Instead of prescribing rules of conduct, it authorizes the making of codes to prescribe them. For that legislative undertaking, § 3 sets up no standards, aside from the statement of the general aims of rehabilitation, correction and expansion described in section one. In view of the scope of that broad declaration, and of the nature of the few restrictions that are imposed, the discretion of the President in approving or prescribing codes, and thus enacting laws for the government of trade and industry throughout the country, is virtually unfettered. We think that the code-making authority thus conferred is an unconstitutional delegation of legislative power.

Third. The question of the application of the provisions of the Live Poultry Code to intrastate transactions.

* * *

These provisions relate to the hours and wages of those employed by defendants in their slaughterhouses in Brooklyn and to the sales there made to retail dealers and butchers.

(1) Were these transactions "*in*" interstate commerce? Much is made of the fact that almost all the poultry coming to New York is sent there from other States. But the code provisions, as here applied, do not concern the transportation of the poultry from other States to New York, or the transactions of the commission men or others to whom it is consigned, or the sales made by such consignees to defendants. When defendants had made their purchases, whether at the West Washington Market in New York City or at the railroad terminals serving the City, or elsewhere, the poultry was trucked to their slaughterhouses in Brooklyn for local disposition. The interstate transactions in relation to that poultry then ended. Defendants held the poultry at their slaughterhouse markets for slaughter and local sale to retail dealers and butchers who in turn sold directly to consumers. Neither the slaughtering nor the sales by defendants were transactions in interstate commerce.

* * *

(2) Did the defendants' transactions directly "*affect*" interstate commerce so as to be subject to federal regulation? . . .

In determining how far the federal government may go in controlling intrastate transactions upon the ground that they "affect" interstate commerce, there is a necessary and well-established distinction between direct and indirect effects. The precise line can be drawn only as individual cases arise, but the distinction is clear in principle. . . .

. . . where the effect of intrastate transactions upon interstate commerce is merely indirect, such transactions remain within the domain of state power. If the commerce clause were construed to reach all enterprises and transactions which could be said to have an indirect effect upon interstate commerce, the federal authority would embrace practically all the activities of the people and the authority of the State over its domestic concerns would exist only by sufferance of the federal government. Indeed, on such a theory, even the development of the State's commercial facilities would be subject to federal control. . . .

. . . the Government argues that hours and wages affect prices; that slaughterhouse men sell at a small margin above operating costs; that labor represents 50 to 60 per cent of these costs; that a slaughterhouse operator paying lower wages or reducing his cost by exacting long hours of work, translates his saving into lower prices; that this results in demands for a cheaper grade of goods; and that the cutting of prices brings about a demoralization of the price structure. Similar conditions may be adduced in relation to other businesses. The argument of the Government proves too much. If the federal government may determine the wages and hours of employees in the internal commerce of a State, because of their relation to cost and prices and their indirect effect upon interstate commerce, it would seem that a similar control might be exerted over other elements of cost, also affecting prices, such as the number of employees, rents, advertising, methods of doing business, etc. All the processes of production and distribution that enter into cost could likewise be controlled. If the cost of doing an intrastate business is in itself the permitted object of federal control, the extent of the regulation of cost would be a question of discretion and not of power.

The Government also makes the point that efforts to enact state legislation establishing high labor standards have been impeded by the belief that unless similar action is taken generally, commerce will be diverted from the States adopting such standards, and that this fear of diversion has led to demands for federal legislation on the subject of wages and hours. The apparent implication is that the federal authority under the commerce clause should be deemed to extend to the establishment of rules to govern wages and hours in intrastate trade and industry generally throughout the country, thus overriding the authority of the States to deal with domestic problems arising from labor conditions in their internal commerce.

It is not the province of the Court to consider the economic advantages or disadvantages of such a centralized system. It is sufficient to say that the Federal Constitution does not provide for it. Our growth and development have called for wide use of the commerce power of the federal government in its control over the expanded activities of interstate commerce, and in protecting that commerce from burdens, interferences, and conspiracies to restrain and monopolize it. But the authority of the federal government may not be pushed to such an extreme as to destroy the distinction, which the commerce clause itself establishes, between commerce "among the several States" and the internal concerns of a State. The same answer must be made to the contention that is based upon the serious economic situation which led to the passage of the Recovery Act,—the fall in prices, the decline in wages and employment, and the curtailment of the market for commodities. Stress is laid upon the great importance of maintaining wage distributions which would provide the necessary stimulus in starting "the cumulative forces making for expanding commercial activity." Without in any way disparaging this motive, it is enough to say that the recuperative efforts of the federal government must be made in a manner consistent with the authority granted by the Constitution.

We are of the opinion that the attempt through the provisions of the Code to fix the hours and wages of employees of defendants in their intrastate business was not a valid exercise of federal power.

The other violations for which defendants were convicted related to the making of local sales. Ten counts, for violation of the provision as to "straight killing," were for permitting customers to make "selections of individual chickens taken from particular coops and half coops." Whether or not this practice is good or bad for the local trade, its effect, if any, upon interstate commerce was only indirect. The same may be said of violations of the Code by intrastate transactions consisting of the sale "of an unfit chicken" and of sales which were not in accord with the ordinances of the City of New York. The requirement of reports as to prices and volumes of defendants' sales was incident to the effort to control their intrastate business.

In view of these conclusions, we find it unnecessary to discuss other questions which have been raised as to the validity of certain provisions of the Code under the due process clause of the Fifth Amendment.

On both the grounds we have discussed, the attempted delegation of legislative power, and the attempted regulation of intrastate transactions which affect interstate commerce only indirectly, we hold the code provisions here in question to be invalid and that the judgment of conviction must be reversed.

* * *

QUESTIONS AND COMMENTS

1 Was *Schechter v. United States* a political decision? If so, how do you explain the fact that the decision was unanimous? Or Cardozo's statement in his concurring opinion (not reported in the text) that "this is delegation running riot." Is it possible that in the midst of a political or ideological conflict between a President and the Court, the Court is capable of making a relatively objective interpretation of the Constitution? Or would such a notion be naive?

2 Later cases on the delegation of legislative power have not generally supported the narrow view of delegation represented in *Schechter*. Cf. *Yakus v. United States,*

(1944); *Arizona v. California,* (1963). Given that the NRA was considered a failure and that President Roosevelt was letting it expire, the unanimous striking of the program is one of those unexplained anomalies with which American constitutional law is replete.

To Determine Supreme Court Jurisdiction

Martin v. Hunter's Lessee (1816)

Ex Parte McCardle (1869)

Courts may be divided into those of general jurisdiction and those of limited jurisdiction. A court in the first category is assumed to have jurisdiction of a case, though under certain conditions an exception may be made. A court falling in the second classification, on the other hand, must be shown in every case to have jurisdiction, i.e., that a controversy comes within the limited jurisdiction which the court possesses. State courts generally fall in the first category, federal courts in the second. We have learned that in a system of delegated powers, government has only the powers delegated by the Constitution. The Constitution establishes the Supreme Court's original and appellate jurisdiction. Appellate jurisdiction, however, is granted "with such exceptions, and under such regulations as the Congress shall make." This has been interpreted to mean that the Court's appellate jurisdiction is subject to congressional control. The two cases in this section test this congressional power on two dimensions: the power of Congress to regulate Supreme Court jurisdiction over state courts, and its power to rescind an appellate jurisdiction previously granted to the Court.

Martin, Heir at Law and Devisee of Fairfax v. Hunter's Lessee

1 Wheaton 304; 4 L. Ed. 97 (1816)
Vote: Unanimous

A Virginia citizen, Lord Fairfax, owned several hundred thousand acres of land in Virginia. The lands were seized by the state during the Revolution. An eventual heir to the lands, Martin, sued to recover them. Rebuffed by Virginia courts, Martin appealed to the Supreme Court, which reversed and established Martin's title to the land. The Virginia Court of Appeals refused to enforce this decision on the ground that the Supreme Court lacked appellate jurisdiction over state courts. The Supreme Court accepted the challenge to its jurisdictional powers in the present case and granted review.

STORY, J., delivered the opinion of the court.

* * *

The constitution of the United States was ordained and established, not by the States in their sovereign capacities, but emphatically, as the preamble of the constitution declares, by "the people of the United States." There can be no doubt that it was competent to the people to invest the general government with all the powers which they might deem proper and necessary; to extend or restrain these powers according to their own good pleasure, and to give them a paramount and supreme authority. As little doubt can there be, that the people had a right to prohibit to the States the exercise of any powers which were, in their judgment, incompatible with the objects of the general compact; to make the powers of the state governments, in given cases, subordinate to those of the nation, or to reserve to themselves those sovereign authorities which they might not choose to delegate to either. The constitution was not, therefore, necessarily carved out of existing state sovereignties, nor a surrender of powers already existing in state institutions, for the powers of the States depend upon their own constitutions; and the people of every State had the right to modify and restrain them, according to their own views of policy or principle. On the other hand, it is perfectly clear that the sovereign powers vested in the state governments, by their respective constitutions, remained unaltered and unimpaired, except so far as they were granted to the government of the United States.

* * *

The government, then, of the United States, can claim no powers which are not granted to it by the constitution, and the powers actually granted must be such as are expressly given or given by necessary implication. On the other hand, this instrument, like every other grant, is to have a reasonable construction, according to the import of its terms; and where a power is expressly given in general terms, it is not to be restrained to particular cases, unless that construction grows out of the context expressly, or by necessary implication. The words are to be taken in their natural and obvious sense, and not in a sense unreasonably restricted or enlarged.

* * *

With these principles in view, principles in respect to which no difference of opinion ought to be indulged, let us now proceed to the interpretation of the constitution, so far as regards the great points in controversy.

The third article of the constitution is that which must principally attract our attention. . . .

This leads us to the consideration of the great question as to the nature and extent of the appellate jurisdiction of the United States.

[The] . . . appellate jurisdiction is given by the constitution to the supreme court in all cases where it has not original jurisdiction, subject, however, to such exceptions and regulations as congress may prescribe. It is, therefore, capable of embracing every case enumerated in the constitution, which is not exclusively to be decided by way of original jurisdiction. But the exercise of appellate jurisdiction is far from being limited by the terms of the constitution to the supreme court. There can be no doubt that congress may create a succession of inferior tribunals, in each of which it may vest appellate as well as original jurisdiction. The judicial power is delegated by the constitution in the most general terms, and may, therefore, be exercised by congress under every variety of form, of appellate or original jurisdiction. And as there is nothing in the constitution which restrains or limits this power, it must, therefore, in all other cases, subsist in the utmost latitude of which, in its own nature, it is susceptible.

As, then, by the terms of the constitution, the appellate jurisdiction is not limited as to the supreme court, and as to this court it may be exercised in all other cases than those of which it has original cognizance, what is there to restrain its exercise over state tribunals in the enumerated cases? The appellate power is not limited by the terms of the third article to any particular courts. The words are, "the judicial power (which includes appellate power) shall extend to all cases," &c, and "in all other cases before mentioned the supreme court shall have appellate jurisdiction." It is the case, then, and not the court, that gives the jurisdiction. If the judicial power extends to the case, it will be in vain to search in the letter of the constitution for any qualification as to the tribunal where it depends. It is incumbent, then, upon those who assert such a qualification to show its existence by necessary implication. If the text be clear and distinct, no restriction upon its plain and obvious import ought to be admitted, unless the inference obvious import ought to be admitted, unless the inference be irresistible.

. . . it is plain that the framers of the constitution did contemplate that cases within the judicial cognizance of the United States not only might but would arise in the state courts, in the exercise of their ordinary jurisdiction. With this view the sixth article declares, that "this constitution, and the laws of the United States which shall be made in pursuance thereof, and all treaties made, or which shall be made, under the authority of the United States, shall be the supreme law of the land, and the judges in every State shall be bound thereby, any thing in the constitution, or laws of any State to the contrary notwithstanding." It is obvious that this obligation is imperative upon the state judges in their official, and not merely in their private, capacities. From the very nature of their judicial duties they would be called upon to pronounce the law applicable to the case in judgment. They were not to decide merely according to the laws or constitution of the State, but according to the constitution, laws, and treaties of the United States, "the supreme law of the land.". . .

. . . the constitution not only contemplated, but meant to provide for cases within the scope of the judicial power of the United States, which might yet depend before state tribunals. It was foreseen that in the exercise of their ordinary jurisdiction, state courts would incidentally take cognizance of cases arising under the constitution, the laws, and treaties of the United States. Yet to all these cases the judicial power, by the very terms of the constitution, is to extend. It cannot extend by original jurisdiction if that was already rightfully and exclusively attached in the state courts, which (as has been already shown) may occur; it must therefore extend by appellate jurisdiction, or not at all. It would seem to follow that the appellate power of the United States must in such cases, extend to state tribunals; and if in such cases, there is no reason why it should not equally attach upon all others within the purview of the constitution.

It has been argued that such an appellate jurisdiction over state courts, is inconsistent with the genius of our governments, and the spirit of the constitution. That the latter was never designed to act upon state sovereignties, but only upon the people, and that, if the power exists, it will materially impair the sovereignty of the States, and the independence of their courts. We cannot yield to the force of this reasoning; it assumes principles which we cannot admit, and draws conclusions to which we do not yield our assent.

It is a mistake that the constitution was not designed to operate upon States, in their corporate capacities. It is crowded with provisions which restrain or annul the sovereignty of the States in some of the highest branches of their prerogatives. The tenth section of the first article contains a long list of disabilities and prohibitions imposed upon the States. Surely, when such essential portions of state sovereignty are taken away, or prohibited to be exercised, it cannot be correctly asserted that the constitution does not act upon the States. The language of the constitution is also imperative upon the States, as to the performance of many duties. It is imperative upon the state legislatures to make laws prescribing the time, places, and manner of holding elections for senators and representatives, and for electors of president and vice-president. And in these, as well as some other cases, congress have a right to revise, amend, or supersede the laws which may be passed by state legislatures. When, therefore, the States are stripped of some of the highest attributes of sovereignty, and the same are given to the United States; when the legislatures of the States are, in some respects, under the control of congress, and in every case are, under the constitution, bound by the paramount authority of the United States; it is certainly difficult to support the argument that the appellate power over the decisions of state courts is contrary to the genius of our institutions. The courts of the United States can, without question, revise the proceedings of the executive and legislative authorities of the States, and if they are found to be contrary to the constitution, may declare them to be of no legal validity. Surely, the exercise of the same right over judicial tribunals is not a higher or more dangerous act of sovereign power.

Nor can such a right be deemed to impair the independence of state judges. It is assuming the very ground in controversy to assert that they possess an absolute independence of the United States. In respect to the powers granted to the United States, they are not independent; they are expressly bound to obedience by the letter of the constitution; and if they should unintentionally transcend their authority, or misconstrue the constitution, there is no more reason for giving their judgments an absolute and irresistible force, than for giving it to the acts of the other coördinate departments of state sovereignty.

The argument urged from the possibility of the abuse of the revising power, is equally unsatisfactory. It is always a doubtful course, to argue against the use or existence of a power, from the possibility of its abuse. It is still more difficult, by such an argument, to ingraft upon a general power, a restriction which is not to be found in the terms in which it is given. From the very nature of things, the absolute right of decision, in the last resort, must rest somewhere— wherever it may be vested it is susceptible of abuse. In all questions of jurisdiction the inferior, or appellate court must pronounce the final judgment; and common sense, as well as legal reasoning, has conferred it upon the latter. . . .

This is not all. A motive of another kind, perfectly compatible with the most sincere respect for state tribunals, might induce the grant of appellate power over their decisions. That motive is the importance, and even necessity of uniformity of decisions throughout the whole United States, upon all subjects within the purview of the constitution. Judges of equal learning and integrity, in different States, might differently interpret a statute, or a treaty of the United States, or even the constitution itself. If there were no revising authority to control these jarring and discordant judgments, and harmonize them into uniformity, the laws, the treaties, and the constitution of the United States would be different in different States, and might, perhaps, never have precisely the same construction, obligation, or efficacy, in any two States. The public mischiefs that would attend such a state of things would be truly deplorable; and it cannot be believed that they could have escaped the enlightened convention which formed the constitution. What, indeed, might then have been only prophecy has now become fact; and the appellate jurisdiction must continue to be the only adequate remedy for such evils.

*   *   *

On the whole, the court are of opinion, that the appellate power of the United States does extend to cases pending in the state courts; and that the 25th section of the Judiciary Act, which authorizes the exercise of this jurisdiction in the specified cases, by a writ of error, is supported by the letter and spirit of the constitution. We find no clause in that instrument which limits this power; and we dare not interpose a limitation where the people have not been disposed to create one.

*   *   *

The next question which has been argued, is, whether the case at bar be within the purview of the 25th section of the Judiciary Act, so that this court may rightfully sustain the present writ of error.

*   *   *

That the present writ of error is founded upon a judgment of the court below, which drew in question and denied the validity of a statute of the United States, is incontrovertible, for it is apparent upon the face of the record.

That this judgment is final upon the rights of the parties is equally true; for if well founded, the former judgment of that court was of conclusive authority, and the former judgment of this court utterly void. The decision was, therefore, equivalent to a perpetual stay of proceedings upon the mandate, and a perpetual denial of all the rights acquired under it. The case, then, falls directly within the terms of the act. It is a final judgment in a suit in a state court, denying the validity of a statute of the United States; and unless a distinction can be made between proceedings under a mandate, and proceedings in an original suit, a writ of error is the proper remedy to revise that judgment. In our opinion no legal distinction exists between the cases.

* * *

It is the opinion of the whole court, that the judgment of the court of appeals of Virginia, rendered on the mandate in this cause, be reversed, and the judgment of the district court, held at Winchester, be, and the same is hereby affirmed.

* * *

Ex Parte McCardle

7 Wall. 506 (1869)
Vote: Unanimous

The facts provided below are taken from the "Statement of the Case."

APPEAL from the Circuit Court for the Southern District of Mississippi.
The case was this:
The Constitution of the United States ordains as follows:

§ 1. The judicial power of the United States shall be vested *in one Supreme Court,* and in such inferior courts as the Congress may from time to time ordain and establish."
§ 2. The judicial power shall extend to all cases in law or equity arising *under this Constitution, the laws of the United States, &c.*

And in these last cases the Constitution ordains that,

The Supreme Court shall have appellate jurisdiction, both as to law and fact, *with such exceptions, and under such regulations, as the Congress shall make.*

With these constitutional provisions in existence, Congress, on the 5th February, 1867, by "An act to amend an act to establish the judicial courts of the United States, approved September 24, 1789," provided that the several courts of the United States, and the several justices and judges of such courts, within their respective jurisdiction, in addition to the authority already conferred by law, should have power to grant writs of *habeas corpus* in all cases where any person may be restrained of his or her liberty in violation of the Constitution, or of any treaty or law of the United States. And that, from the final decision of any judge, justice, or court inferior to the Circuit Court, appeal might be taken to the Circuit Court of the United States for the district in which the cause was heard, and *from the judgment of the said Circuit Court to the Supreme Court of the United States.*

This statute being in force, one McCardle, alleging unlawful restraint by military force, preferred a petition in the court below, for the writ of *habeas corpus.*

The writ was issued, and a return was made by the military commander, admitting the restraint, but denying that it was unlawful.

It appeared that the petitioner was not in the military service of the United States, but was held in custody by military authority for trial before a military commission, upon charges founded upon the publication of articles alleged to be incendiary and libellous, in a newspaper of which he was editor. The custody was alleged to be under the authority of certain acts of Congress.

Upon the hearing, the petitioner was remanded to the military custody; but, upon his prayer, an appeal was allowed him to this court. . . .

[After argument but prior to decision, Congress repealed the statute which gave the Supreme Court jurisdiction in this case. Argument was then heard on the effect of the repealing act.]

The CHIEF JUSTICE delivered the opinion of the court.

The first question necessarily is that of jurisdiction; for, if the act of March, 1868, takes away the jurisdiction defined by the act of February, 1867, it is useless, if not improper, to enter into any discussion of other questions.

It is quite true, as was argued by the counsel for the petitioner, that the appellate jurisdiction of this court is not derived from acts of Congress. It is, strictly speaking, conferred by the Constitution. But it is conferred "with such exceptions and under such regulations as Congress shall make."

It is unnecessary to consider whether, if Congress had made no exceptions and no regulations, this court might not have exercised general appellate jurisdiction under rules prescribed by itself. For among the earliest acts of the first Congress, at its first session, was the act of September 24th, 1789, to establish the judicial courts of the United States. That act provided for the organization of this court, and prescribed regulations for the exercise of its jurisdiction.

The source of that jurisdiction, and the limitations of it by the Constitution and by statute, have been on several occasions subjects of consideration here. In the case of *Durousscau v. The United States,* [1810], particularly, the whole matter was carefully examined, and the court held, that while "the appellate powers of this court are not given by the judicial act, but are given by the Constitution," they are, nevertheless, "limited and regulated by that act, and by such other acts as have been passed on the subject." The court said, further, that the judicial act was an exercise of the power given by the Constitution to Congress "of making exceptions to the appellate jurisdiction of the Supreme Court." "They have described affirmatively," said the court, "its jurisdiction, and this affirmative description has been understood to imply a negation of the exercise of such appellate power as is not comprehended within it."

The principle that the affirmation of appellate jurisdiction implies the negation of all such jurisdiction not affirmed having been thus established, it was an almost necessary consequence that acts of Congress, providing for the exercise of jurisdiction, should come to be spoken of as acts granting jurisdiction, and not as acts making exceptions to the constitutional grant of it.

The exception to appellate jurisdiction in the case before us, however, is not an inference from the affirmation of other appellate jurisdiction. It is made in terms. The provision of the act of 1867, affirming the appellate jurisdiction of this court in cases of *habeas corpus* is expressly repealed. It is hardly possible to imagine a plainer instance of positive exception.

We are not at liberty to inquire into the motives of the legislature. We can only examine into its power under the Constitution; and the power to make exceptions to the appellate jurisdiction of this court is given by express words.

What, then, is the effect of the repealing act upon the case before us? We cannot doubt as to this. Without jurisdiction the court cannot proceed at all in any cause. Jurisdiction is power to declare the law, and when it ceases to exist, the only function remaining to the court is that of announcing the fact and dismissing the cause. And this is not less clear upon authority than upon principle.

Several cases were cited by the counsel for the petitioner in support of the position that jurisdiction of this case is not affected by the repealing act. But none of them, in our judgment, afford any support to it. They are all cases of the exercise of judicial power by the legislature, or of legislative interference with courts in the exercising of continuing jurisdiction.

On the other hand, the general rule, supported by the best elementary writers is, that "when an act of the legislature is repealed, it must be considered, except as to transactions past and closed, as if it never existed." And the effect of repealing acts upon suits under acts repealed, has been determined by the adjudications of this court. The subject was fully considered in *Norris v. Crocker*, [1852], and more recently in *Insurance Company v. Ritchie*, [1867]. In both of these cases it was held that no judgment could be rendered in a suit after the repeal of the act under which it was brought and prosecuted.

It is quite clear, therefore, that this court cannot proceed to pronounce judgment in this case, for it has no longer jurisdiction of the appeal; and judicial duty is not less fitly performed by declining ungranted jurisdiction than in exercising firmly that which the Constitution and the laws confer.

Counsel seem to have supposed, if effect be given to the repealing act in question, that the whole appellate power of the court, in cases of *habeas corpus,* is denied. But this is an error. The act of 1868 does not except from that jurisdiction any cases but appeals from Circuit Courts under the act of 1867. It does not affect the jurisdiction which was previously exercised.

The appeal of the petitioner in this case must be

Dismissed for want of Jurisdiction.

QUESTIONS AND COMMENTS

1 In recent years, it has been *argued* that Congress does not possess the power, via control of appellate jurisdiction, to destroy the essential functions of the Supreme Court—i.e., that its control of appellate jurisdiction is less than absolute. Evaluate that argument.

2 Since the Supreme Court may rule, in appropriate circumstances, on the constitutionality of any congressional repeal of appellate jurisdiction, why should one expect an attempted repeal to be successful?

3 Does *Ex Parte McCardle* reflect judicial activism or judicial restraint? Relate your answer to Canon's dimensions of activism.

4 What would be the consequences of denying the Supreme Court the right to review the decisions of state courts on the constitutionality of state laws? Is this what the framers intended? Why or why not?

To Enforce Racial Policy

Fitzpatrick v. Bitzer (1976)

While Congress may legislate, its laws depend for enforcement on the executive and judicial branches of government. One way in which Congress may assist the enforcing agencies is by attaching sanctions for the violation of national policy. When dealing with state governments, however, Congress must consider the import of the Eleventh Amendment. That amendment denies the citizen of one state the right to sue another state. If this is taken literally, it would mean that a state could violate the constitutional rights of noncitizens without being answerable in any federal court. The Fourteenth Amendment, however, protects the constitutional rights of "persons," and Congress is granted the power to enforce the amendment.

Called upon to resolve this conflict between two amendments, the Supreme Court has broadly interpreted the enforcement powers. In doing so, the Court has serviced the fiction of sovereign immunity by finding a state waiver of its protection against suit either by direct or constructive consent. In the modern day, it is constructive consent that is important. If Congress regulates an activity within its constitutional powers and a state chooses to engage in that activity, the state is said to constructively waive its protection against suit for violation of the regulations if such suit is a remedy provided by the Congress. Such a waiver occurs, the Court has ruled, even if the state explicitly denies its consent to be sued. Thus the Court has given Congress, via interpretation, the power to remove a state's Eleventh Amendment protection under appropriate circumstances.

Fitzpatrick et al. v. Bitzer, Chairman, State Employees Retirement Commission et al.

427 U.S. 445; 96 S. Ct. 2666; 49 L. Ed. 2d 614 (1976)
Vote: 9–0

In 1922, Congress authorized federal courts to award money damages in favor of a private individual against a state government found to have practiced employment discrimination against that person on the basis of "race, color, religion, sex, or national origin" (Title VII, Civil Rights Act of 1964, as amended).

Fitzpatrick was a retired male employee of the state of Connecticut. He brought an action in the federal district court challenging the Connecticut State Employees Retirement Act as a violation of Title VII's ban on sex-based employment discrimination. The court granted an injunction in Fitzpatrick's favor but denied retroactive retirement benefits and attorney's fees on grounds of the Eleventh Amendment and the Supreme Court's decision in *Edelman v. Jordan* (1974).[23] The court of appeals affirmed as to retirement benefits but reversed as to attorney's fees, reasoning that such an award would have slight effect on the state treasury.

MR. JUSTICE REHNQUIST delivered the opinion of the Court.

* * *

In *Edelman v. Jordan,* this Court held that monetary relief awarded by the District Court to welfare plaintiffs, by reason of wrongful denial of benefits which had occurred previous to the entry of the District Court's determination of their wrongfulness, violated the Eleventh Amendment. Such an award was found to be indistinguishable from a monetary award against the State itself which had been prohibited in *Ford Motor Co. v. Department of Treasury,* (1945). It was therefore controlled by that case rather than by *Ex parte Young,* (1908), which permitted suits against state officials to obtain prospective relief against violations of the Fourteenth Amendment.

* * *

All parties in the instant litigation agree with the Court of Appeals that the suit for retroactive benefits by the petitioners is in fact indistinguishable from that sought to be maintained in *Edelman,* since what is sought here is a damages award payable to a private party from the state treasury. . . . The Eleventh Amendment defense is asserted in the context of legislation passed pursuant to Congress' authority under § 5 of the Fourteenth Amendment.

As ratified by the States after the Civil War, that Amendment quite clearly contemplates limitations on their authority. In relevant part, it provides:

> Section 1. . . . No State shall make or enforce any law which shall abridge the privileges or immunities of citizens of the United States; nor shall any State deprive any person of life, liberty, or property, without due process of law; nor deny to any person within its jurisdiction the equal protection of the laws.
>
> Section 5. The Congress shall have power to enforce, by appropriate legislation, the provisions of this article.

The substantive provisions are by express terms directed at the States. Impressed upon them by those provisions are duties with respect to their treatment of private individuals. Standing behind the imperatives is Congress' power to "enforce" them "by appropriate legislation."

The impact of the Fourteenth Amendment upon the relationship between the Federal Government and the States, and the reach of congressional power under § 5, were examined at length by this Court in *Ex parte Virginia,* (1880). A state judge had been arrested and indicted under a federal criminal statute prohibiting the exclusion on the basis of race of any citizen from service as a juror in a state court. The judge claimed that the statute was beyond Congress' power to enact under either the Thirteenth or the Fourteenth Amendment. The Court first observed that these Amendments "were intended to be, what they really are, limitations of the power of the States and enlargements of the power of Congress." It then addressed the relationship between the language of § 5 and the substantive provisions of the Fourteenth Amendment:

> The prohibitions of the Fourteenth Amendment are directed to the States, and they are to a degree restrictions of State power. It is these which Congress is empowered to enforce, and to enforce against State action, however put forth, whether that action be executive, legislative, or judicial. Such enforcement is no invasion of State sovereignty. No law can be, which the people of the States have, by the Constitution of the United States, empowered Congress to enact. . . . It is said the selection of jurors for her courts and the administration of her laws belong to each State; that they are her rights. This is true in the general. But in exercising her rights, a State cannot disregard the limitations which the Federal Constitution has applied to her power. Her rights do not reach to that extent. Nor can she deny to the general government the right to exercise all its granted powers, though they may interfere with the full enjoyment of rights she would have if those powers had not been thus granted. Indeed, every addition of power to the general government involves a corresponding diminution of the governmental powers of the States. It is carved out of them.
>
> The argument in support of the petition for a *habeas corpus* ignores entirely the power conferred upon Congress by the Fourteenth Amendment. Were it not for the fifth section of that amendment, there might be room for argument that the first section is only declaratory of the moral duty of the State. . . . But the Constitution now expressly gives authority for congressional interference and compulsion in the cases embraced within the Fourteenth Amendment. It is but a limited authority, true, extending only to a single class of cases; but within its limits it is complete.

Ex parte Virginia's early recognition of this shift in the federal-state balance has been carried forward by more recent decisions of this Court.

There can be no doubt that this line of cases has sanctioned intrusions by Congress, acting under the Civil War Amendments, into the judicial, executive, and legislative spheres of autonomy previously reserved to the States. The legislation considered in each case was grounded on the expansion of Congress' powers—with the corresponding diminution of state sovereignty—found to be intended by the Framers and made part of the Constitution upon the States' ratification of those Amendments, a phenomenon aptly described as a "carv[ing] out" in *Ex parte Virginia, supra,* at 346.

It is true that none of these previous cases presented the question of the relationship between the Eleventh Amendment and the enforcement power granted to Congress under § 5 of the Fourteenth Amendment. But we think that the Eleventh Amendment, and the principle of state sovereignty which it embodies, are necessarily limited by the enforcement provisions of § 5 of the Fourteenth Amendment. In that section Congress is expressly granted authority to enforce "by appropriate legislation" the substantive provisions of the Fourteenth Amendment, which themselves embody significant limitations on state authority. When Congress acts pursuant to § 5, not only is it exercising legislative authority that is plenary within the terms of the constitutional grant, it is exercising that authority under one section of a constitutional Amendment whose other sections by their own terms embody limitations on state authority. We think that Congress may, in determining what is "appropriate legislation" for the purpose of enforcing the provisions of the Fourteenth Amendment, provide for private suits against States or state officials which are constitutionally impermissible in other contexts.

. . . the state officials contest the Court of Appeals' conclusion that an award of attorneys' fees in this case would under *Edelman* have only an "ancillary effect" on the state treasury and could therefore be permitted as falling outside the Eleventh Amendment under the doctrine of *Ex parte Young,* (1908). We need not address this question, since, given the express congressional authority for such an award in a case brought under Title VII, it follows necessarily . . . that Congress' exercise of power in this respect is also not barred by the Eleventh Amendment. We therefore affirm the Court of Appeals' judgment . . . on this basis.

* * *

QUESTIONS AND COMMENTS

1 If Congress is allowed to provide for monetary damages against a state for violation of federal policy, such damages must be paid, ultimately, by the state's taxpayers. Does this constitute taxation without representation?

2   In deciding that the enforcement provision of the Fourteenth Amendment is a limitation on the Eleventh Amendment rights of the states, the Court must decide the
extent of the limitation. In *Fitzpatrick,* the Eleventh Amendment was limited sufficiently to allow Congress to authorize monetary awards against a state for violating
congressional policy. Where does the Supreme Court discover this particular limitation? Where will it find others? Could Congress allow suits against states, contrary to
Eleventh Amendment language, in all cases involving federal legislation?

To Exercise Inherent or Implied Power

Kansas v. Colorado (1907)

Afroyim v. Rusk (1967)

We saw in *McCulloch v. Maryland* that Congress possesses not only the
powers enumerated in Article I, Section 8, but also the authority to
implement the listed powers as is necessary and proper. The logic is that to
grant a power is to imply the power to use it. The problem is to determine
what is implied by any particular enumerated power.

Some implications of power are fairly obvious. Thus, no one would
question that the power to collect taxes implies the power to punish those
who owe but fail to pay. In *Kansas v. Colorado,* the government's argument
is more complex, and implied authority somewhat more tenuous.

In *Afroyim v. Rusk,* the Court addresses an issue that often has been
controversial, an issue frequently associated with emotion-colored debate—
i.e., congressional control over citizenship.

The Fourteenth Amendment grants citizenship to all persons born or
naturalized in the United States who are subject to United States
jurisdiction. But Congress may establish the conditions under which aliens
are to be naturalized. If these standards are not met, naturalization will not
be granted. While the Fourteenth Amendment does not address the question,
one is free to relinquish citizenship, natural-born or naturalized, should one
choose to do so. The relinquishing must, however, be truly voluntary.[24] In all
events, the rights of a naturalized citizen are equal to those of a natural-born
citizen.

A different question is whether one can lose one's citizenship
involuntarily, and more specifically whether one can lose it at the hands of
the Congress. Prior to *Afroyim* a United States national had been deprived of
citizenship for voting in a Mexican political election, another for desertion in
time of war. Both deprivations occurred under congressional statutes. The
Court upheld the deprivation in the first instance[25] and struck it in the
second.[26] But the uncertainty in the Court over this issue was reflected in the
fact that the first case was decided by a 5–4 vote and the second produced no
majority opinion. That uncertainty is not totally eliminated in *Afroyim v.
Rusk,* since it, too, was decided by a 5–4 vote. But the case does address the
extent to which Congress has implied powers in the area of citizenship, and
it remains good law at this point.

Kansas v. Colorado

206 U.S. 46; 27 S. Ct. 655; 51 L. Ed. 956 (1907)
Vote: 8–0

The state of Colorado was diverting water from the Arkansas River for purposes of irrigation. One result was to reduce the water available to Kansas farther down the river. Kansas sued for an injunction to stop the diversion. The United States sought to intervene on the ground that control of the water was vested in the federal government. The government argued that it had an interest in reclaiming arid lands and that such a goal could not be accomplished at the state level. In the excerpt from the opinion below, the Supreme Court assesses the U.S. claim.

Mr. Justice Brewer . . . delivered the opinion of the court.

* * *

In the Constitution are provisions in separate articles for the three great departments of government—legislative, executive and judicial. But there is this significant difference in the grants of powers to these departments: The first article, treating of legislative powers, does not make a general grant of legislative power. It reads: "Article I, Section 1. All legislative powers herein granted shall be vested in a Congress," etc.; and then in Article VIII mentions and defines the legislative powers that are granted. By reason of the fact that there is no general grant of legislative power it has become an accepted constitutional rule that this is a government of enumerated powers. . . .

Turning now to the controversy as here presented, it is whether Kansas has a right to the continuous flow of the waters of the Arkansas River, as that flow existed before any human interference therewith, or Colorado the right to appropriate the waters of that stream so as to prevent that continuous flow, or that the amount of the flow is subject to the superior authority and supervisory control of the United States. . . .

The primary question is, of course, of national control. For, if the Nation has a right to regulate the flow of the waters, we must inquire what it has done in the way of regulation. . . .

. . . if in the present case the National Government was asserting, as against either Kansas or Colorado, that the appropriation for the purposes of irrigation of the waters of the Arkansas was affecting the navigability of the stream, it would become our duty to determine the truth of the charge. But the Government makes no such contention. On the contrary, it distinctly asserts that the Arkansas River is not now and never was practically navigable beyond Fort Gibson in the Indian Territory, and nowhere claims that any appropriation of the waters by Kansas or Colorado affects its navigability.

It rests its petition of intervention upon its alleged duty of legislating for the reclamation of arid lands; alleges that in or near the Arkansas River, as it runs through Kansas and Colorado, are large tracts of those lands; that the National Government is itself the owner of many thousands of acres; that it has the right to make such legislative provision as in its judgment is needful for the reclamation of all these arid lands and for that purpose to appropriate the accessible waters.

* * *

In other words, the determination of the rights of the two States *inter sese* in regard to the flow of waters in the Arkansas River is subordinate to a superior right on the part of the National Government to control the whole system of the reclamation of arid lands. That involves the question whether the reclamation of arid lands is one of the powers granted to the General Government. As heretofore stated, the constant declaration of this court from the beginning is that this Government is one of enumerated powers. "The Government, then, of the United States, can claim no powers which are not granted to it by the Constitution, and the powers actually granted, must be such as are expressly given, or given by necessary implication.". . .

Turning to the enumeration of the powers granted to Congress by the eighth section of the first article of the Constitution, it is enough to say that no one of them by any implication refers to the reclamation of arid lands. . . .

. . . counsel for the Government relies upon "the doctrine of sovereign and inherent power," adding "I am aware that in advancing this doctrine I seem to challenge great decisions of the court, and I speak with deference." His argument runs substantially along this line: All legislative power must be vested in either the state or the National Government; no legislative powers belong to a state government other than those which affect solely the internal affairs of that State; consequently all powers which are national in their scope must be found vested in the Congress of the United States. But the proposition that there are legislative powers affecting the Nation as a whole which belong to, although not expressed in the grant of powers, is in direct conflict with the doctrine that this is a government of enumerated powers. That this is such a government clearly appears from the Constitution, independently of the Amendments, for otherwise there would be an instrument granting certain specified things made operative to grant other and distinct things. This natural construction of the original body of the Constitution is made absolutely certain by the Tenth Amendment. This amendment, which was seemingly adopted with prescience of just such contention as the present, disclosed the widespread fear that the National Government might, under the pressure of a supposed general welfare, attempt to exercise powers which had not been granted. With equal determination the framers intended that no such assumption should ever find justification in the organic act, and that if in the future further powers seemed necessary they should be granted by the people in the manner they had provided for amending that act. It reads: "The powers not delegated to the United States by the Constitution, nor prohibited by it to the States, are reserved to the States respectively, or to the people." The argument of counsel ignores the principal factor in this article, to wit, "the people." Its principal purpose was not the distribution of power between the United States and the States, but a reservation to the people of all powers not granted. The preamble of the Constitution declares who framed it, "we the people of the United States," not the people of one State, but the people of all the States, and Article X reserves to the people of all the States the powers not delegated to the United States. The powers affecting the internal affairs of the States not granted to the United States by the Constitution, nor prohibited by it to the States, are reserved to the States respectively, and all powers of a national character which are not delegated to the National Government by the Constitution are reserved to the people of the United States. The people who adopted the Constitution knew that in the nature of things they could not foresee all the questions which might arise in the future, all the circumstances which might call for the exercise of further national powers than those granted to the United States, and after making provision for an amendment to the Constitution by which any needed additional powers would be granted, they reserved to themselves all powers not so delegated. This Article X is not to be shorn of its meaning by any narrow or technical construction, but is to be considered fairly and liberally so as to give effect to its scope and meaning.

* * *

The decree which, therefore, will be entered will be one dismissing the petition of the intervenor, without prejudice to the rights of the United States to take such action as it shall deem necessary to preserve or improve the navigability of the Arkansas River. . . .

Afroyim v. Rusk, Secretary of State

387 U.S. 253; 87 S. Ct. 1660; 18 L. Ed. 2d 757 (1967)
Vote: 5–4

The facts are provided in the opinion below.

MR. JUSTICE BLACK delivered the opinion of the Court.

Petitioner, born in Poland in 1893, immigrated to this country in 1912 and became a naturalized American citizen in 1926. He went to Israel in 1950, and in 1951 he voluntarily voted in an election for the Israeli Knesset, the legislative body of Israel. In 1960, when he applied for renewal of his United States passport, the Department of State refused to grant it on the sole ground that he had lost his American citizenship by virtue of § 401 (e) of the Nationality

Act of 1940 which provides that a United States citizen shall "lose" his citizenship if he votes "in a political election in a foreign state." Petitioner then brought this declaratory judgment action in federal district court alleging that § 401 (e) violates both the Due Process Clause of the Fifth Amendment and § 1, cl. 1, of the Fourteenth Amendment which grants American citizenship to persons like petitioner. Because neither the Fourteenth Amendment nor any other provision of the Constitution expressly grants Congress the power to take away that citizenship once it has been acquired, petitioner contended that the only way he could lose his citizenship was by his own voluntary renunciation of it. Since the Government took the position that § 401 (e) empowers it to terminate citizenship without the citizen's voluntary renunciation, petitioner argued that this section is prohibited by the Constitution. The District Court and the Court of Appeals, rejecting this argument, held that Congress has constitutional authority forcibly to take away citizenship for voting in a foreign country based on its implied power to regulate foreign affairs. Consequently, petitioner was held to have lost his American citizenship regardless of his intention not to give it up. This is precisely what this Court held in *Perez v. Brownell,* [1958]. . . .

The fundamental issue before this Court here, as it was in *Perez,* is whether Congress can consistently with the Fourteenth Amendment enact a law stripping an American of his citizenship which he has never voluntarily renounced or given up. The majority in *Perez* held that Congress could do this because withdrawal of citizenship is "reasonably calculated to effect the end that is within the power of Congress to achieve." That conclusion was reached by this chain of reasoning: Congress has an implied power to deal with foreign affairs as an indispensable attribute of sovereignty; this implied power, plus the Necessary and Proper Clause, empowers Congress to regulate voting by American citizens in foreign elections; involuntary expatriation is within the "ample scope" of "appropriate modes" Congress can adopt to effectuate its general regulatory power.

Then, upon summarily concluding that "there is nothing in the . . . Fourteenth Amendment to warrant drawing from it a restriction upon the power otherwise possessed by Congress to withdraw citizenship," the majority specifically rejected the "notion that the power of Congress to terminate citizenship depends upon the citizen's assent."

First we reject the idea expressed in *Perez* that, aside from the Fourteenth Amendment, Congress has any general power, express or implied, to take away an American citizen's citizenship without his assent. This power cannot, as *Perez* indicated, be sustained as an implied attribute of sovereignty possessed by all nations. Other nations are governed by their own constitutions, if any, and we can draw no support from theirs. In our country the people are sovereign and the Government cannot sever its relationship to the people by taking away their citizenship. Our Constitution governs us and we must never forget that our Constitution limits the Government to those powers specifically granted or those that are necessary and proper to carry out the specifically granted ones. The Constitution, of course, grants Congress no express power to strip people of their citizenship, whether in the exercise of the implied power to regulate foreign affairs or in the exercise of any specifically granted power. And even before the adoption of the Fourteenth Amendment, views were expressed in Congress and by this Court that under the Constitution the Government was granted no power, even under its express power to pass a uniform rule of naturalization, to determine what conduct should and should not result in the loss of citizenship. . . .

To uphold Congress' power to take away a man's citizenship because he voted in a foreign election in violation of § 401 (e) would be equivalent to holding that Congress has the power to "abridge," "affect," "restrict the effect of," and "take . . . away" citizenship. Because the Fourteenth Amendment prevents Congress from doing any of these things, we agree with THE CHIEF JUSTICE's dissent in the *Perez* case that the Government is without power to rob a citizen of his citizenship under § 401 (e).

Because the legislative history of the Fourteenth Amendment and of the expatriation proposals which preceded and followed it, like most other legislative history, contains many statements from which conflicting inferences can be drawn, our holding might be unwarranted if it rested entirely or principally upon that legislative history. But it does not. Our holding we think is the only one that can stand in view of the language and the purpose of the Fourteenth Amendment, and our construction of that Amendment, we believe, comports more nearly than *Perez* with the principles of liberty and equal justice to all that the entire Fourteenth Amendment was adopted to guarantee. Citizenship is no light trifle to be jeopardized any moment Congress decides to do so under the name of one of its general or implied grants of power. In some instances, loss of citizenship can mean that a man is left without the protection of citizenship in any country in the world—as a man without a country. Citizenship in this Nation is a part of a cooperative affair. Its citizenry is the country and the country is its citizenry. The very nature of our free government makes it completely incongruous to have a rule of law under which a group of citizens temporarily in office can deprive another group of citizens of their citizenship. We hold that the Fourteenth Amendment was designed to, and does, protect every citizen of this Nation against a congressional forcible destruction of his citizenship, whatever his creed, color, or race. Our holding does no more than to give to this citizen that which is his own, a constitutional right to remain a citizen in a free country unless he voluntarily relinquishes that citizenship.

Perez v. Brownell is overruled. The judgment is

Reversed.

MR. JUSTICE HARLAN, whom MR. JUSTICE CLARK, MR. JUSTICE STEWART, and MR. JUSTICE WHITE join, dissenting.

Almost 10 years ago, in *Perez v. Brownell,* [1958] the Court upheld the constitutionality of § 401 (e) of the Nationality Act of 1940, 54 Stat. 1169. The section deprives of his nationality any citizen who has voted in a foreign political election. The Court reasoned that Congress derived from its power to regulate foreign affairs authority to expatriate any citizen who intentionally commits acts which may be prejudicial to the foreign relations of the United States, and which reasonably may be deemed to indicate a dilution of his allegiance to this country. Congress, it was held, could appropriately consider purposeful voting in a foreign political election to be such an act.

The Court today overrules *Perez,* and declares § 401 (e) unconstitutional, by a remarkable process of circumlocution. First, the Court fails almost entirely to dispute the reasoning in *Perez;* it is essentially content with the conclusory and quite unsubstantiated assertion that Congress is without "any general power, express or implied," to expatriate a citizen "without his assent." Next, the Court embarks upon a lengthy, albeit incomplete, survey of the historical background of the congressional power at stake here, and yet, at the end, concedes that the history is susceptible of "conflicting inferences." The Court acknowledges that its conclusions might not be warranted by that history alone, and disclaims that the decision today relies, even "principally," upon it. Finally, the Court declares that its result is bottomed upon the "language and the purpose" of the Citizenship Clause of the Fourteenth Amendment; in explanation, the Court offers only the terms of the clause itself, the contention that any other result would be "completely incongruous," and the essentially arcane observation that the "citizenry is the country and the country is its citizenry."

I can find nothing in this extraordinary series of circumventions which permits, still less compels, the imposition of this constitutional constraint upon the authority of Congress. I must respectfully dissent.

* * *

The Citizenship Clause thus neither denies nor provides to Congress any power of expatriation; its consequences are, for present purposes, exhausted by its declaration of the classes of individuals to whom citizenship initially attaches. Once obtained, citizenship is of course protected from arbitrary withdrawal by the constraints placed around Congress' powers by the Constitution; it is *not* proper to create from the Citizenship Clause an additional, and entirely unwarranted, restriction upon legislative authority. The construction now placed on the Citizenship Clause rests, in the last analysis, simply on the Court's *ipse dixit,* evincing little more, it is quite apparent, than the present majority's own distaste for the expatriation power.

I believe that *Perez* was rightly decided, and on its authority would affirm the judgment of the Court of Appeals.

QUESTIONS AND COMMENTS

1 Did the government's attorney in *Kansas v. Colorado* show bad judgment in choosing the basis for his implied-power argument? Why or why not?
2 In *Perez,* the congressional power was found in its foreign affairs power. In *Trop,* several justices based their decision on the Eighth Amendment. What role did these provisions play in *Afroyim v. Rusk?*

3 What if Afroyim, born in 1893, had stated on his application for citizenship a birth date of 1903? Different decision?
4 After *Afroyim,* is it possible for Congress to establish any conditions under which one's behavior, other than express denial, may cost one his or her citizenship?
5 Can you find any enumerated power in the Constitution from which the power to denaturalize an American citizen may be implied?

To Veto Executive Action

Immigration and Naturalization Service v. Chadha (1983)

Throughout American history, we have witnessed a fairly constant conflict between the Executive and the Congress over the respective constitutional powers of each. Conflict between the branches of the federal government was intended by the framers, and thus to actually observe it in our governmental system should occasion no surprise. At the same time, for either branch to exercise its legitimate powers effectively there must be some understanding of the margins of power for each. Disagreements about such matters may ultimately end up in the Supreme Court. But most conflicts do not. Congress and the President may seek an accommodation out of expediency or goodwill. Or either may attempt via unilateral action to limit the role of the other in certain policy areas.

In recent history, the Congress, out of concern about the expanding of executive power during and following wars and other domestic crises, has sought to limit presidential prerogatives. An example may be found in the War Powers Resolution adopted in 1973 in the aftermath of the Vietnam War. The act speaks to the limits of a President's power as commander-in-chief of the armed forces and the power given exclusively to Congress to declare war. Congress has not declared war since World War II. Yet, the President ordered hundreds of thousands of American military personnel to fight in Korea and Vietnam, many thousands of whom were killed—over 50,000 alone in the case of Vietnam.

The War Powers Resolution sought to give Congress a greater voice in making decisions to involve United States forces in combat situations. Enacted over President Nixon's veto, it requires the President to inform Congress within 48 hours after sending United States military personnel into certain combat situations. Moreover, the President cannot keep the forces engaged in a combat situation for more than 90 days unless Congress authorizes doing so or formally declares war. In addition, should Congress so desire, it can order the troops home by passing a concurrent resolution. While in this latter case, Congress must take some affirmative action to force the President to withdraw the troops, the withdrawal under the 90-day provision is triggered by congressional inaction. It is this explicit type of "trigger" that is involved in the case reported in this section—a device that has come to be known as the "legislative veto."

The legislative veto originated in 1932 when President Hoover set out to reorganize the executive branch of government. Rather than having to legislate each proposed change, Congress gave the President broad discretion but subjected each reorganization plan to veto by either house of Congress. Subsequently the veto has been inserted in almost every area regulated by federal legislation. Since 1932, over 200 laws have contained over 300 legislative-veto provisions. All this has undoubtedly eased congressional fears over the abuse of executive power. But the comfort accruing from such efforts appears to have been primarily psychological. For the veto has actually been exercised only 230 times in fifty years.[27] Of these 230 cases, 111 have been immigration cases[28]—the same subject matter involved in the *Chadha* case.

When Chadha came before the Supreme Court he had the support of the American Bar Association. Appearing as amicus curiae, the Association argued that the legislative veto violated the separation of powers principle by interfering with the President's responsibility to implement the law. The association also maintained that the Constitution requires legislation by a bicameral body and that legislative action becomes law only when presented to the President for signature or, should the President veto the bill presented, when the veto is overridden by both houses of Congress.

Immigration and Naturalization Service v. Chadha

51 LW 4907 (1983)
Vote: 7–2

Jagdish Rai Chadha was an East Indian born in Kenya. He came to the United States in 1966 on a student visa which expired June 30, 1972. After a hearing before an immigration judge on January 11, 1974, Chadha admitted he was deportable under federal law but asked for suspension of deportation. Such suspension was available under the Immigration and Nationality Act for one who had been "physically present in the United States for a continuous period of not less than seven years . . . [and who had proved that] during all of such period he was and is a person of good moral character; and is a person whose deportation would, in the opinion of the Attorney General, result in extreme hardship to the alien." After a hearing on Chadha's request, the immigration judge found that Chadha met the requirements of the act and suspended deportation.

Under the act, all suspensions had to be reported to Congress, which had the power to veto a suspension of deportation at any time during the session in which it was advised of it or prior to the end of the next congressional session. The veto could be employed by either house of Congress and, if exercised, required the deportation of the alien. After reaching the conclusion that the deportation of Chadha would not impose an "extreme hardship" on him, the House of Representatives vetoed the suspension on December 15, 1975. At a hearing to implement the decision Chadha moved to terminate the proceedings on the ground that Section 244 (c) (2) of the Immigration and Nationality Act, which established the power of Congress to veto suspensions of deportation, was unconstitutional. The immigration judge and the Board of Immigration Appeals both found that they lacked the power to declare an act of Congress unconstitutional. The court of appeals for the ninth circuit, however, held that the House was without power to order the deportation of Chadha—the essence of its holding being that the granting of such power in Section 244 (c) (2) of the act violated the constitutional doctrine of separation of powers. The Supreme Court then granted the petition for certiorari filed by the Immigration and Naturalization Service.

After ruling that it possessed jurisdiction to hear the case, that Chadha had standing to bring the case, that Section 244 (c) (2) was severable (i.e., that the section could be held unconstitutional without affecting the remainder of the act), that the case presented a "case or controversy," and that Chadha had presented no nonjusticiable "political question," the Court reached the main issue.

CHIEF JUSTICE BURGER delivered the opinion of the Court. . . .

We turn now to the question whether action of one House of Congress under § 244 (c) (2) violates strictures of the Constitution. We begin, of course, with the presumption that the challenged statute is valid. Its wisdom is not the concern of the courts; if a challenged action does not violate the Constitution, it must be sustained. . . .

By the same token, the fact that a given law or procedure is efficient, convenient, and useful in facilitating functions of government, standing alone, will not save it if it is contrary to the Constitution. Convenience and efficiency are not the primary objectives—or the hallmarks—of democratic government and our inquiry is sharpened rather than blunted by the fact that Congressional veto provisions are appearing with increasing frequency in statutes which delegate authority to executive and independent agencies. . . .

Explicit and unambiguous provisions of the Constitution prescribe and define the respective functions of the Congress and of the Executive in the legislative process. Since the precise terms of those familiar provisions are critical to the resolution of this case, we set them out verbatim. Art. I provides:

> All legislative Powers herein granted shall be vested in a Congress of the United States, which shall consist of a Senate *and* a House of Representatives." Art. I, § 1. (Emphasis added).
>
> Every Bill which shall have passed the House of Representatives *and* the Senate, *shall,* before it become a Law, be presented to the President of the United States; . . . Art. I, § 7, cl. 2. (Emphasis added).
>
> *Every* Order, Resolution, or Vote to which the Concurrence of the Senate and House of Representatives may be necessary (except on a question of Adjournment) *shall be* presented to the President of the United States; and before the Same shall take Effect, *shall be* approved by him, or being disapproved by him, *shall be* repassed

by two thirds of the Senate and House of Representatives, according to the Rules and Limitations prescribed in the Case of a Bill. Art. I, § 7, cl. 3. (Emphasis added.)

These provisions of Art. I are integral parts of the constitutional design for the separation of powers. We have recently noted that "[t]he principle of separation of powers was not simply an abstract generalization in the minds of the Framers: it was woven into the documents that they drafted in Philadelphia in the summer of 1787." *Buckley v. Valeo, supra,* 424 U.S., at 124. Just as we relied on the textual provision of Art. II, § 2, cl. 2, to vindicate the principle of separation of powers in *Buckley.* We find that the purposes underlying the Presentment Clauses, Art. I, § 7, cls. 2, 3, and the bicameral requirement of Art. I, § 1 and § 7, cl. 2, guide our resolution of the important question presented in this case. The very structure of the articles delegating and separating powers under Arts. I, II, and III exemplify the concept of separation of powers and we now turn to Art. I.

The Presentment Clauses

The records of the Constitutional Convention reveal that the requirement that all legislation be presented to the President before becoming law was uniformly accepted by the Framers. Presentment to the President and the Presidential veto were considered so imperative that the draftsmen took special pains to assure that these requirements could not be circumvented. . . .

The decision to provide the President with a limited and qualified power to nullify proposed legislation by veto was based on the profound conviction of the Framers that the powers conferred on Congress were the powers to be most carefully circumscribed. It is beyond doubt that lawmaking was a power to be shared by both Houses and the President. . . .

The President's role in the lawmaking process also reflects the Framers' careful efforts to check whatever propensity a particular Congress might have to enact oppressive, improvident, or ill-considered measures. The President's veto role in the legislative process was described later during public debate on ratification:

> It establishes a salutary check upon the legislative body, calculated to guard the community against the effects of faction, precipitancy, or of any impulse unfriendly to the public good which may happen to influence a majority of that body. . . . The primary inducement to conferring the power in question upon the Executive is to enable him to defend himself; the secondary one is to increase the chances in favor of the community against the passing of bad laws through haste, inadvertence, or design. The Federalist No. 73, *supra,* at 458 (A. Hamilton). . . .

Bicameralism

The bicameral requirement of Art. I, §§ 1, 7 was of scarcely less concern to the Framers than was the Presidential veto and indeed the two concepts are interdependent. By providing that no law could take effect without the concurrence of the prescribed majority of the Members of both Houses, the Framers reemphasized their belief, already remarked upon in connection with the Presentment Clauses, that legislation should not be enacted unless it has been carefully and fully considered by the Nation's elected officials. In the Constitutional Convention debates on the need for a bicameral legislature, James Wilson, later to become a Justice of this Court, commented:

> Despotism comes on mankind in different shapes. Sometimes in an Executive, sometimes in a military one. Is there danger of a Legislative despotism? Theory & practice both proclaim it. If the Legislative authority be not restrained, there can be neither liberty nor stability; and it can only be restrained by dividing it within itself, into distinct and independent branches. In a single house there is no check, but the inadequate one, of the virtue & good sense of those who compose it.

In *The Federalist,* Hamilton argued that a Congress comprised of a single House was antithetical to the very purposes of the Constitution. Were the Nation to adopt a Constitution providing for only one legislative organ, he warned:

> we shall finally accumulate, in a single body, all the most important prerogatives of sovereignty, and thus entail upon our posterity one of the most execrable forms of government that human infatuation ever contrived. Thus we should create in reality that very tyranny which the adversaries of the new Constitution either are, or affect to be, solicitous to avert.

These observations are consistent with what many of the Framers expressed, none more cogently than Hamilton in pointing up the need to divide and disperse power in order to protect liberty:

> In republican government, the legislative authority necessarily predominates. The remedy for this inconveniency is to divide the legislature into different branches; and to render them, by different modes of election and different principles of action, as little connected with each other as the nature of their common functions and their common dependence on the society will admit.

The Constitution sought to divide the delegated powers of the new federal government into three defined categories, legislative, executive and judicial, to assure, as nearly as possible, that each Branch of government would confine itself to its assigned responsibility. The hydraulic pressure inherent within each of the separate Branches to exceed the outer limits of its power, even to accomplish desirable objectives, must be resisted.

Although not "hermetically" sealed from one another, the powers delegated to the three Branches are functionally identifiable. When any Branch acts, it is presumptively exercising the power the Constitution has delegated to it. When the Executive acts, it presumptively acts in an executive or administrative capacity as defined in Art. II. And when, as here, one House of Congress purports to act, it is presumptively acting within its assigned sphere.

Beginning with this presumption, we must nevertheless establish that the challenged action under §244(c)(2) is of the kind to which the procedural requirements of Art. I, § 7 apply. Not every action taken by either House is subject to the bicameralism and presentment requirements of Art. I.

Whether actions taken by either House are, in law and fact, an exercise of legislative power depends not on their form but upon "whether they contain matter which is properly to be regarded as legislative in its character and effect." S. Rep. No. 1335, 54th Cong., 2d Sess., 8 (1897). . . .

Examination of the action taken here by one House pursuant to §244(c)(2) reveals that it was essentially legislative in purpose and effect. In purporting to exercise power defined in Art. I, § 8, cl. 4 to "establish a uniform Rule of Naturalization," the House took action that had the purpose and effect of altering the legal rights, duties and relations of persons, including the Attorney General, Executive Branch officials and Chadha, all outside the legislative branch. Section 244(c)(2) purports to authorize one House of Congress to require the Attorney General to deport an individual alien whose deportation otherwise would be cancelled under §244. The one-House veto operated in this case to overrule the Attorney General and mandate Chadha's deportation; absent the House action, Chadha would remain in the United States. Congress has *acted* and its action has altered Chadha's status.

The legislative character of the one-House veto in this case is confirmed by the character of the Congressional action it supplants. Neither the House of Representatives nor the Senate contends that, absent the veto provision in §244(c)(2), either of them, or both of them acting together, could effectively require the Attorney General to deport an alien once the Attorney General, in the exercise of legislatively delegated authority, had determined the alien should remain in the United States. Without the challenged provision in §244(c)(2), this could have been achieved, if at all, only by legislation requiring deportation. Similarly, a veto by one House of Congress under §244 as applied to Chadha. Amendment and repeal of statutes, no less than enactment, must conform with Art. I. . . .

Since it is clear that the action by the House under §244(c)(2) was not within any of the express constitutional exceptions authorizing one House to act alone, and equally clear that it was an exercise of legislative power, that action was subject to the standards prescribed in Article I. The bicameral requirement, the Presentment Clauses, the President's veto, and Congress' power to override a veto were intended to erect enduring checks on each Branch and to protect the people from the improvident exercise of power by mandating certain prescribed steps. To preserve those checks, and maintain the separation of powers, the carefully defined limits on the power of each Branch must not be eroded. To accomplish what has been attempted by one House of Congress in this case requires action in conformity with the express procedures of the

Constitution's prescription for legislative action: passage by a majority of both Houses and presentment to the President.

The veto authorized by §244(c)(2) doubtless has been in many respects a convenient shortcut; the "sharing" with the Executive by Congress of its authority over aliens in this manner is, on its face, an appealing compromise. In purely practical terms, it is obviously easier for action to be taken by one House without submission to the President; but it is crystal clear from the records of the Convention, contemporaneous writings and debates, that the Framers ranked other values higher than efficiency. The records of the Convention and debates in the States preceding ratification underscore the common desire to define and limit the exercise of the newly created federal powers affecting the states and the people. There is unmistakable expression of a determination that legislation by the national Congress be a step-by-step, deliberate and deliberative process.

The choices we discern as having been made in the Constitutional Convention impose burdens on governmental processes that often seem clumsy, inefficient, even unworkable, but those hard choices were consciously made by men who had lived under a form of government that permitted arbitrary governmental acts to go unchecked. There is no support in the Constitution or decisions of this Court for the proposition that the cumbersomeness and delays often encountered in complying with explicit Constitutional standards may be avoided, either by the Congress or by the President. See *Youngstown Sheet & Tube Co. v. Sawyer,* (1952). With all the obvious flaws of delay, untidiness, and potential for abuse, we have not yet found a better way to preserve freedom than by making the exercise of power subject to the carefully crafted restraints spelled out in the Constitution.

We hold that the Congressional veto provision in §244(c)(2) is severable from the Act and that it is unconstitutional. Accordingly, the judgment of the Court of Appeals is

Affirmed.

JUSTICE POWELL, concurring in the judgment.

* * *

The Constitution does not establish three branches with precisely defined boundaries. See *Buckley v. Valeo,* (1976) (*per curiam*). Rather, as Justice Jackson wrote. "[w]hile the Constitution diffuses power the better to secure liberty, it also contemplates that practice will integrate the dispersed powers into a workable government. It enjoins upon its branches separateness but interdependence, autonomy but reciprocity." *Youngstown Sheet & Tube Co. v. Sawyer,* (1952) (concurring opinion). The Court thus has been mindful that the boundaries between each branch should be fixed "according to common sense and the inherent necessities of the governmental co-ordination." But where one branch has impaired or sought to assume a power central to another branch, the Court has not hesitated to enforce the doctrine.

Functionally, the doctrine may be violated in two ways. One branch may interfere impermissibly with the other's performance of its constitutionally assigned function. Alternatively, the doctrine may be violated when one branch assumes a function that more properly is entrusted to another.

This case presents the latter situation.

* * *

In deciding whether Chadha deserves to be deported, Congress is not subject to any internal constraints that prevent it from arbitrarily depriving him of the right to remain in this country. Unlike the judiciary or an administrative agency, Congress is not bound by established substantive rules. Nor is it subject to the procedural safeguards, such as the right to counsel and a hearing before an impartial tribunal, that are present when a court or an agency adjudicates individual rights. The only effective constraint on Congress' power is political, but Congress is most accountable politically when it prescribes rules of general applicability. When it decides rights of specific persons, those rights are subject to "the tyranny of a shifting majority."

Chief Justice Marshall observed: "It is the peculiar province of the legislature to prescribe general rules for the government of society; the application of those rules would seem to be the duty of other departments." *Fletcher v. Peck,* (1810). In my view, when Congress undertook to apply its rules to Chadha, it exceeded the scope of its constitutionally prescribed authority. I would not reach the broader question whether legislative vetoes are invalid under the Presentment Clauses.

JUSTICE WHITE, dissenting.

Today the Court not only invalidates §244(c)(2) of the Immigration and Nationality Act, but also sounds the death knell for nearly 200 other statutory provisions in which Congress has reserved a "legislative veto." For this reason the Court's decision is of surpassing importance. And it is for this reason that the Court would have been well-advised to decide the case, if possible, on the narrower grounds of separation of powers, leaving for full consideration the constitutionality of other congressional review statutes operating on such varied matters as war powers and agency rulemaking, some of which concern the independent regulatory agencies.

* * *

During the 1970's the legislative veto was important in resolving a series of major constitutional disputes between the President and Congress over claims of the President to broad impoundment, war, and national emergency powers. The key provision of the War Powers Resolution authorizes the termination by concurrent resolution of the use of armed forces in hostilities. A similar measure resolved the problem posed by Presidential claims of inherent power to impound appropriations. *Congressional Budget and Impoundment Control Act of 1974.* In conference, a compromise was achieved under which permanent impoundments, termed "rescissions," would require approval through enactment of legislation. In contrast, temporary impoundments, or "deferrals," would become effective unless disapproved by one House. This compromise provided the President with flexibility, while preserving ultimate Congressional control over the budget. Although the War Powers Resolution was enacted over President Nixon's veto, the Impoundment Control Act was enacted with the President's approval. These statutes were followed by others resolving similar problems: the National Emergencies Act, (1976), resolving the longstanding problems with unchecked Executive emergency power; the Arms Export Control Act, (1976), resolving the problem of foreign arms sales; and the Nuclear Non-Proliferation Act of 1978, (Supp. IV. 1980), resolving the problem of exports of nuclear technology.

In the energy field, the legislative veto served to balance broad delegations in legislation emerging from the energy crisis of the 1970's. In the educational field, it was found that fragmented and narrow grant programs "inevitably lead to Executive-Legislative confrontations" because they inaptly limited the Commissioner of Education's authority. S. Rep. No. 763, 93d Cong., 2d Sess. 69 (1974). The response was to grant the Commissioner of Education rule-making authority, subject to a legislative veto. In the trade regulation area, the veto preserved Congressional authority over the Federal Trade Commission's broad mandate to make rules to prevent businesses from engaging in "unfair or deceptive acts or practices in commerce."

Even this brief review suffices to demonstrate that the legislative veto is more than "efficient, convenient, and useful." *Ante,* at 23. It is an important if not indispensable political invention that allows the President and Congress to resolve major constitutional and policy differences, assures the accountability of independent regulatory agencies, and preserves Congress' control over lawmaking. Perhaps there are other means of accommodation and accountability, but the increasing reliance of Congress upon the legislative veto suggests that the alternatives to which Congress must now turn are not entirely satisfactory. . . .

If the legislative veto were as plainly unconstitutional as the Court strives to suggest, its broad ruling today would be more comprehensible. But, the constitutionality of the legislative veto is anything but clearcut. The issue divides scholars, courts, attorneys general, and the two other branches of the National Government. If the veto devices so flagrantly disregarded the requirements of Article I as the Court today suggests, I find it incomprehensible that Congress, whose members are bound by oath to uphold the Constitution, would have placed these mechanisms in nearly 200 separate laws over a period of 50 years.

* * *

There is no question that a bill does not become a law until it is approved by both the House and the Senate, and presented to the President. Similarly, I would not hesitate to strike an action of Congress in the form of a concurrent resolution which constituted an exercise of original lawmaking authority. I agree with the Court that the President's qualified veto power is a critical element in the distribution of powers under the Constitution, widely endorsed among the Framers, and intended to serve the President as a defense against legislative encroachment and to check the "passing of bad laws through haste, inadvertence, or design." The Federalist No. 73, at 458 (A. Hamilton). The records of the Convention reveal that it is the first purpose which figured most prominently but I acknowledge the vitality of the second. I also agree that the bicameral approval required by Art. I, §§ 1, 7 "was of scarcely less concern to the Framers than was the Presidential veto," *ante,* at 28, and that the need to divide and disperse legislative power figures significantly in our scheme of Government. All of this . . . does not, however, answer the constitutional question before us. The power to exercise a legislative veto is not the power to write new law without bicameral approval or presidential consideration. The veto must be authorized by statute and may only negative what an Executive department or independent agency has proposed. On its face, the legislative veto no more allows one House of Congress to make law than does the presidential veto confer such power upon the President. . . .

Our cases establish that by virtue of congressional delegation, legislative power can be exercised by independent agencies and Executive departments without the passage of new legislation. For some time, the sheer amount of law—the substantive rules that regulate private conduct and direct the operation of government—made by the agencies has far outnumbered the lawmaking engaged in by Congress through the traditional process. There is no question but that agency rulemaking is lawmaking in any functional or realistic sense of the term. The Administrative Procedure Act provides that a "rule" is an agency statement "designed to implement, interpret, or prescribe law or policy." When agencies are authorized to prescribe law through substantive rulemaking, the administrator's regulation is not only due deference, but is accorded "legislative effect."

These regulations bind courts and officers of the federal government, may pre-empt state law, and grant rights to and impose obligations on the public. In sum, they have the force of law.

If Congress may delegate lawmaking power to independent and executive agencies, it is most difficult to understand Article I as forbidding Congress from also reserving a check on legislative power for itself. Absent the veto, the agencies receiving delegations of legislative or quasi-legislative power may issue regulations having the force of law without bicameral approval and without the President's signature. It is thus not apparent why the reservation of a veto over the exercise of that legislative power must be subject to a more exacting test. In both cases, it is enough that the initial statutory authorizations comply with the Article I requirements.

* * *

I do not suggest that all legislative vetoes are necessarily consistent with separation of powers principles. A legislative check on an inherently executive function, for example that of initiating prosecutions, poses an entirely different question. But the legislative veto device here—and in many other settings—is far from an instance of legislative tyranny over the Executive. It is a necessary check on the unavoidably expanding power of the agencies, both executive and independent, as they engage in exercising authority delegated by Congress.

I regret that I am in disagreement with my colleagues on the fundamental questions that this case presents. But even more I regret the destructive scope of the Court's holding. It reflects a profoundly different conception of the Constitution than that held by the Courts which sanctioned the modern administrative state. Today's decision strikes down in one fell swoop provisions in more laws enacted by Congress than the Court has cumulatively invalidated in its history. I fear it will now be more difficult "to insure that the fundamental policy decisions in our society will be made not by an appointed official but by the body immediately responsible to the people." *Arizona v. California,* (1963) (Harlan, J., dissenting). I must dissent.

QUESTIONS AND COMMENTS

1 Which of the ABA arguments, if any, appears to have been most influential in shaping the Court's opinion in *Chadha*?

2 In your opinion, does the Court's opinion in *Chadha* have implications for the War Powers Resolution of 1973? Which provisions? Explain your answer.

3 In *Chadha,* the Court rules on a single provision of a single congressional statute. That being so, what does Justice White mean by saying that the Court's decision sounds "the death knell for nearly 200 other statutory provisions in which Congress has reserved a 'legislative veto'"? Can you explain why White uses the term "nearly 200" rather than an exact figure?

4 From the standpoint of "making law," can you distinguish the legislative veto from the presidential veto? If one is "law making," why not the other?

5 Is there any significance in the fact that so many members of Congress voted for the legislative veto over a period of fifty years? White asks, in effect, whether so many members of Congress could be wrong. What answer would you give the justice?

6 What effect of this ruling do you see, if any, on democratic political processes in the United States?

7 Is the *Chadha* decision activist or restraintist? If activist, is it supported only by activist justices?

8 Can you think of ways in which Congress might restore its control of executive action consistent with the Court's decision in *Chadha?* Is it worth the effort?

9 Subsequent to *Chadha,* the Supreme Court affirmed court of appeals decisions invalidating legislative veto provisions in two cases, one involving the Federal Trade Commission, and the other, the Federal Regulatory Commission (*Consumer's Union v. F.T.C.,* 691 F. 2d 575, and *Consumer Energy Commission of America v. F.E.R.C.,* 673 F. 2d 425). What does this imply about *Immigration and Naturalization Service v. Chadha?*

NOTES

1 *Hipolite Egg Co. v. United States,* 220 U.S. 45 (1911).
2 *Caminetti v. United States,* 242 U.S. 470 (1917).
3 *Gooch v. United States,* 297 U.S. 124 (1936).
4 *Cleveland v. United States,* 329 U.S. 14 (1946).
5 *Adair v. United States,* 208 U.S. 161 (1908).
6 *Adkins v. Children's Hospital,* 261 U.S. 525 (1923).
7 290 U.S. 398 (1934).
8 291 U.S. 502 (1934).
9 *Railroad Retirement Board v. Alton Ry. Co.,* 295 U.S. 330 (1935).
10 *Schechter Poultry Co. v. United States,* 295 U.S. 495 (1935).
11 *United States v. Butler,* 297 U.S. 1 (1936).
12 *Carter v. Carter Coal Co.,* 298 U.S. 238 (1936).
13 *Morehead v. New York ex rel Tipaldo,* 298 U.S. 587 (1936).
14 *Veazie Bank v. Fenno,* 75 U.S. (8 Wallace) 533 (1869).
15 *Springer v. United States,* 102 U.S. 586 (1880).
16 In *Kahriger,* 345 U.S. 22 (1953), the Court upheld a federal tax levied on persons engaged in the business of accepting wagers. *Kahriger* was overruled in *Marchetti v. United States,* 390 U.S. 39 (1968).
17 301 U.S. 548 (1937).
18 103 U.S. 168 (1881).
19 *Tenney v. Brandhove,* 341 U.S. 367 (1951).
20 *Dombrowski v. Eastland,* 387 U.S. 82 (1967); *Powell v. McCormack,* 395 U.S. 486 (1969).
21 408 U.S. 501 (1972).
22 See *Gibson v. Florida Legislative Investigating Committee,* 372 U.S. 539 (1963), and *Gojack v. United States,* 369 U.S. 749 (1966).
23 415 U.S. 651 (1974).
24 *Kennedy v. Mendozo-Martinez,* 372 U.S. 144 (1963).
25 *Perez v. Brownell,* 356 U.S. 44 (1958).
26 *Trop v. Dulles,* 356 U.S. 86 (1958).
27 "After Shocks of the Fall of the Legislative Veto," 69 *American Bar Association Journal* 1258, 1262 (September 1983).
28 Ibid.

CHAPTER 5

THE POWER OF THE PRESIDENT

To Conduct Foreign Affairs

Missouri v. Holland (1920)

United States v. Curtiss-Wright Export Corp. (1936)

Haig v. Agee (1981)

The Constitution delegates control of United States foreign policy jointly to the President and the Congress. The President has the power to make treaties, but only if two-thirds of the Senate agrees. The same constraint is placed on the President's power to appoint ambassadors. But the constitutional provisions pertaining to foreign affairs are too sketchy to provide a framework for that function. In practice the President has been the nation's primary organ of foreign policy, with most of the presidential power in this area being delegated by Congress.

We noted earlier that Congress may not delegate legislative power, and we have examined some cases which show that the Supreme Court is capable of striking such delegations on occasion. But in the field of foreign affairs, the Court has tended to be more generous in permitting broad delegations of power to the President. The *Curtiss-Wright* case is a good illustration of that tendency on the part of the Court.

Under the supremacy clause of the Constitution, treaties are the law of the land, and any state act or constitutional provision in conflict with a treaty will be held null and void upon appropriate challenge. Likewise, a valid treaty nullifies an earlier congressional statute with which it conflicts, and vice versa, since both are "the law of the land." Thus, the President, through appropriate use of the power to enter into treaties with foreign nations, may—if the Senate agrees—void both state and federal legislation. While the President's ability to do so is limited by the requirement that treaties must involve the foreign relations of the United States, the global relationships of the 1980s make the restriction relatively meaningless. Moreover, the treaty power is enhanced by the fact that the President may use provisions of a particular treaty to promote policies favored by Congress but which Congress lacks authority to pursue under Article I. In this way, in effect, the President can "add to" the enumerated powers. *Missouri v. Holland* illustrates the point.

In conducting foreign affairs, a President obviously does more than negotiate treaties with foreign nations. Indeed, most executive "business" in foreign relations is conducted pursuant to executive orders, rules, regulations, and instructions to the State Department and consular officials. In issuing such administrative rules and regulations, the President normally acts under congressional authorization. Since both the executive and Congress are subject to constitutional constraints in foreign as well as in domestic affairs, it is always possible for one adversely affected to challenge the treatment accorded.

Where the President is acting under congressional statute, a common challenge is that the policy pursued by the President or the President's agents is not the intent of Congress—i.e., the executive has misinterpreted the law. Or one may claim that the delegating statute is invalid under Article I or that the President in carrying out the statute has been careless, thereby invading the constitutional rights of due process, right to travel, free speech, etc. Since the Court gives Congress and the executive greater leeway in dealing with questions of foreign affairs and national security, such claims may have less chance of success than if brought in a different context—say, violation of due process in a criminal trial. But in any event, the "invasions" of liberty must be related to national security, and the Court still sits as a check on the arbitrary exercise of governmental power in both foreign and domestic affairs. *Haig v. Agee* challenges the power of the President at the level of the individual—specifically, the presidential power to revoke passports.

State of Missouri v. Holland, United States Game Warden

252 U.S. 416; 40 S. Ct. 382; 64 L. Ed. 641 (1920)
Vote: 7–2

The facts are given in the opinion.

MR. JUSTICE HOLMES delivered the opinion of the court.

This is a bill in equity brought by the State of Missouri to prevent a game warden of the United States from attempting to enforce the Migratory Bird Treaty Act of July 3, 1918, and the regulations made by the Secretary of Agriculture in pursuance of the same. The ground of the bill is that the statute is an unconstitutional interference with the rights reserved to the States by the Tenth Amendment, and that the acts of the defendant done and threatened under that authority invade the sovereign right of the State and contravene its will manifested in statutes. The State also alleges a pecuniary interest, as owner of the wild birds within its borders and otherwise, admitted by the Government to be sufficient, but it is enough that the bill is a reasonable and proper means to assert the alleged quasi sovereign rights of a State.

A motion to dismiss was sustained by the District Court on the ground that the act of Congress is constitutional. The State appeals.

On December 8, 1916, a treaty between the United States and Great Britain was proclaimed by the President. It recited that many species of birds in their annual migrations traversed certain parts of the United States and of Canada, that they were of great value as a source of food and in destroying insects injurious to vegetation, but were in danger of extermination through lack of adequate protection. It therefore provided for specified close seasons and protection in other forms, and agreed that the two powers would take or propose to their law-making bodies the necessary measures for carrying the treaty out. The above mentioned Act of July 3, 1918, entitled an act to give effect to the convention, prohibited the killing, capturing or selling any of the migratory birds included in the terms of the treaty except as permitted by regulations compatible with those terms, to be made by the Secretary of Agriculture. Regulations were proclaimed on July 31, and October 25, 1918.

It is unnecessary to go into any details, because, as we have said, the question raised is the general one whether the treaty and statute are void as an interference with the rights reserved to the States.

To answer this question it is not enough to refer to the Tenth Amendment, reserving the powers not delegated to the United States, because by Article II, § 2, the power to make treaties is delegated expressly, and by Article VI treaties made under the authority of the United States, along with the Constitution and laws of the United States made in pursuance thereof, are declared the supreme law of the land. If the treaty is valid there can be no dispute about the validity of the statute under Article I, § 8, as a necessary and proper means to execute the powers of the Government. The language of the Constitution as to the supremacy of treaties being general, the question before us is narrowed to an inquiry into the ground upon which the present supposed exception is placed.

It is said that a treaty cannot be valid if it infringes the Constitution, that there are limits, therefore, to the treaty-making power, and that one such limit is that what an act of Congress could not do unaided, in derogation of the powers reserved to the States, a treaty cannot do. An earlier act of Congress that attempted by itself and not in pursuance of a treaty to regulate the killing of migratory birds within the States had been held bad in the District Court.

Those decisions were supported by arguments that migratory birds were owned by the States in their sovereign capacity for the benefit of their people, and that under cases like *Geer v. Connecticut,* [1896], this control was one that Congress had no power to displace. The same argument is supposed to apply now with equal force.

Whether the . . . cases cited were decided rightly or not they cannot be accepted as a test of the treaty power. Acts of Congress are the supreme law of the land only when made in pursuance of the Constitution, while treaties are declared to be so when made under the authority of the United States. It is open to question whether the authority of the United States means more than the formal acts prescribed to make the convention. We do not mean to imply that there are no qualifications to the treaty-making power; but they must be ascertained in a different way. It is obvious that there may be matters of the sharpest exigency for the national well being that an act of Congress could not deal with but that a treaty followed by such an act could, and it is not lightly to be assumed that, in matters requiring national action, "a power which must belong to and somewhere reside in every civilized government" is not to be found. . . .

We are not yet discussing the particular case before us but only are considering the validity of the test proposed. With regard to that we may add that when we are dealing with words that also are a constituent act, like the Constitution of the United States, we must realize that they have called into life a being the development of which could not have been foreseen completely by the most gifted of its begetters. It was enough for them to realize or to hope that they had created an organism; it has taken a century and has cost their successors much sweat and blood to prove that they created a nation. The case before us must be considered in the light of our whole experience and not merely in that of what was said a hundred years ago. The treaty in question does not contravene any prohibitory words to be found in the Constitution. The only question is whether it is forbidden by some invisible radiation from the general terms of the Tenth Amendment. We must consider what this country has become in deciding what that Amendment has reserved.

The State as we have intimated founds its claim of exclusive authority upon an assertion of title to migratory birds, an assertion that is embodied in statute. No doubt it is true that as between a State and its inhabitants the State may

regulate the killing and sale of such birds, but it does not follow that its authority is exclusive of paramount powers. To put the claim of the State upon title
is to lean upon a slender reed. Wild birds are not in the possession of anyone;
and possession is the beginning of ownership. The whole foundation of the
State's rights is the presence within their jurisdiction of birds that yesterday
had not arrived, tomorrow may be in another State and in a week a thousand
miles away. If we are to be accurate we cannot put the case of the State upon
higher ground than that the treaty deals with creatures that for the moment are
within the state borders, that it must be carried out by officers of the United
States within the same territory, and that but for the treaty the State would be
free to regulate this subject itself.

As most of the laws of the United States are carried out within the States
and as many of them deal with matters which in the silence of such laws the
State might regulate, such general grounds are not enough to support Missour-
i's claim. Valid treaties of course "are as binding within the territorial limits
of the States as they are elsewhere throughout the dominion of the United
States." *Baldwin v. Franks,* [1887]. No doubt the great body of private relations
usually fall within the control of the State, but a treaty may override its power.
We do not have to invoke the later developments of constitutional law for this
proposition; it was recognized as early as *Hopkirk v. Bell,* [1806], with regard
to statutes of limitation, and even earlier, as to confiscation, in *Ware v. Hylton,*
[1796]. Further illustration seems unnecessary, and it only remains to consider
the application of established rules to the present case.

Here a national interest of very nearly the first magnitude is involved. It can
be protected only by national action in concert with that of another power. The
subject-matter is only transitorily within the State and has no permanent hab-
itat therein. But for the treaty and the statute there soon might be no birds for
any powers to deal with. We see nothing in the Constitution that compels the
Government to sit by while a food supply is cut off and the protectors of our
forests and our crops are destroyed. It is not sufficient to rely upon the States.
The reliance is vain, and were it otherwise, the question is whether the United
States is forbidden to act. We are of opinion that the treaty and statute must
be upheld.

Decree affirmed.

MR. JUSTICE VAN DEVANTER and JUSTICE PITNEY dissent.

United States v. Curtiss-Wright Export Corporation, et al.

299 U.S. 304; 57 S. Ct. 216; 81 L. Ed. 255 (1936)
Vote: 7–1

A joint resolution adopted by Congress on May 28, 1934, provided that, given certain findings, the President could bar the sales of munitions of war to the countries engaged in armed conflict in the Chaco. The Chaco was an area encompassing a boundary between Bolivia and Paraguay. A dispute over the boundary led to a war between the two countries that lasted from 1932 to 1935. On the same day that the joint resolution was adopted, the President, finding that barring arms sales to the area would enhance the chances for peace, instituted such a ban. In 1935, the ban was revoked.

One day after the joint resolution and presidential proclamation took effect, the Curtiss-Wright Export Corporation conspired to sell fifteen machine guns to Bolivia. An indictment on this charge was returned in 1936. The indictment was challenged by Curtiss-Wright, which claimed, among other things, that the joint resolution represented an invalid delegation of legislative power to the President. The district court upheld the challenge, and the United States appealed.

MR. JUSTICE SUTHERLAND delivered the opinion of the Court.

* * *

It will contribute to the elucidation of the question if we first consider the differences between the powers of the federal government in respect of foreign or external affairs and those in respect of domestic or internal affairs. That there are differences between them, and that these differences are fundamental, may not be doubted.

The two classes of powers are different, both in respect of their origin and their nature. The broad statement that the federal government can exercise no powers except those specifically enumerated in the Constitution, and such implied powers as are necessary and proper to carry into effect the enumerated powers, is categorically true only in respect of our internal affairs. In that field, the primary purpose of the Constitution was to carve from the general mass of legislative powers *then possessed by the states* such portions as it was thought desirable to vest in the federal government, leaving those not included in the enumeration still in the states. *Carter v. Carter Coal Co.,* [1936]. That this doctrine applies only to powers which the states had, is self evident. And since the states severally never possessed international powers, such powers could not have been carved from the mass of state powers but obviously were transmitted to the United States from some other source. . . .

As a result of the separation from Great Britain by the colonies acting as a unit, the powers of external sovereignty passed from the Crown not to the colonies severally, but to the colonies in their collective and corporate capacity as the United States of America. Even before the Declaration, the colonies were a unit in foreign affairs, acting through a common agency—namely the Continental Congress, composed of delegates from the thirteen colonies. That agency exercised the powers of war and peace, raised an army, created a navy, and finally adopted the Declaration of Independence. Rulers come and go; governments end and forms of government change; but sovereignty survives. A political society cannot endure without a supreme will somewhere. Sovereignty is never held in suspense. When, therefore, the external sovereignty of Great Britain in respect of the colonies ceased, it immediately passed to the Union. . . .

It results that the investment of the federal government with the powers of external sovereignty did not depend upon the affirmative grants of the Constitution. The powers to declare and wage war, to conclude peace, to make treaties, to maintain diplomatic relations with other sovereignties, if they had never been mentioned in the Constitution, would have vested in the federal government as necessary concomitants of nationality. Neither the Constitution nor the laws passed in pursuance of it have any force in foreign territory unless in respect of our own citizens, and operations of the nation in such territory must be governed by treaties, international understandings and compacts, and the principles of international law. As a member of the family of nations, the right and power of the United States in that field are equal to the right and power of the other members of the international family. Otherwise, the United States is not completely sovereign.

* * *

Not only, as we have shown, is the federal power over external affairs in origin and essential character different from that over internal affairs, but participation in the exercise of the power is significantly limited. In this vast external realm, with its important, complicated, delicate and manifold problems, the President alone has the power to speak or listen as a representative of the nation. He *makes* treaties with the advice and consent of the Senate; but he alone negotiates. Into the field of negotiation the Senate cannot intrude; and Congress itself is powerless to invade it.

* * *

It is important to bear in mind that we are here dealing not alone with an authority vested in the President by an exertion of legislative power, but with such an authority plus the very delicate, plenary and exclusive power of the President as the sole organ of the federal government in the field of international relations—a power which does not require as a basis for its exercise an act of Congress, but which, of course, like every other governmental power, must be exercised in subordination to the applicable provisions of the Constitution. It is quite apparent that if, in the maintenance of our international relations, embarrassment—perhaps serious embarrassment—is to be avoided and success for our aims achieved, congressional legislation which is to be made effective through negotiation and inquiry within the international field must often accord to the President a degree of discretion and freedom from statutory restriction which would not be admissible were domestic affairs alone involved. Moreover, he, not Congress, has the better opportunity of knowing the conditions which prevail in foreign countries, and especially is this true in time of war. He has his confidential sources of information. He has his agents in the form of diplomatic, consular and other officials. Secrecy in respect of information gathered by them may be highly necessary, and the premature disclosure productive of harmful results.

* * *

When the President is to be authorized by legislation to act in respect of a matter intended to affect a situation in foreign territory, the legislator properly bears in mind the important consideration that the form of the President's action—or, indeed, whether he shall act at all—may well depend, among other things, upon the nature of the confidential information which he has or may thereafter receive, or upon the effect which his action may have upon our foreign relations. . . .

Practically every volume of the United States Statutes contains one or more acts or joint resolutions of Congress authorizing action by the President in respect of subjects affecting foreign relations, which either leave the exercise of the power to his unrestricted judgment, or provide a standard far more general than that which has always been considered requisite with regard to domestic affairs.

* * *

The result of holding that the joint resolution here under attack is void and unenforceable as constituting an unlawful delegation of legislative power would be to stamp this multitude of comparable acts and resolutions as likewise invalid. And while this court may not, and should not, hesitate to declare acts of Congress, however many times repeated, to be unconstitutional if beyond all rational doubt it finds them to be so, an impressive array of legislation such as we have just set forth, enacted by nearly every Congress from the beginning of our national existence to the present day, must be given unusual weight in the process of reaching a correct determination of the problem. A legislative practice such as we have here, evidenced not by only occasional instances, but marked by the movement of a steady stream for a century and a half of time, goes a long way in the direction of proving the presence of unassailable ground for the constitutionality of the practice, to be found in the origin and history of the power involved, or in its nature, or in both combined.

* * *

The uniform, long-continued and undisputed legislative practice . . . disclosed rests upon an admissible view of the Constitution which, even if the practice found far less support in principle than we think it does, we should not feel at liberty at this late day to disturb. . . .

It is enough to summarize by saying that, both upon principle and in accordance with precedent, we conclude there is sufficient warrant for the broad discretion vested in the President to determine whether the enforcement of the statute will have a beneficial effect upon the reestablishment of peace in the affected countries; whether he shall make proclamation to bring the resolution into operation; whether and when the resolution shall cease to operate and to make proclamation accordingly; and to prescribe limitations and exceptions to which the enforcement of the resolution shall be subject.

* * *

The judgment of the court below must be reversed and the cause remanded for further proceedings in accordance with the foregoing opinion.

Reversed.

MR. JUSTICE MCREYNOLDS does not agree. He is of opinion that the court below reached the right conclusion and its judgment ought to be affirmed.

MR. JUSTICE STONE took no part in the consideration or decision of this case.

Alexander M. Haig, Jr., Secretary of State of the United States v. Philip Agee

453 U.S. 280; 101 S. Ct. 2766; 69 L. Ed. 2d 640 (1981)
Vote: 7–2

The facts are given in the opinion.

Chief Justice BURGER delivered the opinion of the Court.

* * *

Philip Agee, an American citizen, currently resides in West Germany. From 1957 to 1968, he was employed by the Central Intelligence Agency. He held key positions in the division of the Agency that is responsible for covert intelligence gathering in foreign countries. In the course of his duties at the Agency, Agee received training in clandestine operations, including the methods used to protect the identities of intelligence employees and sources of the United States overseas. He served in undercover assignments abroad and came to know many Government employees and other persons supplying information to the United States. The relationships of many of these people to our Government are highly confidential; many are still engaged in intelligence gathering.

In 1974, Agee called a press conference in London to announce his "campaign to fight the United States CIA wherever it is operating." He declared his intent "to expose CIA officers and agents and to take the measures necessary to drive them out of the countries where they are operating." Since 1974, Agee has, by his own assertion, devoted consistent effort to that program, and he has traveled extensively in other countries in order to carry it out. To identify CIA personnel in a particular country, Agee goes to the target country and consults sources in local diplomatic circles whom he knows from his prior service in the United States Government. He recruits collaborators and trains them in clandestine techniques designed to expose the "cover" of CIA employees and sources. Agee and his collaborators have repeatedly and publicly identified individuals and organizations located in foreign countries as undercover CIA agents, employees, or sources. The record reveals that the identifications divulge classified information, violate Agee's express contract not to make any public statements about Agency matters without prior clearance by the Agency, have prejudiced the ability of the United States to obtain intelligence, and have been followed by episodes of violence against the persons and organizations identified.

In December 1979, the Secretary of State revoked Agee's passport and delivered an explanatory notice to Agee in West Germany. The notice states in part:

> The Department's action is predicated upon a determination made by the Secretary under the provisions of Section 51.70(b)(4) that your activities abroad are causing or are likely to cause serious damage to the national security or the foreign policy of the United States. The reasons for the Secretary's determination are, in summary, as follows: Since the early 1970's it has been your stated intention to conduct a continuous campaign to disrupt the intelligence operations of the United States. In carrying out that campaign you have traveled in various countries (including, among others, Mexico, the United Kingdom, Denmark, Jamaica, Cuba, and Germany), and your activities in those countries have caused serious damage to the national security and foreign policy of the United States. Your stated intention to continue such activities threatens additional damage of the same kind.

The notice also advised Agee of his right to an administrative hearing and offered to hold such a hearing in West Germany on 5 days' notice.

Agee at once filed suit against the Secretary. He alleged that the regulation invoked by the Secretary, has not been authorized by Congress and is invalid; that the regulation is impermissibly overbroad; the revocation prior to a hearing violated his Fifth Amendment right to procedural due process; and that the revocation violated a Fifth Amendment liberty interest in a right to travel and a First Amendment right to criticize government policies. He sought declaratory and injunctive relief, and he moved for summary judgment on the question of authority to promulgate the regulation and on the constitutional claims. For purposes of that motion, Agee conceded the Government's factual averments and its claim that his activities were causing or were likely to cause serious damage to the national security or foreign policy of the United States. The District Court held that the regulation exceeded the statutory powers of the Secretary under the Passport Act of 1926, granted summary judgment for Agee, and ordered the Secretary to restore his passport. [A court of appeals affirmed. The Supreme Court granted certiorari.]. . .

The history of passport controls since the earliest days of the Republic shows congressional recognition of Executive authority to withhold passports on the basis of substantial reasons of national security and foreign policy. Prior to 1856, when there was no statute on the subject, the common perception was that the issuance of a passport was committed to the sole discretion of the Executive and that the Executive would exercise this power in the interests of the national security and foreign policy of the United States. This derived from the generally accepted view that foreign policy was the province and responsibility of the Executive. From the outset, Congress endorsed not only the underlying premise of Executive authority in the areas of foreign policy and national security, but also its specific application to the subject of passports. Early Congresses enacted statutes expressly recognizing the Executive authority with respect to passports.

The first Passport Act, adopted in 1856, provided that the Secretary of State "shall be authorized to grant and issue passports . . . under such rules as the President shall designate and prescribe for and on behalf of the United States.. . ." This broad and permissive language worked no change in the power of the Executive to issue passports; nor was it intended to do so. The Act was passed to centralize passport authority in the Federal Government and specifically in the Secretary of State.

* * *

The President and the Secretary of State consistently construed the 1856 Act to preserve their authority to withhold passports on national security and foreign policy grounds. Thus, as an emergency measure in 1861, the Secretary issued orders prohibiting persons from going abroad or entering the country without passports; denying passports to citizens who were subject to military service unless they were bonded; and absolutely denying passports to persons "on errands hostile and injurious to the peace of the country and dangerous to the Union. . . ."

By enactment of the first travel control statute in 1918, Congress made clear its expectation that the Executive would curtail or prevent international travel by American citizens if it was contrary to the national security. The legislative history reveals that the principal reason for the 1918 statute was fear that "renegade Americans" would travel abroad and engage in "transference of important military information" to persons not entitled to it. The 1918 statute left the power to make exceptions exclusively in the hands of the Executive, without articulating specific standards. Unless the Secretary had power to apply national security criteria in passport decisions, the purpose of the Travel Control Act would plainly have been frustrated.

[5]   Against this background, and while the 1918 provisions were still in effect, Congress enacted the Passport Act of 1926. The legislative history of the statute is sparse. However, Congress used language which is identical in pertinent part to that in the 1856 statute as amended, and the legislative history clearly shows congressional awareness of the Executive policy. There is no evidence of any intent to repudiate the longstanding administrative construction. Absent such evidence, we conclude that Congress, in 1926, adopted the longstanding administrative construction of the 1856 statute.

The Executive construed the 1926 Act to work no change in prior practice and specifically interpreted it to authorize denial of a passport on grounds of national security or foreign policy. Indeed, by an unbroken line of Executive Orders, regulations, instructions to consular officials, and notices to passport holders, the President and the Department of State left no doubt that likelihood of damage to national security or foreign policy of the United States was the single most important criterion in passport decisions. The regulations are instructive. The 1952 version authorized denial of passports to citizens engaged in activities which would violate laws designed to protect the security of the United States "[i]n order to promote the national interest by assuring that the conduct of foreign relations shall be free from unlawful interference."

The 1956 amendment to this regulation provided that a passport should be denied to any person whose "activities abroad would: (1) Violate the laws of the United States; (b) be prejudicial to the orderly conduct of foreign relations; or (c) otherwise be prejudicial to the interests of the United States." This regulation remained in effect continuously until 1966. . . .

In 1966, the Secretary of State promulgated the regulations at issue in this case.

Closely paralleling the 1956 regulation, these provisions authorize revocation of a passport where "the Secretary determines that the national's activities abroad are causing or are likely to cause serious damage to the national security or the foreign policy of the United States."

Zemel v. Rusk, [1965], recognized that congressional acquiescence may sometimes be found from nothing more than silence in the face of an administrative policy.

Here, however, the inference of congressional approval "is supported by more than mere congressional inaction."

Twelve years after the promulgation of the regulations at issue and 22 years after promulgation of the similar 1956 regulation, Congress enacted the statute making it unlawful to travel abroad without a passport even in peacetime.

Simultaneously, Congress amended the Passport Act of 1926 to provide that "[u]nless authorized by law," in the absence of war, armed hostilities, or imminent danger to travelers, a passport may not be geographically restricted.

*   *   *

The 1978 amendments are weighty evidence of congressional approval of the Secretary's interpretation, particularly that in the 1966 regulations. Despite the longstanding and officially promulgated view that the Executive had the power to withhold passports for reasons of national security and foreign policy, Congress in 1978, "though it once again enacted legislation relating to passports, left completely untouched the broad rule-making authority granted in the earlier Act. . . ."

Agee also attacks the Secretary's action on three constitutional grounds: first, that the revocation of his passport impermissibly burdens his freedom to travel; second, that the action was intended to penalize his exercise of free speech and deter his criticism of government policies and practices; and third, that failure to accord him a prerevocation hearing violated his Fifth Amendment right to procedural due process.

In light of the express language of the passport regulations, which permits their application only in cases involving likelihood of "serious damage" to national security or foreign policy, these claims are without merit.

[8]   Revocation of a passport undeniably curtails travel, but the freedom to travel abroad with a "letter of introduction" in the form of a passport issued by the sovereign is subordinate to national security and foreign policy considerations; as such, it is subject to reasonable governmental regulation. The Court has made it plain that the *freedom* to travel outside the United States must be distinguished from the *right* to travel within the United States. . . .

" 'The constitutional right of interstate travel is virtually unqualified.' "

Griffin v. Breckenridge, [1971].

By contrast the "right" of international travel has been considered to be no more than an aspect of the "liberty" protected by the Due Process Clause of the Fifth Amendment. As such this "right," the Court has held, can be regulated within the bounds of due process.

[9]   It is "obvious and unarguable" that no governmental interest is more compelling than the security of the Nation. *Aptheker v. Secretary of State,* [1964].

Protection of the foreign policy of the United States is a governmental interest of great importance, since foreign policy and national security considerations cannot neatly be compartmentalized. . . .

Not only has Agee jeopardized the security of the United States, but he has endangered the interests of countries other than the United States—thereby creating serious problems for American foreign relations and foreign policy. Restricting Agee's foreign travel, although perhaps not certain to prevent all of Agee's harmful activities, is the only avenue open to the Government to limit these activities.

Assuming *arguendo* that First Amendment protections reach beyond our national boundaries, Agee's First Amendment claim has no foundation. The revocation of Agee's passport rests in part on the content of his speech: specifically, his repeated disclosures of intelligence operations and names of intelligence personnel. Long ago, however, this Court recognized that "No one would question but that a government might prevent actual obstruction to its recruiting service or the publication of the sailing dates of transports or the number and location of troops." *Near v. Minnesota,* (1931), Agee's disclosures, among other things, have the declared purpose of obstructing intelligence operations and the recruiting of intelligence personnel. They are clearly not protected by the Constitution. The mere fact that Agee is also engaged in criticism of the Government does not render his conduct beyond the reach of the law.

[11,12]   To the extent the revocation of his passport operates to inhibit Agee, "it is an inhibition of *action,*" rather than of speech.

Agee is as free to criticize the United States Government as he was when he held a passport—always subject, of course, to express limits on certain rights by virtue of his contract with the Government.

On this record, the Government is not required to hold a prerevocation hearing. In *Cole v. Young,* [1956], we held that federal employees who hold "sensitive" positions "where they could bring about any discernible effects on the Nation's security" may be suspended without a presuspension hearing. For the same reasons, when there is a substantial likelihood of "serious damage" to national security or foreign policy as a result of a passport holder's activities in foreign countries, the Government may take action to ensure that the holder may not exploit the sponsorship of his travels by the United States. "[W]hile the Constitution protects against invasions of individual rights, it is not a suicide pact." *Kennedy v. Mendoza-Martinez,* (1963). The Constitution's due process guarantees call for no more than what has been accorded here: a statement of reasons and an opportunity for a prompt postrevocation hearing.

We reverse the judgment of the Court of Appeals and remand for further proceedings consistent with this opinion.

Reversed and remanded.

* * *

Justice BRENNAN, with whom Justice MARSHALL joins, dissenting. . . .

I suspect that this case is a prime example of the adage that "bad facts make bad law." Philip Agee is hardly a model representative of our Nation. And the Executive Branch has attempted to use one of the only means at its disposal, revocation of a passport, to stop respondent's damaging statements. But just as the Constitution protects both popular and unpopular speech, it likewise protects both popular and unpopular travelers. And it is important to remember that this decision applies not only to Philip Agee, whose activities could be perceived as harming the national security, but also to other citizens who may merely disagree with Government foreign policy and express their views.

The Constitution allocates the lawmaking function to Congress, and I fear that today's decision has handed over too much of that function to the Executive. . . .

QUESTIONS AND COMMENTS

1 In 1952, Senator John Bricker of Ohio proposed that treaties should become effective as internal law only through legislation that would be valid if there were no treaty. The suggestion was rejected in the Senate by a vote of 60 to 31. Had Bricker's proposal been adopted, what would have been the effect on the ability of the President to conduct foreign affairs?

2 Valid treaties must deal with a proper subject of foreign relations. Who is to determine what is proper? Is this a "political question"?

3 In *Curtiss-Wright,* the President acted in accord with congressional policy. What if a President acted contrary to congressional policy—say, by seizing a steel mill in peacetime? See *Youngstown Sheet and Tube v. Sawyer,* 343 U.S. 579 (1952). What if, without congressional authorization, a President ordered a blockade of Cuba and the seizure of all ships entering Cuban harbors? In the absence of a declaration of war by Congress, would such acts be constitutional? See *The Prize Cases,* 2 Black 635 (1863).

4 Does the Tenth Amendment impose any limitations on the use of the treaty power? If yes, give examples.

5 The Supreme Court has held that executive agreements (which do not require the consent of the Senate) may be used to make international agreements in substantially the same fashion as a treaty. What is the source of this power?

6 In *Foster v. Neilson* [27 U.S. (2 Peters) 253 (1829)] the Court distinguished self-executory and executory treaties and held that executory treaties have no effect until implemented by congressional legislation. What is the source of this distinction?

7 Under the Articles of Confederation, treaties were enforceable through state courts, since no national court system was available. When the Treaty of Paris (recognizing American independence) was adopted in 1783, the states were asked to repeal all state laws not consistent with the treaty. The failure of some states to comply was a major factor influencing the framers to vest the treaty power in the national government when they drafted a new Constitution in 1787.

To Appoint and Remove Public Officials

Myers v. United States (1926)

Weiner v. United States (1958)

In order to ensure that the government of the United States would be a "government of laws and not of men,"[1] the framers of the Constitution interlarded that document with numerous "checks and balances." Not only are the powers of the three branches separate, but each branch, in operating in its own sphere, is subject to limitations imposed by the other two branches. For example, Congress may legislate, but the President may veto.

Congress may pass a bill over a presidential veto, but the Supreme Court may decide it is unconstitutional. The Court may nullify a congressional statute, but Congress may redraft the statute, initiate a constitutional amendment, or deprive the Court of the jurisdiction to decide such matters.

The President is given the power, in Article III, Section 2 of the Constitution, to nominate and appoint "ambassadors, other public ministers and consuls, judges of the Supreme Court, and all other officers of the United States, whose appointments are not otherwise provided for, and which shall be established by law." Section 3 adds that the President shall "commission all the officers of the United States." The Supreme Court has defined a public office as "a public station, or employment, conferred by the appointment of government," and said that the term embraces the ideas of "tenure, duration, emolument, and duties."[2]

The Constitution is silent on the power of the President to remove officers of the United States, once appointed or commissioned. But unlike other constitutional silences which the Supreme Court confronted in its early years, the issue of presidential removal power was avoided until the Court's decision in *Myers v. United States*. An interesting sidelight in *Myers* is that the Court's opinion was written by Chief Justice Taft, a former President of the United States. As such, Taft presumably understood the importance of the removal power better than most.

Myers, Administratix, v. United States

272 U.S. 52; 47 S. Ct. 21; 71 L. Ed. 160 (1926)
Vote: 6–3

The facts are given in the opinion below.

MR. CHIEF JUSTICE TAFT delivered the opinion of the Court.

This case presents the question whether under the Constitution the President has the exclusive power of removing executive officers of the United States whom he has appointed by and with the advice and consent of the Senate.

Myers, appellant's intestate, was on July 21, 1917, appointed by the President, by and with the advice and consent of the Senate, to be a postmaster of the first class at Portland, Oregon, for a term of four years. On January 20, 1920, Myers' resignation was demanded. He refused the demand. On February 2, 1920, he was removed from office by order of the Postmaster General, acting by direction of the President. February 10th, Myers sent a petition to the President and another to the Senate Committee on Post Offices, asking to be heard, if any charges were filed. He protested to the Department against his removal, and continued to do so until the end of his term. He pursued no other occupation and drew compensation for no other service during the interval. On

April 21, 1921, he brought this suit in the Court of Claims for his salary from the date of his removal, which, as claimed by supplemental petition filed after July 21, 1921, the end of his term, amounted to $8,838.71. In August, 1920, the President made a recess appointment of one Jones, who took office September 19, 1920.

The Court of Claims gave judgment against Myers, and this is an appeal from that judgment.

* * *

The question where the power of removal of executive officers appointed by the President by and with the advice and consent of the Senate was vested, was presented early in the first session of the First Congress. There is no express provision respecting removals in the Constitution, except as Section 4 of Article II, above quoted, provides for removal from office by impeachment. The subject was not discussed in the Constitutional Convention.

* * *

In the House of Representatives of the First Congress, on Tuesday, May 18, 1789, Mr. Madison moved in the Committee of the Whole that there should be established three executive departments—one of Foreign Affairs, another of the Treasury, and a third of War—at the head of each of which there should be a Secretary, to be appointed by the President by and with the advice and consent of the Senate, and to be removable by the President. . . .

On June 16, 1789, the House resolved itself into a Committee of the Whole on a bill proposed by Mr. Madison for establishing an executive department to be denominated the Department of Foreign Affairs, in which the first clause, after stating the title of the officer and describing his duties, had these words: "to be removable from office by the President of the United States. . . ."

The bill was discussed in the House at length and with great ability. The report of it in the Annals of Congress is extended. James Madison was then a leader in the House, as he had been in the Convention. His arguments in support of the President's constitutional power of removal independently of Congressional provision, and without the consent of the Senate, were masterly, and he carried the House.

It is convenient in the course of our discussion of this case to review the reasons advanced by Mr. Madison and his associates for their conclusion, supplementing them, so far as may be, by additional considerations which lead this Court to concur therein.

First. Mr. Madison insisted that Article II by vesting the executive power in the President was intended to grant to him the power of appointment and removal of executive officers except as thereafter expressly provided in that Article. He pointed out that one of the chief purposes of the Convention was to separate the legislative from the executive functions. He said:

If there is a principle in our Constitution, indeed in any free Constitution, more sacred than another, it is that which separates the Legislative, Executive and Judicial powers. If there is any point in which the separation of the Legislative and Executive powers ought to be maintained with great caution, it is that which relates to officers and offices. . . .

Mr. Madison and his associates in the discussion in the House dwelt at length upon the necessity there was for construing Article II to give the President the sole power of removal in his responsibility for the conduct of the executive branch, and enforced this by emphasizing his duty expressly declared in the third section of the Article to "take care that the laws be faithfully executed. . . ."

As he is charged specifically to take care that they be faithfully executed, the reasonable implication, even in the absence of express words, was that as part of his executive power he should select those who were to act for him under his direction in the execution of the laws. The further implication must be, in the absence of any express limitation respecting removals, that as his selection of administrative officers is essential to the execution of the laws by him, so must be his power of removing those for whom he can not continue to be responsible.

It was urged that the natural meaning of the term "executive power" granted the President included the appointment and removal of executive subordinates. If such appointments and removals were not an exercise of the executive power, what were they? They certainly were not the exercise of legislative or judicial power in government as usually understood.

* * *

Second. The view of Mr. Madison and his associates was that not only did the grant of executive power to the President in the first section of Article II carry with it the power of removal, but the express recognition of the power of appointment in the second section enforced this view on the well approved principle of constitutional and statutory construction that the power of removal of executive officers was incident to the power of appointment. It was agreed by the opponents of the bill, with only one or two exceptions, that as a constitutional principle the power of appointment carried with it the power of removal. . . .

The reason for the principle is that those in charge of and responsible for administering functions of government who select their executive subordinates need in meeting their responsibility to have the power to remove those whom they appoint.

Under section 2 of Article II, however, the power of appointment by the Executive is restricted in its exercise by the provision that the Senate, a part of the legislative branch of the Government, may check the action of the Executive by rejecting the officers he selects. Does this make the Senate part of the removing power? And this, after the whole discussion in the House is read attentively, is the real point which was considered and decided in the negative by the vote already given.

The history of the clause by which the Senate was given a check upon the

President's power of appointment makes it clear that it was not prompted by any desire to limit removals.

* * *

The rejection of a nominee of the President for a particular office does not greatly embarrass him in the conscientious discharge of his high duties in the selection of those who are to aid him, because the President usually has an ample field from which to select for office, according to his preference, competent and capable men. The Senate has full power to reject newly proposed appointees whenever the President shall remove the incumbents. Such a check enables the Senate to prevent the filling of offices with bad or incompetent men or with those against whom there is tenable objection.

The power to prevent the removal of an officer who has served under the President is different from the authority to consent to or reject his appointment. When a nomination is made, it may be presumed that the Senate is, or may become, as well advised as to the fitness of the nominee as the President, but in the nature of things the defects in ability or intelligence or loyalty in the administration of the laws of one who has served as an officer under the President, are facts as to which the President, or his trusted subordinates, must be better informed than the Senate, and the power to remove him may, therefore, be regarded as confined, for very sound and practical reasons, to the governmental authority which has administrative control. The power of removal is incident to the power of appointment, not to the power of advising and consenting to appointment, and when the grant of the executive power is enforced by the express mandate to take care that the laws be faithfully executed, it emphasizes the necessity for including within the executive power as conferred the exclusive power of removal.

* * *

Third. Another argument urged against the constitutional power of the President alone to remove executive officers appointed by him with the consent of the Senate is that, in the absence of an express power of removal granted to the President, power to make provision for removal of all such officers is vested in the Congress by section 8 of Article I. . . .

[And Article II declares that] . . . the Congress may by law vest the appointment of such inferior officers, as they think proper, in the President alone, in the Courts of Law, or in the Heads of Departments." These words, it has been held by this Court, give to Congress the power to limit and regulate removal of such inferior officers by heads of departments when it exercises its constitutional power to lodge the power of appointment with them. Here, then, is an express provision, introduced in words of exception, for the exercise by Congress of legislative power in the matter of appointments and removals in the case of inferior executive officers. The phrase "But Congress may by law vest" is equivalent to "excepting that Congress may by law vest." By the plainest implication it excludes Congressional dealing with appointments or removals of executive officers not falling within the exception, and leaves unaffected the executive power of the President to appoint and remove them.

* * *

It is reasonable to suppose also that, had it been intended to give to Congress power to regulate or control removals in the manner suggested, it would have been included among the specifically enumerated legislative powers in Article I, or in the specified limitations on the executive power in Article II. The difference between the grant of legislative power under Article I to Congress, which is limited to powers therein enumerated, and the more general grant of the executive power to the President under Article II, is significant. The fact that the executive power is given in general terms strengthened by specific terms where emphasis is appropriate, and limited by direct expressions where limitation is needed and that no express limit is placed on the power of removal by the executive, is a convincing indication that none was intended.

* * *

Fourth. Mr. Madison and his associates pointed out with great force the unreasonable character of the view that the Convention intended, without express provision, to give to Congress or the Senate, in case of political or other differences, the means of thwarting the Executive in the exercise of his great powers and in the bearing of his great responsibility, by fastening upon him, as subordinate executive officers, men who by their inefficient service under him, by their lack of loyalty to the service, or by their different views of policy, might make his taking care that the laws be faithfully executed most difficult or impossible. . . .

Made responsible under the Constitution for the effective enforcement of the law, the President needs as an indispensable aid to meet it the disciplinary influence upon those who act under him of a reserve power of removal.

. . . [The President has broad discretion] . . . in determining the national public interest and in directing the action to be taken by his executive subordinates to protect it. In this field his cabinet officers must do his will. He must place in each member of his official family, and his chief executive subordinates, implicit faith. The moment that he loses confidence in the intelligence, ability, judgment or loyalty of any one of them, he must have the power to remove him without delay. To require him to file charges and submit them to the consideration of the Senate might make impossible that unity and coordination in executive administration essential to effective action.

The duties of the heads of departments and bureaus in which the discretion of the President is exercised and which we have described, are the most important in the whole field of executive action of the Government. There is nothing in the Constitution which permits a distinction between the removal of the head of a department or a bureau, when he discharges a political duty of the President or exercises his discretion, and the removal of executive officers engaged in the discharge of their other normal duties. The imperative reasons requiring an unrestricted power to remove the most important of his subordinates in their most important duties must, therefore, control the interpretation of the Constitution as to all appointed by him.

* * *

We come now to consider an argument advanced and strongly pressed on behalf of the complainant, that this case concerns only the removal of a postmaster; that a postmaster is an inferior officer; that such an office was not included within the legislative decision of 1789, which related only to superior officers to be appointed by the President by and with the advice and consent of the Senate. . . .

It is further pressed on us that, even though the legislative decision of 1789 included inferior officers, yet under the legislative power given Congress with respect to such officers, it might directly legislate as to the method of their removal without changing their method of appointment by the President with the consent of the Senate. We do not think the language of the Constitution justifies such a contention.

* * *

The power to remove inferior executive officers, like that to remove superior executive officers, is an incident of the power to appoint them, and is in its nature an executive power. The authority of Congress given by the excepting clause to vest the appointment of such inferior officers in the heads of departments carries with it authority incidentally to invest the heads of departments with power to remove. It has been the practice of Congress to do so and this Court has recognized that power. The Court also has recognized in the *Perkins* case that Congress, in committing the appointment of such inferior officers to the heads of departments, may prescribe incidental regulations controlling and restricting the latter in the exercise of the power of removal. But the Court never has held, nor reasonably could hold, although it is argued to the contrary on behalf of the appellant, that the excepting clause enables Congress to draw to itself, or to either branch of it, the power to remove or the right to participate in the exercise of that power. To do this would be to go beyond the words and implications of that clause and to infringe the constitutional principle of the separation of governmental powers.

Assuming then the power of Congress to regulate removals as incidental to the exercise of its constitutional power to vest appointments of inferior officers in the heads of departments, certainly so long as Congress does not exercise that power, the power of removal must remain where the Constitution places it, with the President, as part of the executive power, in accordance with the legislative decision of 1789 which we have been considering.

* * *

Summing up, then, the facts as to acquiescence by all branches of the Government in the legislative decision of 1789, as to executive officers, whether superior or inferior, we find that from 1789 until 1863, a period of 74 years, there was no act of Congress, no executive act, and no decision of this Court at variance with the declaration of the First Congress, but there was, as we have seen, clear, affirmative recognition of it by each branch of the Government.

Our conclusion on the merits, sustained by the arguments before stated, is that Article II grants to the President the executive power of the Government, i.e., the general administrative control of those executing the laws, including the power of appointment and removal of executive officers—a conclusion confirmed by his obligation to take care that the laws be faithfully executed; that Article II excludes the exercise of legislative power by Congress to provide for appointments and removals, except only as granted therein to Congress in the matter of inferior offices; that Congress is only given power to provide for appointments and removals of inferior officers after it has vested, and on condition that it does vest, their appointment in other authority than the President with the Senate's consent; that the provisions of the second section of Article II, which blend action by the legislative branch, or by part of it, in the work of the executive, are limitations to be strictly construed and not to be extended by implication; that the President's power of removal is further established as an incident to his specifically enumerated function of appointment by and with the advice of the Senate, but that such incident does not by implication extend to removals the Senate's power of checking appointments; and finally that to hold otherwise would make it impossible for the President, in case of political or other differences with the Senate or Congress, to take care that the laws be faithfully executed.

We come now to a period in the history of the Government when both Houses of Congress attempted to reverse this constitutional construction and to subject the power of removing executive officers appointed by the President and confirmed by the Senate to the control of the Senate—indeed, finally, to the assumed power in Congress to place the removal of such officers anywhere in the Government.

This reversal grew out of the serious political difference between the two Houses of Congress and President Johnson. There was a two-thirds majority of the Republican party in control of each House of Congress, which resented what it feared would be Mr. Johnson's obstructive course in the enforcement of the reconstruction measures, in respect of the States whose people had lately been at war against the National Government. This led the two Houses to enact legislation to curtail the then acknowledged powers of the President. . . .

But the chief legislation in support of the reconstruction policy of Congress was the Tenure of Office Act, of March 2, 1867, providing that all officers appointed by and with the consent of the Senate should hold their offices until their successors should have in like manner been appointed and qualified, and that certain heads of departments, including the Secretary of War, should hold their offices during the term of the President by whom appointed and one month thereafter subject to removal by consent of the Senate. The Tenure of Office Act was vetoed, but it was passed over the veto. The House of Representatives preferred articles of impeachment against President Johnson for refusal to comply with, and for conspiracy to defeat, the legislation above referred to, but he was acquitted for lack of a two-thirds vote for conviction in the Senate. . . .

While, in response to this, a bill for repeal of that act passed the House, it failed in the Senate, and, though the law was changed, it still limited the Presidential power of removal. The feeling growing out of the controversy with President Johnson retained the act on the statute book until 1887, when it was repealed.

During this interval, on June 8, 1872, Congress passed an act reorganizing and consolidating the Post Office Department, and provided that the Postmaster General and his three assistants should be appointed by the President by and with the advice and consent of the Senate and might be removed in the same manner.

In 1876 the act here under discussion was passed, making the consent of the Senate necessary both to the appointment and removal of first, second and third class postmasters.

* * *

What, then, are the elements that enter into our decision of this case? We have first a construction of the Constitution made by a Congress which was to provide by legislation for the organization of the Government in accord with the Constitution which had just then been adopted, and in which there were, as representatives and senators, a considerable number of those who had been members of the Convention that framed the Constitution and presented it for ratification. It was the Congress that launched the Government. It was the Congress that rounded out the Constitution itself by the proposing of the first ten amendments which had in effect been promised to the people as a consideration for the ratification. It was the Congress in which Mr. Madison, one of the first in the framing of the Constitution, led also in the organization of the Government under it. It was a Congress whose constitutional decisions have always been regarded, as they should be regarded, as of the greatest weight in the interpretation of that fundamental instrument. This construction was followed by the legislative department and the executive department continuously for seventy-three years, and this although the matter, in the heat of political differences between the Executive and the Senate in President Jackson's time, was the subject of bitter controversy, as we have seen. This Court has repeatedly laid down the principle that a contemporaneous legislative exposition of the Constitution when the founders of our Government and framers of our Constitution were actively participating in public affairs, acquiesced in for a long term of years, fixes the construction to be given its provisions. . . .

We are now asked to set aside this construction, thus buttressed, and adopt an adverse view, because the Congress of the United States did so during a heated political difference of opinion between the then President and the majority leaders of Congress over the reconstruction measures adopted as a means of restoring to their proper status the States which attempted to withdraw from the Union at the time of the Civil War. The extremes to which the majority in both Houses carried legislative measures in that matter are now recognized by all who calmly review the history of that episode in our Government, leading to articles of impeachment against President Johnson, and his acquittal. Without animadverting on the character of the measures taken, we are certainly justified in saying that they should not be given the weight affecting proper constitutional construction to be accorded to that reached by the First Congress of the United States during a political calm and acquiesced in by the whole Government for three-quarters of a century, especially when the new construction contended for has never been acquiesced in by either the executive or the judicial departments. . . .

For the reasons given, we must therefore hold that the provision of the law of 1876, by which the unrestricted power of removal of first class postmasters is denied to the President, is in violation of the Constitution, and invalid. This leads to an affirmance of the judgment of the Court of Claims.

* * *

Judgment affirmed.

Mr. Justice Holmes, dissenting.

My brothers McReynolds and Brandeis have discussed the question before us with exhaustive research and I say a few words merely to emphasize my agreement with their conclusion.

The arguments drawn from the executive power of the President, and from his duty to appoint officers of the United States (when Congress does not vest the appointment elsewhere), to take care that the laws be faithfully executed, and to commission all officers of the United States, seem to me spider's webs inadequate to control the dominant facts.

We have to deal with an office that owes its existence to Congress and that Congress may abolish tomorrow. Its duration and the pay attached to it while it lasts depend on Congress alone. Congress alone confers on the President the power to appoint to it and at any time may transfer the power to other hands. With such power over its own creation, I have no more trouble in believing that Congress has power to prescribe a term of life for it free from any interference than I have in accepting the undoubted power of Congress to decree its end. I have equally little trouble in accepting its power to prolong the tenure of an incumbent until Congress or the Senate shall have assented to his removal. The duty of the President to see that the laws be executed is a duty that does not go beyond the laws or require him to achieve more than Congress sees fit to leave within his power.

The separate opinion of Mr. Justice McReynolds.

* * *

Nothing short of language clear beyond serious disputation should be held to clothe the President with authority wholly beyond congressional control arbitrarily to dismiss every officer whom he appoints except a few judges. There are no such words in the Constitution, and the asserted inference conflicts with the heretofore accepted theory that this government is one of carefully enumerated powers under an intelligible charter. "This instrument contains an enumeration of powers expressly granted." *Gibbons v. Ogden,* [1824]. "Nor should it ever be lost sight of, that the government of the United States is one of limited and enumerated powers, and that a departure from the true import and sense of its powers is *pro tanto* the establishment of a new Constitution. It is doing for the people what they have not chosen to do for themselves. It is usurping the functions of a legislator, and deserting those of an expounder of the law. Arguments drawn from impolicy or inconvenience ought here to be of no weight. The only sound principle is to declare, *ita lex scripta est,* to follow, and to obey. Nor, if a principle so just and conclusive could be overlooked, could there well be found a more unsafe guide in practice than mere policy and convenience."

If the phrase "executive power" infolds the one now claimed, many others heretofore totally unsuspected may lie there awaiting future supposed necessity; and no human intelligence can define the field of the President's permissible activities. "A masked battery of constructive powers would complete the destruction of liberty."

* * *

MR. JUSTICE BRANDEIS, dissenting.

* * *

The separation of the powers of government did not make each branch completely autonomous. It left each, in some measure, dependent upon the others, as it left to each power to exercise, in some respects, functions in their nature executive, legislative and judicial. Obviously the President cannot secure full execution of the laws, if Congress denies to him adequate means of doing so.

* * *

If, in any such way, adequate means are denied to the President, the fault will lie with Congress. The President performs his full constitutional duty, if, with the means and instruments provided by Congress and within the limitations prescribed by it, he uses his best endeavors to secure the faithful execution of the laws enacted.

Checks and balances were established in order that this should be "a government of laws and not of men." As White said in the House, in 1789, an uncontrollable power of removal in the Chief Executive "is a doctrine not to be learned in American governments." Such power had been denied in Colonial Charters, and even under Proprietary Grants and Royal Commissions. It had been denied in the thirteen States before the framing of the Federal Constitution. The doctrine of the separation of powers was adopted by the Convention of 1787, not to promote efficiency but to preclude the exercise of arbitrary power. The purpose was, not to avoid friction, but, by means of the inevitable friction incident to the distribution of the governmental powers among three departments, to save the people from autocracy. In order to prevent arbitrary executive action, the Constitution provided in terms that presidential appointments be made with the consent of the Senate, unless Congress should otherwise provide; and this clause was construed by Alexander Hamilton in The Federalist, No. 77, as requiring like consent to removals. Limiting further executive prerogatives customary in monarchies, the Constitution empowered Congress to vest the appointment of inferior officers, "as they think proper, in the President alone, in the Courts of Law, or in the Heads of Departments." Nothing in support of the claim of uncontrollable power can be inferred from the silence of the Convention of 1787 on the subject of removal. For the outstanding fact remains that every specific proposal to confer such uncontrollable power upon the President was rejected. In America, as in England, the conviction prevailed then that the people must look to representative assemblies for the protection of their liberties. And protection of the individual, even if he be an official, from the arbitrary or capricious exercise of power was then believed to be an essential of free government.

QUESTIONS AND COMMENTS

1 Since Taft had been President and was known to favor the aggrandizement of presidential power, should he have recused himself in *Myers?*

2 Taft could have chosen from a number of alternatives in deciding the *Myers* case. The possibilities include: (1) leaving removal to Congress via its implied powers, (b) allowing the nature of the office to shape the power to remove its occupant, (c) ruling that public officers were to be removed only by impeachment, and (d) ruling that the power to appoint inherently includes the power to remove. Which did Taft choose? Is the evidence for Taft's choice more weighty than the evidence for any other alternative? Does the Court's decision represent judicial activism? If so, which dimension?

3 What is the implication of *Myers* for the tenure of civil servants, which is guaranteed by congressional statute?

* * * * * *

William Howard Taft only lived four years after the Court's decision in *Myers.* Thus he did not live to see what he considered his most important opinion modified substantially in 1935.[3] The modification occurred in a case involving a member of the Federal Trade Commission. The FTC was created by Congress to effectuate legislative policy. Its members could be removed, under the Federal Trade Commission Act, only for inefficiency, malfeasance, or neglect of duty. Humphrey was a conservative Republican who did not share President Roosevelt's policy preferences. At the same time, he gave no evidence of inefficiency, malfeasance, or neglect of duty. But, on the basis of *Myers,* a President did not need to make or prove any such claim in order to remove an officer of the United States who had been appointed by a

President. Thus, Roosevelt simply explained that by removing Humphrey, the President could choose a replacement who would more effectively carry out the policies of his administration.

While *Myers* was undoubtedly the President's justification for his authority to remove Humphrey, the *Myers* case did not involve a member of an "independent regulatory commission." Such commissions, also, were quasi-judicial and quasi-legislative in nature. The postmaster in *Myers* performed neither of these functions. The question in *Humphrey* was whether these distinctions were such as to warrant a different decisional outcome, a question the Court answered in the affirmative. Thus the rule of Humphrey's Case is that presidentially appointed quasi-judicial or quasi-legislative officers cannot be removed by the President except on grounds included in the legislation establishing the office.

The *Weiner* case takes these developments a step further in a fashion that is often associated with activism in the growth of law. While *Humphrey* distinguished quasi-judicial and quasi-legislative functions, *Weiner* raises the level of generality to differentiate executive from nonexecutive functions.

Weiner v. United States

357 U.S. 349; 78 S. Ct. 1275; 2 L. Ed. 2d 1377 (1958)
Vote: Unanimous

The facts are given in the opinion.

MR. JUSTICE FRANKFURTER delivered the opinion of the Court.

This is a suit for back pay, based on petitioner's alleged illegal removal as a member of the War Claims Commission. The facts are not in dispute. By the War Claims Act of 1948, Congress established that Commission with "jurisdiction to receive and adjudicate according to law," § 3, claims for compensating internees, prisoners of war, and religious organizations, §§ 5, 6 and 7, who suffered personal injury or property damage at the hands of the enemy in connection with World War II. The Commission was to be composed of three persons, at least two of whom were to be members of the bar, to be appointed by the President, by and with the advice and consent of the Senate. The Commission was to wind up its affairs not later than three years after the expiration of the time for filing claims, originally limited to two years but extended by successive legislation first to March 1, 1951, and later to March 31, 1952.

This limit on the Commission's life was the mode by which the tenure of the Commissioners was defined, and Congress made no provision for removal of a Commissioner.

Having been duly nominated by President Truman, the petitioner was confirmed on June 2, 1950, and took office on June 8, following. On his refusal to heed a request for his resignation, he was, on December 10, 1958, removed by President Eisenhower in the following terms: "I regard it as in the national interest to complete the administration of the War Claims Act of 1948, as amended, with personnel of my own selection." The following day, the President made recess appointments to the Commission, including petitioner's post. After Congress assembled, the President, on February 15, 1954, sent the names of the new appointees to the Senate. The Senate had not confirmed these nominations when the Commission was abolished, July 1, 1954, by Reorganization Plan No. 1 of 1954, issued pursuant to the Reorganization Act of 1949. Thereupon, petitioner brought this proceeding in the Court of Claims for recovery of his salary as a War Claims Commissioner from December 10, 1953, the day of his removal by the President, to June 30, 1954, the last day of the Commission's existence. A divided Court of Claims dismissed the petition. We brought the case here, because it presents a variant of the constitutional issue decided in *Humphrey's Executor v. United States,* [1935].

Controversy pertaining to the scope and limits of the President's power of removal fills a thick chapter of our political and judicial history. The long stretches of its history, beginning with the very first Congress, with early echoes in the Reports of this Court, were laboriously traversed in *Myers v. United States,* [1926], and need not be retraced.... [In that case, the] Court announced that the President had inherent constitutional power of removal also of officials who have "duties of a quasi-judicial character . . . whose decisions after hearing affect interests of individuals, the discharge of which the President can not in a particular case properly influence or control."

This view of presidential power was deemed to flow from his "constitutional duty of seeing that the laws be faithfully executed. . . ."

Within less than ten years a unanimous Court, in *Humphrey's Executor v. United States,* narrowly confined the scope of the *Myers* decision to include only "all purely executive officers." The Court explicitly "disapproved" the expressions in *Myers* supporting the President's inherent constitutional power to remove members of quasi-judicial bodies.

* * *

Humphrey's case was a *cause célèbre*—and not least in the halls of Congress. And what is the essence of the decision in Humphrey's case? It drew a sharp line of cleavage between officials who were part of the Executive establishment and were thus removable by virtue of the President's constitutional powers, and those who are members of a body "to exercise its judgment without the leave or hindrance of any other official or any department of the government," as to whom a power of removal exists only if Congress may fairly be said to have conferred it. This sharp differentiation derives from the difference in functions between those who are part of the Executive establishment and those whose tasks require absolute freedom from Executive interference. "For it is quite evident," again to quote *Humphrey's Executor,* "that one who holds his office only during the pleasure of another, cannot be depended upon to maintain an attitude of independence against the latter's will."

Thus, the most reliable factor for drawing an inference regarding the President's power of removal in our case is the nature of the function that Congress vested in the War Claims Commission. What were the duties that Congress confided to this Commission? And can the inference fairly be drawn from the failure of Congress to provide for removal that these Commissioners were to remain in office at the will of the President? For such is the assertion of power on which petitioner's removal must rest. The ground of President Eisenhower's removal of petitioner was precisely the same as President Roosevelt's removal of Humphrey. Both Presidents desired to have Commissioners, one on the Federal Trade Commission, the other on the War Claims Commission, "of my own selection." They wanted these Commissioners to be their men. The terms of removal in the two cases are identic and express the assumption that the agencies of which the two Commissioners were members were subject in the discharge of their duties to the control of the Executive. An analysis of the Federal Trade Commission Act left this Court in no doubt that such was not the conception of Congress in creating the Federal Trade Commission. The terms of the War Claims Act of 1948 leave no doubt that such was not the conception of Congress regarding the War Claims Commission.

* * *

The final form of the legislation, . . . left the widened range of claims to be determined by adjudication. Congress could, of course, have given jurisdiction over these claims to the District Courts or to the Court of Claims. The fact that it chose to establish a Commission to "adjudicate according to law" the classes of claims defined in the statute did not alter the intrinsic judicial character of the task with which the Commission was charged. The claims were to be "adjudicated according to law," that is, on the merits of each claim, supported by evidence and governing legal considerations, by a body that was "entirely free from the control or coercive influence, direct or indirect," of either the Executive or the Congress. If, as one must take for granted, the War Claims Act precluded the President from influencing the Commission in passing on a particular claim, a *fortiori* must it be inferred that Congress did not wish to have hang over the Commission the Damocles' sword of removal by the President for no reason other than that he preferred to have on that Commission men of his own choosing.

For such is this case. We have not a removal for cause involving the rectitude of a member of an adjudicatory body, nor even a suspensory removal until the Senate could act upon it by confirming the appointment of a new Commissioner or otherwise dealing with the matter. Judging the matter in all the nakedness in which it is presented, namely, the claim that the President could remove a member of an adjudicatory body like the War Claims Commission merely because he wanted his own appointees on such a Commission, we are compelled to conclude that no such power is given to the President directly by the Constitution, and none is impliedly conferred upon him by statute simply because Congress said nothing about it. The philosophy of *Humphrey's Executor,* in its explicit language as well as its implications, precludes such a claim.

The judgment is

Reversed.

QUESTIONS AND COMMENTS

1 Do Presidents now have the unlimited power to remove purely executive officers they have appointed? Explain your answer.
2 May a President, under any circumstances, remove an officer of the United States if the act creating the office contains no grounds for removal? See *Morgan v. T.V.A.,* 28 F. Supp. 722, 115 F. 2d 900, *cert. denied,* 312 U.S. 701 (1941); *United Public Workers v. Mitchell,* 330 U.S. 75 (1947).

To Impose Restrictions on Persons and Property

Ex Parte Milligan (1866)

Korematsu v. United States (1944)

Youngstown Sheet and Tube Co. v. Sawyer (1952)

The three cases in this section suggest that whether the country is at war or not may influence Supreme Court decisions dealing with presidential power. The Milligan Case was decided in 1866, after the end of the Civil War. *Korematsu* was decided during World War II. The *Youngstown* decision came down in 1952, during peacetime. There is a perfect correlation across these three cases between decision for or against the executive and the formal state of military affairs.

In 1866, President Johnson declared the Civil War over and restored the southern states to the Union. He also suggested that in peacetime, the use of military tribunals was a threat to individual liberties. He made such a suggestion on at least two occasions. But his suggestion was not popular with the military, who felt that conditions in some states were not yet at a point at which military tribunals could be eliminated. The Supreme Court finally settled this disagreement in December 1866 in *Ex Parte Milligan.*

Ex Parte Milligan

71 U.S. 2; 18 L. Ed. 281 (1866)
Vote: Unanimous

The facts are given in the opinion.

Mr. Justice DAVIS delivered the opinion of the court.

On the 10th day of May, 1865, Lambdin P. Milligan presented a petition to the Circuit Court of the United States for the District of Indiana, to be discharged from an alleged unlawful imprisonment. The case made by the petition is this: Milligan is a citizen of the United States; has lived for twenty years in Indiana; and, at the time of the grievances complained of, was not, and never had been in the military or naval service of the United States. On the 5th day of October, 1864, while at home, he was arrested by order of General Alvin P. Hovey, commanding the military district of Indiana; and has ever since been kept in close confinement.

On the 21st day of October, 1864, he was brought before a military commission, convened at Indianapolis, by order of General Hovey, tried on certain charges and specifications; found guilty, and sentenced to be hanged; and the sentence ordered to be executed on Friday, the 19th day of May, 1865.

On the 2d day of January, 1865, after the proceedings of the military commission were at an end, the Circuit Court of the United States for Indiana met at Indianapolis and empanelled a grand jury, who were charged to inquire whether the laws of the United States had been violated; and, if so, to make presentments. The court adjourned on the 27th day of January, having, prior thereto, discharged from further service the grand jury, who did not find any bill of indictment or make any presentment against Milligan for any offence whatever; and, in fact, since his imprisonment, no bill of indictment has been found or presentment made against him by any grand jury of the United States.

Milligan insists that said military commission had no jurisdiction to try him upon the charges preferred, or upon any charges whatever; because he was a citizen of the United States and the State of Indiana, and had not been, since the commencement of the late Rebellion, a resident of any of the States whose citizens were arrayed against the government, and that the right of trial by jury was guaranteed to him by the Constitution of the United States.

The prayer of the petition was, that under the act of Congress, approved March 3d, 1863, entitled, "An act relating to *Habeas corpus* and regulating judicial proceedings in certain cases," he may be brought before the court, and either turned over to the proper civil tribunal to be proceeded against according to the law of the land or discharged from custody altogether.

With the petition were filed the order for the commission, the charges and specifications, the findings of the court, with the order of the War Department reciting that the sentence was approved by the President of the United States, and directing that it be carried into execution without delay. The petition was presented and filed in open court by the counsel for Milligan; at the same time the District Attorney of the United States for Indiana appeared, and, by the agreement of counsel, the application was submitted to the court. The opinions of the judges of the Circuit Court were opposed on three questions, which are certified to the Supreme Court:

1 On the facts stated in said petition and exhibits, ought a writ of *habeas corpus* to be issued?

2 On the facts stated in said petition and exhibits, ought the said Lambdin P. Milligan to be discharged from custody as in said petition prayed?

3 Whether, upon the facts stated in said petition and exhibits, the military commission mentioned therein had jurisdiction legally to try and sentence said Milligan in manner and form as in said petition and exhibits is stated?

* * *

[After determining that it possessed jurisdiction, the Court proceeded to the merits of the case.]

The controlling question in the case is this: Upon the *facts* stated in Milligan's petition, and the exhibits filed, had the military commission mentioned in it *jurisdiction,* legally, to try and sentence him? Milligan, not a resident of one of the rebellious states, or a prisoner of war, but a citizen of Indiana for twenty years past, and never in the military or naval service, is, while at his home, arrested by the military power of the United States, imprisoned, and, on certain criminal charges preferred against him, tried, convicted, and sentenced to be hanged by a military commission, organized under the direction of the military commander of the military district of Indiana. Had this tribunal the *legal* power and authority to try and punish this man?

* * *

The decision of this question does not depend on argument or judicial precedents, numerous and highly illustrative as they are. These precedents inform us of the extent of the struggle to preserve liberty and to relieve those in civil life from military trials. The founders of our government were familiar with the history of that struggle; and secured in a written constitution every right which the people had wrested from power during a contest of ages. By that Constitution and the laws authorized by it this question must be determined. . . .

Have any of the rights guaranteed by the Constitution been violated in the case of Milligan? and if so, what are they?

Every trial involves the exercise of judicial power; and from what source did the military commission that tried him derive their authority? Certainly no part of the judicial power of the country was conferred on them; because the Constitution expressly vests it "in one supreme court and such inferior courts as the Congress may from time to time ordain and establish," and it is not pretended that the commission was a court ordained and established by Congress. They cannot justify on the mandate of the President; because he is controlled by law, and has his appropriate sphere of duty, which is to execute, not to make, the laws; and there is "no unwritten criminal code to which resort can be had as a source of jurisdiction."

But it is said that the jurisdiction is complete under the "laws and usages of war."

It can serve no useful purpose to inquire what those laws and usages are, whence they originated, where found, and on whom they operate; they can never be applied to citizens in states which have upheld the authority of the government, and where the courts are open and their process unobstructed. This court has judicial knowledge that in Indiana the Federal authority was always unopposed, and its courts always open to hear criminal accusations and redress grievances; and no usage of war could sanction a military trial there for any offence whatever of a citizen in civil life, in nowise connected with the military service. Congress could grant no such power; and to the honor of our national legislature be it said, it has never been provoked by the state of the country even to attempt its exercise. One of the plainest constitutional provisions was, therefore, infringed when Milligan was tried by a court not ordained and established by Congress, and not composed of judges appointed during good behavior.

*   *   *

Another guarantee of freedom was broken when Milligan was denied a trial by jury. The great minds of the country have differed on the correct interpretation to be given to various provisions of the Federal Constitution; and judicial decision has been often invoked to settle their true meaning; but until recently no one ever doubted that the right of trial by jury was fortified in the organic law against the power of attack. It is *now* assailed; but if ideas can be expressed in words, and language has any meaning, *this right*—one of the most valuable in a free country—is preserved to every one accused of crime who is not attached to the army, or navy, or militia in actual service. . . .

The discipline necessary to the efficiency of the army and navy . . . [requires] other and swifter modes of trial than are furnished by the common law courts; and, in pursuance of the power conferred by the Constitution, Congress has declared the kinds of trial, and the manner in which they shall be conducted, for offences committed while the party is in the military or naval service. Every one connected with these branches of the public service is amenable to the jurisdiction which Congress has created for their government, and, while thus serving, surrenders his right to be tried by the civil courts. *All other persons,* citizens of states where the courts are open, if charged with crime, are guaranteed the inestimable privilege of trial by jury.

*   *   *

It is claimed that martial law covers with its broad mantle the proceedings of this military commission. The proposition is this: That in a time of war the commander of an armed force (if in his opinion the exigencies of the country demand it, and of which he is to judge), has the power, within the lines of his military district, to suspend all civil rights and their remedies, and subject citizens as well as soldiers to the rule of *his will;* and in the exercise of his lawful authority cannot be restrained, except by his superior officer or the President of the United States.

If this position is sound to the extent claimed, then when war exists, foreign or domestic, and the country is subdivided into military departments for mere convenience, the commander of one of them can, if he chooses, within his limits, on the plea of necessity, with the approval of the Executive, substitute military force for and to the exclusion of the laws, and punish all persons, as he thinks right and proper, without fixed or certain rules.

The statement of this proposition shows its importance; for, if true, republican government is a failure, and there is an end of liberty regulated by law. Martial law, established on such a basis, destroys every guarantee of the Constitution, and effectually renders the "military independent of and superior to the civil power"—the attempt to do which by the King of Great Britain was deemed by our fathers such an offence, that they assigned it to the world as one of the causes which impelled them to declare their independence. Civil liberty and this kind of martial law cannot endure together; the antagonism is irreconcilable; and, in the conflict, one or the other must perish.

* * *

It will be borne in mind that this is not a question of the power to proclaim martial law, when war exists in a community and the courts and civil authorities are overthrown. Nor is it a question what rule a military commander, at the head of his army, can impose on states in rebellion to cripple their resources and quell the insurrection. The jurisdiction claimed is much more extensive. The necessities of the service, during the late Rebellion, required that the loyal states should be placed within the limits of certain military districts and commanders appointed in them; and, it is urged, that this, in a military sense, constituted them the theatre of military operations; and, as in this case, Indiana had been and was again threatened with invasion by the enemy, the occasion was furnished to establish martial law. The conclusion does not follow from the premises. If armies were collected in Indiana, they were to be employed in another locality, where the laws were obstructed and the national authority disputed. On *her* soil there was no hostile foot; if once invaded, that invasion was at an end, and with it all pretext for martial law. Martial law cannot arise from a *threatened* invasion. The necessity must be actual and present; the invasion real, such as effectually closes the courts and deposes the civil administration.

It is difficult to see how the *safety* of the country required martial law in Indiana. If any of her citizens were plotting treason, the power of arrest could secure them, until the government was prepared for their trial, when the courts were open and ready to try them. It was as easy to protect witnesses before a civil as a military tribunal; and as there could be no wish to convict, except on sufficient legal evidence, surely an ordained and established court was better able to judge of this than a military tribunal composed of gentlemen not trained to the profession of the law.

It follows, from what has been said on this subject, that there are occasions when martial rule can be properly applied. If, in foreign invasion or civil war, the courts are actually closed, and it is impossible to administer criminal justice according to law, *then,* on the theatre of active military operations, where war really prevails, there is a necessity to furnish a substitute for the civil authority, thus overthrown, to preserve the safety of the army and society; and as no power is left but the military, it is allowed to govern by martial rule until the laws can have their free course. As necessity creates the rule, so it limits its duration; for, if this government is continued *after* the courts are reinstated, it is a gross usurpation of power. Martial rule can never exist where the courts are open, and in the proper and unobstructed exercise of their jurisdiction. It is also confined to the locality of actual war. Because, during the late Rebellion it could have been enforced in Virginia, where the national authority was overturned and the courts driven out, it does not follow that it should obtain in Indiana, where that authority was never disputed, and justice was always administered. And so in the case of a foreign invasion, martial rule may become a necessity in one state, when, in another, it would be "mere lawless violence."

* * *

To the third question, then, on which the judges below were opposed in opinion, an answer in the negative must be returned.

* * *

The two remaining questions in this case must be answered in the affirmative. The suspension of the privilege of the writ of *habeas corpus* does not suspend the writ itself. The writ issues as a matter of course; and on the return made to it the court decides whether the party applying is denied the right of proceeding any further with it.

* * *

QUESTIONS AND COMMENTS

1 *Ex Parte Milligan* arose in Indiana. Would the Court's decision have been different had the events producing the case transpired in South Carolina or Georgia? Explain your answer.
2 In 1942, the United States tried, by military tribunal, eight German saboteurs who had landed in this country by submarine.[4] In 1946, Japanese General Yamashita was tried by a military commission and put to death for "war crimes."[5] In both cases, civil courts were open and operating. Both were upheld in the Supreme Court. How do you square these rulings with that of *Ex Parte Milligan?*

During World War II, the United States forcibly detained in government camps approximately 112,000 Americans of Japanese descent, most of whom were American citizens. Detention was continued for up to four years. It was based on an executive order issued by President Roosevelt as commander-in-chief, though the order itself was eventually enacted as a congressional statute. The reason for the detention was an alleged fear that persons of Japanese ancestry on the west coast might give aid and comfort to an enemy of the United States in time of war.

The detention order immediately raised a number of constitutional questions about the power of the President in wartime. In *Hirabayashi v. United States*,[6] the Supreme Court was asked to decide whether an order to report to a civil control station for shipment to a detention camp and a curfew imposed on Japanese-Americans, as well as on German and Italian nationals, were unconstitutional. The curfew covered the hours of 8:00 P.M. to 6:00 A.M. and was established by an army general acting under the President's executive order. Deftly sidestepping the issue of "relocation camps," the Court found sufficient "war power" in the President and Congress acting jointly to justify the curfew. Moreover, it did so by a unanimous vote. A year later, the Court agreed to confront the question of "exclusion and detention." Why now and not earlier? One thought, at the time, was that the detention camps were being dismantled and the Court was ready to rule them unconstitutional—possibly being influenced by the fact that the government no longer thought them necessary. But whatever the reason, the *Korematsu* case split the Court 5–4 and left a legacy that has produced considerable soul-searching in subsequent years.

Korematsu v. United States

323 U.S. 214; 65 S. Ct. 193; 89 L. Ed. 194 (1944)
Vote: 6–3

The facts are given in the opinion.

MR. JUSTICE BLACK delivered the opinion of the Court.

The petitioner, an American citizen of Japanese descent, was convicted in a federal district court for remaining in San Leandro, California, a "Military Area," contrary to Civilian Exclusion Order No. 34 of the Commanding General of the Western Command, U. S. Army, which directed that after May 9, 1942, all persons of Japanese ancestry should be excluded from that area. No question was raised as to petitioner's loyalty to the United States. The Circuit Court of Appeals affirmed, and the importance of the constitutional question involved caused us to grant certiorari. . . .

Exclusion Order No. 34, which the petitioner knowingly and admittedly violated, was one of a number of military orders and proclamations, all of which were substantially based upon Executive Order No. 9066.

That order, issued after we were at war with Japan, declared that "the successful prosecution of the war requires every possible protection against espionage and against sabotage to national-defense utilities. . . ."

One of the series of orders and proclamations, a curfew order, which like the exclusion order here was promulgated pursuant to Executive Order 9066, subjected all persons of Japanese ancestry in prescribed West Coast military areas to remain in their residences from 8 p. m. to 6 a. m. As is the case with the exclusion order here, that prior curfew order was designed as a "protection against espionage and against sabotage." In *Hirabayashi v. United States,* [1943], we sustained a conviction obtained for violation of the curfew order. The Hirabayashi conviction and this one thus rest on the same 1942 Congressional Act and the same basic executive and military orders, all of which orders were aimed at the twin dangers of espionage and sabotage.

The 1942 Act was attacked in the *Hirabayashi* case as an unconstitutional delegation of power; it was contended that the curfew order and other orders on which it rested were beyond the war powers of the Congress, the military authorities and of the President, as Commander in Chief of the Army; and finally that to apply the curfew order against none but citizens of Japanese ancestry amounted to a constitutionally prohibited discrimination solely on account of race. To these questions, we gave the serious consideration which their importance justified. We upheld the curfew order as an exercise of the power of the government to take steps necessary to prevent espionage and sabotage in an area threatened by Japanese attack.

In light of the principles we announced in the *Hirabayashi* case, we are unable to conclude that it was beyond the war power of Congress and the Executive to exclude those of Japanese ancestry from the West Coast war area at the time they did. True, exclusion from the area in which one's home is located is a far greater deprivation than constant confinement to the home from 8 p. m. to 6 a. m. Nothing short of apprehension by the proper military authorities of the gravest imminent danger to the public safety can constitutionally justify either. But exclusion from a threatened area, no less than curfew, has a definite and close relationship to the prevention of espionage and sabotage. The military authorities, charged with the primary responsibility of defending our shores, concluded that curfew provided inadequate protection and ordered exclusion. . . .

Like curfew, exclusion of those of Japanese origin was deemed necessary because of the presence of an unascertained number of disloyal members of the group, most of whom we have no doubt were loyal to this country. It was because we could not reject the finding of the military authorities that it was impossible to bring about an immediate segregation of the disloyal from the loyal that we sustained the validity of the curfew order as applying to the whole group. In the instant case, temporary exclusion of the entire group was rested by the military on the same ground. The judgment that exclusion of the whole group was for the same reason a military imperative answers the contention that the exclusion was in the nature of group punishment based on antagonism to those of Japanese origin. That there were members of the group who retained loyalties to Japan has been confirmed by investigations made subsequent to the exclusion. Approximately five thousand American citizens of Japanese ancestry refused to swear unqualified allegiance to the United States and to renounce allegiance to the Japanese Emperor, and several thousand evacuees requested repatriation to Japan.

We uphold the exclusion order as of the time it was made and when the petitioner violated it.

In doing so, we are not unmindful of the hardships imposed by it upon a large group of American citizens. But hardships are part of war, and war is an aggregation of hardships. All citizens alike, both in and out of uniform, feel the impact of war in greater or lesser measure. Citizenship has its responsibilities as well as its privileges, and in time of war the burden is always heavier. Compulsory exclusion of large groups of citizens from their homes, except under circumstances of direst emergency and peril, is inconsistent with our basic governmental institutions. But when under conditions of modern warfare our shores are threatened by hostile forces, the power to protect must be commensurate with the threatened danger.

. . . On May 9, the effective date of the exclusion order, the military authorities had already determined that the evacuation should be effected by assembling together and placing under guard all those of Japanese ancestry, at central points, designated as "assembly centers," in order "to insure the orderly evacuation and resettlement of Japanese voluntarily migrating from Military Area No. 1, to restrict and regulate such migration." And on May 19, 1942, eleven days before the time petitioner was charged with unlawfully remaining in the area, Civilian Restrictive Order No. 1 provided for detention of those of Japanese ancestry in assembly or relocation centers. It is now argued that the validity of the exclusion order cannot be considered apart from the orders requiring him, after departure from the area, to report and to remain in an assembly or relocation center. The contention is that we must treat these separate orders as one and inseparable; that, for this reason, if detention in the assembly or relocation center would have illegally deprived the petitioner of his liberty, the exclusion order and his conviction under it cannot stand. . . .

Since the petitioner has not been convicted of failing to report or to remain in an assembly or relocation center, we cannot in this case determine the validity of those separate provisions of the order. It is sufficient here for us to pass upon the order which petitioner violated. To do more would be to go beyond the issues raised, and to decide momentous questions not contained within the framework of the pleadings or the evidence in this case. It will be time enough to decide the serious constitutional issues which petitioner seeks to raise when an assembly or relocation order is applied or is certain to be applied to him, and we have its terms before us.

Some of the members of the Court are of the view that evacuation and detention in an Assembly Center were inseparable. . . .

It is said that we are dealing here with the case of imprisonment of a citizen in a concentration camp solely because of his ancestry, without evidence or inquiry concerning his loyalty and good disposition towards the United States. Our task would be simple, our duty clear, were this a case involving the imprisonment of a loyal citizen in a concentration camp because of racial prejudice. Regardless of the true nature of the assembly and relocation centers—and we deem it unjustifiable to call them concentration camps with all the ugly connotations that term implies—we are dealing specifically with nothing but an exclusion order. To cast this case into outlines of racial prejudice, without reference to the real military dangers which were presented, merely confuses the issue. Korematsu was not excluded from the Military Area because of hostility to him or his race. He *was* excluded because we are at war with the Japanese Empire, because the properly constituted military authorities feared an invasion of our West Coast and felt constrained to take proper security measures, because they decided that the military urgency of the situation demanded that all citizens of Japanese ancestry be segregated from the West Coast temporarily, and finally, because Congress, reposing its confidence in this time of war in our military leaders—as inevitably it must—determined that they should have the power to do just this. There was evidence of disloyalty on the part of some, the military authorities considered that the need for action was great, and time was short. We cannot—by availing ourselves of the calm perspective of hindsight—now say that at that time these actions were unjustified.

Affirmed.

MR. JUSTICE FRANKFURTER, concurring.

* * *

The provisions of the Constitution which confer on the Congress and the President powers to enable this country to wage war are as much part of the Constitution as provisions looking to a nation at peace. And we have had recent occasion to quote approvingly the statement of former Chief Justice Hughes that the war power of the Government is "the power to wage war successfully." *Hirabayashi v. United States, supra* at 93.

Therefore, the validity of action under the war power must be judged wholly in the context of war. That action is not to be stigmatized as lawless because like action in times of peace would be lawless. . . . If a military order such as that under review does not transcend the means appropriate for conducting war, such action by the military is as constitutional as would be any authorized action by the Interstate Commerce Commission within the limits of the constitutional power to regulate commerce. And being an exercise of the war power explicitly granted by the Constitution for safeguarding the national life by prosecuting war effectively, I find nothing in the Constitution which denies to Congress the power to enforce such a valid military order by making its violation an offense triable in the civil courts.

To find that the Constitution does not forbid the military measures now complained of does not carry with it approval of that which Congress and the Executive did. That is their business, not ours.

MR. JUSTICE ROBERTS.

I dissent, because I think the indisputable facts exhibit a clear violation of Constitutional rights.

This is not a case of keeping people off the streets at night as was *Hirabayashi v. United States,* nor a case of temporary exclusion of a citizen from an area for his own safety or that of the community, nor a case of offering him an opportunity to go temporarily out of an area where his presence might cause danger to himself or to his fellows. On the contrary, it is the case of convicting a citizen as a punishment for not submitting to imprisonment in a concentration camp, based on his ancestry, and solely because of his ancestry, without evidence or inquiry concerning his loyalty and good disposition towards the United States. If this be a correct statement of the facts disclosed by this record, and facts of which we take judicial notice, I need hardly labor the conclusion that Constitutional rights have been violated.

* * *

I would reverse the judgment of conviction.

MR. JUSTICE MURPHY, dissenting.

This exclusion of "all persons of Japanese ancestry, both alien and non-alien," from the Pacific Coast area on a plea of military necessity in the absence of martial law ought not to be approved. Such exclusion goes over "the very brink of constitutional power" and falls into the ugly abyss of racism. . . .

The judicial test of whether the Government, on a plea of military necessity, can validly deprive an individual of any of his constitutional rights is whether the deprivation is reasonably related to a public danger that is so "immediate, imminent, and impending" as not to admit of delay and not to permit the intervention of ordinary constitutional processes to alleviate the danger.

Civilian Exclusion Order No. 34, banishing from a prescribed area of the Pacific Coast "all persons of Japanese ancestry, both alien and non-alien," clearly does not meet that test. Being an obvious racial discrimination, the order deprives all those within its scope of the equal protection of the laws as guaranteed by the Fifth Amendment. It further deprives these individuals of their constitutional rights to live and work where they will, to establish a home where they choose and to move about freely. In excommunicating them without benefit of hearings, this order also deprives them of all their constitutional rights to procedural due process. Yet no reasonable relation to an "immediate, imminent, and impending" public danger is evident to support this racial restriction which is one of the most sweeping and complete deprivations of constitutional rights in the history of this nation in the absence of martial law.

It must be conceded that the military and naval situation in the spring of

1942 was such as to generate a very real fear of invasion of the Pacific Coast, accompanied by fears of sabotage and espionage in that area. The military command was therefore justified in adopting all reasonable means necessary to combat these dangers. In adjudging the military action taken in light of the then apparent dangers, we must not erect too high or too meticulous standards; it is necessary only that the action have some reasonable relation to the removal of the dangers of invasion, sabotage and espionage. But the exclusion, either temporarily or permanently, of all persons with Japanese blood in their veins has no such reasonable relation. And that relation is lacking because the exclusion order necessarily must rely for its reasonablenesss upon the assumption that *all* persons of Japanese ancestry may have a dangerous tendency to commit sabotage and espionage and to aid our Japanese enemy in other ways. It is difficult to believe that reason, logic or experience could be marshalled in support of such an assumption.

That this forced exclusion was the result in good measure of this erroneous assumption of racial guilt rather than bona fide military necessity is evidenced by the Commanding General's Final Report on the evacuation from the Pacific Coast area. In it he refers to all individuals of Japanese descent as "subversive," as belonging to "an enemy race" whose "racial strains are undiluted," and as constituting "over 112,000 potential enemies . . . at large today" along the Pacific Coast. In support of this blanket condemnation of all persons of Japanese descent, however, no reliable evidence is cited to show that such individuals were generally disloyal, or had generally so conducted themselves in this area as to constitute a special menace to defense installations or war industries, or had otherwise by their behavior furnished reasonable ground for their exclusion as a group.

Justification for the exclusion is sought, instead, mainly upon questionable racial and sociological grounds not ordinarily within the realm of expert military judgment, supplemented by certain semi-military conclusions drawn from an unwarranted use of circumstantial evidence. Individuals of Japanese ancestry are condemned because they are said to be "a large, unassimilated, tightly knit racial group, bound to an enemy nation by strong ties of race, culture, custom and religion." They are claimed to be given to "emperor worshipping ceremonies" and to "dual citizenship." Japanese language schools and allegedly pro-Japanese organizations are cited as evidence of possible group disloyalty, together with facts as to certain persons being educated and residing at length in Japan. It is intimated that many of these individuals deliberately resided "adjacent to strategic points," thus enabling them "to carry into execution a tremendous program of sabotage on a mass scale should any considerable number of them have been inclined to do so." The need for protective custody is also asserted. The report refers without identity to "numerous incidents of violence" as well as to other admittedly unverified or cumulative incidents. From this, plus certain other events not shown to have been connected with the Japanese Americans, it is concluded that the "situation was fraught with danger to the Japanese population itself" and that the general public "was ready to take matters into its own hands." Finally, it is intimated, though not directly charged or proved, that persons of Japanese ancestry were responsible for three minor isolated shellings and bombings of the Pacific Coast area, as well as for unidentified radio transmissions and night signalling.

The main reasons relied upon by those responsible for the forced evacuation, therefore, do not prove a reasonable relation between the group characteristics of Japanese Americans and the dangers of invasion, sabotage and espionage. The reasons appear, instead, to be largely an accumulation of much of the misinformation, half-truths and insinuations that for years have been directed against Japanese Americans by people with racial and economic prejudices—the same people who have been among the foremost advocates of the evacuation. . . .

I dissent, therefore, from this legalization of racism. Racial discrimination in any form and in any degree has no justifiable part whatever in our democratic way of life. It is unattractive in any setting but it is utterly revolting among a free people who have embraced the principles set forth in the Constitution of the United States. All residents of this nation are kin in some way by blood or culture to a foreign land. Yet they are primarily and necessarily a part of the new and distinct civilization of the United States. They must accordingly be treated at all times as the heirs of the American experiment and as entitled to all the rights and freedoms guaranteed by the Constitution.

MR. JUSTICE JACKSON, dissenting.

Korematsu was born on our soil, of parents born in Japan. The Constitution makes him a citizen of the United States by nativity and a citizen of California by residence. No claim is made that he is not loyal to this country. There is no suggestion that apart from the matter involved here he is not law-abiding and well disposed. Korematsu, however, has been convicted of an act not commonly a crime. It consists merely of being present in the state whereof he is a citizen, near the place where he was born, and where all his life he has lived.

* * *

A citizen's presence in the locality, however, was made a crime only if his parents were of Japanese birth. Had Korematsu been one of four—the others being, say, a German alien enemy, an Italian alien enemy, and a citizen of American-born ancestors, convicted of treason but out on parole—only Korematsu's presence would have violated the order. The difference between their innocence and his crime would result, not from anything he did, said, or thought, different than they, but only in that he was born of different racial stock.

Now, if any fundamental assumption underlies our system, it is that guilt is personal and not inheritable. Even if all of one's antecedents had been convicted of treason, the Constitution forbids its penalties to be visited upon him, for it provides that "no attainder of treason shall work corruption of blood, or forfeiture except during the life of the person attainted." But here is an attempt to make an otherwise innocent act a crime merely because this prisoner is the son of parents as to whom he had no choice, and belongs to a race from which there is no way to resign. If Congress in peace-time legislation should enact such a criminal law, I should suppose this Court would refuse to enforce it.

* * *

Much is said of the danger to liberty from the Army program for deporting and detaining these citizens of Japanese extraction. But a judicial construction of the due process clause that will sustain this order is a far more subtle blow to liberty than the promulgation of the order itself. A military order, however unconstitutional, is not apt to last longer than the military emergency. Even during that period a succeeding commander may revoke it all. But once a judicial opinion rationalizes such an order to show that it conforms to the Constitution, or rather rationalizes the Constitution to show that the Constitution sanctions such an order, the Court for all time has validated the principle of racial discrimination in criminal procedure and of transplanting American citizens. The principle then lies about like a loaded weapon ready for the hand of any authority that can bring forward a plausible claim of an urgent need. Every repetition imbeds that principle more deeply in our law and thinking and expands it to new purposes. All who observe the work of courts are familiar with what Judge Cardozo described as "the tendency of a principle to expand itself to the limit of its logic. . . ."

Now the principle of racial discrimination is pushed from support of mild measures to very harsh ones, and from temporary deprivations to indeterminate ones. And the precedent which it is said requires us to do so is *Hirabayashi*. The Court is now saying that in *Hirabayashi* we did decide the very things we there said we were not deciding. Because we said that these citizens could be made to stay in their homes during the hours of dark, it is said we must require them to leave home entirely; and if that, we are told they may also be taken into custody for deportation; and if that, it is argued they may also be held for some undetermined time in detention camps. How far the principle of this case would be extended before plausible reasons would play out, I do not know.

I should hold that a civil court cannot be made to enforce an order which violates constitutional limitations even if it is a reasonable exercise of military authority. The courts can exercise only the judicial power, can apply only law, and must abide by the Constitution, or they cease to be civil courts and become instruments of military policy. . . .

My duties as a justice as I see them do not require me to make a military judgment as to whether General DeWitt's evacuation and detention program was a reasonable military necessity. I do not suggest that the courts should have attempted to interfere with the Army in carrying out its task. But I do not think they may be asked to execute a military expedient that has no place in law under the Constitution. I would reverse the judgment and discharge the prisoner.

QUESTIONS AND COMMENTS

1 Is *Korematsu v. United States* still good law?

2 In his *Korematsu* opinion, Justice Black makes much of the "real military dangers" and remarks that "time was short" for making decisions. Are such considerations appropriate for deciding the scope of constitutional liberties? Explain your answer.

3 In a concurring opinion, Justice Frankfurter says that action taken under the war power "is not to be stigmatized as lawless because like action in times of peace would be lawless." In fact, does one have fewer constitutional rights in time of war than in time of peace? Can you justify your answer by reference to the Constitution?

4 How do you explain the fact that one well-known liberal (Black) found no racism in *Korematsu,* while another (Murphy) says the exclusion of Japanese-Americans from the west coast "falls into the ugly abyss of racism"? Do you detect any racism in this case? Explain your answer.

5 The Japanese-American Evacuation Claims Act of 1948 provided compensation to former evacuees for property damages associated with evacuations from their homes and businesses. Federal authorities estimated such losses to total approximately $400 million (not including losses from distress-selling of homes, farms, and business—losses not covered by the 1948 act). Claims under the act totaled $148 million, and $37 million was actually paid out under the provisions of the statute. What do you think prompted Congress to pass such a bill, given that the actions of the federal government in the evacuation program were held constitutional by the Supreme Court in *Korematsu* and other cases?

6 In 1980, Congress established the Wartime Relocation and Internment of Civilians Commission to review the circumstances that produced Executive Order 9066. How would you account for the continued concern of Congress about these matters over thirty-five years after the events, policies, procedures, and Supreme Court rulings germane to wartime relocation of civilians?

7 In February 1983, the commission concluded that the internment of Japanese-Americans in World War II was a "grave injustice" which resulted from careless governmental decisions based on a fear of and anger toward American citizens of Japanese ancestry. In your opinion, can the commission properly reach such a conclusion, given the legality of the evacuation program? Why? Explain your answer. If you think reparations should be paid, how large should the payments be, and who should receive them? Why? (For a thoroughly interesting recent treatment of the Japanese-American internment cases, see Peter Irons, *Justice at War,* Oxford University Press, New York, 1983.)

8 Should the Japanese-American evacuees who are still living, or their heirs, be given reparations for psychological or other nonmonetary losses caused by their relocation experiences? How large should such payments be, and who should receive them? Why?

*   *   *   *   *   *

The background for *Youngstown Sheet and Tube Co. v. Sawyer* is the Korean War. However, only Congress may declare war, and it had not done so. The American forces sent to Korea had been dispatched by President Truman in his capacity as commander-in-chief of the armed forces. Thus, *Youngstown* raises the same question raised in *Ex Parte Milligan;* absent a formal state of war, how broad are the powers of the President, and to what extent may a President constitutionally encroach on persons and property?

Youngstown Sheet and Tube Co. et al. v. Sawyer

343 U.S. 579; 72 S. Ct. 863; 96 L. Ed. 817 (1952)
Vote: 6–3

To prevent a nationwide strike of steel workers in April 1952, President Truman ordered his secretary of commerce to take over and operate most of the steel mills in the country. The President's order was not based on any specific statutory authority. This led the mill owners to challenge the order as "lawmaking"—a function of Congress denied to the President by the Constitution. In response, the President's action was said to be based on all the powers of the executive under the Constitution, including the President's powers as commander-in-chief of the armed forces. According to President Truman, a nationwide steel strike would jeopardize national security.

The secretary of commerce proceeded to seize the mills and ordered their presidents to operate them as managers for the United States. The steel companies sued in a federal district court for injunctive and declaratory relief. The district court issued the injunction, but a court of appeals granted a stay requested by the government. The Supreme Court granted certiorari.

MR. JUSTICE BLACK delivered the opinion of the Court.

* * *

The President's power, if any, to issue the order must stem either from an act of Congress or from the Constitution itself. There is no statute that expressly authorizes the President to take possession of property as he did here. Nor is there any act of Congress to which our attention has been directed from which such a power can fairly be implied. Indeed, we do not understand the Government to rely on statutory authorization for this seizure. There are two statutes which do authorize the President to take both personal and real property under certain conditions. However, the Government admits that these conditions were not met and that the President's order was not rooted in either of the statutes. . . .

It is clear that if the President had authority to issue the order he did, it must be found in some provision of the Constitution. And it is not claimed that express constitutional language grants this power to the President. The contention is that presidential power should be implied from the aggregate of his powers under the Constitution. Particular reliance is placed on provisions in Article II which say that "The executive Power shall be vested in a President. . ."; that "he shall take Care that the Laws be faithfully executed"; and that he "shall be Commander in Chief of the Army and Navy of the United States."

The order cannot properly be sustained as an exercise of the President's military power as Commander in Chief of the Armed Forces. The Government attempts to do so by citing a number of cases upholding broad powers in military commanders engaged in day-to-day fighting in a theater of war. Such cases need not concern us here. Even though "theater of war" be an expanding concept, we cannot with faithfulness to our constitutional system hold that the Commander in Chief of the Armed Forces has the ultimate power as such to take possession of private property in order to keep labor disputes from stopping production. This is a job for the Nation's lawmakers, not for its military authorities.

Nor can the seizure order be sustained because of the several constitutional provisions that grant executive power to the President. In the framework of our Constitution, the President's power to see that the laws are faithfully executed refutes the idea that he is to be a lawmaker. The Constitution limits his functions in the lawmaking process to the recommending of laws he thinks wise and the vetoing of laws he thinks bad. And the Constitution is neither silent nor equivocal about who shall make laws which the President is to execute. The first section of the first article says that "All legislative Powers herein granted shall be vested in a Congress of the United States. . . ." After granting many powers to the Congress, Article I goes on to provide that Congress may "make all Laws which shall be necessary and proper for carrying into Execution the foregoing Powers, and all other Powers vested by this Constitution in the Government of the United States, or in any Department or Officer thereof."

The President's order does not direct that a congressional policy be executed in a manner prescribed by Congress—it directs that a presidential policy be executed in a manner prescribed by the President. The preamble of the order itself, like that of many statutes, sets out reasons why the President believes certain policies should be adopted, proclaims these policies as rules of conduct to be followed, and again, like a statute, authorizes a government official to promulgate additional rules and regulations consistent with the policy proclaimed and needed to carry that policy into execution. The power of Congress to adopt such public policies as those proclaimed by the order is beyond question. It can authorize the taking of private property for public use. It can make laws regulating the relationships between employers and employees, prescribing rules designed to settle labor disputes, and fixing wages and working conditions in certain fields of our economy. The Constitution does not subject this lawmaking power of Congress to presidential or military supervision or control.

It is said that other Presidents without congressional authority have taken possession of private business enterprises in order to settle labor disputes. But even if this be true, Congress has not thereby lost its exclusive constitutional authority to make laws necessary and proper to carry out the powers vested by the Constitution "in the Government of the United States, or any Department or Officer thereof."

The Founders of this Nation entrusted the lawmaking power to the Congress alone in both good and bad times. It would do no good to recall the historical events, the fears of power and the hopes for freedom that lay behind their choice. Such a review would but confirm our holding that this seizure order cannot stand.

The judgment of the District Court is

Affirmed.

* * *

Mr. Justice Frankfurter, concurring.

* * *

Apart from his vast share of responsibility for the conduct of our foreign relations, the embracing function of the President is that "he shall take Care that the Laws be faithfully executed. . . ." Art. II, § 3. The nature of that authority has for me been comprehensively indicated by Mr. Justice Holmes. "The duty of the President to see that the laws be executed is a duty that does not go beyond the laws or require him to achieve more than Congress sees fit to leave within his power." *Myers v. United States,* [1926]. The powers of the President are not as particularized as are those of Congress. But unenumerated powers do not mean undefined powers. The separation of powers built into our Constitution gives essential content to undefined provisions in the frame of our government. . . .

A scheme of government like ours no doubt at times feels the lack of power to act with complete, all-embracing, swiftly moving authority. No doubt a government with distributed authority, subject to be challenged in the courts of law, at least long enough to consider and adjudicate the challenge, labors under restrictions from which other governments are free. It has not been our tradition to envy such governments. In any event our government was designed to have such restrictions.

* * *

Mr. Justice Jackson, concurring in the judgment and opinion of the Court.

* * *

That seems to be the logic of an argument tendered at our bar—that the President having, on his own responsibility, sent American troops abroad derives from that act "affirmative power" to seize the means of producing a supply of steel for them. To quote, "Perhaps the most forceful illustration of the scope of Presidential power in this connection is the fact that American troops in Korea, whose safety and effectiveness are so directly involved here, were sent to the field by an exercise of the President's constitutional powers." Thus, it is said, he has invested himself with "war powers."

I cannot foresee all that it might entail if the Court should indorse this argument. Nothing in our Constitution is plainer than that declaration of a war is entrusted only to Congress. Of course, a state of war may in fact exist without a formal declaration. But no doctrine that the Court could promulgate would seem to me more sinister and alarming than that a President whose conduct of foreign affairs is so largely uncontrolled, and often even is unknown, can vastly enlarge his mastery over the internal affairs of the country by his own commitment of the Nation's armed forces to some foreign venture.

Assuming that we are in a war *de facto,* whether it is or is not a war *de jure,* does that empower the Commander in Chief to seize industries he thinks necessary to supply our army? The Constitution expressly places in Congress power "to raise and *support* Armies" and "to *provide* and *maintain* a Navy." (Emphasis supplied.) This certainly lays upon Congress primary responsibility for supplying the armed forces. Congress alone controls the raising of revenues and their appropriation and may determine in what manner and by what means they shall be spent for military and naval procurement. I suppose no one would doubt that Congress can take over war supply as a Government enterprise. On the other hand, if Congress sees fit to rely on free private enterprise collectively bargaining with free labor for support and maintenance of our armed forces, can the Executive, because of lawful disagreements incidental to that process, seize the facility for operation upon Government-imposed terms?

There are indications that the Constitution did not contemplate that the title Commander in Chief *of the Army and Navy* will constitute him also Commander in Chief of the country, its industries and its inhabitants. He has no monopoly of "war powers," whatever they are. While Congress cannot deprive the President of the command of the army and navy, only Congress can provide him an army or navy to command. . . .

The third clause in which the Solicitor General finds seizure powers is that "he shall take Care that the Laws be faithfully executed. . . ." That authority must be matched against words of the Fifth Amendment that "No person shall be . . . deprived of life, liberty or property, without due process of law. . . ." One gives a governmental authority that reaches so far as there is law, the other gives a private right that authority shall go no farther. These signify about all there is of the principle that ours is a government of laws, not of men, and that we submit ourselves to rulers only if under rules.

The Solicitor General lastly grounds support of the seizure upon nebulous, inherent powers never expressly granted but said to have accrued to the office from the customs and claims of preceding administrations. The plea is for a resulting power to deal with a crisis or an emergency according to the necessities of the case, the unarticulated assumption being that necessity knows no law.

* * *

In the practical working of our Government we already have evolved a technique within the framework of the Constitution by which normal executive powers may be considerably expanded to meet an emergency. Congress may and has granted extraordinary authorities which lie dormant in normal times but may be called into play by the Executive in war or upon proclamation of a national emergency. In 1939, upon congressional request, the Attorney General listed ninety-nine such separate statutory grants by Congress of emergency or wartime executive powers. . . .

In view of the ease, expedition and safety with which Congress can grant and has granted large emergency powers, certainly ample to embrace this crisis, I am quite unimpressed with the argument that we should affirm possession of them without statute. Such power either has no beginning or it has no end. If it exists, it need submit to no legal restraint. I am not alarmed that it would plunge us straightway into dictatorship, but it is at least a step in that wrong direction.

* * *

The Executive, except for recommendation and veto, has no legislative power. The executive action we have here originates in the individual will of the President and represents an exercise of authority without law. No one, perhaps not even the President, knows the limits of the power he may seek to exert in this instance and the parties affected cannot learn the limit of their rights. We do not know today what powers over labor or property would be claimed to flow from Government possession if we should legalize it, what rights to compensation would be claimed or recognized, or on what contingency it would end. With all its defects, delays and inconveniences, men have discovered no technique for long preserving free government except that the Executive be under the law, and that the law be made by parliamentary deliberations.

Such institutions may be destined to pass away. But it is the duty of the Court to be last, not first, to give them up.

* * *

MR. CHIEF JUSTICE VINSON, with whom MR. JUSTICE REED and MR. JUSTICE MINTON join, dissenting.

* * *

Focusing now on the situation confronting the President on the night of April 8, 1952, we cannot but conclude that the President was performing his duty under the Constitution to "take Care that the Laws be faithfully executed"—a duty described by President Benjamin Harrison as "the central idea of the office. . . ."

Much of the argument in this case has been directed at straw men. We do not now have before us the case of a President acting solely on the basis of his own notions of the public welfare. Nor is there any question of unlimited executive power in this case. The President himself closed the door to any such claim when he sent his Message to Congress stating his purpose to abide by any action of Congress, whether approving or disapproving his seizure action. Here, the President immediately made sure that Congress was fully informed of the temporary action he had taken only to preserve the legislative programs from destruction until Congress could act.

The absence of a specific statute authorizing seizure of the steel mills as a mode of executing the laws—both the military procurement program and the anti-inflation program—has not until today been thought to prevent the President from executing the laws. . . .

There is no statute prohibiting seizure as a method of enforcing legislative programs. Congress has in no wise indicated that its legislation is not to be executed by the taking of private property (subject of course to the payment of just compensation) if its legislation cannot otherwise be executed. Indeed, the Universal Military Training and Service Act authorizes the seizure of *any* plant that fails to fill a Government contract or the properties of *any* steel producer that fails to allocate steel as directed for defense production. And the Defense Production Act authorizes the President to requisition equipment and condemn real property needed without delay in the defense effort. Where Congress authorizes seizure in instances not necessarily crucial to the defense program, it can hardly be said to have disclosed an intention to prohibit seizures where essential to the execution of that legislative program.

Whatever the extent of Presidential power on more tranquil occasions, and whatever the right of the President to execute legislative programs as he sees fit without reporting the mode of execution to Congress, the single Presidential purpose disclosed on this record is to faithfully execute the laws by acting in an emergency to maintain the status quo, thereby preventing collapse of the legislative programs until Congress could act. The President's action served the same purposes as a judicial stay entered to maintain the status quo in order to preserve the jurisdiction of a court. In his Message to Congress immediately following the seizure, the President explained the necessity of his action in executing the military procurement and anti-inflation legislative programs and expressed his desire to cooperate with any legislative proposals approving, regulating or rejecting the seizure of the steel mills. Consequently, there is no evidence whatever of any Presidential purpose to defy Congress or act in any way inconsistent with the legislative will.

. . . In this case, there is no statute prohibiting the action taken by the President in a matter not merely important but threatening the very safety of the Nation. Executive inaction in such a situation, courting national disaster, is foreign to the concept of energy and initiative in the Executive as created by the Founding Fathers. The Constitution was itself "adopted in a period of grave emergency. . . . While emergency does not create power, emergency may furnish the occasion for the exercise of power." The Framers knew, as we should know in these times of peril, that there is real danger in Executive weakness. There is no cause to fear Executive tyranny so long as the laws of Congress are being faithfully executed. Certainly there is no basis for fear of dictatorship when the Executive acts, as he did in this case, only to save the situation until Congress could act. . . .

The diversity of views expressed in the six opinions of the majority, the lack of reference to authoritative precedent, the repeated reliance upon prior dissenting opinions, the complete disregard of the uncontroverted facts showing the gravity of the emergency and the temporary nature of the taking all serve to demonstrate how far afield one must go to affirm the order of the District Court.

The broad executive power granted by Article II to an officer on duty 365 days a year cannot, it is said, be invoked to avert disaster. Instead, the President must confine himself to sending a message to Congress recommending action. Under this messenger-boy concept of the Office, the President cannot even act to preserve legislative programs from destruction so that Congress will have something left to act upon. There is no judicial finding that the executive action was unwarranted because there was in fact no basis for the President's finding of the existence of an emergency for, under this view, the gravity of the emergency and the immediacy of the threatened disaster are considered irrelevant as a matter of law.

Seizure of plaintiffs' property is not a pleasant undertaking. Similarly unpleasant to a free country are the draft which disrupts the home and military procurement which causes economic dislocation and compels adoption of price controls, wage stabilization and allocation of materials. . . . A sturdy judiciary should not be swayed by the unpleasantness or unpopularity of necessary executive action, but must independently determine for itself whether the President was acting, as required by the Constitution, to "take Care that the Laws be faithfully executed."

As the District Judge stated, this is no time for "timorous" judicial action. But neither is this a time for timorous executive action. Faced with the duty of executing the defense programs which Congress had enacted and the disastrous effects that any stoppage in steel production would have on those programs, the President acted to preserve those programs by seizing the steel mills.

There is no question that the possession was other than temporary in character and subject to congressional direction—either approving, disapproving or regulating the manner in which the mills were to be administered and returned to the owners. The President immediately informed Congress of his action and clearly stated his intention to abide by the legislative will. No basis for claims of arbitrary action, unlimited powers or dictatorial usurpation of congressional power appears from the facts of this case. On the contrary, judicial, legislative and executive precedents throughout our history demonstrate that in this case the President acted in full conformity with his duties under the Constitution. Accordingly, we would reverse the order of the District Court.

QUESTIONS AND COMMENTS

1 In 1862, President Lincoln suspended the writ of habeas corpus in all cases involving "disloyal" persons. Article I, Section 9 of the Constitution delegates the power to suspend the writ to Congress. Lincoln also based his Emancipation Proclamation on his power as commander in chief. He also promulgated the "Laws of War" for the Union Army without congressional action and in 1863 established his own "reconstruction" program, merely *informing* the Congress after the act. How would the Court that decided *Youngstown* have decided challenges to Lincoln's acts? Why?

2 On the basis of the opinions in *Youngstown,* can you conceive of a situation in which a President could legitimately exercise discretionary executive power to seize private property?

3 Should a President who feels that national security interests require doing so have the power to seize private property? Why or why not?

To Ignore Court Orders

United States v. Nixon (1974)

This is the famous Watergate Tapes Case. It involves the question: Is the President immune from judicial direction? The answer is yes, insofar as the ability of courts to compel performance or enjoin performance by the President is concerned. So the Court held in *Mississippi v. Johnson.*[7] There are good reasons for it. Should a President ignore an order given by the Supreme Court, who would enforce that order? On the other hand, the acts of a President are reviewable, and a court may, upon review, decide that a presidential act is unconstitutional. The pressure to conform to such a court ruling would come from public opinion and the threat of impeachment proceedings in the Congress rather than from any power of courts to enforce their edicts.

The Watergate tapes were recordings of conversations between President Nixon and his subordinates in the White House during 1973. The tapes were alleged to contain evidence of White House involvement in the burglary of

Democratic party offices in the Watergate apartment building in Washington, D.C., and of attempts to suppress that evidence. The tapes and assorted books and papers were subpoenaed by a special prosecutor appointed to investigate the "cover-up." President Nixon interposed the concept of executive privilege.

This concept is related to the ability of Presidents to shield themselves and their subordinates from undue encroachment and harassment by the other branches of the federal government. It is underpinned by the separation of powers doctrine. The question is whether the privilege is absolute or limited. If absolute, its exercise is not subject to review in the courts. If subject to review, it is obviously subject to limitation. If the privilege is not subject to review, the effect would be to put the President above the law.

In general, executive privilege allows the President to decline to divulge confidential communications within the executive branch—i.e., between the President and the President's subordinates. President Nixon not only claimed that the tapes subpoenaed by Special Prosecutor Jaworski were confidential and protected by executive privilege, he asserted, in addition, that the issue was not justiciable. It is worth noting that the second claim, because of its implications for democratic processes, attracted considerably more attention than the first.

United States v. Nixon, President of the United States, et al.

418 U.S. 683; 94 S. Ct. 3090; 41 L. Ed. 2d 1039 (1974)
Vote: 8–0

The facts are provided in the opinion below.

MR. CHIEF JUSTICE BURGER delivered the opinion of the Court.

* * *

On March 1, 1974, a grand jury of the United States District Court for the District of Columbia returned an indictment charging seven named individuals with various offenses, including conspiracy to defraud the United States and to obstruct justice. Although he was not designated as such in the indictment, the grand jury named the President, among others, as an unindicted co-conspirator. On April 18, 1974, upon motion of the Special Prosecutor, a subpoena *duces tecum* was issued pursuant to Rule 17 (c) to the President by the

United States District Court and made returnable on May 2, 1974.* This subpoena required the production, in advance of the September 9 trial date, of certain tapes, memoranda, papers, transcripts, or other writings relating to certain precisely identified meetings between the President and others. The Special Prosecutor was able to fix the time, place, and persons present at these discussions because the White House daily logs and appointment records had been delivered to him. On April 30, the President publicly released edited transcripts of 43 conversations; portions of 20 conversations subject to subpoena in the present case were included. On May 1, 1974, the President's counsel filed a "special appearance" and a motion to quash the subpoena under Rule 17 (c). This motion was accompanied by a formal claim of privilege.

At a subsequent hearing, further motions to expunge the grand jury's action naming the President as an unindicted coconspirator and for protective orders against the disclosure of that information were filed or raised orally by counsel for the President.

On May 20, 1974, the District Court denied the motion to quash and the motions to expunge and for protective orders. It further ordered "the President or any subordinate officer, official, or employee with custody or control of the documents or objects subpoenaed," to deliver to the District Court, on or before May 31, 1974, the originals of all subpoenaed items, as well as an index and analysis of those items, together with tape copies of those portions of the subpoenaed recordings for which transcripts had been released to the public by the President on April 30. The District Court rejected jurisdictional challenges based on a contention that the dispute was nonjusticiable because it was between the Special Prosecutor and the Chief Executive and hence "intra-executive" in character; it also rejected the contention that the Judiciary was without authority to review an assertion of executive privilege by the President. The court's rejection of the first challenge was based on the authority and powers vested in the Special Prosecutor by the regulation promulgated by the Attorney General; the court concluded that a justiciable controversy was presented. The second challenge was held to be foreclosed by the decision in *Nixon v. Sirica,* 159 U. S. App. D. C. 58, 487 F. 2d 700 (173).

The District Court held that the judiciary, not the President, was the final arbiter of a claim of executive privilege. The court concluded that, under the circumstances of this case, the presumptive privilege was overcome by the Special Prosecutor's prima facie "demonstration of need sufficiently compelling to

---

*Rule 17 (c) provides:

"A subpoena may also command the person to whom it is directed to produce the books, papers, documents or other objects designated therein. The court on motion made promptly may quash or modify the subpoena if compliance would be unreasonable or oppressive. The court may direct that books, papers, documents or objects designated in the subpoena be produced before the court at a time prior to the trial or prior to the time when they are to be offered in evidence and may upon their production permit the books, papers, documents or objects or portions thereof to be inspected by the parties and their attorneys."

warrant judicial examination in chambers. . . ." The court held, finally, that the Special Prosecutor had satisfied the requirements of Rule 17 (c). The District Court stayed its order pending appellate review on condition that review was sought before 4 p. m., May 24.

* * *

[The Supreme Court granted certiorari.]

JUSTICIABILITY

In the District Court, the President's counsel argued that the court lacked jurisdiction to issue the subpoena because the matter was an intra-branch dispute between a subordinate and superior officer of the Executive Branch and hence not subject to judicial resolution. That argument has been renewed in this Court with emphasis on the contention that the dispute does not present a "case" or "controversy" which can be adjudicated in the federal courts. The President's counsel argues that the federal courts should not intrude into areas committed to the other branches of Government. He views the present dispute as essentially a "jurisdictional" dispute within the Executive Branch which he analogizes to a dispute between two congressional committees. Since the Executive Branch has exclusive authority and absolute discretion to decide whether to prosecute a case, it is contended that a President's decision is final in determining what evidence is to be used in a given criminal case. Although his counsel concedes that the President has delegated certain specific powers to the Special Prosecutor, he has not "waived nor delegated to the Special Prosecutor the President's duty to claim privilege as to all materials . . . which fall within the President's inherent authority to refuse to disclose to any executive officer."

The Special Prosecutor's demand for the items therefore presents, in the view of the President's counsel, a political question under *Baker v. Carr,* (1962), since it involves a "textually demonstrable" grant of power under Art. II.

* * *

Our starting point is the nature of the proceeding for which the evidence is sought—here a pending criminal prosecution. It is a judicial proceeding in a federal court alleging violation of federal laws and is brought in the name of the United States as sovereign. Under the authority of Art. II, § 2, Congress has vested in the Attorney General the power to conduct the criminal litigation of the United States Government.

It has also vested in him the power to appoint subordinate officers to assist him in the discharge of his duties. Acting pursuant to those statutes, the Attorney General has delegated the authority to represent the United States in these particular matters to a Special Prosecutor with unique authority and tenure. The regulation gives the Special Prosecutor explicit power to contest the invocation of executive privilege in the process of seeking evidence deemed relevant to the performance of these specially delegated duties.

So long as this regulation is extant it has the force of law. . . .

The demands of and the resistance to the subpoena present an obvious controversy in the ordinary sense, but that alone is not sufficient to meet constitutional standards. In the constitutional sense, controversy means more than disagreement and conflict; rather it means the kind of controversy courts traditionally resolve. Here at issue is the production or nonproduction of specified evidence deemed by the Special Prosecutor to be relevant and admissible in a pending criminal case. It is sought by one official of the Executive Branch within the scope of his express authority; it is resisted by the Chief Executive on the ground of his duty to preserve the confidentiality of the communications of the President. Whatever the correct answer on the merits, these issues are "of a type which are traditionally justiciable." *United States v. ICC,* [1970].

The independent Special Prosecutor with his asserted need for the subpoenaed material in the underlying criminal prosecution is opposed by the President with his steadfast assertion of privilege against disclosure of the material. This setting assures there is "that concrete adverseness which sharpens the presentation of issues upon which the court so largely depends for illumination of difficult constitutional questions."

Moreover, since the matter is one arising in the regular course of a federal criminal prosecution, it is within the traditional scope of Art. III power.

* * *

THE CLAIM OF PRIVILEGE

Having determined that the requirements of Rule 17 (c) were satisfied, we turn to the claim that the subpoena should be quashed because it demands "confidential conversations between a President and his close advisors that it would be inconsistent with the public interest to produce." The first contention is a broad claim that the separation of powers doctrine precludes judicial review of a President's claim of privilege. The second contention is that if he does not prevail on the claim of absolute privilege, the court should hold as a matter of constitutional law that the privilege prevails over the subpoena *duces tecum.*

In the performance of assigned constitutional duties each branch of the Government must initially interpret the Constitution, and the interpretation of its powers by any branch is due great respect from the others. . . .

[But] Our system of government "requires that federal courts on occasion interpret the Constitution in a manner at variance with the construction given the document by another branch." *Powell v. McCormack,* [1969]. . . .

Notwithstanding the deference each branch must accord the others, the "judicial Power of the United States" vested in the federal courts by Art. III,

§ 1, of the Constitution can no more be shared with the Executive Branch than the Chief Executive, for example, can share with the Judiciary the veto power, or the Congress share with the Judiciary the power to override a Presidential veto. Any other conclusion would be contrary to the basic concept of separation of powers and the checks and balances that flow from the scheme of a tripartite government.

We therefore reaffirm that it is the province and duty of this Court "to say what the law is" with respect to the claim of privilege presented in this case. *Marbury v. Madison,* [1803].

In support of his claim of absolute privilege, the President's counsel urges two grounds, one of which is common to all governments and one of which is peculiar to our system of separation of powers. The first ground is the valid need for protection of communications between high Government officials and those who advise and assist them in the performance of their manifold duties; the importance of this confidentiality is too plain to require further discussion. Human experience teaches that those who expect public dissemination of their remarks may well temper candor with a concern for appearances and for their own interests to the detriment of the decisionmaking process. Whatever the nature of the privilege of confidentiality of Presidential communications in the exercise of Art. II powers, the privilege can be said to derive from the supremacy of each branch within its own assigned area of constitutional duties. Certain powers and privileges flow from the nature of enumerated powers; the protection of the confidentiality of Presidential communications has similar constitutional underpinnings.

The second ground asserted by the President's counsel in support of the claim of absolute privilege rests on the doctrine of separation of powers. Here it is argued that the independence of the Executive Branch within its own sphere, *Humphrey's Executor v. United States,* [1935], insulates a President from a judicial subpoena in an ongoing criminal prosecution, and thereby protects confidential Presidential communications.

However, neither the doctrine of separation of powers, nor the need for confidentiality of high-level communications, without more, can sustain an absolute, unqualified Presidential privilege of immunity from judicial process under all circumstances. The President's need for complete candor and objectivity from advisers calls for great deference from the courts. However, when the privilege depends solely on the broad, undifferentiated claim of public interest in the confidentiality of such conversations, a confrontation with other values arises. Absent a claim of need to protect military, diplomatic, or sensitive national security secrets, we find it difficult to accept the argument that even the very important interest in confidentiality of Presidential communications is significantly diminished by production of such material for *in camera* inspection with all the protection that a district court will be obliged to provide. . . .

To read the Art. II powers of the President as providing an absolute privilege as against a subpoena essential to enforcement of criminal statutes on no more than a generalized claim of the public interest in confidentiality of non-military and nondiplomatic discussions would upset the constitutional balance of "a workable government" and gravely impair the role of the courts under Art. III.

Since we conclude that the legitimate needs of the judicial process may outweigh Presidential privilege, it is necessary to resolve those competing interests in a manner that preserves the essential functions of each branch.

* * *

A President and those who assist him must be free to explore alternatives in the process of shaping policies and making decisions and to do so in a way many would be unwilling to express except privately. These are the considerations justifying a presumptive privilege for Presidential communications. . . .

But this presumptive privilege must be considered in light of our historic commitment to the rule of law. This is nowhere more profoundly manifest than in our view that "the twofold aim [of criminal justice] is that guilt shall not escape or innocence suffer." *Berger v. United States,* [1942]. We have elected to employ an adversary system of criminal justice in which the parties contest all issues before a court of law. The need to develop all relevant facts in the adversary system is both fundamental and comprehensive. The ends of criminal justice would be defeated if judgments were to be founded on a partial or speculative presentation of the facts. The very integrity of the judicial system and public confidence in the system depend on full disclosure of all the facts, within the framework of the rules of evidence. To ensure that justice is done, it is imperative to the function of courts that compulsory process be available for the production of evidence needed either by the prosecution or by the defense.

* * *

In this case the President challenges a subpoena served on him as a third party requiring the production of materials for use in a criminal prosecution; he does so on the claim that he has a privilege against disclosure of confidential communications. He does not place his claim of privilege on the ground they are military or diplomatic secrets. As to these areas of Art. II duties the courts have traditionally shown the utmost deference to Presidential responsibilities. . . .

No case of the Court, however, has extended this high degree of deference to a President's generalized interest in confidentiality. Nowhere in the Constitution, as we have noted earlier, is there any explicit reference to a privilege of confidentiality, yet to the extent this interest relates to the effective discharge of a President's powers, it is constitutionally based.

The right to the production of all evidence at a criminal trial similarly has constitutional dimensions. The Sixth Amendment explicitly confers upon every defendant in a criminal trial the right "to be confronted with the witnesses against him" and "to have compulsory process for obtaining witnesses in his favor." Moreover, the Fifth Amendment also guarantees that no person shall be deprived of liberty without due process of law. It is the manifest duty of the courts to vindicate those guarantees, and to accomplish that it is essential that all relevant and admissible evidence be produced.

In this case we must weigh the importance of the general privilege of confidentiality of Presidential communications in performance of the President's responsibilities against the inroads of such a privilege on the fair administration of criminal justice. The interest in preserving confidentiality is weighty indeed and entitled to great respect. However, we cannot conclude that advisers will be moved to temper the candor of their remarks by the infrequent occasions of disclosure because of the possibility that such conversations will be called for in the context of a criminal prosecution.

On the other hand, the allowance of the privilege to withhold evidence that is demonstrably relevant in a criminal trial would cut deeply into the guarantee of due process of law and gravely impair the basic function of the courts. A President's acknowledged need for confidentiality in the communications of his office is general in nature, whereas the constitutional need for production of relevant evidence in a criminal proceeding is specific and central to the fair adjudication of a particular criminal case in the administration of justice. Without access to specific facts a criminal prosecution may be totally frustrated. The President's broad interest in confidentiality of communications will not be vitiated by disclosure of a limited number of conversations preliminarily shown to have some bearing on the pending criminal cases.

We conclude that when the ground for asserting privilege as to subpoenaed materials sought for use in a criminal trial is based only on the generalized interest in confidentiality, it cannot prevail over the fundamental demands of due process of law in the fair administration of criminal justice. The generalized assertion of privilege must yield to the demonstrated, specific need for evidence in a pending criminal trial. . . .

Here the District Court treated the material as presumptively privileged, proceeded to find that the Special Prosecutor had made a sufficient showing to rebut the presumption, and ordered an *in camera* examination of the subpoenaed material. On the basis of our examination of the record we are unable to conclude that the District Court erred in ordering the inspection. Accordingly we affirm the order of the District Court that subpoenaed materials be transmitted to that court. . . .

QUESTIONS AND COMMENTS

1 Since the President is delegated the power to execute the laws, which in the case of criminal law means to initiate prosecutions, how can a President be subjected to a federal criminal prosecution or proceedings leading up to that end?

2 Did the Court's ruling in *United States v. Nixon* enhance, diminish, or leave unchanged the power of the Supreme Court in the tripartite system?

3 Does *United States v. Nixon* make it more difficult for a President to ensure that conversations with world leaders or agents of other countries remain confidential? Is that important? Woodrow Wilson favored "open covenants openly arrived at." Is that a good principle to follow in a democracy? Explain your answer and relate it to the Watergate crisis?

4 Are Presidents ever "above the law"? Should they be?

5 Are Supreme Court justices "above the law"? Explain your answer.

NOTES

1 *Myers v. United States,* 272 U.S. 52, 592 (1926).

2 *United States v. Hartwell,* 73 U.S. (6 Wallace) 385, 393 (1860).

3 *Humphrey's Executor v. United States,* 295 U.S. 602 (1935).

4 *Ex Parte Quirin,* 317 U.S. 1 (1942).

5 *In re Yamashita,* 327 U.S. 1 (1946).

6 320 U.S. 81 (1943).

7 71 U.S. (4 Wallace) 475 (1867).

PART TWO

THE PROTECTION OF CONSTITUTIONAL RIGHTS

CHAPTER 6

CONSTITUTIONAL AND CIVIL LIBERTIES

If one were asked what makes the political system in the United States what it is today, a good short answer would be: "the rights of its people against the abuse of governmental power." While these rights were not necessarily "breech-born," the difficulties and impediments which attended their birth can be reasonably described as "hard labor."

CONTENDING FACTIONS IN THE CONSTITUTIONAL DEBATE

The major ideological factions contending over the 1787 Constitution were the Federalists and the Antifederalists.[1] The Federalists were a major force behind the drive for a new government, for a stronger union of the states than that encompassed in the Articles Confederation. The Antifederalists did not necessarily oppose a new union. However, they did not share the Federalist desire for republican government, defined at the time as one structured and operated for the benefit of the people, the ruled, rather than for the benefit of the ruler—primarily, in that day and age, a divine-right monarch. That benefit was to be obtained by pursuing the common good rather than individualism. Our history, however, has revealed a tension between these two thrusts that exists to this day. This is readily seen in the continuing attempt of the Supreme Court to balance the rights of individuals to pursue their own ends with the common or national interest as defined by the justices, law, and the Constitution.

The Antifederalists were akin to those among us today who think that the best government is the least government. Thus, they objected vigorously to the grants of power to the executive and the Senate, to many of the enumerated powers granted to Congress, and to the "implied power" given Congress in the "necessary and proper" clause, i.e., the authority necessary to implement the powers expressly delegated. The Federalists also mistrusted those who exercise governmental power and sought to build a political system in which abuse of power would be discouraged. They were of the view that the structural arrangements in the Constitution provided sufficient protection. The Antifederalists did not agree. Initially, they proposed to remedy the defect, in part, by incorporating a Bill of Rights in the draft Constitution. But their effort was foiled by the argument that the national government was not delegated the power to encroach on the rights of the people and that state constitutions were adequate protection against such encroachment.

ADOPTING A BILL OF RIGHTS

When the Constitution was submitted to the states for ratification, the controversy was revived. At that level, the "rights of the people" proved such a salient issue that the Federalists were forced to agree to add a Bill of Rights in order to assure ratification. In the first Congress under the new government in 1789, twelve amendments were adopted and submitted to the states for approval. Three-fourths of the states ratified the first ten of the amendments by December 1791.

As the cases which follow will make clear, these amendments barred the national government from encroaching on freedom of speech, press, assembly, and religion. They guaranteed the right to bear arms, the right to a fair trial, the right to a jury trial in criminal cases, and in civil cases also if more than $20 was at stake. They prohibited unreasonable searches and seizures, cruel and unusual punishments, compulsory self-incrimination, and putting a person twice in jeopardy for the same crime. Finally, the Tenth Amendment stated flatly that the federal government possessed only the powers delegated to it, all others being reserved to the states or to the people.

Thus, the people got their protections against governmental power written into the Constitution. Yet, what it all meant has raised many difficult issues. Two fundamental questions of a general nature have been: (1) to whom does the Bill of Rights apply, and (2) what precisely is prohibited or guaranteed against government by each of the amendments. In 1791, it was not clear just how these questions were to be answered or by whom. John Marshall provided half an answer in 1803 when he informed us, with the support of his Court, that interpretation of the Constitution is the prerogative of the Supreme Court and that in the exercise of its power, the Court may nullify actions taken by the executive and legislative branches of government.[2] Consequently, the ultimate determination of any claim that Congress has impinged on freedom of speech or other guarantees in the Bill of Rights rests with the Court.

TO WHOM DOES THE BILL OF RIGHTS APPLY?

When the twelve amendments passed by the Congress were first introduced there, it was proposed that the prohibitions and guarantees be operative against both state governments and the federal government. However, for political reasons, protection against the states was dropped before passage. As proposed and ratified, the Bill of Rights appeared to have applicability to the federal government only. Indeed, the First Amendment begins with the words, "Congress shall make no law." The other nine amendments, however, do not incorporate such specific language. But, whatever the intention, the question was a proper one for the Supreme Court—one to which it responded in the case of *Barron v. Baltimore* in 1833.[3]

John Barron, who operated a wharf in Baltimore harbor, was upset with the city of Baltimore because it had redirected several streams and in so doing had damaged his business. He claimed that the city's action had caused sand to accumulate around his wharf, thereby making it inaccessible to ships. This, he alleged, was a taking of private property without adequate or just compensation—a violation of the Fifth Amendment to the Constitution.

The significance of Barron's Case lies in the premise of his argument. Since he was complaining of state rather than federal action, his position necessarily incorporated the view that the Fifth Amendment's just compensation clause applied to both the federal and the state governments. That position was argued vigorously before the Supreme court, which proceeded to reject it. The basis of the Court's decision is simply stated. The framers established a government of delegated and reserved powers. All powers not delegated were reserved to the states or the people unless explicitly prohibited by the Constitution or its amendments. The framers had no qualms about denying the states certain powers. Thus, in Article I, Section 10, all three clauses begin by saying that "No state shall. . .", followed by a list of those things which the states were forbidden to do, essentially negative statements of liberty. Among other things, states may not coin money, grant titles of nobility, lay duties on imports and exports, or keep troops in time of peace without consent of Congress.[4] Examining the Constitution and finding no express prohibition of the kind argued by Barron, the Court rejected his specific claim. However, the Court's opinion stated more broadly that the first ten amendments "contain no expression indicating an intention to apply them to State governments," and its decision settled the issue for over sixty years.

THE CIVIL WAR AMENDMENTS

While the Bill of Rights incorporated the values of primary concern to people in the states in 1791, it should not be read as an exhaustive list of the rights and liberties protected by the Constitution. The original provisions of that document prohibit, among other things, the impairment of contracts[5] and the passage of ex post facto laws[6] or bills of attainder.[7] Suspension of the writ of habeas corpus is also conditioned.[8] Moreover, the passage of time brought home the importance of rights and liberties not fully appreciated by the framers of the Constitution or the Bill of Rights. The Civil War pressed upon the conscience of the American people the values of equality and fair treatment for all people in the United States and was the stimulus for adoption of the Thirteenth, Fourteenth, and Fifteenth Amendments.

The Civil War amendments were designed and adopted primarily to ensure the equality of blacks under the law. In effect they instruct the Supreme Court as to what those rights are, the assumption being that once so instructed the Court can be depended upon to enforce the rights granted. That such instructions were necessary is implied by earlier Supreme Court decisions—that is, the Court showed no predisposition earlier to expand the rights of blacks through the intepretation of constitutional provisions. In 1850, the Court declined to consider whether a slave became free after taking up residence in a free state, holding instead that such matters were questions of state law (*Strader v. Graham,*). In 1857, the Court decided that blacks were not citizens of the United States and therefore lacked standing to bring suits as American citizens in federal court (*Dred Scott v. Sanford*). Yet, although every school-child knows that Abraham Lincoln "freed the slaves," the Supreme Court, in the years since the Civil War, has done more to establish and ensure a meaningful freedom for blacks than any mere Emancipation Proclamation could ever do. The Court's instruments have been the Civil War amendments.

In the long run, these amendments have led to dramatic improvements in the constitutional rights of blacks, and, for that matter, of other Americans. But progress has been analogous to climbing a thousand steps. After climbing for a while, the Court slows the pace of the climb or even stops to rest, but it has always resumed the climb—sometimes slowly, sometimes more rapidly. It would be inaccurate to suggest that the full potential of the Civil War amendments has now been realized. At present, the Court appears to be "catching its breath" or marking time. Future Courts, however, may find a "second wind" and expand further the rights which accrue to all Americans under the Civil War amendments, particularly Amendment XIV.

THE THIRTEENTH AMENDMENT

The Thirteenth Amendment abolished slavery in 1865. It was interpreted by the Supreme Court in 1883 to guarantee the same right to "make and enforce contracts, to sue, be parties, give evidence, and to inherit, purchase, lease, sell and convey property, as is enjoyed by White citizens."[9] At the same time, the Court noted limitations. The amendment, it said, does not apply to all discrimination based on race. Thus, the refusal of private parties to admit blacks to inns and places of public amusement was not forbidden by the Constitution.

In a similar vein, the Court refused to uphold the convictions of several white men who had tried to force several black men to resign their positions in a lumber mill.[10] However, Congress was said to possess the power to enforce the Thirteenth Amendment, i.e., to remove all "badges and symbols" of slavery. In 1866, Congress passed a statute designed to secure to former slaves the right to buy and sell property. Interpreting this right in 1968, the Court held that its ruling in the Lumber Mill Case was mistaken and overruled it.[11] The Court reached this position by suggesting that Congress may determine what badges and symbols of slavery are to be removed and that the behavior complained of in the Lumber Mill Case was barred by the 1866 statute. Other behaviors have not been found to constitute such badges. For example, forced military service,[12] forced labor on public roads,[13] and forced jury service[14] do not violate the amendment.

THE FIFTEENTH AMENDMENT

The Fifteenth Amendment grants the right to vote without abridgment because of race, color, or previous condition of servitude. And, as with the Thirteenth, Congress is given the power to enforce the amendment. This amendment has been an important source of the power to prevent state denial of suffrage to blacks. It has been used specifically to defeat various devices employed by the states to prevent blacks from voting or to dilute that vote when cast.

The Grandfather Clause

In 1898, the Supreme Court upheld the use of literacy tests to qualify voters in state and federal elections. Indeed, the Court approved of a Mississippi law not only mandating literacy but also requiring that a prospective voter be able to "interpret" any provision of the Constitution to the satisfaction of local officials. Also upheld was the notorious poll tax, payment of which was a requirement for all voters—white and black alike.[15] This occurred during an era in which the Court, if it did not assist, certainly did little to ensure that the aims of the Fifteenth Amendment would be accomplished. The Court, at this time, was headed by Chief Justice Melville Fuller. Fuller was a wealthy Democratic attorney when appointed to the Court in 1888 by President Grover Cleveland. Prior to his appointment, he had managed the campaign of Stephen Douglas when he ran against Abraham Lincoln in 1858. He was labeled by his critics as anti-Union, and his nomination drew 20 negative votes in the Senate compared to 41 votes to affirm. Seventeen years later, a Court headed by Chief Justice Edward White, a southern Catholic and Democrat, took a different tack in voiding the use of so-called grandfather clauses.[16]

Between 1895 and 1939, several states had enacted laws or state constitutional provisions that made exceptions to their traditional literacy requirement for all voters. These laws provided that those who were registered voters or descendants of registered voters before some cutoff date could be registered to vote even though they might be illiterate. The cutoff dates chosen were prior to the time when black suffrage existed. The result was that black suffrage was denied while white illiterates were allowed to vote. This practice, in simple form, was held unconstitutional by the Supreme Court in 1915.[17] A more sophisticated version met the same fate in 1939.[18] The grandfather clause decision in 1915 did not signal an abrupt turn by the Court toward greater concern for black suffrage. And the 1915 decision did not put a stop to other efforts to dilute black suffrage. One device which gained popularity in some states was the white primary.

The White Primary and State Action

Between 1940 and 1948, black voting in presidential elections increased from 1 million to 3 million.[19] While, at this time, most blacks lived in the south, the steadily increasing use of the ballot by blacks did not dramatically impact on the southern states or on political life in those states. The reason is a simple one. States in the deep south were basically one-party states. Democrats controlled almost all offices in those states, from local to statewide positions. As a consequence, the winner of the Democratic primary was almost guaranteed to be the winner in the general election that followed. While primary elections were often close, general elections were won by Democrats with such large margins that the increase in the black vote, for Republican candidates, had little effect in changing election outcomes.

The Fifteenth Amendment specifically prohibits the denial or abridgment of the right to vote on account of race, color, or previous condition of servitude by the states or the federal government. But, to find a violation at the state level, one must find "state action." In 1903, the Supreme Court held that statutes attempting to prohibit private interference with the voting rights guaranteed by the Fifteenth Amendment were unconstitutional since the amendment applies only to state or official action.[20]

Commencing in the late twenties, the Court decided several cases which more clearly defined state action. The Fourteenth Amendment declares that no state may deny any person equal protection or due process of law. In 1927, a Texas statute denying blacks the right to vote in primary elections was held to constitute state action and a violation of the equal protection clause of the Fourteenth Amendment.[21] The Fifteenth Amendment was not used by the Court in this case, since the Court was not yet convinced that primaries were elections. In an attempt to escape the constitutional restrictions on state action, the Texas legislature proceeded to vest the decision on participation in primaries in the executive committee of each political party. The executive committee of the Democratic party then adopted a resolution denying blacks the right to vote in the Democratic primary. The Supreme Court found the resolution to represent state action under the Fourteenth Amendment, reasoning that the committee acted under state authority irrespective of the will of the party itself.[22] Thus it became, for all practical purposes, an organ of the state.

Some of the language in the Court's opinion led the Texas legislature to think that a decision by a party convention to bar blacks from the Democratic primary would represent private action, outside the restrictions of the Constitution. Thus, a statute allowing political parties to determine the qualifications of their members was passed. The Democratic convention, acting under its new authority, decided forthwith to limit its membership to white citizens. This approach was tested in the Supreme Court in *Grovey v. Townsend,* decided in 1935.[23] This time, the Court could find no state action. In spite of the fact that the state continued to regulate primary elections, the Court held that the State Democratic Convention was not a mere instrumentality of the state and therefore that its decisions did not constitute state action.

The next case in this series arrived in the Supreme Court in 1944. Between 1935 and 1944, the Court had determined for the first time that, for Fifteenth

Amendment purposes, a primary is the same as a general election if the primary was an integral part of the process by which candidates for federal office were chosen. This occurred in *United States v. Classic.*[24] At the same time, the developing expansion of black rights in the United States made the Texas primary decisions more and more untenable. Three years after *Classic,* in *Smith v. Allwright,*[25] the Supreme Court changed direction—finding that where the primary election was conducted by a political party under state regulation, the party became an agency of the state insofar as it determined who could participate. Thus, the decision of the Democratic party denying blacks the right to vote in the primary constituted state action in violation of the Fifteenth Amendment.

The principle relied upon in *Smith v. Allwright* was not a sufficient rationale for the Court's decision in the next case from Texas challenging the exclusion of blacks from Democratic primaries. After the Court's decision in *Smith,* South Carolina wiped from its books every trace of statutory or constitutional regulation of primaries, reasoning that if state action was based on the nexus or linkage of the state to the primary by its laws, removing such linkages would eliminate state action. This would then permit the continued exclusion of blacks from primaries by the private parties who conducted these elections.

This scheme was nullified by the court of appeals for the fourth circuit as inconsistent with *Smith v. Allwright.* To reach that position, however, the rationale of the Smith Case had to be modified. The circuit court reasoned that any action in pursuit of a "state purpose" or "state function" constitutes state action for Fifteenth Amendment purposes. It then proceeded to find that primaries are an integral part of a general election and that general elections constitute a state function.[26] In so doing, the court provided a basis for the Supreme Court's decision in the next case from Texas—*Terry v. Adams,*[27] the so-called Jaybird Case.

The Jaybird Democratic Association was organized in 1889. Its membership from the outset was limited to whites who were registered voters in Fort Bend County, Texas. No application for membership was necessary. Registered whites were automatically included on the association's rolls. The association conducted the so-called Jaybird primary in May of election years—two months prior to the state Democratic primary. Candidates who participated in the Jaybird primary were first screened by an executive committee named from the county's precincts. Expenses were paid by assessing all candidates who participated. Neither black candidates nor black voters were allowed to take part in these primaries. While winning candidates were not required to enter the state Democratic primary in July, almost all did, and almost all emerged victorious. Between 1889 and 1950, the winners of the Jaybird primary, with one exception, ran unopposed and invariably won in the state Democratic primary and in the general election insofar as countywide offices were concerned. The admitted purpose of all this was to prevent blacks from influencing the choice of county officers.

The challenge presented to the Supreme Court by this case was how to make a ruling consistent with the developing protection of black voting rights and the Court's own recent decisions in this area. The problem lay in the fact that no state action appeared to be involved. Jaybird winners were free to do whatever they chose after the Jaybird primary. The association provided no funds or fees for further political efforts. Jaybird winners who wished to run in the Democratic primary had to file their own application as individuals. On the primary ballot, such candidates had no designation as Jaybird Association members. The association neither availed itself of nor conformed to any state law. Thus, the nexus relied on in *Smith v. Allwright* was missing in *Terry.* Whereas in *Smith,* the Court's ruling had been designed to ensure black participation in the state Democratic primary, that was not the issue in *Terry.* Blacks in Fort Bend County were now participating in both the state primary and the general elections without interference.

The Court had some difficulty in resolving the challenge presented by *Terry.* Three justices seemed to say that any device by which the "purposes" of the Fifteenth Amendment are defeated is a violation of the amendment and implied that this is true even if no state action, strictly speaking, could be identified.[28] One justice assumed that elected county officials participated in the Jaybird primary,[29] thus furnishing the nexus for state action. Four took the position that the Jaybird Association operated as "part and parcel" of the state Democratic party, which in turn was regulated by state law—the necessary linkage for finding state action.[30] One dissented from all this, arguing vigorously that no state action could be found in the facts of this case.[31]

In any event, a close reading of the four opinions in the case makes one thing absolutely clear: blacks are not to be denied the right to vote in primary and general elections, nor are any devices which serve to dilute the influence of blacks in the choice of candidates to be permitted if that dilution is based upon racial considerations. The effect of the ruling in *Terry,* therefore, was to shift the emphasis from state action, technically defined and identified, to state function or purpose and the structure of the procedures, private or public, by which that purpose is to be realized. It should be noted, however, that this analysis is restricted primarily to the voting rights of blacks and that state action remains a viable and necessary requirement in other areas of constitutional law.

Until 1965, Congress left the enforcement of the Fifteenth Amendment primarily to the judiciary. At that point, apparently believing that judicial enforcement of voting rights was porous and piecemeal, Congress passed the Voting Rights Act of 1965. This wide-ranging act effectively transferred enforcement of the Fifteenth Amendment from the courts to the Department of Justice in the executive branch. The provision accomplishing that transfer was upheld by the Supreme Court in *South Carolina v. Katzenbach,*[32] which we have included in this text. It may be noted at this point that the decision in *Katzenbach* established the broad-ranging powers of Congress under the enforcement clause of the Fifteenth Amendment.

THE FOURTEENTH AMENDMENT

In discussing the Fifteenth Amendment, we have noted that, as initially drafted, it protected against federal and state action denying or abridging the right to vote. The Fourteenth, by contrast, protects against state action only. The amendment defines state and federal citizenship, protects the privileges and immunities of United States citizens, and in its most important clause, denies states the right to "deprive any person of life, liberty, or property without due process of law" or "the equal protection of the laws."

Since the rights to due process and equal protection are rights against the states, the Court has been forced, as in the Fifteenth Amendment cases, to address the question of what constitutes state action for due process and equal protection purposes. Thus, this question must be added to any discussion of the Fourteenth Amendment. We wish to know not only what the Court has had to say about citizenship, privileges and immunities, due process, and equal protection, but also what are the conditions under which these concepts have a legal or constitutional significance.

State Action and Fourteenth Amendment Rights

The state-action restriction of the Fourteenth and Fifteenth Amendments was not inserted in these amendments without cause. The philosophical underpinning for the concept relates to individual freedom and the structure of our governmental system. If the limitations of the Constitution are focused primarily on the use of governmental power, we maximize the power of the people to act without undue interference in their private lives. If the rights against governmental power are restricted, however, we enable some regulation of behavior to occur. And by differentiating state and federal action, we permit the federal government to pursue legitimate national policies and the states to regulate behavior in areas in which the federal government has not acted. But given the 1868 historical context in which the Fourteenth and Fifteenth Amendments were adopted, a simpler justification for the state-action restriction is that the states, not the federal government, were engaging in practices which were deplored by the amendment's framers. The amendments gave the abolitionists and other supporters of black rights something that could be used in checking state treatment of newly freed blacks in the United States.

As with the Fifteenth Amendment, cases interpreting the Fourteenth have frequently dealt with the distinction between state and private action. In 1883, the Supreme Court underlined that distinction in ruling that the Civil Rights Act of 1875 was unconstitutional.[33] That act barred all racially based discrimination by private parties with respect to places of lodging, public transportation, and theaters. The Court simply found that the power of Congress to enforce the Fourteenth Amendment did not extend to private action. In later years, however, the Court moved to a less concrete definition of state action. For example, state action is involved when one acts "under color of state law."

This means that one who holds state power (or official state position) and uses that power to violate a right guaranteed by the amendment, engages in state action even if the action has not been authorized by the state. Thus if a county sheriff, a sheriff's deputy, and a police officer beat a black prisoner into unconsciousness and the prisoner later dies, their acts may appropriately be considered as acts of the state.[34] Indeed, the Court has gone so far as to hold that a person who is not an officer of a state engages in state action if he or she participates in an activity conducted by persons who act under color of law.[35]

In our treatment of the Fifteenth Amendment, we discussed several Court decisions based upon the concept of a governmental purpose or function. In *Smith v. Allwright* and *Terry v. Adams,* the Court seemed to say that if an activity is a governmental function, anyone who engages in that activity or has a sufficient nexus to it commits state action. This notion has also been applied to some extent in nonelectoral contexts. Thus, in *Marsh v. Alabama*[36] the Court decided that Jehovah's Witnesses had a right to distribute literature without a license on a sidewalk in Chickasaw, Alabama, even though the town was completely owned by the Gulf Shipbuilding Company. For Chickasaw was the functional equivalent of any other town. That being so, the move by Gulf to restrict handbill distribution was a violation of the First and Fourteenth Amendments.

The Court followed this up with a ruling that a state cannot delegate to the owner of a shopping center the power to ban peaceful picketing.[37] Here the justices found that the picketing would have been protected if it had taken place on a public sidewalk. They reasoned that the shopping center property was the equivalent of public property and that the action of the private property owners constituted state action. However, the extent to which a shopping center is dedicated to public use will determine the scope to be given to constitutional rights.

When a private enterprise assumes all of the attributes of a municipality, as in *Marsh,* clearly its actions in regulating expression constitute state action. However, where the enterprise assumes less than *all* municipal attributes, the question becomes one of judgment. It has been held that one possesses no right to enter a shopping center to distribute handbills concerning Vietnam[38] or, in a separate case, to advertise the purpose of a strike against a shopping center tenant.[39] And a state's acquiescence in a private action does not make it an action of the state for purposes of Fourteenth Amendment analysis.[40] Even where state law authorized a warehouse sale of goods in storage, the sale was held not to involve state action. This ruling seems to imply that the ability of litigants to establish state action in order to plead interference with their Fourteenth Amendment rights varies with the subject matter. The Supreme Court may be seen as more innovative in creating theory to justify a finding of state action in some fields, such as race relations, than in others, such as commercial code transactions.

The discussion of First Amendment rights under a Fourteenth Amendment heading might be somewhat confusing. For we have said earlier that the Bill of Rights, technically speaking, does not apply to the states and the Fourteenth Amendment applies specifically to the states. Possible confusion on this score may be dissipated by showing how the Bill of Rights and the Fourteenth Amendment have, to some extent, been merged.

The Incorporation of the Bill of Rights

Among the amendments to the Constitution suggested to Congress but not passed in 1789 was one declaring that "The equal rights of conscience in freedom of speech or of the press, and the right of trial by jury in criminal cases shall not be infringed by any state."[41] James Madison thought the states should be so restricted because he considered these rights fundamental. Others wanted to impose the same restrictions as those applied to the federal government via the Bill of Rights. We have seen that the Court rejected that argument in 1833. Similar arguments were rejected in *Smith v. Maryland* in 1855,[42] a case involving the Fourth Amendment.

With the adoption of the Fourteenth Amendment in 1868, new arguments became available. That amendment included several abstract concepts, the meaning of which were exceedingly debatable, particularly as applied to specific situations or facts. This opened the opportunity for litigants before the Court to compete for favored interpretations from among the options available to the Court. One line of argument that attracted adherents held that the language of the Fourteenth Amendment "incorporated" or absorbed the first eight amendments to the Constitution. This is known as the theory of "total incorporation." Its proponents argued that such words as "privileges and immunities," "liberty," "due process," and "equal protection" are properly defined to include or protect freedom of speech, press, religion, etc.—i.e., all the rights protected against federal action by the first eight amendments. This view has been expounded by Justices Harlan (I)* Black, Swayne, Field, Bradley, Brewer, Douglas, Murphy, Clifford, Rutledge, and Goldberg.[43] And in one case, four of the nine justices subscribed to this view.[44] But the doctrine has never commanded a majority of the Court.

Of greater significance is the theory of "selective incorporation." It developed from the view that if a majority of the Court could not be persuaded to adopt the theory of total incorporation, perhaps the Court would incorporate selected provisions of the Bill of Rights that could be viewed as "fundamental." Selective incorporation has, in fact, been the major means through which certain provisions of Amendments I through VIII have been applied to the states.

Early attempts were made to employ the privilege and immunities clause to protect against a state-granted monopoly,[45] a state's refusal to license females to practice law,[46] and a state's denial of a woman's right to vote.[47] All these

*Harlan I was the first of two Justice Harlans to serve on the Supreme Court. Harlan II served from 1955 to 1971.

attempts failed. In response, a shift to the due process clause occurred. In 1876, a litigant argued that the clause guaranteed trial by jury in a suit at common law involving more than $20.[48] The argument here was not that the clause incorporated the Seventh Amendment. Rather, it asserted that the due process clause protected such a "fundamental" right as a jury trial in certain civil cases. The Supreme Court thought otherwise and denied relief.

The argument that the fundamental rights described in the first eight amendments are rightly protected from state encroachment by the due process clause was first presented to the Supreme Court in 1887.[49] Similar arguments were presented in 1890,[50] 1891,[51] and 1892.[52] In all cases, they were ignored or rejected. In the third case, however, the doctrine picked up two adherents, Justices Harlan (I) and Brewer. Other justices were added later, most notably in *Adamson v. California,* where Black, arguing the Harlan position in dissent, gained the support of Justices Douglas, Murphy, and Rutledge.

Adamson was a murder case in which the prosecutor was allowed to comment on the failure of the defendant to take the stand and testify in his own defense. While a majority of the justices agreed that this would be a violation of the Fifth Amendment if it occurred in a federal court, they ruled that the Fourteenth Amendment did not absorb the self-incrimination provision of the Fifth Amendment. But this occurred in 1947, long after the Court had begun the process of selective incorporation. Thus, the disagreement in *Adamson* was not only over total versus selective incorporation, but also in contention was the assertion that the Fifth Amendment's self-incrimination provision was one of the fundamental human rights subject to Fourteenth Amendment protection.

Adamson was decided in 1947. The process of selective incorporation began much earlier. In Table 1, we array the cases in which different provisions of the Bill of Rights were declared within the coverage of the Fourteenth Amendment. Some of these are cases in which the Court found a right in the Fourteenth Amendment only because it was in the Bill of Rights. These are the true "incorporation" cases. In other instances, the Court found the right by mere interpretation of the due process clause. In the earliest case in our list, *Chicago, B. and Q. Railway Co. v. City of Chicago,* the Court addressed the meaning of due process in the Fourteenth Amendment without reliance on the due process clause of the Fifth Amendment.

The case involved the condemnation of a certain railroad right-of-way in 1880 by the city of Chicago. The city took the railroad and other private property in order to open and widen some city streets. Property owners who lost property through condemnation procedures were compensated in an amount determined by a lay jury. A jury awarded the railroad exactly $1 for its property but awarded others who lost an equal amount of land approximately $5,000. While agreeing that the due process clause of the Fourteenth Amendment required the city to pay the railroad a "just compensation," the Court decided that the Seventh Amendment prevented it from second-guessing the jury. That amendment states that in suits "where the value in controversy shall exceed

TABLE 1

PROVISIONS OF BILL OF RIGHTS APPLICABLE AGAINST THE STATES THROUGH THE FOURTEENTH AMENDMENT

Date	Amendment no.	Case	Clause
1934	1	*Hamilton v. Regents*, 293 U.S. 245	Religion–free exercise
1940	1	*Cantwell v. Connecticut*, 310 U.S. 296	Religion–free exercise
1947	1	*Everson v. Bd. of Ed.*, 330 U.S. 1	Religion–establishment
1948	1	*Illinois ex rel McCollum*, 333 U.S. 203	Religion–establishment
1925	1	*Gitlow v. New York*, 268 U.S. 652	Freedom of speech
1927	1	*Fiske v. Kansas*, 274 U.S. 380	Freedom of speech
1931	1	*Stromberg v. California*, 283 U.S. 359	Freedom of speech
1931	1	*Near v. Minnesota*, 238 U.S. 697	Free press
1937	1	*Dejonge v. Oregon*, 299 U.S. 353	Freedom of assembly
1937	1	*Dejonge v. Oregon*, 299 U.S. 353	Freedom to petition
1939	1	*Hague v. C.I.O.*, 307 U.S. 496	Freedom to petition
1941	1	*Bridges v. California*, 314 U.S. 252	Freedom to petition
1949	4	*Wolf v. Colorado*, 338 U.S. 25	Search and seizure
1961	4	*Mapp v. Ohio*, 367 U.S. 643	Search and seizure
1969	5	*Benton v. Maryland*, 395 U.S. 784	Double jeopardy
1970	5	*Ashe v. Swenson*, 397 U.S. 436	Double jeopardy
1964	5	*Malloy v. Hogan*, 378 U.S. 1	Self-incrimination
1965	5	*Griffin v. California*, 380 U.S. 609	Self-incrimination
1897	5	*Chicago, B. & Q. Railway Co. v. City of Chicago*, 166 U.S. 226	Just compensation
1967	6	*Klopfer v. North Carolina*, 386 U.S. 213	Speedy trial
1948	6	*In re Oliver*, 333 U.S. 257	Public trial
1968	6	*Duncan v. Louisiana*, 351 U.S. 145	Jury trial
1961	6	*Irvin v. Doud*, 366 U.S. 717	Impartial jury
1961	6	*Turner v. Louisiana*, 379 U.S. 466	Impartial jury
1948	6	*In re Oliver*, 333 U.S. 257	Right to notice
1965	6	*Pointer v. Texas*, 380 U.S. 400	Confrontation of witnesses
1965	6	*Douglas v. Alabama*, 380 U.S. 415	Confrontation of witnesses
1967	6	*Washington v. Texas*, 388 U.S. 14	Compulsory process
1932	6	*Powell v. Alabama*, 287 U.S. 45	Right to counsel
1967	6	*Gideon v. Wainwright*, 372 U.S. 335	Right to counsel
1972	6	*Argersinger v. Hamlim*, 407 U.S. 25	Right to counsel
1947	8	*Louisiana ex rel Francis v. Resweber*, 329 U.S. 459	Cruel and unusual punishment
1962	8	*Robinson v. California*, 370 U.S. 660	Cruel and unusual punishment

Note: In other cases, the Supreme Court has held applicable against the states constitutional rights that cannot be traced to specific wording in an amendment or to a single amendment. Examples are *N.A.A.C.P. v. Alabama,* 357 U.S. 449 (1958), guaranteeing freedom of association against state encroachment, and *Griswold v. Connecticut,* 381 U.S. 479 (1965), extending the right to privacy emanating from the First, Third, Fourth, and Ninth Amendments against the states. Thus, the Court has selectively incorporated not only enumerated guarantees but also certain so-called fundamental rights perhaps implied but not explicitly granted in the Bill of Rights.

Source: Adapted, in part, from Congressional Research Service, *The Constitution of the United States of America,* GPO, Washington, D.C., 1973, pp. 905–906.

twenty dollars . . . , no fact tried by a jury shall be otherwise reexamined in any court of the United States, than according to the rules of the common law."

In the common law (i.e., judge-made law), appellate courts were accustomed to reexamining questions of law only—not questions of fact.[53] Interpreting the Seventh Amendment to apply to state governments as well as to the federal government, the Supreme Court declined to interfere with the Illinois proceedings. In doing so, it reached a decision that would have been reached had there been no Fifth Amendment. However, since the due process clause of the Fourteenth Amendment parallels that of the Fifth, the Court's decision in the case is properly included in a list of cases in which the same right is applicable against both federal and state governments.

Although we have not included the "reexamination of fact" clause of the Seventh Amendment in our list, one could arguably do so. Indeed, it is possible to argue that the *Chicago Railroad Case* "incorporated" that provision of the Seventh Amendment into the due process clause of the Fourteenth, since this was the first time the Supreme Court explicitly declared that the prohibition against reexamination of facts applied to verdicts in state courts. In that event, the same case could represent an example of establishing rights by incorporation and establishing rights by simply declaring them fundamental aspects of due process.

A better example of incorporation, however, is *Wolf v. Colorado,* where the Court decided that the Fourth Amendment protection against unreasonable serches and seizures applied to searches by state as well as federal officers.[54] Clearly, this case arose because of the Fourth Amendment. In earlier cases, the Supreme Court rejected the argument that the Fourteenth Amendment incorporated the Fourth, but in 1949, it finally accepted that argument.

In the same area of law, we find an example of a related phenomenon. In addition to incorporating a right granted specifically in one of the first eight amendments, the Court may decide to make applicable to the states some corollary of an amendment that was initially developed to protect against federal action only. While the Court decided in 1914 that it would exclude or suppress in federal courts all evidence seized by federal agents in violation of the Fourth Amendment,[55] such an "exclusionary rule" was not applied to state courts until 1961.[56] Thus, we see that incorporation may involve not only the rights specifically protected in the first eight amendments but also rights that might be implied by or considered as necessary corollaries of the stated rights.

It may be noted that the rate at which various clauses from the Bill of Rights have been incorporated into the Fourth Amendment or simply defined as fundamental in interpreting that amendment has not been a constant. Historically, the Court has been free to expand or not expand the meaning of the Fourteenth Amendment and to choose the timing of such expansion. That being so, one should not be surprised to find that some Courts have done a lot more "incorporating" than others.

In any discussion of incorporation in the area of civil liberties, special attention must be given to the Court headed by the fourteenth Chief Justice of the

United States—Earl Warren. Warren had been governor of California for three terms and was popular with both Republicans and Democrats in that state. He was appointed to the Court by President Eisenhower, who viewed him as a liberal-conservative. Some newspapers at the time predicted that he would support racial segregation, but others disagreed and labeled him liberal and humanitarian on basic issues. In any event, Warren was destined to lead a due process/equal protection revolution that dramatically changed the face of American constitutional law as it applied to minorities, criminal suspects, and others in our society who are generally considered "underdogs."

In 1954, the Warren Court ruled that segregation of public school children solely on the basis of race was no longer constitutional—a decision based on principles later extended to parks, transportation, golf courses, swimming pools, and other facilities operated by state and local governments. This decision, while highly significant, did not involve incorporation, but it signaled a perspective on the rights of underdogs that was to result in many "new" constitutional rights for criminal suspects. Indeed constitutional protections for such litigants against state action were expanded more in the 16 years under Warren than in the previous 165 years of the Court's existence. This expansion included, among other things, rulings that criminal evidence seized in violation of the search and seizure provisions of the Fourth Amendment is not admissible in state courts, that states cannot put a person twice in jeopardy for the same offense, that one cannot be compelled to give testimony that might be used in a criminal prosecution, that states have to furnish counsel for indigent criminal defendants, that state juries must be impartial, that all criminal defendants must be given a speedy and public trial, that states must give criminal defendants the right to confront witnesses called by the prosecution, and that states may not impose cruel and unusual punishments. While all these rights may seem familiar to us today, none were constitutional rights against the states prior to the Warren era, the 1953 to 1968 terms.

The overall effect of all this activity was to circumscribe considerably the ability of the states to deal with persons subject to state jurisdiction without interference from federal courts. While the Warren Court may not have been the first Supreme Court to increase restrictions on state power, Warren, Douglas, Black, and other justices pursued the idea with greater energy and consequences than any Court sitting earlier. Indeed, the ability of the states to win any civil liberty case in the Warren Court was strikingly diminished when compared with earlier Courts. Recent research on civil liberty cases involving blacks, aliens, criminal defendants, subversives, and labor unions (i.e., underdogs) underscores this point dramatically.

In the period 1903 to 1968, the Supreme Court was headed by seven different Chief Justices: Fuller, White, Taft, Hughes, Stone, Vinson, and Warren. In the Fuller, White, and Taft Courts, the mean percentage of civil liberty cases involving underdogs won by states was approximately 93.6 percent. In the Hughes, Stone, and Vinson Courts, the comparable percentage was 50.2. But in the Warren Court, states won only 24.2 percent of such cases. Thus, while the percentage of civil liberty cases won by the states has steadily declined during this century, support for state authority reached a new low in the Warren era—a figure less than half that associated with the immediately preceding Court, that chaired by Chief Justice Vinson.

Such a disparity correlates with the passage of time, since the Vinson Court sat in the 1946 to 1952 terms and the Warren Court in the following sixteen terms. Consequently, social conditions and cases may have been different for the two Courts. But that distinction is not a sufficient explanation. The makeup of the Warren Court must also be considered. In addition to Warren, who supported the state as litigant only 14.6 percent of the time, that Court contained (at one time or another) Justices Black (24 percent support), Fortas (15.9 percent), Brennan (15.8 percent), Goldberg (14 percent), Marshall (15.1 percent), and Douglas (11.3 percent). Given what we know about these justices, it is unlikely that differences in the cases and the larger environmental context in which they arose account for all the disparity between support for state litigants in the Vinson and Warren periods. A more plausible hypothesis is that judicial sympathies for the underdog were greater in the Warren than in the Vinson Court.

Given our earlier definitions and discussion of activism and restraint in Part I of this volume, it should be evident that a vote to incorporate is activist, while a vote against incorporation is one of restraint. By identifying those Courts that have frequently adopted and applied clauses from the first eight amendments against the states, we can differentiate activist from restraintist Courts. The dimensions of relevance, given our discussion in Part I, are those of interpretive stability and interpretive fidelity. For the Court has frequently overruled or modified earlier precedents or doctrine in incorporating provisions from the first eight amendments into the Fourteenth. And one can certainly argue that the framers of the Constitution had no idea that these developments would occur—thus identifying the "strained" interpretation of words associated with that latter dimension.

An examination of Table 1 shows that of nineteen instances in which a provision in the Bill of Rights was found in the Fourteenth Amendment for the first time, six were found by the Warren Court (1953–1968 terms), five each by the Hughes (1930–1940 terms) and Vinson Courts (1946–1952); one each by the Fuller (1888–1909 terms) and Taft (1921–1929 terms) Courts, and two by the Burger Court (1969 to date). None occurred in the White Court, which sat between the Fuller and Taft Courts (1910–1921 terms).

Thus, the expansion of the protections afforded by the Fourteenth Amendment is a twentieth-century phenomenon which occurred primarily in the period covering Courts headed by three Chief Justices, sitting over a period of thirty-four terms. These three Courts (Hughes, Vinson, Warren) were about equal in the instances in which they expanded the Fourteenth Amendment via discovery that it included provisions parallel to those found in other amendments. Yet if we consider the disparity in the number of years each sat, it is evident that the most activist Court on this dimension was headed by Chief

Justice Vinson, followed by that chaired by Hughes. The Warren Court, which is frequently characterized as one of the most activist Courts ever to sit, comes in third-most-activist insofar as this particular kind of activism is concerned. The Vinson and Warren Courts, which collectively covered the 1946 to 1968 terms, also differed from the Hughes Court, which sat in the 1930 to 1940 terms. In the Hughes Court, four of the five expansions of the Fourteenth Amendment involved rights found in the First Amendment.

In the Vinson and Warren Courts, on the other hand, ten of eleven instances expanded the rights of those being processed in the criminal justice system— i.e., rights parallel to those found in Amendments IV, V, VI, and VIII. We see then that Courts may differ on a given dimension of activism and that those differences may involve not only the degree of activism but also the subject matter to which the activist behavior is directed.

It has probably occurred to the reader that our list of Bill of Rights provisions now available against state action through the Fourteenth Amendment is not exhaustive. Some protections against federal action, still not available against state action insofar as the U.S. Constitution is concerned, include the right to bear arms (Second Amendment), the prohibition against the quartering of troops in homes (Third Amendment), grand jury indictment (Fifth Amendment), jury trial in civil cases (Seventh Amendment), and excessive bail and fines (Eighth Amendment).

Due Process of Law

Although the Fourteenth Amendment guarantees that no state shall deprive any person of life, liberty, or property without due process of law, the guarantee is not self-defining. We must depend on the Supreme Court to tell us what process is due. What it tells us and when will vary depending on the justices on the Court and especially on their attitudes toward incorporation. Nor can internal Court bargaining be ruled out. In telling us what process is due, the Court has utilized two rubrics: procedural due process and substantive due process.

Procedural Due Process   When our forebears founded the United States, they did so against the background of the legal procedures to which they had been accustomed in England. These English processes of law were accepted, with some exceptions, when new governmental and legal structures were established in the United States.

To what processes do we refer? Certainly courtroom procedures but also processes which do not occur in court. Examples would be the collecting of taxes, the deprivation of citizenship, and the drafting of young men to serve in the military forces. In all such cases, the procedures that must be followed are those that are accepted by long usage that are not forbidden by Constitution, statutes, or court rulings. At present, for civil purposes, due process generally requires that basic standards of fairness be observed, i.e., notice, a hearing, an impartial tribunal, the right to call and examine witnesses, the right to a decision based upon the hearing record, and the right to counsel.

In the awarding or taking of benefits, parties must be notified so that they may prepare a proper defense.[57] That defense must be heard. And the body or officer making the decision must hear the parties without bias or malice, i.e., the decision must be impartial. The right to call and cross-examine witnesses is the right to make a case as strongly as possible and to rebut false testimony which might weaken a case if left unattended. By requiring that the decision-maker base his or her decision on the record, we employ a check on bias. The record is there to see, so that it may be decided whether the decision justifiably flowed therefrom. Without this requirement, the discretion of the decision-maker would be considerably enlarged and the threat of partiality potentially more serious. Finally, since civil as well as criminal processes can be exceedingly complex, one has the right to expect assistance in the form of legal counsel. Thus, it all boils down to an attempt to arrive at the truth, to establish objective fact, in settling conflict in a fair and just manner. The procedures we require are those we have found through long experience to maximize the probability of accomplishing that end.

On the criminal side, the requirements of procedural due process are more open-ended and somewhat more extensive. But they relate to the processes sketched above. One must be notified of the crimes charged. Prior to that, however, one must be put on warning by a criminal statute that is neither vague nor unclear as to the nature of the crime. Prosecution must be initiated in particular ways. Examinations and pleadings must accord with well-developed rules and principles. A fair trial must be provided. Prosecutors and defense attorneys must conduct themselves in an appropriate fashion. The rules of evidence and standards of proof to be employed must accord with common usage. Sentencing procedures must be safeguarded to avoid abuse of discretion. And throughout all proceedings, the various rights available in the Constitution must be given to all criminal defendants.

We do not suggest that this general statement is a full definition of criminal due process. It certainly is not a detailed definition but is intended only to alert the reader to the general framework of procedural due process in criminal matters. A number of cases included in Part II of this volume bring into sharper focus just what procedural due process requires in specific criminal situations.

Substantive Due Process: 1890–1936 According to the Fourteenth Amendment, a citizen of the United States has certain privileges and immunities that may not be abridged at the hand of the states. It is possible to interpret the privileges and immunities clause to protect all civil rights. In 1873, however, the Supreme Court differentiated national and state citizenship in the Slaughterhouse Cases. It went on to rule that the privileges and immunities of state citizenship differ from those associated with national citizenship. Included in the former are the rights to "acquire and possess property of every kind, and to pursue and attain happiness and safety, subject, nevertheless, to such restraints as the state government may prescribe for the general good of the whole."

If such rights were defined as rights of national citizenship, the effect would be to delegate to the federal government the responsibility for restraining state encroachment on civil rights in general. Such a conclusion was pressed on the Court in the Slaughterhouse Cases. However, the Court rejected it. Instead, the rights of national citizenship were defined more narrowly and were said to include the right to travel, to assert claims upon the government, and the right to federal protection when in foreign jurisdiction or on the high seas. The theoretical reason for the distinction lies in the conception of the federal system held by the justices in the *Slaughterhouse* majority. They viewed the government of the United States as a federal system of delegated and reserved powers, with the state governments and the national government operating each in their own spheres.

The majority justices thought that were the federal government to become the national police officer for civil rights and the protector of those rights against the states, the balance of powers constructed in the Constitution would be destroyed. The state possessed broad powers to legislate for the protection of public welfare, health, and morals—the so-called police powers—and the privileges and immunities clause was seen as a very limited restriction on those powers. The importance of this choice is hard to exaggerate. For had the majority ruled to the contrary, the massive expansion of civil rights and liberties that occurred many decades later might have occurred much sooner. Justice Miller's conceptualization in *Slaughterhouse* of two autonomous spheres of action—state and federal—was maintained in subsequent cases affirming the right of states to regulate private property in the public interest. In the later cases, however, the attempt to use the Fourteenth Amendment to protect private rights centered on the due process clause. The argument was that in addition to state and federal spheres, there was an area of action in which the citizen was autonomous—an area referred to later by Franklin D. Roosevelt as a "no man's land where no Government—State or Federal—can function."[58] This no man's land was defined by the proposition that no state may deprive a person of life, liberty, or property without due process of law.

Traditionally, this had been viewed as a guarantee that when a state acted against a person, it would do so with procedural regularity. Such an interpretation had been made in the Slaughterhouse Cases. The same interpretation was made in *Munn v. Illinois* four years later when the Court declined to interfere with Illinois legislation regulating rates for the transportation and storage of grain.[59] A year later, in *Davidson v. New Orleans,*[60] the Court upheld an assessment by the city for swampland drainage—on the same interpretation. A short six years later, however, the argument for a sphere of citizen autonomy made some headway. Writing for the Court in *Hurtado v. California,*[61] Justice Matthews asserted that

> . . . the limitations imposed by our constitutional law upon the actions of the governments, both state and national, are essential to the preservation of public and

private rights, not withstanding the representative character of our political institutions. The enforcement of these limitations by judicial process is the device of self governing communities to protect the rights of individuals and minorities, as well as against the power of numbers, as against the violence of public agents transcending the limits of lawful authority, even when acting in the name and wielding the force of the government.[62]

In *Hurtado,* the Court ruled that due process did not require California to use grand jury indictments in capital cases. Two years later, the Court approved a Mississippi statute setting up a railroad commission to regulate rates. The Court's opinion by Justice Waite, however, concluded that such statutes did not "necessarily" deprive the complainant of due process of law, the clear implication being that state regulations of this type were subject to restriction by the due process clause.[63] The following year, in *Mugler v. Kansas,* the Court upheld, against a due process challenge, a state law forbidding the manufacture and sale of intoxicating whiskey.[64] Writing for the majority, Justice Harlan, acknowledging that state police power was broad in scope, noted that it was not unlimited. It is the duty of the courts, he said, to look "at the substance" of things when a state, extensively exercising its police power, is alleged to have violated rights secured under the law of the land.[65]

Finally, in 1890, the Court not only reiterated the substantive due process argument but used it to nullify a Minnesota statute regulating rail rates via a Rail and Warehouse Commission.[66] This was followed in 1898 by a decision nullifying a Nebraska statute directly setting rail rates so low as to represent a deprivation of property without due process of law.[67] At this point, the concept of substantive due process was fully accepted in the Court. States were put on notice that there was a "no man's land" for citizen action as well as one for state and one for federal action. Protection of the citizen could be provided by the federal government without encroaching on the legitimate sphere of the state. For if the state went beyond its authority, it acted illegitimately. Thus, federalism could be maintained while protecting the citizen at the same time. Clearly the Court meant to warn the states that it possessed, and would exercise when appropriate, judicial oversight of all state legislation claimed to be unjust or contrary to the law of the land.

It is commonly said that between 1890 and 1937, the Court used substantive due process to strike both state and federal laws which it found "unwise, improvident, or out of harmony with a particular school of thought."[68] And it is true that during this period, the Court struck down laws interfering with the liberty to contract.[69] Yet during the same period, the Court upheld any number of state laws against substantive due process challenges to health, safety, and morals regulations. For example, the Court approved a state requirement of vaccination against smallpox in *Jacobson v. Massachusetts*[70] and a Tennessee statute prohibiting the sale of cigarettes in *Austin v. Tennessee.*[71]

Declining to either endorse or disagree with the Supreme Court of Tennessee that cigarette smoking was "inherently bad and bad only," the Court said, "At the same time we should be shutting our eyes to what is constantly passing before them were we to affect an ignorance of the fact that a belief in their deleterious effects, particularly upon young people, has become very general, and that communications are constantly finding their way into the public press denouncing their use as fraught with great danger to the youth of both sexes. Without undertaking to affirm or deny their evil effects, we think it within the province of the legislature to say how far they may be sold, or to prohibit their sale entirely,"[72] so long as the statute in question can be viewed as a public health measure. In other words, under the conditions prevailing in Tennessee in 1900, the regulation was reasonable.

Also upheld in the period 1890–1936 were a number of state statutes limiting hours of work[73] and a state sterilization statute. The sterilization case was *Buck v. Bell,*[74] decided in 1927. It involved a Virginia statute which allowed the state to sterilize idiots, imbeciles, the insane, and the feebleminded who were inmates of state institutions. It even permitted the sterilization of those with epilepsy. The state proposed to sterilize Carrie Buck, a 17-year-old feebleminded female and an inmate in a Virginia institution. In ruling on an objection to the proposed sterilization, Justice Holmes, for the Court, found no problem. In a famous and oft-quoted opinion, he wrote: "in order to prevent our being swamped with incompetence ... it is better for all the world, if instead of waiting to execute degenerate offspring for crime, or to let them starve for their imbecility, society can prevent those who are manifestly unfit from continuing their kind. The principle that sustains compulsory vaccination is broad enough to cover cutting the Fallopian tubes."[75] Then, taking note that Carrie's mother was feebleminded and that Carrie had given birth to a mental defective, Holmes added, "Three generations of imbeciles are enough."[76]

Thus, we see that the Court's interest in the period 1890–1936 was not solely in the system of government and the balance of power between state and federal governments referred to by Justice Miller in the Slaughterhouse Cases, nor solely in the theory of citizen's autonomy used successfully by attorneys in such cases as the Chicago Railroad Case and *Smyth v. Ames.* For having established substantive due process as a check on the exercise of state power, the Court proceeded to use it to protect vested economic interests, not systematically, but sporadically, while interfering little with the use of state police power to regulate health, safety, and morals. It cannot be denied that the cases in which the Court used substantive due process to strike state law were cases with highly significant consequences. But since the rulings in those cases were economic in nature, and since the Court has almost abandoned substantive due process as a viable means of interfering with state economic regulation since 1936, the ultimate significance of the concept lies elsewhere.

Substantive Due Process or Its Equivalent: 1937 to the Present In using the concept of substantive due process, the rationale relied on by the Court was the protection of citizen's autonomy, human rights, the rights of humanity, the rights available under the fundamental law or the law of the land—i.e., the

Court approved or disapproved state legislation depending on whether or not it was in accord with abstract principles of justice. Technically, this was determined by deciding whether the legislation was rationally related to a legitimate governmental purpose. At the same time, what is a legitimate purpose depended on the Court's view of property and person.

The view of property which was strongly represented on the Court in the period 1890–1936 has been seen only rarely since 1936. The Court's view of person is reflected in the cases involving health, morals, and welfare. In the period 1890–1936, the states were allowed broad scope for legislation designed to protect or promote the welfare of their citizens. Such an end was considered legitimate, and some restriction on property rights was permitted so long as the safety, health, and welfare of citizens in general were meaningfully enhanced.[77] As the Court said in *Atlantic Coast Line v. Goldsboro,* the state has the power "to establish all regulations that are reasonably necessary to secure the health, safety, good order, comfort, or general welfare of the community; . . . this power can neither be abdicated nor bargained away, and is inalienable even by express grant; and . . . all contract and property rights are held subject to its fair exercise."[78] Consistent with these principles, the Court, in the period 1890–1936, almost always approved of the challenged legislation where public health, safety, and morals were concerned. We can suggest, therefore, that the Court was somewhat sensitive to both property and personal welfare in the 1890 to 1937 era.

A distinction, however, is that property rights were viewed at the individual or corporate level, while personal rights to health, safety, and welfare were treated at the community level. Each vested interest was important to protect, while only collective personal welfare was of much concern to the Court. What is most significant about the Court's cases dealing with public welfare is that the Court did permit such legislation to be challenged and did review it to see if the judge-made requirements of substantive due process were met.

If we concede the power of the Court to act as a censor of state legislation and to judge it by substantive due process considerations, we also must concede the power to (1) emphasize for individualized protection one or more nonproperty rights, and (2) to shift the balance between state and citizen autonomy in favor of the citizen. The Court has done both of these things in the period from 1937 to the present. In this era, we no longer encounter the emphasis on substantive due process as a concept. However, the mode of thinking that characterized the use of that concept has been very much in evidence.

What the Court has done is to substitute the rights of individuals for the vested property interests protected earlier. It has sat as a censor of state legislation (and some federal legislation) which, in the view of a majority of the justices, encroaches on the civil liberties protected by the Constitution. It has found state regulations, proscriptions, or practices a violation of due process much more frequently in the area of civil liberties than it ever did in protecting property rights. The comparison, indeed, is tens of cases at most to literally hundreds of cases in which civil liberties have been violated by state action.

The cases in Part II will illustrate with great detail just how this process has developed. Here, we point to a few cases by way of example.

Freedom of Mind and Conscience   In recent years, the Court has established that government has no power to control the thoughts, perceptions, or state of mind of its citizens.[79] At the individual level, we do not permit the extraction of coerced confessions to a crime. Such confessions must be voluntary to be admitted as evidence. Whether a confession is voluntary is not determined by a mere absence of physical torture in the interrogation process. One must be *mentally* free to confess or deny the crime one is suspected of committing.[80] This means that officials may not engage in any behavior that overbears the suspect's will to resist and causes the suspect to make a confession not truly self-determined.[81] Thus, the Court has held a confession induced by the drug scopolamine (truth serum) inadmissible.[82]

Other cases involving less dramatic inducements, but leading to a confession nevertheless, have led to the same result, i.e., the confessions have been ruled inadmissible. In one case, the suspect was stripped naked and told (falsely) that his cosuspect had confessed;[83] in another the suspect was held for six days, during which he was questioned by relays of officers for nine hours a day without being taken before a magistrate and without being advised of his rights;[84] in a third case, the suspect, an uneducated black, was arrested without a warrant in one county at night, taken to various counties over the next two days, placed in a jail more than 100 miles from his home, and continually threatened by officers with mob violence.[85] In all three cases, there was no physical coercion, but the Court found the confessions inadmissible on grounds of psychological coercion—i.e., the behavior of the officers overbore the free will or free mental state of the defendants. Indeed, the frequency with which the Court was confronted with this kind of problem led it in *Miranda v. Arizona*[86] to lay down, for in-custody interrogations, a strict set of procedural rules.

Freedom of the mind also involves what one is permitted to know and the conditions under which knowledge may be acquired. The Court has not ruled that one may not "know" about obscenity. It has merely held that obscene behavior is not a form of expression protected by the First Amendment. Nor is obscene expression in books, plays, newspapers, or similar sources protected by freedom of the press.[87] The mere dressing up of obscene expression in the clothes of speech and press will not fool the Court; the emperor will be seen as naked, and state action to hide or suppress his nudity will be permitted. However states do not possess unlimited authority to regulate what they define as obscene in any way they choose. A state may not equate obscenity with sex.[88] Nor may it recklessly attempt to control the attitudes and perceptions that one acquires about sex, even if that acquisition is dependent in part on obscene materials.

To say that obscene expression is not protected by the First Amendment is not to say, according to the Supreme Court, that all exposure to such material may be constitutionally banned. Georgia passed, and tried to enforce, just such a law in 1964. Under the Georgia statute, mere knowing possession of obscene materials was made a crime. In reversing a conviction under this statute for a man who was found to have had such materials in his home, the Court found a violation of due process—even though the obscene materials were not protected by the First and Fourteenth Amendments.[89] What is of interest here are the reasons the justices gave for finding a violation.

Concededly, a state may require vaccination against disease as a means of protecting the health of a citizen and consequently that of others. The Court earlier found no merit to the argument that such an intrusion violated substantive due process. In *Stanley v. Georgia,* the state argued that if a state can protect the bodies of its citizens, it can protect their minds, and that its possession statute was merely designed to do that. In other words, Georgia would not permit its citizens' minds to be exposed to such material. To do so would corrupt their morals. The Court, on the other hand, asserted that the Constitution protects the right to receive ideas and information regardless of their social worth, and that the state has no right to control the moral content of a person's private thoughts. In short, mind control by the state is not permissible under the First and Fourteenth Amendments. Since the First Amendment makes no reference to this restriction on governmental power, the Court's ruling was based on an expansive interpretation which reflects the justices' view that one ought to have the "right to be left alone," other things equal; i.e., a right which falls within the "no man's land" referred to by President Roosevelt.

The Supreme Court has confronted several related situations in which governmental autonomy has been denied. A state may not force a criminal defendant to disclose everything that is in his or her mind without running afoul of the Fifth Amendment prohibition against compulsory self-incrimination. Nor may it require an individual to list every organization to which he or she belongs,[90] or to provide postal authorities with identification before receiving mail from foreign countries.[91] Such attempts at probing the contents of mind or knowledge violate the Constitution, for they chill the freedom to learn of and inculcate ideas, theories, attitudes, and beliefs that may not be shared by popular majorities. There is time enough to restrict those with unpopular beliefs when they act or behave in such a way as to violate legitimate law or pose a threat or interference with a legitimate state function. Mere anticipation of such behavior by inference from mere belief is not constitutionally sufficient to support suppressive action by the state.

Freedom of the Body   In this area, the Supreme Court has, in recent years, made a number of decisions underscoring the freedom to use one's body without unreasonable interference from the state. These decisions relate to substantive due process modes of thinking, since they are not based directly on explicit constitutional language. When the Court determines what is a reasonable intrusion on bodily freedom, it is determining what is a legitimate state goal and what is a reasonable means of obtaining it, in a fashion reminiscent of its posture in the "vested interest" cases of the 1890 to 1936 era.

Freedom to use one's body without undue governmental interference comes up in many different contexts. Does one have a right to wear a beard or long hair? Lower courts have differed on the question. The Supreme Court has declined to review the issue of hair-length regulations in public schools, but it has indicated that wearing a beard is not a significant indicator of whether one can get a fair jury trial.[92] Decisions dealing with the use of the body in sexual relations have been plentiful in the Court over the past several decades. In *Griswold v. Connecticut,* the Court upheld the right to use contraceptives in the privacy of the marital bedroom. It nullified a state law carrying a fine of $50 or 60 days in prison, or both, for those who used any "drug, medicinal article or instrument for the purpose of preventing conception."[93] This statute not only interfered with the freedom to use contraceptives, it attempted to shape the decision whether to use genital organs for purposes other than conception. While the Constitution does not directly bar such state regulation, the Supreme Court thought it invaded an area in which people should be left alone—an area of citizen autonomy.

Better known are the so-called abortion decisions of *Roe v. Wade*[94] and subsequent cases.[95] Here the question has been the control of the woman over her body versus the interest of the state in its future citizens. In these cases, the Court has confirmed its pursuit of reproductive autonomy as a goal. It has permitted some state regulation but has carved out some areas in which the decisions by a woman or by a woman and her physician are inviolate.

Related is the case of *Skinner v. Oklahoma,*[96] decided in 1942. It will be recalled that in *Buck v. Bell,* compulsory sterilization at the hands of the state was permitted by the Court, since "three generations of imbeciles . . . [were] enough." Skinner was convicted in 1926 of stealing a chicken. In 1934 and 1935, he was convicted of robbery. These crimes made him a "habitual criminal" under a questionable Oklahoma statute, and an Oklahoma court ordered him sterilized, as permitted under Oklahoma law for habitual criminals! The Supreme Court saved Skinner's reproductive capacity on equal protection grounds. Writing for the majority, Justice Douglas offered the following comment.

> We are dealing here with legislation which involves one of the basic civil rights of man. Marriage and procreation are fundamental to the very existence and survival of the race. The power to sterilize, if exercised, may have subtle, far reaching and devastating effects. In evil or reckless hands it can cause races or types which are inimical to the dominant group to wither and disappear. There is no redemption for the individual whom the law touches. Any experiment which the state conducts is to his irreparable injury. He is forever deprived of a *basic liberty.*[97]

That the use of equal protection to resolve this case was a convenience is suggested by the comments of Chief Justice Stone and Justice Jackson in concurring opinions. More likely, the Court determined that this state intrusion was an unreasonable encroachment on what Douglas called a "basic liberty," the right to reproduce. Such thinking underlay the later abortion decisions and the Court's ruling on the right to use contraceptives.

Contrasted with the question of how one may use one's body is the question of how the state may use it or abuse it. How far may the state intrude into the body in its search for evidence of a crime? American courts have not fully answered this question as yet. Lower courts and the Supreme Court have recently dealt with so-called strip-searches in the setting of state and federal prisons. A strip-search requires the person to be searched to remove all clothing and submit to visual inspection of the body and body cavities. Such searches are considered important in prison environments to prevent the smuggling of weapons, drugs, or other contraband to prison inmates. There are at least two approaches to this problem. One is to strip-search certain family members, friends, and acquaintances who visit the inmates.

The recent policy in Iowa prisons was to give such visitors a choice—submit to a strip-search or be denied access to inmates. The search required, among other things, that the visitor bend over while naked and spread his or her buttocks for a visual inspection of the anal area. A federal court of appeals found such a procedure to violate the Fourth Amendment prohibition against unreasonable searches and seizures when the search was based solely on an uncorroborated and anonymous tip from an inmate.[98]

On the other hand, the U.S. Supreme Court has upheld strip-searches of prison inmates, including requirements that inmates "expose their body cavities for visual inspection."[99] A federal prison in New York City required that all inmates be strip-searched after every contact visit with non-family members, including defense attorneys. The procedure required the inmate to "remove all his or her clothing, spread the buttocks, and display the cavity for inspection by a correctional officer. Women inmates [were required to] . . . assume a suitable posture for vaginal inspection, while men . . . [had to] raise their genitals."[100] These searches were frequently conducted in the presence of other inmates, thereby engendering fear of subsequent sexual assault, one result of which was that some inmates chose to do without nonfamily visits.

A majority of five justices thought such searches were reasonable, given the legitimate security interests of the prison; four justices thought otherwise. But underlying this voting split was a basic disagreement about the role of courts in regulating prison administration. The dissenters were quite willing to tell prison administrators whether they can strip-search inmates. The majority, on the other hand, deplored such a role for courts, saying:

> There was a time not too long ago when the federal judiciary took a completely "hands-off" approach to the problem of prison administration. In recent years, however, these courts largely have discarded this "hands-off" attitude and have waded into this complex area. . . . [M]any of these same courts have, in the name of the Constitution, become increasingly enmeshed in the minutiae of prison operations. Judges, after all, are human. They . . . have a natural tendency to believe that their individual solutions to often intractable problems are better and more workable than those of the persons who are actually charged with and trained in the running of the particular institution under examination. But under the Constitution, the first question to be answered is not whose plan is best, but in what branch of the Government is lodged the authority to initially devise the plan. . . . [T]he inquiry of federal courts

[including the Supreme Court] into prison management must be limited to the issue of whether a particular system violates any prohibition of the Constitution or, in the case of a federal prison, a statute. The wide range of "judgement calls" that meet constitutional and statutory requirements are confided to officials outside of the judicial Branch of Government.[101]

This statement, with which four justices disagreed, reflects considerations of federalism and separation of powers, and may reflect as well the role perceptions which each justice holds for the Supreme Court. Justices do differ about such things, and thus the majority's explanation for its position could be taken at face value. At the same time, one should note that the justices in the majority include those normally considered conservative and basically favorable to government in conflicts with civil liberty claimants, i.e., Rehnquist, who wrote the Court's opinion, and Chief Justice Burger. The four dissenters included justices Brennan and Marshall, justices representing the more liberal wing of the Court. This is entirely consistent with the differences in support of the claims of criminal suspects which numerous studies have shown these justices to exhibit across civil liberty cases generally. Thus, judicial attitudes toward issues and litigants may have played a role here.

The Supreme Court has also permitted police to take scrapings from under a suspect's fingernails by force,[102] the taking of blood over a criminal suspect's objections,[103] and the taking of blood from an unconscious accident victim.[104] In the last two cases, the results of the blood tests were admissible in court. This is no violation of the self-incrimination prohibition, since the Court has ruled that the protection applies to testimonial evidence only.[105] But a bodily intrusion may violate due process if it shows a sufficient lack of respect for traditional standards of justice.[106] Where are those standards to be found?

Justice Frankfurter has told us that the standards "are not authoritatively formulated anywhere as though they were specifics. Due process of law is a summarized constitutional guarantee of respect for those personal immunities which . . . are so rooted in the traditions and conscience of our people as to be ranked as fundamental."[107] The standards of judgment are to be found in the same place that furnished the standards for substantive due process in the period 1890–1936, i.e., in the minds of the justices—in their judgment as to what should be permitted or denied to state authority when dealing with the liberty and property of citizens.

In *Rochin v. California,* the majority of justices agreed that the state went too far in a bodily invasion seeking criminal evidence. Rochin, a resident of Los Angeles, was suspected by police authorities of selling narcotics. On the basis of that possibility, three deputy sheriffs went to Rochin's home, broke down the door to his bedroom, and found him sitting on a bed. On a nightstand beside the bed were two capsules which, upon seeing the officers, Rochin seized and swallowed. The three officers then jumped on Rochin and attempted to extract the capsules. They were unsuccessful. Rochin was then taken in handcuffs to a hospital. A tube was inserted in his stomach against his will. The "stomach pumping" that followed caused Rochin to vomit. In the vomited material, two capsules of morphine were found. Using the capsules as the main evidence of the crime, Rochin was convicted and sentenced to 60 days in prison.

Upon review, the Supreme Court found a violation of due process. Feeling duty bound to determine whether the treatment of Rochin offended due process, i.e., "those canons of decency and fairness which express the notions of justice of English speaking peoples even toward those charged with the most heinous offenses,"[108] the Court reversed the conviction on due process grounds. This, Frankfurter wrote, "is conduct that shocks the conscience. Illegally breaking into the privacy of the petitioner, the struggle to open his mouth and remove what was there, the forcible extraction of his stomach's contents—this course of proceeding by agents of government to obtain evidence is bound to offend even hardened sensibilities. They are methods too close to the rack and screw to permit of constitutional differentiation."[109]

While the cases mentioned do not paint the whole picture and are illustrative only, they are somewhat typical of the Court's use of due process in the period 1937–1984 to protect the area of citizen autonomy from governmental encroachment. The major conceptual device employed to that end has been substantive due process of law, in spite of the Court's avoidance of that phrase, and despite the fact that the populations or interests chosen for protection have been noneconomic in nature.

Equal Protection of the Law

The kind of thinking which has underlain the use of due process to protect civil rights and liberties in recent decades is also seen in equal protection cases. The equal protection clause of the Fourteenth Amendment has reached its present meaning by way of a tortuous journey. Between the enactment of the amendment in 1868 and the turn of the century, the Court ruled against the right of Mrs. Robinson to sit in the "ladies car" on an interstate train,[110] against the claim of Mrs. DeCuir that she could not constitutionally be put in a separate cabin for blacks on a riverboat trip from New Orleans to Vicksburg,[111] and against the claim of Homer Plessy that he could not be forced to sit in a separate car for blacks on a train going from New Orleans to Covington, Louisiana.[112] In Mrs. DeCuir's Case, the Court invalidated a Louisiana statute that protected the right claimed by Mrs. DeCuir on the ground that it was a regulation of interstate commerce. In Mrs. Robinson's Case, a federal act which purportedly protected the right claimed by Mrs. Robinson was held not to reach private discrimination.

The Separate But Equal Doctrine   Homer Plessy's Case is of particular interest, not only for its reach as a precedent, but also because it appears to have been a test case. If so, it would antedate by more than forty years the strategy used so successfully by civil rights organizations in recent decades. The inference that Plessy's Case was contrived is derived from the facts that Plessy was one-eighth black and seven-eighths Caucasian and that the "mixture of colored blood was not discernible in him."[113] Yet, while his status as a "colored person" was not discernible, he was ordered out of a white car and into a car reserved for blacks by a conductor who threatened him with ejection from the train and possible imprisonment should he, Plessy, refuse the command. Indeed, when Plessy declined to obey the conductor's instructions, he was forcibly ejected from the train and imprisoned in the parish jail of New Orleans.

One may surmise that Plessy was known to the conductor or other passengers as a person of color for this series of events to have occurred. If so known, Plessy must have known the probable consequences of his action. Thus, the possibility that there was no live case or controversy, and that Plessy contrived his case to test the Louisiana statute requiring separate seating for whites and blacks on railroad trains, cannot be ruled out. Yet be all that as it may, the Supreme Court did not adopt Plessy's equal protection argument. The Court agreed that Louisiana owed Plessy equal protection of the law but found the Louisiana statute consistent with the state's duty under the Fourteenth Amendment. For, said the majority, the question is merely whether the state law is reasonable—i.e., whether it comports with "the established usages, customs, and traditions of the people, and with a view to the promotion of their comfort, and the preservation of the public peace and good order."[114]

Thus, by a process reminiscent of substantive due process, the Court established the so-called separate but equal doctrine. This doctrine was assumed in later cases challenging the practice of defining Chinese students as blacks, thereby forcing such students to go to black public schools,[115] and a state law prohibiting a private college from teaching whites and blacks in the same facility.[116] No violation was found in either instance.

In 1938, we see the beginning of a process similar to that described in our discussion of the White Primary Cases. It will be recalled that in those cases, the Court reached a decision not by saying that a governing principle was wrong or by overruling such a standard but by accepting the principle and redefining or broadening its coverage. Thus, the proposition that state action was required to invoke the due process clause was accepted but redefined to catch every kind of action that involved a state "function."

Similarly, the Court, in 1938, accepted the separate but equal doctrine but began to ask: What does it require? It answered by making it more and more difficult to practice racial discrimination in public schools and colleges. Thus, the Court held that a state must furnish a law school for blacks if it provided one for its white citizens;[117] that Texas could not send blacks to a separate law school because the intangible benefits to be gained in the white law school could not be made equal in the black law school;[118] and that Oklahoma could not require black students in its law school to be physically separated from white students for instructional purposes.[119] After being forced to admit blacks to its law school, Oklahoma admitted them but set them apart in separate sections of the library, the cafeteria, and classrooms. This, the Court majority ruled, impaired the ability of the black students to study, exchange views, and learn their profession, thus violating their rights under the equal protection clause.

Finally, in 1954, the Warren Court, returning to the "ability to learn" argument, decided that the segregation of black students in public secondary schools, solely on the basis of race, violated equal protection.[120] In doing so, however, the justices abandoned the separate but equal doctrine and overruled *Plessy v. Ferguson,* saying: "Separate educational facilities are inherently unequal."[121] The alert reader will note the similarity between the adoption of the "state function" theory in *Terry v. Adams* and the "inherently unequal" theory here. Both cases illustrate that when the Court is ready to establish a new national policy via the interpretation of constitutional law, it may make proclamations which in effect end debate on matters that might have been controverted for years or decades.

Both before and since the decision in *Brown,* the Court has ruled out racial discrimination in many other areas of national life. Thus a state cannot deduct from a prisoner's pay an amount sufficient to reimburse the state for the "free" trial transcripts furnished to the prisoner unless those given suspended sentences or probation are required to pay for such transcripts.[122] A state may not systematically and solely on the basis of race eliminate or restrict participation in state jury-selection processes.[123] The judicial enforcement of racially restrictive real estate covenants violates the equal protection clause.[124] Racial segregation may not now be required in public beaches and bathhouses,[125] golf courses,[126] or other public facilities.[127] The equal protection clause does not permit a state to bar interracial marriage[128] or interracial cohabitation.[129] A state cannot constitutionally designate a candidate for office on the ballot by race[130] and in elections must treat black and white candidates alike.[131]

Other Invidious Discrimination   The Court has also utilized the equal protection clause in dealing, among other things, with invidious discrimination against aliens, women, illegitimate children, certain classes of voters, and criminal defendants. Invidious discrimination is generally defined as that which is particularly repugnant, frequently involving factors over which the individual has no control. Since the Fourteenth Amendment protects persons, aliens are protected by the equal protection clause. Thus Chinese residents cannot effectively be barred from operating laundries.[132] Nor may a state require employers to discriminate against aliens by requiring some quota of native-born Americans in their workforce,[133] or deny aliens the right to own land.[134] However, some distinctions are permissible. A state may, for example, prohibit aliens from hunting wild game[135] or operating a pool hall.[136]

In the Wild Game Case the legislature had imposed the prohibition on resident unnaturalized aliens in the belief that those so characterized were the primary source of the evil—killing wild game. Justice Holmes, for the Court, declined to hold the legislature's premise untenable, not because he knew it not to be so but because unfamiliarity with local facts suggested that the legislature of Pennsylvania was in a better position to make that judgment than was the Supreme Court of the United States. To overturn the legislation, Holmes suggested, the plaintiff (i.e., the complaining alien) would have to show that the legislature was "manifestly wrong," which was not done in this case. The equal protection clause, then, protects aliens against "plainly irrational" discrimination. But the irrationality must be plainly shown.

In the Pool Hall Case, irrationality was not plainly shown. Here the city of Cincinnati, Ohio, adopted an ordinance prohibiting the operation of pool and billiard parlors by aliens. In his opinion for the Court, Justice Stone, acknowledging that pool and billiard parlors had "harmful and vicious tendencies," suggested that such businesses could constitutionally be forbidden altogether. As for Cincinnati's presumption that aliens in Cincinnati were not as well qualified as citizens to engage in such businesses, Stone found no problem. Here again, it was not that the Court knew the Cincinnati authorities to be "correct" in that view. The Court simply had no basis for precluding "the possibility of a rational basis for legislative judgment." The Court simply had no knowledge of local conditions that would enable it to say that the city was "clearly wrong."

Thus, we see that *plausible* reasons for discrimination against defined classes were, in this era, sufficient to avoid the restrictions of the equal protection clause. Similar kinds of reasoning may be found in later cases involving discrimination. A major difference, however, is that later Supreme Courts have required considerably less evidence to find fatal fault with the premises, assumptions, or beliefs on which legislative bodies have based their discriminatory classifications.

Recently the Court has struck a state probate law giving males preference over females when estate administrators are chosen.[137] And it has required a state to provide free access to its courts for indigent welfare mothers seeking divorce.[138] Illegitimate children can no longer be discriminated against in the gross fashion of earlier days.[139] The right of citizens to equal weight in the electoral process (one person–one vote) has now been established.[140] As noted earlier, criminal defendants have benefited dramatically from equal protection rulings during the era of the Warren Court. For example, a convicted defendant cannot be discriminated against merely because he or she is indigent.[141] The state must provide essentially the same access to its courts and appellate processes for defendants able to pay and those unable to pay court costs and other associated expenses.[142]

The above examples should not lead one to think that the Court always strikes down state action challenged by citizens under the equal protection clause. We have already noted several instances when the challenge failed. Others are readily available. For example, a state may license a private club to sell alcohol even though the club bars blacks,[143] may permit lay judges in some jurisdictions but require law-trained judges in others,[144] or may differentiate day and night students for purposes of unemployment benefits.[145] Evidently, mere classification or differentiation of persons or classes does not necessarily violate the equal protection clause. It is not discrimination per se that is banned. The clause operates only to prohibit "invidious discrimination."

What is "invidious" and what outside the scope of the word is determined by applying the general rules the Court has developed in equal protection cases to the facts of particular situations. Those rules have been summarized in *Morey v. Doud*[146] and read as follows:

> **1** The equal protection clause of the Fourteenth Amendment does not take from the state the power to classify in the adoption of public laws, but admits of the exercise of a wide scope of discretion in that regard, and avoids what is done only when it is without any reasonable basis and therefore is purely arbitrary.
> **2** A classification having some reasonable basis does not offend ... [the equal protection] clause merely because it is not made with mathematical nicety or because in practice it results in some inequality.
> **3** When the classification in ... a law is called in question, if any state of facts reasonably can be conceived that would sustain it, the existence of that state of facts at the time the law was enacted must be assumed.
> **4** One who assails the classification in ... a law must carry the burden of showing that it does not rest upon any reasonable basis, but is essentially arbitrary.[147]

In short, a classification which is neither arbitrary nor unreasonable does not violate the equal protection clause. In applying these general rules to actual cases, the Court has developed and utilized several concepts which have either modified the Constitution or enhanced the discretion of the justices in interpreting that document. Of greatest importance are the concepts of strict scrutiny, compelling state interest, and reasonable fit of means to ends. These concepts come into play where fundamental rights are involved. Otherwise, traditional equal protection analysis is applied and the Court is restrained in finding violations.

Fundamental Rights No provision in the Constitution sets off fundamental rights from other rights protected against governmental action. The distinction is one which the Court has developed. In general, fundamental rights appear to be encroached upon by laws restricting "those political processes which can ordinarily be expected to bring about repeal of undesirable legislation."[148] The quoted words are from Chief Justice Stone's famous footnote in *United States v. Carolene Products Co.* The footnote is famous not because it decided the case in which it appeared. It did not. Yet the ideas expressed in it have had a tremendous impact on the development of constitutional law and doctrine in subsequent years.

In the footnote, Stone illustrated what he meant by fundamental rights: the right to vote, to disseminate information, to participate in political organizations, to peaceably assemble, and to be free from racial and religious discrimination. The first four rights mentioned obviously relate to ability to influence political processes. The last can be seen as an interference with the protection to be afforded minorities—a protection that goes to the very basis for the founding of the American colonies and the governmental systems that later evolved. In later years, the right to vote,[149] the right to interstate travel,[150] and the right to procreation,[151] among others, have been declared by Court majorities to be among the fundamental rights.

The Strict Scrutiny Test   Whenever the Court decides that a fundamental right is involved in a classification, that classification is "suspect." Indicators of suspect classifications include such things as discrimination based on race and national origin—i.e., factors over which individuals have no control, so-called accidental factors. Suspect classifications will not be accorded traditional equal protection analysis, in which the Court is reluctant to overrule state action. Instead the state action will be given "strict scrutiny." When the Court applies strict scrutiny to a classification, the state is likely to be found in violation of equal protection. Indeed, since 1944, for example, no explicit racial discrimination subjected to strict scrutiny has passed the tests employed under that rubric.

The tests applied under strict scrutiny pose two questions: (1) does the government have a compelling interest which necessitates the discrimination? and (2) are the classifications or distinctions reasonably necessary to accomplish a legitimate state end? These tests give the Court several ways in which the state can be found in error. Although a legitimate state goal may be identified, only the Court can determine how "compelling" it is and whether the relationship between means and ends in compelling cases is reasonable. As you read through the cases in Part II of this text, you will become more familiar with these and other tests, such as "rational basis" and "intermediate scrutiny," employed by the Court in deciding civil liberty questions. You will soon learn that the Court's approach in many cases is to first decide which test to apply, followed by a decision as to what the chosen test requires in the given case situation. It is arguable that the "test screening" decision is the more important of the two decisional stages. However, caution must be exercised, since one cannot always predict how the chosen test will be implemented.

In our brief overview of the Civil War amendments and the Bill of Rights, we have suggested (1) that constitutional rights are dynamic, (2) that such rights have been steadily expanded since 1790, (3) that expansion has occurred primarily via Supreme Court interpretation rather than through the amending process, and (4) that through time, the Court has developed a number of concepts and judge-made doctrines to underpin its use of discretion in restricting state and federal action in the area of civil liberties. It is in the reading of civil liberties cases that one gets the fullest sense of the power of the Court to shape the values, practices, relationships, and governmental structures that define the American political system.

NOTES

1 For a more expansive account of the treatment followed here, see Alfred H. Kelly, Winfred A. Harbison, and Herman Belz, *The American Constitution,* 6th ed., Norton, New York, 1983, pp. 107–119.
2 *Marbury v. Madison,* 5 U.S. (1 Cranch) 137 (1803).
3 *Barron v. Baltimore,* 32 U.S. (7 Peters) 243 (1833).
4 Article I, Section 10.
5 Ibid.

 6 Ibid.
 7 Ibid.
 8 Article I, Section 9.
 9 *The Civil Rights Cases,* 109 U.S. 3, 22 (1883).
10 *Hodges v. United States,* 203 U.S. 1 (1966).
11 *Jones v. Alfred H. Mayer Co.,* 392 U.S. 409 (1968).
12 *Robertson V. Baldwin,* 165 U.S. 275 (1897).
13 *Arver v. United States,* 245 U.S. 366 (1918).
14 *Butler v. Perry,* 240 U.S. 328 (1916).
15 *Williams v. Mississippi,* 170 U.S. 213 (1898).
16 *Guinn v. United States,* 238 U.S. 347 (1915).
17 Ibid.
18 *Lane v. Wilson,* 307 U.S. 268 (1939).
19 Alfred H. Kelly and Winfred Harbison, *The American Constitution,* 4th ed., Norton, New York, 1970, p. 948.
20 *James v. Bowman,* 190 U.S. 127 (1903).
21 *Nixon v. Herndon,* 273 U.S. 536 (1927).
22 *Nixon v. Condon,* 286 U.S. 73 (1932).
23 295 U.S. 45 (1935).
24 313 U.S. 299 (1941).
25 321 U.S. 649 (1944).
26 *Rice v. Elmore,* 165 F. 2d 387 (C.A. 4, 1947), *cert. denied,* 333 U.S. 875 (1948).
27 345 U.S. 461 (1953).
28 Justices Black, Douglas, and Burton.
29 Justice Frankfurter.
30 Chief Justice Vinson, Justices Clark, Reed, and Jackson.
31 Justice Minton.
32 383 U.S. 301 (1966).
33 *The Civil Rights Cases,* 109 U.S. 3 (1883).
34 *Screws v. United States,* 325 U.S. 91 (1945).
35 *United States v. Price,* 383 U.S. 787 (1966).
36 326 U.S. 501 (1946).
37 *Amalgamated Food Employees Local 590 v. Logan Valley Plaza,* 391 U.S. 308 (1968).
38 *Lloyd Corporation v. Tanner,* 407 U.S. 551 (1972).
39 *Hudgens v. N.L.R.B.,* 424 U.S. 507 (1976). In *Pruneyard Shopping Center v. Robins,* 447 U.S. 74 (1980), however, the Court held that California constitutional provisions permitting individuals to exercise free speech and petition rights on the property of a privately owned shopping center did not violate the property owner's property or free speech rights under the First, Fifth, and Fourteenth Amendments.
40 *Flagg Brothers Inc. v. Brooks,* 436 U.S. 149 (1978).
41 1 *Annals of Congress* 755 (Aug. 17, 1789).
42 59 U.S. (18 How.) 71 (1855).
43 *Gideon v. Wainwright,* 372 U.S. 335, 345 (1963); *Pointer v. Texas,* 380 U.S. 414 (1965).
44 *Adamson v. California,* 332 U.S. 46 (1947).
45 *The Slaughterhouse Cases,* 83 U.S. (16 Wall.) 36 (1873).
46 *Bradwell v. Illinois,* 83 U.S. (16 Wall.) 130 (1873).
47 *Minor v. Happersett,* 88 U.S. (21 Wall.) 162 (1875).

48 *Walker v. Sauvinet,* 92 U.S. 90 (1876).

49 *Spies v. Illinois,* 123 U.S. 131 (1887).

50 *In re Kemmler,* 136 U.S. 436 (1890).

51 *McElvaine v. Brush,* 142 U.S. 155 (1891).

52 *O'Neil v. Vermont,* 144 U.S. 323 (1892).

53 *The Justices v. Murray,* 76 U.S. (9 Wall.) 274 (1870).

54 338 U.S. 25 (1949).

55 *Weeks v. United States,* 232 U.S. 383 (1914).

56 *Mapp v. Ohio,* 367 U.S. 643 (1961).

57 *Armstrong v. Manzo,* 380 U.S. 545 (1965).

58 Franklin D. Roosevelt, *The Public Papers and Addresses of Franklin D. Roosevelt,* Random House, New York, 1938, p. 192.

59 94 U.S. 113 (1877).

60 96 U.S. 97 (1878).

61 110 U.S. 516 (1884).

62 Ibid., p. 536.

63 *Stone v. Farmer's Loan and Trust Co.,* 116 U.S. 307 (1886).

64 123 U.S. 623 (1887).

65 Ibid., p. 661.

66 *Chicago, Milwaukee and St. Paul Railway Co. v. Minnesota,* 134 U.S. 418 (1890).

67   *Smyth v. Ames,* 169 U.S. 466 (1898).

68 *Williamson v. Lee Optical Co. of Oklahoma,* 348 U.S. 483 (1955).

69 *Adair v. United States,* 208 U.S. 161 (1908); *Allgeyer v. Louisiana,* 165 U.S. 578 (1897); *Lockner v. New York,* 198 U.S. 545 (1905); *Adkins v. Children's Hospital,* 261 U.S. 525 (1923); *Morehead v. New York ex rel Tipaldo,* 298 U.S. 587 (1936).

70 197 U.S. 11 (1905).

71 179 U.S. 343 (1900).

72 Ibid., pp. 348–349.

73 See *Holden v. Hardy,* 169 U.S. 366 (1898); *Miller v. Wilson,* 236 U.S. 373 (1915); *Bosley v. McLaughlin,* 236 U.S. 385 (1915); *Muller v. Oregon,* 208 U.S. 412 (1908); *Bunting v. Oregon,* 243 U.S. 426 (1917).

74 274 U.S. 200 (1927).

75 Ibid., p. 207.

76 Ibid.

77 *Sproles v. Binford,* 286 U.S. 374 (1932).

78 232 U.S. 548, 558 (1914).

79 For a fuller discussion of the rights of privacy and personhood, see Lawrence H. Tribe, *American Constitutional Law,* Foundation Press, Mineola, N.Y., 1978, pp. 886–990.

80 *Lyons v. Oklahoma,* 322 U.S. 596 (1944).

81 *Rogers v. Richmond,* 365 U.S. 534 (1961).

82 *Townsend v. Sain,* 372 U.S. 293 (1963).

83 *Bram v. United States,* 163 U.S. 532 (1897).

84 *Watts v. Indiana,* 338 U.S. 49 (1949).

85 *Ward v. Texas,* 316 U.S. 547 (1942).

86 384 U.S. 436 (1966).

87 *Roth v. United States,* 354 U.S. 476 (1957); *Ginsberg v. United States,* 383 U.S. 463 (1968).

88 *Roth v. United States.*

89 *Stanley v. Georgia,* 394 U.S. 557 (1969).

90 *Shelton v. Tucker,* 364 U.S. 479 (1960).

91 *Lamont v. Postmaster General of the United States,* 381 U.S. 30 (1965).

92 *Hamm v. South Carolina,* 409 U.S. 524 (1973).

93 381 U.S. 479, 480 (1965).

94 410 U.S. 113 (1973).

95 See *Doe v. Bolton,* 410 U.S. 179 (1973); *Planned Parenthood v. Danforth,* 428 U.S. 52 (1976); *Bellotti v. Baird,* 428 U.S. 132 (1976); *Singleton v. Wulff,* 428 U.S. 106 (1976); *Bigelow v. Virginia,* 421 U.S. 809 (1975); *Connecticut v. Menillo,* 423 U.S. 9 (1975); *Maher v. Roe,* 432 U.S. 464 (1977); and *Beal v. Doe,* 432 U.S. 438 (1977).

96 316 U.S. 535 (1942).

97 Ibid., 541 (italics added).

98 *Hunter v. Auger,* 672 F. 2d 668 (1982).

99 *Bell v. Wolfish,* 441 U.S. 561 (1979).

100 Ibid., p. 572.

101 Ibid., p. 562.

102 *Cupp v. Murphy,* 412 U.S. 291 (1973).

103 *Schmerber v. California,* 384 U.S. 757 (1966).

104 *Briethaupt v. Abrams,* 352 U.S. 432 (1967).

105 *Holt v. United States,* 218 U.S. 245 (1910).

106 *Rochin v. California,* 342 U.S. 165 (1952).

107 Ibid., p. 169.

108 Ibid.

109 Ibid., p. 172.

110 *The Civil Rights Cases,* 109 U.S. 3 (1883).

111 *Hall v. DeCuir,* 95 U.S. 485 (1878).

112 *Plessy v. Ferguson,* 163 U.S. 537 (1896).

113 Ibid., p. 538.

114 Ibid., p. 550.

115 *Gong Lum v. Rice,* 275 U.S. 78 (1927).

116 *Berea College v. Kentucky,* 211 U.S. 45 (1908).

117 *Missouri ex rel Gaines v. Canada,* 305 U.S. 337 (1938).

118 *Sweatt v. Painter,* 339 U.S. 629 (1950).

119 *McLauren v. Oklahoma State Regents,* 339 U.S. 637 (1950).

120 *Brown v. Board of Education,* 347 U.S. 483 (1954).

121 Ibid., p. 495.

122 *Rinaldi v. Yeager,* 384 U.S. 305 (1966).

123 *Strauder v. West Virginia,* 100 U.S. 303 (1880); *Smith v. Texas,* 311 U.S. 128 (1940); *Arnold v. North Carolina,* 376 U.S. 773 (1964); *Peters v. Kiff,* 407 U.S. 493 (1972).

124 *Shelley v. Kraemer,* 334 U.S. 1 (1948); *Buchanan v. Warley,* 245 U.S. 60 (1917); *Reitman v. Mulkey,* 387 U.S. 369 (1967).

125 *Mayor and City Council of Baltimore v. Dawson,* 350 U.S. 877 (1955).

126 *Holmes v. Atlanta,* 350 U.S. 879 (1955).

127 *Turner v. Memphis,* 369 U.S. 350 (1962).

128 *Loving v. Virginia,* 388 U.S. 1 (1967).

129 *McLaughlin v. Florida,* 379 U.S. 184 (1964).

130 *Tancil v. Woolls,* 379 U.S. 19 (1964).

131 *Hadnott v. Amos,* 394 U.S. 358 (1971).

132 *Yick Wo v. Hopkins,* 118 U.S. 356 (1886).
133 *Truax v. Raich,* 239 U.S. 33 (1915).
134 *Oyama v. California,* 332 U.S. 633 (1948).
135 *Patsone v. Pennsylvania,* 232 U.S. 138 (1914).
136 *Ohio ex rel Clarke v. Deckebach,* 274 U.S. 392 (1927).
137 *Reed v. Reed,* 404 U.S. 71 (1971).
138 *Boddie v. Connecticut,* 401 U.S. 371 (1971).
139 *Weber v. Aetna Casualty and Surety Co.,* 406 U.S. 164 (1972).
140 *Reynolds v. Sims,* 377 U.S. 533 (1964).
141 *Williams v. Illinois,* 399 U.S. 235 (1970).
142 *Draper v. Washington,* 372 U.S. 487 (1963).
143 *Moose Lodge v. Irvis,* 407 U.S. 163 (1972).
144 *North v. Russell,* 427 U.S. 328 (1976).
145 *Idaho Department of Employment v. Smith,* 434 U.S. 100 (1977).
146 354 U.S. 457 (1957).
147 Ibid., pp. 463–464.
148 *United States v. Carolene Products Co.,* 304 U.S. 144, 152N (1938).
149 *Dunn v. Blumstein,* 405 U.S. 330 (1972).
150 *Shapiro v. Thompson,* 394 U.S. 618 (1969).
151 *Skinner v. Oklahoma ex rel Williamson,* 316 U.S. 535 (1942).

CHAPTER 7

THE FIRST AMENDMENT

Political Expression

Schenck v. United States (1919)

Gitlow v. New York (1925)

Dennis v. United States (1951)

Brandenburg v. Ohio (1969)

Cohen v. California (1971)

Greer v. Spock (1976)

PruneYard Shopping Center v. Robins (1980)

Buckley v. Valeo (1976)

Abood v. Detroit Board of Education (1977)

While freedom of speech as a concept may have intuitive appeal no matter what the content of the speech, its greatest importance lies in the effect it has on the functioning of a democratic political system. For freedom of speech maximizes the opportunities for education and exchange of information and ideas—all of which are necessary if democratic government is to be based on an informed and rational electorate. While the nuts and bolts of democracy are compatible with ignorance, the concept has little appeal absent the assumption of a reasonably informed and responsible citizenry.

As a concept, free speech involves two basic ideas. The first is that one should be free to express oneself without governmental interference before the act. The second idea is that once expression has occurred, there should be no punishment after the fact for anything said or expressed. While the framers of the First Amendment subscribed to the first notion, the second has depended on the Supreme Court for its advancement in more recent years.

In interpreting the Constitution, the Court has never adopted the notion that speech or expression can never be punished. It has held that the circumstances in which the speech or expression is made are considerations of relevance in deciding free speech claims. Whether the speech is political is one such circumstance. In general, the Court has subscribed to the notion that freedom of political speech is essential and that such speech or expression should not be punished absent exigent circumstances. In seeking a test for determining when punishment is warranted, the Court has suggested "clear and present danger," "bad tendency," and "balancing" tests.

The clear and present danger test was mentioned by Holmes in the *Schenck* case. Schenck lost his case by a unanimous vote. Thus the clear and present danger test did not protect him. Nor did it protect Frohwerk[1] and Debs[2] in two subsequent espionage cases—both of which were unanimous and in both of which Justice Holmes wrote for the Court.

Whether expression will be interpreted to create a clear and present danger depends in part on who is doing the interpreting and how direct the connection between the speech and the evils against which government can protect itself. In the case of Schenck, Frohwerk, and Debs, the issue was espionage during wartime, and the circumstances made it easier to see and fear unpopular expression. But in the same year, Holmes cast a dissenting vote in *Abrams v. United States*[3] on the ground that Abrams's speech did not constitute a clear and present danger. And in following years, both Holmes and Brandeis attempted unsuccessfully to convince majorities in the Court that the proper test to employ was clear and present danger. Those majorities, however, preferred the bad tendency test associated with *Gitlow v. New York*. Although the bad tendency test eventually lost out to the clear and present danger test for determining when expression may be punished, *Gitlow* retains its importance as the case in which a majority in the Court read the First Amendment's speech provisions into the Fourteenth Amendment's due process clause.

In the decade of the forties, the clear and present danger test was employed frequently to strike state action punishing expression.[4] But when the test was applied in the era of the so-called Communist menace, it was found wanting. Indeed, *Dennis v. United States* is usually interpreted as diluting, if not discarding, the concept of clear and present danger as a means of determining the legitimacy of punishing expression. The *Dennis* opinion, in effect, adopts a "free-wheeling"[5] version of the test which considerably narrowed the protection for speech. And for the next two decades, the Court preferred to "balance" the interests of society versus those of the individual—permitting invasion of First Amendment rights if the encroachments were partial, conditional, and indirect, and if the state's interest was substantial.[6] In *Brandenburg v. Ohio,* however, we learn that the clear and present danger test still has some life in it, much to the dismay of Justice Douglas.

Schenck v. United States

249 U.S. 47; 39 S. Ct. 247; 63 L. Ed. 470 (1919)
Vote: Unanimous

Schenck, the general secretary of the Socialist party, was charged in a federal district court in Pennsylvania with violating the Espionage Act of June 18, 1917. That act prohibited interference with the recruiting of personnel for the armed forces and the promotion of disloyalty or insubordination in the military services. Schenck was responsible for mailing approximately 15,000 leaflets to young men who had been called and accepted for military duty under the Conscription Act of May 18, 1917. Upon conviction, Schenck appealed to the Supreme Court.

MR. JUSTICE HOLMES delivered the opinion of the Court. . . .

The document in question upon its first printed side recited the first section of the Thirteenth Amendment, said that the idea embodied in it was violated by the Conscription Act and that a conscript is little better than a convict. In impassioned language it intimated that conscription was despotism in its worst form and a monstrous wrong against humanity in the interest of Wall Street's chosen few. It said "Do not submit to intimidation," but in form at least confined itself to peaceful measures such as a petition for the repeal of the act. The other and later printed side of the sheet was headed "Assert Your Rights." It stated reasons for alleging that any one violated the Constitution when he refused to recognize "your right to assert your opposition to the draft," and went on "If you do not assert and support your rights, you are helping to deny or disparage rights which it is the solemn duty of all citizens and residents of the United States to retain." It described the arguments on the other side as coming from cunning politicians and a mercenary capitalist press, and even silent consent to the conscription law as helping to support an infamous conspiracy. It denied the power to send our citizens away to foreign shores to shoot up the people of other lands, and added that words could not express the condemnation such cold-blooded ruthlessness deserves, &c., &c., winding up "You must do your share to maintain, support and uphold the rights of the people of this country." Of course the document would not have been sent unless it had been intended to have some effect, and we do not see what effect it could be expected to have upon persons subject to the draft except to influence them to obstruct the carrying of it out. The defendants do not deny that the jury might find against them on this point.

But it is said, suppose that that was the tendency of this circular, it is protected by the First Amendment to the Constitution. Two of the strongest expressions are said to be quoted respectively from well-known public men. It well may be that the prohibition of laws abridging the freedom of speech is not confined to previous restraints, although to prevent them may have been the main purpose, as intimated in *Patterson v. Colorado,* [1907].

. . . We admit that in many places and in ordinary times the defendants in saying all that was said in the circular would have been within their constitutional rights. But the character of every act depends upon the circumstances in which it is done. . . . The most stringent protection of free speech would not protect a man in falsely shouting fire in a theatre and causing a panic. It does not even protect a man from an injunction against uttering words that may have all the effect of force. *Gompers v. Bucks Stove & Range Co.,* [1911], . . . The question in every case is whether the words used are used in such circumstances and are of such a nature as to create a clear and present danger that they will bring about the substantive evils that Congress has a right to prevent. It is a question of proximity and degree. When a nation is at war many things that might be said in time of peace are such a hindrance to its effort that their utterance will not be endured so long as men fight and that no Court could regard them as protected by any constitutional right. It seems to be admitted that if an actual obstruction of the recruiting service were proved, liability for words that produced that effect might be enforced. The statute of 1917 in § 4 punishes conspiracies to obstruct as well as actual obstruction. If the act, (speaking, or circulating a paper,) its tendency and the intent with which it is done are the same, we perceive no ground for saying that success alone warrants making the act a crime.

Judgements affirmed.

Gitlow v. People of New York

268 U.S. 652; 45 S. Ct. 625; 69 L. Ed. 1138 (1925)
Vote: 7–2

Benjamin Gitlow was indicted, tried, and convicted in New York for violating that state's criminal anarchy statute. The statute made it a felony to advocate the overthrow of government by force or violence. After Gitlow's appeals were rejected by New York appellate courts, Gitlow appealed to the Supreme Court.

MR. JUSTICE SANFORD delivered the opinion of the Court. . . .

The following facts were established on the trial by undisputed evidence and admissions: The defendant is a member of the Left Wing Section of the Socialist Party, a dissenting branch or faction of that party formed in opposition to its dominant policy of "moderate Socialism." Membership in both is open to aliens as well as citizens. The Left Wing Section was organized nationally at a conference in New York City in June, 1919, attended by ninety delegates from twenty different States. The conference elected a National Council, of which the defendant was a member, and left to it the adoption of a "Manifesto." This was published in The Revolutionary Age, the official organ of the Left Wing. The defendant was on the board of managers of the paper and was its business manager. He arranged for the printing of the paper and took to the printer the manuscript of the first issue which contained the Left Wing Manifesto, and also a Communist Program and a Program of the Left Wing that had been adopted by the conference. Sixteen thousand copies were printed, which were delivered at the premises in New York City used as the office of the Revolutionary Age and the headquarters of the Left Wing, and occupied by the defendant and other officials. These copies were paid for by the defendant, as business manager of the paper. Employees at this office wrapped and mailed out copies of the paper under the defendant's direction; and copies were sold from this office. It was admitted that the defendant signed a card subscribing to the Manifesto and Program of the Left Wing, which all applicants were required to sign before being admitted to membership; that he went to different parts of the State to speak to branches of the Socialist Party about the principles of the Left Wing and advocated their adoption; and that he was responsible for the Manifesto as it appeared, that "he knew of the publication, in a general way and he knew of its publication afterwards, and is responsible for its circulation." . . . [The Manifesto] condemned the dominant "moderate Socialism" for its recognition of the necessity of the democratic parliamentary state; repudiated its policy of introducing Socialism by legislative measures; and advocated, in plain and unequivocal language, the necessity of accomplishing the "Communist Revolution" by a militant and "revolutionary Socialism," based on "the class struggle" and mobilizing the "power of the proletariat in action," through mass industrial revolts developing into mass political strikes and "revolutionary mass action," for the purpose of conquering and destroying the parliamentary state and establishing in its place, through a "revolutionary dictatorship of the proletariat," the system of Communist Socialism. The then recent strikes in Seattle and Winnipeg were cited as instances of a development already verging on revolutionary action and suggestive of proletarian dictatorship, in which the strike-workers were "trying to usurp the functions of municipal government"; and revolutionary Socialism, it was urged, must use these mass industrial revolts to broaden the strike, make it general and militant, and develop it into mass political strikes and revolutionary mass action for the annihilation of the parliamentary state. . . .

The precise question presented, and the only question which we can consider . . . is whether the statute, as construed and applied in this case by the state courts, deprived the defendant of his liberty of expression in violation of the due process clause of the Fourteenth Amendment. . . .

For present purposes we may and do assume that freedom of speech and of the press—which are protected by the First Amendment from abridgment by

Congress—are among the fundamental personal rights and "liberties" protected by the due process clause of the Fourteenth Amendment from impairment by the States. We do not regard the incidental statement in *Prudential Ins. Co. v. Check,* [1922], . . . that the Fourteenth Amendment imposes no restrictions on the States concerning freedom of speech, as determinative of this question.

It is a fundamental principle, long established, that the freedom of speech and of the press which is secured by the Constitution, does not confer an absolute right to speak or publish, without responsibility, whatever one may choose, or an unrestricted and unbridled license that gives immunity for every possible use of language and prevents the punishment of those who abuse this freedom.

. . . Reasonably limited, it was said by Story in the passage cited, this freedom is an inestimable privilege in a free government: without such limitation, it might become the scourge of the republic.

That a State in the exercise of its police power may punish those who abuse this freedom by utterances inimical to the public welfare, tending to corrupt public morals, incite to crime, or disturb the public peace, is not open to question. . . .

Thus it was held by this Court in the *Fox Case,* [1915], that a State may punish publications advocating and encouraging a breach of its criminal laws; and, in the *Gilbert Case,* [1920], that a State may punish utterances teaching or advocating that its citizens should not assist the United States in prosecuting or carrying on war with its public enemies.

And, for yet more imperative reasons, a State may punish utterances endangering the foundations of organized government and threatening its overthrow by unlawful means. These imperil its own existence as a constitutional State. Freedom of speech and press, said Story *(supra)* does not protect disturbances to the public peace or the attempt to subvert the government. It does not protect publications or teachings which tend to subvert or imperil the government or to impede or hinder it in the performance of its governmental duties. It does not protect publications prompting the overthrow of government by force; the punishment of those who publish articles which tend to destroy organized society being essential to the security of freedom and the stability of the State.

. . . And a State may penalize utterances which openly advocate the overthrow of the representative and constitutional form of government of the United States and the several States, by violence or other unlawful means.

. . . In short this freedom does not deprive a State of the primary and essential right of self preservation; which, so long as human governments endure, they cannot be denied. . . .

By enacting the present statute the State has determined, through its legislative body, that utterances advocating the overthrow of organized government by force, violence and unlawful means, are so inimical to the general welfare and involve such danger of substantive evil that they may be penalized in the exercise of its police power. That determination must be given great weight. Every presumption is to be indulged in favor of the validity of the statute. *Mugler v. Kansas,* [1887]. And the case is to be considered "in the light of the principle that the State is primarily the judge of regulations required in the interest of public safety and welfare;" and that its police "statutes may only be declared unconstitutional where they are arbitrary or unreasonable attempts to exercise authority vested in the State in the public interest."

. . . That utterances inciting to the overthrow of organized government by unlawful means, present a sufficient danger of substantive evil to bring their punishment within the range of legislative discretion, is clear. Such utterances, by their very nature, involve danger to the public peace and to the security of the State. They threaten breaches of the peace and ultimate revolution. And the immediate danger is none the less real and substantial, because the effect of a given utterance cannot be accurately foreseen. The State cannot reasonably be required to measure the danger from every such utterance in the nice balance of a jeweler's scale. A single revolutionary spark may kindle a fire that, smouldering for a time, may burst into a sweeping and destructive conflagration. It cannot be said that the State is acting arbitrarily or unreasonably when in the exercise of its judgment as to the measures necessary to protect the public peace and safety, it seeks to extinguish the spark without waiting until it has enkindled the flame or blazed into the conflagration. It cannot reasonably be required to defer the adoption of measures for its own peace and safety until the revolutionary utterances lead to actual disturbances of the public peace or imminent and immediate danger of its own destruction; but it may, in the exercise of its judgment, suppress the threatened danger in its incipiency.

. . . Manifestly, the legislature has authority to forbid the advocacy of a doctrine designed and intended to overthrow the government without waiting until there is a present and imminent danger of the success of the plan advocated. If the State were compelled to wait until the apprehended danger became certain, then its right to protect itself would come into being simultaneously with the overthrow of the government, when there would be neither prosecuting officers nor courts for the enforcement of the law. . . .

We cannot hold that the present statute is an arbitrary or unreasonable exercise of the police power of the State unwarrantably infringing the freedom of speech or press; and we must and do sustain its constitutionality . . . the judgement of the Court of Appeals is affirmed.

Mr. Justice Holmes dissenting.

Mr. Justice Brandeis and I are of opinion that this judgment should be reversed. The general principle of free speech, it seems to me, must be taken to be included in the Fourteenth Amendment, in view of the scope that has been given to the word 'liberty' as there used, although perhaps it may be accepted with a somewhat larger latitude of interpretation than is allowed to Congress by the sweeping language that governs or ought to govern the laws of the United States. If I am right, then I think that the criterion sanctioned by the full Court in *Schenck v. United States,* [1919], . . . applies. "The question in every case is whether the words used are used in such circumstances and are of such a nature as to create a clear and present danger that they will bring about the substantive evils that [the State] has a right to prevent." It is true that in my opinion this criterion was departed from in *Abrams v. United States,* [1908], . . . but the convictions that I expressed in that case are too deep for it to be possible for me as yet to believe that it and *Schaefer v. United States,* [1920], . . . have settled the law. If what I think the correct test is applied, it is manifest that there was no present danger of an attempt to overthrow the government by force on the part of the admittedly small minority who shared the defendant's views. It is said that this manifesto was more than a theory, that it was an incitement. Every idea is an incitement. It offers itself for belief and if believed it is acted on unless some other belief outweighs it or some failure of energy stifles the movement at its birth. The only difference between the expression of an opinion and an incitement in the narrower sense is the speaker's enthusiasm for the result. Eloquence may set fire to reason. But whatever may be thought of the redundant discourse before us it had no chance of starting a present conflagration. If in the long run the beliefs expressed in proletarian dictatorship are destined to be accepted by the dominant forces of the community, the only meaning of free speech is that they should be given their chance and have their way.

If the publication of this document had been laid as an attempt to induce an uprising against government at once and not at some indefinite time in the future it would have presented a different question. The object would have been one with which the law might deal, subject to the doubt whether there was any danger that the publication could produce any result, or in other words, whether it was not futile and too remote from possible consequences. But the indictment alleges the publication and nothing more.

Dennis v. United States

341 U.S. 494; 71 S. Ct. 857; 95 L. Ed. 1137 (1951)
Vote: 6–2

On October 14, 1949, Dennis was convicted of violating a federal criminal statute, the Smith Act. That act made it unlawful to organize any group of persons who teach or advocate the overthrow of the United States government by force or violence. It also forbade advocating and teaching the duty and necessity of overthrowing the government by force. Dennis was convicted of conspiring to violate both these prohibitions as a leader of the American Communist party. After conviction was affirmed by the court of appeals, the Supreme Court granted certiorari.

MR. CHIEF JUSTICE VINSON announced the judgment of the Court and an opinion in which MR. JUSTICE REED, MR. JUSTICE BURTON and MR. JUSTICE MINTON join. . . .

It will be helpful in clarifying the issues to treat next the contention that the trial judge improperly interpreted the statute by charging that the statute required an unlawful intent before the jury could convict. . . . We do not agree. . . . We hold that the statute requires as an essential element of the crime proof of the intent of those who are charged with its violation to overthrow the Government by force and violence. . . .

The obvious purpose of the statute is to protect existing Government, not from change by peaceable, lawful and constitutional means, but from change by violence, revolution and terrorism. That it is within the *power* of the Congress to protect the Government of the United States from armed rebellion is a proposition which requires little discussion. Whatever theoretical merit there may be to the argument that there is a "right" to rebellion against dictatorial governments is without force where the existing structure of the government provides for peaceful and orderly change. We reject any principle of governmental helplessness in the face of preparation for revolution, which principle, carried to its logical conclusion, must lead to anarchy. No one could conceive that it is not within the power of Congress to prohibit acts intended to overthrow the Government by force and violence. The question with which we are concerned here is not whether Congress has such *power,* but whether the *means* which it has employed conflict with the First and Fifth Amendments to the Constitution.

One of the bases for the contention that the means which Congress has employed are invalid takes the form of an attack on the face of the statute on the grounds that by its terms it prohibits academic discussion of the merits of Marxism-Leninism, that it stifles ideas and is contrary to all concepts of a free speech and a free press. Although we do not agree that the language itself has that significance, we must bear in mind that it is the duty of the federal courts to interpret federal legislation in a manner not inconsistent with the demands of the Constitution.

The very language of the Smith Act negates the interpretation which petitioners would have us impose on that Act. It is directed at advocacy, not discussion. Thus, the trial judge properly charged the jury that they could not convict if they found that petitioners did "no more than pursue peaceful studies and discussions or teaching and advocacy in the realm of ideas." He further charged that it was not unlawful "to conduct in an American college or university a course explaining the philosophical theories set forth in the books which have been placed in evidence." Such a charge is in strict accord with the statutory language, and illustrates the meaning to be placed on those words. Congress did not intend to eradicate the free discussion of political theories, to destroy the traditional rights of Americans to discuss and evaluate ideas without fear of governmental sanction. Rather Congress was concerned with the very kind of activity in which the evidence showed these petitioners engaged.

But although the statute is not directed at the hypothetical cases which petitioners have conjured, its application in this case has resulted in convictions for the teaching and advocacy of the overthrow of the Government by force and violence, which, even though coupled with the intent to accomplish that overthrow, contains an element of speech. For this reason, we must pay special heed to the demands of the First Amendment marking out the boundaries of speech. . . .

In this case we are squarely presented with the application of the "clear and present danger" test, and must decide what that phrase imports. We first note that many of the cases in which this Court has reversed convictions by use of this or similar tests have been based on the fact that the interest which the State was attempting to protect was itself too insubstantial to warrant restriction of speech.

. . . Overthrow of the Government by force and violence is certainly a substantial enough interest for the Government to limit speech. Indeed, this is the ultimate value of any society, for if a society cannot protect its very structure from armed internal attack, it must follow that no subordinate value can be protected. If, then, this interest may be protected, the literal problem which is presented is what has been meant by the use of the phrase "clear and present danger" of the utterances bringing about the evil within the power of Congress to punish.

Obviously, the words cannot mean that before the Government may act, it must wait until the *putsch* is about to be executed, the plans have been laid and the signal is awaited. If Government is aware that a group aiming at its overthrow is attempting to indoctrinate its members and to commit them to a course whereby they will strike when the leaders feel the circumstances permit, action by the Government is required. The argument that there is no need for Government to concern itself, for Government is strong, it possesses ample powers to put down a rebellion, it may defeat the revolution with ease needs no answer. For that is not the question. Certainly an attempt to overthrow the Government by force, even though doomed from the outset because of inadequate numbers or power of the revolutionists, is a sufficient evil for Congress to prevent. The damage which such attempts create both physically and politically to a nation makes it impossible to measure the validity in terms of the probability of success, or the immediacy of a successful attempt. . . .

The situation with which Justices Holmes and Brandeis were concerned in

Gitlow was a comparatively isolated event, bearing little relation in their minds to any substantial threat to the safety of the community. . . . They were not confronted with any situation comparable to the instant one—the development of an apparatus designed and dedicated to the overthrow of the Government, in the context of world crisis after crisis. . . .

Chief Judge Learned Hand, writing for the majority below, . . . [stated that] "In each case [courts] must ask whether the gravity of the 'evil,' discounted by its improbability, justifies such invasion of free speech as is necessary to avoid the danger." We adopt this statement of the rule. As articulated by Chief Judge Hand, it is as succinct and inclusive as any other we might devise at this time. It takes into consideration those factors which we deem relevant, and relates their significances. More we cannot expect from words.

Likewise, we are in accord with the court below, which affirmed the trial court's finding that the requisite danger existed. The mere fact that from the period 1945 to 1948 petitioners' activities did not result in an attempt to overthrow the Government by force and violence is of course no answer to the fact that there was a group that was ready to make the attempt. The formation by petitioners of such a highly organized conspiracy, with rigidly disciplined members subject to call when the leaders, these petitioners, felt that the time had come for action, coupled with the inflammable nature of world conditions, similar uprisings in other countries, and the touch-and-go nature of our relations with countries with whom petitioners were in the very least ideologically attuned, convince us that their convictions were justified on this score. And this analysis disposes of the contention that a conspiracy to advocate, as distinguished from the advocacy itself, cannot be constitutionally restrained, because it comprises only the preparation. It is the existence of the conspiracy which creates the danger. . . .

There remains to be discussed the question of vagueness—whether the statute as we have interpreted it is too vague, not sufficiently advising those who would speak of the limitations upon their activity. It is urged that such vagueness contravenes the First and Fifth Amendments. This argument is particularly nonpersuasive when presented by petitioners, who, the jury found, intended to overthrow the Government as speedily as circumstances would permit. . . .

We agree that the standard as defined is not a neat, mathematical formulary. Like all verbalizations it is subject to criticism on the score of indefiniteness. But petitioners themselves contend that the verbalization "clear and present danger" is the proper standard. We see no difference, from the standpoint of vagueness, whether the standard of "clear and present danger" is one contained *in haec verba* within the statute, or whether it is the judicial measure of constitutional applicability.

. . . Where there is doubt as to the intent of the defendants, the nature of their activities, or their power to bring about the evil, this Court will review the convictions with the scrupulous care demanded by our Constitution. But we are not convinced that because there may be borderline cases at some time in the future, these convictions should be reversed because of the argument that these petitioners could not know that their activities were constitutionally proscribed by the statute. . . .

We hold that §§ 2 (a) (1), 2 (a) (3) and 3 of the Smith Act do not inherently, or as construed or applied in the instant case, violate the First Amendment and other provisions of the Bill of Rights, or the First and Fifth Amendments because of indefiniteness. Petitioners intended to overthrow the Government of the United States as speedily as the circumstances would permit. Their conspiracy to organize the Communist Party and to teach and advocate the overthrow of the Government of the United States by force and violence created a "clear and present danger" of an attempt to overthrow the Government by force and violence. They were properly and constitutionally convicted for violation of the Smith Act. The judgments of conviction are

Affirmed.

MR. JUSTICE DOUGLAS dissenting.

. . . The Act, as construed, requires the element of intent—that those who teach the creed believe in it. The crime then depends not on what is taught but on who the teacher is. That is to make freedom of speech turn not on *what is said,* but on the *intent* with which it is said. Once we start down that road we enter territory dangerous to the liberties of every citizen.

There was a time in England when the concept of constructive treason flourished. Men were punished not for raising a hand against the king but for thinking murderous thoughts about him. The Framers of the Constitution were alive to that abuse and took steps to see that the practice would not flourish here. Treason was defined to require overt acts—the evolution of a plot against the country into an actual project. The present case is not one of treason. But the analogy is close when the illegality is made to turn on intent, not on the nature of the act. We then start probing men's minds for motive and purpose; they become entangled in the law not for what they did but *for what they thought;* they get convicted not for what they said but for the purpose with which they said it.

Intent, of course, often makes the difference in the law. An act otherwise excusable or carrying minor penalties may grow to an abhorrent thing if the evil intent is present. We deal here, however, not with ordinary acts but with speech, to which the Constitution has given a special sanction.

. . . The First Amendment provides that "Congress shall make no law . . . abridging the freedom of speech." The Constitution provides no exception. This does not mean, however, that the Nation need hold its hand until it is in such weakened condition that there is no time to protect itself from incitement to revolution. Seditious conduct can always be punished. But the command of the First Amendment is so clear that we should not allow Congress to call a halt to free speech except in the extreme case of peril from the speech itself.

The First Amendment makes confidence in the common sense of our people and in their maturity of judgment the great postulate of our democracy. Its philosophy is that violence is rarely, if ever, stopped by denying civil liberties to those advocating resort to force. The First Amendment reflects the philosophy of Jefferson "that it is time enough for the rightful purposes of civil government, for its officers to interfere when principles break out into overt acts against peace and good order." The political censor has no place in our public debates. Unless and until extreme and necessitous circumstances are shown, our aim should be to keep speech unfettered and to allow the processes of law to be invoked only when the provocateurs among us move from speech to action.

Vishinsky wrote in 1938 in The Law of the Soviet State, "In our state, naturally, there is and can be no place for freedom of speech, press, and so on for the foes of socialism."

Our concern should be that we accept no such standard for the United States. Our faith should be that our people will never give support to these advocates of revolution, so long as we remain loyal to the purposes for which our Nation was founded.

Brandenburg v. Ohio

395 U.S. 444; 89 S. Ct. 1827; 23 L. Ed. 2d 430 (1969)
Vote: Unanimous

Brandenburg, a Ku-Klux Klan leader, was convicted of violating a criminal syndicalism statute in Ohio. The statute made it unlawful to advocate sabotage, violence, or other forms of terrorism for the purpose of bringing about industrial or political change. It also forbade assembling with others in order to teach such doctrines. After being fined $1,000 and given a 1 to 10 year prison sentence, Brandenburg claimed a violation of his First and Fourteenth Amendment rights. When Ohio appellate courts afforded him no relief, he appealed to the United States Supreme Court.

PER CURIAM
   ... The record shows that a man, identified at trial as the appellant, telephoned an announcer-reporter on the staff of a Cincinnati television station and invited him to come to a Ku Klux Klan "rally" to be held at a farm in Hamilton County. With the cooperation of the organizers, the reporter and a cameraman attended the meeting and filmed the events. Portions of the films were later broadcast on the local station and on a national network.

   The prosecution's case rested on the films and on testimony identifying the appellant as the person who communicated with the reporter and who spoke at the rally. The State also introduced into evidence several articles appearing in the film, including a pistol, a rifle, a shotgun, ammunition, a Bible, and a red hood worn by the speaker in the films.

One film showed 12 hooded figures, some of whom carried firearms. They were gathered around a large wooden cross, which they burned. No one was present other than the participants and the newsmen who made the film. Most of the words uttered during the scene were incomprehensible when the film was projected, but scattered phrases could be understood that were derogatory of Negroes and, in one instance, of Jews.* Another scene on the same film showed the appellant, in Klan regalia, making a speech. The speech, in full, was as follows:

> This is an organizers' meeting. We have had quite a few members here today which are—we have hundreds, hundreds of members throughout the State of Ohio. I can quote from a newspaper clipping from the Columbus, Ohio Dispatch, five weeks ago Sunday morning. The Klan has more members in the State of Ohio than does any other organization. We're not a revengent organization, but if our President, our Congress, our Supreme Court, continues to suppress the white, Caucasian race, it's possible that there might have to be some revengeance taken.
>
> We are marching on Congress July the Fourth, four hundred thousand strong. From there we are dividing into two groups, one group to march on St. Augustine, Florida, the other group to march into Mississippi. Thank you.

The second film showed six hooded figures one of whom, later identified as the appellant, repeated a speech very similar to that recorded on the first film. The reference to the possibility of "revengeance" was omitted, and one sentence was added, "Personally, I believe the nigger should be returned to Africa, the Jew returned to Israel." Though some of the figures in the films carried weapons, the speaker did not.

The Ohio Criminal Syndicalism Statute was enacted in 1919. From 1917 to 1920, indentical or quite similar laws were adopted by 20 States and two territories. E. Dowell, A History of Criminal Syndicalism Legislation in the United States 21 (1939). In 1927, this Court sustained the constitutionality of California's Criminal Syndicalism Act, the text of which is quite similar to that of the laws of Ohio. *Whitney v. California,* [1927], . . . The Court upheld the

*The significant portions that could be understood were:
"How far is the nigger going to—yeah."
"This is what we are going to do to the niggers."
"A dirty nigger."
"Send the Jews back to Israel."
"Let's give them back to the dark garden."
"Save America."
"Let's go back to constitutional betterment."
"Bury the niggers."
"We intend to do our part."
"Give us our state rights."
"Freedom for the whites."
"Nigger will have to fight for every inch he gets from now on."

statute on the ground that, without more, "advocating" violent means to effect political and economic change involves such danger to the security of the State that the State may outlaw it. . . . But *Whitney* has been thoroughly discredited by later decisions.

. . . These later decisions have fashioned the principle that the constitutional guarantees of free speech and free press do not permit a State to forbid or proscribe advocacy of the use of force or of law violation except where such advocacy is directed to inciting or producing imminent lawless action and is likely to incite or produce such action. As we said in *Noto v. United States,* [1961], . . . "the mere abstract teaching . . . of the moral propriety or even moral necessity for a resort to force and violence, is not the same as preparing a group for violent action and steeling it to such action." . . . A statute which fails to draw this distinction impermissibly intrudes upon the freedoms guaranteed by the First and Fourteenth Amendments. It sweeps within its condemnation speech which our Constitution has immunized from governmental control. . . .

Measured by this test, Ohio's Criminal Syndicalism Act cannot be sustained. The Act punishes persons who "advocate or teach the duty, necessity, or propriety" of violence "as a means of accomplishing industrial or political reform"; or who publish or circulate or display any book or paper containing such advocacy: or who "justify" the commission of violent acts "with intent to exemplify, spread or advocate the propriety of the doctrines of criminal syndicalism"; or who "voluntarily assemble" with a group formed "to teach or advocate the doctrines of criminal syndicalism." Neither the indictment nor the judge's instructions to the jury in any way refined the statute's bald definition of the crime in terms of mere advocacy not distinguished from incitement to imminent lawless action.

Accordingly, we are here confronted with a statute which, by its own words and as applied, purports to punish mere advocacy and to forbid, on pain of criminal punishment, assembly with others merely to advocate the described type of action. Such a statute falls within the condemnation of the First and Fourteenth Amendments. The contrary teaching of *Whitney v. California, supra,* cannot be supported, and that decision is therefore overruled.

Reversed.

MR. JUSTICE DOUGLAS, concurring.

While I join the opinion of the Court, I desire to enter a *caveat.* . . . Though I doubt if the "clear and present danger" test is congenial to the First Amendment in time of a declared war, I am certain it is not reconcilable with the First Amendment in days of peace.

The Court quite properly overrules *Whitney v. California,* [1927], . . . which involved advocacy of ideas which the majority of the Court deemed unsound and dangerous. . . . I see no place in the regime of the First Amendment for any "clear and present danger" test, whether strict and tight as some would make it, or free-wheeling as the Court in *Dennis* rephrased it.

When one reads the opinions closely and sees when and how the "clear and present danger" test has been applied, great misgivings are aroused. First, the threats were often loud but always puny and made serious only by judges so wedded to the *status quo* that critical analysis made them nervous. Second, the test was so twisted and perverted in *Dennis* as to make the trial of those teachers of Marxism an all-out political trial which was part and parcel of the cold war that has eroded substantial parts of the First Amendment.

Action is often a method of expression and within the protection of the First Amendment.

Suppose one tears up his own copy of the Constitution in eloquent protest to a decision of this Court. May he be indicted?

Suppose one rips his own Bible to shreds to celebrate his departure from one "faith" and his embrace of atheism. May he be indicted?

Last Term the Court held in *United States v. O'Brien,* [1968], . . . that a registrant under Selective Service who burned his draft card in protest of the war in Vietnam could be prosecuted. . . .

But O'Brien was not prosecuted for not having his draft card available when asked for by a federal agent. He was indicted, tried, and convicted for burning the card. And this Court's affirmance of that conviction was not, with all respect, consistent with the First Amendment.

The act of praying often involves body posture and movement as well as utterances. It is nonetheless protected by the Free Exercise Clause. Picketing, as we have said on numerous occasions, is "free speech plus."

. . . One's beliefs have long been thought to be sanctuaries which government could not invade. *Barenblatt* is one example of the ease with which that sanctuary can be violated. The lines drawn by the Court between the criminal act of being an "active" Communist and the innocent act of being a nominal or inactive Communist mark the difference only between deep and abiding belief and casual or uncertain belief. But I think that all matters of belief are beyond the reach of subpoenas or the probings of investigators. . . .

The line between what is permissible and not subject to control and what may be made impermissible and subject to regulation is the line between ideas and overt acts.

The example usually given by those who would punish speech is the case of one who falsely shouts fire in a crowded theatre.

This is, however, a classic case where speech is brigaded with action. . . . They are indeed inseparable and a prosecution can be launched for the overt acts actually caused. Apart from rare instances of that kind, speech is, I think, immune from prosecution. Certainly there is no constitutional line between advocacy of abstract ideas . . . and advocacy of political action. . . . The quality of advocacy turns on the depth of the conviction: and government has no power to invade that sanctuary of belief and conscience.

QUESTIONS AND COMMENTS

1 Can you relate anything said in Holmes's *Schenck* opinion to the majority opinion in *Korematsu?*

2 The *Schenck* opinion seems to imply that speech is free until it begins to have some effect, then it may be curbed. Comment on that interpretation.

3 The Court holds for the state in *Gitlow* while announcing that the Fourteenth Amendment incorporates the speech provisions of the First Amendment. Compare this to Marshall's technique in *Marbury v. Madison.* Can you guess why the Court accepted this case for review when a denial of review would have been a victory for New York anyway?

4 In *Dennis,* Chief Justice Vinson focuses on the "substantial" interest of the federal government against forcible overthrow—something he felt lacking in earlier state cases. How are we to determine when an interest is substantial and when insubstantial? Can the Constitution help in answering such a question?

5 In *Yates v. United States* (1957), the Court decided that convictions under the Smith Act for advocating forcible overthrow of the government required a showing that the defendants had promoted *action* in their advocacy. Mere abstract argument pertaining to forcible overthrow was insufficient.

6 According to Justice Douglas, concurring in *Brandenburg,* the clear and present danger test was "twisted and perverted" in *Dennis.* What does he mean? Would he have voted differently in *Dennis* if the test had not been "perverted"? Explain your answer.

7 Conspiracy, the charge in *Dennis,* is defined as an agreement between two or more persons to commit an unlawful act or to accomplish by unlawful means an act that is lawful. The charge has been favored by prosecutors seeking to obtain convictions of dissenters and unorthodox thinkers. Can you guess why?

8 Under the ruling in *Dennis,* which, if any, of the following could be successfully prosecuted?

   a An attorney who, speaking to a bar association meeting, urges all members of the bar to boycott law firms employing female attorneys and expresses the opinion that members of the bar ought to verbally assault female attorneys whenever and wherever encountered.

   b A local paralegal who, speaking to a group of his friends, argues that they should, as a group, block entrance to all law firms employing female paralegals, commencing on Monday next at 8:00 A.M. at the law firm of Dittwillie, Wyler, and Sons.

*   *   *   *   *   *

Once we accept the notion that circumstances may influence the constitutionality of speech or of punishment levied for engaging in speech or other forms of expression, ad hoc judgments involving the totality of the circumstances surrounding expression become necessary. It is not possible to delineate in advance all possible relevant circumstances. But some factors keep turning up in the cases. One of these is *place*—i.e., where the expression occurs. As Justice Holmes implied in *Schenck,* there is nothing wrong with yelling "Fire!" But, as he said, if you do so in a crowded theater in which there is no fire, the utterance is not constitutionally protected. *Cohen, Greer,* and *PruneYard* all involve speech whose constitutionality was related to the place in which the speech occurred. Clearly you have a constitutional right to display the word "fuck" on your jacket while walking around in the privacy of your home. But is it constitutionally protected if you do so in a municipal courthouse? Similarly, one is constitutionally protected in making political speeches. But can one expect such protection on a military base, as in *Greer v. Spock?* Finally a constitutionally protected right to free speech may be limited by other constitutional rights with which the exercise of speech may conflict. In such cases, as in *PruneYard,* a balancing of interests must be undertaken by the Court.

Cohen v. California

403 U.S. 15; 91 S. Ct. 780; 29 L. Ed. 2d 284 (1971)
Vote: 5–4

Paul Cohen was given 30 days in jail for violating California's prohibition against "maliciously and willfully disturbing the peace and quiet of any neighborhood or person . . . by . . . offensive conduct." The statute specifically prohibited disturbing "peace and quiet" by the use of any "vulgar, profane, or indecent language within the presence or hearing of women and children." The Supreme Court agreed to review Cohen's conviction after a California court of appeals denied relief.

MR. JUSTICE HARLAN delivered the opinion of the Court.

This case may seem at first blush too inconsequential to find its way into our books, but the issue it presents is of no small constitutional significance. . . .

> On April 26, 1968, the defendant was observed in the Los Angeles County Courthouse in the corridor outside of division 20 of the municipal court wearing a jacket bearing the words 'Fuck the Draft' which were plainly visible. There were women and children present in the corridor. The defendant was arrested. The defendant testified that he wore the jacket knowing that the words were on the jacket as a means of informing the public of the depth of his feelings against the Vietnam War and the draft.
>
> > The defendant did not engage in, nor threaten to engage in, nor did anyone as the result of his conduct in fact commit or threaten to commit any act of violence. The defendant did not make any loud or unusual noise, nor was there any evidence that he uttered any sound prior to his arrest. . . .

In affirming the conviction the [California] Court of Appeal held that "offensive conduct" means "behavior which has a tendency to provoke *others* to acts of violence or to in turn disturb the peace," and that the State had proved this element because, on the facts of this case, "[i]t was certainly reasonably foreseeable that such conduct might cause others to rise up to commit a violent act against the person of the defendant or attempt to forceably remove his jacket. . . ."

The conviction quite clearly rests upon the asserted offensiveness of the *words* Cohen used to convey his message to the public. The only "conduct" which the State sought to punish is the fact of communication. Thus, we deal here with a conviction resting solely upon "speech," . . . not upon any separately identifiable conduct which allegedly was intended by Cohen to be perceived by others as expressive of particular views but which, on its face, does not necessarily convey any message and hence arguably could be regulated without effectively repressing Cohen's ability to express himself. Further, the State certainly lacks power to punish Cohen for the underlying content of the message the inscription conveyed. At least so long as there is no showing of an intent to incite disobedience to or disruption of the draft, Cohen could not, consistently with the First and Fourteenth Amendments, be punished for asserting the evident position on the inutility or immorality of the draft his jacket reflected.

. . . As it comes to us, this case cannot be said to fall within those relatively few categories of instances where prior decisions have established the power of government to deal more comprehensively with certain forms of individual expression simply upon a showing that such a form was employed. This is not, for example, an obscenity case. Whatever else may be necessary to give rise to the States' broader power to prohibit obscene expression, such expression must be, in some significant way, erotic. . . . It cannot plausibly be maintained that this vulgar allusion to the Selective Service System would conjure up such psychic stimulation in anyone likely to be confronted with Cohen's crudely defaced jacket.

This Court has also held that the States are free to ban the simple use, without a demonstration of additional justifying circumstances, of so-called "fighting words," those personally abusive epithets which, when addressed to the ordinary citizen, are, as a matter of common knowledge, inherently likely to provoke violent reaction. . . . While the four-letter word displayed by Cohen in relation to the draft is not uncommonly employed in a personally provocative fashion, in this instance it was clearly not "directed to the person of the hearer."

. . . No individual actually or likely to be present could reasonably have regarded the words on appellant's jacket as a direct personal insult. Nor do we have here an instance of the exercise of the State's police power to prevent a speaker from intentionally provoking a given group to hostile reaction. . . . There is, as noted above, no showing that anyone who saw Cohen was in fact violently aroused or that appellant intended such a result.

Finally, in arguments before this Court much has been made of the claim that Cohen's distasteful mode of expression was thrust upon unwilling or unsuspecting viewers, and that the State might therefore legitimately act as it did in order to protect the sensitive from otherwise unavoidable exposure to appellant's crude form of protest. Of course, the mere presumed presence of unwitting listeners or viewers does not serve automatically to justify curtailing all speech capable of giving offense.

. . . While this Court has recognized that government may properly act in many situations to prohibit intrusion into the privacy of the home of unwel-

come views and ideas which cannot be totally banned from the public dialogue, *e.g., Rowan v. Post Office Dept.,* [1970], . . . we have at the same time
consistently stressed that "we are often 'captives' outside the sanctuary of the
home and subject to objectionable speech." *Id.,* at 738. The ability of government, consonant with the Constitution, to shut off discourse solely to protect
others from hearing it is, in other words, dependent upon a showing that substantial privacy interests are being invaded in an essentially intolerable manner. Any broader view of this authority would effectively empower a majority
to silence dissidents simply as a matter of personal predilections.

In this regard, persons confronted with Cohen's jacket were in a quite different posture than, say, those subjected to the raucous emissions of sound
trucks blaring outside their residences. Those in the Los Angeles courthouse
could effectively avoid further bombardment of their sensibilities simply by
averting their eyes. And, while it may be that one has a more substantial claim
to a recognizable privacy interest when walking through a courthouse corridor
than, for example, strolling through Central Park, surely it is nothing like the
interest in being free from unwanted expression in the confines of one's own
home. . . . Given the subtlety and complexity of the factors involved, if Coh-
en's "speech" was otherwise entitled to constitutional protection, we do not
think the fact that some unwilling "listeners" in a public building may have
been briefly exposed to it can serve to justify this breach of the peace conviction where, as here, there was no evidence that persons powerless to avoid
appellant's conduct did in fact object to it, and where that portion of the statute
upon which Cohen's conviction rests evinces no concern, either on its face or
as construed by the California courts, with the special plight of the captive
auditor, but, instead, indiscriminately sweeps within its prohibitions all "offensive conduct" that disturbs "any neighborhood or person."

. . . Admittedly, it is not so obvious that the First and Fourteenth Amendments must be taken to disable the States from punishing public utterance of
this unseemly expletive in order to maintain what they regard as a suitable
level of discourse within the body politic. We think, however, that examination and reflection will reveal the shortcomings of a contrary viewpoint. . . .
First, the principle contended for by the State seems inherently boundless.
How is one to distinguish this from any other offensive word? Surely the State
has no right to cleanse public debate to the point where it is grammatically
palatable to the most squeamish among us. Yet no readily ascertainable general principle exists for stopping short of that result were we to affirm the judgment below. For, while the particular four-letter word being litigated here is
perhaps more distasteful than most others of its genre, it is nevertheless often
true that one man's vulgarity is another's lyric. Indeed, we think it is largely
because governmental officials cannot make principled distinctions in this area
that the Constitution leaves matters of taste and style so largely to the
individual.

Additionally, we cannot overlook the fact, because it is well illustrated by
the episode involved here, that much linguistic expression serves a dual com-

municative function: it conveys not only ideas capable of relatively precise, detached explication, but otherwise inexpressible emotions as well. In fact, words are often chosen as much for their emotive as their cognitive force. We cannot sanction the view that the Constitution, while solicitous of the cognitive content of individual speech, has little or no regard for that emotive function which, practically speaking, may often be the more important element of the overall message sought to be communicated. . . .

Finally, and in the same vein, we cannot indulge the facile assumption that one can forbid particular words without also running a substantial risk of suppressing ideas in the process. Indeed, governments might soon seize upon the censorship of particular words as a convenient guise for banning the expression of unpopular views. We have been able, as noted above, to discern little social benefit that might result from running the risk of opening the door to such grave results.

It is, in sum, our judgment that, absent a more particularized and compelling reason for its actions, the State may not, consistently with the First and Fourteenth Amendments, make the simple public display here involved of this single four-letter expletive a criminal offense. Because that is the only arguably sustainable rationale for the conviction here at issue, the judgment below must be

Reversed.

Greer, Commander, Fort Dix Military Reservation, et al. v. Spock, et al.

424 U.S. 828; 96 S. Ct. 1211; 47 L. Ed. 2d 505 (1976)
Vote: 6–2

Fort Dix was (and remains) a federal military installation, with public access limited according to post regulations. While civilian speakers were sometimes invited to speak on the post, partisan political activity was barred. In addition, the distribution or posting of publications of any kind was prohibited without the prior written approval of the adjutant general. On September 9, 1972, Benjamin Spock and Julius Hobson, presidential and vice-presidential candidates of the People's party, informed the post commander of their intention to enter the reservation on September 23 to distribute campaign literature. They also advised him that a meeting to discuss election issues with post personnel was planned.

General David, the commanding officer, rejected the Spock-Hobson request on September 18. Eleven days later, Spock and Hobson sought an order from the federal district court enjoining the enforcement of the regulations governing political speaking and distribution of literature—on the ground that such regulations were impermissible under the First and Fourteenth Amendments. The request for an injunction was denied, but the court of appeals reversed and issued a temporary restraining order. Spock then conducted a political rally in a Fort Dix parking lot on November 4, 1972. Subsequently, the injunction was made permanent. The Supreme Court granted certiorari.

Mr. Justice Stewart delivered the opinion of the Court. . . .

[The court of appeals was mistaken in thinking] . . . that whenever members of the public are permitted freely to visit a place owned or operated by the Government, then that place becomes a "public forum" for purposes of the First Amendment. Such a principle of constitutional law has never existed, and does not exist now. The guarantees of the First Amendment have never meant "that people who want to propagandize protests or views have a constitutional right to do so whenever and however and wherever they please." *Adderley v. Florida,* [1966], . . .

One of the very purposes for which the Constitution was ordained and established was to "provide for the common defence," and this Court over the years has on countless occasions recognized the special constitutional function of the military in our national life, a function both explicit and indispensable. In short, it is "the primary business of armies and navies to fight or be ready to fight wars should the occasion arise." *United States ex rel. Toth v. Quarles,* [1955], . . . And it is consequently the business of a military installation like Fort Dix to train soldiers, not to provide a public forum.

A necessary concomitant of the basic function of a military installation has been "the historically unquestioned power of [its] commanding officer summarily to exclude civilians from the area of his command." *Cafeteria Workers v. McElroy,* [1961], . . . The notion that federal military reservations, like municipal streets and parks, have traditionally served as a place for free public assembly and communication of thoughts by private citizens is thus historically and constitutionally false.

The respondents, therefore, had no generalized constitutional right to make political speeches or distribute leaflets at Fort Dix, and it follows that [the Fort Dix Regulations] . . . are not constitutionally invalid on their face. These regulations, moreover, were not unconstitutionally applied in the circumstances disclosed by the record in the present case.

. . . There is no claim that the military authorities discriminated in any way among candidates for public office based upon the candidates' supposed political views. It is undisputed that, until the appearance of the respondent Spock at Fort Dix on November 4, 1972, as a result of a court order, no candidate of any political stripe had ever been permitted to campaign there.

What the record shows, therefore, is a considered Fort Dix policy, objectively and evenhandedly applied, of keeping official military activities there wholly free of entanglement with partisan political campaigns of any kind. Under such a policy members of the Armed Forces stationed at Fort Dix are wholly free as individuals to attend political rallies, out of uniform and off base. But the military as such is insulated from both the reality and the appearance of acting as a handmaiden for partisan political causes or candidates.

Such a policy is wholly consistent with the American constitutional tradition of a politically neutral military establishment under civilian control. It is a policy that has been reflected in numerous laws and military regulations throughout our history. And it is a policy that the military authorities at Fort Dix were constitutionally free to pursue.

. . . The only publications that a military commander may disapprove are those that he finds constitute "a clear danger to [military] loyalty, discipline, or morale," and he "may not prevent distribution of a publication simply because he does not like its contents," or because it "is critical—even unfairly critical—of government policies or officials. . . ." There is nothing in the Constitution that disables a military commander from acting to avert what he perceives to be a clear danger to the loyalty, discipline, or morale of troops on the base under his command. . . . This case, therefore, simply does not raise any question of unconstitutional application of the regulation to any specific situation. . . .

For the reasons set out in this opinion the judgment is reversed.

It is so ordered.

MR. JUSTICE BRENNAN, with whom MR. JUSTICE MARSHALL concurs, dissenting.

. . . The Court's opinion speaks in absolutes, exalting the need for military preparedness and admitting of no careful and solicitous accommodation of First Amendment interests to the competing concerns that all concede are substantial. It parades general propositions useless to precise resolution of the problem at hand. According to the Court, "it is 'the primary business of armies and navies to fight wars should the occasion arise,'" . . . and "it is consequently the business of a military installation like Fort Dix to train soldiers, not to provide a public forum," . . . .But the training of soldiers does not as a practical matter require exclusion of those who would publicly express their views from streets and theater parking lots open to the general public. Nor does readiness to fight require such exclusion, unless, of course, the battlefields are the streets and parking lots, or the war is one of ideologies and not men.

With similar unenlightening generality, the Court observes: "One of the very purposes for which the Constitution was ordained and established was to 'provide for the common defence,' and this Court over the years has on countless occasions recognized the special constitutional function of the military in our national life, a function both explicit and indispensable. . . ." But the Court overlooks the equally, if not more, compelling generalization that—to paraphrase the Court—one of the very purposes for which the First Amendment was adopted was to "secure the Blessings of Liberty to ourselves and our Posterity," and this Court over the years has on countless occasions recognized the special constitutional function of the First Amendment in our national life, a function both explicit and indispensable. Despite the Court's oversight, if the recent lessons of history mean anything, it is that the First Amendment does not evaporate with mere intonation of interests such as national defense, military necessity, or domestic security. Those interests "cannot be invoked as a talismanic incantation to support any exercise of . . . power." *United States v. Robel,* [1967], . . . In all cases where such interests have been advanced, the inquiry has been whether the exercise of First Amendment rights necessarily must be circumscribed in order to secure those interests. . . .

It is no answer to say that the commander of a military installation has the "historically unquestioned power . . . to exclude civilians from the area of his command."

. . . The Court's reliance on this proposition from *Cafeteria Workers* is misplaced. That case was only concerned with the procedural requisites for revocation of a security clearance on a military base, not with the range of permissible justifications for such revocation and, thereby, exclusion. Indeed, the "privilege" doctrine upon which rested the sweeping powers suggested by that case has long since been repudiated.

. . . But more important that decision specifically recognized that the Government was constrained by specific constitutional limitations, even in the exercise of its proprietary military functions. . . . Where the interference with Fort functions by public expression does not differ from that presented by other activities in unrestricted areas, the Fort command may no more preclude such expression, than " 'Congress may . . . enact a regulation providing that no Republican Jew or Negro shall be appointed to federal office.' " *United Public Workers v. Mitchell,* [1947]. . . .

Similarly, it is no answer to say that the proposed activities in this case may be excluded because similar forms of expression have been evenhandedly excluded. An evenhanded exclusion of all public expression would no more pass constitutional muster than an evenhanded exclusion of all Roman Catholics. . . .

Additionally, prohibiting the distribution of leaflets cannot be justified on the ground that that expression presents a "clear danger to [military] loyalty, discipline, or morale." . . . This standard for preclusion is, in the face of a well-developed line of precedents, constitutionally inadequate. This Court long ago departed from "clear and present danger" as a test for limiting free expression. . . .

Yet the Court today, without reason, would fully reinstate that test and, indeed, would only require that the danger be clear, not even present. . . .

As Mr. Justice Holmes observed in dissent better than a half century ago: "It is only the present danger of immediate evil or an intent to bring it about that warrants . . . setting a limit to the expression of opinion." *Abrams v. United States,* [1919], . . . "Only the emergency that makes it immediately dangerous to leave the correction of evil counsels to time warrants making any exception to the [First Amendment]." . . . Accepting for the moment, however, the validity of a "clear danger" test, I do not see, nor does the Court's opinion demonstrate, how a clear danger is presented in this case. No one has seriously contended that the activities involved here presented such a danger to military loyalty, discipline, or morale.

PruneYard Shopping Center v. Robins

447 U.S. 74; 100 S. Ct. 2035; 64 L. Ed. 2d 741 (1980)
Vote: 9–0

The facts are given fully in the opinion of the Court.

MR. JUSTICE REHNQUIST delivered the opinion of the Court.

Appellant PruneYard is a privately owned shopping center in the city of Campbell, Cal. It covers approximately 21 acres—5 devoted to parking and 16 occupied by walkways, plazas, sidewalks, and buildings that contain more than 65 specialty shops, 10 restaurants, and a movie theater. The PruneYard is open to the public for the purpose of encouraging the patronizing of its commercial establishments. It has a policy not to permit any visitor or tenant to engage in any publicly expressive activity, including the circulation of petitions, that is not directly related to its commercial purposes. This policy has been strictly enforced in a nondiscriminatory fashion. The PruneYard is owned by appellant Fred Sahadi.

Appellees are high school students who sought to solicit support for their opposition to a United Nations resolution against "Zionism." On a Saturday afternoon they set up a card table in a corner of PruneYard's central courtyard. They distributed pamphlets and asked passersby to sign petitions, which were to be sent to the President and Members of Congress. Their activity was peaceful and orderly and so far as the record indicates was not objected to by PruneYard's patrons.

Soon after appellees had begun soliciting signatures, a security guard informed them that they would have to leave because their activity violated PruneYard regulations. The guard suggested that they move to the public sidewalk at the PruneYard's perimeter. Appellees immediately left the premises and later filed this lawsuit in the California Superior Court of Santa Clara County. They sought to enjoin appellants from denying them access to the PruneYard for the purpose of circulating their petitions.

The Superior Court held that appellees were not entitled under either the Federal or California Constitution to exercise their asserted rights on the shopping center property. It concluded that there were "adequate, effective channels of communication for [appellees] other than soliciting on the private property of the [PruneYard]." The California Court of Appeal affirmed.

The California Supreme Court reversed, holding that the California Constitution protects "speech and petitioning, reasonably exercised, in shopping centers even when the centers are privately owned." It concluded that appellees are entitled to conduct their activity on PruneYard property.

. . . Before this Court, appellants contend that their constitutionally established rights under the Fourteenth Amendment to exclude appellees from adverse use of appellants' private property cannot be denied by invocation of a state constitutional provision or by judicial reconstruction of a state's laws of private property. We postponed consideration of the question of jurisdiction until the hearing of the case on the merits. We now affirm. . . .

Appellants first contend that *Lloyd Corp. v. Tanner,* (1972), prevents the State from requiring a private shopping center owner to provide access to persons exercising their state constitutional rights of free speech and petition when adequate alternative avenues of communication are available. *Lloyd* dealt with the question whether under the Federal Constitution a privately owned shopping center may prohibit the distribution of handbills on its property when the handbilling is unrelated to the shopping center's operations. The shopping center had adopted a strict policy against the distribution of handbills within the building complex and its malls, and it made no exceptions to this rule. Respondents in *Lloyd* argued that because the shopping center was open to the public, the First Amendment prevents the private owner from enforcing the handbilling restriction on shopping center premises.

In rejecting this claim we substantially repudiated the rationale of *Food Employees v. Logan Valley Plaza,* (1968), which was later overruled in *Hudgens v. NLRB,* (1976). We stated that property does not "lose its private character merely because the public is generally invited to use it for designated purposes," and that "[t]he essentially private character of a store and its privately owned abutting property does not change by virtue of being large or clustered with other stores in a modern shopping center."

Our reasoning in *Lloyd,* however, does not *ex proprio vigore* limit the authority of the State to exercise its police power or its sovereign right to adopt in its own Constitution individual liberties more expansive than those conferred by the Federal Constitution. *Cooper v. California,* (1967). In *Lloyd, supra,* there was no state constitutional or statutory provision that had been construed to create rights to the use of private property by strangers, comparable to those found to exist by the California Supreme Court here. It is, of course, well established that a State in the exercise of its police power may adopt reasonable restrictions on private property so long as the restrictions do not amount to a taking without just compensation or contravene any other federal constitutional provision.

Lloyd held that when a shopping center owner opens his private property to the public for the purpose of shopping, the First Amendment to the United States Constitution does not thereby create individual rights in expression beyond those already existing under applicable law. . . .

Appellants finally contend that a private property owner has a First Amendment right not to be forced by the State to use his property as a forum for the speech of others. They state that in *Wooley v. Maynard,* (1977), this Court concluded that a State may not constitutionally require an individual to participate in the dissemination of an ideological message by displaying it on his private property in a manner and for the express purpose that it be observed and read by the public. This rationale applies here, they argue, because the message of *Wooley* is that the State may not force an individual to display any message at all.

Wooley, however, was a case in which the government itself prescribed the message, required it to be displayed openly on appellee's personal property that was used "as part of his daily life," and refused to permit him to take any measures to cover up the motto even though the Court found that the display of the motto served no important state interest. Here, by contrast, there are a number of distinguishing factors. Most important, the shopping center by choice of its owner is not limited to the personal use of appellants. It is instead a business establishment that is open to the public to come and go as they please. The views expressed by members of the public in passing out pamphlets or seeking signatures for a petition thus will not likely be identified with those of the owner. Second, no specific message is dictated by the State to be displayed on appellants' property. There consequently is no danger of governmental discrimination for or against a particular message. Finally, as far as appears here appellants can expressly disavow any connection with the message by simply posting signs in the area where the speakers or handbillers stand. Such signs, for example, could disclaim any sponsorship of the message and could explain that the persons are communicating their own messages by virtue of state law.

Appellants also argue that their First Amendment rights have been infringed in light of *West Virginia State Board of Education v. Barnette,* (1943), and *Miami Herald Publishing Co. v. Tornillo,* (1974). *Barnette* is inapposite because it involved the compelled recitation of a message containing an affirmation of belief. This Court held such compulsion unconstitutional because it "require[d] the individual to communicate by word and sign his acceptance" of government-dictated political ideas, whether or not he subscribed to them. Appellants are not similarly being compelled to affirm their belief in any gov-

ernmentally prescribed position or view, and they are free to publicly disso-
ciate themselves from the views of the speakers or handbillers.

Tornillo struck down a Florida statute requiring a newspaper to publish a
political candidate's reply to criticism previously published in that newspaper.
It rests on the principle that the State cannot tell a newspaper what it must
print. The Florida statute contravened this principle in that it "exact[ed] a penalty on the basis of the content of a newspaper." There also was a danger in
Tornillo that the statute would "dampe[n] the vigor and limi[t] the variety of
public debate" by deterring editors from publishing controversial political
statements that might trigger the application of the statute. Thus, the statute
was found to be an "intrusion into the function of editors." These concerns
obviously are not present here.

We conclude that neither appellants' federally recognized property rights
nor their First Amendment rights have been infringed by the California
Supreme Court's decision recognizing a right of appellees to exercise state-pro-
tected rights of expression and petition on appellants' property. The judgment
of the Supreme Court of California is therefore

Affirmed.

QUESTIONS AND COMMENTS

1 Cohen's message was "Fuck the Draft" and therefore susceptible to interpretation as
   political protest. Did that fact have anything to do with the Court's decision? What
   if twenty-five first-grade schoolchildren had been in the courtroom corridor and read
   Cohen's message? Different decision? What if six ardent supporters of the Vietnam
   War had responded to Cohen's message by starting a riot? Would speech still be
   protected?
2 On the basis of *Greer v. Spock,* would you say that the clear and present danger test
   is still alive? Why or why not?
3 What if the military commander in *Greer v. Spock* had permitted political speeches
   on his base for twelve months prior to Spock's request but had decided the day before
   the request that such speeches interfered with discipline or training and issued an
   order banning such speeches? Same decision? Why or why not?
4 Does one have a First Amendment right against being forced to display a particular
   message on one's property? Explain.
5 In *PruneYard,* what if the California Constitution provided no right to free speech
   and petition? Same decision? Explain your answer.

*   *   *   *   *   *

The last two cases in this section raise different kinds of questions and
illustrate the breadth of the coverage sometimes claimed for First
Amendment protection of speech. It will be noted that neither *Buckley v.
Valeo* nor *Abood v. Detroit Board of Education* alleges any direct interference
with an utterance. Both, however, deal with indirect expression of political

views—one through support of one's political party, the other through the withholding of support for social, political, and religious activities that are disapproved.

Buckley et al. v. Valeo, Secretary of the United States Senate et al.

424 U.S. 1; 96 S. Ct. 612; 46 L. Ed. 2d 659 (1976)
Vote: 8–0 (with dissent on some issues)

The Federal Election Campaign Act of 1971, as amended in 1974, limited political contributions to candidates for federal elective office to $1,000 if given by an individual or group and $5,000 if given by a political committee. Furthermore, limits were placed on the expenditures that could be made "relative to" a clearly identified candidate and by candidates or their families. Other provisions required the keeping of detailed records followed by quarterly "disclosure" reports to a Federal Election Commission established by the act.

PER CURIAM.

* * *

GENERAL PRINCIPLES

The Act's contribution and expenditure limitations operate in an area of the most fundamental First Amendment activities. Discussion of public issues and debate on the qualifications of candidates are integral to the operation of the system of government established by our Constitution. The First Amendment affords the broadest protection to such political expression in order "to assure [the] unfettered interchange of ideas for the bringing about of political and social changes desired by the people." *Roth v. United States,* (1957). Although First Amendment protections are not confined to "the exposition of ideas," *Winters v. New York,* (1948), "there is practically universal agreement that a major purpose of that Amendment was to protect the free discussion of governmental affairs, ... of course includ[ing] discussions of candidates. ..." *Mills v. Alabama,* (1966). This no more than reflects our "profound national commitment to the principle that debate on public issues should be uninhibited, robust, and wide-open," *New York Times Co. v. Sullivan,* (1964). In a republic where the people are sovereign, the ability of the citizenry to make informed choices among candidates for office is essential, for the identities of those who are elected will inevitably shape the course that we follow as a nation. As the Court observed in *Monitor Patriot Co. v. Roy,* (1971), "it can hardly be doubted that the constitutional guarantee has its fullest and most urgent application precisely to the conduct of campaigns for political office."

The First Amendment protects political association as well as political expression. The constitutional right of association explicated in *NAACP v. Alabama,* (1958), stemmed from the Court's recognition that "[e]ffective advocacy of both public and private points of view, particularly controversial ones, is undeniably enhanced by group association." Subsequent decisions have made clear that the First and Fourteenth Amendments guarantee " 'freedom to associate with others for the common advancement of political beliefs and ideas,' " a freedom that encompasses " '[t]he right to associate with the political party of one's choice.' " *Kusper v. Pontikes,* (1973), . . .

A restriction on the amount of money a person or group can spend on political communication during a campaign necessarily reduces the quantity of expression by restricting the number of issues discussed, the depth of their exploration, and the size of the audience reached. This is because virtually every means of communicating ideas in today's mass society requires the expenditure of money. The distribution of the humblest handbill or leaflet entails printing, paper, and circulation costs. Speeches and rallies generally necessitate hiring a hall and publicizing the event. The electorate's increasing dependence on television, radio, and other mass media for news and information has made these expensive modes of communication indispensable instruments of effective political speech.

The expenditure limitations contained in the Act represent substantial rather than merely theoretical restraints on the quantity and diversity of political speech. The $1,000 ceiling on spending "relative to a clearly identified candidate," would appear to exclude all citizens and groups except candidates, political parties, and the institutional press from any significant use of the most effective modes of communication. Although the Act's limitations on expenditures by campaign organizations and political parties provide substantially greater room for discussion and debate, they would have required restrictions in the scope of a number of past congressional and Presidential campaigns and would operate to constrain campaigning by candidates who raise sums in excess of the spending ceiling.

By contrast with a limitation upon expenditures for political expression, a limitation upon the amount that any one person or group may contribute to a candidate or political group may contribute to a candidate or political committee entails only a marginal restriction upon the contributor's ability to engage in free communication. A contribution serves as a general expression of support for the candidate and his views, but does not communicate the underlying basis for the support. The quantity of communication by the contributor does not increase perceptibly with the size of his contribution, since the expression rests solely on the undifferentiated, symbolic act of contributing. At most, the size of the contribution provides a very rough index of the intensity of the contributor's support for the candidate. A limitation on the amount of money a person may give to a candidate or campaign organization thus involves little direct restraint on his political communication, for it permits the symbolic expression of support evidenced by a contribution but does not in any way infringe the contributor's freedom to discuss candidates and issues. While contributions may result in political expression if spent by a candidate or an association to present views to the voters, the transformation of contributions into political debate involves speech by someone other than the contributor.

Given the important role of contributions in financing political campaigns, contribution restrictions could have a severe impact on political dialogue if the limitations prevented candidates and political committees from amassing the resources necessary for effective advocacy. There is no indication, however, that the contribution limitations imposed by the Act would have any dramatic adverse effect on the funding of campaigns and political associations. The overall effect of the Act's contribution ceilings is merely to require candidates and political committees to raise funds from a greater number of persons and to compel people who would otherwise contribute amounts greater than the statutory limits to expend such funds on direct political expression, rather than to reduce the total amount of money potentially available to promote political expression.

The Act's contribution and expenditure limitations also impinge on protected associational freedoms. Making a contribution, like joining a political party, serves to affiliate a person with a candidate. In addition, it enables like-minded persons to pool their resources in furtherance of common political goals. The Act's contribution ceilings thus limit one important means of associating with a candidate or committee, but leave the contributor free to become a member of any political association and to assist personally in the association's efforts on behalf of candidates. And the Act's contribution limitations permit associations and candidates to aggregate large sums of money to promote effective advocacy. By contrast, the Act's $1,000 limitation on independent expenditures "relative to a clearly identified candidate" precludes most associations from effectively amplifying the voice of their adherents, the original basis for the recognition of First Amendment protection of the freedom of association. The Act's constraints on the ability of independent associations and candidate campaign organizations to expend resources on political expression "is simultaneously an interference with the freedom of [their] adherents," *Sweezy v. New Hampshire,* (1957) (plurality opinion).

In sum, although the Act's contribution and expenditure limitations both implicate fundamental First Amendment interests, its expenditure ceilings impose significantly more severe restrictions on protected freedoms of political expression and association than do its limitations on financial contributions.

... We agree that in order to preserve the provision against invalidation on vagueness grounds, § 608 (e)(1) must be construed to apply only to expenditures for communications that in express terms advocate the election or defeat of a clearly identified candidate for federal office.

We turn then to the basic First Amendment question—whether § 608 (e)(1), even as thus narrowly and explicitly construed, impermissibly burdens the constitutional right of free expression. . . . The constitutionality of § 608 (e)(1) turns on whether the governmental interests advanced in its support satisfy the exacting scrutiny applicable to limitations on core First Amendment rights of political expression.

We find that the governmental interest in preventing corruption and the appearance of corruption is inadequate to justify § 608 (e)(1)'s ceiling on independent expenditures. First, assuming *arguendo,* that large independent expenditures pose the same dangers of actual or apparent *quid pro quo* arrangements as do large contributions, § 608 (e)(1) does not provide an answer that sufficiently relates to the elimination of those dangers. Unlike the contribution limitations' total ban on the giving of large amounts of money to candidates, § 608 (e)(1) prevents only some large expenditures. So long as persons and groups eschew expenditures that in express terms advocate the election or defeat of a clearly identified candidate, they are free to spend as much as they want to promote the candidate and his views. The exacting interpretation of the statutory language necessary to avoid unconstitutional vagueness thus undermines the limitation's effectiveness as a loophole-closing provision by facilitating circumvention by those seeking to exert improper influence upon a candidate or office-holder. It would naively underestimate the ingenuity and resourcefulness of persons and groups desiring to buy influence to believe that they would have much difficulty devising expenditures that skirted the restriction on express advocacy of election or defeat but nevertheless benefited the candidate's campaign. Yet no substantial societal interest would be served by a loophole-closing provision designed to check corruption that permitted unscrupulous persons and organizations to expend unlimited sums of money in order to obtain improper influence over candidates for elective office.

Second, quite apart from the shortcomings of § 608 (e)(1) in preventing any abuses generated by large independent expenditures, the independent advocacy restricted by the provision does not presently appear to pose dangers of real or apparent corruption comparable to those identified with large campaign contributions. The parties defending § 608 (e)(1) contend that it is necessary to prevent would-be contributors from avoiding the contribution limitations by the simple expedient of paying directly for media advertisements or for other portions of the candidate's campaign activities. They argue that expenditures controlled by or coordinated with the candidate and his campaign might well have virtually the same value to the candidate as a contribution and would pose similar dangers of abuse. Yet such controlled or coordinated expenditures are treated as contributions rather than expenditures under the Act. Section 608 (b)'s contribution ceilings rather than § 608 (e)(1)'s independent expenditure limitation prevent attempts to circumvent the Act through prearranged or coordinated expenditures amounting to disguised contributions. By contrast, § 608(c)(1) limits expenditures for express advocacy of candidates made totally independently of the candidate and his campaign. Unlike contributions, such independent expenditures may well provide little assistance to the candidate's campaign and indeed may prove counterproductive. The absence of prearrangement and coordination of an expenditure with the candidate or his agent not only undermines the value of the expenditure to the candidate, but also alleviates the danger that expenditures will be given as a *quid pro quo* for improper commitments from the candidate. Rather than preventing circumvention of the contribution limitations, § 608 (e)(1) severely restricts all independent advocacy despite its substantially diminished potential for abuse.

While the independent expenditure ceiling thus fails to serve any substantial governmental interest in stemming the reality or appearance of corruption in the electoral process, it heavily burdens core First Amendment expression. For the First Amendment right to " 'speak one's mind . . . on all public institutions' " includes the right to engage in " 'vigorous advocacy' no less than 'abstract discussion.' " *New York Times Co. v. Sullivan,* . . . Advocacy of the election or defeat of candidates for federal office is no less entitled to protection under the First Amendment than the discussion of political policy generally or advocacy of the passage or defeat of legislation.

It is argued, however, that the ancillary governmental interest in equalizing the relative ability of individuals and groups to influence the outcome of elections serves to justify the limitation on express advocacy of the election or defeat of candidates imposed by § 608 (e)(1)'s expenditure ceiling. But the concept that government may restrict the speech of some elements of our society in order to enhance the relative voice of others is wholly foreign to the First Amendment, which was designed "to secure 'the widest possible dissemination of information from diverse and antagonistic sources,' " and " 'to assure unfettered interchange of ideas for the bringing about of political and social changes desired by the people.' " *New York Times Co. v. Sullivan, supra,* . . . The First Amendment's protection against governmental abridgment of free expression cannot properly be made to depend on a person's financial ability to engage in public discussion.

* * *

For the reasons stated, we conclude that § 608 (e)(1)'s independent expenditure limitation is unconstitutional under the First Amendment.

* * *

The ceiling on personal expenditures by candidates on their own behalf, like the limitations on independent expenditures contained in § 608 (e)(1), imposes a substantial restraint on the ability of persons to engage in protected First Amendment expression. The candidate, no less than any other person, has a First Amendment right to engage in the discussion of public issues and vigorously and tirelessly to advocate his own election and the election of other candidates. Indeed, it is of particular importance that candidates have the unfettered opportunity to make their views known so that the electorate may intelligently evaluate the candidates' qualities and their positions on vital public issues before choosing among them on election day.

. . . Indeed, the use of personal funds reduces the candidate's dependence on outside contributions and thereby counteracts the coercive pressures and attendant risks of abuse to which the Act's contribution limitations are directed. . . .

The ancillary interest in equalizing the relative financial resources of candidates competing for elective office, therefore, provides the sole relevant rationale for § 608 (a)'s expenditure ceiling. That interest is clearly not sufficient to justify the provision's infringement of fundamental First Amendment rights. First, the limitation may fail to promote financial equality among candidates. A candidate who spends less of his personal resources on his campaign may nonetheless outspend his rival as a result of more successful fundraising efforts. Indeed, a candidate's personal wealth may impede his efforts to persuade others that he needs their financial contributions or volunteer efforts to conduct an effective campaign. Second, and more fundamentally, the First Amendment simply cannot tolerate § 608 (a)'s restriction upon the freedom of a candidate to speak without legislative limit on behalf of his own candidacy. We therefore hold that § 608 (a)'s restriction on a candidate's personal expenditures is unconstitutional.

* * *

No governmental interest that has been suggested is sufficient to justify the restriction on the quantity of political expression imposed by § 608 (c)'s campaign expenditure limitations.

* * *

There is no indication that the substantial criminal penalties for violating the contribution ceilings combined with the political repercussion of such violations will be insufficient to police the contribution provisions. Extensive reporting, auditing, and disclosure requirements applicable to both contributions and expenditures by political campaigns are designed to facilitate the detection of illegal contributions. Moreover, as the Court of Appeals noted, the Act permits an officeholder or successful candidate to retain contributions in excess of the expenditure ceiling and to use these funds for "any other lawful purpose." This provision undercuts whatever marginal role the expenditure limitations might otherwise play in enforcing the contribution ceilings.

The interest in equalizing the financial resources of candidates competing for federal office is no more convincing a justification for restricting the scope of federal election campaigns. Given the limitation on the size of outside contributions, the financial resources available to a candidate's campaign, like the number of volunteers recruited, will normally vary with the size and intensity of the candidate's support. There is nothing invidious, improper, or unhealthy in permitting such funds to be spent to carry the candidate's message to the electorate. Moreover, the equalization of permissible campaign expenditures might serve not to equalize the opportunities of all candidates, but to handicap a candidate who lacked substantial name recognition or exposure of his views before the start of the campaign.

... The First Amendment denies government the power to determine that spending to promote one's political views is wasteful, excessive, or unwise. In the free society ordained by our Constitution it is not the government, but the people—individually as citizens and candidates and collectively as associations and political committees—who must retain control over the quantity and range of debate on public issues in a political campaign.

MR. JUSTICE WHITE, concurring in part and dissenting in part.

... I dissent from the Court's view that the expenditure limitations of 18 U. S. C. §§ 608 (c) and (e) (1970 ed., Supp. IV) violate the First Amendment.

Concededly, neither the limitations on contributions nor those on expenditures directly or indirectly purport to control the content of political speech by candidates or by their supporters or detractors. What the Act regulates is giving and spending money, acts that have First Amendment significance not because they are themselves communicative with respect to the qualifications of the candidate, but because money may be used to defray the expenses of speaking or otherwise communicating about the merits or demerits of federal candidates for election. The act of giving money to political candidates, however, may have illegal or other undesirable consequences: it may be used to secure the express or tacit understanding that the giver will enjoy political favor if the candidate is elected. Both Congress and this Court's cases have recognized this as a mortal danger against which effective preventive and curative steps must be taken.

Since the contribution and expenditure limitations are neutral as to the content of speech and are not motivated by fear of the consequences of the political speech of particular candidates or of political speech in general, this case depends on whether the nonspeech interests of the Federal Government in regulating the use of money in political campaigns are sufficiently urgent to justify the incidental effects that the limitations visit upon the First Amendment interests of candidates and their supporters.

... As it should be unnecessary to point out, money is not always equivalent to or used for speech, even in the context of political campaigns. I accept the reality that communicating with potential voters is the heart of an election campaign and that widespread communication has become very expensive. There are, however, many expensive campaign activities that are not themselves communicative or remotely related to speech. Furthermore, campaigns differ among themselves. Some seem to spend much less money than others and yet communicate as much as or more than those supported by enormous bureaucracies with unlimited financing. The record before us no more supports the conclusion that the communicative efforts of congressional and Presidential candidates will be crippled by the expenditure limitations than it supports the contrary. The judgment of Congress was that reasonably effective campaigns could be conducted within the limits established by the Act and that the communicative efforts of these campaigns would not seriously suffer. In this posture of the case, there is no sound basis for invalidating the expenditure limitations, so long as the purposes they serve are legitimate and sufficiently substantial, which in my view they are. . . .

The ceiling on candidate expenditures represents the considered judgment of Congress that elections are to be decided among candidates none of whom has overpowering advantage by reason of a huge campaign war chest. At least so long as the ceiling placed upon the candidates is not plainly too low, elections are not to turn on the difference in the amounts of money that candidates have to spend. This seems an acceptable purpose and the means chosen a commonsense way to achieve it. The Court nevertheless holds that a candidate has a constitutional right to spend unlimited amounts of money, mostly that of other people, in order to be elected. The holding perhaps is not that federal candidates have the constitutional right to purchase their election, but many will so interpret the Court's conclusion in this case. I cannot join the Court in this respect.

I also disagree with the Court's judgment that § 608 (a), which limits the amount of money that a candidate or his family may spend on his campaign, violates the Constitution. Although it is true that this provision does not promote any interest in preventing the corruption of candidates, the provision does, nevertheless, serve salutary purposes related to the integrity of federal campaigns. By limiting the importance of personal wealth, § 608 (a) helps to assure that only individuals with a modicum of support from others will be viable candidates. This in turn would tend to discourage any notion that the outcome of elections is primarily a function of money. Similarly, § 608 (a) tends to equalize access to the political arena, encouraging the less wealthy, unable to bankroll their own campaigns, to run for political office.

As with the campaign expenditure limits, Congress was entitled to determine that personal wealth ought to play a less important role in political campaigns than it has in the past. Nothing in the First Amendment stands in the way of that determination.

Abood, et al. v. Detroit Board of Education

431 U.S. 209; 97 S. Ct. 1782; 52 L. Ed. 2d 261 (1977)
Vote: 9–0

Louis Abood and Christine Warczak were teachers in the Detroit public schools. The Detroit Federation of Teachers (a labor union) was the sole representative of teachers in the Detroit school system. As such, it entered into a labor contract with the Detroit Board of Education. One provision of the contract was a so-called agency shop clause. Under the clause, teachers were not required to be union members. However, nonmembers were required to pay a "service charge" equal to regular union dues. Refusal to pay the service charge was grounds for dismissal.

Warczak and Abood filed a complaint against the Board of Education in a state court. The complaint alleged that the union was engaged in various social, political, and religious activities with which they did not agree. Being forced to support financially such activities, the complainants argued, is a violation of First and Fourteenth Amendment rights of association. Having been denied relief at all levels of the Michigan court system, the teachers asked for and received Supreme Court review.

MR. JUSTICE STEWART delivered the opinion of the Court.

The designation of a union as exclusive representative carries with it great responsibilities. The tasks of negotiating and administering a collective-bargaining agreement and representing the interests of employees in settling disputes and processing grievances are continuing and difficult ones. They often entail expenditure of much time and money. The services of lawyers, expert negotiators, economists, and a research staff, as well as general administrative personnel, may be required. Moreover, in carrying out these duties, the union is obliged "fairly and equitably to represent all employees . . . , union and non-union," within the relevant unit [*Machinists v. Street* (1961)]. A union shop arrangement has been thought to distribute fairly the cost of these activities among those who benefit, and it counteracts the incentive that employees might otherwise have to become "free riders"—to refuse to contribute to the union while obtaining benefits of union representation that necessarily accrue to all employees. . . .

To compel employees financially to support their collective-bargaining representative has an impact upon their First Amendment interests. An employee may very well have ideological objections to a wide variety of activities undertaken by the union in its role as exclusive representative. His moral or religious views about the desirability of abortion may not square with the union's policy in negotiating a medical benefits plan. One individual might disagree with a union policy of negotiating limits on the right to strike, believing that to be the road to serfdom for the working class, while another might have economic or political objections to unionism itself. An employee might object to the union's wage policy because it violates guidelines designed to limit inflation, or might object to the union's seeking a clause in the collective-bargaining agreement proscribing racial discrimination. The examples could be multiplied. To be required to help finance the union as a collective-bargaining agent might well be thought, therefore, to interfere in some way with an employee's freedom to associate for the advancement of ideas, or to refrain from doing so, as he sees fit. But the judgment clearly made in [*Railway Employees Dept. v. Hanson* and in *Street*] . . . is that such interference as exists is constitutionally justified by the legislative assessment of the important contribution of the union shop to the system of labor relations established by Congress. "The furtherance of the common cause leaves some leeway for the leadership of the group. As long as they act to promote the cause which justified bringing the group together, the individual cannot withdraw his financial support merely because he disagrees with the group's strategy. If that were allowed, we would be reversing the *Hanson* case, *sub silentio*." *Machinists v. Street,* at 778 (Douglas, J., concurring).

. . . The governmental interests advanced by the agency-shop provision in the Michigan statute are much the same as those promoted by similar provisions in federal labor law. The confusion and conflict that could arise if rival teachers' unions, holding quite different views as to the proper class hours, class sizes, holidays, tenure provisions, and grievance procedures, each sought to obtain the employer's agreement, are no different in kind from the evils that the exclusivity rule in the Railway Labor Act was designed to avoid.

The desirability of labor peace is no less important in the public sector, nor is the risk of "free riders" any smaller.

Our province is not to judge the wisdom of Michigan's decision to authorize the agency shop in public employment. Rather, it is to adjudicate the constitutionality of that decision. The same important government interests recognized in the *Hanson* and *Street* cases presumptively support the impingement upon associational freedom created by the agency shop here at issue. Thus, insofar as the service charge is used to finance expenditures by the Union for the purposes of collective bargaining, contract administration, and grievance adjustment, those two decisions of this Court appear to require validation of the agency-shop agreement before us.

While recognizing the apparent precedential weight of the *Hanson* and *Street* cases, the appellants advance two reasons why those decisions should not control decision of the present case. First, the appellants note that it is *government employment* that is involved here, thus directly implicating constitutional guarantees, in contrast to the private employment that was the subject of the *Hanson* and *Street* decisions. Second, the appellants say that in the public sector collective bargaining itself is inherently "political," and that to require them to give financial support to it is to require the "ideological conformity" that the Court expressly found absent in the *Hanson* case. We find neither argument persuasive.

Because it is employment by the State that is here involved, the appellants suggest that this case is governed by a long line of decisions holding that public employment cannot be conditioned upon the surrender of First Amendment rights. But, while the actions of public employers surely constitute "state action," the union shop, as authorized by the Railway Labor Act, also was found to result from governmental action in *Hanson.* The plaintiffs' claims in

Hanson failed, not because there was no governmental action, but because there was no First Amendment violation. The appellants' reliance on the "unconstitutional conditions" doctrine is therefore misplaced.

The appellants' second argument is that in any event collective bargaining in the public sector is inherently "political" and thus requires a different result under the First and Fourteenth Amendments. This contention rests upon the important and often-noted differences in the nature of collective bargaining in the public and private sectors. A public employer, unlike his private counterpart, is not guided by the profit motive and constrained by the normal operation of the market. Municipal services are typically not priced, and where they are they tend to be regarded as in some sense "essential" and therefore are often price-inelastic. Although a public employer, like a private one, will wish to keep costs down, he lacks an important discipline against agreeing to increases in labor costs that in a market system would require price increases. A public-sector union is correspondingly less concerned that high prices due to costly wage demands will decrease output and hence employment.

The government officials making decisions as the public "employer" are less likely to act as a cohesive unit than are managers in private industry, in part because different levels of public authority—department managers, budgetary officials, and legislative bodies—are involved, and in part because each official may respond to a distinctive political constituency. And the case of negotiating a final agreement with the union may be severely limited by statutory restrictions, by the need for the approval of a higher executive authority or a legislative body, or by the commitment of budgetary decisions of critical importance to others.

Finally, decisionmaking by a public employer is above all a political process. The officials who represent the public employer are ultimately responsible to the electorate, which for this purpose can be viewed as comprising three overlapping classes of voters—taxpayers, users of particular government services, and government employees. Through exercise of their political influence as part of the electorate, the employees have the opportunity to affect the decisions of government representatives who sit on the other side of the bargaining table. Whether these representatives accede to a union's demands will depend upon a blend of political ingredients, including community sentiment about unionism generally and the involved union in particular, the degree of taxpayer resistance, and the views of voters as to the importance of the service involved and the relation between the demands and the quality of service. It is surely arguable, however, that permitting public employees to unionize and a union to bargain as their exclusive representative gives the employees more influence in the decisionmaking process than is possessed by employees similarly organized in the private sector. . . .

There can be no quarrel with the truism that because public employee unions attempt to influence governmental policymaking, their activities—and the views of members who disagree with them—may be properly termed political. But that characterization does not raise the ideas and beliefs of public employees onto a higher plane than the ideas and beliefs of private employees. It is no doubt true that a central purpose of the First Amendment " 'was to protect the free discussion of governmental affairs.' " *Buckley v. Valeo,* [at] 14, and *Mills v. Alabama,* [at] 218. But our cases have never suggested that expression about philosophical, social, artistic, economic, literary, or ethical matters—to take a nonexhaustive list of labels—is not entitled to full First Amendment protection. Union members in both the public and private sectors may find that a variety of union activities conflict with their beliefs.

. . . Nothing in the First Amendment or our cases discussing its meaning makes the question whether the adjective "political" can properly be attached to those beliefs the critical constitutional inquiry.

The differences between public- and private-sector collective bargaining simply do not translate into differences in First Amendment rights. Even those commentators most acutely aware of the distinctive nature of public-sector bargaining and most seriously concerned with its policy implications agree that "[t]he union security issue in the public sector . . . is fundamentally the same issue . . . as in the private sector. . . . No special dimension results from the fact that a union represents public rather than private employees." H. Wellington & R. Winter, Jr., The Unions and the Cities 95–96 (1971). We conclude that the Michigan Court of Appeals was correct in viewing this Court's decisions in *Hanson* and *Street* as controlling in the present case insofar as the service charges are applied to collective-bargaining, contract administration, and grievance-adjustment purposes.

. . . Our decisions establish with unmistakable clarity that the freedom of an individual to associate for the purpose of advancing beliefs and ideas is protected by the First and Fourteenth Amendments. . . . Equally clear is the proposition that a government may not require an individual to relinquish rights guaranteed him by the First Amendment as a condition of public employment. The appellants argue that they fall within the protection of these cases because they have been prohibited, not from actively associating, but rather from refusing to associate. They specifically argue that they may constitutionally prevent the Union's spending a part of their required service fees to contribute to political candidates and to express political views unrelated to its duties as exclusive bargaining representative. We have concluded that this argument is a meritorious one. . . .

The fact that the appellants are compelled to make, rather than prohibited from making, contributions for political purposes works no less an infringement of their constitutional rights. For at the heart of the First Amendment is the notion that an individual should be free to believe as he will, and that in a free society one's beliefs should be shaped by his mind and his conscience rather than coerced by the State. . . .

We do not hold that a union cannot constitutionally spend funds for the expression of political views, on behalf of political candidates, or toward the advancement of other ideological causes not germane to its duties as collective-bargaining representative. Rather, the Constitution requires only that such expenditures be financed from charges, dues, or assessments paid by employees who do not object to advancing those ideas and who are not coerced into doing so against their will by the threat of loss of governmental employment.

. . . The judgment is vacated, and the case is remanded for further proceedings not inconsistent with this opinion.

It is so ordered.

QUESTIONS AND COMMENTS

1 On the basis of your reading of *Buckley,* could a state constitutionally put limits on the amount a corporation can spend to support one side of an issue in a local referendum? See *First National Bank of Boston v. Bellotti,* 435 U.S. 765 (1978). Could a state forbid public utilities to enclose statements describing their position on social or political issues with the monthly bills mailed to their customers? See *Consolidated Edison Co. v. New York Public Service Commission,* 447 U.S. 530 (1980).

2 Does the Court's decision in *Buckley* now make it possible for a candidate to "buy" an election? Explain.

3 Could Section 608 (e) (1) be redrafted in such a way as to meet the Court's objections? If so, how would it be phrased?

4 If the Court had considered the national interest in equalizing the ability of candidates for high political office to communicate, presumably the tangential encroachments on First Amendment rights would have been permitted. Why is the Court's view that the national interest in equalization is insubstantial any better than Justice White's view to the contrary?

5 In *PruneYard Shopping Center v. Robins,* the Court approved the use of private property to promote social views which the shopping center's owners and tenants might oppose—saying, in effect, that the objectors could divorce themselves from such views by posting signs, etc. The use of the property, posting of signs, and similar measures would seem to impose a cost on the shopping center in order to allow the promotion of views to which it might be opposed. In *Abood,* the Court says that one cannot be forced to pay to support social and political views to which one does not subscribe. Are these two cases compatible? Explain your answer.

6 In a recent case involving political expression, the Court struck down a Washington, D.C., ordinance prohibiting the distribution of leaflets and the carrying of signs on the sidewalks surrounding the Supreme Court building [*United States v. Grace,* 51 LW 4444 (1983)].

Rights of the Press

New York Times v. United States (1971)

Bigelow v. Virginia (1975)

Gannett v. Pasquale (1979)

Richmond Newspapers v. Virginia (1980)

New York Times v. Sullivan (1964)

Although the freedom of the press is mentioned specifically in the First Amendment, it is obviously only one aspect of free speech. For freedom of speech has been interpreted to mean freedom of expression in its many and variegated forms. The right to a free press is the right to publish one's thoughts, opinions, arguments, etc., without first getting permission to do so from governmental authority. Such permission was required under English law and has come to be known as "prior restraint" or "censorship."

The early standard regarding prior restraint of publication is developed in *Near v. Minnesota.*[7] In that case a five-member majority of the Court held that Minnesota's "gag law" was unconstitutional. This law allowed the state to permanently enjoin a newspaper from publishing a malicious, scandalous, and defamatory newspaper in the future, once a court had found the paper guilty of such publications in the past. The *Saturday Press* published a series of articles charging, among other things, that "a Jewish gangster was in control of gambling, bootlegging and racketeering in Minneapolis, and that law enforcing officers and agencies were not energetically performing their duties."[8] A permanent injunction against the future publication of such material was then obtained in Minnesota courts.

Noting that in order to avoid a contempt citation in the future, the paper would have to clear all articles in advance with a Minnesota judge, the United States Supreme Court reversed. Observing that state police power does not extend so far, the Court held that the chief purpose of the protection given the press in the First Amendment is to prevent prior restraints upon publication. Even if a publication will cause actionable damage to individuals or groups in the community, or even if the publication will violate a criminal law, it cannot be subjected to prior restraint. None of this is to say, however, that those who publish are not responsible for their acts. It only suggests that they are called to answer for their deed *after the fact.*

In subsequent cases, we find many references to prior restraint, not as an absolute principle, but as a principle which the Court is reluctant to violate. The statement usually encountered is that all prior restraints bear a heavy presumption against their constitutional validity. Thus, a state has been barred from (1) enjoining the distribution of a pamphlet accusing a real estate broker of block-busting,[9] (2) barring the showing of "nudie" movies in drive-ins that can be seen from the street,[10] and (3) barring the media from reporting testimony from public hearings.[11] None of this, however, means that restraints are never permissible. In *Young v. American Mini Theatres,*[12] the Court approved a zoning ordinance prohibiting "adult" theaters within 500 feet of a residential area on the ground that no "impermissible" prior restraint was involved. And in *Near,* the Court suggested that prior restraint on the publication of military information was not in violation of the Constitution. In *New York Times v. United States,* we are not dealing with military information strictly defined. But national security was stressed by the government in its attempt to justify a prior restraint on publication.

New York Times v. United States

403 U.S. 713; 91 S. Ct. 2140; 29 L. Ed. 2d 822 (1971)
Vote: 6–3

This is the famous Pentagon Papers Case. It began on a Sunday when the *New York Times* published several pages of a secret Pentagon study of United States involvement in Vietnam. The study had been given to the *Times* by Daniel Ellsberg, as a protest or an expression of his dissatisfaction over the Vietnam conflict and United States policy regarding the conflict. On Monday, the *Times* refused a request from the government to refrain from further publication of the papers. President Nixon revealed after he left office that a major reason for the government's objection was to protect certain intelligence activities. One of these activities was the planting of a "bug" in an automobile used by the leader of the Soviet Union, Leonid Brezhnev. According to Nixon, some information revealed in the Pentagon Papers could only have come from Brezhnev's automobile.

In any event, the day after the *Time's* refusal, the government persuaded a federal judge to enjoin further publication of the papers. Four days later the injunction was rescinded by the same judge but was restored by a court of appeals. The Supreme Court granted certiorari at the request of the newspaper.

PER CURIAM.

We granted certiorari in these cases in which the United States seeks to enjoin the New York Times and the Washington Post from publishing the contents of a classified study entitled "History of U.S. Decision-Making Process on Viet Nam Policy." . . . "Any system of prior restraints of expression comes to this Court bearing a heavy presumption against its constitutional validity." *Bantam Books, Inc. v. Sullivan,* (1963), . . . see also *Near v. Minnesota,* (1931). . . . The Government "thus carries a heavy burden of showing justification for the imposition of such a restraint." *Organization for a Better Austin v.*

Keefe, (1971), . . . The District Court for the Southern District of New York in the *New York Times* case and the District Court for the District of Columbia and the Court of Appeals for the District of Columbia Circuit in the *Washington Post* case held that the Government had not met that burden. We agree.

The judgment of the Court of Appeals for the District of Columbia Circuit is therefore affirmed. The order of the Court of Appeals for the Second Circuit is reversed and the case is remanded with directions to enter a judgment affirming the judgment of the District Court for the Southern District of New York. The stays entered June 25, 1971, by the Court are vacated. The judgments shall issue forthwith.

So ordered.

MR. JUSTICE BLACK, with whom MR. JUSTICE DOUGLAS joins, concurring. . . .

I adhere to the view that the Government's case against the Washington Post should have been dismissed and that the injunction against the New York Times should have been vacated without oral argument when the cases were first presented to this Court. I believe that every moment's continuance of the injunctions against these newspapers amounts to a flagrant, indefensible, and continuing violation of the First Amendment. Furthermore, after oral argument, I agree completely that we must affirm the judgment of the Court of Appeals for the District of Columbia Circuit and reverse the judgment of the Court of Appeals for the Second Circuit for the reasons stated by my Brothers DOUGLAS and BRENNAN. In my view it is unfortunate that some of my Brethren are apparently willing to hold that the publication of news may sometimes be enjoined. Such a holding would make a shambles of the First Amendment. . . .

In the First Amendment the Founding Fathers gave the free press the protection it must have to fulfill its essential role in our democracy. The press was to serve the governed, not the governors. The Government's power to censor the press was abolished so that the press would remain forever free to censure the Government. The press was protected so that it could bare the secrets of government and inform the people. Only a free and unrestrained press can effectively expose deception in government. And paramount among the responsibilities of a free press is the duty to prevent any part of the government from deceiving the people and sending them off to distant lands to die of foreign fevers and foreign shot and shell. In my view, far from deserving condemnation for their courageous reporting the New York Times, the Washington Post, and other newspapers should be commended for serving the purpose that the Founding Fathers saw so clearly. In revealing the workings of government that led to the Vietnam war, the newspapers nobly did precisely that which the Founders hoped and trusted they would do.

. . . To find that the President has "inherent power" to halt the publication of news by resort to the courts would wipe out the First Amendment and destroy the fundamental liberty and security of the very people the Government hopes to make "secure." No one can read the history of the adoption of the First Amendment without being convinced beyond any doubt that it was injunctions like those sought here that Madison and his collaborators intended to outlaw in this Nation for all time. . . .

MR. JUSTICE DOUGLAS, with whom Mr. Justice Black joins, concurring.

While I join the opinion of the Court I believe it necessary to express my views more fully.

It should be noted at the outset that the First Amendment provides that "Congress shall make no law . . . abridging the freedom of speech or of the press." That leaves, in my view, no room for governmental restraint on the press.

There is, moreover, no statute barring the publication by the press of the material which the Times and the Post seek to use. . . .

So any power that the Government possesses must come from its "inherent power."

The power to wage war is "the power to wage war successfully." See *Hirabayashi v. United States,* [1943], . . . But the war power stems from a declaration of war. The Constitution by Art. I, § 8, gives Congress, not the President, power "[t]o declare War." Nowhere are presidential wars authorized. We need not decide therefore what leveling effect the war power of Congress might have.

These disclosures may have a serious impact. But that is no basis for sanctioning a previous restraint on the press. . . .

As we stated only the other day in *Organization for a Better Austin v. Keefe,* [1971] . . . "[a]ny prior restraint on expression comes to this Court with a 'heavy presumption' against its constitutional validity."

The Government says that it has inherent powers to go into court and obtain an injunction to protect the national interest, which in this case is alleged to be national security.

Near v. Minnesota, . . . repudiated that expansive doctrine in no uncertain terms.

The dominant purpose of the First Amendment was to prohibit the widespread practice of governmental suppression of embarrassing information. It is common knowledge that the First Amendment was adopted against the widespread use of the common law of seditious libel to punish the dissemination of material that is embarrassing to the powers-that-be. . . . The present cases will, I think, go down in history as the most dramatic illustration of that principle. A debate of large proportions goes on in the Nation over our posture in Vietnam. That debate antedated the disclosure of the contents of the present documents. The latter are highly relevant to the debate in progress.

Secrecy in government is fundamentally anti-democratic, perpetuating bureaucratic errors. Open debate and discussion of public issues are vital to our national health. On public questions there should be "uninhibited, robust, and wide-open" debate. *New York Times Co. v. Sullivan,* [1964], . . .

I would affirm the judgment of the Court of Appeals in the *Post* case, vacate the stay of the Court of Appeals in the *Times* case and direct that it affirm the District Court.

The stays in these cases that have been in effect for more than a week constitute a flouting of the principles of the First Amendment as interpreted in *Near v. Minnesota.*

Mr. Justice Brennan, concurring.

I write separately in these cases only to emphasize what should be apparent: that our judgments in the present cases may not be taken to indicate the propriety, in the future, of issuing temporary stays and restraining orders to block the publication of material sought to be suppressed by the Government.

. . . the First Amendment tolerates absolutely no prior judicial restraints of the press predicated upon surmise or conjecture that untoward consequences may result. Our cases, it is true, have indicated that there is a single, extremely narrow class of cases in which the First Amendment's ban on prior judicial restraint may be overridden. Our cases have thus far indicated that such cases may arise only when the Nation "is at war," *Schenck v. United States,* (1919), during which times "[n]o one would question but that a government might prevent actual obstruction to its recruiting service or the publication of the sailing dates of transports or the number and location of troops." *Near v. Minnesota. . . .* Thus, only governmental allegation and proof that publication must inevitably, directly, and immediately cause the occurrence of an event kindred to imperiling the safety of a transport already at sea can support even the issuance of an interim restraining order. In no event may mere conclusions be sufficient: for if the Executive Branch seeks judicial aid in preventing publication, it must inevitably submit the basis upon which that aid is sought to scrutiny by the judiciary. . . . Unless and until the Government has clearly made out its case, the First Amendment commands that no injunction may issue.

Mr Justice Stewart, with whom Mr. Justice White joins, concurring.

In the governmental structure created by our Constitution, the Executive is endowed with enormous power in the two related areas of national defense and international relations. This power, largely unchecked by the Legislative and Judicial branches, has been pressed to the very hilt since the advent of the nuclear missile age. For better or for worse, the simple fact is that a President of the United States possesses vastly greater constitutional independence in these two vital areas of power than does, say, a prime minister of a country with a parliamentary form of government.

In the absence of the governmental checks and balances present in other areas of our national life, the only effective restraint upon executive policy and power in the areas of national defense and international affairs may lie in an enlightened citizenry—in an informed and critical public opinion which alone can here protect the values of democratic government. For this reason, it is perhaps here that a press that is alert, aware, and free most vitally serves the basic purpose of the First Amendment. For without an informed and free press there cannot be an enlightened people.

Yet it is elementary that the successful conduct of international diplomacy and the maintenance of an effective national defense require both confidentiality and secrecy. Other nations can hardly deal with this Nation in an atmosphere of mutual trust unless they can be assured that their confidences will be kept. And within our own executive departments, the development of considered and intelligent international policies would be impossible if those charged with their formulation could not communicate with each other freely, frankly, and in confidence. In the area of basic national defense the frequent need for absolute secrecy is, of course, self-evident.

I think there can be but one answer to this dilemma, if dilemma it be. The responsibility must be where the power is. If the Constitution gives the Executive a large degree of unshared power in the conduct of foreign affairs and the maintenance of our national defense, then under the Constitution the Executive must have the largely unshared duty to determine and preserve the degree of internal security necessary to exercise that power successfully. . . .

But in the cases before us we are asked neither to construe specific regulations nor to apply specific laws. We are asked, instead, to perform a function that the Constitution gave to the Executive, not the Judiciary. We are asked, quite simply, to prevent the publication by two newspapers of material that the Executive Branch insists should not, in the national interest, be published. I am convinced that the Executive is correct with respect to some of the documents involved. But I cannot say that disclosure of any of them will surely result in direct, immediate, and irreparable damage to our Nation or its people. That being so, there can under the First Amendment be but one judicial resolution of the issues before us. I join the judgments of the Court.

Mr. Justice White, with whom Mr. Justice Stewart joins, concurring.

I concur in today's judgments, but only because of the concededly extraordinary protection against prior restraints enjoyed by the press under our constitutional system. I do not say that in no circumstances would the First Amendment permit an injunction against publishing information about government plans or operations. Nor, after examining the materials the Government characterizes as the most sensitive and destructive, can I deny that revelation of these documents will do substantial damage to public interests. Indeed, I am confident that their disclosure will have that result. But I nevertheless agree that the United States has not satisfied the very heavy burden that it must meet to warrant an injunction against publication in these cases, at least in the absence of express and appropriately limited congressional authorization for prior restraints in circumstances such as these.

The Government's position is simply stated: The responsibility of the Executive for the conduct of the foreign affairs and for the security of the Nation is so basic that the President is entitled to an injunction against publication of a newspaper story whenever he can convince a court that the information to be revealed threatens "grave and irreparable" injury to the public interest; and the injunction should issue whether or not the material to be published is classified, whether or not publication would be lawful under relevant criminal statutes enacted by Congress, and regardless of the circumstances by which the newspaper came into possession of the information.

At least in the absence of legislation by Congress, based on its own investigations and findings, I am quite unable to agree that the inherent powers of the Executive and the courts reach so far as to authorize remedies having such sweeping potential for inhibiting publications by the press. . . .

What is more, terminating the ban on publication of the relatively few sensitive documents the Government now seeks to suppress does not mean that the law either requires or invites newspapers or others to publish them or that they will be immune from criminal action if they do. Prior restraints require an unusually heavy justification under the First Amendment; but failure by the Government to justify prior restraints does not measure its constitutional entitlement to a conviction for criminal publication. That the Government mistakenly chose to proceed by injunction does not mean that it could not successfully proceed in another way.

When the Espionage Act was under consideration in 1917, Congress eliminated from the bill a provision that would have given the President broad powers in time of war to proscribe, under threat of criminal penalty, the publication of various categories of information related to the national defense. Congress at that time was unwilling to clothe the President with such far-reaching powers to monitor the press, and those opposed to this part of the legislation assumed that a necessary concomitant of such power was the power to "filter out the news to the people through some man.". . .

The Criminal Code contains numerous provisions potentially relevant to these cases. Section 797 makes it a crime to publish certain photographs or drawings of military installations. Section 798, also in precise language, proscribes knowing and willful publication of any classified information concerning the cryptographic systems or communication intelligence activities of the United States as well as any information obtained from communication intelligence operations. If any of the material here at issue is of this nature, the newspapers are presumably now on full notice of the position of the United States and must face the consequences if they publish. I would have no difficulty in sustaining convictions under these sections on facts that would not justify the intervention of equity and the imposition of a prior restraint. . . . [Congress] has not, however, authorized the injunctive remedy against threatened publication. It has apparently been satisfied to rely on criminal sanctions and their deterrent effect on the responsible as well as the irresponsible press. I am not, of course, saying that either of these newspapers has yet committed a crime or that either would commit a crime if it published all the material now in its possession. That matter must await resolution in the context of a criminal proceeding if one is instituted by the United States. In that event, the issue of guilt or innocence would be determined by procedures and standards quite different from those that have purported to govern these injunctive proceedings.

MR. JUSTICE MARSHALL, concurring.

The problem here is whether in these particular cases the Executive Branch has authority to invoke the equity jurisdiction of the courts to protect what it believes to be the national interest. . . .

The Government argues that in addition to the inherent power of any government to protect itself, the President's power to conduct foreign affairs and his position as Commander in Chief give him authority to impose censorship on the press to protect his ability to deal effectively with foreign nations and to conduct the military affairs of the country. Of course, it is beyond cavil that the President has broad powers by virtue of his primary responsibility for the conduct of our foreign affairs and his position as Commander in Chief. . . . And in some situations it may be that under whatever inherent powers the Government may have, as well as the implicit authority derived from the President's mandate to conduct foreign affairs and to act as Commander in Chief, there is a basis for the invocation of the equity jurisdiction of this Court as an aid to prevent the publication of material damaging to "national security," however that term may be defined.

It would, however, be utterly inconsistent with the concept of separation of powers for this Court to use its power of contempt to prevent behavior that Congress has specifically declined to prohibit. There would be a similar damage to the basic concept of these co-equal branches of Government if when the Executive Branch has adequate authority granted by Congress to protect "national security" it can choose instead to invoke the contempt power of a court to enjoin the threatened conduct. The Constitution provides that Congress shall make laws, the President execute laws, and courts interpret laws. *Youngstown Sheet & Tube Co. v. Sawyer,* [1952], . . .

It did not provide for government by injunction in which the courts and the Executive Branch can "make law" without regard to the action of Congress. It may be more convenient for the Executive Branch if it need only convince a judge to prohibit conduct rather than ask the Congress to pass a law, and it may be more convenient to enforce a contempt order than to seek a criminal conviction in a jury trial. Moreover, it may be considered politically wise to get a court to share the responsibility for arresting those who the Executive Branch has probable cause to believe are violating the law. But convenience and political considerations of the moment do not justify a basic departure from the principles of our system of government. . . .

MR. CHIEF JUSTICE BURGER, dissenting. . . .

Only those who view the First Amendment as an absolute in all circumstances—a view I respect, but reject—can find such cases as these to be simple or easy.

These cases are not simple for another and more immediate reason. We do not know the facts of the cases. No District Judge knew all the facts. No Court of Appeals judge knew all the facts. No member of this court knows all the facts.

Why are we in this posture, in which only those judges to whom the First Amendment is absolute and permits of no restraint in any circumstances or for any reason, are really in a position to act?

I suggest we are in this posture because these cases have been conducted in unseemly haste. MR. JUSTICE HARLAN covers the chronology of events demonstrating the hectic pressures under which these cases have been processed and I need not restate them. The prompt setting of these cases reflects our universal abhorrence of prior restraint. But prompt judicial action does not mean unjudicial haste.

Here, moreover, the frenetic haste is due in large part to the manner in which the Times proceeded from the date it obtained the purloined documents. It seems reasonably clear now that the haste precluded reasonable and deliberate judicial treatment of these cases and was not warranted. The precipitate action of this Court aborting trials not yet completed is not the kind of judicial conduct that ought to attend the disposition of a great issue.

The newspapers make a derivative claim under the First Amendment; they denominate this right as the public "right to know"; by implication, the Times asserts a sole trusteeship of that right by virtue of its journalistic "scoop." The right is asserted as an absolute. Of course, the First Amendment right itself is not an absolute, as Justice Holmes so long ago pointed out in his aphorism concerning the right to shout "fire" in a crowded theater if there was no fire. There are other exceptions, some of which Chief Justice Hughes mentioned by way of example in *Near v. Minnesota*. There are no doubt other exceptions no one has had occasion to describe or discuss. Conceivably such exceptions may be lurking in these cases and would have been flushed had they been properly considered in the trial courts, free from unwarranted deadlines and frenetic pressures. An issue of this importance should be tried and heard in a judicial atmosphere conducive to thoughtful, reflective deliberation, especially when haste, in terms of hours, is unwarranted in light of the long period the Times, by its own choice, deferred publication. . . .

The consequence of all this melancholy series of events is that we literally do not know what we are acting on. As I see it, we have been forced to deal with litigation concerning rights of great magnitude without an adequate record, and surely without time for adequate treatment either in the prior proceedings or in this Court. It is interesting to note that counsel on both sides, in oral argument before this Court, were frequently unable to respond to questions on factual points. Not surprisingly they pointed out that they had been working literally "around the clock" and simply were unable to review the documents that give rise to these cases and were not familiar with them. This Court is in no better posture. I agree generally with MR. JUSTICE HARLAN and MR. JUSTICE BLACKMUN but I am not prepared to reach the merits.

I would affirm the Court of Appeals for the Second Circuit and allow the District Court to complete the trial aborted by our grant of certiorari, meanwhile preserving the status quo in the *Post* case. I would direct that the District Court on remand give priority to the *Times* case to the exclusion of all other business of that court but I would not set arbitrary deadlines. . . .

We all crave speedier judicial processes but when judges are pressured as in these cases the result is a parody of the judicial function.

MR. JUSTICE HARLAN, with whom THE CHIEF JUSTICE and MR. JUSTICE BLACKMUN join, dissenting. . . . With all respect, I consider that the Court has been almost irresponsibly feverish in dealing with these cases. . . .

Forced as I am to reach the merits of these cases, I dissent from the opinion and judgments of the Court. Within the severe limitations imposed by the time constraints under which I have been required to operate, I can only state my reasons in telescoped form, even though in different circumstances I would have felt constrained to deal with the cases in the fuller sweep indicated above.

It is a sufficient basis for affirming the Court of Appeals for the Second Circuit in the *Times* litigation to observe that its order must rest on the conclusion that because of the time elements the Government had not been given an adequate opportunity to present its case to the District Court. At the least this conclusion was not an abuse of discretion. . . .

It is plain to me that the scope of the judicial function in passing upon the activities of the Executive Branch of the Government in the field of foreign affairs is very narrowly restricted. This view is, I think, dictated by the concept of separation of powers upon which our constitutional system rests.

In a speech on the floor of the House of Representatives, Chief Justice John Marshall, then a member of that body, stated:

> The President is the sole organ of the nation in its external relations, and its sole representative with foreign nations. . . .

From that time, shortly after the founding of the Nation, to this, there has been no substantial challenge to this description of the scope of executive power. See *United States v. Curtiss-Wright Corp.,* [1936], . . .

From this constitutional primacy in the field of foreign affairs, it seems to me that certain conclusions necessarily follow. Some of these were stated concisely by President Washington, declining the request of the House of Representatives for the papers leading up to the negotiation of the Jay Treaty:

> The nature of foreign negotiations requires caution, and their success must often depend on secrecy; and even when brought to a conclusion a full disclosure of all the measures, demands, or eventual concessions which may have been proposed or contemplated would be extremely impolitic; for this might have a pernicious influence on future negotiations, or produce immediate inconveniences, perhaps danger and mischief, in relation to other powers. . . .

The power to evaluate the "pernicious influence" of premature disclosure is not, however, lodged in the Executive alone. I agree that, in performance of its duty to protect the values of the First Amendment against political pressures, the judiciary must review the initial Executive determination to the point of satisfying itself that the subject matter of the dispute does lie within the proper compass of the President's foreign relations power. Constitutional considerations forbid "a complete abandonment of judicial control.". . .

Even if there is some room for the judiciary to override the executive determination, it is plain that the scope of review must be exceedingly narrow. I can see no indication in the opinions of either the District Court or the Court of Appeals in the *Post* litigation that the conclusions of the Executive were given even the deference owing to an administrative agency, much less that owing to a co-equal branch of the Government operating within the field of its constitutional prerogative.

Accordingly, I would vacate the judgment of the Court of Appeals for the District of Columbia Circuit on this ground and remand the case for further proceedings in the District Court. Before the commencement of such further proceedings, due opportunity should be afforded the Government for procuring from the Secretary of State or the Secretary of Defense or both an expression of their views on the issue of national security. The ensuing review by the District Court should be in accordance with the views expressed in this opinion. And for the reasons stated above I would affirm the judgment of the Court of Appeals for the Second Circuit.

Pending further hearings in each case conducted under the appropriate ground rules, I would continue the restraints on publication. I cannot believe that the doctrine prohibiting prior restraints reaches to the point of preventing courts from maintaining the *status quo* long enough to act responsibly in matters of such national importance as those involved here.

MR. JUSTICE BLACKMUN, dissenting.

The First Amendment, after all, is only one part of an entire Constitution. Article II of the great document vests in the Executive Branch primary power over the conduct of foreign affairs and places in that branch the responsibility for the Nation's safety. Each provision of the Constitution is important, and I cannot subscribe to a doctrine of unlimited absolutism for the First Amendment at the cost of downgrading other provisions. First Amendment absolutism has never commanded a majority of this Court. . . .

What is needed here is a weighing, upon properly developed standards, of the broad right of the press to print and of the very narrow right of the Government to prevent. Such standards are not yet developed. The parties here are in disagreement as to what those standards should be. But even the newspapers concede that there are situations where restraint is in order and is constitutional. Mr. Justice Holmes gave us a suggestion when he said in *Schenck,*

It is a question of proximity and degree. When a nation is at war many things that might be said in time of peace are such a hindrance to its effort that their utterance will not be endured so long as men fight and that no Court could regard them as protected by any constitutional right.

I therefore would remand these cases to be developed expeditiously, of course, but on a schedule permitting the orderly presentation of evidence from both sides, with the use of discovery, if necessary, as authorized by the rules, and with the preparation of briefs, oral argument, and court opinions of a quality better than has been seen to this point. In making this last statement, I criticize no lawyer or judge. I know from past personal experience the agony of time pressure in the preparation of litigation. But these cases and the issues involved and the courts, including this one, deserve better than has been produced thus far.

QUESTIONS AND COMMENTS

1 In the Pentagon Papers Case, does the Court utilize the clear and present danger test or the balancing test? Explain your answer.
2 In October 1983, a CBS television station proposed to televise a tape of a drug transaction involving John Z. DeLorean. The tape was thought to be part of the evidence to be used by the government in its prosecution of DeLorean. DeLorean's attorney and government prosecutors asked the ninth-circuit court of appeals to enjoin the showing of the tape, arguing that after such showing it would be impossible to find an impartial jury anywhere in the country. Under the doctrine of prior restraint, how should the Court have ruled on this request?
3 In October 1983, United States military forces invaded the Caribbean nation of Grenada. For several days after the invasion, representatives of the news media were not permitted in Grenada. Was this prior restraint?
4 Whatever the outcome of challenges to prior restraints, the Supreme Court has emphasized that such challenged acts must be quickly reviewed in the courts [*Philadelphia Newspapers v. Jerome,* 434 U.S. 241 (1978)].

* * * * * *

Although the First Amendment does not deny freedom to commercial speech or publication, it appears that commercial publication has somewhat less protection than noncommercial expression.[13] In *Bigelow v. Virginia,* the question is not merely commercial expression but commercial advertising, one form of such expression. Prior to *Bigelow,* the Court had held that a city may ban sex-differentiated employment advertising in a newspaper.[14]

Bigelow v. Virginia

421 U.S. 809; 95 S. Ct. 2222; 44 L. Ed. 2d 600 (1975)
Vote: 7–2

The facts are given in the opinion that follows.

MR. JUSTICE BLACKMUN delivered the opinion of the Court. . . .

The Virginia Weekly was a newspaper published by the Virginia Weekly Associates of Charlottesville. It was issued in that city and circulated in Albemarle County, with particular focus on the campus of the University of Virginia. Appellant, Jeffrey C. Bigelow, was a director and the managing editor and responsible officer of the newspaper.

On February 8, 1971, the Weekly's Vol. V, No. 6, was published and circulated under the direct responsibility of the appellant. On page 2 of that issue was the following advertisement:

UNWANTED PREGNANCY
LET US HELP YOU
Abortions are now legal in New York.
There are no residency requirements.
FOR IMMEDIATE PLACEMENT IN ACCREDITED
HOSPITALS AND CLINICS AT LOW COST
Contact
WOMEN'S PAVILION
515 Madison Avenue
New York, N.Y. 10022
or call any time
(212) 371–6670 or (212) 371–6650
AVAILABLE 7 DAYS A WEEK
STRICTLY CONFIDENTIAL. We will make
all arrangements for you and help you
with information and counseling.

It is to be observed that the advertisement announced that the Women's Pavilion of New York City would help women with unwanted pregnancies to obtain "immediate placement in accredited hospitals and clinics at low cost" and would "make all arrangements" on a "strictly confidential" basis; that it offered "information and counseling"; that it gave the organization's address and telephone numbers; and that it stated that abortions "are now legal in New York" and there "are no residency requirements." Although the advertisement did not contain the name of any licensed physician, the "placement" to which it referred was to "accredited hospitals and clinics."

On May 13 Bigelow was charged with violating Va. Code Ann. § 18.1–63 (1960). The statute at that time read:

> If any person, by publication, lecture, advertisement, or by the sale or circulation of any publication, or in any other manner, encourage or prompt the procuring of abortion or miscarriage, he shall be guilty of a misdemeanor.

Shortly after the statute was utilized in Bigelow's case, and apparently before it was ever used again, the Virginia Legislature amended it and changed its prior application and scope.

Appellant was first tried and convicted in the County Court of Albermarle County. He appealed to the Circuit Court of that county where he was entitled to a *de novo* trial. . . . In the Circuit Court he waived a jury and in July 1971 was tried to the judge. The evidence consisted of stipulated facts; an excerpt, containing the advertisement in question, from the Weekly's issue of February 8, 1971; and the June 1971 issue of Redbook magazine, containing abortion information and distributed in Virginia and in Albemarle County. The court rejected appellant's claim that the statute was unconstitutional and adjudged him guilty. He was sentenced to pay a fine of $500, with $350 thereof suspended "conditioned upon no further violation" of the statute. . . .

The Supreme Court of Virginia granted review and, by a 4–2 vote, affirmed Bigelow's conviction.

. . . The court first rejected the appellant's claim that the advertisement was purely informational and thus was not within the "encourage or prompt" language of the statute. It held, instead, that the advertisement "clearly exceeded an informational status" and "constituted an active offer to perform a service, rather than a passive statement of fact."

. . . It then rejected Bigelow's First Amendment claim. This, the court said, was a "commercial advertisement" and, as such, "may be constitutionally prohibited by the state," particularly "where, as here, the advertising relates to the medical-health field." . . . The issue, in the court's view, was whether the statute was a valid exercise of the State's police power. It answered this question in the affirmative, noting that the statute's goal was "to ensure that pregnant women in Virginia who decided to have abortions come to their decisions without the commercial advertising pressure usually incidental to the sale of a box of soap powder." . . .

Bigelow took a timely appeal to this Court. During the pendency of his appeal, *Roe v. Wade,* (1973), and *Doe v. Bolton,* (1973), were decided. We subsequently vacated Bigelow's judgment of conviction and remanded the case for further consideration in the light of *Roe* and *Doe.*

The Supreme Court of Virginia, on such reconsideration, but without further oral argument, again affirmed appellant's conviction, observing that neither *Roe* nor *Doe* "mentioned the subject of abortion advertising," . . . finding nothing in those decisions "which in any way affects our earlier view."

Once again, Bigelow appealed. We noted probable jurisdiction in order to review the important First Amendment issue presented. . . .

The central assumption made by the Supreme Court of Virginia was that the First Amendment guarantees of speech and press are inapplicable to paid commercial advertisements. Our cases, however, clearly establish that speech is not stripped of First Amendment protection merely because it appears in that form.

The fact that the particular advertisement in appellant's newspaper had commercial aspects or reflected the advertiser's commercial interests did not negate all First Amendment guarantees. The State was not free of constitutional restraint merely because the advertisement involved sales or "solicitations," *Murdock v. Pennsylvania,* (1943), or because appellant was paid for printing it, or because appellant's motive or the motive of the advertiser may have involved financial gain, *Thomas v. Collins,* (1945). The existence of "commercial activity, in itself, is no justification for narrowing the protection of expression secured by the First Amendment." *Ginzburg v. United States,* (1966).

Although other categories of speech—such as fighting words, or obscenity, or libel, or incitement—have been held unprotected, no contention has been made that the particular speech embraced in the advertisement in question is within any of these categories. . . .

Viewed in its entirety, the advertisement conveyed information of potential interest and value to a diverse audience—not only to readers possibly in need of the services offered, but also to those with a general curiosity about, or genuine interest in, the subject matter or the law of another State and its development, and to readers seeking reform in Virginia. The mere existence of the Women's Pavilion in New York City, with the possibility of its being typical of other organizations there, and the availability of the services offered, were not unnewsworthy. Also, the activity advertised pertained to constitutional interests.

. . . Thus, in this case, appellant's First Amendment interests coincided with the constitutional interests of the general public.

Moreover, the placement services advertised in appellant's newspaper were legally provided in New York at that time. The Virginia Legislature could not have regulated the advertiser's activity in New York, and obviously could not have proscribed the activity in that State. . . . Neither could Virginia prevent its residents from traveling to New York to obtain those services or, as the State conceded, prosecute them for going there. . . . Virginia possessed no authority to regulate the services provided in New York—the skills and credentials of the New York physicians and of the New York professionals who assisted them, the standards of the New York hospitals and clinics to which patients were referred, or the pratices and charges of the New York referral services.

A State does not acquire power or supervision over the internal affairs of another State merely because the welfare and health of its own citizens may be affected when they travel to that State. It may seek to disseminate information so as to enable its citizens to make better informed decisions when they leave. But it may not, under the guise of exercising internal police powers, bar a citizen of another State from disseminating information about an activity that is legal in that State.

We conclude, therefore, that the Virginia courts erred in their assumptions that advertising, as such, was entitled to no First Amendment protection and that appellant Bigelow had no legitimate First Amendment interest. We need not decide in this case the precise extent to which the First Amendment permits regulation of advertising that is related to activities the State may legitimately regulate or even prohibit.

We conclude that Virginia could not apply Va. Code Ann. § 18.1–63 (1960), as it read in 1971, to appellant's publication of the advertisement in question without unconstitutionally infringing upon his First Amendment rights. The judgment of the Supreme Court of Virginia is therefore reversed.

It is so ordered.

MR. JUSTICE REHNQUIST, with whom MR. JUSTICE WHITE joins, dissenting. . . .

As a threshold matter the advertisement appears to me, as it did to the courts below, to be a classic commercial proposition directed toward the exchange of services rather than the exchange of ideas. It was apparently also so interpreted by the newspaper which published it which stated in apparent apology in its following issue that the " '*Weekly* collective has since learned that this abortion agency . . . as well as a number of other commercial groups are charging women a fee for a service which is done free by Women's Liberation, Planned Parenthood, and others.' " Whatever slight factual content the advertisement may contain and whatever expression of opinion may be laboriously drawn from it does not alter its predominantly commercial content. . . .

Assuming *arguendo* that this advertisement is something more than a normal commercial proposal, I am unable to see why Virginia does not have a legitimate public interest in its regulation. The Court apparently concedes, and our cases have long held, that the States have a strong interest in the prevention of commercial advertising in the health field—both in order to maintain high ethical standards in the medical profession and to protect the public from unscrupulous practices. . . .

Without denying the power of either New York or Virginia to prohibit advertising such as that in issue where both publication of the advertised activity and the activity itself occur in the same State, the Court instead focuses on the multistate nature of this transaction, concluding that a State "may not, under the guise of exercising internal police powers, bar a citizen of another State from disseminating information about an activity that is legal in that State.". . .

Were the Court's statements taken literally, they would presage a standard of the lowest common denominator for commercial ethics and business conduct. Securities issuers could circumvent the established blue-sky laws of States which had carefully drawn such laws for the protection of their citizens by establishing as a situs for transactions those States without such regulations, while spreading offers throughout the country. Loan sharks might well choose States with unregulated small loan industries, luring the unwary with immune commercial advertisements. And imagination would place the only limit on the use of such a "no-man's land" together with artificially created territorial contacts to bilk the public and circumvent long-established state schemes of regulation. . . .

Since the statute in question is a "reasonable regulation that serves a legitimate public interest." I would affirm the judgment of the Supreme Court of Virginia.

QUESTIONS AND COMMENTS

1 Why should commercial expression be differentiated from noncommercial expression insofar as freedom of the press is concerned?

2 If we grant constitutional protection to commercial advertising, are we likely to enhance the dissemination of falsehood? How can we protect ourselves against such a possibility without violating the First Amendment?

3 In *Bigelow,* the Court noted that the advertisements had a noncommercial as well as a commercial content. In *Virginia State Board of Pharmacy v. Virginia Citizen's Consumer Council,* 425 U.S. 748 (1976), the Court, in effect, abandoned the distinction and held that the mere proposing of a commercial transaction is protected. Cf. *Bates v. State Bar of Arizona,* 433 U.S. 350 (1950), upholding advertising by lawyers as a First Amendment right.

* * * * * *

The last two cases in this section deal with the rights of the press when those rights come in conflict with one or more other constitutional rights. The right to fair trial is sometimes used by judges as a basis for denying public access to criminal trials or restricting access to trials or pretrial proceedings and to records. In the two cases which follow, the restrictions were protested by newspaper reporters, who tend to have a strong dislike for any procedure which increases the difficulty of acquiring and reporting the news. At the same time, it must be recognized that members of the press do not base their objections only on grounds of inconvenience. Indeed, they have argued for years that the public has a "right to know" and that reporters are representatives of the public—i.e., the agents with the responsibility of making that right meaningful.

A question implicitly raised by such an argument is whether, if the argument is conceded, news reporters have the same or greater rights of access to judicial proceedings than the public at large. Assuming that reporters have the rights of access claimed, we must still determine whether those rights are absolute. The short answer is that no First Amendment rights are absolute. A balancing of individual and group interests against social interests frequently precedes the settlement of conflict between individuals and governmental authority. But the balancing becomes more complex when the right of a criminal defendant to a fair trial conflicts, in the mind of the judge, with the public's right to know.

Gannett Co., Inc. v. DePasquale, County Court Judge of Seneca County, N.Y. et al.

443 U.S. 368; 99 S. Ct. 2898; 61 L. Ed. 2d 608 (1979)
Vote: 5–4

Wayne Clapp, a 42-year-old resident of Rochester, New York, disappeared on July 16, 1976. Clapp had gone fishing with two male companions in Seneca Lake, 40 miles from Rochester. On the same day, the companions returned without Clapp and drove away in Clapp's pickup truck. On July 19, the police were notified. When the fishing boat used by the three men was examined, it was found to be laced with bulletholes. A search of the lake was then undertaken.

On July 20, two Gannett newspapers ran their first stories on the Clapp case. The next day, police apprehended two males, Greathouse and Jones, in Michigan. On July 25, Greathouse and Jones were arraigned before a Seneca County magistrate on second-degree murder charges. They, and a woman arrested with them, were also arraigned on charges of second-degree grand larceny. The two men were indicted on August 2 for murder, robbery, and grand larceny. The woman was indicted on a single count of grand larceny. At this time, Clapp's body had not been found. At arraignment in the trial court on August 5, Greathouse and Jones entered pleas of not guilty to all charges. Attorneys for the two men were given ninety days to file retrial motions.

On November 4, a hearing was held before Judge DePasquale to suppress statements made to the police by the defendants as well as the gun to which Greathouse had led the Michigan police. At the hearing, defense attorneys, noting the buildup of adverse publicity due to press coverage over the

preceding three months, requested that the public and press be excluded
from the hearing. The request was granted without objection. The next day,
Carol Ritter, a Gannett reporter, wrote Judge DePasquale a letter asking that
she be given access to the transcript of the hearing. In response, the judge
said the hearing had ended and that a decision on release of the transcript
had been postponed. Gannett then moved the court to set aside its
exclusionary order.

At a hearing on Gannett's motion, the judge noted that no representative
of Gannett had objected to the closure motion at the time it was made. He
went on to concede that the press had a constitutional right to access. But,
balancing that right against the right of the defendants to a fair trial,
DePasquale refused to vacate his exclusion order or grant Gannett
immediate access to a transcript of the pretrial hearing.

The next day Gannett filed suit in the supreme court of New York,
challenging the judge's decisions on First, Sixth, and Fourteenth Amendment
grounds. On December 16, 1976, that court found the exclusionary orders to
be in violation of the First and Fourteenth Amendments and, accordingly,
vacated the orders. After the New York court of appeals reversed, the United
States Supreme Court granted certiorari.

Mr. Justice Stewart delivered the opinion of the Court.

The question presented in this case is whether members of the public have
an independent constitutional right to insist upon access to a pretrial judicial
proceeding, even though the accused, the prosecutor, and the trial judge all
have agreed to the closure of that proceeding in order to assure a fair trial.

* * *

While the Sixth Amendment guarantees to a defendant in a criminal case the
right to a public trial, it does not guarantee the right to compel a private trial.
"The ability to waive a constitutional right does not ordinarily carry with it
the right to insist upon the opposite of that right." *Singer v. United States,* 380
U.S. 24, 34–35. But the issue here is not whether the defendant can compel a
private trial. Rather, the issue is whether members of the public have an
enforceable right to a public trial that can be asserted independently of the
parties in the litigation.

There can be no blinking the fact that there is a strong societal interest in
public trials. Openness in court proceedings may improve the quality of testimony, induce unknown witnesses to come forward with relevant testimony,
cause all trial participants to perform their duties more conscientiously, and
generally give the public an opportunity to observe the judicial system. . . . But
there is a strong societal interest in other constitutional guarantees extended to
the accused as well. The public, for example, has a definite and concrete interest in seeing that justice is swiftly and fairly administered. . . . Similarly, the

public has an interest in having a criminal case heard by a jury, an interest distinct from the defendant's interest in being tried by a jury of his peers.

Recognition of an independent public interest in the enforcement of Sixth Amendment guarantees is a far cry, however, from the creation of a constitutional right on the part of the public. In an adversary system of criminal justice, the public interest in the administration of justice is protected by the participants in the litigation. Thus, because of the great public interest in jury trials as the preferred mode of fact-finding in criminal cases, a defendant cannot waive a jury trial without the consent of the prosecutor and judge.

But if the defendant waives his right to a jury trial, and the prosecutor and the judge consent, it could hardly be seriously argued that a member of the public could demand a jury trial because of the societal interest in that mode of fact-finding. Similarly, while a defendant cannot convert his right to a speedy trial into a right to compel an indefinite postponement, a member of the general public surely has no right to prevent a continuance in order to vindicate the public interest in the efficient administration of justice. In short, our adversary system of criminal justice is premised upon the proposition that the public interest is fully protected by the participants in the litigation.

* * *

But even if the Sixth and Fourteenth Amendments could properly be viewed as embodying the common-law right of the public to attend criminal trials, it would not necessarily follow that the petitioner would have a right of access under the circumstances of this case. For there exists no persuasive evidence that at common law members of the public had any right to attend pretrial proceedings; indeed, there is substantial evidence to the contrary. By the time of the adoption of the Constitution, public trials were clearly associated with the protection of the defendant. And pretrial proceedings, precisely because of the same concern for a fair trial, were never characterized by the same degree of openness as were actual trials.

The petitioner also argues that members of the press and the public have a right of access to the pretrial hearing by reason of the First and Fourteenth Amendments. In *Pell v. Procunier, Saxbe v. Washington Post Co.,* and *Houchins v. KQED, Inc.,* this Court upheld prison regulations that denied to members of the press access to prisons superior to that afforded to the public generally. Some Members of the Court, however, took the position in those cases that the First and Fourteenth Amendments do guarantee to the public in general, or the press in particular, a right of access that precludes their complete exclusion in the absence of a significant governmental interest.

The petitioner in this case urges us to narrow our rulings in *Pell, Saxbe,* and *Houchins* at least to the extent of recognizing a First and Fourteenth Amendment right to attend criminal trials. We need not decide in the abstract, however, whether there is any such constitutional right. For even assuming, *arguendo,* that the First and Fourteenth Amendments may guarantee such access in some situations, a question we do not decide, this putative right was given all appropriate deference by the state *nisi prius* court in the present case.

Several factors lead to the conclusion that the actions of the trial judge here were consistent with any right of access the petitioner may have had under the First and Fourteenth Amendments. First, none of the spectators present in the courtroom, including the reporter employed by the petitioner, objected when the defendants made the closure motion. Despite this failure to make a contemporaneous objection, counsel for the petitioner was given an opportunity to be heard at a proceeding where he was allowed to voice the petitioner's objections to closure of the pretrial hearing. At this proceeding, which took place after the filing of briefs, the trial court balanced the "constitutional rights of the press and the public" against the "defendants' right to a fair trial." The trial judge concluded after making this appraisal that the press and the public could be excluded from the suppression hearing and could be denied immediate access to a transcript, because an open proceeding would pose a "reasonable probability of prejudice to these defendants." Thus, the trial court found that the representatives of the press did have a right of access of constitutional dimension, but held, under the circumstances of this case, that this right was outweighed by the defendants' right to a fair trial. In short, the closure decision was based "on an assessment of the competing societal interests involved . . . rather than on any determination that First Amendment freedoms were not implicated." *Saxbe, supra,* at 860 (POWELL, J., dissenting).

Furthermore, any denial of access in this case was not absolute but only temporary. Once the danger of prejudice had dissipated, a transcript of the suppression hearing was made available. The press and the public then had a full opportunity to scrutinize the suppression hearing. Unlike the case of an absolute ban on access, therefore, the press here had the opportunity to inform the public of the details of the pretrial hearing accurately and completely. Under these circumstances, any First and Fourteenth Amendment right of the petitioner to attend a criminal trial was not violated.

We certainly do not disparage the general desirability of open judicial proceedings. But we are not asked here to declare whether open proceedings represent beneficial social policy, or whether there would be a constitutional barrier to a state law that imposed a stricter standard of closure than the one here employed by the New York courts. Rather, we are asked to hold that the Constitution itself gave the petitioner an affirmative right of access to this pretrial proceeding, even though all the participants in the litigation agreed that it should be closed to protect the fair-trial rights of the defendants.

For all of the reasons discussed in this opinion, we hold that the Constitution provides no such right. Accordingly, the judgment of the New York Court of Appeals is affirmed.

It is so ordered.

MR. JUSTICE BLACKMUN, with whom MR. JUSTICE BRENNAN, MR. JUSTICE WHITE, and MR. JUSTICE MARSHALL join, concurring in part and dissenting in part. . . .

Open trials enable the public to scrutinize the performance of police and prosecutors in the conduct of public judicial business. Trials and particularly suppression hearings typically involve questions concerning the propriety of police and government conduct that took place hidden from the public view. Any interest on the part of the prosecution in hiding police or prosecutorial misconduct or ineptitude may coincide with the defendant's desire to keep the proceedings private, with the result that the public interest is sacrificed from both sides.

Public judicial proceedings have an important educative role as well. The victim of the crime, the family of the victim, others who have suffered similarly, or others accused of like crimes, have an interest in observing the course of a prosecution. Beyond this, however, is the interest of the general public in observing the operation of the criminal justice system. Judges, prosecutors, and police officials often are elected or are subject to some control by elected officials, and a main source of information about how these officials perform is the open trial. And the manner in which criminal justice is administered in this country is in and of itself of interest to all citizens. In *Cox Broadcasting Corp. v. Cohn,* . . . it was noted that information about the criminal justice system "appears to us to be of critical importance to our type of government in which the citizenry is the final judge of the proper conduct of public business."

Important in this regard, of course, is the appearance of justice. "Secret hearings—though they be scrupulously fair in reality—are suspect by nature. Public confidence cannot long be maintained where important judicial decisions are made behind closed doors and then announced in conclusive terms to the public, with the record supporting the court's decision sealed from public view." *United States v. Cianfrani,* (CA3 1978). The ability of the courts to administer the criminal laws depends in no small part on the confidence of the public in judicial remedies, and on respect for and acquaintance with the processes and deliberations of those courts. Anything that impairs the open nature of judicial proceedings threatens to undermine this confidence and to impede the ability of the courts to function.

These societal values secured by the public trial are fundamental to the system of justice on both the state and federal levels. As such, they have been recognized by the large majority of both state and federal courts that have considered the issue over the years since the adoption of the Constitution. Indeed, in those States with constitutional provisions modeled on the Sixth Amendment, guaranteeing the right to a public trial literally only to the accused, there has been widespread recognition that such provisions serve the interests of the public as well as those of the defendant.

I therefore conclude that the Due Process Clause of the Fourteenth Amendment, insofar as it incorporates the public-trial provision of the Sixth Amendment, prohibits the States from excluding the public from a proceeding within the ambit of the Sixth Amendment's guarantee without affording full and fair consideration to the public's interests in maintaining an open proceeding. And I believe that the Sixth and Fourteenth Amendments require this conclusion notwithstanding the fact it is the accused who seeks to close the trial. . . .

Before considering whether and under what circumstances a court may conduct a criminal proceeding in private, one must first decide whether the Sixth Amendment, as applied through the Fourteenth, encompasses the type of pretrial hearing contemplated by *Jackson v. Denno,* (1964), and at issue in this case. The Amendment, of course, speaks only of a public "trial." Both the County Court and the New York Court of Appeals emphasized that exclusion from the formal trial on the merits was not at issue, apparently in the belief that the Sixth Amendment's public-trial provision applies with less force, or not at all, to a pretrial proceeding.

I find good reason to hold that even if a State, as it may, chooses to hold a *Jackson v. Denno* or other suppression hearing separate from and prior to the full trial, the Sixth Amendment's public-trial provision applies to that hearing. First, the suppression hearing resembles and relates to the full trial in almost every particular. Evidence is presented by means of live testimony, witnesses are sworn, and those witnesses are subject to cross-examination. Determination of the ultimate issue depends in most cases upon the trier of fact's evaluation of the evidence, and credibility is often crucial. Each side has incentive to prevail, with the result that the role of publicity as a testimonial safeguard, as a mechanism to encourage the parties, the witnesses, and the court to a strict conscientiousness in the performance of their duties, and in providing a means whereby unknown witnesses may become known, are just as important for the suppression hearing as they are for the full trial.

Moreover, the pretrial suppression hearing often is critical, and it may be decisive, in the prosecution of a criminal case. If the defendant prevails, he will have dealt the prosecution's case a serious, perhaps fatal, blow; the proceeding often then will be dismissed or negotiated on terms favorable to the defense. If the prosecution successfully resists the motion to suppress, the defendant may have little hope of success at trial (especially where a confession is in issue), with the result that the likelihood of a guilty plea is substantially increased.

The suppression hearing often is the only judicial proceeding of substantial importance that takes place during a criminal prosecution. In this very case, the hearing from which the public was excluded was the only one in which the important factual and legal issues in the prosecution of respondents Greathouse and Jones were considered. It was the only proceeding at which the conduct of the police, prosecution, and the court itself was exposed to scrutiny.

Indeed, in 1976, when this case was processed, every felony prosecution in Seneca County—and I say this without criticism—was terminated without a trial in the merits. This statistic is characteristic of our state and federal criminal justice systems as a whole, and it underscores the importance of the suppression hearing in the functioning of those systems.

Further, the issues considered at such hearings are of great moment beyond their importance to the outcome of a particular prosecution. A motion to suppress typically involves, as in this case, allegations of misconduct by police and prosecution that raise constitutional issues. Allegations of this kind, although they may prove to be unfounded, are of importance to the public as well as to the defendant. The searches and interrogations that such hearings evaluate do not take place in public. The hearing therefore usually presents the only opportunity the public has to learn about police and prosecutorial conduct, and about allegations that those responsible to the public for the enforcement of laws themselves are breaking it.

A decision to suppress often involves the exclusion of highly relevant evidence. Because this is so, the decision may generate controversy. It is important that any such decision be made on the basis of evidence and argument offered in open court, so that all who care to see or read about the case may evaluate for themselves the propriety of the exclusion.

These factors lead me to conclude that a pretrial suppression hearing is the close equivalent of the trial on the merits for purposes of applying the public-trial provision of the Sixth Amendment. Unlike almost any other proceeding apart from the trial itself, the suppression hearing implicates all the policies that require that the trial be public. For this reason, I would be loath to hold that a State could conduct a pretrial *Jackson v. Denno* hearing in private over the *objection* of the defendant. And for this same reason, the public's interest in the openness of judicial proceedings is implicated fully when it is the accused who seeks to exclude the public from such a hearing. Accordingly, I conclude that the Sixth and Fourteenth Amendments prohibit a State from conducting a pretrial suppression hearing in private, even at the request of the accused, unless full and fair consideration is first given to the public's interest, protected by the Amendments, in open trials.

Richmond Newspapers Inc. et al. v. Virginia et al.
448 U.S. 555; 100 S. Ct. 2814; 65 L. Ed. 2d 973 (1980)
Vote: 7–1

In March 1976, one Stevenson was indicted for the stabbing murder of a hotel manager on December 2, 1975. After one reversal of a conviction and two mistrials, a fourth trial of Stevenson began on September 11, 1978. On that day two reporters from Richmond Newspapers, Inc., were present in court. On the motion of the defense attorneys, the trial judge, without objection from the prosecution, ordered that the "courtroom be kept clear of all parties except the witnesses when they appear." No objection to this order was made by the newspaper reporters at that time. Later that day Richmond Newspapers sought to have the judge's ruling vacated. A hearing on the motion the next day was treated as part of the trial, and the newspaper reporters were again excluded.

At the hearing, the counsel for the newspapers argued that the Constitution required that before ordering closure, consideration must be given to protecting the defendant's rights in some other way. The judge expressed the view that "having people in the courtroom is distracting to the jury" and apparently agreed with the defense counsel that closure was necessary to prevent possibly inaccurate news accounts of the trial proceedings to reach members of the jury. Subsequently, he declined to vacate the closure order. In the closed trial, the jury was excused for technical reasons and the judge found the defendant not guilty. After Richmond Newspapers had failed to get Virginia appellate courts to vacate the closure order, the U.S. Supreme Court granted certiorari.

MR. CHIEF JUSTICE BURGER announced the judgment of the Court and delivered an opinion, in which MR. JUSTICE WHITE and MR. JUSTICE STEVENS joined. . . .

The First Amendment, in conjunction with the Fourteenth, prohibits governments from "abridging the freedom of speech, or of the press; or the right of the people peaceably to assemble, and to petition the Government for a redress of grievances." These expressly guaranteed freedoms share a common core purpose of assuring freedom of communication on matters relating to the functioning of government. Plainly it would be difficult to single out any aspect of government of higher concern and importance to the people than the manner in which criminal trials are conducted.

The Bill of Rights was enacted against the backdrop of the long history of trials being presumptively open. Public access to trials was then regarded as an important aspect of the process itself; the conduct of trials "before as many of the people as chuse to attend" was regarded as one of "the inestimable advantages of a free English constitution of government." 1 Journals 106, 107. In guaranteeing freedoms such as those of speech and press, the First Amendment can be read as protecting the right of everyone to attend trials so as to give meaning to those explicit guarantees. "[T]he First Amendment goes beyond protection of the press and the self-expression of individuals to prohibit government from limiting the stock of information from which members of the public may draw." *First National Bank of Boston v. Belotti,* (1978). Free speech carries with it some freedom to listen. "In a variety of contexts this Court has referred to a First Amendment right to 'receive information and ideas.'" *Klein-*

dienst v. Mandel, (1972). What this means in the context of trials is that the First Amendment guarantees of speech and press, standing alone, prohibit government from summarily closing courtroom doors which had long been open to the public at the time that Amendment was adopted. "For the First Amendment does not speak equivocally. . . . It must be taken as a command of the broadest scope that explicit language, read in the context of a liberty-loving society, will allow." *Bridges v. California,* (1941). . .

It is not crucial whether we describe this right to attend criminal trials to hear, see, and communicate observations concerning them as a "right of access," cf. *Gannett, supra,* at 397 (POWELL, J., concurring); or a "right to gather information," for we have recognized that "without some protection for seeking out the news, freedom of the press could be eviscerated." *Branzburg v. Hayes,* (1972). The explicit, guaranteed rights to speak and to publish concerning what takes place at a trial would lose much meaning if access to observe the trial could, as it was here, be foreclosed arbitrarily.

The right of access to places traditionally open to the public, as criminal trials have long been, may be seen as assured by the amalgam of the First Amendment guarantees of speech and press: and their affinity to the right of assembly is not without relevance. From the outset, the right of assembly was regarded not only as an independent right but also as a catalyst to augment the free exercise of the other First Amendment rights with which it was deliberately linked by the draftsmen.

"The right of peaceable assembly is a right cognate to those of free speech and free press and is equally fundamental." *De Jonge v. Oregon,* (1937). People assemble in public places not only to speak or to take action, but also to listen, observe, and learn; indeed, they may "assembl[e] for any lawful purpose," *Hague v. CIO,* (1939) (opinion of Stone, J.). Subject to the traditional time, place, and manner restrictions, streets, sidewalks, and parks are places traditionally open, where First Amendment rights may be exercised, a trial courtroom also is a public place where the people generally—and representatives of the media—have a right to be present, and where their presence historically has been thought to enhance the integrity and quality of what takes place.

The State argues that the Constitution nowhere spells out a guarantee for the right of the public to attend trials, and that accordingly no such right is protected.

But arguments such as the State makes have not precluded recognition of important rights not enumerated. Notwithstanding the appropriate caution against reading into the Constitution rights not explicitly defined, the Court has acknowledged that certain unarticulated rights are implicit in enumerated guarantees. For example, the rights of association and of privacy, the right to be presumed innocent, and the right to be judged by a standard of proof beyond a reasonable doubt in a criminal trial, as well as the right to travel, appear nowhere in the Constitution or Bill of Rights. Yet these important but unarticulated rights have nonetheless been found to share constitutional protection in common with explicit guarantees. The concerns expressed by Madison and others have thus been resolved; fundamental rights, even though not expressly guaranteed, have been recognized by the Court as indispensable to the enjoyment of rights explicitly defined.

We hold that the right to attend criminal trials is implicit in the guarantees of the First Amendment; without the freedom to attend such trials, which people have exercised for centuries, important aspects of freedom of speech and "of the press could be eviscerated." *Branzburg,* 408 U. S., at 681.

Having concluded there was a guaranteed right of the public under the First and Fourteenth Amendments to attend the trial of Stevenson's case, we return to the closure order challenged by appellants. The Court in *Gannett* made clear that although the Sixth Amendment guarantees the accused a right to a public trial, it does not give a right to a private trial. Despite the fact that this was the fourth trial of the accused, the trial judge made no findings to support closure; no inquiry was made as to whether alternative solutions would have met the need to ensure fairness; there was no recognition of any right under the Constitution for the public or press to attend the trial. In contrast to the pretrial proceeding dealt with in *Gannett,* there exist in the context of the trial itself various tested alternatives to satisfy the constitutional demands of fairness.

There was no suggestion that any problems with witnesses could not have been dealt with by their exclusion from the courtroom or their sequestration during the trial. . . . Nor is there anything to indicate that sequestration of the jurors would not have guarded against their being subjected to any improper information. All of the alternatives admittedly present difficulties for trial courts, but none of the factors relied on here was beyond the realm of the manageable. Absent an overriding interest articulated in findings, the trial of a criminal case must be open to the public. Accordingly, the judgment under review is

Reversed.

* * *

Mr. Justice Brennan, with whom Mr. Justice Marshall joins, concurring in the judgment. . . .

Publicity serves to advance several of the particular purposes of the trial (and, indeed, the judicial) process. Open trials play a fundamental role in furthering the efforts of our judicial system to assure the criminal defendant a fair and accurate adjudication of guilt or innocence. But, as a feature of our governing system of justice, the trial process serves other, broadly political, interests, and public access advances these objectives as well. To that extent, trial access possesses specific structural significance.

The trial is a means of meeting "the notion, deeply rooted in the common law, that 'justice must satisfy the appearance of justice.'" *Offutt v. United States,* (1954). For a civilization founded upon principles of ordered liberty to survive and flourish, its members must share the conviction that they are governed equitably. That necessity underlies constitutional provisions as diverse as the rule against takings without just compensation, and the Equal Protection Clause. It also mandates a system of justice that demonstrates the fairness of the law to our citizens. One major function of the trial, hedged with procedural protections and conducted with conspicuous respect for the rule of law, is to make that demonstration.

Secrecy is profoundly inimical to this demonstrative purpose of the trial process. Open trials assure the public that procedural rights are respected, and that justice is afforded equally. Closed trials breed suspicion of prejudice and arbitrariness, which in turn spawns disrespect for law. Public access is essential, therefore, if trial adjudication is to achieve the objective of maintaining public confidence in the administration of justice. . . .

But the trial is more than a demonstrably just method of adjudicating disputes and protecting rights. It plays a pivotal role in the entire judicial process, and, by extension, in our form of government. Under our system, judges are not mere umpires, but, in their own sphere, lawmakers—a coordinate branch of *government.* While individual cases turn upon the controversies between parties, or involve particular prosecutions, court rulings impose official and practical consequences upon members of society at large. Moreover, judges bear responsibility for the vitally important task of construing and securing constitutional rights. Thus, so far as the trial is the mechanism for judicial fact-finding, as well as the initial forum for legal decisionmaking, it is a genuine governmental proceeding.

It follows that the conduct of the trial is pre-eminently a matter of public interest. More importantly, public access to trials acts as an important check, akin in purpose to the other checks and balances that infuse our system of government. "The knowledge that every criminal trial is subject to contemporaneous review in the forum of public opinion is an effective restraint on possible abuse of judicial power," *In re Oliver,*—an abuse that, in many cases, would have ramifications beyond the impact upon the parties before the court. Indeed, " '[w]ithout publicity, all other checks are insufficient: in comparison of publicity, all other checks are of small account.' "

MR. JUSTICE STEWART, concurring in the judgment. . . .

In conspicuous contrast to a military base, a jail, or a prison, a trial courtroom is a public place. Even more than city streets, sidewalks, and parks as areas of traditional First Amendment activity, a trial courtroom is a place where representatives of the press and of the public are not only free to be, but where their presence serves to assure the integrity of what goes on.

But this does not mean that the First Amendment right of members of the public and representatives of the press to attend civil and criminal trials is absolute. Just as a legislature may impose reasonable time, place, and manner restrictions upon the exercise of First Amendment freedoms, so may a trial judge impose reasonable limitations upon the unrestricted occupation of a courtroom by representatives of the press and members of the public. Much more than a city street, a trial courtroom must be a quiet and orderly place. Moreover, every courtroom has a finite physical capacity, and there may be occasions when not all who wish to attend a trial may do so. And while there exist many alternative ways to satisfy the constitutional demands of a fair trial, those demands may also sometimes justify limitations upon the unrestricted presence of spectators in the courtroom.

Since in the present case the trial judge appears to have given no recognition to the right of representatives of the press and members of the public to be present at the Virginia murder trial over which he was presiding, the judgment under review must be reversed.

It is upon the basis of these principles that I concur in the judgment.

Mr. Justice Blackmun, concurring in the judgment.

My opinion and vote in partial dissent last Term in *Gannett Co. v. DePasquale,* (1979), compels my vote to reverse the judgment of the Supreme Court of Virginia. . . .

The Court's ultimate ruling in *Gannett,* with such clarification as is provided by the opinions in this case today, apparently is now to the effect that there is no *Sixth* Amendment right on the part of the public—or the press—to an open hearing on a motion to suppress. I, of course, continue to believe that *Gannett* was in error, both in its interpretation of the Sixth Amendment generally, and in its application to the suppression hearing, for I remain convinced that the right to a public trial is to be found where the Constitution explicitly placed it—in the Sixth Amendment.

The Court, however, has eschewed the Sixth Amendment route. The plurality turns to other possible constitutional sources and invokes a veritable potpourri of them—the Speech Clause of the First Amendment, the Press Clause, the Assembly Clause, the Ninth Amendment, and a cluster of penumbral guarantees recognized in past decisions. This course is troublesome, but it is the route that has been selected and, at least for now, we must live with it. No purpose would be served by me spelling out at length here the reasons for my saying that the course is troublesome. I need do no more than observe that uncertainty marks the nature—and strictness—of the standard of closure the

Court adopts. The plurality opinion speaks of "an overriding interest articulated in findings," *ante,* at 581; MR. JUSTICE STEWART reserves, perhaps not inappropriately, "reasonable limitations," *ante,* at 600; MR. JUSTICE BRENNAN presents his separate analytical framework; MR. JUSTICE POWELL in *Gannett* was critical of those Justices who, relying on the Sixth Amendment, concluded that closure is authorized only when "strictly and inescapably necessary," 443 U. S., at 339–400; and MR. JUSTICE REHNQUIST continues his flat rejection of, among others, the First Amendment avenue.

Having said all this, and with the Sixth Amendment set to one side in this case, I am driven to conclude, as a secondary position, that the First Amendment must provide some measure of protection for public access to the trial. The opinion in partial dissent in *Gannett* explained that the public has an intense need and a deserved right to know about the administration of justice in general; about the prosecution of local crimes in particular; about the conduct of the judge, the prosecutor, defense counsel, police officers, other public servants, and all the actors in the judicial arena; and about the trial itself.

It is clear and obvious to me, on the approach the Court has chosen to take, that, by closing this criminal trial, the trial judge abridged these First Amendment interests of the public.

I also would reverse, and I join the judgment of the Court.

MR. JUSTICE REHNQUIST, dissenting.

For the reasons stated in my separate concurrence in *Gannett Co. v. DePasquale,* (1979), I do not believe that either the First or Sixth Amendment, as made applicable to the States by the Fourteenth, requires that a State's reasons for denying public access to a trial, where both the prosecuting attorney and the defendant have consented to an order of closure approved by the judge, are subject to any additional constitutional review at our hands. And I most certainly do not believe that the Ninth Amendment confers upon us any such power to review orders of state trial judges closing trials in such situations. . . .

We have at present 50 state judicial systems and one federal judicial system in the United States, and our authority to reverse a decision by the highest court of the State is limited to only those occasions when the state decision violates some provision of the United States Constitution. And that authority should be exercised with a full sense that the judges whose decisions we review are making the same effort as we to uphold the Constitution. As said by Mr. Justice Jackson, concurring in the result in *Brown v. Allen,* (1953), "we are not final because we are infallible, but we are infallible only because we are final."

The proper administration of justice in any nation is bound to be a matter of the highest concern to all thinking citizens. But to gradually rein in, as this Court has done over the past generation, all of the ultimate decisionmaking power over how justice shall be administered, not merely in the federal system but in each of the 50 States, is a task that no Court consisting of nine persons, however gifted, is equal to. Nor is it desirable that such authority be exercised by such a tiny numerical fragment of the 220 million people who compose the population of this country. In the same concurrence just quoted, Mr. Justice Jackson accurately observed that "[t]he generalities of the Fourteenth Amendment are so indeterminate as to what state actions are forbidden that this Court has found it a ready instrument, in one field or another, to magnify federal, and incidentally its own, authority over the states." *Id.,* at 534.

However high-minded the impulses which originally spawned this trend may have been, and which impulses have been accentuated since the time Mr. Justice Jackson wrote, it is basically unhealthy to have so much authority concentrated in a small group of lawyers who have been appointed to the Supreme Court and enjoy virtual life tenure. Nothing in the reasoning of Mr. Chief Justice Marshall in *Marbury v. Madison,* (1803), requires that this Court through ever-broadening use of the Supremacy Clause smother a healthy pluralism which would ordinarily exist in a national government embracing 50 States.

The issue here is not whether the "right" to freedom of the press conferred by the First Amendment to the Constitution overrides the defendant's "right" to a fair trial conferred by other Amendments to the Constitution; it is instead whether any provision in the Constitution may fairly be read to prohibit what the trial judge in the Virginia state-court system did in this case. Being unable to find any such prohibition in the First, Sixth, Ninth, or any other Amendment to the United States Constitution, or in the Constitution itself, I dissent.

QUESTIONS AND COMMENTS

1 On the basis of *Gannett,* could a judge constitutionally announce at the opening of a criminal trial that the public (including reporters) would be barred access, then clear the courtroom and proceed to try and dispose of the case all in a single day? Explain your answer. Could the judge do those things in reference to a pretrial hearing?

2 Did the decision in *Gannett* turn on who was seeking to have the hearing closed? Should it matter? Explain your answer.

3 *Gannett* was decided by a 5–4 vote. What procedures at the lower court level would likely have reduced the number of dissenting votes, even if the judge ultimately closed the hearing?

4 Where is the right of the public to attend criminal trials found in the Constitution? If you cannot find it there, from whence does it come? How probative is an argument that a claimed right cannot be found explicitly in the Constitution?

5 List the differences you detect between the *Gannett* and *Richmond* cases. Are the decisions in these cases consistent with one another? Are the arguments in the majority opinions consistent?

6 In your mind what reasons, conditions, or circumstances would justify closing a criminal trial or portions thereof to the public and the press?

7 In his dissent, Justice Rehnquist refers to the fact that Supreme Court justices are few in number and enjoy virtual life tenure. Of what relevance are such facts to the decision in this case?

8 Does the decision in *Richmond Newspapers* represent activism or restraint? If activism, what dimension?

The final case in this section poses an issue that frequently arises in American society, to wit: how far can the press go in critically reporting the activities of individuals? A typical context in which such issues arise can be illustrated with a recent case in Rhode Island.

At a 1983 school board meeting in Cumberland, Rhode Island, a member of the Cumberland School Committee vehemently condemned what was said to be a disturbing rate of absenteeism among teachers in the Cumberland school system. Thinking this was news, a 16-year-old coeditor of the local high school newspaper not only reported the event but suggested that the facts would not support such a charge and that the committee member making the charge had missed 26 percent of the school board meetings in 1983. In return, the committee member instituted a libel suit for $200,000. These facts pose a conflict between the right of free speech on the one hand and the right to privacy on the other. The problem is that while one may reasonably expect to be protected against defamation, libel laws have the potential of significantly "chilling" rights to speech and press. Up until 1964, libel laws generally provided that anyone who made a statement harmful to another person's reputation was liable for damages unless it could be proved that the statement was true. But recognizing the chilling effect of such a rule on freedom of speech and press, the Supreme Court attempted, in 1964, to provide a better framework for handling disputes of the type represented in the Cumberland Schoolboy case. That attempt was made in *New York Times v. Sullivan.*

New York Times Co. v. Sullivan

376 U.S. 254; 84 S. Ct. 710; 11 L. Ed. 2d 686 (1964)
Vote: 9–0

The facts are given in the opinion below.

MR. JUSTICE BRENNAN delivered the opinion of the Court.

We are required in this case to determine for the first time the extent to which the constitutional protections for speech and press limit a State's power to award damages in a libel action brought by a public official against critics of his official conduct.

Respondent L. B. Sullivan is one of the three elected Commissioners of the City of Montgomery, Alabama. He testified that he was "Commissioner of Public Affairs and the duties are supervision of the Police Department, Fire Department, Department of Cemetery and Department of Scales." He brought this civil libel action against the four individual petitioners, who are Negroes and Alabama clergymen, and against petitioner the New York Times Company, a New York corporation which publishes the New York Times, a daily newspaper. A jury in the Circuit Court of Montgomery County awarded him damages of $500,000, the full amount claimed, against all the petitioners, and the Supreme Court of Alabama affirmed.

Respondent's complaint alleged that he had been libeled by statements in a full-page advertisement that was carried in the New York Times on March 29, 1960. Entitled "Heed Their Rising Voices," the advertisement began by stating that "As the whole world knows by now, thousands of Southern Negro students are engaged in widespread non-violent demonstrations in positive affirmation of the right to live in human dignity as guaranteed by the U. S. Constitution and the Bill of Rights." It went on to charge that "in their efforts to uphold these guarantees they are being met by an unprecedented wave of terror by those who would deny and negate that document which the whole world looked upon as setting the pattern for modern freedom. . . ." Succeeding paragraphs purported to illustrate the "wave of terror" by describing certain alleged events. The text concluded with an appeal for funds for three purposes: support of the student movement, "the struggle for the right-to-vote," and the legal defense of Dr. Martin Luther King, Jr., leader of the movement, against a perjury indictment then pending in Montgomery.

The text appeared over the names of 64 persons, many widely known for their activities in public affairs, religion, trade unions, and the performing arts. Below these names, and under a line reading "We in the south who are struggling daily for dignity and freedom warmly endorse this appeal," appeared the names of the four individual petitioners and of 16 other persons, all but two of whom were identified as clergymen in various Southern cities. The advertisement was signed at the bottom of the page by the "Committee to Defend Martin Luther King and the Struggle for Freedom in the South," and the officers of the Committee were listed.

Of the 10 paragraphs of text in the advertisement, the third and a portion of the sixth were the basis of respondent's claim of libel. They read as follows:

> In Montgomery, Alabama, after students sang "My Country, 'Tis of Thee" on the State Capitol steps, their leaders were expelled from school, and truckloads of police armed with shotguns and tear-gas ringed the Alabama State College Campus. When the entire student body protested to state authorities by refusing to re-register, their dining hall was padlocked in an attempt to starve them into submission.

Sixth paragraph:

> Again and again the Southern violators have answered Dr. King's peaceful protests with intimidation and violence. They have bombed his home almost killing his wife and child. They have assaulted his person. They have arrested him seven times—for 'speeding' 'loitering' and similar 'offenses.' And now they have charged him with 'perjury'—a *felony* under which they could imprison him for *ten years*. . . .

Although neither of these statements mentions respondent by name, he contended that the word "police" in the third paragraph referred to him as the Montgomery Commissioner who supervised the Police Department, so that he was being accused of "ringing" the campus with police. He further claimed that the paragraph would be read as imputing to the police, and hence to him, the padlocking of the dining hall in order to starve the students into submission. . . . We hold that the rule of law applied by the Alabama courts is constitutionally deficient for failure to provide the safeguards for freedom of speech and of the press that are required by the First and Fourteenth Amendments in a libel action brought by a public official against critics of his official conduct. We further hold that under the proper safeguards the evidence presented in this case is constitutionally insufficient to support the judgment for respondent.

We may dispose at the outset of two grounds asserted to insulate the judgment of the Alabama courts from constitutional scrutiny. The first is the proposition relied on by the State Supreme Court—that "The Fourteenth Amendment is directed against State action and not private action." That proposition has no application to this case. . . .

The second contention is that the constitutional guarantees of freedom of speech and of the press are inapplicable here, at least so far as the Times is concerned, because the allegedly libelous statements were published as part of a paid, "commercial" advertisement. The argument relies on *Valentine v. Chrestensen* . . . where the Court held that a city ordinance forbidding street distribution of commercial and business advertising matter did not abridge the First Amendment freedoms, even as applied to a handbill having a commercial message on one side but a protest against certain official action on the other. The reliance is wholly misplaced. The Court in *Chrestensen* reaffirmed the constitutional protection for "the freedom of communicating information and disseminating opinion"; its holding was based upon the factual conclusions that the handbill was "purely commercial advertising" and that the protest against official action had been added only to evade the ordinance.

The publication here was not a "commercial" advertisement in the sense in which the word was used in *Chrestensen.* It communicated information, expressed opinion, recited grievances, protested claimed abuses, and sought financial support on behalf of a movement whose existence and objectives are matters of the highest public interest and concern. See *N. A. A. C. P. v. Button.* . . . That the Times was paid for publishing the advertisement is as immaterial in this connection as is the fact that newspapers and books are sold. . . .

Any other conclusion would discourage newspapers from carrying "editorial advertisements" of this type, and so might shut off an important outlet for the promulgation of information and ideas by persons who do not themselves have access to publishing facilities—who wish to exercise their freedom of speech even though they are not members of the press.

. . . The effect would be to shackle the First Amendment in its attempt to secure "the widest possible dissemination of information from diverse and antagonistic sources." *Associated Press v. United States.* . . . To avoid placing such a handicap upon the freedoms of expression, we hold that if the allegedly libelous statements would otherwise be constitutionally protected from the present judgment, they do not forfeit that protection because they were published in the form of a paid advertisement. . . .

The general proposition that freedom of expression upon public questions is secured by the First Amendment has long been settled by our decisions. The constitutional safeguard, we have said, "was fashioned to assure unfettered interchange of ideas for the bringing about of political and social changes desired by the people." *Roth v. United States.* . . . "The maintenance of the opportunity for free political discussion to the end that government may be responsive to the will of the people and that changes may be obtained by lawful means, an opportunity essential to the security of the Republic, is a fundamental principle of our constitutional system." *Stromberg v. California,* . . . "[I]t is a prized American privilege to speak one's mind, although not always with perfect good taste, on all public institutions," *Bridges v. California,* and this opportunity is to be afforded for "vigorous advocacy" no less than "abstract discussion." *N. A. A. C. P. v. Button.* . . .

The First Amendment, said Judge Learned Hand, "presupposes that right conclusions are more likely to be gathered out of a multitude of tongues, than through any kind of authoritative selection. To many this is, and always will be, folly; but we have staked upon it our all." *United States v. Associated Press,* (D. C. S. D. N. Y. 1943). Mr. Justice Brandeis, in his concurring opinion in *Whitney v. California,* gave the principle its classic formulation:

> Those who won our independence believed . . . that public discussion is a political duty; and that this should be a fundamental principle of the American government. They recognized the risks to which all human institutions are subject. But they knew that order cannot be secured merely through fear of punishment for its infraction; that it is hazardous to discourage thought, hope and imagination; that fear breeds repression; that repression breeds hate; that hate menaces stable government; that the path of safety lies in the opportunity to discuss freely supposed grievances and proposed remedies; and that the fitting remedy for evil counsels is good ones. Believing in the power of reason as applied through public discussion, they eschewed silence coerced by law—the argument of force in its worst form. Recognizing the occasional tyrannies of governing majorities, they amended the Constitution so that free speech and assembly should be guaranteed.

Thus we consider this case against the background of a profound national commitment to the principle that debate on public issues should be uninhibited, robust, and wide-open, and that it may well include vehement, caustic, and sometimes unpleasantly sharp attacks on government and public officials. . . .

The present advertisement, as an expression of grievance and protest on one of the major public issues of our time, would seem clearly to qualify for the constitutional protection. The question is whether it forfeits that protection by the falsity of some of its factual statements and by its alleged defamation of respondent.

Authoritative interpretations of the First Amendment guarantees have consistently refused to recognize an exception for any test of truth—whether administered by judges, juries, or administrative officials—and especially one that puts the burden of proving truth on the speaker. The constitutional protection does not turn upon "the truth, popularity, or social utility of the ideas and beliefs which are offered." . . . That erroneous statement is inevitable in free debate, and that it must be protected if the freedoms of expression are to have the "breathing space" that they "need . . . to survive," *N. A. A. C. P. v. Button,* was also recognized by the Court of Appeals for the District of Columbia Circuit in *Sweeney v. Patterson,* Judge Edgerton spoke for a unanimous court which affirmed the dismissal of a Congressman's libel suit based upon a newspaper article charging him with anti-Semitism in opposing a judicial appointment. . . .

Inquiry to official reputation affords no more warrant for repressing speech that would otherwise be free than does factual error. . . .

If neither factual error nor defamatory content suffices to remove the constitutional shield from criticism of official conduct, the combination of the two elements is no less inadequate. . . .

What a State may not constitutionally bring about by means of a criminal statute is likewise beyond the reach of its civil law of libel. The fear of damage awards under a rule such as that invoked by the Alabama courts here may be markedly more inhibiting than the fear of prosecution under a criminal statute. . . . A rule compelling the critic of official conduct to guarantee the truth of all his factual assertions—and to do so on pain of libel judgments virtually unlimited in amount—leads to a comparable "self-censorship." Allowance of the defense of truth, with the burden of proving it on the defendant, does not mean that only false speech will be deterred. Even courts accepting this defense as an adequate safeguard have recognized the difficulties of adducing legal proofs that the alleged libel was true in all its factual particulars. . . . Under such a rule, would-be critics of official conduct may be deterred from voicing their criticism, even though it is believed to be true and even though it is in fact true, because of doubt whether it can be proved in court or fear of the expense of having to so do. They tend to make only statements which "steer far wider of the unlawful zone." *Speiser v. Randall, supra.* The rule thus dampens the vigor and limits the variety of public debate. It is inconsistent with the First and Fourteenth Amendments.

The constitutional guarantees require, we think, a federal rule that prohibits a public official from recovering damages for a defamatory falsehood relating to his official conduct unless he proves that the statement was made with "actual malice"—that is, with knowledge that it was false or with reckless disregard of whether it was false or not. . . .

We hold today that the Constitution delimits a State's power to award damages for libel in actions brought by public officials against critics of their official conduct. Since this is such an action, the rule requiring proof of actual malice is applicable. While Alabama law apparently requires proof of actual malice for an award of punitive damages, where general damages are concerned malice is "presumed." Such a presumption is inconsistent with the federal rule.

* * *

The judgment of the Supreme Court of Alabama is reversed and the case is remanded to that court for further proceedings not inconsistent with this opinion.

Reversed and remanded.

QUESTIONS AND COMMENTS

1 The Supreme Court has subsequently refined its "public official" doctrine in *Sullivan* to include "public figures"—i.e., those whose position alone commands continuing public interest or who thrust their personalities into the "vortex" of an important public controversy [*Curtis Publishing Co. v. Butts,* 388 U.S. 130, 155 (1967)].
2 Assuming that *New York Times v. Sullivan* will protect our young newspaper editor in the Cumberland, Rhode Island, case, does such protection totally eliminate the chilling effect that libel suits can have on free speech or press? Would Justice Black's position on the meaning of the First Amendment, if adopted, increase or decrease the chilling effect of such suits? Explain your answer.
3 It is said that the Supreme Court in *Sullivan* overturned 100 years of libel law. Does that represent judicial activism? What dimension? What *constitutional* defense of the change can you offer? What other justification?

Obscenity and Nudity

Roth v. United States (1957)

Miller v. California (1973)

F.C.C. v. Pacifica Foundation (1978)

Schad v. Borough of Mount Ephraim (1981)

The freedom of the press as a constitutional issue frequently arises in the area of obscenity. The rule against prior restraint operates in this area as in others. But obscene publication or expression is not protected by the First Amendment, as the Court makes clear in *Roth v. United States.* The problem is to find a workable definition of obscenity so that one may know what is and is not protected expression. *Roth* provides a test for making such determinations.

Between the decisions in *Roth* and *Miller v. California,* the Court decided a large number of obscenity cases. Initially, the *Roth* test was employed, though the Court was not always able to produce a majority opinion. The problem associated with applying the *Roth* test are starkly reflected in Justice Stewart's remark in *Jacobellis v. Ohio.* Complaining that the Court's opinion in *Roth* could be read in a variety of ways, Stewart said:

I imply no criticism of the Court, which in . . . [that case] was faced with the task of trying to define what may be undefinable. I have reached the conclusion, . . . that under the First and Fourteenth Amendments criminal laws in this area are limited to hard-core pornography. I shall not attempt further to define the kinds of material I understand to be embraced within that shorthand description; and perhaps I could never succeed in intelligently doing so. But I know it when I see it, and the motion picture involved in this case is not that.[15]

Such ambiguity in the standards by which obscenity is to be determined has continued to be a problem. In *Miller,* the Court attempts again to enunciate a test for identifying obscene expression which is unprotected by the Constitution. In the process, the question of local and national standards is addressed and resolved. But lest one think that the *Miller* standards have stilled all controversies in this area, it should be noted that many obscenity cases continue to be decided by 5–4 votes in the Burger Court.[16]

Roth v. United States (Alberts v. California)

354 U.S. 476; 77 S. Ct. 1304; 1 L. Ed. 2d 1498 (1957)
Vote: Roth v. United States: 6–3
Alberts v. California: 7–2

The facts are given in the opinion that follows.

MR. JUSTICE BRENNAN delivered the opinion of the Court.

Roth conducted a business in New York in the publication and sale of books, photographs and magazines. He used circulars and advertising matter to solicit sales. He was convicted by a jury in the District Court for the Southern District of New York upon 4 counts of a 26-count indictment charging him with mailing obscene circulars and advertising, and an obscene book, in violation of the federal obscenity statute. His conviction was affirmed by The Court of Appeals for the Second Circuit. We granted certiorari.

Alberts conducted a mail-order business from Los Angeles. He was convicted by the Judge of the Municipal Court of the Beverly Hills Judicial District (having waived a jury trial) under a misdemeanor complaint which charged him with lewdly keeping for sale obscene and indecent books, and with writing, composing and publishing an obscene advertisement of them, in violation of the California Penal Code. The conviction was affirmed by the Appellate Department of the Superior Court of the State of California in and for the County of Los Angeles. We noted probable jurisdiction.

The dispositive question is whether obscenity is utterance within the area of protected speech and press. Although this is the first time the question has been squarely presented to this Court, either under the First Amendment or under the Fourteenth Amendment, expressions found in numerous opinions indicate that this Court has always assumed that obscenity is not protected by the freedoms of speech and press. . . . it is apparent that the unconditional phrasing of the First Amendment was not intended, to protect every utterance. This phrasing did not prevent this Court from concluding that libelous utterances are not within the area of constitutionally protected speech. At the time of the adoption of the First Amendment, obscenity law was not as fully developed as libel law, but there is sufficiently contemporaneous evidence to show that obscenity, too, was outside the protection intended for speech and press.

The protection given speech and press was fashioned to assure unfettered interchange of ideas for the bringing about of political and social changes desired by the people. . . .

All ideas having even the slightest redeeming social importance—unorthodox ideas, controversial ideas, even ideas hateful to the prevailing climate of opinion—have the full protection of the guaranties, unless excludable because they encroach upon the limited area of more important interests. But implicit in the history of the First Amendment is the rejection of obscenity as utterly without redeeming social importance. This rejection for that reason is mirrored in the universal judgment that obscenity should be restrained, reflected in the international agreement of over 50 nations, in the obscenity laws of all of the 48 States, and in the 20 obscenity laws enacted by the Congress from 1842 to 1956. This is the same judgment expressed by this Court in *Chaplinsky v. New Hampshire,* 315 U. S. 568, 571–572:

> . . . There are certain well-defined and narrowly limited classes of speech, the prevention and punishment of which have never been thought to raise any Constitutional problem. *These include the lewd and obscene. . . . It has been well observed that such utterances are no essential part of any exposition of ideas, and are of such slight social value as a step to truth that any benefit that may be derived from them is clearly outweighed by the social interest in order and morality.* . . . (Emphasis added.)

We hold that obscenity is not within the area of constitutionally protected speech or press. . . .

However, sex and obscenity are not synonymous. Obscene material is material which deals with sex in a manner appealing to prurient interest.*. . .

---

*I. e., material having a tendency to excite lustful thoughts. Webster's New International Dictionary (Unabridged, 2d ed., 1949) defines *prurient,* in pertinent part, as follows: ". . . Itching; longing; uneasy with desire or longing; of persons, having itching, morbid, or lascivious longings; of desire, curiosity, or propensity, lewd. . . ."

Pruriency is defined, in pertinent part, as follows: ". . . Quality of being prurient; lascivious desire or thought. . . ."

See also *Mutual Film Corp. v. Industrial Comm'n,* 236 U. S. 230, 242, where this Court said as to motion pictures: ". . . They take their attraction from the general interest, eager and wholesome it may be, in their subjects, but a *purient interest may be excited and appealed to.* . . ." (Emphasis added.)

We perceive no significant difference between the meaning of obscenity developed in the case law and the definition of the A. L. I., Model Penal Code, § 207.10 (2) (Tent. Draft No. 6, 1957), *viz.:*

". . . A thing is obscene if, considered as a whole, its predominant appeal is to prurient interest, i. e., a shameful or morbid interest in nudity, sex, or excretion, and if it goes substantially beyond customary limits of candor in description or representation of such matters. . . ."

The early leading standard of obscenity allowed material to be judged merely by the effect of an isolated excerpt upon particularly susceptible persons. *Regina v. Hicklin,* [1868] L. R. 3 Q. B. 360. Some American courts adopted this standard but later decisions have rejected it and substituted this test: whether to the average person, applying contemporary community standards, the dominant theme of the material taken as a whole appeals to prurient interest. The *Hicklin* test, judging obscenity by the effect of isolated passages upon the most susceptible persons, might well encompass material legitimately treating with sex, and so it must be rejected as unconstitutionally restrictive of the freedoms of speech and press. On the other hand, the substituted standard provides safeguards adequate to withstand the charge of constitutional infirmity.

Both trial courts below sufficiently followed the proper standard. Both courts used the proper definition of obscenity. In addition, in the *Alberts* case, in ruling on a motion to dismiss, the trial judge indicated that, as the trier of facts, he was judging each item as a whole as it would affect the normal person, and in *Roth,* the trial judge instructed the jury as follows:

> . . . The test is not whether it would arouse sexual desires or sexual impure thoughts in those comprising a particular segment of the community, the young, the immature or the highly prudish or would leave another segment, the scientific or highly educated or the so-called worldly-wise and sophisticated indifferent and unmoved. . . .
>
> The test in each case is the effect of the book, picture or publication considered as a whole, not upon any particular class, but upon all those whom it is likely to reach. In other words, you determine its impact upon the average person in the community. . . .

It is argued that the statutes do not provide reasonably ascertainable standards of guilt and therefore violate the constitutional requirements of due process. The federal obscenity statute makes punishable the mailing of material that is "obscene, lewd, lascivious, or filthy . . . or other publication of an indecent character." The California statute makes punishable, *inter alia,* the keeping for sale or advertising material that is "obscene or indecent." The thrust of the argument is that these words are not sufficiently precise because they do not mean the same thing to all people, all the time, everywhere.

Many decisions have recognized that these terms of obscenity statutes are not precise. This Court, however, has consistently held that lack of precision is not itself offensive to the requirements of due process. ". . . [T]he Constitution does not require impossible standards"; all that is required is that the language "conveys sufficiently definite warning as to the proscribed conduct when measured by common understanding and practices. . . ." *United States v. Petrillo,* 332 U. S. 1, 7–8. These words, applied according to the proper standard for judging obscenity, already discussed, give adequate warning of the conduct proscribed and mark ". . . boundaries sufficiently distinct for judges and juries fairly to administer the law. . . . That there may be marginal cases in which it is difficult to determine the side of the line on which a particular fact situation falls is no sufficient reason to hold the language too ambiguous to define a criminal offense. . . ." *Id.,* at 7.

In summary, then, we hold that these statutes, applied according to the proper standard for judging obscenity, do not offend constitutional safeguards against convictions based upon protected material, or fail to give men in acting adequate notice of what is prohibited.

Roth's argument that the federal obscenity statute unconstitutionally encroaches upon the powers reserved by the Ninth and Tenth Amendments to the States and to the people to punish speech and press where offensive to decency and morality is hinged upon his contention that obscenity is expression not excepted from the sweep of the provision of the First Amendment that "*Congress* shall make *no law* . . . abridging the freedom of speech, or of the press. . . ." (Emphasis added.) That argument falls in light of our holding that obscenity is not expression protected by the First Amendment. We therefore hold that the federal obscenity statute punishing the use of the mails for obscene material is a proper exercise of the postal power delegated to Congress by Art. I, § 8, cl. 7. . . .

Alberts argues that because his was a mail-order business, the California statute is repugnant to Art. I, § 8, cl. 7, under which the Congress allegedly preempted the regulatory field by enacting the federal obscenity statute punishing the mailing or advertising by mail of obscene material. The federal statute deals only with actual mailing; it does not eliminate the power of the state to punish "keeping for sale" or "advertising" obscene material. The state statute in no way imposes a burden or interferes with the federal postal functions. . . .

The judgments are

Affirmed.

MR. CHIEF JUSTICE WARREN, concurring in the result.

. . . Under the California law, the prohibited activity must be done "willfully and lewdly." The federal statute limits the crime to acts done "knowingly." In his charge to the jury, the district judge stated that the matter must be "calculated" to corrupt or debauch. The defendants in both these cases were engaged in the business of purveying textual or graphic matter openly advertised to appeal to the erotic interest of their customers. They were plainly engaged in the commercial exploitation of the morbid and shameful craving for materials with prurient effect. I believe that the State and Federal Governments can constitutionally punish such conduct. That is all that these cases present to us, and that is all we need to decide.

I agree with the Court's decision in its rejection of the other contentions raised by these defendants.

MR. JUSTICE HARLAN, concurring in the result in No. 61, and dissenting in No. 582. . . .

I concur in the judgment of the Court in No. 61, *Alberts v. California.*

The question in this case is whether the defendant was deprived of liberty without due process of law when he was convicted for selling certain materials found by the judge to be obscene because they would have a "tendency to deprave or corrupt its readers by exciting lascivious thoughts or arousing lustful desire."

In judging the constitutionality of this conviction, we should remember that our function in reviewing state judgments under the Fourteenth Amendment is a narrow one. We do not decide whether the policy of the State is wise, or whether it is based on assumptions scientifically substantiated. We can inquire only whether the state action so subverts the fundamental liberties implicit in the Due Process Clause that it cannot be sustained as a rational exercise of power. The States' power to make printed words criminal is, of course, confined by the Fourteenth Amendment, but only insofar as such power is inconsistent with our concepts of "ordered liberty." *Palko v. Connecticut,* 302 U. S. 319, 324–325.

What, then, is the purpose of this California statute? Clearly the state legislature has made the judgment that printed words *can* "deprave or corrupt" the reader—that words can incite to antisocial or immoral action. The assumption seems to be that the distribution of certain types of literature will induce criminal or immoral sexual conduct. It is well known, of course, that the validity of this assumption is a matter of dispute among critics, sociologists, psychiatrists, and penologists. There is a large school of thought, particularly in the scientific community, which denies any casual connection between the reading of pornography and immorality, crime, or delinquency. Others disagree. Clearly it is not our function to decide this question. That function belongs to the state legislature. Nothing in the Constitution requires California to accept as truth the most advanced and sophisticated psychiatric opinion. It seems to me clear that it is not irrational, in our present state of knowledge, to consider that pornography can induce a type of sexual conduct which a State may deem obnoxious to the moral fabric of society. In fact the very division of opinion on the subject counsels us to respect the choice made by the State. . . .

What has been said, however, does not dispose of the case. It still remains for us to decide whether the state court's determination that this material should be suppressed is consistent with the Fourteenth Amendment; and that, of course, presents a federal question as to which we, and not the state court, have the ultimate responsibility. And so, in the final analysis, I concur in the judgment because, upon an independent perusal of the material involved, and in light of the considerations discussed above, I cannot say that its suppression would so interfere with the communication of "ideas" in any proper sense of that term that it would offend the Due Process Clause. I therefore agree with the Court that appellant's conviction must be affirmed.

I dissent in No. 582, *Roth v. United States.*

We are faced here with the question whether the federal obscenity statute, as construed and applied in this case, violates the First Amendment to the

Constitution. To me, this question is of quite a different order than one where we are dealing with state legislation under the Fourteenth Amendment. I do not think it follows that state and federal powers in this area are the same, and that just because the State may suppress a particular utterance, it is automatically permissible for the Federal Government to do the same. . . .

Not only is the federal interest in protecting the Nation against pornography attenuated, but the dangers of federal censorship in this field are far greater than anything the States may do. It has often been said that one of the great strengths of our federal system is that we have, in the forty-eight States, forty-eight experimental social laboratories. "State statutory law reflects predominantly this capacity of a legislature to introduce novel techniques of social control. The federal system has the immense advantage of providing forty-eight separate centers for such experimentation." Different States will have different attitudes toward the same work of literature. The same book which is freely read in one State might be classed as obscene in another. And it seems to me that no overwhelming danger to our freedom to experiment and to gratify our tastes in literature is likely to result from the suppression of a borderline book in one of the States, so long as there is no uniform nation-wide suppression of the book, and so long as other States are free to experiment with the same or bolder books.

I judge this case, then, in view of what I think is the attenuated federal interest in this field, in view of the very real danger of a deadening uniformity which can result from nation-wide federal censorship, and in view of the fact that the constitutionality of this conviction must be weighed against the First and not the Fourteenth Amendment. So viewed, I do not think that this conviction can be upheld. . . .

MR. JUSTICE DOUGLAS, with whom MR. JUSTICE BLACK concurs, dissenting.

When we sustain these convictions, we make the legality of a publication turn on the purity of thought which a book or tract instills in the mind of the reader. I do not think we can approve that standard and be faithful to the command of the First Amendment, which by its terms is a restraint on Congress and which by the Fourteenth is a restraint on the States. . . .

The tests by which these convictions were obtained require only the arousing of sexual thoughts. Yet the arousing of sexual thoughts and desires happens every day in normal life in dozens of ways. Nearly 30 years ago a questionnaire sent to college and normal school women graduates asked what things were most stimulating sexually. Of 409 replies, 9 said "music"; 18 said "pictures"; 29 said "dancing"; 40 said "drama"; 95 said "books"; and 218 said "man." Alpert, Judicial Censorship of Obscene Literature, 52 Harv. L. Rev. 40, 73. . . .

The absence of dependable information on the effect of obscene literature on human conduct should make us wary. It should put us on the side of protecting society's interest in literature, except and unless it can be said that the particular publication has an impact on action that the government can control. . . .

Any test that turns on what is offensive to the community's standards is too loose, too capricious, too destructive of freedom of expression to be squared with the First Amendment. Under that test, juries can censor, suppress, and punish what they don't like, provided the matter relates to "sexual impurity" or has a tendency "to excite lustful thoughts." This is community censorship in one of its worst forms.

. . . Unlike the law of libel, wrongfully relied on in *Beauharnais,* there is no special historical evidence that literature dealing with sex was intended to be treated in a special manner by those who drafted the First Amendment. In fact, the first reported court decision in this country involving obscene literature was in 1821. I reject too the implication that problems of freedom of speech and of the press are to be resolved by weighing against the values of free expression, the judgment of the Court that a particular form of that expression has "no redeeming social importance." The First Amendment, its prohibition in terms absolute, was designed to preclude courts as well as legislatures from weighing the values of speech against silence. The First Amendment puts free speech in the preferred position.

Freedom of expression can be suppressed if, and to the extent that, it is so closely brigaded with illegal action as to be an inseparable part of it. As a people, we cannot afford to relax that standard. For the test that suppresses a cheap tract today can suppress a literary gem tomorrow. All it need do is to incite a lascivious thought or arouse a lustful desire. The list of books that judges or juries can place in that category is endless.

I would give the broad sweep of the First Amendment full support. I have the same confidence in the ability of our people to reject noxious literature as I have in their capacity to sort out the true from the false in theology, economics, politics, or any other field.

Miller v. California

413 U.S. 15; 93 S. Ct. 1607; 37 L. Ed. 2d 419 (1973)
Vote: 5–4

The facts of this case are provided in the opinion below.

MR. CHIEF JUSTICE BURGER delivered the opinion of the Court.

This is one of a group of "obscenity-pornography" cases being reviewed by the Court in a re-examination of standards enunciated in earlier cases involving what Mr. Justice Harlan called "the intractable obscenity problem." *Interstate Circuit, Inc. v. Dallas,* (1968) (concurring and dissenting).

Appellant conducted a mass mailing campaign to advertise the sale of illustrated books, euphemistically called "adult" material. After a jury trial, he was convicted of violating California Penal Code § 311.2 (a), a misdemeanor, by knowingly distributing obscene matter, and the Appellate Department, Superior Court of California, County of Orange, summarily affirmed the judgment without opinion. Appellant's conviction was specifically based on his conduct in causing five unsolicited advertising brochures to be sent through the mail in an envolope addressed to a restaurant in Newport Beach, California. The envelope was opened by the manager of the restaurant and his mother. They had not requested the brochures; they complained to the police.

The brochures advertise four books entitled "Intercourse," "Man-Woman," "Sex Orgies Illustrated," and "An Illustrated History of Pornography," and a film entitled "Marital Intercourse." While the brochures contain some descriptive printed material, primarily they consist of pictures and drawings very explicitly depicting men and women in groups of two or more engaging in a variety of sexual activities, with genitals often prominently displayed.

This case involves the application of a State's criminal obscenity statute to a situation in which sexually explicit materials have been thrust by aggressive sales action upon unwilling recipients who had in no way indicated any desire to receive such materials. This Court has recognized that the States have a legitimate interest in prohibiting dissemination or exhibition of obscene material when the mode of dissemination carries with it a significant danger of offending the sensibilities of unwilling recipients or of exposure to juveniles.

It is in this context that we are called on to define the standards which must be used to identify obscene material that a State may regulate without infringing on the First Amendment as applicable to the States through the Fourteenth Amendment. . . . In *Roth v. United States,* (1957), the Court sustained a conviction under a federal statute punishing the mailing of "obscene, lewd, lascivious or filthy. . ." materials. The key to that holding was the Court's rejection of the claim that obscene materials were protected by the First Amendment. Five Justices joined in the opinion. . . .

Nine years later, in *Memoirs v. Massachusetts,* (1966), the Court veered sharply away from the *Roth* concept and, with only three Justices in the plurality opinion, articulated a new test of obscenity. The plurality held that under the *Roth* definition

> as elaborated in subsequent cases, three elements must coalesce: it must be established that (a) the dominant theme of the material taken as a whole appeals to a prurient interest in sex: (b) the material is patently offensive because it affronts contemporary community standards relating to the description or representation of sexual matters; and (c) the material is utterly without redeeming social value.

The sharpness of the break with *Roth,* represented by the third element of the *Memoirs* test and emphasized by MR. JUSTICE WHITE's dissent, *id.,* at 460–462, was further underscored when the *Memoirs* plurality went on to state:

The Supreme Judicial Court erred in holding that a book need not be 'unqualifiedly worthless before it can be deemed obscene.' A book cannot be proscribed unless it is found to be *utterly* without redeeming social value (emphasis in original).

While *Roth* presumed "obscenity" to be "utterly without redeeming social importance," *Memoirs* required that to prove obscenity it must be affirmatively established that the material is "*utterly* without redeeming social value." Thus, even as they repeated the words of *Roth,* the *Memoirs* plurality produced a drastically altered test that called on the prosecution to prove a negative, *i. e.,* that the material was "*utterly* without redeeming social value"—a burden virtually impossible to discharge under our criminal standards of proof. Such considerations caused Mr. Justice Harlan to wonder if the "*utterly* without redeeming social value" test had any meaning at all. . . .

Apart from the initial formulation in the *Roth* case, no majority of the Court has at any given time been able to agree on a standard to determine what constitutes obscene, pornographic material subject to regulation under the States' police power. We have seen "a variety of views among the members of the Court unmatched in any other course of constitutional adjudication." *Interstate Circuit, Inc. v. Dallas,* 390 U. S., at 704–705 (Harlan, j., concurring and dissenting). This is not remarkable, for in the area of freedom of speech and press the courts must always remain sensitive to any infringement on genuinely serious literary, artistic, political, or scientific expression. This is an area in which there are few eternal verities.

The case we now review was tried on the theory that the California Penal Code § 311 approximately incorporates the three-stage *Memoirs* test, *supra.* But now the *Memoirs* test has been abandoned as unworkable by its author, and no Member of the Court today supports the *Memoirs* formulation. . . .

The basic guidelines for the trier of fact must be: (a) whether "the average person, applying contemporary community standards" would find that the work, taken as a whole, appeals to the prurient interest, (b) whether the work depicts or describes, in a patently offensive way, sexual conduct specifically defined by the applicable state law; and (c) whether the work, taken as a whole, lacks serious literary, artistic, political, or scientific value. We do not adopt as a constitutional standard the "*utterly* without redeeming social value" test of *Memoirs v. Massachusetts,* [1966]; that concept has never commanded the adherence of more than three Justices at one time.

If a state law that regulates obscene material is thus limited, as written or construed, the First Amendment values applicable to the States through the Fourteenth Amendment are adequately protected by the ultimate power of appellate courts to conduct an independent review of constitutional claims when necessary.

We emphasize that it is not our function to propose regulatory schemes for the States. That must await their concrete legislative efforts. It is possible, however, to give a few plain examples of what a state statute could define for regulation under part (b) of the standard announced in this opinion, *supra:*

a Patently offensive representations or descriptions of ultimate sexual acts, normal or perverted, actual or simulated.

b Patently offensive representations or descriptions of masturbation, excretory functions, and lewd exhibition of the genitals.

Sex and nudity may not be exploited without limit by films or pictures exhibited or sold in places of public accommodation any more than live sex and nudity can be exhibited or sold without limit in such public places. At a minimum, prurient, patently offensive depiction or description of sexual conduct must have serious literary, artistic, political, or scientific value to merit First Amendment protection. . . .

. . . Today, for the first time since *Roth* was decided in 1957, a majority of this Court has agreed on concrete guidelines to isolate "hard core" pornography from expression protected by the First Amendment. Now we may . . . attempt to provide positive guidance to federal and state courts alike.

This may not be an easy road, free from difficulty. But no amount of "fatigue" should lead us to adopt a convenient "institutional" rationale—an absolutist, "anything goes" view of the First Amendment—because it will lighten our burdens. "Such an abnegation of judicial supervision in this field would be inconsistent with our duty to uphold the constitutional guarantees." *Jacobellis v. Ohio, supra,* at 187–188 (opinion of BRENNAN, J.). Nor should we remedy "tension between state and federal courts" by arbitrarily depriving the States of a power reserved to them under the Constitution, a power which they enjoyed and exercised continuously from before the adoption of the First Amendment to this day.

"Our duty admits of no 'substitute for facing up to the tough individual problems of constitutional judgment involved in every obscenity case.'. . ."

Under a National Constitution, fundamental First Amendment limitations on the powers of the States do not vary from community to community, but this does not mean that there are, or should or can be, fixed, uniform national standards of precisely what appeals to the "prurient interest" or is "patently offensive."

. . . Nothing in the First Amendment requires that a jury must consider hypothetical and unascertainable "national standards" when attempting to determine whether certain materials are obscene as a matter of fact.

It is neither realistic nor constitutionally sound to read the First Amendment as requiring that the people of Maine or Mississippi accept public depiction of conduct found tolerable in Las Vegas, or New York City. People in different States vary in their tastes and attitudes, and this diversity is not to be strangled by the absolutism of imposed uniformity. As the Court made clear in *Mishkin v. New York,* [1966], the primary concern with requiring a jury to apply the standard of "the average person, applying contemporary community standards" is to be certain that, so far as material is not aimed at a deviant group, it will be judged by its impact on an average person, rather than a particularly susceptible or sensitive person—or indeed a totally insensitive one.

We hold that the requirement that the jury evaluate the materials with reference to "contemporary standards of the State of California" serves this protective purpose and is constitutionally adequate.

* * *

In sum, we (a) reaffirm the *Roth* holding that obscene material is not protected by the First Amendment; (b) hold that such material can be regulated by the States, subject to the specific safeguards enunciated above, without a showing that the material is "*utterly* without redeeming social value"; and (c) hold that obscenity is to be determined by applying "contemporary community standards," not "national standards." The judgment of the Appellate Department of the Superior Court, Orange County, California, is vacated and the case remanded to that court for further proceedings not inconsistent with the First Amendment standards established by this opinion.

Vacated and remanded.

Mr. Justice Douglas, dissenting.

Today we leave open the way for California to send a man to prison for distributing brochures that advertise books and a movie under freshly written standards defining obscenity which until today's decision were never the part of any law. . . .

Today the Court retreats from the earlier formulations of the constitutional test and undertakes to make new definitions. This effort, like the earlier ones, is earnest and well intentioned. The difficulty is that we do not deal with constitutional terms, since "obscenity" is not mentioned in the Constitution or Bill of Rights. And the First Amendment makes no such exception from "the press" which it undertakes to protect nor, as I have said on other occasions, is an exception necessarily implied, for there was no recognized exception to the free press at the time the Bill of Rights was adopted which treated "obscene" publications differently from other types of papers, magazines, and books. So there are no constitutional guidelines for deciding what is and what is not "obscene." The Court is at large because we deal with tastes and standards of literature. What shocks me may be sustenance for my neighbor. What causes one person to boil up in rage over one pamphlet or movie may reflect only his neurosis, not shared by others. We deal here with a regime of censorship which, if adopted, should be done by constitutional amendment after full debate by the people. . . .

The idea that the First Amendment permits government to ban publications that are "offensive" to some people puts an ominous gloss on freedom of the press. That test would make it possible to ban any paper or any journal or magazine in some benighted place. The First Amendment was designed "to invite dispute," to induce "a condition of unrest," to "create dissatisfaction with conditions as they are," and even to stir "people to anger." *Terminiello v. Chicago.* The idea that the First Amendment permits punishment for ideas that are "offensive" to the particular judge or jury sitting in judgment is astounding. No greater leveler of speech or literature has ever been designed. To give the power to the censor, as we do today, is to make a sharp and radical break with the traditions of a free society. The First Amendment was not fashioned as a vehicle for dispensing tranquilizers to the people. Its prime function was to keep debate open to "offensive" as well as to "staid" people. The tendency throughout history has been to subdue the individual and to exalt the power of government. The use of the standard "offensive" gives authority to government that cuts the very vitals out of the First Amendment. As is intimated by the Court's opinion, the materials before us may be garbage. But so is much of what is said in political campaigns, in the daily press, on TV, or over the radio. By reason of the First Amendment—and solely because of it— speakers and publishers have not been threatened or subdued because their thoughts and ideas may be "offensive" to some. . . .

Mr. Justice Brennan, with whom Mr. Justice Stewart and Mr. Justice Marshall join, dissenting.

* * *

Since my view in *Paris Adult Theatre I* represents a substantial departure from the course of our prior decisions, and since the state courts have as yet had no opportunity to consider whether a "readily apparent construction suggests itself as a vehicle for rehabilitating the [statute] in a single prosecution," *Dombrowski v. Pfister, supra,* at 491, I would reverse the judgment of the Appellate Department of the Superior Court and remand the case for proceedings not inconsistent with this opinion.

QUESTIONS AND COMMENTS

1 What is the difference between the *Roth* and *Miller* tests for obscenity?
2 In most of the obscenity cases reaching the Supreme Court, the Court has upheld the claim that state or local authorities are violating the First Amendment rights of the claimant. Is that consistent with the proposition that obscenity is not protected by the First Amendment? Is something else going on here? What?
3 In deciding that obscenity is not protected expression, does the Court employ a balancing test, a clear and present danger test, or some other test? Explain your answer.
4 Prior to *Roth,* the states pretty much decided what was obscene and proceeded to ban it via the exercise of police powers. By ruling that obscenity is unprotected, the Court supported state laws banning it. But by choosing to set the standards and definitions to be used in determining obscenity, and reserving to itself the final say as to when these standards are met, the Court has established itself as a national censor in this area. Thus, to establish whether a given motion picture is obscene, the Court often

repairs to its screening room in the Supreme Court building, views the film, and makes a judgment.[17] This is quite similar to what censorship boards did at the community level in earlier days. Is this a proper role for the Court? Why or why not?

5 It has been reported that Justice White has a personal definition of obscenity or hardcore pornography—i.e., "no erect penises, no intercourse, nor oral or anal sodomy. For White, no erections and no insertions equaled no obscenity" (*The Brethren*, p. 193). Would such a test be better or worse than those used in *Roth* and *Miller?* Why or why not?

* * * * * *

The question of obscenity is not restricted to books or adult theaters nor to *indirect* depiction of obscene acts. In *F.C.C. v. Pacifica,* the medium of expression is a significant consideration. The fact that expression may be permitted on a printed page does not ensure that it is protected when made in radio or television programs. In *F.C.C.,* the Court decides whether the medium of expression should affect the scope to be given the First Amendment right to free speech.

In *Schad,* place of expression was also relevant. The alleged obscene act was actually witnessed directly, though through a glass, whereas in most obscenity cases, such acts are read about or witnessed on film. *Schad* also involves a conflict between First Amendment rights and the legitimate authority of municipalities to zone their commercial and residential areas.

Federal Communications Commission v. Pacifica Foundation et al.

438 U.S. 726; 98 S. Ct. 3026; 57 L. Ed. 2d 1073 (1978)
Vote: 5–4

On October 30, 1973, a New York radio station broadcast a 12-minute monologue entitled "Filthy Words." The monologue had been recorded earlier before a live audience by George Carlin, a satiric humorist. A few weeks after the broadcast, the FCC received a complaint from a father whose young son had heard the broadcast.

The Federal Communications Commission is given authority under the Communications Act of 1934 to regulate the use of radio in the public interest. However, it is specifically denied the power to censor radio communications or to interfere with the right of free speech via radio communication [48 Stat. 1091, 47 U.S.C. [at] (326)]. The Pacifica Foundation, owner of the radio station, was asked to comment on the complaint. The foundation explained that listeners had been advised before the broadcast that it included sensitive language which might be offensive to some. At the same time, Carlin was characterized as "a significant social satirist who like Twain and Sahl before him, examines the language of ordinary people. . . . Carlin is not mouthing obscenities, he is merely using words to satirize as harmless and especially silly our attitudes towards those words." The nature of this satire is reflected in the following excerpt from the broadcast.

Aruba-du, ruba-tu, ruba-tu. I was thinking about the curse words and the swear words, the cuss words and the words that you can't say, that you're not supposed to say all the time, 'cause words or people into words want to hear your words. Some guys like to record your words and sell them back to you if they can, (laughter) listen in on the telephone, write down what words you say. A guy who used to be in Washington, knew that his phone was tapped, used to answer, Fuck Hoover, yes, go ahead. (laughter) Okay, I was thinking one night about the words you couldn't say on the public, ah, airwaves, um, the ones you definitely wouldn't say, ever, 'cause I heard a lady say bitch one night on television, and it was cool like she was talking about, you know, as, well, the bitch is the first one to notice that in the litter Johnie right (murmur) Right. And, uh, bastard you can say, and hell and damn so I have to figure out which ones you couldn't and ever and it came down to seven but the list is open to amendment, and in fact, has been changed, uh, by now, has, a lot of people pointed things out to me, and I noticed some myself. The original seven words were, shit, piss, fuck, cunt, cocksucker, motherfucker, and tits. Those are the ones that will curve your spine, grow hair on your hands and (laughter) maybe, even bring us, God help us, peace without honor (laughter) um, and a bourbon. (laughter) And now the first thing that we noticed was that word fuck was really repeated in there because the word motherfucker is a compound word and it's another form of the word fuck. (laughter) You want to be a purist it doesn't really—it can't be on the list of basic words. Also, cocksucker is a compound word and neither half of that is really dirty. The word—the half sucker that's merely suggestive (laughter) and the word cock is a half-way dirty word, 50% dirty—dirty half the time, depending on what you mean by it. (laughter) Uh, remember when you first heard it, like in 6th grade, you used to giggle. And the cock crowed three times, heh (laughter) the cock—three times. It's in the Bible, cock in the Bible. (laughter) And the first time you heard about a cockfight, remember—What? Huh? naw. It ain't that, are you stupid? man. (laughter, clapping) It's chickens, you know, (laughter) Then you have the four letter words from the old Anglo-Saxon fame. Uh, shit and fuck. The word shit, uh, is an interesting kind of word in that the middle class has never really accepted it and approved it. They use it like crazy, but it's not really okay. It's still a rude, dirty, old kind of gushy word. (laughter) They don't like that, but they say it, like, they say it like, a lady now in a middle-class home, you'll hear most of the time she says it as an expletive, you know, it's out of her mouth before she knows. She says, Oh shit oh shit, (laughter) oh shit. If she drops something, Oh, the shit hurt the broccoli. Shit. Thank you.

On February 21, 1975, the commission ordered that the complaint be associated with the station's license file. While no sanctions were imposed, the possibility of future sanctions was left open. Concluding that certain words in the monologue depicted sexual and excretory activities in a patently offensive manner, that the words were broadcast when children were in the audience, and that the offensive words were deliberately repeated over and over, the commission held the language to be indecent and prohibited by federal statute.

A three-judge panel of the U.S. court of appeals for the District of Columbia reversed by a 2–1 vote. One judge found the commission's order to be censorship in violation of the federal Communications Act. A second found a violation of the First Amendment in that the commission's order was too sweeping. The third judge thought the commission had correctly found the broadcast to be "indecent." The Supreme Court then granted certiorari to review the appellate court's decision.

MR. JUSTICE STEVENS delivered the opinion of the Court. . . .

When the issue is narrowed to the facts of this case, the question is whether the First Amendment denies government any power to restrict the public broadcast of indecent language in any circumstances. For if the government has any such power, this was an appropriate occasion for its exercise.

The words of the Carlin monologue are unquestionably "speech" within the meaning of the First Amendment. It is equally clear that the Commission's objections to the broadcast were based in part on its content. The order must therefore fall if, as Pacifica argues, the First Amendment prohibits all governmental regulation that depends on the content of speech. Our past cases demonstrate, however, that no such absolute rule is mandated by the Constitution.

The classic exposition of the proposition that both the content and the context of speech are critical elements of First Amendment analysis is Mr. Justice Holmes' statement for the Court in *Schenck v. United States,* 249 U. S. 47, 52:

> We admit that in many places and in ordinary times the defendants in saying all that was said in the circular would have been within their constitutional rights. But the character of every act depends upon the circumstances in which it is done. . . . The most stringent protection of free speech would not protect a man in falsely shouting fire in a theatre and causing a panic. It does not even protect a man from an injunction against uttering words that may have all the effect of force. . . . The question in every case is whether the words used are used in such circumstances and are of such a nature as to create a clear and present danger that they will bring about the substantive evils that Congress has a right to prevent. . . .

The question in this case is whether a broadcast of patently offensive words dealing with sex and excretion may be regulated because of its content. Obscene materials have been denied the protection of the First Amendment because their content is so offensive to contemporary moral standards. *Roth v. United States,* . . . But the fact that society may find speech offensive is not a sufficient reason for suppressing it. Indeed, if it is the speaker's opinion that gives offense, that consequence is a reason for according it constitutional protection. For it is a central tenet of the First Amendment that the government must remain neutral in the marketplace of ideas. If there were any reason to believe that the Commission's characterization of the Carlin monologue as offensive could be traced to its political content—or even to the fact that it satirized contemporary attitudes about four-letter words—First Amendment protection might be required. But that is simply not this case.

* * *

Although these words ordinarily lack literary, political, or scientific value, they are not entirely outside the protection of the First Amendment. Some uses of even the most offensive words are unquestionably protected. Indeed, we may assume, *arguendo,* that this monologue would be protected in other contexts. Nonetheless, the constitutional protection accorded to a communication containing such patently offensive sexual and excretory language need not be the same in every context. It is a characteristic of speech such as this that both its capacity to offend and its "social value," to use Mr. Justice Murphy's term, vary with the circumstances. Words that are commonplace in one setting are shocking in another. To paraphrase Mr. Justice Harlan, one occasion's lyric is another's vulgarity.

In this case it is undisputed that the content of Pacifica's broadcast was "vulgar," "offensive," and "shocking." Because content of that character is not entitled to absolute constitutional protection under all circumstances, we must consider its context in order to determine whether the Commission's action was constitutionally permissible.

We have long recognized that each medium of expression presents special First Amendment problems. And of all forms of communication, it is broadcasting that has received the most limited First Amendment protection. Thus, although other speakers cannot be licensed except under laws that carefully define and narrow official discretion, a broadcaster may be deprived of his license and his forum if the Commission decides that such an action would serve "the public interest, convenience, and necessity." Similarly, although the First Amendment protects newspaper publishers from being required to print the replies of those whom they criticize, it affords no such protection to broadcasters; on the contrary, they must give free time to the victims of their criticism.

The reasons for these distinctions are complex, but two have relevance to the present case. First, the broadcast media have established a uniquely pervasive presence in the lives of all Americans. Patently offensive, indecent material presented over the airwaves confronts the citizen, not only in public, but also in the privacy of the home, where the individual's right to be left alone plainly outweighs the First Amendment rights on an intruder. Because the broadcast audience is constantly tuning in and out, prior warnings cannot completely protect the listener or viewer from unexpected program content. To say that one may avoid further offense by turning off the radio when he hears indecent language is like saying that the remedy for an assault is to run away after the first blow. One may hang up on an indecent phone call, but that option does not give the caller a constitutional immunity or avoid a harm that has already taken place.

Second, broadcasting is uniquely accessible to children, even those too young to read. Although Cohen's written message might have been incomprehensible to a first grader, Pacifica's broadcast could have enlarged a child's vocabulary in an instant. Other forms of offensive expression may be withheld from the young without restricting the expression at its source. Bookstores and motion picture theaters, for example, may be prohibited from making indecent material available to children. We held in *Ginsberg v. New York,* that the government's interest in the "well-being of its youth" and in supporting "parents' claim to authority in their own household" justified the regulation of otherwise protected expression. The ease with which children may obtain access to broadcast material, coupled with the concerns recognized in *Ginsberg,* amply justify special treatment of indecent broadcasting.

It is appropriate, in conclusion, to emphasize the narrowness of our holding. This case does not involve a two-way radio conversation between a cab driver and a dispatcher, or a telecast of an Elizabethan comedy. We have not decided that an occasional expletive in either setting would justify any sanction or, indeed, that this broadcast would justify a criminal prosecution. The Commission's decision rested entirely on a nuisance rationale under which context is all-important. The concept requires consideration of a host of variables. The time of day was emphasized by the Commission. The content of the program in which the language is used will also affect the composition of the audience, and differences between radio, television, and perhaps closed-circuit transmissions, may also be relevant. As Mr. Justice Sutherland wrote, a "nuisance may be merely a right thing in the wrong place,—like a pig in the parlor instead of the barnyard." *Euclid v. Ambler Realty Co.* We simply hold that when the Commission finds that a pig has entered the parlor, the exercise of its regulatory power does not depend on proof that the pig is obscene.

The judgment of the Court of Appeals is reversed.

It is so ordered.

* * *

MR. JUSTICE POWELL, with whom MR. JUSTICE BLACKMUN joins, concurring in part and concurring in the judgment.

. . . my views are generally in accord with what is said in Part IV–C of MR. JUSTICE STEVENS' opinion. I therefore join that portion of his opinion. I do not join Part IV–B, however, because I do not subscribe to the theory that the Justices of this Court are free generally to decide on the basis of its content which speech protected by the First Amendment is most "valuable" and hence deserving of the most protection, and which is less "valuable" and hence deserving of less protection. In my view, the result in this case does not turn on whether Carlin's monologue, viewed as a whole, or the words that constitute it, have more or less "value" than a candidate's campaign speech. This is a judgment for each person to make, not one for the judges to impose upon him.

The result turns instead on the unique characteristics of the broadcast media, combined with society's right to protect its children from speech generally agreed to be inappropriate for their years, and with the interest of unwilling adults in not being assaulted by such offensive speech in their homes. Moreover, I doubt whether today's decision will prevent any adult who wishes to receive Carlin's message in Carlin's own words from doing so, and from making for himself a value judgment as to the merit of the message and words. These are the grounds upon which I join the judgment of the Court as to Part IV.

MR. JUSTICE BRENNAN, with whom MR. JUSTICE MARSHALL joins, dissenting. . . .

. . . despite the Court's refusal to create a sliding scale of First Amendment protection calibrated to this Court's perception of the worth of a communication's content, and despite our unanimous agreement that the Carlin monologue is protected speech, a majority of the Court nevertheless finds that, on the facts of this case, the FCC is not constitutionally barred from imposing sanctions on Pacifica for its airing of the Carlin monologue. This majority apparently believes that the FCC's disapproval of Pacifica's afternoon broadcast of Carlin's "Dirty Words" recording is a permissible time, place, and manner regulation. Both the opinion of my Brother STEVENS and the opinion of my Brother POWELL rely principally on two factors in reaching this conclusion: (1) the capacity of a radio broadcast to intrude into the unwilling listener's home, and (2) the presence of children in the listening audience.

* * *

Without question, the privacy interests of an individual in his home are substantial and deserving of significant protection. In finding these interests sufficient to justify the content regulation of protected speech, however, the Court commits two errors. First, it misconceives the nature of the privacy interests involved where an individual voluntarily chooses to admit radio communications into his home. Second, it ignores the constitutionally protected interests of both those who wish to transmit and those who desire to receive broadcasts that many—including the FCC and this Court—might find offensive. . . .

Even if an individual who voluntarily opens his home to radio communications retains privacy interests of sufficient moment to justify a ban on protected speech if those interests are "invaded in an essentially intolerable manner," *Cohen v. California, supra,* at 21, the very fact that those interests are threatened only by a radio broadcast precludes any intolerable invasion of privacy; for unlike other intrusive modes of communication, such as sound trucks, "[t]he radio can be turned off," *Lehman v. Shaker Heights,* (1974)— and with a minimum of effort. . . .

Whatever the minimal discomfort suffered by a listener who inadvertently tunes into a program he finds offensive during the brief interval before he can simply extend his arm and switch stations or flick the "off" button, it is surely worth the candle to preserve the broadcaster's right to send, and the right of those interested to receive, a message entitled to full First Amendment protection. To reach a contrary balance, as does the Court, is clearly to follow MR. JUSTICE STEVENS' reliance on animal metaphors, "to burn the house to roast the pig." *Butler v. Michigan,* (1957). . . .

In concluding that the presence of children in the listening audience provides an adequate basis for the FCC to impose sanctions for Pacifica's broadcast of the Carlin monologue, the opinions of my Brother POWELL, and my Brother STEVENS, both stress the time-honored right of a parent to raise his child as he sees fit—a right this Court has consistently been vigilant to protect.

Yet this principle supports a result directly contrary to that reached by the Court. *Yoder* and *Pierce* hold that parents, *not* the government, have the right to make certain decisions regarding the upbringing of their children. As surprising as it may be to individual Members of this Court, some parents may actually find Mr. Carlin's unabashed attitude towards the seven "dirty words" healthy, and deem it desirable to expose their children to the manner in which Mr. Carlin defuses the taboo surrounding the words. Such parents may constitute a minority of the American public, but the absence of great numbers willing to exercise the right to raise their children in this fashion does not alter the right's nature or its existence. Only the Court's regrettable decision does that. . . .

It is quite evident that I find the Court's attempt to unstitch the warp and woof of First Amendment law in an effort to reshape its fabric to cover the patently wrong result the Court reaches in this case dangerous as well as lamentable. Yet there runs throughout the opinions of my Brothers POWELL and STEVENS another vein I find equally disturbing: a depressing inability to appreciate that in our land of cultural pluralism, there are many who think, act, and talk differently from the Members of this Court, and who do not share their fragile sensibilities. It is only an acute ethnocentric myopia that enables the Court to approve the censorship of communications solely because of the words they contain. . . .

Today's decision will thus have its greatest impact on broadcasters desiring to reach, and listening audiences composed of, persons who do not share the Court's view as to which words or expressions are acceptable and who, for a variety of reasons, including a conscious desire to flout majoritarian conventions, express themselves using words that may be regarded as offensive by those from different socio-economic backgrounds. In this context, the Court's decision may be seen for what, in the broader perspective, it really is: another of the dominant culture's inevitable efforts to force those groups who do not share its mores to conform to its way of thinking, acting, and speaking.

Pacifica, in response to an FCC inquiry about its broadcast of Carlin's satire on " 'the words you couldn't say on the public . . . airways.' " explained that "Carlin is not mouthing obscenities, he is merely using words to satirize as harmless and essentially silly our attitudes towards those words." F. C. C. 2d, at 95, 96. In confirming Carlin's prescience as a social commentator by the result it reaches today, the Court evinces an attitude toward the "seven dirty words" that many others besides Mr. Carlin and Pacifica might describe as "silly." Whether today's decision will similarly prove "harmless" remains to be seen. One can only hope that it will. . . .

Schad et al. v. Borough of Mount Ephraim

452 U.S. 61; 101 S. Ct. 2176; 66 L. Ed. 2d 127 (1981)
Vote: 7–2

In 1976, Schad operated an adult bookstore in Mount Ephraim, New Jersey. The store sold adult books, magazines, and films. In addition, the store offered a coin-operated mechanism which permitted a customer to watch a live nude dancer behind a glass panel. The use of property in the commercial zone in which Schad's bookstore was located was regulated by a Mount Ephraim zoning ordinance. In the zone all uses not listed in the ordinance were prohibited. Live dancing was not among the listed uses. Thus, upon complaint, Schad was convicted of violating the ordinance. After state courts refused to interfere with Schad's conviction, the U.S. Supreme Court noted probable jurisdiction.

JUSTICE WHITE delivered the opinion of the Court.

* * *

The First Amendment requires that there be sufficient justification for the exclusion of a broad category of protected expression as one of the permitted commercial uses in the Borough. The justification does not appear on the face of the ordinance since the ordinance itself is ambiguous with respect to whether live entertainment is permitted: § 99–15B purports to specify only the "principal" permitted uses in commercial establishments, and its listing of permitted retail establishments is expressly nonexclusive; yet, § 99–4 declares that all uses not expressly permitted are forbidden. The state courts at least partially resolved the ambiguity by declaring live entertainment to be an impermissible commercial use. In doing so, the County Court, whose opinion was adopted by the Appellate Division of the Superior Court, sought to avoid or to meet the First Amendment issue only by declaring that the restriction on the use of appellants' property was contained in a zoning ordinance that excluded all live entertainment from the Borough, including live nude dancing.

The power of local governments to zone and control land use is undoubtedly broad and its proper exercise is an essential aspect of achieving a satisfactory quality of life in both urban and rural communities. But the zoning power is not infinite and unchallengeable; it "must be exercised within constitutional limits." *Moore v. East Cleveland,* (1977) (STEVENS, J., concurring in judgment). Accordingly, it is subject to judicial review; and as is most often the case, the standard of review is determined by the nature of the right assertedly threatened or violated rather than by the power being exercised or the specific limitation imposed.

Where property interests are adversely affected by zoning, the courts generally have emphasized the breadth of municipal power to control land use and have sustained the regulation if it is rationally related to legitimate state concerns and does not deprive the owner of economically viable use of his property. But an ordinance may fail even under that limited standard of review.

Beyond that, as is true of other ordinances, when a zoning law infringes upon a protected liberty, it must be narrowly drawn and must further a sufficiently substantial government interest. . . .

In this case, however, Mount Ephraim has not adequately justified its substantial restriction of protected activity. None of the justifications asserted in this Court was articulated by the state courts and none of them withstands scrutiny. First, the Borough contends that permitting live entertainment would conflict with its plan to create a commercial area that caters only to the "immediate needs" of its residents and that would enable them to purchase at local stores the few items they occasionally forgot to buy outside the Borough. No evidence was introduced below to support this assertion, and it is difficult to reconcile this characterization of the Borough's commercial zones with the provisions of the ordinance. Section 99–15A expressly states that the purpose of creating commercial zones was to provide areas for "local and *regional* commercial operations." (Emphasis added.) The range of permitted uses goes far beyond providing for the "immediate needs" of the residents. Motels, hardware stores, lumber stores, banks, offices, and car showrooms are permitted in commercial zones. The list of permitted "retail stores" is nonexclusive, and it includes such services as beauty salons, barber shops, cleaners, and restaurants. Virtually the only item or service that may not be sold in a commercial zone is entertainment, or at least live entertainment. The Borough's first justification is patently insufficient.

Second, Mount Ephraim contends that it may selectively exclude commercial live entertainment from the broad range of commercial uses permitted in the Borough for reasons normally associated with zoning in commercial districts, that is, to avoid the problems that may be associated with live entertainment, such as parking, trash, police protection, and medical facilities. The Borough has presented no evidence, and its is not immediately apparent as a matter of experience, that live entertainment poses problems of this nature more significant than those associated with various permitted uses; nor does it appear that the Borough's zoning authority has arrived at a defensible conclusion that unusual problems are presented by live entertainment. We do not find it self-evident that a theater, for example, would create greater parking problems than would a restaurant. Even less apparent is what unique problems would be posed by exhibiting live nude dancing in connection with the sale of adult books and films, particularly since the bookstore is licensed to exhibit nude dancing on films. It may be that some forms of live entertainment would create problems that are not associated with the commercial uses presently permitted in Mount Ephraim. Yet this ordinance is not narrowly drawn to respond to what might be the distinctive problems arising from certain types of live entertainment, and it is not clear that a more selective approach would fail to address those unique problems if any there are. The Borough has not established that its interests could not be met by restrictions that are less intrusive on protected forms of expression.

The Borough also suggests that § 99–15B is a reasonable "time, place, and manner" restriction; yet it does not identify the municipal interests making it reasonable to exclude all commercial live entertainment but to allow a variety of other commercial uses in the Borough. . . .

To be reasonable, time, place, and manner restrictions not only must serve significant state interests but also must leave open adequate alternative channels of communication.

. . . the convictions of these appellants are infirm, and the judgment of the Appellate Division of the Superior Court of New Jersey is reversed and the case is remanded for further proceedings not inconsistent with this opinion.

So ordered.

* * *

CHIEF JUSTICE BURGER, with whom JUSTICE REHNQUIST joins, dissenting.

* * *

The Court depicts Mount Ephraim's ordinance as a ban on live entertainment. But, in terms, it does not mention any kind of entertainment. As applied, it operates as a ban on nude dancing in appellants' "adult" bookstore, and for that reason alone it is here. Thus, the issue *in the case that we have before us* is not whether Mount Ephraim may ban traditional live entertainment, but whether it may ban nude dancing, which is used as the "bait" to induce customers into the appellants' bookstore. When, and if, this ordinance is used to prevent a high school performance of "The Sound of Music," for example, the Court can deal with that problem.

An overconcern about draftsmanship and overbreadth should not be allowed to obscure the central question before us. It is clear that, in passing the ordinance challenged here, the citizens of the Borough of Mount Ephraim meant only to preserve the basic character of their community. It is just as clear that, by thrusting their live nude dancing shows on this community, the appellants alter and damage that community over its objections. As applied in this case, therefore, the ordinance speaks directly and unequivocally. It may be that, as applied in some other case, this ordinance would violate the First Amendment, but, since such a case is not before us, we should not decide it.

Even assuming that the "expression" manifested in the nude dancing that is involved here is somehow protected speech under the First Amendment, the Borough of Mount Ephraim is entitled to regulate it. In *Young v. American Mini-Theatres, Inc.,* (1972), we said:

> The mere fact that the commercial exploitation of material protected by the First Amendment is subject to zoning and other licensing requirements is not a sufficient reason for invalidating these ordinances.

Here, as in *American Mini-Theatres,* the zoning ordinance imposes a minimal intrusion on genuine rights of expression; only by contortions of logic can it be made otherwise. Mount Ephraim is a small community on the periphery of two major urban centers where this kind of entertainment may be found acceptable. The fact that nude dancing has been totally banned in this community is irrelevant. "Chilling" this kind of show business in this tiny residential enclave can hardly be thought to show that the appellants' "message" will be prohibited in nearby—and more sophisticated—cities.

The fact that a form of expression enjoys some constitutional protection does not mean that there are not times and places inappropriate for its exercise. The towns and villages of this Nation are not, and should not be, forced into a mold cast by this Court. Citizens should be free to choose to shape their community so that it embodies their conception of the "decent life." This will sometimes mean deciding that certain forms of activity—factories, gas stations, sports stadia, bookstores, and surely live nude shows—will not be allowed. That a community is willing to tolerate such a commercial use as a convenience store, a gas station, a pharmacy, or a delicatessen does not compel it also to tolerate every other "commercial use," including pornography peddlers and live nude shows.

In Federalist Paper No. 51, p. 160 (R. Fairfield ed. 1966), Madison observed:

> In framing a government which is to be administered by men over men, the great difficulty lies in this: you must first enable the government to control the governed; and in the next place oblidge it to control itself.

This expresses the balancing indispensable in all governing, and the Bill of Rights is one of the checks to control overreaching by government. But it is a check to be exercised sparingly by federal authority over local expressions of choice going to essentially local concerns. . . .

QUESTIONS AND COMMENTS

1 What test of obscenity does the Court employ in *F.C.C. v. Pacifica?*
2 Is Carlin's monologue protected speech? If so, how can it be barred from the airways?
3 Speaking for the Court, Justice Stevens says: "We simply hold that when the Commission finds that a pig has entered the parlor, the exercise of its regulatory power does not depend on proof that the pig is obscene." What is the principle being asserted here?
4 Brennan's dissent suggests that the Court's *attitude* toward the "seven dirty words" had much to do with its decision. For evidence that attitudes toward words might influence votes in cases, see *The Brethren,* pp. 128 ff, dealing with *Cohen v. California.*
5 Does *F.C.C. v. Pacifica* deal with obscenity or indecency? What is the difference insofar as constitutional law and the First Amendment are concerned?
6 Under what test is the dissenting position of Chief Justice Burger and Justice Rehnquist in *Schad* justified? Explain your answer.
7 Would George Carlin be protected if he delivered his "seven dirty words" monologue on cable television? Explain your answer.
8 In *Bolger v. Young Drug Products Inc.,* 51 LW 4961 (1983), the Court held that Congress could not ban the unsolicited mailing of advertisements for contraceptives.

Freedom of Religion

In the Schools

West Virginia Board of Education v. Barnette (1943)

Engel v. Vitale (1962)

Epperson v. Arkansas (1968)

Committee for Public Education v. Nyquist (1973)

The First Amendment says two things about religious freedom. One refers to "an establishment of religion," the other to the "free exercise" of religion, the so-called establishment and free exercise clauses. Congress is barred from legislating in regard to the first and from prohibiting the second. The free exercise clause leaves religious choice to individual preference. The establishment clause guarantees the secular state, or what is sometimes referred to as separation of church and state. Both clauses are now applicable against both the federal and the state governments.[18] Both reflect earlier experience with the English church and state. They also reflect a desire to avoid governmental oppression of religious minorities and oppression of any one faith by those of another through the use of state power.

The problem is that although the United States is a secular nation, its people are religious. And their religious doctrines, beliefs, and practices are exceedingly variegated. The proper role of government in dealing with a religious people on a day-to-day basis is not spelled out in the First Amendment. That role has been delineated through Supreme Court resolution of conflicts between government, on the one hand, and those who charge the government with violating the religion clauses of the First Amendment, on the other. Many of these conflicts have occurred in the context of public education. Such conflicts have not involved religious belief as much as religious practice, which includes not only overt acts but the freedom not to engage in acts which violate one's religious principles. An example of the latter is found in *Minersville School District v. Gobitis.*[19]

In *Minersville,* it was argued that the state could not, consistent with the First Amendment, impose a compulsory classroom flag salute on public school children. The Supreme Court rejected the argument and ruled for the school district. Its reason: flag salutes contribute to the "subtle process of securing effective loyalty to the traditional ideals of democracy."[20] Thus, the flag was seen as a symbol of national unity, the significance of which justified the encroachment. Frankfurter's opinion for the Court was joined by Justices Black, Douglas, and Murphy—all of whom had been on the Court only a short time when the case was decided in 1940. According to Douglas, Frankfurter got the three votes because he and the other two justices were inexperienced, Frankfurter was their hero, and they did not fully understand Frankfurter's position. By 1943, they had it all figured out, deserted Frankfurter and made a new majority in *West Virginia Board of Education v. Barnette.*[21]

West Virginia Board of Education et al. v. Barnette

319 U.S. 624; 63 S. Ct. 1178; 87 L. Ed. 1628 (1943)
Vote: 6–3

The facts are given in the opinion below.

MR. JUSTICE JACKSON delivered the opinion of the Court.

Following the decision by this Court on June 3, 1940, in *Minersville School District v. Gobitis,* the West Virginia legislature amended its statutes to require all schools therein to conduct courses of instruction in history, civics, and in the Constitutions of the United States and of the State "for the purpose of teaching, fostering and perpetuating the ideals, principles and spirit of Americanism, and increasing the knowledge of the organization and machinery of the government." Appellant Board of Education was directed, with advice of the State Superintendent of Schools, to "prescribe the courses of study covering these subjects" for public schools. The Act made it the duty of private, parochial and denominational schools to prescribe courses of study "similar to those required for the public schools."

The Board of Education on January 9, 1942, adopted a resolution containing recitals taken largely from the Court's *Gobitis* opinion and ordering that the salute to the flag become "a regular part of the program of activities in the public schools," that all teachers and pupils "shall be required to participate in the salute honoring the Nation represented by the Flag; provided, however, that refusal to salute the Flag be regarded as an act of insubordination, and shall be dealt with accordingly."

The resolution originally required the "commonly accepted salute to the Flag" which it defined. Objections to the salute as "being too much like Hitler's" were raised by the Parent and Teachers Association, the Boy and Girl Scouts, the Red Cross, and the Federation of Women's Clubs. Some modification appears to have been made in deference to these objections, but no concession was made to Jehovah's Witnesses. What is now required is the "stiff-arm" salute, the saluter to keep the right hand raised with palm turned up while the following is repeated: "I pledge allegiance to the Flag of the United States of America and to the Republic for which it stands; one Nation, indivisible, with liberty and justice for all."

Failure to conform is "insubordination" dealt with by expulsion. Readmission is denied by statute until compliance. Meanwhile the expelled child is "unlawfully absent" and may be proceeded against as a delinquent. His parents or guardians are liable to prosecution, and if convicted are subject to fine not exceeding $50 and jail term not exceeding thirty days.

Appellees, citizens of the United States and of West Virginia, brought suit in the United States District Court for themselves and others similarly situated asking its injunction to restrain enforcement of these laws and regulations against Jehovah's Witnesses. The Witnesses are an unincorporated body teaching that the obligation imposed by law of God is superior to that of laws enacted by temporal government. Their religious beliefs include a literal version of Exodus, Chapter 20, verses 4 and 5, which says: "Thou shalt not make unto thee any graven image, or any likeness of anything that is in heaven above, or that is in the earth beneath, or that is in the water under the earth; thou shalt not bow down thyself to them nor serve them." They consider that the flag is an "image" within this command. For this reason they refuse to salute it.

Children of this faith have been expelled from school and are threatened with exclusion for no other cause. Officials threaten to send them to reformatories maintained for criminally inclined juveniles. Parents of such children have been prosecuted and are threatened with prosecutions for causing delinquency.

The Board of Education moved to dismiss the complaint setting forth these facts and alleging that the law and regulations are an unconstitutional denial of religious freedom, and of freedom of speech, and are invalid under the "due process" and "equal protection" clauses of the Fourteenth Amendment to the Federal Constitution. The cause was submitted on the pleadings to a District Court of three judges. It restrained enforcement as to the plaintiffs and those of that class. The Board of Education brought the case here by direct appeal.

This case calls upon us to reconsider a precedent decision, as the Court throughout its history often has been required to do. . . . The question which underlies the flag salute controversy is whether such a ceremony so touching matters of opinion and political attitude may be imposed upon the individual by official authority under powers committed to any political organization under our Constitution. We examine rather than assume existence of this power and, against this broader definition of issues in this case, reëxamine specific grounds assigned for the *Gobitis* decision.

1. It was said that the flag-salute controversy confronted the Court with "the problem which Lincoln cast in memorable dilemma: 'Must a government of necessity be too *strong* for the liberties of its people, or too *weak* to maintain its own existence?'" and that the answer must be in favor of strength. *Minersville School District v. Gobitis, supra,* at 596.

We think these issues may be examined free of pressure or restraint growing out of such considerations. . . .

Government of limited power need not be anemic government. Assurance that rights are secure tends to diminish fear and jealousy of strong government, and by making us feel safe to live under it makes for its better support. Without promise of a limiting Bill of Rights it is doubtful if our Constitution could have mustered enough strength to enable its ratification. To enforce those rights today is not to choose weak government over strong government. It is only to adhere as a means of strength to individual freedom of mind in preference to officially disciplined uniformity for which history indicates a disappointing and disastrous end.

The subject now before us exemplifies this principle. Free public education, if faithful to the ideal of secular instruction and political neutrality, will not be partisan or enemy of any class, creed, party, or faction. If it is to impose any ideological discipline, however, each party or denomination must seek to control, or failing that, to weaken the influence of the educational system. Observance of the limitations of the Constitution will not weaken government in the field appropriate for its exercise.

2. It was also considered in the *Gobitis* case that functions of educational officers in States, counties and school districts were such that to interfere with their authority "would in effect make us the school board for the country."

[Local School] Boards are numerous and their territorial jurisdiction often small. But small and local authority may feel less sense of responsibility to the Constitution, and agencies of publicity may be less vigilant in calling it to account. The action of Congress in making flag observance voluntary and respecting the conscience of the objector in a matter so vital as raising the Army contrasts sharply with these local regulations in matters relatively trivial to the welfare of the nation. There are village tyrants as well as village Hampdens, but none who acts under color of law is beyond reach of the Constitution.

3. The *Gobitis* opinion reasoned that this is a field "where courts possess no marked and certainly no controlling competence," that it is committed to the

legislatures as well as the courts to guard cherished liberties and that it is constitutionally appropriate to "fight out the wise use of legislative assemblies rather than to transfer such a contest to the judicial arena," since all the "effective means of inducing political changes are left free."

The very purpose of a Bill of Rights was to withdraw certain subjects from the vicissitudes of political controversy, to place them beyond the reach of majorities and officials and to establish them as legal principles to be applied by the courts. One's right to life, liberty, and property, to free speech, a free press, freedom of worship and assembly, and other fundamental rights may not be submitted to vote: they depend on the outcome of no elections.

* * *

4. Lastly, and this is the very heart of the *Gobitis* opinion, it reasons that "National unity is the basis of national security," that the authorities have "the right to select appropriate means for its attainment," and hence reaches the conclusion that such compulsory measures toward "national unity" are constitutional. Upon the verity of this assumption depends our answer in this case.

National unity as an end which officials may foster by persuasion and example is not in question. The problem is whether under our Constitution compulsion as here employed is a permissible means for its achievement.

Struggles to coerce uniformity of sentiment in support of some end thought essential to their time and country have been waged by many good as well as by evil men. Nationalism is a relatively recent phenomenon but at other times and places the ends have been racial or territorial security, support of a dynasty or regime, and particular plans for saving souls. As first and moderate methods to attain unity have failed, those bent on its accomplishment must resort to an ever-increasing severity. As governmental pressure toward unity becomes greater, so strife becomes more bitter as to whose unity it shall be. Probably no deeper division of our people could proceed from any provocation than from finding it necessary to choose what doctrine and whose program public educational officials shall compel youth to unite in embracing. Ultimate futility of such attempts to compel coherence is the lesson of every such effort from the Roman drive to stamp out Christianity as a disturber of its pagan unity, the Inquisition, as a means to religious and dynastic unity, the Siberian exiles as a means to Russian unity, down to the fast failing efforts of our present totalitarian enemies. Those who begin coercive elimination of dissent soon find themselves exterminating dissenters. Compulsory unification of opinion achieves only the unanimity of the graveyard.

It seems trite but necessary to say that the First Amendment to our Constitution was designed to avoid these ends by avoiding these beginnings. There is no mysticism in the American concept of the State or of the nature or origin of its authority. We set up government by consent of the governed, and the Bill of Rights denies those in power any legal opportunity to coerce that consent. Authority here is to be controlled by public opinion, not public opinion by authority.

The case is made difficult not because the principles of its decision are obscure but because the flag involved is our own. Nevertheless, we apply the limitations of the Constitution with no fear that freedom to be intellectually and spiritually diverse or even contrary will disintegrate the social organization. To believe that patriotism will not flourish if patriotic ceremonies are voluntary and spontaneous instead of a compulsory routine is to make an unflattering estimate of the appeal of our institutions to free minds. We can have intellectual individualism and the rich cultural diversities that we owe to exceptional minds only at the price of occasional eccentricity and abnormal attitudes. When they are so harmless to others or to the State as those we deal with here, the price is not too great. But freedom to differ is not limited to things that do not matter much. That would be a mere shadow of freedom. The test of its substance is the right to differ as to things that touch the heart of the existing order.

If there is any fixed star in our constitutional constellation, it is that no official, high or petty, can prescribe what shall be orthodox in politics, nationalism, religion, or other matters of opinion or force citizens to confess by word or act their faith therein. If there are any circumstances which permit an exception, they do not now occur to us.

We think the action of the local authorities in compelling the flag salute and pledge transcends constitutional limitations on their power and invades the sphere of intellect and spirit which it is the purpose of the First Amendment to our Constitution to reserve from all official control.

The decision of this Court in *Minersville School District v. Gobitis* and the holdings of those few *per curiam* decisions which preceded and foreshadowed it are overruled, and the judgment enjoining enforcement of the West Virginia Regulation is

Affirmed.

* * *

MR. JUSTICE FRANKFURTER, dissenting:

One who belongs to the most vilified and persecuted minority in history is not likely to be insensible to the freedoms guaranteed by our Constitution. Were my purely personal attitude relevant I should wholeheartedly associate myself with the general libertarian views in the Court's opinion, representing as they do the thought and action of a lifetime. But as judges we are neither Jew nor Gentile, neither Catholic nor agnostic. We owe equal attachment to the Constitution and are equally bound by our judicial obligations whether we derive our citizenship from the earliest or the latest immigrants to these shores. As a member of this Court I am not justified in writing my private notions of policy into the Constitution, no matter how deeply I may cherish them or how mischievous I may deem their disregard. The duty of a judge who must decide which of two claims before the Court shall prevail, that of a State to enact and enforce laws within its general competence or that of an individual to refuse obedience because of the demands of his conscience, is not that of the ordinary person. It can never be emphasized too much that one's own opinion about the wisdom or evil of a law should be excluded altogether when one is doing one's duty on the bench. The only opinion of our own even looking in that direction that is material is our opinion whether legislators could in reason have enacted such a law. In the light of all the circumstances, including the history of this question in this Court, it would require more daring than I possess to deny that reasonable legislators could have taken the action which is before us for review. Most unwillingly, therefore, I must differ from my brethren with regard to legislation like this. I cannot bring my mind to believe that the "liberty" secured by the Due Process Clause gives this Court authority to deny to the State of West Virginia the attainment of that which we all recognize as a legitimate legislative end, namely, the promotion of good citizenship, by employment of the means here chosen. . . .

This is not dry, technical matter. It cuts deep into one's conception of the democratic process—it concerns no less the practical differences between the means for making these accommodations that are open to courts and to legislatures. A court can only strike down. It can only say "This or that law is void." It cannot modify or qualify, it cannot make exceptions to a general requirement. And it strikes down not merely for a day. At least the finding of unconstitutionality ought not to have ephemeral significance unless the Constitution is to be reduced to the fugitive importance of mere legislation. When we are dealing with the Constitution of the United States, and more particularly with the great safeguards of the Bill of Rights, we are dealing with principles of liberty and justice "so rooted in the traditions and conscience of our people as to be ranked as fundamental"—something without which "a fair and enlightened system of justice would be impossible." *Palko v. Connecticut, Hurtado v. California.* If the function of this Court is to be essentially no different from that of a legislature, if the considerations governing constitutional construction are to be substantially those that underlie legislation, then indeed judges should not have life tenure and they should be made directly responsible to the electorate.

* * *

The essence of the religious freedom guaranteed by our Constitution is . . . this: no religion shall either receive the state's support or incur its hostility. Religion is outside the sphere of political government. This does not mean that all matters on which religious organizations or beliefs may pronounce are outside the sphere of government. Were this so, instead of the separation of church and state, there would be the subordination of the state on any matter deemed within the sovereignty of the religious conscience. . . .

That claims are pressed on behalf of sincere religious convictions does not of itself establish their constitutional validity. Nor does waving the banner of religious freedom relieve us from examining into the power we are asked to deny the states. Otherwise the doctrine of separation of church and state, so cardinal in the history of this nation and for the liberty of our people, would mean not the disestablishment of a state church but the establishment of all churches and of all religious groups.

*   *   *

We are told that a flag salute is a doubtful substitute for adequate understanding of our institutions. The states that require such a school exercise do not have to justify it as the only means for promoting good citizenship in children, but merely as one of diverse means for accomplishing a worthy end. We may deem it a foolish measure, but the point is that this Court is not the organ of government to resolve doubts as to whether it will fulfill its purpose. Only if there be no doubt that any reasonable mind could entertain can we deny to the states the right to resolve doubts their way and not ours.

That which to the majority may seem essential for the welfare of the state may offend the consciences of a minority. But, so long as no inroads are made upon the actual exercise of religion by the minority, to deny the political power of the majority to enact laws concerned with civil matters, simply because they may offend the consciences of a minority, really means that the consciences of a minority are more sacred and more enshrined in the Constitution than the consciences of a majority.

We are told that symbolism is a dramatic but primitive way of communicating ideas. Symbolism is inescapable. Even the most sophisticated live by symbols. But it is not for this Court to make psychological judgments as to the effectiveness of a particular symbol in inculcating concededly indispensable feelings, particularly if the state happens to see fit to utilize the symbol that represents our heritage and our hopes. And surely only flippancy could be responsible for the suggestion that constitutional validity of a requirement to salute our flag implies equal validity of a requirement to salute a dictator. The significance of a symbol lies in what it represents. To reject the swastika does not imply rejection of the Cross. And so it bears repetition to say that it mocks reason and denies our whole history to find in the allowance of a requirement to salute our flag on fitting occasions the seeds of sanction for obeisance to a leader. To deny the power to employ educational symbols is to say that the state's educational system may not stimulate the imagination because this may lead to unwise stimulation.

*   *   *

Saluting the flag suppresses no belief nor curbs it. Children and their parents may believe what they please, avow their belief and practice it. It is not even remotely suggested that the requirement for saluting the flag involves the slightest restriction against the fullest opportunity on the part both of the children and of their parents to disavow as publicly as they choose to do so the meaning that others attach to the gesture of salute. All channels of affirmative free expression are open to both children and parents. Had we before us any act of the state putting the slightest curbs upon such free expression, I should not lag behind any member of this Court in striking down such an invasion of the right to freedom of thought and freedom of speech protected by the Constitution.

* * *

One's conception of the Constitution cannot be severed from one's conception of a judge's function in applying it. The Court has no reason for existence if it merely reflects the pressures of the day. Our system is built on the faith that men set apart for this special function, freed from the influence of immediacy and from the deflections of worldly ambition, will become able to take a view of longer range than the period of responsibility entrusted to Congress and legislatures. We are dealing with matters as to which legislators and voters have conflicting views. Are we as judges to impose our strong convictions on where wisdom lies? That which three years ago had seemed to five successive Courts to lie within permissible areas of legislation is now outlawed by the deciding shift of opinion of two Justices. What reason is there to believe that they or their successors may not have another view a few years hence? Is that which was deemed to be of so fundamental a nature as to be written into the Constitution to endure for all times to be the sport of shifting winds of doctrine? Of course, judicial opinions, even as to questions of constitutionality, are not immutable. As has been true in the past, the Court will from time to time reverse its position. But I believe that never before these Jehovah's Witnesses cases (except for minor deviations subsequently retraced) has this Court overruled decisions so as to restrict the powers of democratic government.

* * *

Of course patriotism can not be enforced by the flag salute. But neither can the liberal spirit be enforced by judicial invalidation of illiberal legislation. Our constant preoccupation with the constitutionality of legislation rather than with its wisdom tends to preoccupation of the American mind with a false value. The tendency of focussing attention on constitutionality is to make constitutionality synonymous with wisdom, to regard a law as all right if it is constitutional. Such an attitude is a great enemy of liberalism. Particularly in legislation affecting freedom of thought and freedom of speech much which should offend a free-spirited society is constitutional. Reliance for the most precious interests of civilization, therefore, must be found outside of their vindication in courts of law. Only a persistent positive translation of the faith of a free society into the convictions and habits and actions of a community is the ultimate reliance against unabated temptations to fetter the human spirit.

QUESTIONS AND COMMENTS

1 In *Barnette,* what test was employed to strike the pledge and flag salute requirements?
2 Did the Court make law when it decided that the right to free speech includes the right to remain silent? Or when it decided to overrule the precedent established in *Gobitis?* Or when it decided what test to employ in evaluating Barnette's claim? Is this activism? What dimension?

3 Judging from Frankfurter's dissent, does he find the First Amendment's religion clauses equally protective against state and federal action? Explain.

4 Frankfurter says that "Our constant preoccupation with the constitutionality of legislation rather than with its wisdom tends to preoccupation of the American mind with a false value." What does he mean here? What role for the Court does Frankfurter envisage?

* * * * * *

If a state may not require a salute and pledge to the flag in its public school rooms, what else may it not require? *Engel v. Vitale* suggests one answer to the question. As with the pledge of allegiance to the flag, this case involves an attempt to inculcate certain values in young schoolchildren. In the case of the flag, the values were secular. But school prayer is religious. And the knife must cut both ways.

In *Epperson v. Arkansas,* the question is inverted, though the effect is the same. By prohibiting certain teachings in a public school, the state leaves the field to other competing teachings. Thus, it promotes the values of these competing teachings. But even if competing teachings are not involved, the denial of the right to teach a given theory, in this case the theory of evolution, promotes the acceptance of competing theories whether these theories are offered in or out of the classroom. Since the most obvious competing theory is found in Christian doctrine, the *Epperson*-type prohibition may violate Jefferson's wall of separation between church and state.[22]

Engel v. Vitale

370 U.S. 421; 82 S. Ct. 1261; 8 L. Ed. 2d 601 (1962)
Vote: 6–1

The facts of this case are provided in the opinion below.

MR. JUSTICE BLACK delivered the opinion of the Court.

The respondent Board of Education of Union Free School District No. 9, New Hyde Park, New York, acting in its official capacity under state law, directed the School District's principal to cause the following prayer to be said aloud by each class in the presence of a teacher at the beginning of each school day:

> Almighty God, we acknowledge our dependence upon Thee, and we beg Thy blessings upon us, our parents, our teachers and our Country.

This daily procedure was adopted on the recommendation of the State Board of Regents, a governmental agency created by the State Constitution to which the New York Legislature has granted broad supervisory, executive, and legislative powers over the State's public school system. These state officials composed the prayer which they recommended and published as a part of their "Statement on Moral and Spiritual Training in the Schools," saying "We believe that this Statement will be subscribed to by all men and women of good will, and we call upon all of them to aid in giving life to our program."

Shortly after the practice of reciting the Regents' prayer was adopted by the School District, the parents of ten pupils brought this action in a New York State Court insisting that use of this official prayer in the public schools was contrary to the beliefs, religions, or religious practices of both themselves and their children. Among other things, these parents challenged the constitutionality of both the state law authorizing the School District to direct the use of prayer in public schools and the School District's regulation ordering the recitation of this particular prayer on the ground that these actions of official governmental agencies violate that part of the First Amendment of the Federal Constitution which commands that "Congress shall make no law respecting an establishment of religion"—a command which was "made applicable to the State of New York by the Fourteenth Amendment of the said Constitution." The New York Court of Appeals, over the dissents of Judges Dye and Fuld, sustained an order of the lower state courts which had upheld the power of New York to use the Regents' prayer as a part of the daily procedures of its public schools so long as the schools did not compel any pupil to join in the prayer over his or his parents' objection. We granted certiorari to review this important decision involving rights protected by the First and Fourteenth Amendments.

* * *

The petitioners contend among other things that the state laws requiring or permitting use of the Regents' prayer must be struck down as a violation of the Establishment Clause because that prayer was composed by governmental officials as a part of a governmental program to further religious beliefs. For this reason, petitioners argue, the State's use of the Regents' prayer in its public school system breaches the constitutional wall of separation between Church and State. We agree with that contention since we think that the constitutional prohibition against laws respecting an establishment of religion must at least mean that in this country it is no part of the business of government to compose official prayers for any group of the American people to recite as a part of a religious program carried on by government. . . .

There can be no doubt that New York's state prayer program officially establishes the religious beliefs embodied in the Regents' prayer. The respondents' argument to the contrary, which is largely based upon the contention that the Regents' prayer is "non-denominational" and the fact that the program, as modified and approved by state courts, does not require all pupils to recite the prayer but permits those who wish to do so to remain silent or be excused from the room, ignores the essential nature of the program's constitutional defects. Neither the fact that the prayer may be denominationally neutral nor the fact that its observance on the part of the students is voluntary can serve to free it from the limitations of the Establishment Clause, as it might from the Free Exercise Clause, of the First Amendment, both of which are operative against the States by virtue of the Fourteenth Amendment. Although these two clauses may in certain instances overlap, they forbid two quite different kinds of governmental encroachment upon religious freedom. The Establishment Clause, unlike the Free Exercise Clause, does not depend upon any showing of direct governmental compulsion and is violated by the enactment of laws which establish an official religion whether those laws operate directly to coerce non-observing individuals or not. This is not to say, of course, that laws officially prescribing a particular form of religious worship do not involve coercion of such individuals. When the power, prestige and financial support of government is placed behind a particular religious belief, the indirect coercive pressure upon religious minorities to conform to the prevailing officially approved religion is plain. But the purposes underlying the Establishment Clause go much further than that. Its first and most immediate purpose rested on the belief that a union of government and religion tends to destroy government and to degrade religion. The history of governmentally established religion, both in England and in this country, showed that whenever government had allied itself with one particular form of religion, the inevitable result had been that it had incurred the hatred, disrespect and even contempt of those who held contrary beliefs. That same history showed that many people had lost their respect for any religion that had relied upon the support of government to spread its faith. The Establishment Clause thus stands as an expression of principle on the part of the Founders of our Constitution that religion is too personal, too sacred, too holy, to permit its "unhallowed perversion" by a civil magistrate. Another purpose of the Establishment Clause rested upon an awareness of the historical fact that governmentally established religions and religious persecutions go hand in hand. The Founders knew that only a few years after the Book of Common Prayer became the only accepted form of religious services in the established Church of England, an Act of Uniformity was passed to compel all Englishmen to attend those services and to make it a criminal offense to conduct or attend religious gatherings of any other kind— a law which was consistently flouted by dissenting religious groups in England and which contributed to widespread persecutions of people like John Bunyan who persisted in holding "unlawful [religious] meetings . . . to the great disturbance and distraction of the good subjects of this kingdom. . . ." And they knew that similar persecutions had received the sanction of law in several of the colonies in this country soon after the establishment of official religions in those colonies. It was in large part to get completely away from this sort of systematic religious persecution that the Founders brought into being our Nation, our Constitution, and our Bill of Rights with its prohibition against any governmental establishment of religion. The New York laws officially prescribing the Regents' prayer are inconsistent both with the purposes of the Establishment Clause and with the Establishment Clause itself.

It has been argued that to apply the Constitution in such a way as to prohibit state laws respecting an establishment of religious services in public schools is to indicate a hostility toward religion or toward prayer. Nothing, of course, could be more wrong. . . . It is neither sacrilegious nor antireligious to say that each separate government in this country should stay out of the business of writing or sanctioning official prayers and leave that purely religious function to the people themselves and to those the people choose to look to for religious guidance.

* * *

The judgment of the Court of Appeals of New York is reversed and the cause remanded for further proceedings not inconsistent with this opinion.

Reversed and remanded.

* * *

MR. JUSTICE STEWART, dissenting.

* * *

The Court does not hold, nor could it, that New York has interfered with the free exercise of anybody's religion. For the state courts have made clear that those who object to reciting the prayer must be entirely free of any compulsion to do so, including any "embarrassments and pressures." Cf. *West Virginia State Board of Education v. Barnette,* 319 U. S. 624. But the Court says that in permitting school children to say this simple prayer, the New York authorities have established "an official religion."

With all respect, I think the Court has misapplied a great constitutional principle. I cannot see how an "official religion" is established by letting those who want to say a prayer say it. On the contrary, I think that to deny the wish of these school children to join in reciting this prayer is to deny them the opportunity of sharing in the spiritual heritage of our Nation. . . .

At the opening of each day's Session of this Court we stand, while one of our officials invokes the protection of God. Since the days of John Marshall our Crier has said, "God save the United States and this Honorable Court." Both the Senate and the House of Representatives open their daily Sessions with prayer. Each of our Presidents, from George Washington to John F. Kennedy, has upon assuming his Office asked the protection and help of God.

The Court today says that the state and federal governments are without constitutional power to prescribe any particular form of words to be recited by any group of the American people on any subject touching religion. One of the stanzas of "The Star-Spangled Banner," made our National Anthem by Act of Congress in 1931, contains these verses:

Blest with victory and peace, may the heav'n rescued land
    Praise the Pow'r that hath made and preserved us a nation!
Then conquer we must, when our cause it is just,
    And this be our motto "In God is our Trust."

In 1954 Congress added a phrase to the Pledge of Allegiance to the Flag so that it now contains the words "one Nation *under God,* indivisible, with liberty and justice for all." In 1952 Congress enacted legislation calling upon the President each year to proclaim a National Day of Prayer. Since 1865 the words "In God We Trust" have been impressed on our coins.

Countless similar examples could be listed, but there is no need to belabor the obvious. It was all summed up by this Court just ten years ago in a single sentence: "We are a religious people whose institutions presuppose a Supreme Being." *Zorach v. Clauson,* 343 U. S. 306, 313.

I do not believe that this Court, or the Congress, or the President has by the actions and practices I have mentioned established an "official religion" in violation of the Constitution. And I do not believe the State of New York has done so in this case. What each has done has been to recognize and to follow the deeply entrenched and highly cherished spiritual traditions of our Nation—traditions which come down to us from those who almost two hundred years ago avowed their "firm Reliance on the Protection of divine Providence" when they proclaimed the freedom and independence of this brave new world.

I dissent.

Epperson v. Arkansas

393 U.S. 97; 89 S. Ct. 266; 21 L. Ed. 2d 228 (1968)
Vote: 9–0

In 1928, Arkansas adopted a statute prohibiting teaching in its public schools and universities that the human race evolved from other species of life. Violation was made a misdemeanor, with dismissal mandated upon conviction. Susan Epperson was a teacher in the Little Rock school system in the fall of 1964. At the start of the 1965 school year, she was confronted with a new biology textbook to be used in her 1965 classes. The book contained a chapter on Darwinian evolution—material condemned by the Arkansas statute. Faced with the dilemma of teaching the text as directed by school authorities, which would subject her to dismissal under the statute, she went to court. She sought and got a ruling that the statute was void as a violation of the First Amendment. On appeal, the supreme court of Arkansas reversed. Appeal was then duly taken to the U.S. Supreme Court.

MR. JUSTICE FORTAS delivered the opinion of the Court.

* * *

Government in our democracy, state and national, must be neutral in matters of religious theory, doctrine, and practice. It may not be hostile to any religion or to the advocacy of no-religion; and it may not aid, foster, or promote one religion or religious theory against another or even against the militant opposite. The First Amendment mandates governmental neutrality between religion and religion, and between religion and nonreligion.

. . . The State's undoubted right to prescribe the curriculum for its public schools does not carry with it the right to prohibit, on pain of criminal penalty, the teaching of a scientific theory or doctrine where that prohibition is based upon reasons that violate the First Amendment. It is much too late to argue that the State may impose upon the teachers in its schools any conditions that it chooses, however restrictive they may be of constitutional guarantees.

In the present case, there can be no doubt that Arkansas has sought to prevent its teachers from discussing the theory of evolution because it is contrary to the belief of some that the Book of Genesis must be the exclusive source of doctrine as to the origin of man. No suggestion has been made that Arkansas' law may be justified by considerations of state policy other than the religious views of some of its citizens. It is clear that fundamentalist sectarian conviction was and is the law's reason for existence. Its antecedent, Tennessee's "monkey law," candidly stated its purpose: to make it unlawful "to teach any theory that denies the story of the Divine Creation of man as taught in the Bible, and to teach instead that man has descended from a lower order of animals." Perhaps the sensational publicity attendant upon the *Scopes* trial induced Arkansas to adopt less explicit language. It eliminated Tennessee's reference to "the story of the Divine Creation of man" as taught in the Bible, but there is no doubt that the motivation for the law was the same: to suppress the teaching of a theory which, it was thought, "denied" the divine creation of man.

Arkansas' law cannot be defended as an act of religious neutrality. Arkansas did not seek to excise from the curricula of its schools and universities all discussion of the origin of man. The law's effort was confined to an attempt to blot out a particular theory because of its supposed conflict with the Biblical account, literally read. Plainly, the law is contrary to the mandate of the First, and in violation of the Fourteenth, Amendment to the Constitution.

The judgment of the Supreme Court of Arkansas is

Reversed.

QUESTIONS AND COMMENTS

1 Does the Court's decision in *Engel* permit any kind of religious prayer in the public school classroom? What if the state required that the prayer given by the chaplain to open congressional sessions be read in each public classroom? Constitutional? What if the chaplain's prayer was given to each student who requested it and 2 minutes was set aside for contemplation? Constitutional?

2 In 1963, the Court struck a Pennsylvania statute requiring Bible reading in public school rooms as a violation of the establishment clause (*School District v. Schempp,* 374 U.S. 203).

3 It is argued that making religious exercises in public school classrooms voluntary sets apart those who choose not to participate and that this is "bad." Do you agree? Why? Consider the view of Irwin Griswold "Absolute Is in the Dark—A Discussion of the Approach of the Supreme Court to Constitutional Questions," 8 *Utah Law Review* 167, 177 (1963). Griswold argues that it is educational to let children who are different know that they are different and that their "differences" are tolerated. Do you agree? Discuss.

Our fourth case falls in an issue area that has frequently involved the Court and one which remains highly controversial today. The question in *Committee v. Nyquist* pertains to the kind and type of financial aid a state may give to religion via the use of its schools or educational policy. Generally, the state, through its legislative enactments, must neither advance nor inhibit religion. It must also proceed in such a way as to avoid excessive governmental entanglement with religion. In all cases, however, it is a judgment call, since no formula exists which will provide objective answers to challenges raised.

In *Everson v. Board of Education,*[23] the Court allowed a state to reimburse parents for the cost of transporting their children to parochial schools. A year later, it denied an Illinois school district the right to give students religious instruction in the schools during school hours, even though the other students were "released" during the time of such instruction.[24] In 1952, however, a released-time program in which students were "released" and given religious instruction off campus was approved.[25] A more recent and more complex case is *Lemon v. Kurtzman.*[26] In that case, the Court, striking state pay supplements to parochial school teachers and other supplements to the schools themselves, enunciated a three-part test for determining an "excessive entanglement with religion": (1) whether the law is intended to achieve a secular legislative purpose, (2) whether its primary effect neither advances nor inhibits religion, and (3) whether the law fosters an excessive entanglement with religion.

Committee for Public Education and Religious Liberty et al. v. Nyquist, Commissioner of Education of New York et al.

413 U.S. 756; 93 S. Ct. 2955; 37 L. Ed. 2d 948 (1973)
Vote: 8–1

New York education and tax laws established several financial aid programs for nonpublic elementary and secondary schools. One provision provided for direct money grants to be used for the maintenance and repair of facilities and equipment to ensure the health and safety of the students. Another established a tuition reimbursement plan for parents of children attending eligible nonpublic schools. A third program allowed each eligible taxpayer parent to take certain deductions from gross income for each child attending eligible schools. Effectively, this lowered the income tax paid to the state by such parents. Almost all the schools eligible for maintenance grants were related to the Roman Catholic church and taught church-related religious doctrine. However, a substantial number of non-Catholic schools were eligible for aid and assistance under the other provisions of the laws.

Challenged as a violation of the establishment clause of the First Amendment, the maintenance, repair, and tuition reimbursement provisions were found invalid by a federal district court. However, the court upheld the income tax provisions. The U.S. Supreme Court agreed to review all three holdings.

MR. JUSTICE POWELL delivered the opinion of the Court.

* * *

Most of the cases coming to this Court raising Establishment Clause questions have involved the relationship between religion and education. Among these religion-education precedents, two general categories of cases may be identified: those dealing with religious activities within the public schools, and those involving public aid in varying forms to sectarian educational institutions. While the New York legislation places this case in the latter category, its resolution requires consideration not only of the several aid-to-sectarian-education cases, but also of our other education precedents and of several important noneducation cases. For the now well-defined three-part test that has emerged from our decisions is a product of considerations derived from the full sweep of the Establishment Clause cases. Taken together, these decisions dictate that to pass muster under the Establishment Clause the law in question, first, must reflect a clearly secular legislative purpose, second, must have a primary effect that neither advances nor inhibits religion, and, third, must avoid excessive government entanglement with religion.

In applying these criteria to the three distinct forms of aid involved in this case, we need touch only briefly on the requirement of a "secular legislative purpose." As the recitation of legislative purposes appended to New York's law indicates, each measure is adequately supported by legitimate, nonsectarian state interests. We do not question the propriety, and fully secular content, of New York's interest in preserving a healthy and safe educational environment for all of its schoolchildren. And we do not doubt—indeed, we fully recognize—the validity of the State's interests in promoting pluralism and diversity among its public and nonpublic schools. Nor do we hesitate to acknowledge the reality of its concern for an already overburdened public school system that might suffer in the event that a significant percentage of children presently attending nonpublic schools should abandon those schools in favor of the public schools.

But the propriety of a legislature's purposes may not immunize from further scrutiny a law which either has a primary effect that advances religion, or which fosters excessive entanglements between Church and State. Accordingly, we must weigh each of the three aid provisions challenged here against these criteria of effect and entanglement.

The "maintenance and repair" provisions of § 1 authorize direct payments to nonpublic schools, virtually all of which are Roman Catholic schools in low-income areas. The grants, totaling $30 or $40 per pupil depending on the age of the institution, are given largely without restriction on usage. So long as expenditures do not exceed 50% of comparable expenses in the public school system, it is possible for a sectarian elementary or secondary school to finance its entire "maintenance and repair" budget from state tax-raised funds. No attempt is made to restrict payments to those expenditures related to the upkeep of facilities used exclusively for secular purposes, nor do we think it possible within the context of these religion-oriented institutions to impose such restrictions. Nothing in the statute, for instance, bars a qualifying school from paying out of state funds the salaries of employees who maintain the school chapel, or the cost of renovating classrooms in which religion is taught, or the cost of heating and lighting those same facilities. Absent appropriate restrictions on expenditures for these and similar purposes, it simply cannot be denied that this section has a primary effect that advances religion in that it subsidizes directly the religious activities of sectarian elementary and secondary schools.

The state officials nevertheless argue that these expenditures for "maintenance and repair" are similar to other financial expenditures approved by this Court. Primarily they rely on *Everson v. Board of Education, supra; Board of Education v. Allen,* (1968); and *Tilton v. Richardson,* (1971). In each of those cases it is true that the Court approved a form of financial assistance which conferred undeniable benefits upon private, sectarian schools. But a close examination of those cases illuminates their distinguishing characteristics. In *Everson,* the Court, in a five-to-four decision, approved a program of reimbursements to parents of public as well as parochial schoolchildren for bus fares paid in connection with transportation to and from school, a program which the Court characterized as approaching the "verge" of impermissible state aid. In *Allen,* decided some 20 years later, the Court upheld a New York law authorizing the provision of *secular* textbooks for all children in grades seven through 12 attending public and nonpublic schools. Finally, in *Tilton,* the Court upheld federal grants of funds for the construction of facilities to be used for clearly *secular* purposes by public and nonpublic institutions of higher learning.

These cases simply recognize that sectarian schools perform secular, educational functions as well as religious functions, and that some forms of aid may be channeled to the secular without providing direct aid to the sectarian. . . . But an indirect and incidental effect beneficial to religious institutions has never been thought a sufficient defect to warrant the invalidation of a state law.

. . . New York's maintenance and repair provisions violate the Establishment Clause because their effect, inevitably, is to subsidize and advance the religious mission of sectarian schools.

* * *

New York's tuition reimbursement program also fails the "effect" test, for much the same reasons that govern its maintenance and repair grants. The state program is designed to allow direct, unrestricted grants of $50 to $100 per child (but no more than 50% of tuition actually paid) as reimbursement to parents in low-income brackets who send their children to nonpublic schools, the bulk of which is concededly sectarian in orientation. To qualify, a parent must have earned less than $5,000 in taxable income and must present a receipted tuition bill from a nonpublic school.

There can be no question that these grants could not, consistently with the Establishment Clause, be given directly to sectarian schools, since they would suffer from the same deficiency that renders invalid the grants for maintenance and repair. In the absence of an effective means of guaranteeing that the state aid derived from public funds will be used exclusively for secular, neutral, and nonideological purposes, it is clear from our cases that direct aid in whatever form is invalid. . . . The controlling question here, then, is whether the fact that the grants are delivered to parents rather than schools is of such significance as to compel a contrary result. The State and intervenor-appellees rely on *Everson* and *Allen* for their claim that grants to parents, unlike grants to institutions, respect the "wall of separation" required by the Constitution. It is true that in those cases the Court upheld laws that provided benefits to children attending religious schools and to their parents: As noted above, in *Everson* parents were reimbursed for bus fares paid to send children to parochial schools, and in *Allen* textbooks were loaned directly to the children. But those decisions make clear that, far from providing a *per se* immunity from examination of the substance of the State's program, the fact that aid is disbursed to parents rather than to the schools is only one among many factors to be considered.

. . . By reimbursing parents for a portion of their tuition bill, the State seeks to relieve their financial burdens sufficiently to assure that they continue to have the option to send their children to religion-oriented schools. And while the other purposes for that aid—to perpetuate a pluralistic educational environment and to protect the fiscal integrity of overburdened public schools—

are certainly unexceptionable, the effect of the aid is unmistakably to provide desired financial support for nonpublic, sectarian institutions.

* * *

Although we think it clear, for the reasons above stated, that New York's tuition grant program fares no better under the "effect" test than its maintenance and repair program, in view of the novelty of the question we will address briefly the subsidiary arguments made by the state officials and intervenors in its defense.

First, it has been suggested that it is of controlling significance that New York's program calls for *reimbursement* for tuition already paid rather than for direct contributions which are merely routed through the parents to the schools, in advance of or in lieu of payment by the parents. The parent is not a mere conduit, we are told, but is absolutely free to spend the money he receives in any manner he wishes. There is no element of coercion attached to the reimbursement, and no assurance that the money will eventually end up in the hands of religious schools. The absence of any element of coercion, however, is irrelevant to questions arising under the Establishment Clause. In *School District of Abington Township v. Schempp,* (1963) it was contended that Bible recitations in public schools did not violate the Establishment Clause because participation in such exercises was not coerced. The Court rejected that argument, noting that while proof of coercion might provide a basis for a claim under the Free Exercise Clause, it was not a necessary element of any claim under the Establishment Clause. . . .

Second, the Majority Leader and President pro tem of the State Senate argues that it is significant here that the tuition reimbursement grants pay only a portion of the tuition bill, and an even smaller portion of the religious school's total expenses. The New York statute limits reimbursement to 50% of any parent's actual outlay. Additionally, intervenor estimates that only 30% of the total cost of nonpublic education is covered by tuition payments, with the remaining coming from "voluntary contribution, endowments and the like." On the basis of these two statistics, appellees reason that the "maximum tuition reimbursement by the State is thus only 15% of educational costs in the nonpublic schools." And, "since the compulsory education laws of the State, by necessity require significantly more than 15% of school time to be devoted to teaching secular courses," the New York statute provides "a statistical guarantee of neutrality." It should readily be seen that this is simply another variant of the argument we have rejected as to maintenance and repair costs, and it can fare no better here. Obviously, if accepted, this argument would provide the foundation for massive, direct subsidization of sectarian elementary and secondary schools. . . .

Finally, the State argues that its program of tuition grants should survive scrutiny because it is designed to promote the free exercise of religion. The State notes that only "low-income parents" are aided by this law, and without state assistance their right to have their children educated in a religious environment "is diminished or even denied." It is true, of course, that this Court has long recognized and maintained the right to choose nonpublic over public education. It is also true that a state law interfering with a parent's right to have his child educated in a sectarian school would run afoul of the Free Exercise Clause. But this Court repeatedly has recognized that tension inevitably exists between the Free Exercise and the Establishment Clauses, and that it may often not be possible to promote the former without offending the latter. As a result of this tension, our cases require the State to maintain an attitude of "neutrality," neither "advancing" nor "inhibiting" religion. In its attempt to enhance the opportunities of the poor to choose between public and nonpublic education, the State has taken a step which can only be regarded as one "advancing" religion. However great our sympathy for the burdens experienced by those who must pay public school taxes at the same time that they support other schools because of the constraints of "conscience and discipline," and notwithstanding the "high social importance" of the State's purposes, neither may justify an eroding of the limitations of the Establishment Clause now firmly emplanted.

Sections 3, 4, and 5 establish a system for providing income tax benefits to parents of children attending New York's nonpublic schools. . . .

Appellees defend the tax portion of New York's legislative package on two grounds. First, they contend that it is of controlling significance that the grants or credits are directed to the parents rather than to the schools. This is the same argument made in support of the tuition reimbursements and rests on the same reading of the same precedents of this Court, primarily *Everson* and *Allen.* Our treatment of this issue is applicable here and requires rejection of this claim. Second, appellees place their strongest reliance on *Walz v. Tax Comm'n,* (1970), in which New York's property tax exemption for religious organizations was upheld. We think that *Walz* provides no support for appellees' position. Indeed, its rationale plainly compels the conclusion that New York's tax package violates the Establishment Clause.

Tax exemptions for church property enjoyed an apparently universal approval in this country both before and after the adoption of the First Amendment. The Court in *Walz* surveyed the history of tax exemptions and found that each of the 50 States has long provided for tax exemptions for places of worship, that Congress has exempted religious organizations from taxation for over three-quarters of a century, and that congressional enactments in 1802, 1813, and 1870 specifically exempted church property from taxation. In sum, the Court concluded that "[f]ew concepts are more deeply embedded in the fabric of our national life, beginning with pre-Revolutionary colonial times, than for the government to exercise at the very least this kind of benevolent neutrality toward churches and religious exercise generally." We know of no historical precedent for New York's recently promulgated tax relief program. Indeed, it seems clear that tax benefits for parents whose children attend parochial schools are a recent innovation, occasioned by the growing financial plight of such nonpublic institutions and designed, albeit unsuccessfully, to tailor state aid in a manner not incompatible with the recent decisions of this Court.

* * *

Our examination of New York's aid provisions, in light of all relevant considerations, compels the judgment that each, as written, has a "primary effect that advances religion" and offends the constitutional prohibition against laws "respecting an establishment of religion." We therefore affirm the three-judge court's holding as to §§ 1 and 2, and reverse as to §§ 3, 4, and 5.

It is so ordered.

* * *

Mr. Justice White, joined in part by The Chief Justice and Mr. Justice Rehnquist, dissenting.

Each of the States regards the education of its young to be a critical matter—so much so that it compels school attendance and provides an educational system at public expense. Any otherwise qualified child is entitled to a free elementary and secondary school education, or at least an education that costs him very little as compared with its cost to the State.

This Court has held, however, that the Due Process Clause of the Fourteenth Amendment to the Constitution entitles parents to send their children to nonpublic schools, secular or sectarian, if those schools are sufficiently competent to educate the child in the necessary secular subjects. About 10% of the Nation's children, approximately 5.2 million students, now take this option and are not being educated in public schools at public expense. Under state law these children have a right to a free public education and it would not appear unreasonable if the State, relieved of the expense of educating a child in the public school, contributed to the expense of his education elsewhere. The parents of such children pay taxes, including school taxes. They could receive in return a free education in the public schools. They prefer to send their children, as they have the right to do, to nonpublic schools that furnish the satisfactory equivalent of a public school education but also offer subjects or other assumed advantages not available in public schools. Constitutional considerations aside, it would be understandable if a State gave such parents a call on the public treasury up to the amount it would have cost the State to educate the child in public school, or, to put it another way, up to the amount the parents save the State by not sending their children to public school.

In light of the Free Exercise Clause of the First Amendment, this would seem particularly the case where the parent desires his child to attend a school that offers not only secular subjects but religious training as well. A State should put no unnecessary obstacles in the way of religious training for the young. "When the state encourages religious instruction . . . it follows the best of our traditions." *Zorach v. Clauson,* (1952).

Positing an obligation on the State to educate its children, which every State acknowledges, it should be wholly acceptable for the State to contribute to the secular education of children going to sectarian schools rather than to insist that if parents want to provide their children with religious as well as secular education, the State will refuse to contribute anything to their secular training. . . .

The Court . . . has not barred all aid to religion or to religious institutions. Rather, it has attempted to devise a formula that would help identify the kind and degree of aid that is permitted or forbidden by the Establishment Clause. Until 1970, the test for compliance with the Clause was whether there was "a secular legislative purpose and a primary effect that neither advances nor inhibits religion. . ."; given a secular purpose, what is "the primary effect of the enactment?" *School District of Abington Township v. Schempp,* (1963); *Board of Education v. Allen.* In 1970, a third element surfaced—whether there is "an excessive government entanglement with religion." *Walz v. Tax Comm'n, supra,* at 674. . . .

But whatever may be the weight and contours of entanglement as a separate constitutional criterion, it is of remote relevance in the cases before us with respect to the validity of tuition grants or tax credits involving or requiring no relationships whatsoever between the State and any church or any church school. So, also, the Court concedes the State's genuine secular purpose underlying these statutes. It therefore necessarily arrives at the remaining consideration in the threefold test which is apparently accepted from prior cases: Whether the law in question has "a primary effect that neither advances nor inhibits religion." *School District of Abington Township v. Schempp, supra.* While purporting to accept the standard stated in this manner, the Court strikes down the New York maintenance law, because its "effect, inevitably, is to subsidize and advance the religious mission of sectarian schools," and for the same reason invalidates the tuition grants. But the test is one of "primary" effect not *any* effect. The Court makes no attempt at that ultimate judgment necessarily entailed by the standard heretofore fashioned in our cases. . . .

The Court's opinion emphasizes a particular kind of parochial school, one restricted to students of particular religious beliefs and conditioning attendance on religious study. Concededly, there are many parochial schools that do not impose such restrictions. Where they do not, it is even more difficult for me to understand why the primary effect of these statutes is to advance religion. I do not think it is and therefore dissent from the Court's judgment invalidating the challenged New York . . . statutes.

QUESTIONS AND COMMENTS

1 In *Mueller v. Allen,* 51 LW 5050 (1983), the Supreme Court upheld a Minnesota law that gave parents of children in public and private schools, sectarian and nonsectarian, an income tax deduction for transportation to and from school, tuition, and textbooks. On the other hand, a university in South Carolina lost its tax exemption because it denied admission, on religious grounds, to applicants who were engaged in interracial marriage [*Bob Jones University v. United States,* 51 LW 4593 (1983)].

2 Of the three tests developed in *Lemon v. Kurtzman,* which were passed/not passed in *Nyquist?*

3 Under the "*Lemon* tests," can a state constitutionally open each day in its legislative body with a prayer paid for by public funds? See *Marsh v. Chambers,* 51 LW 5162 (1983).

4 Can a state constitutionally lend a tape recorder to a student in a parochial school? See *Walman v. Walter,* 433 U.S. 229 (1977).

5 There has been a recent trend in the Court to interpret establishment clause restrictions more leniently. That predisposition may be observed in the *Mueller* and *Marsh* cases as well as in *Lynch v. Donnelly* [52 LW 4317 (1984)]. In *Lynch,* a majority of the justices approved the municipal erection of a Christmas display of a creche or nativity scene in a private park. In doing so, the Court pointed out (a) that the Constitution does not require a complete wall of separation between church and state, (b) that the framers of the First Amendment intended to accommodate religious beliefs, as seen from the use of chaplains in Congress, (c) that all governmental conduct that confers benefits on religion is not a violation of the establishment clause, and (d) that religion is a pervasive part of American life. In regard to the third point, the majority applied *Lemon v. Kurtzman* and found no violation of its three-pronged test, though conceding that the creche displayed had "religious significance."

In *Mueller, Marsh,* and *Lynch,* we can identify a decided and consistent split between the justices who appear to favor modifying the establishment clause restrictions and those who do not. In the first category are Chief Justice Burger and Justices Rehnquist, O'Connor, White, and Powell. All five of these justices were in the majority in *Mueller, Marsh,* and *Lynch.* On the other side, we find Brennan, Marshall, and Stevens, all of whom dissented in these three cases. Blackman also tends to share the views of the dissenters, since he joined them in two of the three cases—*Mueller* and *Lynch,* both decided by 5–4 votes.

Conscientious Objectors

Hamilton v. University of California (1934)

Gillette v. United States (1971)

Johnson v. Robison (1974)

We have noted that religious freedom is not absolute. The question in each case is whether government has a compelling interest in its policy and whether the means chosen to effectuate the encroaching policy is the least restrictive alternative available.[27] One governmental policy area in which religious freedom is frequently an issue pertains to military service and training. Congress has authority under Article I of the Constitution to raise armies and may conscript men and women into the military services if necessary. There is such a compelling governmental interest in procuring personnel for military purposes that few bother to question it. The means chosen to effectuate that interest is another matter.

There are always those who, on religious grounds, object to (1) participation in all wars or (2) participation in "unjust wars." Congress has recognized the legitimacy of the first objection by establishing a "conscientious objector" classification. Those who fall in this class are exempt from military training and service. This implies that the national interest in conscripting everyone is not sufficient to justify the ensuing encroachment on the free exercise rights of those who believe that all war is sinful.

A state has no right to raise armies. States do have a legitimate interest in certain national policies and in promoting the implementation of those policies. Indeed, as seen in *Hamilton v. University of California,* a state and the federal government may collaborate to effectuate a legitimate national goal. Both governments in this case collaborated in the promotion of national security via an ROTC program in a state university. It may be noted that Hamilton's objection was not to any particular or "unjust" war. *Gillette v. United States,* by contrast, turns on precisely that question. Gillette and Negre, apparently, were willing to go to war and to fight and kill if necessary, but not in Vietnam.

The fact that Congress has recognized and exempted from military service those who, on religious grounds, object to participation in all wars does not imply any encouragement for individuals to apply for conscientious objector status. Indeed, the opposite is the case—and for good reason. There is a direct incompatibility between conscripting for military service and exemptions from conscription. These antithetical aims can coexist only if one can assume that the exemptions will be severely limited. One way of fostering such limits is to vary the rewards to be given to those who take the exemption and those who submit to conscription and regular military service. Note that the clear implication of the statute at issue in *Johnson v. Robison* is that active service in the armed forces is more valuable than alternative civilian service as a conscientious objector.

Hamilton et al. v. University of California et al.

293 U.S. 245; 55 S. Ct. 197; 79 L. Ed. 343 (1934)
Vote: 9–0

A California state law required students at the state university to take a course in military science and tactics. In October 1933, Hamilton and others enrolled as students in the university. As such, they complied with all university requirements save one. They refused to take the required courses in the ROTC program. These courses were required by the regents and included rifle marksmanship, scouting and patrolling, drill and command, musketry, combat principles, and use of automatic rifles. Arms, uniforms, and equipment for the courses were supplied by the U.S. government.

The students belonged to the Methodist Episcopal church, members of which believed that participation in war "is a denial of their supreme allegiance to Jesus Christ." The church had officially adopted a resolution calling for the exemption of Methodist students from military service and ROTC programs on grounds of conscientious objection. This ground was used by the students in refusing to take the prescribed courses. In response, the regents suspended the students from the university but indicated a willingness to readmit them anytime they could agree to abide by *all* university rules and regulations.

In court, the students argued that state law and actions taken by the regents to impose compulsory military training violated their rights under the privileges and immunities and due process clauses of the Fourteenth Amendment. State courts denied relief. The Supreme Court accepted the case for review.

MR. JUSTICE BUTLER delivered the opinion of the Court.

* * *

The clauses of the Fourteenth Amendment invoked by appellants declare: "No State shall make or enforce any law which shall abridge the privileges or immunities of citizens of the United States; nor shall any State deprive any person of life, liberty or property, without due process of law." Appellants' contentions are that the enforcement of the order prescribing instruction in military science and tactics abridges some privilege or immunity covered by the first clause and deprives of liberty safeguarded by the second. The "privileges and immunities" protected are only those that belong to citizens of the United States as distinguished from citizens of the States—those that arise from the Constitution and laws of the United States as contrasted with those that spring from other sources. Appellants assert—unquestionably in good faith—that all war, preparation for war, and the training required by the university, are repugnant to the tenets and discipline of their church, to their religion and to their consciences. The "privilege" of attending the university as a student comes not from federal sources but is given by the State. It is not within the asserted protection. The only "immunity" claimed by these students is freedom from obligation to comply with the rule prescribing military training. But that "immunity" cannot be regarded as not within, or as distinguishable from, the "liberty" of which they claim to have been deprived by the enforcement of the regents' order. If the regents' order is not repugnant to the due process clause, then it does not violate the privileges and immunities clause. Therefore we need only decide whether by state action the "liberty" of these students has been infringed.

There need be no attempt to enumerate or comprehensively to define what is included in the "liberty" protected by the due process clause. Undoubtedly it does include the right to entertain the beliefs, to adhere to the principles and to teach the doctrines on which these students base their objections to the order prescribing military training. The fact that they are able to pay their way in this university but not in any other institution in California is without significance upon any constitutional or other question here involved. California has not drafted or called them to attend the university. They are seeking education offered by the State and at the same time insisting that they be excluded from the prescribed course solely upon grounds of their religious beliefs and conscientious objections to war, preparation for war and military education. Taken on the basis of the facts alleged in the petition, appellants' contentions amount to no more than an assertion that the due process clause of the Fourteenth Amendment as a safeguard of "liberty" confers the right to be students in the state university free from obligation to take military training as one of the conditions of attendance.

Viewed in the light of our decisions that proposition must at once be put aside as untenable.

Government, federal and state, each in its own sphere owes a duty to the people within its jurisdiction to preserve itself in adequate strength to maintain peace and order and to assure the just enforcement of law. And every citizen owes the reciprocal duty, according to his capacity, to support and defend government against all enemies.

* * *

In *United States v. Macintosh,* [1930] a . . . naturalization case, the applicant was unwilling, because of the conscientious objections, to take unqualifiedly the statutory oath of allegiance which contains this statement: "That he will support and defend the Constitution and laws of the United States against all enemies, foreign or domestic; and bear true faith and allegiance to the same." His petition stated that he was willing if necessary to take up arms in defense of this country, "but I should want to be free to judge of the necessity." In amplification he said: "I do not undertake to support 'my country, right or wrong' in any dispute which may arise, and I am not willing to promise beforehand, and without knowing the cause for which my country may go to war, either that I will or that I will not 'take up arms in defense of this country,' however 'necessary' the war may seem to be to the government of the day." The opinion of this Court quotes from petitioner's brief a statement to the effect that it is a "fixed principle of our Constitution, zealously guarded by our laws, that a citizen cannot be forced and need not bear arms in a war if he has conscientious religious scruples against doing so." And, referring to that part of the argument in behalf of the applicant, this Court said "This, if it means what it seems to say, is an astonishing statement. Of course, there is no such principle of the Constitution, fixed or otherwise. The conscientious objector is relieved from the obligation to bear arms in obedience to no constitutional provision, express or implied; but because, and only because, it has accorded with the policy of Congress. That body may grant or withhold the exemption as in its wisdom it sees fit; and if it be withheld, the native-born conscientious objector cannot successfully assert the privilege. No other conclusion is compatible with the well-nigh limitless extent of the war powers as above illustrated, which include, by necessary implication, the power, in the last extremity, to compel the armed service of any citizen in the land, without regard to his objections or his views in respect of the justice or morality of the particular war or of war in general. In *Jacobson v. Massachusetts,* this Court [upholding a state compulsory vaccination law] speaking of the liberties guaranteed to the individual by the Fourteenth Amendment, said: '. . . and yet he may be compelled, by force if need be, against his will and without regard to his personal wishes or his pecuniary interests, or even his religious or political convictions, to take his place in the ranks of the army of his country and risk the chance of being shot down in its defense.'"

* * *

Plainly there is no ground for the contention that the regents' order, requiring able-bodied male students under the age of twenty-four as a condition of their enrollment to take the prescribed instruction in military science and tactics, transgresses any constitutional right asserted by these appellants. . . .

Affirmed.

MR. JUSTICE CARDOZO.

Concurring in the opinion I wish to say an extra word.

I assume for present purposes that the religious liberty protected by the First Amendment against invasion by the nation is protected by the Fourteenth Amendment against invasion by the states.

Accepting that premise, I cannot find in the respondents' ordinance an obstruction by the state to "the free exercise" of religion as the phrase was understood by the founders of the nation, and by the generations that have followed.

There is no occasion at this time to mark the limits of governmental power in the exaction of military service when the nation is at peace. The petitioners have not been required to bear arms for any hostile purpose, offensive or defensive, either now or in the future. They have not even been required in any absolute or peremptory way to join in courses of instruction that will fit them to bear arms. If they elect to resort to an institution for higher education maintained with the state's moneys, then and only then they are commanded to follow courses of instruction believed by the state to be vital to its welfare. This may be condemned by some as unwise or illiberal or unfair when there is violence to conscientious scruples, either religious or merely ethical. More must be shown to set the ordinance at naught. In controversies of this order courts do not concern themselves with matters of legislative policy, unrelated to privileges or liberties secured by the organic law. The First Amendment, if it be read into the Fourteenth, makes invalid any state law "respecting an establishment of religion or prohibiting the free exercise thereof." Instruction in military science is not instruction in the practice or tenets of a religion. Neither directly nor indirectly is government establishing a state religion when it insists upon such training. Instruction in military science, unaccompanied here by any pledge of military service, is not an interference by the state with the free exercise of religion when the liberties of the constitution are read in the light of a century and a half of history during days of peace and war.

* * *

For one opposed to force, the affront to conscience must be greater in furnishing men and money wherewith to wage a pending contest than in studying military science without the duty or the pledge of service. Never in our history has the notion been accepted, or even, it is believed, advanced, that acts thus indirectly related to service in the camp or field are so tied to the practice of religion as to be exempt, in law or in morals, from regulation by the state. On the contrary, the very lawmakers who were willing to give release from warlike acts had no thought that they were doing anything inconsistent with the moral claims of an objector, still less with his constitutional immunities, in coupling the exemption with these collateral conditions.

Manifestly a different doctrine would carry us to lengths that have never yet been dreamed of. The conscientious objector, if his liberties were to be thus extended, might refuse to contribute taxes in furtherance of any other end condemned by his conscience as irreligious or immoral. The right of private judgment has never yet been so exalted above the powers and the compulsion of the agencies of government. One who is a martyr to a principle—which may turn out in the end to be a delusion or an error—does not prove by his martyrdom that he has kept within the law.

I am authorized to state that MR. JUSTICE BRANDEIS and MR. JUSTICE STONE join in this opinion.

Gillette v. United States (No. 85)

Negre v. Larsen (No. 325)

401 U.S. 437; 91 S. Ct. 828; 28 L. Ed. 2d 168 (1971)
Vote: 8–1

The facts in these cases are given in the opinion below.

MR. JUSTICE MARSHALL delivered the opinion of the Court.

These cases present the question whether conscientious objection to a particular war, rather than objection to war as such, relieves the objector from responsibilities of military training and service. Specifically, we are called upon to decide whether conscientious scruples relating to a particular conflict are within the purview of established provisions relieving conscientious objectors to war from military service. Both petitioners also invoke constitutional principles barring government interference with the exercise of religion and requiring governmental neutrality in matters of religion.

In No. 85, petitioner Gillette was convicted of wilful failure to report for induction into the armed forces. Gillette defended on the ground that he should have been ruled exempt from induction as a conscientious objector to war. In support of his unsuccessful request for classification as a conscientious objector, this petitioner had stated his willingness to participate in a war of national defense or a war sponsored by the United Nations as a peace-keeping measure, but declared his opposition to American military operations in Vietnam, which he characterized as "unjust." Petitioner concluded that he could not in conscience enter and serve in the armed forces during the period of the Vietnam conflict. Gillette's view of his duty to abstain from any involvement in a war seen as unjust is, in his words, "based on a humanist approach to religion," and his personal decision concerning military service was guided by fundamental principles of conscience and deeply held views about the purpose and obligation of human existence.

The District Court determined that there was a basis in fact to support administrative denial of exemption in Gillette's case. The denial of exemption was upheld, and Gillette's defense to the criminal charge rejected, not because of doubt about the sincerity or the religious character of petitioner's objection to military service but because his objection ran to a particular war. In affirming the conviction, the Court of Appeals concluded that Gillette's conscientious beliefs "were specifically directed against the war in Vietnam," while the relevant exemption provision of the Military Selective Service Act of 1967, "requires opposition 'to participation in war in any form.'"

In No. 325, petitioner Negre, after induction into the Army, completion of basic training, and receipt of orders for Vietnam duty commenced proceedings looking to his discharge as a conscientious objector to war. Application for discharge was denied, and Negre sought judicial relief by habeas corpus. The District Court found a basis in fact for the Army's rejection of petitioners application for discharge. Habeas relief was denied, and the denial was affirmed on appeal, because, in the language of the Court of Appeals, Negre "objects to the war in Vietnam, not to all wars," and therefore does "not qualify for separation [from the Army], as a conscientious objector."

Again, no question is raised as to the sincerity or the religious quality of this petitioner's views. In line with religious counseling and numerous religious texts, Negre, a devout Catholic, believes that it is his duty as a faithful Catholic to discriminate between "just" and "unjust" wars, and to forswear participation in the latter. His assessment of the Vietnam conflict as an unjust war became clear in his mind after completion of infantry training, and Negre is now firmly of the view that any personal involvement in that war would contravene his conscience and "all that I had been taught in my religious training."

We granted certiorari in these cases in order to resolve vital issues concerning the exercise of congressional power to raise and support armies, as affected by the religious guarantees of the First Amendment. We affirm the judgments below in both cases.

Each petitioner claims a nonconstitutional right to be relieved of the duty of military service in virtue of his conscientious scruples. Both claims turn on the proper construction of § 6(j) of the Military Selective Service Act of 1967, 50 U.S.C. App. § 456(j) (1964 ed., Supp. V), which provides:

> Nothing contained in this title * * shall be construed to require any person to be subject to combatant training and service in the armed forces of the United States who, by reason of religious training and belief, is conscientiously opposed to participation in war in any form. . . .

This language, on a straightforward reading, can bear but one meaning; that conscientious scruples relating to war and military service must amount to conscientious opposition to participating personally in any war and all war. . . .

* * *

Both petitioners argue that § 6 (j), construed to cover only objectors to all war, violates the religious clauses of the First Amendment. The First Amendment provides that "Congress shall make no law respecting an establishment of religion, or prohibiting the free exercise thereof * * * *." Petitioners contend that Congress interferes with free exercise of religion by failing to relieve objectors to a particular war from military service, when the objection is religious or conscientious in nature. . . .

Properly phrased, petitioners' contention is that the special statutory status accorded conscientious objection to all war, but not objection to a particular war, works a de facto discrimination among religions. This happens, say petitioners, because some religious faiths themselves distinguish between personal participation in "just" and in "unjust" wars, commending the former and forbidding the latter, and therefore adherents of some religious faiths—and individuals whose personal beliefs of a religious nature include the distinction—cannot object to all wars consistently with what is regarded as the true imperative of conscience. Of course, this contention of de facto religious discrimination, rendering § 6(j) fatally underinclusive, cannot simply be brushed aside. The question of governmental neutrality is not concluded by the observation that § 6(j) on its face makes no discrimination between religions, for the Establishment Clause forbids subtle departures from neutrality, "religious gerrymanders," as well as obvious abuses. *Walz v. Tax Commission,* [1970].

. . . Still a claimant alleging "gerrymander" must be able to show the absence of a neutral, secular basis for the lines government has drawn. See *Epperson v. Arkansas,* [1968].

... We believe that petitioners have failed to make the requisite showing with respect to § 6(j).

We conclude not only that the affirmative purposes underlying § 6(j) are neutral and secular, but also that valid neutral reasons exist for limiting the exemption to objectors to all war, and that the section therefore cannot be said to reflect a religious preference.

Apart from the Government's need for manpower, perhaps the central interest involved in the administration of conscription laws is the interest in maintaining a fair system for determining "who serves when not all serve." When the Government exacts so much, the importance of fair, evenhanded, and uniform decisionmaking is obviously intensified. The Government argues that the interest in fairness would be jeopardized by expansion of § 6(j) to include conscientious objection to a particular war. The contention is that the claim to relief on account of such objection is intrinsically a claim of uncertain dimensions, and that granting the claim in theory would involve a real danger of erratic or even discriminatory decisionmaking in administrative practice.

A virtually limitless variety of beliefs are subsumable under the rubric, "objection to a particular war." All the factors that might go into nonconscientious dissent from policy, also might appear as the concrete basis of an objection that has roots as well in conscience and religion. Indeed, over the realm of possible situations, opposition to a particular war may more likely be political and nonconscientious, than otherwise.

The difficulties of sorting the two, with a sure hand, are considerable. Moreover, the belief that a particular war at a particular time is unjust is by its nature changeable and subject to nullification by changing events. Since objection may fasten on any of an enormous number of variables, the claim is ultimately subjective, depending on the claimant's view of the facts in relation to his judgement that a given factor or congeries of factors colors the character of the war as a whole. In short, it is not at all obvious in theory what sorts of objections should be deemed sufficient to excuse an objector, and there is considerable force in the Government's contention that a program of excusing objectors to particular wars may be "impossible to conduct with any hope of reaching fair and consistent results.   *   *   *"

For their part, petitioners make no attempt to provide a careful definition of the claim to exemption that they ask the courts to carve out and protect. They do not explain why objection to a particular conflict—much less an objection that focuses on a particular facet of a conflict—should excuse the objector from all military service whatever, even from military operations that are connected with the conflict at hand in remote or tenuous ways. They suggest no solution to the problems arising from the fact that altered circumstances may quickly render the objection to military service moot.

To view the problem of fairness and evenhanded decisionmaking, in the present context, as merely a commonplace chore of weeding out "spurious claims," is to minimize substantial difficulties of real concern to a responsible legislative body. For example, under the petitioners' unarticulated scheme for exemption, an objector's claim to exemption might be based on some feature of a current conflict that most would regard as incidental or might be predicted on a view of the facts that most would regard as mistaken. The particular complaint about the war may itself be "sincere," but it is difficult to know how to judge the "sincerity" of the objector's conclusion that the war *in toto* is unjust and that any personal involvement would contravene conscience and religion. To be sure we have ruled, in connection with § 6(j), that "the 'truth' of a belief is not open to question"; rather, the question is whether the objector's beliefs are "truly held." *United States v. Seeger.*

. . . But we must also recognize that "sincerity" is a concept that can bear only so much adjudicative weight.

Ours is a Nation of enormous heterogeneity in respect of political views, moral codes, and religious persuasions. It does not bespeak an establishing of religion for Congress to forgo the enterprise of distinguishing those whose dissent has some conscientious basis from those who simply dissent. There is a danger that as between two would-be objectors, both having the same complaint against a war, that objector would succeed who is more articulate, better educated, or better counseled. There is even a danger of unintended religious discrimination—a danger that a claim's chances of success would be greater the more familiar or salient the claim's connection with conventional religiosity could be made to appear. At any rate, it is true that "the more discriminating and complicated the basis of classification for an exemption—even a neutral one—the greater the potential for state involvement" in determining the character of persons' beliefs and affiliations, thus "entangl[ing] government in difficult classifications of what is or is not religious," or what is or is not conscientious. While the danger of erratic decisionmaking unfortunately exists in any system of conscription that takes individual differences into account, no doubt the dangers would be enhanced if a conscientious objection of indeterminate scope were honored in theory.

. . . Some have perceived a danger that exempting persons who dissent from a particular war, albeit on grounds of conscience and religion in part, would "open the doors to a general theory of selective disobedience to law" and jeopardize the binding quality of democratic decisions.

Other fields of legal obligation aside, it is undoubted that the nature of conscription, much less war itself, requires the personal desires and perhaps the dissenting views of those who must serve to be subordinated in some degree to the pursuit of public purposes. It is also true that opposition to a particular war does depend *inter alia* upon particularistic factual beliefs and policy assessments, beliefs and assessments that presumably were overridden by the government that decides to commit lives and resources to a trial of arms. Further, it is not unreasonable to suppose that some persons who are *not* prepared to assert a conscientious objection, and instead accept the hardships and risks of military service, may well agree at all points with the objector, yet conclude, as a matter of conscience, that they are personally bound by the decision of the democratic process. The fear of the National Advisory Commission on the Selective Service, apparently, is that exemption of objectors to particular wars would weaken the resolve of those who otherwise would feel themselves bound to serve despite personal cost, uneasiness at the prospect of violence, or even serious moral reservations or policy objections concerning the particular conflict.

We need not and do not adopt the view that a categorical, global "interest" in stifling individualistic claims to noncompliance, in respect of duties generally exacted, is the neutral and secular basis of § 6(j). As is shown by the long history of the very provision under discussion, it is not inconsistent with orderly democratic government for individuals to be exempted by law, on account of special characteristics, from general duties of a burdensome nature. But real dangers. . . . might arise if an exemption were made available that in its nature could not be administered fairly and uniformly over the run of relevant fact situations. Should it be thought that those who go to war are chosen unfairly or capriciously, then a mood of bitterness and cynicism might corrode the spirit of public service and the values of willing performance of a citizen's duties that are the very heart of free government. In short, the considerations mentioned in the previous paragraph, when seen in conjunction with the central problem of fairness, are without question properly cognizable by Congress. In light of these valid concerns, we conclude that it is supportable for Congress to have decided that the objector to all war—to all killing in war—has a claim that is distinct enough and intense enough to justify special status, while the objector to a particular war does not.

Petitioners' remaining contention is that Congress interferes with the free exercise of religion by conscripting persons who oppose a particular war on grounds of conscience and religion. Strictly viewed, this complaint does not implicate problems of comparative treatment of different sorts of objectors, but rather may be examined in some isolation from the circumstance that Congress has chosen to exempt those who conscientiously object to all war. And holding that § 6(j) comports with the Establishment Clause does not automatically settle the present issue. For despite a general harmony of purpose between the two religious clauses of the First Amendment, the Free Exercise Clause no doubt has a reach of its own.

Nonetheless, our analysis of § 6(j) for Establishment Clause purposes has revealed governmental interests of a kind and weight sufficient to justify under the Free Exercise Clause the impact of the conscription laws on those who object to particular wars. . . .

The conscription laws, applied to such persons as to others, are not designed to interfere with any religious ritual practice, and do not work a penalty against any theological position. The incidental burdens felt by persons in petitioners' position are strictly justified by substantial governmental interests that relate directly to the very impacts questioned. And more broadly, of course, there is the Government's interest in procuring the manpower necessary for military purposes, pursuant to the constitutional grant of power to Congress to raise support armies. Art. I, § 8.

Since petitioners' statutory and constitutional claims to relief from military service are without merit, it follows that in Gillette's case (No. 85) there was a basis in fact to support administrative denial of exemption, and that in Negre's case (No. 325) there was a basis in fact to support the Army's denial of a discharge. Accordingly, the judgments below are affirmed.

Affirmed.

Mr. Justice BLACK concurs in the Court's judgment and in Part I of the opinion of the Court.

Mr. Justice DOUGLAS, dissenting in No. 85. [Gillette]

* * *

Conscience is often the echo of religious faith. But, as this case illustrates, it may also be the product of travail, meditation, or sudden revelation related to a moral comprehension of the dimensions of a problem, not to a religion in the ordinary sense.

Tolstoy wrote of a man, one Van der Veer, "who, as he himself says, is not a Christian, and who refuses military service, not from religious motives, but from motives of the simplest kind, motives intelligible and common to all men, of whatever religion or nation, whether Catholic, Mohammedan, Buddhist, Confucian, whether Spaniards or Japanese.

> Van der Veer refuses military service, not because he follows the commandment. 'Thou shalt do no murder,' not because he is a Christian, but because he holds murder to be opposed to human nature.

Tolstoy goes on to say:

> Van der Veer says he is not a Christian. But the motives of his refusal and action are Christian. He refuses because he does not wish to kill a brother man; he does not obey, because the commands of his conscience are more binding upon him than the commands of men. * * *   Thereby he shows that Christianity is not a sect or creed which some may profess and others reject; but that it is naught else than a life's following of that light of reason which illumines all men. * * *

... Mr. Justice Black once said: "The First Amendment has lost much if the religious follower and the athiest are no longer to be judicially regarded as entitled to equal justice under law."

We said as much in our recent decision in Epperson v. Arkansas, where we struck down as unconstitutional a state law prohibiting the teaching of the doctrine of evolution in the public schools.

* * *

This is an appropriate occasion to give content to our dictum in West Virginia State Board of Education v. Barnette, *supra,* 319 U.S., at 642,

> [F]reedom to differ is not limited to things that do not matter much. . . . The test of its substance is the right to differ as to things that touch the heart of the existing order.

I would reverse this judgment.

Mr. Justice DOUGLAS, dissenting in No. 325. [Negre]

I approach the facts of this case with some difference, as they involve doctrines of the Catholic Church in which I was not raised. But we have on one of petitioner's briefs an authoritative lay Catholic scholar, Dr. John T. Noonan, Jr., and from that brief I deduce the following:

Under the doctrines of the Catholic Church a person has a moral duty to take part in wars declared by his government so long as they comply with the tests of his church for just wars. Conversely, a Catholic has a moral duty not to participate in unjust wars.

* * *

No one can tell a Catholic that this or that war is either just or unjust. This is a personal decision that an individual must make on the basis of his own conscience after studying the facts.

* * *

Louis Negre is a devout Catholic. In 1951 when he was four, his family immigrated to this country from France. He attended Catholic schools in Bakersfield, California, until graduation from high school. Then he attended Bakersfield Junior College for two years. Following that, he was inducted into the Army.

At the time of his induction he had his own convictions about the Vietnam war and the Army's goals in the war. He wanted, however, to be sure of his convictions. "I agreed to myself that before making any decision or taking any type of stand on the issue, I would permit myself to see and understand the Army's explanation of its reasons for violence in Vietnam. For, without getting an insight on the subject, it would be unfair for me to say anything, without really knowing the answer."

On completion of his advanced infantry training, "I knew that if I would permit myself to go to Vietnam I would be violating my own concepts of natural law and would be going against all that I had been taught in my religious training." Negre applied for a discharge as a conscientious objector. His application was denied. He then refused to comply with an order to proceed for shipment to Vietnam. A general court-martial followed, but he was acquitted. After that he filed this application for discharge as a conscientious objector.

Negre is opposed under his religious training and beliefs to participation in any form in the war in Vietnam. His sincerity is not questioned. His application for a discharge, however was denied because his religious training and beliefs led him to oppose only a particular war which according to his conscience was unjust.

For the reasons I have stated in my dissent in the *Gillette* case decided this day, I would reverse the judgment.

Johnson, Administrator of Veterans' Affairs et al. v. Robison

415 U. S. 361; 94 S. Ct. 1160; 39 L. Ed. 2d 389 (1974)
Vote: 8–1

The facts in this case are incorporated in the opinion below.

MR. JUSTICE BRENNAN delivered the opinion of the Court.

A draftee accorded Class I-O conscientious objector status and completing performance of required alternative civilian service does not qualify under 38 U. S. C. § 1652 (a) (1) as a "veteran who . . . served on active duty" (defined in 38 U. S. C. §101 (21) as "full-time duty in the Armed Forces"), and is therefore not an "eligible veteran" entitled under 38 U. S. C. § 1661 (a) to veterans' educational benefits provided by the Veterans Readjustment Benefits Act of 1966. Appellants, the Veterans' Administration and the Administrator of Veterans' Affairs, for that reason, denied the application for educational assistance of appellee Robison, a conscientious objector who filed his application after he satisfactorily completed two years of alternative civilian service at the Peter Bent Brigham Hospital, Boston. Robison thereafter commenced this class action in the United States District Court for the District of Massachusetts, seeking a declaratory judgment that 38 U. S. C. §§ 101 (21), 1652 (a) (1), and 1661 (a), read together, violated the First Amendment's guarantee of religious freedom and the Fifth Amendment's guarantee of equal protection of the laws.

* * *

The District Court . . . on the merits, rejected appellee's First Amendment claim, but sustained the equal protection claim and entered a judgment declaring "that 38 U. S. C. §§ 1652 (a) (1) and 1661 (a) defining 'eligible veteran' and providing for entitlement to educational assistance are unconstitutional and that 38 U. S. C. § 101 (21) defining 'active duty' is unconstitutional with respect to chapter 34 of Title 38, United States Code, 38 U. S. C. §§ 1651–1697, conferring Veterans' Educational Assistance, for the reason that said sections deny plaintiff and members of his class due process of law in violation of the Fifth Amendment to the Constitution of the United States. . . ."

* * *

. . . the District Court held that, by not including appellee and his class, the challenged sections of the Act create an arbitrary classification in violation of appellee's right to equal protection of the laws. In determining whether, in limiting the class of draftees entitled to benefits to those who serve their country on active duty in the Armed Forces, Congress denied equal protection of the laws to Selective Service registrants who perform alternative civilian service as conscientious objectors, our analysis of the classification proceeds on the basis that, although an individual's right to equal protection of the laws "does not deny . . . the power to treat different classes of persons in different ways[;] . . . [it denies] the power to legislate that different treatment be accorded to persons placed by a statute into different classes on the basis of criteria wholly unrelated to the objective of that statute. A classification 'must be reasonable, not arbitrary, and must rest upon some ground of difference having a fair and substantial relation to the object of the legislation, so that all persons similarly circumstanced shall be treated alike.' *Reed v. Reed,* (1971). . . .

The two groups of draftees are, in fact, not similarly circumstanced. To be sure, a draftee, by definition does not find educational benefits sufficient incentive to enlist. But, military service with educational benefits is obviously more attractive to a draftee than military service without educational benefits. Thus, the existence of educational benefits may help induce a registrant either to volunteer for the draft or not seek a lower Selective Service classification. Furthermore, once drafted, educational benefits may help make military service more palatable to a draftee and thus reduce a draftee's unwillingness to be a soldier. On the other hand, because a conscientious objector bases his refusal to serve in the Armed Forces upon deeply held religious beliefs, we will not assume that educational benefits will make military service more attractive to him. When, as in this case, the inclusion of one group promotes a legitimate governmental purpose, and the addition of other groups would not, we cannot say that the statute's classification of beneficiaries and nonbeneficiaries is invidiously discriminatory.

Finally, appellee argues that the District Court erred in holding that "the challenged exclusion does not abridge [appellee's] free exercise of his religion. He contends that the Act's denial of benefits to alternative service conscientious objectors interferes with his free exercise of religion by increasing the price he must pay for adherence to his religious beliefs. That contention must be rejected in light of our decision in *Gillette v. United States,* (1971).

* * *

The challenged legislation in the present case does not require appellee and his class to make any choice comparable to that required of the petitioners in *Gillette.* The withholding of educational benefits involves only an incidental burden upon appellee's free exercise of religion—if, indeed, any burden exists at all.

. . . the Act was enacted pursuant to Congress' Art. I, § 8, powers to advance the neutral, secular governmental interests of enhancing military service and aiding the readjustment of military personnel to civilian life. Appellee and his class were not included in this class of beneficiaries, not because of any legislative design to interfere with their free exercise of religion, but because to do so would not rationally promote the Act's purposes. Thus, in light of *Gillette,* the Government's substantial interest in raising and supporting armies, Art. I, § 8, is of a "kind and weight" clearly sufficient to sustain the challenged legislation, for the burden upon appellee's free exercise of religion—the denial of the economic value of veterans' educational benefits under the Act—is not nearly of the same order or magnitude as the infringement upon free exercise of religion suffered by petitioners in *Gillette.*

Reversed.

MR. JUSTICE DOUGLAS, dissenting.

* * *

The District Court in the present case said that the penalty which the present Act places on conscientious objectors is of a lesser "order or magnitude" than that which has been upheld in past cases.

That is true; yet the discrimination against a man with religious scruples seems apparent. The present Act derives from a House bill that had as its purpose solely an education program to "help a veteran to follow the educational plan that he might have adopted had he never entered the Armed Forces."

Full benefits are available to occupants of safe desk jobs and the thousands of veterans who performed civilian type duties at home and for whom the rigors of the "war" were far from "totally disruptive," to use the Government's phrase. The benefits are provided, though the draftee did not serve overseas but lived with his family in a civilian community and worked from nine until five as a file clerk on a military base or attended college courses in his off-duty hours. No condition of hazardous duty was attached to the educational assistance program. As Senator Yarborough said, the benefits would accrue even to those who never served overseas, because their "educational progress and opportunity" [have] been impaired in just as serious and damaging a fashion as if they had served on distant shores. Their educational needs are no less than those of their comrades who served abroad."

But the line drawn in the Act is between Class I-O conscientious objectors who performed alternative civilian service and all other draftees. Such conscientious objectors get no educational benefits whatsoever. It is, indeed, demeaning to those who have religious scruples against shouldering arms to suggest, as the Government does, that those religious scruples must be susceptible of compromise before they will be protected. The urge to forgo religious scruples to gain a monetary advantage would certainly be a burden on the Free Exercise Clause in cases of those who were spiritually weak. . . .

We deal with people whose religious scruples are unwavering. Those who would die at the stake for their religious scruples may not constitutionally be penalized by the Government by the exaction of penalties because of their free exercise of religion. Where Government places a price on the free exercise of one's religious scruples it crosses the forbidden line. The issue of "coercive effects," to use another Government phrase, is irrelevant. Government, as I read the Constitution and the Bill of Rights, may not place a penalty on anyone for asserting his religious scruples. That is the nub of the present case and the reason why the judgment below should be affirmed.

QUESTIONS AND COMMENTS

1 Does *Hamilton v. University of California* turn on the religion clauses of the First Amendment? Explain.
2 Would the decision in *Hamilton* be different if Hamilton was required to attend the university? Explain.
3 What if those who took the ROTC training were required to serve in the military forces of the United States for four years upon completion of the training? Different decision?
4 Note that Gillette based his objection to unjust war on a "humanist approach to religion," while Negre was a "devout Catholic." Was that distinction of any significance in this case? Should it have been? What if one's religion is unique and limited to one individual? Any effect?
5 Evaluate the statute in *Gillette* with the three tests from *Lemon v. Kurtzman*. Does the statute pass all tests? Explain.
6 Does the Constitution grant the right not to participate in war on religious grounds? Explain.
7 Could Congress eliminate all exemptions from military training and service? Why or why not?
8 In *Robison*, Justice Douglas argues the unfairness of distinguishing persons for educational benefits on the basis of regular military service versus conscientious-objector service. Essentially, he seems to believe that the benefits could be more equitably distributed if each individual case was decided on an ad hoc basis. What objections can you pose to that argument?

Sunday Closing Laws

McGowan v. Maryland (1961)

In colonial days, it was customary to close all or most commercial establishments on Sunday—the Christian Sabbath. Indeed, so-called blue laws generally required such closings. As the states came into existence, such laws were generally continued. Thus, although separation of church and state was a familiar shibboleth, cooperation between the two was not unknown. As non-protestant minorities (and commercial interests) became larger or more influential, the closing laws came under challenge in the courts. But the Christian values which dominated the culture, the judges, and the courts generally, resulted in a denial of such challenges. In *McGowan v. Maryland,* the Supreme Court assesses a modern challenge to such laws and examines some arguments not encountered in the earlier cases.

McGowan et al. v. Maryland

366 U.S. 420; 81 S. Ct. 1101; 6 L Ed. 2d 393 (1961)
Vote: 8–1

McGowan was an employee of a large department store in Anne Arundel County, Maryland. He was convicted and fined in a Maryland state court for selling a loose-leaf binder, a can of floor wax, a stapler, staples, and a toy. The sales were made on a Sunday in violation of Article 27 of the Maryland Criminal Code. Section 521 of the article prohibited the Sunday sale of all merchandise except the retail sale of tobacco, confectionaries, bread, milk, fruit, gas and oil, greases, drugs, medicines, newspapers, and periodicals. McGowan's allegation that Section 521 imposed the tenets of the Christian religion on him in violation of his constitutional rights was rejected by the Maryland court of appeals. The Supreme Court then granted review.

MR. CHIEF JUSTICE WARREN delivered the opinion of the Court.

The issues in this case concern the constitutional validity of Maryland criminal statutes, commonly known as Sunday Closing Laws or Sunday Blue Laws. These statutes, with exceptions to be noted hereafter, generally proscribe all labor, business and other commercial activities on Sunday. The questions presented are whether the classifications within the statutes bring about a denial of equal protection of the law, whether the laws are so vague as to fail to give reasonable notice of the forbidden conduct and therefore violate due process, and whether the statutes are laws respecting an establishment of religion or prohibiting the free exercise thereof. . . . [Recently amended, the statute at issue here.]

. . . now excepts from the general prohibition the retail sale in Anne Arundel County of all foodstuffs, automobile and boating accessories, flowers, toilet goods, hospital supplies and souvenirs. It now further provides that any retail establishment in Anne Arundel County which does not employ more than one person other than the owner may operate on Sunday.

Although appellants were indicted only under § 521, in order properly to consider several of the broad constitutional contentions, we must examine the whole body of Maryland Sunday laws.

* * *

Appellants argue that the Maryland statutes violate the "Equal Protection" Clause of the Fourteenth Amendment on several counts.

* * *

On the record before us, we cannot say that these statutes do not provide equal protection of the laws.

* * *

The final questions for decision are whether the Maryland Sunday Closing Laws conflict with the Federal constitution's provisions for religious liberty. First, appellants contend here that the statutes applicable to Anne Arundel County violate the constitutional guarantee of freedom of religion in that the statutes' effect is to prohibit the free exercise of religion in contravention of the First Amendment, made applicable to the States by the Fourteenth Amendment. But appellants allege only economic injury to themselves; they do not allege any infringement of their own religious freedoms due to Sunday closing. In fact, the record is silent as to what appellants' religious beliefs are. Since the general rule is that "a litigant may only assert his own constitutional rights or immunities," *United States v. Raines,* [1969] we hold that appellants have no standing to raise this contention.

* * *

Secondly, appellants contend that the statutes violate the guarantee of separation of church and state in that the statutes are laws respecting an establishment of religion contrary to the First Amendment, made applicable to the States by the Fourteenth Amendment. If the purpose of the "establishment" clause was only to insure protection for the "free exercise" of religion, then what we have said above concerning appellants' standing to raise the "free exercise" contention would appear to be true here. However, the writings of Madison, who was the First Amendment's architect, demonstrate that the establishment of a religion was equally feared because of its tendencies to political tyranny and subversion of civil authority. Thus, in *Everson v. Board of Education,* [1947] the Court permitted a district taxpayer to challenge, on "establishment" grounds, a state statute which authorized district boards of education to reimburse parents for fares paid for the transportation of their children to both public and Catholic schools. Appellants here concededly have suffered direct economic injury, allegedly due to the imposition on them of the tenets of the Christian religion. We find that, in these circumstances, these appellants have standing to complain that the statutes are laws respecting an establishment of religion.

The essence of appellants' "establishment" argument is that Sunday is the Sabbath day of the predominant Christian sects; that the purpose of the enforced stoppage of labor on that day is to facilitate and encourage church attendance; that the purpose of setting Sunday as a day of universal rest is to induce people with no religion or people with marginal religious beliefs to join the predominant Christian sects; that the purpose of the atmosphere of tranquility created by Sunday closing is to aid the conduct of church services and religious observance of the sacred day. In substantiating their "establishment" argument, appellants rely on the wording of the present Maryland statutes, on earlier versions of the current Sunday laws and on prior judicial characterizations of these laws by the Maryland Court of Appeals. Although only the constitutionality of § 521, the section under which appellants have been convicted, is immediately before us in this litigation, inquiry into the history of Sunday Closing Laws in our country, in addition to an examination of the Maryland Sunday closing statutes in their entirety and of their history, is relevant to the decision of whether the Maryland Sunday law in question is one respecting an establishment of religion. There is no dispute that the original laws which dealt with Sunday labor were motivated by religious forces. But what we must decide is whether present Sunday legislation, having undergone extensive changes from the earliest forms, still retains its religious character.

* * *

In light of the evolution of our Sunday Closing Laws through the centuries, and of their more or less recent emphasis upon secular considerations, it is not difficult to discern that as presently written and administered, most of them, at least, are of a secular rather than of a religious character, and that presently they bear no relationship to establishment of religion as those words are used in the Constitution of the United States.

Throughout this century and longer, both the federal and state governments have oriented their activities very largely toward improvement of the health, safety, recreation and general well-being of our citizens. Numerous laws affecting public health, safety factors in industry, laws affecting hours and conditions of labor of women and children, week-end diversion at parks and beaches, and cultural activities of various kinds, now point the way toward the good life for all. Sunday Closing Laws, like those before us, have become part and parcel of this great governmental concern wholly apart from their original purposes or connotations. The present purpose and effect of most of them is to provide a uniform day of rest for all citizens; the fact that this day is Sunday, a day of particular significance for the dominant Christian sects, does not bar the State from achieving its secular goals. To say that the States cannot prescribe Sunday as a day of rest for these purposes solely because centuries ago such laws had their genesis in religion would give a constitutional interpretation of hostility to the public welfare rather than one of mere separation of church and State.

We now reach the Maryland statutes under review. The title of the major series of sections of the Maryland Code dealing with Sunday closing—Art. 27, §§ 492—534C—is "Sabbath Breaking"; § 492 proscribes work or bodily labor on the "Lord's day," and forbids persons to "profane the Lord's day" by gaming, fishing et cetera; § 522 refers to Sunday as the "Sabbath day." As has been mentioned above, many of the exempted Sunday activities in the various localities of the State may only be conducted during the afternoon and late evening; most Christian church services, of course, are held on Sunday morning and early Sunday evening. Finally, as previously noted, certain localities do not permit the allowed Sunday activities to be carried on within one hundred yards of any church where religious services are being held. This is the totality of the evidence of religious purpose which may be gleaned from the face of the present statute and from its operative effect.

The predecessors of the existing Maryland Sunday laws are undeniably religious in origin. The first Maryland statute dealing with Sunday activities, enacted in 1649, was entitled "An Act concerning Religion." It made it criminal to "profane the Sabbath or Lord's day called Sunday by frequent swearing, drunkennes or by any uncivil or disorderly recreation, or by working on that day when absolute necessity doth not require it." A 1692 statute entitled "An Act for the Service of Almighty God and the Establishment of the Protestant Religion within this Province," after first stating the importance of keeping the Lord's Day holy and sanctified and expressing concern with the breach of its observance throughout the State, then enacted a Sunday labor prohibition which was the obvious precursor of the present § 492. There was a re-enactment in 1696 entitled "An Act for Sanctifying & keeping holy the Lord's Day Commonly called Sunday."

By 1723, the Sabbath-breaking section of the statute assumed the present form of § 492, omitting the specific prohibition against Sunday swearing and the patently religiously motivated title.

There are judicial statements in early Maryland decisions which tend to support appellants' position. In an 1834 case involving a contract calling for delivery on Sunday, the Maryland Court of Appeals remarked that "Ours is a christian community, and a day set apart as the day of rest, is the day consecrated by the resurrection of our Saviour, and embraces the twenty-four hours next ensuing the midnight of Saturday. . . .

Considering the language and operative effect of the current statutes, we no longer find the blanket prohibition against Sunday work or bodily labor. To the contrary, we find that § 521 of Art. 27, the section which appellants violated, permits the Sunday sale of tobaccos and sweets and a long list of sundry articles which we have enumerated above; we find that § 509 of Art. 27 permits the Sunday operation of bathing beaches, amusement parks and similar facilities; we find that Art. 2B, § 28, permits the Sunday sale of alcoholic beverages, products strictly forbidden by predecessor statutes; we are told that Anne Arundel County allows Sunday bingo and the Sunday playing of pinball machines and slot machines, activities generally condemned by prior Maryland Sunday legislation. Certainly, these are not works of charity or necessity. Section 521's current stipulation that shops with only one employee may remain open on Sunday does not coincide with a religious purpose. These provisions, along with those which permit various sports and entertainments on Sunday, seem clearly to be fashioned for the purpose of providing a Sunday atmosphere of recreation, cheerfulness, repose and enjoyment. Coupled with the general proscription against other types of work, we believe that the air of the day is one of relaxation rather than one of religion.

* * *

After engaging in the close scrutiny demanded of us when First Amendment liberties are at issue, we accept the State Supreme Court's determination that the statutes' present purpose and effect is not to aid religion but to set aside a day of rest and recreation.

But this does not answer all of appellants' contentions. We are told that the State has other means at its disposal to accomplish its secular purpose, other courses that would not even remotely or incidentally give state aid to religion. On this basis, we are asked to hold these statutes invalid on the ground that the State's power to regulate conduct in the public interest may only be executed in a way that does not unduly or unnecessarily infringe upon the religious provisions of the First Amendment. However relevant this argument may be, we believe that the factual basis on which it rests is not supportable. It is true that if the State's interest were simply to provide for its citizens a periodic respite from work, a regulation demanding that everyone rest one day in seven, leaving the choice of the day to the individual, would suffice.

However, the State's purpose is not merely to provide a one-day-in-seven work stoppage. In addition to this, the State seeks to set one day apart from all others as a day of rest, repose, recreation and tranquility—a day which all members of the family and community have the opportunity to spend and enjoy together, a day on which there exists relative quiet and disassociation from the everyday intensity of commercial activities, a day on which people may visit friends and relatives who are not available during working days.

Obviously, a State is empowered to determine that a rest-one-day-in-seven statute would not accomplish this purpose; that it would not provide for a general cessation of activity, a special atmosphere of tranquility, a day which all members of the family or friends and relatives might spend together. . . .

It would seem unrealistic for enforcement purposes and perhaps detrimental to the general welfare to require a State to choose a common day of rest other than that which most persons would select of their own accord. For these reasons, we hold that the Maryland statutes are not laws respecting an establishment of religion.

* * *

Finally, we should make clear that this case deals only with the constitutionality of § 521 of the Maryland statute before us. We do not hold that Sunday legislation may not be a violation of the "Establishment" Clause if it can be demonstrated that its purpose—evidenced either on the face of the legislation, in conjunction with its legislative history, or in its operative effect—is to use the State's coercive power to aid religion.

Accordingly, the decision is

Affirmed.

MR. JUSTICE DOUGLAS, dissenting.

The question is not whether one day out of seven can be imposed by a State as a day of rest. The question is not whether Sunday can by force of custom and habit be retained as a day of rest. The question is whether a State can impose criminal sanctions on those who, unlike the Christian majority that makes up our society, worship on a different day or do not share the religious scruples of the majority.

* * *

Those who fashioned the First Amendment decided that if and when God is to be served, His service will not be motivated by coercive measures of government. "Congress shall make no law respecting an establishment of religion, or prohibiting the free exercise thereof"—such is the command of the First Amendment made applicable to the State by reason of the Due Process Clause of the Fourteenth. This means, as I understand it, that if a religious leaven is to be worked into the affairs of our people, it is to be done by individuals and groups, not by the Government. This necessarily means, *first,* that the dogma, creed, scruples, or practices of no religious group or sect are to be preferred over those of any others; *second,* that no one shall be interfered with by government for practicing the religion of his choice; *third,* that the State may not require anyone to practice a religion or even any religion; and *fourth,* that the State cannot compel one so to conduct himself as not to offend the religious scruples of another. The idea, as I understand it, was to limit the power of government to act in religious matters, not to limit the freedom of religious men to act religiously nor to restrict the freedom of athiests or agnostics. . . .

The issue of these cases would therefore be in better focus if we imagined that a state legislature, controlled by orthodox Jews and Seventh-Day Adventists, passed a law through a state legislature making it a crime to keep a shop open on Fridays. Would the rest of us have to submit under the fear of criminal sanctions?

* * *

The Court picks and chooses language from various decisions to bolster its conclusion that these Sunday laws in the modern setting are "civil regulations." No matter how much is written, no matter what is said, the parentage of these laws is the Fourth Commandment; and they serve and satisfy the religious predispositions of our Christian communities. After all, the labels a State places on its laws are not binding on us when we are confronted with a constitutional decision. We reach our own conclusion as to the character, effect, and practical operation of the regulation in determining its constitutionality.

The conduct held constitutionally criminal today embraces the selling of pure, not impure, food: wholesome, not noxious, articles. Adults, not minors, are involved. The innocent acts, now constitutionally classified as criminal, emphasize the drastic break we make with tradition.

These laws are sustained because, it is said, the First Amendment is concerned with religious convictions or opinion, not with conduct. But it is a strange Bill of Rights that makes it possible for the dominant religious group to bring the minority to heel because the minority, in the doing of acts which intrinsically are wholesome and not antisocial, does not defer to the majority's religious beliefs. Some have religious scruples against eating pork. Those scruples, no matter how bizarre they might seem to some, are within the ambit of the First Amendment. . . . Is it possible that a majority of a state legislature having those religious scruples could make it criminal for the nonbeliever to sell pork? Some have religious scruples against slaughtering cattle. Could a state legislature, dominated by that group, make it criminal to run an abattoir?

The Court balances the need of the people for rest, recreation, late sleeping, family visiting and the like against the command of the First Amendment that no one need bow to the religious beliefs of another. There is in this realm no room for balancing. I see no place for it in the constitutional scheme. A legislature of Christians can no more make minorities conform to their weekly regime than a legislature of Moslems, or a legislature of Hindus.

* * *

The State can, of course, require one day of rest a week: one day when every shop or factory is closed. Quite a few States make that requirement. Then the "day of rest" becomes purely and simply a health measure. But the Sunday laws operate differently. They force minorities to obey the majority's religious feelings of what is due and proper for a Christian community; they provide a coercive spur to the "weaker brethren," to those who are indifferent to the claims of a Sabbath through apathy or scruple. Can there be any doubt that Christians, now aligned vigorously in favor of these laws, would be as strongly opposed if they were prosecuted under a Moslem law that forbade them from engaging in secular activities on days that violated Moslem scruples?

There is an "establishment" of religion in the constitutional sense if any practice of any religious group has the sanction of law behind it. There is an interference with the "free exercise" of religion if what in conscience one can do or omit doing is required because of the religious scruples of the community. Hence I would declare each of those laws unconstitutional as applied to the complaining parties, whether or not they are members of a sect which observes as its Sabbath a day other than Sunday.

QUESTIONS AND COMMENTS

1 While the law in *McGowan* was upheld, i.e., Sunday closing laws are not unconstitutional on their face, the Supreme Court's treatment of the issue in *McGowan* and other cases suggests that such laws must not allow so many exemptions as to become arbitrary or unreasonably discriminating. See *Two Guys from Harrison–Allentown v. McGinley,* 366 U.S. 582 (1961); *Braunfeld v. Brown,* 366 U.S. 599 (1961).
2 What was the "secular purpose" behind the Maryland Sunday-closing statute? Does the Court's ruling in *McGowan* mean that a religious purpose is permissible as long as a secular purpose is also present? Explain.
3 What test does the Court employ to reach its conclusion that the encroachment on the religious beliefs of some persons is justified?
4 Can a Seventh-Day Adventist who refuses to work on Saturday be denied unemployment compensation? See *Sherbert v. Verner,* 374 U.S. 398 (1963).

Religious Expression

Hefron v. International Society for Krishna Consciousness (1981)

This case integrates the right to freely exercise one's religion with the right to free speech. The petitioner concedes that both are subject to restriction by the state but argues that Minnesota cannot constitutionally prevent or suppress behavior that is essential to the Krishna religion.

Hefron, Secretary and Manager of the Minnesota State Agricultural Society Board of Managers, et al. v. International Society for Krishna Consciousness, Inc., et al.

452 U.S. 640; 101 S. Ct. 2559; 69 L. Ed. 2d 298 (1981)
Vote: 5–4

The Minnesota Agricultural Society operated an annual state fair and issued rules for exhibitors and others desiring to participate in fair activities. Rule 6.05 required that all selling, exhibiting, or distributing of materials must be done from fixed locations. The rule permitted agents of organizations to walk about the grounds and communicate their organization's views to fair patrons—face to face.

The day before the opening of the 1977 fair, the Krishnas (ISKCON), a religious society, filed suit seeking to enjoin the enforcement of Rule 6.05. It would, they argued, suppress the practice of "Sankirtan," a religious ritual which requires members to distribute or sell religious literature and solicit donations. The trial court issued orders governing the 1977 fair. Subsequently, the court upheld the constitutionality of Rule 6.05. On appeal, the Minnesota Supreme Court reversed, finding a violation of the Krishnas' First Amendment rights. The U.S. Supreme Court granted certiorari.

JUSTICE WHITE delivered the opinion of the Court.

The question presented for review is whether a State, consistent with the First and Fourteenth Amendments, may require a religious organization desiring to distribute and sell religious literature and to solicit donations at a state fair to conduct those activities only at an assigned location within the fairgrounds even though application of the rule limits the religious practices of the organization.

* * *

The State does not dispute that the oral and written dissemination of the Krishnas' religious views and doctrines is protected by the First Amendment. . . . *Schneider v. State,* (1939). Nor does it claim that this protection is lost because the written materials sought to be distributed are sold rather than given away or because contributions or gifts are solicited in the course of propagating the faith. Our cases indicate as much. *Schaumburg v. Citizens for a Better Environment,* (1980).

It is also common ground, however, that the First Amendment does not guarantee the right to communicate one's views at all times and places or in any manner that may be desired. *Adderley v. Florida.* [1966].

A major criterion for a valid time, place, and manner restriction is that the restriction "may not be based upon either the content or subject matter of speech." *Consolidated Edison Co. v. Public Service Comm'n,* [1980]. Rule 6.05 qualifies in this respect, since, as the Supreme Court of Minnesota observed, the Rule applies evenhandedly to all who wish to distribute and sell written materials or to solicit funds. No person or organization, whether commercial or charitable, is permitted to engage in such activities except from a booth rented for those purposes.

Nor does Rule 6.05 suffer from the more covert forms of discrimination that may result when arbitrary discretion is vested in some governmental authority. The method of allocating space is a straightforward first-come, first-served system. The Rule is not open to the kind of arbitrary application that this Court has condemned as inherently inconsistent with a valid time, place, and manner regulation because such discretion has the potential for becoming a means of suppressing a particular point of view. . . .

A valid time, place, and manner regulation must also "serve a significant governmental interest." *Virginia Pharmacy Board v. Virginia Citizens Consumer Council,* [1976]. Here, the principal justification asserted by the State in support of Rule 6.05 is the need to maintain the orderly movement of the crowd given the large number of exhibitors and persons attending the Fair. . . .

As a general matter, it is clear that a State's interest in protecting the "safety and convenience" of persons using a public forum is a valid governmental objective.

Furthermore, consideration of a forum's special attributes is relevant to the constitutionality of a regulation since the significance of the governmental interest must be assessed in light of the characteristic nature and function of the particular forum involved. . . . This observation bears particular import in the present case since respondents make a number of analogies between the fairgrounds and city streets, which have "immemorially been held in trust for the use of the public and . . . have been used for purposes of assembly, communicating thoughts between citizens, and discussing public questions." *Hague v. CIO,* [1938]. . . . But it is clear that there are significant differences between a street and the fairgrounds. A street is continually open, often uncongested, and constitutes not only a necessary conduit in the daily affairs of a locality's citizens, but also a place where people may enjoy the open air or the company of friends and neighbors in a relaxed environment. The Minnesota Fair, as described above, is a temporary event attracting great numbers of visitors who come to the event for a short period to see and experience the host of exhibits and attractions at the Fair. The flow of the crowd and demands of safety are more pressing in the context of the Fair. As such, any comparisons to public streets are necessarily inexact.

The Minnesota Supreme Court recognized that the State's interest in the orderly movement of a large crowd and in avoiding congestion was substantial and that Rule 6.05 furthered that interest significantly. Nevertheless, the Minnesota Supreme Court declared that the case did not turn on the "importance of the state's undeniable interest in preventing the widespread disorder that would surely exist if no regulation such as Rule 6.05 were in effect" but upon the significance of the State's interest in avoiding whatever disorder would likely result from granting members of ISKCON an exemption from the Rule. Approaching the case in this way, the court concluded that although some disruption would occur from such an exemption, it was not of sufficient concern to warrant confining the Krishnas to a booth. The court also concluded that, in any event, the Rule was not essential to the furtherance of the State's interest in crowd control, which could adequately be served by less intrusive means.

As we see it, the Minnesota Supreme Court took too narrow a view of the State's interest in avoiding congestion and maintaining the orderly movement of fair patrons on the fairgrounds. The justification for the Rule should not be measured by the disorder that would result from granting an exemption solely to ISKCON. That organization and its ritual of Sankirtan have no special claim to First Amendment protection as compared to that of other religions who also distribute literature and solicit funds. None of our cases suggest that the inclusion of peripatetic solicitation as part of a church ritual entitles church members to solicitation rights in a public forum superior to those of members of other religious groups that raise money but do not purport to ritualize the process. . . .

ISKCON desires to proselytize at the fair because it believes it can successfully communicate and raise funds. In its view, this can be done only by intercepting fair patrons as they move about, and if success is achieved, stopping them momentarily or for longer periods as money is given or exchanged for literature. This consequence would be multiplied many times over if Rule 6.05 could not be applied to confine such transactions by ISKCON and others to fixed locations. Indeed, the court below agreed that without Rule 6.05 there would be widespread disorder at the fairgrounds. The court also recognized that some disorder would inevitably result from exempting the Krishnas from the Rule. Obviously, there would be a much larger threat to the State's interest in crowd control if all other religious, nonreligious, and noncommercial organizations could likewise move freely about the fairgrounds distributing and selling literature and soliciting funds at will.

Given these considerations, we hold that the State's interest in confining distribution, selling, and fund solicitation activities to fixed locations is sufficient to satisfy the requirement that a place or manner restriction must serve a substantial state interest. . . .

For Rule 6.05 to be valid as a place and manner restriction, it must also be sufficiently clear that alternative forums for the expression of respondents' protected speech exist despite the effects of the Rule. Rule 6.05 is not vulnerable on this ground. First, the Rule does not prevent ISKCON from practicing Sankirtan anywhere outside the fairgrounds. More importantly, the Rule has not been shown to deny access within the forum in question. Here, the Rule does not exclude ISKCON from the fairgrounds, nor does it deny that organization the right to conduct any desired activity at some point within the forum. Its members may mingle with the crowd and orally propagate their views. The organization may also arrange for a booth and distribute and sell literature and solicit funds from that location on the fairgrounds itself. The Minnesota State Fair is a limited public forum in that it exists to provide a means for a great number of people in an efficient fashion. Considering the limited functions of the Fair and the combined area within which it operates, we are unwilling to say that Rule 6.05 does not provide ISKCON and other organizations with an adequate means to sell and solicit on the fairgrounds. The First Amendment protects the right of every citizen to "reach the minds of willing listeners and to do so there must be opportunity to win their attention." *Kovacs v. Cooper,* (1949). Rule 6.05 does not unnecessarily limit that right within the fairgrounds.

* * *

The judgment of the Supreme Court of Minnesota is reversed, and the case is remanded for further proceedings not inconsistent with this opinion.

So ordered.

JUSTICE BRENNAN, with whom JUSTICE MARSHALL and JUSTICE STEVENS join, concurring in part and dissenting in part.

* * *

The State advances three justifications for its booth Rule. The justification relied upon by the Court today is the State's interest in maintaining the orderly movement of the crowds at the fair. The second justification, relied upon by the dissenting justices below, is the State's interest in protecting its fairgoers from fraudulent, deceptive, and misleading solicitation practices. The third justification, based on the "captive audience" doctrine, is the State's interest in protecting its fairgoers from annoyance and harassment.

I quite agree with the Court that the State has a significant interest in maintaining crowd control on its fairgrounds. I also have no doubt that the State has a significant interest in protecting its fairgoers from fraudulent or deceptive solicitation practices. . . .

. . . accordingly, I join the judgment of the Court insofar as it upholds Rule 6.05's restriction on sales and solicitations. However, because I believe that the booth Rule is an overly intrusive means of achieving the state's interest in crowd control, and because I cannot accept the validity of the State's third asserted justification, I dissent from the Court's approval of Rule 6.05's restriction on the distribution of literature.

* * *

In support of the crowd control justification, petitioners contend that if fairgoers are permitted to distribute literature, large crowds will gather, blocking traffic lanes and causing safety problems.

* * *

But petitioners have failed to provide any support for these assertions. They have made no showing that relaxation of the booth Rule would create additional disorder in a fair that is already characterized by the robust and unrestrained participation of hundreds of thousands of wandering fairgoers. . . .

Relying on a general, speculative fear of disorder, the State of Minnesota has placed a significant restriction on respondents' ability to exercise core First Amendment rights. This restriction is not narrowly drawn to advance the State's interests, and for that reason is unconstitutional.

* * *

JUSTICE BLACKMUN, concurring in part and dissenting in part.

* * *

While I agree with JUSTICE BRENNAN that the State's interest in order does not justify restrictions upon distribution of literature, I think that common-sense differences between literature distribution, on the one hand, and solicitation and sales, on the other, suggest that the latter activities present greater crowd control problems than the former. The distribution of literature does not require that the recipient stop in order to receive the message the speaker wishes to convey; instead, the recipient is free to read the message at a later time. For this reason, literature distribution may present even fewer crowd control problems than the oral proselytizing that the State already allows upon the fairgrounds. In contrast, as the dissent in the Minnesota Supreme Court observed, sales and the collection of solicited funds not only require the fair-goer to stop, but also "engender additional confusion . . . because they involve acts of exchanging articles for money, fumbling for and dropping money, making change, etc."

Rules restricting the exchange of money to booths have been upheld in analogous contexts, see, *e. g., International Society for Krishna Consciousness v. Eaves,* (CA5 1979) (Atlanta airports), and for similar reasons I would uphold Rule 6.05 insofar as it applies to solicitation and sales.

QUESTIONS AND COMMENTS

1 Why is crowd control at a state fair more important than the right of the Krishnas to practice their religion?
2 Can you suggest some way in which the interests of the state could be served without confining the Krishnas to a booth?

NOTES

1 *Frohwerk v. United States,* 249 U.S. 204 (1919).
2 *In re Debs,* 158 U.S. 564 (1895).
3 250 U.S. 616 (1919).
4 *Thornhill v. Alabama,* 310 U.S. 88 (1940); *Terminiello v. Chicago,* 337 U.S. 1 (1949); *Cantwell v. Connecticut,* 310 U.S. 196 (1940).
5 Douglas, dissenting in *Brandenburg v. Ohio,* 395 U.S. 444 (1969).
6 *American Communications Association v. Douds,* 339 U.S. 382 (1950).
7 283 U.S. 697 (1931).
8 *Ibid.,* p. 704.
9 *Organization for a Better Austin v. O'Keefe,* 402 U.S. 415 (1971).
10 *Erznoznik v. Jacksonville,* 422 U.S. 205 (1975).

11 *Nebraska Press Association v. Stuart,* 427 U.S. 539 (1976).

12 427 U.S. 50 (1976).

13 See *Capital Broadcasting Co. v. Mitchell,* 333 F. Supp. 582, *aff'd. per curiam,* 405 U.S. 1000 (1972).

14 *Pittsburgh Press Co. v. Committee on Human Relations,* 413 U.S. 376 (1973).

15 *Jacobellis v. Ohio,* 378 U.S. 184 (1964).

16 See *Marks v. United States,* 430 U.S. 188 (1977); *Smith v. United States,* 431 U.S. 291 (1977); *Splawn v. California,* 431 U.S. 595 (1977); *Ward v. Illinois,* 431 U.S. 767 (1977).

17 It is alleged that clerks to the justices frequently used to mock Justice Stewart in the screening room by calling out, "That's it, that's it, I know it when I see it" (Bob Woodward and Scott Armstrong, *The Brethren,* Simon & Schuster, New York, 1979, p. 198).

18 *Cantwell v. Connecticut,* 310 U.S. 296 (1940); *Everson v. Board of Education,* 330 U.S. 1 (1947).

19 310 U.S. 586 (1940).

20 Ibid., p. 598.

21 According to Justice Douglas in *The Court Years 1939–1975,* Random House, New York, 1980 pp. 45–46.

22 *Reynolds v. United States,* 98 U.S. 145 (1879), re the "wall of separation."

23 330 U.S. 1 (1947).

24 *Illinois ex rel McCollum v. Board of Education,* 333 U.S. 203 (1948).

25 *Zorach v. Clausen,* 343 U.S. 306 (1952).

26 403 U.S. 602 (1971).

27 *Sherbert v. Verner,* 374 U.S. 398 (1963).

CHAPTER 8

THE RIGHTS OF CRIMINAL SUSPECTS

Protection Against Unreasonable Search and Seizure

The Exclusionary Rule

Mapp v. Ohio (1961)

While the Fourth Amendment ensures the "right of the people to be secure in their persons, houses, papers, and effects against unreasonable searches and seizures," it does not specify what is to be done if the right is violated. In *Weeks v. United States,*[1] the Supreme Court came up with one answer to the question. In order to discourage violations of the amendment the Court decided that any evidence obtained as a result of a violation would be suppressed or excluded in criminal prosecutions. Violation of this "exclusionary rule," on the other hand, would lead to the reversal on appeal of any conviction obtained thereby. Since *Weeks* involved a federal agent, and the Fourth Amendment had not yet been applied to the states, the case stands for the proposition that evidence illegally obtained may not be used in a federal court. In the 1949 case of *Wolf v. Colorado,*[2] the Supreme Court declared the search and seizure provision of the Fourth Amendment applicable to the states through the Fourteenth Amendment. However, the Court declined to impose the exclusionary rule. *Mapp v. Ohio* reexamines the Court's judgment on this point.

Mapp v. Ohio

367 U.S. 643; 81 S. Ct. 1684; 6 L. Ed. 2d 1981 (1961)
Vote: 6–3

The facts of this case are given in the opinion below.

MR. JUSTICE CLARK delivered the opinion of the Court.

Appellant stands convicted of knowingly having had in her possession and under her control certain lewd and lascivious books, pictures, and photographs in violation of § 2905.34 of Ohio's Revised Code. As officially stated in the syllabus to its opinion, the Supreme Court of Ohio found that her conviction was valid though "based primarily upon the introduction in evidence of lewd and lascivious books and pictures unlawfully seized during an unlawful search of defendant's home. . . ."

On May 23, 1957, three Cleveland police officers arrived at appellant's residence in that city pursuant to information that "a person [was] hiding out in the home, who was wanted for questioning in connection with a recent bombing, and that there was a large amount of policy paraphernalia being hidden in the home." Miss Mapp and her daughter by a former marriage lived on the top floor of the two-family dwelling. Upon their arrival at that house, the officers knocked on the door and demanded entrance but appellant, after telephoning her attorney, refused to admit them without a search warrant. They advised their headquarters of the situation and undertook a surveillance of the house.

The officers again sought entrance some three hours later when four or more additional officers arrived on the scene. When Miss Mapp did not come to the door immediately, at least one of the several doors to the house was forcibly opened and the policemen gained admittance. Meanwhile Miss Mapp's attorney arrived, but the officers, having secured their own entry, and continuing in their defiance of the law, would permit him neither to see Miss Mapp nor to enter the house. It appears that Miss Mapp was halfway down the stairs from the upper floor to the front door when the officers, in this highhanded manner, broke into the hall. She demanded to see the search warrant. A paper, claimed to be a warrant, was held up by one of the officers. She grabbed the "warrant" and placed it in her bosom. A struggle ensued in which the officers recovered the piece of paper and as a result of which they handcuffed appellant because she had been "belligerent" in resisting their official rescue of the "warrant" from her person. Running roughshod over appellant, a policeman "grabbed" her, "twisted [her] hand," and she "yelled [and] pleaded with him" because "it was hurting." Appellant, in handcuffs, was then forcibly taken upstairs to her bedroom where the officers searched a dresser, a chest of drawers, a closet and some suitcases. They also looked into a photo album and through personal papers belonging to the appellant. The search spread to the rest of the second floor including the child's bedroom, the living room, the kitchen and a dinette. The basement of the building and a trunk found therein were also searched. The obscene materials for possession of which she was ultimately convicted were discovered in the course of that widespread search.

At the trial no search warrant was produced by the prosecution, nor was the failure to produce one explained or accounted for. At best, "There is, in the record, considerable doubt as to whether there ever was any warrant for the search of defendant's home."

The Ohio Supreme Court believed a "reasonable argument" could be made that the conviction should be reversed "because the 'methods' employed to obtain the [evidence] . . . were such as to 'offend "a sense of justice." '" but the court found determinative the fact that the evidence had not been taken "from defendant's person by the use of brutal or offensive physical force against defendant."

The State says that even if the search were made without authority, or otherwise unreasonably, it is not prevented from using the unconstitutionally seized evidence at trial, citing *Wolf v. Colorado,* (1949), in which this Court did indeed hold "that in a prosecution in a State court for a State crime the Fourteenth Amendment does not forbid the admission of evidence obtained by an unreasonable search and seizure." On this appeal, of which we have noted probable jurisdiction, it is urged once again that we review that holding.

. . . In the year 1914, in the *Weeks* case, this Court "for the first time" held that "in a federal prosecution the Fourth Amendment barred the use of evidence secured through an illegal search and seizure. . . ."

In 1949, 35 years after *Weeks* was announced, this Court, in *Wolf v. Colorado,* again for the first time, discussed the effect of the Fourth Amendment upon the States through the operation of the Due Process Clause of the Fourteenth Amendment. It said:

> [We] have no hesitation in saying that were a State affirmatively to sanction such police incursion into privacy it would run counter to the guaranty of the Fourteenth Amendment.

Nevertheless, after declaring that the "security of one's privacy against arbitrary intrusion by the police" is "implicit in 'the concept of ordered liberty' and as such enforceable against the States through the Due Process Clause," cf. *Polko v. Connecticut,* (1937) and announcing that it "stoutly adher[d]" to the *Weeks* decision, the Court decided that the *Weeks* exclusionary rule would not then be imposed upon the States as "an essential ingredient of the right. . . ."

The Court in *Wolf* first stated that "[t]he contrariety of views of the States' on the adoption of the exclusionary rule of *Weeks* was "particularly impressive" and, in this connection, that it could not "brush aside the experience of States which deem the incidence of such conduct by the police too slight to call for a deterrent remedy . . . by overriding the [States'] relevant rules of evidence." While in 1949, prior to the *Wolf* case, almost two-thirds of the States were opposed to the use of the exclusionary rule, now, despite the *Wolf* case, more than half of those since passing upon it, by their own legislative or judicial decision, have wholly or partly adopted or adhered to the *Weeks* rule. See *Elkins v. United States,* (1960). . . .

It, therefore, plainly appears that the factual considerations supporting the failure of the *Wolf* Court to include the *Weeks* exclusionary rule when it recognized the enforcability of the right to privacy against the States in 1949, while not basically relevant to the constitutional consideration, could not, in any analysis, now be deemed controlling.

* * *

. . . Only last Term, after again carefully re-examining the *Wolf* doctrine in *Elkins v. United States,* the Court pointed out that "the controlling principles" as to search and seizure and the problem of admissibility "seemed clear" until the announcement in *Wolf* "that the Due Process Clause of the Fourteenth Amendment does not itself require state courts to adopt the exclusionary rule" of the *Weeks* case. At the same time, the Court pointed out, "the underlying constitutional doctrine which *Wolf* established . . . that the Federal Constitution . . . prohibits unreasonable searches and seizures by state officers" had undermined the "foundation upon which the admissibility of state-seized evidence in a federal trial originally rested. . . ."

The Court concluded that it was therefore obliged to hold, although it chose the narrower ground on which to do so, that all evidence obtained by an unconstitutional search and seizure was inadmissible in a federal court regardless of its source. Today we once again examine *Wolf's* constitutional documentation of the right to privacy free from unreasonable state intrusion, and, after its dozen years on our books, are led by it to close the only courtroom door remaining open to evidence secured by official lawlessness in flagrant abuse of that basic right, reserved to all persons as a specific guarantee against that very same unlawful conduct. We hold that all evidence obtained by searches and seizures in violation of the Constitution is, by that same authority, inadmissible in a state court. . . .

. . . Our holding that the exclusionary rule is an essential part of both the Fourth and Fourteenth Amendment is not only the logical dictate of prior cases, but it also makes very good sense. There is no war between the Constitution and common sense. Presently, a federal prosecutor may make no use of evidence illegally seized, but a State's attorney across the street may; although he supposedly is operating under the enforceable prohibitions of the same Amendment. Thus the State, by admitting evidence unlawfully seized, serves to encourage disobedience to the Federal Constitution which it is bound to uphold. Moreover, as was said in *Elkins*, "[t]he very essence of a healthy federalism depends upon the avoidance of needless conflict between state and federal courts."

... Yet the double standard recognized until today hardly put such a thesis into practice. In nonexclusionary States, federal officers, being human, were by it invited to and did, as our cases indicate, step across the street to the State's attorney with their unconstitutionally seized evidence. Prosecution on the basis of that evidence was then had in a state court in utter disregard of the enforceable Fourth Amendment. ...

[Now] Federal-state cooperation in the solution of crime under constitutional standards will be promoted, if only by recognition of their now mutual obligation to respect the same fundamental criteria in their approaches.

* * *

There are those who say, as did Justice (then Judge) Cardozo, that under our constitutional exclusionary doctrine "[t]he criminal is to go free because the constable has blundered." *People v. Defore,* 242 N. Y., at 21, 150 N. E., at 587. In some cases this will undoubtedly be the result. But, as was said in *Elkins,* "there is another consideration—the imperative of judicial integrity." The criminal goes free, if he must, but it is the law that sets him free.

* * *

Having once recognized that the right to privacy embodied in the Fourth Amendment is enforceable against the States, and that the right to be secure against rude invasions of privacy by state officers is, therefore, constitutional in origin, we can no longer permit that right to remain an empty promise. Because it is enforceable in the same manner and to like effect as other basic rights secured by the Due Process Clause, we can no longer permit it to be revocable at the whim of any police officer who, in the name of law enforcement itself, chooses to suspend its enjoyment. Our decision, founded on reason and truth, gives to the individual no more than that which the Constitution guarantees him, to the police officer no less than that to which honest law enforcement is entitled, and, to the courts, that judicial integrity so necessary in the true administration of justice.

The judgment of the Supreme Court of Ohio is reversed and the cause remanded for further proceedings not inconsistent with this opinion.

Reversed and remanded.

* * *

Mr. Justice Harlan, whom Mr. Justice Frankfurter and Mr. Justice Whittaker join, dissenting.

In overruling the *Wolf* case the Court, in my opinion, has forgotten the sense of judicial restraint which, with due regard for *stare decisis,* is one element that should enter into deciding whether a past decision of this Court should be overruled. Apart from that I also believe that the *Wolf* rule represents sounder Constitutional doctrine than the new rule which now replaces it.

From the Court's statement of the case one would gather that the central, if not controlling, issue on this appeal is whether illegally state-seized evidence is Constitutionally admissible in a state prosecution, an issue which would of course face us with the need for re-examining *Wolf.* However, such is not the situation. For, although that question was indeed raised here and below among appellant's subordinate points, the new and pivotal issue brought to the Court by this appeal is whether § 2905.34 of the Ohio Revised Code making criminal the *mere* knowing possession or control of obscene material, and under which appellant has been convicted, is consistent with the rights of free thought and expression assured against state action by the Fourteenth Amendment. That was the principal issue which was decided by the Ohio Supreme Court, which was tendered by appellant's Jurisdictional Statement, and which was briefed and argued in this Court. . . .

In this posture of things, I think it fair to say that five members of this Court have simply "reached out" to overrule *Wolf.* With all respect for the views of the majority, and recognizing that *stare decisis* carries different weight in Constitutional adjudication than it does in nonconstitutional decision, I can perceive no justification for regarding this case as an appropriate occasion for re-examining *Wolf.*

The action of the Court finds no support in the rule that decision of Constitutional issues should be avoided wherever possible. For in overruling *Wolf* the Court, instead of passing upon the validity of Ohio's § 2905.34, has simply chosen between two Constitutional questions. Moreover, I submit that it has chosen the more difficult and less appropriate of the two questions. The Ohio statute which, as construed by the State Supreme Court, punishes knowing possession or control of obscene material, irrespective of the purposes of such possession or control (with exceptions not here applicable) and irrespective of whether the accused had any reasonable opportunity to rid himself of the material after discovering that it was obscene, surely presents a Constitutional question which is both simpler and less far-reaching than the question which the Court decides today. It seems to me that justice might well have been done in this case without overturning a decision on which the administration of criminal law in many of the States has long justifiably relied.

* * *

I am bound to say that what has been done is not likely to promote respect either for the Court's adjudicatory process or for the stability of its decisions. Having been unable, however, to persuade any of the majority to a different procedural course, I now turn to the merits of the present decision. . . .

First, it is said that "the factual grounds upon which *Wolf* was based" have since changed, in that more States now follow the *Weeks* exclusionary rule than was so at the time *Wolf* was decided. While that is true, a recent survey indicates that at present one-half of the States will adhere to the common-law non-exclusionary rule, and one, Maryland, retains the rule as to felonies.

But in any case surely all this is beside the point, as the majority itself indeed seems to recognize. Our concern here, as it was in *Wolf*, is not with the desirability of that rule but only with the question whether the States are Constitutionally free to follow it or not as they may themselves determine, and the relevance of the disparity of views among the States on this point lies simply in the fact that the judgment involved is a debatable one. Moreover, the very fact on which the majority relies, instead of lending support to what is now being done, points away from the need of replacing a voluntary state action with federal compulsion.

The preservation of a proper balance between state and federal responsibility in the administration of criminal justice demands patience on the part of those who might like to see things move faster among the States in this respect. Problems of criminal law enforcement vary widely from State to State. One State, in considering the totality of its legal picture, may conclude that the need for embracing the *Weeks* rule is pressing because other remedies are unavailable or inadequate to secure compliance with the substantive Constitutional principle involved. Another, though equally solicitous of Constitutional rights, may choose to pursue one purpose at a time, allowing all evidence relevant to guilt to be brought into a criminal trial, and dealing with Constitutional infractions by other means. Still another may consider the exclusionary rule too rough-and-ready a remedy in that it reaches only unconstitutional intrusions which eventuate in criminal prosecution of the victims. Further, a State after experimenting with the *Weeks* rule for a time may, because of unsatisfactory experience with it, decide to revert to a non-exclusionary rule. And so on. From the standpoint of Constitutional permissibility in pointing a State in one direction or another, I do not see at all why "time has set its face against" the considerations which led Mr. Justice Cardozo, then chief judge of the New York Court of Appeals, to reject for New York in *People v. Defore,* the *Weeks* exclusionary rule. For us the question remains, as it has always been, one of state power, not one of passing judgment on the wisdom of one state course or another. In any view this Court should continue to forbear from fettering the States with an adamant rule which may embarrass them in coping with their own peculiar problems in criminal law enforcement.

Further, we are told that imposition of the *Weeks* rule on the States makes "very good sense," in that it will promote recognition by state and federal officials of their "mutual obligation to respect the same fundamental criteria" in their approach to law enforcement, and will avoid " 'needless conflict between state and federal courts.'" Indeed the majority now finds an incongruity in *Wolf's* discriminating perception between the demands of "ordered liberty" as respects the basic right of "privacy" and the means of securing it among the States. That perception, resting both on a sensitive regard for our federal system and a sound recognition of this Court's remoteness from particular state problems, is for me the strength of that decision.

* * *

Finally, it is said that the overruling of *Wolf* is supported by the established doctrine that the admission in evidence of an involuntary confession renders a state conviction Constitutionally invalid. Since such a confession may often be entirely reliable, and therefore of the greatest relevance to the issue of the trial, the argument continues, this doctrine is ample warrant in precedent that the way evidence was obtained, and not just its relevance, is Constitutionally significant to the fairness of a trial. I believe this analogy is not a true one. The "coerced confession" rule is certainly not a rule that any illegally obtained statements may not be used in evidence. I would suppose that a statement which is procured during a period of illegal detention, *Mc.Nabb v. United States,* is, as much as unlawfully seized evidence, illegally obtained, but this Court has consistently refused to reverse state convictions resting on the use of such statements. . . .

The point, then, must be that in requiring exclusion of an involuntary statement of an accused, we are concerned not with an appropriate remedy for what the police have done, but with something which is regarded as going to the heart of our concepts of fairness in judicial procedure. The operative assumption of our procedural system is that "Ours is the accusatorial as opposed to the inquisitorial system. Such has been the characteristic of Anglo-American criminal justice since it freed itself from practices borrowed by the Star Chamber from the Continent whereby the accused was interrogated in secret for hours on end."

The pressures brought to bear against an accused leading to a confession, unlike an unconstitutional violation of privacy, do not, apart from the use of the confession at trial, necessarily involve independent Constitutional violations. What is crucial is that the trial defense to which an accused is entitled should not be rendered an empty formality by reason of statements wrung from him, for then "a prisoner . . . [has been] made the deluded instrument of his own conviction."

That this is a *procedural right,* and that its violation occurs at the time his improperly obtained statement is admitted at trial, is manifest. For without this right all the careful safeguards erected around the giving of testimony, whether by an accused or any other witness, would become empty formalities in a procedure where the most compelling possible evidence of guilt, a confession, would have already been obtained at the unsupervised pleasure of the police.

This, and not the disciplining of the police, as with illegally seized evidence, is surely the true basis for excluding a statement of the accused which was unconstitutionally obtained. In sum, I think the coerced confession analogy works strongly *against* what the Court does today.

* * *

I regret that I find so unwise in principle and so inexpedient in policy a decision motivated by the high purpose of increasing respect for Constitutional rights. But in the last analysis I think this Court can increase respect for the Constitution only if it rigidly respects the limitations which the Constitution places upon it, and respects as well the principles inherent in its own processes. In the present case I think we exceed both, and that our voice becomes only a voice of power, not of reason.

QUESTIONS AND COMMENTS

1 Whether the exclusionary rule discourages violations of the prohibition against unreasonable search and seizure is controversial. At the same time, alternatives are available under present law, and new legislation or administrative rules could incorporate different means to accomplish the same purpose. Assess the following possibilities for enforcing the Fourth Amendment as alternatives to the exclusionary rule:
   a Criminal prosecution of the officer violating the right (this may entail defining the violation as a crime under state law).
   b Disciplinary action by police departments against those who violate the Fourth Amendment's search and seizure provisions.
   c Reducing or restricting budgetary allocations to police departments frequently found to violate the amendment.
   d Civil suits (tort actions) against officers who violate the amendment.
   e Modifying the exclusionary rule to require suppression of evidence only when the police officer acts in the knowledge that the action is unconstitutional (this essentially is the position taken by Justice White in *Stone v. Powell* [428 U.S. 465 (1976)].

Search Incident to Arrest

Chimel v. California (1969)

United States v. Robinson (1973)

South Dakota v. Opperman (1976)

It may be noted that the Fourth Amendment only prohibits unreasonable searches and seizures conducted without a warrant. To obtain a warrant to search, the applying officer must satisfy a judge or magistrate that there is probable cause to believe a crime has been committed and produce sufficient evidence to justify such a belief. The warrant itself must specify with particularity the place to be searched and the persons or things to be seized. Most problems in this area of law arise over warrantless searches. Such searches are reasonable if based on probable cause and usually if it is not practicable to obtain a warrant. The three cases in this section deal with two kinds of exceptions to the warrant requirement: searches incident to arrest and automobile searches.

Chimel v. California

395 U.S. 752; 89 S. Ct. 2034; 23 L. Ed. 2d 685 (1969)
Vote: 7–2

The facts are included in the opinion provided below.

MR. JUSTICE STEWART delivered the opinion of the Court.

This case raises basic questions concerning the permissible scope under the Fourth Amendment of a search incident to a lawful arrest.

The relevant facts are essentially undisputed. Late in the afternoon of September 13, 1965, three police officers arrived at the Santa Ana, California, home of the petitioner with a warrant authorizing his arrest for the burglary of a coin shop. The officers knocked on the door, identified themselves to the petitoner's wife, and asked if they might come inside. She ushered them into the house, where they waited 10 or 15 minutes until the petitioner returned home from work. When the petitioner entered the house, one of the officers handed him the arrest warrant and asked for permission to "look around." The petitioner objected, but was advised that "on the basis of the lawful arrest," the officers would nonetheless conduct a search. No search warrant had been issued.

Accompanied by the petitioner's wife, the officers then looked through the entire three-bedroom house, including the attic, the garage, and a small workshop. In some rooms the search was relatively cursory. In the master bedroom and sewing room, however, the officers directed the petitioner's wife to open drawers and "to physically move contents of the drawers from side to side so that [they] might view any items that would have come from [the] burglary." After completing the search, they seized numerous items—primarily coins, but also several medals, tokens, and a few other objects. The entire search took between 45 minutes and an hour.

At the petitioner's subsequent state trial on two charges of burglary, the items taken from his house were admitted into evidence against him, over his objection that they had been unconstitutionally seized. He was convicted, and the judgments of conviction were affirmed by both the California Court of Appeal, and the California Supreme Court.

Both courts accepted the petitioner's contention that the arrest warrant was invalid because the supporting affidavit was set out in conclusory terms, but held that since the arresting officers had procured the warrant "in good faith," and since in any event they had had sufficient information to constitute probable cause for the petitioner's arrest, that arrest had been lawful. From this conclusion the appellate courts went on to hold that the search of the petitioner's home had been justified, despite the absence of a search warrant, on the ground that it had been incident to a valid arrest. We granted certiorari in order to consider the petitioner's substantial constitutional claims.

Without deciding the question, we proceed on the hypothesis that the California courts were correct in holding that the arrest of the petitioner was valid under the Constitution. This brings us directly to the question whether the warrantless search of the petitioner's entire house can be constitutionally justified as incident to that arrest.

* * *

When an arrest is made, it is reasonable for the arresting officer to search the person arrested in order to remove any weapons that the latter might seek to use in order to resist arrest or effect his escape. Otherwise, the officer's safety might well be endangered, and the arrest itself frustrated. In addition, it is entirely reasonable for the arresting officer to search for and seize any evidence on the arrestee's person in order to prevent its concealment or destruction. And the area into which an arrestee might reach in order to grab a weapon or evidentiary items must, of course, be governed by a like rule. A gun on a table or in a drawer in front of one who is arrested can be as dangerous to the arresting officer as one concealed in the clothing of the person arrested. There is ample justification, therefore, for a search of the arrestee's person and the area "within his immediate control"—construing that phrase to mean the area from within which he might gain possession of a weapon or destructible evidence.

There is no comparable justification, however, for routinely searching any room other than that in which an arrest occurs—or, for that matter, for searching through all the desk drawers or other closed or concealed areas in that room itself. Such searches, in the absence of well-recognized exceptions, may be made only under the authority of a search warrant. The "adherence to judicial processes" mandated by the Fourth Amendment requires no less.

* * *

Application of sound Fourth Amendment principles to the facts of this case produces a clear result. The search here went far beyond the petitioner's person and the area from within which he might have obtained either a weapon or something that could have been used as evidence against him. There was no constitutional justification, in the absence of a search warrant, for extending the search beyond that area. The scope of the search was, therefore, "unreasonable" under the Fourth and Fourteenth Amendments, and the petitioner's conviction cannot stand.

Reversed.

* * *

MR. JUSTICE WHITE, with whom MR. JUSTICE BLACK joins, dissenting.

The issue in this case is not the breadth of the search, since there was clearly probable cause for the search which was carried out. No broader search than if the officers had a warrant would be permitted. The only issue is whether a search warrant was required as a precondition to that search. It is agreed that such a warrant would be required absent exigent circumstances. I would hold that the fact of arrest supplies such an exigent circumstance, since the police had lawfully gained entry to the premises to effect the arrest and since delaying the search to secure a warrant would have involved the risk of not recovering the fruits of the crime.

The majority today proscribes searches for which there is probable cause and which may prove fruitless unless carried out immediately. This rule will have no added effect whatsoever in protecting the rights of the criminal accused at trial against introduction of evidence seized without probable cause.

Nor does the majority today give any added protection to the right of privacy of those whose houses there is probable cause to search. A warrant would still be sworn out for those houses, and the privacy of their owners invaded. The only possible justification for the majority's rule is that in some instances arresting officers may search when they have no probable cause to do so and that such unlawful searches might be prevented if the officers first sought a warrant from a magistrate. Against the possible protection of privacy in that class of cases, in which the privacy of the house has already been invaded by entry to make the arrest—an entry for which the majority does not assert that any warrant is necessary—must be weighed the risk of destruction of evidence for which there is probable cause to search, as a result of delays in obtaining a search warrant. Without more basis for radical change than the Court's opinion reveals, I would not upset the balance of these interests which has been struck by the former decisions of this Court.

In considering searches incident to arrest, it must be remembered that there will be immediate opportunity to challenge the probable cause for the search in an adversary proceeding. The suspect has been apprised of the search by his very presence at the scene, and having been arrested, he will soon be brought into contact with people who can explain his rights.

... A search contemporaneous with a warrantless arrest is specially safeguarded since "[s]uch an arrest may constitutionally be made only upon probable cause, the existence of which is subject to judicial examination, and such an arrest demands the prompt bringing of the person arrested before a judicial officer, where the existence of probable cause is to be inquired into. . . . *Mallory v. United States,* [1956].

... [Recently] the Court has imposed on state and federal officers alike the duty to warn suspects taken into custody, before questioning them, of their right to a lawyer. *Miranda v. Arizona,* (1966).

An arrested man, by definition conscious of the police interest in him, and provided almost immediately with a lawyer and a judge, is in an excellent position to dispute the reasonableness of his arrest and contemporaneous search in a full adversary proceeding. I would uphold the constitutionality of this search contemporaneous with an arrest since there were probable cause both for the search and for the arrest, exigent circumstances involving the removal or destruction of evidence, and satisfactory opportunity to dispute the issues of probable cause shortly thereafter. In this case, the search was reasonable.

United States v. Robinson

414 U.S. 218; 94 S. Ct. 467; 38 L. Ed. 2d 427 (1973)
Vote: 6–3

The facts are provided in the opinion below.

MR. JUSTICE REHNQUIST delivered the opinion of the Court.

* * *

On April 23, 1968, at approximately 11 p.m., Officer Richard Jenks, a 15-year veteran of the District of Columbia Metropolitan Police Department, observed the respondent driving a 1965 Cadillac near the intersection of 8th and C Streets, N.E., in the District of Columbia. Jenks, as a result of previous investigation following a check of respondent's operator's permit four days earlier, determined there was reason to believe that respondent was operating a motor vehicle after the revocation of his operator's permit. This is an offense defined by statute in the District of Columbia which carries a mandatory minimum jail term, a mandatory minimum fine, or both.

Jenks signaled respondent to stop the automobile, which respondent did, and all three of the occupants emerged from the car. At that point Jenks informed respondent that he was under arrest for "operating after revocation and obtaining a permit by misrepresentation." It was assumed by the Court of Appeals and is conceded by the respondent here, that Jenks had probable cause to arrest respondent, and that he effected a full-custody arrest.

In accordance with procedures prescribed in police department instructions, Jenks then began to search respondent. He explained at a subsequent hearing that he was "face-to-face" with the respondent, and "placed [his] hands on [the respondent], my right-hand to his left breast like this (demonstrating) and proceeded to pat him down thus [with the right hand]." During this patdown,

Jenks felt an object in the left breast pocket of the heavy coat respondent was wearing, but testified that he "couldn't tell what it was" and also that he "couldn't actually tell the size of it." Jenks then reached into the pocket and pulled out the object, which turned out to be a "crumpled up cigarette package." Jenks testified that at this point he still did not know what was in the package:

> As I felt the package I could feel objects in the package but I couldn't tell what they were. . . . I knew they weren't cigarettes.

The officer then opened the cigarette pack and found 14 gelatin capsules of white powder which he thought to be, and which later analysis proved to be, heroin. Jenks then continued his search of respondent to completion, feeling around his waist and trouser legs, and examining the remaining pockets. The heroin seized from the respondent was admitted into evidence at the trial which resulted in his conviction in the District Court.

[A court of appeals reversed.]

*   *   *

It is well settled that a search incident to a lawful arrest is a traditional exception to the warrant requirement of the Fourth Amendment. This general exception has historically been formulated into two distinct propositions. The first is that a search may be made of the *person* of the arrestee by virtue of the lawful arrest. The second is that a search may be made of the area within the control of the arrestee.

Examination of this Court's decisions shows that these two propositions have been treated quite differently. The validity of the search of a person incident to a lawful arrest has been regarded as settled from its first enunciation, and has remained virtually unchallenged until the present case. The validity of the second proposition, while likewise conceded in principle, has been subject to differing interpretations as to the extent of the area which may be searched.

*   *   *

Throughout the series of cases in which the Court has addressed the second proposition relating to a search incident to a lawful arrest—the permissible area beyond the person of the arrestee which such a search may cover—no doubt has been expressed as to the unqualified authority of the arresting authority to search the person of the arrestee. . . .

In its decision of this case, the Court of Appeals decided that even after a police officer lawfully places a suspect under arrest for the purpose of taking him into custody, he may not ordinarily proceed to fully search the prisoner. He must, instead, conduct a limited frisk of the outer clothing and remove such weapons that he may, as a result of that limited frisk, reasonably believe and ascertain that the suspect has in his possession. While recognizing that *Terry v. Ohio,* (1968), dealt with a permissible "frisk" incident to an investigative stop based on less than probable cause to arrest, the Court of Appeals felt that the principles of that case should be carried over to this probable-cause arrest for driving while one's license is revoked. Since there would be no further evidence of such a crime to be obtained in a search of the arrestee, the court held that only a search for weapons could be justified. . . .

The Court of Appeals in effect determined that the *only* reason supporting the authority for a *full* search incident to lawful arrest was the possibility of discovery of evidence or fruits. Concluding that there could be no evidence or fruits in the case of an offense such as that with which respondent was charged, it held that any protective search would have to be limited by the conditions laid down in *Terry* for a search upon less than probable cause to arrest. Quite apart from the fact that *Terry* clearly recognized the distinction between the two types of searches, and that a different rule governed one than governed the other, we find additional reason to disagree with the Court of Appeals. . . .

The justification or reason for the authority to search incident to a lawful arrest rests quite as much on the need to disarm the suspect in order to take him into custody as it does on the need to preserve evidence on his person for later use at trial. The standards traditionally governing a search incident to lawful arrest are not, therefore, commuted to the stricter *Terry* standards by the absence of probable fruits or further evidence of the particular crime for which the arrest is made.

Nor are we inclined, on the basis of what seems to us to be a rather speculative judgment, to qualify the breadth of the general authority to search incident to a lawful custodial arrest on an assumption that persons arrested for the offense of driving while their licenses have been revoked are less likely to possess dangerous weapons than are those arrested for other crimes.* It is scarcely open to doubt that the danger to an officer is far greater in the case of the extended exposure which follows the taking of a suspect into custody and transporting him to the police station than in the case of the relatively fleeting contact resulting from the typical *Terry*-type stop. This is an adequate basis for treating all custodial arrests alike for purposes of search justification.

---

*Such an assumption appears at least questionable in light of the available statistical data concerning assaults on police officers who are in the course of making arrests. The danger to the police officer flows from the fact of the arrest, and its attendant proximity, stress, and uncertainty, and not from the grounds for arrest. One study concludes that approximately 30% of the shootings of police officers occur when an officer stops a person in an automobile. Bristow, Police Officer Shootings—A Tactical Evaluation, 54 J. Crim. L.C. & P.S. 93 (1963), cited in *Adams v. Williams,* 407 U.S. 143, 148 (1972). The Government in its brief notes that the Uniform Crime Reports, prepared by the Federal Bureau of Investigation, indicate that a significant percentage of murders of police officers occurs when the officers are making traffic stops. Brief for the United States 23. Those reports indicate that during January–March 1973, 35 police officers were murdered; 11 of those officers were killed while engaged in making traffic stops. *Ibid.*

But quite apart from these distinctions, our more fundamental disagreement with the Court of Appeals arises from its suggestion that there must be litigated in each case the issue of whether or not there was present one of the reasons supporting the authority for a search of the person incident to a lawful arrest. We do not think the long line of authorities of this Court dating back to *Weeks,* or what we can glean from the history of practice in this country and in England, requires such a case-by-case adjudication. A police officer's determination as to how and where to search the person of a suspect whom he has arrested is necessarily a quick *ad hoc* judgment which the Fourth Amendment does not require to be broken down in each instance into an analysis of each step in the search. The authority to search the person incident to a lawful custodial arrest, while based upon the need to disarm and to discover evidence, does not depend on what a court may later decide was the probability in a particular arrest situation that weapons or evidence would in fact be found upon the person of the suspect. A custodial arrest of a suspect based on probable cause is a reasonable intrusion under the Fourth Amendment; that intrusion being lawful, a search incident to the arrest requires no additional justification. It is the fact of the lawful arrest which establishes the authority to search, and we hold that in the case of a lawful custodial arrest a full search of the person is not only an exception to the warrant requirement of the Fourth Amendment, but is also a "reasonable" search under that Amendment.

The search of respondent's person conducted by Officer Jenks in this case and the seizure from him of the heroin, were permissible under established Fourth Amendment law. While thorough, the search partook of none of the extreme or patently abusive characteristics which were held to violate the Due Process Clause of the Fourteenth Amendment in *Rochin v. California,* (1952). Since it is the fact of custodial arrest which gives rise to the authority to search, it is of no moment that Jenks did not indicate any subjective fear of the respondent or that he did not himself suspect that respondent was armed. Having in the course of a lawful search come upon the crumpled package of cigarettes, he was entitled to inspect it; and when his inspection revealed the heroin capsules, he was entitled to seize them as "fruits, instrumentalities or contraband" probative of criminal conduct.

The judgment of the Court of Appeals holding otherwise is

Reversed.

* * *

Mr. Justice Marshall, with whom Mr. Justice Douglas and Mr. Justice Brennan join, dissenting.

* * *

The majority . . . suggests that the Court of Appeals reached a novel and unprecedented result by imposing qualifications on the historically recognized authority to conduct a full search incident to a lawful arrest. Nothing could be further from the truth, as the Court of Appeals itself was so careful to point out. . . .

The majority states that "[a] police officer's determination as to how and where to search the person of a suspect whom he has arrested is necessarily a quick *ad hoc* judgment which the Fourth Amendment does not require to be broken down in each instance into an analysis of each step in the search." No precedent is cited for this broad assertion—not surprisingly, since there is none. Indeed, we only recently rejected such "a rigid all-or-nothing model of justification and regulation under the Amendment, [for] it obscures the utility of limitations upon the scope, as well as the initiation, of police action as a means of constitutional regulation. This Court has held in the past that a search which is reasonable at its inception may violate the Fourth Amendment by virtue of its intolerable intensity and scope." *Terry v. Ohio,*

As we there concluded, "in determining whether the seizure and search were 'unreasonable' our inquiry is a dual one—whether the officer's action was justified at its inception, and whether it was reasonably related in scope to the circumstances which justified the interference in the first place."

The majority relies on statistics indicating that a significant percentage of murders of police officers occurs when the officers are making traffic stops. But these statistics only confirm what we recognized in *Terry*—that "American criminals have a long tradition of armed violence, and every year in this country many law enforcement officers are killed in the line of duty, and thousands more are wounded." As the very next sentence in *Terry* recognized, however, "[v]irtually all of these deaths and a substantial portion of the injuries are inflicted with guns and knives."

The statistics relied on by the Government in this case support this observation. Virtually all of the killings are caused by guns and knives, the very type of weapons which will not go undetected in a properly conducted weapons frisk. It requires more than citation to these statistics, then, to support the proposition that it is reasonable for police officers to conduct more than a *Terry*-type frisk for weapons when seeking to disarm a traffic offender who is taken into custody.

The majority opinion fails to recognize that the search conducted by Officer Jenks did not merely involve a search of respondent's person. It also included a separate search of effects found on his person. And even were we to assume, *arguendo,* that it was reasonable for Jenks to remove the object he felt in respondent's pocket, clearly there was no justification consistent with the Fourth Amendment which would authorize his opening the package and looking inside.

To begin with, after Jenks had the cigarette package in his hands, there is no indication that he had reason to believe or did in fact believe that the package contained a weapon. More importantly, even if the crumpled-up cigarette package had in fact contained some sort of small weapon, it would have been impossible for respondent to have used it once the package was in the officer's hands. Opening the package, therefore, did not further the protective purpose of the search. Even the dissenting opinion in the Court of Appeals conceded that "since the package was now in the officer's possession, any risk of the prisoner's use of a weapon in this package had been eliminated."

* * *

The Government argues that it is difficult to see what constitutionally protected "expectation of privacy" a prisoner has in the interior of a cigarette pack. One wonders if the result in this case would have been the same were respondent a businessman who was lawfully taken into custody for driving without a license and whose wallet was taken from him by the police. Would it be reasonable for the police officer, because of the possibility that a razor blade was hidden somewhere in the wallet, to open it, remove all the contents, and examine each item carefully? Or suppose a lawyer lawfully arrested for a traffic offense is found to have a sealed envelope on his person. Would it be permissible for the arresting officer to tear open the envelope in order to make sure that it did not contain a clandestine weapon—perhaps a pin or a razor blade?

Would it not be more consonant with the purpose of the Fourth Amendment and the legitimate needs of the police to require the officer, if he has any question whatsoever about what the wallet or letter contains, to hold on to it until the arrestee is brought to the precinct station?

I, for one, cannot characterize any of these intrusions into the privacy of an individual's papers and effects as being negligible incidents to the more serious intrusion into the individual's privacy stemming from the arrest itself. Nor can any principled distinction be drawn between the hypothetical searches I have posed and the search of the cigarette package in this case. The only reasoned distinction is between warrantless searches which serve legitimate protective and evidentiary functions and those that do not.

The search conducted by Officer Jenks in this case went far beyond what was reasonably necessary to protect him from harm or to ensure that respondent would not effect an escape from custody. In my view, it therefore fell outside the scope of a properly drawn "search incident to arrest" exception to the Fourth Amendment's warrant requirement. I would affirm the judgment of the Court of Appeals holding that the fruits of the search should have been suppressed at respondent's trial.

South Dakota v. Opperman

428 U.S. 364; 96 S. Ct. 3092; 49 L. Ed. 2d 1000 (1976)
Vote: 5–4

The facts are given in the opinion below.

MR. CHIEF JUSTICE BURGER delivered the opinion of the Court.

We review the judgment of the supreme court of South Dakota, holding that local police violated the Fourth Amendment to the Federal Constitution, as applicable to the States under the Fourteenth Amendment, when they conducted a routine inventory search of an automobile lawfully impounded by police for violations of municipal parking ordinances.

Local ordinances prohibit parking in certain areas of downtown Vermillion, S.D., between the hours of 2 a.m. and 6 a.m. During the early morning hours of December 10, 1973, a Vermillion police officer observed respondent's unoccupied vehicle illegally parked in the restricted zone. At approximately 3 a.m. the officer issued an overtime parking ticket and placed it on the car's windshield. The citation warned:

> Vehicles in violation of any parking ordinance may be towed from the area.

At approximately 10 o'clock on the same morning, another officer issued a second ticket for an overtime parking violation. These circumstances were routinely reported to police headquarters, and after the vehicle was inspected, the car was towed to the city impound lot.

From outside the car at the impound lot, a police officer observed a watch on the dashboard and other items of personal property located on the back seat and back floorboard. At the officer's direction, the car door was then unlocked and, using a standard inventory form pursuant to standard police procedures, the officer inventoried the contents of the car, including the contents of the glove compartment, which was unlocked. There he found marijuana contained in a plastic bag. All items, including the contraband, were removed to the police department for safekeeping. During the late afternoon of December 10, respondent appeared at the police department to claim his property. The marijuana was retained by police.

Respondent was subsequently arrested on charges of possession of marijuana. His motion to suppress the evidence yielded by the inventory search was denied; he was convicted after a jury trial and sentenced to a fine of $100 and 14 days' incarceration in the county jail. On appeal, the Supreme Court of South Dakota reversed the conviction. The court concluded that the evidence had been obtained in violation of the Fourth Amendment prohibition against unreasonable searches and seizures. We granted certiorari, and we reverse.

This Court has traditionally drawn a distinction between automobiles and homes or offices in relation to the Fourth Amendment. Although automobiles are "effects" and thus within the reach of the Fourth Amendment, warrantless examinations of automobiles have been upheld in circumstances in which a search of a home or office would not.

The reason for this well-settled distinction is twofold. First, the inherent mobility of automobiles creates circumstances of such exigency that, as a practical necessity, rigorous enforcement of the warrant requirement is impossible. But the Court has also upheld warrantless searches where no immediate danger was presented that the car would be removed from the jurisdiction. Besides the element of mobility, less rigorous warrant requirements govern because the expectation of privacy with respect to one's automobile is significantly less than that relating to one's home or office.

* * *

In applying the reasonableness standard adopted by the Framers, this Court has consistently sustained police intrusions into automobiles impounded or otherwise in lawful police custody where the process is aimed at securing or protecting the car and its contents. In *Cooper v. California, supra,* the Court upheld the inventory of a car impounded under the authority of a state forfeiture statute. Even though the inventory was conducted in a distinctly criminal setting and carried out a week after the car had been impounded, the Court nonetheless found that the car search, including examination of the glove compartment where contraband was found, was reasonable under the circumstances. This conclusion was reached despite the fact that no warrant had been issued and probable cause to search for the contraband in the vehicle had not been established. The Court said in language explicitly applicable here:

> It would be unreasonable to hold that the police, having to retain the car in their custody for such a length of time, had no right, even for their own protection, to search it.

In the following Term, the Court in *Harris v. United States,* (1968), upheld the introduction of evidence, seized by an officer who, after conducting an inventory search of a car and while taking means to safeguard it, observed a car registration card lying on the metal stripping of the car door. Rejecting the argument that a warrant was necessary, the Court held that the intrusion was justifiable since it was "taken to protect the car while it was in police custody."

Finally, in *Cady v. Dombrowski,* [1973], the Court upheld a warrantless search of an automobile towed to a private garage even though no probable cause existed to believe that the vehicle contained fruits of a crime. The sole justification for the warrantless incursion was that it was incident to the caretaking function of the local police to protect the community's safety. Indeed, the protective search was instituted solely because local police "were under the impression" that the incapacitated driver, a Chicago police officer, was required to carry his service revolver at all times; the police had reasonable grounds to believe a weapon might be in the car, and thus available to vandals. The Court carefully noted that the protective search was carried out in accordance with *standard procedures* in the local police department, a factor tending to ensure that the intrusion would be limited in scope to the extent necessary to carry out the caretaking function. In reaching this result, the Court in *Cady* distinguished *Preston v. United States,* (1964), on the grounds that the holding, invalidating a car search conducted after a vagrancy arrest, "stands only for the proposition that the search challenged there could not be justified as one incident to an arrest." *Preston* therefore did not raise the issue of the constitutionality of a protective inventory of a car lawfully within police custody.

The holdings in *Cooper, Harris,* and *Cady* point the way to the correct resolution of this case. None of the three cases, of course, involves the precise situation presented here; but, as in all Fourth Amendment cases, we are obliged to look to all the facts and circumstances of this case in light of the principles set forth in these prior decisions.

* * *

The Vermillion police were indisputably engaged in a caretaking search of a lawfully impounded automobile.

The inventory was conducted only after the car had been impounded for multiple parking violations. The owner, having left his car illegally parked for an extended period, and thus subject to impoundment, was not present to make other arrangements for the safekeeping of his belongings. The inventory itself was prompted by the presence in plain view of a number of valuables inside the car. As in *Cady,* there is no suggestion whatever that this standard procedure, essentially like that followed throughout the country, was a pretext concealing an investigatory police motive.

On this record we conclude that in following standard police procedures, prevailing throughout the country and approved by the overwhelming majority of courts, the conduct of the police was not "unreasonable" under the Fourth Amendment.

The judgment of the South Dakota Supreme Court is therefore reversed, and the case is remanded for further proceedings not inconsistent with this opinion.

Reversed and remanded.

* * *

MR. JUSTICE MARSHALL, with whom MR. JUSTICE BRENNAN and MR. JUSTICE STEWART join, dissenting.

* * *

Because the record in this case shows that the procedures followed by the Vermillion police in searching respondent's car fall far short of . . . [Fourth

Amendment] standards, in my view the search was impermissible and its fruits must be suppressed. First, so far as the record shows, the police in this case had no reason to believe that the glove compartment of the impounded car contained particular property of any substantial value. Moreover, the owner had apparently thought it adequate to protect whatever he left in the car overnight on the street in a business area simply to lock the car, and there is nothing in the record to show that the impoundment lot would prove a less secure location against pilferage, particularly when it would seem likely that the owner would claim his car and its contents promptly, at least if it contained valuables worth protecting. Even if the police had cause to believe that the impounded car's glove compartment contained particular valuables, however, they made no effort to secure the owner's consent to the search. Although the Court relies, as it must, upon the fact that respondent was not present to make other arrangements for the care of his belongings, in my view that is not the end of the inquiry. Here the police readily ascertained the ownership of the vehicle, yet they searched it immediately without taking any steps to locate respondent and procure his consent to the inventory or advise him to make alternative arrangements to safeguard his property. Such a failure is inconsistent with the rationale that the inventory procedure is carried out for the benefit of the owner.

The Court's result in this case elevates the conservation of property interests—indeed mere possibilities of property interests—above the privacy and security interests protected by the Fourth Amendment. For this reason I dissent.

QUESTIONS AND COMMENTS

1 *Coolidge v. New Hampshire* [403 U.S. 443 (1971)] found four justices taking a position at odds with that taken by the majority in *Chimel.* But in 1978, the Court reaffirmed *Chimel* in *Mincey v. Arizona* [437 U.S. 385 (1978)].
2 In *United States v. Robinson,* the officer was required to arrest Robinson and take him into custody. What if the offense had been one for which it is customary to issue a citation or summons? Different decision? See *Gustafson v. Florida,* 414 U.S. 260 (1973).
3 Compare the rationale for the limitation placed on the search in *Chimel* with the rationale for searching the cigarette package in *United States v. Robinson.* Are these two cases compatible?
4 What is the theory used by the Court to justify the kind of inventory search of seized automobiles that occurred in *South Dakota v. Opperman?* What if no valuables in the car were in plain view? Different decision? Did the mobility of the car have anything to do with the decision in this case? Explain.
5 In *Opperman,* why were the police not required to obtain a warrant? Wasn't it practicable to do so?

Stop and Frisk

Terry v. Ohio (1968)

In many cases, the police officer may not have sufficient evidence to make an arrest, to obtain a warrant for search and seizure, or to support a probable-cause search. Yet an officer whose suspicions are aroused by someone's behavior may feel that further investigation is warranted. This kind of situation has led to a procedure known as the "stop and frisk," which the Supreme Court examined in *Terry v. Ohio.*

Terry v. Ohio

392 U.S. 1; 88 S. Ct. 1868; 20 L. Ed. 2d 889 (1968)
Vote: 8–1

Terry and Chilton were convicted of carrying concealed weapons in Cleveland, Ohio, on October 31, 1963. For this crime they were sentenced to 1 to 3 years in the state penitentiary. The primary evidence used against them was two revolvers seized by Cleveland police detective Martin McFadden. McFadden, a detective with thirty years experience, had observed Terry and his codefendant engaged in what he thought were suspicious activities. The two men took turns walking down the street, pausing and looking in a store window. They repeated this routine with the same store, five or six times each, eventually stopping to confer with a third man. Thinking something was amiss, McFadden approached the men and asked for their names. When the response was "mumbled," McFadden grabbed Terry and patted down the outside of his overcoat. Feeling a pistol, he removed Terry's coat and retrieved a .38-caliber revolver. Patting down the other two men, McFadden found a revolver on Chilton but nothing on the other man. All three men were arrested. Terry and Chilton were convicted of carrying concealed weapons after their motions to suppress the evidence at trial were denied. The Ohio Supreme Court dismissed the defendants' appeal. The U.S. Supreme Court granted certiorari.

MR. CHIEF JUSTICE WARREN delivered the opinion of the Court.

* * *

We have recently held that "the Fourth Amendment protects people, not places," *Katz v. United States,* (1967), and wherever an individual may harbor a reasonable "expectation of privacy," he is entitled to be free from unreasonable governmental intrusion. Of course, the specific content and incidents of this right must be shaped by the context in which it is asserted. For "what the Constitution forbids is not all searches and seizures, but unreasonable searches and seizures." *Elkins v. United States,* (1960). Unquestionably petitioner was entitled to the protection of the Fourth Amendment as he walked down the street in Cleveland. . . . The question is whether in all the circumstances of this on-the-street encounter, his right to personal security was violated by an unreasonable search and seizure.

* * *

Our first task is to establish at what point in this encounter the Fourth Amendment becomes relevant. That is, we must decide whether and when Officer McFadden "seized" Terry and whether and when he conducted a "search." There is some suggestion in the use of such terms as "stop" and "frisk" that such police conduct is outside the purview of the Fourth Amendment because neither action rises to the level of a "search" or "seizure" within the meaning of the Constitution. We emphatically reject this notion. It is quite plain that the Fourth Amendment governs "seizures" of the person which do not eventuate in a trip to the station house and prosecution for crime—"arrests" in traditional terminology. It must be recognized that whenever a police officer accosts an individual and restrains his freedom to walk away, he has "seized" that person. And it is nothing less than sheer torture of the English language to suggest that a careful exploration of the outer surfaces of a person's clothing all over his or her body in an attempt to find weapons is not a "search." Moreover, it is simply fantastic to urge that such a procedure performed in public by a policeman while the citizen stands helpless, perhaps facing a wall with his hands raised, is a "petty indignity." It is a serious intrusion upon the sanctity of the person, which may inflict great indignity and arouse strong resentment, and it is not to be undertaken lightly.

The danger in the logic which proceeds upon distinctions between a "stop" and an "arrest," or "seizure" of the person, and between a "frisk" and a "search" is two-fold. It seeks to isolate from constitutional scrutiny the initial stages of the contact between the policeman and the citizen. And by suggesting a rigid all-or-nothing model of justification and regulation under the Amendment, it obscures the utility of limitations upon the scope, as well as the initiation, of police action as a means of constitutional regulation. . . .

The distinctions of classical "stop-and-frisk" theory thus serve to divert attention from the central inquiry under the Fourth Amendment—the reasonableness in all the circumstances of the particular governmental invasion of a citizen's personal security. "Search" and "seizure" are not talismans. We therefore reject the notions that the Fourth Amendment does not come into play at all as a limitation upon police conduct if the officers stop short of something called a "technical arrest" or a "full-blown search."

In this case there can be no question, then, that Officer McFadden "seized" petitioner and subjected him to a "search" when he took hold of him and patted down the outer surfaces of his clothing. We must decide whether at that point it was reasonable for Officer McFadden to have interfered with petitioner's personal security as he did. . . .

Certainly it would be unreasonable to require that police officers take unnecessary risks in the performance of their duties. American criminals have a long tradition of armed violence, and every year in this country many law enforcement officers are killed in the line of duty, and thousands more are wounded. Virtually all of these deaths and a substantial portion of the injuries are inflicted with guns and knives.

In view of these facts, we cannot blind ourselves to the need for law enforcement officers to protect themselves and other prospective victims of violence in situations where they may lack probable cause for an arrest. When an officer is justified in believing that the individual whose suspicious behavior he is investigating at close range is armed and presently dangerous to the officer or to others, it would appear to be clearly unreasonable to deny the officer the power to take necessary measures to determine whether the person is in fact carrying a weapon and to neutralize the threat of physical harm. . . .

We must now examine the conduct of Officer McFadden in this case to determine whether his search and seizure of petitioner were reasonable, both at their inception and as conducted.

. . . When Officer McFadden approached the three men gathered before the display window at Zucker's store he had observed enough to make it quite reasonable to fear that they were armed; and nothing in their response to his hailing them, identifying himself as a police officer, and asking their names served to dispel that reasonable belief. We cannot say his decision at that point to seize Terry and pat his clothing for weapons was the product of a volatile or inventive imagination, or was undertaken simply as an act of harassment; the record evidences the tempered act of a policeman who in the course of an investigation had to make a quick decision as to how to protect himself and others from possible danger, and took limited steps to do so.

The manner in which the seizure and search were conducted is, of course, as vital a part of the inquiry as whether they were warranted at all. The Fourth Amendment proceeds as much by limitations upon the scope of governmental action as by imposing preconditions upon its initiation. . . .

We need not develop at length in this case, however, the limitations which the Fourth Amendment places upon a protective seizure and search for weapons. These limitations will have to be developed in the concrete factual circumstances of individual cases. See *Sibron v. New York* . . . decided today. Suffice it to note that such a search, unlike a search without a warrant incident to a lawful arrest, is not justified by any need to prevent the disappearance or destruction of evidence of crime. See *Preston v. United States* (1964). The sole justification of the search in the present situation is the protection of the police officer and others nearby, and it must therefore be confined in scope to an intrusion reasonably designed to discover guns, knives, clubs, or other hidden instruments for the assault of the police officer.

The scope of the search in this case presents no serious problem in light of these standards. Officer McFadden patted down the outer clothing of petitioner and his two companions. He did not place his hands in their pockets or under the outer surface of their garments until he had felt weapons, and then he merely reached for and removed the guns.

Officer McFadden confined his search strictly to what was minimally necessary to learn whether the men were armed and to disarm them once he discovered the weapons. He did not conduct a general exploratory search for whatever evidence of criminal activity he might find.

We conclude that the revolver seized from Terry was properly admitted in evidence against him. At the time he seized petitioner and searched him for weapons, Officer McFadden had reasonable grounds to believe that petitioner was armed and dangerous, and it was necessary for the protection of himself and others to take swift measures to discover the true facts and neutralize the threat of harm if it materialized. The policeman carefully restricted his search to what was appropriate to the discovery of the particular items which he sought. Each case of this sort will, of course, have to be decided on its own facts. We merely hold today that where a police officer observes unusual conduct which leads him reasonably to conclude in light of his experience that criminal activity may be afoot and that the persons with whom he is dealing may be armed and presently dangerous, where in the course of investigating this behavior he identifies himself as a policeman and makes reasonable inquiries, and where nothing in the initial stages of the encounter serves to dispel his reasonable fear for his own or others' safety, he is entitled for the protection of himself and others in the area to conduct a carefully limited search of the outer clothing of such persons in an attempt to discover weapons which might be used to assault him. Such a search is a reasonable search under the Fourth Amendment, and any weapons seized may properly be introduced in evidence against the person from whom they were taken.

Affirmed.

* * *

MR. JUSTICE DOUGLAS, dissenting.

I agree that petitioner was "seized" within the meaning of the Fourth Amendment. I also agree that frisking petitioner and his companions for guns was a "search." But it is a mystery how that "search" and that "seizure" can be constitutional by Fourth Amendment standards, unless there was "probable cause" to believe that (1) a crime had been committed or (2) a crime was in the process of being committed or (3) a crime was about to be committed.

The opinion of the Court disclaims the existence of "probable cause." If loitering were in issue and that was the offense charged, there would be "probable cause" shown. But the crime here is carrying concealed weapons; and there is no basis for concluding that the officer had "probable cause" for believing that that crime was being committed. Had a warrant been sought, a magistrate would, therefore, have been unauthorized to issue one, for he can act only if there is a showing of "probable cause." We hold today that the police have greater authority to make a "seizure" and conduct a "search" than a judge has to authorize such action. We have said precisely the opposite over and over again.

* * *

To give the police greater power than a magistrate is to take a long step down the totalitarian path. Perhaps such a step is desirable to cope with modern forms of lawlessness. But if it is taken, it should be the deliberate choice of the people through a constitutional amendment.

* * *

There have been powerful hydraulic pressures throughout our history that bear heavily on the Court to water down constitutional guarantees and give the police the upper hand. That hydraulic pressure has probably never been greater than it is today.

Yet if the individual is no longer to be sovereign, if the police can pick him up whenever they do not like the cut of his jib, if they can "seize" and "search" him in their discretion, we enter a new regime. The decision to enter it should be made only after a full debate by the people of this country.

QUESTIONS AND COMMENTS

1 What does *Terry* hold regarding the seizure of the person stopped? Was he unreasonably seized?
2 What if the officer's "fear" had been unfounded? Same decision? What if the "object" had been soft rather than hard? Same decision?
3 What if the suspect, when asked to stop, replied "Go to hell" and continued on his way? What action could the officer have reasonably taken? Cf. *Brown v. Texas,* 443 U.S. 47 (1979).
4 The Court has held that when a police officer validly stops a car for a traffic violation and then notices a bulge under the driver's jacket, the police officer may conduct a "*Terry* frisk." [*Pennsylvania v. Mimms,* 434 U.S. 106 (1977)].

Third-Party Search

Zurcher v. Stanford Daily (1978)

This case is sometimes classified as a free press case, since it subjected the press as a third party to the needs of law enforcement. However, it can readily be classified as a third-party search case, since it raises the question of whether the Fourth Amendment protects a party not suspected of a crime against a search based upon a search warrant. In reading this case, keep in mind that the Fourth Amendment permits reasonable searches of persons and places and that the case takes on particular importance because it involves the press.

Zurcher, Chief of Police of Palo Alto, et al. v. Stanford Daily et al.

436 U.S. 547; 98 S. Ct. 1970; 56 L. Ed. 2d 525 (1978)
Vote: 5–3

The facts are provided in the opinion below.

MR. JUSTICE WHITE delivered the opinion of the Court.

* * *

Late in the day on Friday, April 9, 1971, officers of the Palo Alto Police Department and of the Santa Clara County Sheriff's Department responded to a call from the director of the Stanford University Hospital requesting the removal of a large group of demonstrators who had seized the hospital's administrative offices and occupied them since the previous afternoon. After several futile efforts to persuade the demonstrators to leave peacefully, more drastic measures were employed. The demonstrators had barricaded the doors at both ends of a hall adjacent to the administrative offices. The police chose to force their way in at the west end of the corridor. As they did so, a group of demonstrators emerged through the doors at the east end and, armed with sticks and clubs, attacked the group of nine police officers stationed there. One officer was knocked to the floor and struck repeatedly on the head; another suffered a broken shoulder. All nine were injured. There were no police photographers at the east doors, and most bystanders and reporters were on the west side. The officers themselves were able to identify only two of their assailants, but one of them did see at least one person photographing the assault at the east doors.

On Sunday, April 11, a special edition of the Stanford Daily, . . . a student newspaper published at Stanford University, carried articles and photographs devoted to the hospital protest and the violent clash between demonstrators and police. The photographs carried the byline of a Daily staff member and indicated that he had been at the east end of the hospital hallway where he could have photographed the assault on the nine officers. The next day, the Santa Clara County District Attorney's Office secured a warrant from the Municipal Court for an immediate search of the Daily's offices for negatives, film, and pictures showing the events and occurrences at the hospital on the evening of April 9. The warrant issued on a finding of "just, probable and reasonable cause for believing that: Negatives and photographs and films, evidence material . . . relevant to the identity of the perpetrators of felonies, to wit. Battery on a Peace Officer, and Assault with Deadly Weapon, will be located [on the premises of the Daily]."

The warrant affidavit contained no allegation or indication that members of the Daily staff were in any way involved in unlawful acts at the hospital.

The search pursuant to the warrant was conducted later that day by four police officers and took place in the presence of some members of the Daliy staff. The Daily's photographic laboratories, filing cabinets, desks, and wastepaper baskets were searched. Locked drawers and rooms were not opened. The officers apparently had opportunity to read notes and correspondence during the search; but, contrary to claims of the staff, the officers denied that they had exceeded the limits of the warrant. They had not been advised by the staff that the areas they were searching contained confidential materials. The search revealed only the photographs that had already been published on April 11, and no materials were removed from the Daily's office. . . .

[Later, the Daily and some of its staff members filed a civil suit in federal district court alleging that the search had deprived them of First, Fourth, and Fourteenth Amendment rights. The court found the search illegal, holding that the Fourth and Fourteenth Amendments forbade the issuance of a warrant to search for materials of one not suspected of crime unless there is probable cause to believe that a subpoena would be impractical. Impracticality could be shown, the court held, only by establishing that the possessor of the material would disregard a court order not to remove or destroy them. The Court of Appeals affirmed. The Supreme Court granted certiorari.]

It is an understatement to say that there is no direct authority in this or any other federal court for the District Court's sweeping revision of the Fourth Amendment. Under existing law, valid warrants may be issued to search *any* property, whether or not occupied by a third party, at which there is probable cause to believe that fruits, instrumentalities, or evidence of a crime will be found. Nothing on the face of the Amendment suggests that a third-party search warrant should not normally issue. The Warrant Clause speaks of search warrants issued on "probable cause" and "particularly describing the place to be searched, and the persons or things to be seized." In situations where the State does not seek to seize "persons" but only those "things" which there is probable cause to believe are located in the place to be searched, there is no apparent basis in the language of the Amendment for also imposing the requirements for a valid arrest—probable cause to believe that the third party is implicated in the crime. . . .

Against this background, it is untenable to conclude that property may not be searched unless its occupant is reasonably suspected of crime and is subject to arrest. And if those considered free of criminal involvement may nevertheless be searched or inspected under civil statutes, it is difficult to understand why the Fourth Amendment would prevent entry onto their property to recover evidence of a crime not committed by them but by others. As we understand the structure and language of the Fourth Amendment and our cases expounding it, valid warrants to search property may be issued when it is satisfactorily demonstrated to the magistrate that fruits, instrumentalities, or evidence of crime is located on the premises. The Fourth Amendment has itself struck the balance between privacy and public need, and there is no occasion or justification for a court to revise the Amendment and strike a new balance by denying the search warrant in the circumstances present here and by insisting that the investigation proceed by subpoena *duces tecum,* whether on the theory that the latter is a less intrusive alternative or otherwise.

This is not to question that "reasonableness" is the overriding test of compliance with the Fourth Amendment or to assert that searches, however or whenever executed may never be unreasonable if supported by a warrant issued on probable cause and properly identifying the place to be searched and the property to be seized. We do hold, however, that the courts may not, in the name of Fourth Amendment reasonableness, prohibit the States from issuing warrants to search for evidence simply because the owner or possessor of the place to be searched is not then reasonably suspected of criminal involvement.

*   *   *

The District Court held, and respondents assert here, that whatever may be true of third-party searches generally, where the third party is a newspaper, there are additional factors derived from the First Amendment that justify a nearly *per se* rule forbidding the search warrant and permitting only the subpoena *duces tecum.* The general submission is that searches of newspaper offices for evidence of crime reasonably believed to be on the premises will seriously threaten the ability of the press to gather, analyze, and disseminate news. This is said to be true for several reasons: First, searches will be physically disruptive to such an extent that timely publication will be impeded. Second, confidential sources of information will dry up, and the press will also lose opportunities to cover various events because of fears of the participants that press files will be readily available to the authorities. Third, reporters will be deterred from recording and preserving their recollections for future use if such information is subject to seizure. Fourth, the processing of news and its dissemination will be chilled by the prospects that searches will disclose internal editorial deliberations. Fifth, the press will resort to self-censorship to conceal its possession of information of potential interest to the police.

It is true that the struggle from which the Fourth Amendment emerged "is largely a history of conflict between the Crown and the press." *Stanford v. Texas,* (1965), and that in issuing warrants and determining the reasonableness of a search, state and federal magistrates should be aware that "unrestricted power of search and seizure could also be an instrument for stifling liberty of expression." *Marcus v. Search Warrant,* (1961). Where the materials sought to be seized may be protected by the First Amendment, the requirements of the Fourth Amendment must be applied with "scrupulous exactitude."

"A seizure reasonable as to one type of material in one setting may be unreasonable in a different setting or with respect to another kind of material." *Roaden v. Kentucky,* (1973). Hence, in *Stanford v. Texas,* the Court invalidated a warrant authorizing the search of a private home for all books, records, and other materials relating to the Communist Party, on the ground that whether or not the warrant would have been sufficient in other contexts, it authorized the searchers to rummage among and make judgments about books and papers and was the functional equivalent of a general warrant, one of the principal targets of the Fourth Amendment. Where presumptively protected materials are sought to be seized, the warrant requirement should be administered to leave as little as possible to the discretion or whim of the officer in the field.

Similarly, where seizure is sought of allegedly obscene materials, the judgment of the arresting officer alone is insufficient to justify issuance of a search warrant or a seizure without a warrant incident to arrest. The procedure for determining probable cause must afford an opportunity for the judicial officer to "focus searchingly on the question of obscenity." *Heller v. New York,* (1973).

Neither the Fourth Amendment nor the cases requiring consideration of First Amendment values in issuing search warrants, however, call for imposing the regime ordered by the District Court. Aware of the long struggle between Crown and press and desiring to curb unjustified official intrusions, the Framers took the enormously important step of subjecting searches to the test of reasonableness and to the general rule requiring search warrants issued by neutral magistrates. They nevertheless did not forbid warrants where the press was involved, did not require special showings that subpoenas would be impractical, and did not insist that the owner of the place to be searched, if connected with the press, must be shown to be implicated in the offense being investigated. Further, the prior cases do no more than insist that the courts apply the warrant requirements with particular exactitude when First Amendment interests would be endangered by the search. As we see it, no more than this is required where the warrant requested is for the seizure of criminal evidence reasonably believed to be on the premises occupied by a newspaper. Properly administered, the preconditions for a warrant—probable cause, specificity with respect to the place to be searched and the things to be seized, and overall reasonableness—should afford sufficient protection against the harms that are assertedly threatened by warrants for searching newspaper offices.

There is no reason to believe, for example, that magistrates cannot guard against searches of the type, scope, and intrusiveness that would actually interfere with the timely publication of a newspaper. Nor, if the requirements of specificity and reasonableness are properly applied, policed, and observed, will there be any occasion or opportunity for officers to rummage at large in newspaper files or to intrude into or to deter normal editorial and publication decisions. The warrant issued in this case authorized nothing of this sort. Nor are we convinced, any more than we were in *Branzburg v. Hayes,* (1972), that confidential sources will disappear and that the press will suppress news because of fears of warranted searches. Whatever incremental effect there may be in this regard if search warrants, as well as subpoenas, are permissible in proper circumstances, it does not make a constitutional difference in our judgment.

We note finally that if the evidence sought by warrant is sufficiently connected with the crime to satisfy the probable-cause requirement, it will very likely be sufficiently relevant to justify a subpoena and to withstand a motion to quash. Further, Fifth Amendment and state shield-law objections that might be asserted in opposition to compliance with a subpoena are largely irrelevant to determining the legality of a search warrant under the Fourth Amendment. Of course, the Fourth Amendment does not prevent or advise against legislative or executive efforts to establish nonconstitutional protections against possible abuses of the search warrant procedure, but we decline to reinterpret the Amendment to impose a general constitutional barrier against warrants to search newspaper premises, to require resort to subpoenas as a general rule, or to demand prior notice and hearing in connection with the issuance of search warrants.

We accordingly reject the reasons given by the District Court and adopted by the Court of Appeals for holding the search for photographs at the Stanford Daily to have been unreasonable within the meaning of the Fourth Amendment and in violation of the First Amendment. Nor has anything else presented here persuaded us that the Amendments forbade this search. It follows that the judgment of the Court of Appeals is reversed.

So ordered.

* * *

Mr. Justice Stevens, dissenting.

The novel problem presented by this case is an outgrowth of the profound change in Fourth Amendment law that occurred in 1967, when *Warden v. Hayden,* was decided. The question is what kind of "probable cause" must be established in order to obtain a warrant to conduct an unannounced search for documentary evidence in the private files of a person not suspected of involvement in any criminal activity. The Court holds that a reasonable belief that the files contain relevant evidence is a sufficient justification. This holding rests on a misconstruction of history and of the Fourth Amendment's purposely broad language. . . .

In the pre-*Hayden* era warrants were used to search for contraband, weapons, and plunder, but not for "mere evidence." The practical effect of the rule prohibiting the issuance of warrants to search for mere evidence was to narrowly limit not only the category of objects, but also the category of persons and the character of the privacy interests that might be affected by an unannounced police search.

Just as the witnesses who participate in an investigation or a trial far outnumber the defendants, the persons who possess evidence that may help to identify an offender, or explain an aspect of a criminal transaction, far outnumber those who have custody of weapons or plunder. Countless law-abiding citizens—doctors, lawyers, merchants, customers, bystanders—may have documents in their possession that relate to an ongoing criminal investigation. The consequences of subjecting this large category of persons to unannounced police searches are extremely serious. The *ex parte* warrant procedure enables the prosecutor to obtain access to privileged documents that could not be examined if advance notice gave the custodian an opportunity to object. The search for the documents described in a warrant may involve the inspection of files containing other private matter. The dramatic character of a sudden search may cause an entirely unjustified injury to the reputation of the persons searched.

Of greatest importance, however, is the question whether the offensive intrusion on the privacy of the ordinary citizen is justified by the law enforcement interests it is intended to vindicate. Possession of contraband or the proceeds or tools of crime gives rise to two inferences: that the custodian is involved in the criminal activitity, and that, if given notice of an intended search, he will conceal or destroy what is being sought. The probability of criminal culpability justifies the invasion of his privacy; the need to accomplish the law enforcement purpose of the search justifies acting without advance notice and by force, if necessary. By satisfying the probable-cause standard appropriate for weapons. or plunder, the police effectively demonstrate that no less intrusive method of investigation will succeed.

Mere possession of documentary evidence, however, is much less likely to demonstrate that the custodian is guilty of any wrongdoing or that he will not honor a subpoena or informal request to produce it. In the pre-*Hayden* era, evidence of that kind was routinely obtained by procedures that presumed that the custodian would respect his obligation to obey subpoenas and to cooperate in the investigation of crime. These procedures had a constitutional dimension. For the innocent citizen's interest in the privacy of his papers and possessions is an aspect of liberty protected by the Due Process Clause of the Fourteenth Amendment. Notice and an opportunity to object to the deprivation of the citizen's liberty are, therefore, the constitutionally mandated general rule. An exception to that rule can only be justified by strict compliance with the Fourth Amendment. That Amendment flatly prohibits the issuance of any warrant unless justified by probable cause.

A showing of probable cause that was adequate to justify the issuance of a warrant to search for stolen goods in the 18th century does not automatically satisfy the new dimensions of the Fourth Amendment in the post-*Hayden* era. In *Hayden* itself, the Court recognized that the meaning of probable cause should be reconsidered in the light of the new authority it conferred on the police. The only conceivable justification for an unannounced search of an innocent citizen is the fear that, if notice were given, he would conceal or destroy the object of the search. Probable cause to believe that the custodian is a criminal, or that he holds a criminal's weapons, spoils, or the like, justifies that fear, and therefore such a showing complies with the Clause. But if nothing said under oath in the warrant application demonstrates the need for an unannounced search by force, the probable-cause requirement is not satisfied. In the absence of some other showing of reasonableness, the ensuing search violates the Fourth Amendment.

In this case, the warrant application set forth no facts suggesting that respondents were involved in any wrongdoing or would destroy the desired evidence if given notice of what the police desired. I would therefore hold that the warrant did not comply with the Warrant Clause and that the search was unreasonable within the meaning of the first Clause of the Fourth Amendment.

I respectfully dissent.

QUESTIONS AND COMMENTS

1 What are the implications of the Court's ruling in *Stanford Daily* for other private relationships (lawyer-client, doctor-patient, etc.) in the United States? Are these implications worrisome insofar as privacy rights are concerned? What would you do, if anything, to protect rights of privacy from the implications of *Stanford Daily*?

Warrantless Search of Homes

Payton v. New York (1980)

Generally speaking, an arrest without a warrant is valid if the crime was committed in the arresting officer's presence or if the officer had probable cause to believe the suspect committed the crime. In *United States v. Watson,*[3] a postal inspector arrested Watson without a warrant for suspected possession of stolen credit cards. The probable cause was based on an informant's tip that Watson had the cards in his possession. The arrest took place in a public restaurant at midday. As it turned out, Watson did not have the cards on him. But with Watson's consent, a search of his nearby car revealed the cards in question. Watson's conviction was reversed by the court of appeals on the ground that a warrant should have been obtained. The Supreme Court disagreed, saying that as long as the arrest is made in a *public place,* upon probable cause, it may be made without a warrant even if there was sufficient time to obtain one.

This decision may be contrasted with others holding that a warrant must be obtained to search a private place.[4] Since an arrest is a seizure, and thus covered by the Fourth Amendment, one may see a certain inconsistency here. But in *Watson,* the arrest was in a *public place,* and the Court expressly reserved the question "whether and under what circumstances an officer may enter a suspect's home to make a warrantless arrest."[5] That question is confronted in *Payton v. New York.*

Payton v. New York

445 U.S. 573; 100 S. Ct. 1371; 63 L. Ed. 2d 639 (1980)
Vote: 6–3

The facts are given in the opinion below.

MR. JUSTICE STEVENS delivered the opinion of the Court.

* * *

On January 14, 1970, after two days of intensive investigation, New York detectives had assembled evidence sufficient to establish probable cause to believe that Theodore Payton had murdered the manager of a gas station two days earlier. At about 7:30 A.M. on January 15, six officers went to Payton's apartment in the Bronx, intending to arrest him. They had not obtained a warrant. Although light and music emanated from the apartment there was no response to their knock on the metal door. They summoned emergency assistance and about 30 minutes later, used crowbars to break open the door and enter the apartment. No one was there. In plain view, however, was a .30-caliber shell casing that was seized and later admitted into evidence at Payton's murder trial.

In due course Payton surrendered to the police, was indicted for murder, and moved to suppress the evidence taken from his apartment. The trial judge held that the warrantless and forcible entry was authorized by the New York Code of Criminal Procedure, and that the evidence in plain view was properly seized. He found that exigent circumstances justified the officers' failure to announce their purpose before entering the apartment as required by the statute. He had no occasion, however, to decide whether those circumstances also would have justified the failure to obtain a warrant, because he concluded that the warrantless entry was adequately supported by the statute without regard to the circumstances. The Appellate Division, First Department, summarily affirmed. . . . Our analysis in this case may therefore properly commence with rules that have been well established in Fourth Amendment litigation involving tangible items. As the Court reiterated just a few years ago, the "physical entry of the house is the chief evil against which the wording of the Fourth Amendment is directed." *United States v. United States District Court,* [1972].

And we have long adhered to the view that the warrant procedure minimizes the danger of needless intrusions of that sort.

It is a "basic principle of Fourth Amendment law" that searches and seizures inside a home without a warrant are presumtively unreasonable. . . .

The majority of the New York Court of Appeals, however, suggested that there is a substantial difference in the relative intrusiveness of an entry to search for property and an entry to search for a person. It is true that the area that may legally be searched is broader when executing a search warrant than when executing an arrest warrant in the home. This difference may be more theoretical than real, however, because the police may need to check the entire premises for safety reasons, and sometimes they ignore the restrictions on searches incident to arrest.

But the critical point is that any differences in the intrusiveness of entries to search and entries to arrest are merely ones of degree rather than kind. The two intrusions share this fundamental characteristic: the breach of the entrance to an individual's home. The Fourth Amendment protects the individual's privacy in a variety of settings. In none is the zone of privacy more clearly defined than when bounded by the unambiguous physical dimensions of an individual's home—a zone that finds its roots in clear and specific constitutional terms: "The right of the people to be secure in their . . . houses . . . shall not be violated." That language unequivocally establishes the proposition that "[a]t the very core [of the Fourth Amendment] stands the right of a man to retreat into his own home and there be free from unreasonable governmental intrusion." *Silverman v. United States,* [1960].

In terms that apply equally to seizures of property and to seizures of persons, the Fourth Amendment has drawn a firm line at the entrance to the house. Absent exigent circumstances that threshold may not reasonably be crossed without a warrant.

* * *

A majority of the States that have taken a position on the question permit warrantless entry into the home to arrest even in the absence of exigent circumstances. At this time 24 States permit such warrantless entries: 15 States clearly prohibit them, though 3 States do so on federal constitutional grounds alone; and 11 States have apparently taken no position on the question.

But these current figures reflect a significant decline during the last decade in the number of States permitting warrantless entries for arrest. Recent dicta in this Court raising questions about the practice and Federal Courts of Appeals' decisions on point have led state courts to focus on the issue. Virtually all of the state courts that have had to confront the constitutional issue directly have held warrantless entries into the home to arrest to be invalid in the absence of exigent circumstances.

Three state courts have relied on Fourth Amendment grounds alone, while seven have squarely placed their decisions on both federal and state constitutional grounds. A number of other state courts, though not having had to confront the issue directly, have recognized the serious nature of the constitutional question. Apparently, only the Supreme Court of Florida and the New York Court of Appeals in this case have expressly upheld warrantless entries to arrest in the face of a constitutional challenge.

A longstanding, widespread practice is not immune from constitutional scrutiny. But neither is it to be lightly brushed aside. This is particularly so when the constitutional standard is as amorphous as the word "reasonable" and when custom and contemporary norms necessarily play such a large role in the constitutional analysis. In this case, although the weight of state-law authority is clear, there is by no means the kind of virtual unanimity on this question that was present in *United States v. Watson,* with regard to warrantless arrests in public places.

Only 24 of the 50 States currently sanction warrantless entries into the home to arrest, and there is an obvious declining trend. Further, the strength of the trend is greater than the numbers alone indicate. Seven state courts have recently held that warrantless home arrests violate their respective *State* Constitutions.

That is significant because by invoking a state constitutional provision, a state court immunizes its decision from review by this Court. This heightened degree of immutability underscores the depth of the principle underlying the result. . . .

The parties have argued at some length about the practical consequences of a warrant requirement as a precondition to a felony arrest in the home. In the absence of any evidence that effective law enforcement has suffered in those States that already have such a requirement, we are inclined to view such arguments with skepticism. More fundamentally, however, such arguments of policy must give way to a constitutional command that we consider to be unequivocal.

Finally, we note the State's suggestion that only a search warrant based on probable cause to believe the suspect is at home at a given time can adequately protect the privacy interests at stake, and since such a warrant requirement is manifestly impractical, there need be no warrant of any kind. We find this ingenious argument unpersuasive. It is true that an arrest warrant requirement may afford less protection than a search warrant requirement, but it will suffice to interpose the magistrate's determination of probable cause between the zealous officer and the citizen. If there is sufficient evidence of a citizen's participation in a felony to persuade a judicial officer that his arrest is justified, it is constitutionally reasonable to require him to open his doors to the officers of the law.

Thus, for Fourth Amendment purposes, an arrest warrant founded on probable cause implicitly carries with it the limited authority to enter a dwelling in which the suspect lives when there is reason to believe the suspect is within.

Because no arrest warrant was obtained in either of these cases, the judgments must be reversed and the cases remanded to the New York Court of Appeals for further proceedings not inconsistent with this opinion.

It is so ordered.

* * *

[MR. JUSTICE WHITE, dissenting.]

The history of the Fourth Amendment does not support the rule announced today. At the time that Amendment was adopted the constable possessed broad inherent powers to arrest. The limitations on those powers derived, not from a warrant "requirement," but from the generally ministerial nature of the constable's office at common law.

* * *

Today's decision rests, in large measure, on the premise that warrantless arrest entries constitute a particularly severe invasion of personal privacy. I do not dispute that the home is generally a very private area or that the common law displayed a special "reverence . . . for the individual's right of privacy in his house." *Miller v. United States.* [1957].

However, the Fourth Amendment is concerned with protecting people, not places, and no talismanic significance is given to the fact that an arrest occurs in the home rather than elsewhere. . . . The inquiry in the present case, therefore, is whether the incremental intrusiveness that results from an arrest's being made *in the dwelling* is enough to support an inflexible constitutional role requiring warrants for such arrests whenever exigent circumstances are not present.

Today's decision ignores the carefully crafted restrictions on the common-law power of arrest entry and thereby overestimates the dangers inherent in that practice. At common law, absent exigent circumstances, entries to arrest could be made only for felony. Even in cases of felony, the officers were required to announce their presence, demand admission, and be refused entry before they were entitled to break doors. Further, it seems generally accepted that entries could be made only during daylight hours. And, in my view, the officer entering to arrest must have reasonable grounds to believe, not only that the arrestee has committed a crime, but also that the person suspected is present in the house at the time of the entry.

These four restrictions on home arrests—felony, knock and announce, daytime, and stringent probable cause—constitute powerful and conplementary protections for the privacy interests associated with the home. The felony requirement guards against abusive or arbitrary enforcement and ensures that invasions of the home occur only in case of the most serious crimes. The knock-and-announce and daytime requirements protect individuals against the fear, humiliation, and embarrassment of being roused from their beds in states of partial or complete undress. And these requirements allow the arrestee to surrender at his front door, thereby maintaining his dignity and preventing the officers from entering other rooms of the dwelling. The stringent probable-cause requirement would help ensure against the possibility that the police would enter when the suspect was not home, and, in searching for him, frighten members of the family or ransack parts of the house, seizing items in plain view. In short, these requirements, taken together, permit an individual suspected of a serious crime to surrender at the front door of his dwelling and thereby avoid most of the humiliation and indignity that the Court seems to believe necessarily accompany a house arrest entry.

* * *

The Court substitutes, in one sweeping decision, a rigid constitutional rule in place of the common-law approach, evolved over hundreds of years, which achieved a flexible accommodation between the demands of personal privacy and the legitimate needs of law enforcement.

* * *

Our cases establish that the ultimate test under the Fourth Amendment is one of "reasonableness." *Marshall v. Barlow's, Inc.,* (1978). I cannot join the Court in declaring unreasonable a practice which has been thought entirely reasonable by so many for so long. It would be far preferable to adopt a clear and simple rule: after knocking and announcing their presence, police may enter the home to make a daytime arrest without a warrant when there is probable cause to believe that the person to be arrested committed a felony and is present in the house. This rule would best comport with the common-law background, with the traditional practice in the States, and with the history and policies of the Fourth Amendment. Accordingly, I respectfully dissent.

QUESTIONS AND COMMENTS

1 The majority opinion in *Payton* characterizes the word "reasonable," as in "reasonable search and seizure," as "amorphous." What does that imply about judicial decision-making in the area of search and seizure law?

2 The Court makes a survey, in *Payton,* of what the states have done with the issue of

warrantless home entries. What does that have to do with deciding the meaning of a constitutional provision? Could the evidence from the state experiences be used to support a different decision? How?

3 The majority opinion rejects New York's policy argument and says such arguments "must give way to a constitutional command that we consider to be unequivocal." If the constitutional command is so unequivocal and so probative of the issue, why does the Court pay so much attention to the policy of the fifty states?

4 Conceding that the Fourth Amendment contains some "amorphous" words, what test is impliedly used to reach decision in *Payton*? Clear and present danger, balancing, intent of the framers, or what? Explain your answer.

Protection Against Self-Incrimination

In State Courts

Brown v. Mississippi (1936)

Miranda Rights

Miranda v. Arizona (1966)

Harris v. New York (1971)

Rhode Island v. Innis (1980)

Like many of the provisions in the Bill of Rights, the Fifth Amendment's proviso that a person may not be "compelled in any Criminal Case to be a witness against himself" stems from the experiences of our Puritan forebears in England. Prior to the seventeenth century, English defendants could be forced to incriminate themselves, and torture was commonly applied if a defendant's response to questions did not satisfy the accusers. This practice stopped in 1641 when Lilburne's Case[6] established the rule that one could not be forced to testify against oneself. The adoption of the Fifth Amendment simply reaffirmed the principle, which had already been incorporated into many state constitutions of the day.

We know from the Fifth Amendment that the self-incrimination prohibition applies to criminal trials. But that does not begin to exhaust the questions that have been raised about this protection. Among the questions resolved by Supreme Court decisions over the years are the following:

1 Does the amendment apply to the federal government only?
2 Is the protection available in civil prosecutions?
3 Does a coerced confession constitute a violation of the Fifth Amendment?
4 Is the protection available if government grants immunity from prosecution?

Generally speaking, the Fifth Amendment privilege is available in both civil and criminal proceedings as long as the testimony requested may be used in a criminal prosecution. Governments frequently need testimony before legislative committees, executive commissions, and in other civil and criminal settings. The concept of "immunity" has been developed largely as a response to such needs. A government may wish to grant immunity from prosecution to a witness whose testimony it considers to be of greater value than prosecution for the offense committed.

In 1893, Congress passed a statute which permitted the granting of *transactional immunity* in exchange for testimony in certain situations. Transactional immunity provides that once testimony is given under a grant of immunity, the witness may not be prosecuted for the offense admitted in the testimony. In 1896, the Court held the 1893 Statute constitutional, and the concept of transactional immunity was the norm for immunity statutes for over seventy-five years.

In 1970, Congress adopted a *use immunity* statute. Use immunity provides that when one testifies about an offense, that testimony cannot be used in any respect. However, evidence of the offense acquired independently of the testimony may furnish the basis for prosecution. While it is obvious that use immunity gives less protection than transactional immunity, the Supreme Court has held that use immunity does not violate the Fifth Amendment's prohibition against self-incrimination.[7]

Like many self-incrimination cases, *Brown v. Mississippi* involved a coerced confession. Yet no violation of the Fifth Amendment was found in *Brown.* That amendment's protection against self-incrimination was not available as a basis for complaint against a state until *Malloy v. Hogan,*[8] twenty-eight years after the decision in *Brown.* Thus, in deciding *Brown,* the Court was forced to rely on another provision of the Constitution, the Fourteenth Amendment's due process clause.

After 1964, the Court frequently docketed state cases in which pretrial treatment of criminal suspects was alleged to violate the Fifth Amendment's self-incrimination clause. Within two years of *Malloy,* the Court, under the leadership of Chief Justice Earl Warren, recognized explicitly that what transpires before trial may determine the outcome of a criminal prosecution—that merely outlawing physical abuse in obtaining confessions is not enough. In deciding *Miranda v. Arizona,* therefore, the Court moved to ensure that criminal suspects would henceforth be interrogated in accordance with specific principles.

The problem recognized in *Miranda* can be found as early as 1897 in the case of *Bram v. United States.* Bram was a ship captain accused of murder on the high seas. A police detective who eventually had custody of Bram forced him to strip naked with only the detective present. He then informed Bram that a witness, who had been at the wheel of the ship, had seen Bram commit the murder. Thereupon Bram replied: "He could not see me from there." The Supreme Court held this "confession" inadmissible as a violation of the self-incrimination clause.

It is just such subtle aspects of interrogation that the Court sought to deal with in *Miranda.* Subsequently, it has been discovered that there is, seemingly, no end to subtlety. And the Court has been called on repeatedly to provide progressively refined interpretations of its ruling in *Miranda.* Two such decisions occurred in *Harris v. New York* and *Rhode Island v. Innis.*

Brown et al. v. Mississippi

297 U.S. 278; 56 S. Ct. 461; 80 L. Ed. 682 (1936)
Vote: Unanimous

The facts are given in the opinion below.

MR. CHIEF JUSTICE HUGHES delivered the opinion of the Court.

The question in this case is whether convictions, which rest solely upon confessions shown to have been extorted by officers of the State by brutality and violence, are consistent with the due process of law required by the Fourteenth Amendment of the Constitution of the United States.

Petitioners were indicted for the murder of one Raymond Stewart, whose death occurred on March 30, 1934. They were indicted on April 4, 1934, and were then arraigned and pleaded not guilty. Counsel were appointed by the court to defend them. Trial was begun the next morning and was concluded on the following day, when they were found guilty and sentenced to death.

* * *

"The crime with which these defendants, all ignorant negroes, are charged, was discovered about one o'clock p.m. on Friday, March 30, 1934. On that night one Dial, a deputy sheriff, accompanied by others, came to the home of Ellington, one of the defendants, and requested him to accompany them to the house of the deceased, and there a number of white men were gathered, who began to accuse the defendant of the crime. Upon his denial they seized him, and with the participation of the deputy they hanged him by a rope to the limb of a tree, and having let him down, they hung him again, and when he was let down the second time, and he still protested his innocence, he was tied to a tree and whipped, and still declining to accede to the demands that he confess, he was finally released and he returned with some difficulty to his home, suffering intense pain and agony. The record of the testimony shows that the signs of the rope on his neck were plainly visible during the so-called trial. A day or two thereafter the said deputy, accompanied by another, returned to the home of the said defendant and arrested him, and departed with the prisoner towards the jail in an adjoining county, but went by a route which led into the State of Alabama; and while on the way, in that State, the deputy stopped and again severely whipped the defendant, declaring that he would continue the whipping until he confessed, and the defendant then agreed to confess to such a statement as the deputy would dictate, and he did so, after which he was delivered to jail.

"The other two defendants, Ed Brown and Henry Shields, were also arrested and taken to the same jail. On Sunday night, April 1, 1934, the same deputy, accompanied by a number of white men, one of whom was also an officer, and by the jailer, came to the jail, and the two last named defendants were made to strip and they were laid over chairs and their backs were cut to pieces with a leather strap with buckles on it, and they were likewise made by the said deputy definitely to understand that the whipping would be continued unless and until they confessed, and not only confessed, but confessed in every matter of detail as demanded by those present; and in this manner the defendants confessed the crime, and as the whippings progressed and were repeated, they changed or adjusted their confession in all particulars of detail so as to conform to the demands of their torturers. When the confessions had been obtained in the exact form and contents as desired by the mob, they left with the parting admonition and warning that, if the defendants changed their story at any time in any respect from that last stated, the perpetrators of the outrage would administer the same or equally effective treatment. . . .

"All this having been accomplished, on the next day, that is, on Monday, April 2, when the defendants had been given time to recuperate somewhat from the tortures to which they had been subjected, the two sheriffs, one of the county where the crime was committed, and the other of the county of the jail in which the prisoners were confined, came to the jail, accompanied by eight other persons, some of them deputies, there to hear the free and voluntary confession of these miserable and abject defendants.

* * *

"The evidence upon which the conviction was obtained was the so-called confessions. Without this evidence a peremptory instruction to find for the defendants would have been inescapable. The defendants were put on the stand, and by their testimony the facts and the details thereof as to the manner by which the confessions were extorted from them were fully developed, and it is further disclosed by the record that the same deputy, Dial, under whose guiding hand and active participation the tortures to coerce the confessions were administered, was actively in the performance of the supposed duties of a court deputy in the courthouse and in the presence of the prisoners during what is denominated, in complimentary terms, the trial of these defendants. This deputy was put on the stand by the state in rebuttal, and admitted the whippings. It is interesting to note that in his testimony with reference to the whipping of the defendant Ellington, and in response to the inquiry as to how severely he was whipped, the deputy stated, 'Not too much for a negro; not as much as I would have done if it were left to me.' Two others who had participated in these whippings were introduced and admitted it—not a single witness was introduced who denied it. The facts are not only undisputed, they are admitted, and admitted to have been done by officers of the state, in conjunction with other participants, and all this was definitely well known to every-body connected with the trial, and during the trial, including the state's prosecuting attorney and the trial judge presiding."

1. The State stresses the statement in *Twining v. New Jersey,* [1908], that "exemption from compulsory self-incrimination in the courts of the States is not secured by any part of the Federal Constitution," and the statement in *Snyder v. Massachusetts,* [1934] that "the privilege against self-incrimination may be withdrawn and the accused put upon the stand as a witness for the State." But the question of the right of the State to withdraw the privilege against self-incrimination is not here involved. The compulsion to which the quoted statements refer is that of the processes of justice by which the accused may be called as a witness and required to testify. Compulsion by torture to extort a confession is a different matter.

The State is free to regulate the procedure of its courts in accordance with its own conceptions of policy, unless in so doing it "offends some principle of justice so rooted in the traditions and conscience of our people as to be ranked as fundamental."

The State may abolish trial by jury. It may dispense with indictment by a grand jury and substitute complaint or information. But the freedom of the State in establishing its policy is the freedom of constitutional government and is limited by the requirement of due process of law. Because a State may dispense with a jury trial, it does not follow that it may substitute trial by ordeal. The rack and torture chamber may not be substituted for the witness stand. The State may not permit an accused to be hurried to conviction under mob domination—where the whole proceeding is but a mask—without supplying corrective process. The State may not deny to the accused the aid of counsel. Nor may a State, through the action of its officers, contrive a conviction through the pretense of a trial which in truth is "but used as a means of depriving a defendant of liberty through a deliberate deception of court and jury by the presentation of testimony known to be perjured." *Mooney v. Holohan,* [1935]. And the trial equally is a mere pretense where the state authorities have contrived a conviction resting solely upon confessions obtained by violence. The due process clause requires "that state action, whether through one agency or another, shall be consistent with the fundamental principles of liberty and justice which lie at the base of all our civil and political institutions." *Hebert v. Louisiana,* [1926]. It would be difficult to conceive of methods more revolting to the sense of justice than those taken to procure the confessions of these petitioners, and the use of the confessions of these petitioners, and the use of the confessions thus obtained as the basis for conviction and sentence was a clear denial of due process.

2. It is in this view that the further contention of the State must be considered. That contention rests upon the failure of counsel for the accused, who had objected to the admissibility of the confessions, to move for their exclusion after they had been introduced and the fact of coercion had been proved. . . .

It is not a question of state practice, or whether counsel assigned to petitioners were competent or mistakenly assumed that their first objections were sufficient. . . .

In an earlier case the Supreme Court of the State had recognized the duty of the court to supply corrective process where due process of law had been denied. In *Fisher v. State,* the Court said: "Coercing the supposed state's criminals into confessions and using such confessions so coerced from them against them in trials has been the curse of all countries. It was the chief inequity, the crowning infamy of the Star Chamber, and the Inquisition, and other similar institutions. The constitution recognized the evils that lay behind these practices and prohibited them in this country. . . . The duty of maintaining constitutional rights of a person on trial for his life rises above mere rules of procedure and wherever the court is clearly satisfied that such violations exist, it will refuse to sanction such violations and will apply the corrective."

In the instant case, the trial court was fully advised by the undisputed evidence of the way in which the confessions had been procured. The trial court knew that there was no other evidence upon which conviction and sentence could be based. Yet it proceeded to permit conviction and to pronounce sentence. The conviction and sentence were void for want of the essential elements of due process, and the proceeding thus vitiated could be challenged in any appropriate manner. It was challenged before the Supreme Court of the State by the express invocation of the Fourteenth Amendment. That court entertained the challenge, considered the federal question thus presented, but declined to enforce petitioners' constitutional right. The court thus denied a federal right fully established and specially set up and claimed and the judgment must be. . . .

Reversed.

Miranda v. Arizona

384 U.S. 436; 86 S. Ct. 1602; 16 L. Ed. 2d 694 (1966)
Vote: 6–3

Ernesto Mirando, 23, was arrested on March 13, 1963, in Phoenix, Arizona, and charged with rape, robbery, and kidnapping. He had previously been convicted of car theft and had served a year in a federal prison. After his arrest on March 13, Miranda was taken to police interrogation room #2 in the Phoenix Detective Bureau and questioned by two officers for two hours. He was not advised that he had a right to have an attorney present during questioning. At the end of the session, Miranda signed a written confession to kidnapping and rape. At the top of the confession document was a typed statement that the confession was made voluntarily without threats or promises of immunity and "with full knowledge of my legal rights, understanding any statement I make may be used against me."

During prearraignment processing, Miranda requested and was denied a lawyer. At arraignment he was provided with an attorney—a 73-year-old man who had practiced no criminal law (virtually) for sixteen years.

At trial, Miranda was convicted of rape and kidnapping on the basis of the written confession in spite of defense objections that the confession was obtained illegally. A sentence of 20 to 30 years imprisonment was then imposed. On appeal, the supreme court of Arizona found no constitutional violations. The court emphasized that Miranda had not specifically requested counsel during the interrogation session. The U.S. Supreme Court granted certiorari.

MR. CHIEF JUSTICE WARREN delivered the opinion of the Court.

Our holding is this: the prosecution may not use statements, whether exculpatory or inculpatory, stemming from custodial interrogation of the defendant unless it demonstrates the use of procedural safeguards effective to secure the privilege against self-incrimination. By custodial interrogation, we mean questioning initiated by law enforcement officers after a person has been taken into custody or otherwise deprived of his freedom of action in any significant way. As for the procedural safeguards to be employed, unless other fully effective means are devised to inform accused persons of their right of silence and to assure a continuous opportunity to exercise it, the following measures are required. Prior to any questioning, the person must be warned that he has a right to remain silent, that any statement he does make may be used as evidence against him, and that he has a right to the presence of an attorney, either retained or appointed. The defendant may waive effectuation of these rights, provided the waiver is made voluntarily, knowingly and intelligently. If, however, he indicates in any manner and at any stage of the process that he wishes to consult with an attorney before speaking there can be no questioning. Likewise, if the individual is alone and indicates in any manner that he does not wish to be interrogated, the police may not question him. The mere fact that he may have answered some questions or volunteered some statements on his own does not deprive him of the right to refrain from answering any further inquiries until he has consulted with an attorney and thereafter consents to be questioned.

* * *

. . . The modern practice of in-custody interrogation is psychologically rather than physically oriented. As we have stated before, "Since *Chambers v. Florida,* [1940], this Court has recognized that coercion can be mental as well as physical, and that the blood of the accused is not the only hallmark of an unconstitutional inquisition." *Blackburn v. Alabama,* (1960). Interrogation still takes place in privacy. Privacy results in secrecy and this in turn results in a gap in our knowledge as to what in fact goes on in the interrogation rooms. A valuable source of information about present police practices, however, may be found in various police manuals and texts which document procedures employed with success in the past, and which recommend various other effective tactics. These texts are used by law enforcement agencies themselves as guides. It should be noted that these texts professedly present the most enlightened and effective means presently used to obtain statements through custodial interrogation. By considering these texts and other data, it is possible to describe procedures observed and noted around the country.

The officers are told by the manuals that the "principal psychological factor contributing to a successful interrogation is *privacy*—being alone with the person under interrogation." The efficacy of this tactic has been explained as follows:

> If at all practicable, the interrogation should take place in the investigator's office or at least in a room of his own choice. The subject should be deprived of every psychological advantage. In his own home he may be confident, indignant, or recalcitrant. He is more keenly aware of his rights and more reluctant to tell of his indiscretions or criminal behavior within the walls of his home. Moreover his family and other friends are nearby, their presence lending moral support. In his own office, the investigator possesses all the advantages. The atmosphere suggests the invincibility of the forces of the law.

To highlight the isolation and unfamiliar surroundings, the manuals instruct the police to display an air of confidence in the suspect's guilt and from outward appearance to maintain only an interest in confirming certain details. The guilt of the subject is to be posited as a fact. The interrogator should direct his comments toward the reasons why the subject committed the act, rather than court failure by asking the subject whether he did it. Like other men, perhaps the subject has had a bad family life, had an unhappy childhood, had too much to drink, had an unrequited childhood, had too much to drink, had an unrequited desire for women. The officers are instructed to minimize the moral seriousness of the offense, to cast blame on the victim or on society. These tactics are designed to put the subject in a psychological state where his story is but an elaboration of what the police purport to know already—that he is guilty. Explanations to the contrary are dismissed and discouraged.

The texts thus stress that the major qualities an interrogator should possess are patience and perseverance.

* * *

The interrogators sometimes are instructed to induce a confession out of trickery. The technique here is quite effective in crimes which require identification or which run in series. In the identification situation, the interrogator may take a break in his questioning to place the subject among a group of men in a line-up. "The witness or complainant (previously coached, if necessary) studies the line-up and confidently points out the subject as the guilty party." Then the questioning resumes "as though there were now no doubt about the guilt of the subject." A variation on this technique is called the "reverse line-up":

> The accused is placed in a line-up, but this time he is identified by several fictitious witnesses or victims who associated him with different offenses. It is expected that the subject will become desperate and confess to the offense under investigation in order to escape from the false accusations.

The manuals also contain instructions for police on how to handle the individual who refuses to discuss the matter entirely, or who asks for an attorney or relatives. The examiner is to concede him the right to remain silent. "This usually has a very undermining effect. First of all, he is disappointed in his expectation of an unfavorable reaction on the part of the interrogator. Secondly, a concession of this right to remain silent impresses the subject with the apparent fairness of his interrogator." After this psychological conditioning, however, the officer is told to point out the incriminating significance of the suspect's refusal to talk:

> Joe, you have a right to remain silent. That's your privilege and I'm the last person in the world who'll try to take it away from you. If that's the way you want to leave this, O. K. But let me ask you this. Suppose you were in my shoes and I were in yours and you called me in to ask me about this and I told you, "I don't want to answer any of your questions." You'd think I had something to hide, and you'd probably be right in thinking that. That's exactly what I'll have to think about you, and so will everybody else. So let's sit here and talk this whole thing over.

Few will persist in their initial refusal to talk, it is said, if this monologue is employed correctly.

In the event that the subject wishes to speak to a relative or an attorney, the following advice is tendered:

> [T]he interrogator should respond by suggesting that the subject first tell the truth to the interrogator himself rather than get anyone else involved in the matter. If the request is for an attorney, the interrogator may suggest that the subject save himself or his family the expense of any such professional service, particularly if he is innocent of the offense under investigation. The interrogator may also add, "Joe, I'm only looking for the truth, and if you're telling the truth, that's it. You can handle this by yourself."

From these representative samples of interrogation techniques, the setting prescribed by the manuals and observed in practice becomes clear. In essence, it is this: To be alone with the subject is essential to prevent distraction and to deprive him of any outside support. The aura of confidence in his guilt undermines his will to resist. He merely confirms the preconceived story the police seek to have him describe. Patience and persistence, at times relentless questioning, are employed. To obtain a confession, the interrogator must "patiently maneuver himself or his quarry into a position from which the desired objective may be attained." When normal procedures fail to produce the needed result, the police may resort to deceptive stratagems such as giving false legal advice. It is important to keep the subject off balance, for example, by trading on his insecurity about himself or his surroundings. The police then persuade, trick, or cajole him out of exercising his constitutional rights. . . .

It is obvious that such an interrogation environment is created for no purpose other than to subjugate the individual to the will of his examiner. This atmosphere carries its own badge of intimidation. To be sure, this is not physical intimidation, but it is equally destructive of human dignity. The current practice of incommunicado interrogation is at odds with one of our Nation's most cherished principles—that the individual may not be compelled to incriminate himself. Unless adequate protective devices are employed to dispel the compulsion inherent in custodial surroundings, no statement obtained from the defendant can truly be the product of his free choice.

From the foregoing, we can readily perceive an intimate connection between the privilege against self-incrimination and police custodial questioning.

. . . In order to . . . permit a full opportunity to exercise the privilege against self-incrimination, the accused must be adequately and effectively apprised of his rights and the exercise of those rights must be fully honored.

* * *

At the outset, if a person in custody is to be subjected to interrogation, he must first be informed in clear and unequivocal terms that he has the right to remain silent. For those unaware of the privilege, the warning is needed simply to make them aware of it—the threshold requirement for an intelligent decision as to its exercise. More important, such a warning is an absolute prerequisite in overcoming the inherent pressures of the interrogation atmosphere. It is not just the subnormal or woefully ignorant who succumb to an interrogator's imprecations, whether implied or expressly stated, that the interrogation will continue until a confession is obtained or that silence in the face of accusation is itself damning and will bode ill when presented to a jury. Further, the warning will show the individual that his interrogators are prepared to recognize his privilege should he choose to exercise it.

The Fifth Amendment privilege is so fundamental to our system of constitutional rule and the expedient of giving an adequate warning as to the availability of the privilege so simple, we will not pause to inquire in individual cases whether the defendant was aware of his rights without a warning being given. Assessments of the knowledge the defendant possessed, based on information as to his age, education, intelligence, or prior contact with authorities, can never be more than speculation; a warning is a clearcut fact. More important, whatever the background of the person interrogated, a warning at the time of the interrogation is indispensable to overcome its pressures and to insure that the individual knows he is free to exercise the privilege at that point in time.

The warning of the right to remain silent must be accompanied by the explanation that anything said can and will be used against the individual in court. This warning is needed in order to make him aware not only of the privilege, but also of the consequences of forgoing it. It is only through an awareness of these consequences that there can be any assurance of real understanding and intelligent exercise of the privilege. Moreover, this warning may serve to make the individual more acutely aware that he is faced with a phase of the adversary system—that he is not in the presence of persons acting solely in his interest.

The circumstances surrounding in-custody interrogation can operate very quickly to overbear the will of one merely made aware of his privilege by his interrogators. Therefore, the right to have counsel present at the interrogation is indispensable to the protection of the Fifth Amendment privilege under the system we delineate today. Our aim is to assure that the individual's right to choose between silence and speech remains unfettered throughout the interrogation process. A once-stated warning, delivered by those who will conduct the interrogation, cannot itself suffice to that end among those who most require knowledge of their rights. A mere warning given by the interrogators is not alone sufficient to accomplish that end. Prosecutors themselves claim that the admonishment of the right to remain silent without more "will benefit only the recidivist and the professional."

Even preliminary advice given to the accused by his own attorney can be swiftly overcome by the secret interrogation process. Thus, the need for counsel to protect the Fifth Amendment privilege comprehends not merely a right to consult with counsel prior to questioning, but also to have counsel present during any questioning if the defendant so desires.

The presence of counsel at the interrogation may serve several significant subsidiary functions as well. If the accused decides to talk to his interrogators, the assistance of counsel can mitigate the dangers of untrustworthiness. With a lawyer present the likelihood that the police will practice coercion is reduced, and if coercion is nevertheless exercised the lawyer can testify to it in court. The presence of a lawyer can also help to guarantee that the accused gives a fully accurate statement to the police and that the statement is rightly reported by the prosecution at trial.

An individual need not make a pre-interrogation request for a lawyer. While such request affirmatively secures his right to have one, his failure to ask for a lawyer does not constitute a waiver. No effective waiver of the right to counsel during interrogation can be recognized unless specifically made after the warnings we here delineate have been given. The accused who does not know his rights and therefore does not make a request may be the person who most needs counsel.

* * *

Accordingly we hold that an individual held for interrogation must be clearly informed that he has the right to consult with a lawyer and to have the lawyer with him during interrogation under the system for protecting the privilege we delineate today. As with the warnings of the right to remain silent and that anything stated can be used in evidence against him, this warning is an absolute prerequisite to interrogation. No amount of circumstantial evidence that the person may have been aware of this right will suffice to stand in its stead. Only through such a warning is there ascertainable assurance that the accused was aware of this right.

* * *

In order fully to apprise a person interrogated of the extent of his rights under this system then, it is necessary to warn him not only that he has the right to consult with an attorney, but also that if he is indigent a lawyer will be appointed to represent him. Without this additional warning, the admonition of the right to consult with counsel would often be understood as meaning only that he can consult with a lawyer if he has one or has the funds to obtain one. The warning of a right to counsel would be hollow if not couched in terms that would convey to the indigent—the person most often subjected to interrogation—the knowledge that he too has a right to have counsel present. As with the warnings of the right to remain silent and of the general right to counsel, only by effective and express explanation to the indigent of this right can there be assurance that he was truly in a position to exercise it.

Once warnings have been given, the subsequent procedure is clear. If the individual indicates in any manner, at any time prior to or during questioning, that he wishes to remain silent, the interrogation must cease. At this point he has shown that he intends to exercise his Fifth Amendment privilege; any statement taken after the person invokes his privilege cannot be other than the product of compulsion, subtle or otherwise. Without the right to cut off questioning, the setting of in-custody interrogation operates on the individual to overcome free choice in producing a statement after the privilege has been once invoked. If the individual states that he wants an attorney, the interrogation must cease until an attorney is present. At that time, the individual must have an opportunity to confer with the attorney and to have him present during any subsequent questioning. If the individual cannot obtain an attorney and he indicates that he wants one before speaking to police, they must respect his decision to remain silent.

* * *

In dealing with statements obtained through interrogation, we do not purport to find all confessions inadmissible. Confessions remain a proper element in law enforcement. Any statement given freely and voluntarily without any compelling influences is, of course, admissible in evidence. The fundamental import of the privilege while an individual is in custody is not whether he is allowed to talk to the police without the benefit of warnings and counsel, but whether he can be interrogated. There is no requirement that police stop a person who enters a police station and states that he wishes to confess to a crime, or a person who calls the police to offer a confession or any other statement he desires to make. Volunteered statements of any kind are not barred by the Fifth Amendment and their admissibility is not affected by our holding today.

To summarize, we hold that when an individual is taken into custody or otherwise deprived of his freedom by the authorities in any significant way and is subjected to questioning, the privilege against self-incrimination is jeopardized. Procedural safeguards must be employed to protect the privilege, and unless other fully effective means are adopted to notify the person of his right of silence and to assure that the exercise of the right will be scrupulously honored, the following measures are required. He must be warned prior to any questioning that he has the right to remain silent, that anything he says can be used against him in a court of law, that he has the right to the presence of an attorney, and that if he cannot afford an attorney one will be appointed for him prior to any questioning if he so desires. Opportunity to exercise these rights must be afforded to him throughout the interrogation. After such warnings have been given, and such opportunity afforded him, the individual may knowingly and intelligently waive these rights and agree to answer questions or make a statement. But unless and until such warnings and waiver are demonstrated by the prosecution at trial, no evidence obtained as a result of interrogation can be used against him.

* * *

[At Miranda's] . . . trial before a jury, the written confession was admitted into evidence over the objection of defense counsel, and the officers testified to the prior oral confession made by Miranda during the interrogation. Miranda was found guilty of kidnapping and rape. He was sentenced to 20 to 30 years' imprisonment on each count, the sentences to run concurrently. On appeal, the Supreme Court of Arizona held that Miranda's constitutional rights were not violated in obtaining the confession and affirmed the conviction.

In reaching its decision, the court emphasized heavily the fact that Miranda did not specifically request counsel.

We reverse. From the testimony of the officers and by the admission of respondent, it is clear that Miranda was not in any way apprised of his right to consult with an attorney and to have one present during the interrogation, nor was his right not to be compelled to incriminate himself effectively protected in any other manner. Without these warnings the statements were inadmissible. The mere fact that he signed a statement which contained a typed-in clause stating that he had "full knowledge" of his "legal rights" does not approach the knowing and intelligent waiver required to relinquish constitutional rights. . . .

MR. JUSTICE HARLAN, whom MR. JUSTICE STEWART and MR. JUSTICE WHITE join, dissenting.

I believe the decision of the Court represents poor constitutional law and entails harmful consequences for the country at large. How serious these consequences may prove to be only time can tell. But the basic flaws in the Court's justification seem to me readily apparent now once all sides of the problem are considered.

INTRODUCTION

At the outset, it is well to note exactly what is required by the Court's new constitutional code of rules for confessions. . . .

The new rules are not designed to guard against police brutality or other unmistakably banned forms of coercion. Those who use third-degree tactics and deny them in court are equally able and destined to lie as skillfully about warnings and waivers. Rather, the thrust of the new rules is to negate all pressures, to reinforce the nervous or ignorant suspect, and ultimately to discourage any confession at all. The aim in short is toward "voluntariness" in a utopian sense, or to view it from a different angle, voluntariness with a vengeance.

To incorporate this notion into the Constitution requires a strained reading of history and precedent and a disregard of the very pragmatic concerns that alone may on occasion justify such strains. I believe that reasoned examination will show that the Due Process Clauses provide an adequate tool for coping with confessions and that, even if the Fifth Amendment privilege against self-incrimination be invoked, its precedents taken as a whole do not sustain the present rules. Viewed as a choice based on pure policy, these new rules prove to be a highly debatable, if not one-sided, appraisal of the competing interests, imposed over widespread objection, at the very time when judicial restraint is most called for by the circumstances.

* * *

The Court's opinion in my view reveals no adequate basis for extending the Fifth Amendment's privilege against self-incrimination to the police station. Far more important, it fails to show that the Court's new rules are well supported, let alone compelled, by Fifth Amendment precedents. . . .

Having decided that the Fifth Amendment privilege does apply in the police station, the Court reveals that the privilege imposes more exacting restrictions than does the Fourteenth Amendment's voluntariness test. It then emerges from a discussion of *Escobedo* that the Fifth Amendment requires for an admissible confession that it be given by one distinctly aware of his right not to speak and shielded from "the compelling atmosphere" of interrogation. From these key premises, the Court finally develops the safeguards of warning, counsel, and so forth. I do not believe these premises are sustained by precedents under the Fifth Amendment.

The more important premise is that pressure on the suspect must be eliminated though it be only the subtle influence of the atmosphere and surroundings. The Fifth Amendment, however, has never been thought to forbid *all* pressure to incriminate one's self in the situations covered by it. On the contrary, it has been held that failure to incriminate one's self can result in denial of removal of one's case from state to federal court. *Maryland v. Soper,* [1925], in refusal of a military commission, *Orloff v. Willoughby,* [1951], in denial of a discharge in bankruptcy, and in numerous other adverse consequences.

This is not to say that short of jail or torture any sanction is permissible in any case; policy and history alike may impose sharp limits. See, *e. g., Griffin v. California,* [1964]. However, the Court's unspoken assumption that *any* pressure violates the privilege is not supported by the precedents and it has failed to show why the Fifth Amendment prohibits that relatively mild pressure the Due Process Clause permits.

* * *

POLICY CONSIDERATIONS

Examined as an expression of public policy, the Court's regime proves so dubious that there can be no due compensation for its weakness in constitutional law.

* * *

The Court's new rules aim to offset . . . minor pressures and disadvantages intrinsic to any kind of police interrogation. The rules do not serve due process interests in preventing blatant coercion since, as I noted earlier, they do nothing to contain the policeman who is prepared to lie from the start. The rules work for reliability in confessions almost only in the Pickwickian sense that they can prevent some from being given at all. In short, the benefit of this new regime is simply to lessen or wipe out the inherent compulsion and inequalities to which the Court devotes some nine pages of description.

What the Court largely ignores is that its rules impair, if they will not eventually serve wholly to frustrate, an instrument of law enforcement that has long and quite reasonably been thought worth the price paid for it. There can be little doubt that the Court's new code would markedly decrease the number of confessions. To warn the suspect that he may remain silent and remind him that his confession may be used in court are minor obstructions. To require also an express waiver by the suspect and an end to questioning whenever he demurs must heavily handicap questioning. And to suggest or provide counsel for the suspect simply invites the end of the interrogation.

How much harm this decision will inflict on law enforcement cannot fairly be predicted with accuracy. Evidence on the role of confessions is notoriously incomplete, and little is added by the Court's reference to the FBI experience and the resources believed wasted in interrogation.

We do know that some crimes cannot be solved without confessions, that ample expert testimony attests to their importance in crime control, and that the Court is taking a real risk with society's welfare in imposing its new regime on the country. The social costs of crime are too great to call the new rules anything but a hazardous experimentation. . . .

In conclusion: Nothing in the letter or the spirit of the Constitution or in the precedents squares with the heavy-handed and one-sided action that is so precipitously taken by the Court in the name of fulfilling its constitutional responsibilities. The foray which the Court makes today brings to mind the wise and farsighted words of Mr. Justice Jackson in *Douglas v. Jeannette,* [1941]. "This Court is forever adding new stories to the temples of constitutional law, and the temples have a way of collapsing when one story too many is added."

MR. JUSTICE WHITE, with whom MR. JUSTICE HARLAN and MR. JUSTICE STEWART join, dissenting.

* * *

The obvious underpinning of the Court's decision is a deep-seated distrust of all confessions. As the Court declares that the accused may not be interrogated without counsel present, absent a waiver of the right to counsel, and as the Court all but admonishes the lawyer to advise the accused to remain silent, the result adds up to a judicial judgment that evidence from the accused should not be used against him in any way, whether compelled or not. This is the not so subtle overtone of the opinion—that it is inherently wrong for the police to gather evidence from the accused himself. And this is precisely the nub of this dissent. I see nothing wrong or immoral, and certainly nothing unconstitutional, in the police's asking a suspect whom they have reasonable cause to arrest whether or not he killed his wife or in confronting him with the evidence on which the arrest was based, at least where he has been plainly advised that he may remain completely silent, see *Escobedo v. Illinois,* [1964], (dissenting opinion). Until today, "the admissions or confessions of the prisoner, when voluntarily and freely made, have always ranked high in the scale of incriminating evidence." *Brown v. Walker,* [1895].

Particularly when corroborated, as where the police have confirmed the accused's disclosure of the hiding place of implements or fruits of the crime, such confessions have the highest reliability and significantly contribute to the certitude with which we may believe the accused is guilty. Moreover, it is by no means certain that the process of confessing is injurious to the accused. To the contrary it may provide psychological relief and enhance the prospects for rehabilitation.

This is not to say that the value of respect for the inviolability of the accused's individual personality should be accorded no weight or that all confessions should be indiscriminately admitted. This Court has long read the Constitution to proscribe compelled confessions, a salutary rule from which there should be no retreat. But I see no sound basis, factual or otherwise, and the Court gives none, for concluding that the present rule against the receipt of coerced confessions is inadequate for the task of sorting out inadmissible evidence and must be replaced by the *per se* rule which is now imposed. Even if the new concept can be said to have advantages of some sort over the present law, they are far outweighed by its likely undesirable impact on other very relevant and important interests.

The most basic function of any government is to provide for the security of the individual and of his property. These ends of society are served by the criminal laws which for the most part are aimed at the prevention of crime. Without the reasonably effective performance of the task of preventing private violence and retaliation, it is idle to talk about human dignity and civilized values.

The modes by which the criminal laws serve the interest in general security are many. First the murderer who has taken the life of another is removed from the streets, deprived of his liberty and thereby prevented from repeating his offense. . . .

Secondly, the swift and sure apprehension of those who refuse to respect the personal security and dignity of their neighbor unquestionably has its impact on others who might be similarly tempted. . . .

Thirdly, the law concerns itself with those whom it has confined. The hope and aim of modern penology, fortunately, is as soon as possible to return the convict to society a better and more law-abiding man than when he left. Sometimes there is success, sometimes failure. But at least the effort is made, and it should be made to the very maximum extent of our present and future capabilities.

The rule announced today will measurably weaken the ability of the criminal law to perform these tasks. It is a deliberate calculus to prevent interrogations, to reduce the incidence of confessions and pleas of guilty and to increase the number of trials.

* * *

I have no desire whatsoever to share the responsibility for any such impact on the present criminal process.

* * *

Applying the traditional standards to the cases before the Court, I would hold these confessions voluntary.

Harris v. New York

401 U.S. 222; 91 S. Ct. 643; 28 L. Ed. 2d 1 (1971)
Vote: 5–4

Harris was convicted of selling heroin to an undercover police officer. After his arrest, Harris made certain incriminating statements to the police. These statements were not introduced at trial initially since they were obtained in violation of Harris's *Miranda* rights. At trial, Harris took the stand and admitted the sale. However, he claimed that the glassine bag sold to the undercover officer contained baking powder. On cross-examination, he was asked whether he had made certain contradictory statements to the police earlier. Harris replied that he could not remember most of the questions and answers recited by the prosecution. At the request of Harris's counsel, the list of questions and answers from which the prosecutor had read was placed in the record for use on appeal. The transcript was not given to the jury.

At trial, the prosecutor made no attempt to use the incriminating questions and answers to establish the defendant's guilt. After trial, Harris appealed his conviction on the ground that the use of the incriminating statements to impeach his credibility violated his *Miranda* rights. After New York courts denied relief the U.S. Supreme Court granted certiorari.

MR. CHIEF JUSTICE BURGER delivered the opinion of the Court.

* * *

Some comments in the *Miranda* opinion can indeed be read as indicating a bar to use of an uncounseled statement for any purpose, but discussion of that issue was not at all necessary to the Court's holding and cannot be regarded as controlling. *Miranda* barred the prosecution from making its case with statements of an accused made while in custody prior to having or effectively waiving counsel. It does not follow from *Miranda* that evidence inadmissible against an accused in the prosecution's case in chief is barred for all purposes, provided of course that the trustworthiness of the evidence satisfies legal standards.

* * *

Every criminal defendant is privileged to testify in his own defense, or to refuse to do so. But that privilege cannot be construed to include the right to commit perjury. See *United States v. Knox,* (1969); ... Having voluntarily taken the stand, petitioner was under an obligation to speak truthfully and accurately, and the prosecution here did no more than utilize the traditional truth-testing devices of the adversary process. Had inconsistent statements been made by the accused to some third person, it could hardly be contended that the conflict could not be laid before the jury by way of cross-examination and impeachment.

The shield provided by *Miranda* cannot be perverted into a license to use perjury by way of a defense, free from the risk of confrontation with prior inconsistent utterances. We hold, therefore, that petitioner's credibility was appropriately impeached by use of his earlier conflicting statements.

Affirmed.

MR. JUSTICE BLACK dissents.

MR. JUSTICE BRENNAN, with whom MR. JUSTICE DOUGLAS and MR. JUSTICE MARSHALL join, dissenting.

It is conceded that the question-and-answer statement used to impeach petitioner's direct testimony was, under *Miranda v. Arizona,* (1966), constitutionally inadmissible as part of the State's direct case against petitioner. I think that the Constitution also denied the State the use of the statement on cross-examination to impeach the credibility of petitioner's testimony given in his own defense.

* * *

The State's case against Harris depended upon the jury's belief of the testimony of the undercover agent that petitioner "sold" the officer heroin on January 4 and again on January 6. Petitioner took the stand and flatly denied having sold anything to the officer on January 4. He countered the officer's testimony as to the January 6 sale with testimony that he had sold the officer two glassine bags containing what appeared to be heroin, but that actually the bags contained only baking powder intended to deceive the officer in order to obtain $12. The statement contradicted petitioner's direct testimony as to the events of both days. The statement's version of the events on January 4 was that the officer had used petitioner as a middleman to buy some heroin from a third person with money furnished by the officer. The version of the events on January 6 was that petitioner had again acted for the officer in buying two bags of heroin from a third person for which petitioner received $12 and a part of the heroin. Thus, it is clear that the statement was used to impeach petitioner's direct testimony not on collateral matters but on matters directly related to the crimes for which he was on trial.

* * *

The objective of deterring improper police conduct is only part of the larger objective of safeguarding the integrity of our adversary system. The "essential mainstay" of that system is the privilege against self-incrimination, which for that reason has occupied a central place in our jurisprudence since before the Nation's birth. . . .

. . . It is monstrous that courts should aid or abet the law-breaking police officer. It is abiding truth that "[n]othing can destroy a government more quickly than its failure to observe its own laws, or worse, its disregard of the charter of its own existence." *Mapp v. Ohio,* (1961). Thus, even to the extent that *Miranda* was aimed at deterring police practices in disregard of the Constitution, I fear that today's holding will seriously undermine the achievement of that objective. The Court today tells the police that they may freely interrogate an accused incommunicado and without counsel and know that although any statement they obtain in violation of *Miranda* cannot be used on the State's direct case, it may be introduced if the defendant has the temerity to testify in his own defense. This goes far toward undoing much of the progress made in conforming police methods to the Constitution. I dissent.

Rhode Island v. Innis

446 U.S. 291; 100 S. Ct. 1682; 64 L. Ed. 2d 297 (1980)
Vote: 6–3

The facts are given in the opinion below.

MR. JUSTICE STEWART delivered the opinion of the Court.

* * *

On the night of January 12, 1975, John Mulvaney, a Providence, R.I., taxicab driver, disappeared after being dispatched to pick up a customer. His body was discovered four days later buried in a shallow grave in Coventry, R.I. He had died from a shotgun blast aimed at the back of his head.

On January 17, 1975, shortly after midnight, the Providence police received a telephone call from Gerald Aubin, also a taxicab driver, who reported that he had just been robbed by a man wielding a sawed-off shotgun. Aubin further reported that he had dropped off his assailant near Rhode Island College in a section of Providence known as Mount Pleasant. While at the Providence police station waiting to give a statement, Aubin noiced a picture of his assailant on a bulletin board. Aubin so informed one of the police officers present. The officer prepared a photo array, and again Aubin identified a picture of the same person. That person was the respondent. Shortly thereafter, the Providence police began a search of the Mount Pleasant area.

At approximately 4:30 A.M. on the same date, Patrolman Lovell, while cruising the streets of Mount Pleasant in a patrol car, spotted the respondent standing in the street facing him. When Patrolman Lovell stopped his car, the respondent walked towards it. Patrolman Lovell then arrested the respondent, who was unarmed, and advised him of his so-called *Miranda* rights. While the two men waited in the patrol car for other police officers to arrive, Patrolman Lovell did not converse with the respondent other than to respond to the latter's request for a cigarette.

Within minutes, Sergeant Sears arrived at the scene of the arrest, and he also gave the respondent the *Miranda* warnings. Immediately thereafter, Captain Leyden and other police officers arrived. Captain Leyden advised the respondent of his *Miranda* rights. The respondent stated that he understood those rights and wanted to speak with a lawyer. Captain Leyden then directed that the respondent be placed in a "caged wagon," a four-door police car with a wire screen mesh between the front and rear seats, and be driven to the central police station. Three officers, Patrolmen Gleckman, Williams, and McKenna, were assigned to accompany the respondent to the central station. They placed the respondent in the vehicle and shut the doors. Captain Leyden then instructed the officers not to question the respondent or intimidate or coerce him in any way. The three officers then entered the vehicle, and it departed.

While en route to the central station, Patrolman Gleckman initiated a conversation with Patrolman McKenna concerning the missing shotgun. As Patrolman Gleckman later testified:

> A. At this point, I was talking back and forth with Patrolman McKenna stating that I frequent this area while on patrol and [that because a school for handicapped children is located nearby,] there's a lot of handicapped children running around in this area, and God forbid one of them might find a weapon with shells and they might hurt themselves.

Patrolman McKenna apparently shared his fellow officer's concern:

> A. I more or less concurred with him [Gleckman] that it was a safety factor and that we should, you know, continue to search for the weapon and try to find it.

* * *

The respondent then interrupted the conversation, stating that the officers should turn the car around so he could show them where the gun was located. At this point, Patrolman McKenna radioed back to Captain Leyden that they were returning to the scene of the arrest, and that the respondent would inform them of the location of the gun. At the time the respondent indicated that the officers should turn back, they had traveled no more than a mile, a trip encompassing only a few minutes.

The police vehicle then returned to the scene of the arrest where a search for the shotgun was in progress. There, Captain Leyden again advised the respondent of his *Miranda* rights. The respondent replied that he understood those rights but that he "wanted to get the gun out of the way because of the kids in the area in the school." The respondent then led the police to a nearby field, where he pointed out the shotgun under some rocks by the side of the road.

* * *

[After conviction on the basis of the shotgun evidence and statements made regarding the shotgun, having been denied relief by Rhode Island courts, Innis requested and was granted review by the U.S. Supreme Court.]

In the present case, the parties are in agreement that the respondent was fully informed of his *Miranda* rights and that he invoked his *Miranda* right to counsel when he told Captain Leyden that he wished to consult with a lawyer. It is also uncontested that the respondent was "in custody" while being transported to the police station.

The issue, therefore, is whether the respondent was "interrogated" by the police officers in violation of the respondent's undisputed right under *Miranda* to remain silent until he had consulted with a lawyer. In resolving this issue, we first define the term "interrogation" under *Miranda* before turning to a consideration of the facts of this case.

The starting point for defining "interrogation" in this context is, of course, the Court's *Miranda* opinion. There the Court observed that "[b]y custodial interrogation, we mean *questioning* initiated by law enforcement officers after a person has been taken into custody or otherwise deprived of his freedom of action in any significant way." (Emphasis added.) This passage and other references throughout the opinion to "questioning" might suggest that the *Miranda* rules were to apply only to those police interrogation practices that involve express questioning of a defendant while in custody. . . .

We do not, however, construe the *Miranda* opinion so narrowly. The concern of the Court in *Miranda* was that the "interrogation environment" created by the interplay of interrogation and custody would "subjugate the individual to the will of his examiner" and thereby undermine the privilege against compulsory self-incrimination. The police practices that evoked this concern included several that did not involve express questioning. For example, one of the practices discussed in *Miranda* was the use of line-ups in which a coached witness would pick the defendant as the perpetrator. This was designed to establish that the defendant was in fact guilty as a predicate for further interrogation. A variation on this theme discussed in *Miranda* was the so-called "reverse line-up" in which a defendant would be identified by coached witnesses as the perpetrator of a fictitious crime, with the object of inducing him to confess to the actual crime of which he was suspected in order to escape the false prosecution. The Court in *Miranda* also included in its survey of interrogation practices the use of psychological ploys, such as "posi[t]" "the guilt of the subject," to "minimize the moral seriousness of the offense," and "to cast blame on the victim or on society."

It is clear that these techniques of persuasion, no less than express questioning, were thought, in a custodial setting, to amount to interrogation. . . .

We conclude that the *Miranda* safeguards come into play whenever a person in custody is subjected to either express questioning or its functional equivalent. That is to say, the term "interrogation" under *Miranda* refers not only to express questioning, but also to any words or actions on the part of the police (other than those normally attendant to arrest and custody) that the police should know are reasonably likely to elicit an incriminating response from the suspect.

* * *

Turning to the facts of the present case, . . . it cannot be fairly concluded that the respondent was subjected to the "functional equivalent" of questioning. It cannot be said, in short, that Patrolmen Gleckman and McKenna should have known that their conversation was reasonably likely to elicit an incriminating response from the respondent. There is nothing in the record to suggest that the officers were aware that the respondent was peculiarly susceptible to an appeal to his conscience concerning the safety of handicapped children. Nor is there anything in the record to suggest that the police knew that the respondent was unusually disoriented or upset at the time of his arrest.

The case thus boils down to whether, in the context of a brief conversation, the officers should have known that the respondent would suddenly be moved to make a self-incriminating response. Given the fact that the entire conversation appears to have consisted of no more than a few offhand remarks, we cannot say that the officers should have known that it was reasonably likely that Innis would so respond. This is not a case where the police carried on a lengthy harangue in the presence of the suspect. Nor does the record support the respondent's contention that, under the circumstances, the officers' comments were particularly "evocative." It is our view, therefore, that the respondent was not subjected by the police to words or actions that the police should have known were reasonably likely to elicit an incriminating response from him.

* * *

For the reasons stated, the judgment of the Supreme Court of Rhode Island is vacated, and the case is remanded to that court for further proceedings not inconsistent with this opinion.

It is so ordered.

* * *

MR. JUSTICE MARSHALL, with whom MR. JUSTICE BRENNAN joins, dissenting.

I am substantially in agreement with the Court's definition of "interrogation" within the meaning of *Miranda v. Arizona,* (1966). In my view, the *Miranda* safeguards apply whenever police conduct is intended or likely to produce a response from a suspect in custody. As I read the Court's opinion, its definition of "interrogation" for *Miranda* purposes is equivalent, for practical purposes, to my formulation, since it contemplates that "where a police practice is designed to elicit an incriminating response from the accused, it is unlikely that the practice will not also be one which the police should have known was reasonably likely to have that effect.". . .

I am utterly at a loss, however, to understand how this objective standard as applied to the facts before us can rationally lead to the conclusion that there was no interrogation. . . .

One can scarcely imagine a stronger appeal to the conscience of a suspect—*any* suspect—that the assertion that if the weapon is not found an innocent person will be hurt or killed. And not just any innocent person, but an innocent child—a little girl—a helpless, handicapped little girl on her way to school. The notion that such an appeal could not be expected to have any effect unless the suspect were known to have some special interest in handicapped children verges on the ludicrous. . . .

I firmly believe that this case is simply an aberration, and that in future cases the Court will apply the standard adopted today in accordance with its plain meaning.

Mr. Justice Stevens, dissenting.

* * *

The Court holds that police conduct is not the "functional equivalent" of direct questioning unless the police should have known that what they were saying or doing was likely to elicit an incriminating response from the suspect. This holding represents a plain departure from the principles set forth in *Miranda.*

. . . To give full protection to a suspect's right to be free from any interrogation at all, the definition of "interrogation" must include any police statement or conduct that has the same purpose or effect as a direct question. Statements that appear to call for a response from the suspect, as well as those that are designed to do so, should be considered interrogation. By prohibiting only those relatively few statements or actions that a police officer should know are likely to elicit an incriminating response, the Court today accords a suspect considerably less protection. Indeed, since I suppose most suspects are unlikely to incriminate themselves even when questioned directly, this new definition will almost certainly exclude every statement that is not punctuated with a question mark from the concept of "interrogation."

. . . The Court's test creates an incentive for police to ignore a suspect's invocation of his rights in order to make continued attempts to extract information from him. If a suspect does not appear to be susceptible to a particular type of psychological pressure, the police are apparently free to exert that pressure on him despite his request for counsel, so long as they are careful not to punctuate their statements with question marks. And if, contrary to all reasonable expectations, the suspect makes an incriminating statement, that statement can be used against him at trial. The Court thus turns *Miranda*'s unequivocal rule against any interrogation at all into a trap in which unwary suspects may be caught by police deception.

* * *

Under my view of the correct standard, the judgment of the Rhode Island Supreme Court should be affirmed because the statements made within Innis' hearing were as likely to elicit a response as a direct question. However, even if I were to agree with the Court's much narrower standard, I would disagree with its disposition of this particular case because the Rhode Island courts should be given an opportunity to apply the new standard to the facts of this case.

QUESTIONS AND COMMENTS

1 Is *Brown v. Mississippi,* activist? On which dimensions? Explain your answer with reference to the case.

2 *Miranda* provides that defendants who do so voluntarily and intelligently may waive their "*Miranda* rights." How can the Court know in a particular case that these conditions have been met? If the suspect signs a waiver statement, how can the Court know that the signature was not coerced? Can you think of any sure-fire solution to this problem? Is it possible to give an "intelligent" waiver, or would it be unwise to waive one's rights anytime one is in custody? It may be suggested that confessions should be outlawed for use in criminal trials. Why do you think the Supreme Court has not adopted such a rule?

3 In *Miranda,* the Supreme Court seems to assume that interrogating officers will give all warnings and make a good-faith effort to see that defendants understand them. Further, it seems to assume that if the warnings are understood, criminal suspects will act rationally in their own best interests. These assumptions are violated on a fairly broad scale. See Project, "Interrogations in New Haven: The Impact of Miranda," 76 *Yale Law Journal* 1519 (1967); Griffiths and Ayres, "A Postscript to the Miranda Project: Interrogation of Draft Protesters," 77 *Yale Law Journal* 300 (1967); Medalie, Letz, and Alexander, "Custodial Police Interrogation in Our Nation's Capital: The Attempt to Implement Miranda," 66 *Michigan Law Review* 1347 (1968); Burger and Wettick, "Miranda in Pittsburgh—A Statistical Study," 29 *University of Pittsburgh Law Review* 1 (1967).

4 Given that the *Miranda* warnings are not found in the Constitution and are merely Court-made rules, could Congress constitutionally enact legislation permitting the states to dispense with the warnings in all circumstances? In certain circumstances? Explain.

5 The *Miranda* procedure was essentially in use by the FBI prior to the *Miranda* decision, though there is no evidence that this fact influenced Chief Justice Warren and his Court.

6 In *Miranda,* Warren says that "any evidence that an accused was . . . tricked, or cajoled into a waiver will . . . show that the defendant did not voluntarily waive his privilege." Does *Innis* meet this standard? Explain.

7 Can you think of a way in which the officers might have acquired the gun with Innis's help without violating his *Miranda* rights?

8 In *Estelle v. Smith* [451 U.S. 454 (1981)], *Miranda* rights were extended to sentencing procedures and questioning by a state psychiatrist.

9 In *Harris v. New York,* Chief Justice Burger concedes that some comments in the *Miranda* opinion bar using an "uncounseled statement for any purpose." Why, then, does he proceed to rule to the contrary? Why are these *Miranda* "comments" not controlling?

10 In *Innis,* what if the police officer's conversation had taken place in the station house? Same decision?

11 In *South Dakota v. Neville* [459 U.S. 553 (1981)], police officers stopped a man who had run a stop sign and asked him to submit to a blood alcohol test. The man replied: "I'm too drunk, I won't pass the test." A South Dakota statute permitted evidence of this nature to be admitted in court. Under Supreme Court rulings, is such evidence constitutionally permissible? Cite cases to support your answer.

Protection Against Double Jeopardy

Palko v. Connecticut (1937)

In addition to the self-incrimination clause, the Fifth Amendment says that for the same offense, no one may "be twice put in jeopardy of life or limb." This means essentially that one may not be tried twice for the same crime or on the same charge. However, one who appeals a conviction is said to waive this right. Thus, there are many instances in which one is tried and convicted, obtains a reversal on appeal, and then is tried again for the same crime, convicted, and sentenced.

In *Palko v. Connecticut,* the Court confronts the argument that the first eight amendments apply to both state and federal governments and that the double jeopardy provision of the Fifth Amendment is a limitation on Connecticut.

Palko v. Connecticut

302 U.S. 319; 58 S. Ct. 149; 82 L. Ed. 288 (1937)
Vote: 8–1

The facts are provided in the opinion excerpted below.

MR. JUSTICE CARDOZO delivered the opinion of the Court.

A statute of Connecticut permitting appeals in criminal cases to be taken by the state is challenged by appellant as an infringement of the Fourteenth Amendment of the Constitution of the United States. Whether the challenge should be upheld is now to be determined.

Appellant was indicted in Fairfield County, Connecticut, for the crime of murder in the first degree. A jury found him guilty of murder in the second degree, and he was sentenced to confinement in the state prison for life. Thereafter the State of Connecticut, with the permission of the judge presiding at the trial, gave notice of appeal to the Supreme Court of Errors. . . .

Upon such appeal, the Supreme Court of Errors reversed the judgment and ordered a new trial. It found that there had been error of law to the prejudice of the state (1) in excluding testimony as to a confession by defendant; (2) in excluding testimony upon cross-examination of defendant to impeach his credibility, and (3) in the instructions to the jury as to the difference between first and second degree murder.

Pursuant to the mandate of the Supreme Court of Errors, defendant was brought to trial again. Before a jury was impaneled and also at later stages of the case he made the objection that the effect of the new trial was to place him twice in jeopardy for the same offense, and in so doing to violate the Fourteenth Amendment of the Constitution of the United States. Upon the overruling of the objection the trial proceeded. The jury returned a verdict of murder in the first degree, and the court sentenced the defendant to the punishment of death. The Supreme Court of Errors affirmed the judgment of conviction. . . .

The case is here upon appeal.

1. The execution of the sentence will not deprive appellant of his life without the process of law assured to him by the Fourteenth Amendment of the Federal Constitution.

The argument for appellant is that whatever is forbidden by the Fifth Amendment is forbidden by the Fourteenth also. The Fifth Amendment, which is not directed to the states, but solely to the federal government, creates immunity from double jeopardy. No person shall be "subject for the same offense to be twice put in jeopardy of life or limb." The Fourteenth Amendment ordains, "nor shall any State deprive any person of life, liberty, or property, without due process of law." To retry a defendant, though under one indictment and only one, subjects him, it is said, to double jeopardy in violation of the Fifth Amendment, if the prosecution is one on behalf of the United States. From this the consequence is said to follow that there is a denial of life or liberty without due process of law, if the prosecution is one on behalf of the People of a State. Thirty-five years ago a like argument was made to this court in *Dreyer v. Illinois,* [1902], and was passed without consideration of its merits as unnecessary to a decision. The question is now here.

* * *

We have said that in appellant's view the Fourteenth Amendment is to be taken as embodying the prohibitions of the Fifth. His thesis is even broader. Whatever would be a violation of the original bill of rights (Amendments I to VIII) if done by the federal government is now equally unlawful by force of the Fourteenth Amendment if done by a state. There is no such general rule.

The Fifth Amendment provides, among other things, that no person shall be held to answer for a capital or otherwise infamous crime unless on presentment or indictment of a grand jury. This court has held that, in prosecutions by a state, presentment or indictment by a grand jury may give way to informations at the instance of a public officer. The Fifth Amendment provides also that no person shall be compelled in any criminal case to be a witness against himself. This court has said that, in prosecutions by a state, the exemption will fail if the state elects to end it.

The Sixth Amendment calls for a jury trial in criminal cases and the Seventh for a jury trial in civil cases at common law where the value in controversy shall exceed twenty dollars. This court has ruled that consistently with those amendments trial by jury may be modified by a state or abolished altogether. . . .

On the other hand, the due process clause of the Fourteenth Amendment may make it unlawful for a state to abridge by its statutes the freedom of speech which the First Amendment safeguards against encroachment by the Congress, or the like freedom of the press, or the free exercise of religion, or the right of peaceable assembly, without which speech would be unduly trammeled, or the right of one accused of crime to the benefit of counsel. In these and other situations immunities that are valid as against the federal government by force of the specific pledges of particular amendments have been found to be implicit in the concept of ordered liberty, and thus, through the Fourteenth Amendment, become valid as against the states.

The line of division may seem to be wavering and broken if there is a hasty catalogue of the cases on the one side and the other. Reflection and analysis will induce a different view. There emerges the perception of a rationalizing principle which gives to discrete instances a proper order and coherence. The right to trial by jury and the immunity from prosecution except as the result of an indictment may have value and importance. Even so, they are not of the very essence of a scheme of ordered liberty. To abolish them is not to violate a "principle of justice so rooted in the traditions and conscience of our people as to be ranked as fundamental." *Brown v. Mississippi,* [1936].

Few would be so narrow or provincial as to maintain that a fair and enlightened system of justice would be impossible without them. What is true of jury trials and indictments is true also, as the cases show, of the immunity from compulsory self-incrimination. *Twining v. New Jersey, supra.* This too might be lost, and justice still be done. Indeed, today as in the past there are students of our penal system who look upon the immunity as a mischief rather than a benefit, and who would limit its scope, or destroy it altogether. No doubt there would remain the need to give protection against torture, physical or mental. Justice, however, would not perish if the accused were subject to a duty to respond to orderly inquiry. The exclusion of these immunities and privileges from the privileges and immunities protected against the action of the states has not been arbitrary or casual. It has been dictated by a study and appreciation of the meaning, the essential implications, of liberty itself.

We reach a different plane of social and moral values when we pass to the privileges and immunities that have been taken over from the earlier articles of the federal bill of rights and brought within the Fourteenth Amendment by a process of absorption. These in their origin were effective against the federal government alone. If the Fourteenth Amendment has absorbed them, the process of absorption has had its source in the belief that neither liberty nor justice would exist if they were sacrificed. This is true, for illustration, of freedom of thought, and speech.

* * *

Our survey of the cases serves, we think, to justify the statement that the dividing line between them, if not unfaltering throughout its course, has been true for the most part to a unifying principle. On which side of the line the case made out by the appellant has appropriate location must be the next inquiry and the final one. Is that kind of double jeopardy to which the statute has subjected him a hardship so acute and shocking that our policy will not endure it? Does it violate those "fundamental principles of liberty and justice which lie at the base of all our civil and political institutions"? *Hebert v. Louisiana,* [1926]. The answer surely must be "no." What the answer would have to be if the state were permitted after a trial free from error to try the accused over again or to bring another case against him, we have no occasion to consider. We deal with the statute before us and no other. The state is not attempting to wear the accused out by a multitude of cases with accumulated trials. It asks no more than this, that the case against him shall go on until there shall be a trial free from the corrosion of substantial legal error.

This is not cruelty at all, nor even vexation in any immoderate degree. If the trial had been infected with error adverse to the accused, there might have been review at his instance, and as often as necessary to purge the vicious taint. . . .

There is here no seismic innovation. The edifice of justice stands, its symmetry, to many, greater than before.

2. The conviction of appellant is not in derogation of any privileges or immunities that belong to him as a citizen of the United States.

There is argument in his behalf that the privileges and immunities clause of the Fourteenth Amendment as well as the due process clause has been flouted by the judgment.

Maxwell v. Dow, supra, gives all the answer that is necessary.

The judgment is

Affirmed.

MR. JUSTICE BUTLER dissents.

QUESTIONS AND COMMENTS

1 *Palko v. Connecticut* was overruled in *Benton v. Maryland,* 395 U.S. 784 (1969).
2 In *Palko,* the Court finds that putting one twice in jeopardy of life or limb for the same offense is not so shocking as to "violate those fundamental principles of liberty and justice which lie at the base of all our civil and political institutions." Does this suggest that the Court's decision is activist or restrained? Explain.

Right to a Fair Trial

Chandler et al. v. Florida (1981)

It is now assumed that a criminal defendant has the right to a "fair trial" at the hands of the state. Such an assumption is based on the fact that, beginning in the 1920s, the Supreme Court incorporated a number of trial and pretrial rights from the Bill of Rights into the Fourteenth Amendment. It must be kept in mind, however, that the Fourteenth Amendment guarantees due process against the state, and that due process is broader than the provisions of the Bill of Rights incorporated into it. Thus, while one has the right to counsel, the right to a speedy trial, the right to suppress tainted evidence, and so on, the state must follow procedures that ensure that a defendant is not treated "unfairly," i.e., is given a "fair trial."

What is fair or unfair cannot always be specified in advance, for we cannot know in advance all the circumstances of the trial and the trial setting that may impinge on fairness. *Chandler v. Florida* is properly viewed as one case in which the fairness issue is raised—a case involving circumstances that could not have been known to the framers.

Chandler et al. v. Florida

449 U.S. 560; 101 S. Ct. 802; 66 L. Ed. 2d 16 (1981)
Vote: 8–0

Under a canon, 3A (7), promulgated by the Florida Supreme Court, controlled electronic media and still-photography coverage of judicial proceedings was permitted, Chandler and others were convicted in Florida courts on burglary and related charges. During one entire afternoon of the trial, a television camera was present and operating in the courtroom. Almost three minutes of the coverage was broadcast—all of which depicted the prosecution's side of the case.

The appellants' motion for a new trial argued that the television coverage denied them a fair and impartial trial. The Florida district court of appeals affirmed. Review was denied by the Florida Supreme Court but granted by the U.S. Supreme Court.

CHIEF JUSTICE BURGER delivered the opinion of the Court.

The question presented on this appeal is whether, consistent with constitutional guarantees, a state may provide for radio, television, and still photographic coverage of a criminal trial for public broadcast, notwithstanding the objection of the accused. . . .

Appellants rely chiefly on *Estes v. Texas,* (1965), and Chief Justice Warren's separate concurring opinion in that case. They argue that the televising of criminal trials is inherently a denial of due process, and they read *Estes* as announcing a *per se* constitutional rule to that effect.

* * *

If appellants' reading of *Estes* were correct, we would be obliged to apply that holding and reverse the judgment under review. . . . [After reviewing the six opinions written in that case, the Court concluded] . . . *Estes* is not to be read as announcing a constitutional rule barring still photographic, radio, and television coverage in all cases and under all circumstances. It does not stand as an absolute ban on state experimentation, with an evolving technology, which, in terms of modes of mass communication, was in its relative infancy in 1964, and is, even now, in a state of continuing change.

Since we are satisfied that *Estes* did not announce a constitutional rule that all photographic or broadcast coverage of criminal trials is inherently a denial of due process, we turn to consideration, as a matter of first impression, of the appellants' suggestions that we now promulgate such a *per se* rule.

Any criminal case that generates a great deal of publicity presents some risks that the publicity may compromise the right of the defendant to a fair trial. Trial courts must be especially vigilant to guard against any impairment of the defendant's right to a verdict based solely upon the evidence and the relevant law. Over the years, courts have developed a range of curative devices to prevent publicity about a trial from infecting jury deliberations. See *e. g., Nebraska Press Assn. v. Stuart,* (1976).

An absolute constitutional ban on broadcast coverage of trials cannot be justified simply because there is a danger that, in some cases, prejudicial broadcast accounts of pretrial and trial events may impair the ability of jurors to decide the issue of guilt or innocence uninfluenced by extraneous matter. The risk of juror prejudice in some cases does not justify an absolute ban on news coverage of trials by the printed media; so also the risk of such prejudice does not warrant an absolute constitutional ban on all broadcast coverage. A case attracts a high level of public attention because of its intrinsic interest to the public and the manner of reporting the event. The risk of juror prejudice is present in any publication of a trial, but the appropriate safeguard against such prejudice is the defendant's right to demonstrate that the media's coverage of his case—be it printed or broadcast—compromised the ability of the particular jury that heard the case to adjudicate fairly. . . .

In confronting the difficult and sensitive question of the potential psychological prejudice associated with broadcast coverage of trials, we have been aided by *amici* briefs submitted by various state officers involved in law enforcement, the Conference of Chief Justices, and the Attorneys General of 17 States in support of continuing experimentation such as that embarked upon by Florida, the American College of Trial Lawyers, and various members of the defense bar representing essentially the views expressed by the concurring Justices in *Estes.*

Not unimportant to the position asserted by Florida and other states is the change in television technology since 1962, when Estes was tried. It is urged, and some empirical data are presented, that many of the negative factors found in *Estes*—cumbersome equipment, cables, distracting lighting, numerous camera technicians—are less substantial factors today than they were at that time.

It is also significant that safeguards have been built into the experimental programs in state courts, and into the Florida program, to avoid some of the most egregious problems envisioned by the six opinions in the *Estes* case. Florida admonishes its courts to take special pains to protect certain witnesses—for example, children, victims of sex crimes, some informants, and even the very timid witness or party—from the glare of publicity and the tensions of being "on camera."

The Florida guidelines place on trial judges positive obligations to be on guard to protect the fundamental right of the accused to a fair trial.

* * *

Inherent in electronic coverage of a trial is the risk that the very awareness by the accused of the coverage and the contemplated broadcast may adversely affect the conduct of the participants and the fairness of the trial, yet leave no evidence of how the conduct or the trial's fairness was affected. Given this danger, it is significant that Florida requires that objections of the accused to coverage be heard and considered on the record by the trial court.

* * *

To say that the appellants have not demonstrated that broadcast coverage is inherently a denial of due process is not to say that the appellants were in fact accorded all of the protections of due process in their trial. As noted earlier, a defendant has the right on review to show that the media's coverage of his case—printed or broadcast—compromised the ability of the jury to judge him fairly. Alternatively, a defendant might show that broadcast coverage of his particular case had an adverse impact on the trial participants sufficient to constitute a denial of due process. Neither showing was made in this case.

To demonstrate prejudice in a specific case a defendant must show something more than juror awareness that the trial is such as to attract the attention of broadcasters. No doubt the very presence of a camera in the courtroom made the jurors aware that the trial was thought to be of sufficient interest to the public to warrant coverage. Jurors, forbidden to watch all broadcasts, would have had no way of knowing that only fleeting seconds of the proceeding would be reproduced. But the appellants have not attempted to show with any specificity that the presence of cameras impaired the ability of the jurors to decide the case on only the evidence before them or that their trial was affected adversely by the impact on any of the participants of the presence of cameras and the prospect of broadcast.

* * *

It is not necessary either to ignore or to discount the potential danger to the fairness of a trial in a particular case in order to conclude that Florida may permit the electronic media to cover trials in its state courts. Dangers lurk in this, as in most experiments, but unless we were to conclude that television coverage under all conditions is prohibited by the Constitution, the states must be free to experiment. We are not empowered by the Constitution to oversee or harness state procedural experimentation; only when the state action infringes fundamental guarantees are we authorized to intervene. We must assume state courts will be alert to any factors that impair the fundamental rights of the accused.

The Florida program is inherently evolutional in nature; the initial project has provided guidance for the new canons which can be changed at will, and application of which is subject to control by the trial judge. The risk of prejudice to particular defendants is ever present and must be examined carefully as cases arise. Nothing of the "Roman circus" or "Yankee Stadium" atmosphere, as in *Estes,* prevailed here, however, nor have appellants attempted to show that the unsequestered jury was exposed to "sensational" coverage, in the sense of *Estes* or of *Sheppard v. Maxwell,* (1966). Absent a showing of prejudice of constitutional dimensions to these defendants, there is no reason for this Court either to endorse or to invalidate Florida's experiment.

In this setting, because this Court has no supervisory authority over state courts, our review is confined to whether there is a constitutional violation. We hold that the Constitution does not prohibit a state from experimenting with the program authorized by revised Canon 3A(7).

Affirmed.

Justice Stevens took no part in the decision of this case.

Justice Stewart, concurring in the result.

Although concurring in the judgment, I cannot join the opinion of the Court because I do not think the convictions in this case can be affirmed without overruling *Estes v. Texas,* . . .

I believe now, as I believed in dissent then, that *Estes* announced a *per se* rule that the Fourteenth Amendment "prohibits all television cameras from a state courtroom whenever a criminal trial is in progress." Accordingly, rather than join what seems to me a wholly unsuccessful effort to distinguish that decision, I would now flatly overrule it. . . .

The constitutional violation perceived by the *Estes* Court did not, therefore, stem from physical disruption that might one day disappear with technological advances in television equipment. The violation inhered, rather, in the hypothesis that the mere presence of cameras and recording devices might have an effect on the trial participants prejudicial to the accused. . . .

It can accurately be asserted that television technology has advanced in the past 15 years, and that Americans are now much more familiar with that medium of communication. It does not follow, however, that the "subtle capacities for serious mischief" are today diminished, or that the "imponderables of the trial arena" are now less elusive. . . .

The Court in *Estes* found the admittedly unobtrusive presence of television cameras in a criminal trial to be inherently prejudicial, and thus violative of due process of law. Today the Court reaches precisely the opposite conclusion. I have no great trouble in agreeing with the Court today, but I would acknowledge our square departure from precedent.

JUSTICE WHITE, concurring in the judgment.

* * *

Whether the decision in *Estes* is read broadly or narrowly, I agree with JUSTICE STEWART that it should be overruled. I was in dissent in that case, and I remain unwilling to assume or conclude without more proof than has been marshaled to date that televising criminal trials is inherently prejudicial even when carried out under properly controlled conditions. A defendant should, of course, have ample opportunity to convince a judge that televising his trial would be unfair to him, and the judge should have the authority to exclude cameras from all or part of the criminal trial. But absent some showing of prejudice to the defense, I remain convinced that a conviction obtained in a state court should not be overturned simply because a trial judge refused to exclude television cameras and all or part of the trial was televised to the public.

* * *

QUESTIONS AND COMMENTS

1 Under *Chandler,* would one have a right to have one's appeal hearing in the Supreme Court televised if the televising was done with decorum? Explain your answer.
2 The opinion of Chief Justice Burger says that "We must assume state courts will be alert to any factors that impair the fundamental rights of the accused." How realistic is this statement? Explain your answer.

Jury Trial

Right to in State Courts

Duncan v. Louisiana (1968)

The trial by petit jury in England began in the reign of Henry III. The jury became a trier of evidence in the reign of Henry VI, and by the seventeenth century was viewed as a basic protection for those accused of committing a crime. In this country, the constitutions of all the original states included the right, as do Article III and the Sixth Amendment to the United States Constitution. Such provisions seek to protect individuals against governmental oppression and corruption—against the governmental use of false charges to eliminate or punish critics of the regime, political opponents, insular minorities, and others who might be out of governmental favor at some point in time.

The right is sparsely described in the Constitution and has gained its current meaning through Supreme Court interpretation. Basically, the jury must be drawn from a cross-section of the community in such a way as to be representative and impartial. At the least, this means that blacks,[9] Mexican-Americans,[10] and women[11] cannot be systematically excluded from petit juries solely on the basis of race or sex. This does not mean that every petit jury must include blacks, Mexican-Americans, or women if they exist in the community. But such parties may not be denied the opportunity to be chosen for jury service equally with others in the community.

The right to a jury trial is available only in trials for "serious offenses," which the Court has defined as offenses carrying a possible punishment of six months or longer.[12] The right to a public trial, while stated flatly in the Sixth Amendment, is not absolute. A judge, who thinks doing so is necessary to ensure a fair trial for the defendant, may close a criminal trial to the public. The argument here is that the right to a public trial is a right of the defendant and that it is reasonable to impinge upon one right to ensure a more important protection. We have encountered discussion of such questions earlier in the free press cases, *Gannett v. Pasquale* and *Richmond Newspapers v. Virginia.*

A major question not touched on in these introductory remarks is whether the Sixth Amendment right to jury trial applies against the states. The Court confronts that question in *Duncan v. Louisiana.*

Duncan v. Louisiana

391 U.S. 145; 88 S. Ct. 1444; 20 L. Ed. 2d 491 (1968)
Vote 7–2

The facts are presented in the opinion below.

MR. JUSTICE WHITE delivered the opinion of the Court.

Appellant, Gary Duncan, was convicted of simple battery in the Twenty-fifth Judicial District Court of Louisiana. Under Louisiana law simple battery is a misdemeanor, punishable by a maximum of two years' imprisonment and a $300 fine. Appellant sought trial by jury, but because the Louisiana Constitution grants jury trials only in cases in which capital punishment or imprisonment at hard labor may be imposed, the trial judge denied the request. Appellant was convicted and sentenced to serve 60 days in the parish prison and pay a fine of $150. Appellant sought review in the Supreme Court of Louisiana, asserting that the denial of jury trial violated rights guaranteed to him by the United States Constitution. The Supreme Court, finding "[n]o error of law in the ruling complained of," denied appellant a writ of certiorari. Pursuant to 28 U.S.C. § 1257 (2) appellant sought review in this Court, alleging that the Sixth and Fourteenth Amendments to the United States Constitution secure the right to jury trial in state criminal prosecutions where a sentence as long as two years may be imposed. We noted probable jurisdiction, and set the case for oral argument.

Appellant was 19 years of age when tried. While driving on Highway 23 in Plaquemines Parish on October 18, 1966, he saw two younger cousins engaged in a conversation by the side of the road with four white boys. Knowing his cousins, Negroes who had recently transferred to a formerly all-white high school, had reported the occurrence of racial incidents at the school, Duncan stopped the car, got out, and approached the six boys. At trial the white boys and a white onlooker testified, as did appellant and his cousins. The testimony was in dispute on many points, but the witnesses agreed that appellant and the white boys spoke to each other, that appellant encouraged his cousins to break off the encounter and enter his car, and that appellant was about to enter the car himself for the purpose of driving away with his cousins. The whites testified that just before getting in the car appellant slapped Herman Landry, one of the white boys, on the elbow. The Negroes testified that appellant had not slapped Landry, but had merely touched him. The trial judge concluded that the State had proved beyond a reasonable doubt that Duncan had committed simple battery, and found him guilty.

The Fourteenth Amendment denies the States the power to "deprive any person of life, liberty, or property, without due process of law." In resolving conflicting claims concerning the meaning of this spacious language, the Court has looked increasingly to the Bill of Rights for guidance; many of the rights guaranteed by the first eight Amendments to the Constitution have been held to be protected against state action by the Due Process Clause of the Fourteenth Amendment. That clause now protects the right to compensation for property taken by the State;* the rights of speech, press, and religion covered by the First Amendment;† the Fourth Amendment rights to be free from unreasonable searches and seizures and to have excluded from criminal trials any evidence illegally seized;‡ the right guaranteed by the Fifth Amendment to be free of compelled self-incrimination;¶ and the Sixth Amendment rights to counsel,§ to a speedy** and public†† trial, to confrontation of opposing witnesses,‡‡ and to compulsory process for obtaining witnesses.§§

The test for determining whether a right extended by the Fifth and Sixth Amendments with respect to federal criminal proceedings is also protected against state action by the Fourteenth Amendment has been phrased in a variety of ways in the opinions of this Court. The question has been asked whether a right is among those " 'fundamental principles of liberty and justice which lie at the base of all our civil and political institutions,' " *Powell v. Alabama*, (1932); whether it is "basic in our system of jurisprudence," *In re Oliver*, (1948); and whether it is "a fundamental right, essential to a fair trial," *Gideon v. Wainwright*, (1963); *Malloy v. Hogan*, (1964); *Pointer v. Texas*, (1965). The claim before us is that the right to trial by jury guaranteed by the Sixth Amendment meets these tests. The position of Louisiana, on the other hand, is that the Constitution imposes upon the States no duty to give a jury trial in any criminal case, regardless of the seriousness of the crime or the size of the punishment which may be imposed. Because we believe that trial by jury in criminal cases is fundamental to the American scheme of justice, we hold that the Fourteenth Amendment guarantees a right of jury trial in all criminal cases which—were they to be tried in a federal court—would come within the Sixth Amendment's guarantee. Since we consider the appeal before us to be such a case, we hold that the Constitution was violated when appellant's demand for jury trial was refused.

The history of trial by jury in criminal cases has been frequently told. It is sufficient for present purposes to say that by the time our Constitution was written, jury trial in criminal cases had been in existence in England for several centuries and carried impressive credentials traced by many to Magna Carta.

Chicago, B. & Q. R. Co. v. Chicago, 166 U.S. 226 (1897).
†See, *e.g., Fiske v. Kansas*, 274 U.S. 380 (1927).
‡See *Mapp v. Ohio*, 367 U.S. 643 (1961).
§*Malloy v. Hogan*, 378 U.S. 1 (1964).
¶*Gideon v. Wainwright*, 372 U.S. 335 (1963).
**Klopfer v. North Carolina*, 386 U.S. 213 (1967).
††*In re Oliver*, 333 U.S. 257 (1948).
‡‡*Pointer v. Texas*, 380 U.S. 400 (1965).
§§*Washington v. Texas*, 388 U.S. 14 (1967).

Its preservation and proper operation as a protection against arbitrary rule were among the major objectives of the revolutionary settlement which was expressed in the Declaration and Bill of Rights of 1689. . . .

The constitutions adopted by the original States guaranteed jury trial. Also, the constitution of every State entering the Union thereafter in one form or another protected the right to jury trial in criminal cases.

Even such skeletal history is impressive support for considering the right to jury trial in criminal cases to be fundamental to our system of justice, an importance frequently recognized in the opinions of this Court.

* * *

Jury trial continues to receive strong support. The laws of every State guarantee a right to jury trial in serious criminal cases; no State has dispensed with it; nor are there significant movements underway to do so. Indeed, the three most recent state constitutional revisions, in Maryland, Michigan, and New York, carefully preserved the right of the accused to have the judgment of a jury when tried for a serious crime.

We are aware of prior cases in this Court in which the prevailing opinion contains statements contrary to our holding today that the right to jury trial in serious criminal cases is a fundamental right and hence must be recognized by the States as part of their obligation to extend due process of law to all persons within their jurisdiction. Louisiana relies especially on *Maxwell v. Dow,* (1900); *Palko v. Connecticut,* (1937); and *Snyder v. Massachusetts,* (1934). None of these cases, however, dealt with a State which had purported to dispense entirely with a jury trial in serious criminal cases.

* * *

The State of Louisiana urges that holding that the Fourteenth Amendment assures a right to jury trial will cast doubt on the integrity of every trial conducted without a jury. Plainly, this is not the import of our holding. Our conclusion is that in the American States, as in the federal judicial system, a general grant of jury trial for serious offenses is a fundamental right, essential for preventing miscarriages of justice and for assuring that fair trials are provided for all defendants.

Louisiana's final contention is that even if it must grant jury trials in serious criminal cases, the conviction before us is valid and constitutional because here the petitioner was tried for simple battery and was sentenced to only 60 days in the parish prison. We are not persuaded. It is doubtless true that there is a category of petty crimes or offenses which is not subject to the Sixth Amendment jury trial provision and should not be subject to the Fourteenth Amendment jury trial requirement here applied to the States. Crimes carrying possible penalties up to six months do not require a jury trial if they otherwise qualify as petty offenses, *Cheff v. Schnackenberg,* (1966). But the penalty autho-rized for a particular crime is of major relevance in determining whether it is serious or not and may in itself, if severe enough, subject the trial to the man-dates of the Sixth Amendment.

In the case before us the Legislature of Louisiana has made simple battery a criminal offense punishable by imprisonment for up to two years and a fine. The question, then, is whether a crime carrying such a penalty is an offense which Louisiana may insist on trying without a jury.

We think not. . . .

In determining whether the length of the authorized prison term or the seri-ousness of other punishment is enough in itself to require a jury trial, we are counseled by *District of Columbia v. Clawans,* [1936], to refer to objective cri-teria, chiefly the existing laws and practices in the Nation. In the federal sys-tem, petty offenses are defined as those punishable by no more than six months in prison and a $500 fine. In 49 of the 50 States crimes subject to trial without a jury, which occasionally include simple battery, are punishable by no more than one year in jail. Moreover, in the late 18th century in America crimes triable without a jury were for the most part punishable by no more than a six-month prison term, although there appear to have been exceptions to this rule. We need not, however, settle in this case the exact location of the line between petty offenses and serious crimes. It is sufficient for our purposes to hold that a crime punishable by two years in prison is, based on past and contemporary standards in this country, a serious crime and not a petty offense. Conse-quently, appellant was entitled to a jury trial and it was error to deny it.

The judgment below is reversed and the case is remanded for proceedings not inconsistent with this opinion.

* * *

MR. JUSTICE HARLAN, whom MR. JUSTICE STEWART joins, dissenting.

Every American jurisdiction provides for trial by jury in criminal cases. The question before us is not whether jury trial is an ancient institution, which it is; nor whether it plays a significant role in the administration of criminal jus-tice, which it does; nor whether it will endure, which it shall. The question in this case is whether the State of Louisiana, which provides trial by jury for all felonies, is prohibited by the Constitution from trying charges of simple battery to the court alone. In my view, the answer to that question, mandated alike by our constitutional history and by the longer history of trial by jury, is clearly "no."

* * *

The Court's approach to this case is an uneasy and illogical compromise among the views of various Justices on how the Due Process Clause should be interpreted. The Court does not say that those who framed the Fourteenth

Amendment intended to make the Sixth Amendment applicable to the States. And the Court concedes that it finds nothing unfair about the procedure by which the present appellant was tried. Nevertheless, the Court reverses his conviction; it holds, for some reason not apparent to me, that the Due Process Clause incorporates the particular clause of the Sixth Amendment that requires trial by jury in federal criminal cases—including, as I read its opinion, the sometimes trivial accompanying baggage of judicial interpretation in federal contexts. I have raised my voice many times before against the Court's continuing undiscriminating insistence upon fastening on the States federal notions of criminal justice, and I must do so again in this instance. With all respect, the Court's approach and its reading of history are altogether topsy-turvy.

I believe I am correct in saying that every member of the Court for at least the last 135 years has agreed that our Founders did not consider the requirements of the Bill of Rights so fundamental that they should operate directly against the States. They were wont to believe rather that the security of liberty in America rested primarily upon the dispersion of governmental power across a federal system. The Bill of Rights was considered unnecessary by some but insisted upon by others in order to curb the possibility of abuse of power by the strong central government they were creating.

* * *

A few members of the Court have taken the position that the intention of those who drafted the first section of the Fourteenth Amendment was simply, and exclusively, to make the provisions of the first eight Amendments applicable to state action. This view has never been accepted by this Court. In my view, often expressed elsewhere, the first section of the Fourteenth Amendment was meant neither to incorporate, nor to be limited to, the specific guarantees of the first eight Amendments. The overwhelming historical evidence marshalled by Professor Fairman demonstrates, to me conclusively, that the Congressmen and state legislators who wrote, debated, and ratified the Fourteenth Amendment did not think they were "incorporating" the Bill of Rights and constitutional straitjacket with respect to their own development in the administration of criminal or civil law.

Although I therefore fundamentally disagree with the total incorporation view of the Fourteenth Amendment, it seems to me that such a position does at least have the virtue, lacking in the Court's selective incorporation approach, of internal consistency; we look to the Bill of Rights, word for word, clause for clause, precedent for precedent because, it is said, the men who wrote the Amendment wanted it that way. For those who do not accept this "history," a different source of "intermediate premises" must be found. The Bill of Rights is not necessarily irrelevant to the search for guidance in interpreting the Fourteenth Amendment, but the reason for and the nature of its relevance must be articulated.

* * *

Today's Court still remains unwilling to accept the total incorporationists' view of the history of the Fourteenth Amendment. This, if accepted, would afford a cogent reason for applying the Sixth Amendment to the States. The Court is also, apparently, unwilling to face the task of determining whether denial of trial by jury in the situation before us, or in other situations, is fundamentally unfair. Consequently, the Court has compromised on the ease of the incorporationist position, without its internal logic. It has simply assumed that the question before us is whether the Jury Trial Clause of the Sixth Amendment should be incorporated into the Fourteenth, jot-for-jot and case-for-case, or ignored. Then the Court merely declares that the clause in question is "in" rather than "out.". . .

Even if I could agree that the question before us is whether Sixth Amendment jury trial is totally "in" or totally "out," I can find in the Court's opinion no real reasons for concluding that it should be "in." The basis for differentiating among clauses in the Bill of Rights cannot be that only some clauses are in the Bill of Rights, or that only some are old and much praised, or that only some have played an important role in the development of federal law. These things are true of all. The Court says that some clauses are more "fundamental" than others, but it turns out to be using this word in a sense that would have astonished Mr. Justice Cardozo and which, in addition, is of no help. The word does not mean "analytically critical to procedural fairness" for no real analysis of the role of the jury in making procedures fair is even attempted. Instead, the word turns out to mean "old," "much praised," and "found in the Bill of Rights." The definition of "fundamental" thus turns out to be circular.

* * *

This Court, other courts, and the political process are available to correct any experiments in criminal procedure that prove fundamentally unfair to defendants. That is not what is being done today; instead, and quite without reason, the Court has chosen to impose upon every State one means of trying criminal cases; it is a good means, but it is not the only fair means, and it is not demonstrably better than the alternative States might devise.

I would affirm the judgment of the Supreme Court of Louisiana.

QUESTIONS AND COMMENTS

1 Justice Harlan, in dissent, says, regarding the inclusion of the Sixth Amendment in the Fourteenth: "I can find in the Court's opinion no real reasons for concluding that it should be 'in.'" Can you find any? Explain.
2 The majority opinion observes that "The laws of every State guarantee a right to jury trial in serious criminal cases." How is that fact relevant to determining the constitutional question in this case?

Jury Size

Ballew v. Georgia (1978)

Once the Court decided that the Sixth Amendment right to jury trial was applicable against the states, it became germane to ask just what that right involved. Earlier Court decisions had delineated some answers to this question, but the question of the required size of the jury in a criminal case had not been addressed for many years. In 1898, the Court decided that a petit jury meant a jury of twelve persons.[13] But after *Duncan v. Louisiana,* the question became more pressing. Upon reexamination in *Williams v. Florida,*[14] the Court decided that the number twelve was a historical accident and that states were not required by the Sixth Amendment to provide juries of exactly that size. At the same time, the Court did not specify what size jury would be appropriate. In *Williams,* it held that a jury of six was permissible. One could assume, therefore, that any number greater than five would be constitutional. The Court reserved judgment on jury trial by less than six persons. In *Ballew v. Georgia,* that question is finally confronted.

Ballew v. Georgia

435 U.S. 223; 98 S. Ct. 1029; 55 L. Ed. 2d 234 (1978)
Vote: Unanimous

The facts are given in the opinion below.

MR. JUSTICE BLACKMUN announced the judgment of the Court and delivered an opinion in which MR. JUSTICE STEVENS joined.

* * *

In November 1973 petitioner Claude Davis Ballew was the manager of the Paris Adult Theatre at 320 Peachtree Street, Atlanta, Ga. On November 9 two investigators from the Fulton County Solicitor General's office viewed at the theater a motion picture film entitled "Behind the Green Door." After they had seen the film, they obtained a warrant for its seizure, returned to the theater, viewed the film once again, and seized it. Petitioner and a cashier were arrested. Investigators returned to the theater on November 26, viewed the film in its entirety, secured still another warrant, and on November 27 once again viewed the motion picture and seized a second copy of the film.

On September 14, 1974, petitioner was charged in a two-count misdemeanor accusation with distributing obscene materials in violation of Georgia Code Section 26-2101 in that the said accused did, knowing the obscene nature thereof, exhibit a motion picture film entitled 'Behind the Green Door' that contained obscene and indecent scenes. . . .

Petitioner was brought to trial in the Criminal Court of Fulton County. After a jury of 5 persons had been selected and sworn, petitioner moved that the court impanel a jury of 12 persons. That court, however, tried its misdemeanor cases before juries of five persons pursuant to Ga. Const. Art. 6. § 16. . . . Petitioner contended that for an obscenity trial, a jury of only five was constitutionally inadequate to assess the contemporary standards of the community. He also argued that the Sixth and Fourteenth Amendments required a jury of at least six members in criminal cases.

The motion for a 12-person jury was overruled, and the trial went on to its conclusion before the 5-person jury that had been impaneled. At the conclusion of the trial, the jury deliberated for 38 minutes and returned a verdict of guilty on both counts of the accusation.

* * *

[After Georgia courts denied relief, Ballew brings his case here.]

In his petition for certiorari . . . petitioner raised three issues: the unconstitutionality of the five-person jury; the constitutional sufficiency of the jury instructions on scienter and constructive, rather than actual, knowledge of the contents of the film; and obscenity *vel non.* We granted certiorari. Because we now hold that the five-member jury does not satisfy the jury trial guarantee of the Sixth Amendment, as applied to the States through the Fourteenth, we do not reach the other issues.

* * *

In *Williams v. Florida,* [1970], the Court reaffirmed that the "purpose of the jury trial, as we noted in *Duncan,* is to prevent oppression by the Government. 'Providing an accused with the right to be tried by a jury of his peers gave him an inestimable safeguard against the corrupt or overzealous prosecutor and against the compliant, biased, or eccentric judge.' *Duncan v. Louisiana,* [1968]. This purpose is attained by the participation of the community in determinations of guilt and by the application of the common sense of laymen who, as jurors, consider the case.

* * *

When the Court in *Williams* permitted the reduction in jury size—or, to put it another way, when it held that a jury of six was not unconstitutional—it expressly reserved ruling on the issue whether a number smaller than six passed constitutional scrutiny.

The Court refused to speculate when this so-called "slippery slope" would become too steep. We face now, however, the two-fold question whether a further reduction in the size of the state criminal trial jury does make the grade too dangerous, that is, whether it inhibits the functioning of the jury as an institution to a significant degree, and, if so, whether any state interest counterbalances and justifies the disruption so as to preserve its constitutionality.

* * *

... Recent empirical data suggest that progressively smaller juries are less likely to foster effective group deliberations. At some point, this decline leads to inaccurate fact-finding and incorrect application of the common sense of the community to the facts. Generally, a positive correlation exists between group size and the quality of both group performance and group productivity. A variety of explanations have been offered for this conclusion. Several are particularly applicable in the jury setting. The smaller the group, the less likely are members to make critical contributions necessary for the solution of a given problem. Because most juries are not permitted to take notes, ... memory is important for accurate jury deliberations. As juries decrease in size, then, they are less likely to have members who remember each of the important pieces of evidence or argument. Furthermore, the smaller the group, the less likely it is to overcome the biases of its members to obtain an accurate result. When individual and group decisionmaking were compared, it was seen that groups performed better because prejudices of individuals were frequently counterbalanced, and objectivity resulted. Groups also exhibited increased motivation and self-criticism. All these advantages, except, perhaps, self-motivation, tend to diminish as the size of the group diminishes. ... Statistical studies suggest that the risk of convicting an innocent person ... rises as the size of the jury diminishes. Because the risk of not convicting a guilty person ... increases with the size of the panel, an optimal jury size can be selected as a function of the interaction between the two risks. ...

Another doubt about progressively smaller juries arises from the increasing inconsistency that results from the decreases.

* * *

Third, the data suggest that the verdicts of jury deliberation in criminal cases will vary as juries become smaller, and that the variance amounts to an imbalance to the detriment of one side, the defense. ...

Fourth, what has just been said about the presence of minority viewpoint as juries decrease in size foretells problems not only for jury decisionmaking, but also for the representation of minority groups in the community. The Court repeatedly has held that meaningful community participation cannot be attained with the exclusion of minorities or other identifiable groups from jury service.

* * *

Fifth, several authors have identified in jury research methodological problems tending to mask differences in the operation of smaller and larger juries. For example, because the judicial system handles so many clear cases, decisionmakers will reach similar results through similar analyses most of the time. One study concluded that smaller and larger juries could disagree in their verdicts in no more than 14% of the cases. Disparities, therefore, appear in only small percentages. Nationwide, however, these small percentages will represent a large number of cases. And it is with respect to those cases that the jury trial right has its greatest value. When the case is close, and the guilt or innocence of the defendant is not readily apparent, a properly functioning jury system will insure evaluation by the sense of the community and will also tend to insure accurate factfinding.

* * *

While we adhere to, and reaffirm our holding in *Williams v. Florida*, ... studies, ... made since *Williams* was decided in 1970, lead us to conclude that the purpose and functioning of the jury in a criminal trial is seriously impaired, and to a constitutional degree, by a reduction in size to below six members. We readily admit that we do not pretend to discern a clear line between six members and five. But the assembled data raise substantial doubt about the reliability and appropriate representation of panels smaller than six. Because of the fundamental importance of the jury trial to the American system of criminal justice, any further reduction that promotes inaccurate and possibly biased decisionmaking, that causes untoward differences in verdicts, and that prevents juries from truly representing their communities, attains constitutional significance.

Georgia here presents no persuasive argument that a reduction to five does not offend important Sixth Amendment interests. First, its reliance on *Johnson v. Louisiana,* (1972), for the proposition that the Court previously has approved the five-person jury is misplaced. In *Johnson* the petitioner challenged the Louisiana statute that permitted felony convictions on less-than-unanimous verdicts. The prosecution had to garner only nine votes of the 12-member jury to convict in a felony trial. The Court held that the statute did not violate the due process guarantee by diluting the reasonable-doubt standard. The only discussion of the five-person panels, which heard less serious offenses, was with respect to the petitioner's equal protection challenge. He contended that requiring only nine members of a 12-person panel to convict in a felony case was a deprival of equal protection when a unanimous verdict was required from the 5-member panel used in a misdemeanor trial. The Court held merely that the classification was not invidious. Because the issue of the constitutionality of the five-member jury was not then before the Court, it did not rule upon it.

Second, Georgia argues that its use of five-member juries does not violate the Sixth and Fourteenth Amendments because they are used only in misdemeanor cases. If six persons may constitutionally assess the felony charge in *Williams,* the State reasons, five persons should be a constitutionally adequate number for a misdemeanor trial. The problem with this argument is that the purpose and functions of the jury do not vary significantly with the importance of the crime. In *Baldwin v. New York,* (1970), the Court held that the right to a jury trial attached in both felony and misdemeanor cases. Only in cases concerning truly petty crimes, where the deprivation of liberty was minimal, did the defendant have no constitutional right to trial by jury. In the present case the possible deprivation of liberty is substantial. . . .

Third, the retention by Georgia of the unanimity requirement does not solve the Sixth and Fourteenth Amendment problem. Our concern has to do with the ability of the smaller group to perform the functions mandated by the Amendments. That a five-person jury may return a unanimous decision does not speak to the questions whether the group engaged in meaningful deliberation, could remember all the important facts and arguments, and truly represented the sense of the entire community. Despite the presence of the unanimity requirement, then, we cannot conclude that "the interest of the defendant in having the judgment of his peers interposed between himself and the officers of the State who prosecute and judge him is equally well served" by the five-person panel.

Fourth, Georgia submits that the five-person jury adequately represents the community because there is no arbitrary exclusion of any particular class. We agree that it has not been demonstrated that the Georgia system violates the Equal Protection Clause by discriminating on the basis of race or some other improper classification.

But [there is] substantial doubt about the ability of juries truly to represent the community as membership decreases below six. If the smaller and smaller juries will lack consistency, as the cited studies suggest, then the sense of the community will not be applied equally in like cases. Not only is the representation of racial minorities threatened in such circumstances, but also majority attitude or various minority positions may be misconstrued or misapplied by the smaller groups. Even though the facts of this case would not establish a jury discrimination claim under the Equal Protection Clause, the question of representation does constitute one factor of several that, when combined, create a problem of constitutional significance under the Sixth and Fourteenth Amendments.

* * *

With the reduction in the number of jurors below six creating a substantial threat to Sixth and Fourteenth Amendment guarantees, we must consider whether any interest of the State justifies the reduction. We find no significant state advantage in reducing the number of jurors from six to five.

The States utilize juries of less than 12 primarily for administrative reasons. Savings in court time and in financial costs are claimed to justify the reductions. The financial benefits of the reduction from 12 to 6 are substantial; this is mainly because fewer jurors draw daily allowances as they hear cases. On the other hand, the asserted saving in judicial time is not so clear. [One] ... study found little reduction in the time for *voir dire* with the six-person jury because many questions were directed at the veniremen as a group. Total trial time did not diminish, and court delays and backlogs improved very little. The point that is to be made, of course, is that a reduction in size from six to five or four or even three would save the States little. They could reduce slightly the daily allowances, but with a reduction from six to five the saving would be minimal. If little time is gained by the reduction from 12 to 6, less will be gained with a reduction from 6 to 5. Perhaps this explains why only two States, Georgia and Virginia, have reduced the size of juries in certain nonpetty criminal cases to five. Other States appear content with six members or more. In short, the State has offered little or no justification for its reduction to five members.

Petitioner, therefore, has established that his trial on criminal charges before a five-member jury deprived him of the right to trial by jury guaranteed by the Sixth and Fourteenth Amendments.

The judgment of the Court of Appeals is reversed, and the case is remanded for further proceedings not inconsistent with this opinion.

It is so ordered.

* * *

QUESTIONS AND COMMENTS

1 Identify the reasons given by the Court for outlawing juries of less than six persons and show that these reasons are applicable as between five and six but not at any other cutting point (such as six and seven or four and five) on the numerical scale.

2 In *Ballew,* five members of the Court expressed the view that decision by five persons raised "sufficiently substantial doubts as to the fairness of the proceedings and proper functioning of the jury to warrant drawing the line at 6." In their minds, violation of "fairness" meant interfering with group deliberation, with obtaining a fair cross-section of the community, and with the assurance that the jury would be free from intimidation. This is to suggest that a group of five cannot deliberate as well as a group of six, that six is a much better cross-section of the community than five, and that five can be much more easily intimidated than six. In terms of plausibility, how would you rank these three propositions? Defend your answer.

Decision Rule

Johnson v. Louisiana (1972)

It may be noted that in *Ballew v. Georgia,* the Court was unanimous—i.e., though the slope was "slippery," all the justices stopped sliding at the same place on the hill. But having decided appropriately just what the Sixth Amendment implied about jury size, they were now called on to determine the implications of the amendment for jury decision rules. In common law, the twelve-member jury had been required to decide criminal cases unanimously. And that practice had always been followed in the federal system. But the states used various rules—a variation of less consequence in the days when one had no federal constitutional right to a jury trial in state courts.

In *Apodaca v. Oregon,*[15] a case involving a trial after *Duncan v. Louisiana,* the Supreme Court decided that unanimity was not required and approved the Oregon practice of verdict by a 10–2 or 11–1 vote. But having decided that 10–2 is permissible, the Court did not specify what other sized majorities would pass muster. Justice Blackmun indicated, however, that in his view, a division closer than 9–3 (such as 8–4) would not be constitutional.

The question arose again in *Johnson v. Louisiana,* a case in which the trial occurred prior to *Duncan.* The issue, therefore, was whether the due process clause, not the Sixth Amendment, would permit a state to employ jury verdicts of 9–3.

Johnson v. Louisiana

406 U.S. 356; 92 S. Ct. 1620; 32 L. Ed. 2d 152 (1972)
Vote: 5–4

The facts are given in the opinion below.

Mr. Justice White delivered the opinion of the Court.

Under both the Louisiana Constitution and Code of Criminal Procedure, criminal cases in which the punishment is necessarily at hard labor are tried to a jury of 12, and the vote of nine jurors is sufficient to return either a guilty or not guilty verdict. . . .

Appellant Johnson was arrested at his home on January 20, 1968. There was no arrest warrant, but the victim of an armed robbery had identified Johnson from photographs as having committed the crime. He was then identified at a lineup, at which he had counsel, by the victim of still another robbery. The latter crime is involved in this case. Johnson pleaded not guilty, was tried on May 14, 1968, by a 12-man jury and was convicted by a nine-to-three verdict. His due process and equal protection challenges to the Louisiana constitutional and statutory provisions were rejected by the Louisiana courts and he appealed here. We noted probable jurisdiction. Conceding that under *Duncan v. Louisiana,* (1968), the Sixth Amendment is not applicable to his case, appellant presses his equal protection and due process claims, together with a Fourth Amendment claim also rejected by the Louisiana Supreme Court. We affirm.

* * *

. . . It is our view that the fact of three dissenting votes to acquit raises no question of constitutional substance about either the integrity or the accuracy of the majority verdict of guilt. Appellant's contrary argument breaks down into two parts, each of which we shall consider separately: first, that nine individual jurors will be unable to vote conscientiously in favor of guilt beyond a reasonable doubt when three of their colleagues are arguing for acquittal, and second, that guilt cannot be said to have been proved beyond a reasonable doubt when one or more of a jury's members at the conclusion of deliberation still possess such a doubt. Neither argument is persuasive.

Numerous cases have defined a reasonable doubt as one " 'based on reason which arises from the evidence or lack of evidence.' "

* * *

In considering the first branch of appellant's argument, we can find no basis for holding that the nine jurors who voted for his conviction failed to follow their instructions concerning the need for proof beyond such a doubt or that the vote of any one of the nine failed to reflect an honest belief that guilt had been so proved. Appellant, in effect, asks us to assume that, when minority jurors express sincere doubts about guilt, their fellow jurors will nevertheless ignore them and vote to convict even if deliberation has not been exhausted and minority jurors have grounds for acquittal which, if pursued, might persuade members of the majority to acquit. But the mere fact that three jurors voted to acquit does not in itself demonstrate that, had the nine jurors of the majority attended further to reason and the evidence, all or one of them would have developed a reasonable doubt about guilt. We have no grounds for believing that majority jurors, aware of their responsibility and power over the liberty of the defendant, would simply refuse to listen to arguments presented to them in favor of acquittal, terminate dicussion, and render a verdict. On the contrary it is far more likely that a juror presenting reasoned argument in favor of acquittal would either have his arguments answered or would carry enough other jurors with him to prevent conviction. A majority will cease discussion and outvote a minority only after reasoned discussion has ceased to have persuasive effect or to serve any other purpose—when a minority, that is, continues to insist upon acquittal without having persuasive reasons in support of its position. At that juncture there is no basis for denigrating the vote of so large a majority of the jury or for refusing to accept their decision as being, at least in their minds, beyond a reasonable doubt. Indeed, at this point, a "dissenting juror should consider whether his doubt was a reasonable one . . . [when it made] no impression upon the minds of so many men, equally honest, equally intelligent with himself." *Allen v. United States,* (1896). Appellant offers no evidence that majority jurors simply ignore the reasonable doubts of their colleagues or otherwise act irresponsibly in casting their votes in favor of conviction, and before we alter our own longstanding perceptions about jury behavior and overturn a considered legislative judgment that unanimity is not essential to reasoned jury verdicts, we must have some basis for doing so other than unsupported assumptions.

We conclude, therefore, that, as to the nine jurors who voted to convict, the State satisfied its burden of proving guilt beyond any reasonable doubt. The remaining question under the Due Process Clause is whether the vote of three jurors for acquittal can be said to impeach the verdict of the other nine and to demonstrate that guilt was not in fact proved beyond such doubt. We hold that it cannot.

Of course, the State's proof could perhaps be regarded as more certain if it had convinced all 12 jurors instead of only nine; it would have been even more compelling if it had been required to convince and had, in fact, convinced 24 or 36 jurors. But the fact remains that nine jurors—a substantial majority of the jury—were convinced by the evidence. In our view disagreement of three jurors does not alone establish reasonable doubt, particularly when such a heavy majority of the jury, after having considered the dissenters' views, remains convinced of guilt. That rational men disagree is not in itself equivalent to a failure of proof by the State, nor does it indicate infidelity to the reasonable-doubt standard.

* * *

Appellant also attacks as violative of the Equal Protection Clause the provisions of Louisiana law requiring unanimous verdicts in capital and five-man jury cases, but permitting less-than-unanimous verdicts in cases such as his. We conclude, however, that the Louisiana statutory scheme serves a rational purpose and is not subject to constitutional challenge.

* * *

The judgment of the Supreme Court of Louisiana is therefore

Affirmed.

* * *

MR. JUSTICE DOUGLAS, with whom MR. JUSTICE BRENNAN and MR. JUSTICE MARSHALL concur, dissenting.

* * *

The plurality approves a procedure which diminishes the reliability of a jury. First, it eliminates the circumstances in which a minority of jurors (a) could have rationally persuaded the entire jury to acquit, or (b) while unable to persuade the majority to acquit, nonetheless could have convinced them to convict only on a lesser-included offense. Second, it permits prosecutors in . . . Louisiana to enjoy a conviction-acquittal ratio substantially greater than that ordinarily returned by unanimous juries.

The diminution of verdict reliability flows from the fact that nonunanimous juries need not debate and deliberate as fully as must unanimous juries. As soon as the requisite majority is attained, further consideration is not required . . . by Louisiana even though the dissident jurors might, if given the chance, be able to convince the majority. Such persuasion does in fact occasionally occur in States where the unanimous requirement applies: "In roughly one case in ten, the minority eventually succeeds in reversing an initial majority, and these may be cases of special importance." One explanation for this phenomenon is that because jurors are often not permitted to take notes and because they have imperfect memories, the forensic process of forcing jurors to defend their conflicting recollections and conclusions flushes out many nuances which otherwise would go overlooked. This collective effort to piece together the puzzle of historical truth, however, is cut short as soon as the requisite majority is reached in . . . Louisiana. Indeed, if a necessary majority is immediately obtained, then no deliberation at all is required.

* * *

The Court now extracts from the jury room this automatic check against hasty factfinding by relieving jurors of the duty to hear out fully the dissenters.

* * *

It is my belief that a unanimous jury is necessary if the great barricade known as proof beyond a reasonable doubt is to be maintained. This is not to equate proof beyond a reasonable doubt with the requirement of a unanimous jury. That would be analytically fallacious since a deadlocked jury does not bar, as double jeopardy, retrial for the same offense. Nevertheless, one is necessary for a proper effectuation of the other.

Suppose a jury begins with a substantial minority but then in the process of deliberation a sufficient number changes to reach the required 9:3 or 10:2 for a verdict. Is not there still a lingering doubt about that verdict? Is it not clear that the safeguard of unanimity operates in this context to make it far more likely that guilt is established beyond a reasonable doubt.

* * *

Today the Court approves a nine-to-three verdict. Would the Court relax the standard of reasonable doubt still further by resorting to eight-to-four verdicts, or even a majority rule? Moreover, in light of today's holdings and that of *Williams v. Florida,* in the future would it invalidate three-to-two or even two-to-one convictions?

* * *

The vast restructuring of American law which is entailed in today's decisions is for political not for judicial action. Until the Constitution is rewritten, we have the present one to support and construe. It has served us well. We lifetime appointees, who sit here only by happenstance, are the last who should sit as a Committee of Revision on rights as basic as those involved in the present cases.

Proof beyond a reasonable doubt and unanimity of criminal verdicts and the presumption of innocence are basic features of the accusatorial system. What we do today is not in that tradition but more in the tradition of the inquisition. Until amendments are adopted setting new standards, I would let no man be fined or imprisoned in derogation of what up to today was indisputably the law of the land.

QUESTIONS AND COMMENTS

1 Having approved jury verdicts of 9–3 and 10–2 and 11–1, the Court left open a question similar to that posed regarding jury size—i.e., what other voting breakdowns are permissible? Additional light was shed on this issue in *Burch v. Louisiana*[16] when the Court ruled that a 5–1 verdict violated the Sixth and Fourteenth Amendments. Thus, at this point we know that the Sixth and Fourteenth Amendments require state courts in criminal trials to (a) employ juries composed of at least six persons, and (b) require unanimous verdicts if the jury is composed of the minimum number of persons—six. We also know that decision rules requiring nine-twelfths, ten-twelfths, or eleven-twelfths in twelve-number juries are permissible.

   We do not know about other possible breakdowns, since the Court has yet to rule on all possibilities. It would not be straining to characterize the Court's decisions in this area as activism running rampant. But that is not to say, necessarily, that these decisions disserve the system or that they are inconsistent with the spirit of the Constitution. What do you think?

2 Does a verdict of guilty by a vote of 9–3 constitute proof of guilt beyond reasonable doubt? How about a vote of 8–4? or 7–5? Explain your answers.

3 *Apodaca v. Oregon* and *Johnson v. Louisiana* were argued twice—in two different years. These cases were held over because, first time around, Justices Douglas, Brennan, Stewart, and Marshall thought juries must decide criminal cases unanimously, while Burger, Blackmun, Black, and White thought otherwise. The ninth justice, Harlan, felt that juries should be unanimous in federal trials but not in state trials.[17] The second time around, in *Johnson* and *Apodaca,* the first four justices dissented, consistent with their position a year earlier. Burger, Stewart, and White were also consistent in both cases. But between the two terms, Black and Harlan died and were replaced by Rehnquist and Powell. These two justices took their oath of office on January 7, 1972. The two cases were reargued on January 10, 1972, and decided in May of that year. Rehnquist joined the White opinion in both cases, along with Burger and Blackmun. Powell joined the White opinion in *Johnson* but concurred with the judgment only in *Apodaca,* taking the position that the Sixth Amendment applies with different force to state and federal governments. All this points up the significance of Court composition in policy-making cases and, indeed, the importance of a single justice in such contexts.

Indigents and the Right to Counsel

Gideon v. Wainwright (1963)

Argersinger v. Hamlin (1972)

In 1931, nine young black youths were charged in Alabama with raping two white prostitutes. The defendants were without counsel at the beginning of the trial. Later they were "assisted" by an out-of-state attorney and a member of the local bar, both of whom volunteered their services. However, neither was appointed or paid, and neither had prepared the case for trial. Reviewing seven of the convictions in *Powell v. Alabama*,[18] the Supreme Court found that the failure to provide the defendants with "reasonable time and opportunity to secure counsel" violated the due process clause of the Fourteenth Amendment. The ruling also emphasized the failure of the trial judge to timely appoint effective counsel.

Powell was a capital case, and one of the defendants was given the death penalty. Ten years later in *Betts v. Brady*,[19] the Court ruled that in a noncapital case, states were not required to see that defendants were represented by counsel. This ruling came down in spite of the fact that in the federal courts, indigent defendants were provided with counsel at governmental expense in all criminal cases. The distinction between the rights of indigents in capital and noncapital cases was still being maintained when the Court docketed *Gideon v. Wainwright* twenty years later.

In the interim, the capital-noncapital distinction had been subjected to frequent criticism by Justices Black and Douglas as well as by off-the-Court commentators.[20] By 1963, the Court was ready to reassess the question. This is indicated by the fact that Abe Fortas, a leading attorney in Washington, D.C., and later a justice of the Supreme Court, was appointed to handle Gideon's appeal. Gideon was also supported by twenty-two states, arguing as amici curiae. There is some irony in the fact that the majority opinion in *Gideon* was written by Justice Black, one of only two justices on the Court who had sat and dissented twenty years earlier in *Betts v. Brady*.

Gideon v. Wainwright

372 U.S. 335; 83 S. Ct. 792; 9 L. Ed. 2d 799 (1963)
Vote: Unanimous

The facts are given in the opinion below.

MR. JUSTICE BLACK delivered the opinion of the Court.

Petitioner was charged in a Florida state court with having broken and entered a poolroom with intent to commit a misdemeanor. This offense is a felony under Florida law. Appearing in court without funds and without a lawyer, petitioner asked the court to appoint counsel for him, whereupon the following colloquy took place:

> The COURT: Mr. Gideon, I am sorry, but I cannot appoint Counsel to represent you in this case. Under the laws of the State of Florida, the only time the Court can appoint Counsel to represent a Defendant is when that person is charged with a capital offense. I am sorry, but I will have to deny your request to appoint Counsel to defend you in this case.
>
> The DEFENDANT: The United States Supreme Court says I am entitled to be represented by Counsel.

Put to trial before a jury, Gideon conducted his defense about as well as could be expected from a layman. He made an opening statement to the jury, cross-examined the State's witnesses, presented witnesses in his own defense, declined to testify himself, and made a short argument "emphasizing his innocence to the charge contained in the Information filed in this case." The jury returned a verdict of guilty, and petitioner was sentenced to serve five years in the state prison. Later, petitioner filed in the Florida Supreme Court this habeas corpus petition attacking his conviction and sentence on the ground that the trial court's refusal to appoint counsel for him denied him rights "guaranteed by the Constitution and the Bill of Rights by the United States Government." Treating the petition for habeas corpus as properly before it, the State Supreme Court, "upon consideration thereof" but without an opinion, denied all relief. Since 1942, when *Betts v. Brady,* was decided by a divided Court, the problem of a defendant's federal constitutional right to counsel in a state court has been a continuing source of controversy and litigation in both state and federal courts. To give this problem another review here, we granted certiorari. Since Gideon was proceeding *in forma pauperis,* we appointed counsel to represent him and requested both sides to discuss in their briefs and oral arguments the following: "Should this Court's holding in *Betts v. Brady,* be reconsidered?"

The facts upon which Betts claimed that he had been unconstitutionally denied the right to have counsel appointed to assist him are strikingly like the facts upon which Gideon here bases his federal constitutional claim. Betts was indicted for robbery in a Maryland state court. On arraignment, he told the trial judge of his lack of funds to hire a lawyer and asked the court to appoint one for him. Betts was advised that it was not the practice in that county to appoint counsel for indigent defendants except in murder and rape cases. He then pleaded not guilty, had witnesses summoned, cross-examined the State's witnesses, examined his own, and chose not to testify himself. He was found guilty by the judge, sitting without a jury and sentenced to eight years in prison. Like Gideon, Betts sought release by habeas corpus, alleging that he had been denied the right to assistance of counsel in violation of the Fourteenth Amendment. Betts was denied any relief, and on review this Court affirmed. It was held that a refusal to appoint counsel for an indigent defendant charged with a felony did not necessarily violate the Due Process Clause of the Fourteenth Amendment, which for reasons given the Court deemed to be the only applicable federal constitutional provision. The Court said:

> Asserted denial [of due process] is to be tested by an appraisal of the totality of facts in a given case. That which may, in one setting, constitute a denial of fundamental fairness, shocking to the universal sense of justice, may, in other circumstances, and in the light of other considerations, fall short of such denial.

Treating due process as "a concept less rigid and more fluid than those envisaged in other specific and particular provisions of the Bill of Rights," the Court held that refusal to appoint counsel under the particular facts and circumstances in the *Betts* case was not so "offensive to the common and fundamental idea of fairness" as to amount to a denial of due process. Since the facts and circumstances of the two cases are so nearly indistinguishable, we think the *Betts v. Brady* holding if left standing would require us to reject Gideon's claim that the Constitution guarantees him the assistance of counsel. Upon full reconsideration we conclude that *Betts v. Brady* should be overruled.

The Sixth Amendment provides, "In all criminal prosecutions, the accused shall enjoy the right . . . to have the Assistance of Counsel for his defence." We have construed this to mean that in federal courts counsel must be provided for defendants unable to employ counsel unless the right is competently and intelligently waived.

* * *

. . . The *Betts* Court refused to accept the contention that the Sixth Amendment's guarantee of counsel for indigent federal defendants was extended to or, in the words of that Court, "made obligatory upon the States by the Fourteenth Amendment." Plainly had the Court concluded that appointment of counsel for an indigent criminal defendant was "a fundamental right essential to a fair trial," it would have held that the Fourteenth Amendment requires appointment of counsel in a state court, just as the Sixth Amendment requires in a federal court.

* * *

In many cases other than *Betts,* this Court has looked to the fundamental nature of original Bill of Rights guarantees to decide whether the Fourteenth Amendment makes them obligatory on the States. Explicitly recognized to be of this "fundamental nature" and therefore made immune from state invasion by the Fourteenth, or some part of it, are the First Amendment's freedoms of speech, press, religion, assembly, association, and petition for redress of grievances. For the same reason, though not always in precisely the same terminology, the Court has made obligatory on the States the Fifth Amendment's command that private property shall not be taken for public use without just compensation, the Fourth Amendment's prohibition of unreasonable searches and seizures, and the Eighth's ban on cruel and unusual punishment. On the other hand, this Court in *Palko v. Connecticut,* (1937), refused to hold that the Fourteenth Amendment made the double jeopardy provision of the Fifth Amendment obligatory on the States. . . .

We accept *Betts v. Brady's* assumption, based as it was on our prior cases, that a provision of the Bill of Rights which is "fundamental and essential to a fair trial" is made obligatory upon the States by the Fourteenth Amendment. We think the Court in *Betts* was wrong, however, in concluding that the Sixth Amendment's guarantee of counsel is not one of these fundamental rights.

* * *

. . . Reason and reflection require us to recognize that in our adversary system of criminal justice, any person haled into court, who is too poor to hire a lawyer, cannot be assured a fair trial unless counsel is provided for him. This seems to us to be an obvious truth. Governments, both state and federal, quite properly spend vast sums of money to establish machinery to try defendants accused of crime. Lawyers to prosecute are everywhere deemed essential to protect the public's interests in an orderly society. Similarly, there are few defendants charged with crime, few indeed, who fail to hire the best lawyers they can get to prepare and present their defenses. That government hires lawyers to prosecute and defendants who have the money hire lawyers to defend are the strongest indications of the widespread belief that lawyers in criminal courts are necessities, not luxuries. The right of one charged with crime to counsel may not be deemed fundamental and essential to fair trials in some countries, but it is in ours. From the very beginning, our state and national constitutions and laws have laid great emphasis on procedural and substantive safeguards designed to assure fair trials before impartial tribunals in which every defendant stands equal before the law. This noble ideal cannot be realized if the poor man charged with crime has to face his accusers without a lawyer to assist him. A defendant's need for a lawyer is nowhere better stated than in the moving words of Mr. Justice Sutherland in *Powell v. Alabama:*

> The right to be heard would be, in many cases, of little avail if it did not comprehend the right to be heard by counsel. Even the intelligent and educated layman has small and sometimes no skill in the science of law. If charged with crime, he is incapable, generally, of determining for himself whether the indictment is good or bad. He is unfamiliar with the rules of evidence. Left without the aid of counsel he may be put on trial without a proper charge, and convicted upon incompetent evidence, or evidence irrelevant to the issue or otherwise inadmissible. He lacks both the skill and knowledge adequately to prepare his defense, even though he have a perfect one. He requires the guiding hand of counsel at every step in the proceedings against him. Without it, though he be not guilty, he faces the danger of conviction because he does not know how to establish his innocence.

The Court in *Betts v. Brady* departed from the sound wisdom upon which the Court's holding in *Powell v. Alabama* rested. Florida, supported by two other States, has asked that *Betts v. Brady* be left intact. Twenty-two States, as friends of the Court, argue that *Betts* was "an anachronism when handed down" and that it should now be overruled. We agree.

The judgment is reversed and the cause is remanded to the Supreme Court of Florida for further action not inconsistent with this opinion.

Reversed.

After the Court's decision that indigent criminal defendants in felony prosecutions have the right to state-furnished counsel in state courts, a quite normal and frequent process occurred. That process is one in which a newly enunciated principle is explored to see what its limits might be. Such explorations proceed by changing some part or condition of the new rule and asking the Supreme Court to accept the change. Thus, if indigent criminal defendants have a right to state-appointed counsel in felony cases, maybe the condition "felony case" is not crucial and the Court will apply the rule to misdemeanor prosecutions. That is precisely what Argersinger's attorneys proposed to the Court in *Argersinger v. Hamlin.*

Argersinger v. Hamlin, Sheriff

407 U.S. 25; 92 S. Ct. 2006; 32 L. Ed. 2d 530 (1972)
Vote: Unanimous

The facts are provided in the opinion below.

MR. JUSTICE DOUGLAS delivered the opinion of the Court.

Petitioner, an indigent, was charged in Florida with carrying a concealed weapon, an offense punishable by imprisonment up to six months, a $1,000 fine, or both. The trial was to a judge, and petitioner was unrepresented by counsel. He was sentenced to serve 90 days in jail, and brought this habeas corpus action in the Florida Supreme Court, alleging that, being deprived of his right to counsel, he was unable as an indigent layman properly to raise and present to the trial court good and sufficient defenses to the charge for which he stands convicted. The Florida Supreme Court by a four-to-three decision, in ruling on the right to counsel, followed the line we marked out in *Duncan v. Louisiana,* [1968], as respects the right to trial by jury and held that the right to court-appointed counsel extends only to trials "for non-petty offenses punishable by more than six months imprisonment."

The case is here on a petition for certiorari, which we granted. We reverse.

* * *

In *Gideon v. Wainwright, supra* (overruling *Betts v. Brady,* [1942]), we dealt with a felony trial. But we did not so limit the need of the accused for a lawyer. . . . [The Gideon] rationale has relevance to any criminal trial, where an accused is deprived of his liberty. . . .

The requirement of counsel may well be necessary for a fair trial even in a petty-offense prosecution. We are by no means convinced that legal and constitutional questions involved in a case that actually leads to imprisonment even for a brief period are any less complex than when a person can be sent off for six months or more.

* * *

Beyond the problem of trials and appeals is that of the guilty plea, a problem which looms large in misdemeanor as well as in felony cases. Counsel is needed so that the accused may know precisely what he is doing, so that he is fully aware of the prospect of going to jail or prison, and so that he is treated fairly by the prosecution.

In addition, the volume of misdemeanor cases, far greater in number than felony prosecutions, may create an obsession for speedy dispositions, regardless of the fairness of the result. The Report by the President's Commission on Law Enforcement and Administration of Justice, The Challenge of Crime in a Free Society (1967), states:

> For example, until legislation last year increased the number of judges, the District of Columbia Court of General Sessions had four judges to process the preliminary stages of more than 1,500 felony cases, 7,500 serious misdemeanor cases, and 38,000 petty offenses and an equal number of traffic offenses per year. An inevitable consequence of volume that large is the almost total preoccupation in such a court with the movement of cases. The calendar is long, speed often is substituted for care, and casually arranged out-of-court compromise too often is substituted for adjudication. Inadequate attention tends to be given to the individual defendant, whether in protecting his rights, sifting the facts at trial, deciding the social risk he presents, or determining how to deal with him after conviction. . . .

We . . . conclude . . . that the problems associated with misdemeanor and petty offenses often require the presence of counsel to insure the accused a fair trial.

. . . We need not consider the requirements of the Sixth Amendment as regards the right to counsel where loss of liberty is not involved, however, for here petitioner was in fact sentenced to jail. And, as we said in *Baldwin v. New York,* [1970], the prospect of imprisonment for however short a time will seldom be viewed by the accused as a trivial or 'petty' matter and may well result in quite serious repercussions affecting his career and his reputation.

We hold, therefore, that absent a knowing and intelligent waiver, no person may be imprisoned for any offense, whether classified as petty, misdemeanor, or felony, unless he was represented by counsel at his trial.

* * *

Under the rule we announce today, every judge will know when the trial of a misdemeanor starts that no imprisonment may be imposed, even though local law permits it, unless the accused is represented by counsel. He will have a measure of the seriousness and gravity of the offense and therefore know when to name a lawyer to represent the accused before the trial starts.

The run of misdemeanors will not be affected by today's ruling. But in those that end up in the actual deprivation of a person's liberty, the accused will receive the benefit of "the guiding hand of counsel" so necessary when one's liberty is in jeopardy.

Reversed.

* * *

QUESTIONS AND COMMENTS

1 The Sixth Amendment fully protects the right of criminal defendants to retain counsel of their own choice.[21] But recent cases deal primarily with the rights of indigent defendants.
2 In *Gideon* and *Argersinger,* the Court suggests that defendants are not capable of serving as their own counsel, though they may legally do so under proper conditions. Do you agree? Would an indigent member of the local bar be incapable of serving as his or her own attorney? Since the providing of attorneys to indigents is a cost to the state, would it be better to require the state to do so only after determining that the defendant requires such a service? Would such a determination depend on the nature of the charge?
3 In both these cases, the Court emphasized that counsel is necessary to ensure a "fair trial." If that is so, how do you explain the fact that *Argersinger* does not require counsel in all misdemeanor cases? Does the Court's position imply that an unfair trial in noncovered cases is acceptable? In that connection, is imprisonment worse than a fine which leads to bankruptcy? Even if the maximum possible imprisonment is one hour—to take an extreme example? Can you find the Court's distinction in the Constitution?

Capital Punishment

Francis v. Resweber (1947)

Gregg v. Georgia (1976)

While the Eighth Amendment bars cruel and unusual punishments, it does not define those terms. Thus, we are left with such questions as: What is forbidden, only punishments considered cruel and unusual at the time the amendment was adopted or does the amendment prohibit any punishment considered cruel and unusual by the community at the moment the punishment is challenged? Is punishment cruel because it is unusual, or because it degrades human dignity, or because it is disproportionate to the crime committed? In *Francis v. Resweber,* the Court suggests that the "infliction of unnecessary pain" or the "wanton infliction of pain" is forbidden by the Fourteenth Amendment's due process clause. But it finds no such inflictions in the facts of the case.

Much clearer answers to our questions are to be found in a series of capital punishment cases which began with *Furman v. Georgia* in 1972.[22] While in 1892 the Court held that the Eighth Amendment did not apply to the states,[23] *Francis v. Resweber* hints that it does, and *Robinson v. California*[24] disposes of that question. Thus, the cases beginning with *Furman* determine whether state capital punishment statutes and procedures violate the Eighth and Fourteenth Amendments. These cases establish that the amendment draws its meaning from the "evolving standards of decency that mark the progress of a maturing society"[25]—standards found in public opinion, legislative enactments, court rulings, and jury decisions. And since such things change over time, the meaning of the Eighth Amendment is dynamic, not static.

Furman implies that the death penalty per se is not unconstitutional. However, beginning with *Furman*, the Court has struck a number of death penalty statutes, while upholding others. In 1976, the Court upheld capital punishment statutes in Georgia, Texas, and Florida. *Gregg v. Georgia* was one of these cases. In reading the case, one should be alert for answers to the questions posed above.

Louisiana ex rel. Francis v. Resweber

329 U.S. 459; 67 S. Ct. 673; 91 L. Ed. 1295 (1947)

Vote: 5–4
The facts are given in the opinion below.

MR. JUSTICE REED announced the judgment of the Court in an opinion in which THE CHIEF JUSTICE, MR. JUSTICE BLACK and MR JUSTICE JACKSON join.

This writ of certiorari brings before the Court a unique situation. The petitioner, Willie Francis, is a colored citizen of Louisiana. He was duly convicted of murder and in September, 1945, sentenced to be electrocuted for the crime. Upon a proper death warrant , Francis was prepared for execution and on May 3, 1946, pursuant to the warrant, was placed in the official electric chair of the State of Louisiana in the presence of the authorized witnesses.

. . . Of the proceedings on that day the Supreme Court of Louisiana has said:

. . . between the Hours of 12:00 o'clock noon and 3:00 o'clock p.m., Willie Francis was strapped in the electric chair and an attempt was made to electrocute him, but, because of some defect in the apparatus failed to function, and after an unsuccessful attempt to electrocute Francis he was removed from the chair.

Of the same proceedings, the State's brief says:

> Through a latent electrical defect, the attempt to electrocute Francis failed, the State contending no current whatsoever reached Francis' body, the relator contending a current of electricity did pass through his body; but in any event, Willie Francis was not put to death.*

. . . He was thereupon removed from the chair and returned to prison where he now is. A new death warrant was issued by the Governor of Louisiana, fixing the execution for May 9, 1946.

Applications to the Supreme Court of the state were filed for writs of certiorari, mandamus, prohibition and habeas corpus, directed to the appropriate officials in the state. Execution of the sentence was stayed. By the applications petitioner claimed the protection of the due process clause of the Fourteenth Amendment on the ground that an execution under the circumstances detailed would deny due process to him because of the double jeopardy provision of the Fifth Amendment and the cruel and unusual punishment provision of the Eighth Amendment.† These federal constitutional protections, petitioner claimed, would be denied because he had once gone through the difficult preparation for execution and had once received through his body a current of electricity intended to cause death. The Supreme Court of Louisiana denied the applications on the ground of a lack of any basis for judicial relief. That is, the state court concluded there was no violation of state or national law alleged in the various applications. It spoke of the fact that no "current of sufficient intensity to cause death" passed through petitioner's body. It referred specifically to the fact that the applications of petitioner invoked the provisions of the Louisiana Constitution against cruel and inhuman punishments and putting one in jeopardy of life or liberty twice for the same offense. We granted certiorari on a petition setting forth the aforementioned contentions, to consider the alleged violations of rights under the Federal Constitution in the unusual circumstances of this case.

* * *

To determine whether or not the execution of the petitioner may fairly take place after the experience through which he passed, we shall examine the circumstances under the assumption, but without so deciding, that violation of the principles of the Fifth and Eighth Amendments, as to double jeopardy and cruel and unusual punishment, would be violative of the due process clause of the Fourteenth Amendment. As nothing has been brought to our attention to suggest the contrary, we must and do assume that the state officials carried out

---

Author's note: These statements from the Court and the State's brief are taken from the dissenting opinion.

†Fifth Amendment: ". . . nor shall any person be subject for the same offence to be twice put in jeopardy of life or limb. . . ."

Eighth Amendment: "Excessive bail shall not be required, nor excessive fines imposed, nor cruel and unusual punishments inflicted."

their duties under the death warrant in a careful and humane manner. Accidents happen for which no man is to blame. We turn to the question as to whether the proposed enforcement of the criminal law of the state is offensive to any constitutional requirements to which reference has been made.

First. Our minds rebel against permitting the same sovereignty to punish an accused twice for the same offense. But where the accused successfully seeks review of a conviction, there is no double jeopardy upon a new trial.

Even where a state obtains a new trial after conviction because of errors, while an accused may be placed on trial a second time, it is not the sort of hardship to the accused that is forbidden by the Fourteenth Amendment. *Palko v. Connecticut,* [1937]. As this is a prosecution under state law, so far as double jeopardy is concerned, the *Palko* case is decisive. For we see no difference from a constitutional point of view between a new trial for error of law at the instance of the state that results in a death sentence instead of imprisonment for life and an execution that follows a failure of equipment. When an accident, with no suggestion of malevolence, prevents the consummation of a sentence, the state's subsequent course in the administration of its criminal law is not affected on that account by any requirement of due process under the Fourteenth Amendment. We find no double jeopardy here which can be said to amount to a denial of federal due process in the proposed execution.

Second. We find nothing in what took place here which amounts to cruel and unusual punishment in the constitutional sense. The case before us does not call for an examination into any punishments except that of death. See *Weems v. United States,* [1900]. The traditional humanity of modern Anglo-American law forbids the infliction of unnecessary pain in the execution of the death sentence. Prohibition against the wanton infliction of pain has come into our law from the Bill of Rights of 1688. The identical words appear in our Eighth Amendment. The Fourteenth would prohibit by its due process clause execution by a state in a cruel manner.

Petitioner's suggestion is that because he once underwent the psychological strain of preparation for electrocution, now to require him to undergo this preparation again subjects him to a lingering or cruel and unusual punishment. Even the fact that petitioner has already been subjected to a current of electricity does not make his subsequent execution any more cruel in the constitutional sense than any other execution. The cruelty against which the Constitution protects a convicted man is cruelty inherent in the method of punishment, not the necessary suffering involved in any method employed to extinguish life humanely. The fact that an unforeseeable accident prevented the prompt consummation of the sentence cannot, it seems to us, add an element of cruelty to a subsequent execution. There is no purpose to inflict unnecessary pain nor any unnecessary pain involved in the proposed execution. The situation of the unfortunate victim of this accident is just as though he had suffered the identical amount of mental anguish and physical pain in any other occurrence, such as, for example, a fire in the cell block. We cannot agree that the hardship imposed upon the petitioner rises to that level of hardship denounced as denial of due process because of cruelty.

* * *

On this record, we see nothing upon which we could conclude that the constitutional rights of petitioner were infringed.

Affirmed.

MR. JUSTICE FRANKFURTER, concurring.

* * *

One must be on guard against finding in personal disapproval a reflection of more or less prevailing condemnation. Strongly drawn as I am to some of the sentiments expressed by my brother BURTON, I cannot rid myself of the conviction that were I to hold that Louisiana would transgress the Due Process Clause if the State were allowed, in the precise circumstances before us, to carry out the death sentence, I would be enforcing my private view rather than that consensus of society's opinion which, for purposes of due process, is the standard enjoined by the Constitution.

. . . Since I cannot say that it would be "repugnant to the conscience of mankind," for Louisiana to exercise the power on which she here stands, I cannot say that the Constitution withholds it.

MR. JUSTICE BURTON, with whom MR. JUSTICE DOUGLAS, MR. JUSTICE MURPHY and MR. JUSTICE RUTLEDGE concur, dissenting.

* * *

In determining whether the proposed procedure is unconstitutional, we must measure it against a lawful electrocution. The contrast is that between instantaneous death and death by installments—caused by electric shocks administered after one or more intervening periods of complete consciousness of the victim. Electrocution, when instantaneous, *can* be inflicted by a state in conformity with due process of law.

* * *

The all-important consideration is that the execution shall be so instantaneous and substantially painless that the punishment shall be reduced, as nearly as possible, to no more than that of death itself. Electrocution has been approved only in a form that eliminates suffering.

* * *

If the state officials deliberately and intentionally had placed the relator in the electric chair five times and, each time, had applied electric current to his body in a manner not sufficient, until the final time, to kill him, such a form of torture would rival that of burning at the stake. Although the failure of the first attempt, in the present case, was unintended, the reapplication of the electric current will be intentional. How many deliberate and intentional reapplications of electric current does it take to produce a cruel, unusual and unconstitutional punishment? While five applications would be more cruel and unusual than one, the uniqueness of the present case demonstrates that, today, two separated applications are sufficiently "cruel and unusual" to be prohibited. If five attempts would be "cruel and unusual," it would be difficult to draw the line between two, three, four and five. It is not difficult, however, as we here contend, to draw the line between the one continuous application prescribed by statute and any other application of the current.

* * *

In determining whether a case of cruel and unusual punishment constitutes a violation of due process of law, each case must turn upon its particular facts. The record in this case is not limited to an instance where a prisoner was placed in the electric chair and released before being subjected to the electric current. It presents more than a case of mental anguish, however severe such a case might be.

. . . The petition contains the unequivocal allegation that the official electrocutioner "turned on the switch and a current of electricity was caused to pass through the body of relator, all in the presence of the official witnesses." This allegation must be read in the light of the Louisiana statute which authorized the electrocutioner to apply to the body of the relator only such an electric current as was of "sufficient intensity to cause death." On that record, denial of relief means that the proposed repeated, and at least second, application to the relator of an electric current sufficient to cause death is not, under present circumstances, a cruel and unusual punishment violative of due process of law. It exceeds any punishment prescribed by law. There is no precedent for it. What then is it, if it be not cruel, unusual and unlawful? In spite of the constitutional issue thus raised, the Supreme Court of Louisiana treated it as an executive question not subject to judicial review. We believe that if the facts are as alleged by the relator the proposed action is unconstitutional. We believe also that the Supreme Court of Louisiana should provide for the determination of the facts and then proceed in a manner not inconsistent with this opinion.

* * *

The remand of this cause to the Supreme Court of Louisiana in the manner indicated would not mean that the relator necessarily is entitled to a complete release. It would mean merely that the courts of Louisiana must examine the facts, both as to the actual nature of the punishment already inflicted and that proposed to be inflicted and, if the proposed punishment amounts to a violation of due process of law under the Constitution of the United States, then the State must find some means of disposing of this case that will not violate that Constitution.

For the reasons stated, we are unable to concur in the judgment of this Court which affirms the judgment below.

Gregg v. Georgia

428 U.S. 153; 96 S. Ct. 2909; 49 L. Ed. 2d 859 (1976)
Vote: 7–2

The facts are given in the opinion below.

Judgment of the Court, and opinion of MR. JUSTICE STEWART, MR. JUSTICE POWELL, and MR. JUSTICE STEVENS, announced by MR. JUSTICE STEWART.

The issue in this case is whether the imposition of the sentence of death for the crime of murder under the law of Georgia violates the Eighth and Fourteenth Amendments.

The petitioner, Troy Gregg, was charged with committing armed robbery and murder. In accordance with Georgia procedure in capital cases, the trial was in two stages, a guilt stage and a sentencing stage. The evidence at the guilt trial established that on November 21, 1973, the petitioner and a traveling companion, Floyd Allen, while hitchhiking north in Florida were picked up by Fred Simmons and Bob Moore. Their car broke down, but they continued north after Simmons purchased another vehicle with some of the cash he was carrying. While still in Florida, they picked up another hitchhiker, Dennis Weaver, who rode with them to Atlanta, where he was let out about 11 P.M. A short time later the four men interrupted their journey for a rest stop along the highway. The next morning the bodies of Simmons and Moore were discovered in a ditch nearby.

. . . The next afternoon, the petitioner and Allen, while in Simmons' car, were arrested in Ashville, N.C. In the search incident to the arrest a .25-caliber pistol, later shown to be that used to kill Simmons and Moore, was found in the petitioner's pocket. After receiving the warnings required by *Miranda v. Arizona,* (1966), and signing a written waiver of his rights, the petitioner signed a statement in which he admitted shooting, then robbing Simmons and Moore. He justified the slayings on grounds of self-defense. The next day, while being transferred to Lawrenceville, Ga., the petitioner and Allen were taken to the scene of the shootings. Upon arriving there, Allen recounted the events leading to the slayings. His version of these events was as follows: After Simmons and Moore left the car, the petitioner stated that he intended to rob them. The petitioner then took his pistol in hand and positioned himself on the car to improve his aim. As Simmons and Moore came up an embankment toward the car, the petitioner fired three shots and the two men fell near a ditch. The petitioner, at close range, then fired a shot into the head of each. He robbed them of valuables and drove away with Allen.

[At trial, Gregg] . . . indicated that he had shot Simmons and Moore because of fear and in self-defense, testifying they had attacked Allen and him, one wielding a pipe and the other a knife. . . .

The jury found the petitioner guilty of two counts of armed robbery and two counts of murder.

At the penalty stage, which took place before the same jury, neither the prosecutor nor the petitioner's lawyer offered any additional evidence. Both counsel, however, made lengthy arguments dealing generally with the propriety of capital punishment under the circumstances and with the weight of the evidence of guilt. The trial judge instructed the jury that it could recommend either a death sentence or a life prison sentence on each count. The judge further charged the jury that in determining what sentence was appropriate the jury was free to consider the facts and circumstances, if any, presented by the parties in mitigation or aggravation.

Finally, the judge instructed the jury that it "would not be authorized to consider [imposing] the penalty of death" unless it first found beyond a reasonable doubt one of these aggravating circumstances:

> One—That the offense of murder was committed while the offender was engaged in the commission of two other capital felonies, to-wit the armed robbery of [Simmons and Moore].
>
> Two—That the offender committed the offense of murder for the purpose of receiving money and the automobile described in the indictment.
>
> Three—The offense of murder was outrageously and wantonly vile, horrible and inhuman, in that they [sic] involved the depravity of [the] mind of the defendant.

Finding the first and second of these circumstances, the jury returned verdicts of death on each count.

The Supreme Court of Georgia affirmed the convictions and the imposition of the death sentences for murder.

* * *

The death sentences imposed for armed robbery, however, were vacated on the grounds that the death penalty had rarely been imposed in Georgia for that offense and that the jury improperly considered the murders as aggravating circumstances for the robberies after having considered the armed robberies as aggravating circumstances for the murders.

We granted the petitioner's application for a writ of certiorari limited to his challenge to the imposition of the death sentences in this case as "cruel and unusual" punishment in violation of the Eighth and the Fourteenth Amendments.

* * *

We address initially the basic contention that the punishment of death for the crime of murder is, under all circumstances, "cruel and unusual" in violation of the Eighth and Fourteenth Amendments of the Constitution.

... Until *Furman v. Georgia,* (1972), the Court never confronted squarely the fundamental claim that the punishment of death always, regardless of the enormity of the offense or the procedure followed in imposing the sentence, is cruel and unusual punishment in violation of the Constitution. Although this issue was presented and addressed in *Furman,* it was not resolved by the Court. Four Justices would have held that capital punishment is not unconstitutional *per se;* two Justices would have reached the opposite conclusion; and three Justices, while agreeing that the statutes then before the Court were invalid as applied, left open the question whether such punishment may ever be imposed. We now hold that the punishment of death does not invariably violate the Constitution.

* * *

The imposition of the death penalty for the crime of murder has a long history of acceptance both in the United States and in England. The common-law rule imposed a mandatory death sentence on all convicted murderers. *McGautha v. California,* (1971). And the penalty continued to be used into the 20th century by most American States, although the breadth of the common-law rule was diminished, initially by narrowing the class of murders to be punished by death and subsequently by widespread adoption of laws expressly granting juries the discretion to recommend mercy. See *Woodson v. North Carolina.*

It is apparent from the text of the Constitution itself that the existence of capital punishment was accepted by the Framers. At the time the Eighth Amendment was ratified, capital punishment was a common sanction in every State. Indeed, the First Congress of the United States enacted legislation providing death as the penalty for specified crimes.

The Fifth Amendment, adopted at the same time as the Eighth, contemplated the continued existence of the capital sanction by imposing certain limits on the prosecution of capital cases. ...

And the Fourteenth Amendment, adopted over three-quarters of a century later, similarly contemplates the existence of the capital sanction in providing that no State shall deprive any person of "life, liberty, or property" without due process of law.

For nearly two centuries, this Court, repeatedly and often expressly, has recognized that capital punishment is not invalid *per se.* ...

Four years ago, the petitioners in *Furman* and its companion cases predicated their argument primarily upon the asserted proposition that standards of decency had evolved to the point where capital punishment no longer could be tolerated. The petitioners in those cases said, in effect, that the evolutionary process had come to an end, and that standards of decency required that the Eighth Amendment be construed finally as prohibiting capital punishment for any crime regardless of its depravity and impact on society. This view was accepted by two Justices. ...

The petitioners in the capital cases before the Court today renew the "standards of decency" argument, but developments during the four years since *Furman* have undercut substantially the assumptions upon which their argument rested. Despite the continuing debate, dating back to the 19th century, over the morality and utility of capital punishment, it is now evident that a large proportion of American society continues to regard it as an appropriate and necessary criminal sanction.

The most marked indication of society's endorsement of the death penalty for murder is the legislative response to *Furman*. The legislatures of at least 35 States have enacted new statutes that provide for the death penalty for at least some crimes that result in the death of another person. And the Congress of the United States, in 1974, enacted a statute providing the death penalty for aircraft piracy that results in death. These recently adopted statutes have attempted to address the concerns expressed by the Court in *Furman* primarily (i) by specifying the factors to be weighed and the procedures to be followed in deciding when to impose a capital sentence, or (ii) by making the death penalty mandatory for specified crimes. But all of the post-*Furman* statutes make clear that capital punishment itself has not been rejected by the elected representatives of the people.

* * *

There is no question that death as a punishment is unique in its severity and irrevocability. When a defendant's life is at stake, the Court has been particularly sensitive to insure that every safeguard is observed. But we are concerned here only with the imposition of capital punishment for the crime of murder, and when a life has been taken deliberately by the offender, we cannot say that the punishment is invariably disproportionate to the crime. It is an extreme sanction, suitable to the most extreme of crimes.

We hold that the death penalty is not a form of punishment that may never be imposed, regardless of the circumstances of the offense, regardless of the character of the offender, and regardless of the procedure followed in reaching the decision to impose it.

We now consider whether Georgia may impose the death penalty on the petitioner in this case.

While *Furman* did not hold that the infliction of the death penalty *per se* violates the Constitution's ban on cruel and unusual punishments, it did recognize that the penalty of death is different in kind from any other punishment imposed under our system of criminal justice. Because of the uniqueness of the death penalty, *Furman* held that it could not be imposed under sentencing procedures that created a substantial risk that it would be inflicted in an arbitrary and capricious manner.

... The concerns expressed in *Furman* that the penalty of death not be imposed in an arbitrary or capricious manner can be met by a carefully drafted statute that ensures that the sentencing authority is given adequate information and guidance. As a general proposition these concerns are best met by a system that provides for a bifurcated proceeding at which the sentencing authority is apprised of the information relevant to the imposition of sentence and provided with standards to guide its use of the information.

* * *

We now turn to consideration of the constitutionality of Georgia's capital-sentencing procedures. In the wake of *Furman,* Georgia amended its capital punishment statute, but chose not to narrow the scope of its murder provisions. Thus, now as before *Furman,* in Georgia "[a] person commits murder when he unlawfully and with malice aforethought, either express or implied, causes the death of another human being." Ga. Code Ann., § 26-1101 (a) (1972). All persons convicted of murder "shall be punished by death or by imprisonment for life." § 26-1101 (e) (1972).

Georgia did act, however, to narrow the class of murderers subject to capital punishment by specifying 10 statutory aggravating circumstances, one of which must be found by the jury to exist beyond a reasonable doubt before a death sentence can ever be imposed. In addition, the jury is authorized to consider any other appropriate aggravating or mitigating circumstances. The jury is not required to find any mitigating circumstance in order to make a recommendation of mercy that is binding on the trial court, but it must find a *statutory* aggravating circumstance before recommending a sentence of death.

These procedures require the jury to consider the circumstances of the crime and the criminal before it recommends sentence. No longer can a Georgia jury do as Furman's jury did: reach a finding of the defendant's guilt and then, without guidance or direction, decide whether he should live or die. Instead, the jury's attention is directed to the specific circumstances of the crime: Was it committed in the course of another capital felony? Was it committed for money? Was it committed upon a peace officer or judicial officer? Was it committed in a particularly heinous way or in a manner that endangered the lives of many persons? In addition, the jury's attention is focused on the characteristics of the person who committed the crime: Does he have a record of prior convictions for capital offenses? Are there any special facts about this defendant that mitigate against imposing capital punishment (*e. g.,* his youth, the extent of his cooperation with the police, his emotional state at the time of the crime). As a result, while some jury discretion still exists, "the discretion to be exercised is controlled by clear and objective standards so as to produce non-discriminatory application." *Coley v. State,* 204 S.E. 2d 612, 615 (1974).

As an important additional safeguard against arbitrariness and caprice, the Georgia statutory scheme provides for automatic appeal of all death sentences to the State's Supreme Court. That court is required by statute to review each sentence of death and determine whether it was imposed under the influence of passion or prejudice, whether the evidence supports the jury's finding of a statutory aggravating circumstance, and whether the sentence is disproportionate compared to those sentences imposed in similar cases.

In short, Georgia's new sentencing procedures require as a prerequisite to the imposition of the death penalty, specific jury findings as to the circumstances of the crime or the character of the defendant. Moreover, to guard further against a situation comparable to that presented in *Furman,* the Supreme Court of Georgia compares each death sentence with the sentences imposed on similarly situated defendants to ensure that the sentence of death in a particular case is not disproportionate. On their face these procedures seem to satisfy the concerns of *Furman.* No longer should there be "no meaningful basis for distinguishing the few cases in which [the death penalty] is imposed from the many cases in which it is not."

The petitioner contends, however, that the changes in the Georgia sentencing procedures are only cosmetic, that the arbitrariness and capriciousness condemned by *Furman* continue to exist in Georgia—both in traditional practices that still remain and in the new sentencing procedures adopted in response to *Furman.*

First, the petitioner focuses on the opportunities for discretionary action that are inherent in the processing of any murder case under Georgia law. He notes that the state prosecutor has unfettered authority to select those persons whom he wishes to prosecute for a capital offense and to plea bargain with them. Further, at the trial the jury may choose to convict a defendant of a lesser included offense rather than find him guilty of a crime punishable by death, even if the evidence would support a capital verdict. And finally, a defendant who is convicted and sentenced to die may have his sentence commuted by the Governor of the State and the Georgia Board of Pardons and Paroles.

The existence of these discretionary stages is not determinative of the issues before us. At each of these stages an actor in the criminal justice system makes a decision which may remove a defendant from consideration as a candidate for the death penalty. *Furman,* in contrast, dealt with the decision to impose the death sentence on a specific individual who had been convicted of a capital offense. Nothing in any of our cases suggests that the decision to afford an individual defendant mercy violates the Constitution. *Furman* held only that, in order to minimize the risk that the death penalty would be imposed on a capriciously selected group of offenders, the decision to impose it had to be guided by standards so that the sentencing authority would focus on the particularized circumstances of the crime and the defendants. . . .

Finally, the Georgia statute has an additional provision designed to assure that the death penalty will not be imposed on a capriciously selected group of convicted defendants. The new sentencing procedures require that the State Supreme Court review every death sentence to determine whether it was imposed under the influence of passion, prejudice, or any other arbitrary factor, whether the evidence supports the findings of a statutory aggravating circumstance, and "[w]hether the sentence of death is excessive or disproportionate to the penalty imposed in similar cases, considering both the crime and the defendant.". . .

In performing its sentence-review function, the Georgia court has held that "if the death penalty is only rarely imposed for an act or it is substantially out of line with sentences imposed for other acts it will be set aside as excessive."

* * *

It is apparent that the Supreme Court of Georgia has taken its review responsibilities seriously. In *Coley,* it held that "[t]he prior cases indicate that the past practice among juries faced with similar factual situations and like aggravating circumstances has been to impose only the sentence of life imprisonment for the offense of rape, rather than death."

It thereupon reduced Coley's sentence from death to life imprisonment. Similarly, although armed robbery is a capital offense under Georgia law, the Georgia court concluded that the death sentences imposed in this case for that crime were "unusual in that they are rarely imposed for [armed robbery]. Thus, under the test provided by statute, . . . they must be considered to be excessive or disproportionate to the penalties imposed in similar cases."

The court therefore vacated Gregg's death sentences for armed robbery and has followed a similar course in every other armed robbery death penalty case to come before it.

* * *

The basic concern of *Furman* centered on those defendants who were being condemned to death capriciously and arbitrarily. Under the procedures before the Court in that case, sentencing authorities were not directed to give attention to the nature or circumstances of the crime committed or to the character or record of the defendant. Left unguided, juries imposed the death sentence in a way that could only be called freakish. The new Georgia sentencing procedures, by contrast, focus the jury's attention on the particularized nature of the crime and the particularized characteristics of the individual defendant. While the jury is permitted to consider any aggravating or mitigating circumstances, it must find and identify at least one statutory aggravating factor before it may impose a penalty of death. In this way the jury's discretion is channeled. No longer can a jury wantonly and freakishly impose the death sentence; it is always circumscribed by the legislative guidelines. In addition, the review function of the Supreme Court of Georgia affords additional assurance that the concerns that prompted our decision in *Furman* are not present to any significant degree in the Georgia procedure applied here.

For the reasons expressed in this opinion, we hold that the statutory system under which Gregg was sentenced to death does not violate the Constitution. Accordingly, the judgment of the Georgia Supreme Court is affirmed.

It is so ordered.

* * *

Mr. Justice Brennan, dissenting.

The Cruel and Unusual Punishments Clause "must draw its meaning from the evolving standards of decency that mark the progress of a maturing society."

* * *

In *Furman v. Georgia,* (1972) (concurring opinion), I read "evolving standards of decency" as requiring focus upon the essence of the death penalty itself and not primarily or solely upon the procedures under which the determination to inflict the penalty upon a particular person was made. . . . That continues to be my view. For the Clause forbidding cruel and unusual punishments under our constitutional system of government embodies in unique degree moral principles restraining the punishments that our civilized society may impose on those persons who transgress its laws. Thus, I too say: "For myself, I do not hesitate to assert the proposition that the only way the law has progressed from the days of the rack, the screw and the wheel is the development of moral concepts, or, as stated by the Supreme Court . . . the application of 'evolving standards of decency'. . . ."

This Court inescapably has the duty, as the ultimate arbiter of the meaning of our Constitution, to say whether, when individuals condemned to death stand before our Bar, "moral concepts" require us to hold that the law has progressed to the point where we should declare that the punishment of death, like punishments on the rack, the screw, and the wheel, is no longer morally tolerable in our civilized society. My opinion in *Furman v. Georgia* concluded that our civilization and the law had progressed to this point and that therefore the punishment of death, for whatever crime and under all circumstances, is "cruel and unusual" in violation of the Eighth and Fourteenth Amendments of the Constitution. . . .

The fatal constitutional infirmity in the punishment of death is that it treats "members of the human race as nonhumans, as objects to be toyed with and discarded. [It is] thus inconsistent with the fundamental premise of the clause that even the vilest criminal remains a human being possessed of common human dignity." As such it is a penalty that "subjects the individual to a fate forbidden by the principle of civilized treatment guaranteed by the [Clause]." I therefore would hold, on that ground alone, that death is today a cruel and unusual punishment prohibited by the Clause. "Justice of this kind is obviously no less shocking than the crime itself, and the new 'official' murder, far from offering redress for the offense committed against society, adds instead a second defilement to the first."

* * *

MR. JUSTICE MARSHALL, dissenting.

* * *

In *Furman* I concluded that the death penalty is constitutionally invalid for two reasons. First, the death penalty is excessive. And second, the American people, fully informed as to the purposes of the death penalty and its liabilities, would in my view reject it as morally unacceptable.

* * *

The death penalty, unnecessary to promote the goal of deterrence or to further any legitimate notion of retribution, is an excessive penalty forbidden by the Eighth and Fourteenth Amendments. I respectfully dissent from the Court's judgment upholding the sentences of death imposed upon the petitioners in these cases.

QUESTIONS AND COMMENTS

1 Should capital punishment be permitted in the United States? Under what circumstances?

2 Supreme Court justices have taken a number of different positions on capital punishment and the Eighth Amendment. Some have held that capital punishment is forbidden by the amendment, others that it cannot be applied in a discriminatory, wanton, freakish, or arbitrary manner, or so infrequently that it serves no legitimate end. However, the Court has mustered enough votes to hold (a) that mandatory death penalties are unconstitutional,[26] (b) that a death penalty for murder is not per se cruel and unusual punishment,[27] (c) that the procedure by which a death penalty is derived must be structured to maximize fairness and the guided use of discretion by the sentencing agency—particularly where that agency is a petit jury,[28] and (d) that the death penalty must be proportionate to the crime for which it is imposed.[29] For additional insights on the Court's current position, cf. *Lockett v. Ohio,* 438 U.S. 585 (1978); *Bell v. Ohio,* 438 U.S. 637 (1978); *Eddings v. Oklahoma,* 455 U.S. 104 (1982); *Adams v. Texas,* 448 U.S. 38 (1980); *Godfrey v. Georgia,* 446 U.S. 42 (1980); *Beck v. Alabama,* 447 U.S. 625 (1980); *Bullington v. Missouri,* 451 U.S. 430 (1981); *Estelle v. Smith,* 451 U.S. 454 (1981); *Coker v. Georgia,* 433 U.S. 584 (1977).

3 In your opinion, how would the Court that decided *Gregg v. Georgia* have decided *Francis v. Resweber?* Explain your answer.

4 On April 22, 1983, John Louis Evans, a convicted murderer, died in Alabama's electric chair. The electrocution required three different electrical charges of 1900 volts of electricity for a half-minute each—because Evans was not dead after the first and second charges. At the first charge, an electrode on Evans's leg exploded in smoke and flame. The second charge was given while Evans was limp. The third charge was given because a heartbeat could be faintly detected and, according to Alabama Prison

Commissioner Fred Smith, "so they could be exactly sure he was dead" (Mark C. Winne, "Evans Dies in the Electric Chair," *Atlanta Constitution,* April 23, 1983, p. 10A). Was that cruel and unusual punishment? Explain your answer.

FOOTNOTES

1 232 U.S. 383 (1914).
2 338 U.S. 25 (1949).
3 423 U.S. 44 (1976).
4 *Katz v. United States,* 389 U.S. 347 (1967).
5 Ibid., p. 418, N6.
6 16 Car. I, chap. 10.
7 *Kastigar v. United States,* 406 U.S. 441 (1972).
8 378 U.S. 1 (1964).
9 *Strauder v. West Virginia,* 100 U.S. 303 (1880).
10 *Castenada v. Partida,* 430 U.S. 482 (1977).
11 *Taylor v. Louisiana,* 419 U.S. 522 (1975).
12 *Baldwin v. New York,* 399 U.S. 66 (1970).
13 *Thompson v. Utah,* 170 U.S. 343 (1895).
14 399 U.S. 78 (1970).
15 406 U.S. 404 (1972).
16 441 U.S. 130 (1979).
17 According to *The Brethren,* p. 222.
18 287 U.S. 45 (1932).
19 316 U.S. 455 (1942).
20 See Paul Freund, *On Understanding the Supreme Court,* Little, Brown, Boston, 1951.
21 *Chandler v. Fretag,* 348 U.S. 3 (1954).
22 408 U.S. 238 (1972) (see note 2 post).
23 *O'Neil v. Vermont,* 144 U.S. 323 (1892).
24 370 U.S. 660 (1962).
25 *Trop v. Dulles,* 356 U.S. 86 (1958) (plurality opinion by Warren).
26 *Woodson v. North Carolina,* 428 U.S. 280 (1976).
27 *Jurek v. Texas,* 428 U.S. 262 (1976).
28 *Furman v. Georgia,* 408 U.S. 238 (1972).
29 *Enmund v. Florida,* 458 U.S. 782 (1982).

CHAPTER 9

FREEDOM FROM INVIDIOUS DISCRIMINATION

Race Discrimination
In Public Schools

Brown v. Board of Education (1954)

Swann v. Charlotte-Mecklenburg Board of Education (1971)

Milliken v. Bradley (1974)

With the adoption of the Fourteenth Amendment and its equal protection clause in 1868, blacks ostensibly gained protection against racial discrimination at the hands of the states. But for many years, that protection was somewhat diluted and less than what most black leaders thought required by the amendment. The tone was set in 1896 with the separate but equal doctrine enunciated by the Supreme Court in *Plessy v. Ferguson.* That doctrine held that segregation by race was acceptable under the equal protection clause as long as the separated facilities (in this case rail transportation) were equal. That doctrine was the major support for segregation by race in public schools for fifty-eight years. In *Brown v. Board of Education,* the Court reassesses the separate but equal rule.

Brown et al. v. Board of Education of Topeka et al.

347 U.S. 483; 74 S. Ct. 686; 98 L. Ed. 873 (1954)
Vote: 9–0

The facts are given in the opinion below.

MR. CHIEF JUSTICE WARREN delivered the opinion of the Court.

These cases come to us from the States of Kansas, South Carolina, Virginia, and Delaware. They are premised on different facts and different local conditions, but a common legal question justifies their consideration together in this consolidated opinion.*

*In the Kansas case, *Brown v. Board of Education,* the plaintiffs are Negro children of elementary school age residing in Topeka. They brought this action in the United States District Court for the District of Kansas to enjoin enforcement of a Kansas statute which permits, but does not require, cities of more than 15,000 population to maintain separate school facilities for Negro and white students. Kan. Gen. Stat. § 72–1724 (1949). Pursuant to that authority, the Topeka Board of Education elected to establish segregated elementary schools. Other public schools in the community, however, are operated on a nonsegregated basis. The three-judge District Court, convened under 28 U. S. C. §§ 2281 and 2284, found that segregation in public education has a detrimental effect upon Negro children, but denied relief on the ground that the Negro and white schools were substantially equal with respect to buildings, transportation, curricula, and educational qualifications of teachers. 98 F. Supp. 797. The case is here on direct appeal under 28 U. S. C. § 1253.

In the South Carolina case, *Briggs v. Elliot,* the plaintiffs are Negro children of both elementary and high school age residing in Clarendon County. They brought this action in the United States District Court for the Eastern District of South Carolina to enjoin enforcement of provisions in the state constitution and statutory code which require the segregation of Negroes and whites in public schools. S. C. Const., Art. XI, § 7; S. C. Code § 5377 (1942). The three-judge District Court, convened under 28 U. S. C. §§ 2281 and 2284, denied the requested relief. The court found that the Negro schools were inferior to the white schools and ordered the defendants to begin immediately to equalize the facilities. But the court sustained the validity of the contested provisions and denied the plaintiffs admission to the white schools during the equalization program. 98 F. Supp. 529. This Court vacated the District Court's judgment and remanded the case for the purpose of obtaining the Court's views on a report filed by the defendants concerning the progress made in the equalization program. 342 U. S. 350. On remand, the District Court found that substantial equality had been achieved except for buildings and that the defendants were proceeding to rectify this inequality as well. 103 F. Supp. 920. The case is again here on direct appeal under 28 U. S. C. § 1253.

In the Virginia case, *Davis v. County School Board,* the plaintiffs are Negro children of high school age residing in Prince Edward County. They brought this action in the United States District Court for the Eastern District of Virginia to enjoin enforcement of provisions in the state constitution and statutory code which require the segregation of Negroes and whites in public school. Va. Const., § 140; Va. Code § 22–221 (1950). The three-judge District Court, convened under 28 U. S. C. §§ 2281 and 2284, denied the requested relief. The court found the Negro school inferior in physical plant, curricula, and transportation, and ordered the defendants forthwith to provide substantially equal curricula and transportation and to "proceed with all reasonable diligence and dispatch to remove" the inequality in physical plant. But, as in the South Carolina case, the court sustained the validity of the contested provisions and denied the plaintiffs admission to the white schools during the equalization program. 103 F. Supp. 337. The case is here on direct appeal under 28 U. S. C. § 1253.

In the Delaware case, *Gebhart v. Belton,* the plaintiffs are Negro children of both elementary and high school age residing in New Castle County. They brought this action in the Delaware Court of Chancery to enjoin enforcement of provisions in the state constitution and statutory code which require the segregation of Negroes and whites in public schools. Del. Const., Art. X, § 2; Del Rev.

In each of the cases, minors of the Negro race, through their legal representatives, seek the aid of the courts in obtaining admission to the public schools of their community on a nonsegregated basis. In each instance, they had been denied admission to schools attended by white children under laws requiring or permitting segregation according to race. This segregation was alleged to deprive the plaintiffs of the equal protection of the laws under the Fourteenth Amendment. In each of the cases, other than the Delaware case, a three-judge federal district court denied relief to the plaintiffs on the so-called "separate but equal" doctrine announced by this Court in *Plessy v. Ferguson,* [1896]. Under that doctrine, equality of treatment is accorded when the races are provided substantially equal facilities, even though these facilities be separate. In the Delaware case, the Supreme Court of Delaware adhered to that doctrine, but ordered that the plaintiffs be admitted to the white schools because of their superiority to the Negro schools.

The plaintiffs contend that segregated public schools are not "equal" and cannot be made "equal," and that hence they are deprived of the equal protection of the laws. Because of the obvious importance of the question presented, the Court took jurisdiction. Argument was heard in the 1952 Term, and reargument was heard this Term on certain questions propounded by the Court.

Reargument was largely devoted to the circumstances surrounding the adoption of the Fourteenth Amendment in 1868. It covered exhaustively consideration of the Amendment in Congress, ratification by the states, then existing practices in racial segregation, and the views of proponents and opponents of the Amendment. This discussion and our own investigation convince us that, although these sources cast some light, it is not enough to resolve the problem with which we are faced. At best, they are inconclusive. The most avid proponents of the post-War Amendments undoubtedly intended them to remove all legal distinctions among "all persons born or naturalized in the United States." Their opponents, just as certainly, were antagonistic to both the letter and the spirit of the Amendments and wished them to have the most limited effect. What others in Congress and the state legislatures had in mind cannot be determined with any degree of certainty.

* * *

In the first cases in this Court construing the Fourteenth Amendment, decided shortly after its adoption, the Court interpreted it as proscribing all

---

Code § 2631 (1935). The Chancellor gave judgment for the plaintiffs and ordered their immediate admission to schools previously attended only by white children, on the ground that the Negro schools were inferior with respect to teacher training, pupil-teacher ratio, extracurricular activities, physical plant, and time and distance involved in travel. 87 A. 2d 862. The Chancellor also found that segregation itself results in an inferior education for Negro children (see note 10, *infra*), but did not rest his decision on that ground. *Id.,* at 865. The Chancellor's decree was affirmed by the Supreme Court of Delaware, which intimated, however, that the defendants might be able to obtain a modification of the decree after equalization of the Negro and white schools had been accomplished. 91 A. 2d 137, 152. The defendants, contending only that the Delaware courts had erred in ordering the immediate admission of the Negro plaintiffs to the white schools, applied to this Court for certiorari. The writ was granted, 344 U. S. 891. The plaintiffs, who were successful below, did not submit a cross-petition.

state-imposed discriminations against the Negro race. The doctrine of "separate but equal" did not make its appearance in this Court until 1896 in the case of *Plessy v. Ferguson,* involving not education but transportation. American courts have since labored with the doctrine for over half a century. In this Court, there have been six cases involving the "separate but equal" doctrine in the field of public education. In *Cumming v. County Board of Education,* [1899], and *Gong Lum v. Rice,* [1927], the validity of the doctrine itself was not challenged. In more recent cases, all on the graduate school level, inequality was found in that specific benefits enjoyed by white students were denied to Negro students of the same educational qualifications. *Missouri ex rel. Gaines v. Canada,* [1938]; *Sipuel v. Oklahoma,* [1948]; *Sweatt v. Painter,* [1950]; *McLaurin v. Oklahoma State Regents,* [1950]. In none of these cases was it necessary to re-examine the doctrine to grant relief to the Negro plaintiff. And in *Sweatt v. Painter,* the court expressly reserved decision on the question whether *Plessy v. Ferguson* should be held inapplicable to public education.

In the instant cases, that question is directly presented. Here, unlike *Sweatt v. Painter,* there are findings below that the Negro and white schools involved have been equalized, or are being equalized, with respect to buildings, curricula, qualifications and salaries of teachers, and other "tangible" factors. Our decision, therefore, cannot turn on merely a comparison of these tangible factors in the Negro and white schools involved in each of the cases. We must look instead to the effect of segregation itself on public education.

In approaching this problem, we cannot turn the clock back to 1868 when the Amendment was adopted, or even to 1896 when *Plessy v. Ferguson* was written. We must consider public education in the light of its full development and its present place in American life throughout the Nation. Only in this way can it be determined if segregation in public schools deprives these plaintiffs of the equal protection of the laws.

Today, education is perhaps the most important function of state and local governments. Compulsory school attendance laws and the great expenditures for education both demonstrate our recognition of the importance of education to our democratic society. It is required in the performance of our most basic public responsibilities, even service in the armed forces. It is the very foundation of good citizenship. Today it is a principal instrument in awakening the child to cultural values, in preparing him for later professional training, and in helping him to adjust normally to his environment. In these days, it is doubtful that any child may reasonably be expected to succeed in life if he is denied the opportunity of an education. Such an opportunity, where the state has undertaken to provide it, is a right which must be made available to all on equal terms.

We come then to the question presented: Does segregation of children in public schools solely on the basis of race, even though the physical facilities and other "tangible" factors may be equal, deprive the children of the minority group of equal educational opportunities? We believe that it does. . . .

To separate them from others of similar age and qualifications solely because of their race generates a feeling of inferiority as to their status in the community that may affect their hearts and minds in a way unlikely ever to be undone. The effect of this separation on their educational opportunities was well stated by a finding in the Kansas case by a court which nevertheless felt compelled to rule against the Negro plaintiffs:

> Segregation of white and colored children in public schools has a detrimental effect upon the colored children. The impact is greater when it has the sanction of the law; for the policy of separating the races is usually interpreted as denoting the inferiority of the negro group. A sense of inferiority affects the motivation of a child to learn. Segregation with the sanction of the law, therefore, has a tendency to [retard] the educational and mental development of negro children and to deprive them of some of the benefits they would receive in a racial[ly] integrated school system.

Whatever may have been the extent of psychological knowledge at the time of *Plessy v. Ferguson,* this finding is amply supported by modern authority. Any language in *Plessy v. Ferguson* contrary to this finding is rejected.

We conclude that in the field of public education the doctrine of "separate but equal" has no place. Separate educational facilities are inherently unequal. Therefore, we hold that the plaintiffs and others similarly situated for whom the actions have been brought are, by reason of the segregation complained of, deprived of the equal protection of the laws guaranteed by the Fourteenth Amendment. This disposition makes unnecessary any discussion whether such segregation also violates the Due Process Clause of the Fourteenth Amendment.

Because these are class actions, because of the wide applicability of this decision, and because of the great variety of local conditions, the formulation of decrees in these cases presents problems of considerable complexity. On reargument, the consideration of appropriate relief was necessarily subordinated to the primary question—the constitutionality of segregation in public education. We have now announced that such segregation is a denial of the equal protection of the laws. In order that we may have the full assistance of the parties in formulating decrees, the cases will be restored to the docket, and the parties are requested to present further argument on Questions 4 and 5 previously propounded by the Court for the reargument this Term.* The Attorney

*"4. Assuming it is decided that segregation in public schools violates the Fourteenth Amendment

"(*a*) would a decree necessarily follow providing that, within the limits set by normal geographic school districting, Negro children should forthwith be admitted to schools of their choice, or

"(*b*) may this Court, in the exercise of its equity powers, permit an effective gradual adjustment to be brought about from existing segregated systems to a system not based on color distinctions?

"5. On the assumption on which questions 4 (*a*) and (*b*) are based, and assuming further that this Court will exercise its equity powers to the end described in question 4 (*b*),

"(*a*) should this Court formulate detailed decrees in these cases:

"(*b*) if so, what specific issues should the decrees reach;

"(*c*) should this Court appoint a special master to hear evidence with a view to recommending specific terms for such decrees;

"(*d*) should this Court remand to the courts of first instance with directions to frame decrees in these cases, and if so what general directions should the decrees of this Court include and what procedures should the courts of first instance follow in arriving at the specific terms of more detailed decrees?"

General of the United States is again invited to participate. The Attorneys General of the states requiring or permitting segregation in public education will also be permitted to appear as *amici curiae* upon request to do so by September 15, 1954, and submission of briefs by October 1, 1954.

It is so ordered.

QUESTIONS AND COMMENTS

1 In implementing *Brown,* the Court was forced to make a number of policy choices. These included decisions
  a to turn enforcement of its mandate over to federal district courts,
  b to allow *Brown* to be heard as a class-action suit, and
  c to require that public schools cease to segregate students by race "with all deliberate speed" [*Brown II,* 349 U.S. 394 (1955)]. From the standpoint of hindsight, which of these choices were wise or unwise? Why?
2 *Brown* is sometimes said to have been decided on the basis of sociological evidence. Can you develop an argument that it was decided consistent with past Supreme Court precedents? A good approach here is to assess the strength of *Plessy v. Ferguson* as precedent in 1954.
3 To the extent that the Court based its decision on social, political, and psychological factors, how much of a departure was its approach from that used in other cases? Can you give examples of cases that illustrate your answer? Conversely, can you cite cases which indicate that such an approach was entirely proper?
4 In addition to the four state cases decided in *Brown,* the Court also decided at the same time a case from the District of Columbia *Bolling v. Sharpe,* 347 U.S., 497 (1954). The decisions in *Bolling* and *Brown* were the same, but *Bolling* was decided on the basis of the Fifth Amendment. Can you explain why?

*   *   *   *   *   *

Brown and *Bolling* clearly ruled out racial segregation in the public schools if such segregation was mandated by law—so-called de jure segregation. But segregation of the races can also be accomplished less directly through the siting of schools, the assignment of students and teachers, the zoning of school boundaries, etc. Whether the segregation is de jure or not, federal district courts have the authority to fashion appropriate remedies, such remedies being subject to review by the Supreme Court. *Swann v Charlotte-Mecklenburg Board of Education* and *Milliken v. Bradley* specifically illustrate the great discretion granted the district courts in dealing with or fashioning appropriate desegregation measures. At the same time, they make the point that this discretion is not unlimited.

Swann et al. v. Charlotte-Mecklenburg County Board of Education et al.

402 U.S. 1; 91 S. Ct. 1267; 28 L. Ed. 2d 554 (1971)
Vote: Unanimous

The facts are given in the opinion below.

MR. CHIEF JUSTICE BURGER delivered the opinion of the Court.

We granted certiorari in this case to review important issues as to the duties of school authorities and the scope of powers of federal courts under this Court's mandates to eliminate racially separate public schools established and maintained by state action. *Brown v. Board of Education,* (1954) (*Brown I*).

This case and those argued with it arose in States having a long history of maintaining two sets of schools in a single school system deliberately operated to carry out a governmental policy to separate pupils in schools solely on the basis of race. That was what *Brown v. Board of Education* was all about. These cases present us with the problem of defining in more precise terms than heretofore the scope of the duty of school authorities and district courts in implementing *Brown I* and the mandate to eliminate dual systems and establish unitary systems at once. . . .

The Charlotte-Mecklenburg school system, the 43d largest in the Nation, encompasses the city of Charlotte and surrounding Mecklenburg County, North Carolina. The area is large—550 square miles—spanning roughly 22 miles east-west and 36 miles north-south. During the 1968–1969 school year the system served more than 84,000 pupils in 107 schools. Approximately 71% of the pupils were found to be white and 29% Negro. As of June 1969 there were approximately 24,000 Negro students in the system, of whom 21,000 attended schools within the city of Charlotte. Two-thirds of those 21,000— approximately 14,000 Negro students—attended 21 schools which were either totally Negro or more than 99% Negro.

This situation came about under a desegregation plan approved by the District Court at the commencement of the present litigation in 1965, based upon geographic zoning with a free-transfer provision.

* * *

In April 1969 the District Court ordered the school board to come forward with a plan for both faculty and student desegregation. Proposed plans were accepted by the court in June and August 1969 on an interim basis only, and the board was ordered to file a third plan by November 1969. In November the board moved for an extension of time until February 1970, but when that was denied the board submitted a partially completed plan. In December 1969 the District Court held that the board's submission was unacceptable and appointed an expert in education administration, Dr. John Finger, to prepare a desegregation plan. Thereafter in February 1970, the District Court was presented with two alternative pupil assignment plans—the finalized "board plan" and the "Finger plan.". . .

The board plan proposed substantial assignment of Negroes to nine of the system's 10 high schools, producing 17% to 36% Negro population in each. The projected Negro attendance at the 10th school, Independence, was 2%. The proposed attendance zones for the high schools were typically shaped like wedges of a pie, extending outward from the center of the city to the suburban and rural areas of the county in order to afford residents of the center city area access to outlying schools.

As for junior high schools, the board plan rezoned the 21 school areas so that in 20 the Negro attendance would range from 0% to 38%. The other school, located in the heart of the Negro residential area, was left with an enrollment of 90% Negro.

The board plan with respect to elementary schools relied entirely upon gerrymandering of geographic zones. More than half of the Negro elementary pupils were left in nine schools that were 86% to 100% Negro; approximately half of the white elementary pupils were assigned to schools 86% to 100% white.

The Finger Plan. The plan submitted by the court-appointed expert, Dr. Finger, adopted the school board zoning plan for senior high schools with one modification: it required that an additional 300 Negro students be transported from the Negro residential area of the city to the nearly all-white Independence High School.

The Finger plan for the junior high schools employed much of the rezoning plan of the board, combined with the creation of nine "satellite" zones.* Under the satellite plan, inner-city Negro students were assigned by attendance zones to nine outlying predominantly white junior high schools, thereby substantially desegregating every junior high school in the system.

The Finger plan departed from the board plan chiefly in its handling of the system's 76 elementary schools. Rather than relying solely upon geographic zoning, Dr. Finger proposed use of zoning, pairing, and grouping techniques, with the result that student bodies throughout the system would range from 9% to 38% Negro.

The District Court described the plan thus:

> Like the board plan, the Finger plan does as much by rezoning school attendance lines as can reasonably be accomplished. However, unlike the board plan, it does not stop there. It goes further and desegregates all the rest of the elementary schools by the technique of grouping two or three outlying schools with one black inner city

---

*A "satellite zone" is an area which is not contiguous with the main attendance zone surrounding the school.

school; by transporting black students from grades one through four to the outlying white schools; and by transporting white students from the fifth and sixth grades from the outlying white schools to the inner city black schools.

Under the Finger plan, nine inner-city Negro schools were grouped in this manner with 24 suburban white schools.

[After completion of assorted court proceedings, a modified version of the Finger Plan received the approval of the district court on August 7, 1970. The court of appeals affirmed in part.]

* * *

Over the 16 years since *Brown II,* many difficulties were encountered in implementation of the basic constitutional requirement that the State not discriminate between public school children on the basis of their race. Nothing in our national experience prior to 1955 prepared anyone for dealing with changes and adjustments of the magnitude and complexity encountered since then. Deliberate resistance of some to the Court's mandates has impeded the good-faith efforts of others to bring school systems into compliance. The detail and nature of these dilatory tactics have been noted frequently by this Court and other courts. . . .

The problems encountered by the district courts and courts of appeals make plain that we should now try to amplify guidelines, however incomplete and imperfect, for the assistance of school authorities and courts.

* * *

We turn now to the problem of defining with more particularity the responsibilities of school authorities in desegregating a state-enforced dual school system in light of the Equal Protection Clause.

* * *

The central issue in this case is that of student assignment, and there are essentially four problem areas:

1 to what extent racial balance or racial quotas may be used as an implement in a remedial order to correct a previously segregated system;

2 whether every all-Negro and all-white school must be eliminated as an indispensable part of a remedial process of desegregation;

3 what the limits are, if any, on the rearrangement of school districts and attendance zones, as a remedial measure; and

4 what the limits are, if any, on the use of transportation facilities to correct state-enforced racial school segregation.

Racial Balances or Racial Quotas

The constant theme and thrust of every holding from *Brown I* to date is that state-enforced separation of races in public schools is discrimination that violates the Equal Protection Clause. The remedy commanded was to dismantle dual school systems.

We are concerned in these cases with the elimination of the discrimination inherent in the dual school systems, not with myriad factors of human existence which can cause discrimination in a multitude of ways on racial, religious, or ethnic grounds. . . .

Our objective in dealing with the issues presented by these cases is to see that school authorities exclude no pupil of a racial minority from any school, directly or indirectly, on account of race; it does not and cannot embrace all the problems of racial prejudice, even when those problems contribute to disproportionate racial concentrations in some schools.

In this case it is urged that the District Court has imposed a racial balance requirement of 71%–29% on individual schools. The fact that no such objective was actually achieved—and would appear to be impossible—tends to blunt that claim, yet in the opinion and order of the District Court of December 1, 1969, we find that court directing

> that efforts should be made to reach a 71–29 ratio in the various schools so that there will be no basis for contending that one school is racially different from the others . . . , [t]hat pupils of all grades [should] be assigned in such a way that as nearly as practicable the various schools at various grade levels have about the same proportion of black and white students.

The District Judge went on to acknowledge that variation "from that norm may be unavoidable." This contains intimations that the "norm" is a fixed mathematical racial balance reflecting the pupil constituency of the system. If we were to read the holding of the District Court to require, as a matter of substantive constitutional right, any particular degree of racial balance or mixing, that approach would be disapproved and we would be obliged to reverse. The constitutional command to desegregate schools does not mean that every school in every community must always reflect the racial composition of the school system as a whole. . . .

. . . The use made of mathematical ratios was no more than a starting point in the process of shaping a remedy, rather than an inflexible requirement. From that starting point the District Court proceeded to frame a decree that was within its discretionary powers, as an equitable remedy for the particular circumstances. As we said . . . a school authority's remedial plan or a district court's remedial decree is to be judged by its effectiveness. Awareness of the racial composition of the whole school system is likely to be a useful starting point in shaping a remedy to correct past constitutional violations. In sum, the very limited use of mathematical ratios was within the equitable remedial discretion of the District Court.

One-Race Schools

The record in this case reveals the familiar phenomenon that in metropolitan areas minority groups are often found concentrated in one part of the city. In some circumstances certain schools may remain all or largely of one race until new schools can be provided or neighborhood patterns change. Schools all or predominantly of one race in a district of mixed population will require close scrutiny to determine that school assignments are not part of state-enforced segregation.

* * *

An optional majority-to-minority transfer provision has long been recognized as a useful part of every desegregation plan. Provision for optional transfer of those in the majority racial group of a particular school to other schools where they will be in the minority is an indispensable remedy for those students willing to transfer to other schools in order to lessen the impact on them of the state-imposed stigma of segregation. In order to be effective, such a transfer arrangement must grant the transferring student free transportation and space must be made available in the school to which he desires to move. The court orders in this and the companion *Davis* case now provide such an option.

Remedial Altering of Attendance Zones

The maps submitted in these cases graphically demonstrate that one of the principal tools employed by school planners and by courts to break up the dual school system has been a frank—and sometimes drastic—gerrymandering of school districts and attendance zones. An additional step was pairing, "clustering," or "grouping" of schools with attendance assignments made deliberately to accomplish the transfer of Negro students out of formerly segregated Negro schools and transfer of white students to formerly all-Negro schools. More often than not, these zones are neither compact nor contiguous; indeed they may be on opposite ends of the city. As an interim corrective measure, this cannot be said to be beyond the broad remedial powers of a court.

* * *

Transportation of Students

The scope of permissible transportation of students as an implement of a remedial decree has never been defined by this Court and by the very nature of the problem it cannot be defined with precision. No rigid guidelines as to student transportation can be given for application to the infinite variety of problems presented in thousands of situations. Bus transportation has been an integral part of the public education system for years, and was perhaps the single most important factor in the transition from the one-room schoolhouse to the consolidated school. Eighteen million of the Nation's public school children, approximately 39%, were transported to their schools by bus in 1969–1970 in all parts of the country.

The importance of bus transportation as a normal and accepted tool of educational policy is readily discernible in this and the companion case. The Charlotte school authorities did not purport to assign students on the basis of geographically drawn zones until 1965 and then they allowed almost unlimited transfer privileges. The District Court's conclusion that assignment of children to the school nearest their home serving their grade would not produce an effective dismantling of the dual system is supported by the record.

Thus the remedial techniques used in the District Court's order were within that court's power to provide equitable relief; implementation of the decree is well within the capacity of the school authority.

* * *

The Court of Appeals, searching for a term to define the equitable remedial power of the district courts, used the term "reasonableness."...

On the facts of this case, we are unable to conclude that the order of the District Court is not reasonable, feasible and workable. However, in seeking to define the scope of remedial power or the limits on remedial power of courts in an area as sensitive as we deal with here, words are poor instruments to convey the sense of basic fairness inherent in equity. Substance, not semantics, must govern, and we have sought to suggest the nature of limitations without frustrating the appropriate scope of equity.

At some point, these school authorities and others like them should have achieved full compliance with this Court's decision in *Brown I.* The systems would then be "unitary" in the sense required by our decisions in *Green* and *Alexander.*

It does not follow that the communities served by such systems will remain demographically stable, for in a growing, mobile society, few will do so. Neither school authorities nor district courts are constitutionally required to make year-by-year adjustments of the racial composition of student bodies once the affirmative duty to desegregate has been accomplished and racial discrimination through official action is eliminated from the system. This does not mean that federal courts are without power to deal with future problems; but in the absence of a showing that either the school authorities or some other agency of the State has deliberately attempted to fix or alter demographic patterns to affect the racial composition of the schools, further intervention by a district court should not be necessary.

For the reasons herein set forth, the judgment of the Court of Appeals is affirmed as to those parts in which it affirmed the judgment of the District Court. The order of the District Court, dated August 7, 1970, is also affirmed.

It is so ordered.

Milliken, Governor of Michigan et al. v. Bradley et al.

418 U.S. 717; 94 S. Ct. 3112; 41 L. Ed. 2d 1069 (1974)
Vote: 5–4

Bradley and others brought this class action, charging that the Detroit public school system was racially segregated as a result of official policy. They sought a plan to eliminate racial segregation from the Detroit public school system. A federal district court ordered state officials to submit desegregation plans encompassing a three-county metropolitan area in spite of the fact that eighty-five school districts in the outlying areas of the counties were not parties to the suit and there was no allegation that they had committed constitutional violations. When Detroit-only plans were submitted, all were rejected. The judge concluded that only a metropolitan plan would suffice and appointed a panel to draw up such a plan for Detroit and fifty-three of the eighty-five school districts. At the same time, the court ordered the Detroit School Board to purchase 295 school buses to provide transportation under an interim plan to be used in the school year 1972–73.

A court of appeals upheld these actions, holding that constitutional violations had occurred, that the district court was required to desegregate the Detroit school system, and that a metropolitan-area plan embracing the fifty-three outlying districts was within the district court's power, even though no evidence was introduced to show that the outlying districts had committed acts of de jure segregation. The U.S. Supreme Court granted certiorari to review the decision of the appellate court.

MR. CHIEF JUSTICE BURGER delivered the opinion of the Court.

We granted certiorari in these consolidated cases to determine whether a federal court may impose a multidistrict, areawide remedy to a single-district de jure segregation problem absent any finding that the other included school districts have failed to operate unitary school systems within their districts, absent any claim or finding that the boundary lines of any affected school district were established with the purpose of fostering racial segregation in public schools, absent any finding that the included districts committed acts which effected segregation within the other districts, and absent a meaningful opportunity for the included neighboring school districts to present evidence or be heard on the propriety of a multidistrict remedy or on the question of constitutional violations by those neighboring districts.

* * *

Ever since *Brown v. Board of Education,* (1954), judicial consideration of school desegregation cases has begun with the standard:

> [I]n the field of public education the doctrine of "separate but equal" has no place. Separate educational facilities are inherently unequal.

This has been reaffirmed time and again as the meaning of the Constitution and the controlling rule of law.

The target of the *Brown* holding was clear and forthright: the elimination of state-mandated or deliberately maintained dual school systems with certain schools for Negro pupils and others for white pupils. This duality and racial segregation were held to violate the Constitution in the cases subsequent to 1954, including particularly *Green v. County School Board of New Kent County,* (1968); *Raney v. Board of Education,* (1968); *Monroe v. Board of Comm'rs,* (1968); *Swann v. Charlotte-Mecklenburg Board of Education,* (1971); *Wright v. Council of the City of Emporia,* (1972); *United States v. Scotland Neck Board of Education,* (1972).

* * *

In *Brown v. Board of Education, (Brown II),* the Court's first encounter with the problem of remedies in school desegregation cases, the Court noted:

> In fashioning and effectuating the decrees, the courts will be guided by equitable principles. Traditionally, equity has been characterized by a practical flexibility in shaping its remedies and by a facility for adjusting and reconciling public and private needs.

In further refining the remedial process, *Swann* held, the task is to correct, by a balancing of the individual and collective interests, "the condition that offends the Constitution." A federal remedial power may be exercised "only on the basis of a constitutional violation" and, "[a]s with any equity case, the nature of the violation determines the scope of the remedy."

Proceeding from these basic principles, we first note that in the District Court the complainants sought a remedy aimed at the *condition* alleged to offend the Constitution—the segregation within the Detroit City School District. The court acted on this theory of the case and in its initial ruling on the "Desegregation Area" stated:

> The task before this court, therefore, is now, and . . . has always been, how to desegregate the Detroit public schools.

Thereafter, however, the District Court abruptly rejected the proposed Detroit-only plans on the ground that "while [they] would provide a racial mix more in keeping with the Black-White proportions of the student population [they] would accentuate the racial identifiability of the [Detroit] district as a Black school system, and would not accomplish desegregation." "[T]he racial composition of the student body is such," said the court, "that the plan's implementation would clearly make the entire Detroit public school system racially identifiable" "leav[ing] many of its schools 75 to 90 percent Black." Consequently, the court reasoned, it was imperative to "look beyond the limits of the Detroit school district for a solution to the problem of segregation in the Detroit public schools . . ." since "[s]chool district lines are simply matters of political convenience and may not be used to deny constitutional rights." Accordingly, the District Court proceeded to redefine the relevant area to include areas of predominantly white pupil population in order to ensure that "upon implementation, no school, grade or classroom [would be] substantially disproportionate to the overall pupil racial composition" of the entire metropolitan area.

While specifically acknowledging that the District Court's findings of a condition of segregation were limited to Detroit, the Court of Appeals approved the use of a metropolitan remedy largely on the grounds that it is

> impossible to declare 'clearly erroneous' the District Judge's conclusion that any Detroit only segregation plan will lead directly to a single segregated Detroit school district overwhelmingly black in all of its schools, surrounded by a ring of suburbs and suburban school districts overwhelmingly white in composition in a State in which the racial composition is 87 percent white and 13 percent black.

Viewing the record as a whole, it seems clear that the District Court and the Court of Appeals shifted the primary focus from a Detroit remedy to the metropolitan area only because of their conclusion that total desegregation of Detroit would not produce the racial balance which they perceived as desirable. Both courts proceeded on an assumption that the Detroit schools could not be truly desegregated—in their view of what constituted desegregation—unless the racial composition of the student body of each school substantially reflected the racial composition of the population of the metropolitan area as a whole. The metropolitan area was then defined as Detroit plus 53 of the outlying school districts. . . .

The District Court's approach to what constituted "actual desegregation" raises the fundamental question, not presented in *Swann,* as to the circumstances in which a federal court may order desegregation relief that embraces more than a single school district. The Court's analytical starting point was its conslusion that school district lines are no more than arbitrary lines on a map drawn "for political convenience." Boundary lines may be bridged where there has been a constitutional violation calling for interdistrict relief, but the notion that school district lines may be casually ignored or treated as a mere administrative convenience is contrary to the history of public education in our country. No single tradition in public education is more deeply rooted than local control over the operation of schools; local autonomy has long been thought essential both to the maintenance of community concern and support for public schools and to quality of the educational process.

Thus, in *San Antonio School District v. Rodriguez,* (1973); we observed that local control over the educational process affords citizens an opportunity to participate in decisionmaking, permits the structuring of school programs to fit local needs, and encourages "experimentation, innovation, and a healthy competition for educational excellence."

* * *

The controlling principle consistently expounded in our holdings is that the scope of the remedy is determined by the nature and extent of the constitutional violation. Before the boundaries of separate and autonomous school districts may be set aside by consolidating the separate units for remedial purposes or by imposing a cross-district remedy, it must first be shown that there has been a constitutional violation within one district that produces a significant segregative effect in another district. Specifically, it must be shown that racially discriminatory acts of the state or local school districts, or of a single school district have been a substantial cause of interdistrict segregation.

* * *

The record before us, voluminous as it is, contains evidence of *de jure* segregated conditions only in the Detroit schools; indeed, that was the theory on which the litigation was initially based and on which the District Court took evidence. With no showing of significant violation by the 53 outlying school districts and no evidence of any interdistrict violation or effect, the court went beyond the original theory of the case framed by the pleadings and mandated a metropolitan area remedy. To approve the remedy ordered by the court would impose on the outlying districts, not shown to have committed any constitutional violation, a wholly impermissible remedy based on a standard not hinted at in *Brown I* and *II* or any holding of this Court.

* * *

The constitutional right of the Negro respondents residing in Detroit is to attend a unitary school system in that district. Unless petitioners drew the district lines in a discriminatory fashion, or arranged for white students residing in the Detroit District to attend schools in Oakland and Macomb Counties, they were under no constitutional duty to make provisions for Negro students to do so. The view of the dissenters, that the existence of a dual system in Detroit can be made the basis for a decree requiring cross-district transportation of pupils, cannot be supported on the grounds that it represents merely the devising of a suitably flexible remedy for the violation of rights already established by our prior decisions. It can be supported only by drastic expansion of the constitutional right itself, an expansion without any support in either constitutional principle or precedent.

* * *

We conclude that the relief ordered by the District Court and affirmed by the Court of Appeals was based upon an erroneous standard and was unsupported by record evidence that acts of the outlying districts effected the discrimination found to exist in the schools of Detroit. Accordingly, the judgment of the Court of Appeals is reversed and the case is remanded for further proceedings consistent with this opinion leading to prompt formulation of a decree directed to eliminating the segregation found to exist in Detroit city schools, a remedy which has been delayed since 1970.

Reversed and remanded.

* * *

MR. JUSTICE DOUGLAS, dissenting.

* * *

When we rule against the metropolitan area remedy we take a step that will likely put the problems of the blacks and our society back to the period that antedated the "separate but equal" regime of *Plessy v. Ferguson,* [1896]. The reason is simple. The inner core of Detroit is now rather solidly black; and the blacks, we know, in many instances are likely to be poorer, just as were the Chicanos in *San Antonio School District v. Rodriguez.* By that decision the poorer school districts must pay their own way. It is therefore a foregone conclusion that we have now given the States a formula whereby the poor must pay their own way.

Today's decision, given *Rodriguez,* means that there is no violation of the Equal Protection Clause though the schools are segregated by race and though the black schools are not only "separate" but "inferior."

So far as equal protection is concerned we are now in a dramatic retreat from the 7-to-1 decision in 1896 that blacks could be segregated in public facilities, provided they received equal treatment.

As I indicated in *Keyes v. School District No. 1 Denver, Colorado,* [1973], there is so far as the school cases go no constitutional difference between *de facto* and *de jure* segregation. Each school board performs state action for Fourteenth Amendment purposes when it draws the lines that confine it to a given area, when it builds schools at particular sites, or when it allocates students. The creation of the school districts in Metropolitan Detroit either maintained existing segregation or caused additional segregation. Restrictive covenants maintained by state action or inaction build black ghettos. It is state action when public funds are dispensed by housing agencies to build racial ghettos. Where a community is racially mixed and school authorities segregate schools, or assign black teachers to black schools or close schools in fringe areas and build new schools in black areas and in more distant white areas, the State creates and nurtures a segregated school system, just as surely as did those States involved in *Brown v. Board of Education,* when they maintained dual school systems.

All these conditions and more were found by the District Court to exist. The issue is not whether there should be racial balance but whether the State's use of various devices that end up with black schools and white schools brought the Equal Protection Clause into effect. Given the State's control over the educational system in Michigan, the fact that the black schools are in one district and the white schools are in another is not controlling—either constitutionally or equitably. No specific plan has yet been adopted. We are still at an interlocutory stage of a long drawn-out judicial effort at school desegregation. It is conceivable that ghettos develop on their own without any hint of state action. But since Michigan by one device or another has over the years created black school districts and white school districts, the task of equity is to provide a unitary system for the affected area where, as here, the State washes its hands of its own creations.

* * *

Mr. Justice Marshall, with whom Mr. Justice Douglas, Mr. Justice Brennan, and Mr. Justice White join, dissenting.

In *Brown v. Board of Education,* this Court held that segregation of children in public schools on the basis of race deprives minority group children of equal educational opportunities and therefore denies them the equal protection of the laws under the Fourteenth Amendment. This Court recognized then that remedying decades of segregation in public education would not be an easy task. Subsequent events, unfortunately, have seen that prediction bear bitter fruit. But however imbedded old ways, however ingrained old prejudices, this Court has not been diverted from its appointed task of making "a living truth" of our constitutional ideal of equal justice under law. *Cooper v. Aaron,* (1958).

After 20 years of small, often difficult steps toward that great end, the Court today takes a giant step backwards. Notwithstanding a record showing widespread and pervasive racial segregation in the educational system provided by the State of Michigan for children in Detroit, this Court holds that the District Court was powerless to require the State to remedy its constitutional violation in any meaningful fashion. Ironically purporting to base its result on the principle that the scope of the remedy in a desegregation case should be determined by the nature and the extent of the constitutional violation, the Court's answer is to provide no remedy at all for the violation proved in this case, thereby guaranteeing that Negro children in Detroit will receive the same separate and inherently unequal education in the future as they have been unconstitutionally afforded in the past.

I cannot subscribe to this emasculation of our constitutional guarantee of equal protection of the laws and must respectfully dissent. Our precedents, in my view, firmly establish that where, as here, state-imposed segregation has been demonstrated, it becomes the duty of the State to eliminate root and branch all vestiges of racial discrimination and to achieve the greatest possible degree of actual desegregation. I agree with both the District Court and the Court of Appeals that, under the facts of this case, this duty cannot be fulfilled unless the State of Michigan involves outlying metropolitan area school districts in its desegregation remedy.

* * *

The rights at issue in this case are too fundamental to be abridged on grounds as superficial as those relied on by the majority today. We deal here with the right of all of our children, whatever their race, to an equal start in life and to an equal opportunity to reach their full potential as citizens. Those children who have been denied that right in the past deserve better than to see fences thrown up to deny them that right in the future. Our Nation, I fear, will be ill served by the Court's refusal to remedy separate and unequal education, for unless our children begin to learn together, there is little hope that our people will ever learn to live together.

The great irony of the Court's opinion and, in my view, its most serious analytical flaw may be gleaned from its concluding sentence, in which the Court remands for "prompt formulation of a decree directed to eliminating the segregation found to exist in Detroit city schools, a remedy which has been delayed since 1970."

The majority, however, seems to have forgotten the District Court's explicit finding that a Detroit-only decree, the only remedy permitted under today's decision, "would not accomplish desegregation."

* * *

We cautioned in *Swann,* of course, that the dismantling of a segregated school system does not mandate any particular racial balance. We also concluded that a remedy under which there would remain a small number of racially identifiable schools was only presumptively inadequate and might be justified. But this is a totally different case. The flaw of a Detroit-only decree is not that it does not reach some ideal degree of racial balance or mixing. It simply does not promise to achieve actual desegregation at all. It is one thing to have a system where a small number of students remain in racially identifiable schools. It is something else entirely to have a system where all students continue to attend such schools.

The continued racial identifiability of the Detroit schools under a Detroit-only remedy is not simply a reflection of their high percentage of Negro students. What is or is not a racially identifiable vestige of *de jure* segregation must necessarily depend on several factors.

Foremost among these should be the relationship between the schools in question and the neighboring community. For these purposes the city of Detroit and its surrounding suburbs must be viewed as a single community.

* * *

Desegregation is not and was never expected to be an easy task. Racial attitudes ingrained in our Nation's childhood and adolescence are not quickly thrown aside in its middle years. But just as the inconvenience of some cannot be allowed to stand in the way of the rights of others, so public opposition, no matter how strident, cannot be permitted to divert this Court from the enforcement of the constitutional principles at issue in this case. Today's holding, I fear, is more a reflection of a perceived public mood that we have gone far enough in enforcing the Constitution's guarantee of equal justice than it is the product of neutral principles of law. In the short run, it may seem to be the easier course to allow our great metropolitan areas to be divided up each into two cities—one white, the other black—but it is a course, I predict, our people will ultimately regret. I dissent.

QUESTIONS AND COMMENTS

1 In *Green v. School Board of New Kent County,* 319 U.S. 430 (1968), the Court held that the time for implementing desegregation had run out, and rather than desegregate "with all deliberate speed," the school board was required to do so "now."

2 In your opinion, has the Supreme Court allowed the district courts too little or too much flexibility in eliminating racial segregation in the schools? Explain your answer.

In Employment Practices

Washington v. Davis (1976)
United Steelworkers of America v. Weber (1979)

In controversies dealing with race discrimination, a key legal concept is "intent." The fact that the Supreme Court has declared it unconstitutional to discriminate on the basis of race does not mean that enforcement of that prohibition will be automatic. It remains up to the affected individual or group to bring a legal complaint and to prove that government is guilty of racial discrimination. How is that proof to be established? Prior to *Davis,* a number of lower courts had held that when a government policy has a disproportionate impact on a class, race discrimination is proved without regard to intent or motive unless the classification can be justified by the government. A contrary view holds that race discrimination is unconstitutional only if intent or motive to discriminate is established. In *Davis,* the Supreme Court chooses between these two positions in the area of employment.

In the Weber Case, we observe policy-making in a nonconstitutional context. *Weber* turns on the correct interpretation of Title VII of the Civil Rights Act of 1964. It is an "affirmative action" case. In *Brown v. Board of Education* and other cases decided between 1954 and 1985, the Court has firmly established that under certain conditions racial discrimination violates the equal protection clause. Almost always the cases have dealt with discrimination against blacks. Nevertheless, it was widely assumed, as Justice Harlan asserted in his *Plessy* dissent, that the Constitution is color-blind.

Under a color-blind test, discrimination on the basis of white skin color is just as unconstitutional as discrimination based on black skin color. But given the 300 years of racial discrimination to which blacks had been subjected, the suggestion that "we ought to do something for blacks" proved appealing in the 1960s. Thus, the affirmative action provisions of the 1964 Civil Rights Act.

Conceptually, however, there is some logical tension between color-blindness on the one hand and doing something affirmative for blacks on the other. This tension brought several cases to the Supreme Court in the seventies. While most of these cases were denied plenary review, one, *Regents of the University of California v. Bakke,* produced a decision of some note. In *Bakke,* a 32-year-old white male sought admission to the medical school at the University of California at Davis. Allan Bakke's grade-point average and medical school admissions test scores were exceptionally high. On grades and scores alone, Bakke would have gained admittance. However, because the medical school had an affirmative action program which allocated sixteen places for disadvantaged minority applicants, Bakke's application was denied. On review, the Supreme Court ordered Bakke's admission and condemned the use of numerical quotas. At the same time, the Court appeared to approve race consciousness in selecting students for professional programs so long as race was only one of the factors considered relevant to attaining a diverse student body.

Bakke concerned state or public policy, since a state university was involved. *Weber,* on the other hand, raises affirmative action questions in a private or nonpublic context. The Weber Court, therefore, restricts its discussion and its decision to the meaning of Title VII.

Washington, Mayor of Washington, D.C. et al. v. Davis et al.

426 U.S. 229; 96 S. Ct. 2040; 48 L. Ed. 2d 597 (1976)
Vote: 7–2

On April 19, 1970, two black police officers filed suit against the chief of police and other officials in Washington, D.C., alleging that promotion policies were racially discriminatory. They sought a declaratory judgment to that effect, and an injunction. Later two additional persons (Harley and Sellers) were allowed to intervene. The amended complaint alleged that Harley's and Seller's applications to become police officers had been rejected and that the department's recruiting procedure discriminated against black applicants. The practices described included a written personnel test which excluded a disproportionately high number of black applicants. These practices were challenged as a violation of Fifth Amendment due process rights. The plaintiffs' motion for a summary judgment that the test was unconstitutional was rejected in the district court. The court of appeals reversed and directed summary judgment in favor of Harley and Sellers. The U.S. Supreme Court granted certiorari.

MR. JUSTICE WHITE delivered the opinion of the Court.

This case involves the validity of a qualifying test administered to applicants for positions as police officers in the District of Columbia Metropolitan Police Department. The test was sustained by the District Court but invalidated by the Court of Appeals. We are in agreement with the District Court and hence reverse the judgment of the Court of Appeals. . . .

According to the findings and conclusions of the District Court, to be accepted by the Department and to enter an intensive 17-week training program, the police recruit was required to satisfy certain physical and character standards, to be a high school graduate or its equivalent, and to receive a grade of at least 40 out of 80 on "Test 21," which is "an examination that is used generally throughout the federal service, which "was developed by the Civil Service Commission, not the Police Department," and which was "designed to test verbal ability, vocabulary, reading and comprehension."

The validity of Test 21 was the sole issue before the court on the motions for summary judgment. The District Court noted that there was no claim of "an intentional discrimination or purposeful discriminatory acts" but only a claim that Test 21 bore no relationship to job performance and "has a highly discriminatory impact in screening out black candidates." Respondents' evidence, the District Court said, warranted three conclusions: "(a) The number of black police officers, while substantial, is not proportionate to the population mix of the city. (b) A higher percentage of blacks fail the Test than whites. (c) The Test has not been validated to establish its reliability for measuring subsequent job performance." This showing was deemed sufficient to shift the burden of proof to the defendants in the action, petitioners here; but the court nevertheless concluded that on the undisputed facts respondents were not entitled to relief. The District Court relied on several factors. Since August 1969, 44% of new police force recruits had been black; that figure also represented the proportion of blacks on the total force and was roughly equivalent to 20- to 29-year-old blacks in the 50-mile radius in which the recruiting efforts of the Police Department had been concentrated. It was undisputed that the Department had systematically and affirmatively sought to enroll black officers many of whom passed the test but failed to report for duty. The District Court rejected the assertion that Test 21 was culturally slanted to favor whites and was "satisfied that the undisputable facts prove the test to be reasonably and directly related to the requirements of the police recruit training program and that it is neither so designed nor operates [sic] to discriminate against otherwise qualified blacks." It was thus not necessary to show that Test 21 was not only a useful indicator of training school performance but had also been validated in terms of job performance—"The lack of job performance validation does not defeat the Test, given its direct relationship to recruiting and the valid part it plays in this process." The District Court ultimately concluded that "[t]he proof is wholly lacking that a police officer qualifies on the color of his skin rather than ability" and that the Department "should not be required on this showing to lower standards or to abandon efforts to achieve excellence."

Having lost on both constitutional and statutory issues in the District Court, respondents brought the case to the Court of Appeals claiming that their summary judgment motion, which rested on purely constitutional grounds, should have been granted. The tendered constitutional issue was whether the use of Test 21 invidiously discriminated against Negroes and hence denied them due process of law contrary to the commands of the Fifth Amendment. The Court of Appeals, addressing that issue, announced that it would be guided by *Griggs v. Duke Power Co.,* (1971), a case involving the interpretation and application of Title VII of the Civil Rights Act of 1964, and held that the statutory standards elucidated in that case were to govern the due process question tendered in this one.

The court went on to declare that lack of discriminatory intent in designing and administering Test 21 was irrelevant; the critical fact was rather that a far greater proportion of blacks—four times as many—failed the test then did whites. This disproportionate impact, standing alone and without regard to whether it indicated a discriminatory purpose, was held sufficient to establish a constitutional violation, absent proof by petitioners that the test was an adequate measure of job performance in addition to being an indicator of probable success in the training program, a burden which the court ruled petitioners had failed to discharge. That the Department had made substantial efforts to recruit blacks was held beside the point and the fact that the racial distribution of recent hirings and of the Department itself might be roughly equivalent to the racial makeup of the surrounding community, broadly conceived, was put aside as a "comparison [not] material to this appeal."

The Court of Appeals, over a dissent, accordingly reversed the judgment of the District Court and directed that respondents' motion for partial summary judgment be granted. We granted the petition for certiorari, filed by the District of Columbia officials.

Because the Court of Appeals erroneously applied the legal standards applicable to Title VII cases in resolving the constitutional issue before it, we reverse its judgment in respondents' favor. Although the petition for certiorari did not present this ground for reversal, our Rule 40 (1) (d) (2) provides that we "may notice a plain error not presented"; and this is an appropriate occasion to invoke the Rule.

As the Court of Appeals understood Title VII, employees or applicants proceeding under it need not concern themselves with the employer's possibly discriminatory purpose but instead may focus solely on the racially differential impact of the challenged hiring or promotion practices. This is not the constitutional rule. We have never held that the constitutional standard for adjudicating claims of invidious racial discrimination is identical to the standards applicable under Title VII, and we decline to do so today.

The central purpose of the Equal Protection Clause of the Fourteenth Amendment is the prevention of official conduct discriminating on the basis of race. It is also true that the Due Process Clause of the Fifth Amendment contains an equal protection component prohibiting the United States from invidiously discriminating between individuals or groups. *Bolling v. Sharpe,* (1954). But our cases have not embraced the proposition that a law or other official act, without regard to whether it reflects a racially discriminatory purpose, is unconstitutional *solely* because it has a racially disproportionate impact.

* * *

The school desegregation cases have also adhered to the basic equal protection principle that the invidious quality of a law claimed to be racially discriminatory must ultimately be traced to a racially discriminatory purpose. That there are both predominantly black and predominantly white schools in a community is not alone violative of the Equal Protection Clause. The essential element of *de jure* segregation is "a current condition of segregation resulting from intentional state action." *Keyes v. School Dist. No. 1,* (1973). "The differentiating factor between *de jure* segregation and so-called *de facto* segregation . . . is *purpose* or *intent* to segregate." The Court has also recently rejected allegations of racial discrimination based solely on the statistically disproportionate racial impact of various provisions of the Social Security Act because "[t]he acceptance of appellants' constitutional theory would render suspect each difference in treatment among the grant classes, however lacking in racial motivation and however otherwise rational the treatment might be." *Jefferson v. Hackney,* (1972).

This is not to say that the necessary discriminatory racial purpose must be express or appear on the face of the statute, or that a law's disproportionate impact is irrelevant in cases involving Constitution-based claims of racial discrimination. A statute, otherwise neutral on its face, must not be applied so as invidiously to discriminate on the basis of race. *Yick Wo v. Hopkins,* (1886). It is also clear from the cases dealing with racial discrimination in the selection of juries that the systematic exclusion of Negroes is itself such an "unequal application of the law . . . as to show intentional discrimination." *Akins v. Texas,* [1944]. A prima facie case of discriminatory purpose may be proved as well by the absence of Negroes on a particular jury combined with the failure of the jury commissioners to be informed of eligible Negro jurors in a community, *Hill v. Texas,* (1942), or with racially nonneutral selection procedures, *Whitus v. Georgia,* (1967). With a prima facie case made out, "the burden of proof shifts to the State to rebut the presumption of unconstitutional action by showing that permissible racially neutral selection criteria and procedures have produced the monochromatic result."

Necessarily, an invidious discriminatory purpose may often be inferred from the totality of the relevant facts, including the fact, if it is true, that the law bears more heavily on one race than another. It is also not infrequently true that the discriminatory impact—in the jury cases for example, the total or seriously disproportionate exclusion of Negroes from jury venires—may for all practical purposes demonstrate unconstitutionality because in various circumstances the discrimination is very difficult to explain on nonracial grounds. Nevertheless, we have not held that a law, neutral on its face and serving ends otherwise within the power of government to pursue, is invalid under the Equal Protection Clause simply because it may affect a greater proportion of one race than of another. Disproportionate impact is not irrelevant, but it is not the sole touchstone of an invidious racial discrimination forbidden by the Constitution. Standing alone, it does not trigger the rule, *McLaughlin v. Florida,* (1964), that racial classifications are to be subjected to the strictest scrutiny and are justifiable only by the weightiest of considerations.

* * *

As we have indicated, it was error to direct summary judgment for respondents based on the Fifth Amendment. . . .

The judgment of the Court of Appeals accordingly is reversed.

So ordered.

* * *

QUESTIONS AND COMMENTS

1 Assume that a municipality adopts a policy which impacts more severely on blacks than on whites. Assume further that its purposes were six in number, one of which was racial discrimination, but five of which were perfectly legitimate purposes. Under *Davis,* would the policy be struck? Note that the policy might be the same even if the city had no racial purpose. See the 1977 case, *Village of Arlington Heights v. Metropolitan Housing Development Corporation,* 429 U.S. 252.

2 Other things equal, can intent to discriminate on the basis of race be inferred from disproportionate impact? Give evidence for your answer.

United Steelworkers of America v. Weber

443 U.S. 193 (1979)
Vote: 5–2

The facts are given in the opinion.

MR. JUSTICE BRENNAN delivered the opinion of the Court.

* * *

In 1974 petitioner United Steelworkers of America (USWA) and petitioner Kaiser Aluminum & Chemical Corporation (Kaiser) entered into a master collective-bargaining agreement covering terms and conditions of employment at

15 Kaiser plants. The agreement contained, *inter alia* an affirmative action plan designed to eliminate conspicuous racial imbalances in Kaiser's then almost exclusively white craft work forces. Black craft hiring goals were set for each Kaiser plant equal to the percentage of blacks in the respective local labor forces. To enable plants to meet these goals, on-the-job training programs were established to teach unskilled production workers—black and white—the skills necessary to become craft workers. The plan reserved for black employees 50% of the openings in these newly created in-plant training programs.

This case arose from the operation of the plan at Kaiser's plant in Gramercy, La. Until 1974 Kaiser hired as craft workers for that plant only persons who had had prior craft experience. Because blacks had long been excluded from craft unions, few were able to present such credentials. As a consequence, prior to 1974 only 1.83% (five out of 273) of the skilled craft workers at the Gramercy plant were black, even though the work force in the Gramercy area was approximately 39% black.

Pursuant to the national agreement Kaiser altered its craft hiring practice in the Gramercy plant. Rather than hiring already trained outsiders, Kaiser established a training program to train its production workers to fill craft openings. Selection of craft trainees was made on the basis of seniority, with the proviso that at least 50% of the new trainees were to be black until the percentage of black skilled craft workers in the Gramercy plant approximated the percentage of blacks in the local labor force.

During 1974, the first year of the operation of the Kaiser-USWA affirmative action plan, 13 craft trainees were selected from Gramercy's production work force. Of these, 7 were black and 6 white. The most junior black selected into the program had less seniority than several white production workers whose bids for admission were rejected. Thereafter one of those white production workers, respondent Brian Weber, instituted this class action in the United States District Court for the Eastern District of Louisiana.

The complaint alleged that the filling of craft trainee positions at the Gramercy plant pursuant to the affirmative action program had resulted in junior black employees receiving training in preference to more senior white employees, thus discriminating against respondent and other similarly situated white employees in violation of §§ 703 (a) and (d) of Title VII. The District Court held that the plan violated Title VII, entered a judgment in favor of the plaintiff class, and granted a permanent injunction prohibiting Kaiser and the USWA "from denying plaintiffs, Brian F. Weber and all other members of the class, access to on-the-job training programs on the basis of race." A divided panel of the Court of Appeals for the Fifth Circuit affirmed, holding that all employment preferences based upon race, including those preferences incidental to bona fide affirmative action plans, violated Title VII's prohibition against racial discrimination in employment. We granted certiorari. We reverse.

* * *

The only question before us is the narrow statutory issue of whether Title VII *forbids* private employers and unions from voluntarily agreeing upon bona fide affirmative action plans that accord racial preferences in the manner and for the purpose provided in the Kaiser-USWA plan. That question was expressly left open in *McDonald v. Santa Fe Trail Trans. Co.,* which held, in a case not involving affirmative action, that Title VII protects whites as well as blacks from certain forms of racial discrimination.

Respondent argues that Congress intended in Title VII to prohibit all race-conscious affirmative action plans. Respondent's argument rests upon a literal interpretation of §§ 703 (a) and (d) of the Act. Those sections make it unlawful to "discriminate ... because of ... race" in hiring and in the selection of apprentices for training programs. Since, the argument runs, *McDonald v. Santa Fe Trans. Co., supra,* settled that Title VII forbids discrimination against whites as well as blacks, and since the Kaiser-USWA affirmative action plan operates to discriminate against white employees solely because they are white, it follows that the Kaiser-USWA plan violates Title VII.

Respondent's argument is not without force. But it overlooks the significance of the fact that the Kaiser-USWA plan is an affirmative action plan voluntarily adopted by private parties to eliminate traditional patterns of racial segregation. In this context respondent's reliance upon a literal construction of § 703 (a) and (d) upon *McDonald* is misplaced. It is a "familiar rule, that a thing may be within the letter of the statute and yet not within the statute, because not within its spirit, nor within the intention of its makers." The prohibition against racial discrimination in § 703 (a) and (d) of Title VII must therefore be read against the background of the legislative history of Title VII and the historical context from which the Act arose. Examination of those sources makes clear that an interpretation of the sections that forbade all race-conscious affirmative action would "bring about an end completely at variance with the purpose of the statute" and must be rejected.

Congress' primary concern in enacting the prohibition against racial discrimination in Title VII of the Civil Rights Act of 1964 was with "the plight of the Negro in our economy." Before 1964, blacks were largely relegated to "unskilled and semi-skilled jobs." Because of automation the number of such jobs was rapidly decreasing. As a consequence "the relative position of the Negro worker [was] steadily worsening. In 1947 the non-white unemployment rate was only 64 percent higher than the white rate; in 1962 it was 124 percent higher." Congress considered this a serious social problem. As Senator Clark told the Senate:

> The rate of Negro unemployment has gone up consistently as compared with white unemployment for the past 15 years. This is a social malaise and a social situation which we should not tolerate. That is one of the principal reasons why this bill should pass.

Congress feared that the goals of the Civil Rights Act—the integration of blacks into the mainstream of American society—could not be achieved unless this trend were reversed. And Congress recognized that that would not be possible unless blacks were able to secure jobs "which have a future." As Senator Humphrey explained to the Senate.

What good does it do a Negro to be able to eat in a fine restaurant if he cannot afford to pay the bill? What good does it do him to be accepted in a hotel that is too expensive for his modest income? How can a Negro child be motivated to take full advantage of integrated educational facilities if he has no hope of getting a job where he can use that education?

* * *

Without a job, one cannot afford public convenience and accommodations. Income from employment may be necessary to further a man's education, or that of his children. If his children have no hope of getting a good job, what will motivate them to take advantage of educational opportunities.

These remarks echoed President Kennedy's original message to Congress upon the introduction of the Civil Rights Act in 1963.

There is little value in a Negro's obtaining the right to be admitted to hotels and restaurants if he has no cash in his pocket and no job.

Accordingly, it was clear to Congress that "the crux of the problem [was] to open employment opportunities for Negroes in occupations which have been traditionally closed to them," and it was to this problem that Title VII's prohibition against racial discrimination in employment was primarily addressed.

It plainly appears from the House Report accompanying the Civil Rights Act that Congress did not intend wholly to prohibit private and voluntary affirmative action efforts as one method of solving this problem. The Report provides:

No bill can or should lay claim to eliminating all of the causes and consequences of racial and other types of discrimination against minorities. There is reason to believe, however, that national leadership provided by the enactment of Federal legislation dealing with the most troublesome problems *will create an atmosphere conducive to voluntary or local resolution of other forms of discrimination.*

Given this legislative history, we cannot agree with respondent that Congress intended to prohibit the private sector from taking effective steps to accomplish the goal that Congress designed Title VII to achieve. The very statutory words intended as a spur or catalyst to cause "employers and unions to self-examine and to self-evaluate their employment practices and to endeavor to eliminate, so far as possible, the last vestiges of an unfortunate and ignominious page in this country's history," cannot be interpreted as an absolute prohibition against all private, voluntary, race-conscious affirmative action efforts to hasten the elimination of such vestiges. It would be ironic indeed if a law triggered by a Nation's concern over centuries of racial injustice and intended to improve the lot of those who had "been excluded from the American dream for so long" constituted the first legislative prohibition of all voluntary, private, race-conscious efforts to abolish traditional patterns of racial segregation and hierarchy.

Our conclusion is further reinforced by examination of the language and legislative history of § 703 (j) of Title VII. Opponents of Title VII raised two related arguments against the bill. First, they argued that the Act would be interpreted to *require* employers with racially imbalanced work forces to grant preferential treatment to racial minorities in order to integrate. Second, they argued that employers with racially imbalanced work forces would grant preferential treatment to racial minorities, even if not required to do so by the Act. Had Congress meant to prohibit all race-conscious affirmative action, as respondent urges, it easily could have answered both objections by providing that Title VII would not require or *permit* racially preferential integration efforts. But Congress did not choose such a course. Rather Congress added § 703 (j) which addresses only the first objection. The section provides that nothing contained in Title VII "shall be interpreted to *require* any employer . . . to grant preferential treatment . . . to any group because of the race . . . of such . . . group on account of " a defacto racial imbalance in the employer's work force. The section does *not* state "nothing in Title VII shall be interpreted to *permit* " voluntary affirmative efforts to correct racial imbalances. The neutral inference is that Congress chose not to forbid all voluntary race-conscious affirmative action.

The reasons for this choice are evident from the legislative record. Title VII could not have been enacted into law without substantial support from legislators in both Houses who traditionally resisted federal regulation of private business. Those legislators demanded as a price for their support that "management prerogatives and union freedoms . . . be left undisturbed to the greatest extent possible." Section 703 (j) was proposed by Senator Dirksen to allay any fears that the Act might be interpreted in such a way as to upset this compromise. The section was designed to prevent § 703 of Title VII from being interpreted in such a way as to lead to undue "Federal Government interference with private business because of some Federal employee's ideas about racial balance or imbalance." Clearly, a prohibition against all voluntary, race-conscious, affirmative action efforts would disserve these ends. Such a prohibition would augment the powers of the Federal Government and diminish traditional management prerogatives while at the same time impeding attainment of the ultimate goals. In view of this legislative history and in view of Congress' desire to avoid undue federal regulation of private businesses, use of the word "require" rather than the phrase "require or permit" in § 703 (j) fortifies the conclusion that Congress did not intend to limit traditional business freedom to such a degree as to prohibit all voluntary, race-conscious affirmative action plans.

* * *

MR. CHIEF JUSTICE BURGER dissenting.

* * *

Until today, I had thought the Court was of the unanimous view that "discriminatory preference for any group, minority or majority, is precisely and only what Congress has proscribed" in Title VII. *Griggs v. Duke Power Co.*

Had Congress intended otherwise, it very easily could have drafted language allowing what the Court permits today. Far from doing so, Congress expressly *prohibited* in §§ 703 (a) and (d) the discrimination against Brian Weber the Court approves now. If "affirmative action" programs such as the one presented in this case are to be permitted, it is for Congress, not this Court, to so direct.

It is often observed that hard cases make bad law. I suspect there is some truth to that adage, for the "hard" cases always tempt judges to exceed the limits of their authority, as the Court does today by totally rewriting a crucial part of Title VII to reach a desirable result. Cardozo no doubt had this type of case in mind when he wrote:

> The judge, even when he is free, is still not wholly free. He is not to innovate at pleasure. He is not a knight-errant, roaming at will in pursuit of his own ideal of beauty or of goodness. He is to draw his inspiration from consecrated principles. He is not to yield to spasmodic sentiment, to vague and unregulated benevolence. He is to exercise a discretion informed by tradition, methodized by analogy, disciplined by system, and subordinated to 'the primordial necessity of order in the social life.' Wide enough in all conscience is the field of discretion that remains.

What Cardozo tells us is beware the "good result," achieved by judicially unauthorized or intellectually dishonest means on the appealing notion that the desirable ends justify the improper judicial means. For there is always the danger that the seeds of precedent sown by good men for the best motives will yield a rich harvest of unprincipled acts of others also aiming at "good ends."

MR. JUSTICE REHNQUIST, with whom the CHIEF JUSTICE joins, dissenting.

In a very real sense, the Court's opinion is ahead of its time: it could more appropriately have been handed down five years from now, in 1984, a year coinciding with the title of a book from which the Court's opinion borrows, perhaps subconsciously, at least one idea. Orwell describes in his book a governmental official of Oceania, one of the three great world powers, denouncing the current enemy, Eurasia, to an assembled crowd:

> It was almost impossible to listen to him without being first convinced and then maddened. . . . The speech had been proceeding for perhaps twenty minutes when a messenger hurried onto the platform and a scrap of paper was slipped into the speaker's hand. He unrolled and read it without pausing in his speech. Nothing altered in his voice or manner, or in the content of what he was saying, but suddenly the names were different. Without words said, a wave of understanding rippled through the crowd. Oceania was at war with Eastasia! . . . The banners and posters with which the square was decorated were all wrong! . . .
>
> [T]he speaker had switched from one line to the other actually in midsentence, not only without a pause, but without even breaking the syntax.

Today's decision represents an equally dramatic and equally unremarked switch in this Court's interpretation of Title VII.

The operative sections of Title VII prohibit racial discrimination in employment *simpliciter.* Taken in its normal meaning, and as understood by all Members of Congress who spoke to the issue during the legislative debates . . . this language prohibits a covered employer from considering race when making an employment decision, whether the race be black or white. Several years ago, however, a United States District Court held that "the dismissal of white employees charged with misappropriating company property while not dismissing a similarly charged Negro employee does not raise a claim upon which Title VII relief may be granted." *McDonald v. Santa Fe Trail Transp. Co.* This Court unanimously reversed, concluding from the "uncontradicted legislative history" that "Title VII prohibits racial discrimination against the white petitioners in this case upon the same standards as would be applicable were they Negroes. . . ."

We have never wavered in our understanding that Title VII "Prohibits *all* racial discrimination in employment, without exception for any particular employees." In *Griggs v. Duke Power Co.,* our first occasion to interpret Title VII, a unanimous court observed that "[d]iscriminatory preference, for any group, minority or majority, is precisely and only what Congress has proscribed." And in our most recent discussion of the issue, we uttered words seemingly dispositive of this case: "It is clear beyond cavil that the obligation imposed by Title VII is to provide an equal opportunity for *each* applicant regardless of race, without regard to whether members of the applicant's race are already proportionately represented in the work force." *Furnco Construction Corp v. Waters.*

Today, however, the Court behaves much like the Orwellian speaker earlier described, as if it had been handed a note indicating that Title VII would lead to a result unacceptable to the Court if interpreted here as it was in our prior decisions. Accordingly, without even a break in syntax, the Court rejects "a literal construction of § 703 (a)" in favor of newly discovered "legislative history," which leads it to a conclusion directly contrary to that compelled by the "uncontradicted legislative history" unearthed in *McDonald* and our other prior decisions. Now we are told that the legislative history of Title VII shows that employers are free to discriminate on the basis of race: an employer may, in the Court's words, "trammel the interests of white employees" in favor of black employees in order to eliminate "racial imbalance." Our earlier interpretations of Title VII, like the banners and posters decorating the square in Oceania, were all wrong.

As if this were not enough to make a reasonable observer question this Court's adherence to the oft-stated principle that our duty is to construe rather than rewrite legislation, the Court also seizes upon § 703 (j) of Title VII as an independent, or at least partially independent, basis for its holding. Totally ignoring the wording of that section, which is obviously addressed to those charged with the responsibility of interpreting the law rather than those who are subject to its proscriptions, and totally ignoring the months of legislative debates preceding the section's introduction and passage, which demonstrate clearly that it was enacted to prevent precisely what occurred in this case, the

Court infers from § 703 (j) that "Congress chose not to forbid all voluntary race-conscious affirmative action."

Thus, by a *tour de force* reminiscent not of jurists such as Hale, Holmes, and Hughes, but of escape artists such as Houdini, the Court eludes clear statutory language, "Uncontradicted" legislative history, and uniform precedent in concluding that employers are, after all, permitted to consider race in making employment decisions. It may be that one or more of the principal sponsors of Title VII would have preferred to see a provision allowing preferential treatment of minorities written into the bill. Such a provision, however, would have to have been expressly or impliedly excepted from Title VII's explicit prohibition on all racial discrimination in employment. There is no such exception in the Act. And a reading of the legislative debates concerning Title VII, in which proponents and opponents alike uniformly denounced discrimination in favor of, as well as discrimination against, Negroes, demonstrates clearly that any legislator harboring an unspoken desire for such a provision could not possibly have succeeded in enacting it into law.

QUESTIONS AND COMMENTS

1 In the opinion for the majority in *Weber,* Justice Brennan holds that discrimination against whites is barred by a literal reading of Title VII but not by the "spirit" of the statute. Is the concept of "substantive due process" of any relevance here? Explain.
2 The Brennan opinion suggests that "the prohibition against racial discrimination [in Title VII] does not condemn all private race-conscious affirmative action plans." What is the difference between a plan that discriminates on the basis of race and one that is merely race-conscious?
3 In his dissent, Justice Rehnquist accuses the majority of activism on at least two of the dimensions of activism discussed on page 34. Which two? Are Rehnquist's changes valid? Give specific evidence from the majority opinion.

In Legislative Reapportionment

United Jewish Organizations v. Carey (1977)

While the Fifteenth Amendment assures the right to vote, that right is protected from invidious discrimination by the Fourteenth Amendment's equal protection clause. In order to overcome the effects of racial discrimination in the past, the Supreme Court has permitted government to take "affirmative action"—i.e., to take invidious or suspect classification into consideration in formulating policy. But it is one thing to take affirmative action to remedy past discrimination and something else if some class is given preference in the awarding of a public good. Moreover, the Court has distinguished "taking race into consideration" and using it as a "criterion," as we saw in *Bakke.*[1] In *United Jewish Organization v. Carey,* the Court tries to sort out some of the complexities involved in relating affirmative action to a state policy not designed to remedy past discrimination.

United Jewish Organizations of Williamsburgh, Inc., et al. v. Carey, Governor of New York et al.

430 U.S. 144; 97 S. Ct. 996; 51 L. Ed. 2d 229 (1977)
Vote: 8–1

The facts are provided in the opinion that follows.

MR. JUSTICE WHITE announced the judgment of the Court and filed an opinion in which MR. JUSTICE STEVENS joined; Parts I, II, and III of which are joined by MR. JUSTICE BRENNAN and MR. JUSTICE BLACKMUN; and Parts I and IV of which are joined by MR. JUSTICE REHNQUIST.

Section 5 of the Voting Rights Act of 1965 prohibits a State or political subdivision subject to § 4 of the Act from implementing a legislative reapportionment unless it has obtained a declaratory judgment from the District Court for the District of Columbia, or a ruling from the Attorney General of the United States, that the reapportionment "does not have the purpose and will not have the effect of denying or abridging the right to vote on account of race or color. . . .

* * *

Kings County, N. Y., together with New York (Manhattan) and Bronx Counties, became subject to §§ 4 and 5 of the Act, by virtue of a determination by the Attorney General that a literacy test was used in these three counties as of November 1, 1968, and a determination by the Director of the Census that fewer than 50% of the voting-age residents of these three counties voted in the Presidential election of 1968. Litigation to secure exemption from the Act was unsuccessful, and it became necessary for New York to secure the approval of the Attorney General or of the United States District Court for the District of Columbia for its 1972 reapportionment statute insofar as that statute concerned Kings, New York, and Bronx Counties. On January 31, 1974, the provisions of the statute districting these counties for congressional, state senate, and state assembly seats were submitted to the Attorney General. . . .

On April 1, 1974, the Attorney General concluded that, as to certain districts in Kings County covering the Bedford-Stuyvesant area of Brooklyn, the State had not met the burden placed on it by § 5 and the regulations thereunder to demonstrate that the redistricting had neither the purpose nor the effect of abridging the right to vote by reason of race or color.

* * *

A revised plan, submitted to the Attorney General on May 31, 1974, in its essentials did not change the number of districts with nonwhite majorities in most of those districts. Under the 1972 plan, Kings County had three state senate districts with nonwhite majorities of approximately 91%, 61%, and 53%; under the revised 1974 plan, there were again three districts with non-white majorities, but now all three were between 70% and 75% nonwhite. As for state assembly districts, both the 1972 and the 1974 plans provided for seven districts with nonwhite majorities. However, under the 1972 plan, there were four between 85% and 95% nonwhite, and three were approximately 76%,61%, and 52%, respectively; under the 1974 plan, the two smallest non-white majorities were increased to 65% and 67.5%, and the two largest non-white majorities were decreased from greater than 90% to between 80% and 90%. The report of the legislative committee on reapportionment stated that these changes were made "to overcome Justice Department objections" by cre-ating more "substantial nonwhite majorities" in two assembly districts and two senate districts.

One of the communities affected by these revisions in the Kings County reapportionment plan was the Williamsburgh area, where about 30,000 Has-idic Jews live. Under the 1972 plan, the Hasidic community was located entirely in one assembly district (61% nonwhite) and one senate district (37% nonwhite); in order to create substantial nonwhite majorities in these districts, the 1974 revisions split the Hasidic community between two senate and two assembly districts. A staff member of the legislative reapportionment commit-tee testified that in the course of meetings and telephone conversations with Justice Department officials, he "got the feeling . . . that 65 percent would be probably an approved figure" for the nonwhite population in the assembly dis-trict in which the Hasidic community was located, a district approximately 61% nonwhite under the 1972 plan. To attain the 65% figure, a portion of the white population, including part of the Hasidic community, was reassigned to an adjoining district.

Shortly after the State submitted this revised redistricting plan for Kings County to the Attorney General, petitioners sued on behalf of the Hasidic Jew-ish community of Williamsburgh, alleging that the 1974 plan "would dilute the value of each plaintiff's franchise by halving its effectiveness," solely for the purpose of achieving a racial quota and therefore in violation of the Fourteenth Amendment. Petitioners also alleged that they were assigned to electoral dis-tricts solely on the basis of race, and that this racial assignment diluted their voting power in violation of the Fifteenth Amendment. Petitioners sought an injunction restraining New York officials from enforcing the new redistricting plan and a declaratory judgment that the Attorney General of the United States had used unconstitutional and improper standards in objecting to the 1972 plan.

* * *

The District Court granted . . . motions to dismiss the complaint, reasoning that petitioners enjoyed no constitutional right in reapportionment to separate community recognition as Hasidic Jews, that the redistricting did not disenfranchise petitioners, and that racial considerations were permissible to correct past discrimination.

A divided Court of Appeals affirmed. . . .

. . . It is evident that the Act's prohibition against instituting new voting procedures without the approval of the Attorney General or the three-judge District Court is not dependent upon proving past unconstitutional apportionments and that in operation the Act is aimed at preventing the use of new procedures until their capacity for discrimination has been examined by the Attorney General or by a court. Although recognizing that the "stringent new remedies," including § 5, were "an uncommon exercise of congressional power," we nevertheless sustained the Act as a "permissibly decisive" response to "the extraordinary stratagem of contriving new rules of various kinds for the sole purpose of perpetrating voting discrimination in the face of adverse federal court decrees." *South Carolina v. Katzenbach,* [1966].

* * *

In *Beer v. United States,* (1976), the Court considered the question of what criteria a legislative reapportionment must satisfy under § 5 of the Voting Rights Act to demonstrate that it does not have the "effect" of denying or abridging the right to vote on account of race. *Beer* established that the Voting Rights Act does not permit the implementation of a reapportionment that "would lead to a retrogression in the position of racial minorities with respect to their effective exercise of the electoral franchise." This test was satisfied where the reapportionment increased the percentage of districts where members of racial minorities protected by the Act were in the majority. But if this test were not met, clearance by the Attorney General or the District Court for the District of Columbia could not be given, and the reapportionment could not be implemented. . . .

The Court has taken a similar approach in applying § 5 to the extension of city boundaries through annexation. Where the annexation has the effect of reducing the percentage of blacks in the city, the proscribed "effect" on voting rights can be avoided by a post-annexation districting plan which "fairly reflects the strength of the Negro community as it exists after the annexation" and which "would afford [it] representation reasonably equivalent to [its] political strength in the enlarged community." *City of Richmond v. United States,* (1975).

In *City of Richmond,* the Court approved an annexation which reduced the proportion of blacks in the city from 52% to 42%, because the postannexation ward system created four out of nine wards with substantial black majorities of 64%.

Implicit in *Beer* and *City of Richmond,* then, is the proposition that the Constitution does not prevent a State subject to the Voting Rights Act from deliberately creating or preserving black majorities in particular districts in order to ensure that its reapportionment plan complies with § 5. That proposition must be rejected and § 5 held unconstitutional to that extent if we are to accept petitioners' view that racial criteria may never be used in redistricting or that they may be used, if at all, only as a specific remedy for past unconstitutional apportionments. We are unwilling to overturn our prior cases, however. Section 5 and its authorization for racial redistricting where appropriate to avoid abridging the right to vote on account of race or color are constitutional. Contrary to petitioners' first argument, neither the Fourteenth nor the Fifteenth Amendment mandates any *per se* rule against using racial factors in districting and apportionment. Nor is petitioners' second argument valid. The permissible use of racial criteria is not confined to eliminating the effects of past discriminatory districting or apportionment.

. . . In the process of drawing black majority districts in order to comply with § 5, the State must decide how substantial those majorities must be in order to satisfy the Voting Rights Act. The figure used in drawing the *Beer* plan, for example, was 54% of registered voters. At a minimum and by definition, a "black majority district" must be more than 50% black. But whatever the specific percentage, the State will inevitably arrive at it as a necessary means to ensure the opportunity for the election of a black representative and to obtain approval of its reapportionment plan. Unless we adopted an unconstitutional construction of § 5 in *Beer* and *City of Richmond,* a reapportionment cannot violate the Fourteenth or Fifteenth Amendment merely because a State uses specific numerical quotas in establishing a certain number of black majority districts. Our cases under § 5 stand for at least this much.

* * *

In the absence of any evidence regarding nonwhite voting strength under the 1966 apportionment, the creation of substantial nonwhite majorities in approximately 30% of the senate and assembly districts in Kings County was reasonably related to the constitutionally valid statutory mandate of maintaining nonwhite voting strength. The percentage of districts with nonwhite majorities was less than the percentage of nonwhites in the county as a whole (35%). The size of the nonwhite majorities in those districts reflected the need to take account of the substantial difference between the nonwhite percentage of the total population in a district and the nonwhite percentage of the voting-age population. Because, as the Court said in *Beer,* the inquiry under § 5 focuses ultimately on "the position of racial minorities with respect to their effective exercise of the electoral franchise," the percentage of eligible voters by district is of great importance to that inquiry. In the redistricting plan approved in *Beer,* for example, only one of the two districts with a black population majority also had a black majority of registered voters. We think it was reasonable for the Attorney General to conclude in this case that a *substantial* nonwhite population majority—in the vicinity of 65%—would be required to achieve a nonwhite majority of eligible voters.

* * *

... Additional argument, however, affords a second, and independent, ground for sustaining the particulars of the 1974 plan for Kings County. Whether or not the plan was authorized by or was in compliance with § 5 of the Voting Rights Act, New York was free to do what it did as long as it did not violate the Constitution, particularly the Fourteenth and Fifteenth Amendments; and we are convinced that neither Amendment was infringed.

There is no doubt that in preparing the 1974 legislation, the State deliberately used race in a purposeful manner. But its plan represented no racial slur or stigma with respect to whites or any other race, and we discern no discrimination violative of the Fourteenth Amendment nor any abridgment of the right to vote on account of race within the meaning of the Fifteenth Amendment. ...

Where it occurs, voting for or against a candidate because of his race is an unfortunate practice. But it is not rare; and in any district where it regularly happens, it is unlikely that any candidate will be elected who is a member of the race that is in the minority in that district. However disagreeable this result may be, there is no authority for the proposition that the candidates who are found racially unacceptable by the majority, and the minority voters supporting those candidates, have had their Fourteenth or Fifteenth Amendment rights infringed by this process. ...

Districting plans would be vulnerable under our cases if "*racial or political groups* have been fenced out of the political process and their voting strength invidiously minimized," *id.,* at 754 (emphasis added); but that was not the case there, and no such purpose or effect may be ascribed to New York's 1974 plan. Rather, that plan can be viewed as seeking to alleviate the consequences of racial voting at the polls and to achieve a fair allocation of political power between white and nonwhite voters in Kings County.

* * *

The judgment is

Affirmed.

* * *

Mr. Chief Justice Burger, dissenting.

* * *

I begin with this Court's holding in *Gomillion v. Lightfoot,* (1960), the first case to strike down a state attempt at racial gerrymandering. If *Gomillion* teaches anything, I had thought it was that drawing of political boundary lines with the sole, explicit objective of reaching a predetermined racial result cannot ordinarily be squared with the Constitution. The record before us reveals—and it is not disputed—that this is precisely what took place here. In drawing up the 1974 reapportionment scheme, the New York Legislature did not consider racial composition as merely *one* of several political characteristics; on the contrary, race appears to have been the one and only criterion applied.

The principal opinion notes that after the 1972 apportionment plan was rejected, New York officials conferred with the Justice Department as to what plan could obtain the Attorney General's approval. One New York official testified that he " 'got the feeling [from a Justice Department spokesman] . . . that 65 percent would be probably an approved figure.' " Further testimony by that same official is revealing:

> Q: So that your reason for dividing the Ha[s]idic community was to effect compliance with the Department of Justice determination, and the minimum standards they impose—they appear to impose?
>
> A: *That was the sole reason.* We spent over a full day right around the clock, attempting to come up with some other type of districting plan that would maintain the Ha[s]idic community as one entity, *and I think that is evidenced clearly by the fact that that district is exactly 65 percent, and it's because we went block by block, and didn't go higher or lower than that,* in order to maintain as much of the community as possible. (Emphasis added.)

This official also testified that apportionment solutions which would have kept the Hasidic community within a single district, but would have resulted in a 63.4% nonwhite concentration, were rejected for fear that, falling short of "exactly 65 percent," they "would not be acceptable" to the Justice Department.

The words "racial quota" are emotionally loaded and must be used with caution. Yet this undisputed testimony shows that the 65% figure was viewed by the legislative reapportionment committee as so firm a criterion that even a fractional deviation was deemed impermissible. I cannot see how this can be characterized otherwise than a strict quota approach and I must therefore view today's holding as casting doubt on the clear-cut principles established in *Gomillion.*

My second inquiry is whether the action of the State of New York becomes constitutionally permissible because it was taken to comply with the remedial provisions of the federal Voting Rights Act.

On the present sparse record, . . . I cannot find support in the Voting Rights Act for the arbitrary process followed by the New York Legislature.

The record is devoid of any evidence that the 65% figure was a reasoned response to the problem of past discrimination. It is, rather, clear that under the time pressure of upcoming elections, and "in an atmosphere of hasty dickering," 510 F. 2d 512, 525, 526 (CA2 1975) (Frankel, J., dissenting), the New

York Legislature simply accepted the standard formula from the Department of Justice and treated it as mandatory. Moreover, the formula appears to be based upon factually unsupportable assumptions. For example, it would make no sense to assure nonwhites a majority of 65% in a voting district unless it were assumed that nonwhites and whites vote in racial blocs, and that the blocs vote adversely to, or independently of, one another. Not only is the record in this case devoid of any evidence that such bloc voting has taken or will take place in Kings County, but such evidence as there is points in the opposite direction: We are informed that four out of five "safe" (65%+) nonwhite districts established by the 1974 plan have since elected white representatives.

* * *

The result reached by the Court today in the name of the Voting Rights Act is ironic. The use of a mathematical formula tends to sustain the existence of ghettos by promoting the notion that political clout is to be gained or maintained by marshaling particular racial, ethnic, or religious groups in enclaves. It suggests to the voter that only a candidate of the same race, religion, or ethnic origin can properly represent that voter's interests, and that such candidate can be elected only from a district with a sufficient minority concentration. The device employed by the State of New York, and endorsed by the Court today, moves us one step farther away from a truly homogeneous society. This retreat from the ideal of the American "melting pot" is curiously out of step with recent political history—and indeed with what the Court has said and done for more than a decade. The notion that Americans vote in firm blocs has been repudiated in the election of minority members as mayors and legislators in numerous American cities and districts overwhelmingly white. Since I cannot square the mechanical racial gerrymandering in this case with the mandate of the Constitution, I respectfully dissent from the affirmance of the judgment of the Court of Appeals.

QUESTIONS AND COMMENTS

1 In the opinion for the Court, Justice White identifies the relevant classes as white and nonwhite (or black). Why does he not choose Hasidic Jews as a relevant class for discrimination analysis? Would the decision be different had he done so?

2 A well-known case dealing with reverse discrimination is *Regents of the University of California v. Bakke* (438 U.S. 265). In 1973 and 1974, the medical school at Davis had 100 positions to fill each year in its entering class. It set aside 16 of these positions in both years to be filled via a special admissions program for disadvantaged and minority students (blacks, Chicanos, American Indians, Asians, etc.). In both 1973 and 1974, the medical school denied admission to Allan Bakke, a white male. In the same years, it admitted applicants under its special admissions program who had lower-caliber credentials than Bakke.

Bakke brought suit seeking admission and vindication of his rights under the Fourteenth Amendment's equal protection clause and Title VI of the Civil Rights Act of 1964. The California Supreme Court ordered admission on equal protection grounds. The U.S. Supreme Court also ordered admission. The meaning of the Court's decision for constitutional law and policy-making, however, is somewhat unclear. Four justices based their ruling on Title VI. Four others found no violation, constitutional or statutory. The case was decided, therefore, by the fifth justice, who adopted neither position. The decision in the case, therefore, is what we call a "judgment." Such a judgment does not establish any general principle of constitutional law. The Bakke Case does establish that a state may not use a racial quota to deny a student admission to a state medical school.

Does the quota in *Bakke* differ from the quota referred to by Chief Justice Burger in *United Jewish Organizations?* How?

3 In *Plyler v. Doe* [50 LW 4650 (1982)], schoolchildren of Mexican origin who could not demonstrate their legal admission to the United States were denied enrollment in public schools. The school district decided that such a policy was necessary because the state (Texas) would financially support only children who were legally residents of the state. Noting that the Fourteenth Amendment protects "persons," a majority in the Supreme Court held the policy unconstitutional. The dissent of four justices is of particular interest because of the basis of the dissent. All four agreed that the Court was making social policy—and they agreed with the policy being made, i.e., that schoolchildren should not be deprived of an education. But noting that "The Equal Protection Clause does not mandate identical treatment of different categories of persons," the dissenters emphasized that "the Constitution does not constitute us as 'Platonic Guardians' nor does it vest in this Court the authority to strike down laws because they do not meet our standards of desirable social policy, 'wisdom' or 'common sense'. . . . We trespass on the assigned function of the political branches under our structure of limited and separated powers when we assume a policy making role as the Court does today."

a Can you think of any compelling state interests which would justify a position contrary to that taken by the majority in this case?

b What counterargument can you suggest in rebuttal to the argument offered by the four dissenting justices?

Sex Discrimination

And State Police Power

Craig v. Boren (1976)

Michael M. v. Superior Court of Sonoma County (1981)

While the Supreme Court has long been sensitive to discrimination against blacks, it has only recently become concerned about discrimination against women. Legislation protecting women from long hours of work, low wages, and substandard working conditions has been a part of the national scene for many years. And congressional legislation prohibiting discrimination on the basis of gender is a staple in modern efforts to see that women are treated fairly. But the Court has shown a decidedly greater interest in eliminating racial discrimination than in equating the rights of males and females under the Fourteenth Amendment.

In 1873, the Court upheld an Illinois statute prohibiting women from practicing law and declared the female sex unfit "for many of the occupations of life."[2] The attitude reflected in that case has long since passed from the Court. Yet, a gender-based equal protection claim still does not trigger the studied interest the Court has shown in racial discrimination cases. It will be recalled that in deciding equal protection claims, the Court uses several different levels of analysis. If a classification is suspect, it will be subjected to strict scrutiny. This makes justification much more difficult to establish, since an overriding and legitimate state interest must be shown.

The Court has also labeled some rights fundamental, and has generally required a compelling state interest and proof that the classification is necessary to accomplish the state's interest before it will permit an encroachment on such rights. Any classification based on race is suspect, and the right to be free of racial discrimination has been declared a fundamental right. Traditionally, by contrast, a sexual classification has not been suspect. It has been analyzed in the Court with "traditional equal protection standards." That test requires that the classification be reasonable and that the linkage between the classification and a legitimate state object not be arbitrary. Moreover, one who brings a challenge triggering this test has had the burden of proving that the classification is arbitrary. And the Court traditionally has been quite restrained in overruling the use of state police power in such cases.

Craig v. Boren is a case involving the use of state police power to legislate in the interest of social welfare. This is an important and legitimate power guaranteed by the Tenth Amendment. But the Constitution not only grants power, it also limits it. In *Craig* and in *Michael M. v. Superior Court,* the question is whether these limits have been exceeded.

Craig et al. v. Boren, Governor of Oklahoma et al.

429 U.S. 190: 97 S. Ct. 451; 50 L. Ed. 2d 397 (1976)
Vote: 7–2

An Oklahoma statute (Sections 241 and 245) prohibited the sale of "nonintoxicating" 3.2 beer to males under 21 and females under 18 years of age. Craig was an underage male. Whitener was a female vendor of 3.2 beer. They brought suit in a three-judge federal court seeking a declaration that the statutes violated the equal protection clause of the Fourteenth Amendment and injunctive relief. The federal court sustained the constitutionality of the statutes. The U.S. Supreme Court noted probable jurisdiction.

Mr. Justice Brennan delivered the opinion of the Court.

* * *

We first address a preliminary question of standing. Appellant Craig attained the age of 21 after we noted probable jurisdiction. Therefore, since only declaratory and injunctive relief against enforcement of the gender-based differential is sought, the controversy has been rendered moot as to Craig. See, *e. g., DeFunis v. Odegaard,* (1974). The question thus arises whether appellant Whitener, the licensed vendor of 3.2% beer, who has a live controversy against enforcement of the statute, may rely upon the equal protection objections of males 18–20 years of age to establish her claim of unconstitutionality of the age-sex differential. We conclude that she may. . . .

[The statute] plainly has inflicted "injury in fact" upon appellant sufficient to guarantee her "concrete adverseness," *Baker v. Carr,* (1962), and to satisfy the constitutionally based standing requirements imposed by Art. III. The legal duties created by the statutory sections under challenge are addressed directly to vendors such as appellant. She is obliged either to heed the statutory discrimination, thereby incurring a direct economic injury through the constriction of her buyers' market, or to disobey the statutory command and suffer, in the words of Oklahoma's Assistant Attorney General, "sanctions and perhaps loss of license." This Court repeatedly has recognized that such injuries establish the threshold requirements of a "case or controversy" mandated by Art. III. See, *e. g., Singleton v. Wulff,* [1972]. . . .

As a vendor with standing to challenge the lawfulness of [the statute], appellant Whitener is entitled to assert those concomitant rights of third parties that would be "diluted or adversely affected" should her constitutional challenge fail and the statutes remain in force. *Griswold v. Connecticut,* (1965). . . . Otherwise, the threatened imposition of governmental sanctions might deter appellant Whitener and other similarly situated vendors from selling 3.2% beer to young males, thereby ensuring that "enforcement of the challenged restriction against the [vendor] would result indirectly in the violation of third parties' rights." *Warth v. Seldin,* (1975).

* * *

We therefore hold that Whitener has standing to raise relevant equal protection challenges to Oklahoma's gender-based law. . . .

Analysis may appropriately begin with the reminder that *Reed* emphasized that statutory classifications that distinguish between males and females are "subject to scrutiny under the Equal Protection Clause." To withstand constitutional challenge, previous cases establish that classifications by gender must serve important governmental objectives and must be substantially related to achievement of those objectives. Thus, in *Reed,* the objectives of "reducing the workload on probate courts," and "avoiding intrafamily controversy," were deemed of insufficient importance to sustain use of an overt gender criterion in the appointment of administrators in intestate decedents' estates. Decisions following *Reed* similarly have rejected administrative ease and convenience as sufficiently important objectives to justify gender-based classifications, cf. *Schlesinger v. Ballard*, (1975). And only two Terms ago, *Stanton v. Stanton*, (1975), expressly stating that *Reed v. Reed* was "controlling," held that *Reed* required invalidation of a Utah differential age-of-majority statute, notwithstanding the statute's coincidence with and furtherance of the State's purpose of fostering "old notions" of role typing and preparing boys for their expected performance in the economic and political worlds. . . .

In this case, too, "*Reed*, we feel, is controlling . . . ," *Stanton v. Stanton*, *supra*, at 13. We turn then to the question whether, under *Reed*, the difference between males and females with respect to the purchase of 3.2% beer warrants the differential in age drawn by the Oklahoma statute. We conclude that it does not.

* * *

We accept for purposes of discussion the District Court's identification of the objective underlying [the statute as] . . . the enhancement of traffic safety. Clearly, the protection of public health and safety represents an important function of state and local governments. However, appellees' statistics in our view cannot support the conclusion that the gender-based distinction closely serves to achieve that objective and therefore the distinction cannot under *Reed* withstand equal protection challenge.

The appellees introduced a variety of statistical surveys. First, an analysis of arrest statistics for 1973 demonstrated that 18–20-year-old male arrests for "driving under the influence" and "drunkenness" substantially exceeded female arrests for that same age period. Similarly, youths aged 17–21 were found to be overrepresented among those killed or injured in traffic accidents, with males again numerically exceeding females in this regard. Third, a random roadside survey in Oklahoma City revealed that young males were more inclined to drive and drink beer than were their female counterparts. Fourth, Federal Bureau of Investigation nationwide statistics exhibited a notable increase in arrests for "driving under the influence." Finally, statistical evidence gathered in other jurisdictions, particularly Minnesota and Michigan, was offered to corroborate Oklahoma's experience by indicating the pervasiveness of youthful participation in motor vehicle accidents following the imbibing of alcohol. Conceding that "the case is not free from doubt," the District Court nonetheless concluded that this statistical showing substantiated "a rational basis for the legislative judgment underlying the challenged classification."

Even were this statistical evidence accepted as accurate, it nevertheless offers only a weak answer to the equal protection question presented here. The most focused and relevant of the statistical surveys, arrests of 18–20-year-olds for alcohol-related driving offenses, exemplifies the ultimate unpersuasiveness of this evidentiary record. Viewed in terms of the correlation between sex and the actual activity that Oklahoma seeks to regulate—driving while under the influence of alcohol—the statistics broadly establish that .18% of females and 2% of males in that age group were arrested for that offense. While such a disparity is not trivial in a statistical sense, it hardly can form the basis for employment of a gender line as a classifying device. Certainly if maleness is to serve as a proxy for drinking and driving, a correlation of 2% must be considered an unduly tenuous "fit." Indeed, prior cases have consistently rejected the use of sex as a decisionmaking factor even though the statutes in question certainly rested on far more predictive empirical relationships than this. . . .

There is no reason to belabor this line of analysis. It is unrealistic to expect either members of the judiciary or state officials to be well versed in the rigors of experimental or statistical technique. But this merely illustrates that proving broad sociological propositions by statistics is a dubious business, and one that inevitably is in tension with the normative philosophy that underlies the Equal Protection Clause. Suffice to say that the showing offered by the appellees does not satisy us that sex represents a legitimate, accurate proxy for the regulation of drinking and driving. In fact, when it is further recognized that Oklahoma's statute prohibits only the selling of 3.2% beer to young males and not their drinking the beverage once acquired (even after purchase by their 18–20-year-old female companions), the relationship between gender and traffic safety becomes far too tenuous to satisfy *Reed's* requirement that the gender-based difference be substantially related to achievement of the statutory objective.

We hold, therefore, that under *Reed,* Oklahoma's 3.2% beer statute invidiously discriminates against males 18–20 years of age. . . .

We conclude that the gender-based differential contained in Okla. Stat., Tit. 37, § 245 (1976 Supp.) constitutes a denial of the equal protection of the laws to males aged 18–20 and reverse the judgment of the District Court.

It is so ordered.

* * *

Mr. Justice Stevens, concurring.

There is only one Equal Protection Clause. It requires every State to govern impartially. . . .

In this, case, the classification is not as obnoxious as some the Court has condemned, nor as inoffensive as some the Court has accepted. It is objectionable because it is based on an accident of birth, because it is a mere remnant of the now almost universally rejected tradition of discriminating against males in this age bracket, and because, to the extent it reflects any physical difference between males and females, it is actually perverse. The question then is whether the traffic safety justification put forward by the State is sufficient to make an otherwise offensive classification acceptable.

The classification is not totally irrational. For the evidence does indicate that there are more males than females in this age bracket who drive and also more who drink. Nevertheless, there are several reasons why I regard the justification as unacceptable. It is difficult to believe that the statute was actually intended to cope with the problem of traffic safety, since it has only a minimal effect on access to a not very intoxicating beverage and does not prohibit its consumption. Moreover, the empirical data submitted by the State accentuate the unfairness of treating all 18–20-year-old males as inferior to their female counterparts. The legislation imposes a restraint on 100% of the males in the class allegedly because about 2% of them have probably violated one or more laws relating to the consumption of alcoholic beverages. It is unlikely that this law will have a significant deterrent effect either on that 2% or on the law-abiding 98%. But even assuming some such slight benefit, it does not seem to me that an insult to all of the young men of the State can be justified by visiting the sins of the 2% on the 98%.

* * *

Mr. Justice Stewart, concurring in the judgment.

* * *

The disparity created by these Oklahoma statutes amounts to total irrationality. For the statistics upon which the State now relies, whatever their other shortcomings, wholly fail to prove or even suggest that 3.2% beer is somehow more deleterious when it comes into the hands of a male aged 18–20 than of a female of like age. The disparate statutory treatment of the sexes here, without even a colorably valid justification or explanation, thus amounts to invidious discrimination. See *Reed v. Reed,* [1971].

* * *

Mr. Justice Rehnquist, dissenting.

The Court's disposition of this case is objectionable on two grounds. First is its conclusion that *men* challenging a gender-based statute which treats them less favorably than women may invoke a more stringent standard of judicial review than pertains to most other types of classifications. Second is the Court's enunciation of this standard, without citation to any source, as being that "classifications by gender must serve *important* governmental objectives and must be *substantially* related to achievement of those objectives." (Emphasis added.) The only redeeming feature of the Court's opinion, to my mind, is that it apparently signals a retreat by those who joined the plurality opinion in *Frontiero v. Richardson,* (1973), from their view that sex is a "suspect" classification for purposes of equal protection analysis. I think the Oklahoma statute challenged here need pass only the "rational basis" equal protection analysis expounded in cases such as *McGowan v. Maryland,* (1961), and *Williamson v. Lee Optical Co.,* (1955), and I believe that it is constitutional under that analysis.

* * *

The Court's conclusion that a law which treats males less favorably than females "must serve important governmental objectives and must be substantially related to achievement of those objectives" apparently comes out of thin air. The Equal Protection Clause contains no such language, and none of our previous cases adopt that standard. I think we have had enough difficulty with the two standards of review which our cases have recognized—the norm of "rational basis," and the "compelling state interest" required where a "suspect classification" is involved—so as to counsel weightily against the insertion of still another "standard" between those two. How is this Court to divine what objectives are important? How is it to determine whether a particular law is "substantially" related to the achievement of such objective, rather than related in some other way to its achievement? Both of the phrases used are so diaphanous and elastic as to invite subjective judicial preferences or prejudices relating to particular types of legislation, masquerading as judgments whether such legislation is directed at "important" objectives or, whether the relationship to those objectives is "substantial" enough.

I would have thought that if this Court were to leave anything to decision by the popularly elected branches of the Government, where no constitutional claim other than that of equal protection is invoked, it would be the decision as to what governmental objectives to be achieved by law are "important," and which are not. As for the second part of the Court's new test, the Judicial Branch is probably in no worse position than the Legislative or Executive Branches to determine if there is *any* rational relationship between a classification and the purpose which it might be thought to serve. But the introduction of the adverb "substantially" requires courts to make subjective judgments as to operational effects, for which neither their expertise nor their access to data fits them. And even if we manage to avoid both confusion and the mirroring of our own preferences in the development of this new doctrine, the thousands of judges in other courts who must interpret the Equal Protection Clause may not be so fortunate.

* * *

The rationality of a statutory classification for equal protection purposes does not depend upon the statistical "fit" between the class and the trait sought to be singled out. It turns on whether there may be sufficiently higher incidence of the trait within the included class than in the excluded class to justify different treatment. Therefore the present equal protection challenge to this gender-based discrimination poses only the question whether the incidence of drunk driving among young men is sufficiently greater than among young women to justify differential treatment. Notwithstanding the Court's critique of the statistical evidence, that evidence suggests clear differences between the drinking and driving habits of young men and women. Those differences are grounds enough for the State reasonably to conclude that young males pose by far the greater drunk-driving hazard, both in terms of sheer numbers and in terms of hazard on a per-driver basis. The gender-based difference in treatment in this case is therefore not irrational.

The Court's argument that a 2% correlation between maleness and drunk driving is constitutionally insufficient therefore does not pose an equal protection issue concerning discrimination between males and females. The clearest demonstration of this is the fact that the precise argument made by the Court would be equally applicable to a flat bar on such purchases by *anyone,* male or female, in the 18–20 age group; in fact it would apply *a fortiori* in that case given the even more "tenuous 'fit' " between drunk-driving arrests and femaleness. The statistics indicate that about 1% of the age group population as a whole is arrested. What the Court's argument is relevant to is not equal protection, but due process—whether there are enough persons in the category who drive while drunk to justify a bar against purchases by all members of the group. . . .

The Oklahoma Legislature could have believed that 18–20-year-old males drive substantially more, and tend more often to be intoxicated than their femal counterparts; that they prefer beer and admit to drinking and driving at a higher rate than females; and that they suffer traffic injuries out of proportion to the part they make up of the population. Under the appropriate rational-basis test for equal protection, it is neither irrational nor arbitrary to bar them from making purchases of 3.2% beer, which purchases might in many cases be made by a young man who immediately returns to his vehicle with the beverage in his possession. The record does not give any good indication of the true proportion of males in the age group who drink and drive (except that it is no doubt greater than the 2% who are arrested), but whatever it may be I cannot see that the mere purchase right involved could conceivably raise a due process question. There being no violation of either equal protection or due process, the statute should accordingly be upheld.

Michael M. v. Superior Court of Sonoma County

450 U.S. 464; 101 S. Ct. 1200; 67 L. Ed. 2d 437 (1981)
Vote: 5–4

The facts are given in the opinion below.

Justice REHNQUIST announced the judgment of the Court and delivered an opinion in which THE CHIEF JUSTICE, Justice STEWART, and Justice POWELL joined.

The question presented in this case is whether California's "statutory rape" law, § 261.5 of the California Penal Code, violates the Equal Protection Clause of the Fourteenth Amendment. Section 261.5 defines unlawful sexual intercourse as "an act of sexual intercourse accomplished with a female not the wife of the perpetrator, where the female is under the age of 18 years." The statute thus makes men alone criminally liable for the act of sexual intercourse.

In July 1978, a complaint was filed in the Municipal Court of Sonoma County, Cal., alleging that petitioner, then a 17½ year old male, had had unlawful sexual intercourse with a female under the age of 18, in violation of § 261.5. The evidence, adduced at a preliminary hearing showed that at approximately midnight on June 3, 1978, petitioner and two friends approached Sharon, a 16½ year old female, and her sister as they waited at a bus stop. Petitioner and Sharon, who had already been drinking, moved away from the others and began to kiss. After being struck in the face for rebuffing petitioner's initial advances. Sharon submitted to sexual intercourse with petitioner. Prior to trial, petitioner sought to set aside the information on both state and federal constitutional grounds, asserting that § 261.5 unlawfully discriminated on the basis of gender. The trial court and the California Court of Appeal denied petitioner's request for relief and petitioner sought review in the Supreme Court of California.

The Supreme Court, held that "Section 261.5 discriminates on the basis of sex because only females may be victims, and only males may violate the section." The court then subjected the classification to "strict scrutiny," stating that it must be justified by a compelling state interest. It found that the classification was "supported not by mere social convention but by the immutable physiological fact that it is the female exclusively who can become pregnant." Canvassing "the tragic human cost of illegitimate teenage pregnancies," including the large number of teenage abortions, the increased medical risk associated with teenage pregnancies, and the social consequences of teenage child bearing, the court concluded that the state has a compelling interest in preventing such pregnancies. Because males alone can "physiologically cause the result which the law properly seeks to avoid" the court further held that the gender classification was readily justified as a means of identifying offender and victim. For the reasons stated below, we affirm the judgment of the California Supreme Court. . . .

. . . A legislature may not "make overbroad generalizations based on sex which are entirely unrelated to any differences between men and women or which demean the ability or social status of the affected class." *Parham v. Hughes,* (1979) (STEWART, J., plurality). But because the Equal Protection Clause does not "demand that a statute necessarily apply equally to all persons" or require "things which are different in fact . . . to be treated in law as though they were the same," *Rinaldi v. Yeager,* (1969), . . . this Court has consistently upheld statutes where the gender classification is not invidious, but rather realistically reflects the fact that the sexes are not similarly situated in certain circumstances. *Califano v. Webster,* (1977); . . .

As the Court has stated, a legislature may "provide for the special problems of women." *Weinberger v. Wiesenfeld,* (1975).

Applying those principles to this case, the fact that the California Legislature criminalized the act of illicit sexual intercourse with a minor female is a sure indication of its intent or purpose to discourage that conduct. Precisely why the legislature desired that result is of course somewhat less clear. This Court has long recognized that "inquiries into congressional motives or purposes are a hazardous matter," *Palmer v. Thompson,* (1970), and the search for the "actual" or "primary" purpose of a statute is likely to be elusive. *Arlington Heights v. Metropolitan Housing Corp.,* (1977).

Here, for example, the individual legislators may have voted for the statute for a variety of reasons. Some legislators may have been concerned about preventing teenage pregnancies, others about protecting young females from physical injury or from the loss of "chastity," and still others about promoting various religious and moral attitudes towards premarital sex.

The justification for the statute offered by the State, and accepted by the Supreme Court of California, is that the legislature sought to prevent illegitimate teenage pregnancies. That finding, of course, is entitled to great deference. *Reitman v. Mulkey,* (1967). And although our cases establish that the State's asserted reason for the enactment of a statute may be rejected, "if it could not have been a goal of the legislation," *Weinberger v. Wiesenfeld, supra,* this is not such a case.

We are satisfied not only that the prevention of illegitimate pregnancy is at least one of the "purposes" of the statute, but that the State has a strong interest in preventing such pregnancy. At the risk of stating the obvious, teenage pregnancies, which have increased dramatically over the last two decades, have significant social, medical and economic consequences for both the mother and her child, and the State. Of particular concern to the State is that approximately half of all teenage pregnancies end in abortion. And of those children who are born, their illegitimacy makes them likely candidates to become wards of the State.

We need not be medical doctors to discern that young men and young women are not similarly situated with respect to the problems and the risks of sexual intercourse. Only women may become pregnant and they suffer disproportionately the profound physical, emotional and psychological consequences of sexual activity. The statute at issue here protects women from sexual intercourse at an age when those consequences are particularly severe.

The question thus boils down to whether a State may attack the problem of sexual intercourse and teenage pregnancy directly by prohibiting a male from having sexual intercourse with a minor female. We hold that such a statute is sufficiently related to the State's objectives to pass constitutional muster. . . .

We are unable to accept petitioner's contention that the statute is impermissibly underinclusive and must, in order to pass judicial scrutiny, be *broadened* so as to hold the female as criminally liable as the male. It is argued that this statute is not *necessary* to deter teenage pregnancy because a gender-neutral statute, where both male and female would be subject to prosecution, would serve that goal equally well. The relevant inquiry, however, is not whether the statute is drawn as precisely as it might have been, but whether the line chosen by the California Legislature is within constitutional limitations. *Kahn v. Shevin,* [1974].

In any event, we cannot say that a gender-neutral statute would be as effective as the statute California has chosen to enact. The State persuasively contends that a gender-neutral statute would frustrate its interest in effective enforcement. Its view is that a female is surely less likely to report violations of the statute if she herself would be subject to criminal prosecution. In an area already fraught with prosecutorial difficulties, we decline to hold that the Equal Protection Clause requires a legislature to enact a statute so broad that it may well be incapable of enforcement.

We similarly reject petitioner's argument that § 261.5 is impermissibly overbroad because it makes unlawful sexual intercourse with prepubescent females, who are, by definition, incapable of becoming pregnant. Quite apart from the fact that the statute could well be justified on the grounds that very young females are particularly susceptible to physical injury from sexual intercourse, it is ludicrous to suggest that the Constitution requires the California Legislature to limit the scope of its rape statute to older teenagers and exclude young girls.

There remains only petitioner's contention that the statute is unconstitutional as it is applied to him because he, like Sharon, was under 18 at the time of sexual intercourse. Petitioner argues that the statute is flawed because it presumes that as between two persons under 18, the male is the culpable aggressor. We find petitioner's contentions unpersuasive. Contrary to his assertions, the statute does not rest on the assumption that males are generally the aggressors. It is instead an attempt by a legislature to prevent illegitimate teenage pregnancy by providing an additional deterrent for men. The age of the man is irrelevant since young men are as capable as older men of inflicting the harm sought to be prevented.

In upholding the California statute we also recognize that this is not a case where a statute is being challenged on the grounds that it "Invidiously discriminates" against females. To the contrary, the statute places a burden on males which is not shared by females. But we find nothing to suggest that men, because of past discrimination or peculiar disadvantages, are in need of the special solicitude of the courts. Nor is this a case where the gender classification is made "solely . . . for administrative convenience," as in *Frontiero v. Richardson,* (1970) or rests on "the baggage of sexual stereotypes" as in *Orr v. Orr,* (1979). As we have held, the statute instead reasonably reflects the fact that the consequences of sexual intercourse and pregnancy fall more heavily on the female than on the male.

Accordingly, the judgment of the California Supreme Court is affirmed.

Affirmed.

* * *

Justice STEWART, concurring.

* * *

. . . the Equal Protection Clause does not mean that the physiological differences between men and women must be disregarded. While those differences must never be permitted to become a pretext for invidious discrimination, no such discrimination is presented by this case. The Constitution surely does not require a State to pretend that demonstrable differences between men and women do not really exist.

* * *

Justice BRENNAN, with whom Justices WHITE and MARSHALL join, dissenting.

It is disturbing to find the court so splintered on a case that presents such a straightforward issue: whether the admittedly gender-based classification in Cal. Penal Code § 261.5 bears a sufficient relationship to the State's asserted goal of preventing teenage pregnancies to survive the "mid-level" constitutional scrutiny mandated by *Craig v. Boren,* (1976). Applying the analytical framework provided by our precedents, I am convinced that there is only one proper resolution of this issue: the classification must be declared unconstitutional. I fear that the plurality and Justices STEWART and BLACKMUN reach the opposite result by placing too much emphasis on the desirability of achieving the State's asserted statutory goal—prevention of teenage pregnancy—and not enough emphasis on the fundamental question of whether the sex-based discrimination in the California statute is *substantially* related to the achievement of the goal.

* * *

... There are at least two serious flaws in the State's assertion that law enforcement problems created by a gender-neutral statutory rape law would make such a statute less effective than a gender-based statute in deterring sexual activity.

First, the experience of other jurisdictions, and California itself, belies the plurality's conclusion that a gender-neutral statutory rape law "may well be incapable of enforcement." There are now at least 37 States that have enacted gender-neutral statutory rape laws. Although most of these laws protect young persons (of either sex) from the sexual exploitation of older individuals, the laws of Arizona, Florida, and Illinois permit prosecution of both minor females and minor males for engaging in mutual sexual conduct. California has introduced no evidence that those states have been handicapped by the enforcement problems the plurality finds so persuasive. Surely, if those States could provide such evidence, we might expect that California would have introduced it.

* * *

The second flaw in the State's assertion is that even assuming that a gender-neutral statute would be more difficult to enforce, the State has still not shown that those enforcement problems would make such a statute less effective than a gender-based statute in deterring minor females from engaging in sexual intercourse. Common sense, however, suggests that a gender-neutral statutory rape law is potentially a *greater* deterrent of sexual activity than a gender-based law, for the simple reason that a gender-neutral law subjects both men and women to criminal sanctions and thus arguably has a deterrent effect on twice as many potential violators. Even if fewer persons were prosecuted under the gender-neutral law, as the State suggest, it would still be true that twice as many persons would be *subject* to arrest. The State's failure to prove that a gender-neutral law would be a less effective deterrent than a gender-based law, like the State's failure to prove that a gender-neutral law would be difficult to enforce, should have led this Court to invalidate § 261.5.

Until very recently, no California court or commentator had suggested that the purpose of California's statutory rape law was to protect young women from the risk of pregnancy. Indeed, the historical development of § 261.5 demonstrates that the law was initially enacted on the premise that young women, in contrast to young men, were to be deemed legally incapable of consenting to an act of sexual intercourse. Because their chastity was considered particularly precious, those young women were felt to be uniquely in need of the State's protection. In contrast, young men were assumed to be capable of making such decisions for themselves; the law therefore did not offer them any special protection.

It is perhaps because the gender classification in California's statutory rape law was initially designed to further these outmoded sexual stereotypes, rather than to reduce the incidence of teenage pregnancies, that the State has been unable to demonstrate a substantial relationship between the classification and its newly asserted goal. But whatever the reason, the State has not shown that Cal.Penal Code § 261.5 is any more effective than a gender-neutral law would be in deterring minor females from engaging in sexual intercourse. It has therefore not met its burden of proving that the statutory classification is substantially related to the achievement of its asserted goal.

I would hold that § 261.5 violates the Equal Protection Clause of the Fourteenth Amendment and I would reverse the judgment of the California Supreme Court.

Justice STEVENS, dissenting.

* * *

In my judgment, the fact that a class of persons is especially vulnerable to a risk that a statute is designed to avoid is a reason for making the statute applicable to that class. The argument that a special need for protection provides a rational explanation for an exemption is one I simply do not comprehend.*

*A hypothetical racial classification will illustrate my point. Assume that skin pigmentation provides some measure of protection against cancer caused by exposure to certain chemicals in the atmosphere and, therefore, that white employees confront a greater risk than black employees in certain industrial settings. Would it be rational to require black employees to wear protective clothing but to exempt whites from that requirement? It seems to me that the greater risk of harm to white workers would be a reason for including them in the requirement—not for granting them an exemption.

In this case, the fact that a female confronts a greater risk of harm than a male is a reason for applying the prohibition to her—not a reason for granting her a license to use her own judgment on whether or not to assume the risk. Surely, if we examine the problem from the point of view of society's interest in preventing the risk-creating conduct from occurring at all, it is irrational to exempt 50% of the potential violators. See Dissent of Justice BRENNAN, *ante, . . .* And, if we view the government's interest as that of a *parens patriae* seeking to protect its subjects from harming themselves, the discrimination is actually perverse. Would a rational parent making rules for the conduct of twin children of opposite sex simultaneously forbid the son and authorize the daughter to engage in conduct that is especially harmful to the daughter? That is the effect of this statutory classification.

If pregnancy or some other special harm is suffered by one of the two participants in the prohibited act, that special harm no doubt would constitute a legitimate mitigating factor in deciding what, if any, punishment might be appropriate in a given case. But from the standpoint of fashioning a general preventive rule—or, indeed, in determining appropriate punishment when neither party in fact has suffered any special harm—I regard a total exemption for the members of the more endangered class as utterly irrational.

* * *

Nor do I find at all persuasive the suggestion that this discrimination is adequately justified by the desire to encourage females to inform against their male partners. Even if the concept of a wholesale informant's exemption were an acceptable enforcement device, what is the justification for defining the exempt class entirely by reference to sex rather than by reference to a more neutral criterion such as relative innocence? Indeed, if the exempt class is to be composed entirely of members of one sex, what is there to support the view that the statutory purpose will be better served by granting the informing license to females rather than to males? If a discarded male partner informs on a promiscuous female, a timely threat of prosecution might well prevent the precise harm the statute is intended to minimize.

Finally, even if my logic is faulty and there actually is some speculative basis for treating equally guilty males and females differently, I still believe that any such speculative justification would be outweighed by the paramount interest in evenhanded enforcement of the law. A rule that authorizes punishment of only one of two equally guilty wrongdoers violates the essence of the constitutional requirement that the sovereign must govern impartially.

I respectfully dissent.

QUESTIONS AND COMMENTS

1 What test was used in deciding *Craig v. Boren?* Is this a new test? Explain how it is similar to or different from earlier tests. Does the choice of test in this case have anything to do with the fact that the discrimination complained of is against males?

2 Would Oklahoma have had a better chance of getting approval for its law if it had chosen some justification other than "traffic safety"? Any suggestions?

3 Writing in concurrence, Justice Stevens describes Oklahoma's law as "an insult to all of the young men of the State," since it imposes a restriction on 98 percent of the males for the sins of 2 percent. He finds the insult unjustified. Rehnquist, on the other hand, says that on that argument, Oklahoma could not totally ban the purchase of 3.2 beer to males and females. Who has the best of this exchange? Explain your answer.

4 The concept of statistical significance speaks to the probability that an observed difference in a sample of cases also exists in the total population from which the sample is drawn. Oklahoma's statistics indicate that the probability is high—i.e., that there is a real or nonchance difference between male and female behavior relevant to its statute. The concept of predictability is quite different. It asks how well one variable will predict the other, given a correlation between the two variables. In this case, if we know that one is a male or a female aged 18 to 20, how well can we predict whether he or she will be arrested for drunk driving, or be killed or maimed in a traffic accident? As between Brennan and Rehnquist, which is concerned with the mere difference between classes and which with the magnitude of the difference? Which approach, in your mind, is most appropriate? Why?

5 How would you answer the question posed by Justice Stevens in his footnote on page 751? Why?

In Military Contexts

Frontiero v. Richardson (1973)

Massachusetts v. Feeney (1979)

Rostker v. Goldberg (1981)

In the modern day, gender discrimination claims are being made in a number of different areas of life. The three cases in this section focus on certain military contexts in which claims of gender discrimination have been made. *Frontiero v. Richardson* and *Rostker v. Goldberg* raise Fifth Amendment due process questions, but that clause of the amendment has been held to incorporate an equal protection dimension. Thus, for all practical purposes, these cases may be equated with *Massachusetts v. Feeney*. All three are subjected by the Court to equal protection analysis.

Frontiero et vir v. Richardson, Secretary of Defense, et al.

411 U.S. 677; 93 S. Ct. 1764; 36 L. Ed. 2d 583 (1973)
Vote: 8–1

The facts are given in the opinion below.

Mr. Justice Brennan announced the judgment of the Court and an opinion in which Mr. Justice Douglas, Mr. Justice White, and Mr. Justice Marshall join.

The question before us concerns the right of a female member of the uniformed services to claim her spouse as a "dependent" for the purposes of obtaining increased quarters allowances and medical and dental benefits under 37 U. S. C. §§ 1072, 1076, on an equal footing with male members. Under these statutes, a serviceman may claim his wife as a "dependent" without regard to whether she is in fact dependent upon him for any part of her support.

A servicewoman, on the other hand, may not claim her husband as a "dependent" under these programs unless he is in fact dependent upon her for over one-half of his support.

* * *

Appellant Sharron Frontiero, a lieutenant in the United States Air Force, sought increased quarters allowances, and housing and medical benefits for her husband, appellant Joseph Frontiero, on the ground that he was her "dependent." Although such benefits would automatically have been granted with respect to the wife of a male member of the uniformed services, appellant's application was denied because she failed to demonstrate that her husband was dependent on her for more than one-half of his support. Appellants then commenced this suit, contending that, by making this distinction, the statutes unreasonably discriminate on the basis of sex in violation of the Due Process Clause of the Fifth Amendment. In essence, appellants asserted that the discriminatory impact of the statutes is twofold: first, as a procedural matter, a female member is required to demonstrate her spouse's dependency, while no such burden is imposed upon male members; and, second, as a substantive matter, a male member who does not provide more than one-half of his wife's support receives benefits, while a similarly situated female member is denied such benefits. Appellants therefore sought a permanent injunction against the continued enforcement of these statutes and an order directing the appellees to provide Lieutenant Frontiero with the same housing and medical benefits that a similarly situated male member would receive.

* * *

[Failing to get relief in the district court, Frontiero appealed directly to the Supreme Court.]

At the outset, appellants contend that classifications based upon sex, like classifications based upon race, alienage, and national origin, are inherently suspect and must therefore be subjected to close judicial scrutiny. We agree and, indeed, find at least implicit support for such an approach in our unanimous decision only last Term in *Reed v. Reed,* (1971).

In *Reed,* the Court considered the constitutionality of an Idaho statute providing that, when two individuals are otherwise equally entitled to appointment as administrator of an estate, the male applicant must be preferred to the female. Appellant, the mother of the deceased, and appellee, the father, filed competing petitions for appointment as administrator of their son's estate. Since the parties, as parents of the deceased, were members of the same entitlement class, the statutory preference was invoked and the father's petition was therefore granted. Appellant claimed that this statute, by giving a mandatory preference to males over females without regard to their individual qualifications, violated the Equal Protection Clause of the Fourteenth Amendment.

. . . The Court held the statutory preference for male applicants unconstitutional. In reaching this result, the Court implicitly rejected appellee's apparently rational explanation of the statutory scheme, and concluded that, by ignoring the individual qualifications of particular applicants, the challenged statute provided "dissimilar treatment for men and women who are . . . similarly situated."

The Court therefore held that, even though the State's interest in achieving administrative efficiency "is not without some legitimacy," "[t]o give a mandatory preference to members of either sex over members of the other, merely to accomplish the elimination of hearings on the merits, is to make the very kind of arbitrary legislative choice forbidden by the [Constitution]. . . ."

This departure from "traditional" rational-basis analysis with respect to sex-based classifications is clearly justified.

There can be no doubt that our Nation has had a long and unfortunate history of sex discrimination. Traditionally, such discrimination was rationalized by an attitude of "romantic paternalism" which, in practical effect, put women, not on a pedestal, but in a cage. Indeed, this paternalistic attitude became so firmly rooted in our national consciousness that, 100 years ago, a distinguished Member of this Court was able to proclaim:

> Man is, or should be, woman's protector and defender. The natural and proper timidity and delicacy which belongs to the female sex evidently unfits it for many of the occupations of civil life. The constitution of the family organization, which is founded in the divine ordinance, as well as in the nature of things, indicates the domestic sphere as that which properly belongs to the domain and functions of womanhood. The harmony, not to say identity, of interests and views which belong, or should belong, to the family institution is repugnant to the idea of a woman adopting a distinct and independent career from that of her husband. . . .
> . . . The paramount destiny and mission of woman are to fulfil the noble and

benign offices of wife and mother. This is the law of the Creator. *Bradwell v. State,* (1873), (Bradley, J., concurring).

As a result of notions such as these, our statute books gradually became laden with gross, stereotyped distinctions between the sexes and, indeed, throughout much of the 19th century the position of women in our society was, in many respects, comparable to that of blacks under the pre-Civil War slave codes. Neither slaves nor women could hold office, serve on juries, or bring suit in their own names, and married women traditionally were denied the legal capacity to hold or convey property or to serve as legal guardians of their own children. And although blacks were guaranteed the right to vote in 1870, women were denied even that right—which is itself "preservative of other basic civil and political rights"—until adoption of the Nineteenth Amendment half a century later.

It is true, of course, that the position of women in America has improved markedly in recent decades. Nevertheless, it can hardly be doubted that, in part because of the high visibility of the sex characteristic, women still face pervasive, although at times more subtle, discrimination in our educational institutions, in the job market and, perhaps most conspicuously, in the political arena.

Moreover, since sex, like race and national origin, is an immutable characteristic determined solely by the accident of birth, the imposition of special disabilities upon the members of a particular sex because of their sex would seem to violate "the basic concept of our system that legal burdens should bear some relationship to individual responsibility. . . ." *Weber v. Aetna Casualty & Surety Co.,* (1972). And what differentiates sex from such nonsuspect statuses as intelligence or physical disability, and aligns it with the recognized suspect criteria, is that the sex characteristic frequently bears no relation to ability to perform or contribute to society. As a result, statutory distinctions between the sexes often have the effect of invidiously relegating the entire class of females to inferior legal status without regard to the actual capabilities of its individual members. . . .

. . . We can only conclude that classifications based upon sex, like classifications based upon race, alienage, or national origin, are inherently suspect, and must therefore be subjected to strict judicial scrutiny. Applying the analysis mandated by that stricter standard of review, it is clear that the statutory scheme now before us is constitutionally invalid.

The sole basis of the classification established in the challenged statutes is the sex of the individuals involved.

* * *

Moreover, the Government concedes that the differential treatment accorded men and women under these statutes serves no purpose other than mere "administrative convenience." In essence, the Government maintains that, as an empirical matter, wives in our society frequently are dependent upon their husbands, while husbands rarely are dependent upon their wives. Thus, the Government argues that Congress might reasonably have concluded that it would be both cheaper and easier simply conclusively to presume that wives of male members are financially dependent upon their husbands, while burdening female members with the task of establishing dependency in fact.

The Government offers no concrete evidence, however, tending to support its view that such differential treatment in fact saves the Government any money. . . .

In any case, our prior decisions make clear that, although efficacious administration of governmental programs is not without some importance, "the Constitution recognizes higher values than speed and efficiency." *Stanley v. Illinois,* (1972). . . . any statutory scheme which draws a sharp line between the sexes, *solely* for the purpose of achieving administrative convenience, necessarily commands "dissimilar treatment for men and women who are . . . similarly situated," and therefore involves the "very kind of arbitrary legislative choice forbidden by the [Constitution]. . . ." *Reed v. Reed,* . . . . We therefore conclude that, by according differential treatment to male and female members of the uniformed services for the sole purpose of achieving administrative convenience, the challenged statutes violate the Due Process Clause of the Fifth Amendment insofar as they require a female member to prove the dependency of her husband.

Reversed.

* * *

MR. JUSTICE POWELL, with whom THE CHIEF JUSTICE and MR. JUSTICE BLACKMUN join, concurring in the judgment.

I agree that the challenged statutes constitute an unconstitutional discrimination against servicewomen in violation of the Due Process Clause of the Fifth Amendment, but I cannot join the opinion of MR. JUSTICE BRENNAN, which would hold that all classifications based upon sex, "like classifications based upon race, alienage, and national origin," are "inherently suspect and must therefore be subjected to close judicial scrutiny."

It is unnecessary for the Court in this case to characterize sex as a suspect classification, with all of the far-reaching implications of such a holding. *Reed v. Reed,* (1971), which abundantly supports our decision today, did not add sex to the narrowly limited group of classifications which are inherently suspect. In my view, we can and should decide this case on the authority of *Reed* and reserve for the future any expansion of its rationale.

* * *

QUESTIONS AND COMMENTS

1 Justice Brennan's holding in *Frontiero* that sex is a suspect classification, it should be noted, was adopted by only three other Justices—Douglas, Marshall, and White.

2 In deciding *Frontiero*, does the Court employ the suspect classification test, the strict
scrutiny test, or the traditional equal protection test?
3 Can you conceive of any situation in which a "little sex discrimination" would be
justified by a "great deal of administrative convenience"? Would the Court's position
in *Frontiero* be consistent with your position? Explain.

Personnel Administrator of Massachusetts et al. v. Feeney

442 U.S. 256; 99 S. Ct. 2282; 60 L. Ed. 2d 870 (1979)
Vote: 7–2

The facts are provided in the opinion below.

MR. JUSTICE STEWART delivered the opinion of the Court.

This case presents a challenge to the constitutionality of the Massachusetts
veterans' preference statute, Mass. Gen. Laws Ann., ch. 31, § 23, on the ground
that it discriminates against women in violation of the Equal Protection Clause
of the Fourteenth Amendment. Under ch. 31, § 23, all veterans who qualify
for state civil service positions must be considered for appointment ahead of
any qualifying nonveterans. The preference operates overwhelmingly to the
advantage of males.

The appellee Helen B. Feeney is not a veteran. She brought this action pursuant to 42 U. S. C. § 1983, alleging that the absolute-preference formula established in ch. 31, § 23, inevitably operates to exclude women from consideration
for the best Massachusetts civil service jobs and thus unconstitutionally denies
them the equal protection of the laws. The three-judge District Court agreed,
one judge dissenting.

The District Court found that the absolute preference afforded by Massachusetts to veterans has a devastating impact upon the employment opportunities of women. Although it found that the goals of the preference were worthy
and legitimate and that the legislation had not been enacted for the purpose of
discriminating against women, the court reasoned that its exclusionary impact
upon women was nonetheless so severe as to require the State to further its
goals through a more limited form of preference. Finding that a more modest
preference formula would readily accommodate the State's interest in aiding
veterans, the court declared ch. 31, § 23, unconstitutional and enjoined its
operation.

Upon an appeal taken by the Attorney General of Massachusetts, this Court
vacated the judgment and remanded the case for further consideration in light
of our intervening decision in *Washington v. Davis,* [1976]. *Massachusetts v.
Feeney,* [1977]. The *Davis* case held that a neutral law does not violate the

Equal Protection Clause solely because it results in a racially disproportionate impact; instead the disproportionate impact must be traced to a purpose to discriminate on the basis of race.

Upon remand, the District Court, one judge concurring and one judge again dissenting, concluded that a veterans' hiring preference is inherently nonneutral because it favors a class from which women have traditionally been excluded, and that the consequences of the Massachusetts absolute-preference formula for the employment opportunities of women were too inevitable to have been "unintended." Accordingly, the court reaffirmed its original judgment.

The Attorney General again appealed to this Court pursuant to 28 U. S. C. § 1253, and probable jurisdiction of the appeal was noted. . . .

The appellee has lived in Dracut, Mass., most of her life. She entered the work force in 1948, and for the next 14 years worked at a variety of jobs in the private sector. She first entered the state civil service system in 1963, having competed successfully for a position as Senior Clerk Stenographer in the Massachusetts Civil Defense Agency. There she worked for four years. In 1967, she was promoted to the position of Federal Funds and Personnel Coordinator in the same agency. The agency, and with it her job, was eliminated in 1975.

During her 12-year tenure as a public employee, Ms. Feeney took and passed a number of open competitive civil service examinations. On several she did quite well, receiving in 1971 the second highest score on an examination for a job with the Board of Dental Examiners, and in 1973 the third highest on a test for an Administrative Assistant position with a mental health center. Her high scores, however, did not win her a place on the certified eligible list. Because of the veterans' preference, she was ranked sixth behind five male veterans on the Dental Examiner list. She was not certified, and a lower scoring veteran was eventually appointed. On the 1973 examination, she was placed in a position on the list behind 12 male veterans, 11 of whom had lower scores. Following the other examinations that she took, her name was similarly ranked below those veterans who had achieved passing grades.

Ms. Feeney's interest in securing a better job in state government did not wane. Having been consistently eclipsed by veterans, however, she eventually concluded that further competition for civil service positions of interest to veterans would be futile. In 1975, shortly after her civil defense job was abolished, she commenced this litigation.

* * *

The first Massachusetts veterans' preference statute defined the term "veterans" in gender-neutral language. . . .

When the first general veterans' preference statute was adopted in 1896, there were no women veterans. The statute, however, covered only Civil War veterans. Most of them were beyond middle age, and relatively few were actively competing for public employment. Thus, the impact of the preference upon the employment opportunities of nonveterans as a group and women in particular was slight.

Notwithstanding the apparent attempts by Massachusetts to include as many military women as possible within the scope of the preference, the statute today benefits an overwhelmingly male class. This is attributable in some measure to the variety of federal statutes, regulations, and policies that have restricted the number of women who could enlist in the United States Armed Forces, and largely to the simple fact that women have never been subjected to a military draft.

When this litigation was commenced, then, over 98% of the veterans in Massachusetts were male; only 1.8% were female. And over one-quarter of the Massachusetts population were veterans. During the decade between 1963 and 1973 when the appellee was actively participating in the State's merit selection system, 47,005 new permanent appointments were made in the classified official service. Forty-three percent of those hired were women, and 57% were men. Of the women appointed, 1.8% were veterans, while 54% of the men had veteran status. A large unspecified percentage of the female appointees were serving in lower paying positions for which males traditionally had not applied. . . .

The sole question for decision on this appeal is whether Massachusetts in granting an absolute lifetime preference to veterans, has discriminated against women in violation of the Equal Protection Clause of the Fourteenth Amendment. . . .

When a statute gender-neutral on its face is challenged on the ground that its effects upon women are disproportionably adverse, a twofold inquiry is thus appropriate. The first question is whether the statutory classification is indeed neutral in the sense that it is not gender based. If the classification itself, covert or overt, is not based upon gender, the second question is whether the adverse effect reflects invidious gender-based discrimination. In this second inquiry, impact provides an "important starting point," but purposeful discrimination is "the condition that offends the Constitution." *Swann v. Charlotte-Mecklenburg Board of Education,* [1971].

It is against this background of precedent that we consider the merits of the case before us.

* * *

If the impact of this statute could not be plausibly explained on a neutral ground, impact itself would signal that the real classification made by the law was in fact not neutral. See *Arlington Heights v. Metropolitan Housing Dev.*

Corp., [1976]. But there can be but one answer to the question whether this
veteran preference excludes significant numbers of women from preferred state
jobs because they are women or because they are nonveterans. Apart from the
facts that the definition of "veterans" in the statute has always been neutral as
to gender and that Massachusetts has consistently defined veteran status in a
way that has been inclusive of women who have served in the military, this is
not a law that can plausibly be explained only as a gender-based classification.
Indeed, it is not a law that can rationally be explained on that ground. Veteran
status is not uniquely male. Although few women benefit from the preference,
the nonveteran class is not substantially all female. To the contrary, significant
numbers of nonveterans are men, and all nonveterans—male as well as
female—are placed at a disadvantage. Too many men are affected by ch. 31, §
23, to permit the inference that the statute is but a pretext for preferring men
over women.

  Moreover, as the District Court implicitly found, the purposes of the statute
provide the surest explanation for its impact. Just as there are cases in which
impact alone can unmask an invidious classification, cf. *Yick Wo v. Hopkins,*
[1886], there are others, in which—notwithstanding impact—the legitimate
noninvidious purposes of a law cannot be missed. This is one. The distinction
made by ch. 31, §23, is, as it seems to be, quite simply between veterans and
nonveterans, not between men and women.

The contention that this veterans' preference is "inherently nonneutral" or
"gender-biased" presumes that the State, by favoring veterans, intentionally
incorporated into its public employment policies the panoply of sex-based and
assertedly discriminatory federal laws that have prevented all but a handful of
women from becoming veterans. There are two serious difficulties with this
argument. First, it is wholly at odds with the District Court's central finding
that Massachusetts has not offered a preference to veterans for the purpose of
discriminating against women. Second, it cannot be reconciled with the
assumption made by both the appellee and the District Court that a more limited hiring preference for veterans could be sustained. Taken together, these
difficulties are fatal.

  To the extent that the status of veteran is one that few women have been
enabled to achieve, every hiring preference for veterans, however modest or
extreme, is inherently gender-biased. If Massachusetts by offering such a preference can be said intentionally to have incorporated into its state employment
policies the historical gender-based federal military personnel practices, the
degree of the preference would or should make no constitutional difference.
Invidious discrimination does not become less so because the discrimination
accomplished is of a lesser magnitude. Discriminatory intent is simply not
amenable to calibration. It either is a factor that has influenced the legislative

choice or it is not. The District Court's conclusion that the absolute veterans' preference was not originally enacted or subsequently reaffirmed for the purpose of giving an advantage to males as such necessarily compels the conclusion that the State intended nothing more than to prefer "veterans." Given this finding, simple logic suggests that an intent to exclude women from significant public jobs was not at work in this law. To reason that it was, by describing the preference as "inherently nonneutral" or "gender-biased," is merely to restate the fact of impact, not to answer the question of intent.

To be sure, this case is unusual in that it involves a law that by design is not neutral. The law overtly prefers veterans as such. As opposed to the written test at issue in *Davis,* it does not purport to define a job-related characteristic. To the contrary, it confers upon a specifically described group—perceived to be particularly deserving—a competitive headstart. But the District Court found, and the appellee has not disputed, that this legislative choice was legitimate. The basic distinction between veterans and nonveterans, having been found not gender-based, and the goals of the preference having been found worthy, ch. 31 must be analyzed as is any other neutral law that casts a greater burden upon women as a group than upon men as a group. The enlistment policies of the Armed Services may well have discriminated on the basis of sex. . . . cf. *Schlesinger v. Ballard,* [1975]. But the history of discrimination against women in the military is not on trial in this case.

The appellee's ultimate argument rests upon the presumption, common to the criminal and civil law, that a person intends the natural and forseeable consequences of his voluntary actions. Her position was well stated in the concurring opinion in the District Court:

> Conceding . . . that the goal here was to benefit the veteran, there is no reason to absolve the legislature from awareness that the means chosen to achieve this goal would freeze women out of all those state jobs actively sought by men. To be sure, the legislature did not wish to harm women. But the cutting-off of women's opportunities was an inevitable concomitant of the chosen scheme—as inevitable as the proposition that if tails is up, heads must be down. Where a law's consequences are *that* inevitable, can they meaningfully be described as unintended?

This rhetorical question implies that a negative answer is obvious, but it is not. The decision to grant a preference to veterans was of course "intentional." So, necessarily, did an adverse impact upon nonveterans follow from that decision. And it cannot seriously be argued that the Legislature of Massachusetts could have been unaware that most veterans are men. It would thus be disingenuous to say that the adverse consequences of this legislation for women were unintended, in the sense that they were not volitional or in the sense that they were not forseeable.

"Discriminatory purpose," however, implies more than intent as volition or intent as awareness of consequences. See *United Jewish Organizations v. Carey,* [1977], (concurring opinion). It implies that the decisionmaker, in this case a state legislature, selected or reaffirmed a particular course of action at least in part "because of," not merely "in spite of," its adverse effects upon an identifiable group. Yet nothing in the record demonstrates that this preference for veterans was originally devised or subsequently re-enacted because it would accomplish the collateral goal of keeping women in a stereotypic and prede-fined place in the Massachusetts Civil Service.

To the contrary, the statutory history shows that the benefit of the prefer-ence was consistently offered to "any person" who was a veteran. That benefit has been extended to women under a very broad statutory definition of the term veteran. The preference formula itself, which is the focal point of this challenge, was first adopted—so it appears from this record—out of a per-ceived need to help a small group of older Civil War veterans. It has since been reaffirmed and extended only to cover new veterans. When the totality of leg-islative actions establishing and extending the Massachusetts veterans' pref-erence are considered, the law remains what it purports to be: a preference for veterans of either sex over nonveterans of either sex, not for men over women. . . .

The substantial edge granted to veterans by ch. 31, § 23, may reflect unwise policy. The appellee, however, has simply failed to demonstrate that the law in any way reflects a purpose to discriminate on the basis of sex.

The judgment is reversed, and the case is remanded for further proceedings consistent with this opinion.

It is so ordered.

Mr. Justice Stevens, with whom Mr. Justice White joins, concurring.

While I concur in the Court's opinion, I confess that I am not at all sure that there is any difference between the two questions posed *ante.* If a classi-fication is not overtly based on gender, I am inclined to believe the question whether it is covertly gender based is the same as the question whether its adverse effects reflect invidious gender-based discrimination. However the question is phrased, for me the answer is largely provided by the fact that the number of males disadvantaged by Massachusetts' veterans preference (1,867,000) is sufficiently close to the number of disadvantaged females (2,954,000)—to refute the claim that the rule was intended to benefit males as a class over females as a class.

Mr. Justice Marshall, with whom Mr. Justice Brennan joins, dissenting.

Although acknowledging that in some circumstances, discriminatory intent may be inferred from the inevitable or forseeable impact of a statute, the Court concludes that no such intent has been established here. I cannot agree. In my judgment, Massachusetts' choice of an absolute veterans' preference system evinces purposeful gender-based discrimination. And because the statutory scheme bears no substantial relationship to a legitimate governmental objective, it cannot withstand scrutiny under the Equal Protection Clause. . . .

Although neutral in form, the statute is anything but neutral in application. It inescapably reserves a major sector of public employment to "an already established class which, as a matter of historical fact, is 98% male." Where the foreseeable impact of a facially neutral policy is so disproportionate, the burden should rest on the State to establish that sex-based considerations played no part in the choice of the particular legislative scheme. Cf. *Castaneda v. Partida,* (1977). Clearly, that burden was not sustained here.

* * *

The Court's conclusion . . . —that "nothing in the record" evinces a "collateral goal of keeping women in a stereotypic and predefined place in the Massachusetts Civil Service," *ante,*—displays a singularly myopic view of the facts established below. . . .

In its present unqualified form, the veterans' preference statute precludes all but a small fraction of Massachusetts women from obtaining any civil service position also of interest to men.

Given the range of alternatives available, this degree of preference is not constitutionally permissible.

I would affirm the judgment of the court below.

QUESTIONS AND COMMENTS

1 What test did the Court use in deciding *Massachusetts v. Feeney,* strict scrutiny or traditional analysis? Explain.
2 How would you evaluate the methods by which the Court finds no discriminatory purpose?
3 Can a state constitutionally bar males from a nursing program in a state-supported all-female university? Or, broader still, may a state operate or substantially support universities limited to students of one sex? See *Mississippi University for Women v. Hogan,* 50 LW 5068 (1982).

Bernard Rostker, Director of Selective Service v. Robert L. Goldberg et al.

453 U.S. 57; 101 S. Ct. 2646; 69 L. Ed. 2d 478 (1981)
Vote: 6–3

The Military Selective Service Act (MSSA) authorizes the President to require males to register for possible military service. In 1980, President Carter sought funds for that purpose from Congress. He also asked Congress to change the law to permit the registration and conscription of both men and women. Congress declined to make the change but did authorize funds for registering males. The President subsequently ordered the registration of certain specified groups of men. Goldberg and others (all males) challenged the act as a violation of the Fifth Amendment's due process clause. Their claim was upheld by a three-judge district court. The United States appealed.

Justice REHNQUIST delivered the opinion of the Court.

* * *

On Friday, July 18, 1980, three days before registration was to commence, the District Court issued an opinion finding that the Act violated the Due Process Clause of the Fifth Amendment and permanently enjoined the Government from requiring registration under the Act. The court initially determined that the plaintiffs had standing and that the case was ripe, determinations which are not challenged here by the Government. Turning to the merits, the court rejected plaintiffs' suggestions that the equal protection claim should be tested under "strict scrutiny," and also rejected defendants' argument that the deference due Congress in the area of military affairs required application of the traditional "minimum scrutiny" test. Applying the "important government interest" test articulated in *Craig v. Boren,* (1976), the court struck down the MSSA. The court stressed that it was not deciding whether or to what extent women should serve in combat, but only the issue of registration, and felt that this "should dispel any concern that we are injecting ourselves in an inappropriate manner in military affairs."

The court then proceeded to examine the testimony and hearing evidence presented to Congress by representatives of the military and the Executive Branch, and concluded on the basis of this testimony that "military opinion, backed by extensive study, is that the availability of women registrants would materially increase flexibility, not hamper it." It rejected Congress' contrary determination in part because of what it viewed as Congress' "inconsistent positions" in declining to register women yet spending funds to recruit them and expand their opportunities in the military.

The United States immediately filed a notice of appeal and the next day, Saturday, July 19, 1980, Justice BRENNAN, acting in his capacity as Circuit Justice for the Third Court, stayed the District Court's order enjoining commencement of registration.

Registration began the next Monday. . . .

The case arises in the context of Congress' authority over national defense and military affairs, and perhaps in no other area has the Court accorded Congress greater deference. In rejecting the registration of women, Congress explicitly relied upon its constitutional powers under Art. I, § 8, cls. 12-14. The "specific findings" section of the Report of the Senate Armed Services Committee, later adopted by both Houses of Congress, began by stating:

Article I, section 8 of the Constitution commits exclusively to the Congress the powers to raise and support armies, provide and maintain a Navy, and make rules for Government and regulation of the land and naval forces, and pursuant to these powers it lies within the discretion of the Congress to determine the occasions for expansion of our Armed Forces, and the means best suited to such expansion should it prove necessary.

This Court has consistently recognized Congress' "broad constitutional power" to raise and regulate armies and navies, *Schlesinger v. Ballard,* 1975. . . .

Not only is the scope of Congress' constitutional power in this area broad, but the lack of competence on the part of the courts is marked. In *Gilligan v. Morgan,* (1973), the Court noted:

> It is difficult to conceive of an area of governmental activity in which the courts have less competence. The complex, subtle, and professional decisions as to the composition, training, equipping, and control of a military force are essentially professional military judgments, subject always to civilian control of the Legislative and Executive branches. . . .

The Solicitor General argues, largely on the basis of the foregoing cases emphasizing the deference due Congress in the area of military affairs and national security, that this Court should scrutinize the MSSA only to determine if the distinction drawn between men and women bears a rational relation to some legitimate government purpose, see *United States Railroad Retirement Board v. Fritz,* (1980), and should not examine the Act under the heightened scrutiny with which we have approached gender-based discrimination, see *Michael M. v. Superior Court of Sonoma County,* (1981); . . . We do not think that the substantive guarantee of due process or certainty in the law will be advanced by any further "refinement" in the applicable tests as suggested by the Government. Announced degrees of "deference" to legislative judgments, just as levels of "scrutiny" which this Court announces that it applies to particular classifications made by a legislative body, may all too readily become facile abstractions used to justify a result. In this case the courts are called upon to decide whether Congress, acting under an explicit constitutional grant of authority, has by that action transgressed an explicit guarantee of individual rights which limits the authority so conferred. Simply labeling the legislative decision "military" on the one hand or "gender-based" on the other does not automatically guide a court to the correct constitutional result.

No one could deny that under the test of *Craig v. Boren,* the Government's interest in raising and supporting armies is an "important governmental interest." Congress and its committees carefully considered and debated two alternative means of furthering that interest: the first was to register only males for potential conscription, and the other was to register both sexes. Congress chose the former alternative. When that decision is challenged on equal protection grounds, the question a court must decide is not which alternative it would have chosen, had it been the primary decisionmaker, but whether that chosen by Congress denies equal protection of the laws.

Nor can it be denied that the imposing number of cases from this Court previously cited suggest that judicial deference to such congressional exercise of authority is at its apogee when legislative action under the congressional authority to raise and support armies and make rules and regulations for their governance is challenged. As previously noted, deference does not mean abdication. The reconciliation between the deference due Congress and our own constitutional responsibility is perhaps best instanced in *Schlesinger v. Ballard.*

> This Court has recognized that "it is the primary business of armies and navies to fight or be ready to fight wars should the occasion arise."
>
> . . . The responsibility for determining how best our Armed Forces shall attend to that business rests with Congress, and with the President. See U.S. Const., Art. II, § 2, cl. 1. We cannot say that, in exercising its broad constitutional power here, Congress has violated the Due Process Clause of the Fifth Amendment.

* * *

The MSSA established a plan for maintaining "adequate armed strength . . . to ensure the security of [the] nation."

Registration is the first step "in a united and continuous process designed to raise an army speedily and efficiently," *Falbo v. United States,* (1944).

. . . Under the MSSA induction is interlocked with registration: only those registered may be drafted, and registration serves no purpose beyond providing a pool for the draft. Any assessment of the congressional purpose and its chosen means must therefore consider the registration scheme as a prelude to a draft in a time of national emergency. Any other approach would not be testing the Act in light of the purposes Congress sought to achieve.

Congress determined that any future draft, which would be facilitated by the registration scheme, would be characterized by a need for combat troops. The Senate Report explained, in a specific finding later adopted by both Houses, that "if mobilization were to be ordered in a wartime scenario, the primary manpower need would be for combat replacements."

This conclusion echoed one made a year before by the same Senate Committee, . . . As Senator Jepsen put it, "The shortage would be in the combat arms. That is why you have drafts."

Congress' determination that the need would be for combat troops if a draft took place was sufficiently supported by testimony adduced at the hearings so that the courts are not free to make their own judgment on the question. . . . The purpose of registration, therefore, was to prepare for a draft of *combat troops.*

Women as a group, however, unlike men as a group, are not eligible for combat. The restrictions on the participation of women in combat in the Navy and Air Force are statutory. Under 10 U.S.C. § 6015 "women may not be assigned to duty on vessels or in aircraft that are engaged in combat missions," and under 10 U.S.C. § 8549 female members of the Air Force "may not be assigned to duty in aircraft engaged in combat missions." The Army and Marine Corps preclude the use of women in combat as a matter of established policy. Congress specifically recognized and endorsed the exclusion of women from combat in exempting women from registration. In the words of the Senate Report:

> The principle that women should not intentionally and routinely engage in combat is fundamental, and enjoys wide support among our people. It is universally supported by military leaders who have testified before the Committee. . . . Current law and policy exclude women from being assigned to combat in our military forces, and the Committee reaffirms this policy.

The Senate Report specifically found that "Women should not be intentionally or routinely placed in combat positions in our military services."

The President expressed his intent to continue the current military policy precluding women from combat. . . . and appellees present their argument concerning registration against the background of such restrictions on the use of women in combat. . . .

The existence of the combat restrictions clearly indicates the basis for Congress' decision to exempt women from registration. The purpose of registration was to prepare for a draft of combat troops. Since women are excluded from combat, Congress concluded that they would not be needed in the event of a draft, and therefore decided not to register them.

* * *

The District Court stressed that the military need for women was irrelevant to the issue of their registration. As that court put it: "Congress could not constitutionally require registration under MSSA of only black citizens or only white citizens, or single out any political or religious group simply because those groups contained sufficient persons to fill the needs of the Selective Service System."

This reasoning is beside the point. The reason women are exempt from registration is not because military needs can be met by drafting men. This is not a case of Congress arbitrarily choosing to burden one of two similarly situated groups, such as would be the case with an all-black or all-white, or an all-Catholic or all-Lutheran, or an all-Republican or all-Democratic registration. Men and women, because of the combat restrictions on women, are simply not similarly situated for purposes of a draft or registration for a draft.

Congress' decision to authorize the registration of only men, therefore, does not violate the Due Process Clause. The exemption of women from registration is not only sufficiently but closely related to Congress' purpose in authorizing registration.

The fact that Congress and the Executive have decided that women should not serve in combat fully justifies Congress in not authorizing their registration, since the purpose of registration is to develop a pool of potential combat troops. . . .

In light of the foregoing, we conclude that Congress acted well within its constitutional authority when it authorized the registration of men, and not women, under the Military Selective Service Act. The decision of the District Court holding otherwise is accordingly

Reversed.

*   *   *

Justice MARSHALL, with whom Justice BRENNAN joins, dissenting.

*   *   *

By now it should be clear that statutes like MSSA, which discriminate on the basis of gender, must be examined under the "heightened" scrutiny mandated by *Craig v. Boren,* (1976). Under this test, a gender-based classification cannot withstand constitutional challenge unless the classification is substantially related to the achievement of an important governmental objective. *Kirchberg v. Feenstra,* (1981). This test applies whether the classification discriminates against males or females. *Caban v. Mohammed,* (1979). . . .

The party defending the challenged classification carries the burden of demonstrating both the importance of the governmental objective it serves and the substantial relationship between the discriminatory means and the asserted end.

Consequently, before we can sustain the MSSA, the Government must demonstrate that the gender-based classification it employs bears "a close and substantial relationship to [the achievement of] important governmental objectives," *Personnel Administrator of Massachusetts v. Feeney,* (1979).

The MSSA states that "an adequate armed strength must be achieved and maintained to insure the security of this Nation." I agree with the majority, *ante,* that "none could deny that . . . the Government's interest in raising and supporting armies is an 'important governmental interest.' " Consequently, the first part of the *Craig v. Boren,* test is satisfied. But the question remains whether the discriminatory means employed itself substantially serves the statutory end. . . . the Government's task in this case is to demonstrate that excluding women from registration substantially furthers the goal of preparing for a draft of combat troops. Or to put it another way, the Government must show that registering women would substantially impede its efforts to prepare for such a draft. Under our precedents, the Government cannot meet this burden without showing that a gender neutral statute would be a less effective means of attaining this end. See *Wengler v. Druggist Mutual Ins. Co.,* [1980].

*   *   *

In this case, the Government makes no claim that preparing for a draft of combat troops cannot be accomplished just as effectively by *registering* both men and women but *drafting* only men if only men turn out to be needed. Nor can the Government argue that this alternative entails the additional cost and administrative inconvenience of registering women. This Court has repeatedly stated that the administrative convenience of employing a gender classification is not an adequate constitutional justification under the *Craig v. Boren* test.

* * *

In concluding that the Government has carried its burden in this case, the Court adopts "an appropriately deferential examination of *Congress'* evaluation of [the] evidence," (emphasis in the original). The majority then proceeds to supplement Congress' actual findings with those the Court apparently believes Congress could (and should) have made. Beyond that, the Court substitutes hollow shibboleths about "deference to legislative decisions" for constitutional analysis. It is as if the majority has lost sight of the fact that "it is the responsibility of this Court to act as the ultimate interpreter of the Constitution." *Powell v. McCormack.*

Congressional enactments in the area of military affairs must, like all other laws, be *judged* by the standards of the Constitution. For the Constitution is the supreme law of the land and *all* legislation must conform to the principles it lay down. . . .

Furthermore, "[w]hen it appears that an Act of Congress conflicts with [a constitutional] provisio[n], we have no choice but to enforce the paramount commands of the Constitution. We are sworn to do no less. We cannot push back the limits of the Constitution merely to accommodate challenged legislation." *Trop v. Dulles,* (1958), (plurality opinion). In some 106 instances since this Court was established it has determined that congressional action exceeded the bounds of the Constitution. I believe the same is true of this statute. In an attempt to avoid its constitutional obligation, the Court today "pushes back the limits of the Constitution" to accommodate an Act of Congress.

I would affirm the judgment of the District Court.

QUESTIONS AND COMMENTS

1 Could Congress constitutionally exclude all Mexican-Americans from the military draft? Explain your answer.
2 What test is used to decide *Rostker v. Goldberg*?
3 After reading this case, would you say that Congress has more power to discriminate against women than against a state? Explain your answer.
4 Title IX of the Education Act Amendments of 1972 prohibits sex discrimination in "any education program or activity receiving federal financial assistance." And the federal government is permitted to terminate financial assistance to any program in which sexual discrimination is found. The Supreme Court has interpreted these provisions to permit the termination of Basic Educational Opportunity Grants paid directly to students in a college which received no direct federal aid when the college refuses to guarantee affirmatively that it is not practicing sex discrimination [*Grove City College v. Bell,* 52 LW 4283 (1984)]. In dissent, Justice Stevens called the majority's opinion "an advisory opinion." Do you agree? Why or why not?

Other Discrimination

Against Noncitizens and Nonresidents

Hampton v. Wong (1976)

Nyquist v. Mauclet (1977)

Shapiro v. Thompson (1968)

The rights guaranteed against government in the Fourteenth Amendment are rights guaranteed to *persons.* Therefore, it is quite legitimate for an alien or noncitizen to bring an equal protection or due process claim. Viewing alienage as a suspect category requiring strict scrutiny, the Supreme Court has upheld many such claims. A violation of equal protection has been found in a San Francisco ordinance which effectively barred Chinese from operating laundries,[3] in an Arizona statute requiring that if a state employer had more than five workers on the payroll, 80 percent of them had to be native-born citizens,[4] and in a California ban on the issuing of fishing licences to alien Japanese.[5] However, all use of alienage as a classification for state legislative purposes is not unconstitutional.[6] Even a suspect category or classification, after being given strict scrutiny, may pass muster if the discrimination is not unreasonable or arbitrary and serves some compelling state interest.

In *Hampton v. Wong,* the Court's decision turns, technically, on the power of the United States Civil Service Commission, but questions of the type raised in the cases mentioned above are lurking in the background.

Nyquist v. Mauclet addresses discrimination against aliens at the state level.

Hampton, Chairman, U.S. Civil Service Commission et al. v. Mon Sun Wong et al.

426 U.S. 88; 96 S. Ct. 1895; 48 L. Ed. 2d 495 (1976)
Vote: 5–4

The facts are provided in the body of the opinion below.

Mr. Justice Stevens delivered the opinion of the Court.

Five aliens, lawfully and permanently residing in the United States, brought this litigation to challenge the validity of a policy, adopted and enforced by the Civil Service Commission and certain other federal agencies, which excludes all persons except American citizens and natives of American Samoa from employment in most positions subject to their respective jurisdictions. Because the policy, the law, and the identity of the parties have changed somewhat since the litigation commenced, we state the facts in detail before addressing the important question which we granted certiorari to resolve.

Each of the five plaintiffs was denied federal employment solely because of his or her alienage. They were all Chinese residents of San Francisco and each was qualified for an available job.

After performing satisfactory work for the Post Office Department for 10 days, respondent Kae Cheong Lui was terminated because his personnel record disclosed that he was not a citizen. Respondents Mow Sun Wong and Siu Hung Mok also demonstrated their ability to perform on the job; they both participated in the California Supplemental Training and Education Program (STEP) and were assigned to federal agencies until the STEP program ended. As a noncitizen, Mow Sun Wong, who had been an electrical engineer in China, was ineligible for employment as a janitor for the General Services Administration. Siu Hung Mok, who had 18 years' experience as a businessman in China, could not retain his job as a file clerk with the Federal Records Center of GSA.

Respondent Francene Lum was not permitted to take an examination for a position as evaluator of educational programs in the Department of Health, Education, and Welfare. Her background included 15 years of teaching experience, a master's degree in education, and periods of graduate study at four universities. Anna Yu, the fifth plaintiff, who is not a respondent because she did not join in the appeal from the adverse decision of the District Court, sought a position as a clerk-typist, but could not take the typing test because she was not a citizen.

Two of the plaintiffs, Mow Sun Wong and Siu Hung Mok, had filed declarations of intent to become citizens; the other three had not. They were all lawfully admitted, Francene Lum in 1946, Anna Yu in 1965, Siu Hung Mok and Kae Cheong Lui in 1968, and Mow Sun Wong in 1969.

On December 22, 1970, they commenced this class action in the Northern District of California. As defendants they named the Chairman and the Commissioners of the Civil Service Commission and the heads of the three agencies which had denied them employment.

* * *

Plaintiffs . . . alleged that the advantage given to citizens seeking federal civil service positions is arbitrary and violates the Due Process Clause of the Fifth Amendment to the United States Constitution and Executive Order No. 11,478, which forbids discrimination in federal employment on the basis of "national origin." The complaint sought declaratory and injunctive relief. . . . the District Court held that the Commission's discrimination against aliens was constitutional. . . . The Court of Appeals reversed. . . .

We granted certiorari to decide the following question presented by the petition:

Whether a regulation of the United States Civil Service Commission that bars resident aliens from employment in the federal competitive civil service is constitutional.

We now address that question.

Petitioners have chosen to argue on the merits a somewhat different question. In their brief, the petitioners rephrased the question presented as "[w]hether the Civil Service Commission's regulation . . . is within the constitutional powers of Congress and the President and hence not a constitutionally forbidden discrimination against aliens."

This phrasing of the question assumes that the Commission regulation is one that was mandated by the Congress, the President, or both. On this assumption, the petitioners advance alternative arguments to justify the discrimination as an exercise of the plenary federal power over immigration and naturalization. First, the petitioners argue that the equal protection aspect of the Due Process Clause of the Fifth Amendment is wholly inapplicable to the exercise of federal power over aliens, and therefore no justification for the rule is necessary. Alternatively, the petitioners argue that the Fifth Amendment imposes only a slight burden of justification on the Federal Government, and that such a burden is easily met by several factors not considered by the District Court or the Court of Appeals.

* * *

When the Federal Government asserts an overriding national interest as justification for a discriminatory rule which would violate the Equal Protection Clause if adopted by a State, due process requires that there be a legitimate basis for presuming that the rule was actually intended to serve that interest. If the agency which promulgates the rule has direct responsibility for fostering or protecting that interest, it may reasonably be presumed that the asserted interest was the actual predicate for the rule. That presumption would, of course, be fortified by an appropriate statement of reasons identifying the relevant interest. Alternatively, if the rule were expressly mandated by the Congress or the President, we might presume that any interest which might rationally be served by the rule did in fact give rise to its adoption.

In this case the petitioners have identified several interests which the Congress or the President might deem sufficient to justify the exclusion of noncitizens from the federal service. They argue, for example, that the broad exclusion may facilitate the President's negotiation of treaties with foreign powers by enabling him to offer employment opportunities to citizens of a given foreign country in exchange for reciprocal concessions—an offer he could not make if those aliens were already eligible for federal jobs. Alternatively, the petitioners argue that reserving the federal service for citizens provides an appropriate incentive to aliens to qualify for naturalization and thereby to participate more effectively in our society. They also point out that the citizenship requirement has been imposed in the United States with substantial consistency for over 100 years and accords with international law and the practice of most foreign countries. Finally, they correctly state that the need for undivided loyalty in certain sensitive positions clearly justifies a citizenship requirement in at least some parts of the federal service, and that the broad exclusion serves the valid administrative purpose of avoiding the trouble and expense of classifying those positions which properly belong in executive or sensitive categories.

The difficulty with all of these arguments except the last is that they do not identify any interest which can reasonably be assumed to have influenced the Civil Service Commission, the Postal Service, the General Services Administration, or the Department of Health, Education, and Welfare in the administration of their respective responsibilities or, specifically, in the decision to deny employment to the respondents in this litigation. We may assume with the petitioners that if the Congress or the President had expressly imposed the citizenship requirement, it would be justified by the national interest in providing an incentive for aliens to become naturalized, or possibly even as providing the President with an expendable token for treaty negotiating purposes; but we are not willing to presume that the Chairman of the Civil Service Commission, or any of the other original defendants, was deliberately fostering an interest so far removed from his normal responsibilities. Consequently, before evaluating the sufficiency of the asserted justification for the rule, it is important to know whether we are reviewing a policy decision made by Congress and the President or a question of personnel administration determined by the Civil Service Commission.

It is perfectly clear that neither the Congress nor the President has ever *required* the Civil Service Commission to adopt the citizenship requirement as a condition of eligibility for employment in the federal civil service. On the other hand, in view of the fact that the policy has been in effect since the Commission was created in 1883, it is fair to infer that both the Legislature and the Executive have been aware of the policy and have acquiesced in it. . . .

We have no doubt that the statutory directive which merely requires such regulations "as will best promote the efficiency of [the] Service," as well as the pertinent Executive Order, gives the Civil Service Commission the same discretion that the Postal Service has actually exercised; the Commission may either retain or modify the citizenship requirement without further authorization from Congress or the President. We are therefore persuaded that our inquiry is whether the national interests which the Government identifies as justifications for the Commission rule are interests on which that agency may properly rely in making a decision implicating the constitutional and social values at stake in this litigation.

We think the petitioners accurately stated the question presented in their certiorari petition. The question is whether the regulation of the United States Civil Service Commission is valid. We proceed to a consideration of that question, assuming, without deciding, that the Congress and the President have the constitutional power to impose the requirement that the Commission has adopted.

It is the business of the Civil Service Commission to adopt and enforce regulations which will best promote the efficiency of the federal civil service. That agency has no responsibility for foreign affairs, for treaty negotiations, for establishing immigration quotas or conditions of entry, or for naturalization policies. Indeed, it is not even within the responsibility of the Commission to be concerned with the economic consequences of permitting or prohibiting the participation by aliens in employment opportunities in different parts of the national market. On the contrary, the Commission performs a limited and specific function.

The only concern of the Civil Service Commission is the promotion of an efficient federal service. In general it is fair to assume that its goal would be best served by removing unnecessary restrictions on the eligibility of qualified applicants for employment. With only one exception, the interests which the petitioners have put forth as supporting the Commission regulation at issue in this case are not matters which are properly the business of the Commission. That one exception is the administrative desirability of having one simple rule excluding all noncitizens when it is manifest that citizenship is an appropriate and legitimate requirement for some important and sensitive positions. Arguably, therefore, administrative convenience may provide a rational basis for the general rule.

For several reasons that justification is unacceptable in this case. The Civil Service Commission, like other administrative agencies, has an obligation to perform its responsibilities with some degree of expertise, and to make known the reasons for its important decisions. There is nothing in the record before us, or in matter of which we may properly take judicial notice, to indicate that the Commission actually made any considered evaluation of the relative desirability of a simple exclusionary rule on the one hand, or the value to the service of enlarging the pool of eligible employees on the other. Nor can we reasonably infer that the administrative burden of establishing the job classifications for which citizenship is an appropriate requirement would be a particularly onerous task for an expert in personnel matters; indeed, the Postal Service apparently encountered no particular difficulty in making such a classification. Of greater significance, however, is the quality of the interest at stake. Any fair balancing of the public interest in avoiding the wholesale deprivation of employment opportunities caused by the Commission's indiscriminate policy, as opposed to what may be nothing more than a hypothetical justification, requires rejection of the argument of administrative convenience in this case.

In sum, assuming without deciding that the national interests identified by the petitioners would adequately support an explicit determination by Congress or the President to exclude all noncitizens from the federal service, we conclude that those interests cannot provide an acceptable rationalization for such a determination by the Civil Service Commission. . . .

By broadly denying this class substantial opportunities for employment, the Civil Service Commission rule deprives its members of an aspect of liberty. Since these residents were admitted as a result of decisions made by the Congress and the President, implemented by the Immigration and Naturalization Service acting under the Attorney General of the United States, due process requires that the decision to impose that deprivation of an important liberty be made either at a comparable level of government or, if it is to be permitted to be made by the Civil Service Commission, that it be justified by reasons which are properly the concern of that agency. We hold that § 338.101 (a) of the Civil Service Commission Regulations has deprived these respondents of liberty without due process of law and is therefore invalid.

The judgment of the Court of Appeals is

Affirmed.

* * *

MR. JUSTICE REHNQUIST, with whom THE CHIEF JUSTICE, MR. JUSTICE WHITE, and MR. JUSTICE BLACKMUN join, dissenting. . . .

At the outset it is important to recognize that the power of the federal courts is severely limited in the areas of immigration and regulation of aliens. As we reiterated recently in *Kleindienst v. Mandel,* (1972):

> "The power of Congress to exclude aliens altogether from the United States, or to prescribe the terms and conditions upon which they may come to this country, and to have its declared policy in that regard enforced exclusively through executive officers, without judicial intervention, is settled by our previous adjudications." Quoting from *Lem Moon Sing v. United States,* (1895).

It is also clear that the exclusive power of Congress to prescribe the terms and conditions of entry includes the power to regulate aliens in various ways once they are here. *E. g., Hines v. Davidowitz,* (1941). Indeed the Court, by holding that the regulation in question would presumptively have been valid if "expressly mandated by the Congress," concedes the congressional power to exclude aliens from employment in the civil service altogether if it so desires or to limit their participation.

* * *

[Here] Congress and the President . . . took a power which they possessed and, instead of exercising it directly, chose to delegate it. This is the process by which all federal regulations are promulgated and to forbid it would be to necessarily dismantle the entire structure of the Executive Branch. But the majority does not challenge the procedure as to all cases. Rather, the challenge seems to be leveled only at policies which rais[e] . . . constitutional questions."

In those cases it becomes necessary for the agency, which was concededly acting within the scope of its delegated power, to provide reasons which will justify its actions in the eyes of the courts.

But, as previously discussed, such a holding overlooks the basic principle that a decision to exclude aliens from the civil service is a political decision reserved to Congress, the wisdom of which may not be challenged in the courts. Once it is determined that the agency in question was properly delegated the power by Congress to make decisions regarding citizenship of prospective civil servants, then the reasons for which that power was exercised are as foreclosed from judicial scrutiny as if Congress had made the decision itself. The fact that Congress has delegated a power does not provide a back door through which to attack a policy which would otherwise have been immune from attack. . . .

Since I do not believe that the Court is correct in concluding that the regulation promulgated by the Civil Service Commission is invalid because of any lack of authority in the Commission to promulgate the rule, I must address the question of whether "the national interests" identified by the petitioners would adequately support a "determination . . . to exclude all noncitizens from the federal service." This question was saved in both *Sugarman v. Dougall,* (1973), and *In re Griffiths,* (1973), and I agree with the Court that "the paramount federal power over immigration and naturalization forecloses a simple extension of the holding in *Sugarman* as decisive of this case."

> For reasons long recognized as valid, the responsibility for regulating the relationship between the United States and our alien visitors has been committed to the political branches of the Federal Government. *Mathews v. Diaz,* [1976]. [A]ny policy toward aliens is vitally and intricately interwoven with contemporaneous policies in regard to conduct of foreign relations, the war power, and the maintenance of a republican form of government. Such matters are so exclusively entrusted to the political branches of government as to be largely immune from judicial inquiry or interference. *Harisiades v. Shaughnessy,* [1951].

I conclude therefore that Congress, in the exercise of its political judgment, could have excluded aliens from the civil service. The fact that it chose, in a separate political decision, to allow the Civil Service Commission to make this determination does not render the governmental policy any less "political" and, consequently, does not render it any more subject to judicial scrutiny under the reasoning of *Diaz.* The regulations here, enforced without question for nearly a century, do not infringe upon any constitutional right of these respondents. I would therefore reverse the judgment of the Court of Appeals.

Nyquist, Commissioner of Education of New York, et al. v. Mauclet et al.

432 U.S. 1; 97 S. Ct. 2120; 53 L. Ed. 2d 63 (1977)
Vote: 5–4

The facts are given in the opinion below.

MR. JUSTICE BLACKMUN delivered the opinion of the Court.

New York, by statute, bars certain *resident* aliens from state financial assistance for higher education. This litigation presents a constitutional challenge to that statute. . . .

Appellee Jean-Marie Mauclet is a citizen of France and has lived in New York since April 1969. He has been a permanent resident of the United States since November of that year. He is married to a United States citizen and has a child by that marriage. The child is also a United States citizen. Mauclet by affidavit stated: "Although I am presently qualified to apply for citizenship and intend to reside permanently in the United States, I do not wish to relinquish my French citizenship at this time." He applied for a tuition assistance award to aid in meeting the expenses of his graduate studies at the State University of New York at Buffalo. Because of his refusal to apply for United States citizenship, his application was not processed.

Appellee Alan Rabinovitch is a citizen of Canada. He was admitted to this country in 1964 at the age of nine as a permanent resident alien. He is unmarried and, since his admission, has lived in New York with his parents and a younger sister, all of whom are Canadian citizens. He registered with Selective Service on his 18th birthday. He graduated in 1973 from the New York public school system. As a result of a commendable performance on the competitive Regents Qualifying Examinations, Rabinovitch was informed that he was qualified for, and entitled to, a Regents college scholarship and tuition assistance. He later was advised, however, that the offer of the scholarship was withdrawn since he intended to retain his Canadian citizenship.

Rabinovitch entered Brooklyn College without financial aid from the State. He states that he "does not intend to become a naturalized American, but . . . does intend to continue to reside in New York."

Mauclet and Rabinovitch each brought suit in United States District Court (Mauclet in the Western District of New York and Rabinovitch in the Eastern District), alleging that the citizenship bar of § 661 (3) was unconstitutional. The same three-judge court was convened for each of the cases. Subsequently, it was ordered that the cases be heard together.

After cross motions for summary judgment, the District Court in a unanimous opinion ruled in appellees' favor. It held that § 661 (3) violated the Equal Protection Clause of the Fourteenth Amendment in that the citizenship requirement served to discriminate unconstitutionally against resident aliens. Its enforcement was enjoined in separate judgments.

Appellants—the various individuals and corporate entities responsible for administering the State's educational assistance programs—challenge this determination. We noted probable jurisdiction. . . .

The Court has ruled that classifications by a State that are based on alienage are "inherently suspect and subject to close judicial scrutiny." *Graham v. Richardson,* (1971); *Sugarman v. Dougall,* (1973). In undertaking this scrutiny, "the governmental interest claimed to justify the discrimination is to be carefully examined in order to determine whether that interest is legitimate and substantial, and inquiry must be made whether the means adopted to achieve the goal are necessary and precisely drawn." Alienage classifications by a State that do not withstand this stringent examination cannot stand.

Appellants claim that § 661 (3) should not be subjected to such strict scrutiny because it does not impose a classification based on alienage. Aliens who have applied for citizenship, or, if not qualified for it, who have filed a statement of intent to apply as soon as they are eligible, are allowed to participate in the assistance programs. Hence, it is said, the statute distinguishes "only within the 'heterogeneous' class of aliens" and "does not distinguish between citizens and aliens *vel non.*" Only statutory classifications of the latter type, appellants assert, warrant strict scrutiny.

. . . [But the] fact that the statute is not an absolute bar does not mean that it does not discriminate against the class.

Appellants also assert that there are adequate justifications for § 661 (3). First, the section is said to offer an incentive for aliens to become naturalized. Second, the restriction on assistance to only those who are or will become eligible to vote is tailored to the purpose of the assistance program, namely, the enhancement of the educational level of the electorate. Both justifications are claimed to be related to New York's interest in the preservation of its "political community."

The first purpose offered by the appellants, directed to what they describe as some "degree of national affinity," however, is not a permissible one for a State. Control over immigration and naturalization is entrusted exclusively to the Federal Government, and a State has no power to interfere. U. S. Const., Art I, § 8, cl. 4. See *Mathews v. Diaz,* (1976). But even if we accept, *arguendo,* the validity of the proffered justifications, we find them inadequate to support the ban.

In *Sugarman v. Dougall,* the Court recognized that the State's interest "in establishing its own form of government to those who are within 'the basic conception of a political community' " might justify some consideration of alienage. But as *Sugarman* makes quite clear, the Court had in mind a State's historical and constitutional powers to define the qualifications of voters, or of "elective or important nonelective" officials "who participate directly in the formulation, execution, or review of broad public policy. . . ."

Certainly, the justifications for § 661 (3) offered by appellants sweep far beyond the confines of the exception defined in *Sugarman.* If the encouragement of naturalization through these programs were seen as adequate, then every discrimination against aliens could be similarly justified. The exception would swallow the rule. *Sugarman* clearly does not tolerate that result. Nor does the claimed interest in educating the electorate provide a justification; although such education is a laudable objective, it hardly would be frustrated by including resident aliens, as well as citizens, in the State's assistance programs.

Resident aliens are obligated to pay their full share of the taxes that support the assistance programs. There thus is no real unfairness in allowing resident aliens an equal right to participate in programs to which they contribute on an equal basis. And although an alien may be barred from full involvement in the political arena, he may play a role—perhaps even a leadership role—in other areas of import to the community. The State surely is not harmed by providing resident aliens the same educational opportunity it offers to others.

Since we hold that the challenged statute violates the Fourteenth Amendment's equal protection guarantee, we need not reach appellees' claim that it also intrudes upon Congress' comprehensive authority over immigration and naturalization. *Truax v. Raich,* (1915).

The judgments of the District Court are affirmed.

It is so ordered.

* * *

MR. JUSTICE REHNQUIST, with whom THE CHIEF JUSTICE joins, dissenting.

* * *

Under this New York statute, a resident alien has, at all times, the power to remove himself from one classification and to place himself in the other, for, at all times, he may become entitled to benefits either by becoming a citizen *or* by declaring his intention to become a citizen as soon as possible. Here, unlike the other cases, the resident alien is not a member of a discrete and insular minority for purposes of the classification, even during the period that he must remain an alien, because he has at all times the means to remove himself immediately from the disfavored classification. There is no temporal disability since the resident alien may declare an intent, thereby at once removing himself from the disabled class, even if the intent cannot come to fruition for some period of time. Unlike the situation in ... *Sugarman,* and *Graham,* there exists no period of disability, defined by status, from which the alien cannot escape. The alien is not, therefore, for any period of time, forced into a position as a discrete and insular minority.

Since the New York statute under challenge in this case does *not* create a discrete and insular minority by placing an inevitable disability based on status, the Court's heightened judicial scrutiny is unwarranted. The reason for the more rigorous constitutional test having ceased, the applicability of the test should likewise cease. Applying the rational-basis test, it is obvious that the statutory scheme in question should be sustained. The funds that New York wishes to spend on its higher education assistance programs are, of course, limited. New York's choice to distribute these limited funds to resident citizens and to resident aliens who intend to become citizens, while denying them to aliens who have no intention of becoming citizens, is a natural legislative judgment. By limiting the available pool of recipients to resident citizens and aliens who will become citizens, New York is able to give such recipients a larger payment from the same quantum of funds than would be the case were other aliens recipients as well. A State is entitled to decide, in distributing benefits, that resident citizens, whether or not they will remain residents of New York, are more likely to contribute to the future well-being of the State, either directly (by settling there) or indirectly (by living in some other State, but maintaining economic or social ties with New York or by improving the general well-being of the United States) than are aliens who are unwilling to renounce citizenship in a foreign country, and who may be thought more likely to return there. New York may also decide, in providing student loans pursuant to N. Y. Educ. Law §§ 680–684, that it will be easier to collect repayment sums from citizens than from aliens, should these loans be defaulted upon. These are permissible legislative judgments. When we deal, as we do here, with questions of economic legislation, our deference to the actions of a State is extremely great. New York's decision to deny educational monetary benefits to aliens who do not wish to become citizens and other resident aliens, is rational, and should be sustained.

QUESTIONS AND COMMENTS

1 Which of the following concepts are important in *Hampton v. Wong*—i.e., influenced the Court in reaching a decision? (a) political questions, (b) federalism, (c) delegation of legislative power, (d) due process of law. Explain your answer.

2 Note that Wong was Chinese and Mauclet was French. Was that distinction of any consequence in these two cases? Explain.

3 Note that *Hampton* involved federal power while *Nyquist v. Mauclet* involved state power. Was that distinction of any consequence in these two cases? Explain.

4 New York maintains that it makes no distinctions between aliens and nonaliens per se. Yet the Court chooses those two classes for comparative equal protection analysis. Why? Is the Court's choice arbitrary?

5 Can you suggest any justifications for the New York statute that might have satisfied the Supreme Court? Do you think the constitutionality of state statutes might turn on the imagination of the state's attorney?

6 Can you explain or suggest any good reason for the Court to decide *Hampton v. Wong* on the basis of Fourteenth Amendment equal protection rather than on the power given Congress in Article I to regulate immigration and naturalization?

* * * * * *

Given a federal system with fifty states, one may expect some differences in cultural values, social and political practices, and economic well-being. In the area of public welfare, such differences combine to produce a wide array of social welfare policies across the fifty states. The states that are most generous in responding to the needs of the unemployed, the sick, and the destitute are somewhat like magnets. They are apt to attract those who fall in such classes away from the states where attitudes or economic considerations support less generous policies. It is obvious, however, that no state could afford to service all in the nation who fall in the deprived classes it identifies. That is to say, there must be some limit to the numbers of people to be served by the state policies.

The problem for the magnet states is to find some way to limit those numbers. When enacted, state policy may take into consideration the number of probable welfare recipients in the state. What cannot be known is how many welfare cases will be attracted to the state because of the policy. A simple solution might be to close state borders to all prospective residents who cannot support themselves. But, as we saw in *Edwards v. California,* to do so would violate the constitutional right to travel.[7] As a consequence, a state must seek some less absolute means of discouraging the entry of indigents. One not uncommon approach is a residency requirement of the sort featured in *Shapiro v. Thompson.* But as we see in that case, this may bring charges of invidious discrimination in violation of the equal protection clause.

Shapiro, Commissioner of Welfare of Connecticut v. Thompson

394 U.S. 618; 89 S. Ct. 1322; 22 L. Ed. 2d 600 (1968)
Vote: 6–3

The facts are given in the opinion below.

MR. JUSTICE BRENNAN delivered the opinion of the Court.

* * *

In No. 9, the Connecticut Welfare Department invoked § 17–2d of the Connecticut General Statutes to deny the application of appellee Vivian Marie Thompson for assistance under the program for Aid to Families with Dependent Children (AFDC). She was a 19-year-old unwed mother of one child and pregnant with her second child when she changed her residence in June 1966 from Dorchester, Massachusetts, to Hartford, Connecticut, to live with her mother, a Hartford resident. She moved to her own apartment in Hartford in August 1966, when her mother was no longer able to support her and her infant son. Because of her pregnancy, she was unable to work or enter a work training program. Her application for AFDC assistance, filed in August, was denied in November solely on the ground that, as required by § 17–2d, she had not lived in the State for a year before her application was filed. She brought this action in the District Court for the District of Connecticut where a three-judge court, one judge dissenting, declared § 17–2d unconstitutional. The majority held that the waiting-period requirement is unconstitutional because it "has a chilling effect on the right to travel." The majority also held that the provision was a violation of the Equal Protection Clause of the Fourteenth Amendment because the denial of relief to those resident in the State for less than a year is not based on any permissible purpose but is solely designed, as "Connecticut states quite frankly," "to protect its . . . [fiscal health] by discouraging entry of those who come needing relief." We noted probable jurisdiction.

* * *

Primarily, appellants justify the waiting-period requirement as a protective device to preserve the fiscal integrity of state public assistance programs. It is asserted that people who require welfare assistance during their first year of residence in a State are likely to become continuing burdens on state welfare programs. Therefore, the argument runs, if such people can be deterred from entering the jurisdiction by denying them welfare benefits during the first year, state programs to assist long-time residents will not be impaired by a substantial influx of indigent newcomers. . . .

We do not doubt that the one-year waiting-period device is well suited to discourage the influx of poor families in need of assistance. An indigent who desires to migrate, resettle, find a new job, and start a new life will doubtless hesitate if he knows that he must risk making the move without the possibility of falling back on state welfare assistance during his first year of residence, when his need may be most acute. But the purpose of inhibiting migration by needy persons into the State is constitutionally impermissible.

This Court long ago recognized that the nature of our Federal Union and our constitutional concepts of personal liberty unite to require that all citizens be free to travel throughout the length and breadth of our land uninhibited by statutes, rules, or regulations which unreasonably burden or restrict this movement. . . .

We have no occasion to ascribe the source of this right to travel interstate to a particular constitutional provision. It suffices that, as MR. JUSTICE STEWART said for the Court in *United States v. Guest,* (1966):

> The constitutional right to travel from one State to another . . . occupies a position fundamental to the concept of our Federal Union. It is a right that has been firmly established and repeatedly recognized.
>
> . . . [T]he right finds no explicit mention in the Constitution. The reason, it has been suggested, is that a right so elementary was conceived from the beginning to be a necessary concomitant of the stronger Union the Constitution created. In any event, freedom to travel throughout the United States has long been recognized as a basic right under the Constitution.

Thus, the purpose of deterring the in-migration of indigents cannot serve as justification for the classification created by the one-year waiting period, since that purpose is constitutionally impermissible. If a law has "no other purpose . . . than to chill the assertion of constitutional rights by penalizing those who choose to exercise them, then it [is] patently unconstitutional." *United States v. Jackson,* (1968).

* * *

. . . Fundamentally, a State may no more try to fence out those indigents who seek higher welfare benefits than it may try to fence out indigents generally. Implicit in any such distinction is the notion that indigents who enter a State with the hope of securing higher welfare benefits are somehow less deserving than indigents who do not take this consideration into account. But we do not perceive why a mother who is seeking to make a new life for herself and her children should be regarded as less deserving because she considers, among other factors, the level of a State's public assistance. Surely such a mother is no less deserving than a mother who moves into a particular State in order to take advantage of its better educational facilities.

Appellants argue further that the challenged classification may be sustained as an attempt to distinguish between new and old residents on the basis of the contribution they have made to the community through the payment of taxes. We have difficulty seeing how long-term residents who qualify for welfare are making a greater present contribution to the State in taxes than indigent residents who have recently arrived.

* * *

Appellants' reasoning would logically permit the State to bar new residents from schools, parks, and libraries or deprive them of police and fire protection. Indeed it would permit the State to apportion all benefits and services to the past tax contributions of its citizens. The Equal Protection Clause prohibits such an apportionment of state services.

We recognize that a State has a valid interest in preserving the fiscal integrity of its programs. It may legitimately attempt to limit its expenditures, whether for public assistance, public education, or any other program. But a State may not accomplish such a purpose by invidious distinctions between classes of its citizens. It could not, for example, reduce expenditures for education by barring indigent children from its schools. Similarly, in the cases before us, appellants must do more than show that denying welfare benefits to new residents saves money. The saving of welfare costs cannot justify an otherwise invidious classification.

In sum, neither deterrence of indigents from migrating to the State nor limitation of welfare benefits to those regarded as contributing to the State is a constitutionally permissible state objective.

Appellants next advance as justification certain administrative and related governmental objectives allegedly served by the waiting-period requirement. They argue that the requirement (1) facilitates the planning of the welfare budget; (2) provides an objective test of residency; (3) minimizes the opportunity for recipients fraudulently to receive payments from more than one jurisdiction; and (4) encourages early entry of new residents into the labor force.

The argument that the waiting-period requirement facilitates budget predictability is wholly unfounded. The record . . . [is] utterly devoid of evidence that . . . [Connecticut] in fact uses the one-year requirement as a means to predict the number of people who will require assistance in the budget year. . . . [Connecticut does not] take a census of new residents or collect any other data that would reveal the number of newcomers in the State less than a year. Nor are new residents required to give advance notice of their need for welfare assistance. Thus, the welfare authorities cannot know how many new residents come into the jurisdiction in any year, much less how many of them will require public assistance. In these circumstances, there is simply no basis for the claim that the one-year waiting requirement serves the purpose of making the welfare budget more predictable. . . . Finally, the claim that a one-year waiting requirement is used for planning purposes is plainly belied by the fact that the requirement is not also imposed on applicants who are long-term residents, the group that receives the bulk of welfare payments. . . .

The argument that the waiting period serves as an administratively efficient rule of thumb for determining residency similarly will not withstand scrutiny. The residence requirement and the one-year waiting-period requirement are distinct and independent prerequisites for assistance under these three statutes, and the facts relevant to the determination of each are directly examined by the welfare authorities. Before granting an application, the welfare authorities investigate the applicant's employment, housing, and family situation and in the course of the inquiry necessarily learn the facts upon which to determine whether the applicant is a resident.

Similarly, there is no need for a State to use the one-year waiting period as a safeguard against fraudulent receipt of benefits; for less drastic means are available, and are employed, to minimize that hazard. Of course, a State has a valid interest in preventing fraud by any applicant, whether a newcomer or a long-time resident. It is not denied, however, that the investigations now conducted entail inquiries into facts relevant to that subject provides no rational basis for imposing a one-year waiting-period restriction on new residents only.

We conclude therefore that appellants in these cases do not use and have no need to use the one-year requirement for the governmental purposes suggested. Thus, even under traditional equal protection tests a classification of welfare applicants according to whether they have lived in the State for one year would seem irrational and unconstitutional. But, of course, the traditional criteria do not apply in these cases. Since the classification here touches on the fundamental right of interstate movement, its constitutionality must be judged by the stricter standard of whether it promotes a *compelling* state interest. Under this standard, the waiting-period requirement clearly violates the Equal Protection Clause. . . .

Affirmed.

MR. JUSTICE HARLAN, dissenting.

*   *   *   *

In upholding the equal protection argument, the Court has applied an equal protection doctrine of relatively recent vintage: the rule that statutory classifications which either are based upon certain "suspect" criteria or affect "fundamental rights" will be held to deny equal protection unless justified by a "compelling" governmental interest.

The "compelling interest" doctrine, which today is articulated more explicitly than ever before, constitutes an increasingly significant exception to the long-established rule that a statute does not deny equal protection if it is rationally related to a legitimate governmental objective. The "compelling interest" doctrine has two branches. The branch which requires that classifications based upon "suspect" criteria be supported by a compelling interest apparently had its genesis in cases involving racial classifications, which have, at least since *Korematsu v. United States,* (1944), been regarded as inherently "suspect." The criterion of "wealth" apparently was added to the list of "suspects" as an alternative justification for the rationale in *Harper v. Virginia Bd. of Elections,* (1966), in which Virginia's poll tax was struck down. The criterion of political allegiance may have been added in *Williams v. Rhodes,* (1968). Today the list apparently has been further enlarged to include classifications based upon recent interstate movement, and perhaps those based upon the exercise of *any* constitutional right, for the Court states, *ante,* at 634:

> The waiting-period provision denies welfare benefits to otherwise eligible applicants solely because they have recently moved into the jurisdiction. But in moving . . . appellees were exercising a constitutional right, and any classification which serves to penalize the exercises of that right, unless shown to be necessary to promote a *compelling* governmental interest, is unconstitutional.

I think that this branch of the "compelling interest" doctrine is sound when applied to racial classifications, for historically the Equal Protection Clause was largely a product of the desire to eradicate legal distinctions founded upon race. However, I believe that the more recent extensions have been unwise. . . .

The second branch of the "compelling interest" principle is even more troublesome. For it has been held that a statutory classification is subject to the "compelling interest" test if the result of the classification may be to affect a "fundamental right," regardless of the basis of the classification. . . .

I think this branch of the "compelling interest" doctrine particularly unfortunate and unnecessary. It is unfortunate because it creates an exception which threatens to swallow the standard equal protection rule. Virtually every state statute affects important rights. This Court has repeatedly held, for example, that the traditional equal protection standard is applicable to statutory classifications affecting such fundamental matters as the right to pursue a particular occupation, the right to receive greater or smaller wages or to work more or less hours, and the right to inherit property. Rights such as these are in principle indistinguishable from those involved here, and to extend the "compelling interest" rule to all cases in which such rights are affected would go far toward making this Court a "super-legislature." This branch of the doctrine is also unnecessary. When the right affected is one assured by the Federal Constitution, any infringement can be dealt with under the Due Process Clause. But when a statute affects only matters not mentioned in the Federal Constitution and is not arbitrary or irrational, I must reiterate that I know of nothing which entitles this Court to pick out particular human activities, characterize them as "fundamental," and give them added protection under an unusually stringent equal protection test.

* * *

The next issue, which I think requires fuller analysis than that deemed necessary by the Court under its equal protection rationale, is whether a one-year welfare residence requirement amounts to an undue burden upon the right of interstate travel. . . .

. . . The right to travel interstate is a "fundamental" right which, for present purposes, should be regarded as having its source in the Due Process Clause of the Fifth Amendment.

The next questions are: (1) To what extent does a one-year residence condition upon welfare eligibility interfere with this right to travel? and (2) What are the governmental interests supporting such a condition? The consequence of the residence requirements is that persons who contemplate interstate changes of residence, and who believe that they otherwise would qualify for welfare payments, must take into account the fact that such assistance will not be available for a year after arrival. The number or proportion of persons who are actually deterred from changing residence by the existence of these provisions is unknown. If one accepts evidence put forward by the appellees, to the effect that there would be only a minuscule increase in the number of welfare applicants were existing residence requirements to be done away with, it follows that the requirements do not deter an appreciable number of persons from moving interstate.

Against this indirect impact on the right to travel must be set the interests of the States, and of Congress with respect to the District of Columbia, in imposing residence conditions. There appear to be four such interests. First, it is evident that a primary concern of Congress and the Pennsylvania and Connecticut Legislatures was to deny welfare benefits to persons who moved into the jurisdiction primarily in order to collect those benefits. This seems to me an entirely legitimate objective. A legislature is certainly not obliged to furnish welfare assistance to every inhabitant of the jurisdiction, and it is entirely rational to deny benefits to those who enter primarily in order to receive them, since this will make more funds available for those whom the legislature deems more worthy of subsidy.

A second possible purpose of residence requirements is the prevention of fraud. A residence requirement provides an objective and workable means of determining that an applicant intends to remain indefinitely within the jurisdiction. It therefore may aid in eliminating fraudulent collection of benefits by nonresidents and persons already receiving assistance in other States. There can be no doubt that prevention of fraud is a valid legislative goal. Third, the requirement of a fixed period of residence may help in predicting the budgetary amount which will be needed for public assistance in the future. While none of the appellant jurisdictions appears to keep data sufficient to permit the making of detailed budgetary predictions in consequence of the requirement, it is probable that in the event of a very large increase or decrease in the number of indigent newcomers the waiting period would give the legislature time to make needed adjustments in the welfare laws. Obviously, this is a proper objective. Fourth, the residence requirements conceivably may have been predicated upon a legislative desire to restrict welfare payments financed in part by state tax funds to persons who have recently made some contribution to the State's economy, through having been employed, having paid taxes, or having spent money in the State. This too would appear to be a legitimate purpose.

The next question is the decisive one: whether the governmental interests served by residence requirements outweigh the burden imposed upon the right to travel. In my view, a number of considerations militate in favor of constitutionality. First, as just shown, four separate, legitimate governmental interests are furthered by residence requirements. Second, the impact of the requirements upon the freedom of individuals to travel interstate is indirect and, according to evidence put forward by the appellees themselves, insubstantial. Third, these are not cases in which a State or States, acting alone, have attempted to interfere with the right of citizens to travel, but one in which the States have acted within the terms of a limited authorization by the National Government, and in which Congress itself has laid down a like rule for the District of Columbia. Fourth, the legislatures which enacted these statutes have been fully exposed to the arguments of the appellees as to why these residence requirements are unwise, and have rejected them. This is not, therefore, an instance in which legislatures have acted without mature deliberation.

Fifth, and of longer-range importance, the field of welfare assistance is one in which there is a widely recognized need for fresh solutions and consequently for experimentation. Invalidation of welfare residence requirements might have the unfortunate consequence of discouraging the Federal and State Governments from establishing unusually generous welfare programs in particular areas on an experimental basis, because of fears that the program would cause an influx of persons seeking higher welfare payments. Sixth and finally, a strong presumption of constitutionality attaches to statutes of the types now before us. . . .

Taking all of these competing considerations into account, I believe that the balance definitely favors constitutionality. In reaching that conclusion, I do not minimize the importance of the right to travel interstate. However, the impact of residence conditions upon that right is indirect and apparently quite insubstantial. On the other hand, the governmental purposes served by the requirements are legitimate and real, and the residence requirements are clearly suited to their accomplishment. To abolish residence requirements might well discourage highly worthwhile experimentation in the welfare field. The statutes come to us clothed with the authority of Congress and attended by a correspondingly heavy presumption of constitutionality. Moreover, although the appellees assert that the same objectives could have been achieved by less restrictive means, this is an area in which the judiciary should be especially slow to fetter the judgment of Congress and of some 46 state legislatures in the choice of methods. Residence requirements have advantages, such as administrative simplicity and relative certainty, which are not shared by the alternative solutions proposed by the appellees. In these circumstances, I cannot find that the burden imposed by residence requirements upon ability to travel outweighs the governmental interests in their continued employment. Nor do

I believe that the period of residence required in these cases—one year—is so excessively long as to justify a finding of unconstitutionality on that score.

I conclude with the following observations. Today's decision, it seems to me, reflects to an unusual degree the current notion that this Court possesses a peculiar wisdom all its own whose capacity to lead this Nation out of its present troubles is contained only by the limits of judicial ingenuity in contriving new constitutional principles to meet each problem as it arises. For anyone who, like myself, believes that it is an essential function of this Court to maintain the constitutional divisions between state and federal authority and among the three branches of the Federal Government, today's decision is a step in the wrong direction. This resurgence of the expansive view of "equal protection" carries the seeds of more judicial interference with the state and federal legislative process, much more indeed than does the judicial application of "due process" according to traditional concepts (see my dissenting opinion in *Duncan v. Louisiana,* (1968), about which some members of this Court have expressed fears as to its potentialities for setting us judges "at large." I consider it particularly unfortunate that this judicial roadblock to the powers of Congress in this field should occur at the very threshold of the current discussions regarding the "federalizing" of these aspects of welfare relief.

QUESTIONS AND COMMENTS

1 Based on your reading of the Court's opinion in *Shapiro,* what are the circumstances, if any, under which a state could constitutionally employ the type of one-year residency law enacted by Connecticut?

2 What test does the Court use in judging whether Connecticut's interest justifies its residency requirement?

3 Harlan, in dissent, says that protection against racial discrimination is more important than protection against discrimination based on wealth. Do you agree or disagree? Why?

4 Could a state simply eliminate the *particular* welfare policy that is attracting most indigents from out of state? Explain your answer.

*   *   *   *   *   *

Against Indigents

Boddie v. Connecticut (1971)

Although *Shapiro v. Thompson* was focused on indigents who might come into the state seeking welfare relief, a state may have a similar interest in denying services to indigent residents no matter how long they have been in the state. In both cases, protection of the state budget may be the primary motivating factor. In *Shapiro,* we learned that a state cannot invidiously discriminate on the basis of wealth. In *Boddie v. Connecticut,* we also encounter discrimination based on wealth, but the case involves access to the courts, which triggers Fourteenth Amendment due process analysis. As Black obliquely suggests in his dissent, the facts in *Boddie* could have been analyzed under equal protection had the Court been so inclined.

Boddie et al. v. Connecticut et al.

401 U.S. 371; 91 S. Ct. 780; 28 L. Ed. 2d 113 (1971)
Vote: 8–1

The facts are reported in the opinion below.

MR. JUSTICE HARLAN delivered the opinion of the Court.

Appellants, welfare recipients residing in the State of Connecticut, brought this action in the Federal District Court for the District of Connecticut on behalf of themselves and others similarly situated, challenging, as applied to them, certain state procedures for the commencement of litigation, including requirements for payment of court fees and costs for service of process, that restrict their access to the courts in their effort to bring an action for divorce.

It appears from the briefs and oral argument that the average cost to a litigant for bringing an action for divorce is $60. Section 52–259 of the Connecticut General Statutes provides: "There shall be paid to the clerks of the supreme court or the superior court, for entering each civil cause, forty-five dollars. . . ." An additional $15 is usually required for the service of process by the sheriff, although as much as $40 or $50 may be necessary where notice must be accomplished by publication.

There is no dispute as to the inability of the named appellants in the present case to pay either the court fees required by statute or the cost incurred for the service of process. The affidavits in the record establish that appellants' welfare income in each instance barely suffices to meet the costs of the daily essentials of life and includes no allotment that could be budgeted for the expense to gain access to the courts in order to obtain a divorce. Also undisputed is appellants' "good faith" in seeking a divorce.

Assuming, as we must on this motion to dismiss the complaint, the truth of the *undisputed* allegations made by the appellants, it appears that they were unsuccessful in their attempt to bring their divorce actions in the Connecticut courts, simply by reason of their indigency. The clerk of the Superior Court returned their papers "on the ground that he could not accept them until an entry fee had been paid." Subsequent efforts to obtain a judicial waiver of the fee requirement and to have the court effect service of process were to no avail.

Appellants thereafter commenced this action in the Federal District Court seeking a judgment declaring that Connecticut's statute and service of process provisions, "requiring payment of court fees and expenses as a condition precedent to obtaining court relief [are] unconstitutional [as] applied to these indigent [appellants] and all other members of the class which they represent." As further relief, appellants requested the entry of an injunction ordering the appropriate officials to permit them "to proceed with their divorce actions without payment of fees and costs." A three-judge court was convened pursuant to 28 U. S. C. § 2281, and on July 16, 1968, that court concluded that "a state [may] limit access to its civil courts and particularly in this instance, to its divorce courts, by the requirement of a filing fee or other fees which effectively bar persons on relief from commencing actions therein."

We noted probable jurisdiction. . . .

We now reverse. Our conclusion is that, given the basic position of the marriage relationship in this society's hierarchy of values and the concomitant state monopolization of the means for legally dissolving this relationship, due process does prohibit a State from denying, solely because of inability to pay, access to its courts to individuals who seek judicial dissolution of their marriages.

At its core, the right to due process reflects a fundamental value in our American constitutional system. Our understanding of that value is the basis upon which we have resolved this case.

Perhaps no characteristic of an organized and cohesive society is more fundamental than its erection and enforcement of a system of rules defining the various rights and duties of its members, enabling them to govern their affairs and definitively settle their differences in an orderly, predictable manner. Without such a "legal system," social organization and cohesion are virtually impossible; with the ability to seek regularized resolution of conflicts individuals are capable of interdependent action that enables them to strive for achievements without the anxieties that would beset them in a disorganized society. Put more succinctly, it is this injection of the rule of law that allows society to reap the benefits of rejecting what political theorists call the "state of nature."

American society, of course, bottoms its systematic definition of individual rights and duties, as well as its machinery for dispute settlement, not on custom or the will of strategically placed individuals, but on the common-law model. It is to courts, or other quasi-judicial official bodies, that we ultimately look for the implementation of a regularized, orderly process of dispute settlement. Within this framework, those who wrote our original Constitution, in the Fifth Amendment, and later those who drafted the Fourteenth Amendment recognized the centrality of the concept of due process in the operation of this system. Without this guarantee that one may not be deprived of his rights, neither liberty nor property, without due process of law, the State's monopoly over techniques for binding conflict resolution could hardly be said to be acceptable under our scheme of things. Only by providing that the social enforcement mechanism must function strictly within these bounds can we hope to maintain an ordered society that is also just. It is upon this premise that this Court has through years of adjudication put flesh upon the due process principle. . . .

Recognition of this theoretical framework illuminates the precise issue presented in this case. As this Court on more than one occasion has recognized, marriage involves interests of basic importance in our society.

It is not surprising, then, that the States have seen fit to oversee many aspects of that institution. Without a prior judicial imprimatur, individuals may freely enter into and rescind commercial contracts, for example, but we are unaware of any jurisdiction where private citizens may covenant for or dissolve marriages without state approval. Even where all substantive requirements are concededly met, we know of no instance where two consenting adults may divorce and mutually liberate themselves from the constraints of legal obligations that go with marriage, and more fundamentally the prohibition against remarriage, without invoking the State's judicial machinery.

Thus, although they assert here due process rights as would-be plaintiffs, we think appellants' plight, because resort to the state courts is the only avenue to dissolution of their marriages, is akin to that of defendants faced with exclusion from the only forum effectively empowered to settle their disputes. Resort to the judicial process by these plaintiffs is no more voluntary in a realistic sense than that of the defendant called upon to defend his interests in court. For both groups this process is not only the paramount dispute-settlement technique, but, in fact, the only available one. In this posture we think that this appeal is properly to be resolved in light of the principles enunciated in our due process decisions that delimit rights of defendants compelled to litigate their differences in the judicial forum.

*   *   *

Prior cases establish . . . that due process requires, at a minimum, that absent a countervailing state interest of overriding significance, persons forced to settle their claims of right and duty through the judicial process must be given a meaningful opportunity to be heard.

*   *   *

Our cases further establish that a statute or a rule may be held constitutionally invalid as applied when it operates to deprive an individual of a protected right although its general validity as a measure enacted in the legitimate exercise of state power is beyond question. Thus, in cases involving religious freedom, free speech or assembly, this Court has often held that a valid statute was unconstitutionally applied in particular circumstances because it interfered with an individual's exercise of those rights. . . .

Drawing upon the principles established by the cases . . . we conclude that the State's refusal to admit these appellants to its courts, the sole means in Connecticut for obtaining a divorce, must be regarded as the equivalent of denying them an opportunity to be heard upon their claimed right to a dissolution of their marriages, and, in the absence of a sufficient countervailing justification for the State's action, a denial of due process.

The arguments for this kind of fee and cost requirement are that the State's interest in the prevention of frivolous litigation is substantial, its use of court fees and process costs to allocate scarce resources is rational, and its balance between the defendant's right to notice and the plaintiff's right to access is reasonable.

In our opinion, none of these considerations is sufficient to override the interest of these plaintiff-appellants in having access to the only avenue open for dissolving their allegedly untenable marriages. Not only is there no necessary connection between a litigant's assets and the seriousness of his motives in bringing suit, but it is here beyond present dispute that appellants bring these actions in good faith. Moreover, other alternatives exist to fees and cost requirements as a means for conserving the time of courts and protecting parties from frivolous litigation, such as penalties for false pleadings or affidavits, and actions for malicious prosecution or abuse of process, to mention only a few. . . .

We are thus left to evaluate the State's asserted interest in its fee and cost requirements as a mechanism of resource allocation or cost recoupment. Such a justification was offered and rejected in *Griffin v. Illinois,* (1956). In *Griffin* it was the requirement of a transcript beyond the means of the indigent that blocked access to the judicial process. While in *Griffin* the transcript could be waived as a convenient but not necessary predicate to court access, here the State invariably imposes the cost as a measure of allocating its judicial resources. Surely, then, the rationale of *Griffin* covers this case.

In concluding that the Due Process Clause of the Fourteenth Amendment requires that these appellants be afforded an opportunity to go into court to obtain a divorce, we wish to re-emphasize that we go no further than necessary to dispose of the case before us, a case where the *bona fides* of both appellants' indigency and desire for divorce are here beyond dispute. We do not decide that access for all individuals to the courts is a right that is, in all circumstances, guaranteed by the Due Process Clause of the Fourteenth Amendment so that its exercise may not be placed beyond the reach of any individual, for, as we have already noted, in the case before us this right is the exclusive precondition to the adjustment of a fundamental human relationship. The requirement that these appellants resort to the judicial process is entirely a state-created matter. Thus we hold only that a State may not, consistent with the obligation imposed on it by the Due Process Clause of the Fourteenth Amendment, pre-empt the right to dissolve this legal relationship without affording all citizens access to the means it has prescribed for doing so.

Reversed.

* * *

MR. JUSTICE BLACK, dissenting.

This is a strange case and a strange holding. Absent some specific federal constitutional or statutory provision, marriage in this country is completely under state control, and so is divorce. When the first settlers arrived here the power to grant divorces in Great Britain was not vested in that country's courts but in its Parliament. And as recently as 1888 this Court in *Maynard v. Hill* upheld a divorce granted by the Legislature of the Territory of Oregon. Since that time the power of state legislatures to grant divorces or vest that power in their courts seems not to have been questioned. It is not by accident that marriage and divorce have always been considered to be under state control. The institution of marriage is of peculiar importance to the people of the States. It is within the States that they live and vote and rear their children under laws passed by their elected representatives. The States provide for the stability of their social order, for the good morals of all their citizens, and for the needs of children from broken homes. The States, therefore, have particular interests in the kinds of laws regulating their citizens when they enter into, maintain, and dissolve marriages. The power of the States over marriage and divorce is complete except as limited by specific constitutional provisions.

* * *

It is true, as the majority points out, that the Court did hold in *Griffin v. Illinois,* (1956), that indigent defendants in criminal cases must be afforded the same right to appeal their convictions as is afforded to a defendant who has ample funds to pay his own costs. But in *Griffin* the Court studiously and carefully refrained from saying one word or one sentence suggesting that the rule there announced to control rights of criminal defendants would control in the quite different field of civil cases. And there are strong reasons for distinguishing between the two types of cases.

Criminal defendants are brought into court by the State or Federal Government to defend themselves against charges of crime. They go into court knowing that they may be convicted, and condemned to lose their lives, their liberty, or their property, as a penalty for their crimes. Because of this great governmental power the United States Constitution has provided special protections for people charged with crime. They cannot be convicted under bills of attainder or ex post facto laws. And numerous provisions of the Bill of Rights—the right to counsel, the right to be free from coerced confessions, and other rights—shield defendants in state courts as well as federal courts.

With all of these protections safeguarding defendants charged by government with crime, we quite naturally and quite properly held in *Griffin* that the Due Process and Equal Protection Clauses both barred any discrimination in criminal trials against poor defendants who are unable to defend themselves against the State. Had we not so held we would have been unfaithful to the explicit commands of the Bill of Rights, designed to wrap the protections of the Constitution around all defendants upon whom the mighty powers of government are hurled to punish for crime.

Civil lawsuits, however, are not like government prosecutions for crime. Civil courts are set up by government to give people who have quarrels with their neighbors the chance to use a neutral governmental agency to adjust their differences. In such cases the government is not usually involved as a party, and there is no deprivation of life, liberty, or property as punishment for crime. Our Federal Constitution, therefore, does not place such private disputes on the same high level as it places criminal trials and punishment. There is consequently no necessity, no reason, why government should in civil trials be hampered or handicapped by the strict and rigid due process rules the Constitution has provided to protect people charged with crime.

* * *

One more thought about the Due Process and Equal Protection Clauses: neither, in my judgment, justifies judges in trying to make our Constitution fit the times, or hold laws constitutional or not on the basis of a judge's sense of fairness. The Equal Protection Clause is no more appropriate a vehicle for the "shock the conscience" test than is the Due Process Clause. See, *e. g.,* my dissent in *Harper v. Virginia Board of Elections,* (1966). The rules set out in the Constitution itself provide what is governmentally fair and what is not. Neither due process nor equal protection permits state laws to be invalidated on any such nonconstitutional standard as a judge's personal view of fairness. The people and their elected representatives, not judges, are constitutionally vested with the power to amend the Constitution. Judges should not usurp that power in order to put over their own views. Accordingly, I would affirm this case.

QUESTIONS AND COMMENTS

1 Would the decision in *Boddie* have been different if the petitioner had been indigent but male?
2 What if, without paying court fees, Boddie had wished to sue General Motors for violating her civil rights under state law? Same decision? Explain.
3 What relationships can you identify in modern society that would be as fundamental as the marriage relationship on which the Court placed so much emphasis? Doctor-patient? Lawyer-client? Employer-worker? Others?
4 If Boddie had wished to sue to enforce her rights of consortium, would the Court have reached the same decision? Is the maintenance of a marriage relationship more or less important or "fundamental" than the right to rend such a relationship "asunder"?

5 By limiting its holding essentially to the facts of this case, is the Supreme Court "legislating" or "interpreting the Constitution"? Can you state the Court's holding in such a general way as to avoid a charge of "lawmaking"?
6 Is the distinction between a criminal defendant forced into court and a civil litigant who goes to court voluntarily—which Black offers—one that should lead to different legal outcomes? Defend your answer with reasons not offered by Black.

Against Unwed Mothers

Califano v. Boles (1979)

A claim that equal protection has been violated via invidious discrimination at the hands of government is essentially a claim that one or more individual members of an identifiable class have been treated differently from the members of some other class and that the distinctions made cannot be justified in law. The choice of the classes to be compared for equal protection analysis is one for the Court to make. How that choice is made can determine whether the complaining party is awarded the remedy sought. In *Califano v. Boles,* the Supreme Court notes that "The proper classification for purposes of equal protection analysis is not an exact science." Nevertheless, the Court reviews the classifications adopted by the district court and determines for itself whether that court erred in making its nonscientific choices.

Califano, Secretary of Health, Education and Welfare v. Boles et al.
443 U.S. 282; 99 S. Ct. 2767; 61 L. Ed. 2d 541 (1979)
Vote: 5–4

The facts are provided in the opinion below.

Mr. Justice Rehnquist delivered the opinion of the Court.
　. . . Appellees Norman J. Boles and Margaret Gonzales represent a nationwide class of all illegitimate children and their mothers who are allegedly ineligible for insurance benefits under the SSA [Social Security Act] because in each case the mother was never married to the wage earner who fathered her child. Section 202 (g) (1) of the SSA, as amended, 42 U. S. C. § 402 (g) (1), only makes "mother's insurance benefits" available to widows and divorced wives.

By virtue of this Court's decision in *Weinberger v. Wiesenfeld,* (1975), "mother's insurance benefits" are available to widowers, leaving the title of these benefits a misnomer. There we held that the provision of such benefits only to women violated the Due Process Clause of the Fifth Amendment.

Norman W. Boles died in 1971. He left a widow, Nancy L. Boles, and their two children, who were each promptly awarded child's insurance benefits. Nancy Boles receives mother's insurance benefits. Appellee Gonzales lived with Norman W. Boles for three years before his marriage to Nancy Boles and bore a son by him, Norman J. Boles. Gonzales sought mother's insurance benefits for herself and child's benefits for her son. Her son was granted benefits, but her personal request was denied because she had never been married to the wage earner.

Gonzales exhausted her administrative remedies and then filed this suit in the United States District Court for the Western District of Texas. The District Court certified a class of "all illegitimate children and their mothers who are presently ineligible for Mother's Insurance Benefits solely because 42 U. S. C. § 402 (g) (1) restricts such benefits to women who were once married to the fathers of their children." The District Court found that § 202 (g) (1) of the SSA was unconstitutional. There were three steps in its logic.

First, it read *Weinberger v. Wiesenfeld, supra,* as holding that mother's insurance benefits are chiefly for the benefit of the child. It quoted from a passage in that opinion where this Court observed:

> [Section] 402 (g), linked as it is directly to responsibility for minor children, was intended to permit women to elect not to work and to devote themselves to the care of children. . . .
>
> That the purpose behind § 402 (g) is to provide children deprived of one parent with the opportunity for the personal attention of the other could not be more clear in the legislative history. 420 U. S., at 648–649.

On the basis of this language it then concluded that for purposes of equal protection analysis, the pertinent discrimination in this case is not unequal treatment of unwed mothers, but rather discrimination against illegitimate children. In its final step the District Court held that the application of § 202 (g) (1) at issue here is unconstitutional, relying on cases of this Court invalidating on constitutional grounds legislation that discriminated against illegitimates solely because of their status at birth.

We noted probable jurisdiction, and now conclude that the District Court incorrectly analyzed the equal protection issue in this case. We accordingly reverse.

As this Court noted in *Weinberger v. Wiesenfeld,* at 202 (8) "was added to the Social Security Act in 1939 as one of a large number of amendments designed to 'afford more adequate protection to the family as a unit.' The benefits created in 1939 "were intended to provide persons dependent on the wage earner with protection against the economic hardship occasioned by loss of the wage earner's support." *Califano v. Jobst.* Specifically, § 202 (g) "was intended to permit women [and now men] to elect not to work and to devote themselves to care of children." The animating concern was the economic dislocation that occurs when the wage earner dies and the surviving parent is left with the choice to stay home and care for the children or to go to work, a hardship often exacerbated by years outside the labor force. "Mother's insurance benefits" were intended to make the choice to stay home easier. But the program was not designed to be, and we think is not now, a general system for the dispensing of child-care subsidies. Instead, Congress sought to limit the category of beneficiaries to those who actually suffer economic dislocation upon the death of a wage earner and are likely to be confronted at that juncture with the choice between employment or the assumption of full-time child-care responsibilities.

In this light there is an obvious logic in the exclusion from § 202 (g) of women or men who have never married the wage earner. "Both tradition and common experience support the conclusion that marriage is an event which normally marks an important change in economic status." *Califano v. Jobst, supra,* at 53. Congress could reasonably conclude that a woman who has never been married to the wage earner is far less likely to be dependent upon the wage earner at the time of his death. He was never legally required to support her and therefore less likely to have been an important source of income. Thus, the possibility of severe economic dislocation upon his death is more remote.

* * *

. . . When Congress seeks to alleviate hardship and inequity under the Social Security laws, it may quite rightly conceive its task to be analogous to painting a fence, rather than touching up an etching. We have repeatedly stated that there is no constitutional requirement that "a statutory provision . . . filte[r] out those, and only those, who are in the factual position which generated the congressional concern reflected in the statute." *Weinberger v. Salfi,* [1975]. In sum, we conclude that the denial of mother's insurance benefits to a woman who never married the wage earner bears a rational relation to the Government's desire to ease economic privation brought on by the wage earner's death.

But the appellees argue that to characterize the problem in this fashion is to miss the point because at root this case involves discrimination against illegitimate children. Quite naturally, those who seek benefits denied them by statute will frame the constitutional issue in a manner most favorable to their claim. The proper classification for purposes of equal protection analysis is not an exact science, but scouting must begin with the statutory classification itself. Only when it is shown that the legislation has a substantial disparate impact on classes defined in a different fashion may analysis continue on the basis of the impact on those classes.

We conclude that the legislation in this case does not have the impact on illegitimates necessary to warrant further inquiry whether § 202 (g) is the product of discriminatory purposes.

* * *

The SSA and its amendments are the product of hard choices and counter-vailing pressures. The desire to alleviate hardship wherever it is found is tempered by the concern that the social security system in this country remain a contributory insurance plan and not become a general welfare program. General welfare objectives are addressed through public assistance legislation. In light of the limited resources of the insurance fund, any expansion of the class of beneficiaries invariably poses the prospect of reduced benefits to individual claimants. We need look no further than the facts of this case for an illustration. The benefits available to Norman W. Boles' beneficiaries under that Act are limited by his earnings record. The effect of extending benefits to Gonzales may be to deprive Nancy Boles of a meaningful choice between full-time employment and staying home with her children, thereby undermining the express legislative purpose of mother's insurance benefits. We think Congress could rationally choose to concentrate limited funds where the need is likely to be greatest. . . .

The judgment of the District Court is accordingly,

Reversed.

MR. JUSTICE MARSHALL, with whom MR. JUSTICE BRENNAN, MR. JUSTICE WHITE, and MR. JUSTICE BLACKMUN join, dissenting.

* * *

Statutes that foreclose opportunities solely because of a child's status at birth represent a particularly invidious form of discrimination. . . . To penalize an illegitimate child for conduct he could not prevent and a status he cannot alter is both "illogical and unjust." *Weber v. Aetna Casualty & Surety Co.* Accordingly, classifications based on legitimacy violate the equal protection requirements of the Fifth Amendment unless they bear a close and substantial relationship to a permissible governmental interest.

In arguing that § 202 (g) meets this test, the Secretary suggests that legitimate children as a class are more likely than illegitimates to be dependent on the insured wage earner at the time of his death. Therefore, because the statute establishes a maximum amount payable to any one wage earner's survivors, the Secretary contends that the exclusion of illegitimates is an appropriate means of allocating finite resources to those most likely to have suffered economically from the insured's death.

The threshold difficulty with this argument is that § 202 (g)'s marital restriction bars recovery by illegitimates regardless of whether any other individuals are eligible to claim benefits on a particular wage earner's account. Thus, the restriction defended here as a rationing device withholds assistance to illegitimates even when there are no competing claimants among whom to ration. Insofar as the exclusion of illegitimates is designed to allocate limited funds on the basis of need, it is not carefully tailored to achieve that objective.

* * *

We cannot, of course, expect perfect congruence between legislative ends and means in the administration of a complex statutory scheme. But neither should we give our imprimatur to distinctions needlessly predicated on a disfavored social status, particularly one beyond an individual's power to affect. Although a "blanket and conclusive exclusion" of illegitimate children may be an administratively expedient means of screening for dependence under § 202 (g), it is also inaccurate, unjust, and, under this Court's settled precedents, unconstitutional.

I respectfully dissent.

QUESTIONS AND COMMENTS

1 In this case, the district court thought the appropriate classes were legitimate versus illegitimate children, while the Supreme Court chose wedded versus unwedded mothers. Do the two courts use the same or different methods in making their class determinations? What are the methods in each case? Any activism here?

2 The Rehnquist opinion for the Court asserts that Congress "may quite rightly conceive its task to be analogous to painting a fence, rather than touching up an etching." What is the principle of constitutional analysis reflected in this colorful expression? See *Weinberger v. Salfi,* 422 U.S. 749, 769 (1975).

NOTES

1 *Regents of the University of California v. Bakke,* 438 U.S. 265 (1978).
2 *Bradwell v. Illinois,* 83 U.S. (16 Wallace) 130 (1873).
3 *Yick Wo v. Hopkins,* 118 U.S. 356 (1886).
4 *Truax v. Raich,* 239 U.S. 33 (1915).
5 *Takahashi v. Fish & Game Commission,* 334 U.S. 410 (1948).
6 *Oyama v. California,* 332 U.S. 633 (1948).
7 314 U.S. 160 (1941).

CHAPTER 10

THE RIGHT TO MAKE PERSONAL DECISIONS

The Use of Contraceptives

Griswold v. Connecticut (1965)

Abortion

Roe v. Wade (1973)

Planned Parenthood v. Danforth (1976)
Harris v. McRae (1980)

The kind of "personal" decisions with which we are concerned in this chapter are those traditionally considered quite intimate—decisions that we have been inclined to think are not the business of government. Such decisions would include (1) whether to procreate, and (2) whether to abort the reproductive process once that process has been set into play. With the development of the modern state and its penchant for ever expanding regulation of human activity, conflict with certain traditional practices in this area was inevitable. One such conflict arose in 1965 when the Court was asked to strike a Connecticut statute prohibiting the use of contraceptives and making it a crime for anyone to assist or abet such use.

Griswold et al. v. Connecticut

381 U.S. 479; 85 S. Ct. 1678; 14 L. Ed. 2d 510 (1965)
Vote: 7–2

The facts are given in the opinion below.

MR. JUSTICE DOUGLAS delivered the opinion of the Court.

Appellant Griswold is Executive Director of the Planned Parenthood League of Connecticut. Appellant Buxton is a licensed physician and a professor at the Yale Medical School who served as Medical Director for the League at its Center in New Haven—a center open and operating from November 1 to November 10, 1961, when appellants were arrested.

They gave information, instruction, and medical advice to *married persons* as to the means of preventing conception. They examined the wife and prescribed the best contraceptive device or material for her use. Fees were usually charged, although some couples were serviced free.

The statutes whose constitutionality is involved in this appeal are §§ 53–32 and 54–196 of the General Statutes of Connecticut (1958 rev.). The former provides:

> Any person who uses any drug, medical article or instrument for the purpose of preventing conception shall be fined not less than fifty dollars or imprisoned not less than sixty days nor more than one year or be both fined and imprisoned.

Section 54–196 provides:

> Any person who assists, abets, counsels, causes, hires or commands another to commit any offense may be prosecuted and punished as if he were the principal offender.

The appellants were found guilty as accessories and fined $100 each, against the claim that the accessory statute as so applied violated the Fourteenth Amendment. The Appellate Division of the Circuit Court affirmed. The Supreme Court of Errors affirmed that judgment. We noted probable jurisdiction.

* * *

By *Pierce v. Society of Sisters,* [1924], the right to educate one's children as one chooses is made applicable to the States by the force of the First and Fourteenth Amendments. By *Meyer v. Nebraska,* [1923], the same dignity is given the right to study the German language in a private school. In other words, the State may not, consistently with the spirit of the First Amendment, contract the spectrum of available knowledge. The right of freedom of speech and press includes not only the right to utter or to print, but the right to distribute, the right to receive, the right to read, and freedom of inquiry, freedom of thought, and freedom to teach—indeed the freedom of the entire university community, *Baggett v. Bullitt,* [1963]. Without those peripheral rights the specific rights would be less secure. And so we reaffirm the principle of the *Pierce* and the *Meyer* cases.

In *NAACP v. Alabama,* [1958], we protected the "freedom to associate and privacy in one's associations," noting that freedom of association was a peripheral First Amendment right. Disclosure of membership lists of a constitutionally valid association, we held, was invalid "as entailing the likelihood of a substantial restraint upon the exercise by petitioner's members of their right to freedom of association." In other words, the First Amendment has a penumbra where privacy is protected from governmental intrusion.

* * *

. . . Specific guarantees in the Bill of Rights have penumbras, formed by emanations from those guarantees that help give them life and substance. See *Poe v. Ullman,* [1961], (dissenting opinion). Various guarantees create zones of privacy. The right of association contained in the penumbra of the First Amendment is one, as we have seen. The Third Amendment in its prohibition against the quartering of soldiers "in any house" in time of peace without the consent of the owner is another facet of that privacy. The Fourth Amendment explicitly affirms the "right of the people to be secure in their persons, houses, papers, and effects, against unreasonable searches and seizures." The Fifth Amendment in its Self-Incrimination Clause enables the citizen to create a zone of privacy which government may not force him to surrender to his detriment. The Ninth Amendment provides: "The enumeration in the Constitution, of certain rights, shall not be construed to deny or disparage others retained by the people."

* * *

The present case . . . concerns a relationship lying within the zone of privacy created by several fundamental constitutional guarantees. And it concerns a law which, in forbidding the *use* of contraceptives rather than regulating their manufacture or sale, seeks to achieve its goals by means having a maximum destructive impact upon that relationship. Such a law cannot stand in light of the familiar principle, so often applied by this Court, that a "governmental purpose to control or prevent activities constitutionally subject to state regulation may not be achieved by means which sweep unnecessarily broadly and thereby invade the area of protected freedoms." Would we allow the police to search the sacred precincts of marital bedrooms for telltale signs of the use of contraceptives? The very idea is repulsive to the notions of privacy surrounding the marriage relationship.

We deal with a right of privacy older than the Bill of Rights—older than our political parties, older than our school system. Marriage is a coming together for better or for worse, hopefully enduring, and intimate to the degree of being sacred. It is an association that promotes a way of life, not causes; a harmony in living, not political faiths; a bilateral loyalty, not commercial or social projects. Yet it is an association for as noble a purpose as any involved in our prior decisions.

Reversed.

MR. JUSTICE GOLDBERG, whom THE CHIEF JUSTICE and MR. JUSTICE BRENNAN join, concurring.

I agree with the Court that Connecticut's birth-control law unconstitutionally intrudes upon the right of marital privacy, and I join in its opinion and judgment. Although I have not accepted the view that "due process" as used in the Fourteenth Amendment incorporates all of the first eight Amendments, . . .

I do agree that the concept of liberty protects those personal rights that are fundamental, and is not confined to the specific terms of the Bill of Rights. My conclusion that the concept of liberty is not so restricted and that it embraces the right of marital privacy though that right is not mentioned explicitly in the Constitution is supported both by numerous decisions of this Court, referred to in the Court's opinion, and by the language and history of the Ninth Amendment.

* * *

The Ninth Amendment to the Constitution may be regarded by some as a recent discovery and may be forgotten by others, but since 1791 it has been a basic part of the Constitution which we are sworn to uphold. To hold that a right so basic and fundamental and so deep-rooted in our society as the right of privacy in marriage may be infringed because that right is not guaranteed in so many words by the first eight amendments to the Constitution is to ignore the Ninth Amendment and to give it no effect whatsoever. Moreover, a judicial construction that this fundamental right is not protected by the Constitution because it is not mentioned in explicit terms by one of the first eight amendments or elsewhere in the Constitution would violate the Ninth Amendment, which specifically states that

[t]he enumeration in the Constitution, of certain rights, shall not be *construed* to deny or disparage others retained by the people. (Emphasis added.)

* * *

I do not mean to imply that the Ninth Amendment is applied against the States by the Fourteenth. Nor do I mean to state that the Ninth Amendment constitutes an independent source of rights protected from infringement by either the States or the Federal Government. Rather, the Ninth Amendment shows a belief of the Constitution's authors that fundamental rights exist that are not expressly enumerated in the first eight amendments and an intent that the list of rights included there not be deemed exhaustive. As any student of this Court's opinions knows, this Court has held, often unanimously, that the Fifth and Fourteenth Amendments protect certain fundamental personal liberties from abridgment by the Federal Government or the States. The Ninth Amendment simply shows the intent of the Constitution's authors that other fundamental personal rights should not be denied such protection or disparaged in any other way simply because they are not specifically listed in the first eight constitutional amendments.

Although the Constitution does not speak in so many words of the right of privacy in marriage, I cannot believe that it offers these fundamental rights no protection. The fact that no particular provision of the Constitution explicitly forbids the State from disrupting the traditional relation of the family—a relation as old and as fundamental as our entire civilization—surely does not show that the Government was meant to have the power to do so. Rather, as the Ninth Amendment expressly recognizes, there are fundamental personal rights such as this one, which are protected from abridgment by the Government though not specifically mentioned in the Constitution.

* * *

In a long series of cases this Court has held that where fundamental personal liberties are involved, they may not be abridged by the States simply on a showing that a regulatory statute has some rational relationship to the effectuation of a proper state purpose. "Where there is a significant encroachment upon personal liberty, the State may prevail only upon showing a subordinating interest which is compelling," *Bates v. Little Rock,* [1960]. The law must be shown "necessary, and not merely rationally related, to the accomplishment of a permissible state policy." *McLaughlin v. Florida,* [1964].

Although the Connecticut birth-control law obviously encroaches upon a fundamental personal liberty, the State does not show that the law serves any "subordinating [state] interest which is compelling" or that it is "necessary . . . to the accomplishment of a permissible state policy." The State, at most, argues that there is some rational relation between this statute and what is admittedly a legitimate subject of state concern—the discouraging of extramarital relations. It says that preventing the use of birth-control devices by married persons helps prevent the indulgence by some in such extra-marital relations. The rationality of this justification is dubious, particularly in light of the admitted widespread availability to all persons in the State of Connecticut, unmarried as well as married, of birth-control devices for the prevention of disease, as distinguished from the prevention of conception. . . .

But, in any event, it is clear that the state interest in safeguarding marital fidelity can be served by a more discriminately tailored statute, which does not, like the present one, sweep unnecessarily broadly, reaching far beyond the evil sought to be dealt with and intruding upon the privacy of all married couples.

* * *

In sum, I believe that the right of privacy in the marital relation is fundamental and basic—a personal right "retained by the people" within the meaning of the Ninth Amendment. Connecticut cannot constitutionally abridge this fundamental right, which is protected by the Fourteenth Amendment from infringement by the States. I agree with the Court that petitioners' convictions must therefore be reversed.

MR. JUSTICE HARLAN, concurring in the judgment.

I fully agree with the judgment of reversal, but find myself unable to join the Court's opinion. The reason is that it seems to me to evince an approach to this case very much like that taken by my Brothers BLACK and STEWART in dissent, namely: the Due Process Clause of the Fourteenth Amendment does not touch this Connecticut statute unless the enactment is found to violate some rights assured by the letter or penumbra of the Bill of Rights.

In other words, what I find implicit in the Court's opinion is that the "incorporation" doctrine may be used to *restrict* the reach of Fourteenth Amendment Due Process. For me this is just as unacceptable constitutional doctrine as is the use of the "incorporation" approach to *impose* upon the States all the requirements of the Bill of Rights as found in the provisions of the first eight amendments and in the decisions of this Court interpreting them.

In my view, the proper constitutional inquiry in this case is whether this Connecticut statute infringes the Due Process Clause of the Fourteenth Amendment because the enactment violates basic values "implicit in the concept of ordered liberty," *Palko v. Connecticut,* [1937].

For reasons stated at length in my dissenting opinion in *Poe v. Ullman, supra,* I believe that it does. While the relevant inquiry may be aided by resort to one or more of the provisions of the Bill of Rights, it is not dependent on them or any of their radiations. The Due Process Clause of the Fourteenth Amendment stands, in my opinion, on its own bottom.

A further observation seems in order respecting the justification of my Brothers BLACK and STEWART for their "incorporation" approach to this case. Their approach does not rest on historical reasons, which are of course wholly lacking . . . but on the thesis that by limiting the content of the Due Process Clause of the Fourteenth Amendment to the protection of rights which can be found elsewhere in the Constitution, in this instance in the Bill of Rights, judges will thus be confined to "interpretation" of specific constitutional provisions, and will thereby be restrained from introducing their own notions of constitutional right and wrong into the "vague contours of the Due Process Clause." *Rochin v. California,* [1952].

While I could not more heartily agree that judicial "self restraint" is an indispensable ingredient of sound constitutional adjudication, I do submit that the formula suggested for achieving it is more hollow than real. "Specific" provisions of the Constitution, no less than "due process," lend themselves as readily to "personal" interpretations by judges whose constitutional outlook is simply to keep the Constitution in supposed "tune with the times." Need one go further than to recall last Term's reapportionment cases, *Wesberry v. Sanders,* [1964] and *Reynolds v. Sims,* [1964], where a majority of the Court "interpreted" "by the People" (Art. I, § 2) and "equal protection" (Amdt. 14) to command "one person, one vote," an interpretation that was made in the face of irrefutable and still unanswered history to the contrary? . . .

Judicial self-restraint will not, I suggest, be brought about in the "due process" area by the historically unfounded incorporation formula long advanced by my Brother BLACK, and now in part espoused by my Brother STEWART. It will be achieved in this area, as in other constitutional areas, only by continual insistence upon respect for the teachings of history, solid recognition of the basic values that underlie our society, and wise appreciation of the great roles that the doctrines of federalism and separation of powers have played in establishing and preserving American freedoms.

* * *

MR. JUSTICE WHITE, concurring in the judgment.

In my view this Connecticut law as applied to married couples deprives them of "liberty" without due process of law, as that concept is used in the Fourteenth Amendment. I therefore concur in the judgment of the Court reversing these convictions under Connecticut's aiding and abetting statute.

* * *

MR. JUSTICE BLACK, with whom MR. JUSTICE STEWART joins, dissenting.

* * *

The Court talks about a constitutional "right of privacy, as though there is some constitutional provision or provisions forbidding any law ever to be passed which might abridge the "privacy" of individuals. But there is not. There are, of course, guarantees in certain specific constitutional provisions which are designed in part to protect privacy at certain times and places with respect to certain activities. Such, for example, is the Fourth Amendment's guarantee against "unreasonable searches and seizures." But I think it belittles that Amendment to talk about it as though it protects nothing but "privacy." To treat it that way is to give it a niggardly interpretation, not the kind of liberal reading I think any Bill of Rights provision should be given. The average man would very likely not have his feelings soothed any more by having his property seized openly than by having it seized privately and by stealth. He simply wants his property left alone. And a person can be just as much, if not more, irritated, annoyed and injured by an unceremonious public arrest by a policeman as he is by a seizure in the privacy of his office or home.

One of the most effective ways of diluting or expanding a constitutionally guaranteed right is to substitute for the crucial word or words of a constitutional guarantee another word or words, more or less flexible and more or less restricted in meaning. This fact is well illustrated by the use of the term "right of privacy" as a comprehensive substitute for the Fourth Amendment's guarantee against "unreasonable searches and seizures." "Privacy" is a broad, abstract and ambiguous concept which can easily be shrunken in meaning but which can also, on the other hand, easily be interpreted as a constitutional ban against many things other than searches and seizures. I have expressed the view many times that First Amendment freedoms, for example, have suffered from a failure of the courts to stick to the simple language of the First Amendment in construing it, instead of invoking multitudes of words substituted for those the Framers used. For these reasons I get nowhere in this case by talk about a constitutional "right of privacy" as an emanation from one or more constitutional provisions. I like my privacy as well as the next one, but I am nevertheless compelled to admit that government has a right to invade it unless prohibited by some specific constitutional provision. For these reasons I cannot agree with the Court's judgment and the reasons it gives for holding this Connecticut law unconstitutional.

* * *

My Brother GOLDBERG has adopted the recent discovery that the Ninth Amendment as well as the Due Process Clause can be used by this Court as authority to strike down all state legislation which this Court thinks violates "fundamental priciples of liberty and justice," or is contrary to the "traditions and [collective] conscience of our people." He also states, without proof satisfactory to me, that in making decisions on this basis judges will not consider "their personal and private notions." One may ask how they can avoid considering them. Our Court certainly has no machinery with which to take a Gallup Poll.* And the scientific miracles of this age have not yet produced a gadget which the Court can use to determine what traditions are rooted in the "[collective] conscience of our people." Moreover, one would certainly have to look far beyond the language of the Ninth Amendment to find that the Framers vested in this Court any such awesome veto powers over lawmaking, either by the States or by the Congress. Nor does anything in the history of the Amendment offer any support for such a shocking doctrine. The whole history of the adoption of the Constitution and Bill of Rights points the other way, and the very material quoted by my Brother GOLDBERG shows that the Ninth Amendment was intended to protect against the idea that "by enumerating particular exceptions to the grant of power" to the Federal Government, "those rights which were not singled out, were intended to be assigned into the hands of the General Government [The United States], and were consequently insecure." That Amendment was passed, not to broaden the powers of this Court or any other department of "the General Government," but, as every

---

*Of course one cannot be oblivious to the fact that Mr. Gallup has already published the results of a poll which he says show that 46% of the people in this country believe schools should teach about birth control. Washington Post, May 21, 1965, p. 2, col. 1. I can hardly believe, however, that Brother GOLDBERG would view 46% of the persons polled as so overwhelming a proportion that this Court may now rely on it to declare that the Connecticut law infringes "fundamental" rights, and overrule the long-standing view of the people of Connecticut expressd through their elected representatives.

student of history knows, to assure the people that the Constitution in all its provisions was intended to limit the Federal Government to the powers granted expressly or by necessary implication. If any broad, unlimited power to hold laws unconstitutional because they offend what this Court conceives to be the "[collective] conscience of our people," is vested in this Court by the Ninth Amendment, the Fourteenth Amendment, or any other provision of the Constitution, it was not given by the Framers, but rather has been bestowed on the Court by the Court. This fact is perhaps responsible for the peculiar phenomenon that for a period of a century and a half no serious suggestion was ever made that the Ninth Amendment, enacted to protect state powers against federal invasion, could be used as a weapon of federal power to prevent state legislatures from passing laws they consider appropriate to govern local affairs. Use of any such broad, unbounded judicial authority would make of this Court's members a day-to-day constitutional convention.

* * *

So far as I am concerned, Connecticut's law as applied here is not forbidden by any provision of the Federal Constitution as that Constitution was written, and I would therefore affirm.

MR. JUSTICE STEWART, whom MR. JUSTICE BLACK joins, dissenting.

Since 1879 Connecticut has had on its books a law which forbids the use of contraceptives by anyone. I think this is an uncommonly silly law. As a practical matter, the law is obviously unenforceable, except in the oblique context of the present case. As a philosophical matter, I believe the use of contraceptives in the relationship of marriage should be left to personal and private choice, based upon each individual's moral, ethical, and religious beliefs. As a matter of social policy, I think professional counsel about methods of birth control should be available to all, so that each individual's choice can be meaningfully made. But we are not asked in this case to say whether we think this law is unwise, or even asinine. We are asked to hold that it violates the United States Constitution. And that I cannot do.

In the course of its opinion the Court refers to no less than six Amendments to the Constitution: the First, the Third, the Fourth, the Fifth, the Ninth, and the Fourteenth. But the Court does not say which of these Amendments, if any, it thinks is infringed by this Connecticut law. . . .

As to the First, Third, Fourth, and Fifth Amendments, I can find nothing in any of them to invalidate this Connecticut law, even assuming that all those Amendments are fully applicable against the States. It has not even been argued that this is a law "respecting an establishment of religion, or prohibiting the free exercise thereof." And surely, unless the solemn process of constitutional adjudication is to descend to the level of a play on words, there is not involved here any abridgment of "the freedom of speech, or of the press; or the right of the people peaceably to assemble, and to petition the Government for a redress of grievances." No soldier has been quartered in any house. There has been no search, and no seizure. Nobody has been compelled to be a witness against himself.

The Court also quotes the Ninth Amendment, and my Brother GOLDBERG'S concurring opinion relies heavily upon it. But to say that the Ninth Amendment has anything to do with this case is to turn somersaults with history.

* * *

What provision of the Constitution, then, does make this state law invalid? The Court says it is the right of privacy "created by several fundamental constitutional guarantees." With all deference, I can find no such general right of privacy in the Bill of Rights, in any other part of the Constitution, or in any case ever decided by this Court.

* * *

QUESTIONS AND COMMENTS

1 Which amendment to the Constitution does the Court say is violated in *Griswold?* Support your answer with evidence. Can you identify any amendments, the words of which conflict with Connecticut's statute or its goal? Can you identify any amendment, the implications of which require the striking of the statute? Explain how you derive such implications.
2 Can a state prohibit the use of contraceptives
   a by nonmarried persons,
   b outside the marital bedroom,
   c in a public place, such as a parking lot or a movie theater?
      Support your answers.
3 Did the means of enforcing the Connecticut statute influence the Court's decision to strike it? Explain.

* * * * * *

To use *Griswold* as a precedent in future cases, a lower court would have to ascertain the principle for which that case stands. Given the six opinions written in the case and the fact that the decision did not turn on any specific words in the Constitution, that may not be an easy task. It would have been simpler if the Court had adopted Justice Goldberg's position that the right denied by Connecticut was a "fundamental" right or Justice Harlan's argument that the statute violates basic values "implicit in the concept of ordered liberty," in contradiction of Fourteenth Amendment due process. But, absent such holdings, the best guide is the Supreme Court's own interpretation of the right to privacy in a later case.

In *Eisenstadt v. Baird,* Justice Brennan defined the right of privacy as "the right of an individual, married or single, to be free of unwanted governmental intrusions into matters so fundamentally affecting a person as the decision whether to bear or beget a child."[1] Given this reading, *Griswold* is consistent with *Skinner v. Oklahoma,*[2] holding that the right to reproduce—reproductive autonomy—is a basic constitutional right, but inconsistent with *Buck v. Bell,* upholding the states' right to sterilize imbeciles. Relating *Griswold* and *Skinner,* we can say that one has a right to engage in sexual intercourse to procreate, to engage in sexual intercourse while preventing procreation, and to halt the reproductive process resulting from sexual intercourse after that process has begun.

In the three abortion cases included in this section, we shall learn that the meaning of the third right listed is exceedingly complex. The complicating factor is the meaning of life and the problem of determining when life begins. For the right to abort a pregnancy may or may not be the right to take another life—depending on one's definition of life. If life begins at conception, we confront principles that may be irrelevant if life begins at a later point and one aborts a pregnancy before that point has been reached. In *Roe v. Wade,* the Court attempts to sort out the principles it believes should govern abortion decisions and the reach of State power to control or influence those decisions.

Roe et al. v. Wade, District Attorney of Dallas County

410 U.S. 113; 93 S. Ct. 705; 35 L. Ed. 2d 147 (1973)
Vote: 7–2

The facts are given in the opinion below.

MR. JUSTICE BLACKMUN delivered the opinion of the Court.

* * *

The Texas statutes that concern us here are Arts. 1191–1194 and 1196 of the State's Penal Code. These make it a crime to "procure an abortion," as therein defined, or to attempt one, except with respect to "an abortion procured or attempted by medical advice for the purpose of saving the life of the mother." Similar statutes are in existence in a majority of the States.

Jane Roe, a single woman who was residing in Dallas County, Texas, instituted this federal action in March 1970 against the District Attorney of the county. She sought a declatory judgment that the Texas criminal abortion statutes were unconstitutional on their face, and an injunction restraining the defendant from enforcing the statutes.

Roe alleged that she was unmarried and pregnant; that she wished to terminate her pregnancy by an abortion "performed by a competent, licensed physician, under safe, clinical conditions"; that she was unable to get a "legal" abortion in Texas because her life did not appear to be threatened by the continuation of her pregnancy; and that she could not afford to travel to another jurisdiction in order to secure a legal abortion under safe conditions. She claimed that the Texas statutes were unconstitutionally vague and that they abridged her right of personal privacy, protected by the First, Fourth, Fifth, Ninth, and Fourteenth Amendments. By an amendment to her complaint Roe purported to sue "on behalf of herself and all other women" similarly situated. . . .

On the merits, the District Court held that the "fundamental right of single women and married persons to choose whether to have children is protected by the Ninth Amendment, through the Fourteenth Amendment," and that the Texas criminal abortion statutes were void on their face because they were both unconstitutionally vague and constituted an overbroad infringement of the plaintiffs' Ninth Amendment rights. The court then held that abstention was warranted with respect to the requests for an injunction. It therefore . . . declared the abortion statutes void, and dismissed the application for injunctive relief. . . .

[Roe and other appellants in this case appealed the denial of injunctive relief to the Supreme Court. That Court denied standing to the other appellants and proceeded to decision in *Roe v. Wade.*]

The principle thrust of appellant's attack on the Texas statutes is that they improperly invade a right, said to be possessed by the pregnant woman, to choose to terminate her pregnancy. Appellant would discover this right in the concept of personal "liberty" embodied in the Fourteenth Amendment's Due Process Clause; or in personal, marital, familial, and sexual privacy said to be protected by the Bill of Rights or its penumbras, see *Eisenstadt v. Baird,* (1972); or among those rights reserved to the people by the Ninth Amendment, *Griswold v. Connecticut,* [1965]. . . .

Three reasons have been advanced to explain historically the enactment of criminal abortion laws in the 19th century and to justify their continued existence.

It has been argued occasionally that these laws were the product of a Victorian social concern to discourage illicit sexual conduct. Texas, however, does not advance this justification in the present case, and it appears that no court or commentator has taken the argument seriously. . . .

A second reason is concerned with abortion as a medical procedure. When most criminal abortion laws were first enacted, the procedure was a hazardous one for the woman. . . .

Thus, it has been argued that a State's real concern in enacting a criminal abortion law was to protect the pregnant woman, that is, to restrain her from submitting to a procedure that placed her life in serious jeopardy.

Modern medical techniques have altered this situation. Appellants and various *amici* refer to medical data indicating that abortion in early pregnancy, that is, prior to the end of the first trimester, although not without its risk, is now relatively safe. Mortality rates for women undergoing early abortions, where the procedure is legal, appear to be as low as or lower than the rates for normal childbirth. Consequently, any interest of the State in protecting the woman from an inherently hazardous procedure, except when it would be equally dangerous for her to forgo it, has largely disappeared. Of course, important state interests in the areas of health and medical standards do remain. The State has a legitimate interest in seeing to it that abortion, like any other medical procedure, is performed under circumstances that insure maximum safety for the patient. This interest obviously extends at least to the performing physician and his staff, to the facilities involved, to the availability of after-care, and to adequate provision for any complication or emergency that might arise. The prevalence of high mortality rates at illegal "abortion mills" strengthens, rather than weakens, the State's interest in regulating the conditions under which abortions are performed. Moreover, the risk to the woman increases as her pregnancy continues. Thus, the State retains a definite interest in protecting the woman's own health and safety when an abortion is proposed at a late stage of pregnancy.

The third reason is the State's interest—some phrase it in terms of duty—in protecting prenatal life. Some of the argument for this justification rests on the theory that a new human life is present from the moment of conception. The State's interest and general obligation to protect life then extends, it is argued, to prenatal life. Only when the life of the pregnant mother herself is at stake, balanced against the life she carries within her, should the interest of the embryo or fetus not prevail. Logically, of course, a legitimate state interest in this area need not stand or fall on acceptance of the belief that life begins at conception or at some other point prior to live birth. In assessing the State's interest, recognition may be given to the less rigid claim that as long as at least *potential* life is involved, the State may assert interests beyond the protection of the pregnant woman alone. . . .

The Constitution does not explicitly mention any right of privacy. In a line of decisions, however, going back perhaps as far as *Union Pacific R. Co. v. Bots-*

ford, (1891), the Court has recognized that a right of personal privacy, or a guarantee of certain areas or zones of privacy, does exist under the Constitution.

* * *

This right of privacy, whether it be founded in the Fourteenth Amendment's concept of personal liberty and restrictions upon state action, as we feel it is, or, as the District Court determined, in the Ninth Amendment's reservation of rights to the people, is broad enough to encompass a woman's decision whether or not to terminate her pregnancy. The detriment that the State would impose upon the pregnant woman by denying this choice altogether is apparent. Specific and direct harm medically diagnosable even in early pregnancy may be involved. Maternity, or additional offspring, may force upon the woman a distressful life and future. Psychological harm may be imminent. Mental and physical health may be taxed by child care. There is also the distress, for all concerned, associated with the unwanted child, and there is the problem of bringing a child into a family already unable, psychologically and otherwise, to care for it. In other cases, as in this one, the additional difficulties and continuing stigma of unwed motherhood may be involved. All these are factors the woman and her responsible physician necessarily will consider in consultation.

On the basis of elements such as these, appellant and some *amici* argue that the woman's right is absolute and that she is entitled to terminate her pregnancy at whatever time, in whatever way, and for whatever reason she alone chooses. With this we do not agree. Appellant's arguments that Texas either has no valid interest at all in regulating the abortion decision, or no interest strong enough to support any limitation upon the woman's sole determination, are unpersuasive. The Court's decisions recognizing a right of privacy also acknowledge that some state regulation in areas protected by that right is appropriate. As noted above, a State may properly assert important interests in safeguarding health, in maintaining medical standards, and in protecting potential life. At some point in pregnancy, these respective interests become sufficiently compelling to sustain regulation of the factors that govern the abortion decision. The privacy right involved, therefore, cannot be said to be absolute. . . .

We, therefore, conclude that the right of personal privacy includes the abortion decision, but that this right is not unqualified and must be considered against important state interests in regulation.

. . . Most . . . courts have argued that the right of privacy, however based, is broad enough to cover the abortion decision; that the right, nonetheless, is not absolute and is subject to some limitations; and that at some point the state interests as to protection of health, medical standards, and prenatal life, become dominant. We agree with this approach. . . .

The appellee and certain *amici* argue that the fetus is a "person" within the language and meaning of the Fourteenth Amendment. In support of this, they outline at length and in detail the well-known facts of fetal development. If this suggestion of personhood is established, the appellant's case, of course, collapses, for the fetus' right to life would then be guaranteed specifically by the Amendment. The appellant conceded as much on reargument. On the other hand, the appellee conceded on reargument that no case could be cited that holds that a fetus is a person within the meaning of the Fourteenth Amendment.

* * *

In nearly all . . . instances, the use of the word is such that it has application only postnatally. None indicates, with any assurance, that it has any possible pre-natal application.

* * *

This conclusion, however, does not of itself fully answer the contentions raised by Texas, and we pass on to other considerations.

* * *

Texas argues that, apart from the Fourteenth Amendment, life begins at conception and is present throughout pregnancy, and that, therefore, the State has a compelling interest in protecting that life from and after conception. We need not resolve the difficult question of when life begins. When those trained in the respective disciplines of medicine, philosophy, and theology are unable to arrive at any consensus, the judiciary, at this point in the development of man's knowledge, is not in a position to speculate as to the answer.

It should be sufficient to note briefly the wide divergence of thinking on this most sensitive and difficult question. There has always been strong support for the view that life does not begin until live birth. This was the belief of the Stoics. It appears to be the predominant, though not the unanimous, attitude of the Jewish faith. It may be taken to represent also the position of a large segment of the Protestant community, insofar as that can be ascertained; organized groups that have taken a formal position on the abortion issue have generally regarded abortion as a matter for the conscience of the individual and her family.

. . . Physicians and their scientific colleagues have regarded that event with less interest and have tended to focus either upon conception, upon live birth, or upon the interim point at which the fetus becomes "viable," that is, potentially able to live outside the mother's womb, albeit with artificial aid. Viability is usually placed at about seven months (28 weeks) but may occur earlier, even at 24 weeks. The Aristotelian theory of "mediate animation," that held sway throughout the Middle Ages and the Renaissance in Europe, continued to be official Roman Catholic dogma until the 19th century, despite opposition to this "ensoulment" theory from those in the Church who would recognize the existence of life from the moment of conception. The latter is now, of course, the official belief of the Catholic Church. As one brief *amicus* discloses, this is a view strongly held by many non-Catholics as well, and by many physicians.

* * *

In view of all this, we do not agree that, by adopting one theory of life, Texas may override the rights of the pregnant woman that are at stake. We repeat, however, that the State does have an important and legitimate interest in preserving and protecting the health of the pregnant woman, whether she be a resident of the State or a nonresident who seeks medical consultation and treatment there, and that it has still *another* important and legitimate interest in protecting the potentiality of human life. These interests are separate and distinct. Each grows in substantiality as the woman approaches term and, at a point during pregnancy, each becomes "compelling."

With respect to the State's important and legitimate interest in the health of the mother, the "compelling" point, in the light of present medical knowledge, is at approximately the end of the first trimester. This is so because of the now-established medical fact, referred to above, . . . that until the end of the first trimester mortality in abortion may be less than mortality in normal childbirth. It follows that, from and after this point, a State may regulate the abortion procedure to the extent that the regulation reasonably relates to the preservation and protection of maternal health. Examples of permissible state regulation in this area are requirements as to the qualifications of the person who is to perform the abortion; as to the licensure of that person; as to the facility in which the procedure is to be performed, that is, whether it must be a hospital or may be a clinic or some other place of less-than-hospital status; as to the licensing of the facility; and the like.

This means, on the other hand, that, for the period of pregnancy prior to this "compelling" point, the attending physician, in consultation with his patient, is free to determine, without regulation by the State, that, in his medical judgment, the patient's pregnancy should be terminated. If that decision is reached, the judgment may be effectuated by an abortion free of interference by the State.

With respect to the State's important and legitimate interest in potential life, the "compelling" point is at viability. This is so because the fetus then presumably has the capability of meaningful life outside the mother's womb. State regulation protective of fetal life after viability thus has both logical and biological justifications. If the State is interested in protecting fetal life after viability, it may go so far as to proscribe abortion during that period, except when it is necessary to preserve the life or health of the mother.

Measured against these standards, Art. 1196 of the Texas Penal Code, in restricting legal abortions to those "procured or attempted by medical advice for the purpose of saving the life of the mother," sweeps too broadly. The statute makes no distinction between abortions performed early in pregnancy and those performed later, and it limits to a single reason, "saving" the mother's life, the legal justification for the procedure. The statute, therefore, cannot survive the constitutional attack made upon it here. . . .

To summarize and to repeat:

1 A state criminal abortion statute of the current Texas type, that excepts from criminality only a *life-saving* procedure on behalf of the mother, without regard to pregnancy stage and without recognition of the other interests involved, is violative of the Due Process Clause of the Fourteenth Amendment.

   a For the stage prior to approximately the end of the first trimester, the abortion decision and its effectuation must be left to the medical judgment of the pregnant woman's attending physician.

   b For the stage subsequent to approximately the end of the first trimester, the State, in promoting its interest in the health of the mother, may, if it chooses, regulate the abortion procedure in ways that are reasonably related to maternal health.

   c For the stage subsequent to viability, the State in promoting its interest in the potentiality of human life may, if it chooses, regulate, and even proscribe, abortion except where it is necessary, in appropriate medical judgment, for the preservation of the life or health of the mother.

2 The State may define the term "physician," as it has been employed in the preceding paragraphs of . . . Part XI of this opinion, to mean only a physician currently licensed by the State, and may proscribe any abortion by a person who is not a physician as so defined.

* * *

Our conclusion that Art. 1196 is unconstitutional means, of course, that the Texas abortion statutes, as a unit, must fall. The exception of Art. 1196 cannot be struck down separately, for then the State would be left with a statute proscribing all abortion procedures no matter how medically urgent the case.

Although the District Court granted appellant Roe declaratory relief, it stopped short of issuing an injunction against enforcement of the Texas statutes. The Court has recognized that different considerations enter into a federal court's decision as to declaratory relief, on the one hand, and injunctive relief, on the other. *Dombrowski v. Pfister,* (1965). We are not dealing with a statute that, on its face, appears to abridge free expression, an area of particular concern under *Dombrowski* and refined in *Younger v. Harris,* [1970].

We find it unnecessary to decide whether the District Court erred in withholding injunctive relief, for we assume the Texas prosecutorial authorities will give full credence to this decision that the present criminal abortion statutes of that State are unconstitutional.

The judgment of the District Court as to [Roe is, in all other respects, affirmed.]

* * *

Mr. Justice Rehnquist, dissenting.

The Court's opinion brings to the decision of this troubling question both extensive historical fact and a wealth of legal scholarship. While the opinion thus commands my respect, I find myself nonetheless in fundamental disagreement with those parts of it that invalidate the Texas statute in question, and therefore dissent. . . .

The Due Process Clause of the Fourteenth Amendment undoubtedly does place a limit, albeit a broad one, on legislative power to enact laws such as this. If the Texas statute were to prohibit an abortion even where the mother's life is in jeopardy, I have little doubt that such a statute would lack a rational relation to a valid state objective under the test stated in *Williamson, supra.* But the Court's sweeping invalidation of any restrictions on abortion during the first trimester is impossible to justify under that standard, and the conscious weighing of competing factors that the Court's opinion apparently substitutes for the established test is far more appropriate to a legislative judgment than to a judicial one.

The Court eschews the history of the Fourteenth Amendment in its reliance on the "compelling state interest" test. See *Weber v. Aetna Casualty & Surety.* . . .

As in . . . cases applying substantive due process standards to economic and social welfare legislation, the adoption of the compelling state interest standard will inevitably require this Court to examine the legislative policies and pass on the wisdom of these policies in the very process of deciding whether a particular state interest put forward may or may not be "compelling." The decision here to break pregnancy into three distinct terms and to outline the permissible restrictions the State may impose in each one, for example, partakes more of the judicial legislation than it does of a determination of the intent of the drafters of the Fourteenth Amendment.

The fact that a majority of the States reflecting, after all, the majority sentiment in those States, have had restrictions on abortions for at least a century is a strong indication, it seems to me, that the asserted right to an abortion is not "so rooted in the traditions and conscience of our people as to be ranked as fundamental," *Snyder v. Massachusetts,* (1934). Even today, when society's views on abortion are changing, the very existence of the debate is evidence that the "right" to an abortion is not so universally accepted as the appellant would have us believe.

To reach its result, the Court necessarily has had to find within the scope of the Fourteenth Amendment a right that was apparently completely unknown to the drafters of the Amendment. As early as 1821, the first state law dealing directly with abortion was enacted by the Connecticut Legislature.

By the time of the adoption of the Fourteenth Amendment in 1868, there were at least 36 laws enacted by state or territorial legislatures limiting abortion. While many States have amended or updated their laws, 21 of the laws on the books in 1868 remain in effect today. Indeed, the Texas statute struck down today was, as the majority notes, first enacted in 1857 and "has remained substantially unchanged to the present time."

There apparently was no question concerning the validity of this provision or of any of the other state statutes when the Fourteenth Amendment was adopted. The only conclusion possible from this history is that the drafters did not intend to have the Fourteenth Amendment withdraw from the States the power to legislate with respect to this matter. . . .

I respectfully dissent.

QUESTIONS AND COMMENTS

1 What is the basis of the Court's decision that the state's interest in protecting a fetus is secondary to the woman's right to abort her pregnancy during the first trimester of the pregnancy? Moral? Religious? Legal? Medical? Social? Other? Explain your answer.

2 If a state cannot tell a woman whether she can abort a pregnancy in the first trimester, could it constitutionally tell a man whether he can have a vasectomy? Explain your answer.

3 What arguments can you advance for or against the proposition that decisions about abortion should be made via the political process and not by the courts?

4 Would you say that the Court's decision in *Roe v. Wade* was proabortion or antiabortion? Why?

5 On which dimension of activism does decision in *Roe v. Wade* fall? Explain your answer.

6 The American Medical Association generally opposed induced abortions as early as 1859.[3] Resolutions to that effect were adopted in 1859, 1871, and 1967. In 1967, the association's House of Delegates adopted a policy of opposition to abortion except
   a to save the mental and physical health or life of the mother, and
   b to prevent serious physical or mental deficiency in the child.
   However, in 1970, the profession was polarized on the issue, which the AMA described as controversial. It is possible that the Court was influenced by this shift. It is reported that Justice Blackmun, who wrote the Court's opinion in *Roe,* did extensive research in the library of the Mayo Clinic in the summer preceding decision in *Roe.* He was seeking, among other things, to understand the position of the medical profession. And the trimester division which Blackmun ultimately adopted was not uncommon among physicians practicing in this area of medicine. Is abortion a medical question? Should the medical profession be used as the primary source for determining the constitutionality of abortion? Should any weight by given to the medical profession's view as to whether abortion should be permitted? If yes, how much? On what justification?

*   *   *   *   *   *

In the last two cases in this chapter, we see that *Roe v. Wade* left many questions unanswered. Indeed, by choosing to decide, in effect, that a woman has a right to abortion under certain conditions or circumstances, the Court guaranteed extensive litigation involving the presence or absence of those conditions or the validity of the conditions imposed on the exercise of the right itself.[4] In *Planned Parenthood* and other cases, the Court revealed a willingness to examine the most minute details of state abortion laws. The general thrust has been to impose more and more restrictions on state regulation of abortion. However, when the question is federal rather than state power, as in *Harris v. McRae,* earlier cases in other fields have taught us to be careful in predicting similar outcomes.

Planned Parenthood of Central Missouri et al. v. Danforth, Attorney General of Missouri et al.

428 U.S. 52; 96 S. Ct. 2831; 49 L. Ed. 2d 788 (1976)
Vote: 5–4

Two Missouri physicians who performed or supervised abortions at Planned Parenthood challenged certain provisions of the Missouri abortion statute. The challenges were directed to Section 2 (2), defining viability as that point at which the unborn child could live outside the womb indefinitely; Section 3 (2), requiring that before submitting to an abortion in the first twelve weeks of pregnancy, a woman must consent in writing to the procedure and certify that her consent is informed and freely given; Section 3 (3), requiring, for the first twelve weeks of a pregnancy, a signed consent from her spouse unless a physician certifies that the abortion is necessary to save the woman's life; Section 3 (4), requiring for the same period the written consent of a parent or guardian to the abortion of an unmarried woman under 18 years of age; Section 6 (1), requiring the physician to seek to preserve the life of the fetus and making the physician guilty of manslaughter and liable for damages if he or she does not do so; Section 7, declaring an infant delivered in an abortion not necessary to save the mother's life a ward of the state with parental rights denied to the mother and a consenting father; Section 9, prohibiting saline amniocentesis beyond the twelfth week of pregnancy; and Sections 10 and 11, requiring record-keeping and reporting by physicians performing abortions.

A three-judge district court found Section 6 (1) unconstitutionally overbroad but ruled for the state regarding all other challenges. The U.S. Supreme Court noted probable jurisdiction, later ruling that the parties had standing to sue in regard to all but Section 7 of the statute, which the Court declined to decide.

Mr. Justice Blackmun delivered the opinion of the Court.

* * *

In *Roe v. Wade* the Court concluded that the "right of privacy, whether it be founded in the Fourteenth Amendment's concept of personal liberty and

restrictions upon state action, as we feel it is, or, as the District Court determined, in the Ninth Amendment's reservation of rights to the people, is broad
enough to encompass a woman's decision whether or not to terminate her
pregnancy." It emphatically rejected, however, the proffered argument "that
the woman's right is absolute and that she is entitled to terminate her pregnancy at whatever time, in whatever way, and for whatever reason she alone
chooses.". . .

The Definition of Viability   Section 2 (2) of the Act defines "viability" as
"that stage of fetal development when the life of the unborn child may be continued indefinitely outside the womb by natural or artificial life-supportive systems." Appellants claim that this definition violates and conflicts with the discussion of viability in our opinion in *Roe*. In particular, appellants object to
the failure of the definition to contain any reference to a gestational time
period, to its failure to incorporate and reflect the three stages of pregnancy, to
the presence of the word "indefinitely," and to the extra burden of regulation
imposed. It is suggested that the definition expands the Court's definition of
viability as expressed in *Roe,* and amounts to a legislative determination of
what is properly a matter for medical judgment. It is said that the "mere possibility of momentary survival is not the medical standard of viability."

In *Roe,* we used the term "viable," properly we thought, to signify the point
at which the fetus is "potentially able to live outside the mother's womb, albeit
with artificial aid," and presumably capable of "meaningful life outside the
mother's womb," 163. We noted that this point "is usually placed" at about
seven months or 28 weeks, but may occur earlier.

* * *

We thus do not accept appellants' contention that a specified number of
weeks in pregnancy must be fixed by statute as the joint of viability. . . .

We therefore hold that the Act's definition of "viability" comports with *Roe*
and withstands the constitutional attack made upon it in this litigation.

* * *

[As for patient's consent, we] . . . do not disagree with the result reached by
the District Court as to § 3 (2). It is true that *Doe* and *Roe* clearly establish that
the State may not restrict the decision of the patient and her physician regarding abortion during the first stage of pregnancy. Despite the fact that apparently
no other Missouri statute, with the exceptions referred to in n. 6, *supra,*
requires a patient's prior written consent to a surgical procedure, the imposition by § 3 (2) of such a requirement for termination of pregnancy even during
the first stage, in our view, is not in itself an unconstitutional requirement. The
decision to abort, indeed, is an important, and often a stressful one, and it is
desirable and imperative that it be made with full knowledge of its nature and

consequences. The woman is the one primarily concerned, and her awareness of the decision and its significance may be assured, constitutionally, by the State to the extent of requiring her prior written consent.

We could not say that a requirement imposed by the State that a prior written consent for any surgery would be unconstitutional. As a consequence, we see no constitutional defect in requiring it only for some types of surgery as, for example, an intracardiac procedure, or where the surgical risk is elevated above a specified mortality level, or, for that matter, for abortions.

In *Roe* and *Doe* we specifically reserved decision on the question whether a requirement for consent by the father of the fetus, by the spouse, or by the parents, or a parent, of an unmarried minor, may be constitutionally imposed. We now hold that the State may not constitutionally require the consent of the spouse, as is specified under § 3 (3) of the Missouri Act, as a condition for abortion during the first 12 weeks of pregnancy. We thus agree with the dissenting judge in the present case, and with the courts whose decisions are cited above, that the State cannot "delegate to a spouse a veto power which the state itself is absolutely and totally prohibited from exercising during the first trimester of pregnancy." Clearly, since the State cannot regulate or proscribe abortion during the first stage, when the physician and his patient make that decision, the State cannot delegate authority to any particular person, even the spouse, to prevent abortion during that same period.

. . . We recognize that the decision whether to undergo or to forgo an abortion may have profound effects on the future of any marriage, effects that are both physical and mental, and possibly deleterious. Notwithstanding these factors, we cannot hold that the State has the constitutional authority to give the spouse unilaterally the ability to prohibit the wife from terminating her pregnancy, when the State itself lacks that right.

We conclude that § 3 (3) of the Missouri Act is inconsistent with the standards enunciated in *Roe v. Wade,* and is unconstitutional.

* * *

[In regard to parental consent, the] . . . District Court majority recognized that, in contrast to § 3 (3), the State's interest in protecting the mutuality of a marriage relationship is not present with respect to § 3 (4). It found "a compelling basis," however, in the State's interest "in safeguarding the authority of the family relationship." 392 F. Supp., at 1370. The dissenting judge observed that one could not seriously argue that a minor must submit to an abortion if her parents insist, and he could not see "why she would not be entitled to the same right of self-determination now explicitly accorded to adult women, provided she is sufficiently mature to understand the procedure and to make an intelligent assessment of her circumstances with the advice of her physician. . . ." Other courts that have considered the parental-consent issue in the light of *Roe* and *Doe,* have concluded that a statute like § 3 (4) does not withstand constitutional scrutiny.

We agree with appellants and with the courts whose decisions have just been cited that the State may not impose a blanket provision, such as § 3 (4), requiring the consent of a parent or person *in loco parentis* as a condition for abortion of an unmarried minor during the first 12 weeks of her pregnancy. Just as with the requirement of consent from the spouse, so here, the State does not have the constitutional authority to give a third party an absolute, and possibly arbitrary, veto over the decision of the physician and his patient to terminate the patient's pregnancy, regardless of the reason for withholding the consent. . . .

Saline amniocentesis   Section 9 of the statute prohibits the use of saline amniocentesis, as a method or technique of abortion, after the first 12 weeks of pregnancy. It describes the method as one whereby the amniotic fluid is withdrawn and "a saline or other fluid" is inserted into the amniotic sac. The statute imposes this proscription on the ground that the technique "is deleterious to maternal health," and places it in the form of a legislative finding. . . .

We held in *Roe* that after the first stage, "the State, in promoting its interest in the health of the mother, may, if it chooses, regulate the abortion procedure in ways that are reasonably related to maternal health." The question with respect to § 9 therefore is whether the flat prohibition of saline amniocentesis is a restriction which "reasonably relates to the preservation and protection of maternal health."

* * *

[The District Court] . . . in reaching its conclusion, failed to appreciate and to consider several significant facts. First, it did not recognize the prevalence, as the record conclusively demonstrates, of the use of saline amniocentesis as an accepted medical procedure in this country; the procedure, as noted above, is employed in a substantial majority (the testimony from both sides ranges from 68% to 80%) of all post-first-trimester abortions. Second, it failed to recognize that at the time of trial, there were severe limitations on the availability of the prostaglandin technique, which, although promising, was used only on an experimental basis until less than two years before. See *Wolfe v. Schroering,* where it was said that at that time (1974), there were "no physicians in Kentucky competent in the technique of prostaglandin amnio infusion." And appellees offered no evidence that prostaglandin abortions were available in Missouri. Third, the statute's reference to the insertion of "a saline or other fluid" appears to include within its proscription the intra-amniotic injection of prostaglandin itself and other methods that may be developed in the future and that may prove highly effective and completely safe. Finally, the majority did not consider the anomaly inherent in § 9 when it proscribes the use of saline but does not prohibit techniques that are many times more likely to result in maternal death. . . . As a practical matter [the State] . . . forces a woman and her physician to terminate her pregnancy by methods more dangerous to her health than the method outlawed.

As so viewed, particularly in the light of the present unavailability—as demonstrated by the record—of the prostaglandin technique, the outright legislative proscription of saline fails as a reasonable regulation for the protection of maternal health. It comes into focus, instead, as an unreasonable or arbitrary regulation designed to inhibit, and having the effect of inhibiting, the vast majority of abortions after the first 12 weeks. As such, it does not withstand constitutional challenge.

* * *

Appellants object to reporting and recordkeeping provisions on the ground that they, too, impose an extra layer and burden of regulation, and that they apply throughout all stages of pregnancy. . . .

Recordkeeping and reporting requirements that are reasonably directed to the preservation of maternal health and that properly respect a patient's confidentiality and privacy are permissible. This surely is so for the period after the first stage of pregnancy, for then the State may enact substantive as well as recordkeeping regulations that are reasonable means of protecting maternal health. As to the first stage, one may argue forcefully, as the appellants do, that the State should not be able to impose any recordkeeping requirements that significantly differ from those imposed with respect to other, and comparable, medical or surgical procedures. We conclude, however, that the provisions of §§ 10 and 11, while perhaps approaching impermissible limits, are not constitutionally offensive in themsleves. Recordkeeping of this kind, if not abused or overdone, can be useful to the State's interest in protecting the health of its female citizens, and may be a resource that is relevant to decisions involving medical experience and judgment. The added requirements for confidentiality, with the sole exception for public health officers, and for retention for seven years, a period not unreasonable in length, assist and persuade us in our determination of the constitutional limits. As so regarded, we see no legally significant impact or consequence on the abortion decision or on the physician-patient relationship.

* * *

Standard of Care   Appellee Danforth in No. 74–1419 appeals from the unanimous decision of the District Court that § 6 (1) of the Act is unconstitutional.

* * *

. . . We are unable to accept the appellee's . . . interpretation of the statute. Section 6 (1) requires the physician to exercise the prescribed skill, care, and diligence to preserve the life and health of the *fetus*. It does not specify that such care need be taken only after the stage of viability has been reached. As the provision now reads, it impermissibly requires the physician to preserve the life and health of the fetus, whatever the stage of pregnancy. The fact that the second sentence of § 6 (1) refers to a criminal penalty where the physician fails "to take such measures to encourage or to sustain the life of the *child,* and the death of the *child* results" (emphasis supplied), simply does not modify the duty imposed by the previous sentence or limit that duty to pregnancies that have reached the stage of viability.

The appellees finally argue that if the first sentence of § 6 (1) does not survive constitutional attack, the second sentence does, and, under the Act's severability provision, § B, is severable from the first. The District Court's ruling of unconstitutionality, made specific reference to the first sentence, but its conclusion of law and its judgment invalidated all of § 6 (1). Appellee Danforth's motion to alter or amend the judgment, so far as the second sentence of § 6 (1) was concerned, was denied by the District Court.

We conclude, as did the District Court, that § 6 (1) must stand or fall as a unit. Its provisions are inextricably bound together. And a physician's or other person's criminal failure to protect a liveborn infant surely will be subject to prosecution in Missouri under the State's criminal statutes.

The judgment of the District Court is affirmed in part and reversed in part, and the case is remanded for further proceedings consistent with this opinion. *It is so ordered.*

* * *

MR. JUSTICE WHITE, with whom THE CHIEF JUSTICE and MR. JUSTICE REHNQUIST join, concurring in part and dissenting in part. . . .

Section 3 (3) of the [Missouri] Act provides that a married woman may not obtain an abortion without her husband's consent. The Court strikes down this statute in one sentence. It says that "since that State cannot . . . proscribe abortion . . . the State cannot delegate authority to any particular person, even the spouse, to prevent abortion. . . ." But the State is not—under § 3 (3)—delegating to the husband the power to vindicate the *State's* interest in the future life of the fetus. It is instead recognizing that the husband has an interest of his own in the life of the fetus which should not be extinguished by the unilateral decision of the wife. It by no means follows, from the fact that the mother's interest in deciding "whether or not to terminate her pregnancy" outweighs the *State's* interest in the potential life of the fetus, that the husband's interest is also outweighed and may not be protected by the State. A father's interest in having a child—perhaps his only child—may be unmatched by any other interest in his life. See *Stanley v. Illinois,* 405 (1972). . . .

Section 3 (4) requires that an unmarried woman under 18 years of age obtain the consent of a parent or a person *in loco parentis* as a condition to an abortion. . . . The Court rejects the notions that the *State* has an interest in strengthening the family unit, or that the *parent* has an "independent interest" in the abortion decision, sufficient to justify § 3 (4) and apparently concludes that the provision is therefore unconstitutional. But the purpose of the parental-consent requirement is not merely to vindicate any interest of the parent or of the State. The purpose of the requirement is to vindicate the very right created in *Roe v. Wade, supra*—the right of the pregnant woman to decide "whether *or not* to terminate her pregnancy."

The abortion decision is unquestionably important and has irrevocable consequences whichever way it is made. Missouri is entitled to protect the minor unmarried woman from making the decision in a way which is not in her own best interests, and it seeks to achieve this goal by requiring parental consultation and consent. This is the traditional way by which States have sought to protect children from their own immature and improvident decisions; and there is absolutely no reason expressed by the majority why the State may not utilize that method here.

Section 9 of the Act prohibits abortion by the method known as saline amniocentesis—a method used at the time the Act was passed for 70% of abortions performed after the first trimester. . . .

The Court nevertheless reverses the decision of the District Court sustaining § 9 against unconstitutional challenge. It does so apparently because saline amniocentesis was widely used before the Act was passed; because the prostaglandin method was seldom used and was not generally available; and because other abortion techniques more dangerous than saline amniocentesis were not banned. At bottom the majority's holding—as well as the concurrence—rests on its *factual* finding that the prostaglandin method is unavailable to the women of Missouri. It therefore concludes that the ban on the saline method is "an unreasonable or arbitrary regulation designed to inhibit, and having the effect of inhibiting, the vast majority of abortions after the first 12 weeks."

* * *

The majority relies on the testimony of one doctor that prostaglandin had been available on an experimental basis only until January 1, 1974; and that its manufacturer, the Upjohn Co., restricted its sales to large medical centers for the following six months, after which sales were to be unrestricted.

In what manner this evidence supports the proposition that prostaglandin is unavailable to the women of Missouri escapes me. . . .

In any event, the point of § 9 is to change the practice under which most abortions were performed under the saline amniocentesis method and to make the safer prostaglandin method generally available. It promises to achieve that result, if it remains operative, and the evidence discloses that the result is a desirable one or at least that the legislature could have so viewed it. That should end our inquiry, unless we purport to be not only the country's continuous constitutional convention but also its *ex officio* medical board with powers to approve or disapprove medical and operative practices and standards throughout the United States. . . .

If this section is read in any way other than through a microscope, it is plainly intended to require that, where a "fetus [may have] the capability of meaningful life outside the mother's womb," *Roe v. Wade,* the abortion be handled in a way which is designed to preserve that life notwithstanding the mother's desire to terminate it. Indeed, even looked at through a microscope the statute seems to go no further. It requires a physician to exercise "*that* degree of professional skill . . . to preserve the . . . fetus," which he would be required to exercise if the mother wanted a live child. Plainly, if the pregnancy is to be terminated at a time when there is no chance of life outside the womb, a physician would not be required to exercise any care or skill to preserve the life of the fetus during abortion no matter what the mother's desires. The statute would appear then to operate only in the gray area after the fetus *might* be viable but while the physician is still able to certify "with reasonable medical certainty that the fetus is not viable. . . ." Since the State has a compelling interest, sufficient to outweigh the mother's desire to kill the fetus, when the "fetus . . . has the capability of meaningful life outside the mother's womb," *Roe v. Wade, supra,* at 163, the statute is constitutional. . . .

I join the judgment and opinion of the Court insofar as it upholds the other portions of the Act against constitutional challenge.

MR. JUSTICE STEVENS, concurring in part and dissenting in part. . . .

In my opinion, . . . the parental-consent requirement is consistent with the holding in *Roe.* The State's interest in the welfare of its young citizens justifies a variety of protective measures. Because he may not foresee the consequences of his decision, a minor may not make an enforceable bargain. He may not lawfully work or travel where he pleases, or even attend exhibitions of constitutionally protected adult motion pictures. Persons below a certain age may not marry without parental consent. Indeed, such consent is essential even when the young woman is already pregnant. The State's interest in protecting a young person from harm justifies the imposition of restraints on his or her freedom even though comparable restraints on adults would be constitutionally impermissible. Therefore, the holding in *Roe v. Wade* that the abortion decision is entitled to constitutional protection merely emphasizes the importance of the decision; it does not lead to the conclusion that the state legislature has no power to enact legislation for the purpose of protecting a young pregnant woman from the consequences of an incorrect decision.

The abortion decision is, of course, more important than the decision to attend or to avoid an adult motion picture, or the decision to work long hours in a factory. It is not necessarily any more important than the decision to run away from home or the decision to marry. But even if it is the most important kind of a decision a young person may ever make, that assumption merely enhances the quality of the State's interest in maximizing the probability that the decision be made correctly and with full understanding of the consequences of either alternative.

* * *

If there is no parental-consent requirement, many minors will submit to the abortion procedure without ever informing their parents. An assumption that the parental reaction will be hostile, disparaging, or violent no doubt persuades many children simply to bypass parental counsel which would in fact be loving, supportive, and, indeed, for some indispensable. It is unrealistic, in my judgment, to assume that every parent-child relationship is either (a) so perfect that communication and accord will take place routinely or (b) so imperfect that the absence of communication reflects the child's correct prediction that the parent will exercise his or her veto arbitrarily to further a selfish interest rather than the child's interest. A state legislature may conclude that most parents will be primarily interested in the welfare of their children, and further, that the imposition of a parental-consent requirement is an appropriate method of giving the parents an opportunity to foster that welfare by helping a pregnant distressed child to make and to implement a correct decision.

* * *

In short, the State's interest in the welfare of its young citizens is sufficient, in my judgment, to support the parental-consent requirement.

Harris, Secretary of Health and Human Services v. McRae et al.

448 U.S. 297; 100 S. Ct. 2671; 65 L. Ed. 2d 784 (1980)
Vote: 5–4

The facts are given in the opinion below.

Mr. Justice Stewart delivered the opinion of the Court.

* * *

The Medicaid program was created in 1965, when Congress added Title XIX to the Social Security Act, for the purpose of providing federal financial assistance to States that choose to reimburse certain costs of medical treatment for needy persons. Although participation in the Medicaid program is entirely optional, once a State elects to participate, it must comply with the require-ments of Title XIX.

One such requirement is that a participating State agree to provide financial assistance to the "categorically needy" with respect to five general areas of medical treatment: (1) inpatient hospital services, (2) outpatient hospital ser-vices, (3) other laboratory and X-ray services, (4) skilled nursing facilities ser-vices, periodic screening and diagnosis of children, and family planning ser-vices, and (5) services of physicians.

Although a participating State need not "provide funding for all medical treatment falling within the five general categories, [Title XIX] does require that [a] state Medicaid pla[n] establish 'reasonable standards . . . for determin-ing . . . the extent of medical assistance under the plan which . . . are consistent with the objectives of [Title XIX].' "

Since September 1976, Congress has prohibited—either by an amendment to the annual appropriations bill for the Department of Health, Education, and Welfare or by a joint resolution—the use of any federal funds to reimburse the cost of abortions under the Medicaid program except under certain specified circumstances. This funding restriction is commonly known as the "Hyde Amendment," after its original congressional sponsor, Representative Hyde. . . .

On September 30, 1976, the day on which Congress enacted the initial ver-sion of the Hyde Amendment, these consolidated cases were filed in the Dis-trict Court for the Eastern District of New York. The plaintiffs—Cora McRae, a New York Medicaid recipient then in the first trimester of a pregnancy that she wished to terminate, the New York City Health and Hospitals Corp., a public benefit corporation that operates 16 hospitals, 12 of which provide abor-tion services, and others—sought to enjoin the enforcement of the funding restriction on abortions. They alleged that the Hyde Amendment violated the First, Fourth, Fifth, and Ninth Amendments of the Constitution insofar as it limited the funding of abortions to those necessary to save the life of the mother, while permitting the funding of costs associated with childbirth. Although the sole named defendant was the Secretary of Health, Education, and Welfare, the District Court permitted Senators James L. Buckley and Jesse A. Helms and Representative Henry J. Hyde to intervene as defendants. . . .

[After several legal proceedings involving the Supreme Court and lower fed-eral courts, a District Court] . . . concluded that the Hyde Amendment, though valid under the Establishment Clause, violates the equal protection component of the Fifth Amendment's Due Process Clause and the Free Exercise Clause of the First Amendment. With regard to the Fifth Amendment, the District Court noted that when an abortion is "medically necessary to safeguard the pregnant woman's health, . . . the disentitlement to [M]edicaid assistance impinges directly on the woman's right to decide, in consultation with her physician and in reliance on his judgment, to terminate her pregnancy in order to preserve her health." *McRae v. Califano,* 491 F. Supp. 630, 737. The court concluded that the Hyde Amendment violates the equal protection guarantee because, in its view, the decision of Congress to fund medically necessary services generally but only certain medically necessary abortions serves no legitimate governmental interest. As to the Free Exercise Clause of the First Amendment, the court held that insofar as a woman's decision to seek a medically necessary abortion may be a product of her religious beliefs under certain Protestant and Jewish tenets, the funding restrictions of the Hyde Amendment violate that constitutional guarantee as well.

Accordingly, the District Court ordered the Secretary to "[c]ease to give effect" to the various versions of the Hyde Amendment insofar as they forbid payments for medically necessary abortions. It further directed the Secretary to "[c]ontinue to authorize the expenditure of federal matching funds [for such abortions]." In addition, the court recertified the *McRae* case as a nationwide class action on behalf of all pregnant and potentially pregnant women eligible for Medicaid who wish to have medically necessary abortions, and of all authorized providers of abortions for such women.

The Secretary then applied to this Court for a stay of the judgment pending direct appeal of the District Court's decision. We denied the stay, but noted probable jurisdiction of this appeal. . . .

We address first the appellees' argument that the Hyde Amendment, by restricting the availability of certain medically necessary abortions under Medicaid, impinges on the "liberty" protected by the Due Process Clause as recognized in *Roe v. Wade,* [1973] and its progeny. . . .

Regardless of whether the freedom of a woman to choose to terminate her pregnancy for health reasons lies at the core or the periphery of the due process liberty recognized in *Wade,* it simply does not follow that a woman's freedom of choice carries with it a constitutional entitlement to the financial resources to avail herself of the full range of protected choices. . . . Although government may not place obstacles in the path of a woman's exercise of her freedom of choice, it need not remove those not of its own creation. Indigency falls in the latter category. The financial constraints that restrict an indigent woman's ability to enjoy the full range of constitutionally protected freedom of choice are the product not of governmental restrictions on access to abortions, but rather of her indigency. Although Congress has opted to subsidize medically necessary services generally, but not certain medically necessary abortions, the fact remains that the Hyde Amendment leaves an indigent woman with at least the same range of choice in deciding whether to obtain a medically necessary abortion as she would have had if Congress had chosen to subsidize no health care costs at all. We are thus not persuaded that the Hyde Amendment impinges on the constitutionally protected freedom of choice recognized in *Wade.*

* * *

Whether freedom of choice that is constitutionally protected warrants federal subsidization is a question for Congress to answer, not a matter of constitutional entitlement. Accordingly, we conclude that the Hyde Amendment does not impinge on the due process liberty recognized in *Wade.*

The appellees also argue that the Hyde Amendment contravenes rights secured by the Religion Clauses of the First Amendment. It is the appellees' view that the Hyde Amendment violates the Establishment Clause because it incorporates into law the doctrines of the Roman Catholic Church concerning the sinfulness of abortion and the time at which life commences. Moreover, insofar as a woman's decision to seek a medically necessary abortion may be a product of her religious beliefs under certain Protestant and Jewish tenets, the appellees assert that the funding limitations of the Hyde Amendment impinge on the freedom of religion guaranteed by the Free Exercise Clause. . . .

Although neither a State nor the Federal Government can constitutionally "pass laws which aid one religion, aid all religions, or prefer one religion over another," *Everson v. Board of Education,* [1947], it does not follow that a statute violates the Establishment Clause because it "happens to coincide or harmonize with the tenets of some or all religions." *McGowan v. Maryland,* [1961].

That the Judaeo-Christian religions oppose stealing does not mean that a State or the Federal Government may not, consistent with the Establishment Clause, enact laws prohibiting larceny. The Hyde Amendment, as the District Court noted, is as much a reflection of "traditionalist" values toward abortion, as it is an embodiment of the views of any particular religion. In sum, we are convinced that the fact that the funding restrictions in the Hyde Amendment may coincide with the religious tenets of the Roman Catholic Church does not, without more, contravene the Establishment Clause.

We need not address the merits of the appellees' arguments concerning the Free Exercise Clause, because the appellees lack standing to raise a free exercise challenge to the Hyde Amendment. . . .

It remains to be determined whether the Hyde Amendment violates the equal protection component of the Fifth Amendment. This challenge is premised on the fact that, although federal reimbursement is available under Medicaid for medically necessary services generally, the Hyde Amendment does not permit federal reimbursement of all medically necessary abortions. The District Court held, and the appellees argue here, that this selective subsidization violates the constitutional guarantee of equal protection.

The guarantee of equal protection under the Fifth Amendment is not a source of substantive rights or liberties, but rather a right to be free from invidious discrimination in statutory classifications and other governmental activity. It is well settled that where a statutory classification does not itself impinge on a right or liberty protected by the Constitution, the validity of classification must be sustained unless "the classification rests on grounds wholly irrelevant to the achievement of [any legitimate governmental] objective."

This presumption of constitutional validity, however, disappears if a statutory classification is predicted on criteria that are, in a constitutional sense, "suspect," the principle example of which is a classification based on race, *e. g., Brown v. Board of Education,* [1954].

For the reasons stated above, we have already concluded that the Hyde Amendment violates no constitutionally protected substantive rights. We now conclude as well that it is not predicated on a constitutionally suspect classification.

* * *

The remaining question then is whether the Hyde Amendment is rationally related to a legitimate governmental objective. It is the Government's position that the Hyde Amendment bears a rational relationship to its legitimate interest in protecting the potential life of the fetus. We agree.

... The Hyde Amendment, by encouraging childbirth except in the most urgent circumstances, is rationally related to the legitimate governmental objective of protecting potential life. By subsidizing the medical expenses of indigent women who carry their pregnancies to term while not subsidizing the comparable expenses of women who undergo abortions (except those whose lives are threatened), Congress has established incentives that make childbirth a more attractive alternative than abortion for persons eligible for Medicaid. These incentives bear a direct relationship to the legitimate congressional interest in protecting potential life. Nor is it irrational that Congress has authorized federal reimbursement for medically necessary services generally, but not for certain medically necessary abortions. Abortion is inherently different from other medical procedures, because no other procedure involves the purposeful termination of a potential life.

* * *

For the reasons stated in this opinion, we hold that a State that participates in the Medicaid program is not obligated under Title XIX to continue to fund those medically necessary abortions for which federal reimbursement is unavailable under the Hyde Amendment. We further hold that the funding restrictions of the Hyde Amendment violate neither the Fifth Amendment nor the Establishment Clause of the First Amendment. It is also our view that the appellees lack standing to raise a challenge to the Hyde Amendment under the Free Exercise Clause of the First Amendment. Accordingly, the judgment of the District Court is reversed, and the case is remanded to that court for further proceedings consistent with this opinion.

It is so ordered.

* * *

MR. JUSTICE BRENNAN, with whom MR. JUSTICE MARSHALL and MR. JUSTICE BLACKMUN join, dissenting.

I agree entirely with my Brother STEVENS that the State's interest in protecting the potential life of the fetus cannot justify the exclusion of financially and medically needy women from the benefits to which they would otherwise be entitled solely because the treatment that a doctor has concluded is medically necessary involves an abortion. . . .

When viewed in the context of the Medicaid program to which it is appended, it is obvious that the Hyde Amendment is nothing less than an attempt by Congress to circumvent the dictates of the Constitution and achieve indirectly what *Roe v. Wade* said it could not do directly. Under Title XIX of the Social Security Act, the Federal Government reimburses participating States for virtually all medically necessary services it provides to the categorically needy. The sole limitation of any significance is the Hyde Amendment's prohibition against the use of any federal funds to pay for the costs of abortions (except where the life of the mother would be endangered if the fetus were carried to term). As my Brother STEVENS persuasively demonstrates, exclusion of medically necessary abortions from Medicaid coverage cannot be justified as a cost-saving device. Rather, the Hyde Amendment is a transparent attempt by the Legislative Branch to impose the political majority's judgment of the morally acceptable and socially desirable preference on a sensitive and intimate decision that the Constitution entrusts to the individual. Worse yet, the Hyde Amendment does not foist that majoritarian viewpoint with equal measure upon everyone in our Nation, rich and poor alike; rather, it imposes that viewpoint only upon that segment of our society which, because of its position of political powerlessness, is least able to defend its privacy rights from the encroachments of state-mandated morality. The instant legislation thus calls for more exacting judicial review than in most other cases.

* * *

The Court's . . . belief [is] that "[t]he financial constraints that restrict an indigent woman's ability to enjoy the full range of constitutionally protected freedom of choice are the product not of governmental restrictions on access to abortions, but rather of her indigency." Accurate as this statement may be, it reveals only half the picture. For what the Court fails to appreciate is that it is not simply the woman's indigency that interferes with her freedom of choice, but the combination of her own property and the Government's unequal subsidization of abortion and childbirth.

A poor woman in the early stages of pregnancy confronts two alternatives: she may elect either to carry the fetus to term or to have an abortion. In the abstract, of course, this choice is hers alone, and the Court rightly observes that the Hyde Amendment "places no governmental obstacle in the path of a woman who chooses to terminate her pregnancy."

But the reality of the situation is that the Hyde Amendment has effectively removed this choice from the indigent woman's hands. By funding all of the expenses associated with childbirth and none of the expenses incurred in terminating pregnancy, the Government literally makes an offer that the indigent woman cannot afford to refuse. It matters not that in this instance the Government has used the carrot rather than the stick. What is critical is the realization that as a practical matter, many poverty-stricken women will choose to carry their pregnancy to term simply because the Government provides funds for the associated medical services, even though these same women would have chosen to have an abortion if the Government had also paid for that option, or indeed if the Government had stayed out of the picture altogether and had defrayed the costs of neither procedure. . . . If the state may compel the surrender of one constitutional right as a condition of its favor, it may, in like manner, compel a surrender of all. It is inconceivable that guaranties embedded in the Constitution of the United States may thus be manipulated out of existence."

I respectfully dissent.

* * *

Mr. Justice Stevens, dissenting. . . .

If a woman has a constitutional right to place a higher value on avoiding either serious harm to her own health or perhaps an abnormal childbirth than on protecting potential life, the exercise of that right cannot provide the basis for the denial of a benefit to which she would otherwise be entitled. The Court's sterile equal protection analysis evades this critical though simple point. The Court focuses exclusively on the "legitimate interest in protecting the potential life of the fetus." It concludes that since the Hyde Amendments further that interest, the exclusion they create is rational and therefore constitutional. But it is misleading to speak of the Government's legitimate interest in the fetus without reference to the context in which that interest was held to be legitimate. For *Roe v. Wade* squarely held that the States may not protect that interest when a conflict with the interest in a pregnant woman's health exists. It is thus perfectly clear that neither the Federal Government nor the States may exclude a woman from medical benefits to which she would otherwise be entitled solely to further an interest in potential life when a physician, "in appropriate medical judgment," certifies that an abortion is necessary "for the preservation of the life or health of the mother."

The Court totally fails to explain why this reasoning is not dispositive here.

* * *

Nor can it be argued that the exclusion of this type of medically necessary treatment of the indigent can be justified on fiscal grounds. There are some especially costly forms of treatment that may reasonably be excluded from the program in order to preserve the assets in the pool and extend its benefits to the maximum number of needy persons. Fiscal considerations may compel certain difficult choices in order to improve the protection afforded to the entire benefited class. But, ironically, the exclusion of medically necessary abortions harms the entire class as well as its specific victims. For the records in both *McRae* and *Zbaraz** demonstrate that the cost of an abortion is only a small fraction of the costs associated with childbirth.† Thus, the decision to tolerate harm to indigent persons who need an abortion in order to avoid "serious and long-lasting health damage" is one that is financed by draining money out of the pool that is used to fund all other necessary medical procedures. Unlike most invidious classifications, this discrimination harms not only its direct victims but also the remainder of the class of needy persons that the pool was designed to benefit. . . .

QUESTIONS AND COMMENTS

1 To what extent are the Court's decisions in *Planned Parenthood* and *Harris v. McRae* required by stare decisis? Explain.
2 Can you distinguish, during the first trimester of a pregnancy, the interest of the state from that of the spouse? Should that difference be reflected in law? How?
3 In your judgment, is a court of law the appropriate body for determining such questions as whether saline amniocentesis is deleterious to maternal health? Explain your answer.

**Williams and Diamond v. Zbaraz*, 448 U.S. 358 (1980).

†In the *Zbaraz* case, Judge Grady found that the average cost to the State of Illinois of an abortion was less than $150 as compared with the cost of a childbirth which exceeded $1,350.Indeed, based on an estimated cost of providing support to children of indigent parents together with their estimate of the number of medically necessary abortions that would be funded but for the Hyde Amendment, appellees in the *Zbaraz* case contend that in the State of Illinois alone the effect of the Hyde Amendment is to impose a cost of about $20,000,000 per year on the public fisc.

See also Judge Dooling's conclusion:

"While the debate [on the Hyde Amendment] in both years was on a rider to the departmental appropriations bill, it was quickly established that the restriction on abortion funding was not an economy measure; it was recognized that if an abortion was not performed for a medicaid eligible woman, the medicaid and other costs of childbearing and nurture would greatly exceed the cost of abortion. Opponents of funding restriction were equally at pains, however, to make clear that they did not favor funding abortion as a means of reducing the Government's social welfare costs."

4 In *Harris,* the Court emphasizes the importance of protecting "potential life." Is this emphasis more or less supportive of abortion than the emphasis in *Roe v. Wade?* Explain your answer.

5 On the question of discrimination based on wealth, how would you distinguish the Court's position in *Boddie v. Connecticut* [401 U.S. 371 (1971)]? In *Griffin v. Illinois* [351 U.S. 12, 17 (1956)], the Court held that one convicted in a criminal trial cannot be denied a transcript of trial proceedings because of indigency. In a plurality opinion, Justice Black said that in criminal trials, a state "can no more discriminate on account of poverty than on account of religion, race, or color." Compare this position with that in *Harris.* Any conflict?

NOTES

1 405 U.S. 438, 453 (1972).
2 316 U.S. 535 (1942).
3 Lionel H. Frankel, *Law, Power, and Personal Freedom,* West, St. Paul, Minn., 1975, pp. 382–383.
4 *Doe v. Bolton,* 410 U.S. 179 (1973).

Chapter 11

VOTING RIGHTS

Malapportionment of Legislative Bodies

Wesberry v. Sanders (1963)

Reynolds v. Sims (1964)

In Chapter 1, we discussed the concept of "political questions" and the use of that concept to insulate certain kinds of issues from judicial questioning. Until 1962 and the Court's decision in *Baker v. Carr* (included in the text, pp. 81ff), the setting of geographical boundaries for legislative election purposes was considered a political question not subject to judicial action. In *Baker v. Carr,* however, we learned that such questions are indeed justiciable. A federal court's refusal to hear a complaint about a Tennessee statute apportioning the state legislature was reversed by the Supreme Court on the ground that the complaint stated a cause of action on which appellants had a right to a trial and a decision.

One year later in *Gray v. Sanders,*[1] the Court struck down Georgia's county unit system for electing governors as a violation of equal protection. The Georgia system allowed a majority of voters in counties with one-third of the state's population to determine the outcomes of statewide elections. But though the Court nullified this system, others with similar consequences remained in effect in other states. While Douglas coined his famous "one man, one vote" equation in *Gray,* the implications of that proposition were not developed. The phrase seemed to imply equal numbers of voters in election districts, but exact equality is not practical. And the Court gave no precise guidance on permissible and impermissible departures from exact equality.

In 1964, the Court handed down seven decisions which, in toto, had the effect of altering legislative bodies all across the country. Two of these cases were *Wesberry v. Sanders* and *Reynold v. Sims.* The first dealt with apportionment of congressional districts, the second with inequality of representation in the Alabama legislature.

Wesberry et al. v. Sanders, Governor of Georgia et al.

376 U.S. 1; 84 S. Ct. 526; 11 L. Ed. 2d 481 (1964)
Vote: 6–3

The facts are given in the opinion below.

MR. JUSTICE BLACK delivered the opinion of the Court.

Appellants are citizens and qualified voters of Fulton County, Georgia, and as such are entitled to vote in congressional elections in Georgia's Fifth Congressional District. That district, one of ten created by a 1931 Georgia statute, includes Fulton, DeKalb, and Rockdale Counties and has a population according to the 1960 census of 823,680. The average population of the ten districts is 394,312, less than half that of the Fifth. One district, the Ninth, has only 272,154 people, less than one-third as many as the Fifth. Since there is only one Congressman for each district, this inequality of population means that the Fifth District's Congressman has to represent from two to three times as many people as do Congressmen from some of the other Georgia districts.

Claiming that these population disparities deprived them and voters similarly situated of a right under the Federal Constitution to have their votes for Congressmen given the same weight as the votes of other Georgians, the appellants brought this action under 42 U.S.C. §§ 1983 and 1988 and 28 U.S.C. § 1343 (3) asking that the Georgia statute be declared invalid and that the appellees, the Governor and Secretary of State of Georgia, be enjoined from conducting elections under it. The complaint alleged that appellants were deprived of the full benefit of their right to vote, in violation of (1) Art. I, § 2, of the Constitution of the United States, which provides that "The House of Representatives shall be composed of Members chosen every second Year by the People of the several States. . ."; (2) the Due Process, Equal Protection, and Privileges and Immunities Clauses of the Fourteenth Amendment; and (3) that part of Section 2 of the Fourteenth Amendment which provides that "Representatives shall be apportioned among the several States according to their respective numbers. . . ."

The case was heard by a three-judge District Court, which found unanimously, from facts not disputed, that:

> It is clear by any standard . . . that the population of the Fifth District is grossly out of balance with that of the other nine congressional districts of Georgia and in fact, so much so that the removal of DeKalb and Rockdale Counties from the District, leaving only Fulton with a population of 556,326, would leave it exceeding the average by slightly more than forty per cent.

Notwithstanding these findings, a majority of the court dismissed the complaint, citing as their guide, Mr. Justice Frankfurter's minority opinion in *Cole-*

grove v. Green, [1946], an opinion stating that challenges to apportionment of congressional districts raised only "political" questions, which were not justiciable. Although the majority below said that the dismissal here was based on "want of equity" and not on nonjusticiability, they relied on no circumstances which were peculiar to the present case; instead, they adopted the language and reasoning of Mr. Justice Frankfurter's *Colegrove* opinion in concluding that the appellants had presented a wholly "political" question. . . .

The right to vote is too important in our free society to be stripped of judicial protection by such an interpretation of Article I. This dismissal can no more be justified on the ground of "want of equity" than on the ground of "nonjusticiability." We therefore hold that the District Court erred in dismissing the complaint.

This brings us to the merits. We agree with the District Court that the 1931 Georgia apportionment grossly discriminates against voters in the Fifth Congressional District. A single Congressman represents from two to three times as many Fifth District voters as are represented by each of the Congressmen from the other Georgia congressional districts. The apportionment statute thus contracts the value of some votes and expands that of others. If the Federal Constitution intends that when qualified voters elect members of Congress each vote be given as much weight as any other vote, then this statute cannot stand.

We hold that, construed in its historical context, the command of Art. I, § 2, that Representatives be chosen "by the people of the several States" means that as nearly as is practicable one man's vote in a congressional election is to be worth as much as another's. This rule is followed automatically, of course, when Representatives are chosen as a group on a statewide basis, as was a widespread practice in the first 50 years of our Nation's history. It would be extraordinary to suggest that in such statewide elections the votes of inhabitants of some parts of a State, for example, Georgia's thinly populated Ninth District, could be weighed at two or three times the value of the votes of people living in more populous parts of the State, for example, the Fifth District around Atlanta. Cf. *Gray v. Sanders,* [1963].

We do not believe that the Framers of the Constitution intended to permit the same vote-diluting discrimination to be accomplished through the device of districts containing widely varied numbers of inhabitants. To say that a vote is worth more in one district than in another would not only run counter to our fundamental ideas of democratic government, it would cast aside the principle of a House of Representatives elected "by the People," a principle tenaciously fought for and established at the Constitutional Convention. The history of the Constitution, particularly that part of it relating to the adoption of Art. I, § 2, reveals that those who framed the Constitution meant that, no matter what the mechanics of an election, whether statewide or by districts, it was population which was to be the basis of the House of Representatives.

* * *

. . . The Constitutional Convention of 1787, [was] called for "the sole and express purpose of revising the Articles of Confederation. . ." When the Convention met in May, this modest purpose was soon abandoned for the greater challenge of creating a new and closer form of government than was possible under the Confederation. Soon after the Convention assembled, Edmund Randolph of Virginia presented a plan not merely to amend the Articles of Confederation but to create an entirely new National Government with a National Executive, National Judiciary, and a National Legislature of two Houses, one house to be elected by "the people," the second house to be elected by the first.

The question of how the legislature should be constituted precipitated the most bitter controversy of the Convention. One principle was uppermost in the minds of many delegates: that, no matter where he lived, each voter should have a voice equal to that of every other in electing members of Congress. . . .

The delegates who wanted every man's vote to count alike were sharp in their criticism of giving each State, regardless of population, the same voice in the National Legislature. Madison entreated the Convention "to renounce a principle wch. was confessedly unjust," and Rufus King of Massachusetts "was prepared for every event, rather than sit down under a Govt. founded in a vicious principle of representation and which must be as shortlived as it would be unjust."

* * *

The debates at the Convention make at least one fact abundantly clear: that when the delegates agreed that the House should represent "people" they intended that in allocating Congressmen the number assigned to each State should be determined solely by the number of the State's inhabitants. The Constitution embodied Edmund Randolph's proposal for a periodic census to ensure "fair representation of the people," an idea endorsed by Mason as assuring that "number of inhabitants" should always be the measure of representation in the House of Representatives. The Convention also overwhelmingly agreed to a resolution offered by Randolph to base future apportionment squarely on numbers and to delete any reference to wealth. And the delegates defeated a motion made by Elbridge Gerry to limit the number of Representatives from newer Western States so that it would never exceed the number from the original States.

It would defeat the principle solemnly embodied in the Great Compromise—equal representation in the House for equal numbers of people—for us to hold that, within the States, legislatures may draw the lines of congressional districts in such a way as to give some voters a greater voice in choosing a Congressman than others. . . .

It is in the light of such history that we must construe Art. I, § 2, of the Constitution, which, carrying out the ideas of Madison and those of like views, provides that Representatives shall be chosen "by the People of the several States" and shall be "apportioned among the several States . . . according to their respective Numbers." It is not surprising that our Court has held that this Article gives persons qualified to vote a constitutional right to vote and to have their votes counted. Not only can this right to vote not be denied outright, it cannot, consistently with Article I, be destroyed by alteration of ballots, or diluted by stuffing of the ballot box. No right is more precious in a free country than that of having a voice in the election of those who make the laws under which, as good citizens, we must live. Other rights, even the most basic, are illusory if the right to vote is undermined. Our Constitution leaves no room for classification of people in a way that unnecessarily abridges this right.

While it may not be possible to draw congressional districts with mathematical precision, that is no excuse for ignoring our Constitution's plain objective of making equal representation for equal numbers of people the fundamental goal for the House of Representatives. That is the high standard of justice and common sense which the Founders set for us.

Reversed and remanded.

* * *

MR. JUSTICE HARLAN, dissenting.

* * *

Disclaiming all reliance on other provisions of the Constitution, in particular those of the Fourteenth Amendment on which the appellants relied below and in this Court, the Court holds that the provision in Art. I, § 2, for election of Representatives "by the People" *means* that congressional districts are to be "as nearly as is practicable" equal in population. Stripped of rhetoric and a "historical context," which bears little resemblance to the evidence in the pages of history, the Court's opinion supports its holding only with the bland assertion that "the principle of a House of Representatives elected 'by the People' " would be "cast aside" if "a vote is worth more in one district than in another," *i. e.,* if congressional districts within a State, each electing a single Representative, are not equal in population. The fact is, however, that Georgia's 10 Representatives *are* elected "by the People" of Georgia, just as Representatives from other States are elected "by the People of the several States." This is all that the Constitution requires.

Although the Court finds necessity for its artificial construction of Article I in the undoubted importance of the right to vote, that right is not involved in this case. All of the appellants do vote. The Court's talk about "debasement" and "dilution" of the vote is a model of circular reasoning, in which the premises of the argument feed on the conclusion. Moreover, by focusing exclusively on numbers in disregard of the area and shape of a congressional district as well as party affiliations within the district, the Court deals in abstractions which will be recognized even by the politically unsophisticated to have little relevance to the realities of political life.

* * *

There is a further basis for demonstrating the hollowness of the Court's assertion that Article I requires "one man's vote in a congressional election . . . to be worth as much as another's." Nothing that the Court does today will disturb the fact that although in 1960 the population of an average congressional district was 410,481, the States of Alaska, Nevada, and Wyoming each have a Representative in Congress, although their respective populations are 226,167, 285,278, and 330,066. In entire disregard of population, Art. I, § 2, guarantees each of these States and every other State "at Least one Representative." It is whimsical to assert in the face of this guarantee that an absolute principle of "equal representation in the House for equal numbers of people" is "solemnly embodied" in Article I. All that there is is a provision which bases representation in the House, generally but not entirely, on the population of the States. The provision for representation of *each State* in the House of Representatives is not a mere exception to the principle framed by the majority; it shows that no such principle is to be found.

* * *

Reynolds, Judge, et al. v. Sims et al.

377 U.S. 533; 84 S. Ct. 1362; 12 L. Ed. 2d 506 (1964)
Vote: 8–1

Sims and others were residents, taxpayers, and voters in Jefferson County, Alabama, who challenged the apportionment of the Alabama legislature. Their suit, filed in August 1961, alleged a deprivation of rights under the equal protection clause of the Fourteenth Amendment. The claim rested on the fact that the apportionment of the legislature was based on the 1900 federal census and had not been changed since 1903. As a consequence of growth in population since that time, Jefferson County was said to be the victim of serious discrimination with respect to the allocation of legislative representation. A three-judge district court found the inequality of representation to be a violation of the equal protection clause in July 1962. The U.S. Supreme Court then noted probable jurisdiction.

MR. CHIEF JUSTICE WARREN delivered the opinion of the Court.

* * *

On July 21, 1962, the District Court held that the inequality of the existing representation in the Alabama Legislature violated the Equal Protection Clause of the Fourteenth Amendment, a finding which the Court noted had been "generally conceded" by the parties to the litigation, since population growth and shifts had converted the 1901 scheme, as perpetuated some 60 years later, into an invidiously discriminatory plan completely lacking in rationality. Under the existing provisions, applying 1960 census figures, only 25.1% of the State's total population resided in districts represented by a majority of the members of the Senate, and only 25.7% lived in counties which could elect a majority of the members of the House of Representatives. Population-variance ratios of up to about 41-to-1 existed in the Senate, and up to about 16-to-1 in the House. Bullock County, with a population of only 13,462, and Henry County, with a population of only 15,286, each were allocated two seats in the Alabama House, whereas Mobile County, with a population of 314,301, was given only three seats, and Jefferson County, with 634,864 people, had only seven representatives. With respect to senatorial apportionment, since the pertinent Alabama constitutional provisions had been consistently construed as prohibiting the giving of more than one Senate seat to any one county, Jefferson County, with over 600,000 people, was given only one senator, as was Lowndes County, with a 1960 population of only 15,417, and Wilcox County, with only 18,739 people. . . .

Undeniably the Constitution of the United States protects the right of all qualified citizens to vote, in state as well as in federal elections.

* * *

The right to vote freely for the candidate of one's choice is of the essence of a democratic society, and any restrictions on that right strike at the heart of representative government. And the right of suffrage can be denied by a debasement or dilution of the weight of a citizen's vote just as effectively as by wholly prohibiting the free exercise of the franchise.

In *Baker v. Carr,* [1962], we held that a claim asserted under the Equal Protection Clause challenging the constitutionality of a State's apportionment of seats in its legislature, on the ground that the right to vote of certain citizens was effectively impaired since debased and diluted, in effect presented a justiciable controversy subject to adjudication by federal courts. . . .

In *Gray v. Sanders,* [1963], we held that the Georgia county unit system, applicable in statewide primary elections, was unconstitutional since it resulted in a dilution of the weight of the votes of certain Georgia voters merely because of where they resided. . . .

In *Wesberry v. Sanders,* [1964], decided earlier this Term, we held that attacks on the constitutionality of congressional districting plans enacted by state legislatures do not present nonjusticiable questions and should not be dismissed generally for "want of equity." We determined that the constitutional test for the validity of congressional districting schemes was one of substantial equality of population among the various districts established by a state legislature for the election of members of the Federal House of Representatives.

* * *

Gray and *Wesberry* are of course not dispositive of or directly controlling on our decision in these cases involving state legislative apportionment controversies. Admittedly, those decisions, in which we held that, in statewide and in congressional elections, one person's vote must be counted equally with those of all other voters in a State, were based on different constitutional considerations and were addressed to rather distinct problems. But neither are they wholly inapposite. *Gray,* though not determinative here since involving the weighting of votes in statewide elections, established the basic principle of equality among voters within a State, and held that voters cannot be classified, constitutionally, on the basis of where they live, at least with respect to voting in statewide elections. And our decision in *Wesberry* was of course grounded on that language of the Constitution which prescribes that members of the Federal House of Representatives are to be chosen "by the People," while attacks on state legislative apportionment schemes, such as that involved in the instant cases, are principally based on the Equal Protection Clause of the Fourteenth Amendment. Nevertheless, *Wesberry* clearly established that the fundamental principle of representative government in this country is one of equal representation for equal numbers of people, without regard to race, sex, economic status, or place of residence within a State. Our problem, then, is to ascertain, in the instant cases, whether there are any constitutionally cognizable principles which would justify departures from the basic standard of equality among voters in the apportionment of seats in state legislatures.

A predominant consideration in determining whether a State's legislative apportionment scheme constitutes an invidious discrimination violative of rights asserted under the Equal Protection Clause is that the rights allegedly impaired are individual and personal in nature. . . .

Legislators represent people, not trees or acres. Legislators are elected by voters, not farms or cities or economic interests. As long as ours is a representative form of government, and our legislatures are those instruments of government elected directly by and directly representative of the people, the right to elect legislators in a free and unimpaired fashion is a bedrock of our political system. . . .

With respect to the allocation of legislative representation, all voters, as citizens of a State, stand in the same relation regardless of where they live. Any suggested criteria for the differentiation of citizens are insufficient to justify any discrimination, as to the weight of their votes, unless relevant to the permissible purposes of legislative apportionment. Since the achieving of fair and effective representation for all citizens is concededly the basic aim of legislative apportionment, we conclude that the Equal Protection Clause guarantees the opportunity for equal participation by all voters in the election of state legislators. Diluting the weight of votes because of place of residence impairs basic constitutional rights under the Fourteenth Amendment just as much as invidious discriminations based upon factors such as race, *Brown v. Board of Education,* [1954], or economic status, *Griffin v. Illinois,* [1956].

* * *

We hold that, as a basic constitutional standard, the Equal Protection Clause requires that the seats in both houses of a bicameral state legislature must be apportioned on a population basis. Simply stated, an individual's right to vote for state legislators is unconstitutionally impaired when its weight is in a substantial fashion diluted when compared with votes of citizens living in other parts of the State. Since, under neither the existing apportionment provisions nor either of the proposed plans* was either of the houses of the Alabama Legislature apportioned on a population basis, the District Court correctly held that all three of these schemes were constitutionally invalid. . . .

By holding that as a federal constitutional requisite both houses of a state legislature must be apportioned on a population basis, we mean that the Equal Protection Clause requires that a State make an honest and good faith effort to construct districts, in both houses of its legislature, as nearly of equal population as is practicable. We realize that it is a practical impossibility to arrange legislative districts so that each one has an identical number of residents, or citizens, or voters. Mathematical exactness or precision is hardly a workable constitutional requirement.

In *Wesberry v. Sanders,* the Court stated that congressional representation must be based on population as nearly as is practicable. In implementing the basic constitutional principle of representative government as enunciated by the Court in *Wesberry*—equality of population among districts—some distinctions may well be made between congressional and state legislative representation. Since, almost invariably, there is a significantly larger number of

*The Court also considered and rejected plans proposed in Alabama to meet the complaints of petitioners.

seats in state legislative bodies to be distributed within a State than congressional seats, it may be feasible to use political subdivision lines to a greater extent in establishing state legislative districts than in congressional districting while still affording adequate representation to all parts of the State. To do so would be constitutionally valid, so long as the resulting apportionment was one based substantially on population and the equal-population principle was not diluted in any significant way.

* * *

History indicates, however, that many States have deviated, to a greater or lesser degree, from the equal-population principle in the apportionment of seats in at least one house of their legislatures. So long as the divergences from a strict population standard are based on legitimate considerations incident to the effectuation of a rational state policy, some deviations from the equal-population principle are constitutionally permissible with respect to the apportionment of seats in either or both of the two houses of a bicamarel state legislature. But neither history alone, nor economic or other sorts of group interests, are permissible factors in attempting to justify disparities from population-based representation. Citizens, not history or economic interests, cast votes. Considerations of area alone provide an insufficient justification for deviations from the equal-population principle. Again, people, not land or trees or pastures, vote. Modern developments and improvements in transportation and communications make rather hollow, in the mid-1960's, most claims that deviations from population-based representation can validly be based solely on geographical considerations. Arguments for allowing such deviations in order to insure effective representation for sparsely settled areas and to prevent legislative districts from becoming so large that the availability of access of citizens to their representatives is impaired are today, for the most part, unconvincing. . . .

Although general provisions of the Alabama Constitution provide that the apportionment of seats in both houses of the Alabama Legislature should be on a population basis, other more detailed provisions clearly make compliance with both sets of requirements impossible. With respect to the operation of the Equal Protection Clause, it makes no difference whether a State's apportionment scheme is embodied in its constitution or in statutory provisions. In those States where the alleged malapportionment has resulted from noncompliance with state constitutional provisions which, if complied with, would result in an apportionment valid under the Equal Protection Clause, the judicial task of providing effective relief would appear to be rather simple. We agree with the view of the District Court that state constitutional provisions should be deemed violative of the Federal Constitution only when validly asserted constitutional rights could not otherwise be protected and effectuated.

Clearly, courts should attempt to accommodate the relief ordered to the apportionment provisions of state constitutions insofar as it is possible. But it is also quite clear that a state legislative apportionment scheme is no less violative of the Federal Constitution when it is based on state constitutional provisions which have been consistently complied with than when resulting from a non-compliance with state constitutional requirements. When there is an unavoidable conflict between the Federal and a State Constitution, the Supremacy Clause of course controls.

* * *

... We affirm the judgment below and remand the cases for further proceedings consistent with the views stated in this opinion.

It is so ordered.

* * *

MR. JUSTICE HARLAN, dissenting.

* * *

The Court's elaboration of its new "constitutional" doctrine indicates how far—and how unwisely—it has strayed from the appropriate bounds of its authority. The consequence of today's decision is that in all but the handful of States which may already satisfy the new requirements the local District Court or, it may be, the state courts, are given blanket authority and the constitutional duty to supervise apportionment of the State Legislatures. It is difficult to imagine a more intolerable and inappropriate interference by the judiciary with the independent legislatures of the States. . . .

Generalities cannot obscure the cold truth that cases of this type are not amenable to the development of judicial standards. No set of standards can guide a court which has to decide how many legislative districts a State shall have, or what the shape of the districts shall be, or where to draw a particular district line. No judicially manageable standard can determine whether a State should have single-member districts or multimember districts or some combination of both. No such standard can control the balance between keeping up with population shifts and having stable districts. In all these respects, the courts will be called upon to make particular decisions with respect to which a principle of equally populated districts will be of no assistance whatsoever. Quite obviously, there are limitless possibilities for districting consistent with such a principle. Nor can these problems be avoided by judicial reliance on legislative judgments so far as possible. Reshaping or combining one or two districts, or modifying just a few district lines, is no less a matter of choosing among many possible solutions, with varying political consequences, than reapportionment broadside. . . .

Although the Court—necessarily, as I believe—provides only generalities in elaboration of its main thesis, its opinion nevertheless fully demonstrates how far removed these problems are from fields of judicial competence. Recognizing that "indiscriminate districting" is an invitation to "partisan gerrymandering," the Court nevertheless excludes virtually every basis for the formation of electoral districts other than "indiscriminate districting.". . .

So far as presently appears, the *only* factor which a State may consider, apart from numbers, is political subdivisions. . . . [The] Court says . . . that "legislators represent people, not trees or acres," that "citizens, not history or economic interests, cast votes,"; that "people, not land or trees or pastures, vote." All this may be conceded. But it is surely equally obvious, and, in the context of elections, more meaningful to note that people are not ciphers and that legislators can represent their electors only by speaking for their interests—economic, social, political—many of which do reflect the place where the electors live. The Court does not establish, or indeed even attempt to make a case for the proposition that conflicting interests within a State can only be adjusted by disregarding them when voters are grouped for purposes of representation.

* * *

Finally, these decisions give support to a current mistaken view of the Constitution and the constitutional function of this Court. This view, in a nutshell, is that every major social ill in this country can find its cure in some constitutional "principle," and that this Court should "take the lead" in promoting reform when other branches of government fail to act. The Constitution is not a panacea for every blot upon the public welfare, nor should this Court, ordained as a judicial body, be thought of as a general haven for reform movements. The Constitution is an instrument of government, fundamental to which is the premise that in a diffusion of governmental authority lies the greatest promise that this Nation will realize liberty for all its citizens. This Court, limited in function in accordance with that premise, does not serve its high purpose when it exceeds its authority, even to satisfy justified impatience with the slow workings of the political process. For when, in the name of constitutional interpretation, the Court *adds* something to the Constitution that was deliberately excluded from it, the Court in reality substitutes its view of what should be so for the amending process.

* * *

QUESTIONS AND COMMENTS

1 Identify the constitutional bases of the Court's decisions in *Wesberry* and *Reynolds.* Why did the Court choose different bases for decision? What, if any, are the implications of the Court's choices?

2 In *Wesberry,* the Court required the states to structure their congressional districts in such a way as to equalize votes across districts, "as nearly as practicable." What did the Court mean by that phrase? Did it mean "one person, one vote?"

3 Dissenting in *Wesberry,* Justice Harlan says that "The Court's talk about 'debasement' and 'dilution' of the vote is a model of circular reasoning, in which the premises of the argument feed on the conclusion." What does he mean? Can you identify the evidence on which Harlan bases this proposition?

4 What argument can be made to rebut Black's assertion in *Wesberry* that the framers intended the number of congressional representatives assigned each state to be determined by "the number of the state's inhabitants?"

5 On your reading of *Wesberry* and *Reynolds,* which of the following departures from the mathematical ideal of exact equality would be unconstitutional?

   a Most populous congressional district 3.13 percent above, least populous 2.84 percent below.[2]

   b Most populous district 2.43 percent above, least populous 1.7 percent below.[3]

   c Most populous .086 percent above, least populous .063 percent below.[4]

   d Most overrepresented state legislative district exceeded mathematical exactness by 6.8 percent, most underrepresented by 9.6 percent.[5]

6 Having considered question 5, what inference would you draw regarding the subjectivity or objectivity of Supreme Court decision-making?

Regulating Voting Rights

South Carolina v. Katzenbach (1966)

Richardson v. Ramirez (1974)

The reapportionment cases speak to the right to have one's vote count equally with those of others. Most voting rights cases, however, concern racial discrimination and the denial or dilution of voting rights on the basis of race. We have already discussed the white primary cases and shown how the Supreme Court steadily thwarted the efforts of some states to deny suffrage to blacks. Congress added its authority to that effort with the passage of the Voting Rights Act in 1965. In *South Carolina v. Katzenbach,* that statute is put to the constitutional test.

South Carolina v. Katzenbach, Attorney General

383 U.S. 301; 86 S. Ct. 803; 15 L. Ed. 2d 769 (1966)
Vote: 8–1

South Carolina asked the Supreme Court to declare certain sections of the federal Voting Rights Act of 1965 unconstitutional and to enjoin the enforcement of the challenged provisions by the attorney general. One section of the act provides for the suspension of voting tests or devices after appropriate administrative determinations. Under this section, South Carolina's literacy tests were suspended. The act provides that during such a suspension, the affected state may not apply new voting rules unless the attorney general offers no objection within 60 days of their submission. South Carolina wished to adopt new rules without complying with this section.

Other sections of the act allow the attorney general, given appropriate conditions, to approve the appointment of voting examiners by the Civil Service Commission. These examiners are empowered to go into a state where voting tests have been suspended and register qualified voters. Under these provisions, voting examiners were appointed in two South Carolina counties. South Carolina objected to these procedures and mounted a general attack on the constitutionality of the act.

Mr. Chief Justice Warren delivered the opinion of the Court.

* * *

The Voting Rights Act was designed by Congress to banish the blight of racial discrimination in voting, which has infected the electoral process in parts of our country for nearly a century. The Act creates stringent new remedies for voting discrimination where it persists on a pervasive scale, and in addition the statute strengthens existing remedies for pockets of voting discrimination elsewhere in the country. Congress assumed the power to prescribe these remedies from § 2 of the Fifteenth Amendment, which authorizes the National Legislature to effectuate by "appropriate" measures the constitutional prohibition against racial discrimination in voting. We hold that the sections of the Act which are properly before us are an appropriate means for carrying out Congress' constitutional repsponsibilities and are consonant with all other provisions of the Constitution. We therefore deny South Carolina's request that enforcement of these sections of the Act be enjoined.

The constitutional propriety of the Voting Rights Act of 1965 must be judged with reference to the historical experience which it reflects. . . .

The Fifteenth Amendment to the Constitution was ratified in 1870. Promptly thereafter Congress passed the Enforcement Act of 1870, which made it a crime for public officers and private persons to obstruct exercise of the right to vote. The statute was amended in the following year to provide for detailed federal supervision of the electoral process, from registration to the certification of returns. As the years passed and fervor for racial equality waned, enforcement of the laws became spotty and ineffective, and most of their provisions were repealed in 1894. The remnants have had little significance in the recently renewed battle against voting discrimination.

Meanwhile, beginning in 1890, the States of Alabama, Georgia, Louisiana, Mississippi, North Carolina, South Carolina, and Virginia enacted tests still in use which were specifically designed to prevent Negroes from voting. Typically, they made the ability to read and write a registration qualification and also required completion of a registration form. These laws were based on the fact that as of 1890 in each of the named States, more than two-thirds of the adult Negroes were illiterate while less than one-quarter of the adult whites were unable to read or write. At the same time, alternate tests were prescribed in all of the named States to assure that white illiterates would not be deprived of the franchise. These included grandfather clauses, property qualifications, "good character" tests, and the requirement that registrants "understand" or "interpret" certain matter.

The course of subsequent Fifteenth Amendment litigation in this Court demonstrates the variety and persistence of these and similar institutions designed to deprive Negroes of the right to vote. Grandfather clauses were invalidated in *Guinn v. United States,* [1914], and *Myers v. Anderson,* [1915]. Procedural hurdles were struck down in *Lane v. Wilson,* [1938]. The white primary was outlawed in *Smith v. Allwright,* [1944], and *Terry v. Adams,* [1952]. Improper challenges were nullified in *United States v. Thomas,* [1969]. Racial gerrymandering was forbidden by *Gomillion v. Lightfoot,* [1960]. Finally, discriminatory application of voting tests was condemned in *Louisiana v. United States,* [1964].

According to the evidence in recent Justice Department voting suits, the latter stratagem is now the principal method used to bar Negroes from the polls. Discriminatory administration of voting qualifications has been found in all eight Alabama cases, in all nine Louisiana cases, and in all nine Mississippi cases which have gone to final judgment. Moreover, in almost all of these cases, the courts have held that the discrimination was pursuant to a widespread "pattern of practice." White applicants for registration have often been excused altogether from the literacy and understanding tests or have been given easy versions, have received extensive help from voting officials, and have been registered despite serious errors in their answers. Negroes, on the other hand, have typically been required to pass difficult versions of all the tests, without any outside assistance and without the slightest error. The good-morals requirement is so vague and subjective that it has constituted an open invitation to abuse at the hands of voting officials. Negroes obliged to obtain vouchers from registered voters have found it virtually impossible to comply in areas where almost no Negroes are on the rolls.

In recent years, Congress has repeatedly tried to cope with the problem by facilitating case-by-case litigation against voting discrimination. The Civil Rights Act of 1957 authorized the Attorney General to seek injunction against public and private interference with the right to vote on racial grounds. Perfecting amendments in the Civil Rights Act of 1960 permitted the joinder of States as parties defendant, gave the Attorney General access to local voting records, and authorized courts to register voters in areas of systematic discrimination. Title I of the Civil Rights Act of 1964 expedited the hearing of voting cases before three-judge courts and outlawed some of the tactics used to disqualify Negroes from voting in federal elections.

Despite the earnest efforts of the Justice Department and of many federal judges, these new laws have done little to cure the problem of voting discrimination. According to estimates by the Attorney General during hearings of the Act, registration of voting-age Negroes in Alabama rose only from 14.2% to 19.4% between 1958 and 1964; in Louisiana it barely inched ahead from 31.7% to 31.8% between 1956 and 1965; and in Mississippi it increased only from 4.4% to 6.4% between 1954 and 1964. In each instance, registration of voting-age whites ran roughly 50 percentage points or more ahead of Negro registration.

The previous legislation has proved ineffective for a number of reasons. Voting suits are unusually onerous to prepare, sometimes requiring as many as 6000 manhours spent combing through registration records in preparation for trial. Litigation has been exceedingly slow, in part because of the ample opportunities for delay afforded voting officials and others involved in the proceedings. Even when favorable decisions have finally been obtained, some of the States affected have merely switched to discriminatory devices not covered by the federal decrees or have enacted difficult new tests designed to prolong the existing disparity between white and Negro registration. Alternatively, certain local officials have defied and evaded court orders or have simply closed their registration offices to freeze the voting rolls. The provision of the 1960 law authorizing registration by federal officers has had little impact on local maladministration because of its procedural complexities.

* * *

Coverage Formula

The remedial sections of the Act assailed by South Carolina automatically apply to any State, or to any separate political subdivision such as a county or parish, for which two findings have been made: (1) the Attorney General has determined that on November 1, 1964, it maintained a "test or device," and (2) the Director of the Census has determined that less than 50% of its voting-age residents were registered on November 1, 1964, or voted in the presidential election of November 1964. These findings are not reviewable in any court and are final upon publication in the Federal Register. As used throughout the Act, the phrase "test or device" means any requirement that a registrant or voter must "(1) demonstrate the ability to read, write, understand, or interpret any matter, (2) demonstrate any educational achievement or his knowledge of any particular subject, (3) possess good moral character, or (4) prove his qualifications by the voucher of registered voters or members of any other class."

Statutory coverage of a State or political subdivision under § 4 (b) is terminated if the area obtains a declaratory judgment from the District Court for the District of Columbia, determining that tests and devices have not been used during the preceding five years to abridge the franchise on racial grounds. The Attorney General shall consent to entry of the judgment if he has no reason to believe that the facts are otherwise. For the purposes of this section, tests and devices are not deemed to have been used in a forbidden manner if the incidents of discrimination are few in number and have been promptly corrected, if their continuing effects have been abated, and if they are unlikely to recur in the future.

On the other hand, no area may obtain a declaratory judgment for five years after the final decision of a federal court (other than the denial of a judgment under this section of the Act), determining that discrimination through the use of tests or devices has occurred anywhere in the State, or political subdivision. These declaratory judgment actions are to be heard by a three-judge panel, with direct appeal to this Court.

South Carolina was brought within the coverage formula of the Act on August 7, 1965, pursuant to appropriate administrative determinations which have not been challenged in this proceeding. On the same day, coverage was also extended to Alabama, Alaska, Georgia, Louisiana, Mississippi, Virginia, 26 counties in North Carolina, and one county in Arizona. Two more counties in Arizona, one county in Hawaii, and one county in Idaho were added to the list on November 19, 1965. Thus far Alaska, the three Arizona counties, and the single county in Idaho have asked the District Court for the District of Columbia to grant a declaratory judgment terminating statutory coverage.

Suspension of Tests

In a State or political subdivision covered by § 4 (b) of the Act, no person may be denied the right to vote in any election because of his failure to comply with a "test or device."

On account of this provision, South Carolina is temporarily barred from enforcing the portion of its voting laws which requires every applicant for registration to show that he:

Can both read and write any section of [the State] Constitution submitted to [him] by the registration officer or can show that he owns, and has paid all taxes collectible during the previous year on, property in this State assessed at three hundred dollars or more.

The Attorney General has determined that the property qualification is inseparable from the literacy test, and South Carolina makes no objection to this finding. Similar tests and devices have been temporarily suspended in the other sections of the country listed above.

Review of New Rules

In a State or political subdivision covered by § 4 (b) of the Act, no person may be denied the right to vote in any election because of his failure to comply with a voting qualification or procedure different from those in force on November 1, 1964. This suspension of new rules is terminated, however, under either of the following circumstances: (1) if the area has submitted the rules to the Attorney General, and he has not interposed an objection within 60 days, or (2) if the area has obtained a declaratory judgment from the District Court for the District of Columbia, determining that the rules will not abridge the franchise on racial grounds. These declaratory judgment actions are to be heard by a three-judge panel, with direct appeal to this Court.

South Carolina altered its voting laws in 1965 to extend the closing hour at polling places from 6:00 P.M. to 7:00 P.M. The State has not sought judicial review of this change in the District Court for the District of Columbia, nor has it submitted the new rule to the Attorney General for his scrutiny, although at our hearing the Attorney General announced that he does not challenge the amendment. There are indications in the record that other sections of the country listed above have also altered their voting laws since November 1, 1964.

Federal Examiners

In any political subdivision covered by § 4 (b) of the Act, the Civil Service Commission shall appoint voting examiners whenever the Attorney General certifies either of the following facts: (1) that he has received meritorious written complaints from at least 20 residents alleging that they have been disenfranchised under color of law because of their race, or (2) that the appointment of examiners is otherwise necessary to effectuate the guarantees of the Fifteenth Amendment. In making the latter determination, the Attorney General must consider, among other factors, whether the registration ratio of non-whites to whites seems reasonably attributable to racial discrimination, or whether there is substantial evidence of good-faith efforts to comply with the Fifteenth Amendment. These certifications are not reviewable in any court and are effective upon publication in the Federal Register.

The examiners who have been appointed are to test the voting qualifications of applicants according to regulations of the Civil Service Commission prescribing times, places, procedures, and forms. Any person who meets the voting requirements of state law, insofar as these have not been suspended by the Act, must promptly be placed on a list of eligible voters. Examiners are to transmit their lists at least once a month to the appropriate state or local officials, who in turn are required to place the listed names on the official voting polls. Any person listed by an examiner is entitled to vote in all elections held more than 45 days after his name has been transmitted.

A person shall be removed from the voting list by an examiner if he has lost his eligibility under valid state law, or if he has been successfully challenged through the procedure prescribed in § 9 (1) of the Act. The challenge must be filed at the office within the State designated by the Civil Service Commission; must be submitted within 10 days after the listing is made available for public inspection; must be supported by the affidavits of at least two people having personal knowledge of the relevant facts; and must be served on the person challenged by mail or at his residence. A hearing officer appointed by the Civil Service Commission shall hear the challenge and render a decision within 15 days after the challenge is filed. A petition for review of the hearing officer's decision must be submitted within an additional 15 days after service of the decision on the person seeking review. The court of appeals for the circuit in which the person challenged resides is to hear the petition and affirm the hearing officer's decision unless it is clearly erroneous. Any person listed by an examiner is entitled to vote pending a final decision of the hearing officer or the court.

The listing procedures in a political subdivision are terminated under either of the following circumstances: (1) if the Attorney General informs the Civil Service Commission that all persons listed by examiners have been placed on the official voting rolls, and that there is no longer reasonable cause to fear abridgment of the franchise on racial grounds, or (2) if the political subdivision has obtained a declaratory judgment from the District Court for the District of Columbia, ascertaining the same facts which govern termination by the Attorney General, and the Director of the Census has determined that more than 50% of the non-white residents of voting age are registered to vote. A political subdivision may petition the Attorney General to terminate listing procedures or to authorize the necessary census, and the District Court itself shall request the census if the Attorney General's refusal to do so is arbitrary or unreasonable, § 13 (a). The determinations by the Director of the Census are not reviewable in any court and are final upon publication in the Federal Register.

On October 30, 1965, the Attorney General certified the need for federal examiners in two South Carolina counties, and examiners appointed by the Civil Service Commission have been serving there since November 8, 1965. Examiners have also been assigned to 11 counties in Alabama, five parishes in Louisiana, and 19 counties in Mississippi. The examiners are listing people found eligible to vote, and the challenge procedure has been employed extensively. No political subdivision has yet sought to have federal examiners withdrawn through the Attorney General or the District Court for the District of Columbia.

* * *

The Voting Rights Act of 1965 reflects Congress' firm intention to rid the country of racial discrimination in voting. . . .

These provisions of the Voting Rights Act of 1965 are challenged on the fundamental ground that they exceed the powers of Congress and encroach on an area reserved to the States by the Constitution. . . .

The ground rules for resolving this question are clear. The language and purpose of the Fifteenth Amendment, the prior decisions construing its several provisions, and the general doctrines of constitutional interpretation, all point to one fundamental principle. As against the reserved powers of the States, Congress may use any rational means to effectuate the constitutional prohibition of racial discrimination in voting. Cf. our rulings last Term, sustaining Title II of the Civil Rights Act of 1964, in *Heart of Atlanta Motel v. United States,* [1964], and *Katzenbach v. McClung,* [1964]. We turn now to a more detailed description of the standards which govern our review of the Act.

Section 1 of the Fifteenth Amendment declares that "[t]he right of citizens of the United States to vote shall not be denied or abridged by the United States or by any State on account of race, color, or previous condition of servitude." This declaration has always been treated as self-executing and has repeatedly been construed, without further legislative specification, to invalidate state voting qualifications or procedures which are discriminatory on their face or in practice.

These decisions have been rendered with full respect for the general rule, reiterated last Term in *Carrington v. Rash,* [1965], that States "have broad powers to determine the conditions under which the right of suffrage may be exercised." The gist of the matter is that the Fifteenth Amendment supersedes contrary exertions of state power. "When a State exercises power wholly within the domain of state interest, it is insulated from federal judicial review. But such insulation is not carried over when state power is used as an instrument for circumventing a federally protected right." *Gomillion v. Lightfoot,* [1960].

* * *

After enduring nearly a century of widespread resistance to the Fifteenth Amendment, Congress has marshalled an array of potent weapons against the evil, with authority in the Attorney General to employ them effectively. Many of the areas directly affected by this development have indicated their willingness to abide by any restraints legitimately imposed upon them. We here hold that the portions of the Voting Rights Act properly before us are a valid means for carrying out the commands of the Fifteenth Amendment. Hopefully, millions of non-white Americans will now be able to participate for the first time on an equal basis in the government under which they live. We may finally look forward to the day when truly "[t]he right of citizens of the United States to vote shall not be denied or abridged by the United States or by any State on account of race, color, or previous condition of servitude."

The bill of complaint is

Dismissed.

* * *

MR. JUSTICE BLACK, concurring and dissenting.

I agree with substantially all of the Court's opinion sustaining the power of Congress under § 2 of the Fifteenth Amendment to suspend state literacy tests and similar voting qualifications and to authorize the Attorney General to secure the appointment of federal examiners to register qualified voters in various sections of the country. . . .

I have no doubt whatever as to the power of Congress under § 2 to enact the provisions of the Voting Rights Act of 1965 dealing with the suspension of state voting tests that have been used as notorious means to deny and abridge voting rights on racial grounds. This same congressional power necessarily exists to authorize appointment of federal examiners. I also agree with the judgment of the Court upholding § 4 (b) of the Act which sets out a formula for determining when and where the major remedial sections of the Act take effect. I reach this conclusion, however, for a somewhat different reason than that stated by the Court, which is that "the coverage formula is rational in both practice and theory." I do not base my conclusion on the fact that the formula is rational, for it is enough for me that Congress by creating this formula has merely exercised its hitherto unquestioned and undisputed power to decide when, where, and upon what conditions its laws shall go into effect. By stating in specific detail that the major remedial sections of the Act are to be applied in areas where certain conditions exist, and by granting the Attorney General and the Director of the Census unreviewable power to make the mechanical determination of which areas come within the formulas of § 4 (b), I believe that Congress has acted within its established power to set out preconditions upon which the Act is to go into effect.

Though, as I have said, I agree with most of the Court's conclusions, I dissent from its holding that every part of § 5 of the Act is constitutional. Section 4 (a), to which § 5 is linked, suspends for five years all literacy tests and similar devices in those States coming within the formula of § 4 (b). Section 5 goes on to provide that a State covered by §4 (b) can in no way amend its constitution or laws relating to voting without first trying to persuade the Attorney General of the United States or the Federal District Court for the District of Columbia that the new proposed laws do not have the purpose and will not have the effect of denying the right to vote to citizens on account of their race or color. I think this section is unconstitutional on at least two grounds.

(a)   The Constitution gives federal courts jurisdiction over cases and controversies only. If it can be said that any case or controversy arises under this section which gives the District Court for the District of Columbia jurisdiction to approve or reject state laws or constitutional amendments, then the case or controversy must be between a State and the United States Government. But it is hard for me to believe that a justiciable controversy can arise in the constitutional sense from a desire by the United States Government or some of its officials to determine in advance what legislative provisions a State may enact or what constitutional amendments it may adopt. If this dispute between the Federal Government and the States amounts to a case or controversy it is a far cry from the traditional constitutional notion of a case or controversy as a dispute over the meaning of enforceable laws or the manner in which they are applied.

* * *

(b)   My second and more basic objection to § 5 is that Congress has here exercised its power under § 2 of the Fifteenth Amendment through the adoption of means that conflict with the most basic principles of the Constitution. As the Court says the limitations of the power granted under § 2 are the same as the limitations imposed on the exercise of any of the powers expressly granted Congress by the Constitution. . . .

Section 5, by providing that some of the States cannot pass state laws or adopt state constitutional amendments without first being compelled to beg federal authorities to approve their policies, so distorts our constitutional structure of government as to render any distinction drawn in the Constitution between state and federal power almost meaningless.

. . . Moreover, it seems to me that § 5 which gives federal officials power to veto state laws they do not like is in direct conflict with the clear command of our Constitution that "The United States shall guarantee to every State in this Union a Republican Form of Government." I cannot help but believe that the inevitable effect of any such law which forces any one of the States to entreat federal authorities in far-away places for approval of local laws before they can become effective is to create the impression that the State or States treated in this way are little more than conquered provinces.

* * *

Of course I do not mean to cast any doubt whatever upon the indisputable power of the Federal Government to invalidate a state law once enacted and operative on the ground that it intrudes into the area of supreme federal power. But the Federal Government has heretofore always been content to exercise this power to protect federal supremacy by authorizing its agents to bring lawsuits against state officials once an operative state law has created an actual case and controversy. A federal law which assumes the power to compel the States to submit in advance any proposed legislation they have for approval by federal agents approaches dangerously near to wiping the States out as useful and effective units in the government of our country. I cannot agree to any constitutional interpretation that leads inevitably to such a result.

* * *

In this and other prior Acts Congress has quite properly vested the Attorney General with extremely broad power to protect voting rights of citizens against discrimination on account of race or color. Section 5 viewed in this context is of very minor importance and in my judgment is likely to serve more as an irritant to the States than as an aid to the enforcement of the Act. I would hold § 5 invalid for the reasons stated above with full confidence that the Attorney General has ample power to give vigorous, expeditious and effective protection to the voting rights of all citizens.

QUESTIONS AND COMMENTS

1 Compare the "prior approval" for states covered by the Voting Rights Act to change their voting rules and regulations with the "prior restraint" denied to government when dealing with restrictions on the press. Is such a comparison equivalent to comparing apples and oranges? Or can the theory underlying one of these concepts, at some level of generality, be applied to the other? Explain your answer.

2 Of the various arguments used by Justice Black in concluding that some parts of the Voting Rights Act were unconstitutional, which do you consider
   a the most telling and
   b the least probative?
   Explain your reasons.

3 The Voting Rights Act of 1965 was extended in 1970, 1975, and 1982, and is still in effect at this time (1985).

4 The Voting Rights Act was adopted at a time when black leaders were militantly attempting to improve the treatment accorded blacks. The threat of collective violence was in the air. It was coupled with a general recognition that many of the black complaints had merit and that the day of temporizing over such irritants was over. Can you find any evidence in the Court's opinion that suggests an awareness of the context in which the case was docketed?

* * * * * *

Finally, in *Richardson v. Ramirez,* we come to the claim that voting rights may not be denied to convicted felons who have completed their sentences. In 1973, the Court struck a state statute prohibiting absentee registration and voting by unconvicted jail inmates, basing its decision on the equal protection clause.[7] *Richardson* also turns on the Fourteenth Amendment. But the case is notable for the Court's failure to employ equal protection analysis.

Richardson, County Clerk and Registrar of Voters of Mendocino County v. Ramirez et al.

418 U.S. 24; 94 S. Ct. 2655; 41 L. Ed. 2d 551 (1974)
Vote: 6–3

Three individuals, convicted of felonies in three different California counties, completed their sentences and paroles. When they then attempted to register to vote, they were denied the privilege. The California Constitution at that time provided that "no person convicted of any infamous crime . . . shall ever exercise the privileges of an elector in this state." State statutes required the disqualification of any person convicted of a felony. After being refused registration, the respondents asked the California Supreme Court to order their registration on the ground that the voting restrictions violated their rights under the equal protection and due process clauses of the Fourteenth Amendment. The California court upheld the equal protection claim.

Viola Richardson was the county clerk of Mendocino County. Since the original complaint was treated by the California Supreme Court as a class action, Richardson was bound to register all ex-felons in her county who met the usual voter requirements, even though her county was not involved in the original suit. Richardson thought there had been collusion between the secretary of state and the original plaintiffs and asked to intervene. The California court then made her a defendant in the original suit. In that status, Richardson sought and was granted review of the California Supreme Court decision in the U.S. Supreme Court.

MR. JUSTICE REHNQUIST delivered the opinion of the Court.

* * *

Unlike most claims under the Equal Protection Clause, for the decision of which we have only the language of the Clause itself as it is embodied in the Fourteenth Amendment, respondents' claim implicates not merely the language of the Equal Protection Clause of § 1 of the Fourteenth Amendment, but also the provisions of the less familiar § 2 of the Amendment:

> Representatives shall be apportioned among the several States according to their respective numbers, counting the whole number of persons in each State, excluding Indians not taxed. But when the right to vote at any election for the choice of electors for President and Vice President of the United States, Representatives in Congress, the Executive and Judicial officers of a State, or the members of the Legislature thereof, is denied to any of the male inhabitants of such State, being twenty-one years of age, and citizens of the United States, or in any way abridged, *except for participation in rebellion, or other crime,* the basis of representation therein shall be reduced

in the proportion which the number of such male citizens shall bear to the whole number of male citizens twenty-one years of age in such State. (Emphasis supplied.)

Petitioner contends that the italicized language of § 2 expressly exempts from the sanction of that section disenfranchisement grounded on prior conviction of a felony. She goes on to argue that those who framed and adopted the Fourteenth Amendment could not have intended to prohibit outright in § 1 of that Amendment that which was expressly exempted from the lesser sanction of reduced representation imposed by § 2 of the Amendment. This argument seems to us a persuasive one unless it can be shown that the language of § 2, "except for participation in rebellion, or other crime," was intended to have a different meaning than would appear from its face.

The problem of interpreting the "intention" of a constitutional provision is, as countless cases of this Court recognize, a difficult one. Not only are there deliberations of congressional committees and floor debates in the House and Senate, but an amendment must thereafter be ratified by the necessary number of States. The legislative history bearing on the meaning of the relevant language of § 2 is scant indeed; the framers of the Amendment were primarily concerned with the effect of reduced representation upon the States, rather than with the two forms of disenfranchisement which were exempted from that consequence by the language with which we are concerned here. Nonetheless, what legislative history there is indicates that this language was intended by Congress to mean what it says.

* * *

Further light is shed on the understanding of those who framed and ratified the Fourteenth Amendment, and thus on the meaning of § 2, by the fact that at the time of the adoption of the Amendment, 29 States had provisions in their constitutions which prohibited, or authorized the legislature to prohibit, exercise of the franchise by persons convicted of felonies or infamous crimes.

More impressive than the mere existence of the state constitutional provisions disenfranchising felons at the time of the adoption of the Fourteenth Amendment is the congressional treatment of States readmitted to the Union following the Civil War. For every State thus readmitted, affirmative congressional action in the form of an enabling act was taken, and as a part of the readmission process the State seeking readmission was required to submit for the approval of the Congress its proposed state constitution. In March 1867, before any State was readmitted, Congress passed "An act to provide for the more efficient Government of the Rebel States," the so-called Reconstruction Act. Section 5 of the Reconstruction Act established conditions on which the former Confederate States would be readmitted to representation in Congress.

* * *

[The Act stated flatly that electors for the conventions to frame new state constitutions need not include those who] *may be disenfranchised for participation in the rebellion or for felony at common law, . . .*

Despite this settled historical and judicial understanding of the Fourteenth Amendment's effect on state laws disenfranchising convicted felons, respondents argue that our recent decisions invalidating other state-imposed restrictions on the franchise as violative of the Equal Protection Clause require us to invalidate the disenfranchisement of felons as well. They rely on such cases as *Dunn v. Blumstein,* (1972), to support the conclusions of the Supreme Court of California that a State must show a "compelling state interest" to justify exclusion of ex-felons from the franchise and that California has not done so here.

As we have seen, however, the exclusion of felons from the vote has an affirmative sanction in § 2 of the Fourteenth Amendment, a sanction which was not present in the case of the other restrictions on the franchise which were invalidated in the cases on which respondents rely. We hold that the understanding of those who adopted the Fourteenth Amendment, as reflected in the express language of § 2 and in the historical and judicial interpretation of the Amendment's applicability to state laws disenfranchising felons, is of controlling significance in distinguishing such laws from those other state limitations on the franchise which have been held invalid under the Equal Protection Clause by this Court.

* * *

Pressed upon us by the respondents, and by *amici curiae,* are contentions that these notions are outmoded, and that the more modern view is that it is essential to the process of rehabilitating the ex-felon that he be returned to his role in society as a fully participating citizen when he has completed the serving of his term. We would by no means discount these arguments if addressed to the legislative forum which may properly weigh and balance them against those advanced in support of California's present constitutional provisions. But it is not for us to choose one set of values over the other. If respondents are correct, and the view which they advocate is indeed the more enlightened and sensible one, presumably the people of the State of California will ultimately come around to that view. And if they do not do so, their failure is some evidence, at least, of the fact that there are two sides to the argument.

We therefore hold that the Supreme Court of California erred in concluding that California may no longer, consistent with the Equal Protection Clause of the Fourteenth Amendment, exclude from the franchise convicted felons who have completed their sentences and paroles.

* * *

Accordingly, we reverse and remand for further proceedings not inconsistent with this opinion.

It is so ordered.

Mr. Justice Marshall, with whom Mr. Justice Brennan joins, dissenting.

* * *

In my view, the disenfranchisement of ex-felons must be measured against the requirements of the Equal Protection Clause of § 1 of the Fourteenth Amendment. That analysis properly begins with the observation that because the right to vote "is of the essence of a democratic society, and any restrictions on that right strike at the heart of representative government," *Reynolds v. Sims,* [1964], voting is a "fundamental" right.

* * *

[I]fa challenged statute grants the right to vote to some citizens and denies the franchise to others, "the Court must determine whether the exclusions are *necessary* to promote a *compelling* state interest. . . ."

I think it clear that the State has not met its burden of justifying the blanket disenfranchisement of former felons presented by this case. There is certainly no basis for asserting that ex-felons have any less interest in the democratic process than any other citizen. Like everyone else, their daily lives are deeply affected and changed by the decisions of government. . . .

It is argued that disenfranchisement is necessary to prevent vote frauds. Although the State has a legitimate and, in fact, compelling interest in preventing election fraud, the challenged provision is not sustainable on that ground. First, the disenfranchisement provisions are patently both overinclusive and underinclusive. The provision is not limited to those who have demonstrated a marked propensity for abusing the ballot by violating election laws. Rather, it encompasses all former felons and there has been no showing that ex-felons generally are more likely to abuse the ballot than the remainder of the population.

In contrast, many of those convicted of violating election laws are treated as misdemeanants and are not barred from voting at all. It seems clear that the classification here is not tailored to achieve its articulated goal, since it crudely excludes large numbers of otherwise qualified voters. . . .

The public purposes asserted to be served by disenfranchisement have been found wanting in many quarters. When this suit was filed, 23 States allowed ex-felons full access to the ballot. Since that time, four more States have joined their ranks. Shortly after federal courts sustained New York's and Florida's disenfranchisement provisions, the legislatures repealed those laws. Congress has recently provided for the restoration of felons' voting rights at the end of sentence or parole in the District of Columbia.

The National Conference on Uniform State Laws, the American Law Institute, the National Probation and Parole Association, the National Advisory Commission on Criminal Justice Standards and Goals, the President's Commission on Law Enforcement and the Administration of Justice, the California League of Women Voters, the National Democratic Party, and the Secretary of State of California have all strongly endorsed full suffrage rights for former felons.

The disenfranchisement of ex-felons had "its origin in the fogs and fictions of feudal jurisprudence and doubtless has been brought forward into modern statutes without fully realizing either the effect of its literal significance or the extent of its infringement upon the spirit of our system of government." I think it is clear that measured against the standards of this Court's modern equal protection jurisprudence, the blanket disenfranchisement of ex-felons cannot stand.

I respectfully dissent.

* * *

QUESTIONS AND COMMENTS

1 In this case, Justice Rehnquist for the Court writes: ". . . it is not for us to choose one set of values over the other." Does the Court do so in this case? In other cases? Explain your answer.
2 Should felons who have completed their sentences be allowed to vote? If your answer is affirmative,
 a give your reasons, and
 b indicate how you would get around the Supreme Court's holding in *Richardson*.

NOTES

1 372 U.S. 368 (1963).
2 *Kirkpatrick v. Preisler,* 394 U.S. 526 (1969).
3 *White v. Weiser,* 412 U.S. 783 (1973).
4 Ibid.
5 *Mahan v. Howell,* 410 U.S. 315 (1973).
6 *White v. Regester,* 412 U.S. 755 (1973); *Connor v. Finch,* 431 U.S. 407 (1977).
7 *Goosby v. Osser,* 409 U.S. 512 (1973).

THE CONSTITUTION OF THE UNITED STATES OF AMERICA

We the People of the United States, in Order to form a more perfect Union, establish Justice, insure domestic Tranquility, provide for the common defence, promote the general Welfare, and secure the Blessings of Liberty to ourselves and our Posterity, do ordain and establish this CONSTITUTION for the United States of America.

ARTICLE I

Section 1 All legislative Powers herein granted shall be vested in a Congress of the United States, which shall consist of a Senate and House of Representatives.

Section 2 [1] The House of Representatives shall be composed of Members chosen every second Year by the People of the several States, and the Electors of the most numerous Branch of the State Legislature.

[2] No Person shall be a Representative who shall not have attained to the Age of twenty-five Years, and been seven Years a Citizen of the United States, and who shall not, when elected, be an Inhabitant of that State in which he shall be chosen.

[3] Representatives and direct Taxes shall be apportioned among the several States which may be included within this Union, according to their respective Numbers, which shall be determined by adding to the whole Number of free Persons, including those bound to Service for a Term of Years, and excluding Indians not taxed, three fifths of all other Persons. The actual Enumeration shall be made within three Years after the first Meeting of the Congress of the United States, and within every subsequent Term of ten Years, in such Manner as they shall by Law direct. The Number of Representatives shall not exceed one for every thirty Thousand, but each State shall have at Least one Representative; and until such enumeration shall be made, the State of New Hampshire shall be entitled to chuse three, Massachusetts eight, Rhode-Island and Providence Plantations one, Connecticut five, New York six, New Jersey four, Pennsylvania eight, Delaware one, Maryland six, Virginia ten, North Carolina five, South Carolina five, and Georgia three.

[4] When vacancies happen in the Representation from any State, the Executive Authority thereof shall issue Writs of Election to fill such Vacancies.

[5] The House of Representatives shall chuse their Speaker and other Officers; and shall have the sole Power of Impeachment.

Section 3   [1] The Senate of the United States shall be composed of two Senators from each State, chosen by the Legislature thereof, for six Years; and each Senator shall have one Vote.

[2] Immediately after they shall be assembled in Consequence of the first Election, they shall be divided as equally as may be into three Classes. The Seats of the Senators of the first Class shall be vacated at the Expiration of the Second Year, of the second Class at the Expiration of the fourth Year, and of the third Class at the Expiration of the sixth Year, so that one-third may be chosen every second Year; and if Vacancies happen by Resignation, or otherwise, during the Recess of the Legislature of any State, the Executive therof may make temporary Appointments until the next Meeting of the Legislature which shall then fill such Vacancies.

[3] No person shall be a Senator who shall not have attained to the Age of thirty Years, and been nine Years a Citizen of the United States, and who shall not when elected be an Inhabitant of that State for which he shall be chosen.

[4] The Vice President of the United States shall be President of the Senate, but shall have no Vote, unless they be equally divided.

[5] The Senate shall chuse their other Officers, and also a President pro tempore, in the absence of the Vice President, or when he shall exercise the Office of President of the United States.

[6] The Senate shall have the sole Power to try all Impeachments When sitting for that Purpose, they shall be on Oath or Affirmation. When the President of the United States is tried, the Chief Justice shall preside: And no Person shall be convicted without the Concurrence of two-thirds of the Members present.

[7] Judgment in Cases of Impeachment shall not extend further than to removal from Office, and disqualification to hold and enjoy any Office of honor, Trust, or Profit under the United States: but the Party convicted shall nevertheless be liable and subject to Indictment, Trial, Judgment, and Punishment, according to Law.

Section 4   [1] The Times, Places and Manner of holding Elections for Senators and Representatives, shall be prescribed in each State by the Legislature thereof; but the Congress may at any time by Law make or alter such Regulations, except as to the Places of chusing Senators.

[2] The Congress shall assemble at least once in every Year, and such Meeting shall be on the first Monday in December, unless they shall by Law appoint a different Day.

Section 5   [1] Each House shall be the Judge of the Elections, Returns, and Qualifications of its own Members, and a Majority of each shall constitute a Quorum to do Business; but a smaller Number may adjourn from day to day, and may be authorized to compel the Attendance of absent Members, in such Manner, and under such Penalties as each House may provide.

[2] Each House may determine the Rules of its Proceedings, punish its Members for disorderly Behavior, and, with the Concurrence of two thirds, expel a Member.

[3] Each House shall keep a Journal of its Proceedings, and from time to time publish the same, excepting such Parts as may in their judgment require Secrecy; and the Yeas and Nays of the Members of either House on any question shall, at the Desire of one fifth of those Present, be entered on the Journal.

[4] Neither House, during the Session of Congress, shall, without the Consent of the other adjourn for more than three days, nor to any other Place than that in which the two Houses shall be sitting.

Section 6   [1] The Senators and Representatives shall receive a Compensation for their Services to be ascertained by Law, and paid out of the Treasury of the United States. They shall in all Cases, except Treason, Felony and Breach of the Peace, be privileged from Arrest during their Attendance at the Session of their respective Houses, and in going to and returning from the same; and for any Speech or Debate in either House, they shall not be questioned in any other Place.

[2] No Senator or Representative shall, during the Time for which he was elected, be appointed to any civil Office under the Authority of the United States, which shall have been created, or Emoluments whereof shall have been encreased during such time; and no Person holding any Office under the United States, shall be a Member of either House during his Continuance in Office.

Section 7   [1] All Bills for raising Revenue shall originate in the House of Representatives; but the Senate may propose or concur with Amendments as on other Bills.

[2] Every Bill which shall have passed the House of Representatives and the Senate, shall, before it become a Law, be presented to the President of the United States; if he approve he shall sign it, but if not he shall return it, with his Objections to that House in which it shall have originated, who shall enter the Objections at large on their Journal, and proceed to reconsider it. If after such Reconsideration two thirds of that House shall agree to pass the Bill, it shall be sent, together with the Objections, to the other House, by which it shall likewise be reconsidered, and if approved by two thirds of that House, it shall become a Law. But in all such cases the Votes of both Houses shall be determined by Yeas and Nays, and the Names of the Persons voting for and against the Bill shall be entered on the Journal of each House respectively. If any Bill shall not be returned by the President within ten Days (Sundays excepted) after it shall have been presented to him, the Same shall be a Law, in like Manner as if he had signed it, unless the Congress by their Adjournment prevent its Return, in which Case it shall not be a Law.

[3] Every Order, Resolution, or vote to which the Concurrence of the Senate and House of Representatives may be necessary (except on a question of

Adjournment) shall be presented to the President of the United States; and before the Same shall take Effect, shall be approved by him, or being disapproved by him, shall be repassed by two thirds of the Senate and House of Representatives, according to the Rules and Limitations prescribed in the Case of a Bill.

Section 8   The Congress shall have Power [1] To lay and collect Taxes, Duties, Imposts and Excises, to pay the Debts and provide for the common Defence and general Welfare of the United States; but all Duties, Imposts and Excises shall be uniform throughout the United States;

[2] To borrow money on the credit of the United States;

[3] To regulate Commerce with foreign Nations, and among the several States, and with the Indian Tribes;

[4] To establish an uniform Rule of Naturalization, and uniform Laws on the subject of Bankruptcies throughout the United States;

[5] To coin Money, regulate the Value thereof, and of foreign Coin, and fix the Standard of Weights and Measures;

[6] To provide for the Punishment of counterfeiting the Securities and current Coin of the United States;

[7] To establish Post Offices and post Roads;

[8] To promote the Progress of Science and useful Arts, by securing for limited Times to Authors and Inventors the exclusive Right to their respective Writings and Discoveries;

[9] To constitute Tribunals inferior to the Supreme Court;

[10] To define and punish Piracies and Felonies committed on the high Seas, and Offenses against the Law of Nations;

[11] To declare War, grant Letters of Marque and Reprisal, and make Rules concerning Captures on Land and Water;

[12] To raise and support Armies, but no Appropriation of Money to that Use shall be for a longer Term than two Years;

[13] To provide and maintain a Navy;

[14] To make Rules for the Government and Regulation of the land and naval Forces;

[15] To provide for calling forth the Militia to execute the Laws of the Union, suppress Insurrections and repel Invasions;

[16] To provide for organizing, arming, and disciplining the Militia, and for governing such Part of them as may be employed in the Service of the United States, reserving to the States respectively, the Appointment of the Officers, and Authority of training the Militia according to the discipline prescribed by Congress;

[17] To exercise exclusive Legislation in all Cases whatsoever, over such District (not exceeding ten Miles square) as may, by Cession of particular States, and the acceptance of Congress, become the Seat of the Government of the United States, and to exercise like Authority over all Places purchased by the Consent of the Legislature of the State in which the Same shall be, for the

Erection of Forts, Magazines, Arsenals dock-Yards, and other needful Buildings;—And

[18] To make all Laws which shall be necessary and proper for carrying into Execution the foregoing Powers, and all other Powers vested by this Constitution in the Government of the United States, or in any Department or Officer thereof.

Section 9 [1] The Migration or Importation of Such Persons as any of the States now existing shall think proper to admit, shall not be prohibited by the Congress prior to the Year one thousand eight hundred and eight, but a tax or duty may be imposed on such Importation, not exceeding ten dollars for each Person.

[2] The privilege of the Writ of Habeas Corpus shall not be suspended, unless when in Cases of Rebellion or Invasion the public Safety may require it.

[3] No Bill of Attainder or ex post facto Law shall be passed.

[4] No capitation, or other direct, Tax shall be laid unless in Proportion to the Census or Enumeration herein before directed to be taken.

[5] No Tax or Duty shall be laid on Articles exported from any State.

[6] No preference shall be given by any Regulation of Commerce or Revenue to the Ports of one State over those of another: nor shall Vessels bound to, or from, one State be obliged to enter, clear, or pay Duties in another.

[7] No money shall be drawn from the Treasury, but in Consequence of Appropriations made by Law; and a regular Statement and Account of the Receipts and Expenditures of all public Money shall be published from time to time.

[8] No Title of Nobility shall be granted by the United States: And no Person holding any Office of Profit or Trust under them, shall, without the Consent of the Congress, accept of any present, Emolument, Office, or Title, of any kind whatever, from any King, Prince, or foreign State.

Section 10 [1] No State shall enter into any Treaty, Alliance, or Confederation; grant Letters of Marque and Reprisal; coin Money; emit Bills of Credit; make any Thing but gold and silver Coin a Tender in Payment of Debts; pass any Bill of Attainder, ex post facto Law, or Law impairing the Obligation of Contracts, or grant any Title of Nobility.

[2] No State shall, without the Consent of the Congress, lay any Imposts or Duties on Imports or Exports, except what may be absolutely necessary for executing its inspection Laws: and the net Produce of all Duties and Imposts, laid by any State on Imports or Exports, shall be for the Use of the Treasury of the United States; and all such Laws shall be subject to the Revision and Control of the Congress.

[3] No State shall, without the Consent of Congress, lay any duty of Tonnage, keep Troops, or Ships of War in time of Peace, enter into any Agreement or Compact with another State, or with a foreign Power or engage in War,

unless actually invaded, or in such imminent Danger as will not admit of delay.

ARTICLE II

Section 1 [1] The executive Power shall be vested in a President of the United States of America. He shall hold his Office during the Term of four Years, and, together with the Vice President, chosen for the same Term, be elected, as follows:

[2] Each State shall appoint, in such Manner as the Legislature thereof may direct, a Number of Electors, equal to the whole Number of Senators and Representatives to which the State may be entitled in the Congress: but no Senator or Representative, or Person holding an Office of Trust or Profit under the United States, shall be appointed an Elector.

[3] The Electors shall meet in their respective States, and vote by Ballot for two persons of whom one at least shall not be an Inhabitant of the same State with themselves. And they shall make a List of all the Persons voted for, and of the Number of Votes for each; which List they shall sign and certify, and transmit sealed to the Seat of the Government of the United States, directed to the President of the Senate. The President of the Senate shall, in the Presence of the Senate and House of Representatives, open all the Certificates, and the Votes shall then be counted. The Person having the greatest Number of Votes shall be the President, if such Number be a Majority of the whole Number of Electors appointed; and if there be more than one who have such Majority, and have an equal Number of Votes, then the House of Representatives shall immediately chuse by Ballot one of them for President; and if no Person have a Majority, then from the five highest on the List the said House shall in like Manner chuse the President. But in chusing the President, the Votes shall be taken by States, the Representation from each State having one Vote; A quorum for this Purpose shall consist of a Member or Members from two-thirds of the States, and a Majority of all the States shall be necessary to a Choice. In every Case, after the Choice of the President, the Person having the greatest Number of Votes of the Electors shall be the Vice President. But if there should remain two or more who have equal Votes, the Senate shall chuse from them by Ballot the Vice President.

[4] The Congress may determine the Time of chusing the Electors and the Day on which they shall give their Votes; which Day shall be the same throughout the United States.

[5] No person except a natural born Citizen, or a Citizen of the United States, at the time of the Adoption of this Constitution, shall be eligible to the Office of President; neither shall any Person be eligible to that Office who shall not have attained to the Age of thirty-five Years, and been fourteen Years a Resident within the United States.

[6] In case of the removal of the President from Office, or of his Death, Resignation, or Inability to discharge the Powers and Duties of the said Office,

the same shall devolve on the Vice President, and the Congress may by Law Provide for the Case of Removal, Death, Resignation or Inability, both of the President and Vice President, declaring what Office shall then act as President, and such Officer shall act accordingly, until the Disability be removed, or a President shall be elected.

[7] The President shall, at stated Times, receive for his Services, a Compensation, which shall neither be encreased nor diminished during the Period for which he shall have been elected, and he shall not receive within that Period any other Emolument from the United States, or any of them.

[8] Before he enter on the Execution of his Office, he shall take the following Oath or Affirmation:—"I do solemnly swear (or affirm) that I will faithfully execute the Office of President of the United States, and will to the best of my Ability, preserve, protect and defend the Constitution of the United States."

Section 2   [1] The President shall be Commander in Chief of the Army and Navy of the United States, and of the Militia of the several States, when called into the actual Service of the United States; he may require the Opinion, in writing, of the principle Officer in each of the executive Departments, upon any subject relating to the Duties of their respective Offices, and he shall have Power to grant Reprieves and Pardons for Offenses against the United States, except in Cases of Impeachment.

[2] He shall have Power, by and with the Advice and Consent of the Senate, to make Treaties, provided two-thirds of the Senators present concur; and he shall nominate, and by and with the Advice and Consent of the Senate, shall appoint Ambassadors, other public Ministers and Consuls, Judges of the Supreme Court, and all other Officers of the United States, whose Appointments are not herein otherwise provided for, and which shall be established by Law; but the Congress may by Law vest the Appointment of such inferior Officers, as they think proper, in the President alone, in the Courts of Law, or in the Heads of Departments.

[3] The President shall have Power to fill up all Vacancies that may happen during the Recess of the Senate, by granting Commissions which shall expire at the End of their next Session.

Section 3   He shall from time to time give to the Congress Information of the State of the Union, and recommend to their Consideration such Measures as he shall judge necessary and expedient; he may, on extraordinary Occasions, convene both Houses, or either of them, and in Case of Disagreement between them, with Respect to the Time of Adjournment, he may adjourn them to such Time as he shall think proper; he shall receive Ambassadors and other public Ministers; he shall take Care that the Laws be faithfully executed, and shall Commission all the Officers of the United States.

Section 4   The President, Vice President and all civil Officers of the United States, shall be removed from Office on Impeachment for, and Conviction of, Treason, Bribery, or other high Crimes and Misdemeanors.

ARTICLE III

Section 1 The judicial Power of the United States, shall be vested in one supreme Court, and in such inferior Courts as the Congress may from time to time ordain and establish. The Judges, both of the supreme and inferior Courts, shall hold their Offices during good Behaviour, and shall, at stated Times, receive for their Services a Compensation which shall not be diminished during their Continuance in Office.

Section 2 [1] The judicial Power shall extend to all Cases, in Law and Equity, arising under this Constitution, the Laws of the United States, and Treaties made, or which shall be made, under their Authority;—to all Cases affecting Ambassadors, other public Ministers and Consuls;—to all Cases of admiralty and maritime Jurisdiction;—Controversies to which the United States shall be a Party;—to Controversies between two or more States;—between a State and Citizens of another State;—between Citizens of different States;—between Citizens of the same State claiming Lands under Grants of different States, and between a State, or the Citizens thereof, and foreign States, Citizens or Subjects.

[2] In all Cases affecting Ambassadors, other public Ministers and Consuls, and those in which a State shall be Party, the supreme Court shall have original Jurisdiction. In all the other Cases before mentioned, the supreme Court shall have appellate Jurisdiction, both as to Law and Fact, with such Exceptions, and under such Regulations as the Congress shall make.

[3] The trial of all Crimes, except in Cases of Impeachment, shall be by Jury; and such Trial shall be held in the State where the said Crimes shall have been committed; but when not committed within any State, the Trial shall be at such Place or Places as the Congress may by Law have directed.

Section 3 [1] Treason against the United States, shall consist only in levying War against them, or, in adhering to their Enemies, giving them Aid and comfort. No Person shall be convicted of Treason unless on the Testimony of two Witnesses to the same overt Act, or on Confession in open Court.

[2] The Congress shall have power to declare the Punishment of Treason, but no Attainder of Treason shall work Corruption of Blood, or Forfeiture except during the Life of the Person attainted.

ARTICLE IV

Section 1 Full Faith and Credit shall be given in each State to the public Acts, Records, and judicial Proceedings of every other State. And the Congress may by general Laws prescribe the Manner in which such Acts, Records and Proceedings shall be proved and the Effect thereof.

Section 2 [1] The Citizens of each State shall be entitled to all Privileges and Immunities of Citizens in the several States.

[2] A Person charged in any State with Treason, Felony, or other Crime, who shall flee from Justice, and be found in another State, shall on demand of the executive Authority of the State from which he fled, be delivered up, to be removed to the State having Jurisdiction of the Crime.

[3] No Person held to Service or Labour in one State, under the Laws thereof, escaping into another, shall, in Consequence of any law or Regulation therein, be discharged from such Service or Labour, but shall be delivered up on Claim of the Party to whom such Service or Labour may be due.

Section 3 [1] New States may be admitted by the Congress into this Union; but no new State shall be formed or erected within the Jurisdiction of any other State; nor any State be formed by the Junction of two or more States, or parts of States, without the Consent of the Legislatures of the States concerned as well as of the Congress.

[2] The Congress shall have Power to dispose of and make all needful Rules and Regulations respecting the Territory or other Property belonging to the United States; and nothing in this Constitution shall be so construed as to Prejudice any Claims of the United States, or of any particular State.

Section 4 The United States shall guarantee to every State in this Union a Republican Form of Government, and shall protect each of them against Invasion; and on Application of the Legislature, or of the Executive (when the Legislature cannot be convened) against domestic Violence.

ARTICLE V

The Congress, whenever two-thirds of both Houses shall deem it necessary shall propose Amendments to this Constitution, or, on the Application of the Legislatures of two-thirds of the several States, shall call a Convention for proposing Amendments, which, in either Case, shall be valid to all Intents and Purposes, as part of this Constitution, when ratified by the Legislatures of three-fourths of the several States, or by Conventions in three-fourths thereof, as the one or the other Mode of Ratification may be proposed by the Congress; Provided that no Amendment which may be made prior to the Year One thousand eight hundred and eight shall in any Manner affect the first and fourth Clauses in the Ninth Section of the first Article; and that no State, without its Consent, shall be deprived of its equal Suffrage in the Senate.

ARTICLE VI

[1] All Debts contracted and Engagements entered into, before the Adoption of this Constitution shall be as valid against the United States under this Constitution, as under the Confederation.

[2] This Consitution, and the Laws of the United States which shall be made in Pursuance thereof; and all Treaties made, or which shall be made, under the

Authority of the United States, shall be the supreme Law of the Land; and the Judges in every State shall be bound thereby, any Thing in the Constitution or Laws of any State to the Contrary notwithstanding.

[3] The Senators and Representatives before mentioned, and the Members of the several State Legislatures, and all executive and judicial Officers, both of the United States and of the several States, shall be bound by Oath or Affirmation, to support this Constitution; but no religious Test shall ever be required as a Qualification to any Office or public Trust under the United States.

ARTICLE VII

The Ratification of the Conventions of nine States shall be sufficient for the Establishment of this Constitution between the States so ratifying the Same.

ARTICLES IN ADDITION TO, AND AMENDMENT OF, THE CONSTITUTION OF THE UNITED STATES OF AMERICA, PROPOSED BY CONGRESS, AND RATIFIED BY THE LEGISLATURES OF THE SEVERAL STATES, PURSUANT TO THE FIFTH ARTICLE OF THE ORIGINAL CONSTITUTION

AMENDMENT I [1791]

Congress shall make no law respecting an establishment of religion, or prohibiting the free exercise thereof; or abridging the freedom of speech, or of the press; or the right of the people peaceably to assemble and to petition the Government for a redress of grievances.

AMENDMENT II [1791]

A well regulated Militia, being necessary to the security of a free State, the right of the people to keep and bear Arms, shall not be infringed.

AMENDMENT III [1791]

No Soldier shall, in time of peace be quartered in any house, without the consent of the Owner, nor in time of war, but in a manner to be prescribed by Law.

AMENDMENT IV [1791]

The right of the people to be secure in their persons, houses, papers, and effects, against unreasonable searches and seizures, shall not be violated, and no Warrants shall issue, but upon probable cause, supported by Oath or affirmation, and particularly describing the place to be searched, and the persons or things to be seized.

AMENDMENT V [1791]

No person shall be held to answer for a capital, or otherwise infamous crime, unless on a presentment or indictment of a Grand Jury, except in cases arising in the land or naval forces, or in the Militia, when in actual service in time of War or public danger; nor shall any person be subject for the offence to be twice put in jeopardy of life, liberty, or property, without due process of law; nor shall private property be taken for public use, without just compensation.

AMENDMENT VI [1791]

In all criminal prosecutions, the accused shall enjoy the right to a speedy and public trial, by an impartial jury of the State and district wherein the crime shall have been committed, which district shall have been previously ascertained by law, and to be informed of the nature and cause of the accusation; to be confronted with the witnesses against him; to have compulsory process for obtaining witnesses in his favor, and to have the Assistance of Counsel for his defence.

AMENDMENT VII [1791]

In suits at common law, where the value in controversy shall exceed twenty dollars, the right of trial by jury shall be preserved, and no fact tried by jury, shall be otherwise reexamined in any Court of the United States, than according to the rules of the common law.

AMENDMENT VIII [1791]

Excessive bail shall not be required, nor excessive fines imposed, nor cruel and unusual punishments inflicted.

AMENDMENT IX [1791]

The enumeration in the Constitution, of certain rights, shall not be construed to deny or disparage others retained by the people.

AMENDMENT X [1791]

The powers not delegated to the United States by the Constitution, nor prohibited by it to the States, are reserved to the States respectively, or to the people.

AMENDMENT XI [1798]

The Judicial power of the United States shall not be construed to extend to any suit in law or equity, commenced or prosecuted against one of the United States by Citizens of another State, or by Citizens or Subjects of any Foreign State.

AMENDMENT XII [1804]

The electors shall meet in their respective states and vote by ballot for President and Vice-President, one of whom, at least, shall not be an inhabitant of the same state with themselves; they shall name in their ballots the person voted for as President, and in distinct ballots the person voted for as Vice-President, and they shall make distinct lists of all persons voted for as President, and of all persons voted for as Vice-President, and of the number of votes for each, which lists they shall sign and certify, and transmit sealed to the seat of the government of the United States, directed to the President of the Senate;—The President of the Senate shall, in presence of the Senate and House of Representatives, open all the certificates and the votes shall then be counted;—The person having the greatest number of votes for President shall be the President, if such number be a majority of the whole number of Electors appointed; and if no person have such majority, then from the persons having the highest numbers not exceeding three on the list of those voted for as President, the House of Representatives shall choose immediately, by ballot, the President. But in choosing the President, the votes shall be taken by states, the representation from each state having one vote; a quorum for this purpose shall consist of a member or members from two-thirds of the states, and a majority of all the states shall be necessary to a choice. And if the House of Representatives shall not choose a President whenever the right of choice shall devolve upon them, before the fourth day of March next following, then the Vice-President shall act as President, as in the case of the death or other constitutional disability of the President.—The person having the greatest number of votes as Vice-President, shall be the Vice-President, if such number be a majority of the whole number of Electors appointed, and if no person have a majority, then from the two highest numbers on the list, the Senate shall choose the Vice-President; a quorum for the purpose shall consist of two-thirds of the whole number of Senators, and a majority of the whole number shall be necessary to a choice. But no person constitutionally ineligible to the office of President shall be eligible to that of Vice-President of the United States.

AMENDMENT XIII [1865]

Section 1 Neither slavery nor involuntary servitude, except as a punishment for crime whereof the party shall have been duly convicted, shall exist within the United States, or any place subject to their jurisdiction.

Section 2   Congress shall have power to enforce this article by appropriate legislation.

AMENDMENT XIV [1868]

Section 1   All persons born or naturalized in the United States, and subject to the jurisdiction thereof, are citizens of the United States and of the State wherein they reside. No State shall make or enforce any law which shall abridge the privileges or immunities of citizens of the United States; nor shall any State deprive any person of life, liberty, or property, without due process of law; nor deny to any person within its jurisdiction the equal protection of the laws.

Section 2   Representatives shall be apportioned among the several States according to their respective numbers, counting the whole number of persons in each State, excluding Indians not taxed. But when the right to vote at any election for the choice of electors for President and Vice-President of the United States, Representatives in Congress, the Executive and Judicial officers of a State, or the members of the Legislature thereof, is denied to any of the male inhabitants of such State, being twenty-one years of age, and citizens of the United States, or in any way abridged, except for participation in rebellion, or other crime, the basis of representation therein shall be reduced in the proportion which the number of such male citizens shall bear to the whole number of male citizens twenty-one years of age in such State.

Section 3   No person shall be a Senator or Representative in Congress, or elector of President and Vice-President, or hold any office, civil or military, under the United States, or under any State, who, having previously taken an oath, as a member of Congress, or as an officer of the United States, or as a member of any State legislature, or as an executive or judicial officer of any State, to support the Constitution of the United States, shall have engaged in insurrection or rebellion against the same, or given aid or comfort to the enemies thereof. But Congress may by a vote of two-thirds of each House, remove such disability.

Section 4   The validity of the public debt of the United States, authorized by law, including debts incurred for payment of pensions and bounties for services in suppressing insurrection or rebellion, shall not be questioned. But neither the United States nor any State shall assume or pay any debt or obligation incurred in aid of insurrection or rebellion against the United States, or any claim for the loss or emancipation of any slave; but all such debts, obligations and claims shall be held illegal and void.

Section 5   The Congress shall have power to enforce, by appropriate legislation, the provisions of this article.

AMENDMENT XV [1870]

Section 1 The right of citizens of the Unites States to vote shall not be denied or abridged by the United States or by any State on account of race, color, or previous condition of servitude.

Section 2 The Congress shall have power to enforce this article by appropriate legislation.

AMENDMENT XVI [1913]

The Congress shall have power to lay and collect taxes on incomes, from whatever source derived, without apportionment among the several States, and without regard to any census or enumeration.

AMENDMENT XVII [1913]

The Senate of the United States shall be composed of two Senators from each State, elected by the people thereof, for six years; and each Senator shall have one vote. The electors in each State shall have the qualifications requisite for electors of the most numerous branch of the State legislatures.

When vacancies happen in the representation of any State in the Senate, the executive authority of such State shall issue writs of election to fill such vacancies: *Provided,* That the legislature of any State may empower the executive thereof to make temporary appointments until the people fill the Vacancies by election as the legislature may direct.

This amendment shall not be so construed as to the affect the election or term of any Senator chosen before it becomes valid as part of the Constitution.

AMEMDMENT XVIII [1919]

Section 1 After one year from the ratification of this article the manufacture, sale, or transportation of intoxicating liquors within, the importation thereof into, or the exportation thereof from the United States and all territory subject to the Jurisdiction thereof for beverage purposes is hereby prohibited.

Section 2 The Congress and the several States shall have concurrent power to enforce this article by appropriate legislation.

Section 3 This article shall be inoperative unless it shall have been ratified as an amendment to the Constitution by the legislatures of the several States, as provided in the Constitution, within seven years from the date of the submission hereof to the States by the Congress.

AMENDMENT XIX [1920]

The right of citizens of the United States to vote shall not be denied or abridged by the United States or by any State on account of sex.

Congress shall have the power to enforce this article by appropriate legislation.

AMENDMENT XX [1933]

Section 1   The terms of the President and Vice President shall end at noon on the 20th day of January, and the terms of Senators and Representatives at noon on the 3d day of January, of the years in which such terms would have ended if this article had not been ratified; and the terms of their successors shall then begin.

Section 2   The Congress shall assemble at least once in every year, and such meeting shall begin at noon on the 3d day of January, unless they shall by law appoint a different day.

Section 3   If, at the time fixed for the beginning of the term of the President, the President elect shall have died, the Vice President elect shall become President. If a President shall not have been chosen before the time fixed for the beginning of his term, or if the President elect shall have failed to qualify, then the Vice President elect shall act as President until a President shall have qualified; and the Congress may by law provide for the case wherein neither a President elect nor a Vice President elect shall have qualified, declaring who shall then act as President, or the manner in which one who is to act shall be selected, and such person shall act accordingly until a President or Vice President shall have qualified.

Section 4   The Congress may by law provide for the case of death of any of the persons from whom the House of Representatives may choose a President whenever the right of choice shall have devolved upon them, and for the case of the death of any of the persons from whom the Senate may choose a Vice President whenever the right of choice shall have devolved upon them.

Section 5   Sections 1 and 2 shall take effect on the 15th day of October following the ratification of this article.

Section 6   This article shall be inoperative unless it shall have been ratified as an amendment to the Constitution by the legislatures of three-fourths of the several States within seven years from the date of its submission.

AMENDMENT XXI [1933]

Section 1   The eighteenth article of amendment to the Constitution of the United States is hereby repealed.

Section 2   The transportation or importation into any State, Territory, or possession of the United States for delivery of use therein of intoxicating liquors, in violation of the laws thereof, is hereby prohibited.

Section 3   This article shall be inoperative unless it shall have been ratified as an amendment to the Constitution by conventions in the several States, as provided in the Constitution, within seven years from the date of the submission hereof to the States by the Congress.

AMENDMENT XXII [1951]

Section 1   No person shall be elected to the offce of President more than twice, and no person who has held the office of President, or acted as President, for more than two years of a term to which some other person was elected President shall be elected to the office of the President more than once. But this Article shall not apply to any person holding the office of President when this Article was proposed by the Congress, and shall not prevent any person who may be holding the office of President, or acting as President, during the term within which the Article becomes operative from holding the office of President or acting as President during the remainder of such term.

Section 2   This article shall be inoperative unless it shall have been ratified as an amendment to the Constitution by the legislature of three-fourths of the several States within seven years from the date of its submission to the States by the Congress.

AMENDMENT XXIII [1961]

Section 1   The District constituting the seat of Government of the United States shall appoint in such manner as the Congress may direct:
A number of electors of President and Vice President equal to the whole number of Senators and Representatives in Congress to which the District would be entitled if it were a State, but in no event more than the least populous State; they shall be in addition to those appointed by the States, but they shall be considered, for the purposes of election of President and Vice President, to be electors appointed by a State; and they shall meet in the District and perform such duties as provided by the twelfth article of amendment.

Section 2 The Congress shall have power to enforce this article by appropriate legislation.

AMENDMENT XXIV [1964]

Section 1 The right of citizens of the United States to vote in any primary or other election for President or Vice President, for elector for President or Vice President, or for Senator or Representative in Congress, shall not be denied or abridged by the United States or any State by reason of failure to pay any poll tax or other tax.

Section 2 The Congress shall have power to enforce this article by appropriate legislation.

AMENDMENT XXV [1967]

Section 1 In case of the removal of the President from office or his death or resignation, the Vice President shall become President.

Section 2 Whenever there is a vacancy in the office of the Vice President, the President shall nominate a Vice President who shall take the Office upon confirmation by a majority vote of both houses of Congress.

Section 3 Whenever the President transmits to the President pro tempore of the Senate and the Speaker of the House of Representatives his written declaration that he is unable to discharge the powers and duties of his office, and until he transmits to them a written declaration to the contrary, such powers and duties shall be discharged by the Vice President as Acting President.

Section 4 Whenever the Vice President and a majority of either the principal officers of the executive departments, or of such other body as Congress may by law provide, transmit to the President pro tempore of the Senate and the Speaker of the House of Representatives their written declaration that the President is unable to discharge the powers and duties of his office, the Vice President shall immediately assume the powers and duties of the office as Acting President.

Thereafter, when the President transmits to the President pro tempore of the Senate and the Speaker of the House of Representatives his written declaration that no inability exists, he shall resume the powers and duties of his office unless the Vice President and a majority of either the principle officers of the executive department, or of such other body as Congress may by law provide, transmit within four days to the President pro tempore of the Senate and the Speaker of the House of Representatives their written declaration that the President is unable to discharge the powers and duties of his office. Thereupon Congress shall decide the issue, assembling within 48 hours for that purpose if not in session. If the Congress, within 21 days after receipt of the latter written declaration, or, if Congress is not in session within 21 days after Congress is required to assemble, determines by two-thirds vote of both houses that the President is unable to discharge the powers and duties of his office, the Vice President shall continue to discharge the same as Acting President; otherwise, the President shall resume the powers and duties of his office.

AMENDMENT XXVI [1971]

Section 1 The right of citizens of the United States, who are eighteen years of age, or older, to vote shall not be denied or abridged by the United States or any state on account of age.

Section 2 The Congress shall have the power to enforce this article by appropriate legislation.

TABLE OF CASES

Opinions of the Court appear at the **boldface** page numbers.

885